C0-ATR-197

The
INTERNATIONAL CRITICAL COMMENTARY
on the Holy Scriptures of the Old and New Testaments

HOSEA

A CRITICAL AND EXEGETICAL COMMENTARY

ON

HOSEA

BY

A. A. MACINTOSH, B.D.
President of St. John's College, Cambridge

T&T CLARK
EDINBURGH

T&T CLARK LTD
59 GEORGE STREET
EDINBURGH EH2 2LQ
SCOTLAND

First published 1997

ISBN 0 567 08545 7

British Library Cataloguing-in-Publication Data
A catalogue record for this book is available from the British Library

Typeset by Aslan Ltd, Girton, Cambridge
in Adobe Times, Linguists' Hebraica and Aslan Greek

Printed in Great Britain by Page Brothers, Norwich
Bound by Bookcraft, Avon

לולרי
ולעם ישׂראל

For Valerie
and her people

PREFACE

The editors of the series have allowed me considerable freedom in respect of the form of the commentary. As a consequence I have resolved to keep something of the traditional divisions of the ICC in the hope that the commentary may be useful to different sorts of readers. Accordingly each verse is translated from the Hebrew and notes justifying the translation are provided. The translation seeks to give as clearly as possible in English the meaning of the Hebrew but no attempt has been made at a literary or polished version. In the notes Hebrew words are reproduced in Hebrew script. Secondly, there are the more general comments on each verse and they are printed in larger type; here Hebrew words are transliterated. Thirdly, there are the sections marked 'Text and Versions' in which the more recondite material is set out in smaller type for those who are interested by it.

I am grateful to the editors, J. A. Emerton and C. E. B. Cranfield, for entrusting the work to me. I have been fortunate in that the Master and Fellows of my College have graciously allowed me, subject to the performance of my primary duties, to concentrate exclusively on this particular work. In the nature of the case it has taken over fifteen years to complete.

It is impossible to cover everything in a modern commentary on a biblical author. My own priority has been to attempt an accurate account of the meaning of Hosea's words; for on this, it seems to me, everything else depends. In many cases it will be for others (if they approve the particulars of what I have done) to draw out the implications for other branches of Old Testament scholarship. Yet even in respect of what I regard as my primary task I have been unable to use everything that has become available. For example, the commentary had already reached an advanced stage when D. Barthélemy's important *Critique textuelle de l'AT* on Hosea, in many respects similar in its emphasis and interest, appeared in 1992 (see the Bibliography).

For the rest I wish to record my heartfelt thanks as follows: to my teachers, †J. S. Bezzant, †J. G. Essame, H. St J. Hart and †D. W. Thomas; to colleagues and friends, J. A. Crook, G. I. Davies, R. P. Gordon, Ruth Kartun-Blum, Ora Lipschitz, S. C.

Reif, for much helpful advice; to D. R. de Lacey, who has read the manuscript and made many valuable suggestions, has worked hard to produce camera-ready copy, and has also revealed to me the mysteries of computer techniques so that I have been able to make my own corrections; to B. A. Mastin of the University of Wales, Bangor, who has painstakingly read and criticised the entire manuscript of this book and made many valuable suggestions, to whom I owe a very special debt of gratitude; mistakes and infelicities which survive are emphatically mine and not his; to Valerie Collis for her warm and long-suffering generosity in converting all my original hand-written autographs into typescript and in her sustained help in reading proofs; and to Mary, my beloved wife, for her constant support and encouragement.

Cambridge, *St John's Day*, 1996. AAM

CONTENTS

THE CHAPTERS AND THEIR CONTENTS

1.1 Superscription and title:
exilic or post-exilic classification of the prophecy.

1.2–9 A retrospective account of Hosea's marriage and children:
the chronology of his message:
its burden, the deterioration of the relationship between Yahweh and Ephraim.

2.1–3 Recapitulation:
a prayer for the reversal of the burden of 1.2–9.

2.4–15 Remonstration with Israel under the figure of a wayward wife and mother:
syncretism between Yahwism and Canaanite religion;
the fertility of the land and its author.

2.16–25 The offer of a new beginning:
a prayer for a new beginning in the relationship between Yahweh and Israel under the figure of the marriage of husband and wife;
a new entry to the land from the desert;
the fertility of the land and its author.

3.1–5 A personal testimony of Hosea:
his marriage and its deterioration, compared with that of the state;
his and Yahweh's attempt to redeem the situation;
contemporary Israelite religion.

Excursus on Hosea's marriage.

4.1–19 Yahweh's indictment of Israel:
the responsibility of the priests;
contemporary Israelite religion;
syncretism between Yahwism and Canaanite religion;
sacrificial feasting and the cult;
(cultic) women and prostitutes;
idolatry.

9.1–9 **The effects of Yahweh's sentence of judgement:**
the failure of agricultural endeavour and the repudiation of Ephraim's relationship with Yahweh;
reversal of the exodus theme;
the banishment of Ephraim from the worship of Yahweh;
the Assyrian invasions of 733 BC and King Hoshea's *volte-face* of 725 BC;
the vindication of Hosea's message;
the corruption of the state compared with the Benjamite outrage of Gibeah.

9.10–17 **What must be, contrasted with what was and might have been:**
Yahweh's gracious initiative in his love for Israel, contrasted with Israel's age-old ingratitude;
Baal-Peor;
the loss of fecundity;
Yahweh's withdrawal from Ephraim, no longer his people;
Lo-Ammi alluded to;
the death throes of the state;
Gilgal and (?) Menahem or Shallum;
Lo-Ruḥamah alluded to;
divine sorrow at the imminent end of Ephraim;
contemporary history.

10.1–8 **The demise of the state, its cult and its king:**
Ephraim a damaged vine, its fruit the multiplication of cultic centres;
Ephraim's dissimulation entails the end of such centres;
the debilitating weakness of the monarchy in its commitment to intrigue and corruption;
proper government reduced to poisonous weeds;
the resources of the calf-cult diminished by the payment of tribute to Assyria;
its fate is banishment at the hands of the Assyrians;
Ephraim's disgrace;
the fate of its monarchy and its national sanctuaries.

10.9–15 The failure of the nation to fulfil its destiny: its inevitable fall to Assyria;
Ephraim's guilt and punishment compared with that of the Benjamites following the outrage of Gibeah;
Ephraim's commitment to wicked intention and action contrasted with vocation under figures of agricultural endeavour;
King Hoshea's misplaced confidence in his policies;
the tumult and horror of war;
the end of the monarchy and the national cult.

11.1–11 Consistent love and consistent ingratitude:
Yahweh's son called from Egypt;
Ephraim's craven overtures to Egypt;
Yahweh's protection of his young son;
his care for Israel compared with that of the good farmer for his beast;
Hosea's modification of earlier prophecies;
exile in Assyria envisaged for an unrepentant nation;
the awful reality of Assyrian invasion;
the nation's inherent inability to repent;
Yahweh's reluctance to punish;
his deep compassion;
his ultimate purpose to restore his people from the exile that they had imposed on themselves.

12.1–15 Ephraim and its patriarchal ancestor Jacob: correction with judgement;
Israel's congenital deceit and treachery is exemplified is switches of foreign policy;
Egypt and Assyria;
the inevitability of Yahweh's punishment;
Jacob's congenital ruthlessness and hybris;
Jacob becomes Israel and Yahweh corrects him;
the resulting divine promise to Jacob and his descendants at Bethel;
the contemporary nation, then, should repent;
Ephraimite and Jacobite guilt in the economics of extortion;
improper attempts at self-justification;
Yahweh's corrective intervention;
the nation to return to the tents of the desert;
the mode by which, through the prophets, Yahweh had sought to correct the nation;

Gilead and Gilgal, exemplars of contemporary corruption, now totally discredited by the will of Yahweh;
Jacob's penitential flight to Paddan-aram;
his love for Rachel and its redeeming effect;
its reflection of Yahweh's love for his people mediated through Moses;
Ephraim's manifest provocation and blood-guilt openly indicted;
Yahweh's effective control of the events of contemporary history.

13.1–14.1 The final rupture:
Ephraim's disruption of Israel from the time of Jeroboam I;
its syncretistic policies;
the increase of idolatry;
the fate of idolatrous artefacts;
Yahweh, God of the exodus and the desert, the only saviour;
Ephraim's arrogance and ingratitude;
Yahweh's terrible reaction compared with the ferocity of the lion, the leopard and the she-bear;
the radical incapacity of the monarchy and of the establishment;
the inherent weakness itself a judgement of Yahweh upon it;
Ephraim's iniquity indelibly recorded;
its senseless immorality entails death, the death of a still-born son;
Yahweh's anguish at the punishment that he must inflict;
death and Sheol;
Ephraim's ancient blessing reversed;
the assault of Assyria likened to the east wind;
Samaria's guilt and its terrible punishment in the horrors of invasion;
the reality of the end.

14.2–9 Hosea's prayer *de profundis*:
that his people would return to Yahweh in penitence and contrition;
that they would confess that he alone provides the care and protection that Israel needs;
that he would heal their delinquency;

his care likened to the dew and Israel to the lily, the olive and the trees of Lebanon;
his people to revive successful agriculture;
Ephraim's and Yahweh's dialogue of mutual understanding;
Yahweh's attentive care and Ephraim's fruitful security.

14.10 Epilogue:
an exilic or post-exilic indication of the way in which Hosea's prophecies should be read and understood.

BIBLIOGRAPHY

COMMENTARIES CITED

Andersen, F. I. and Freedman, D. N.	*Hosea. A New Translation with Commentary.* The Anchor Bible (Garden City, New York, 1980). AF
Bauer, G. L.	*Die kleinen Propheten übersetzt und mit Commentarien erläutert* vol. 1 (Leipzig, 1786).
Cheyne, T. K.	*Hosea with Notes and Introduction* (Cambridge, 1884).
Dathe, J. A.	*Prophetae minores* (Halle, 1790).
Davies, G. I.	*Hosea.* New Century Bible Commentary (London and Grand Rapids, 1992).
Deden, D.	*De kleine Profeten.* I and II De Boeken van het Oude Testament (Roermond, 1953 and 1956).
Duhm, B.	*Die zwölf Propheten, in den Versmassen der Urschrift übersetzt* (Tübingen, 1910).
Ewald, H.	*Die Propheten des Alten Bundes* (2nd edn., Göttingen, 1867).
Frey, H.	*Das Buch des Werbens Gottes um seine Kirche. Der Prophet Hosea.* Die Botschaft des AT 23/ii (Stuttgart, 1957).
Gelderen, C. van and Gispen, W. H.	*Het Boek Hosea* (Kampen, 1953).
Guthe, H. et al. (edd.)	*Hosea bis Chronik.* HSAT E. Kautzsch (ed.) (4th edn., Tübingen, 1923).
Harper, W. R.	*Amos and Hosea.* ICC (Edinburgh, 1905).
Hitzig, F.	*Die zwölf kleinen Propheten* (4th edn., Leipzig, 1881).

Hoonacker, A. van — *Les douze petits prophètes*. Études bibliques (Paris, 1908).

Jerome (c. 342–420) — *PL* 25, ed. J.-P. Migne (Paris, 1845). *CC* lxxvi (Turnhout, 1969).

Jeremias, J. — *Der Prophet Hosea*. ATD xxiv 1 (Göttingen, 1983).

Keil, C. F. — *Biblischer Commentar über die zwölf kleinen Propheten* (3rd edn., Leipzig, 1888).

Knight, G. A. F. — *Hosea*. Torch Bible Commentary (London, 1960).

Lippl, J. — *Die zwölf kleinen Propheten*. HSAT viii (Bonn, 1937).

Manger, S. H. — *Commentarius in librum propheticum Hoseae* (Campis, 1782).

Marti, K. — *Dodekapropheton*. KHAT xiii (Tübingen, 1904).

Mauchline, J. — *The Book of Hosea* in The Interpreter's Bible VI (New York/Nashville, 1956).

Mays, J. L. — *Hosea: A Commentary* (London, 1969).

Newcome, W. — *An Attempt towards an Improved Version of the Twelve Minor Prophets* (London, 1836).

Nowack, W. — *Die kleinen Propheten*. HAT (3rd edn., Göttingen, 1922).

Orelli, C. von — *Die zwölf kleinen Propheten* (3rd edn., Munich, 1908).

Procksch, O. — *Die kleinen prophetischen Schriften vor dem Exil*. Erläuterung zum AT 3 (Stuttgart, 1910).

Qyl, J. — קיל, י. תרי־עשר (הושע־יונה) (Jerusalem, 1973).

Reuss, E. — *Das AT übersetzt, eingeleitet und erläutert* vol. 2 (Braunschweig, 1892).

Ridderbos, J.	*De kleine Profeten* (2nd edn., Kampen, 1952).
Riessler, P.	*Die kleinen Propheten* (Rottenberg, 1911).
Robinson, T. H. and Horst, F.	*Die zwölf kleinen Propheten.* HAT xiv/1 (second edn., Tübingen, 1954).
Rosenmüller, E. F. C.	*Scholia in VT*, 7, 1 (Leipzig, 1812).
Rudolph, W.	*Hosea.* KAT xiii 1 (Gütersloh, 1966).
Scholz, A.	*Commentar zum Buche des Propheten Hosea* (Würzburg, 1882).
Sellin, E.	*Das Zwölfprophetenbuch.* KAT xii/1 (2nd and 3rd ednn., Leipzig, 1929).
Simson, A.	*Der Prophet Hosea erklärt und übersetzt* (Hamburg, 1851).
Smith, G. A.	*The Book of the Twelve Prophets.* Expositor's Bible (2nd edn., London, 1928).
Umbreit, F. W. C.	*Praktischer Commentar über die kleinen Propheten* vol. 4 (Hamburg, 1844).
Valeton, J. J. P.	*Amos et Hosea* (Nijmegen, 1894).
Weiser, A.	*Das Buch der zwölf kleinen Propheten.* ATD 24 (Göttingen, 1949).
Wellhausen, J.	*Skizzen und Vorarbeiten* 5. *Die kleinen Propheten übersetzt und erklärt* (3rd edn., Berlin, 1892; 4th edn., Berlin, 1898).
Wolff, H. W.	*Dodekapropheton 1 Hosea.* BKAT xiv/1 (Neukirchen-Vluyn, 1961); ET, *Hosea.* Hermeneia – A Critical and Historical Commentary on the Bible (Philadelphia, 1974).
Wünsche, A.	*Der Prophet Hosea übersetzt und erklärt unter Benutzung der Targumim, der jüdischen Ausleger etc.* (Leipzig, 1868).

OTHER WORKS CITED

Ackroyd, P. R.	'Hosea and Jacob' *VT* 13 (1963), pp. 245–259.
Ackroyd, P. R.	'Goddesses, Woman and Jezebel'; see Cameron *Images*, pp. 249–253.
Ackroyd, P. R. and Evans, C. F. (edd.)	*The Cambridge History of the Bible* vol. 1 (Cambridge, 1970). *CHB*
Ackroyd, P. R. and Lindars, B. (edd.)	*Words and Meanings: Essays presented to David Winton Thomas* (Cambridge, 1968).
Aharoni, Y.	*The Arad Inscriptions*. Israel Exploration Society (Jerusalem, 1981).
Aistleitner, J.	*Wörterbuch der Ugaritischen Sprache* (3rd edn., Berlin, 1967).
Albright, W. F.	*Archaeology and the Religion of Israel* (Baltimore, 1956).
Albright, W. F., Alt, A. and Caspari, W. (edd.)	*Beiträge zur Religionsgeschichte und Archäologie Palästinas. Festschrift E. Sellin* (Leipzig, 1927).
Alt, A.	*Der Gott der Väter*. BWANT III 12 (Stuttgart, 1929) *DGV* = *KS* vol. I (Munich, 1954), pp. 1–79; ET 'The God of the Fathers'. *Essays on Old Testament History and Religion* (Oxford,1966), pp. 1–77.
Alt, A.	'Hosea 5:8–6:6. Ein Krieg und seine Folgen in prophetischer Beleuchtung' *Kleine Schriften* vol. II (Munich, 1954), pp. 163–187. *KS*
Alt, A.	'Das System der assyrischen Provinzen' *Kleine Schriften* vol. II (Munich, 1954), pp. 202–205. *KS*
Anderson, G. W. et al. (edd.)	*Hebräische Wortforschung. Festschrift W. Baumgartner*. SVT 16 (Leiden, 1967).

Arndt, W. F. and Gingrich, F. W.	*A Greek–English Lexicon of the NT and other early Christian Literature* (Cambridge and Chicago, 1957).
Artzi, P. and Malamat, A.	'The Great King'; see Cohen, M. E. et al., *Studies in honor of W. W. Hallo*, pp. 28–38.
Bachmann, J.	*AT Untersuchungen* (Berlin, 1894).
Baly, D.	*The Geography of the Bible* (London, 1957).
Barr, J.	*Comparative Philology and the Text of the OT* (Oxford, 1968). *CPOT*
Barr, J.	*The Variable Spellings of the Hebrew Bible* (Oxford, 1989).
Barth, J.	*Die Nominalbildung in den semitischen Sprachen* (Leipzig, 1894).
Barthélemy, D.	*Critique textuelle de l'AT*. Orbis biblicus et orientalis 50/3 (Fribourg and Göttingen, 1992), pp. 497ff.
Barthélemy, D.	*Les devanciers d'Aquila. Première publication integrale du texte des fragments du Dodecapropheton.* SVT X (Leiden, 1963).
Bauer, H. and Leander, P.	*Historische Grammatik der Hebräischen Sprache des AT* (Halle, 1922, photographically reproduced, Hildesheim, 1962). BL
Baumgartner, W.	*Festschrift W. Baumgartner*; see Anderson.
Baumgartner, W. et al. (edd.)	*Festschrift Alfred Bertholet* (Tübingen, 1950).
Ben Yehudah, E.	*Thesaurus totius hebraitatis et veteris et recentioris* (Berlin, later Jerusalem, 1908–59).
Bentzen, A.	'The Weeping of Jacob' *VT* 1 (1951), pp. 58f.

Bernarkadis, G. N. *Plutarchi Chaeronensis Moralia* 2 (Leipzig, 1889).

Bertholet, A. *Bertholet Festschrift*; see Baumgartner.

Beyer, K. *Die Aramäischen Texte vom Toten Meer* (Göttingen, 1984).

Borbone, P. G. *Il libro del Profeta Osea. Edizione critica del testo ebraico* (Turin, 1987).

Borée, W. *Die alten Ortsnamen Palästinas* (Hildesheim, 1968).

Branden, A. van den *Les inscriptions thamudiennes* (Louvain, 1950).

Brockelmann, C. *Grundriss der vergleichenden Grammatik der semitischen Sprachen* (2 vols., Berlin, 1908–13).

Brockelmann, C. *Hebräische Syntax* (Neukirchen, 1956).

Brockington, L. H. *The Hebrew Text of the OT: the readings adopted by the translators of the NEB* (Oxford and Cambridge, 1973).

Brown, F., Driver, S. R. and Briggs, C. A. *A Hebrew and English Lexicon of the OT* (Oxford, 1907; reprinted with corrections, 1953). BDB

Bruno, A. *Das Buch der Zwölf. Eine rhythmische und textkritische Untersuchung* (Stockholm, 1957).

Buber, M. *The Prophetic Faith* (New York, 1949).

Budde, K. (ed.) *Vom AT: K. Marti zum 70 Geburtstag gewidmet*. BZAW 41 (Giessen, 1925).

Budde, K. 'Zu Text und Auslegung des Buches Hosea' *JBL* 45 (1926), pp. 280–297 (on chapter 4); *JPOS* 14 (1934), pp. 1–41 (on chapters 5, 6); *JBL* 53 (1934), pp. 118–133 (on chapters 6–7.2).

Burrows, Millar *The Basis of Israelite Marriage* (New York, 1966).

Caquot, A. and Delcor, M. (edd.) *Mélanges bibliques et orientaux en l'honneur de M. Henri Cazelles*. AOAT 212 (Neukirchen-Vluyn, 1981).

Caquot, A., Légasse, S. and Tardieu, M. (edd.) *Mélanges bibliques et orientaux en l'honneur de M. Mathias Delcor*. AOAT 215 (Neukirchen-Vluyn, 1985).

Cameron, A. and Kuhrt, A. (edd.) *Images of Women in Antiquity* (London, 1983).

Cappell(us), L. *Critica sacra, sive de variis quae in sacris VT libris ...* (3 vols., Halae Magdaburgicae, 1775–86).

Cathcart, K. J. and Gordon, R. P. *The Targum of the Minor Prophets*. The Aramaic Bible vol. 14 (Wilmington, Delaware, 1989).

Clements, R. E. *God and Temple. The Idea of the Divine Presence in Ancient Israel* (Oxford, 1965).

Clements, R. E. *Isaiah 1–39*. New Century Bible Commentary (London and Grand Rapids, 1980).

Clements, R. E. *Prophecy and Tradition* (Oxford, 1975). *PT*

Clines, D. J. A. 'Hosea 2: Structure and Interpretation' in E. A. Livingstone (ed.) *Studia Biblica 1978* (Sheffield, 1979), pp. 83–103.

Cogan, M. and Tadmor, H. *II Kings*. The Anchor Bible (Garden City, New York, 1988).

Cohen, M. E., Snell, D. C. and Weisberg, D. B. *The Tablet and the Scroll. Near Eastern Studies in honor of William W. Hallo* (Bethesda, Maryland, 1993).

Cowley, A. *Aramaic Papyri of the Fifth Century B.C.* (Oxford, 1923).

Cross, F. M. *Canaanite Myth and Hebrew Epic* (Cambridge, Mass., 1973). *CMHE*

Cyril of Alexandria (d. AD 444); Pusey, P. E. (ed.) *Cyrilli archiepiscopi Alexandrini in xii prophetas* (2 vols., Oxford, 1868).

Dahood, M.	*Proverbs and N.W. Semitic Philology* (Rome, 1963).
Dalley, Stephanie	'Foreign chariotry and cavalry in the armies of Tiglath-pileser III and Sargon II' *Iraq* 47 (1985), pp. 31–48.
Dalman, G.	*Arbeit und Sitte in Palästina* (6 vols., Gütersloh, 1928–39). *AUS*
Danby, H.	*The Mishnah* (Oxford, 1933).
Davies, G. I.	*Ancient Hebrew Inscriptions. Corpus and Concordance* (Cambridge, 1991). *AHI*
Day, J.	*Molech: A God of Human Sacrifice in the OT* (Cambridge, 1989).
Day, J., Gordon, R. P. and Williamson, H. G. M.	*Wisdom in Ancient Israel. Essays in honour of J. A. Emerton* (Cambridge, 1995).
Delcor, M. Mathias	*Delcor Festschrift*; see Caquot.
Delekat, L.	'Zum hebräischen Wörterbuch' *VT* 14 (1964), pp. 7–66.
Deroche, M.	'The Reversal of Creation in Hosea' *VT* 31 (1981), pp. 400–409.
Dietrich, M., Lorenz, O. and Sanmartin, J.	*Die keilalphabetischen Texte aus Ugarit.* AOAT 24 (Neukirchen-Vluyn, 1976). *KTU*
Dozy, R.	*Supplément aux dictionnaires arabes* (Paris, 1927).
Driver, G. R.	'Linguistic and Textual Problems. Minor Prophets I' *JTS* 39 (1938), pp. 154–186.
Driver, G. R.	*Canaanite Myths and Legends* (Edinburgh, 1956). See also Gibson. *CML*
Driver, G. R.	'Glosses in the Hebrew Text of the OT' *OBL* I (1957), pp. 123–161.
Driver, G. R.	*The Judaean Scrolls* (Oxford, 1965).
Driver, G. R.	*Hebrew Studies presented to*; see McHardy.

Driver, G. R. and Miles, J. C.	*The Assyrian Laws* (Oxford, 1935). *AL*
Driver, G. R. and Miles, J. C.	*The Babylonian Laws* (2 vols., Oxford, 1952/1955). *BL*
Driver, S. R.	*A Treatise on the Use of the Tenses in Hebrew etc.* (3rd edn., Oxford, 1892).
Driver, S. R.	*Deuteronomy*. ICC (Edinburgh, 1895).
Driver, S. R.	*The Book of Genesis* (9th edn., London, 1913).
Driver, S. R.	*An Introduction to the Literature of the OT* (9th edn., Edinburgh, 1913).
Driver, S. R.	*Notes on the Hebrew Text of the Books of Samuel* (2nd edn., Oxford, 1913).
Ehrlich, A. B.	מקרא כפשטו *Miqrâ ki-Pheschutô* vol. 3, H. M. Orlinsky (ed.) Library of Biblical Studies (New York, 1969; first published, Berlin, 1901). *Miq.*
Ehrlich, A. B.	*Randglossen zur Hebräischen Bibel* vol. 5 (Leipzig, 1912). *RG*
Eissfeldt, O.	*Kleine Schriften* (6 vols., Tübingen, 1962–1979). *KS*
Eissfeldt, O.	*Einleitung in das Alte Testament* (3rd edn., Tübingen, 1964); ET, *The Old Testament: An Introduction* (Oxford, 1965).
Eitan, I.	'Biblical Studies I. Philological Studies in Hosea'. *HUCA* 14 (1939), pp. 1–5.
Emerton, J. A.	*Essays in honour of* ; see Day.
Emmerson, G. I.	*Hosea: An Israelite Prophet in Judean Perspective* (Sheffield, 1984).
Eslinger, L. M.	'Hosea 12:5a and Genesis 32:29' *JSOT* 18 (1980), pp. 91–99.
Eusebius	*Onomasticon*, F. Larsow and G. Parthey (edd.), *Eusebii Onomasticon* (Berlin, 1862).

Evenari, M., Shanan, L. and Tadmore, N. *The Negev: The Challenge of a Desert* (2nd edn., Cambridge, Mass. and London, 1982).

Felix, Y. פליקס, י. עולם הצומח המקראי (Tel-Aviv, 1957).

Finkelstein, L. *Siphrê on Deuteronomy* (Berlin, 1939; reprinted New York, 1969).

Fohrer, G. *Die symbolischen Handlungen der Propheten* (Zürich, 1953). *SH*

Fohrer, G. *Geschichte der Israelitischen Religion* (Berlin, 1968); ET, *History of Israelite Religion* (London, 1973). *HIR*

Frey, H. 'Der Aufbau der Gedichte Hoseas' *Wort und Dienst* NF 5 (1957), pp. 9–103.

Friedmann, M. *Sifre debe Rab* (1864, photographically reproduced, Jerusalem, 1962).

Fück, J. 'Hosea Kapitel 3' *ZAW* 39 (1921), pp. 283–290.

Galling, K. (ed.) *Biblisches Reallexikon* (Tübingen, 1937). *Bibl. Real.*

Gardner, W. R. W. 'Notes on certain passages in Hosea' *AJSL* 18 (1902), pp. 178–183.

Garr, W. Randall *Dialect Geography of Syria-Palestine, 1000–586 BCE* (Philadelphia, 1965).

Gaster, T. H. *Anniversary Volume*; see Schindler.

Gelston, A. 'Kingship in the Book of Hosea' *OTS* 19 (1974), pp. 71–85.

Gelston, A. *The Peshiṭta of the Twelve Prophets* (Oxford, 1987).

Gertner, M. 'An attempt at an interpretation of Hosea xii' *VT* 10 (1960), pp. 272–284.

Gesenius, W. and Buhl, F. *Hebräisches und Aramäisches Handwörterbuch über das AT* (16th edn. Leipzig, 1915).

Gesenius-Kautzsch — *Gesenius' Hebrew Grammar*, E. Kautzsch and A. E. Cowley (edd.) (2nd edn., Oxford, 1910). GK

Geus, C. H. J. de — *The Tribes of Israel* (Assen and Amsterdam, 1976).

Gibson, J. C. L. — *Canaanite Myths and Legends* (2nd edn., Edinburgh, 1978); see Driver for 1st edn. *CML*

Giesebrecht, F. — *Beiträge zur Jesaiakritik* (Göttingen, 1890).

Ginsberg, H. L. — 'Studies in Hosea 1–3' in *Kaufmann Jubilee Volume*, pp. 50–69.

Ginsberg, H. L. — 'The Omrid-Davidid Alliance and its Consequences' in *Fourth World Congress of Jewish Studies, Papers*. vol. 1 (Jerusalem, 1967), pp. 92–93.

Glueck, N. — *Essays in honor of* ; see Sanders.

Goldschmidt, L. — *Der Babylonische Talmud* (9 vols., Berlin, 1897–1935).

Gordis, R. — 'Hosea's Marriage and Message' *HUCA* 25 (1954), pp. 9–35.

Gordis, R. — 'The Text and Meaning of Hosea xiv 3' *VT* 5 (1955), pp. 89–90.

Gordon, C. H. — *Ugaritic Grammar* (Rome,1940). *UG*

Gordon, C. H. — *Ugaritic Handbook* (Rome, 1947). *UH*

Gordon, C. H. — *Introduction to OT Times* (Ventnor, 1953). *IOTT*

Gordon, C. H. — *Ugaritic Textbook* (Rome, 1965). *UT*

Gordon, R. P. — *Studies in the Targum to the Twelve Prophets*. SVT 51 (Leiden, New York and Cologne, 1994).

Gottwald, N. K. — *All the Kingdoms of the Earth* (New York, 1964).

Grätz, H. — *Emendationes in plerosque sacrae scripturae VT libros* (Breslau, 1893).

Grätz, H. *Geschichte der Juden* vol. 2, 1 (1st and 2nd ednn., Leipzig, 1875, 1902).

Gray, J. *I and II Kings*. OT Library (2nd edn., London, 1970).

Greenfield, J. 'Aramaic *hnṣl* and some Biblical Passages' in I. Seybold (ed.) *Meqor Hajjim. Festschrift G. Molin* (Graz, 1983), pp. 115–119.

Gressmann, H. *Altorientalische Bilder zum AT* (2nd edn., Berlin, Leipzig, 1927). *AOB*

Gressmann, H. *Der Messias* (Göttingen, 1929).

Gröndahl, F. *Die Personennamen der Texte aus Ugarit* (Rome, 1967).

Gruber, M. I. 'The *qādēš* in the Book of Kings and in Other Sources' *Tarbiz* 52 (1982–83), pp. 167–176.

Gruber, M. I. 'Hebrew *Qᵉdēšāh* and her Canaanite and Akkadian Cognates' *UF* 18 (1986), pp. 133–148.

Guillaume, A. 'Hebrew and Arabic Lexicography' *Abr-Nahrain* I (1959–60), pp. 1–35; II (1960–61), pp. 5–35; III (1961–62), pp. 1–10.

Gunkel, H. *Die Psalmen* (5th edn., Göttingen, 1968).

Halévy, J. 'Le livre d'Osée' *RS* 10 (1902), pp. 1–12, 97–133, 193–212, 289–304.

Haran, M. (ed.) *Y. Kaufmann Jubilee Volume* (Jerusalem and New York, 1960).

Hatch, E. and Redpath, H. A. *A Concordance to the Septuagint* (2 vols., Oxford, 1897).

Hengstenberg, E. W. *Die Christologie des AT* vol. 3 (Berlin, 1835).

Herdner, A. *Corpus des tablettes en cunéiformes alphabétiques découvertes à Ras Shamra-Ugarit* (Paris, 1963). *CTA*

Herrmann, S. *Herrmann Festschrift*; see Liwak.

Hölscher, G.	*Die Profeten* (Leipzig, 1914).
Holladay, W. L.	*The root šûbh in the Old Testament* (Leiden, 1958).
Holladay, W. L.	'Chiasmus, the key to Hosea xii 3–6' *VT* 16 (1966), pp. 53–64.
Horovitz, H. S.	*Sifre Numbers* (Leipzig, 1917; revised edn., Jerusalem, 1966).
Houtsma, M. T.	'Bijdrage tot de kritiek en verklaring van Hosea' *ThT* 9 (1875), pp. 55–75.
Hultsch, F.	*Griechische und Römische Metrologie* (Berlin, 1862).
Hvidberg, F. F.	*Weeping and Laughter in the OT* (Leiden, 1962).
Janssen, E.	*Judah in Exilzeit*. FRLANT 69 (Göttingen, 1956).
Jastrow, M.	*A Dictionary of the Targumim, the Talmud Babli and Yerushalmi, and the Midrashic Literature* (2 vols., New York, 1950; first published 1903).
Jepsen, A.	'Zur Chronologie des Könige von Israel und Juda' BZAW 88 (1964), pp. 1–47.
Johnson, A. R.	*The Cultic Prophet in Ancient Israel* (2nd edn., Cardiff, 1962).
Jones, G. H.	*1 and 2 Kings*. New Century Bible Commentary (London and Grand Rapids, 1988).
Junker, H. and Botterweck, J.	*AT Studien Friedrich Nötscher gewidmet* (Bonn, 1950).
Kahle, P. E.	*The Cairo Genizah* (2nd edn., Oxford, 1959).
Kallai, Z.	*The Historical Geography of the Bible* (Jerusalem, 1986). *HGB*
Kallai, Z.	'Beth-el–Luz and Beth-aven' in *Herrmann Festschrift*, pp. 171–188. *Bethaven*

Kaufmann, Y. — *Kaufmann Jubilee Volume*; see Haran.

Kitchen, K. A. — *The Third Intermediate Period in Egypt* (Warminster, 1973).

Kittel, G. and Friedrich, G. (edd.) — *Theologisches Wörterbuch zum NT* (Stuttgart, 1933–78); ET, *Theological Dictionary of the NT* (trans. G. W. Bromiley, Grand Rapids, 1964–76). *TDNT*

Kittel, R. — *Die Bücher der Könige*. HAT (Göttingen, 1900).

Kittel, R. — *Geschichte des Volkes Israel* vol. 2 (6th edn., Gotha, 1925).

Knudtzon, J. A. — *Die El-Amarna Tafeln* (Leipzig, 1915).

Köhler, L. — *Der Hebräische Mensch* (Tübingen, 1953); ET, *Hebrew Man* (trans. P. R. Ackroyd, London, 1956). *Mensch/Man*

Köhler, L. and Baumgartner, W. — *Lexicon in VT libros* (Leiden, 1953). KB

Köhler, L. and Baumgartner, W. — *Hebräisches und Aramäisches Lexicon zum AT* (3rd edn., Leiden, 1967–96). KB^3

König, E. — *Historisch-kritisches Lehrgebäude (– comparative Syntax) der hebräischen Sprache* (Leipzig, 1897).

König, E. — *Hebräisches und aramäisches Wörterbuch zum AT* (Leipzig, 1910; 7th edn., 1936).

Kraeling, E. G. — *The Brooklyn Museum Aramaic Papyri* (New Haven, 1953).

Kraus, H.-J. — *Gottesdienst in Israel* (Munich, 1962); ET, *Worship in Israel* (Oxford, 1966).

Kuenen, A. — *National Religions and Universal Religion* (London, 1882).

Kuhnigk, W. — *Nordwestsemitische Studien zum Hoseabuch*. Biblica et Orientalia 27 (Rome, 1974).

Kutscher, E. Y.	*The Language and Linguistic Background of the Isaiah Scroll* (Leiden, 1974). *Is.*
Kutscher, E. Y.	*A History of the Hebrew Language* (Jerusalem, 1982).
Lane, E. W.	*An Arabic–English Lexicon* (8 vols., London, 1863–77).
Lemche, N. P.	*The Canaanites and their Land* (Sheffield, 1991).
Liddell, H. G. and Scott, R., revised Jones, H. S.	*A Greek–English Lexicon* (2 vols., Oxford, 1940).
Lindblom, J.	*Hosea, literarisch untersucht* (Åbo, 1927). *HLU*
Lindblom, J.	*Prophecy in Ancient Israel* (Oxford, 1962). *PAI*
Lipschitz, O.	*Hosea – A Classified Bibliography.* Simor Bible Bibliographies (Jerusalem, forthcoming).
Liwak, R. and Wagner, S.	*Prophetie und geschichtliche Wirklichkeit im alten Israel* (Stuttgart, 1991).
Macintosh, A. A.	*Isaiah xxi: A Palimpsest* (Cambridge, 1980).
Macintosh, A. A.	'Hosea and the Wisdom Tradition' in *Essays in Honour of J. A. Emerton*, ed. J. Day et al., pp. 124–132.
Marti, K.	*Festschrift Marti*; see Budde.
Mazar, A.	'The "Bull Site". An Iron Age I Open Cult Place' *BASOR* 247 (1982), pp. 27–40.
McHardy, W. D. and Thomas, D. W. (edd.)	*Hebrew and Semitic Studies presented to Godfrey Rolles Driver* (Oxford, 1963).
McKane, W.	*Proverbs.* OT Library (London, 1970).
McKane, W.	*Jeremiah* vol. 1 ICC (Edinburgh, 1986).

McKenzie, J. L. 'Divine Passion in Osee' *CBQ* 17 (1955), pp. 287–299.

McKenzie, S. L. 'The Jacob Tradition in Hosea xii 4–5' *VT* 36 (1986), pp. 311–322.

Meinhold, J. *Studien zur israelitischen Religionsgeschichte* (Bonn, 1963).

Michaelis, J. D. *Supplementa ad Lexica Hebraica* (Göttingen, 1792).

Miller, J. M. 'The Fall of the House of Ahab' *VT* 17 (1967), pp. 307–324.

Moor, J. C. de *The Seasonal Pattern in the Ugaritic Myth of Ba'lu*. AOAT 16 (Neukirchen-Vluyn, 1971).

Morag, S. לשאלת ייחוד לשונו של הושע *Tarbiz* 53 (1984), pp. 489–511.

Muraoka, T. הערות על תרגום השבעים לספר הושע in Ch. Rabin et al. (edd.) *Studies in the Bible and the Hebrew Language offered to M. Wallenstein* (Jerusalem, 1979)[1].

Muraoka, T. 'Hosea iv in the Septuagint Version' *AJBI* 9 (1983), pp. 24–64.

Muraoka, T. 'Hosea v in the Septuagint Version' *Abr-Nahrain* 24 (1986), pp. 120–138.

Muraoka, T. and Shavitsky, Z. 'Abraham Ibn Ezra's Biblical Hebrew Lexicon: The Minor Prophets I' *Abr-Nahrain* 28 (1990), pp. 53–75 and II 29 (1991), pp. 106–128.

Neef, H.-D. 'Der Septuaginta-Text und der Masoreten-Text des Hoseabuches im Vergleich' *Biblica* 67 (1986), pp. 195–220.

Neher, A. *L'essence du prophétisme* (Paris, 1955).

Neubauer, A. *The Book of the Hebrew Roots* (Oxford, 1875).

[1] The article concerns Hos 2 only.

Nicholson, E. W. *Jeremiah 1–25*. The Cambridge Bible Commentary (Cambridge, 1973).

Nicholson, E. W. *God and His People* (Oxford, 1986). *GP*

Nötscher, F. *Nötscher Festschrift*; see Junker.

Noth, M. *Die israelitischen Personennamen im Rahmen der gemeinsemitischen Namengebung*. BWANT 46 (Stuttgart, 1928). *Pers.*

Noth, M. *Überlieferungsgeschichte des Pentateuch* (Darmstadt, 1928); ET, *A History of Pentateuchal Traditions* (Eaglewood Cliffs, 1972). *UP*

Noth, M. *Die Welt des AT* (3rd edn., Berlin, 1957); ET, *The OT World* (Philadelphia, 1966). *WAT*

Noth, M. *Geschichte Israels* (4th edn., Göttingen, 1959). *GI*; ET, *The History of Israel* (2nd edn., London and New York, 1958). *History*

Noth, M. *Das zweite Buch Mose, Exodus*. ATD 5 (Göttingen, 1959); ET, *Exodus*. OT Library (London, 1962).

Noth, M. *Das dritte Buch Mose, Leviticus*. ATD 6 (Göttingen, 1962); ET, *Leviticus*. OT Library (London, 1977).

Nyberg, H. *Studien zum Hoseabuche* (Uppsala, 1935).

Östborn, G. 'Yahweh and Baal' *LUÅ* NF 1, 51.6 (1956).

Oesterley, W. E. O. 'The Old Latin Texts of the Minor Prophets' *JTS* 5 (1904), pp. 76–88.

Oettli, A. *Amos und Hosea. Zwei Zeugen gegen die Anwendung der Evolutionstheorie und die Religion Israels*. BFChrTh 4 (Gütersloh, 1901).

Oort, H. *Textus hebraici emendationes* (Leiden, 1900). *Em*

Otzen, B. *Studien über Deuterosacharja* (Copenhagen, 1964).

Patterson, G. H. 'The Septuagint Text of Hosea compared with the MT' *Hebraica* 7 (1890–91), pp. 190–221.

Paul, S. M. 'The image of the oven and the cake in Hosea vii' *VT* 18 (1968), pp. 114–120.

Payne Smith, R. *Thesaurus Syriacus* (Oxford, 1879–1901).

Pedersen, J. *Israel: its Life and Culture* vols. 3–4 (London and Copenhagen, 1959).

Perles, F. *Analekten zur Textkritik des AT* (Munich, 1895).

Perlitt, L. *Bundestheologie im AT*. WMANT 36 (Neukirchen-Vluyn, 1969).

Pritchard, J. B. *Ancient Near Eastern Texts relating to the OT* (3rd edn., Princeton, N.J., 1969). *ANET*

Rabin, Ch. לשנם של הושע ועמוס in B. Z. Luria (ed.) איונים בספר תרי־עשר (Jerusalem, 1981), pp. 115–132.

Rad, G. von *Die Theologie des AT* (2 vols., Munich, 1957); ET, *OT Theology* (2 vols., London and Edinburgh, 1962).

Rendsburg, G. A. *Linguistic Evidence for the Northern Origin of selected Psalms* (Atlanta, 1990).

Richter, G. *Erläuterungen zu dunkeln Stellen in den kleinen Propheten*. BFChrTh 18 (Gütersloh, 1914), pp. 3–4.

Riedel, W. *AT Untersuchungen* (Leipzig, 1902).

Robertson Smith, W. *The Religion of the Semites* (London, 1889).

Robinson, H. W. *Two Hebrew Prophets* (London, 1948).

Rofé, A. 'The vineyard of Naboth: the origin and message of the story' *VT* 38 (1988), pp. 89–104.

Rowley, H. H. — 'The Marriage of Hosea' *BJRL* 39 (1956), pp. 200–233 = *Men of God* (London and Edinburgh, 1963), pp. 66–97. *MG*

Rowley, H. H. (ed.) — *Studies in Old Testament Prophecy presented to T. H. Robinson* (Edinburgh, 1950).

Ruben, P. — *Critical Remarks upon some Passages of the OT* (London, 1896).

Rudolph, W. — *Chronikbücher*. HAT i/21 (Tübingen, 1955).

Rudolph, W. — *Jeremia*. HAT 12 (2nd and 3rd ednn., Tübingen, 1958, 1968).

Rudolph, W. — *Joel, Amos etc.* BKAT xiii 2 (Gütersloh, 1971).

Rykmanns, G. R. — *Les noms propres sud-sémitiques* 1/3 (Löwen, 1934–5).

Sanders, J. A. (ed.) — *Essays in honor of Nelson Glueck* (Garden City, New York, 1970).

Schärf, R. R. — *Die Gestalt des Satans im AT* (Zürich, 1948).

Schindler, B. and Marmorstein, A. (edd.) — *Occident and Orient. Gaster Anniversary Volume* (London, 1936).

Schleusner, J. F. — *Opuscula critica ad versiones Graecas VT pertinentes* (Leipzig, 1812).

Schmoller, O. — *Die Propheten Hosea, Joel und Amos* (Leipzig, 1872).

Schroeder, N. G. — *Observationes selectae ad origines Hebraeas* (Groningen, 1762).

Schultens, A. — *Animadvertiones philologicae et criticae ad varia loca VT* (Leiden, 1769).

Schunck, K.-D. — *Benjamin*. BZAW 86 (Berlin, 1963).

Sebök, M. — *Die syrische Übersetzung der zwölf kleinen Propheten* (Breslau, 1887).

Sellin, E. *Sellin Festschrift*; see Albright et al.

Seow, C. L. 'Hosea 14.10 and the Foolish People Motif' *CBQ* 44 (1982), pp. 212–224.

Simons, J. *The Geographical and Topographical Texts of the OT* (Leiden, 1959).

Smolar, L. and Aberbach, M. *Studies in Targum Jonathan to the Prophets* (New York, 1983).

Soggin, J. A. *Judges*. OT Library (London, 1981).

Soggin, J. A. *Storia d'Israele* (Brescia, 1985); ET, *A History of Israel* (London, 1984). *H*

Strugnell, J. 'Notes en marge du vol. V des "Discoveries in the Judaean Desert"' *RQ* 26 (1970), pp. 163–276.

Theis, J. *Sumerisches im AT* (Trier, 1912).

Thomas, D. W. *Documents from OT Times* (Edinburgh and London, 1958). *DOTT*

Thomas, D. W. *Archaeology and OT Study* (Oxford, 1967). *AOTS*

Thomas, D. W. *Essays presented to*; see Ackroyd.

Torczyner, N. H. *The Lachish Letters* (London and Oxford, 1938).

Tov, E. *The Text-Critical Use of the Septuagint in Biblical Research* (Jerusalem, 1981).

Treitel, L. 'Die Septuaginta zu Hosea' *MGWJ* 41 (1897), pp. 433–454.

Tur-Sinai, N. H. (=Torczyner) *The Book of Job* (Jerusalem, 1957).

Tur-Sinai, N. H. הלשון והספר (3 vols., Jerusalem, 1948–1955). *LS*

Tushingham, A. D. 'A Reconsideration of Hosea Chapters 1–3' *JNES* 12 (1953), pp. 150–159.

Ubach, B. *Miscellanea Biblica* (Montserrat, 1953).

Ussishkin, D. and Woodhead, J. 'Excavations at Tel Jezreel 1990–91', *Tel Aviv* 19 (1992), pp. 3–53.

Vaux, R. de	*Les institutions de l'Ancien Testament* (2 vols., Paris, 1958–60). *IAT*; ET, *Ancient Israel: its Life and Institutions* (London, 1961). *IAI*
Vaux, R. de	*Histoire ancienne d'Israël* (2 vols., Paris, 1971–73). *HAI*; ET, *The Early History of Israel* (London, 1978). *EHI*
Vilnay, Z.	*The Guide to Israel* (23rd edn., Jerusalem, 1984).
Vollers, K.	'Das Dodekapropheton der Alexandriner' *ZAW* 3 (1883), pp. 219–272; 4 (1884), pp. 1–20.
Volz, P.	*Die vorexilische Jahweprophetie und der Messias* (Göttingen, 1897).
Vriezen, Th. C.	*Hosea: profeet en cultuur* (Groningen, 1941).
Wechter, P.	*Ibn Barūn's Arabic works on Hebrew Grammar and Lexicography* (Philadelphia, 1964).
Wehr, H., and Cowan, J. M. (edd.)	*A Dictionary of Modern Written Arabic* (Wiesbaden, 1979).
Wellhausen, J.	*Prolegomena zur Geschichte Israels* (Berlin, 1883).
Wenning, R. and Zenger, E.	'Ein bäuerliches Baal-Heiligtum im samarischen Gebirge aus der Zeit der Anfänge Israels' *ZDPV* 102 (1986), pp. 75–86.
Westermann, C.	*Genesis*. BKAT I/1–3 (3 vols., Neukirchen-Vluyn, 1974–1982).
Wevers, J. W.	*Ezekiel*. New Century Bible Commentary (London, 1969).
Wickes, W.	*A Treatise on the Accentuation of the Twenty-One so-called Prose Books of the OT* (Oxford, 1887).
Williams, R. J.	*Hebrew Syntax: An Outline* (Toronto, 1967).

Williamson, H. G. M. — *Israel in the Books of Chronicles* (Cambridge, 1977). *IBC*

Williamson, H. G. M. — *1 and 2 Chronicles*. New Century Bible Commentary (London and Grand Rapids, 1982).

Williamson, H. G. M. — *Ezra and Nehemiah*. OT Guides (Sheffield, 1987).

Williamson, H. G. M. — 'Jezreel in the Biblical Texts' *Tel Aviv* 18 (1991), pp. 72–92.

Williamson, H. G. M. — 'Tel Jezreel and the Dynasty of Omri' *PEQ* 128 (1996), pp. 41–51.

Winckler, H. — *Alttestamentliche Untersuchungen* (Leipzig, 1892).

Wolff, H. W. — 'Der grosse Jesreeltag' *EvTh* 12 (1952–53), pp. 78–104, reprinted in *Gesammelte Studien zum AT* (Munich, 1964), pp. 151–181.

Wutz, F. X. — *Die Transkriptionen von der Septuaginta bis zu Hieronymus. Beiträge zur Wissenschaft vom AT* NF 9 (2 Lieferungen. Berlin, Stuttgart and Leipzig, 1925–33).

Yadin, Y., Lewis, N. and Greenfield, J. C. (edd.) — *The Documents from the Bar Kokhba Period in the Cave of Letters* (Jerusalem, 1989).

Ziegler, J. — 'Beiträge zum griechischen Dodekapropheton' *Nachrichten von der Akademie der Wissenschaften in Göttingen* (Nr. 10, Göttingen, 1943), pp. 345–412, reprinted in *idem, Sylloge. Gesammelte Aufsätze zur Septuaginta* (Göttingen, 1971), pp. 71–138. *Bei.*

Ziegler, J. — 'Studien zur Verwertung der Septuaginta im Zwölfprophetenbuch' *ZAW* 60 (1944), pp. 107–131.

Zimmerli, W. *Ezechiel.* BKAT 13 (2 vols., Neukirchen-Vluyn, 1969); ET, *Ezekiel.* Hermeneia – A Critical and Historical Commentary on the Bible (2 vols., Philadelphia, 1979–83).

Zimmerli, W. 'Ich bin Yahweh' in *Gottes Offenbarung* (Munich, 1969); ET, *I am Yahweh* (Atlanta, 1982). *IBY/IAY*

Zobel, H.-J. *Stammesspruch und Geschichte.* BZAW 95 (Berlin, 1965).

EDITIONS CITED

THE (HEBREW) MASSORETIC TEXT

Alt, A. and Eissfeldt, O. (edd.) — *Biblia Hebraica* (3rd edn., Stuttgart, 1937). *BH*

Elliger, K. and Rudolph, W. (edd.) — *Biblia Hebraica Stuttgartensia* (Stuttgart, 1977). *BHS*

Kennicott, B. (ed.) — *VT Hebraicum cum variis lectionibus* (2 vols., Oxford, 1776–80).

Rossi, G. B. de — *Variae lectiones VT* (Parmae, 1784–99).

THE DEAD SEA SCROLLS

Specimens of Cave 4 Hosea fragments can currently be viewed on the Internet. Graphics browsers can be directed at http://sunsite.unc.edu/expo/deadsea.scrolls.exhibit/intro.html.

Allegro, J. M. — *Qumrân Cave 4 I (4Q158–4Q186)* (Oxford, 1968). *DJD* 5; cf. Strugnell, J. 'Notes en marge du vol. V des "Discoveries in the Judaean Desert"' *RQ* 26 (1970), pp. 163–276.

Benoit, P., Milik, J. T. and Vaux, R. de — *Les Grottes de Murabba'ât* (Oxford, 1961). *DJD* 2

Fuller, R. E. — 'A Critical Note on Hos. 12:10 and 13:4' *RB* 98 (1991), pp. 341–357. (4QXII^{c})

Sinclair, L. A. — 'A Qumran Biblical Fragment. Hos. 1:7–2:5' *BASOR* 239 (1980), pp. 61–65. (4QXII^{d})

Testuz, M. — 'Deux fragments inédits des manuscripts de la Mer Morte' *Semitica* 5 (1955), pp. 37–38. (4QXII? = 4QXII^{c})

Tov, E. — *The Greek Minor Prophets' Scroll from Naḥal Ḥever* (Oxford, 1990). (8ḤevXIIgr) *DJD* 8

Zeitlin, S. — *The Zadokite Fragments: Facsimile of the MSS in the Cairo Genizah Collection in the possession of the University Library, Cambridge, England* (Philadelphia, 1952). *CD*

THE LXX

Swete, H. B. — *An Introduction to the OT in Greek* (2nd edn., Cambridge, 1902).

Swete, H. B. (ed.) — *The OT in Greek according to the Septuagint* vol. 3 (Cambridge, 1912).

Ziegler, J. (ed.) — *Duodecim Prophetae* (2nd edn., Göttingen, 1967).

THE MINOR GREEK VERSIONS (AQUILA, THEODOTION, SYMMACHUS AND QUINTA)

Field, F. — *Origenis Hexaplorum quae supersunt* vol. 2 (Oxford, 1867).

THE VULGATE

Weber, R. et al. (edd.) — *Biblia Sacra iuxta Vulgatam Versionem* vol. 2 (Stuttgart, 1969; 2nd edn. 1975).

THE TARGUM

Sperber, A. (ed.) — *The Bible in Aramaic etc.: The Latter Prophets* vol. 3 (Leiden, 1962; 2nd edn. 1975). See also Cathcart under 'Other Works Cited'.

THE PESHIṬTA

Gelston, A. (ed.)	*Vetus Testamentum Syriace* III 4 (Leiden, 1980). See also Gelston under 'Other Works Cited'.
Gelston, A.	in Dirksen, P. B. and Mulder, M. J. *The Peshiṭta: its early text and history* (Leiden, New York, Copenhagen and Cologne, 1988), pp. 267–269, 290–292.

TALMUD

Goldschmidt, L.	*Der Babylonische Talmud* (9 vols., Berlin, 1897–1935).
The Babylonian Talmud translated into English	ed. I. Epstein (Soncino, London, 1938–1961).
Jerusalem/Palestinian	תלמוד ירושלמי (Krotoshin, 1866; photographically reproduced, Jerusalem, 1969).
Schwab, M.	*Le Talmud de Jérusalem* vol. 7 (Paris, 1885).

MIDRASH

	מדרש רבה Section 2 (Exodus–Deuteronomy) (Vilna 1878).

RABBINIC AUTHORITIES AND COMMENTARIES CITED

Abarbanel, R. Isaac (15th Cent.)	פירוש על הנביאים האחרונים (Amsterdam, 1641).

Eliezer, R., of Beaugency (12th Cent.), S. Poznanski (ed.)	*Kommentar zu Ezechiel und den xii kleinen Propheten* vol. 2 (Warsaw, 1910).
Ibn Barun, R. Abu Ibrahim Isḥaḳ (11th–12th Cents.)	See Wechter under 'Other Works Cited'.
Ibn Ezra, R. Abraham (11th–12th Cents.)	מקראות גדולות (Warsaw, 1860–69).
Ibn Janaḥ, R. Jonah Abu 'l-Walīd Marwan (10th–11th Cents.)	See Neubauer under 'Other Works Cited'.
Kimchi, R. David (12th–13th Cents.)	מקראות גדולות (Warsaw, 1860–69).
Metsudat Zion = R. Yehiel ben David Altschul (mid–17th Cent.)	מקראות גדולות (Warsaw, 1860–69).
Nachmanides = R. Moses ben Nahman, Gerondi (12th–13th Cents.)	C. B. Chavel (ed.) *Commentary on the Torah* vol. 1 (Jerusalem, 1959).
Rashi, R. Solomon ben Isaac (11th–12th Cents.)	מקראות גדולות (Warsaw, 1860–69).
Saadya, ben Joseph al-Fayyumi ('ha-Gaon') (9th–10th Cents.)	His comments on Hosea survive only in quotations by other rabbinic commentators, notably Kimchi.

ABBREVIATIONS

AAM	A. A. Macintosh
AASOR	See *BASOR*
AF	See Andersen and Freedman under 'Commentaries Cited'
AJBA	*Australian Journal of Biblical Archaeology*
AJBI	*Annual of the Japanese Biblical Institute*
AJSL	*American Journal of Semitic Languages and Literatures*
ANET	See Pritchard under 'Other Works Cited'
AO	*Archiv für Orientforschung*
AOAT	Alter Orient und AT; see (1) de Moor, (2) Dietrich, (3) Caquot/Delcor, (4) Caquot/Légasse/Tardieu under 'Other Works Cited'
AOB	See Gressmann under 'Other Works Cited'
Aq.	Aquila; see Field under 'Editions Cited – Minor Greek Versions'
ARW	*Archiv für Religionswissenschaft*
ASB	The Alternative Service Book 1980 (translation of the Psalms)
ATD	Das Alte Testament Deutsch
AUS	See Dalman under 'Other Works Cited'
AV	The Authorized (King James) Version of the Bible
B/AASOR	*Bulletin/Annual of the American Schools of Oriental Research*
BDB	See Brown under 'Other Works Cited'
BFChrTh	Beiträge zur Förderung Christlicher Theologie
BH	*Biblia Hebraica*; see 'Editions Cited – Hebrew Text'

BHS	*Biblia Hebraica Stuttgartensia*; see 'Editions Cited – Hebrew Text'
Bibl. Real.	See Galling under 'Other Works Cited'
BJRL	*Bulletin of the John Rylands Library*
BKAT	Biblischer Kommentar Altes Testament
BL	See Bauer under 'Other Works Cited'
BO	*Bibliotheca Orientalis*
BWANT	Beiträge zur Wissenschaft vom AT und NT
BZ	*Biblische Zeitschrift*
BZAW	Beihefte zur *ZAW*
CAD	*Chicago Assyrian Dictionary*
CBQ	*Catholic Biblical Quarterly*
CC	*Corpus Christianorum*
CD	See Zeitlin under 'Editions Cited – Dead Sea Scrolls'
CHB	*The Cambridge History of the Bible*; see Ackroyd under 'Other Works Cited'
CTA	See Herdner under 'Other Works Cited'
DJD	See Allegro (*DJD* 5), Benoit (*DJD* 2) and Tov (*DJD* 8) under 'Editions Cited – Dead Sea Scrolls'
ETL	*Ephemerides Theologicae Lovanienses*
EV	English version(s)
EvTh	*Evangelische Theologie*
ExpT	*Expository Times*
FRLANT	Forschungen zur Religion und Literatur des AT und NT
GK	See Gesenius-Kautzsch under 'Other Works Cited'
HAT	Handkommentar zum AT
HDB	*Hastings' Dictionary of the Bible*
HSAT	Die heilige Schrift des AT
HUCA	*Hebrew Union College Annual*
JAOS	*Journal of the American Oriental Society*

JBL	*Journal of Biblical Literature*
JJS	*Journal of Jewish Studies*
JNES	*Journal of Near Eastern Studies*
JQR	*Jewish Quarterly Review*
JPOS	*Journal of the Palestine Oriental Society*
JSOT	*Journal for the Study of the Old Testament*
JSS	*Journal of Semitic Studies*
JTS	*Journal of Theological Studies*
KAT	Kommentar zum AT
KB	See Köhler under 'Other Works Cited'
KHAT	Kurzer Handcommentar zum AT
KTU	See Dietrich under 'Other Works Cited'
LUÅ	*Lund Universitets Årsskrift*
LXX	The Septuagint; see Swete and Ziegler under 'Editions Cited – The LXX'
LXX[Luc]	The Lucianic recension of the LXX; see Ziegler, pp. 70–89, under 'Editions Cited – The LXX'
MGWJ	*Monatsschrift für Geschichte und Wissenschaft des Judentums*
NAG	*Nachrichten der Akademie der Wissenschaften in Göttingen*
NEB	The New English Bible
NJPS	The Prophets. A New Translation of the Holy Scriptures according to the Masoretic Text (Jewish Publication Society, Philadelphia, 1978)
NT	*Novum Testamentum*
NThT	*Nederlands Theologisch Tijdschrift*
OBL	*Orientalia et Biblica Lovaniensia*
OL	Vetus Latina or Old Latin translation of the LXX
OLZ	*Orientalistische Literaturzeitung*
OTS	*Oudtestamentische Studien*

PEQ	*Palestine Exploration Quarterly*
Pesh.	Peshiṭta; see Gelston under 'Editions Cited – Peshiṭta'
PJ	*Palästinajahrbuch*
PL	*Patrologiae Latinae*; see Jerome under 'Commentaries Cited'
QIs[a]	4QIs[a]; see Allegro under 'Editions Cited – Dead Sea Scrolls'
RB	*Revue Biblique*
RE	*Realencyklopädie für protestantische Theologie und Kirche* (3rd edn., 24 vols., Leipzig, 1896–1913)
REB	The Revised English Bible
REJ	*Revue des études juives*
RGG	*Die Religion in Geschichte und Gegenwart* (3rd edn., Tübingen, 1957–1965)
RHPhR	*Revue d'histoire et de philosophie religieuses*
RQ	*Revue de Qumran*
RS	*Revue sémitique*
RSO	*Revista degli Studi Orientali*
RSV	The Revised Standard Version of the Bible
RV	The Revised Version of the Bible
SDB	*Supplément au dictionnaire de la Bible*
SEL	*Studi Epigrafici e Linguistici*
SH	*Scripta Hierosolymitana*
SJOT	*Scandinavian Journal of the OT*
SVT	Supplements to VT
Symm.	Symmachus; see Field under 'Editions Cited – Minor Greek Versions'
Targ.	The Targum; see Sperber under 'Editions Cited – The Targum'
TDNT	*Theological Dictionary of the NT*; see Kittel under 'Other Works Cited'
ThBl	*Theologische Blätter*

Theod.	Theodotion; see Field under 'Editions Cited – Minor Greek Versions'
ThLZ	*Theologische Literaturzeitung*
ThR	*Theologische Rundschau*
ThT	*Theologisch Tijdschrift*
ThV	*Theologia Viatorum*
ThZ	*Theologische Zeitschrift*
TSK	*Theologische Studien und Kritiken*
UF	*Ugarit-Forschungen*
VT	*Vetus Testamentum*
Vulg.	The Vulgate; see Weber under 'Editions Cited – The Vulgate'
WMANT	Wissenschaftliche Monographien zum Alten und Neuen Testament
WO	*Welt des Orients*
ZAW	*Zeitschrift für die alttestamentliche Wissenschaft*
ZDMG	*Zeitschrift der Deutschen Morgenländischen Gesellschaft*
ZDPV	*Zeitschrift des deutschen Palästina-Vereins*
ZThK	*Zeitschrift für Theologie und Kirche*

INTRODUCTION

THE PLACE OF THE BOOK OF HOSEA IN THE CANON OF SCRIPTURE

According to all witnesses, the 'book' of Hosea comes first in that collection of works which together comprise what was regarded by long tradition (see below) as a single book, *viz.* 'The Twelve Minor Prophets'.

The earliest reference to this book or collection is that in the early second century BC book of Ecclesiasticus (49.10). There Jesus ben Sira, in his 'Praise of the Fathers', after reviewing the work of Isaiah, Jeremiah and Ezekiel, mentions the Twelve Prophets (שנים עשר הנביאים/ ...τῶν δώδεκα προφητῶν) and expresses the hope that their bones may 'send forth new life from the ground where they lie' (NEB).

The MT reflects this same order of arrangement since the book of the Twelve is placed amongst the Latter Prophets immediately following the book of Ezekiel. That this was not universally or always the case is apparent from a number of sources. First, B. *Baba Bathra* 14b (ET, p. 70 in *Neziḳin* II) records that the Rabbis listed the order of the prophets thus: 'Jeremiah, Ezekiel, Isaiah and the Twelve'. The debate with R. Joḥanan recorded in this passage suggests that a number of considerations were deployed by the eastern communities of the diaspora to explain this their tradition. Thus, the order Kings, Jeremiah, Ezekiel and Isaiah reflects a thematic sequence, i.e. from the two first books which proclaimed destruction, to the third which initially proclaimed destruction but ended with comfort; and, finally, to Isaiah, which was understood as a book of undiminished comfort. Again, recognition of the principle of the correct chronological order is clearly reflected in the question posed: why should Isaiah precede Hosea? In answer to that question, there is acknowledgement that Hosea's work was already bound up with the other shorter prophecies some of which (Haggai, Zechariah and Malachi) were chronologically amongst the last of the prophets. The question why the early prophecy of Hosea should have been bound up with these late prophecies is answered by the consideration that, being so short, it could easily have been lost (Aramaic אידא דזוטר מירכיס), i.e. if it had been circulated independently on a short scroll.

Recognition of the chronological priority of Hosea is linked in this same passage to the phrase of Hosea 1.2 תחלת דבר יהוה בהושע, 'the beginning of Yahweh's speaking' and this is interpreted in a relative sense, i.e. amongst the contemporaries Hosea, Isaiah, Amos and Micah, it was to Hosea that the Lord first spoke (cf. Jerome on 1.2). Although the interpretation refers explicitly to the eighth century prophets, it is likely also to reflect the prior place accorded to Hosea in the quite different category of the Twelve or Minor Prophets.

Secondly, while the Vulgate and the Targum reflect (where the prophets are concerned) the same order and arrangement as the MT, the LXX and the Peshiṭta do not. In the LXX the Twelve precede the prophecies of Isaiah, Jeremiah and Ezekiel (but see Swete *Introduction*, p. 227 for א etc.); in the Peshiṭta they appear between Isaiah and Jeremiah. The various considerations advanced in *Baba Bathra* (see above) may give some clue to the reasons behind such variations. Where the order of the prophecies within the Twelve is concerned, the versions agree with the MT except for the LXX, which presents a different order for the first six (*viz.* Hosea, Amos, Micah, Joel, Obadiah and Jonah as against the MT's Hosea, Joel, Amos, Obadiah, Jonah and Micah). In the tradition of the MT the chronological criterion for determining the order of prophecies within the Twelve appears to have been determinative (so Eissfeldt *Introduction*, p. 383; *Einleitung*, p. 517): Hosea, Joel, Amos, Obadiah, Jonah and Micah are reckoned to belong to the second half of the eighth century BC; Nahum, Habakkuk and Zephaniah to the second half of the seventh century BC and Haggai, Zechariah and Malachi to the sixth/fifth centuries BC. In respect of the principle underlying the LXX, the length of the various books appears to have been determinative except that Jonah comes at the end despite being longer than Obadiah, because, being concerned with a narrative about a prophet, it is *sui generis* (cf. *CHB* 1, p. 142).

The date of the compilation of the Twelve is relatively easy to determine. The *terminus ad quem* is the notice of ben Sira quoted above; he is dated at the beginning of the second century BC. The *terminus a quo* is determined by the date of the latest of the component parts of the Twelve. Joel and Zechariah 9–14 cannot be much earlier than *c.* 350 BC. Thus, the compilation or collection together of the Twelve is likely to have taken place during the third century BC.

Continuing recognition of the Twelve as a unit may be inferred from the statement of B. *Megillah* 24a (ET, p. 144 in *Mo'ed* IV) where it is said that, in reading, skipping (מדלגים) from one prophet to another is not permitted, except that in the case of the Twelve it is permitted. Similarly, in the prologue to the Twelve of the Vulgate, Jerome emphasises his view that *unum librum esse duodecim prophetarum.* Christian tradition, e.g. Melito (second century), Athanasius (fourth century) and Epiphanius (fourth century) all speak of the Twelve as *one* book (for references, see Swete *Introduction*, pp. 203ff).

The Aramaic equivalent name for the Twelve (תרי עסר) is attested in *Numbers Rabba* (Vilna edn. 18.21) and it was this rather than the Hebrew title which, in the course of time, became (and remains) prevalent in Jewish circles. In the tradition which depends upon the LXX, the Greek equivalent title οἱ δώδεκα προφῆται is commonly attested (e.g. Melito, Origen, Athanasius), though apparently Epiphanius was the first to use the composite title τὸ Δωδεκαπρόφητον.

The title 'the Minor Prophets', commonly used in modern times, goes back to Augustine (*De civitate dei*, xviii, 29) who explains that the term refers to the small size of the prophecies as compared with those of Isaiah, Jeremiah and Ezekiel. In no way is the title to be taken to mean that these shorter prophecies were of minor importance. The same sentiments are likely to lie behind the prayer enunciated by ben Sira quoted above.

THE LANGUAGE OF HOSEA

The opening words of Jerome's commentary on Hosea aptly characterise the unique difficulties which scholars have universally experienced when faced with his prophecies: 'If in the interpretation of all the prophets we stand in need of the intervention of the Holy Spirit ... how much more should the Lord be invoked in interpreting Hosea and in St. Peter's words should it be said, "Expound for us this parable" (Mt 15.15); more especially is this the case since the author himself wrote at its end, "Whoso is wise, let him understand these things" ... thereby giving a precise indication of the obscurity of the book'.

Whereas the prevailing scholarly view of the first three-quarters of the twentieth century has attributed the difficulties of the book to the 'corrupt state of the text'[1], it now seems likely that they are due rather to our unfamiliarity with the prophet's language and dialect. Since Hosea is the only prophet from the Northern Kingdom whose written words have come down to us, it is not surprising that this should be the case. On this view of the matter

[1] So, e.g., Harper (1905), Rudolph (1966), cf. Mays (1969).

the Massoretic Text may not be as corrupt as was formerly supposed. Rather, it is likely to have preserved faithfully words and expressions which were unfamiliar to its later readers. Indeed, there are reasons for supposing that, even at a relatively early stage, those who received the prophet's words in the Southern Kingdom, and who were destined further to transmit them, experienced at least some difficulty in understanding them.

Yet it is not enough merely to assert that the language of Hosea is dialectal and specifically northern for most of the obvious Shibboleths[2] by which northern dialect is readily identified are strangely absent from Hosea's writings. Thus, and most important, there is not a single instance of the relative particle *š* in place of the familiar *'šr* of Standard Biblical Hebrew[3] (the latter occurs about ten times in the book, cf. Rabin, p. 122). Again, the form *št* 'year' (cf. Aramaic *št'* and contrast the regular *šnh*), so clearly attested in the approximately contemporary Samaria Ostraca, is not mirrored by any comparable form in the book of Hosea.

If, then, there are no immediately obvious indications of a northern dialectal usage, the question arises whether Hosea's words have been the object of standardisation, i.e. the judicious bringing of his words into line with the language of the South by the scribes who received them there (see under Composition, pp. lxx–lxxiv).

The manifest peculiarities of Hosea's language seem to preclude any such possibility, for it cannot be said that there is in this respect any marked affinity between his words and the language of Judah or a later standardised biblical Hebrew. Rather, the reader has the impression that the language of the book in its very peculiarity accurately represents something of the prophet's own creation. This assessment would seem to find confirmation in the existence within the text of some ten early glosses[4] whose function was to translate or otherwise to elucidate certain particularly difficult words or expressions (see p. lvii below). Standardisation of the language on the one hand and provision of glosses on the other are mutually inconsistent

[2] There are no instances in Hosea of *s* replacing *š* in accordance with what appears *prima facie* to be Ephraimite usage as depicted in Judges 12. In any case the theory that proto-semitic *ṯ* underlies the phoneme in question has been discounted by Kutscher (p. 15). The phenomenon is likely to be a matter of phonology or pronunciation, cf. Emerton *Delcor Festschrift*, pp. 149–157.

[3] For the concept 'Standard Biblical Hebrew', see Kutscher, pp. 12ff.

[4] For a treatment of the phenomenon in general, see G. R. Driver 'Glosses' (1957).

activities. Since the text shows clear evidence of the latter we may safely discount any wholesale deployment of the former.

If the text shows no evidence of consistent standardisation on the one hand and if, on the other, there are no obvious Shibboleths which indicate northern dialect, the language of Hosea, being both intelligible (for there are only approximately ten explanatory glosses) and difficult (for the evidence of the same glosses is present none the less), must be defined in a way which on the one hand avoids understanding it as mere 'Samaritan slang' (Rabin's term) and on the other as a work very largely shaped by later editors and scribes.

The truth would seem to lie in the supposition that the book of Hosea represents a literary work[5] which was more or less complete before it went south to Judah following the fall of Samaria. It is cast in a language in general not so different from that of Judah and Jerusalem, the language which was to become Standard Biblical Hebrew. At the same time the work has clearly not been revised to conform to that language and the general uniformity throughout the book, particularly of style and vocabulary, suggests that much of it accurately represents of the language of the prophet himself, an authentic literary language of the North which contained elements discernibly different from that of Jerusalem and the South.

Transmission of Hosea's prophecies through Judah has naturally left some mark on the language and text. Apart from the addition of the translational glosses, the influence is probably to be detected rather in phonology and morphology than in vocabulary (cf. Morag, p. 491). It may be assumed, for example, that the monosyllabic *yodh* with *tsere*, attested by the Samaria Ostraca, cf. Amos 8.5, was replaced by the diphthong *pataḥ* and *ḥireq* with *yodh*, typical of Judaean speech[6]. Again that two forms of the infinitive absolute of the same verb are found in 4.2 (*'lh*)[7] and 10.4 (*'lwt*) suggests that in the latter case the form may have been modified to approximate more closely to the Judaean infinitive construct. Here, as in the case of the

[5] The vexed problem of the connection between the spoken words of a prophet and the written record of them is well described by M. Haran, *apud* Rabin, pp. 130f. Cf. also H. M. Barstad *JSOT* 57 (1993), pp. 58f.

[6] Cf. Kutscher, p. 66; *yayin* (south) and *yēn* (north) is the standard example. The name Ephraim (not Ephrēm) may be a case in point; the name Diblayim (1.3), though it is unlikely ever to have been Diblēm, may represent the southern predilection for this sound (cf. the familiar Yerušā*lēm*/Yerušā*layim*) which in turn rendered possible the Judaean interpretation of the name in terms of the dual Israel and Judah (see p. 13 below).

[7] For another form in *h*, not standardised, cf. *'śh* in Ps 101.3.

translational glosses where the distribution is also uneven, there is no evidence of rigid consistency and, for example, the more radically dialectal form of the infinitive construct of a verb *lamedh yodh* (i.e. in *yodh*) occurring in 6.9 appears to have escaped alteration or else was not correctly understood.

The clearest evidence for the dialectal character of the language of Hosea is to be found in his vocabulary. There are, however, a number of other elements which point in this direction and it is convenient to mention them first: (1) Of the variant forms of the infinitive, see above. (2) The tendency for *Hiphil/Yiphil* forms to appear where *Qal* forms are found in Standard Biblical Hebrew; e.g. in 4.10, 18; 7.5, 12; 8.9f and 11.4. For further details and for reference to Morag's treatment of the phenomenon, see on 8.9 below. (3) An instance of a *Pe'al'al* form but with the additional repetition of the third plural ending in 4.18 (*'hbwhbw*), together with similar reduplicated forms such as *šbbym* in 8.6 and *znwnym* in 1.2, 2.4 (EV 2) and *n'pwpyh* in 2.4 (EV 2), the latter terms reflecting Hosea's predilection for emphatic or intensive forms when speaking of love and sexual intercourse; cf. Morag, pp. 498ff. (4) Examples of peculiarities of syntax may be cited as follows: a predilection for asyndeton, see 4.7, 18; 5.3, 6, 10; 6.10; 7.12, 16; 9.6, 9, 15; 10.1, 2, 11;14.4f; cf. S. R. Driver *Introduction*, p. 306, and, for the possibility that the phenomenon was a particular feature of Aramaic, Rabin, p. 126[8]. Secondly, the particular and succinct construction of comparative clauses in 4.7; 10.1 and 11.2, cf. Morag, p. 490. Thirdly, the use of *'th* 'now' asyndetically to introduce punishment as inevitable in a particular situation, see 4.16; 5.7; 8.8, 13; 10.2; cf. Driver, loc. cit. Fourthly, the repetition of the verb in rhetorical style in 2.4, 23 (EV 2, 21); 9.7; for a comparison with a similar usage in spoken Arabic, cf. Rabin, p. 126. Fifthly, the use of the negative *bly*, cf. *bl*, familiar from Phoenician, in compound phrases, 7.8; 8.7; 9.16. Sixthly, the use of *'l* in close association with nouns to form 'syntactic descriptions', 9.1 (*'l-gyl*), 9.13 (*'l-hrg*), 11.7 (*'l-'l*); cf. Morag, p. 491.

It is, however, Hosea's vocabulary as it survives in the text of his prophecies which points most clearly to the dialectal character of his language. It is not simply that there are a number of *hapax legomena*, for manifestly these occur in other biblical books where there is no suspicion of dialectal usage. Rather the situation may be characterised as analogous to that obtaining between British and American English and (in

[8] Cf. Brockelmann *Grundriss* II, pp. 476f.

G. Bernard Shaw's phrase) to 'peoples divided by a common language'[9]. Thus, Hosea makes use of words which are perfectly well-known to us from books written in Standard Biblical Hebrew; but the sense which they convey is, in his usage, clearly different. Examples of this latter phenomenon are: *z'm* in 7.16, denoting 'offensive words', i.e. blasphemy against God, cf. the standard meaning 'anger', 'indignation'; *ṣph* in 9.8 with the sense of confrontation, cf. its usual meaning 'to watch', 'to look out'. In both these cases explanatory glosses have been added within the text in order to elucidate these words; in the first instance the glossator understood the word *z'm* correctly; in the second he sought to invest *ṣph* with its usual, standard sense and consequently his mistake has effected what many scholars have judged to be a corrupt text. For other instances see category B in the table of vocabulary, pp. 585ff.

A second category of words indicating the dialectal character of Hosea's Hebrew is that in which, again, the words/roots are reasonably well-known to us from Standard Biblical Hebrew, and yet the particular forms in Hosea are different. Thus, for example, in 13.2 there is uniquely a masculine form of the word *tbwnh* 'skill'; in 2.14 (EV 12) the unique form *'tnh* (cf. the usual *'tnn*) with the sense 'gift', 'present' (to a prostitute) is confirmed as correct by the word-play with *t'nh* 'fig' which occurs in close proximity. In 13.3 the verbal form *ys'r*, meaning 'remove', occurs spelt with *s*; cf. Ps 58.10 where, with the same meaning, it occurs with *ś*. By contrast, in 9.12 it is likely that we are presented with a verbal form of the well-known root *swr* spelt with *ś* rather than with *s*. That *swr* (i.e. with *s*) occurs in 2.4, 19 (EV 2, 17); 4.18, may indicate a degree of Judaean standardisation from which 9.12 escaped. For further instances, see category A in the table of vocabulary.

Thirdly, there occur a number of words, many *hapax legomena*, whose meaning and etymology is not readily apparent. Here, as in comparable cases occurring in other biblical works whose dialect seems to differ from Standard Biblical Hebrew (especially, for example, the book of Job), the meanings are often established by the familiar technique of comparing words and roots from cognate languages. The dangers attending this process are now generally recognised and more especially since the important work of J. Barr *CPOT* (1968). Accordingly I have chosen to rely heavily on the meticulous work of the rabbinic

[9] E.g. 'I'm mad about my flat' in England means that I am pleased with my apartment; in America the same simple words mean that I am exasperated because I have a puncture.

commentators (e.g. Rashi, ibn Ezra and Kimchi) and especially upon the tenth/eleventh century authority Rabbi Abu 'l-Walīd Marwan ibn Janāḥ. His *Kitāb al Uṣūl* ('The Book of the Roots'), written in Arabic, is a masterly forerunner of the modern Hebrew lexicon. Of his work ibn Janāḥ wrote (*Uṣūl*, root *bll*, Neubauer col 93): 'My explanation belongs to the sum of what I have produced of unusual thoughts and noteworthy opinions which no one else has expressed or noticed'. If this implies that he undertook what today is called original research into Hebrew lexicography, that is not to imply that he was other than careful in recording the views of earlier authorities. Indeed, it is this faithfulness in recording received traditions, together with the assiduous attempts critically to evaluate them, which gives to him (as also to the other rabbinic authorities) his unique importance.

That ibn Janāḥ thought and wrote in his native Arabic is of cardinal importance. For here is a scholar who had applied himself tirelessly to the Hebrew scriptures and who, knowing them intimately, uses all the vast resources of another Semitic language to describe the semantic range of the Hebrew words of which he treats. His method is not restricted simply to the direct comparison of Hebrew and Arabic cognate words. That method, indeed, is exemplified in the work of his contemporary Isḥāḳ ibn Barūn (see Wechter) with his *Book of Comparisons* and he has made at least seven important contributions to the understanding of Hosea's vocabulary by it. Ibn Janāḥ, by contrast, does not in the majority of instances even mention or refer to the relevant Arabic cognate words. Rather he seeks to find comparable usages elsewhere in the bible and then, by rendering the Hebrew words or expressions with a number of Arabic synonyms, determines and fixes their meaning within a particular semantic range. In this connection it is frequently the case that the parallel instances from the scriptures which he cites are different from those, generally established, which have survived into the standard modern lexica. Indeed, his work still contains 'thoughts and noteworthy opinions which no one else has expressed or noticed'.

A few examples of such contributions are listed; for further instances, see the table of vocabulary. (1) *zkr* 'fragrance', 'renown' in 14.8 (EV 7). No Arabic cognate is mentioned; the semantic range of Arabic *'rf* is cited. Reference is made to Ps 20.4 (EV 3) for comparable usage. (2) *nblth* 'vile corruption' in 2.12 (EV 10). No Arabic cognate is mentioned. Reference to Nah 3.6 and Job 42.8 establishes the sense. (3) *bwqq* 'damaged' in 10.1. No Arabic cognate is mentioned. Reference to Nah 2.3 establishes the basic sense. (4) Instances where ibn Janāḥ refers to or makes use of Arabic cognates are: *'nh* (2.17, 23, 24; EV 15, 21, 22; 14.9, EV 8); *prd* (4.14); *hbhby* (8.13); *r'h* (9.2; 12.2, EV 1, cf. 10.15); *rtt* (13.1); *tl'bwt* (13.5).

In many such cases the modern commentator, by reference to cognate languages, is able to give further precision to ibn Janāḥ's contributions and to provide philological support for them. In the main, so it seems, Aramaic/Syriac and Arabic are the languages which prove most useful in this endeavour. That does not preclude the possibility that other languages, such as Ugaritic and Accadian, may also prove useful. Lexicographers will no doubt supply further information in those instances where they judge the contributions of this commentary to be correct. Nor should the fact that the three languages mentioned above are those which are predominantly cited here be taken as evidence of itself that Hosea's dialect was closer to Aramaic or Arabic than that of Jerusalem or of Standard Biblical Hebrew. For there are, of course, many very common words in the latter which are closely paralleled by cognate words in these particular languages.

The use of comparative philology has not been restricted entirely to words whose meaning has been posited on other grounds by such rabbinic authorities. There are some five instances where proposals made by more recent scholars (Michaelis, Schultens, A. J. Arnold, G. R. Driver, Morag) have seemed to me to be correct.

A final category consists of words in the prophecy which are possibly to be judged Aramaisms (category D in the table of vocabulary). Here, however, very great caution is necessary. It would seem that 'in the districts of Ephraim and Samaria the influence of Aramaic was considerably greater than in Judah, yet in respect of Hosea the general impression that one gains is that his language does not reveal traits of vocabulary which are attributable in the main to the influence of Aramaic' (Morag, p. 509; my translation). If the Samaria Ostraca reveal forms which are close to those occurring in Aramaic (e.g. *št* 'year' for *šnh*), such forms are not immediately apparent in Hosea's writings. And if Hosea uses words which are clearly attested in Aramaic (e.g. *r'h* 'think', 'give attention') that does not of itself justify the supposition that they are not also authentic words of a literary Hebrew which belonged to the Northern Kingdom. Accordingly there are no more than four instances in the table of vocabulary where words are judged possible Aramaisms.

If heavy reliance upon the work of the medieval rabbinic commentators serves as a proper defence against arbitrary or subjective use of the methods of comparative philology[10], it has the added advantage that it often illuminates the traditions of interpretation upon which the renderings of the ancient versions are based. Two examples may be set out: 7.16, where the renderings of all the versions become intelligible in the light of ibn Janāḥ's treatment of the word *z'm*; 11.6, where the renderings of the LXX, Peshiṭta and Symmachus (cf. Vulgate/Jerome) become intelligible in the light of the same commentator's account of the word *bdym*; without it these renderings are unexplained and, unexplained, have prompted scholars to propose emendations to the MT. Other examples are detectable in 8.3; 9.2; 10.17; 11.4; 12.9, 15 (EV 8, 14); 13.3, 14, 15; 14.6, 9 (EV 5, 8).

There are a very few instances where renderings from amongst the ancient versions coincide precisely with estimates as to meaning made on the basis of comparative philology and adopted in this commentary; they are *ṣw* in 5.11 (LXX/G. R. Driver); *hbhby* in 8.13 (Symmachus/ibn Janāḥ); *'mgnk* in 11.8 (Symmachus/KB^3); *rd* in 12.1 (Aquila/ibn Janāḥ); *'wn* in 12.9 (LXX/AAM). Accordingly, as witnesses to the meaning of difficult words and expressions in Hosea's prophecies, the ancient versions cannot be said to have the same 'prime exegetical significance' which McKane finds for them in the case of Jeremiah (see p. xv of the sister volume in the ICC). The Hebrew text which they translated seems to have differed little from that of the MT (cf. Borbone, p. 53) and the ears of none of them seem to have been tuned in any noticeable or consistent way to the peculiarities of Hosea's language[11].

[10] Nyberg's work on Hosea's vocabulary is a case in point; while it is imaginative and addresses real problems, it none the less fails substantially because he seeks, by comparative philology, to make the text conform to his own estimates of contemporary Israelite religion. Similar criticisms *mutatis mutandis* may be levelled at Kuhnigk's study. In ways familiar from the work of his mentor, M. Dahood, Kuhnigk refers wholesale most problems of the text of Hosea to Ugaritic and the Ugaritic Texts, where parallels in vocabulary, usage and religion are fulsomely claimed.

[11] Cf. the judicious comments of Gelston in respect of the Peshiṭta (pp. 146f). On the likelihood that the LXX reflects lack of familiarity with Hosea's language, cf. Treitel, p. 441; in agreeing with this judgement, I am not committed to Treitel's view that the LXX is worthless as an aid to tackling the textual problems of MT nor to the conclusion (Nyberg, p. 116) that the characteristic traits of the LXX as a translation are desperation and arbitrariness. As Neef has shown (pp. 219f), the version displays evidence of the exercise of great care and responsibility both in respect of its *Vorlage* and of the audience to which it was directed, cf. Patterson, p. 220.

The fourth column of the table of vocabulary seeks (where possible) to name those biblical books apart from Hosea where, in each case, similar words or forms occur. The intention is not to attempt any exhaustive account but merely to give some general impression as to affinity of language. (Exact references are provided in particular cases and when it is necessary to indicate which part of a book is involved, e.g., Psalms, Isaiah.) The book most mentioned in the table is Job (ten times) and this is not surprising in view of the generally acknowledged dialectal character of that work. That Nahum is mentioned as many as four times accords with the tentative judgement of S. R. Driver (*Introduction*, p. 335) 'if Nahum were of Galilaean origin, certain slight peculiarities of his diction might be explained as provincialisms' (*sic*, in connection with the possibility that Nahum was by birth a Galilaean). Proverbs, mentioned four times, reflects the international endeavours of the wise and its Arabisms and Aramaisms are very widely recognised. Similar considerations apply to Ecclesiastes (mentioned twice), famous for its Aramaisms and important as evidence for the verb *'nh* II. In the case of Jeremiah (mentioned five times) and Ezekiel (also five times), the preponderance of similar forms occurs in the context of promiscuity and unfaithfulness, themes which are likely to reflect the influence of Hosea upon these prophets.

FORM AND STYLE

The Talmud records the adage (B. *Sanhedrin* 89a; ET, p. 592 in *Neziḳin* III) that, while form and matter may be common to any number of prophets, the individual style of each is always unique. The force of the observation depends on the two different senses of the word *sgnwn* which it deploys (i.e. 'form/matter', but also individual 'style' – so Qyl, p. 25, following Rashi); and it may be brought into relation with the talmudic saying that Hosea was the greatest of all the early prophets (i.e. those of the eighth century; see B. *Pesaḥim* 87a; ET, p. 460 in *Mo'ed* II; see also *Leviticus Rabba* 6.6–Vilna edn.).

If such observations characterise the uniqueness, even the mystery, of Hosea's speech, they may be said accurately to indicate the massive artistic skill with which his prophecies have been composed. He is simply a master of language.

It is not, of course, his own sentiments to which he gives such eloquent expression. Hosea, perhaps more than any other prophet, speaks in the name of his God and first person pronouns used in this sense occur with the utmost frequency. Thus 'I' occurs some twenty times (10 instances of *'ny* and 11 of *'nky*); 'me' (in various combinations) occurs some seventeen times (cf. Qyl, p. 26). The divine speech to which Hosea gives expression explicitly reflects his own personal experience (cf. 1.2 and 3.1), and with relentless vigour he recounts both the hopeless pain of despair and, *mirabile dictu*, the survival of a hope that will not be extinguished. Indeed, as it has been said, '(where mental process is concerned), there is no difference at all between Hosea and his God' (so Ora Lipschitz in a private communication). If divine speech predominates, there are, however, occasions where prophetic speech (i.e. speech about Yahweh in the third person) obtrudes (4.6–15; 8.10–13; 12.1–15, EV 11.12–12.14) and the result is what Wolff (p. xxiii) has described as 'lively alternation'.

Another important and related form of speech deployed by Hosea is that of prayer. Yet his prayers are not the straightforward intercessions offered to Yahweh by a prophet on behalf of his people as witnessed, for example, in the contemporary Amos 7.2, 5. Hosea's prayers are expressed by a remarkable combination of exhortation directed to Ephraim (6.1a; 14.2f, EV 1f), and model, ideal confession by Ephraim of her dependence upon Yahweh (6.1b; 14.3b, EV 2b), the latter comprising (third person) assurance of his immediate and favourable response (6.3b) or else, expressed separately in direct speech, a personal (first person) assurance of that same response (14.5ff, EV 4ff). Such consummate artistry serves again to emphasise the radical unity of purpose that exists between Hosea and his God.

That forms of speech whose *Sitz im Leben* is the law court occur in Hosea's prophecies is highly probable. The word *ryb* with its forensic overtones in 4.1; 12.3 (EV 2) and the frequent use of *'th* (see p. lvi), introducing the inevitability of punishment following accusation or announcement of judgement, both point in this direction. On the other hand, the wholesale commitment of a large number of Hosea's sayings to varied and complex forensic categories (e.g. *Schlichtungsvorschlag* = 'proposal to reach a settlement', for 4.15) typical of Wolff's commentary, smacks of over-interpretation. There is no need to suppose that Israelite prophets were unable to communicate other than in clichés and the supposition that Hosea should have done so is, in view of the infinitely rich texture of his craft, most unlikely. In general the familiar forms of prophetic condemnation are to be found in chapters 4–8.

In the later chapters (9–13) as also in chapter 2.4–25 (EV 2–23), Hosea's oracles are characterised by a deeply meditative tone. That the material of chapter 2 had its origins in public pronouncements delivered by Hosea seems likely, yet its present form suggests that this material has been reworked and stamped with the prophet's personal reflections upon its significance (see p. lxix and pp. 114ff below). Certainly its placement between chapters 1 and 3 confirms that impression. Where the later chapters are concerned, the meditations or soliloquies are replete with references to earlier pronouncements and judgements and thereby testify to further personal reflection upon the terrible implications of the message of Yahweh that Hosea had been obliged to record. Again the rapid change of subject, so typical of Hosea, whereby, e.g., third person plural descriptions alternate with second person singular interjections (chapter 9), serves well to convey the despair as also (e.g. 12.7, EV 6) *de profundis* the hope which the prophet felt and which he dared to presume was felt in equal measure by his God. For further observations on the forms used by the prophet, see under Composition below.

As has been generally noted, no other prophet uses as many similes as Hosea does. At times he presses remorselessly the vehicle of his similes; thus, in chapter 7, the rulers of Ephraim are compared with an oven no less than three times (vv. 4, 6, 7) and the impression gained is that the particulars of the simile answer very precisely (for reasons not now apparent) to the intrigues of the conspirators. In other cases it is enough for him merely to present similes in the knowledge that a single mention of the vehicle suffices to produce immediate and powerful effect (see, e.g., 4.16; 5.14; 6.4; 8.8; 9.10; 10.7; 11.11; 13.3; 14.6, 7, 9, EV 5, 6, 8). Characteristic of Hosea's metaphors is his description of moral deviation in terms of sickness and disease (see, e.g., 5.13; 6.1; 7.1; 11.3; 14.5, EV 4), as well as of sexual promiscuity and unfaithfulness (see, e.g., 7.4; 8.9f; 9.1). Again, the natural world and agriculture are used extensively as a rich quarry for similes and metaphors and there can be no doubt that Hosea was knowledgeable and even technically competent in this field. For knowledge of fruit trees and vines, see, e.g., 9.10, 13, 16; 10.1; 14.6, EV 5; for the use of technical details of domestic animals, ploughing and agriculture see, e.g., 4.16; 8.7; 10.4, 10ff.

Most striking, perhaps, are Hosea's similes for Yahweh; combined, they depict the twin aspects of the nation's God. On the one hand Yahweh, in his anger, is compared with a lion, a leopard, a she-bear and also with wasting disease (see 5.14; 13.7f; 5.12), on the other hand, in his forbearance and love, with life-giving rain and with dew (6.3; 14.6, EV 5).

Other devices much favoured by the prophet include:

(1) Asyndeton: see p. lvi above.

(2) The repetition of words, rhetorical in style, for emphasis, see 2.23f, EV 21f (*'nh*); 3.4 and 4.1 (*'yn*); 9.14 (*ntn*); 14.6ff, EV 5ff, (Lebanon). In this connection, there are instances where words, alike in form but different, and even radically different, follow each other in close sequence. Thus 10.15, *r't r'tkm*, and particularly chapter 4: *ryb/yrb/mryby* (4.1, 4); *'mk/'my* together with *khn/mkhn/kkhn* (4.4–9); *wkšlt/wkšl, wdmyty/ndmw, m'st/ w'm's'k, wtškḥ/'škḥ* (4.5f); *ḥṭ'w/ḥṭ't* together with *y'klw/w'klw* (4.7–10); and especially *znwt/znwnym/wyznw/tznynh/tn'pnh/ tn'pnh/tznynh/hznwt/znh/hznh/hznw* (4.11–18); in chapter 7, similarly, *wr'wt/r'tm/br'tm* (7.1–3).

(3) Alliteration and assonance: 4.16 *srrh srr yśr'l* (*samech/sin*), cf. 9.15; 10.10 *w'srm w'spw b'srm* (*aleph/samech*); further, 5.1 (*pe*); 5.7 (*ḥeth*); 9.6 (*mem*); 9.11 (*aleph/pe, ayin/pe*); 10.11, 14 and 11.4 (*aleph/ayin*); 11.8f (*aleph*); 12.2, EV 1 (*resh*); 12.12, EV 11 (*gimel/lamedh*).

(4) Word-play: the name Ephraim (*'prym*), so central to Hosea's prophecies, is also the word most subjected to word-play. In 8.9, cf 13.15, the word is juxtaposed with *pr'* 'wild ass' and thereby the behaviour of the nation is forcefully characterised. Similarly in 4.6f the name suggests to Hosea *prh* 'a heifer', stubborn and intractable. Elsewhere (9.16) 'Ephraim' prompts Hosea to the judgement that the nation is radically unfruitful (*pry bly*) and indeed has reversed the original blessing of fruitfulness associated with the naming of eponymous Ephraim (Gen 41.52, cf. 49.22–26). In 11.3 Ephraim is said to be unaware that Yahweh had proffered his prophylactic care (*rp'tym*). Other examples of word-play may be listed as follows: 1.4f Israel/Jezreel (*yśr'l/yzr''l*); 2.13 (EV 11) *whšbty/wšbth*; 2.14 (EV 12) *t'nth/'tnh*; 4.7 *krbm/kbwdm*; 4.16, 18f *srrh/srr/sr*; 6.9 *škmh*; 7.4 *mn'pym/'ph*; 7.14f *yswrw/ysrty*; 8.11 *hrbh/rbw*; 9.13 *bnwh/bnyw*; 9.15 *śryhm/srrym*; 10.5 *ygylw/glh*; 10.10 *w'srm/w'spw/b'srm*; 11.5 *yšwb/lšwb*; 12.1, 15 (EV 11.12, 12.14) *mrmh/tmrwrym*; 12.5 (EV 4) *wyśr 'l/yśr'l*; 12.9 (EV 8) *'wn/'wn*; 12.7, 13f (EV 6, 12f) *šmr/nšmr*; 14.4, 9 (EV 3, 8) *'swr/w'swrnw*. There is necessarily some overlap between the categories 2–4 listed above.

In conclusion, Jerome's observation on Hosea's style remains entirely apposite: 'Hosea is broken up into clauses, and speaks as if in aphorisms' (*commaticus est et quasi per sententias loquens*). Again, and typically, S. R. Driver's comments (*Introduction*, p. 305), written one hundred years ago, cannot be bettered: 'Hosea's style seems to be the expression of the emotion which is stirring in his heart: his sensitive soul is full of love and sympathy for his people; and his keen perception of their moral decay, and of the destruction towards which they are hastening, produces in consequence a conflict of emotions, which is reflected in the pathos, and force, and artless rhythm of sighs and sobs, which characterise his prophecy.' If that judgement testifies to Hosea's ability to address himself to the terrible realities of his nation's situation, then, by contrast, his prayers and meditations, often extended and lyrical in character (see, e.g., 2.16ff, EV 14ff; 12; 14), testify equally to his limitless faith in the power of love and in the God who is its source.

As is generally agreed, our knowledge of the workings of Hebrew poetry is scanty and, consequently, I have chosen to refrain from attempting any analysis in respect of the received text of Hosea's prophecies. It seems probable that Wolff (p. xxiv) is right to suggest that Hosea's words, as they are represented in the massoretic text, reflect 'elevated prose that frequently changes into stricter poetic forms'. Certainly parallelism is a marked feature, synonymous parallelism being more common than the synthetic or (rare) antithetic varieties. Again, Wolff's judgement that Hosea's words have a rhythmic structure accords with my own impressions. That structure is detectable in, e.g., the predominant bicola and in the tricola which occur especially at the beginnings and ends of units (see, e.g., 5.1; 9.3; 12.7, EV 6; 14.1b, EV 13.16b).

THE COMPOSITION OF THE BOOK OF HOSEA

Consideration of the language and style of the prophecies of Hosea has suggested the conclusion that the work is fundamentally literary in character. If, then, there are no particular indications of Northern or Ephraimite dialectal *speech*, there are in the prophecies no explicit reports of the prophet engaging in conversation or dialogue with anyone; nor (with the likely exception of a quotation in 9.7) is there any report of words spoken to the prophet by his contemporaries. In the case of the contemporary prophets, Amos and Isaiah (as well as of a number of later prophets), there are, by contrast, explicit reports of the prophets' dialogues with their contemporaries as well as equally explicit records that these prophets were called to address their contemporaries in sermons and speeches prompted by Yahweh. What we are told in respect of Hosea is that he was instructed by Yahweh initially to marry Gomer and, at a later stage (so I suppose), to renew his love in redeeming her from a harsh situation. That was to be done in order to reflect and set forth the parallel situation that obtained as between Yahweh and the nation. We are also told that he was to mark the progressively deteriorating state of the nation by reference to the births of his three children and by naming them accordingly. The reports on these matters are contained in chapters 1 and 3 and, as has been argued in the Excursus on Hosea's marriage (pp. 113–126), the former chapter appears to be essentially personal and retrospective in character (even if it is the work of a redactor) and the latter to be an *Ichbericht* or first person memorandum by the prophet himself. Both chapters are, then, by nature private in character, the one because it is retrospective, the other because it records an instruction from Yahweh which is personal. In neither is there recorded explicitly any further instruction to speak about these matters.

The important verse 9.7 proclaims that the days of reckoning and of retribution have come upon the nation which will now perceive whether 'the prophet is a knave, the inspired man deranged'. Here we are presented with a quotation which reflects the attitude and reaction of Hosea's opponents. From this it is clear that Hosea, like other prophets, practised a public ministry and that at least some of his contemporaries were aware of his opinions. With this the opening words of chapters 4 and 5 are consistent, for they contain solemn calls to the nation, its priests and rulers, to hear Yahweh's indictment of them. Similarly 8.1 constitutes an instruction from Yahweh to the prophet to deliver a solemn warning of imminent invasion, like that of a trumpet. It seems likely that, generally speaking, the words which Hosea delivered publicly are reflected and predominate in chapters 2 and 4–8. It is unlikely, however, that these passages contain accurate transcriptions (as of a stenographer) of the prophet's *ipsissima verba*. Examination of the language and style has prompted the conclusion that we are confronted with what is a literary endeavour. That is to say that when Hosea (or a scribe) sat down to write an account of the oracles which he had spoken he produced something different, *viz.* a literary work in the literary language of the North. Contents and form may be said to confirm this impression. In this connection the following considerations are set forth.

The book of Hosea (especially from chapter 9) is replete with mature, distilled judgement upon the implications of what has been said elsewhere more shortly. Chapter 9, for example, contains in its two parts systematic and extended meditations, the first upon the sentence of judgement in 8.13b, the second upon the theme of what might have been as contrasted with the reality of the situation. In the latter case, too, there are reasons for supposing that elements of Hosea's personal life are alluded to and give particular shape to what is said. Chapter 10, like chapter 9, is meditative in character and treats of implications of the state's demise, its cult and its king. Chapter 11, with its careful cross-references to earlier oracles, is a sustained meditation upon the theme of consistent love and consistent ingratitude. Chapter 12, too, while it contains specific indictments of Ephraim's behaviour which may derive from public pronouncements (vv. 3, 8), is deeply reflective in character. Its theme, based upon a complex evaluation of Ephraim's fault by reference to the personality and vicissitudes of its eponymous ancestor Jacob, is theological, even prayerful, in character. The supposition that Jacob's character was redeemed by love for a woman (v. 13) again matches aspects of the prophet's personal life and becomes the premise upon which Hosea's hope for Ephraim is based. Such complex musings with their cross-references to earlier sayings (vv. 10b, 12) are not the stuff of public pronouncements; they take us to the prophet's mind, to the inner source of his inspiration and genius. Chapter 13 (to 14.1) is not so much a prophetic proclamation of the final rupture; rather it seeks to perceive the *débâcle* as through the eyes of Yahweh and to depict the pain within the heart of God. Indeed it is, surprisingly perhaps, of a sort with the prayer that follows it, the one meditation prompting its successor; the successor pleading for the reversal of its predecessor. Chapter 14.2–9 takes the form of a prayer offered by the prophet for his people in their terrible straits. It reflects Hosea's personal reaction to the stark, final horror of 14.1 and to the doom which *ex prophetae officio* he had been constrained to mediate. Here again what is presented (with its studied element of recapitulation[12]) differs markedly from what we know from other prophetic books of the oracles of public ministry as also from formal prayers associated with the prophetic office (cf. and contrast Amos 7.2, 5).

If such mature, expansive meditations of the prophet contain within them echoes of words spoken during the course of his public ministry and at times explicit and studied cross-references to them, then those passages listed above which more nearly reflect his public utterances are in turn punctuated with meditative, prayerful expansions. Most noticeable in this respect is 6.1–6 which interrupts, as an aside, the sustained indictments of the nation, its priests and cult (chapters 4–5.7), the

[12] For a definition of the sense in which this term is used, see p. 33.

characterisation of the strife between Ephraim and Judah as a manifestation of divine judgement (5.8ff) and the portrayal of the hideous palace intrigues of Ephraim (6.7ff) together with meretricious courting of foreign alliances (7.8ff). This lyrical expression of yearning for a penitence which alone could right the situation, together with its penetrating appraisal of the nation's inner moral flaw, serves to interpret the oracles into which it obtrudes by reference to Hosea's deeply personal reactions to what he had proclaimed publicly. And since it is Hosea's prayer it is also, so to speak, the prayer of Yahweh.

For observations on chapter 2, see ad loc and the Excursus (pp. 114f). Here it is important to note that v. 15 (EV 13), sealed with the formula 'Oracle of Yahweh', marks the end of a unit in which the parable of the wronged husband is deployed in order to indict Ephraim's treacherous unfaithfulness to Yahweh. In the section which immediately follows (vv. 16–25; EV 14–23) the soliloquy continues, yet the mood changes. Coercion and threats of punishment are replaced by the theme of coercion through love. The language takes on a lyrical beauty and the contents indicate what is a personal song of love. Here again what was initially proclaimed publicly as a telling parable, becomes part of a complete composition in which is expressed a prayer for reconciliation and the renewal of love between Yahweh and Ephraim. That Hosea should give expression to such longing independently of his own experience is unthinkable. Yahweh's longing is, then, also Hosea's.

Much the same prayerful tone marks the unit 2.1–3 (EV 1.10–2.1), which sets forth a recapitulation of the pronouncements of chapter 1 and, like them, is linked with the names of Hosea's children. Again, like chapter 1, the unit reflects the personal, private aspects of Hosea's endeavours.

Throughout such estimates of the literary character of the book of Hosea a distinction is made between elements that are private and personal and elements which were likely to have been proclaimed publicly, the literary composition *ex hypothesi* being a fusion of the two elements. There is, of course, no explicit evidence in favour of this distinction. One verse, however, may afford indirect evidence in this sense. In 5.15 Yahweh announces, 'I shall retreat to my place until, suffering punishment, they seek my presence and, in their distress, they resort eagerly to me'. This withdrawal by Yahweh forms part of his punitive action; withdrawn, yet remaining totally in control of events, he awaits a response from his people. The inexorable doom has been set in motion; behind its workings there lay its cause: the complete rupture of Yahweh's relationship with his people. Without their repentance nothing whatsoever could or would change. The remarkable unity of purpose as between the prophet and his God has been noted elsewhere (p. lxii). It is not unreasonable, then, to suppose that Hosea also withdrew, and, in particular, ceased to speak publicly; so, secluded 'in his place', he meditated further upon the word of Yahweh that had come to him and that came to him, filling out the implications of its effect in the continuing decline and eclipse of his nation and always by reference to the remarkable coincidence of the events of his own life (cf. the explicit notice of Isaiah's similar withdrawal in Isa 8.16–18).

Such fusion between what is personal on the one hand and what was proclaimed publicly on the other also accounts for the placing of chapters 1 and 3 at the beginning of the work. Indeed, that chapter 2 intervenes constitutes a miniature fusion within the greater fusion that is the whole. As is argued below (Excursus, pp. 116f), chapters 1 and 3 constitute a *mise-en-scène*; by means of this literary device the reader is permitted to look behind the parable of the wronged husband in chapter 2 much as the reader of the book of Job, taken by the prologue to the court of heaven, knows what lies behind the poems that follow. That this miniature fusion assumed a form which is complete in itself (thereby prompting many scholars to speak of the unit as radically distinct from the rest of the book) depends, of course, on the particular and immediate connection between the public discourses which lie behind chapter 2 and Hosea's personal life. Yet the placing of it before the bulk of Hosea's prophecies enables the reader, by means of this literary device, to see why Hosea spoke and thought as he did throughout the turbulent days of his ministry. Here we are close indeed to perceiving the purpose of the literary work as a whole. It is a written testimony that Hosea and his family, like his southern contemporary Isaiah and his children, were authentic 'signs and wonders in Israel from the Lord of hosts' (Isa 8.18); that the burden of his message reflected accurately the mind and purpose of the God he knew so well.

If then the book of Hosea represents what is fundamentally a literary composition, forged from a blend of the matter of his public oracles, of his personal amplifications and of his meditations upon them, there can be no doubt that Hosea himself was the author and composer. That does not preclude the possibility that, like Jeremiah, he was assisted by a personal scribe or that his endeavour was promoted by some redactional activity (see, e.g., on 2.1ff and 3.5).

The notion, too, that, like other prophets (cf. Isa 8.16), Hosea revealed the totality of his thoughts to a circle of disciples who received and guarded them should not be excluded. If there is no explicit evidence in its favour, the notion goes some way to explaining what is incontrovertible, *viz.* that Hosea's work found its way to Judah at or after the final collapse of Samaria in 722/1 BC (see below). Whatever the precise circumstances, the massive unity of purpose which has been detected in the work is most naturally attributed to a single mind and a single author; and, if he was assisted in his endeavour by such a person or persons as have been indicated above, then they knew that mind and author so well that their contribution will have served only to promote the unity of purpose that was his.

The circumstances by which Hosea's work reached Judah are not known to us. His final indication of what the fall of Samaria entailed (14.1, EV 13.16) suggests either that he had witnessed it or, more probably, that he knew of its imminent reality. Whether Hosea survived the final end of his nation, we do not know. At all events, speculation concerning Hosea's circumstances at and after the fall of Samaria can be no more than speculation. Such characterises Wolff's bold pronouncements (pp. 210f, 224) on the matter: for him Hosea and his entourage, consisting of a levitical/prophetic circle, their aspirations for the future increasingly transferred to Judah, may have witnessed the fall of Samaria from the Benjamite border area and then proceeded to settle in Judah itself.

Recognition that Hosea's work was received in Judah depends first upon the consideration that, had it not done so, it is likely that it would have been lost to us. More directly, the (late) superscription of 1.1, with its clear Judaean emphasis, testifies clearly to this mode of transmission. For the rest, the text displays a number of references to Judah which, strictly inconsistent with the context in which they are found, are judged to be glosses or alterations made by Judaean redactors with the purpose of giving Hosea's words a longer perspective following the fall of Samaria. That Hosea himself believed Judah to be an integral part of Israel, of the people of Yahweh, seems clear from 2.2 (EV 1.11); 5.8–14; 6.4; 8.14, passages which include Judah (whether for weal or for woe) in announcements of Yahweh's disposition towards his people. The fall of Samaria will have vindicated Hosea's fundamental message that Ephraim's idolatry and unfaithfulness brought about its doom and so, *mutatis mutandis*, it will have become a paradigm in the eyes of the Yahwists of Judah to be deployed in their own fight against such evils. But, additionally, the irrepressible hope for the future and the unquenchable faith in the goodness of Yahweh so characteristic of Hosea will also have commended themselves to such circles and they will have appropriated for their own case those of his prayers which expressed this sense. If Ephraim had failed to live up to its true vocation, Judah now had the chance to do so. Hosea's writings, then, authenticated by history, were redirected to a new situation. He was, in Emmerson's phrase, 'an Israelite prophet in Judean perspective'.

The contributions of the Judaean redactors are listed as follows, together with rough estimates of their dates:

(A) 1.7. Judah, in contrast to the 'House of Israel', will be saved by faith in Yahweh alone. A late seventh century addition.

(B) 3.5. To Hosea's words two phrases are added: 'and David their king' and 'in the days to come'. The words are a recapitulation (see p. lxvii n. 12) of the contents of v. 4 'without king' and 'without feasting etc.' Restoration becomes specifically that of the king of Jerusalem and that of the Jerusalem cult. Earliest date: late seventh century; possibly post-exilic.

(C) 4.5. Two glosses are added. The first, showing some verbal identity with a similar gloss in 5.5, extends the judgement of the priests to the prophets. The second is exegetical and serves to explain that the people, destroyed for lack of knowledge, is equated with the mother of chapter 2. The first may reflect condemnation of the false prophets who opposed Jeremiah. Earliest date: late seventh century; possibly post-exilic.

(D) 4.15. A substantial modification of words from Hosea which incorporates phrases from the prophecies of Amos. Judah should not follow the example of Ephraim. Date: ? late eighth century/early seventh century.

(E) 5.5. A gloss added to the end of the verse so as to assert that Judah is as guilty as Ephraim in respect of pride. Date: as D.

(F) 6.11a. An addition which extends Hosea's condemnation to include Judah. Date: late seventh century.

(G) 6.11b. An addition (later than v. 11a) which creates of the whole verse a prophecy of weal for Judah and which is built upon the opening words of 7.1. Date: exilic.

(H) 9.4. The concluding sentence of the verse is added to Hosea's words in order to elucidate their meaning in the light of later experience and understanding. Date: exilic.

(I) 10.11. The gloss 'Judah' is added in order specifically to include Judah in the call of Israel as a whole. A less likely alternative is that an original 'Israel', the other name of Jacob, is replaced by 'Judah' for the same purpose, the original triple nomenclature facilitating the alteration. Date: late eighth century/seventh century.

(J) 11.10. An addition, constructed on the basis of Hosea's words in v. 11, which gives expression to Judaean eschatology of salvation with its notion of Yahweh's call to the exiles far and wide to return to Zion. Date: post-exilic.

(K) 12.1. An original 'and he' (referring to Ephraim) has been replaced by 'and Judah'. Hosea's indictment of Ephraim's treachery is extended to the glossator's Judah and possibly reinterpreted in a favourable sense. Date: late eighth century/seventh century.

(L) 12.3. An original 'with Israel' is replaced by 'with Judah'. Date: as I above.

(M, N) The addition of the superscription (1.1) and of the epilogue (14.10, EV 14.9) respectively reminds the reader of the historical background of the book and invites him to understand it as a scriptural witness to the ethical basis which underlies Yahweh's ordering of history. Date: exilic or post-exilic.

Examination of these contributions prompts the conclusion that they were made piecemeal over the course of some two centuries but, tentatively, that the greater number are to be dated in the seventh century BC. If that judgement is correct, an important stage in the (Judaean) redaction of Hosea's prophecies may be more or less contemporary and parallel with the redaction of (Ur-) Deuteronomy or Josiah's book of the Law, promulgated in 621 BC. Its origins, like Hosea, are generally regarded as northern. For further observations on the relationship between Hosea's writings and the tradition behind Deuteronomy, see the introduction to Wolff's commentary (p. xxxi).

A second category of glosses is that discussed under 'Language' above and 'Text and Versions' below. It consists of the linguistic and exegetical glosses whose function was to render Hosea's dialectal Hebrew more understandable to the Judaean circles which received them and to interpret his more difficult or obscure references. These glosses are listed on p. lxxv in categories d and e. Their nature is such that they do not afford any clear evidence as to their date. That the majority of the changes made by Judaean redactors are likely to have been made in the late eighth or seventh century may be held to indicate that this second category belonged also to this time.

In conclusion, my estimate of the stages by which the book of Hosea reached its current form may be set out as follows:

(1) Hosea's public oracles: in them he attacked the cultic exuberance and syncretistic worship of the affluent period towards the end of the reign of Jeroboam II. His words are reflected predominantly in chapters 4 and 5.1–7 and in the original parable of the wronged husband set out in 2.4–15 (EV

2–13). He proclaimed the internecine strife between Ephraim and Judah at the time of the Syro-Ephraimite War (*c*. 733 BC) to be a judgement of Yahweh upon both nations for their unfaithfulness. His words are reflected in chapter 5.8–14. Other instances of public pronouncements are to be detected in 6.7–7.7, where he condemns the circumstances of Pekah's accession, and 7.8–8.14, in which Ephraim's reliance upon foreign alliances is seen to be of a sort with the state's fundamental unfaithfulness in idolatry.

(2) Hosea, *c*. 733 BC, withdrew from his public ministry (cf. on 5.15 and p. lxviii) and wrote up his public oracles, incorporating their metaphors and figures of speech, making of them a literary piece by expanding them with meditative amplifications of a more personal kind and, particularly, by incorporating his insights into the mind of Yahweh. In general his endeavour is reflected in chapters 2 and 4–8. In the case of chapter 2, 4–25 (EV 2–23) the original parable of the wronged husband which had featured in a public oracle (cf. the parable of the vineyard in Isa 5) was reworked in the light of events in the prophet's own life; for by then Gomer's adulterous behaviour had mirrored precisely the unfaithfulness of Ephraim, thereby giving Hosea his most profound insight into the heart of God (cf. chapter 3).

(3) Withdrawn to 'his place', Hosea composed further meditations (chapters 9–14) which drew out the implications of what had earlier been revealed to him and was seen to be correct in the hastening decline of the rump of Ephraim during the days of Hoshea ben Elah and of the siege of Samaria.

(4) During this period, too, he revealed to his disciples the circumstances of his personal life as 'a scene within a play that comes near the large circumstance' (after *Hamlet* III 2 80).

(5) Hosea (or, acting on his instructions, his scribe/redactor) composed a unit (chapters 1–3) made up of various personal recollections and of his (expanded) speech on the wronged husband (see the Excursus, pp. 113–116) which then served the purposes of indicating the fundamental mode by which Yahweh had spoken to him *throughout* his ministry and of authenticating the validity and truth of that revelation.

(6) This special unit was prefixed to the residue of the literary account of his oracles and meditations.

(7) The whole was transmitted to Judah at or soon after the fall of Samaria in 722/1 BC.

(8) The Judaean redactors of the seventh century modified the work to meet their own particular needs.

(9) Exilic and post-exilic glosses were added.

(10) The superscription and epilogue served to catalogue the work and to indicate that it should be regarded as (what we may call) authoritative scripture.

TEXT AND VERSIONS

W. R. Harper in his ICC commentary of 1905 concluded that 'the text of Hosea is one of the most corrupt in the OT'. He further stated (pp. clxxiiif), 'Hosea's reputation for obscurity is due in large measure to the corrupt form in which the text of his message has reached us'. Accordingly he believed it right to seek to restore the original text, deriving 'much help ... from the versions, but in many cases' resorting, as of necessity, 'to critical conjecture'. Judging the text of the LXX to be preferable in some forty instances, he thereby corrected the MT. Aquila was used similarly in one instance; Symmachus in two instances (but within the same verse); Theodotion in three instances; the Peshiṭta in eleven instances. The Vulgate and the Targum were not used at all (i.e. independently of other versions). For the rest, and relying on the work of earlier scholars, he deployed the faculty of critical conjecture to restore the text. Whether his restoration is supported by one or more of the ancient versions or not, he judged the mistakes to have arisen under the following headings: (a) changes in pointing, thirty-three instances; (b) incorrect word divisions, eight instances; (c) dittography and haplography, seventeen instances; (d) confusion of various letters (e.g., *r/d*, *ś/š*, etc.), twenty-one instances; (e) transpositions of letters, six instances; (f) omission or insertion of *aleph*, five instances; (g) confusion of suffixes, five instances; (h) omission or insertion of the copula, seven instances; (i) theological changes, two instances; (j) miscellaneous corruptions, thirty-eight instances.

In this commentary some four consonantal emendations have been adopted; in one instance (4.4) the correction is made on the grounds of an assumed dittography; in two instances, on the grounds of assumed confusion of suffixes (8.13 and 11.3); and in one, of the confusion of verbal forms (11.11)[13]. Of these corrections only those in 11.3 and 11.11 are supported by any of the ancient versions. Secondly, MS readings at variance with what is printed in *BHS* have been adopted on three occasions (2.8, EV 6; 4.6; 7.14); in 2.8 (EV 6) the variant is that of a Dead

[13] Since vowel letters alone are involved, this may not be strictly a consonantal emendation; cf. Jer 32.37.

Sea Scroll fragment (4QpHos[a]). Another fragment (4Qp Hos[b]) possibly gives support to a variant form of the word *šbbym* (8.6), i.e. the *Kethib* of Jer 50.6, *šwbbym*, adopted in 8.6 as preferable. Thirdly, *Qere* has been judged preferable to *Kethib* in two instances (4.6 and 10.10). Fourthly, corrections to the pointing have been made in seven instances (4.4; 5.2; 7.14; 8.10, 12; 12.5, EV 4) and of these there is possible versional support in three (7.14; 8.10; 12.5, EV 4).

For the rest, apart from the categories listed above, alterations to the text, made after it came to Judah, have been detected in a number of places and they may be listed as follows: (a) substitution of Judah for another word: three instances (10.11; 12.1, 3, EV 11.12, 12.2); (b) the addition of as little as one word or as much as a whole verse by Judaean redactors of Hosea's oracles (see pp. xxiff): nine instances; (c) a gloss or dittograph: one instance (5.5, 'and Israel'); (d) the addition of glosses whose function is to elucidate difficult words or phrases: six instances (2.8, EV 6; 7.14ff; 8.13; 13.1); (e) the addition of other exegetical or expansive glosses: four instances (9.8, 11, 13; 12.5, EV 4); (f) exilic or post-exilic glosses: three instances (6.11b; 9.4; 11.10), together with the superscription (1.1) and the epilogue (14.10, EV 9). In the case of categories (d) and (e), it is arguable that 13.1 belongs to (e) rather than to (d) and that 9.8 belongs to (d) rather than (e). On the other hand, 13.1 is closely connected with the use of what is demonstrably a very rare word and hence the function of the gloss is of a sort with the others in category (d). The gloss of 9.8 interprets (as I suppose, mistakenly) the word *ṣph* in its standard sense and not in the sense which Hosea intended; hence its purpose is exegetical rather than 'translational' as in category (d).

The large reduction in the number of proposed emendations to the MT in this commentary *vis à vis* that of my distinguished predecessor is due to the following considerations: first, the greater reluctance of contemporary scholarship to resort to emendation on the grounds that it is often arbitrary and subjective in character (cf. Barr *CPOT*, pp. 72ff). Secondly, and more particularly, the recognition that Hosea's vocabulary is dialectal and cannot be treated as if it were Standard Biblical Hebrew. Thirdly, and related to the second consideration, the judgement that the ancient versions of Hosea were, in the main, confronted with a Hebrew text which differed little from our received text and that the ears of the translators, tuned more or less to Standard Biblical Hebrew, do not seem to have been tuned to his particular language and vocabulary. Fourthly, the identification of a number of early glosses within the text which, unidentified, have led scholars to suppose that the text in such instances is corrupt.

If emendation has its dangers, so too does wholesale resort to the methods of comparative philology (cf., again, Barr *CPOT*). Accordingly I have sought to rely heavily on the medieval rabbinic authorities and especially on ibn Janāḥ (for the simple reason that his particular views are so often convincing) in the attempt to relate my interpretations to established Jewish traditions and to the expertise of those uniquely at home with them. By contrast I have used sparingly suggestions of the sort more recently associated with the names of G. R. Driver and D. W. Thomas. See further pp. lvii–lix above.

The text of Hosea to which the MT and the ancient versions witness is likely to have reached roughly the form in which we have received it during post-exilic times[14]. When post-exilic glosses are excluded we may suppose that the consonantal text approximates to what left the pen of the Judaean redactors. In so far as we are able to identify their contributions and to exclude or to reverse them, we have some approximation to the text which arrived in Judah from Ephraim (see further pp. lxxif)[15].

The LXX

As the oldest of the ancient versions, whose origins stretch back to the Greek-speaking Jews of Alexandria in the third century BC, the LXX has long been regarded as a particularly important witness to the Hebrew text of the bible. Not least in importance is the consideration that the LXX antedates the normative standardisation of the consonantal Hebrew text, a process which had its origins in the first century BC, which reached its final form *c.* AD 100, and which was further confirmed by the vocalisation of the text, concluded by the middle of the first millennium.

[14] Cf., though from a different standpoint, the comments of Borbone.

[15] Borbone, in his recent study of the text of Hosea, believes that the various witnesses (MT, versions, etc.) must be used critically to reconstruct the exemplar or achetype of the text of Hosea (already corrupt by the time of the LXX) and thereafter, by conjecture, to reconstruct the 'original' text of Hosea, i.e. the text written 'by Judaic authors after the exile'. Borbone's text is, then, in the full sense of the word an eclectic text, and with that there need be *a priori* no disagreement; yet it is constructed on the basis of considerable reliance on the LXX and of a tendency to discount the value of MT. While there are clearly a few instances in which the versions indicate a text superior to MT (e.g. 11.3), generally they do not do so. The MT remains the best guide for any attempt to understand the message of the eighth century prophet and provides a solid basis for retrieving the text which that message brought to birth (so essentially Nyberg).

Recent studies of the Peshiṭta and the Targum of the Twelve Prophets are unfortunately not matched by any similar major endeavour in respect of the LXX version of the Twelve (or of Hosea in particular). It is possible, consequently, to give here only impressions gained as a result of the writing of a commentary on the Hebrew text[16].

While the LXX version of Hosea clearly shows considerable differences from the MT, it cannot be said to indicate a *Vorlage* which differed often or substantially from what has come down to us in the MT. It seems to have been the practice of the translator, particularly when confronted with difficult passages, to render the text word for word and without regard to the overall sense; thus, he extracts meanings which are often quite inappropriate (e.g. *ʿnh* in 2.17, EV 15, and 14.9). This very deficiency has, at times, the merit that it facilitates the careful analysis which reveals that, more often than not, he was confronted with the Hebrew consonantal text with which we are confronted (so Ziegler 'Verwertung', pp. 107f; cf. Neef, p. 219).

Secondly, if the translator is at times painfully literal (e.g. 2.1, EV 1.10, *bmqwm ʾšr*; 1.6 *lʾ ʾwsyp*; 8.9 *ʿlw*) and, at others, free and expansive (e.g. 5.13 and the addition of 'elders'; 7.13 *šd*), he very frequently resorts to approximate, 'rough' translations (e.g. 3.2 *wʾkrh*; 4.14 *yprdw*; 5.12 *ʿš*; 5.13 *yghh*; 9.2 *yrʿm*, if *r* was read; 13.5 *tlʾbwt*; 13.10, 14 *ʾhy*; 13.15 *ypryʾ*; 14.6, EV 5, *wyk*). The existence of what are explicable as approximate renderings of the Hebrew serves as a warning against too hasty a use (for the purpose of claiming a different *Vorlage*) of other renderings whose relationship to MT is less amenable to explanation. To claim, for example, that the LXX at 1.6 suggests forms of the root *śnʾ* rather than the MT's forms of the root *nśʾ* may be rejected; cf., further, 4.18 *mgnyh*; 7.12 *ʿdtm*; 8.13 *hbhby*; 9.2 *yrʿm*; 10.9 *ʿlwh*; 10.15 *byt ʾl, rʿtkm*; 11.3 *qḥm*; 12.1 (EV 11.12) *rd*; 12.9 (EV 8) *ygyʿy*. On the other hand, at 11.3 (*zrwʿty*) and 11.11 (*whšbwtym*) the LXX does seem to witness to a different and better *Vorlage*.

If, for example, compared with that of Samuel, the LXX of Hosea is of much less use for correcting errors in the MT (so Eissfeldt *Einleitung/Introduction*, pp. 957/705), it remains important in its own right as the earliest translation of Hosea's prophecies[17]. In this connection, the following points may be made: (1) The version testifies occasionally to word division which differs from MT (e.g. 9.13 *štwlh*; 12.1, EV 11.12, *ʿd rd ʿm ʾl*) and, more frequently, to a different

16 Muraoka's notes on the LXX of Hos 2, 4, 5, and on its rendering of *hapax legomena* reflect what he calls a 'wholistic' approach to the version. His endeavour suffers from the disadvantage that he is not moved to come to any particular conclusions nor to offer any judgements on the all-important question of the nature of the LXX's *Vorlage* as compared with the MT. For a balanced attempt to weigh such matters and to formulate some conclusions, see Neef, pp. 214–220.

17 See further the reasoned statement of Neef (pp. 219f).

construction of the words (called sometimes 'sense division'); for example, 4.10f (adopted here in preference to MT); 4.18; 6.5; 11.2. (2) In the light of the investigations of this commentary into the meaning of various Hebrew words, the LXX seems at times to deploy translations which accord with later exegetical traditions: e.g. 10.7 *qṣp* 'chip', 'stick', cf. ibn Ezra, Kimchi; 11.6 *bdyw* 'hands', cf. ibn Janāḥ, ibn Ezra, Kimchi. (3) Again, the version often seems to reflect knowledge of Standard Biblical Hebrew rather than the dialectal usage of Hosea. Examples are: *'nh* (2.17, EV 15; 14.9, EV 8); *šmr* (4.10; 12.13, EV 12); *śmḥ* (7.3); *bll* (7.8); *'lh* (8.9); *qbṣ* (8.10); *hbhb* (8.13); *ṣph* (9.8); *ḥlq* (10.2); *'br* (10.11); *r'h* (10.15, 12.2, EV 1); *mgn* (11.8); *tmrwrym* (12.15, EV 14). (4) On the other hand, there are a number of rare words which the LXX seems to have rendered more or less correctly. Since some of the instances may be characterised as approximate translations (and are here marked 'A'), it is difficult to judge whether the translator made his decisions on the basis of knowledge or on that of intelligent guess-work. Examples are: *nblt* (2.12, EV 10); *w'krh* A(3.2); *prd* (4.14); *ṣw* (5.11); *'š* A(5.12); *ghh* A(5.13); *z'm* A(7.16); *r'h* A(9.2), if *r* was read; *'lwh* A(10.9); *s'r* (13.3); *tl'bwt* A(13.5); *'hy* (13.10, 14); *nḥm* A(13.14); *bwš* A(13.15); *wyk* A(14.6, EV 5). (5) Finally there are a number of renderings which may be judged to be inaccurate: they include *nś'* (1.6); *ḥdš* (5.7); *hw'yl* (5.11); *'dtm* (7.12); *bśwry* (9.12); *bšnh* (10.6); *trgl* (11.3). (6) The glosses identified in this commentary are all reproduced in the LXX except that, in the case of 7.15, where a rare word in the MT is immediately followed by a gloss in the form of a synonym, the LXX has but one word. It is conceivable that the *Vorlage* of the LXX represents a textual tradition in which the gloss was not included. More likely, however, is the supposition that the translator rendered the word familiar to him from Standard Biblical Hebrew and chose to ignore the word (*ysrty*) with which he was unfamiliar.

Mention may be made of the following editions of the text of the LXX published since Harper's commentary: *Septuaginta* A. Rahlfs (ed.) (6th edition, Stuttgart, 1959); *Duodecim Prophetae* (Göttingen, 1st edition, 1943; 2nd edition,1967).

The Old Latin Version

The Old Latin version, or *Vetus Latina*, is a translation of the LXX which dates from the second and third centuries AD in North Africa, Gaul and Italy. It was used by Latin-speaking Christians and is important in that it ante-dates the recensions of the LXX of the third and fourth centuries. It has survived only in fragments, as witnessed by three useful MSS (Codex Wirceburgensis, sixth century; Codex Constantiensis, fifth century; Fragmenta Sangallensia, ninth century). Readings from these MSS are included by Ziegler in the apparatus of his edition of the LXX. The fragments are: 1.1–4.12a (S); 1.1b–2.13a,

15a (W); 4.14–7.1a (W); 7.16c–9.17 (C); 8.1–14.10 (S); 13.4c–14.4a (C). Jerome, in his Commentary, normally and verse by verse provides a Latin translation of the LXX and, when he does not, he writes *LXX similiter*, thereby implying that there is no essential variation from his Vulgate text. This translation is styled by Ziegler (p. 17) '*ein altlateinischer fortlaufender Bibeltext*'.

The OL version is occasionally helpful to the task of understanding the LXX (e.g. 3.1) and from time to time throws light on traditions of interpretation (e.g. 1.4, Jezreel and Jehu; 1.6, 8, Lo-Ruḥamah; 14.6, 7). Jerome's translation of the LXX is similarly useful in places (e.g. 5.2; 7.2; 9.16; 10.4, 6; 11.11). There is at present no edition of the OL version, though reference may be made to W. O. E. Oesterley's compilation which is now, naturally, somewhat out-of-date.

The Minor Greek Versions

The versions by Aquila (*c.* AD 130), Symmachus (late second century AD) and Theodotion (second century AD) originated as a result of the increasing disfavour in which the LXX was held in Jewish circles. It is likely that those versions made use of earlier attempts of the same sort and in the case of the Minor Prophets there are substantial fragments of a leather scroll containing a Greek translation from Naḥal Ḥever (Wādi Murabba'at) in the Judaean desert and dated tentatively by P. J. Parsons to the later first century BC[18]. Quinta[19], probably of Jewish origin, is quoted from time to time in Origen's Hexapla (AD 240–245).

Aquila's version of Hosea shares the characteristics generally discernible elsewhere, *viz.* a predilection for pedantic literalness. Theodotion's rendering is a revision of the LXX by reference to the Hebrew text, while Symmachus sought to avoid the over-literalness of Aquila by expressing the sense of the Hebrew in good Greek. Of the three versions Jerome and Lucian of Antioch showed a preference for that of Symmachus.

J. Ziegler's 'Beiträge zum griechischen Dodekapropheton' (1943), pp. 345ff, represents one of the few attempts to evaluate a number of readings of the text of Hosea in the minor Greek versions. Ziegler is at pains to note that a large number of the readings were transmitted only in Syriac (i.e. in the Syro-Hexapla) and hence an element of conjecture in estimating which Greek words lay behind the Syriac adds to the difficulties. In general, however, he concludes that the *Vorlage* used by these versions was generally identical to the *Textus Receptus* (i.e. MT).

[18] See Barthélemy *RB* 60 (1953), pp. 18ff and *Les devanciers* pp. 67f; P. Kahle *ThLZ* 79 (1954), cols 81ff and *Cairo Geniza*, pp. 225ff. See *DJD* 8 for the published edition.

[19] Barthélemy *ThZ* 16 (1960), pp. 342ff.

Apparent discrepancies as between the MT and these versions, such as singular/plural forms or in the rendering of the tenses of verbs cannot be said necessarily to point to a different *Vorlage* but must be carefully evaluated in the light of what can be established about the translators' techniques. After such evaluation, Ziegler believes that it is possible to point to a different Hebrew *Vorlage* only in isolated instances, e.g. in 10.4 where Symmachus and Theodotion (in common with the LXX) seem to have read *kdš(')* for MT's *kr'š*. For the rest, these versions point to a Hebrew *Vorlage* which contains minor differences from MT (i.e. in vocalisation, confusion of letters and metathesis). Examples include: 5.7, Symm. *yldw*; 6.8, Theod. *'qbh*; 7.16, Symm. *'l* (vocalisation); 8.10, Theod. *mmś'*; 9.13, Theod. *bnwh* (confusion of letters).

For the few instances where renderings of the Minor Greek Versions (notably Symmachus) coincide with estimates here adopted as to the meaning of difficult words in Hosea, see above p. lx. The readings of the Minor Versions are taken from F. Field *Origenis Hexaplorum quae supersunt* II (Oxford, 1867).

The Peshiṭta

An edition of this version (of the Minor Prophets) has recently been prepared by A. Gelston under the auspices of the Leiden project with the title *The Old Testament in Syriac/Vetus Testamentum Syriace* (III 4, 1980). *Dodekapropheton.* Gelston's companion volume *The Peshiṭta of the Twelve Prophets* (Oxford, 1987) is a thorough evaluation of the data which emerged from his collation and evaluation of the biblical MSS of the Peshiṭta of the Twelve and scholars owe a considerable debt of gratitude to him for his painstaking and important work. It is not necessary here to do other than indicate Gelston's general conclusions. He finds (pp. 116, 118) but one instance in the text of Hosea where the Peshiṭta presupposes a significant extant non-massoretic reading (4.16, cf. *CD* i 13–14); he concludes that the Hebrew *Vorlage* presupposed by the Peshiṭta was closely similar to the MT though word-division occasionally, and vocalisation more often, differed from that of the later Massoretic tradition; investigation of the translation methods adopted in the Peshiṭta reveals that some of the apparent agreements of the Peshiṭta with variant readings in later Hebrew MSS etc. are probably to be attributed to the initiative of the translators rather than to derivation from a Hebrew *Vorlage* distinct from MT; other readings are to be attributed to the influence of the LXX or of the exegetical traditions attested also in the Targum. He concludes, 'the Peshiṭta of the Dodekapropheton has thus only a limited contribution to make to the reconstruction of a putative original Hebrew text' (p. 192). Gelston proves that the Peshiṭta knew and made use of the LXX and supposes that agreements between the Peshiṭta and the Targum reveal 'a common exegetical tradition or common linguistic factors rather than ... a relationship of direct literary dependence on either side' (p. 192).

As to the origin of the version, Gelston concludes that it was probably made within a Jewish community in the middle or late first century AD and that several translators contributed to the work. His careful and well-founded conclusions agree substantially with the impression on the matter gained in the course of preparing this commentary.

The Targum

The text quoted in this commentary is that edited by A. Sperber (Leiden, 1975) under the general title *The Bible in Aramaic. III. The Latter Prophets according to Targum Jonathan*. A translation, with notes and an Introduction, was published in 1989 under the title *The Targum of the Minor Prophets* (Wilmington, Delaware) by K. J. Cathcart and R. P. Gordon (C/G), the former being responsible for Targum Jonathan to Hosea[20].

The distinctive features of the Targum to Hosea are those of the Targum in general; the rendering is very free, at times amounting to paraphrase, serving the purpose of presenting to the ordinary reader or hearer a version which is uniformly intelligible. The originality and vitality of the original text is often lost to 'sameness and jejuneness' (C/G, p. 2). Again, metaphors frequently become similes and prophetic symbolic actions, such as the all-important Hos 1.2 and 3.1, are replaced by bland theological substitutes. Explanatory words and phrases are very frequently added and stock theological expressions abound; e.g., the *Memra* or 'word' of God appears frequently as the agent of his will and his *Shekinah* or presence as a symbol of his favour; the more direct personal relationship between God and his people is replaced by a definition in terms of the service or worship of God; the ubiquitous *mn qdm*, 'from before (God)', serves to remove any lingering traces of anthropomorphism which, in any case, is always replaced by paraphrase. The orthodox beliefs of rabbinic Judaism (e.g., Messiah, the Law, Resurrection, Repentance) often find expression in the version and the process of rendering the MT is made to serve this purpose.

The Targum of Hosea, in common with the generality of such Targums, represents essentially the massoretic text-form (so C/G, p. 10). Two examples of non-massoretic readings are suggested by them (6.5, *mšpṭy*; 13.10, *'yh*); both suggestions are discounted in this commentary. For the rest C/G's caution concerning the use of the Targum to establish non-

20 The translation appeared after I had made considerable progress with the commentary and I have not always harmonised my own translations with those of Cathcart.

massoretic readings is noteworthy: 'many a non-Massoretic reading has been reconstructed in the modern period by scholars whose skill in retroversion has not been matched by awareness of the characteristics of the Targum which render such exercises generally inadvisable'. (C/G, p. 11).

As regards the date and provenance of the Targum to the Minor Prophets, C/G conclude that, though the case for considering it as a Palestinian composition in origin is strong, the case for editorial activity in Babylon is even stronger (C/G, p. 14); they suppose that the evidence points to a post-AD 70 date for the 'significant work of composition or editing', though they acknowledge the generally held assumption that the version had an oral prehistory (C/G, pp. 16, 18).

The Vulgate

St Jerome's Latin version of what he called the *Hebraica veritas* was made in Bethlehem between AD 390 and AD 405. Although it is late, in general it witnesses to a stage of the Hebrew text which still antedates the final form with its fixed vocalisation. The version was declared *textus auctoritate plenus* by the Council of Trent in 1546.

The version of Hosea follows the MT very closely but is at times influenced by the Greek versions, especially the LXX and Symmachus. While sometimes it follows the literalness of Aquila (e.g. 8.13 *hbhby*), more frequently Jerome prefers to convey the sense with judicious freedom. Of considerable importance in evaluating his translation of Hosea is his own commentary on the prophecy, which clearly reflects his Christian standpoint and, replete with references to the New Testament, becomes at times devotional in character. An example of lyrical beauty is his comparison of 2.9 (EV 7) with the parable of the Prodigal Son of Lk 15.11–32. If the commentary is marked by such characteristics, there remains much useful material on textual matters. Jerome begins each verse by rendering from the Hebrew and follows at once with a rendering of the LXX version. Thereafter he frequently mentions the renderings of the Minor Greek Versions. Examples of his predilection for the *Hebraica veritas*, as of his care in recording details of the Hebrew text, may be found at 8.6, where he argues against the LXX and Theodotion (*sababum* with *waw*) in favour of the Hebrew *sababim*, i.e. with *yodh*; 9.13, where the Hebrew *ṣwr* is defended against the LXX which he supposes mistakenly read *sud* (√צוד I).

Such examples in particular, as well as the general impressions gained from the Vulgate of Hosea and Jerome's commentary upon it, suggest that Jerome's Hebrew *Vorlage* differed little, if at all, from the MT. That, in view of conclusions gained from a study of the earlier versions, is hardly surprising. There can be no doubt that Jerome found Hosea's Hebrew very difficult (see p. liii above). Yet his work is important in that, having learnt Hebrew from Jews in (Syrian) Chalcis and Bethlehem, he is sometimes a witness to contemporary Jewish traditions concerning the meaning of words. As an example, 11.6 may be cited; he is aware that *bdyw*, rendered literally by Symmachus 'arms', 'branches', is capable of a metaphorical sense.

The Vulgate displays no particular or consistent knowledge of Hosea's dialect and no textual variant not found in the earlier versions is adopted in this commentary on the basis of this version.

The editions used here are *Biblia Sacra iuxta Vulgatam Versionem* II, R. Weber et al. (edd.) (Stuttgart, 1969 and 1975).

THE HISTORICAL BACKGROUND[21]

With the superscription of 1.1 and its statement that the word of the Lord first came to Hosea in the days of Jeroboam II of Israel (787–747 BC), the contents of chapter 1 and its reference (v. 4) to the imminent end of the House of Jehu (Jeroboam's great-grandfather) are consistent. The pain expressed in the unit 13.1–14.1, culminating in the brutal objectivity of 14.1 (EV 13.16), suggests that the piece was written shortly before the fall of Samaria in 722/1 BC. Hosea's writings, then, reflect a period of some thirty years beginning *c.* 750 BC.

The accession of Tiglath-pileser III (known as Pul in the OT) to the throne of Assyria in 745 BC marked a decisive turning point in the history of the Ancient Near East. This able and vigorous soldier began the definitive process by which, for the next hundred years and more, Assyria was to become the power which completely dominated the region of which Israel/Palestine formed part. To be sure, he followed a pattern established by some of his predecessors, notably Shalmaneser III, who, in 841 BC, had cut through Syria and reached the Lebanese coast to the north of Beirut (*ANET*, p. 280, cols 1f). The initial purpose of such expeditions seems to have been to appropriate the plentiful timber resources of the region (cf. *ANET*, p. 278, col 1). Such incursions were never consolidated and Shalmaneser, after the last such incursion in 838 BC, withdrew from Syria without establishing any permanent garrison (cf. *ANET*, p. 280, col 2).

The Assyrian withdrawal at once freed Israel's neighbour and adversary Syria to renew her efforts to gain control of the territory of Ephraim/Manasseh to the east of the Jordan (cf. Amos 1.3) and, under her ruthlessly successful king Hazael, she

21 The reader is referred to the Table of Dates on pp. xcviii f.

largely succeeded in her endeavour (2 Kgs 10.32f). Hazael, moreover, encouraged the Philistines in their attacks on Israel and Judah (? Amos 1.6) and, at the same time, the Ammonites in Transjordan seized the opportunity to 'enlarge their border' in Gilead, south of the Jabbok (Amos 1.13).

Such border disputes between the smaller nations, in which clearly Israel (and Judah) were the losers, were abruptly brought to an end in 796 BC when the Assyrian king Adadnirari III followed the pattern set by his predecessors, invaded Syria and, encircling Damascus, forced its king to pay tribute[22]. The expedition seems to have caused the fortunes of Damascus to decline appreciably and, in consequence, those of Hamath in central Syria to improve. With Damascus now weak, Israel was able to enter a period of peace and prosperity and Jeroboam II's father Jehoash began to retrieve the cities and settlements in Transjordan which had been purloined by the Syrians (2 Kgs 13.22ff). The endeavour was furthered by Jeroboam II, whose forty-year reign began in 787 (789) BC. He is credited with restoring 'the frontier of Israel from the pass of Hamath as far as the sea of the Arabah' (i.e. the Dead Sea, 2 Kgs 14.25), and his achievement lies in his having secured the length of the eastern frontier of Israel, i.e. the frontier which obtained in the time of David and Solomon and which included land east of the Jordan encompassing Ramoth-gilead. That land to the south of the Jabbok was also returned to Ephraim's control from that of the Ammonites may be deduced from Hos 6.8ff and from the likelihood that Pekah, with assistance from the city of Gilead in this area, mounted thence his successful bid for the throne of Samaria (2 Kgs 15.25).

The prophecies of Hosea and Amos bear ample witness to the freedom and prosperity of Ephraim during Jeroboam II's long reign. Free from external assaults and the necessity to pay tribute, the nation was able to enjoy the fruits of its agricultural endeavours and the success of its economy (cf. 2.7, 10, EV 5, 8; 12.9, EV 8; Amos 3.15; 5.11). More particularly, enjoyment of prosperity and plenty manifested itself in exuberant and lavish cultic worship, with its attendant feasting, drinking and sexual licence (cf. 2.13, 15, EV 11, 13; 4.11, 13; 8.13; Amos 2.7f; 4.4; 5.21ff etc). Again, a strong measure of independence encouraged the expression of nationalistic pride (cf. 5.5) and, in Israel, this seems to have been associated with the royal cult of the 'calf of Samaria' (8.4ff), introduced by Jeroboam I some one hundred

22 See A. R. Millard *PEQ* 105 (1973), pp. 161ff and W. T. Pitard *Ancient Damascus* (Winona Lake, 1987), pp. 160–165.

and forty years earlier for just such purposes (1 Kgs 12.28). Despite the strong condemnation of this king's action by the later Deuteronomists, for whom it was the paradigmatic act of idolatry, it seems clear that Jeroboam I intended to foster an authentic cult of Yahweh in the north in order, for political and religious reasons, to diminish the claims of Judaean Jerusalem.

Israel's freedom from external threat during Jeroboam II's reign was matched by a similar freedom in Judah. The two states had engaged in border disputes during the early ninth century BC but the aggressive dominance of Syria during the period of the dynasty of Omri in the second half of the century prompted the kings of that dynasty to bury the hatchet and to co-operate with the smaller Judaean kingdom against what they perceived to be a common danger. Indeed, such co-operative endeavour is reflected in the marriage between Ahab's daughter, Athaliah and Jehoram of Judah (2 Kgs 8.18). One incident only seems to have interrupted the tranquil co-existence of the two states, *viz.* the battle of Beth-shemesh early in the eighth century, when the Judaean Amaziah challenged the military supremacy of Jehoash of Israel and was soundly beaten (2 Kgs 14.8ff). The Israelites plundered the treasuries of Judah and damaged part of the wall of Jerusalem, but the incident seems to have had no perceptible consequences other than, perhaps, to confirm the status of the Northern Kingdom as the more powerful of the two. At all events the long reign of Uzziah of Judah (787–736 BC), contemporary with Jeroboam II, marked for the former, as for the latter, a time of relative calm and prosperity.

Tiglath-pileser III began to implement his policy of subjugating the whole area of Syria/Palestine with his attacks on Syria in 740 BC and 738 BC. Northern Syria and the central Syrian state of Hamath were at this time appropriated and turned into Assyrian provinces (*ANET*, p. 282, col 2 – p. 283, col 1)[23]. A number of neighbouring rulers, including 'Menahem of Samaria' and 'Rezon of Damascus' (= Rezin of 2 Kgs 15.37 etc.), acknowledged Assyrian ascendancy by paying tribute and thereby, for the time being, escaped the more radical fate of having their kingdoms reduced to Assyrian provinces (*ANET*, p. 283, col 1). Menahem of Samaria had but recently usurped the throne, following the murder of the last king of the dynasty of Jehu, and 2 Kgs 15.19f suggests that his motive in paying tribute lay in his need for external support in the confirmation of his position. The same passage agrees with the testimony of Tiglath-

[23] On the question of lines 103–119 of this text, see N. Na'aman *BASOR* 214 (1974), pp. 25–39.

pileser concerning the payment of tribute and it makes clear that Menahem had collected a thousand talents of silver from the landowners of Ephraim.

In 734 BC Tiglath-pileser, not content with what he had achieved previously, mounted an expedition to Philistia which reached as far as Gaza and the Wādi el-Arish where he established a garrison, thereby making it difficult for the small states of the area to appeal to Egypt for help. In the course of this expedition the Assyrians secured their route through central Syria to the coast whence, turning south along the coastal plain, they reached their objective (cf. *ANET*, p. 283, col 2 – p. 284, col 1). It is probable that that part of the coastal plain which belonged to Israel was at this time appropriated by Tiglath-pileser in order to secure his lines of communication[24].

Meanwhile, in 736 BC Pekah had mounted his successful bid for the throne of Samaria (Hos 6.7ff; 2 Kgs 15.25) and, shortly thereafter, he began to involve himself in a conspiracy to rebel against the Assyrians under the leadership of Rezin of Damascus. The events that followed are commonly styled the Syro-Ephraimite War of 733 BC. 2 Kings 15.37; 16.5; Isa 7.1ff record that Israel and Syria, having failed to win the support of Ahaz of Jerusalem for their plot, resolved to depose him and place a Syrian sympathetic to their cause in his place. To that end they marched south and laid siege to Jerusalem. According to Isa 7.1, however, they were unable to provoke a decisive battle against the Judaeans. In the meantime, Ahaz appealed to Tiglath-pileser of Assyria for help, sending to him extensive inducements in the form of gifts from the treasuries of the Temple and of the palace. Whether the Assyrian king needed such inducements is questionable, since his campaign of 734 BC revealed his clear intention to subjugate the whole of Syria and Palestine. With large parts of northern and central Syria in his possession, Damascus and Israel were the only remaining powers to be neutralised. At all events, Tiglath-pileser first attacked Israel and, in 733 BC, moving southward along the upper Jordan, he fanned out and conquered Galilee to the west and Gilead to the east (cf. 2 Kgs 15.29). He records that he had conquered 'all the cities' (*sc.* of Israel) and that Samaria with its king (i.e. Pekah) alone escaped this fate (*ANET*, p. 283, col 2). The conquered areas were organised as three Assyrian provinces named after the principal towns in them, thus: the province of Megiddo, comprising Galilee and the plain of Jezreel; the province of Dor, comprising that part of the coastal plain south of Carmel; the

24 Alt *KS* II, pp. 150ff.

province of Gilead, comprising Israelite land east of the Jordan. In accordance with their practice, the upper classes from these areas were deported to Assyria and replaced by similar elements from elsewhere in the empire. The following year saw Damascus suffer the same fate. Henceforth the whole of Syria-Palestine was in Assyrian hands save only the strongly fortified city of Samaria and the mountains of Ephraim south of the Jezreel valley. Judah had submitted and, as a small state off the beaten track of the Assyrian lines of communication, it was, for the time being, left alone.

Pekah of Israel, discredited by Tiglath-pileser's successes, was assassinated in 732 BC by Hoshea, who became the last king of Samaria (2 Kgs 15.30, cf. *ANET*, p. 283, col 2 – p. 284, col 1). His vassal status is clear from the fact that he paid substantial tribute and from Tiglath-pileser's own statement, 'I placed Hoshea as king over them'. In 725 BC Hoshea, probably in concert with other states, sought help from the Egyptians in a bid to shake off the Assyrian yoke. The Assyrian response was swift: Hoshea, presumably travelling outside Samaria, was seized in person and the siege of Samaria began.

Tiglath-pileser died in 727 BC and his successor Shalmaneser V reigned for four years. Samaria finally fell in 722/1 BC, shortly before the accession of Sargon II, who claimed the title 'conqueror of Samaria' (*ANET*, p. 284, col 1)[25]. Thereafter Samaria became an Assyrian province of that name from which, again, the upper classes were deported and to which comparable elements were imported (cf. 2 Kgs 17.24 and *ANET*, p. 284, col 2 – p. 285, col 1). The moment marked the end of the Northern Kingdom; from then on it ceased to exist.

THE ESSENCE OF HOSEA'S THOUGHT

Any account of Hosea's ministry as a prophet must be constructed from the literary work which bears his name. That literary work testifies to the prophet's interpretation of the decline and imminent fall of the kingdom of Ephraim and, made from a blend of the matter of his public oracles and of his personal amplifications and meditations upon them (p. lxix), constitutes what has become a prophetic interpretation of some thirty years of the history of his times. It has been argued above (p. lxix) that the work as a whole reflects Hosea's thinking after he had withdrawn from his public ministry and that it is largely

[25] Cf. Cogan and Tadmor, p. 199.

retrospective. The book, then, constitutes a record of the authentication of the prophet's judgements and perceptions by reference to the events which led to the fall of Samaria in 722/1 BC. Thereafter, modified by Judaean redactors, the work became, in turn, a statement of their understanding of the fall and demise of Ephraim (pp. lxxff).

Hosea's function as a prophet exercising a public ministry (cf. 9.7 and p. lxvi) was clearly to warn his people that the kingdom of Ephraim, unreformed, was doomed to perdition. His view seems to have been formulated initially in the prosperous times which marked the closing years of the reign of Jeroboam II. He believed that, for all the outward signs of well-being and plenty, the present constitution of the state, personified in the dynasty of Jehu, was established upon the reprehensible basis of bloodthirsty cruelty and self-serving fanaticism (1.4). The judgement is the more remarkable in that it is based on criteria which are more sophisticated than those which were inclined to see in Jehu's overthrow of the dynasty of Omri simply a triumph of Yahwism over the encroaches of Baalism.

If the state was tainted by murder in the establishment of the dynasty of Jehu, then the mode by which that dynasty was replaced by a succession of *coups d'état* was not less dishonourable or debilitating. In the short period between the death of Jeroboam II (747 BC) and the fall of Samaria (722/1 BC), no fewer than six kings ascended the throne; four were assassinated.

For Hosea these events were symptomatic of the disease which raged in the very constitution of his nation. Yet he did not equate the symptoms with the disease itself. To be sure, the symptoms in all their unpleasantness reflected Yahweh's creation of a moral order which, abused, must necessarily result in their manifestation. Accordingly, for Hosea, the rapid succession of *coups d'état* was seen as a punishment inflicted by a God of consistency whose moral order had been abused (8.4; 13.11). For all this the prophet does not seem to have condemned in principle the institution of the Ephraimite monarchy itself (cf. Gelston, 'Kingship'). On the contrary, he may in this respect have shared the sentiments expressed in what is generally regarded as an Ephraimite psalm – 80.18, EV 17 (so Davies, p. 32). With this, 7.5 and its apparently favourable, if transient, reference to 'our king' may be compared. On the view here adopted that 2.2 (EV 1.11) accurately reflects Hosea's views, the use of the word 'head' to describe the leader of a restored, united and single Israel is tentative in character (cf. Gelston, *op. cit.*, p. 78); it accords with the prophet's prayer for a new beginning, a new constitution of the people of Yahweh, a creation untainted by the corrupt manifestations of leadership which he had known; its unity expressed in loyalty to a common single leader, defined in terms of the pre-monarchical past. It is unlikely that Hosea looked to Judah and Jerusalem for the fulfilment of his prayer, though clearly the Judaean redactors of his work were disposed to interpret it in this sense (see on 3.5).

Hosea's indictment of the official state religion of Ephraim (8.4ff) is closely connected with his diagnosis of the diseased nature of the monarchy of his times . The calf of Samaria (i.e. the calf of the kingdom of which Samaria was the capital) was worshipped as an expression of the particular identity and aspirations of the Northern Kingdom. There can be no doubt that it was, on the one hand, intentionally and intimately connected with Yahweh, the God who brought his people from Egypt; but it testified also to a national (8.6) policy of syncretism, undertaken by Jeroboam I for the purpose of consolidating the independence of Ephraim and of uniting the Israelite and Canaanite elements of its population. It is perhaps significant that Hosea's judgement (with its reference to *one* calf) belongs to the later stages of his ministry (i.e. after 733 BC and the loss of Dan) and to his retrospective meditations (10.5); for the calf and Ephraim as it existed were virtually synonymous. The imminent total collapse of Ephraim (9.7) is quite in step with the imminent annihilation of the calf which epitomised its whole endeavour (8.5f; 10.6). The judgement, then, that the calf was a mere idol comparable in every respect to the idolatrous artefacts made and worshipped by his contemporaries (8.4, 6; 13.2; cf. 2.10, EV 8), may represent a very particular and personal insight on Hosea's part. If he understood and knew that Ephraim was doomed, he understood, too, that the state's false perceptions of itself and of its God, epitomised in the calf of Samaria, had proved illusory and bankrupt (8.5). This insight is summarised thus (10.1): 'Israel is a damaged vine whose fruit fails him. At the time that his fruit should have been prolific, he was prolific with altars; when his land should have been at its best, they excelled with sacred pillars.' At any rate, so clear is Hosea's insight that, following the collapse of Ephraim in 722/1 BC, his words became normative as an explanation for that collapse. So it was that the Deuteronomists applied the lesson inherited from Hosea and characterised the apostasy of Jeroboam I as the cardinal sin of Ephraim and by reference to it they judged all his successors in the history which eventually they edited.

If the calf of Samaria represented the syncretistic policy of the state, Hosea's own preaching to his contemporaries, the individual members of that state (2.4ff, EV 2ff), seems at an earlier stage to have made much the same point. The all-important and definitive statement of 2.18 (EV 16), expressed in the context of Hosea's longing for a new beginning, reveals that his contemporaries individually were disposed to think of Yahweh as if he were Baal, the Canaanite god of fertility. It is possible that worship of this deity survived in Ephraim after the prophetic reforms of the ninth century BC[26]. Yet it is significant, perhaps, that, according to 2 Kgs 13.6, it was the cult of Asherah which remained in Samaria during the reign of Jehoahaz, son of Jehu, the latter being the commander of the force which pressed to its bloodthirsty conclusion the specifically Yahwistic reforms of Elijah and Elisha. The now famous pithos inscription of the first half of the eighth century BC from the Ephraimite outpost of Kuntillet 'Ajrud (in the Egyptian Sinai desert) with its invocation of a blessing by 'Yahweh of Samaria and his Asherah' accords well with Hosea's precise definition of 2.18 (EV 16). Thus, at Kuntillet 'Ajrud it is Yahweh and his Asherah that are invoked and not Baal and his Asherah[27]. Accordingly, the force of Hosea's words in chapter 2 does not suggest that, like Elijah, he was obliged to confront the religion of Baal head on. Rather, the corrupt, syncretistic forms of Yahwism, according to which the national God was perceived as fulfilling the functions of Baal in ensuring the fertility of the land, produced in the minds of his contemporaries a type of schizophrenia which Hosea chose to indict by the rhetorical expedient of accusing his contemporaries of regression to the worship of Baal while, at the same time, retaining a nominal allegiance to Yahweh, cf. 2.15, 9b (EV 13, 7b). The same point is made in the prophet's later meditation upon his people's proclivity to gross ingratitude. Making use of traditions which emerge in Num 25, he points (9.10) to the incident at (Beth-) Baal-peor as a *locus classicus* in which Yahweh's generous love for his people is betrayed by their fathers' immediate surrender to a desire to accommodate themselves to the seductive charms of a religion so closely associated with the cultivated land (cf. Gilgal in 9.15; 12.12, EV 11).

In all this (and here is the root of the matter) it is his people's faulty perceptions which are the real cause of the national malaise. Their minds in times of plenty had been infected by a promiscuous impulse (4.12; 5.4) and this manifested itself most

26 See p. 80 below for the evidence of the Samaria Ostraca.

27 For references to the literature on Kuntillet 'Ajrud and Khirbet el-Qom, see on 14.9.

directly in their addiction to cultic exuberance, to the sensual pleasures of endless (8.13) feasting and drinking which were more typical of the worship of Baal than that of Yahweh (4.10–19). On the tops of the hills, under the shade of the trees, their consciences eased by sanctions of religious observance, they indulged in sexual orgies with the prostitutes and cult-women who were wont to associate themselves with the sanctuaries (see on 4.14). For Hosea such indulgence robbed men of their reason (4.11); they failed to see that it was their own society which suffered the resulting damage (4.13) and their own nation whose moral perception was disastrously atrophied. Accordingly their depravity had become in all respects of a sort with that associated long ago with Gibeah and the notorious wickedness perpetrated by the Benjamites (9.9; 10.9). A large part of the blame was to be laid at the doors of the priests who presided over such abominable and dangerous practices; those whose function was properly to impart knowledge, i.e. within the context of Yahwism, *conscientia* or sound evaluation of moral truth (cf. on *'l 'l*, 11.7), had rejected it for the easy life of self-centred indulgence (4.4ff, cf. 5.1).

The cancer of false perception, easily contracted in the affluent times of Jeroboam II, was to spread ever wider within the constitution of Ephraim. Promiscuity, caught in the cult and in its associated idolatry, was for Hosea the term which best epitomised all the nation's depraved and immoral behaviour. As the events of 736 BC drew on, he concluded that the national establishment, in its monarchy and priesthood, had quite failed Ephraim, now itself defiled and trapped in the toils of its own hopeless inadequacy (5.3). In this state Ephraim was incapable of redemption (5.4, cf. 11.7), of finding her way back to the only source of healing. The anti-Assyrian Syro-Ephraimite confederation, following Menahem's submission to Assyria of 738 BC, marked the beginnings of Ephraim's political pursuit of futility (5.11); and the resulting *débâcle*, both in a civil war between elements of the very people of Yahweh and in the reduction by the Assyrians of Ephraim to a rump state in 733 BC, was a terrible consequence of it. By now, indeed, Yahweh's full fury was manifest; he, so consistently and wrongly diminished in the perception of his people, had repudiated them and became in truth the emaciating disease which was destroying their being; the lion who mauled them and ripped them to pieces (5.12, 14).

For Hosea promiscuity (6.10) also characterises the monstrous circumstances of the conspiracy by which Pekah, renouncing divinely sanctioned allegiance (6.7), snatched the throne of Ephraim (6.7–7.2). Promiscuity, akin to mental aberration, defiled the name of Israel (6.10) and led it, as a silly dove (7.11), to revert first to pro-Egyptian and then, again, to pro-Assyrian policies. Such vacillation, such fleeting commitments, first to one policy and then to its opposite, marked another aspect of the nation's disregard of its God and is characterised by Hosea as the meretricious love-affairs of promiscuity (8.9f).

If what has been set out so far represents Hosea's prophetic indictment and condemnation of his people, there remains to be contrasted with it his positive teachings. In the nature of the case warning and condemnation belonged to his public ministry and to the urgent need to try to bring his people to their senses. By contrast, his positive teaching is largely to be found in the prayers and meditations which belong, as I suppose, to the period in which he had withdrawn from that public ministry. To be sure, elements of the parable of the unfaithful wife of chapter 2 are necessarily positive in character; thus, it is clear that the wife's unfaithfulness stands in contrast to the caring love of her husband (2.10, EV 8) and points to Yahweh's consistent graciousness. Indeed, the husband's very interventions, even the harsh ones, are designed to restore the wife to the love where alone she will find her security. Again, Hosea's prayer for the nation's penitence (6.1–3), deeply personal in its character, introduces a strongly positive note within the context of unrelieved judgement and condemnation. If Yahweh must of necessity smite, maul, destroy, he alone, properly honoured, was capable of healing, restoration and salvation.

If false perceptions of the nation's God constituted the root cause of the sickness which raged within it, the antidote lay always to hand and it consisted of the correct understanding of ethical reality and of Yahweh who had defined and created it. The all-important phrase is, for Hosea, 'knowledge of Yahweh' (4.6; 6.3, 6). From the nation's personal experience of Yahweh's actions and initiatives, from recognition of their unique salutary effect, there followed, or there should have followed, that whole knowledge and integrity of thought, associated closely with allegiance to him, to be defined by later philosophers and theologians as *conscientia*[28]. The proper attitudes of gratitude and allegiance to Yahweh brought with them, necessarily and as a reflection of his nature, his particular gift of *ḥesed* (2.21, EV 19), 'kindness/goodness', which, like charity, is 'the very bond of peace and of all virtues' and which alone could ensure the wholesome fabric of society and of the nation. If, for the

[28] A. E. Taylor *The Faith of a Moralist*, single vol. edn., London, 1951; I, pp. 208ff and II, pp. 239ff.

philosopher Kant, 'there is nothing wholly good without qualification either in the world or without it except the good will'[29], then for Hosea, too, knowledge of Yahweh has as its supreme importance that it informs the reason, shapes intention and thus ensures actions which are consistent with conscience. Accordingly, in 10.12, he urges his contemporaries, forswearing evil intention and policy (10.10), to grasp the opportunity to seek Yahweh and, in so doing, to co-operate, as if in agricultural endeavour, in the good and edifying intentions which are consistent with social righteousness, justice and kindness (2.21, EV 19). Indeed, intention is the only real and necessary precondition of a process which, once it is initiated, continues as surely as does sequence in the natural world, which accurately reflects it and which also, properly understood, is a distinctive gift of Yahweh (cf. 6.3; 10.12; 2.23ff, EV 21ff).

If all such teaching is radically consistent with what, in the Christian tradition, is described as a doctrine of grace (cf. 12.7, EV 6), Hosea judged his contemporaries to be wretchedly incapable of responding to it. Though they were summoned to higher things, yet they prevaricated in regard to returning to Yahweh. If they adopted any change of heart, it was contaminated by false perception and thus deflected from its proper direction (*'l 'l*, 11.7, cf. 7.16). To this problem Hosea also pays attention, and he does so more particularly by reference to the vicissitudes of the nation's eponymous ancestor Jacob (12.3ff, EV 2ff), who was, from the moment of his birth, driven by motives of self-assertion and greed. Yet, although in his mature years he sought even to dominate God in the furtherance of his own ambition, he found himself face to face with none other than Yahweh, the God of Hosts, who could not but prevail (12.4ff, EV 3ff). He was the God who, at Bethel, encountered Jacob and vouchsafed the promise that he and his descendants would return to inherit the land. Jacob, then, having been fundamentally corrected, fled to Syrian exile and, in his unselfish devotion to a woman which he formed there, he became, with her and in accordance with the dispositions of Yahweh's providence, the worthy forbear of Israel itself. The devotion shown by the patriarch was of a sort with Yahweh's devotion shown to the nation through the prophet Moses in the events of the exodus (12.14, EV 13).

Yahweh, the God of Hosts, was also described by Hosea in the laconic phrase 'I am Yahweh your God, from the Land of Egypt'

[29] *Grundlegung zur Metaphysik der Sitten* (Riga, 1785); see K. Rosenkranz (ed.) *Geschichte der Kant'schen Philosophie* (Leipzig, 1838), p. 11.

(13.4). There can be no doubt of the fundamental importance for Hosea of the exodus. In this respect he utilises the traditions which were predominantly associated with the north (cf., e.g., with Davies, p. 32, the northern psalms 80.9ff, EV 8ff; and 81.6ff, 11, EV 5ff, 10), and especially with the sanctuary of Bethel (cf. 1 Kgs 12.28f), the sanctuary where Yahweh had initially spoken his definitive words to Jacob, and so to his descendants (12.5, EV 4). For Hosea, the exodus from Egypt marked the supreme act of Yahweh's grace in that he chose a mere child, small and vulnerable and, loving him, adopted him as his own son (11.1). Applying himself assiduously to Ephraim, he took him in his arms, extending to him the totality of his protective care (11.3). Here, indeed, lies the significance of the very name of Yahweh itself. As does Exod 3.14, Hosea understands the name by reference to the meaning of the verb *hyh*. Thus the verb implies that Yahweh had *intervened* on Israel's behalf to become her protector and helper (cf. the negative formulation of this Hosea's understanding in the condemnation of 1.9). In so doing he saw the fundamental relationship between God and people as a covenant, a notion later expressed by P in the definitive formula 'I will take you to myself as a people, and I will be your God' (Exod 6.7).

Closely connected with the exodus is the sojourn in the wilderness, the geographical proximity reflecting, so typically for Hosea, the temporal or sequential aspect of the matter. The desert was the place where Israel, now in early maturity (2.17, EV 15), was first known by Yahweh (13.5, cf. 2.22, EV 20). If the location changes, then so does the metaphor. Israel in the desert is Yahweh's bride; or else, defined in relation to its individual components, the nation's fathers, found, appreciated and savoured as if a *bonne bouchée* of desert grapes or a fig ripe in early summer (9.10). Yahweh's renewed election of Israel in the desert differs in character from that which obtained in the exodus; in the exodus the election was wholly compassionate, akin to the parental adoption of an orphan (14.4, EV 3); in the desert the election reflects, mysteriously, Yahweh's falling in love with his people, his calling her to enter a covenant of love[30] in which he requires of her, now mature, to share a common endeavour to which she must commit herself (cf. 2.17, EV 15, and the verb

[30] For the argument that the (later) full doctrine of Yahweh's covenant with Israel owes its origins, as a fundamental concept, to the teachings of Hosea, see Nicholson *GP*, pp. 187f. 8.1 and its reference to 'my covenant' seems to indicate that Hosea knew of an early or emerging form of the 'Mosaic' covenant in Exod 24.1–11.

'nh). Moving from the vehicle of the metaphor, in which Yahweh's bride-price consists of equity, justice, kindness, compassion and steadfastness (2.21f, EV 19f), thereby indicating the nature and quality of the marriage offered, the endeavour, in the tenor of the metaphor, may be said to consist in the creation of an Israel, of a nation, whose very life is to be characterised by just these qualities (again, 2.21f, EV 19f)[31].

This, Israel's vocation, is also defined by yet another metaphor: she is likened to a biddable heifer whose potential for the mature and responsible work of ploughing is readily noted by Yahweh (10.11). For Hosea ploughing, with sowing and reaping – themselves a metaphor for intention and resolution – defines again the task of realising Yahweh's design for the establishment of a nation called by his name and characterised by the qualities which reflected his nature. So Israel is urged, 'Your sowing shall be in accordance with what is right; your reaping in accordance with goodness; give yourselves to ploughing the fallow. And then there is the season to seek Yahweh till he comes to rain down blessing for you' (10.12)[32].

Here again is a geographical and temporal connection. From the wilderness Israel passed to the land, to the sphere of agricultural endeavour (2.17, EV 15). In reality that migration had been marked by the momentous failure of (Beth-) Baal-peor (9.10), of Gilgal (9.15; 12.12, EV 11), of the disobedience and trouble of the Valley of Achor (2.17, EV 15). Yet Hosea's vision of a new beginning, an 'Entry of Hope', is based upon his recognition of Yahweh's design as it was intended. What should have been was marred alone by the people's failure; what should have been is defined by reference to the reality of what, in

31 The relationship between these concepts and that of Yahweh's (written) *tôrah*, 'law/instruction/teaching', is, unfortunately, not clarified by Hosea. He seems quite naturally to take for granted the existence of such a corpus and reference to 4.2 may suggest that it included a form of the Ten Commandments. 4.4ff may imply that the priests, whose proper function included the promotion of 'knowledge (of Yahweh)', were the natural custodians of his law and interpreters of it. It should be noted that Moses is connected specifically with the events of the exodus rather than with those of the desert (12.14, EV 13), and that Hosea makes no mention whatsoever of Sinai/Horeb. On the other hand the Ephraimite psalm 81 (cf. Davies, p. 32) can speak naturally of the religious observances imposed on Israel in connection with commemoration of the exodus as a 'statute' and an 'ordinance' (*ḥq/'dwt*, vv. 5f, EV 4f). Moreover, mention there of Meribah (in the desert) and of the 'secret place of thunder' (v. 8, EV 7), together with insights such as Hosea's, may have furnished elements in the later formulation which associated *tôrah* with Moses and Sinai/Horeb.

32 For a treatment of this passage in connection with Wisdom traditions, see my essay in *Essays in honour of J. A. Emerton*, pp. 129–131.

Yahweh's volition and creation, had, aside from that failure, obtained. So, too, the renewal of Israel's mysterious intimacy with Yahweh in the desert for which Hosea longed (2.21ff, EV 19ff) was but a renewal of an intimacy which, marred only by the nation's unfaithfulness, had once been effected.

The possession of the land by his people marks the culmination of Yahweh's fundamental purpose and endeavour. It is upon the basis of his knowledge of his people in the desert (13.5) and of their knowledge of him (2.22, EV 20) that that possession should have been and now, in Hosea's fervent wish, could yet be accomplished. It was Yahweh alone who controlled the fertility of the land (2.10, EV 8) and not, as the people were disposed to believe (2.18, EV 16), Yahweh conceived of as approximate to Baal and his consort. Here, there can be no doubt, Hosea chose courageously and with great skill to redefine the religious ideas indigenous to Canaan. For him the fertility of the land was indeed reflected in a fundamental *hieros gamos*. Yet that was emphatically not defined in terms of the raw promptings of nature, of Baal, whose triumph over death (Mot), over the dry sterility of summer, culminated in his coupling with Anath, reflected perhaps by the sympathetic imitations of his worshippers and indicative of the coming of the rains and the fertility of the crops. Rather, for Hosea, the only efficacious marriage was that between Yahweh and his people, proposed and, as it were, consummated in the desert (2.21f, EV 19f) and characterised by mutual commitment. That marriage carried as a concomitant feature Yahweh's covenant with the natural world (2.23f, EV 21f) by means of which his people, protected from all harm, would be nourished by the corn and wine and oil which his attentive care alone ensured. Thus, the workings of the natural world, properly understood, mirror precisely the attentive dependence upon Yahweh which is the vocation of his people (see on the root *'nh* in 2.17, 23f, EV 15, 21f). Here, again, Hosea's thought is characterised by rapid oscillation between the past as it should have been and the future as it should be. Or again, the disasters which should not have been could yet be redeemed in recapitulation (see chapter 14 *passim*), the latter in all respects a reverse image of what, in his anger, Yahweh had decreed. Israel, in the desert, fleetingly and before her corruption, had once shown a proper attentive dependence upon Yahweh (2.17, EV 15); and for that, in the future, Yahweh (and Hosea) longed. Accordingly, in the darkest of times before the fall of Samaria, when Hosea could do nothing but give expression *de profundis* to his prayer, he knew intuitively of Yahweh's constant love which required only his people's repentant return to him

(14.2, EV 1). The constancy of that love, tried to the uttermost, was yet revealed by the divine *cri de cœur*, 'How can I hand you over, Ephraim? How can I deliver you up, O Israel? ... My own heart recoils; at once my compassion is aroused' (11.8). The only response that is required of Israel is the simple response of renewed commitment, expressed indeed in those words which are, in all respects, equal in Yahweh's sight to the costly sacrifice of young bulls (14.3, EV 2, cf. 6.6). Such words, in which the renunciation of false perceptions, of political intrigue and of idolatry, is matched by the resumption of the archetypal confession of total dependence, as by the orphan Israel at the exodus, are immediately and wholly effective of the restored marriage of God and people (14.4, EV 3). So again Yahweh will guard Ephraim with single-minded attention (14.9, EV 8; again *'nh*) and Israel, no longer inclined to idolatry, will flourish as a luxuriant juniper, its fruitfulness assured. Here, in the lyrical culmination of his vision and prayer, in the dialogue of love between God and people, Hosea may have redefined even the crude syncretistic doctrine of 'Yahweh and his Asherah'. Israel, now safe in the security of its true marriage, will effect, in the persons of its citizens, the revival of the land's fertility (14.8, EV 7); so doing, Israel's vocation and destiny as Yahweh's people and nation will find their fulfilment.

There can be no doubt, it seems to me, that Hosea's thinking, as reflected in the literary work that bears his name, was greatly and consistently influenced by the events of his personal life. Hosea's marriage to Gomer, his taking her to wife (*lqḥ*) was, according to his own testimony, planned and ordained by Yahweh and it marked the beginning of his prophetic insight (1.2). It was thus planned and ordained as a vehicle of Yahweh's revelation of himself. In this respect ibn Ezra has an important point to make notwithstanding his wholesale allegorical interpretation, devised on the *a priori* grounds that it was inconceivable for God to prompt a prophet to have dealings with a promiscuous woman. He suggests that for Hosea to *take* such a wife was to take to heart, to understand[33] the true nature and significance of his marriage. The birth and naming of the children of his marriage, its subsequent deterioration and his attempts to save it reflect for Hosea, step by step and accurately, the deterioration of the relationship between Yahweh and Ephraim as well as Yahweh's consistent desire to redeem the situation. The details of this remarkable personal testimony are set out in the Excursus on Hosea's marriage (pp. 113ff).

[33] For this sense of *lqḥ*, see p. 9, n. 3.

TABLE OF DATES RELATING TO HOSEA

	Israel	Judah
871	Ahab 871–852	Jehoshaphat 868–847
853	Battle of Karkar: Israel and Syria against Shalmaneser III of Assyria; Assyrian incursions temporarily checked	
852	Ahaziah 852–851 Jehoram 851–845 (842)	Jehoram 852 (851)–845 (843) Ahaziah 845 (843–842)
845	Battles between Israel and Syria at Ramoth-gilead	Ahaziah assists Israel at Ramoth-gilead
845 (842)	Jehu's revolt; Jehoram and Jezebel killed at Jezreel	Ahaziah killed at Ibleam
	Jehu 845 (842)–818 (814)	Athaliah 845 (842)–840 (836)
841	Shalmaneser III reaches Lebanese coast	
	Jehu pays tribute to Assyria	Joash 840 (836)–801 (798)
838	Shalmaneser III withdraws to Assyria Jehoahaz 818 (817)–802 (800) Jehoash 802 (800)–787 (784)	Amaziah 801 (798)–773 (769)
796	Ben-hadad III of Syria defeated at Aphek and territories restored to Israel	
788	Jehoash defeats Amaziah at Beth-shemesh	
	Jeroboam II 787 (789)–747 (748)	Uzziah 787 (785)–736 (733) Jotham (regent) 759 or 756 (758)–744 or 741 (743)

	Israel	**Judah**
750–740	Hosea's marriage and children Zechariah 747 (748–747) Shallum 747 Menahem 747–738 (747–737)	Ahaz 736 (743)–729 (727)
745	Tiglath-pileser III accedes to the Assyrian throne	
738	Menahem pays tribute to Tiglath-pileser III Pekahiah 737–736 (737–735)	
736/5	Pekah's revolt	
	Pekah 735–732 (733)	
733	Syro-Ephraimite coalition and attack on Jerusalem; Ahaz appeals to Assyria for help; Judah becomes a vassal of Assyria; Tiglath-pileser annexes Galilee and Gilead	
732	Damascus captured by Assyria Hoshea's revolt against Pekah Hoshea 731 (733)–723 (724)	
730	Hoshea pays tribute to Shalmaneser V	Hezekiah 728 or 725 (727)–700 or 697 (698)
725	Hoshea rebels against Assyria with Egyptian support; is imprisoned by Shalmaneser V	
722/1	The fall of Samaria	
700		Hezekiah besieged in Jerusalem by Sennacherib

The dates are those of A. Jepsen 'Chronologie'; the dates set out in Cogan and Tadmor, pp. 12–15, are recorded in brackets.

CHAPTER 1.1

SUPERSCRIPTION AND TITLE

1.1 **The word of Yahweh which came to Hosea, son of Beeri, in the time[a] of Uzziah, Jotham, Ahaz, Hezekiah, kings of Judah, and in that of Jeroboam, son of Joash, King of Israel.**

[a] Lit. 'days'.

The opening formula 'the word of Yahweh which came to ...' is found in the superscriptions of other prophetic books; see Joel, Micah, Zephaniah, Ezekiel (1.3), Jonah, Zechariah and Haggai. The prophets to whom such revelations came are named, together with their fathers' names, in the superscriptions of Isaiah, Jeremiah, Ezekiel, Joel, Jonah, Zephaniah and Zechariah. The dating of the prophet's ministry by reference to the contemporary kings of Judah occurs in Isaiah, Jeremiah (1.2), Micah and Zephaniah. The superscription to the prophecies of Amos is the only one (other than Hosea) which mentions both kings of Judah and Israel.

Mention here of the kings of both Israel and Judah immediately raises a number of questions. First, since it is abundantly clear from his writings that Hosea was a northern prophet, why should his work have been dated in the first instance by reference to kings of Judah? Secondly, since the time span indicated by the list of these kings extends for at least twenty years and perhaps just over thirty years beyond the time of Jeroboam II, what is to be made of the lack of synchronism? Again, if the time span indicated by the kings of Judah is substantially correct as an indication of the period in which Hosea's prophecies are set, why is Jeroboam II (here 'son of Joash') alone mentioned, rather than all the kings up to and including Hoshea ben Elah, the last of them?

Some of these problems were already seen in talmudic times. Thus, B. *Pesaḥim* 87b (ET, p. 462 in *Mo'ed* II) records that R. Johanan noticed that Jeroboam II was the only Israelite king mentioned in 1.1 (alongside the kings of Judah); he supposed that Jeroboam alone deserved mention on the grounds that he was not inclined to listen to Amaziah's calumny against Amos (Amos 7.10). In modern times, it has been suggested (e.g. van Gelderen and Frey) that mention of Jeroboam II accords with the author's view that he alone was legitimate (i.e. as opposed to his successors, who were not). Such views are hardly satisfying in the form in which they are presented, the latter not least because Jeroboam's son and successor was legitimate (cf. Rudolph).

More satisfactory is the view, widely held in modern times, that the verse is a late addition to the prophecies of Hosea, a superscription whose function is to label and to date what follows. As mentioned, the formula 'the word of Yahweh which came to ...' is found at the beginning of a number of prophetic collections and should be distinguished from another formula 'the words of (prophet's name)' which introduces the prophecies of Amos and Jeremiah. The latter is likely to be earlier; the former, reflecting the theological appraisal that it is Yahweh's word which the prophet's written words contain and convey, is later (e.g. Marti *ad loc.*). Since it is Deuteronomy and the circles associated with it that first sought to promulgate this doctrine by reference to the written prophetic works in their possession[1], the formula, as it appears in Hos 1.1, is essentially exilic or post-exilic. Rudolph's objection to this view rests upon the consideration that the words of the formula are found in a number of passages which are clearly pre-Deuteronomic (e.g. Gen 15.1; 2 Sam 7.4; 24.11 etc.). His case is, however, hardly convincing since such verses are not superscriptions. It is not denied that the phrase is older than Deuteronomy; what is asserted is that as a formula within superscriptions it is characteristic of the editorial work of such exilic and post-exilic redactors. If the work of the Deuteronomists suggests a *terminus a quo* for the composition of Hos 1.1, the form in which the name Hezekiah is written (יחזקיה) may present particular reasons to suggest that the notice is rather later. E. Y. Kutscher's (*Is.*, pp. 104ff) careful analysis of the four forms of the name as it occurs in the Hebrew bible (יחזקיה/יחזקיהו/חזקיה/חזקיהו) concludes that forms with an initial *yodh* belong to the Second Temple period. יחזקיהו (with final *waw*) is typical of Chronicles and reflects conscious archaism in reference to kings of the First Temple period. יחזקיה (without *waw*) is reserved in Chronicles to names which do not fall within this category and the form is likely to reflect general contemporary usage. The Deuteronomic history (i.e. 2 Kings) and Isaiah contain more than seventy instances of the name without initial *yodh* (and only one instance each with it). It seems likely, then, that Hos 1.1 with the spelling יחזקיה (cf. Mic 1.1) represents a transitional stage between what the Deuteronomists and their successors received from pre-exilic

[1] Cf. E. Janssen, pp. 84ff, Lindblom *PAI*, pp. 279f.

times and the consistent orthography of the Chronicler. The date therefore falls at some time between the mid-sixth century BC and the mid-fourth century BC.

I conclude, therefore, that the author of 1.1 belonged to the tradition of those who, in the times following the fall of Jerusalem in 587 BC, sought to edit a number of pre-exilic prophetic writings. They perceived that such older prophetic sayings of judgement, in some cases long authenticated by the fall of the Northern Kingdom, were confirmed finally by the demise of the Kingdom of Judah through which they had been transmitted and to which they had also served as a warning (so, e.g., Wolff; cf. Kimchi's remark to the effect that Hosea's prophecies, as God's words, were directed to Israel and Judah for their wrong-doing, 'in the days of the kings').

If this judgement is essentially correct, then it is at once clear why the primary dating of Hosea's work is made by reference to the kings of Judah rather than to those of his native Israel. The actual list coincides precisely with that found in Isa 1.1 and seems to make the redactor's point that Hosea is a contemporary of Isaiah and (translated) that his work belongs to the second half of the eighth century BC. The contents of Hosea's writings agree with this assessment since they reflect knowledge of events up to the time just before the fall of Samaria in 722/1 BC. Accordingly it is probable that the author of the superscription devised his chronological formula as a result of his perusal of Hosea's work.

The secondary formula, dating Hosea's work to the reign of Jeroboam II of Israel, is less precise; indeed it is strictly inconsistent with the primary formula (see above). Its presence, however, is to be seen as a recognition by the author of Hosea's northern provenance, since Amos 1.1, in respect of another prophet whose ministry was set in the north, is the only other example. In the case of Amos, that Jeroboam II alone is mentioned accords with the comparatively short period of his ministry (*c*. 765–750 BC) within that king's reign. Here in Hos 1.1 the reference is made in order to indicate that Amos and Hosea were more or less contemporary. Again, the author's knowledge of the contents of Hosea's prophecies and in particular of the prophet's early pronouncement of the fall of the House of Jehu (1.4) would have afforded ample grounds for this estimate (cf. Marti). The talmudic tradition already noted is suggestive of the conclusion that, in a secondary and less precise chronological notice, Jeroboam II, enjoying the only significantly long and successful reign before the monarchy deteriorated into a succession of shameful palace revolts, alone was worthy of mention.

In conclusion, it seems likely that the superscription gives a roughly accurate indication of the date of Hosea's ministry. That the first king of Judah mentioned is Uzziah (787–736 BC) rather than his predecessor Amaziah, also (just) a contemporary of Jeroboam II (787–747 BC), suggests that Hosea's ministry began in *c.* 750 BC. Mention of Hezekiah, the date of whose accession is not known with certainty, is an indication that Hosea was still prophesying in *c.* 725 BC (cf. Rudolph). Such considerations accord with the contents of the prophecy (see further the introduction, p. lxxxiii).

The superscription of 1.1 records the information, not mentioned in the rest of the book of Hosea or elsewhere in the bible, that Hosea was the 'son of Beeri' and this has led some scholars (e.g. Wolff and Rudolph) to suppose that this information, together with the reference to Jeroboam II, originally belonged to v. 2. Accordingly they suggest that both references were taken thence to form part of the (final) superscription of 1.1. On this theory, mention of Jeroboam II in connection with an explicit reference to the *beginning* (v. 2) of Hosea's prophecies, indicates that the information originally related only to chapters 1–3 (or 1 alone) and not to the whole collection of Hosea's prophecies. The theory, attractive in some respects, is, however, untenable (see on v. 2 below).

How, then, is the knowledge of the name of Hosea's father to be explained? Since it is a feature of many (but not all) superscriptions of prophetic books to include the names of the fathers of the prophets concerned (see above), and without those names occurring in the subsequent text, the conclusion is inevitable that the authors of these superscriptions had access to independent information or to written titles which they chose to discard in favour of their own compositions. On the latter supposition and by reference to Amos 1.1 or Jer 1.1, the conjecture may be hazarded that Hosea's prophecies, in the form in which they were received, were introduced by some such short title as 'the words of Hosea, son of Beeri' (cf. Marti).

The author of 1.1 wishes to make the point that the importance of Hosea's oracles lies in their testimony to the word of God. That word is indicative both of his nature and of his will. The circumstances of its coming are set forth in the description of particular prophets and of the times in which they lived. Thus, here as elsewhere, the word of God is mediated through a particular person and at a particular time and place. It is not arbitrary or purposeless in its coming; it is no timeless myth even though its origin is transcendent. It is perceived in a concrete historical situation (so, rightly, Rudolph). To perceive the operation of God's word in history, to know 'his ways' is to be wise and discriminating (see on 14.10); to be attuned to the consistent ethical nature of God is to see things aright and it ensures the salvation of the reader.

Hosea's name (הוֹשֵׁעַ) appears to be a shortened form of the fuller הוֹשַׁעְיָה (Neh 12.32; Jer 42.1; 43.2) and to mean 'Yahweh has helped' or 'Yahweh, help!' (see Noth *Pers.*, p. 32). The massoretic pointing seems to indicate an infinitive absolute (cf. Rosenmüller, Harper) which is capable of either of the interpretations listed above (cf. Rudolph)[2]. The name occurs elsewhere in the bible, most notably as the name of the last of the kings of Israel; in the English tradition (cf. AV) the name is distinguished from that of the prophet by the (more accurate) transliteration *Hoshea*. Numbers 13.16 (cf. 13.8; Deut 32.44) contains the notice[3] that Joshua (of the conquest) was originally named Hosea but that Moses was responsible for giving him the name by which he was subsequently known (יהושע). The two names may be (cf. BDB in contrast to KB) more or less equivalent in meaning but in form they are quite different. Certainly הושע (Hosea) is no dialectal variant of יהושע (Joshua) since in the latter case the theophoric element introduces the name; in the former, when present, it concludes it (cf. Rudolph, *contra* KB and van Gelderen). The name also occurs widely in inscriptions and other non-biblical sources[4].

Beeri, the name of Hosea's father, is also attested as a personal name elsewhere in the bible (Gen 26.34) as well as in non-biblical sources (the Tell el-Amarna Letters[5] and the Elephantine Papyri[6]). A possible meaning 'my Spring', given to a child by exultant parents, is held to be understandable (cf. Noth *Pers.*, p. 224) as an expression of continuity and new life (cf. Wolff). A number of scholars have sought to connect the name with the Benjamite place-name Beeroth (Josh 18.25) and to assume that Hosea's father is thus styled by a gentilic name, i.e. 'the man

[2] It is possible that the pointing (i.e. with *tsere*) represents a lengthening of *pathaḥ* in the interests of euphony, i.e. to create *fermata* (to use a musical term).

[3] 'Unhistorical'; so Rudolph BZAW 68 (1938), p. 80; Eissfeldt *Essays presented to D. W. Thomas*, p. 77, regards it as 'an historical reminiscence which informs us that after the adoption of the cult of Yahweh ... such changes of name actually took place'.

[4] Cf. Wolff and KB[3] *ad locc.* and G. I. Davies *AHI*, pp. 333f.

[5] Knudtzon, 174, 3.

[6] Cowley, p. 158.

from Beeroth' (Hölscher, pp. 205f, cf. Wolff). Objections to this 'bold conjecture' (*sic* Hölscher) are, however, insuperable (Sellin, cf. Rudolph); thus בְּאֵרֹתִי is clearly attested for this designation (2 Sam 4.2, 5; 23.37) as is also בֵּרֹתִי (1 Chr 11.39). There is, then, no evidence from Hos 1.1 to link Hosea with Benjamite Beeroth (so Rudolph *contra* Wolff). It remains possible that *Beeri* originally made reference to a place of origin (for Hosea's father or for his family). באר/*Beer* (meaning a 'well') is attested as a place-name in the desert (Num 21.16) and as a refuge for Jotham in Judg 9.21. In the Samaria Ostraca (No. 1) a certain Shemaryau is stated to be from בארים, perhaps to be located within sight of the Sea of Galilee (? El-Bireh, north of Beth-Shean)[7]. Yet all such considerations are necessarily speculative and, in the end, not much more plausible than the supposition (quoted in the name of Hayitṣḥaqi[8] and repudiated by ibn Ezra) that Hosea ben Beeri is identical with Hoshea ben Elah, the last of the Israelite kings, because Beeri and Elah can *mirabile dictu* be equated.

Text and Versions

הושע LXX Ὡσῆε; Vulg. *Osee.*

[7] See Davies *AHI*, p. 39, and J. N. Schofield in D. W. Thomas (ed.) *DOTT*, p. 206.

[8] The identification of this scholar is not certain; a definitive article has been promised by the Israeli scholar U. Simon.

CHAPTER 1.2–9

A RETROSPECTIVE ACCOUNT OF HOSEA'S MARRIAGE AND CHILDREN: ITS AND THEIR SIGNIFICANCE

1.2 **When Yahweh first spoke[a] to[b] Hosea, he said this to him: Go, marry[c] a promiscuous wife[d] and have children of promiscuity. For the nation[e] has turned from Yahweh[f] in gross[g] promiscuity.**

[a]Lit. 'the beginning of that Yahweh spoke ...'. For a construct followed by a clause with a finite verb in place of a *nomen rectum* GK 130d and cf., e.g., Gen 1.1 (Rashi *ad loc.* and cf. NEB), Isa 29.1 and Ps 81.6. Another view (so Kimchi) which produces the same sense is that דבר is a noun like שִׁלֵּם (Deut 32.5), קִטֵּר (Jer 44.21) and, especially, הַדִּבֵּר (Jer 5.13). On this understanding the phrases are juxtaposed in parataxis, thus: 'The beginning of Yahweh's speaking to Hosea. He said to him ...'. In either case the essential point is that תְּחִלַּת introduces an adverbial clause (with determination of time) related to the main verb ויאמר 'he said (this)'. A number of modern scholars (notably Rudolph; cf. Marti and Wolff, whose views are nonetheless somewhat ambivalent) are inclined to repudiate the connection described above between v. 2a and 2b. They prefer to see in 2a a superscription to the prophecies of Hosea shortened, in its present form, from an original: 'The beginning of Yahweh's speaking to Hosea, son of Beeri, in the days of Jeroboam, son of Joash'. The principal grounds for their objection to seeing a grammatical connection between 2a and 2b is the unnecessary repetition of the two proper names, Yahweh and Hosea, where pronouns would have sufficed. Yet an exact parallel occurs in Exod 6.28 where there is repetition of the two proper names, Yahweh and Moses. Indeed, such repetition may be held to contribute to the precise formality characteristic of solemn accounts of Yahweh's initiative in revealing himself (see further below).

[b]The most likely force of the preposition ב is 'to' or 'with' (so, e.g., Rashi), cf. Num 12.2, 6 and 8; Zech 1.9, 13f and the following ויאמר אל. What is conveyed is intimate personal speech, cf. Marti, who by reference to 2 Sam 23.2; 1 Kgs 22.28 and Zech 1.9ff suggests that the voice of God is heard in the inner consciousness of the prophet. Rashi (on 2 Sam 23.2): 'all expressions of prophecy comprise speech; speech because the spirit enters a prophet and speaks with him.' The view that the preposition indicates that Yahweh spoke *through* Hosea seems to me to be less likely. Had this been intended, the expression ביד 'through', 'by the agency of' might have been expected (BDB p. 391, col 1, 5 d).

The case for 'through' is argued by Kimchi who quotes the Numbers texts cited above together with 2 Sam 23.2 and comments that divine speech associated with prophecy is often construed with *beth hashimush*. Kimchi makes an exegetical point; for Yahweh's speaking to Hosea constitutes and marks the beginning of his message through Hosea to the nation. Jerome draws out the complementary character of the prepositions used in the verse thus: 'It is one thing for the Lord to speak in (*in*) Hosea; it is another thing for him to speak to (*ad*) Hosea. In speaking in (*in*) Hosea he is speaking not to Hosea himself, but through (*per*) Hosea to others; but in speaking to (*ad*) Hosea it is clear that he conveys his message to the man himself.'

[c]The verb לקח construed with *dativus commodi* (לך) denotes marriage, cf. with Rosenmüller Gen 4.19; 24.3, 67; 34.4; Jer 29.6. The second object of the verb לקח, *viz.* 'children of promiscuity' indicates that the saying is marked by zeugma and means that the prophet is to take on a promiscuous wife and consequently is by her to become the father of 'children of promiscuity', the latter being so called because they partake of the character of their mother (so Kimchi[1]). Recognition of zeugma and of the force of the preposition ל precludes the notion that Hosea married a woman who already had children by previous partners.

[d]Lit. 'wife of promiscuity'[2]. The word זְנוּנִים is an abstract plural and the phrase may be compared with אִישׁ־דָּמִים 'sanguinary man' (e.g. 2 Sam 16.7f) and with אֵשֶׁת־מִדְוָנִים/מִדְיָנִים 'a contentious, nagging wife' (e.g. Prov 21.9; 25.24; 27.15). The expression indicates characteristic behaviour, in this case behaviour that was later manifested. The instruction, recorded by the redactor on the testimony of Hosea, alludes to the subsequent rather than to the present behaviour of the woman (for the verse refers retrospectively to the situation 'when Yahweh first spoke to Hosea') and therefore the expression in Yahweh's mouth is here proleptic. See further on 2.18 below.

[e]Lit. 'land', i.e. 'all the inhabitants of the land (of Israel)' – so ibn Ezra; cf. Kimchi 'Israel and its descendants in those days'.

[f]No difficulty is occasioned by reference to Yahweh (third person) within a speech of Yahweh; cf. e.g. Hos 1.7; Zeph 1.5, 6.

[g]The infinitive absolute (זנה) emphasises the frequentative imperfect (תזנה) and this describes the present situation (so Rashi). The nation has turned from Yahweh in and through its grossly promiscuous behaviour.

[1] They will incur 'the suspicion of bastardy' (so Rashi).

[2] For similar expressions, cf., with AF, אֵשֶׁת נְעוּרִים 'wife of youth', i.e. referring to a lasting marriage, contracted early in life (Prov 5.18; Isa 54.6; Mal 2.14f); אֵשֶׁת חֵיק 'bosom wife', referring to a loving and satisfactory marriage (Deut 13.7; 28.54; 2 Sam 12.8).

The third person account of the beginning of Hosea's reception of Yahweh's message is likely to rest upon an authentic recollection of the prophet himself. That the notice speaks of the *beginning* of Yahweh's revelation to Hosea (see note a) implies the prophet's knowledge of at least part of the rest of that revelation and consequently the words are best understood as the result of Hosea's reflecting retrospectively on his experiences and his message (cf. Jer 1.4ff and Isa 6). In other words, Hosea recalls that the beginning of Yahweh's message was associated with the circumstances of his marriage to Gomer. This marriage, together with the children born to it, constitute a parable or sign (cf. the Hebrew word *mšl*) of the nation's apostasy together with its inevitable results. The marriage is not contracted in order to illustrate the message; it constitutes the beginning of the message itself[3]; for it is an outward sign or representation of the relationship between God and his people, and it is the means by which God began to communicate to Hosea his message to the nation. One might compare Isa 7.3; 8.3 for a similar association of members of a prophet's family with the message of the prophet. It may be noted that there are few, if any, biographical details in Isaiah's account of his children. It is as persons with God-given names that they signify and represent the divine message. The reference of the sign is to Israel and it is Israel's promiscuity that is set forth by it. Since, then, the emphasis is upon the reference of the sign, and upon the continuity between the sign and its reference, there is lacking the precise biographical detail about Hosea's wife and the circumstances of his marriage which are so avidly desired by modern commentators and which by much ingenuity they seek to supply.

In these circumstances ibn Ezra's comment has some force; if Hosea had sought a suitable wife, he would not have found one since the land (i.e. the entirety of its inhabitants) had turned from God in gross promiscuity. On the other hand this observation forms part of ibn Ezra's view that the marriage was wholly visionary and that view fails to do justice to the reality of the circumstances (including, e.g., the precise naming of Hosea's wife) in which Yahweh began to speak with the prophet.

The essential point of the verse is the continuity between the sign and what is symbolised by it.

As to the theory (see note a above) that 2a is a superscription two further objections may be raised: first, there is no other

[3] Ibn Ezra and Rashi see in the use of the word *lqḥ* a reference to mental reception, i.e. learning or taking to heart (BDB p. 543, col 1 f and the noun *lqḥ* 'learning/teaching').

instance when the noun *tḥlh* 'beginning' is used in a superscription to prophetic material. Secondly, the meaning postulated ('the beginning of Yahweh's speaking to Hosea ...'), if understood absolutely as a self-contained superscription, would be otiose. Indeed, both Wolff and Rudolph are at pains to emphasise that 'the beginning' has a relative and not an absolute sense, i.e. it relates either to the passage 2b–9 (Wolff) or to the whole section, chapters 1–3 (Rudolph). Yet if a redactor of Hosea's words expressly wished to 'begin his account of God's revelation to Hosea by relating how, in Jeroboam's time and at Yahweh's command, he married ...' (so Rudolph in a paraphrase), that is no reason to question a grammatical connection with the following main verb in 2b 'he said (this)'. Indeed, Rudolph's paraphrase would seem to concede the point.

Such considerations tell against the theory that the verse was intended as a superscription and that 'Jeroboam' and 'Beeri' originally belonged to it. To affirm the plain sense of the verse (note a), *viz.* that Yahweh's revelations to Hosea began at the time of his marriage, is not to claim that this beginning constituted his call to the prophetic office (cf. Rowley *BJRL*, pp. 231f).

Text and Versions

דבר. LXX, Pesh. and Targ. appear to have read the word as a substantive (דְּבַר) and Vulg. as a verbal noun (דַּבֵּר); Aq. follows MT in reading it as a finite verb.

בהושע LXX ἐν or πρός (on this variant reading, arising by attraction to πρός in 2b, see Ziegler); Theod. ἐν; Vulg. *in*; Pesh. *'l*; Targ. ב. Targ. renders the verse thus: 'The beginning of the word of the Lord to Hosea was when the Lord said to Hosea, "Go, prophesy against the inhabitants of the idolatrous city who continue to sin since the residents of the land turn to idolatry from the worship of the Lord"'. The translation is of interest in that it interprets the verse wholly in terms of idolatry and avoids all reference to the marriage of Hosea. Kimchi specifically approves this allegorical interpretation.

1.3 **So he went and married Gomer, the daughter of Diblaim[a], and she conceived and bore him a son.**

[a]Gomer, daughter of Diblaim: these names are best understood as the actual names of Hosea's wife and of his father-in-law (cf. 2 Sam 11.3 where exactly the same formula is used to describe 'Bathsheba, daughter

of Eliam'). The prophet does not appear to see any significance in these names as, by contrast, he does in the names of his children. In the latter case the significance is explained and the naming is a symbolic act, expressive of the message of Yahweh. The significance of Gomer is her promiscuous nature and her marriage to Hosea and not the name by which she was known at the time of that marriage. Since the marriage marks the beginning of Yahweh's message, and in the absence of any notice that she was re-named in this connection, it seems likely that we have a straightforward and factual statement of the name of the woman whom the prophet married (cf. Kimchi).

Since at least talmudic times attempts have been made to give the names significance. Thus, she was called Gomer because all could gratify their lust on her (הכל גומרין בה) and Bath Diblaim because she could be readily squeezed like a press of figs (ודשין בה כדבלה)[4]. Ibn Ezra and Jerome, by reference to the root גמר ('to complete', 'to bring to an end'), see her as completed, perfect in seductive promiscuity (גמורה בזנות, τετελεσμένη, *consummata in fornicatione et perfecta filia voluptatis*), the figs (Diblaim) being for Jerome a symbol of seductive sweetness[5]. Amongst modern commentators who attempt similar interpretations of the names, mention may be made of E. Nestle[6] and Tur-Sinai[7]; for the former the name Diblaim, by reference to parallels in Latin literature, implies that Gomer's services could be had for as little as (the price of) two figs; for the latter, by reference to the Arabic cognate *ǧamratun* 'a hot coal', the name Gomer implies that she burned with lust. For further interpretations of the names, see Harper.

The name Gomer occurs also as the name of a man both in the OT (Gen 10.2f etc.) and in the contemporary Samaria Ostraca[8]. It is probably best compared with the names גמריה and גמריהו which are known to us from Jer 29.3 and 36.10, 12, 25 as well as from the Lachish Ostraca[9], the Arad Ostraca[10] and the Elephantine Papyri[11]. The meaning is apparently 'Yahweh has accomplished' (*sc.* the successful birth of the child)[12].

4 B. *Pesaḥim* 87b, ET, pp. 460f in *Mo'ed* II.

5 Ibn Ezra sees the dual ending of Diblaim as an allusion to Judah and Israel.

6 *ZAW* 29 (1909), pp. 233f, followed by W. Baumgartner *ZAW* 33 (1913), p. 78.

7 *LS* 2, pp. 316f; cf. KB[3].

8 See W. F. Albright in *ANET*, p. 321 and Davies *AHI*, pp. 326f; that a name is attested both for a man and a woman presents no problem, cf. Noth *Pers.*, p. 61.

9 1[1] in Torczyner, cf. Davies *AHI*, p. 1.

10 Aharoni *ad loc.*; cf. Davies *AHI*, pp. 22ff.

11 See Cowley, p. 281.

12 Cf. Noth *Pers.*, p. 175; L. Köhler *ZAW* 32 (1912), p. 8 believes that the name indicates a command, i.e. 'let this be the end (*sc.* of producing female children)'. A name compounded of an imperative addressed to a god and having this meaning seems most unlikely.

If the massoretic pointing is based upon reliable tradition (NB that the LXX appears to confirm it), the name of Hosea's wife may be defined as a short form (i.e. without the theophoric element) of a name such as גמריהו adapted hypocoristically to the pattern of a segholate noun. With this we may compare Shemer, the original owner of the site of Samaria in 1 Kgs 16.24 as a short form of the fuller שמריהו[13]. Alternatively, the name may simply denote a personal attribute (Noth *Pers.*, pp. 228f). In either case the meaning is probably perfection, consummation (of, i.e. vouchsafed by, a divinity). That the theophoric element is now missing leaves open the question whether the deity honoured was Yahweh or Baal. It is possible to argue that the circumstances of the marriage point to the latter (cf. Wolff).

Diblaim has been understood as the name of Gomer's father and/or as the name of her place of birth or residence. The latter proposal presents the difficulty that בן or בת as opposed to בני or בנות are never used elsewhere to define a person's birthplace or place of residence (cf. Wolff). On the other hand the place-name Diblathaim in Moab is known to us from Num 33.46f and Jer 48.22 as well as from Mesha's Moabite Stone (Beth-diblathen, line 30; *ANET*, p. 321).

The root *dbl* occurs in a proper name on an Ammonite seal (seventh–sixth centuries BC) in the form *dblks* whereas *ks* may be a variant spelling of the Edomite/north Arabian deity Qōs[14]. In this connection it may be recalled that Ammon was subject either to the Northern Kingdom or to Damascus until the Assyrian invasions in 733 BC. It is possible, then, that there were cultural links and inter-marriage between the two kingdoms. Further there is the name *dbl nar/nur* from the Thamudic Inscriptions[15], where *nr* is the well-attested Palmyrene deity. Not a little uncertainty prevails as to the meaning of *dbl* in these names[16], but it should be noted that the *d* is *ḏ* and not *d*. The guess may be hazarded that the root is cognate to and illuminated by the well-known Ugaritic and Hebrew root *zbl* 'to be exalted' found in particular in the noun *z*^{e}*bul* 'prince' occurring, e.g., in the title *zbl ym* 'Prince Sea' in the Ugaritic Texts[17], and in the presumably short-form names *z*^{e}*bul(un)* in Hebrew.

It is well known that *ḏ* corresponds to both *daleth* and *zayin* in Hebrew and consequently the possibility arises that *dbl* in the name Diblaim represents a variant or dialectal spelling (akin to the names attested from trans-Jordan) of the verb *zbl*. On that hazardous guess, we may suggest (cf. Rudolph) that the name expresses the exaltation of a

[13] For 'o' type segholate names, cf. אֹצֶם, בֹּעַז, קֹרַח.

[14] Albright in Ubach, p. 134. N. Avigad reads the name *dblbs*; see *Essays in honour of Nelson Glueck*, p. 293 n. 10 and, further, W. E. Aufrecht in *BASOR* 266 (1987), p. 88. *dbl*, at any rate, seems reasonably secure.

[15] van den Branden, p. 274.

[16] Rykmanns *ad loc.* tentatively compares Arabic *ḏbl* = 'se flétrir', but adds a question mark.

[17] *CTA*, 2.III.8, 16, 23; *KTU* 1.2 (p. 8); Gröndahl, pp. 104, 144, 316.

god (? Yam, cf. *'bdym* as a proper name from Ugarit[18], Akhiyami in Taanach Letter 2.2 and Abijam in 1 Kgs 14.31[19]) or gods (hence the apparent dual[20] or plural ending).

The Moabite place-name mentioned above may be seen as a reflection of this element and as representing a dedication to the god(s) whose title was compounded of the root *dbl*.

In conclusion, it may be said that Diblaim is a proper name designating Hosea's father-in-law. The dual ending, though common in place-names, is not attested elsewhere for personal names. Although it is confirmed as early as the LXX it had probably by that stage lost its original point of reference and has been taken, e.g., as an allusion to the two kingdoms of Israel and Judah (cf. ibn Ezra and Ezek 23). What little evidence there is suggests that the name may have its origins in trans-Jordan and have a North Arabian character[21]. That does not, of course, allow any inference for the circumstances or particulars of Gomer's immediate family.

The verse records Hosea's obedient response to the divine command and the consequential conception and birth of his first son. The word *lw* 'to him' (see Text and Versions) precludes the possibility that the child was fathered by any other than Hosea. It is he that is instructed both to take on a promiscuous wife and also to become the father of children who were inescapably to inherit their mother's designation.

Text and Versions

לו The pronoun is not present in 3 Kennicott and 1 de Rossi MSS, nor is it represented in 2 LXX MSS (V, 764). Rudolph concludes that this represents a harmonising tendency which has brought the verse into agreement with vv. 6 and 8 where the pronoun is not found. The pronoun is not represented in Vulg.; Borbone omits.

18 *KTU* 4.103:18, *CTA* 82.A.18; *KTU* 4.103:47, *CTA* 82.B.15; *KTU* 3.3:10 and *KTU* 4.341:3.

19 For the Taanach Letters of the fifteenth century BC and for Abijam, see W. F. Albright *BASOR* 94 (1944), p. 20.

20 Shaḥar/Shalim or Yam/Nahar? Against this latter supposition is the consideration that quasi-dual endings in place-names may represent secondary expansions of earlier monosyllabic forms typical of the Jerusalem dialect, cf. GK 88c and for the comparable ֵין/ַיִן, Introduction, p. lv.

21 The names Ahab and Omri in the Northern Kingdom are also thought to be of Arabian origin; cf. Noth *Pers.*, p. 63.

1.4 **And Yahweh said to him: Call him by the name Jezreel, for in the near future[a] I will punish[b] the blood-guilt[c] of Jezreel upon the dynasty of Jehu and I will bring to an end the kingdom of the house of Israel[d].**

[a]Cf. Exod 17.4; Jer 51.33; Hag 2.6; Ps 37.10 and GK 112oo, 143d (for the following perfect consecutive).

[b]פקד 'to punish', cf. Deut 5.9; Amos 3.2, 14 and Hos 2.15; 12.3.

[c]Originally a plural of result or of local extension, but early acquiring the sense 'blood-guilt'; cf. GK 124n.

[d]The noun ממלכות is found only in the construct. The word can mean both '(geographical) state' (Josh 13.12) and the 'exercise of kingship', 'reign' or 'royal power' (1 Sam 15.28; 2 Sam 16.3; Jer 26.1). Wolff argues for the latter sense and regards the phrase as an indication that, with the demise of the dynasty of Jehu, the monarchy as an institution of the Northern Kingdom is to end[22]. If, however, the monarchy is to be brought to an end then so too is the state of which it is the head. Thus the 'House of Israel' refers to the nation, i.e. the people of the Northern Kingdom (cf. 1.6; 12.1, EV 11.12). By reference to 5.1, where 'House of Israel' is parallel to 'House of the King', I conclude that it is the whole establishment of the state that is to be terminated (cf. Rudolph).

Following the birth of his son, Hosea receives another command from Yahweh: he is to name his son in reference to the guilt of the royal dynasty founded by Jehu of which Jeroboam II was the contemporary exemplar. The name was also to express the inevitability and near approach of Yahweh's punishment of that dynasty and of the resulting collapse of the Israelite state of which the monarchy was the established head. For *talis rex, qualis grex*.

That Hosea named the child is a further indication that he was the father[23]. This was a technical prophetic act to which Isaiah's naming of Maher-shalal-hash-baz (Isa 8.3) is exactly parallel. The child so named becomes a living sign or expression of the divine message and to his natural growth is inexorably bound the fulfilment of the message that he bears[24]. In the case of Isaiah's son the time span is expressed precisely: the fulfilment of the message will be accomplished by the time the child learns the

22 For ibn Ezra בית ישראל is parallel to and means בית יהוא. With Zechariah's murder at Ibleam in 747 BC the dynasty of Jehu ended.

23 For fathers rather than mothers naming children, cf. Gen 16.15; 17.19; 35.18; Exod 2.22; 2 Sam 12.24 (*K^e thib*) and Isa 8.3.

24 For ibn Ezra and Kimchi the fact that he is a boy specifically signifies the strength of Jeroboam II's reign. Cf. below, the latter's comment on Hosea's daughter.

rudiments of speech (Isa 8.4). Here the time span is apparently less precisely delineated but it may be assumed to be very similar. If the event is correctly dated at *c.* 750 BC (see on 1.1), then there were in fact some two years before Jehu's dynasty was to end.

Again the naming of the child is a technical prophetic action and *sui generis*. The name is not elsewhere attested as a personal name and, with Noth *Pers.*, p. 9, we may conclude that Jezreel and other such symbolic names were literary and contrived rather than actual names in daily use.

Jezreel is attested as the name of two settlements, the one in Judah (site unknown) and the other on the north-western spur of Mount Gilboa at the eastern entrance of the great plain (called *'mq yzr''l* in the Old Testament and Ezdraelon by Josephus) which separates the mountains of Samaria from those of Galilee[25]. The ruined Arab village of Zer'in (adjacent to the modern Kibbutz Jezreel) is thought to have preserved the ancient name[26]. On the assumption that Hosea refers here to this site (rather than to the valley of the same name, cf. the following verse), it is generally assumed that he has in mind the events recounted in 2 Kgs 9f and Jehu's bloodthirsty revolt against the house of Omri. These chapters, while clearly shaped by the Deuteronomists, are generally thought to depend upon a reliable and near contemporary source for the events there described[27]. According to this source, Jehu, an important military officer, was charged with the defence of Ramoth-gilead following the wounding at this place of King Jehoram by the Syrians and his subsequent retreat to Jezreel for convalescence. In Ramoth-gilead, apparently encouraged by some prophetic sanction, Jehu resolved to make his bid for the throne and, moving on Jezreel, slew Jehoram of Israel and Ahaziah of Judah (also present in Jezreel)

25 For a description of the site, see Ussishkin and Woodhead, pp. 3ff.

26 The place-name Jezreel is of itself likely to constitute a reference to the highly fertile land of the area and of the valley which was to bear its name. Whether the verbal element is to be understood as a frequentative imperfect 'God/El sows', as a preterite 'God/El has sown' or as a jussive 'Let God/El sow' is very difficult to determine. For similar place-names, compounded of a verb (imperfect) with theophoric element, see Borée *ad loc.*

27 This assessment is usually made within the context of the vexed question of the nature and provenance of the story of Naboth's vineyard in 1 Kgs 21. The version of Naboth's death recorded in 2 Kgs 9 is held to be inherently more plausible and this, together with other considerations, lends support to the conclusion that 2 Kgs 9f reflects a reliable and near contemporary source while 1 Kgs 21 is suggestive of a late novelette; see J. M. Miller, pp. 307–324; A. Rofé, pp. 89–104; Williamson, *Jezreel*, pp. 79–104; for recent commentaries, cf. Gray, G. H. Jones, Cogan and Tadmor, *ad locc.*

who had come out to meet him. Having entered the settlement, he apparently slew the queen-mother, Jezebel, and then proceeded, by messenger, to intimidate those in Samaria charged with the care of Ahab's remaining descendants into murdering them and sending their heads in baskets to Jezreel. At some stage he captured and exterminated a small force of Judaean allies of the Israelite king before finally entering Samaria, ascending the throne, and, by trickery, slaughtering the worshippers of Baal and destroying their temple. Whether his motivation in the whole enterprise was simply 'zeal for Yahweh' (2 Kgs 10.16), a view no doubt congenial to the Deuteronomists, or whether his actions reflected the aims of a party favouring a charismatic as opposed to a dynastic monarchy (so Miller) cannot here be determined.

At the time of writing, recent archaeological discoveries at Jezreel are not inconsistent with the possibility (cf. 1 Kgs 4.12) of a tenth century settlement of the site[28]. More particularly, they have revealed an iron-age enclosure and (?) a casemate wall but little else. Ussishkin and Woodhead are inclined to speak of a 'royal enclosure' similar in some respects to that of the Israelite royal enclosure at Samaria. They conclude tentatively that the enclosure 'was built either by Omri (882–871 BCE) or by Ahab (873–852) and was then used by Ahab's sons Ahaziah (852–851) and Jehoram (851–842)'; and, further, that the evidence of forcible destruction 'should be assigned to Jehu's *coup d'état* of 842 BCE and is probably reflected in Hosea 1.4'. Whether these conclusions are justified will have to await further evidence and evaluation. For an assessment of the biblical data in relation to the archaeological evidence, see Williamson *Jezreel* and note his conclusion that 'so far as the time of Ahab is concerned the site should be excavated with a completely open mind as to whether there is a palace to be found there or not'.

More recently in lectures, both Ussishkin and Williamson have suggested that the enclosure at Jezreel may have had a military significance, the 'elevated, level surface' (Ussishkin, p. 52) comprising a barracks for horses and chariots. With this view two biblical notices are not inconsistent: in 2 Kgs 8.29, cf. 9.15, Jehoram, on active service at Ramoth-gilead, withdrew to Jezreel to convalesce from his wounds. Jezreel, situated near the main highway from Megiddo to Beth-shean (and so on to Ramoth-gilead), commanded also the road from the valley of Jezreel to

[28] Cf. Williamson *Jezreel*, p. 78 and Ussishkin and Woodhead, p. 50. There is no evidence that the city was Canaanite or that it existed before the time of the Israelite settlement, cf. Alt *KS* 3, pp. 260, 265, 268. NB Williamson, *PEQ* 128 (1996), pp. 41–51, has just appeared.

Samaria and would thus constitute a convenient and strategically important military installation; and, according to 1 Kgs 18.45f, Ahab drove on a chariot some 25 kilometres from Carmel to Jezreel before the heavy rains made the roads impassable. In this connection it is worth recording that nowhere does the bible characterise Jezreel as a 'city'.

Jezreel, then, whatever its precise status, is clearly defined by 2 Kgs 9f as the place from which Jehu mounted his ruthless and bloody putsch against the house of Omri. Its laconic mention by Hosea is paralleled perhaps by his mention of Adam and Gilead (6.7f) as places from which, in his own time, Pekah was to mount his bloodthirsty bid for the throne.

Such is the blood-guilt of Jezreel, and it is this that is condemned by Yahweh in the mouth of Hosea and in the person and name of his infant son. Since early times, attempts to reconcile the contradiction between Hosea's condemnation of events one hundred years earlier and explicit approval of them in the Deuteronomic history (2 Kgs 10.30) have been undertaken. Thus the Targum, followed by ibn Ezra, Rashi and Kimchi, observes that Jehu, despite his purge of Baalism, in fact continued in the idolatries of Jeroboam I and was for this reason deemed to be guilty of shedding innocent blood in the prophetic revolution. In other words, his residual and persistent idolatry rendered culpable the bloodthirsty deeds which, without it, would have incurred no guilt.

This somewhat casuistic argument indicates, perhaps, a deeper appreciation of the matter. Thus ibn Ezra comments that the blood-guilt of Jezreel comprises for Hosea that of Ahab's dynasty as well as that of Jehu's, and thus the Israelite monarchy was totally corrupt, murderous and unacceptable to Yahweh. Similarly Kimchi, quoting 2 Kgs 10.32, 'In those days (i.e. Jehu's reign) the Lord began to cut Israel short', underlines the ancient historian's accurate assessment of the early beginnings of the inexorable collapse of the Northern Kingdom.

For all this, Hosea's unambiguous condemnation, one hundred years after the events, of a movement approved and instigated by Elisha, if not Elijah, is worthy of notice. Murder is murder and it is by their fruits that kings are known. Ends do not justify means and, as Hosea says elsewhere (8.7) and in another context, when the wind is sown it is the whirlwind that is reaped. Such is the reality of the moral order and of the consistent creator who devised it. As Marti comments, Hosea will have nothing to do with the suppression of conscience in the interests of fanatical Yahwism; true Yahwism recognises what is ethically good and reflects the ethical nature of Yahweh.

If the name Jezreel has a clear reference to atrocities committed by the Israelite monarchy, it is also chosen in order to set forth the judgement and punishment of Yahweh upon those atrocities. In this connection the name is likely to have been chosen because of its near approach in form[29] and sound to Israel. Thus Israel has become Jezreel. The latter characterises the corruption of the former[30]. The murderous behaviour associated with Jezreel typifies and exemplifies what Israel has become. Secondly, where punishment is concerned, the name is likely to have implied the scattering of the inhabitants of the kingdom[31] for such a meaning is attested for *zrʿ* in Zech 10.9, 'I will scatter (lit. 'sow') them among the peoples'[32], and it is indicated by the prophecy of recapitulation[33]: 'I will sow her in the land' (Hos 2.25, EV 23). Such a sinister connotation of sowing, though clearly having agricultural reference, may be detected also in the Ugaritic Texts[34] where Anat, having killed Mot, scatters (*ḏrʿ*) his remains across the land.

Such is the sign constituted by the infant Jezreel. In respect of the demise of Jehu's dynasty, the prophecy found its fulfilment in 747 BC with the assassination of the last of the line, i.e. Zechariah, son of Jeroboam II, probably at Ibleam some thirteen kilometres from Jezreel on the road to Samaria[35].

The monarchy was to survive for another thirty years or so, but its effective force at the head of a stable state was henceforth seriously weakened both by a series of bloody palace revolts and, from 738 BC, by the imposition of tribute on the part of increasingly dominant invaders. Yahweh's promise that 'in the near future' the effective establishment of Israel would come to an end was confirmed by such circumstances and, confirmed, it was recorded as the beginning (v. 2) of his revelation to Hosea. But further, recorded, it will have been seen, whether by Hosea or his readers, to have had its final corroboration in the fall of Samaria in 722/1 BC.

29 Imperfect/jussive followed by theophoric element, cf. Noth *Pers.*, p. 27; cf. also the readings of OL in Text and Versions.

30 See e.g. Rosenmüller and cf. Bethaven for Bethel in Hos 4.15.

31 So the Targum, 'call their name "scattered ones"'.

32 If in this prophecy of restoration Zechariah is dependent on Hosea, then he represents an early testimony to the meaning of the word in Hosea.

33 I.e. the prophecy which sets forth the opposite to this one.

34 *CTA* 6.II.31ff; 6.V.12ff (pp. 40, 42); *KTU* 1.6; cf. Gibson, pp. 77, 79 (6, col ii, 31ff; cf. col v, 12ff).

35 2 Kgs 15.10; see Gray *ad loc.*

Text and Versions

אליו A single Hebrew MS (K 224) reads אלי. With Wolff we may suppose that the *waw* was inadvertently omitted, *contra* F. S. North[36], who believes that the first person reading was original.

יזרעאל LXX[V] ιεσραελ, cf. OL[S*W] *israhel* – as in vv. 5 and 2.2.

יהוא Some important LXX MSS read ιουδα (*BAQC*), cf. OL[W] *iudae*. Jerome in his commentary regards this as arising from unfamiliarity with the name Jehu. The reading may possibly indicate a tradition going back to the time of the Judaean appropriation of the prophecy of Hosea (see p. lxx) and represent the tendency then to apply the prophecy to the Southern Kingdom.

1.5 **And[a] on that day I will break the bow[b] of Israel in the valley of Jezreel[c].**

[a]Cf. GK 112y for והיה in the announcement of a future event.

[b]A symbol of military might, cf. Gen 49.24; Jer 49.35; Job 29.20. For a later aphoristic statement about Ephraim and the bow, cf., with Jerome, Ps 78.9; cf. p. 26 below and *contra* J. Day *VT* 36 (1986), pp. 1ff.

[c]The town gives its name to the broad fertile valley which runs east to west from the Jordan valley to the Kishon valley behind Carmel; cf. 2.2, 24, EV 1.11, 2.22; Josh 17.16 and Judg 6.33.

Kimchi sees a direct connection between this verse and what precedes it (so AF); thus: On that day, i.e. on the day that I punish the house of Jehu for the blood-guilt of Jezreel, I will break the bow of Israel ... For him the *waw* consecutive form *wšbrty* follows the verb *whšbty* in v. 4. On this view the verse spells out the consequences of the fall of Jehu's dynasty; that fall, with the consequent weakening of the state, will lead to the destruction of Israel's military capability; that, in turn, to the demise of the kingdom in the face of the growing Assyrian world power. This view of the verse is consistent with the case argued above for the meaning of v. 4b and the thought is the same as that expressed in vv. 6 and 9. Since Meinhold, however, this verse has been considered by a number of scholars to be a later addition. Thus, e.g., Marti regards 'And on that day' as properly an introductory formula which, placed here, arouses suspicion. Secondly, 'the valley of Jezreel' corresponds with the

[36] *VT* 8 (1958), pp. 429ff.

name of Hosea's child less well than the straight-forward reference to the city in v. 4.

A compromise position is advocated by Wolff for whom the verse is authentic but added later by Hosea and specifically in connection with the events of 733 BC when the Assyrian invaders under Tiglath-pileser III appropriated[37] all the Northern Kingdom except for Mount Ephraim and Samaria.

There is some cumulative force in such arguments for the secondary character of the verse. On this view the reference to the valley of Jezreel, if not a *vaticinium ex eventu*, at least approximates to being such. It is possible, as Rudolph observes, that the emphasis of the verse may be general, i.e. less concerned with concrete historical events than with the prophetic insight into the requirements of justice and the notion that punishment should be meted out at the scene of the sins which prompt it. On the other hand, there are two considerations which might have led Hosea to designate in advance the valley of Jezreel as the place of Yahweh's final judgement for the deeds wrought in the city of that name. Since at least the first half of the fifteenth century BC when Thutmose III fought victoriously here (1479 BC), the valley of Jezreel became the veritable battleground of Palestine. Here Deborah fought Sisera, Gideon the Midianites[38] and Saul the Philistines (on nearby Mount Gilboa – but Jezreel is mentioned by name, 1 Sam 29.1, 11)[39]. The valley of Jezreel, then, may have been a synonym for the decisive battlefield of the future in the way that Megiddo at its western end (according to some authorities) was to become the Armageddon of Christian apocalyptic. In association with such a view there is also the further possibility that Hosea himself saw the valley of Jezreel as a proper place for Israel's punishment. If it was to be the site of Israel's future military defeat, then, bearing the name Jezreel, poetic justice would coincide with divine justice (cf. Keil, Wolff and Rudolph).

Text and Versions

No significant readings.

[37] Noth *History*, pp. 260f; *GI*, pp. 235f.

[38] 'The day of Midian' in Isa 9.3 is a reference to this battle as a paradigm of deliverance.

[39] Cf. Keil and Wolff. Keil rightly draws attention to decisive battles here even in modern times; we may add Allenby's defeat of the Turks at Megiddo in 1918.

1.6 **And she conceived again and bore[a] a daughter. And he [*sc.* Yahweh] said to him, Call her by the name Lo-Ruḥamah[b]. For I will show no more[c] forbearance[d] towards the House of Israel. Indeed I will annihilate them completely[e].**

[a]The pronoun 'to him' is not present in the account of this child's birth, and this has been taken by some scholars (see Harper, p. 208 for references) as an indication that Hosea was not her father. More likely, however, is the explanation which suggests natural economy of language in the report of the birth of a second and third child. As Keil observes the word 'again' is not used in the account of the birth of the third child (v. 8).

[b]The name is compounded of the negative adverb and a third feminine singular perfect *Pual* verbal form and means lit. 'she is not pitied/loved'. The *qametz* beneath the *ḥeth* is pausal. For a similar form, cf. Isa 54.11, 'she is not comforted' (לֹא נֻחָמָה).

[c]For the asyndetic juxtaposition of two finite verbs, see GK 120c, and cf. Isa 47.1; 52.1 and Prov 23.35.

[d]The verb is denominative from רֶחֶם 'womb', cf. the abstract plural רַחֲמִים 'compassion'. It describes the natural love of a mother (Isa 49.15) and of a father (Ps 103.13) for their offspring and frequently that of God for his people; e.g. Exod 33.19; Deut 13.18; Isa 9.16. In Aramaic the cognate verb means 'to love', and in the Targum answers to Hebrew אהב. Such a meaning has been detected in the verb in Ps 18.2 (EV 18.1). In this particular context and with the 'House of Israel' as its object the sense is that 'I will no longer show the (compassionate, caring) forbearance that I have shown hitherto'. Cf. LXX[V] and OL in Text and Versions below.

[e]The view here taken of the meaning of נָשֹׂא אֶשָּׂא לָהֶם is that of ibn Janāḥ (cf. ibn Ezra) who compares specifically Job 32.22 'my maker would sweep me away', cf. BDB p. 671 col 1, 3 b, and gives to the phrase in question the meaning 'I will uproot them and annihilate them' (Arabic *'ql'hm w'st'ṣlhm*)[40]. This sense differs little from that listed in BDB and KB³, 'to carry off', 'to take away' and finds support in the Peshiṭta (see Text and Versions); and it is found in Hos 5.14. Some difficulty is occasioned by the preposition ל which follows rather than the expected direct object. The rabbinic authorities quoted argue that the ל is a variant for the accusative particle and for this ibn Ezra (e.g.) compares 2 Sam 3.30 הרגו לאבנר (cf. GK 117n)[41]. A variant on this interpretation and one which lessens the difficulty of the ל following is that of Wolff[42]. For him the direct object of the verb can be understood as implied from

40 Qyl compares also Ps 102.11.

41 For ל used to mark the accusative in early Hebrew, cf. König, 289.

42 The suggestion is built upon the work of earlier scholars, e.g. Hengstenberg (p. 43) who posited the translation 'I will remove (*sc.* everything) from them'.

what precedes (i.e. pity, compassion) and the ל has the well-attested sense 'in respect of them' (cf. Jer 49.29); the resulting sense is 'on the contrary I will sweep it (i.e. my compassion, pity) away completely in respect of them'. Wolff admits that no precise parallel is found elsewhere, though he notes the existence of the phrases שׂים/נתן רחמים ל. The suggestion is attractive and based on sound principles. In the absence, however, of any ancient traditions to support it, ibn Janāḥ's interpretation is to be preferred. The latter has the merit that it furnishes a more straightforward sense[43] and does not involve the contention that the phrase is marked by somewhat complicated ellipsis.

The verb נשׂא followed by ל frequently has the sense 'to remove the guilt of (ל) a person'[44] and this sense has been detected here, cf. the Targum and ibn Ezra (so Borbone); the latter explicitly prefers the explanation adopted above but mentions this as a possibility. Accordingly the finite verb is a frequentative imperfect with past reference and the sense is 'for (hitherto) I was utterly forgiving towards them'. The suggestion has the merit that it fits well with the sense of the preceding words ('I will no longer show forbearance'). On the other hand reference to vv. 4 and 9 suggests that the words here are likely to convey an element of the punishment to come rather than an explanation of the background to that punishment.

An alternative under this heading is to assume that the force of the negative in the preceding words carries over to this phrase (so, e.g., Qyl, AF). Hence, 'For/surely I will in no way forgive them' (cf. NEB). Here considerable difficulty is occasioned by the supposition that the negative sense can carry over the intervening conjunction כי.

Kimchi invests the verb נשׂא here with the meaning 'I will raise up (*sc.* an enemy against you to lead you into captivity and devastate your land)'. He does not produce any parallels though Qyl, reviewing the theory, refers to a similar phrase in Deut 28.49 'the Lord will bring (יִשָּׂא) a nation against thee'. The suggestion amounts to a possibility, though this particular elliptical usage is not elsewhere attested and accordingly, in this particular context, requires a very substantial assumption[45].

The verse recounts the birth and naming of Hosea's second child in language similar to that used for his first-born. Here, however, there is no reference to an interval of time before the divine message (of which the infant girl is a living sign) will take

43 Cf. in v. 4 the concluding punishment 'I will bring to an end the kingdom of the House of Israel', and in v. 9, 'I will be no longer (your God)'.

44 The figure of speech arises from ellipsis of עון, cf. the standard dictionaries.

45 One further Jewish tradition concerning the phrase is that of Abarbarnel. For him the phrase is marked by an ellipsis of the word יד 'hand', and the meaning is 'I have solemnly sworn (this) for them' (lit. 'I have raised my hand, *sc.* in oath)'. The solution has not won much support.

effect. Rather from the moment of her birth Yahweh will show no more forbearance towards the kingdom of Israel. If he is no longer to show forbearance then the assumption is a natural one that hitherto he had shown such gracious forbearance.

There is no indication of the interval of time between the birth of Jezreel and that of Lo-Ruḥamah. For ibn Ezra and Kimchi (cf. Jerome) the girl, being of the weaker sex, signifies and represents the weakness of the kings and the kingdom following the extinction of the dynasty of Jehu. Whether they are right in this particular respect, their understanding of the temporal connection between the girl and Yahweh's withdrawal of his care for the state is surely correct. It was from the moment when the short reign of Zechariah ended in his assassination that the monarchy of Israel was marked by the instability of frequent palace revolts and, consequently, by weakness in the face of the growing Assyrian menace.

The account of the birth of his children is to some extent retrospective (see p. 9 above). It is likely, then, that Hosea saw in his daughter Lo-Ruḥamah a living parable of the accelerating decline of the kingdom following the demise of the dynasty of Jehu in 747 BC. It may be suggested that the child was born early in, and (in Hosea's understanding) reflects, the period *c.* 747–740 BC.

As has been indicated, the withdrawal by Yahweh of his compassion implies that hitherto he had shown it. Such an understanding of the history of the period is reflected also in the Deuteronomic history where the view is set forth that Yahweh had shown forbearance in respect of every single king of the dynasty of Jehu (other than Zechariah). For Jehu, see 2 Kgs 10.30; for Jehoahaz 2 Kgs 13.4f; for Joash 2 Kgs 13.23 (including the verb *rḥm*) for Jeroboam II 2 Kgs 14.25f.

There is, of course, no need to suppose that Hosea showed anything other than normal paternal love for his daughter. As noted above, the naming of the child is a technical prophetic action and the name has a literary and contrived character. The essential testimony of the verse is to Hosea's perception, at Yahweh's behest, that the period following the birth of his daughter marked the withdrawal from Israel of Yahweh's favour and forbearance. The inevitable corollary of that decision is expressed in the final phrase ('for/surely I will completely annihilate them'). The threat is marked by a substantial increase in severity over that expressed in v. 4 (i.e. 'I will bring to an end the kingdom of the house of Israel'). What is implied in the earlier verse is drawn out expressly in this; such increased precision of expression may reflect a growing appreciation on the prophet's part of the final outcome of the judgement he had earlier perceived more tentatively; cf. further on 9.15.

Text and Versions

ויאמר לו Pesh.+ *mry*', cf. LXX[Luc], in the interests of clarity in translation; + יהוה (Borbone); Pesh. *ly* might imply MT לי, but is more likely a natural mistake, cf. Gelston, p. 137.

לא רוחמה/ארחם LXX οὐκ ἠλεημένη/ἐλεῆσαι; LXX[V] οὐκ ἠγαπημένη, cf. OL[SW] (and at v. 8); Vulg. *absque misericordia/misereri*; Pesh. *l' 'trḥmt/lmrḥmw*; Targ. דלא רחימין[46]/לרחמא.

כי נשׂא אשׂא להם LXX ἀλλ' ἢ ἀντιτασσόμενος ἀντιτάξομαι αὐτοῖς; Aq. ἐπιλήσομαι αὐτῶν; Vulg. *sed oblivione obliviscar eorum*; Pesh. *mšql šql'n lhm* (cf. Gelston, p. 145); Targ. משבוק אשבק להון. The LXX means 'but I will set myself against them'. *BH* suggests on the basis of this שָׂנֹא אֶשְׂנָא. As Wolff notes, however, it is μισεῖν that always answers to Hebrew שׂנא. Aq. and Vulg. may have read 'I will utterly forget them'. The root is נשׁה II for which a parallel form נשׁא is attested in Jer 23.39. If the meaning of the verb רחם has been accurately determined, the meaning 'forget' for נשׂא appears to me to be weak if not virtually tautologous. For observations on Targ. ('forgive', cf. Cathcart) and Pesh. ('carry off'), see note e above.

1.7 **(But I will show forbearance towards the House of Judah[a] and I will save them by[b] Yahweh their God. I will not save them by bow or sword or weapons of war[c], by horses or chariot horses[d].)**

[a]The phrase 'House of Judah' is an old one, referring to the confederation of six southern tribes which is likely to have existed before David's time (cf. 2 Sam 4 and Noth *History*, pp. 58f (*GI*, p. 59), and de Vaux *EHI* 2, pp. 549, 737 = *HAI* 1, p. 487, 2, p. 54).

[b]The preposition ב must have the same force (*instrumenti*) as it has in the second half of the verse. Attempts to see it as *essentiae* are designed to lessen the awkwardness of the phrase in translation. For such attempts, see J. Lippl.

[c]See Ps 76.4 and ibn Ezra's comment on it; also the translations of NEB and ASB.

[d]In texts of the seventh century BC and earlier פרשׁ is more likely to denote chariot horses; cf. Galling *ZThK* 53 (1956), pp. 129f, Mowinkel *VT* 12 (1962), pp. 278ff, 291 and KB[3] *ad loc.* On this view, according

[46] The Targum explicitly interprets the child of the (plural) people.

to KB[3], סוסים is a more general term and is defined more precisely by the following פרשים. For a full treatment of the Assyrian evidence, see S. Dalley, pp. 31ff. According to her, cavalry (in the sense of the unit, a single soldier on a single horse[47]) began to be developed by the Assyrians during the reign of Sargon while Samaria was distinctive for possessing chariotry without cavalry. By the seventh century cavalry may have been familiar and hence 'riders' (i.e. cavalry) may possibly have been intended by the writer.

The verse is generally regarded as a Judaean gloss, i.e. it was added to Hosea's prophecy after that prophecy had found its way to the Southern Kingdom and had been there appropriated (see p. lxxi on the transmission of Hosea's oracles).

For the rabbinic commentators Yahweh's compassionate forbearance is shown to Judah from the fall of Samaria in 722/1 BC and the contemporary reign of Hezekiah until the fall of Jerusalem in 587 BC (Rashi and Kimchi). In particular the salvation mentioned is thought by these authorities to reflect the deliverance of Judah from the menace of the Assyrian empire and especially the events of 701/700 BC when, in apparently miraculous circumstances and with no military endeavour on Judah's part, the army of Sennacherib withdrew from the siege of Jerusalem (ibn Ezra and Kimchi, 2 Kgs 19.32–35; Isa 29.5ff; 30.27ff).

This view of the matter is likely to be substantially correct[48]. The absence within the text of any notice of a *terminus ad quem* for Yahweh's forbearance to Judah suggests that the interpolation had been made well before 587 BC.

The appropriation of Hosea's oracles and their use by Yahwistic circles in Judah gives to the prophecies of Hosea a longer perspective and may constitute the beginning of an important element of Judaean faith, *viz.* that Yahweh's election of his chosen people was narrowed to Judah following his rejection of the Northern Kingdom. The prophecies, so appropriated, serve as a warning to the South not to follow the disastrous idolatry and unfaithfulness which had characterised the Northern Kingdom and thereby to avoid the judgement that their northern kinsmen had so justly incurred. It is generally recognised that a parallel and important appropriation by Judah of a tradition which was originally northern is to be found in the

47 See further M. A. Littauer and J. H. Crouwel, *Wheeled vehicles and ridden animals in the ANE* (Leiden, 1979).

48 For criticisms of it and for an attempt to understand the verse (though secondary) as consistent with Hosea's views on Judah, see Emmerson, pp. 88ff.

book of Deuteronomy; the reference in Ps 114.2 'Judah became his sanctuary and Israel his dominion', where Judah has the primacy and is recognised as the site of the only sanctuary, is likely to belong to the period immediately following Josiah's reform and its sentiments are consistent with those of Hos 1.7. Further, Ps 78[49], which at its end explicitly sets forth the election of Judah following Ephraim's demise and which also proclaims the supremacy of the Jerusalem sanctuary, is added evidence of the same doctrine in Judah in the seventh century. Finally, in a passage of Jeremiah (3.6–11), clearly dependent on Hosea, Judah is castigated for not learning the lessons of the north. This revelation, it is said (v. 6), came to Jeremiah 'in the reign of Josiah'. Even if the passage is a later composition by the Deuteronomic editors of Jeremiah[50] it furnishes evidence that the sentiments it sets forth were later regarded as appropriate to the reign of Josiah.

Hosea 1.7, then, is a Judaean gloss of the seventh century BC. The sentiments are attested independently for the period following Josiah's reform of 621 BC. It is possible, however, that the doctrine of Hos 1.7 was formulated before it became an accepted commonplace and found its way into the psalms mentioned above. I conclude that the verse belongs to the period *c*. 650–620 BC.

Text and Versions

No significant readings. The (Dead Sea Scroll) fragment 4QXII[d] (Hos 1.7–2.5) appears to agree with MT; for a reconstruction, see Sinclair.

1.8 and 9 (8) **And after she had weaned Lo-Ruḥamah she conceived and bore a son.** (9) **And he [Yahweh] said, Call him by the name Lo-Ammi for you are not my people and I will not be [Yahweh] for you.**

The form of the two verses and the language used follow closely the notices of the birth of the previous children, though this time the style is more abrupt (see Text and Versions for the amplifications in the LXX and Peshiṭta). The absence of *lw* ('to him', *sc.* to Hosea) following the verb 'she bore' together with

49 For observations on the dating of these psalms, see Gunkel *ad loc.*
50 Cf. Nicholson and McKane *ad locc.*

the name 'not my people' has suggested to some scholars[51] that Hosea was not the child's father and that it was at this point that Gomer's adultery became apparent[52]. As, however, there is no other difference between the notice of this child's birth and those of the other children, the presumption remains that the same circumstances obtained and that Hosea's child bore in his person the final and most severe of the judgements of Yahweh in respect of the kingdom of Ephraim. It is the fate of Ephraim that the child represents; that fate is sealed from the moment of his birth; his birth marks the beginning of the inexorable consequences of Yahweh's final repudiation of Ephraim. The birth of the child and the circumstances of it do not prompt Hosea to perceive Yahweh's message. Yahweh's message is received directly by Hosea and then, at Yahweh's behest, tied to or associated with the birth of his son by the process of naming him in accordance with the message.

The name 'not my people' has as its point of reference the nation and not the child[53]. It sets forth the reversal of the terms of the covenant by which Yahweh adopted Israel as his people; cf. Exod 3.7, 10 and especially (as later formulated) 6.7[54]. Similarly the phrase *w'nky l' 'hyh lkm* reverses Yahweh's undertaking to become Israel's national God expressed in the formula *'hyh 'šr 'hyh* (Exod 3.14) which has the function of offering an interpretation of the tetragrammaton. In this latter verse the word or name *'hyh* is also construed as the subject of the following verb 'thou shalt then say unto the children of Israel, I AM (*'hyh*) has sent me to you'. Accordingly, and noting the *maqqeph*, Wolff construes the phrase here *l' 'hyh* (lit. 'I will not be') as a noun predicative of *'nky* (= I am), parallel to *l' ʿmy* ('not my people') and having the literal meaning 'I am "not I will be" for you (anymore)'. While such an assessment of the syntax is probably correct, that does not preclude the likelihood that other senses or nuances pertain to the phrase. Thus, as Rosenmüller observes, a number of texts from the Psalms throw light on the matter: (1) Ps 124.1, 'if Yahweh had not been (*šhyh*) on our side'; (2) Ps 118.6 (cf. Ps 56.10), 'the Lord is on my side (*yhwh ly*), I will not fear'. The former text (if not the latter) clearly makes a play on the divine name and, like Exod 3.14,

51 E.g. Procksch, p. 23 and Qyl. Both authors detect and emphasise the sense of close relationship and love in the word עם.

52 An alternative explanation of the absence of לו is suggested by Qyl – that the elliptical style alludes to the imminent complete break between Yahweh and his people.

53 See above for the literary and contrived nature of symbolic names.

54 For the negative form of the name, see on Lo-Ruḥamah above.

connects it with the verb *hyh* 'to be/become'; it has the meaning 'if Yahweh had not become (*sc.* our defender in the face of hostile threats)'[55].

The phrase before us, then, means lit. 'I am (from now on) not '*hyh* (I will be) for you' (cf. Symmachus). That highly epigrammatic saying has the force 'I am from this moment no longer Yahweh to you'. In turn this phrase implies that Yahweh will no longer act as the nation's God in supporting, defending and sustaining a people who, by the same tokens, have forfeited their status as his covenant people[56]. The break is complete.

For ibn Ezra and Rashi (following the Targum) the significance of the name 'not my people' lies in its allusion to the hopelessness of the children of those exiled from the Northern Kingdom and their fatalistic reluctance or inability to return to their land. In this they forfeited their status as members of Yahweh's people. More directly in accord with the rabbinic interpretations of the prophet's previous children is that of Kimchi. Lo-Ruḥamah's period at the breast depicts the feebleness of the kingdom in the period from Zechariah until Pekah (747–735 BC). The latter king strengthened the kingdom, ruled 'for twenty years'[57] and, with Rezin, King of Damascus, prevailed over Judah killing 'twelve thousand men in a day' (cf. 2 Chr 28.6). It is to this king that the allusion is made by the phrase 'she conceived and bore a son'.

Kimchi's assessment of Pekah's reign as a strong one (NB the third child is a boy) does not altogether accord with historical reality. For it was in his reign that Tiglath-pileser III subjugated extensive Israelite territory (733 BC). On the other hand the events surrounding the Syro-Ephraimite conspiracy in which Pekah played a leading role, and the consequential arrival of the Assyrians in 733 BC marked the beginning of the end for the Northern Kingdom and substantial deportations of its citizens[58]. From this moment the kingdom was reduced in size to the Ephraimite hill country and its capital Samaria. Menahem had paid tribute to the Assyrians in 738 and this, no doubt, already served as a portent of what was to come. Kimchi's view, then, of the significance of Hosea's third child who bore the severest statement of Yahweh's repudiation of the Northern Kingdom is a telling one. Accordingly, by reference to the historical evidence,

[55] Rudolph doubts that Hosea knew Exod 3.14 since it is a late text; see his commentary and further his article in BZAW 68 (1938), p. 9.

[56] It follows from this account of the phrase that emendation is unnecessary. For proposals to emend, see, e.g., Harper *ad loc.*

[57] Cf. 2 Kgs 15.27 and Gray's comments on the chronology (pp. 64f and 626).

[58] Noth *History*, pp. 260f (*GI*, pp. 235f).

the birth of Lo-Ammi best fits the early part of the decade 747–740 BC[59], and his growth to manhood reflects the period from then until 733 BC. Cf. further 9.12.

According to the understanding of the prophet's children as 'signs' set forth above, the child and his name represent and proclaim Yahweh's particular judgement and punishment of his people. As the child grows, the message he bears inexorably finds fulfilment. In this particular case, the only temporal reference is to the time that elapsed between Lo-Ruḥamah's birth and her being weaned. The evidence for the time between birth and weaning in ancient Israel is about three years[60]. I conclude that Hosea, some three years after his recognition that Yahweh's forbearance towards the Northern Kingdom was at an end (Lo-Ruḥamah), perceived that Yahweh had repudiated his particular covenant relationship with the Northern Kingdom of Israel.

Text and Versions

ותהר LXX adds ἔτι and Pesh. *twb*; this does not constitute evidence that עוד followed ותהר. The versions are likely to represent a tendency to harmonise the verse with v. 6.

ואנכי לא אהיה לכם LXX καὶ ἐγὼ οὐκ εἰμὶ ὑμῶν; Symm. οὐδὲ ἐγὼ ἔσομαι ὑμῖν· οὐδὲ γὰρ ὑμεῖς λαός μου; Vulg. *et ego non ero vester*; Pesh. *w'n' l' 'hw' lkwn*; Targ. ומימרי לא הוה בסעדיכון, 'my word has not been your support'; Symm. inverts the order of the phrases in MT, presumably because the resulting line is (in Greek) more felicitous. LXX's ὑμῶν (genitive) indicates that Εἰμί (*sic* with capital, so Ziegler) is not a verb but a name (cf. אהיה, MT Exod 3.14); cf. P. Katz *ThLZ* 20 (1936), p. 286. → אלהיכם (Borbone, after LXX MS 764, cf. OL[S] and *BHS*); אהלכם 'your father', Hirschberg *VT* 11 (1961), p. 374.

59 Cf. Rudolph; the interval of time suggested by the events of chapter 1 is 'five or six years'.

60 Cf. with Wolff 2 Macc 7.27; 'The (Egyptian) Instruction of Ani', Wilson *ANET*, p. 420, and 1 Sam 1.23ff, where Samuel is presented to the sanctuary of Shiloh after being weaned. The presumption is that for the child to leave his mother and lead an independent life he must have been nearer five than three years old.

CHAPTER 2.1–3

A PROPHECY OF RECAPITULATION: HOPE FOR THE FUTURE ASSOCIATED WITH THE NAMES OF HOSEA'S CHILDREN

NB The English Versions add verses 2.1–2 to chapter 1; hence the numbering of the verses in chapter 2 (English Versions) is two behind that of MT. Elsewhere in the commentary the difference is noted, but not in the commentary on chapter 2.

(1) **In future[a] the number of the Israelites shall be as the sand of the sea which cannot be measured[b] or counted[b]. And where[c] it was said of them 'You are not my people', in the future[a] it will be said of them 'You are sons of the living God'.** (2) **Then the Judaeans will assemble[d] in unity with the Israelites and they will appoint[e] a single ruler[f] and they [g]will flourish on the land[g]; for great is the day of Jezreel.** (3) **Say to your brothers 'My people'** [Hebrew Ammi] **and to your sisters 'Beloved'[h]** [Hebrew Ruḥamah].

[a]וְהָיָה is a common prophetic expression for events in the future; its use here implies transition from the preceding prophecy of judgement to a prophecy of recapitulation. The word is used elsewhere by Hosea in 1.5; 2.18, 23.

[b]*Niphal tolerativum*, GK 51c; i.e. sand which does not permit of measurement, which cannot be quantified.

[c]Ibn Ezra (cf. Kimchi and GK 130c) notes that the phrase בִּמְקוֹם אֲשֶׁר 'in the place where', is capable of meaning 'instead of' (תַּחַת אֲשֶׁר). The Targum and Peshiṭta interpret the phrase more literally, i.e. the increase in numbers will occur in the place of exile. Rudolph, comparing the versions and Rom 9.26, prefers to think specifically of Jezreel as the place; cf. AF.

[d]The verb נקבצו has a concrete meaning and depicts assembly as a prelude (in this case) to the appointment of a single ruler. Wolff's view that the word means abstractly 'be united' fails to convey the image. It is יחד(ו) 'together', 'in unity' (cf. Ps 133.1) which denotes what Wolff looks for in the verb.

[e]Cf. Deut 17.15 and 1 Sam 8.5 for the verb שׂים 'to appoint' (a king).

[f]Lit. 'a single head'. The word ראשׁ denotes a leader, cf. Num 14.4; Judg 11.8.

g—g The words form a notorious *crux*. Broadly speaking, there are three main types of solution. First, the traditional Jewish view (cf. the Peshiṭta, Targum, Kimchi and Qyl) is that the words mean 'they will go up (the usual verb for journeys to Israel) from the land, *sc*. of their captivity'. The insuperable difficulty arises that 'the land' (הארץ) naturally denotes Israel and not a foreign country[1]. The interpretation harmonises with prophecies current in exilic times (cf. especially Ezek 37.15ff) and is best regarded as evidence as to the way in which the verse was read from these times onwards. For ibn Ezra's different view, see the commentary below.

Secondly, from a comparison with Exod 1.10 where the same words are found in Pharaoh's mouth, M. Lambert[2] proposed that the words in both passages denote 'and they will gain ascendancy over the land'. Lambert's theory has been convincingly repudiated by K. Rupprecht[3] and should be set aside as having no philological basis (Rupprecht p. 443)[4].

A variation on Lambert's view is that of H. Gressmann (p. 235) for whom the phrase in question means 'they will swamp the land' (lit. 'they will go higher than the land'). The theory rests on another of J. Theis (pp. 14ff) in relation to Gen 2.6 and requires the assumption that the מן is comparative. Rupprecht's criticisms of this theory are equally (or more) devastating and demonstrate clearly Gressmann's misunderstanding and arbitrary use of the theories of both Theis and Lambert.

A more recent theory which links Exod 1.10 with this verse is that of W. L. Holladay[5] for whom ארץ denotes the underworld. For this sense he compares Gen 2.6 and 1 Sam 28.13 where, again, the verb עלה is

1 'From the earth', i.e. from the countries of the world, is a variation on this theme; cf. Wolff's criticism of this particular theory. Ibn Ezra, despite his somewhat forced solution to the problem, perceived that the word must mean Israel.

2 *REJ* 39 (1899), p. 300; Lambert's theory has been accepted by a surprisingly large number of modern authorities; e.g. Wolff, KB, NEB etc.

3 *ZAW* 82 (1970), pp. 442ff.

4 To this I would add that Lambert's appeal to the talmudic view of Exod 1.10 (quoted by ibn Ezra, Rashi and Naḥmanides *ad loc.*) prompted this erroneous conclusion. What is there said is that עלה מן הארץ is an impersonal construction with the meaning 'we will vacate the land'; thus '(the Hebrews will join our enemies and fight against us) and one (we) will vacate the land'. The consequence will be that the Hebrews will take possession of it. From this it is quite clear that the authority cited by the Talmud believed that the verb עלה had the usual meaning 'we (the Egyptians) will go up from the land' (i.e. vacate it) and that Pharaoh did not, in the circumstances, need to expand his sentence by saying 'with the result that the Hebrews will take possession of it'. Lambert thus conflated two distinct talmudic arguments about the meaning of Exod 1.10 and, as a consequence, made a conjecture about the precise meaning of the verb which was unwarranted; see B. *Soṭah* 11a (ET, p. 54 in *Nashim* III).

5 *VT* 19 (1969), pp. 123f. The theory is adopted by AF in conjunction with the exodus motif.

used. The literal sense both there and in Exod 1.10 is 'they will come up from the underworld' and the meaning here and in Exod 1.10 is that the Israelites will experience a national resurrection or revival. The suggestion is in some respects attractive but there lacks firm evidence in favour of so sophisticated a meaning for such straightforward words. Thus in both Gen 2.6 and 1 Sam 28.13 there is no need to suppose that the words עלה and ארץ do not have their usual sense of 'go up from the earth'. Further, as Rupprecht observes (p. 446 n.), Holladay's theory depends in no small part on Lambert's assumption that the phrase in Exod 1.10 and Hos 2.2 has a particular and special meaning which is one and the same[6].

Thirdly, there are the solutions which give to the words עלה and ארץ their usual meanings but decline to see the same significance in the words in what are taken to be the different contexts of Exod 1.10 and the verse before us (so Rupprecht). Where Exod 1.10 is concerned attention may be drawn to Naḥmanides' contention that עלה here has the force 'go up' in a military sense. Hence any alliance between the Hebrews and the external enemies of Pharaoh will enable the former to mount an attack from within the land[7]. Alternatively, there is Rupprecht's view that the phrase in Pharaoh's mouth is anachronistic and alludes to the events of the exodus. What Pharaoh fears is proleptically what was to happen: there is the danger that the Hebrews will 'go up' (*sc.* flee) from the land (*sc.* of Egypt). Where Hos 2.2 is concerned the words are found in the different context of a prophecy depicting the restoration of a united and prosperous state upon the land of Israel. With this in mind, two theories may be noted. First, Wolff, *EvTh* 12 (1952/3), pp. 94ff, proposed the view that the words depicted a pilgrimage undertaken by representatives of the united kingdom of Judah and Israel to a common covenant sanctuary. Thus they will go up (to the sanctuary) from the (whole, united) land. By the time that he had written his commentary on Hosea, Wolff had abandoned this view on the grounds that (1) the words do not express clearly enough such a cultic event and (2) the name of the pilgrimage site is not given. With these criticisms of his earlier theory we may agree.

Further, under this heading, there is the suggestion of Th. C. Vriezen[8] that the verb עלה here has the sense 'to shoot up', 'grow up' (as of a plant). Drawing attention to Deut 29.22 and to Hos 2.25a ('I will sow

[6] If it be insisted that the phrase here and in Exod 1.10 has the same meaning, then the only account of עלה which begins to fit both texts is that advocated by Naḥmanides for Exod 1.10, *viz.* 'to mount an attack'. Here, on this view of the matter, the words would seem to mean that the united population of Judah and Israel under a single ruler will 'go up from the (whole) land' to fight its invaders.

[7] Whether generally of Egypt or specifically (so Naḥmanides) of Goshen.

[8] Pp. 13 and 22. His suggestion is accepted by Rudolph; Wolff too takes up the suggestion in his commentary but combines it with Lambert's interpretation of the precise meaning of the phrase.

her in the land')[9], Vriezen's theory suggests that the words here depict the vigorous repopulation of the land by the Israelites under the figure of Yahweh's gracious blessing of it in relation to its fertility and growth. Such a view of the matter has the advantage that it accords with Hosea's thought (so, here, his view of the Day of Jezreel; see also especially 2.20ff) as well as being consistent with linguistic considerations which amount to a real possibility.

[h]For a discussion of the meaning of this word and for the difficulties of translating it, see on 1.6. The sense is that Yahweh's loving care is restored.

The verses are closely related in content to the verses that precede them, though the sense appears to be exactly the opposite. For this reason the prophecy as a unit has been regarded either as a later (post exilic) composition akin to that of Ezek 37.21f[10] or as a prophecy of recapitulation (i.e. reversal of the original sense) composed by Hosea[11] at a later stage in his ministry.

The difficulty presented by the verses has long been recognised. Thus Rosenmüller states laconically *moris prophetarum est, ut laeta tristibus admisceant*. A radical solution to the problem was advocated by ibn Ezra for whom the verses, following the oracles of doom in chapter 1 and preceding the oracle 'strive with your mother', were wholly oracles of doom[12]. Thus the large numbers of the Israelites depict their increase in exile where, claiming to be sons of the living God, they were actually not his people. The 'gathering' is that of Sennacherib when he deported the inhabitants of the fortified cities of Judah; he is the single head appointed over them, and theirs is the going up (*sc.* the departure) from the land. The day of Jezreel is thus great by reason of the greatness of the doom which it brought, and the command to style brothers 'my people' etc. is wholly sarcastic and ironic in tone.

Ibn Ezra's interpretation is forced in most respects. Yet his insistence upon the unity of the verses with what precedes them is valuable and, as we are now accustomed to see it, points rather to the ambivalent character of some early prophetic oracles whose import, *more prophetarum*, whether for weal or for woe,

9 See, e.g., BDB p. 748, col 2 4; for an example of the verb predicated metaphorically of a person, see Isa 53.2.

10 So, e.g., Procksch, Marti, Harper.

11 So, e.g., Wolff. Mays takes the similar but not identical view that the verses were added by a contemporary editor, well acquainted with Hosea's work.

12 The same interpretation may lie behind the Peshitta's introduction of 'if' – 'if the number of the children of Israel shall be like the sand ...'.

is dependent upon the response of those to whom they are addressed (cf. the prophecies of Emmanuel and Shear-Jashub in Isaiah and the formula of Isa 1.19f). In other words, the prophecies of judgement in chapter 1, if effective of true repentance, can be turned under divine providence to the benefit of the nation.

The view that these verses are genuine depends upon the consideration that the thought contained in them is consistent with that elsewhere expressed by Hosea (cf. Rudolph). Indeed the verses constitute a precise recapitulation of Yahweh's judgement as announced by Hosea; thus (so Mays) Israel's increase coincided with increased sinfulness and the result is that their growth shall cease (4.10; 9.12, 16; 14.1, EV 13.16); the covenant is repudiated (1.9; 8.1); the Syro-Ephraimite War is the occasion of Yahweh's wrath (5.8–14); the fertility of the land will cease (2.11, 12, 14; 4.3). Since the verses are explicitly a recapitulation of these aspects of judgement, it is understandable that the linguistic features are to an extent contrived and even prolix. Secondly, as has been widely recognised, in content and sentiment the verses are of a sort with what is contained in 2.23–25. Indeed, it has been suggested (so, e.g., Wolff)[13] that the unit 2.1–3 originally found its place amongst these sayings and that the editor who compiled chapter 1 removed it to follow the specific words of judgement at the end of chapter 1 in order to display there the full range, effect and purpose of Yahweh's judgement. If he could not abandon his people to annihilation (cf. 11.9) then judgement served as the means whereby his people, purified of their wickedness, might be restored to the status to which they were called (cf. Deut 4.30f).

The point is well illuminated by Rashi who quotes B. *Pesaḥim* 87b (ET, p. 462 in *Mo'ed* II) to the effect that Hosea realised that he had exaggerated the harshness of Yahweh's judgement and that he must needs express equally firmly the element of divine pity. Similarly he quotes Rab (*Sifre Numbers* 25.1)[14] as suggesting that the juxtaposition in Hosea of sentiments of judgement and consolation, as different in character as east is from west, is explained by the story of a certain king who in a moment of exasperation at his wife's behaviour summoned a scribe to execute a divorce. The latter was late in coming and,

[13] The theory is mentioned by, e.g., Marti who dismisses it. Appeal to Rom 9.25f where Hos 2.25 (EV 23) is quoted, preceding a quotation of Hos 2.1, does not constitute evidence, for, as Marti rightly observes, St Paul is free to juxtapose quotations in any way convenient to him.

[14] See Horovitz, § 131, p. 170.

during this time, the king was reconciled to his wife. Wishing to avoid the scribe's thinking him indecisive at heart, the king resolved to tell him that he had been summoned to write a second (confirmatory) marriage certificate.

It seems best to regard the verses in the form that we have them as the work of the redactor of Hosea's sayings. That is not to say, of course, that they are not wholly consistent with the thought of Hosea as it developed in the light of the historical judgements which he witnessed. Whether he actually wrote them or whether his redactor wrote them in his name is difficult to resolve and, in any case, is bound up with the more general question of the history of the composition of the book which bears his name.

On the view, then, that the verses represent Hosea's understanding of God's mercy prevailing over his judgement, they are best dated in the period following Tiglath-pileser III's subjugation of a large part of the Northern Kingdom in 733 BC[15] and before the final collapse of Samaria in 722/721 BC which, in respect of Ephraim at least, precluded the possibility of any such prophecy of weal on Hosea's lips. They are of a sort with the prophet's lyrical prayer for his people as it is expressed in the words of chapter 14 (*q.v.*).

VERSE 1

The words suggest the possibility of a gracious and miraculous reversal of the decline in the population of Israel following the deportation of the urban upper classes by Tiglath-pileser in 733 BC[16].

'Sons of Israel' appears as a designation for the Northern Kingdom in 3.1, 4, 5 as in 4.1 and evokes, as does the simile of the sand (Gen 22.17, cf. 13.16), the promise to the patriarchs of old. The essential point is that the promise will prevail even over the horrific judgement. *bmqwm 'šr* denotes primarily the reversal

[15] For details, see Noth *History*, pp. 260f; *GI*, pp. 235f. The important point is that while Tiglath-pileser conquered and annexed Gilead and Galilee, he left Samaria with the Ephraimite hill country in the hands of the usurper Hoshea.

[16] According to Sargon II's Display Inscription (*ANET*, p. 285) some 27,000 were deported from Samaria and the Ephraimite hill country in 721 BC. 2 Kgs 15.19f records that in 738 BC the kingdom had a total taxable strength of 60,000 land owners. We may assume that a substantial portion of these latter must have been deported in 733 BC when Galilee and the Jezreel valley were reorganised as the Assyrian province of Megiddo. These figures give at least some impression of the extent of the disaster.

of the judgement of depopulation but is likely to have been chosen to imply the repopulation specifically of Jezreel and Galilee whence Tiglath-pileser's deportations of 733 BC were made.

The judgement expressed by the name Not-my-people is the repudiation of the covenant. The recapitulation of that judgement and the renewal of the covenant is expressed in the name 'sons of the living God' which may also effect a contrast with Israel designated in 1.2 'sons of promiscuity'. The relationship between Israel and God indicated by the word 'sons' is that of single-minded loyalty within the covenant, cf. Deut 14.1, 'You are sons of the Lord your God'. The term 'living God' is likely specifically to denote Yahweh in contradistinction to false gods (so Kimchi) and to emphasise his effective reality (cf. 1 Sam 17.26; Ps 42.3; 84.3). The complete expression 'sons of the living God' constitutes an instructive, carefully contrived antithesis to 'Not-my-people' (1.9) and suggests that, restored to the covenant relationship, Israel will be infused with life by the author of life and hence will be blessed with fertility and strength (cf. 6.2).

VERSE 2

In this new situation Israel and Judah will assemble in unity to appoint a common leader. The contrast is to the enmity between the two states at the time of the Syro-Ephraimite War, regarded by Hosea as a manifestation of their sinfulness and of the ensuing judgement upon them (cf. 5.8–14). The image of assembly recalls the ancient traditions of the unity of Yahweh's people (cf. with AF, Gen 49.1f and Deut 33.5) as does the appointment of a single head or leader (Hebrew *r'š*, cf. Num 14.4, and Judg 11.8). Hosea avoids the word 'king' for the reason that the institution, where the Northern Kingdom is concerned, is totally discredited (cf. 8.4) and because the blander title 'head' delineates the future in terms of the pre-monarchical past[17].

On the view taken of the phrase here, the united and restored people will flourish on the land since the covenant is restored, and the blessing of Yahweh effects the luxuriant growth of his obedient people (cf. 2.20ff). Such a view accords with the converted sense of Jezreel. So far from being a name indicating

[17] For the possibility that Hosea viewed with favour the future restoration of a Davidic (southern) king, cf. Rudolph and especially Emmerson, p. 110.

judgement and punishment, now it conveys its original sense that God (*sc.* for Hosea, Yahweh) is the author of the blessing of fertility and growth associated initially with the geographical area but now transferred metaphorically to the covenant people[18].

So clear is this vision to its author, so exact its power of recapitulation, that the event is to become proleptically a paradigm of blessing and good fortune. 'Great is the day of Jezreel' – as great in its import as the classic military victory of Gideon over the Midianites (Judg 7) named by Isaiah (9.3) with the comparable phrase 'the day of Midian'.

VERSE 3

The imperative[19] of the phrase that follows ('say to your brothers ...') expresses the prophet's assurance (cf. GK 110c) that the citizens of the united realm will greet each other in warm friendship. Such friendly relations mark the reverse of the enmity which prevailed at the time of the Syro-Ephraimite War and constitute a manifestation of the restoration of the covenant between Yahweh and his people. The latter are now once again 'my people' and 'beloved'. Where Hosea's second son and his daughter had set forth and represented the repudiation of the covenant (Not-my-people and Not-beloved, see on vv. 9 and 6 of chapter 1 above), now the people, described as brothers and sisters (i.e. compatriots), are restored to their erstwhile status. In a prophecy of recapitulation with its necessary prolixity and exactitude, it is not surprising that the plural forms ('brothers' and 'sisters') are used and attempts (e.g. Harper and Marti) to emend on the basis of the LXX are unwarranted (see Text and Versions).

There is no need to follow Rudolph in his judgement that the verse is to be attributed to the Judaean redactor of chapters 1–3. The verse represents simply a recapitulation of the names Lo-Ruḥamah (1.6) and Lo-Ammi (1.9); where these names were used in chapter 1 of the Northern Kingdom, here the (positive) names refer to a future united kingdom, including Judah. The

18 For the name Jezreel see above p. 15. For the metaphor, cf. especially 2.25a.

19 For the Targum, the prophets are addressed and they are to speak to 'your brothers'. Kimchi reports Saadya as supposing that Judah and Benjamin are addressed and that they are to speak to the (other) ten tribes; cf. Jerome in his commentary. The interpretation is instructive and may reflect the later (Jewish) appropriation and use of the prophecies of Hosea.

prophet speaks of his assurance that all the citizens of the future realm will have friendly relations with each other.

Rudolph's argument depends upon his misunderstanding of the nature of the command 'say to your brothers'. For him the evidence is provided by the juxtaposition of 1.6 and 7 where in the latter verse Judah is said by the Judaean redactor to be exempt from the judgement ('Lo-Ruḥamah') of the Northern Kingdom (v. 6). A united realm, as prophesied in 2.2, would render such a distinction otiose and hence the command is an encouragement specifically to Judaeans to welcome back the northerners to friendly relations.

Rudolph thinks that, since v. 3 presupposes the contents of 1.7, it too must be the work of the Judaean redactor; with this Jerome's understanding that the Judaeans are addressed in 2.3 is consistent.

If, however, the imperative expresses Hosea's assurance (see above) of the future reconciliation of all the elements of an ideal Israel, there is no need to pose the question which particular element is addressed in the imperative. The evidence of Jerome (and of the rabbinic commentators) is valuable testimony to the way the verse was understood in Judah when Hosea's prophecies were received there (cf. fn 19, p. 37 above).

Text and Versions

והיה (2.1) LXX καὶ ἦν (not supported by 4QXII[d]) suggesting ויהי, though for the second והיה, καὶ ἔσται. The former reading may represent an attempt to link the verse with what precedes it (so Wolff) thereby suggesting that repudiation of the covenant follows a time of numerical strength.

Pesh. inserts *w'n* 'and if' at the beginning of the verse, presumably to alleviate the sudden transition from woe to weal in MT; see the commentary above.

ראש (2.2) LXX ἀρχὴν which is translational.

הארץ 4QXII[d] הרץ without א; see Sinclair, p. 64.

לאחיכם/ולאחותיכם (2.3) LXX has the nouns in the singular (τῷ ἀδελφῷ/τῇ ἀδελφῇ), probably in order to harmonise the verse with the (singular) son and daughter of Hosea in chapter 1. Vulg. *fratribus/sorori* gives a plural noun followed by a singular, presumably not understanding אֲחוֹתֵיכֶם to be an alternative plural form of the more correct אַחְיֹתֵיכֶם (for which, see the comments of Kimchi and of GK p. 284). Aq., with plural 'sisters', seems in part to confirm MT.

CHAPTER 2.4–15

REMONSTRATION WITH AND THREATS TO ISRAEL UNDER THE FIGURE OF A WAYWARD WIFE AND MOTHER

2.4 **Remonstrate[a], remonstrate with your mother; [tell her] that[b] she is not my wife and that I am not her husband. Let her[c] give up her brazen promiscuity[d] and her adulterous embraces[d].**

[a]The verb ריב followed by the preposition ב denotes 'strive with words' and so here 'to remonstrate'. For the usage, cf. Gen 31.36. Construed with עם (e.g. Exod 17.2; Jer 2.9) the word often means 'to quarrel' (cf. the Syriac cognate 'to quarrel noisily', so, e.g., BDB *ad loc.*). Kimchi defines the usage as indicating moral correction (so the Targum).

[b]The particle כי is understood (so the Targum) as introducing a quotation, cf. Ps 148.13: 'praise the Lord', כי נשגב שמו i.e. '(with these very words) his name is exalted', cf. also Jer 30.5.

[c]ותסר A simple *waw* with jussive expressing purpose or wish, GK 165a.

[d–d]Lit. 'her promiscuity from her face and her adulteries from between her breasts'. The expressions are a blend of abstract and concrete. They are understood to denote attitude and behaviour defined by reference to the bodily parts named. It is a feature of biblical Hebrew to name particular parts of the body in the depiction, for instance, of mental attitudes, of personal action or of general or characteristic behaviour; e.g., 'hands hang slack' = to lose heart, be discouraged (רפה); 'to lift the face' = to show favour (נשא); high eyes, heavy ears = pride and insensitivity (see עין and אזן). Both זנוניה and נאפופיה are abstract plurals, cf. GK 124d and f. The face, then, associated with the abstract noun denoting promiscuous behaviour, indicates the brazen, unashamed nature of that behaviour and for this we may compare Jer 3.3 ('thou hadst a whore's forehead, thou refusest to be ashamed')[1]. Similarly the breasts indicate the intimacy of a mother's body from which adulterous couplings must be banished. The image of breasts, compressed and bruised, are similarly used by Ezekiel (23.8 etc.) to depict the sexual initiation and defloration of virgin Israel by her Egyptian lovers (cf. Kimchi on Ezekiel; Kimchi on Hosea explicitly compares Ezek 23).

[1] Gen 38.15 indicates that, veiled, Tamar was not recognised by Judah; not that, so clad, she was wearing the distinctive dress of a prostitute; cf. S. R. Driver *Genesis ad loc.*

The alternative view is to regard the abstracts as *abstracta pro concretis* and to interpret them of the ornaments with which a whore adorns herself and which, by metonymy, indicate her promiscuous behaviour. For this usage, Rosenmüller, e.g., compares Ps 93.1 'the Lord has put on strength' where עז is an *abstractum pro concreto* indicating 'weapons'. Amongst the rabbinic commentators Kimchi thinks specifically of cosmetics applied to the face and Abarbarnel of jewelry suspended from the neck between the breasts[2].

More recently, Mays and Wolff have argued for jewelry (or other identifying marks) worn in connection with the Baal cult for which they compare v. 15 of the present chapter. Such an interpretation seems to me less likely on the following grounds: Hosea in fact uses abstract nouns; that he should do so in order to denote concrete artefacts which then in turn signify reprehensible behaviour is too convoluted to be likely. There is also no evidence that jewelry attached to the face or suspended between the breasts identifies specifically whores or sacred prostitutes of the Baal cult and v. 15 constitutes no exception to this view (cf. Marti).

The abstracts, then, are best taken to denote the wife's behaviour and it is this, rather than alleged symbols of that behaviour, which she is urged to forswear.

The section 2.4–15 suggests a prophetic speech (cf. Wolff's 'kerygmatic sermon') of Hosea in which he makes use of the parable of a wayward wife and mother in order to indict the perversity of his nation (for further assessment, see pp. 114 and 118). The words are spoken by Yahweh and addressed to the children. The latter are bidden to remonstrate with their wayward and adulterous mother and the expressed intention ('let her give up') is that she forswear her waywardness and return to the marriage bond. According to the rabbinic commentators (Rashi, ibn Ezra and Kimchi) the mother indicates the present generation and the children those who are to succeed it and with this view we may compare their observations on the children of Hosea in chapter 1 (see especially on 1.6 above). Kimchi suggests a slightly variant view: the mother stands for the people of Israel as a whole, the children for its individual citizens who are urged to bring their neighbours back to rectitude (so, e.g., Marti, Mays). The urgency of Yahweh's exhortation is emphasised by the judgement that the children are urged in their father's name to put to their mother; by her adulterous behaviour she is effectively bringing to an end the marriage to which they were born. The words constitute, then, the grounds upon which the exhortation, appropriated by the children, is to be based (cf. note

[2] Qyl too thinks of jewelry and cosmetics, citing Jer 4.30; cf. Rudolph and AF.

b). They are not used absolutely (so Rosenmüller); rather they serve to indicate the implications of the mother's perversity for the unity and well-being of the family. The mother is to be reminded that what she does sets in train the destruction of the marriage to which she belongs. Since the mother is herself effectively the agent of this process and since appeal to her reason is urged in order to impede it, the statement 'she is not my wife etc.' cannot be understood as a quotation of a divorce formula[3] (*contra*, e.g., Wolff; other references below) nor even as a threat of divorce (so, as a possibility, Qyl). Indeed, the specific threats which follow (v. 5), including those of ruin and death, are quite inconsistent with divorce. The purpose of Yahweh's judgement concerning what is happening is set forth clearly in the words that follow: 'let her give up her brazen promiscuity etc.' (cf. the Targum which rightly links the two sentences). Such considerations tell against the judgement (e.g. Harper) that 'she is not my wife etc.' is a gloss or editorial explanation.

In these circumstances the scene which Hosea envisages is that of a family quarrel rather than that of a law court (*contra* Wolff, Rudolph; cf. AF). The closest parallel is Gen 31.36 where Jacob in a family quarrel remonstrates with Laban. In the parable the father seeks to utilize the support of his children in his desperate quest to preserve his marriage and his family. The only hope is for his wife to forswear her promiscuous infidelities. As applied,

[3] Review of the evidence concerning divorce formulae supports the view expressed above that this verse does not contain such a formula. The words 'she is not my wife etc.' are not attested elsewhere in the OT as a formula of divorce. According to Gordis (p. 30, n. 30a; cf. Rowley *BJRL*, p. 227) they do not feature in Talmudic treatments of adultery and divorce. He argues from B. *Gittin* 9, 3 that the essential purpose of a bill of divorce is that it renders a woman free to become the wife of another man; cf. with Rudolph, the bill of divorce from the Murabba'at Caves (second century BC) where the relative clause 'you who were formerly my wife' is found (*DJD* 2, pp. 104ff). In the Elephantine Papyri the (positive) contract of marriage is expressed three times by 'she is my wife and I am her husband' (Cowley, p. 4, no. 4; Kraeling, pp. 3f, no. 2, p. 4 no. 7). The typical (negative) divorce formula features the verb שׂנא 'to hate' (i.e. 'to divorce'), e.g. 'I hate/divorce my husband/wife' (Cowley, p. 23, no. 15; p. 27, no. 15; Kraeling, p. 9, no. 2; p. 7, no. 2). In one instance this is expanded by the addition of the words '(I hate/divorce my wife), she shall be no longer my wife' (Kraeling, pp. 21ff, no. 7). In Accadian divorce formulae (C. von Kuhl *ZAW* 52, 1934, pp. 104f; cf. C. H. Gordon in *ZAW* 54, 1936, p. 277) there occurs either 'thou art not my wife' or 'thou art not my husband' but apparently the two are never combined. Accordingly Hosea's words are not to be understood as the quotation of a divorce formula; rather they form (in the parable) part of a husband's urgent appeal to his wife, directed through his children, not to indulge in behaviour which will destroy a marriage to which, for his part, he is committed (cf. the NEB which renders the phrase 'Is she not my wife? etc.').

the parable constitutes an invitation to individual Israelites to rise in condemnation of the idolatry and corruption of the nation as a whole and to work for its return to the covenant relationship with Yahweh, who alone legitimately holds sovereignty over it. It is difficult to be more precise about the significance of the children. However, the view presented by the rabbinic commentators, *viz.* that the younger generations will have cause to enter into controversy with their seniors (unless the nation repents), is consistent with a motif detectable in chapter 1 of the prophecy and accords with the view that the purpose of the present oracle is to address an urgent warning to the nation and its leaders.

Text and Versions

ריבו LXX κρίθητε, Aq. and Symm. (2°) δικάσασθε, Vulg. *iudicate*, Pesh. *dwnw*, all suggest 'judge'; Targ. אוכחו 'rebuke' is perhaps more accurate in this context.

ריבו ... כי Targ. אוכחו ... ואמרו לה ארי expresses accurately, if freely, the syntax of MT.

ותסר LXX καὶ ἐξαρῶ ... ἐκ προσώπου μου; the first person (*sc.* Yahweh) interpretation is likely to represent a (mis)understanding of the text which avoids the difficult combination of abstract and concrete predicated of the mother in MT. In favour of MT is the consideration that the next verse constitutes a threat which, then, is preceded by an exhortation (so Wolff).

מפניה The suffix is unpointed in *BHS* (*sic* L); many MSS supply the pointing.

נאפופים/זנונים are, as ibn Ezra notes, formed by the gemination of the second radical and third radical respectively; for the first he compares הגיג (from הגה) in Ps 5.2, and for the second סַגְרִיר (from סגר) in Prov 27.15; cf. GK 55g–d.

2.5 **Lest I strip[a] her naked and exhibit her[b] as she was on the day of her birth; and make her like the desert, [c]like a dried up land[d] and let her die of thirst.**

[a]The verb פשט is used, e.g., of the violent stripping of Joseph (Gen 37.23).

[b]Ibn Ezra compares Gen 30.38 where the verb יצג is used of Jacob setting up his rods so that they should be seen by the flocks; cf. also Job 17.6.

[c]The verb ושתיה is synonymous with the preceding 'make her' (ושׂמתיה) and is not here rendered in English (cf. NEB).

[d]The parallelistic phrase defines the desert as being utterly waterless. ציה defines a totally desolate place (cf. Jer 2.6; Joel 2.20; Ezek 19.13; Ps 63.2) whereas a מדבר could allow (especially in autumn) pasturing of animals (cf. Qyl, Isa 5.17; Mic 2.12).

There follows a statement of the threat which the children and the mother are to take to heart in the event that the plea of the former falls on deaf ears. That threat is depicted in terms of the harsh realities of the punishments available to the wronged husband.

According to Ezek 16.39f (which, together with Jeremiah, may be represented as an early commentary on Hosea) the stripping and humiliation[4] of an adulteress was the prelude to her execution by stoning (cf. Jn 8.5) or by the sword[5]. Such preliminaries are attested in the Talmud (B. *Sotaḥ* 7a–8b; ET, pp. 30–38 in *Nashim* III) as well as, e.g., amongst the ancient Germans[6]. For further biblical references, see Jer 13.26f; Nah 3.4f.

In this highly sophisticated simile the details of the punishments threatened are matched in the second part of the verse by indications of their meaning for the referent *viz.* Israel in her land. In turn such indications of meaning render possible interpretations of the details of the humiliation set forth initially. Whether Yahweh (according to Hosea) compassionately avoids reference to the final fate of an adulteress (so Wolff) or whether the last phrase ('let her die of thirst') suggests it under the cipher of the nation is difficult to judge. It is clear, however, that the action of stripping is parallel to Yahweh's threat to despoil the nation in its land, i.e. to destroy the benefits of fertility and plenty which Israel had known. If unrepentant, Israel and her land will become like a waterless desert just as a divorced adulteress is reduced to nakedness.

4 *Sic* rather than the husband's formal renunciation of his duty to clothe his wife (*contra*, e.g., Wolff and Mays, citing Exod 21.10). With imminent death in prospect, such a renunciation is otiose. For evidence from Accadian texts (Emar) to the effect that before remarriage widows were stripped of their clothing to signify the end of their dependence upon their dead husbands' families, see J. Huehnergard 'New Akkadian Texts from Emar' *CBQ* 47 (1985), pp. 431–434. Huehnergard's attempt to illuminate the present verse by means of this evidence is implausible since Hosea is in no way concerned with the preliminaries to the remarriage of a widow.

5 Lev 20.10 and Deut 22.22 speak of death as the punishment for an adulteress.

6 Tacitus *Germania* xix.

The rabbinic commentators (so also Jerome) refer to Ezek 16.4ff as an indication of the significance of the 'day of her birth'. Yahweh is represented as finding the new-born Israel naked and still unclean from the blood and the mess of her after-birth. It is from such squalid and utterly wretched beginnings[7] that Yahweh graciously rescued his intended bride and lavished upon her her clothing and possessions. Accordingly for Kimchi the metaphor of the 'day of birth' depicts the origins of Israel in the abject slavery of Egypt. Hence the stripping of the mother and being exhibited as on the day of her birth conveys the notion that Yahweh will remove from unrepentant Israel all that he has given her and all that he has made her (cf. Marti).

In the second part of the verse the reference is rather to Israel in its land than to the mother of the parable, though the link between the two is indicated by the continuation of the third feminine suffix and the final phrase 'I will let her die of thirst', where the form of words seems to refer once again to the mother. For Rosenmüller, indeed, this last phrase is a decisive pointer in favour of construing the whole of the second part of the verse in terms of the woman who is to be placed *as in* the desert *as in* a dried-up land *as on* the day of her birth (where *kmdbr* stands for *kbmdbr*; *kywm* for *kbywm* and *k'rṣ* for *kb'rṣ*), to which place, when she is returned, she (and not the desert) will be left to die of thirst. The matter is, according to Rosenmüller, seen aright by Rashi who quotes Num 14.35 'in this wilderness they will come to an end and there they shall die'.

Rosenmüller's argument carries some force but it fails to do justice to the poet's conscious confusing of parable and referent. The complexity of ideas and associations is rich indeed and the words interact with each other to convey those ideas. Accordingly the verse may be analysed as follows:

(1) 'Lest I strip her naked and exhibit her as she was on the day of her birth.' The threat to strip the adulterous mother suggests, as a concomitant, the reversion of Israel to its miserable beginnings.

(2) 'And make her like the desert, like a dried-up land'. The words suggest Yahweh's threat to destroy the fertility and prosperity of the land of Israel which, by use of the third feminine suffix, is identified with the adulterous mother.

(3) 'And let her die of thirst'. The phrase reverts to a description of the mother who is threatened with a cruel death; however, its juxtaposition to the preceding phrases is suggestive

[7] The description suggests the exposure of an unwanted female child, cf. Wevers *Ezekiel ad loc.*

of drought by means of which the fertility of the land of Israel will be destroyed.

The threats are issued by Yahweh in his capacity as a wronged husband[8] and as the true author of the fertility and prosperity of the land of Israel. It was Israel's mistaken and self-indulgent (v. 10) belief that her lovers, the Baals, were the donors of the fertility of the nation on its land (cf. v. 7) and that recourse to them (i.e. in the idolatrous fertility cult) was her guarantee of such fertility. Yahweh as its real author threatens to reveal himself as such by the most devastating and conclusive of proofs. That is nothing less than the total ruin of Israel (i.e. the nation in its land) which he alone could initiate just as it was he alone who brought about the prosperity which by mistaken judgements had so mislead her.

The verse constitutes an important testimony to Hosea's use and adaptation of Canaanite motifs concerning the land's fertility and its author and to his insistence that Yahweh, so far from being merely the God of the exodus and of the desert, was the God of Israel in her settled agricultural existence on the land which was his (so Wolff, following Vriesen, p. 8).

Text and Versions

פן LXX ὅπως ἄν 'in order that' hardly fits the context. MT is followed by Aq., Symm. and Theod. with εἴ πως.

כארץ For Rosenmüller's interpretation, see the commentary above; for the more radical resort to emendation in this sense (ב for כ) see Grätz and Halévy.

ארץ ציה Vulg. *terram inviam*, cf. perhaps Targ. אשוי ארעא צדיא, 'I will make the land desolate'.

2.6 **And to her children also I will show no forbearance, for they are children of promiscuity.**

For comments on the translation of the terms used, see on 1.2, 6 above.

8 Such an interpretation is entirely natural and consistent with the parable. Insistence on a formal law court scene involves the necessary and strained exegesis that Yahweh's role changes from that of plaintiff to that of judge.

With Yahweh's initial plea to the children to remonstrate with their mother, the momentum of the speech is established and now he is represented as musing in soliloquy (so AF) on the inevitable fate of the children themselves. As has been noted, the rabbinic commentators are probably correct in interpreting the children as subsequent generations (so ibn Ezra) or as individual citizens (so Kimchi) whose fate is determined by the wickedness of Israel, the mother of the parable. The thought is thus not so different, *mutatis mutandis*, from that expressed by the proverb 'the fathers have eaten sour grapes and the children's teeth are set on edge' (Jer 31.29). The children are tainted by the waywardness of their mother; from her, if unrepentant, they will inherit the proclivity to waywardness and consequently they will share inexorably in the punishment that will be hers. Although the words are a soliloquy, they constitute a threat directed urgently and primarily to the mother whose wickedness brings misery not only to herself but also to her children. They are thus children of promiscuity because their mother is promiscuous (cf. Jerome, *filii fornicationis sunt et mali ex malis geniti*).

The words are likely to be prior to those of 1.2 and 6 since the latter are part of Hosea's retrospective account of his marriage composed in the light of events as they unfolded. Here the reference is more general in that it is not connected explicitly with the circumstances of Hosea's family (although he is likely, even at this early date, to have been conscious of the parallel circumstances, see pp. 117 below). The parable is fixed by reference to the opening phrases of the speech (v. 4) and the threat is directed to the wayward mother in respect of her children; the reference is to the nation which, while enjoying great prosperity under the reign of Jeroboam II, is by its idolatry and wickedness doomed (unless repentant) to a judgement which will afflict not only the present establishment of the nation but also the rising generations (cf. the sequence Jezreel to Lo-Ammi in chapter 1 of the prophecy).

If the threat is formally a part of that directed to the mother, the appeal is to those younger people to repent, to repudiate the idolatrous behaviour of their seniors and further to remonstrate with them in the hope that they too will repent. The sense of the present verse, then, reflects the *de facto* failure of this appeal (so, e.g., Rudolph) or else it sets forth, somewhat as does Isa 6.10, in apparently fatalistic terms the likely failure of the appeal. The latter is more likely since the phrase 'children of promiscuity'[9]

[9] Cf., with Rudolph, Num 17.25; Hos 10.9 where *bny* indicates identification with a class of persons.

implies that inevitably the sons will be disgraced (so AF) by their mother's wickedness and that consequently, unless they repent, Yahweh will eventually show no more forbearance towards them.

Recognition of the priority of the words in this verse over those of chapter 1.2, 6 in their present form suggests that the argument for regarding this verse as a gloss[10] based on them is ill-founded. In particular the point is generally made that the form of the words in this verse is inconsistent with Yahweh's appeal in what precedes them. Once, however, it is recognised that the words are not those of a law court and that an element of soliloquy supervenes over a father's appeal to preserve his family the argument loses its force.

The argument that the words of this verse are prior to those of 1.2 and 6 must include the definition 'in their present form'. If chapter 1 in its present form is a retrospective account, that is not to say that its substance is not early. Since Hosea explicitly states that the birth of the children there recounted was the beginning of Yahweh's revelation to him, it is likely that the phrases of this verse had their origins in Hosea's consciousness at the time of the birth of his daughter (so, e.g., Rudolph); and that they have found their way both into the retrospective account of that birth, and also into the present highly sophisticated speech where the reference is primarily to the relationship between Yahweh and the younger generation (the sons of the mother). If there is any element of amplification or of harmonisation then it is likely to be found in the retrospective account (i.e. chapter 1) where the link between Hosea's marriage and what it signified is explained. If this definition is correct, Harper and Wolff (e.g.) are mistaken in supposing that the present verse is a gloss made on the basis of chapter 1.2 and 6. On the other hand, Rudolph goes too far in supposing that the phrases 'wife of promiscuity' and 'children of promiscuity' in 1.2 are wholly dependent on chapter 2.6, though his insight that 2.6 is prior is substantially correct[11].

Text and Versions

No significant readings.

[10] So Harper; Marti regards 6b alone as a gloss and Wolff both 6 and 7 as 'a new rhetorical unit ... joined to the foregoing as a gloss'.

[11] There appears to be an inconsistency between this his general view of the matter and his statement (on 2.6) that '2.6 auf 1.6 zurückgreift'.

2.7 **For their mother has acted promiscuously, she who conceived them[a] has behaved shamefully[b]. For she said, I will go after[c] my lovers[d] who provide my bread and my water, my wool and my flax[e], my oil and my drink[f].**

[a] A parallelistic expression for 'mother', cf. Ct 3.4.

[b] An internal *Hiphil*, GK 53d, metaplastically formed from the root בוש, GK 72x, 78b.

[c] The phrase, here translated literally, is used elsewhere of commitment both to Yahweh (Deut 13.5; 1 Kgs 14.8) and to false gods (e.g. Deut 4.3; 6.14 *et passim*). The cohortative should be noted (cf. Marti) as conveying resolution.

[d] The root אהב originally denoted passionate desire. The *Piel* participle is used almost exclusively of adulterous affairs; whether (so Wolff) as intensive, thereby denoting their passionate character, or whether as causative, indicating that the paramours caused her to love them by their gifts (so ibn Ezra and Rosenmüller) is difficult to resolve[12].

[e] פשתי The form is found only here and in v. 11. By analogy with other names for agricultural products (חטה//חטים; שערה/שערים) and because the usual forms are פשתה/פשתים, it is suggested that the form here should be pointed as a plural: פִּשְׁתַּי, so Ehrlich, cf. W. F. Albright *BASOR* 92 (1943), p. 22 and D. N. Freedman *JBL* 74 (1955), p. 275. On the other hand, the form אִשְׁתַּי from אשה (i.e. not אִשְׁתִּי) may indicate the possibility that the Massoretes preserved an authentic dialectal form.

[f] The word שקויי (from the root שקה 'give to drink') occurs also in Prov 3.8 and Ps 102.10 (+ לחם). For Kimchi, the word denotes wine and other drinks and for ibn Ezra it corresponds to תירוש 'new wine' (in 2.11) as opposed to water. In Prov 3.8 the word is paralleled by רפאות 'healing', 'refreshment'. The word, then, may denote here tonics or potions or else (alcoholic) drinks having a tonic effect[13].

The soliloquy continues and the reason for the threatened repudiation of the sons is traced to the initial wilful promiscuity of the mother. The nation, i.e. its leaders and establishment at the time of Jeroboam II, had displayed a wanton faithlessness to Yahweh, meretriciously attributing to the Baals (the lovers) the rich prosperity of the times.

The phrase *'lkh 'ḥry* 'I will go after' is itself neutral (see note c above) but in this context conveys the mother's resolution to indulge in the promiscuity which (it is convenient for her to suppose) brings the additional benefits of luxurious comfort.

12 On the word, see D. W. Thomas *ZAW* 57 (1939), pp. 57ff.
13 Cf. McKane *Proverbs ad loc.*

These are comprehensively defined from the staple requirements of life, bread and water (cf. with ibn Ezra, 1 Kgs 18.13 and Deut 9.9, 18) to the wool and flax from which clothing is made[14] and beyond to the olive oil[15] and tonic potions[16] associated with the cultivation of beauty and health.

The supposition that the lovers are the Baals, i.e. manifestations of the god Baal associated with particular areas and their sanctuaries (cf. Wolff) rather than the foreign nations, Egypt and Assyria (so Jerome and Kimchi), fits better the times of Jeroboam II and a period not associated with foreign alliances. The attitude displayed by the mother/the nation is well illustrated by Jer 44.15ff where the women of Jerusalem argue that their cult of the queen of heaven had ensured their material welfare, and that its cessation had occasioned immediate famine and disaster (so Kimchi, in relation to his father's view, that the lovers were the astral deities).

It is clear that the image of 'going after lovers' has as its primary reference the idolatrous fertility cults of the Northern Kingdom. It is in the historical reality of the nation's concern to appropriate the lore of the land (2 Kgs 17.26), i.e. the correct understanding of the land and its agriculture (which was seen as possessing a religious dimension), that the temptation to idolatry arose. Whether that is defined in terms of the wholesale and unequivocal worship of Baal (so Wolff) or in terms of syncretistic worship of Yahweh as a Baal (so, e.g., Harper and Rudolph) is disputed. The latter view seems to me to be more likely; first, because sayings of Hosea clearly indicate that the worship of Yahweh (in name at least) continued (5.6 and 8.2); secondly, because in 2.18 Hosea explicitly appeals for Israel no longer to call Yahweh 'my Baal'; and, thirdly, because the imagery of promiscuous adultery, used by Hosea, implies that Israel was committing adultery not by forswearing her husband but by deceiving him. Her promiscuity was characterised by wanton lust and self-interest[17], by a desire to have the best of both worlds. In terms of the nation's establishment and its behaviour in matters of worship, the idolatry was not that of abandoning the worship of Yahweh for the alternative worship of Baal; it was rather the worship of Yahweh as if he were a Baal. That such worship involved both sacrificial festivities and sexual

[14] Wool (for warm clothing, Job 31.20) and flax (for cool clothing, Ezek 44.17f) are both woven by the resourceful wife, Prov 31.13 (so Wolff).

[15] Cf. Ps 104.15; Mic 6.15.

[16] See note f above and cf. Ps 104.15; for wine as a medicine, 1 Tim 5.23.

[17] NB with AF, 'my bread', etc.

promiscuity is clear from, e.g., 4.13ff. Yet for Hosea it is the lasting effect of such promiscuity upon the minds of the people (the 'sons' of the parable) that needs so urgently to be set forth. For in such worship, and by the self-indulgent fantasy that such worship brought the rewards of luxurious plenty, the moral sensibilities of the people were atrophied and dulled (cf. 4.1ff). Hence the sons are sons of promiscuity because their mother's wanton waywardness will have or has had, inexorably, that effect.

Text and Versions

שקויי LXX πάντα ὅσα μοι καθήκει, cf. Pesh. *wkl dmtb'' ly* and Targ. כל פרנוסי 'all my provisions'; Aq. ποτισμόν 'my drink', cf. Vulg. *potum meum.* The translations 'all that belongs/is necessary for me,' (LXX etc.) offer generalisations (cf. Borbone) and do not presuppose a different text (*contra* Nyberg). In Prov 3.8 LXX displays the same tendency with ἐπιμέλεια 'care', 'attention'. For emendations of MT, see, e.g., Sellin, Driver *JTS* 39 (1938), p. 155.

2.8 **Accordingly[a] I shall obstruct[b] her way[c] with thorns[d] and I will block her path[e] with a wall so that she can no longer find her old ways[f].**

[a]לכן is used frequently by the prophets to express, on Yahweh's behalf, the sentence of judgement following conviction (cf. Wolff for statistical details). Here in a soliloquy, however, the action proposed (הנני שׂך) is a direct response to the expressed attitude and intention of the mother of the parable.

[b]The root שׂוך appears to be a variant form of סוך II and to be connected with the root שׂכך II/סכך II (cf., with BDB, Arabic *skk* 'to close up', 'stop up'). The verb occurs in Job 1.10 (שׂוך) and in Job 38.8; 3.23 (סוך) and, as Rashi observes, denotes enclosure as in Isa 5.5 where the cognate noun משׂוכה is the hedge protecting a vineyard.

[c]Hebrew 'thy way'; see Text and Versions.

[d]Cf., with ibn Ezra, the tangled thorns in Nah 1.10.

[e]Lit. 'I will build up her wall'. Since the participle of the verb גדר is attested with the meaning 'wall builder' (2 Kgs 12.13; 22.6) it is likely to be a denominative from the noun גָּדֵר 'wall' (cf. GK 117r). The suffix ('her wall') has an objective sense, *viz.* a wall for her, against her. For the *schema etymologicum*, cf. GK 117p, q. An alternative view, based upon the absence of the phrase in 4QpHos[a], is to regard it as an early

explanation of the rare form שׂך (note b). For other such translations within the text of Hosea, see on 7.14ff; 8.13. On this view the phrase will have the effect '... I will obstruct thy/her way, i.e. I will block off her way' (cf. the LXX), or '... I will obstruct thy/her way, i.e. I will block-her-path with a wall' (cf. MT); see further under Text and Versions.

[f]Cf. the NEB for this translation. The paths are those which the adulteress was accustomed to walk in meeting her lovers and which Israel treads when she indulges in the idolatrous worship of the various shrines. The word indicates also conduct and behaviour as a path of life, cf. BDB p. 677, col 1 2.

The father's reflection upon the mother's self-indulgent resolution to seek her lovers prompts him to declare his intention to stop her. 'Accordingly' (note a) denotes the father's response to the situation and introduces his longing to frustrate his wife's wrong-headed and self-indulgent attitude. Thus he resolves to obstruct the paths used by the mother in her promiscuous quest. The words express a goal and the image is designed to match that of the preceding verse in which the mother's intentions and attitude are expressed. In these circumstances the verse does not express a punishment nor (as so often elsewhere) does *lkn* introduce a juridical sentence[18]. Again, it is best to understand the verse in terms of a husband's concern to preserve his marriage and family.

The details of the image are clear and portray the cultivation of a thorn hedge or the erection of a stone wall[19] for the purpose of obliterating a hitherto well-used footpath. Lam 3.7, 9; Job 19.8 (wall) and Prov 15.19; Job 3.23 (thorns) clearly indicate that these images were used of the frustration of human traffic (and therefore metaphorically of human intentions and goals) whether or not originally they had to do with the containment of wild or of wayward domestic animals (so, e.g., Marti).

Where the relation between Yahweh and Israel is concerned, again the verse is best understood in terms of the former's aim and goal, *viz.* to bring an end to Israel's resort to idolatrous worship. The question how this is to be effected is answered[20] in vv. 11ff where Yahweh, alone the controller of the fertility of the land, will bring about its infertility in order to repudiate the self-

[18] *Contra*, e.g., Marti, Wolff, Rudolph.

[19] *AUS* 2, pp. 319ff (thorns) and 59f for stone walls of a metre in height, marking the boundaries of vineyards.

[20] *Contra* Rudolph for whom, because the verse is an announcement of punishment, no answer is possible.

indulgent rationalisation of the mother of the parable (v. 7; cf. v. 10).

Text and Versions

דַּרְכֵּךְ LXX (αὐτης) suggests דַּרְכָּהּ (so *BHS*, Borbone); Pesh. *'wrḥth* and Targ. אורחתיך suggest the plural דְּרָכֶיהָ/ךְ though this may have arisen by attraction to נְתִיבוֹתֶיהָ below. Qyl defends MT on the grounds that change of personal pronoun is common in scripture. In the context of a soliloquy there may be some force to his argument (cf. Ct 1.2), though in translation it is perhaps preferable to emend to the third feminine singular suffix.

וגדרתי Targ. ואפסיק 'and I will cut them (*sc.* roads) off as one does with a wall' is translational and does not presuppose וגזרתי (*contra* Sebök); cf. LXX ἀνοικοδομήσω τὰς ὁδούς αὐτῆς, 'I will wall up her roads'; Vulg. *sepiam eam maceria* 'I will fence her with a wall', on the basis of which Grätz suggests אִתָּהּ גְּדֵרָה; 4QpHos[a] omits וגדרתי את גדרה (so Borbone); on the alternative explanation suggested above (note e) the tendency of the textual development may have been somewhat as follows:

... הנני שך את דרכך בסירים ונתיבותיה (cf. 4QpHos[a]): Stage 1
... הנני שך את דרכך בסירים (גדרתי) ונתיבותיה (cf. LXX): Stage 2
... הנני שך את דרכה ... וגדרתי את דרכה ונתיבותיה (cf. MT and LXX): Stage 3
... הנני שך את דרכך ... וגדרתי את גדרה ונתיבותיה (cf. MT): Stage 4

2.9 **Then, when she hankers after[a] her lovers, she will not be able to reach them, when she seeks[b] them she will not find them[c]. And she will conclude[d], I shall return[e] to my husband[f] for it was better for me then than now[g].**

[a]The *Piel* ורדפה is intensive implying 'to pursue ardently' or here more figuratively 'to aim to secure'; cf. BDB p. 923, col 1 and, with Rashi, Prov 12.11. The tenses (*waw* consecutive and perfects) imply endeavour (so Qyl) and the imperfects are conative (hence in translation 'she will not be able to'), cf. GK 107n.

[b]For בקש used of seeking Yahweh in the cult, see 5.6, 15; for the phrase as used here, cf. Isa 41.12.

[c]See Text and Versions.

[d]ואמרה here denotes thought rather than speech; cf. BDB p. 56, col 1 2.

[e]אלכה ואשובה cf. GK 120d; the second verb introduces the principal idea.

[f]Lit. 'to my first (i.e. original) man', cf. Deut 24.4. In English, where the language requires 'husband', the sense is best conveyed, perhaps, by this word alone.

[g]For the phrase, cf. the somewhat similar Jer 22.15f.

Again it is the father's aim that is expressed, and the verse follows closely upon what precedes it. When the mother's resort to her lovers (*sc.* Israel's resort to idolatrous worship) is precluded, as it were, by wall and hedge, then she will see sense and resolve to return to her true husband. Jerome rightly draws a comparison with the sentiments of the prodigal son (Lk 15.17f) which are similarly based upon sensible recognition of the realities of the situation, 'How many of my father's paid servants have more food than they can eat, and here am I starving to death; I will set off and go to my father, and say to him, "Father, I have sinned ..."'. He concludes. 'From this we may deduce how in God's providence calamities often befall us so that our lusts may not be gratified and, accordingly, oppressed by the various woes and miseries of this life, we are constrained to return to the service of God.'

Clines seeks to define the matter more precisely; for him genuine repentance is not expressed by these words. With that view I agree. The husband of the parable seeks to utilise what Clines characterises as 'an easy and unthinking reaction'; I would prefer to define the reaction as essentially selfish rather than 'unthinking'.

The reference in the parable to the happier past ('it was better for me then than now') is, as frequently in Hosea, to the period in the wilderness when Israel was alone with her God (cf. 11.1–3) and before she succumbed to the temptations of Canaanite belief and practice.

Marti regards 9b[21] as a later insertion which reflects the exiles' conclusion that they would do better to live in Palestine. A similar view of the significance of the words may be seen in Kimchi's observation that they were not said until long into the exile since, had they been said in Israel, there would have been no exile and therefore no need to say them. Marti's argument rests primarily on the view that the words with their allusion to repentance ruin the context and are at odds with vv. 10ff in which there is no trace of the element of repentance. Against this is the consideration that the words form part of a statement of the ultimate aims of the father of the parable, the most important

21 For Lindblom's denial of the authenticity of the words, see *PAI*, p. 58.

element of which is that the mother should come to her senses and see the advantage of returning to her family. Kimchi's view of the matter, however, may reflect the way in which the words were interpreted in later exilic times.

Text and Versions

תמצא LXX and Pesh. supply (third person plural) objects on the basis of which (e.g.) Marti (cf. Borbone) suggests תמצאם. For a defence of the text and the indications of progressive abbreviation, cf. van Gelderen (i.e. in 9a, את־מאהביה followed by אתם, then ם, then absence of suffix; so facilitating תמצא without suffix).

2.10 **For her part, she[a] does not acknowledge[b] that it was I who provided her with her grain, new wine and oil; I who multiplied for her silver [c](and gold which they consecrated to Baal/they made into a statue of Baal)[c].**

[a]The use of the third feminine singular pronoun is emphatic and suggests to ibn Ezra in the context the sense 'up till now' (i.e. the moment of repentance; see further below).

[b]Cf. with Rosenmüller Isa 1.3. Rashi paraphrases with 'paid no attention, but gave the appearance of ignorance'. For ידע, 'admit', 'confess', cf. BDB p. 394, col 1 f. The context suggests that the perfect of this stative verb should here be translated by the present tense.

[c—c]As the text stands it is perhaps easier to understand עשׂו לבעל as a short relative sentence following זהב. An alternative view (van Hoonacker) is to take עשׂו as the main verb of a single sentence in which הרביתי לה is a short relative clause, thus: 'and the silver which I multiplied for her, and the gold they have consecrated to Baal'.

The view that the words עשׂו לבעל represent a marginal gloss which has found its way into the text (so Wellhausen, Nowack, Harper, and more recently, Wolff, cf. Mays) has some force. First, the change to a third masculine plural verb in a passage which otherwise uniformly speaks of the mother/Israel in the third feminine singular gives grounds for suspicion. Secondly, elsewhere in this passage Baal is referred to or appears in the plural, not the singular (2.7, 9, 15). Thirdly, mention of the actions of Israelites in a verse which is concerned with Yahweh's actions seems unlikely.

In these circumstances the phrase is best seen as an early definition of Israel's sin made by reference to such texts as 8.4 and 13.2, where the making of idols from silver or gold is explicitly mentioned.

Marti's argument that וזהב 'gold' also forms part of the gloss is telling; for if genuine it would more likely follow the word וכסף 'silver'. On the other hand the separation of 'silver' and 'gold' may constitute a feature of a poetic oracle. Such considerations apply whether the translation 'they have made into (a statue of) Baal' (so the Targum, the rabbinic commentators and Jerome) is adopted or whether the alternative 'they have consecrated to Baal' (so Rosenmüller, cf. 2 Chr 24.7). On the other hand, if it be denied that the last phrase is an intrusive gloss, the alternative translation may be held to be preferable (cf. Rudolph).

Ibn Ezra's observation that the phrase 'she does not acknowledge' implies 'until this time' (i.e. until the moment that she came to her senses) is surely correct (see note a). His observation is designed to facilitate the transition from the thought of the previous verse. A more radical solution to the problem is that proposed by a number of scholars[22], *viz.* to suggest that this verse originally followed v. 7. Hence the present verse repudiates the sentiments expressed in v. 7, 'I will go after my lovers who provide me with my bread ...'. Yet to acknowledge that v. 10 negates specifically the argument of v. 7 does not of itself require the conclusion that the verse originally followed v. 7. If ibn Ezra's understanding of the matter is followed, then we may suppose that, following the father's recollection of the mother's promiscuous behaviour and of her intentions in so behaving, he should be prompted to express at once his ultimate concern, *viz.* to bring an end to her promiscuous actions and to lead her to acknowledge on very practical grounds her faulty reasoning (v. 8). On this view 'and she will conclude' (v. 9) matches precisely 'for she said' in v. 7[23]; it is the father's intention and goal that, as a result of his intervention, his wife should be compelled to think correctly and acknowledge the truth of the situation.

Verses 8f, then, express his reaction and his ultimate intention. Verse 10 reverts to a further description of the mother's (wilfully) mistaken thinking and allows the father to proceed to describe the measures of discipline by which he will achieve his intention and goal (vv. 11ff).

Yahweh reflects that the mother/Israel was not simply ignorant but rather, in keeping with her self-indulgent fantasies, was wilfully unprepared to acknowledge (even to herself) that it was Yahweh alone who provided (for *ntn* cf. 2.17) the blessings of fertility and plenty. She preferred to attribute such blessings to

22 E.g. Volz, Nowack, Marti, Wolff, Rudolph.
23 So, correctly, AF.

her lovers, the fertility and plenty of the land to the syncretistic cultus of the sanctuaries. It was convenient for her to forget (cf. 2.15b) the realities of the situation. It was Yahweh alone who created all things and who had given the land with its products in accordance with his promise to the patriarchs. Corn, wine and oil are the chief agricultural products of the land and are similarly listed in the Ugaritic Texts[24]. The use of the article indicates their staple character. The terms used denote these products in an unmanufactured state – relatively (*tyrwš*), if not absolutely (*dgn*, *yṣhr*); *dgn* not *ḥṭym*, *tyrwš* not *yyn*, *yṣhr* not *šmn*. *tyrwš*, though not entirely unfermented or harmless (Hos 4.11), was nevertheless a much fresher extract of the grape than *yyn* (cf. Judg 9.13; Mic 6.15; Isa 65.8[25]). In Deuteronomy (7.12f; 11.13f; 12.17 etc.; cf. Jer 31.12) these gifts of Yahweh are vouchsafed to his people in so far as they keep the covenant laws imposed upon them. Silver and gold are not products of the land but represent wealth acquired by virtue of the success of the agricultural and business endeavours of the people. Similarly, notice of wealth of this sort is recorded in the eighth century BC by Isaiah (2.7) in respect of Judah[26]. In Deuteronomy the growth of economic wealth (again both in respect of agriculture and more generally) is specified as an eventuality which must not be allowed to tempt Israel to forget Yahweh (cf. Deut 8.13ff). Such sentiments are likely to represent an accurate reflection and expansion of the words expressed here by Hosea.

Text and Versions

וזהב עשו לבעל LXX begins a new sentence αὐτὴ δὲ ἀργυρᾶ καὶ χρυσᾶ ἐποίησε τῇ Βααλ and harmonises the plural verb of MT with the (feminine) singular of the beginning of the verse; for the feminine article before Βααλ, cf. Tob 1.5 τῇ Βααλ τῇ δαμάλει; its origin is likely to derive from the reading ἡ αἰσχύνη 'shame' (cf. the frequent בֹּשֶׁת for בַּעַל of MT; so O. Eissfeldt *ZAW* 58, 1940/41, pp. 201ff). J. Huesman *Biblica* 31 (1950), p. 294 attempts to retain the consonants עשו in the

24 *ANET*, p. 148 and *CTA* 16.III (pp. 74f); *KTU* 1.16 (p. 50). The rain of Baal, 'sweet to the earth', is awaited because 'spent is the breadcorn from their jars, the wine from their skin-bottles and the oil from their jugs'. For Dagan and Tirsu as Philistine and Canaanite gods, cf. BDB p. 186 and W. F. Albright *BASOR* 139 (1955), p. 18.

25 So S. R. Driver on Deut 7.13; cf. Köhler *ZAW* 46 (1928), pp. 218ff. For a recent treatment, see S. Naeh and M. P. Weitzman *VT* 44 (1994), pp. 115–119.

26 The mention in the next verse of the increase of idolatry may suggest that possession of silver and gold occasioned the increased manufacture of representations of divinities; cf. Deut 8.19.

face of the argument that a third masculine plural verb is out of place by reading an infinitive absolute עָשׂוֹ with (here) the force עָשְׂתָה. The argument is ingenious rather than plausible. In 4QpHos[a] two or more letters preceding עשו have been erased. The last of these seems to have been ה. והב is clearly present; see *DJD* 5, p. 31, Allegro in *JBL* 78 (1959), p. 145 and further J. Strugnell *RQ* 26 (1970), pp. 163ff.

2.11 **Accordingly[a] I will take back[b] my corn when it is ripe[c] and my new wine at the vintage[d]; and I will remove[e] the wool and the flax which I gave her [f]to cover her nakedness[f].**

[a]Cf. note a on 2.8.

[b]The verb שוב has a wide range of meanings. Amongst them, in places as here, it denotes reverse action; cf. BDB p. 998, col 1 8 and Josh 2.23; 2 Kgs 13.25; Deut 30.3 etc. For a different definition, see Rudolph.

[c]Lit. 'in its season', i.e. when it is ripe; cf. Ps 1.3 'which gives its fruit in season'. Rashi comments 'at the time when the corn is ripe'; cf. also Jer 5.24; Job 5.26.

[d]Lit. 'in its appointed season', i.e. the vintage. The word מועד has the connotation of festivals, of set feasts (cf. Num 9.2f), here associated specifically with the vintage which *Succoth* (Booths) celebrated.

[e]The word והצלתי is a strong one, lit. 'to snatch away'; cf., with Rashi, Gen 31.9, 16. For the view that the word is an Aramaism, see J. Greenfield and Morag (p. 511 n.).

[f–f]Lit. 'my wool and my flax (designed) to cover her nakedness'; cf. Exod 28.42 and Ezek 16.8. For the elliptical construction, cf. Gen 24.23; 1 Sam 30.4; Mic 7.11; Eccles 3.2. For 'flax', see note e on 2.7.

Yahweh, the father of the parable, responds to the mother's (Israel's) wilful failure to acknowledge the truth by proposing (*lkn*, note a) to counter (note b) this attitude. The seasonal regularity of the staple agricultural products was seen as a particular blessing comparable to the regularity of the rain which was tied to its seasons (cf. Deut 11.14; 28.12; Lev 26.4)[27]. The thought is most clearly set forth in Jer 5.24, 'They do not think, Let us fear Yahweh our God who gives us the rains of autumn and the spring showers in their turn, who brings us unfailingly fixed seasons of harvest'. It is the reversal (note b above) of

27 The grain harvest began in April and May. The vintage took place in August to early October and culminated in the feast of *Succoth* (Booths).

precisely these benefits that Yahweh sets forth as his intention, thereby to demonstrate finally who is the giver of the land's fertility. In this connection the use of the first person pronominal suffix ('my corn' etc.) should be noted; in v. 7 Israel had used it wantonly, 'my lovers, who give me my bread' etc.; here the sober truth is asserted, the corn etc. are Yahweh's to bestow or to withhold as he pleases. The means by which this catastrophe will take place are not specified; for ibn Ezra the crops will be plundered by hostile invaders, for Kimchi a curse (presumably of drought or crop disease) is envisaged. The mention of wool and flax (cf. v. 7) and of their specific function in providing clothes to cover nakedness suggests that here the specific threat of v. 5 is renewed, 'I will strip her naked'. (See also the following verse.) There the threat comprehends not merely the punishment of the adulterous mother but also the drought which is to devastate the land. It seems, then, that Kimchi's view is the more likely to be correct. Similarly in Deut 11.17 disobedience on Israel's part leads specifically to Yahweh's withholding rain and the consequence is that the land will not yield its produce. Jerome expresses well the sense of total desolation, 'It is a greater blow when, at the time of harvest and vintage, the expected fruits and flax are removed and whatever is ripe is somehow snatched from one's hands. If, then, there is total dearth at the very season of threshing-floor, of winepress and olive press, when the earth transforms the past barrenness by new fruits, how are we to appraise the rest of the year, the time when the old fruits are stored?'

Text and Versions

לכסות Targ. דיהבית לה לכסאה, 'that I gave her to cover', cf. Pesh. *dyhbt lh* (Gelston, p. 186), is an expansion *ad sensum* and rightly links the infinitive to the preceding nouns. LXX τοῦ μὴ καλύπτειν links the infinitive with the verb and consequently adds a negative 'so as not to cover'; cf. מלכסות in 4QpHos[a] → מלכסות (Borbone, cf. Qyl). Dahood *Biblica* (1965), p. 330 makes the unlikely (cf. the following verse) suggestion that לכסות has a privative sense 'to lay bare'.

2.12 **Now is the time[a] for me to expose her lewd behaviour/vile corruption[b] in the sight of her lovers and no one will deliver her from me.**

[a]ועתה A common expression in Hosea indicating the imminence of (divine) action.

[b]נבלתה The word is a *hapax legomenon*. For the translations of the versions, see below. There are four main derivations of the word: first, it is connected with the root נבל II (BDB p. 614, col 2, cf. KB³, p. 626, col 2) and is taken to be a variant form[28] of the noun נבלה which denotes 'senseless folly', 'disgraceful deed' (especially of sexual misdeeds, cf., e.g., Gen 34.7; Judg 19.23; 2 Sam 13.12). This is Jerome's view of the matter: folly (Vulgate *stultitia*) is an alternative description of foulness (*turpitudo*) for the former is characteristic of the latter. Secondly, ibn Ezra takes a similar but not identical view for 'when nakedness is uncovered, there is senseless folly (נבלה)'. For him the use of the verb אֲגַלֶּה implies that 'nakedness' (ערוה) is uncovered and, indeed, the verb is very commonly construed with nakedness as its object (cf. BDB p. 163, col 1 1 a and especially Ezek 16.37). According to this view of the matter, נבלת, denoting disgraceful behaviour, is construed metaphorically with גָּלָה 'to strip', 'expose', and the phrase means 'I will expose her disgusting behaviour'; cf. Ezek 23.18 where 'her whoredoms' (תזנותיה) is construed with the same verb.

Thirdly, ibn Janāḥ appears to connect the word with the root נבל III 'to sink', 'drop down', 'languish', and the noun נבלה 'corpse' (BDB p. 615, col 1, KB³, pp. 626f)[29]. He does not give an Arabic translation of this verse but is content to link it in meaning with Nah 3.6 and Job 42.8. In the former case the *Piel* verb נבלתיך is parallel to 'I will cast loathsome filth over you'. Ibn Janāḥ, then, appears to invest the verb here with the meaning 'I will treat you as filthy, unclean, corrupt'. Since he believes the usage in Hosea is similar, the translation 'I will expose your corruption' (i.e. your corrupt, grossly unclean behaviour) is listed as a possibility; cf. Kimchi 'her unseemliness (כיעורה) and her evil deeds will be exposed'.

Fourthly, since the time of Michaelis (cf. the Peshiṭta below) the word has been taken to mean *pudendum muliebre*. Michaelis relies entirely on his view that this meaning fits the context whether the word is derived from 'vileness' (cf. Nah 3.6), or from נבלה which would indicate the part of the body with which the lewd folly was committed; or whether from נבל 'to wither', having the sense shrivelled *pudendum*. In conclusion he suggests *membrum pudendum sed emarcidum*, i.e. vile and shrivelled. More recently Steininger *ZAW* 24 (1904), pp. 141f, has argued that

28 For this form of the noun, ibn Ezra compares ילדות and שחרות in Eccles 11.10.

29 Ibn Barūn's criticism (see Wechter, p. 13) of ibn Janāḥ's theory that the root נבל has the basic meaning 'to swell up', 'to distend' (as a corpse) does not affect his argument that the words in Hosea and Nahum are connected with the well-attested meanings of נבל 'sink down/corpse' etc. A similar view of נבלת is taken by van Hoonacker (apparently independently of ibn Janāḥ) who argues that the context requires the meaning 'l'état d'abjection, d'épuisement'.

נבלות is a *Naf'ul* form of the root בלת, cf. Accadian *baltu* with the same meaning[30]. Such a meaning, while it can be said to fit the context in a rather gratuitously blunt way, does not have the merit of the preceding view, *viz.* that it is the grossly disgusting behaviour of the woman (rather than her privy parts) which is to be revealed to her erstwhile lovers. Nor does the theory have the merit, as does the second view, of close parallels in Ezek 23. and elsewhere. Lastly the etymological theories on which the translation is founded are contrived and far from certainly correct.

The link between this verse and that which precedes it is on the one hand narrowly forged and consists of a development of the theme of clothing and nakedness. On the other hand, the connection is one which consists in the logical development of thought. The removal of the agricultural products including the wool and flax designed for clothing suggests initially and naturally the consequential exposure of the mother's nakedness. Yet that exposure is a parable of the exposure of her faulty reasoning and moral turpitude (cf. vv. 7 and 10 above). For this reason the interpretation of *nblt* specifically in terms of *pudendum muliebre* seems to me to be unlikely, quite apart from the etymological difficulties (see above).

The withdrawal by Yahweh of his gifts serves his aim: that Israel, under the figure of the adulterous wife, should be driven to her senses and to repudiate her stupidity (cf. v. 9 above). Where the parable is concerned, the stripping of the wife is the punishment previously threatened (v. 5) by the husband and now executed in the very sight of her lovers[31]. The punishment itself is conceived as a modification of the sins which prompted it; cf., with Rudolph, *Mishnah Sotaḥ* 1.7 'she laid herself bare for transgression – the Almighty likewise laid her bare' (Danby, p. 294). The lovers who, as such, had witnessed her wanton nakedness, now see that nakedness as an exposition of her shame and corruption in the presence of her wronged husband and as the mark of the final termination of their illicit relationships. Not one of them is able to rescue her (cf. Deut 32.39), none snatches her away (note the verb is that used in the previous verse, *q.v.*) from her naked humiliation at her husband's hands. Their impotence and craven immorality is shewn in sharp focus by the event, cf. Lam 1.8 'All those who had honoured her held her cheap, for they had seen her nakedness', and Jerome 'whom clothed they desired, naked they spurned'.

[30] The theory is justly criticised by I. Willi-Plein BZAW 123 (1979), p. 122.
[31] For parallels, cf. Isa 47.3; Jer 13.26; Ezek 16.37; Nah 3.5.

Where the nation is concerned, Yahweh's withholding of the fertility of the land demonstrates the impotence of the Baals and consequently the stupidity of the mother (Israel) in having supposed that it was their cultus that effected it. Reduced to the nakedness of disaster, her folly is exposed together with the tainting corruption which it brought about.

Such is the general sense of the verse, whatever the precise etymology of the word *nblt* (note b). In the context the word denotes the moral turpitude of the mother (Israel) whether that is defined in terms of her stupidity or whether in terms of its tainting corruption.

Text and Versions

נבלתה LXX ἀκαθαρσίαν 'impurity'; Vulg. *stultitiam* 'folly'; Targ. קלנה 'shame'; Pesh. *pwrsyh* 'nakedness', '*pudenda*' (Gelston, p. 140).

2.13 **I will bring an end[a] to all her revelry[b], her annual festivals[c], her new moons[d] and sabbaths and all her festive occasions[e].**

[a]Cf. 1.4; NB the word play שבתה ... והשבתי[32].

[b]משוש 'joy', 'exultation' as of a bridegroom (Isa 62.5); the opposite of mourning (Lam 5.15).

[c]חג The word is, like those that follow, a collective singular and, since the true singular can refer to any one of them[33], it is likely to denote here the three annual pilgrimage festivals (רגלים, cf. Exod 23.14; Num 22.28, 32f; i.e. Passover, Weeks, Booths)[34]. In talmudic times, *Succoth* (Booths) was described as the festival *par excellence*, cf. 1 Kgs 8.2, 12.32 which refer to the annual autumn festival. Kimchi, referring to 1 Kgs 8.65 suggests that not every חג was a מועד but could be a spontaneous festival (in this particular case lasting fourteen days).

[d]חדש Festivals which marked the beginning of each month 'when the moon renews itself' (so ibn Ezra); cf. 1 Sam 20.4ff, 24. Sabbaths, often linked with new moons (2 Kgs 4.23; Isa 1.13; Amos 8.5 etc.) were in pre-exilic times evidently days of cultic observance (including sacrifices, cf. Isa 1.11) on which trade ceased (Amos 8.5). According to some authorities, the word in early pre-exilic times denotes specifically full-moon festivals and accordingly is linked with the new-moon festivals.

32 For the view that the verb is denominative, see R. North *Biblica* 36 (1955), pp. 182ff.

33 Cf. Exod 12.14; 23.14ff; 34.22; Deut 16.13ff.

34 So Saadya as reported by Kimchi.

From such an original form it evolved into a weekly festival, independent of the moon[35]. The emphasis on rest from ordinary labours is probably later and connected with the centralization of the cult and the circumstances of the exile.

[e]מועדה The word is a more general term which specifically denotes an appointed time or place (root יעד). Here the collective singular is used finally and comprehensively to denote all the nation's festivities. The word is used of the Sabbath (Lev 23.2f), the Passover (Lev 23.4f), New Moon (Ps 104.19), the Year of Release (Deut 31.10) and the Feasts of *Matzoth* (Lev 23.6) and of *Succoth* (Deut 31.10; Hos 12.10, EV 9). Marti's view that this last phrase is a gloss is surely erroneous, for Hos 9.5 links חג and מועד.

The words move naturally from the parable to its referent, Israel. The third feminine singular suffix (required by the parable), 'her' yearly festivals etc., provides the link. Stripped of the fertility of its land, the nation will no longer be able to observe the various festivals which celebrate it, from the great yearly festivals through to the monthly and weekly observances. (Cf. Ezek 45.17 for a similarly comprehensive list.) From the context it seems that these festivals are the trysts of the wife with her lovers (cf. vv. 14ff) and this furnishes another clear link with what precedes and follows. The festivals are 'her' festivals since they are conducted at her instigation and provide an opportunity for her to earn her bonus from her lovers. It is here that her rejoicing (*mśwśh*) is manifest, all her self-indulgent delight in her affairs. Where the state is concerned the relaxed and self-confident revelry of its citizens is depicted in times of affluence and plenty (cf. Jer 7.34; Lam 1.4; Amos 8.10). Naturally Yahweh finds all this totally abhorrent and loathsome. All the state's religious observances were tainted by idolatry, and in them he was confused with the Baals (cf. v. 18). Increasingly his character and demands were obscured and forgotten in the self-indulgent syncretism which prevailed, and the cancer spread out into the moral and political life of the nation. For similar prophetic condemnation of the pre-exilic cultus, with its distinctively merry and festive character and its implications for the moral life of Judah and Israel, cf. Isa 1.12ff; Amos 5.21ff. It is this that is to cease as a natural consequence of Yahweh's intervention; cf. for the sense Isa 24.11 'all revelry is darkened and mirth is banished from the land'.

[35] So, e.g., Harper; see further S. R. Driver in *HDB* 4 (1902), pp. 317ff; de Vaux *IAT*, pp. 371ff (*IAI*, pp. 475ff) and J. Briend *SDB* 10, pp. 1131ff.

Text and Versions

מועדה 4QpHos[a] reads מועדיה (plural), cf. LXX, Vulg. and Pesh.; the reading is adopted by Borbone. All the nouns are plural in LXX, cf. Pesh. (except for 'revelry' which is singular); for 'sabbath' (singular) a plural reading is attested (see Gelston).

2.14 **And I will destroy[a] her vines[b] and her fig-trees[b] of which she was inclined to think[c], they are a present[d] for me which my lovers have given me. I will reduce them to scrub[e] and the wild animals will devour them[f].**

[a]I.e. lay waste, cf. Lev 26.32.

[b]Collective singulars, as in the previous verse. It is possible that by synecdoche the words denote the fruit of these trees (so Rosenmüller, cf. the Targum). On the other hand, the destruction of the trees themselves may indicate the totally radical character of Yahweh's intervention which precludes the possibility of a mere one year's dearth (so Rudolph).

[c]Lit. 'of which she said'. It is, however, the attitude of mind that is set forth here, cf. on vv. 7 and 9 above. Rudolph notes that the words are put in Israel's mouth by Yahweh, here the speaker, to indicate his estimation of her thinking.

[d]The more common word for a prostitute's fee is אתנן (cf., e.g., Deut 23.19; Isa 23.18; Hos 9.1). The form of the word here אתנה, *hapax legomenon*, is almost certainly prompted by the context and achieves the resulting word-play, תאנתה/אתנה/נתנו; for ibn Janāḥ (so Kimchi) the root of both words is תנה and (with prosthetic *aleph*) the form אתנן is a variant (with ן for ה[36]). For the meaning he compares Hos 8.9ff and the verbs התנו/יתנו 'Ephraim has given her favours (to Assyria, and the nations)'. אתנה, connected in meaning, denotes a whore's wages.

Morag (p. 503) makes much the same philological observations though he goes further by linking the words with the root תנה[37] 'to repeat', 'celebrate', 'praise'. The primary meaning in the context of love and sexual relations is 'to recount the praise' (of the girl or of the act of love). Hence אתנה (properly אתנת אהבים) denotes, by metonymy, a gift or present offered as a tangible expression of appreciation of a girl or of the sexual act. From its use in the sphere of (true) love, where appreciation is expressed by a present, the same word is debased to denote the fee of a prostitute. Morag notes that תנה occurs only in texts

36 For this he compares שריה and the variant שריון from the root שרה.

37 Cf. BDB p. 1072, col 1. Morag compares Arabic *tny* 'to celebrate', 'praise' (IVth theme) and BDB's caution on the point may safely be set aside.

with a northern connection (cf. 'regular' Hebrew's use of שׁנה) and concludes that Hosea's usage is dialectal.

Ibn Janāḥ's account of the matter (as amplified by Morag) is highly satisfactory and is here accepted. BDB tentatively list two separate roots (תנה and תנן) both possibly connected with the well-known root נתן 'to give'. It is conceivable that Hosea (whether or not 'scientifically') proposes by his word-play in this verse to link the word with the root נתן[38].

Hengstenberg[39] has suggested ('form criticism' pressed to extremes) that the word derives from the language of the brothel where, to the question 'what will you give me?' the client replies 'I will give you' (אתננה), cf. Gen 38.16, 18. As Rudolph justly observes the suggestion is more ingenious than convincing.

[e]For יער 'scrub country' (so ibn Janāḥ, Arabic *š'ry*), see Macintosh *Isaiah XXI*, p. 55. The term is used to denote harsh desert areas (Isa 21.13) and places, once cultivated and now neglected, which are covered with briars and thorns (cf. Isa 7.2; 29.17; 32.15; Jer 5.6; Mic 3.12).

[f]The suffix refers to the vines and fig-trees; for the use of the masculine suffix (and the masculine המה preceding) to refer to feminine antecedents, see König, 14.

The withdrawal by Yahweh of the staple agricultural products (v. 11) brings, as a consequence, the end of the feasts and festive occasions. Yet he is to destroy also those very symbols of peace, independence and affluence, the vines and fig-trees, whose fruits enrich men's diet (Kimchi) and contribute directly to the nation's sense of festive plenty[40]. The grape and fig harvests in August and September were the prelude to the great autumnal festival, and hence the connection of thought between this verse and what precedes it. Israel, under the figure of the adulterous wife, had supposed (note c) that such gifts were a present (note d) due to her from her lovers, the Baals, for her services rather than the liberal gifts of her God given as to a wife (so Jerome). Once again the verse lays bare the muddled thinking of the mother (Israel) who, for selfish reasons and with disastrous consequences, wishes to confuse, adulterously, the worship of Yahweh and of the Baals.

The destruction of the vines and fig-trees with their fruits is designed to indicate clearly the truth of the situation and the identity of the true giver, as in v. 11 (cf. Kimchi). Again the

[38] Against this derivation is the consideration that the Massora does not indicate a *daghesh* in the ת (so Morag, p. 503 n.).

[39] Quoted in Keil.

[40] Jerome suggests that the vine stands for rejoicing, the fig for pleasantness.

mode of the destruction is not clear though in the wild animals Jerome and Kimchi see the possibility of a reference to foreign invaders. Whether by drought or by enemy action, the vineyards with their fig-trees[41] will be reduced to scrub country (note e) infested with the uninhibited growth of briars and thorns, visited only by wild animals who will consume what little is left (cf. Ps 80.14; Isa 34.13; contrast Hos 2.17 below). The free range of increased numbers of wild animals is a not infrequent aspect of God's curse upon the land, cf. Lev 26.22[42]; Deut 32.24.

Text and Versions

גפנה ותאנתה Targ. פירי גופנה ותינה, 'the fruits of her vine and fig'.

אתנה המה 4QpHos[a] has אתנם הם.

ליער LXX reads εἰς μαρτύριον 'for a witness' (which, since Jerome, has been taken to imply לעד). The reading does not fit the context[43].

חית השדה LXX adds καὶ τὰ πετεινὰ τοῦ οὐρανοῦ καὶ τὰ ἑρπετὰ τῆς γῆς 'the birds of the air and the creeping things of the ground' in harmony with v. 20 below. The reading is unlikely on the grounds that it does not fit this particular context; for arguments in favour, see Sellin.

2.15 **And so I will punish her for the days of the Baals when[a] she offered sacrifices[b] to them, and adorned herself with her ear-rings[c] and necklaces[d] and went after her lovers, quite forgetting me[e]. Oracle of Yahweh[f].**

[a]The relative is here taken to refer to the days rather than to the Baals. The latter alternative is, however, possible and (e.g.) was followed by the Vulgate (*quibus accendebat incensum*).

[b]The tense is a frequentative imperfect, i.e. she was accustomed to do it (so Rashi). The verb קטר, outside the Priestly literature, never denotes the offering of incense. In the *Piel* and *Hiphil* (lit. 'to send up in smoke'), it can, again outside P, denote the making of either animal sacrifices or meal-offerings whether or not seasoned by the addition of sweet-smelling spices. That such seasoning was practised by the priests in order to ameliorate the thick smoke of burning flesh is likely. For a full treatment, see M. Haran *VT* 10 (1960), pp. 113ff. For the sense of the word it is instructive to compare Arabic *quṭār*[un] 'aroma of cooked food', and Gen 8.21.

41 For fig-trees in vineyards (as today in Palestine/Israel), see Lk 13.6.

42 For the reverse, Lev 26.6.

43 For a defence of it, see Mauchline.

[c]נזם Ear- or nose-rings; cf. BDB and KB^3 *ad locc.* Jerome favours the former; Kimchi and Rosenmüller favour the latter.

[d]חליתה, a *hapax legomenon* (root III חלה = 'adorn', BDB), is perhaps best taken as 'necklace', so ibn Ezra; cf. Ct 7.2; Prov 25.12 (חלי). For an argument in favour of ear-rings, see *AUS* 5, p. 349; Kimchi suggests more generally 'a type of jewelry' (cf. Rudolph).

[e]Lit. 'and me (emphatically expressed by inversion) she forgot'. The translation offered here seeks to express the meaning in relation to the context.

[f]So literally; the phrase often in prophetic literature seals a prophecy as 'the very word of the Lord' (NEB).

The language of the verse is a blend of phrases from the parable and of the idolatrous practices to which the parable refers. For the first time the lovers are specifically identified as the Baals, the local manifestations of the fertility god of that name. The days of the Baals are the festivals and other occasions, the trysts of the parable, to which Yahweh has already referred (v. 13), rather than more generally the time (i.e. from the settlement) during which Israel had practised idolatry (an exilic interpretation?)[44]. On these days the people had participated in sacrificial worship (note b), decked in their jewelry and ornaments (for the wearing of ornaments in the cult, cf. Exod 3.22; 33.4). Here the parable again obtrudes and adulterous Israel, seductively adorning herself with her jewelry (cf. Jer 4.30), goes off to her lovers and in so doing forgets her husband because for the moment she dismisses such responsibilities from her mind. It is again the mental attitude of the mother/Israel that is primarily described by the phrase 'she went after her lovers' though, in respect of the nation, the phrase may well suggest resort to the sanctuaries. At all events, such considerations militate against Wolff's view that formal processions within the sanctuary are here depicted. Further, on general grounds, it is the idolatrous tendency of the ostensible worship of Yahweh that Hosea attacks rather than wholesale apostasy to Baal[45]. It is in the seductive smell of sacrificial worship (see note b), in its excitement, unrestrained glamour and immediacy that faithfulness

[44] So Rosenmüller and more recently van Hoonacker. Kimchi, too, takes this view and sees in the exile the long punishment for the pre-exilic days of idolatry. Such an interpretation (with which the Targum is not inconsistent) may well indicate the way in which the prophecy was understood from exilic times.

[45] Cf. especially Rudolph.

to Yahweh and his demands is dismissed from the minds of his people.

It is this that prompts Yahweh to act in punishment. To punish Israel, to visit the days of the Baals upon her, implies Yahweh's sorrowful but determined response, cf. 1.4 above.

Since the time of Oort, it has been argued (recently, e.g., by Rudolph)[46] that vv. 8 and 9 have been misplaced and that their original setting was here (following v. 15). The reasons include the considerations, (1) that notices of punishment (vv. 10 and 11) do not follow well the practical repentance of 9b; (2) that the 'therefore' (*lkn*) of v. 16 does not fit the previous words 'me she forgot' but does fit the practical repentance of 9b[47]. While considerations of logic may prompt such rearrangement, and while the possibility is instructive in elucidating the prophet's thought, retention of the text in the form we have it can be defended on the general grounds; first, that Hosea sets forth the urgent pleadings and reasoning of Yahweh, the wronged husband, and that such pleadings need not and would not be shaped by the dictates of strict logical progression. Further, it is a feature of the author, especially in this chapter, to confuse the parable and the referent of the parable as also, *more prophetarum*, sticks and carrots, threats and cajolements. What is reflected here is the genuinely persistent conflict – the thoughts somewhat disconnected – within the prophet himself, who again and again attempts to declare the will of a God who cannot abandon his faithless people[48]. See further on v. 16 below[49].

The historical setting of the substance of the section (2.4–15) is determined by the notice of the affluence of the nation in v. 10. This, together with the references to the extravagant celebration of feasts and festivals, points to the early years of Hosea's ministry in the last years of Jeroboam II, the period reflected also in Amos' prophecies. Freedom from foreign domination and economic prosperity lasted until Jeroboam's death in 747 BC; from that moment the situation began to decline.

46 See further J. Halévy, p. 10, Humbert BZAW 41 (1925), p. 158, Procksch.

47 It is interesting to note that ibn Ezra expressly draws attention to the close connection of thought between 9b and 16 though for him, of course, there is no question of re-ordering the text.

48 So Wolff, though on his supposition (which is not mine) that the forms of speech are derived from the law court. A more radical solution to the problem is to suggest that vv. 8f are a later gloss, see, e.g., Harper and, with variations, Marti.

49 For a vigorous defence of the structure of MT, see Clines, pp. 83ff.

Text and Versions

תקטיר Nowack's suggestion (so *BH* and Wolff) that a *Piel* form (תְּקַטֵּר) be read is unnecessary; cf. Harper and Haran (*op. cit.*) for indications that the *Hiphil* was clearly used in pre-exilic literature.

CHAPTER 2.16–25

THE OFFER OF A NEW BEGINNING

2.16 **Accordingly[a] I[b] shall woo her[c] myself[b] and lead her to the desert and comfort her[d].**

[a]For לכן cf. v. 9 above. The meaning is 'according to such conditions', and the adverb introduces, as frequently in the prophets, Yahweh's declaration of intent or reaction (so BDB, p. 486). Rosenmüller, seeking to come to terms with the sudden transition from punishment to promise, suggests that the adversive force of Arabic *lākinn*, 'however', 'yet', is to be detected here. There is no reason, however, to depart from the usual understanding of the adverb especially when the significance of the verses of promise following notices of punishment is properly evaluated, see below.

[b]הנה אנכי emphasises the subject (Yahweh) in place of the blander הנני.

[c]The participle מפתיה is that of imminent action (GK 116p). The *yodh* occurring before the third person feminine singular suffix is the third radical (Kimchi, GK 93ss). The verb is used of deceit (1 Kgs 22.20ff; Jer 20.7; Ezek 14.9) and, between the sexes, of seduction and enticement (Exod 22.15; Judg 14.15; 16.5). The usage here is striking.

[d]Lit. 'I shall speak to her heart'. Like the preceding verb, the phrase denotes especially talk between a man and a woman. The former reassures the latter with words of love, tenderness and encouragement, cf. particularly Gen 34.3 and Judg 19.3; further Gen 50.21 and Isa 40.1. The translation 'comfort' is not entirely satisfactory, but is chosen to meet the needs of the context (cf. the Targum below).

The soliloquy continues but the mood changes abruptly from punishment and coercion to coercion through love. The transition, abrupt as it is, does not break the underlying unity of thought (*contra*, e.g., Rudolph, cf. AF). Yahweh seeks, as it were, to win back his erring wife and to do so he will try everything and anything. The punishments and coercion that hitherto he has proposed should bring her at least to the common-sense conclusion of v. 9b 'I will return to my husband for it was better for me then than now'. Logically, then, as ibn Ezra noted long ago, the threats and punishments are devised solely to bring her to the point where she is amenable to reason. At this point

Yahweh, as a husband, will be able to cajole and woo her (notes c and d above) to complete repentance, to a new start to the marriage. The Targum and rabbinic commentators forcefully recognised the unity between what precedes this verse and what follows it. Israel is to be subjugated anew to the Law (Targum); 'after she has recognised that all these calamities came upon her because she forgot me ... then I will allure her' (ibn Ezra); 'a man who reasons with (*pth*) his friend makes him change his attitude, from that which he had to a new one' (Kimchi). It is in recognition that the whole soliloquy is directed to the goal of Israel's coming to her senses, to her repentance, to her changing fundamentally her attitude of mind, that its unity is apparent. Thus the opening adverb 'accordingly' (see note a above) refers to the whole punishment for the days of the Baals, the punishment that was designed to bring Israel to the position where she was amenable to reason (stated in 9b).

At this point, then, Yahweh announces his intention to complete the process that he has begun, by wooing (note c) Israel, by comforting her[1] (note d) as a man reassures a confused woman. To do so he will lead her to the desert, the solitary place of lovers (cf. Ct 8.5; 3.6; Jer 2.2). Here once again a word that is entirely appropriate to the parable suggests the way in which the parable is to be interpreted. The desert indicates the origins of the Israelite nation, the place where, following the exodus, she found her beginnings and her initial marriage with Yahweh in the days of her youth (see next verse, cf. Jer 2.2, 6)[2], still uncorrupted by the idolatry of Canaan. There in the desert, purged of the pernicious presence of her lovers, her confusion is dispersed in the warmth of her husband's love.

The desert is interpreted somewhat differently by the rabbinic commentators. For ibn Ezra, it is the land of Israel reduced by Yahweh to a desert that constitutes the site of her repentance (cf. v. 5 above). For Rashi and Kimchi it is the exile to which Yahweh will lead Israel and there she will learn that it was better for her then than now. Both interpretations are of interest and deserve attention. Both views have the merit that they see the unity of punishment and loving exhortation as well as providing a concrete definition of what is involved in a return to the desert. For Hosea, in mentioning a leading to the desert, is clearly using a highly poetic and complex metaphor. In ibn Ezra's view, the

[1] With Rudolph, the view of A. Neher *RHPhR* 34 (1954), pp. 32 n. 4, 43 that these phrases have forcible overtones is to be rejected.

[2] So the Targum 'I will do for her wonders and mighty acts as I did for her in the desert'.

devastation of the land by Yahweh (cf. v. 5) constitutes the return to the desert and the possibility of Israel's repentance, leading to a new and properly based repossession of the land (cf. vv. 17ff).

The interpretation of Rashi and Kimchi is of a sort with that of ibn Ezra but with a longer perspective of history. It is likely that reference to the 'desert of the exile' reflects the way that Hosea's prophecies were read at that time. The sermon that is thereby preached endeavours to exhort the exiles to see in their lot the harshness of the way through the desert which was, and will again be, the prelude to possession of the promised land (cf. with Kimchi especially Ezek 20.35 and, more generally, e.g. Deut 1.19; 8.15)[3].

Text and Versions

והלכתיה המדבר LXX καὶ τάξω αὐτὴν εἰς ἔρημον 'I will arrange her into/as a desert'; Ziegler (p. 121) suggests an inner LXX corruption whereby κατάξω → τάξω 'I will lead' (and εἰς → ὡς).

ודברתי על־לבה Targ. אמליל תנחומין על לבה, 'I will speak comfort to her heart'.

2.17 **And I will give her her vineyards from that moment[a], turning[b] the Valley of Achor into an Entry[c] of Hope. And she will be wholly attentive[d] there[e] as in the days of her youth, when she came up from the land of Egypt.**

[a]Lit. 'from there' (i.e. from the desert). The word implies the situation in which Israel has been led back to the desert; it is from that situation and so 'from that moment' that her vineyards can be restored by Yahweh. See further below. For שם in a temporal sense 'then', cf., with Rosenmüller, Ps 132.17; Judg 5.11; Isa 48.16. Rudolph objects to the attempt to invest משם with a temporal sense on the grounds that שמה later in the verse has a spatial meaning and that two different senses are unlikely in a single verse. I suggest, however, that the sense of משם here derives from the context, i.e. from (her situation) there → from that moment. For a similar usage, cf. 13.4.

[b]The main verb ונתתי 'to make' or 'turn' as well as 'to give' governs the accusative 'valley' and in English 'turning' is supplied *ad sensum*.

[3] For later interpretations of the same sort at Qumran, see the War Scroll I 2; E. L. Sukenik *Oṣar hammegilloth haggenuzoth* (Jerusalem, 1954), plate 16; ET, T. H. Gaster *The Dead Sea Scriptures* (New York, 1964), p. 301.

[c]For the noun פתח used to describe the way(s) into a country, cf. Mic 5.5 (EV 5.6).

[d]The question of the meaning and derivation of this word presents very considerable difficulties and, consequently, there have been a large number of attempts at its solution. Not least among the difficulties is the fact that at least four roots ענה are attested in biblical Hebrew. For the evidence of the versions, see below. Jerome, ibn Ezra and Kimchi consider that the word means 'to sing', and for this Exod 15.21 is cited. The allusion is to Israel's singing praise following her new redemption just as did Miriam for Israel after the exodus. (For a recent exposition of this view, cf. Qyl.) Rashi and ibn Barūn give the word the meaning 'to dwell', for which they compare the noun מעון 'habitation' as in Nah 2.12; Ps 90.1. The supposition is unlikely on the grounds that מעון is to be derived from the root עון[4] (cf. ibn Ezra's and Rosenmüller's criticisms). Amongst modern commentators reference is frequently made to ענה I 'to answer', 'respond' and the meaning is taken to be 'and there shall she respond/be responsive' (so, e.g., BDB, Harper, Rudolph, Wolff, AF). A more precise definition of this theory is given by L. Delekat, *VT* 14 (1964), pp. 41f, and the verb is taken to mean 'to respond to', i.e. 'accommodate herself to her husband's desires'[5]. Such a meaning is not unattractive in that it fits the context well in relation to the parable of the husband and wife. On the other hand, no clear parallel is adduced to the meaning 'to be responsive' which is alleged for the verb in this verse. In this connection Delekat (p. 41) lists a number of verses in which God calls (קרא) and there is no answer (ענה). That such words imply attention and obedience is not denied, but the standard word 'answer' fits these verses perfectly well and there is no need to posit the somewhat extended meaning 'be responsive'. In any case, for the verb with the meaning 'be responsive' predicated specifically of a woman in relation to a man there is no parallel at all. Secondly, while it is true that the evidence of two of the ancient versions (see on Aquila and Theodotion below) is consistent with this view of the matter, it is

[4] Ibn Barūn observes that Hos 2.17 contains a different root from עון; for both, however, he compares Arabic *ġny* = to dwell. For a more recent presentation of this theory, see I. Eitan *HUCA* 14 (1939), p. 1. That Israel should be depicted as dwelling contentedly in the wilderness in the permanent sense which attaches to this verb is inconsistent with the theme of return to the land.

[5] For the verb as illuminating the name of the goddess Anat and having the meaning 'to give oneself in sexual intercourse', see A. Deem *JSS* 23 (1978), pp. 25ff. For the meaning 'to perform one's marital duties' by comparison with the obscure עֹנָה in Exod 21.10, see P. Humbert *Marti Festschrift*, p. 165. These views seem to me to be based on philological arguments which are at least uncertain (cf. Rudolph's criticisms) and to furnish a sense which is gratuitously crude. In any case it is argued here and elsewhere that Hosea refers to the sexual theme by analogy and that he is at pains to show that Israel's relations with Yahweh are like those of a husband and wife, and even very like them, but are not the same.

striking that not one of the rabbinic commentators even mentions the possibility. If it be urged that out of reverence to God they could not be expected to have done so, it is equally possible to retort that they could have referred to ענה 'answer' having here the overtones of obedience[6]. Thirdly, while it is possible that the verb in this verse has a meaning different from that which (apparently) the same verb contains in vv. 23f, it is more likely that it does not. The meaning 'to answer' cannot be said to fit satisfactorily the context of vv. 23f, and an element of special pleading seems to attach to all attempts to make it do so (see below on v. 23).

For the verb ענה as it occurs in vv. 23f ibn Janāḥ gives the meaning 'to attend to', 'occupy oneself with' (*sc.* the heavens, the earth etc.), see below. On the view that the meaning of the verb here is likely to be the same or closely related to that in vv. 23f[7] (cf. 14.9, EV 8) it seems probable that its meaning here is 'and there she will be attentive'. Since no object of the verb is expressed, the sense is likely to denote the single-minded attitude of attentiveness, or pre-occupation, cf. Eccles 5.19 (*Hiphil*) 'God makes him pre-occupied, busy, attentive, with joy of heart'[8]. That this sense is elsewhere attested for ענה only in Ecclesiastes is perhaps an indication of the dialectal character of Hosea's Hebrew. For the compatible view that ענה II (so BDB, KB³ ענה III) is an Aramaic loan-word, see Delekat, p. 38, cf. Beyer, p. 662. If the usage is dialectal it is easy to see why knowledge of it was obscured and why the majority of the rabbinic commentators seek to explain the word by reference to the better known roots and words. Ibn Janāḥ is the exception and while he makes no mention of this verse in the course of his explanation of ענה in vv. 23f, it is not unreasonable to suppose that he invests the word with virtually the same meaning since, elsewhere, he makes no mention of this verse whatsoever.

[c] For שמה with the force שם, see BDB p. 1027, col 2 3 c, cf. König, 331h. The usage may derive from the point of view of the speaker, i.e. in colloquial English 'over there'.

Once Israel is returned to the desert, free from the idolatry which tainted her in the land, the process of recapitulation can begin. The vineyards which Yahweh had destroyed (v. 14) will, from this moment (see note a) be restored to her. Where the parable is concerned, the vineyards may denote a bridal gift (Rudolph) or be simply a token of the renewed love (cf. with Qyl, Ct 7.11ff). It is unlikely here that they represent Israel as does the vineyard

[6] Cf. the Targum 'they will be given there to my word'.

[7] So Morag, pp. 496f, but with a differing meaning, 'show fruitfulness' (see on v. 23).

[8] Cf. KB³ under ענה III. For the *Qal* in a similar sense, cf. Eccles 1.13; 3.10, and BDB under ענה II.

of Isa 5 (so Qyl as an alternative) for here they are restored to Israel[9]. It is equally unlikely that 'from there' (see note a) implies that the vines will grow from the soil of the desert, even in a miraculous way[10], for the presence of Israel 'in the desert' is not literal but metaphorical. On the other hand it is possible that there is an allusion in these words to the sort of agricultural operations in the Negev desert clearly attested in Nabataean and Byzantine times[11]. In any case the restoration of Israel's agricultural productivity (as typified by the vineyards) is seen by Hosea to have its starting point (again, note a) in Israel's exclusive presence with Yahweh and in her recognition that it is he alone who can effect it. If the vineyards of the land, styled the corrupt present for the harlot, have been destroyed, they will be replaced by new vineyards, a result of the sojourn in the desert, i.e. the gifts of love granted by him who alone can give them.

The reconstituted possession of the agricultural land by Israel is expressed in the words that follow. The Valley of Achor is to become the Entry of Hope (see note c) through which Israel will pass on her way from the desert to that repossession of the land. It is likely that Hosea refers here quite generally to the lower end of the Jordan valley or, perhaps, to the plain of Nebi Musa (so Kallai) whence he envisages access to central Palestine/Israel. His main concern is clearly thematic and it is the change of name, i.e. Valley of Trouble (Hebrew *'kwr*, 'trouble') to Entry of Hope[12], that is the burden of his message. According to Josh 7 the Valley of Achor featured in the traditions of Israel concerning her original possession of the land and for that reason is most likely to have been located in the area around Jericho and Ai. In the traditions concerning the partition of the land, the valley marks part of the northern boundary of the territory of Judah with Benjamin (Josh 15.7). Wolff's suggestion that it is one of the bay-type valleys north-west of Jericho (possibly the Wadi en Nuwe'ime) has the merit that it accords with the similar view of Eusebius (*Onomasticon*, pp. 186f)[13], though it meets the

[9] So also Jerome, but see Text and Versions.

[10] *Contra* Sellin; cf. Rudolph.

[11] See M. Evenari, pp. 120ff. I have myself tasted grapes from the bedouin gardens in the mountains surrounding St Catherine's monastery in Sinai.

[12] So, e.g., E. Reuss, comparing Pss 23.4 and 84.7. For the imaginative use of the name Petaḥ Tiqva in modern times to describe the earliest Jewish agricultural settlement (originally intended for the Jericho area) in Palestine *c*. 1878, see Z. Vilnay *Israel Guide ad loc.*

[13] For Noth's arguments in favour of the Buqe'a, 20 kilometres south of Jericho, Qumran and Khirbet Mird, see *ZDPV* 71 (1955), pp. 42ff, and 73 (1957),

fatal objection that it is too far to the north (so Noth, Kallai). If the final identification of the Valley of Achor remains uncertain, its significance for Hosea is clear. The repossession of the land will be marked not, as of old, by the trouble (Hebrew 'Achor') occasioned by Achan's disobedience but by joyful and confident hope. 'Where once desperation, there now hope' (Jerome).

Kimchi records his father's view that the Valley of Achor denotes here the Valley of Jezreel where Israel has recently been troubled. While such a view is unlikely to have been uppermost in Hosea's use of the expression, the interpretation is useful in indicating that, for Hosea, the image of repossession by reference to the Valley of Achor concerns repossession of the whole land and that such repossession will include the redemption of Jezreel (cf. vv. 2 and 23ff). For a similar statement of the redemption of the whole land containing a reference to Achor, cf. Isa 65.10. For Rashi and Kimchi the Valley of Achor symbolises the depths of misery and distress occasioned by the exile. Again it seems highly likely that this interpretation reflects the way in which the prophecy was interpreted from exilic times.

It is from Israel's situation 'in the desert' that repossession of the land will take place and it is from that moment that her agriculture will successfully begin anew. There in the desert, free from idolatry and isolated from her lovers, she will display single-minded attentiveness to Yahweh (see note d) as she did in the days of her youth when, redeemed from slavery in Egypt, she loved him with 'unfailing devotion' (*ḥsd*, Jer 2.2). Here, as Rudolph observes (though on a different understanding of *'nh*), the stipulations of the first commandment find their place and Israel's single-minded commitment is with all her heart, with all

pp. 4f; further, F. M. Cross and J. T. Milik *BASOR* 142 (1956), p. 17 and J. M. Allegro *The Treasure of the Copper Scroll* (London, 1960), p. 64. The evidence of the Copper Scroll points to an identification made at the time (AD 68) which may well have been artificial; cf. the identification of Gerizim and Ebal with mountains behind Jericho, see Allegro, *op. cit.*, pp. 75f. For Wolff's view, see *ZDPV* 70 (1954), pp. 76ff and for his telling arguments (so Rudolph) against Noth's identification, see his commentary *ad loc.* Of these the following may be singled out: first, it is difficult to envisage the territory of Benjamin extending as far south as the Buqe'a, cf. K-D. Schunck BZAW 86 (1963), pp. 39ff, 144ff, 161 and Kallai, p. 120. Secondly, Josh 7.24ff does not imply as great a distance from Jericho for the execution of Achan (and it may be suggested further that that execution is likely to have taken place, for propitiatory purposes, on the route of the abortive expedition which brought it about). If Cross and Milik's argument is correct that the three ruins in the Buqe'a are to be identified with Middin etc. then it is surprising that they are not mentioned in connection with Achor in Josh 15.7. For a detailed review of the evidence, see Simons, § 463, p. 271 and Kallai, pp. 119f.

her soul and with all her strength. If this is an accurate assessment of Hosea's use of *'nh*, he may be said to describe specifically the relationship of Israel to Yahweh and, where the parable which reflects it is concerned, the renewed commitment of a wife to her husband in a marriage that has been repaired. It seems to me that Hosea, by his use of these words, does not, even at the level of the parable, depict a crudely sexual aspect of the relationship. Yet the larger nuances of the word *'nh* (made possible by the various and distinguishable homonyms[14]) may in this context enable Hosea, as it were, to redeem Israel's relationship with Yahweh from the crudity of the sexual presentation of it in Baalism. If in vv. 23ff the relationship of Yahweh with the heavens, and the heavens with the earth, is to reflect the single-mindedness and orderly preoccupation of the one with the other (so *'nh* in these verses, see below), that correct definition is made against the corrupt and idolatrous view that the relationship was a crudely sexual one. It is possible that a similar redemption of the word *yd'* 'to know' from a crudely sexual meaning is represented by Hosea's use of it to depict Israel's knowledge of Yahweh in v. 22 below (*q.v.*).

The image of Israel as an attentive and loving bride is but one (even if the most important) which Hosea uses. In 11.1, 3 Israel is Yahweh's son whom he summoned from Egypt and on whom he lavished his parental care. What is common to both images is the relationship of love, trust and obedience which they seek to portray.

Rudolph suggests that 17b originally stood before 17a. While the suggestion is attractive in the sense that Israel's renewed obedience is thereby clearly seen as a pre-condition of Yahweh's renewal of his gifts of fertility, it is hardly necessary to go so far as to propose textual rearrangement. The unity of the verse and of the thought contained in it is sufficiently clear; the gifts of Yahweh and the renewal of Israel's obedience are seen by Hosea as two aspects of the situation arising from her presence 'in the desert'.

Text and Versions

כרמיה LXX τὰ κτήματα αὐτῆς 'her possessions'; the agricultural emphasis of MT is here adapted to the needs of the urban congregations

[14] If Hosea is making an allusion to such a sexual sense (only to oppose it) it is difficult to determine which of the homonyms he has in mind, for there are a number of possibilities (for some of them, see p. 72 above); but there are no certainties.

of the diaspora (so Wolff); Vulg. *vinitores* 'vinedressers' (? reading כֹּרְמֶיהָ) in accordance with Jerome's view that Israel is the vine); Targ. פרנסהא 'her leaders' – as in the previous verse God speaks comfort to Israel by his servants the prophets.

משם A number of emendations are proposed on the view that the word is here awkward. See, e.g., Marti, G. R. Driver *JTS* 39 (1938), p. 155 and Humbert in *Marti Festschift*, p. 165. Further suggestions are listed in Rudolph *ad loc.*

לפתח תקוה LXX διανοῖξαι σύνεσιν αὐτῆς → לִפְתֹּחַ תְּבוּנָהּ (Oettli); cf. Pesh.'s *dtpth swklh* 'that her understanding may be opened' and Vulg. *ad aperiendam spem.* All are likely to be interpretative translations rather than translations presupposing a different Hebrew text. See further, Gelston, p. 162.

וענתה LXX καὶ ταπεινωθήσεται, cf. Symm. κακωθήσεται and Pesh. *wttmkk* = ענה III in BDB; Aq. καὶ ὑπακούσει = ענה I or ענה II as explained above; Theod. ἀποκριθήσεται = ענה I; Vulg. *et canet* = ענה IV.

2.18 **And so[a] on that day, Oracle of Yahweh, you will call out 'My husband'[b] and no longer will you call me 'My Baal'[b].**

[a]Lit. 'and it will come to pass'; the verb is followed by *waw* consecutive with the perfect (cf. Amos 8.9; Mic 5.9; Isa 22.20; Hos 1.5) or, as here, by a simple imperfect. Wolff notes that the former usage is more typical of the older literature (cf. 2.23, Isa 7.18, Jer 4.9) and therefore the usage here is not (*contra* Robinson), of itself, evidence indicating a later redactor.

[b]Hebrew phonetically *Ishi/Baali* respectively.

'And so on that day' is a common expression in prophecy and is generally, but not exclusively, used to introduce a promise of good things to come. In Hosea there are three occurrences (1.5, here and 2.23, cf. 2.20); in the first it introduces a threat and here, and in the verses that follow, promises. Since the phrase does not occur elsewhere in the book it is likely that the three pericopes (beginning with vv. 18, 20, 23) are additions to the kerygmatic piece which precedes[15]. With this supposition the contents of the verses seem to agree, for in each case nothing fundamentally new is said but rather there is amplification and

[15] The use of the second feminine singular of this verse does not match the third feminine singular of the following; this may indicate composition of originally independent short oracles or fragments (cf. Wolff *ad loc.*), or else it accords with the rapid and emotionally charged change of subject for which Ct 1.2 may be cited; see further under Text and Versions.

illumination of motifs which have appeared in the preceding material. (For discussion of vv. 20ff and 23ff see below; also p. lxvi for conclusions in regard to the composition of the book.)

In the case of vv. 18 and 19, the verses follow naturally enough the image of Yahweh and Israel in the desert under the parable of man and wife in a renewed marriage. Free from the pernicious influences of her lovers and now wholly attentive to Yahweh, Israel's restored understanding of the truth of the situation is reflected in her mode of address for her husband[16]. Already Yahweh has been described as Israel's *Ish*, husband, both in the remonstration of v. 4, and in the pragmatic wish to return to her husband (v. 9). It seems unlikely that in everyday speech there was any practical distinction between the two synonyms for husband, *Ish* and *Baal* (cf. especially 2 Sam 11.26 and Joel 1.8). Where Hosea is concerned, in that he can speak of Yahweh as Israel's true *Ish*/husband (lit. 'original husband' in v. 9), there is the implication that Israel was inclined to call her lovers by the same name. Jerome, too, records that in his day *Baali* (my husband) was in common usage both amongst the Jews[17] and the Syrians. It is likely, then, that attempts[18] to draw a distinction between the two names on the basis of everyday usage are mistaken. It is, as Rudolph rightly observes, the relationship between Yahweh and Israel that is defined by the distinction made in this verse between the two synonyms. Yahweh, Israel's God, is not now ever again to be confused with the Canaanite fertility god called by the title Baal. The point of reference in the words is to the Israelites' mistaken understanding (v. 10 above) and the words represent Hosea's urgent attempt to inculcate in his countrymen a proper understanding on which the moral life of the nation may be rebuilt. It is supremely here in this verse that the source of Israel's sinfulness is defined and indicated by Hosea; it is faulty reasoning based upon self-indulgent fantasies that lie behind the decline and fall of the nation.

16 Wolff (so Rudolph) sees the verse as a verbal expression of Israel's response (i.e. ענה I = 'to answer', in the previous verse). The theory is not unattractive and may indicate, again, the wealth of nuances rendered possible by Hosea's use of the root(s) ענה. It does not, however, constitute evidence that the ענה in the previous verse is exclusively or primarily used to denote 'response'.

17 As indeed in spoken Hebrew continuously, to Israel of the present day.

18 E.g. Rashi, *'yš* is appropriate to long-lasting marriage; *b'l* to mastery and fear. He quotes the rabbinic adage 'like a bride in her father-in-law's house as opposed to a bride in her father's house'. Wolff suggests that *b'l* denotes the legal owner of a wife, while *'yš* denotes a loving partner. Knight believes that *'yš* is used in monogamy; *b'l* in polygamy. Such suggestions are speculative.

If, then, Israel had deluded herself by calling Yahweh Baal, by treating him as if he were the Canaanite fertility god of that name, it is likely that the titles *Ishi* and *Baali* are used here to define Hosea's attempt to correct that delusion. Now it is axiomatic that throughout these early chapters Hosea portrays the love of Yahweh for Israel in terms of the love of a husband for his wife. To have done so was to sail close to the wind. For a central theme of the Canaanite religion was that the sexual principle was reflected in nature and personified in the licentious fertility god Baal. In this situation Hosea seeks to redeem the notion of love between man and woman from the murky confusion into which Baalism had dragged it and to exalt it to a representation of the faithful love of the just and true God for the people that he had chosen of old. In so doing he was able to use and refine some of the concepts that were known to Baalism (see, e.g., on 'wholly attentive', v. 17 and 'to know', v. 22), to redeem them and so to define them as representations of the truth. Or, conversely, his task was to show that Yahweh, the God of the exodus and of the desert, was also the God of creation who controlled the land's fertility. If Hosea was able to use some of the concepts of Baalism, he was emphatically concerned to repudiate others. Above all it is the grossly and licentiously sexual element that he repudiates. That element was personified in Baal, but it is likely that it was also associated with the cognate verb *b'l* (see especially, with KB³, Prov 30.23[19] and Isa 62.4f). Indeed such is the conservatism of language that some three centuries later the author of Isa 62.4f can refer to Jerusalem and the land as *Be'ulah*, i.e. consummated (and so repopulated) and compare, using the same verb, Yahweh's re-possession of his inheritance with the proper consummation of a marriage between a young man and a virgin[20]. The use of such language may indicate that, by Trito-Isaiah's time, the malignant aspects of the word had been successfully purged, rather as terms (such as *ashteroth* = increase of flocks) pertaining originally to the Canaanite fertility cult were later used by the orthodox Deuteronomists[21]. At all events the problem that Hosea faced was immediate and pressing. His response was to repudiate what in the Canaanite religion was totally incompatible with Yahweh while subtly refining and adapting what was compatible. For him

[19] Cf. Metsudat Zion's comments upon this verse.

[20] Cf. especially Kimchi's comments on Isa 62.5.

[21] Deut 7.13 etc. As is well known, modern Arabic to this day uses the expressions *b'l* and *'ṯrt* to denote land watered by heaven.

the name Baal and what it implied fell clearly and unequivocally into the former category.

The confusion between Yahweh and Baal prevalent in early Israel can be illustrated from personal names. In 1 Chr 12.16 the name Bealiah, compounded with Yahweh and Baal, is suggestive of an explicit identification (even if the meaning intended is 'Yahweh is Lord', cf. Noth *Pers.*, p. 121). Further individuals whose allegiance to Yahweh was paramount also name their children with names compounded with Baal, e.g., in Saul's family, Ishbaal, and Meribaal; in David's, Beeliada (changed to Eliada in 2 Sam 5.16)[22]. In the Samaria Ostraca of the eighth century BC (thus more or less contemporary with Hosea) eleven names are compounded with Yahweh, eight with Baal[23]. To this we may add the evidence of the Elephantine Papyri of the fifth century BC where Yahweh is worshipped syncretistically with a female consort Anathyahu or Anathbethel, names compounded with the title of the consort of Baal in the Ugaritic Texts[24].

Text and Versions

תקראי (both occurrences) LXX καλέσει με, so Aq. (Jerome), Vulg. and Pesh. 'she will call me → תקרא לי (Borbone and NEB) yet the reading may have arisen in accordance with a harmonising tendency. MT's *difficilior lectio* is *potior*. Theod. and Symm. καλέσεις, at least in the second occurrence.

בעלי LXX βααλιμ; Symm. and Theod. βααλειμ; the plural represents an attempt to harmonise the verse with the following. Aq. translates the name, ἔχων με 'owning me'; cf. Jerome's commentary.

2.19 **And I will remove the names of the Baals from her mouth and they will not be invoked[a] any more by their names.**

[a]Cf. Joseph Blau *VT* 11 (1961), p. 85. The verb זכר, usually translated 'remember', has here a cultic, religious significance, cf. Exod 23.13; Jer 3.16; Ps 20.8.

22 For the Chronicler's avoidance of the scribal tradition by which Baal names were concealed, see Rudolph's commentary (on Chronicles), 1 Chr 8.33f; 9.39f; 14.7 and, as an exception, 1 Chr 3.8.

23 A. Lemaire *Inscriptions hébraiques*, Paris, 1977, p. 55.

24 For the Elephantine Papyri, see Cowley, no. 22 line 125 and no. 44 line 3.

'Once a sinner repents, God helps him and restores him with all his heart'; so aptly ibn Ezra on this verse. Once Israel has taken the initial step, i.e. of repudiating her wrong-headed notion that Yahweh and Baal were interchangeable gods, the resulting deductions from that initial premise are swift to follow and appear as an initiative of Yahweh himself. Totally dedicated to Yahweh, Israel will no longer, as if by inertia, have recourse to the Baals, the local manifestations of the god of that name. She will not invoke them by name in the feasts and ceremonies of the local shrines with the aim of coercing the forces of nature to fulfil her needs. No longer will Israel be associated with the Baals, nor the Baals with Israel and, atrophied by their neglect, they will fade into oblivion (cf. Isa 2.18 – so Rashi, and Zech 13.2).

Text and Versions

בשמם LXX τὰ ὀνόματα αὐτῶν, making the names plural as in the first part of the verse; a harmonising tendency (Wolff).

2.20 **And I will make a covenant for them[a] on that day with the wild animals, with the birds and with the reptiles. Bow, sword and weapons of war[b] will I break and I will banish them[c] from the land[d], and I will make them[e] lie down in safety.**

[a]להם 'for their (*sc.* the Israelites') benefit', cf. BDB p. 515, col 1 (b) α.

[b]So Kimchi; see on 1.7.

[c]Supplied *ad sensum*; lit. 'I will break ... from the land', i.e. a pregnant construction.

[d]I.e. the land of Israel; see Wolff's analysis of the use of the word by Hosea.

[e]Presumably the Israelites (so, e.g., Rudolph) rather than the animals (so e.g. NEB) since the latter, without Yahweh's covenant, constitute a threat to the former.

The verse marks the beginning of the second 'on that day' pericope. Its contents represent the recapitulation of v. 14 where Israel's vines are to be destroyed by the wild animals. The restoration by Yahweh of the land's fertility, promised her 'in the desert', will not be impeded by any subsequent imbalance of nature. For a similar promise associated with the covenant, see

Lev 26.6. Not only the wild animals but also the birds (including grasshoppers, so Kimchi) and the reptiles (e.g. snakes and scorpions, Kimchi) will be so ordered that no harm shall befall the Israelites or the crops on which their well-being depends[25]. For a notice of an abnormal plague of lions, see 2 Kgs 17.25. For similar prophecies, see Isa 11.6ff; 35.9; 65.25 and Ezek 34.25, 28.

The mode of this ordering of nature is described as a covenant instituted by Yahweh which effects an agreement between Israel and the world of nature, and is thus distinguishable from a covenant made directly by Yahweh with his people (cf. Nicholson *GP*, pp. 92, 116). Here as in Gen 3.15 the disposition is imposed by Yahweh upon two parties who are dependent on him and for the benefit specifically of the more important of them (see note a above)[26].

If the balance of nature is ordered for Israel's benefit, then the other scourge with which she was threatened, *viz.* invasion by hostile neighbours, is also to be removed by the God who alone can control them. Again the promise matches the specific threat of a previous verse (1.5) where the military might of Israel is to be smashed. In this particular context, as in Amos 5.11 and Zeph 1.13, the horror of invasions is seen specifically in terms of the resulting plunder and damage to crops and property. Yahweh will smash the weapons of such invaders and rid the land of their menace (cf. Isa 2.4; 9.3f; Mic 5.4f; Zech 9.10), allowing its inhabitants a life of peace and well-being. The latter sentiment is expressed in the phrase 'and I will make them lie down in safety', cf. Lev 26.6 'you shall lie down to sleep with no one to terrify you'. That some elements of this picture belong to traditional aspirations expressed in the cult is likely in view of the following parallels; first, nature: see the parallel prophetic texts listed above; secondly, the destruction of weapons of war: Pss 46.10; 76.4; thirdly, personal safety and freedom to sleep in peace: Ps 4.9. The texts which combine these elements are Lev 26.6 and Ezek 34.25 and it is possible that they are composed on the basis of this verse of Hosea (so Wolff).

25 For observations on this verse in relation to 4.3 and the motifs of creation and the reverse of creation, see Deroche.

26 See Wolff *VT* 6 (1956), pp. 316ff; for a parallel from the Mari Texts, see his commentary and M. Noth *Gesammelte Studien zum AT*, 2nd edn. (Munich, 1960), pp. 142–154; ET *The Laws in the Pentateuch and Other Essays* (Edinburgh/London, 1966) pp. 108–117.

Text and Versions

אשבור Targ. אבטיל 'abolish', cf. Pesh. *'bṭl* = אשבית according to Sebök. It is more likely that the renderings seek to lessen the difficulty of the pregnant construction in MT; cf. further Gelston, p. 184.

והשכבתים LXX κατοικιῶ σε, cf. Symm. κατοικίσω αὐτούς and Theod. κατοικιῶ αὐτούς → הוֹשַׁבְתִּים (Oettli); Aq. κοιμήσω αὐτούς is very literal; the preceding renderings are somewhat free.

2.21 and 22 (21) **And I will betroth you[a] for ever; I will betroth you to myself with [gifts of][b] equity and justice, of kindness and compassion.** (22) **I will betroth you with [the gift of][b] steadfastness and you will know Yahweh.**

[a] Second feminine singular suffix.

[b] *Beth pretii* of the price paid for a bride, cf. BDB and KB³ on ארש. For an alternative view, see below.

The suffixes change from reference to the Israelites under the third person plural to reference to Israel under the second feminine singular. Thus the parable of husband and wife again obtrudes and the covenant relationship between Yahweh and his people, to which the previous verse alludes, is now defined in terms of a betrothal. The verb denotes the legal act by which the various parties (bridegroom, bride, bride's father) contract and settle a forthcoming marriage. The verb *lqḥ* (Deut 20.7; cf. Hos 1.2) denotes the beginning of the marriage itself, involving the bride leaving her father's house as well as the consummation of the marriage. The binding, legal act of settlement is marked by the payment of the bride-price (*mohar*) to the bride's father (Exod 22.15f; 1 Sam 18.25; 2 Sam 3.14[27]). Such a payment constitutes a guarantee of the good faith of the bridegroom in his proposal of lasting marriage ('for ever' *l'wlm*[28]).

It is against this background that the verses are to be understood. Yahweh's thrice repeated declaration that he will betroth Israel emphasises its solemn and legal character. His gifts, i.e. the bride-price that he pays (see note b), are equity and justice, kindness and compassion and reliable steadfastness. Such gifts

27 Further, Deut 22.23ff; Gen 34.12, Millar Burrows *The Basis of Israelite Marriage*; E. Kutsch BZAW 87 (1963), pp. 29f.

28 On עולם as a legal term denoting life-long commitment, cf. Exod 21.6 and E. Jenni *ZAW* 65 (1953), p. 13.

indicate the quality of the marriage that he offers and they are concomitants to it. Where the nation is concerned, the parable indicates that, once Israel's relationship with Yahweh is re-established, then the life of the nation will be characterised by these qualities rather than by those deriving from idolatrous syncretism, i.e. the selfish nihilism and bloodthirsty anarchy described in 4.1ff. Such an understanding is consistent with a doctrine of grace and with the fundamental belief of Hosea that Israel's correct relationship with her God is the precondition of the restoration of justice and peace to the nation's life. That relationship is restored by God's gracious initiative (so especially v. 16); he is the guarantor of righteousness (cf. Jer 23.6).

An alternative view is that the betrothal will be effected by means of (*beth instrumenti*) equity etc. (so, e.g., Rosenmüller, comparing Isa 1.27[29]). Thus, e.g., Kimchi states that only future redemption (under the figure of betrothal) will be 'for ever' because in the past Israel's redemptions have been marred by her failures to observe justice, equity etc. The interpretation seems to me to be more in accord with later Jewish understanding than with the fundamental emphasis of Hosea.

For 'equity' (*ṣdq*)[30], the proper concern for individuals in society, see Hos 10.12; Amos 5.7, 24; 6.12; Ps 98.2; for justice (*mšpṭ*)[31], the ordering of society through proper legal decisions, see Hos 5.11; 6.5; 10.4; Amos 5.7, 24; 6.12. Kindness (*ḥsd*)[32], thoughtful and generous concern, is illustrated by Hos 4.1; 6.4, 6; 10.12; 12.7, EV 6; Jer 2.2; Josh 2.12 etc. On compassion, pity (*rḥmym*) see the commentary on 1.6. Steadfastness (*'mwnh*)[33] denotes the qualities of reliability and integrity which reflect the very personality of Yahweh. In all, the qualities or gifts of Yahweh here listed constitute the fabric of the restored nation which will reflect the God who created it and who, now, will not again need to chastise it.

When Israel receives Yahweh as her bridegroom together with the gifts that he brings, she will know him. The phrase here expresses the opposite of 'she forgot me' (v. 15) and 'she did not know' (v. 10) and implies Israel's single-minded recognition (cf. again *'nh* in v. 17 above) of Yahweh's claims as her true husband. Again it is likely that Hosea sails close to the wind by

[29] Cf. Qyl who mentions the possibility that the phrases are stipulations or conditions set out in a marriage contract.

[30] K. H. Fahlgren *Sᵉdaka* (Uppsala, 1932), p. 78, K. Koch *ZThK* 52 (1955), p. 2.

[31] L. Köhler *Mensch*, pp. 143ff; ET *Man*, pp. 149ff.

[32] H. J. Stoebe *VT* 2 (1952), pp. 244ff.

[33] A. Weiser *TDNT* 6, p. 185.

the use of this term for, where the parable of marriage is concerned, the word is likely to have had the nuance of sexual knowledge[34] and thus of the consummation of the marriage. Again, however, Hosea seeks to show that the relationship between Yahweh and Israel is like that between a husband and wife, and even very like it, but it is not identical. What emphatically it is not like is the licentious couplings of the idolatrous fertility cult. Its characteristics are rather those of the gifts – kindness, faithfulness and compassion. As in v. 17 and his use of the verb 'be attentive' and as in vv. 23ff and his description of the rain, Hosea here seeks to redeem the true significance of sexual love from the mire of Canaanite depravity and to exalt it to a representation of God's love for his people. If, then, a sexual element remains, it belongs, by Hosea's careful definition, to the mysterious privacy[35] of faithfulness and kindness, since that is its true place.

It is significant that in a speech by Yahweh, Israel is to 'know Yahweh' (i.e. rather than 'me'). Thus it is the name and nature of her God that Israel will perceive, will take to heart, will attend to with single-minded devotion. Such knowledge of Yahweh corresponds to Israel's corrected understanding whereby no longer is she inclined to the perversity of calling Yahweh 'my Baal' (v. 18); indeed knowledge of Yahweh is consistent alone with the repudiation of Baal.

In all this there can be no doubt of the miraculous and lyrical nature of what is portrayed. The earlier elements of the parable, in which the promiscuous wife is threatened and later wooed, seem to recede into the background and the new start is emphasised and set forth in terms of a marriage *de novo* (cf. perhaps Isa 62.5). For the rest, as Wolff observes, where the verses proclaim a renewed covenant recognition of his people by Yahweh (cf. Nicholson *GP*, p. 63) there are the makings of Jeremiah's developed doctrine of the new covenant in which, again, knowledge of Yahweh finds a central place (Jer 31.31ff).

Text and Versions

את־יהוה 45 MSS read כִּי אֲנִי י״, cf. Vulg. *quia ego Dominus* '... that I am Yahweh', perhaps under the influence of Ezekiel (so Wolff *EvTh* 15, 1955, pp. 428ff) and II Isaiah.

[34] Instances of the verb predicated of women, Gen 19.8; Num 31.17; Judg 11.39; 21.12.

[35] According to the parable, 'in the desert'.

2.23 and 24 **And so[a] on that day, Oracle of Yahweh, I will attend to[b] the heavens, and they will attend to the land.** (24) **Then the land will attend to the corn and new wine and oil, and they will attend to[b] Jezreel.**

[a]Lit. 'and it will come to pass'. See on v. 18 above.

[b]The verb is repeated in the MT for emphasis and the two occurrences in v. 23 are separated by 'Oracle of Yahweh', cf. Pss 29.1; 93.3 and see Text and Versions below. The translation offered above represents the view taken of the meaning of the verb ענה here by ibn Janāḥ. In essence his theory is that the verb is to be identified with ענה II (see on v. 17). Specifically Hosea's use of ענה in this passage is to be compared with the phrase in Eccles 10.19 והכסף יענה את הכל, which means 'money attends to everything (in procuring it)', (cf. the colloquial American phrase 'money takes care of everything')[36]. He believes that the usage is similar to that of the cognate Arabic verb *'ny* which denotes 'intention', 'purpose', 'business', 'concern' (Arabic *'lqṣd*[37]) and so 'to concern oneself with', 'to busy oneself with ...'. According to ibn Janāḥ a secondary meaning of the same verb in Arabic, when predicated of the earth, is 'to bring forth vegetation', 'to sprout' (Arabic *nbt*) and this meaning is to be detected in the one phrase of Hosea, *viz.* 'the land will attend to [i.e. bring forth] the corn, wine and oil'. This secondary meaning, he says, is derived from the first or primary meaning, *viz.*, *'lqṣd* 'intention', 'concern', 'business', so that when the earth is busy it is preoccupied and concerned with bringing forth vegetation. This theory has the advantage over others in that it gives a coherent and consistent account of the verb in this particular context. First, from the philological point of view, the particular root is established in biblical Hebrew and the Arabic cognate mentioned by ibn Janāḥ has long been identified as illuminating the Hebrew verb and derivative nouns, particularly as they occur in Ecclesiastes. If Delekat (p. 38) is right in supposing that the word is an Aramaic loan-word, its use by Hosea points to the northern dialectal features of his language. Secondly, the theory has the merit that it is able to give to the verb, predicated of the earth in this passage, a particular meaning which, consistent and connected with its primary meaning, fits the context with precision (*sc.* 'to sprout', 'to bring forth

36 So ibn Ezra whose brief comments seem to match the fuller statement of ibn Janāḥ.

37 For *qṣd* Lane gives 'he directed himself' or 'his cause' or 'aim to', 'he made him [or it] his object', 'he sought', 'endeavoured after', 'pursued'.

vegetation')[38]. Thirdly, while he does not explicitly mention v. 17 in the course of his treatment of the subject, ibn Janāḥ's theory has the merit that it fits this verse also. It is surely very unlikely that Hosea would use separate or distinct roots within the space of a few verses and in a passage where subject matter is relatively homogeneous. Fourthly, alternative theories all seem to suffer from the defect that an element of the contrived attends their attempts to make another root ענה fit every occurrence. Thus, the majority view that ענה I 'to answer' lies behind Hosea's usage prompts Kimchi (so more recently Qyl and Rudolph) to suggest that God answers, as it were, a request from the heavens to be permitted to rain; that the earth, personified, asks the heavens for rain and that they answer etc. Wolff prefers to shift the argument to the field of form criticism and to urge that 'to answer' is appropriate to what he believes is here an oracle of favourable response (*Erhörungswort*). The NEB translates the verb 'to answer for' which, I submit, seeks the meaning advocated by ibn Janāḥ, but by reference to ענה I.

The third 'on that day' pericope sets forth in uncompromising terms Yahweh's total control over the forces of nature. In this particular context that control is seen as the positive recapitulation of his earlier threat to disrupt those forces (vv. 11ff). Yahweh's single-minded attentiveness (note b above) towards the forces of nature matches precisely Israel's newly-found attentiveness to him 'in the desert' (v. 17 above). If Yahweh the creator concerns himself with nature, the interdependence of its component parts will flourish and with speed and regularity the land will produce the staple agricultural crops desired by his people. As ibn Ezra observes, the sense of the passage is the exact opposite of Lev 26.19 where, incensed at

[38] A. Guillaume *JTS* NS 5 (1964), pp. 57ff and S. Morag, who do not appear to know ibn Janāḥ's contribution, have detected this particular meaning in all the occurrences of ענה of this particular passage. Ibn Janāḥ's theory is, however, far superior for it incorporates satisfactorily the particular meaning (*viz.* 'sprout' etc.) without attempting to extend that meaning to fit every occurrence in this passage and in v. 17. For this, without positing, e.g., *Hiphil* forms, it does not do satisfactorily. The evidence from Arabic suggests that the word, with this meaning, is used of the earth and of the earth alone. Morag suggests that the meaning 'flow' (of a water-bottle or of blood oozing), also attested for the Arabic cognate, is detectable, but this hardly provides clear evidence that the word might be used in Hebrew or Arabic of the heavens pouring rain. Indeed Lane suggests that the primary sense of the verb in these instances is 'to appear'. Morag's further suggestion that v. 17 contains a reference to Israel sprouting, or producing fruit cannot be correct even if the verb is understood in a causative sense, or figuratively, as a reference to a new life. The evidence of the Arabic *'ny* is that the earth 'sprouts', 'produces vegetation' and this is understandable; that Israel (whether the nation, or the woman of the parable) should be said to do so is clearly wrong if not ludicrous.

Israel's disobedience, Yahweh will 'make the sky above you like iron and the earth beneath you like bronze'. The attentive concern of Yahweh as the prime-mover[39] is first and foremost with the heavens described in Deuteronomy (28.12) as his rich treasure house which, opened by him, give rain upon the land at the proper time. They in turn attend to the land and the land busies itself with production of corn, wine and oil (see note b above). Lastly the corn and oil and wine attend to the repopulation of Jezreel, earlier threatened with desolation and depopulation following defeat in war (1.5 and commentary). As in 1.4 the name Jezreel, being in form and sound similar, alludes to Israel (see on 1.4 above). Israel, wholly attentive to Yahweh, is herself 'sown in the land' (v. 25 below) so that on her land she can be designated Jezreel (lit. 'God sows') and the mutual interdependence of land and people constitute a veritable Jezreel, i.e. the whole concept of Israel in her land is exemplified in that most fertile of her valleys.

The emphasis, then, upon Yahweh as the sole author and prime-mover of nature's fertility marks Hosea's vision of a time to come when Yahweh is no longer confused in Israel's thinking with Baal. Again it is this that is conveyed by the verb *'nh*, repeated five times, matching as it does Israel's single-minded attention to Yahweh in v. 17. By use of words which may have their origin in an incantation of rogation[40] and by adapting them to portray the total dependence of nature upon Yahweh, Hosea gains the high ground for Yahwism in its battle against Canaanite syncretism. Yahweh, the God of the exodus and of Israel's origins, is recognised alone as the Lord of Nature and of the Sown, of the settled agricultural land of Israel/Palestine.

Another element that is clearly to be detected in these verses is an allusion to the ominous naming of Hosea's first son by the name Jezreel. If now Jezreel is Israel fulfilled and restored to Yahweh, that emphasises the enormous contrast to the Jezreel which was Israel at the time of the birth of Hosea's first son. For then Jezreel signified the murderous anarchy and misery to which Israel was reduced. Here, then, Hosea sets forth the massively powerful redemptive activity of his God who, on the basis of repentance, can change the most horrific consequences of sin and folly to salvation and blessedness. On the recapitulation of the

[39] So Rudolph, rightly. His words are even more appropriate if ענה is understood in ibn Janāḥ's way.

[40] So, e.g., Wolff and Rudolph, on the basis of the chain reaction implied by the words. For a parallel in Babylonia (relating to toothache!), see Speiser *ANET*, p. 100.

ominous names of Hosea's children (including Jezreel) see on the following verse.

Wolff's attempt to date these verses specifically in the period following the disasters of 733 BC is unlikely to be correct. His view depends upon the supposition that the words find their place in connection with a particular drought in this period for which there is otherwise no evidence. Rudolph is surely correct in his statement that Hosea's words here are general and fundamental to his teaching.

Text and Versions

אענה (first occurrence) is not represented by LXX and Pesh. and is omitted by Borbone. Indications of style (see note b above) suggest the authenticity of MT. The versions mentioned probably omitted the word as redundant. Wolff's view that MT's repetition represents a secondary amplification of a catchword or reflects oral discourse is contrived and unlikely to be correct.

והם (first occurrence) LXX (most MSS) reads ὁ οὐρανός, but B has αὐτός which Ziegler (p. 132) thinks is original.

2.25 And I[a] will sow[b] her in the land and I will show forbearance to Lo-Ruḥamah[c] and will say to Lo-Ammi[c], 'You are my people'. And he[d] will say, 'My God'.

[a]Lit. 'I will sow her for myself', where לי is *dativus commodi*, BDB p. 515, col 1 (b) α, or *dativus ethicus*, GK 119s.

[b]Such is the straightforward meaning of the Hebrew verb זרע. It is used in an agricultural metaphor of the repopulation of the land by Israel (see commentary below). Rudolph's theory that the word denotes 'I will impregnate her' and that the metaphor is genetic and refers to mother Israel's fecundity in the land seems to me to be incorrect. The word זרע in the *Qal* is never used with a woman as the object and with the meaning to make pregnant (would not rather the *Hiphil* of ילד be appropriate to convey this sense?). Objects of the verb are either the ground or soil in which seed is planted or else the seed sown (i.e. a cognate accusative). Jer 31.27, 'I will sow Israel and Judah with the seed of man and the seed of cattle', cited by, e.g., Marti and Rudolph in support of their view, is clearly another metaphorical usage and denotes not the impregnation of the House of Israel, but the wide and full dissemination of men and cattle within its confines, i.e. the increase in numbers of both (cf. Kimchi's comments *ad loc.*). Decisive evidence against Rudolph's view is Jer 32.41 'with all my heart and soul I will

plant them (ונטעתים) in this land'. Cf. further on 2.2 where 'they will flourish on the land' represents the most plausible view of the Hebrew phrase ועלו מן הארץ.

[c]For the meaning of the names, see on 1.6 and 9 above and the commentary below.

[d]The masculine pronoun is required by the reference to the name of Hosea's third child, a boy. That a feminine pronominal suffix occurs at the beginning of the verse constitutes grounds rather for admiration of the author's skill than for attempts to emend the text. See further below.

The verse concludes the chapter with a prophecy of recapitulation in respect of the ominous names of Hosea's second and third children (see above 1.6, 9). The link between this verse and the preceding one is formed by the use of the word *zr'* as it occurs in Jezreel (v. 24) and in the verbal form here 'I will sow her in the land' (see note b above, and cf. especially Jer 32.41). Thus the land will be repopulated. By Yahweh's gracious initiative the forces of nature will be harnessed to provide the staple agricultural crops which will support a prosperous and increasing population. It is 'from the desert' that Israel will take possession of her inheritance and 'from the desert', which symbolises the fully restored relationship between Yahweh and his people, that Yahweh will sow his people (her[41]) in the land (see especially on v. 17 above). The reference is to the nation, the mother of the individual citizens who make up the population, and reflects the thought of chapter 1. The emphasis in this particular verse is, then, not upon the bride of Yahweh nor does the language used constitute the last reference in the passage to the marriage and children expected of it (*contra* Rudolph). As is to be expected in a verse which explicitly refers to the second and third children of Hosea's marriage, the prophecy depicts the changed fortunes of the nation which will follow inexorably its restored relationship with Yahweh. The parable of Yahweh and his bride does not therefore here obtrude, for the prophet's concern at the end of the passage is, as in chapter 1, with the realities of the historical situation; he is ready now to indicate more directly the results which will flow from the nation's corrected understanding. The climax is the nation's acknowledgement that Yahweh alone is its God (*sic*; this and this alone, now without parable).

41 Wolff's concern that the third feminine singular suffix has no antecedent and his speculation that such an antecedent has been lost is out of place as is Wellhausen's emendation to a third masculine singular suffix in order to find an antecedent in Jezreel.

Yahweh's initiative effects the nation's repossession of the land; he sows her there for himself in such a way that the action must be recognised as totally his and as existing for his benefit (note a above). There can be no recurrence of the debilitating misunderstanding that Baal was involved or, more precisely, had a part in the provision of the crops which sustained the nation's possession of the land. The exclusion of this mistaken understanding from Israel was effected by Yahweh's chastisement through which the nation was compelled to recognise the truth (cf. v. 9). More particularly Hosea's three children signified and represented aspects of that chastisement as it unfolded within the history of the nation from the moment that Yahweh first began to speak to the prophet (1.2).

Now that the essential relationship is rightly restored (v. 21), chastisement is converted to blessing and, in the wisdom of hindsight, of corrected understanding, the former is seen to be productive of the latter. Accordingly the names of the children now signify blessing rather than chastisement. Formerly the moral anarchy and bloody strife represented by Jezreel prompted Yahweh no longer to show forbearance to his people and ultimately utterly to repudiate his covenant with them. Now, however, where Jezreel had brought the scattering of the nation and its depopulation (1.4f), the nation is sown on its land and there it flourishes (2.2). Kimchi comments aptly, 'In the time of punishment he called Israel Jezreel because they were sown among the nations; in the time of deliverance he calls them again Jezreel in that they are sown in their land'. Sustained by regular and abundant crops and free from external hostility, the nation enjoys the perennial care of Yahweh (the verb *rḥm*), a care which, before, in exasperation, he had abandoned (Lo-Ruḥamah 1.6). Above all, rooted and grounded in unequivocal loyalty to Yahweh, Israel becomes again his people (*ammi*) and in adoration of him makes the massively simple confession: 'My God'[42]. Here the joy matches precisely the depths of darkness and horror implied by Yahweh's repudiation of the covenant (Lo-Ammi, 1.9) and of his removal from the nation of the very efficacy of his name ('I will not be [Yahweh] for you', 1.9). The contrast makes a fitting and powerful climax to the chapter and is a testimony to the skill of the author.

[42] Cf. (with a longer formulation) Jn 20.28.

Text and Versions

אלהי LXX expands the confession to a full form κύριος ὁ θεός μου εἶ σύ, cf. Vulg. *Dominus meus es tu*, where κύριος/*Dominus* reflect the usage of synagogue and church.

CHAPTER 3.1–5

A PERSONAL TESTIMONY OF HOSEA

3.1 **And Yahweh said to me, Go again[a] love a woman [at present] in an adulterous relationship[b], just as Yahweh loves[c] the Israelites while they turn to other gods and are lovers of raisin-cakes/wine flagons[d].**

[a] So, apparently, the LXX, Vulgate and Peshiṭta[1]. The Targum is ambivalent. An alternative translation is 'And Yahweh said to me again, Go love a woman'. אלי is marked by the disjunctive massoretic accent *rebhia'*; but עוד is also marked by the disjunctive accent *jethib*, and consequently the Massoretes appear to show no preference[2]. Clear parallels can be cited for either translation; for 'said to me again', see Exod 4.6; for 'Go again', Zech 11.15. BDB p. 729, col 1 c cites a majority of instances where עוד follows the verb with which it is connected but also seven instances (in Hosea and Jeremiah) when it precedes the verb[3]. Usage, then, like accentuation, does not constitute decisive evidence. In view of Zech 11.15 (a specifically prophetic parallel) the balance of probability may tilt towards 'Go again'. It is possible, on the one hand, that the composer of this section of the book (as opposed to Hosea) saw in the word עוד a convenient reference for his introduction at chapter 1.2, 'when Yahweh first spoke to Hosea, he said ...'. Consequently it may have been his intention that עוד should signify 'said to me again'[4]. On this view the compiler's point must be that Yahweh said something similar on this second occasion to what he had said on the first. Since the acquisition of a wife is the substance of what he said, the problem of the significance of עוד may be more apparent than real. Thus, there is little real distinction between notice of a renewed command and notice that the substance of the command is renewed.

1 Amongst recent commentators, e.g. Harper, Wolff, Qyl favour this view.

2 Cf. Wickes *Accentuation*, pp. 10, 19, 106 and R. Gordis *HUCA* 25 (1954), p. 29. Qyl argues that the accentuation favours 'Go again'.

3 Gordis' observation that these seven are restricted to imperfects with a future reference and his assumption that they may not be cited here is hardly convincing; for an imperative like an imperfect has future reference. (NB Zech 11.15 also contains an imperative.) Gordis has not assembled all the OT examples of the usage and so his statistics are scarcely reliable.

4 Cf. Kimchi; עוד 'because he has already told him to marry a promiscuous wife and now he speaks another parable to him'. Amongst recent commentators, e.g. Rudolph, Mays and Gordis favour 'said to me again'.

ᵇLit. 'a woman loved of a paramour and adulterous'. The phrase אהבת רע as a whole is understood to define a specific relationship having financial and domestic implications. For the form of the phrase, cf. Isa 3.3 where נְשׂוּא פנים, 'men of rank', defines a specific class or group within society and Deut 25.10, where חלוץ הנעל denotes the legal designation of a person who has failed to show proper affection and responsibility to his family *in re* the Levirate Marriage[5]. The verb אהב like 'to love' in English has a wide variety of meanings. Here the passive participle like the similar, and dissimilar, בעולה in Isa 54.1 and 62.4 denotes the woman as the object of sexual love or desire. This is defined by the following absolute רע which indicates a lover or paramour (cf. Jer 3.1), i.e. an associate[6] or male friend[7] who has a sexual relationship with the woman outside marriage (cf. the Samaritan woman, Jn 4.18). The interpretation of the Targum that רע means 'husband' (i.e. loved by her husband but adulterous) is followed by a number of commentators[8] who cite Jer 3.20 ('like a woman who deceives her husband', or 'acts deceitfully away from her husband'). That either מרע or רע (with מן) in this passage denotes husband has been vigorously challenged and it is likely that Jeremiah's phrase should be translated 'like a woman who deceives (her husband) on account of her lover'[9]. There is no other evidence from the OT that רע can be used to denote 'husband' and consequently the theory must be rejected.

A number of scholars[10] have noted ibn Ezra's exegesis that the woman 'loved a friend with whom she committed adultery' and have suggested that the participle be read as an active אֹהֶבֶת (cf. the evidence of the LXX and Peshitta below). It is quite clear, however, that ibn Ezra read אֲהוּבַת, i.e. the passive participle, for, following his explanation, he says so explicitly (וזה הוא אהובת רע). His explanation is consistent with an understanding of the passive participle as frequently having an active or middle force (cf. Ps 103.14 זכור 'mindful' and GK 50f).

The translation '(at present) in an adulterous relationship' seeks to convey the objective description of the situation implied by Hosea's use of the words. These words do not of themselves reveal whether the initiative in the affair lay with the woman or her lover nor whether love

5 Further, see Isa 33.24; Joel 1.8; Prov 14.2; cf. J. Barth *Nominalbildung*, pp. 175ff and GK 116k.

6 Such is the basic meaning of the root רעה II; see the standard dictionaries. There is no evidence that the word had a technical cultic meaning, i.e. a paramour in the sense of a lover acting as a deputy or substitute of the god; *contra* van Selms *JNES* 9 (1950), pp. 71ff and Tushingham *JNES* 12 (1953), p. 150.

7 Cf. rightly AF 'neighbour', 'member of the same community', as in the decalogue.

8 E.g. Rashi, Kimchi (but 'in that you will love her and become her friend'), Gordis, Qyl.

9 Cf. Ehrlich *Miq.*, p. 247, *RG*, p. 171; Rudolph (*Jer.*) and McKane.

10 Michaelis, Harper, T. H. Robinson, Wolff.

(in a relatively good sense) played any part in it. See further in the commentary below.

[c]The word אַהֲבַת is an infinitive construct as is indicated by the accusative particle את following, GK 115d, and BDB p. 13, col 1 5 (b). For mention of Yahweh's name within a speech from his lips, cf. 1.2. For proposed emendation, see Text and Versions below.

[d]The translation 'raisin-cakes' goes back to the LXX (see Text and Versions). On this view the root אשׁשׁ denotes 'to compress', 'compact'[11] and the noun אשׁישׁה indicates a cake made of compressed grapes. An alternative theory is proposed by ibn Janāḥ according to which the expression is elliptical and stands for אשׁישׁי יין ענבים which means 'flagons of the wine of grapes'. Ibn Ezra (cf. Rashi and Kimchi) takes a similar view though he states that אשׁישׁי means the wine itself. Neither authority gives a philological account of the word with this meaning[12]. Some uncertainty, therefore, must attend any attempt to translate the word. On the other hand it is safe to assume that an aspect of the practice of idolatry (having specifically something to do with grapes or wine) is named and that, by metonymy, the idolatrous cult itself is depicted (see further below).

It is the compiler of chapters 1–3 who has placed Hosea's own oracle here in order to set forth a connection with the initial command to marry Gomer which, in his own recollection, marked the beginning of Hosea's prophetic ministry. What the compiler placed here was a first person account already complete. By placing it here he connected it with his recollections of Hosea's marriage in chapter 1. It follows, therefore, that there is no reason whatsoever why the first person account should itself contain reference to the beginning of Hosea's ministry[13]. Indeed the events which Hosea describes here are described in order

11 W. Riedel *Untersuchungen*, pp. 15f.

12 G. R. Driver *Bertholet Festschrift*, p. 144 compares Arabic *'tyṯ* (*herba luxurians*) and, by reference to the LXX at Ct 2.5, suggests that אשׁישׁה means the inflorescence of the vine and specifically 'raisin-cakes' as resembling the clump of grapes pressed into a solid mass. Jastrow gives for the mishnaic word אשׁישׁא 'jug' and Driver suggests that this word is also connected with inflorescence and specifically with the spadix of the palm tree used as a drinking vessel. Rosenmüller suggests (tentatively) that the word means flagons into which wine, pressed from grapes, is poured. Ehrlich (*Miq.*, p. 365) proceeds rather differently and compares the phrase דמי חנם (1 Kgs 2.31); he suggests that אשׁישׁי ענבים constitutes an adjectival definition of the people's love. Their love of idolatry is strong enough to induce sickness (cf. Ct 2.5) for which the antidote is raisin-cakes. Their love is a sick love because it is a love (characterised by the need for) raisin-cakes.

13 So, rightly, Wolff, 'as the writer of chapter 3, Hosea does not presuppose any knowledge of chapter 1'.

simply and explicitly to signify Yahweh's immense love for wayward Israel; the piece is, apart from the context in which it is placed, a sufficient and self-contained oracle originating from the prophet himself. Arguments[14], then, to the effect that if Hosea was referring to Gomer he would not have used the indefinite expression 'a woman' (cf. fn.18 below) but would rather have said explicitly 'your wife' or 'Gomer' are misconceived and have no force. Chapter 3 must be interpreted in terms of the situation obtaining specifically when Hosea wrote it and must not be confused with the evidence of chapter 1 which is quite different in character in that (1) it is written in the third person and (2) it is explicitly a retrospective account of the beginnings of Hosea's prophetic life and ministry[15]. It is then the compiler who, by the act of placing Hosea's own self-contained oracle here, and by describing (in chapter 1) the initial moment when Yahweh commanded Hosea to marry a 'promiscuous wife', suggests an identification between Gomer of chapter 1 and the 'woman' of chapter 3. That that identification is not made more explicitly is due to the nature of compiler's methods and, in particular, to this compiler's use (in chapter 3) of an oracle which had already been written by Hosea and which he had to hand.

The question arises whether the word *'wd* (see note a above)[16] was present in the first person account which the compiler received. It is possible that he added it to the text in order the better to link chapter 3 with chapter 1. Thus 'when Yahweh first spoke to Hosea, he said' (1.2) and 'And Yahweh said to me again' (3.1). On the other hand, if the compiler's recollection of the beginning of Hosea's ministry (with which the command to marry Gomer was connected) is essentially accurate, then Hosea in his first person oracle (referring to an event later in his life) may well have used the word *'wd*. In any case such considerations suggest to me that the compiler wished to say that Yahweh had commanded Hosea to renew his love for Gomer by attempting to win her back and that the compiler's testimony reflects accurately the events of Hosea's life and the prophet's own understanding of them.

Turning now to the evidence of Hosea's own first person account and seeking to understand it primarily as a self-contained

[14] E.g. Rudolph, with his customary lucidity.

[15] Such considerations need in no way cast doubt on the general accuracy of the recollections of chapter 1. Indeed, it is likely that the third person account was written by the compiler shortly after the end of Hosea's ministry.

[16] Attempts to excise *'wd* from the text have frequently been made particularly by scholars who seek to demonstrate that chapters 1 and 3 refer to the same incident.

oracle (and then secondarily in connection with chapter 1) the words are reasonably clear. Hosea is commanded to 'go again, love a woman'; he is to renew his efforts (*'wd qḥ*, Zech 11.15) to show the caring love of a husband towards his wife[17] who is characterised as 'a woman (at present) in an adulterous relationship' (note b above)[18]. That she is 'adulterous' indicates clearly that she was properly married for, as Rashi observes on Exod 20.14, 'there cannot be adultery except when a man's wife is involved'. It seems to me inconceivable that Hosea should be prompted to enter a relationship with another man's wife (even if it were 'platonic' or non sexual or symbolic) and *a fortiori* so when that relationship is to signify Yahweh's love for Israel. It follows, then, that the adulterous woman was his wife. In reference to Yahweh's command to Hosea to 'love', Kimchi aptly compares the powerfully simple statement of Gen 29.18 'and Jacob loved Rachel'. Such is the love of Yahweh for Israel; it is absolute and exclusive 'for no other woman does a man love equally when she is the object of his affection'. It is simply 'a great love'. Yahweh's command is made explicitly to the end that Hosea's action should reflect and symbolise Yahweh's love for his people, a people who had turned[19], as if adulterously, to the worship of other gods which, with its licentious practices (see note d above), they were incautiously and thoughtlessly inclined for the moment to enjoy. Such is the import of the mysterious phrase 'raisin-cakes/flagons of wine' (see note d above and Text and Versions). The word occurs in 2 Sam 6.19 where each person receives an *'šyšh* from David in connection with the Jerusalem cult and in Ct 2.5 where the lover refreshes his girl with *'šyšwt*. Jerome, commenting on the LXX's translation 'raisin-cakes', notes that similar cakes were 'offered to idols' (cf. Jer 7.18; 44.19) and refers to the similar πόπανα of Greek sacrificial worship. For the rabbinic commentators the reference is to wine with which the Israelites loved to get drunk (Rashi) and which inhibits wise behaviour (Kimchi, comparing Prov 20.1). At all events there can be no doubt that the other gods are those of Canaan and that the *'šyšy* denote an aspect of the vine and its products, so prevalent in Canaanite culture, and typical of

17 The notion that Yahweh can command 'love' (rather than an 'action') is difficult indeed (cf. M. Buber, p. 112; unless indeed the command relates to Hosea's feelings for one who is his wife. For Hosea's and Yahweh's love as true concern, cf. Wolff.

18 For 'indeterminateness for the sake of amplification', see GK 125c. For another example within the text of Hosea, cf. 12.13 (EV 12) where the indefinite 'woman' is clearly Rachel.

19 For פנה of apostasy, cf. Deut 31.18, 20; Lev 19.4.

the cultus at its shrines. Rudolph's observation that Hosea here reflects the understanding of his contemporaries is illuminating; within the context of adulterous idolatry, their love of *'šyšym*, i.e. of Canaanite cult practices, did not preclude their simultaneous reliance upon Yahweh nor, according to their thoughtless stupidity, would it affect Yahweh's love for them. Indeed his use of 'love' (*'hb*) four times in this verse is polemic against this understanding.

The stark simplicity of Yahweh's command and the revelation to Hosea of its significance suggest that this may have been the decisive and most profound of Hosea's prophetic experiences in relation to his marriage. Indeed, it is noteworthy that his account of it is the only one which he himself wrote. If that estimate is correct then chapter 1 represents a later retrospective view of his marriage on the part of the prophet which the compiler has accurately reproduced. In other words Rudolph's argument that 1.2b (promiscuous wife) was added by the compiler in the light of other material with which he was dealing (especially 2.4, EV 2) is right but not quite so. More likely is the supposition that Hosea began to perceive, as a result of the experiences that he recounts in chapter 3, that the whole of his marriage signified and represented Yahweh's love for Israel and that, in retrospect, he saw the very beginning of his marriage to have been instituted by his God. To this the work of the compiler may be held to bear witness. For a similar retrospective account of a call (this time *in utero*), coupled with an account of its import for the prophet's whole life, cf. Jer 1.4ff.

Text and Versions

אהבת רע LXX (so Pesh.) ἀγαπῶσαν πονηρά (*rḥm' byšt'*) which suggests that they may have read the consonants as אֹהֶבֶת רֵעַ/רַע002 'loving evil' (so *BH*, cf. *BHS*, but see note b above). Pesh. inverts this phrase and the next word, 'adulterous and loving evil'; Aq. and Symm. (ἠγαπημένην τῷ πλησίον/ἀφ' ἑτέρου) presuppose MT as does Vulg. *dilectam amico*; Targ. דרחימא על בעלה 'that was loved of her husband'; → אֹהֶבֶת (Wolff, Jeremiah, cf. *BHS*).

כאהבת יהוה → כאהבתי 'like my love' (*BH*).

אשישי ענבים LXX πέμματα μετὰ σταφίδων (Aq. -ος) raisin-cakes (OL[S] *uva passa*), see above; Pesh. *dbwš' d'pšt'* 'honey (cakes) of raisins', which Michaelis (p. 142) believes denotes a syrup concocted from grapes and 'widely known in the east'. Jerome discusses the readings of Aq. (παλαιά) and Symm. (ἀκάρπους) and believes that they refer to the old or sterile grapes (i.e. the husks or skins) signifying that, in their love of idolatry, the Israelites loved what was useless refuse. Similarly Vulg. *vinacea uvarum*, i.e. mere grape skins which held no wine and have lost their pristine goodness. Targ. seems to connect אשישי with איש 'man': ויהון דמן לגבר דאשתלי 'they have become like a man who errs (and said something while drunk with wine)'. For the phrase as a whole, N. H. Tur-Sinai *Debīr* 2 (1923), p. 85 has proposed the emendation ואהב אשת עגבים comparing Ezek 33.31f 'and so I loved a woman of lust'. Yet he himself later proposed the modification אשת → אשיש 'I loved a woman of broad hips', *LS*, p. 313, comparing Arabic *'ṯṯ* 'abundant'; see further H. H. Hirschberg *VT* 11 (1961), p. 379. It may be suggested that all such emendations are out of place.

3.2 So at the cost[a] of fifteen shekels[b] of silver, a *ḥomer*[c] and a *lethek*[c] of barley, I gained possession of her[d].

[a]*Beth pretii*, GK 119p.

[b]For 'silver' meaning 'shekels of silver', see BDB p. 494, col 1 8 b and König, 314h.

[c]A *ḥomer* is a dry measure used for wheat, barley etc. equivalent to ten *ephahs*. Modern estimates have been offered at 393.9 litres (Hultsch *Metrologie* 2, pp. 448, 452f) and 394 litres (*Bibl. Real.*, pp. 367ff). A *lethek* (which occurs only here in the Hebrew bible) is a similar measure equivalent, according to Jerome, to half a *ḥomer*. Mishnaic references (e.g. *Shebuoth* 6.3, Danby, p. 417) indicate only that a *lethek* is less than a *kor* which, according to Jerome, is equivalent to a *ḥomer*. The cost of barley is attested at one shekel per 2 *seahs* (where a *seah* = $\frac{1}{30}$ of a *ḥomer*) in time of scarcity following a siege (2 Kgs 7.1, 16, 18). It is estimated that in normal times a *seah* would fetch $\frac{1}{3}$ shekel, so that $1\frac{1}{2}$ *ḥomers* of barley would be cost 15 shekels. The total cost to Hosea of the transaction would be 30 shekels[20] which according to Exod 21.32 is the worth of a slave. Rudolph, however, rightly questions the reliability of these calculations on the grounds of a number of prevailing uncertainties (e.g. the value of the *lethek*, and the assumption that Exod 21.32 determines the fixed value of a slave as distinct from a payment compensating for his loss). The calculations are set forth here on the grounds that some estimate is better than none.

[d]Considerable uncertainty attends attempts to give an account of ואכרה. First, Jerome (cf. Aquila) and Rashi understand it to be derived from כרה I 'to dig'. For Jerome the allusion is to Israel as a vine dug in, implanted (cf. Isa 5). That such a metaphor should find a place in so straightforward an account of the woman is most unlikely. For Rashi 'to dig' sometimes has the force 'to buy' as in Gen 50.5 'in the grave

20 So, e.g., Harper, Wolff; cf. *Bibl. Real.*, pp. 177f.

which I have dug/bought for myself in Canaan'. He notes the talmudic[21] adage that 'in the sea towns they call a sale a כִּרָה which accounts for כריתי in Gen 50.5'. Again the theory is unlikely to be correct as it probably rests upon a confusion of homonymous or similar roots. Rosenmüller (p. 103) suggests the possibility that there is a reference to the digging or perforation of a slave's ear as a ratification of his willingness to remain in his master's employment (Exod 21.6; Deut 15.17, cf. Ps 40.7). This, however, hardly fits the following notice of a financial transaction as Rosenmüller himself observes.

The majority view is that the verb is from the root כרה II cognate with Arabic *kry* 'to hire', 'let for hire' with the meaning 'to buy'. Ibn Janāḥ (comparing Ruth 4.10 where קנה is used) and Kimchi subscribe to this view and ibn Ezra mentions it but with the proviso that it is uncertain. All these authorities compare Deut 2.6 'from them ... you may buy (תכרו) water'. The difficulty arises that this usage may indicate 'digging' rather than 'buying' (cf. NEB fn. 'from them ... you may dig for water')[22], and other parallels from Job 6.27 and 40.30 are far from certainly so[23]. Secondly, the MT points the *kaph* with a *dagesh forte* which, on this view of the word, is *dagesh forte dirimens* (so, e.g., Kimchi, cf. GK 20h). Again the difficulty arises that such a usage is comparatively rare. In any case the *shewa* here is not sounded but silent and therefore the *dagesh* is inconsistent with *dirimens* (cf. Tushingham and Morag).

The third possibility and perhaps the most likely is that suggested by ibn Ezra, *viz.* that the root in question is נכר and that it denotes the legal transfer of a person from one sphere of authority to another. From the basic sense of 'recognition' (BDB נכר I), Morag (e.g.) detects such an extended meaning in 1 Sam 23.7 where the *Piel* denotes 'God has delivered/sold him into (*sc.* caused him to be recognised as in) my power'. Accordingly the *Qal* (as here and only here) means 'I gained possession of her', 'I gained the legal recognition that she was mine'[24]. The general sense is well caught by the Peshiṭta and Targum (see below) with words denoting 'ransom', 'redemption'.

[21] *Rosh Hashanah* 26a; ET, p. 118 in *Mo'ed* IV.

[22] So, e.g., Morag (p. 499); it is reasonable to infer a shift in meaning from 'digging wells' to 'digging for water' and so, by metonymy, to 'obtaining water'.

[23] Ibn Janāḥ, who holds the view cited above, nonetheless connects Job 40.30 with כרה III 'give a feast' and NEB at Job 6.7 has 'hurl yourself upon'.

[24] The arguments are set out by Gordis (p. 25) and Tushingham, p. 153 and more recently by Morag (p. 499). For the use of *Qal* and *Piel*, Gordis aptly compares the Aramaic word זבן; *Peal* 'to buy', *Pael* 'to sell', and קנה in Mishnaic Hebrew: *Qal* 'to acquire', 'buy'; *Hiphil* 'to sell', 'transfer ownership'. Gordon's supposition that נכר is Ugaritic, *JBL* 57 (1938), pp. 407ff, and means to re-marry by paying a price is dubious; cf. Aistleitner, p. 206 and Driver *CML*, p. 156 (Gibson, p. 153) for very different views. Gordon himself is inconsistent: in *UG* and *HUCA* 25 (1954), p. 25 n. 37 he sets out his original view; in *UH* and *UT* he offers a different view.

Hosea reports his actions following receipt of the divine command to repair his marriage. The nature of the financial transaction is unfortunately far from clear. The most likely interpretation of the verb concerned is that it denotes the transfer of Gomer from the adulterous relationship in which she found herself to the house and jurisdiction of Hosea (see note d above). The questions arise: why should a husband make a payment for recognition of an ownership which was his by right? Secondly, on the (unlikely, cf. 2.4, EV 2) view that he had divorced Gomer but now wished to take her back, such a practice is condemned explicitly by Deut 24.1ff and Jer 3.1 as well as by later talmudic law[25].

Such considerations are undoubtedly important and may well constitute negative evidence. For the rest the only evidence that is available has to be gleaned from 2.4ff (EV 2ff) where the emphasis is upon Yahweh and Israel under the figure of husband and wife rather than upon Hosea's relationship with Gomer. There can be no doubt, however, that this extended poem bears some relationship to Hosea's personal experiences for it is clearly the work of a man who has extensive knowledge of and insight into the nature of marriage, of the forces which may destroy it and of the remonstrations, pleadings and devotion which may save it[26]. Further, the whole poem with its parable of a man's love for his faithless wife is totally consistent with the fundamental and formative insight recorded by Hosea himself (in 3.1) that his love for 'the woman' was a reflection of Yahweh's love for Israel. Tentatively, then, it may be suggested that, while no divorce proceedings were undertaken by Hosea, he had been moved to complain of the *de facto* end of his marriage as a result of his wife's behaviour (2.4, EV 2); secondly, that Gomer's infidelity was prompted by her thoughtless and short-sighted belief that therein lay, amongst other things, material advantages greater than those which her marriage could offer (2.7, 14; EV 5, 12); thirdly, that eventually Gomer's circumstances were such that Hosea could envisage her coming to the

[25] B. *Sotah* 28a (ET, pp. 138f in *Nashim* III) and *Sifre Numbers*, § 7, Friedmann p. 4a.

[26] *Contra* Rudolph (p. 60). With his contention that this material has its origin in Hosea's public speeches and not in an account of his marriage there need be no disagreement. Such speeches may be said to reflect deep insight into marriage and marital problems. That they were public need not imply that the hearers (at that stage) knew of Hosea's personal problems nor that he was guilty of unnecessary cruelty in speaking publicly of his wife. The fact remains that his marriage was explicitly to reflect Yahweh's love for Israel.

conclusion recorded of Israel in 2.9 (EV 7) 'I wish to return to my husband, for things were better for me then than now'.

In the light of such considerations the phrase 'at present in an adulterous relationship' (3.1) suggests that Gomer's infidelities had eventually betrayed her into a liaison from whose financial and domestic implications she could not readily escape. Whether those implications should be defined as concubinage or as slavery cannot be known[27]. It is in any case probable that, as in all times and in all places, financial arrangements attended all such relationships. Certainly Prov 6.35 refers to a lover's attempts to buy off the wrath of a cuckolded husband. Judges 19.2ff is instructive in that, while it does not specify financial transactions, there is reference to a Levite and his concubine, to her leaving him for her father's house following a domestic row[28] and to the Levite's wooing her (cf. Hos 2.16, EV 14) back to him. While no exact parallel is afforded at least there is in the latter text precedent for a woman's taking the initiative in leaving a stable relationship and for her lover's vigorous attempts to restore it. Again, while no formal procedure in the bible is recorded for a husband's forgiving his erring wife, Assyrian and Babylonian codes make specific provision for it[29].

In any case, however, life does not always conform to precedents or to codified canons of behaviour. Hosea believed himself to be commanded by Yahweh to gain possession of Gomer and this he did at the cost to himself of silver and barley. Whether this was done to redeem Gomer from financial liability or from slavery or whether to facilitate and speed his objectives by judicious payments cannot be known.

Text and Versions

ואכרה LXX καὶ ἐμισθωσάμην 'I hired (her)'; Aq. καὶ ἔσκαψα αὐτήν, 'dug her in', cf. Vulg. *et fodi eam*; Pesh. *wzbnth* 'redeemed', cf. Targ. ופרקתינון 'I redeemed them', interpreting MT's 'her'.

ולתך שערים LXX καὶ νέβελ οἴνου 'and a flagon of wine' → נבל יין (e.g. Grätz, Borbone). Rudolph's suggestion that the origins of the

[27] For slavery see, e.g., Budde *ThBl* 13 (1934), pp. 337ff and Rowley *MG*, p. 90 n. 2. For observations on Tushingham's views that she was redeemed from cult prostitution, see Excursus p. 125.

[28] So, e.g., Soggin, p. 284, following G. R. Driver *ETL* 26 (1950), p. 348 and KB³ (*q.v.*), interprets *wtznh*; it is possible that the word denotes unfaithfulness; so, e.g., Kimchi *ad loc.*

[29] Cf. with Rowley *MG*, p. 91, Code of Hammurabi, § 129 and Assyrian Code, Tablet A, § 15 (Driver/Miles *BL* II, pp. 50ff and *AL*, pp. 388f).

reading are to be found in אשישי ענבים at the end of v. 1 is likely to be correct; thus a marginal gloss indicating an alternative translation of that phrase has found its way by mistake into the text here apparently displacing the translation of לחך שערים. For the less satisfactory theory that there is here a genuine variant (*sc.* to MT), see Nyberg *ZAW* 52 (1954), pp. 241ff. There is no need to delete MT's reading (so *BH*) since repetition of the *nomen rectum* when it refers to two co-ordinated nouns is known from Gen 5.5, cf. König, 275a.

3.3 **And I said to her: you shall remain mine[a] for an extended period[b]. You shall not act promiscuously[c] nor enter a relationship with any man[d]. And I too will refrain from you[e].**

[a]For ישב in the sense 'to remain', see Gen 38.11, 'remain as a widow in your father's house'. For the verb construed with ל, the closest parallel is found in Jer 3.2 'you took up your position on the wayside for them (*sc.* lovers)', i.e. to be ready to meet them (Rashi), 'to catch them' (NEB). Here ל would seem to correspond to the usage noted in BDB p. 514, col 2 g where the preposition means 'with reference to', 'on account of' and designates a cause or occasion. Here, the preposition, denoting cause, indicates 'you shall remain because of me' and, as Rudolph suggests, it has the force of strengthening the command. Alternatively, there is the view of ibn Ezra and Kimchi that the preposition denotes exclusive possession. Ibn Ezra defines such possession in terms of the woman's consent, 'if you consent to being mine, you shall stay ...' and Kimchi, in terms of the legal status of marriage "לי indicates that she will be called by Hosea's name rather than by that of another man'. Either of the alternative translations seems to me to be possible. The view[30] that לי is *dativus commodi* 'for my benefit' (*sc.* for later consummation) is rightly challenged by Rudolph on the grounds of its inconsistency with vv. 3b and 4.

[b]Lit. 'for many days'.

[c]The verb זנה, while it often denotes prostitution, can, as Num 25.1 makes clear, denote promiscuous sexual intercourse.

[d]The phrase היה ל, as Lev 21.3 and Ezek 16.8 indicate, denotes a more formal relationship (including marriage) than is implied by casual promiscuity.

[e]Lit. 'and also I to you'. Ibn Ezra (so Kimchi) suggests that the force of the negative in the previous phrases is carried over into this and, further,

[30] E.g. Vulgate (see below), van Hoonacker and van Gelderen.

that the phrase is elliptical[31] for וגם אני (לא אבוא) אליך, 'and I, too, will not come in to you', i.e. I will refrain from sexual intercourse with you. The understanding has the merit that reasonable sense is procured without emendation of the text. A number of scholars have judged the phrase to be awkward and have proposed emendations, e.g., for אֵלֶיךָ, אֵלֵךְ (Bruno, comparing 5.14) 'and I will go away'; אֵלַי 'and I will live for myself' (Ehrlich *RG*, p. 171; *Miq.*, p. 366); אַאֲלֶךָ 'I will place you under a curse', Hirschberg *VT* 11 (1961), p. 379; עָלֶיךָ 'I will be against you', (Wunsche)[32]. See Text and Versions.

Hosea continues to give an account of his actions following Yahweh's initial command. For an indefinite period, though not for ever (for which Hosea uses לעולם, cf. 2.21, EV 19), Gomer must remain quietly under Hosea's discipline whether that is said explicitly or whether it is implied by her situation as exclusively his ('mine', see note a above). She is not to indulge in promiscuous sexual encounters nor to enter again a more permanent relationship with another man (see notes c and d). The period of discipline also affects Hosea in that he is to refrain from normal marital relations. All this is an expression of Hosea's caring love and is a reflection of Yahweh's love for Israel, a love which expresses itself in correction and discipline. With Hosea's actions in the sphere of his marriage elements of Yahweh's care for Israel, as expressed in chapter 2, are to be compared. Thus his actions are designed to remove all temptation from Gomer's life just as the thorns and the wall (2.8, EV 6) prevent the mother of the parable from pursuing her lovers. Gomer is isolated from her lovers just as Israel is isolated in the desert: her confusion is resolved by the physical absence of the Baals and the reassuring presence of Yahweh (2.16ff, EV 14ff). There Israel, comforted, was led to a reappraisal of the truth of her situation; here Gomer in the presence of her faithful husband is corrected with quiet discipline and led, without urgency, to understand that things could be better now than they had been and, as earlier still, they once were (2.9, EV 7).

Kimchi (so, tentatively, AF) suggests that Gomer is to live in *'lmnwt ḥywt* 'living widowhood' (2 Sam 20.3) as David's concubines were constrained to do following their desecration by Absalom in his unsuccessful revolt. That this phrase (probably to

[31] The ellipsis may be euphemistic in character; the phrase reflecting the natural courtesy (apparent in most languages) by which sexual intercourse is defined without crudity. See BDB p. 98, col 1 e. This solution is adopted by, e.g., Rudolph and Qyl. For emendations, see Text and Versions.

[32] For further suggestions, see Rowley *MG*, p. 69 n. 1 and Rudolph.

be pointed אַלְמְנוֹת חַיּוּת 'living widows')[33] indicates a parallel in custom or in terminology is perhaps doubtful. Where David's action is concerned, the decision is explicitly for life and with this the term 'widowhood/widows' conforms; in Hosea, Gomer is to live in the way defined 'for many days' and so (even if for a long time) temporarily, and with this the term 'widowhood/widow' conforms less well.

Text and Versions

תשבי לי LXX καθήσῃ ἐπ' ἐμοί (Aq. ... μοι) 'you shall remain with me, in my power'; Vulg. *expectabis me*, cf. Symm. προσδοκήσεις με 'you will wait for me'.

לאיש LXX ἀνδρί; + ἑτέρῳ (AQ) *ad sensum* (cf. Borbone), rather than implying that they read אחר *contra BH*; cf., with Ziegler, LXX Deut 24.2; Jer 3.1.

וגם אני אליך LXX understands the phrase as positive and as continuing the sense of καθήσῃ ἐπ' ἐμοί earlier in the verse, καὶ ἐγὼ ἐπὶ σοί 'and I (will remain) with you', cf. Pesh. *w'n' 'hw' lwtky*; Vulg. and Symm., too, follow the sense of the beginning of the speech *et ego expectabo te*, ἀλλὰ καὶ ἐγὼ σοί 'and I will wait for you' → + לא אלך (*BH*), +לא אבוא (Wellhausen, cf. *BHS*).

3.4 **Because for an indefinite period[a] the Israelites shall live[b] without[c] king, without prince, without feasting, without sacred pillar, without Ephod or Teraphim.**

[a] See note b on 3.3.

[b] The word is the same as that translated 'remain' in 3.3.

[c] אין for מאין, cf. Exod 21.11; Num 20.19; Deut 32.4.

The reason (*ky*) for Hosea's actions is now revealed. Those actions set forth and represent *more prophetarum* Yahweh's will for his people. The discipline of true love in the context of Hosea's marriage reflects precisely the discipline of Yahweh's true love for his wayward people of the Northern Kingdom. They are to live for an indefinite period without the support and benefit of the establishment, i.e. of the state as constituted by the monarchy with its ancillary officers and the cult. In theory such an establishment was a guarantee and expression of the nation's

33 Cf. S. R. Driver *Samuel ad loc.*

well-being and independence. In practice the whole was so utterly corrupt that its disintegration was assured. From the primary sin of idolatry, so closely paralleled by his wife's adultery, the cancer of moral decline had infected the whole life of the nation so that murder, adultery and perfidy were its hallmarks (4.1f).

The five-fold repetition of 'without' emphasises the comprehensive nature of the disintegration envisaged (for a similar notice, cf. 2 Chr 15.3). The monarchy, the pinnacle of the establishment, was, for Hosea, particularly characterised by disloyalty to Yahweh (cf. 5.1; 8.4, 10; 10.15; 13.10f). The 'princes', similarly corrupt, are mentioned a number of times (7.3, 16; 8.4, 10; 13.10) and indicate the military and court officials of the monarchy.

Where the cult is concerned, the whole is described by metonymy. The feasts are the communal acts of worship and of eating in Yahweh's presence (cf. 6.6; 8.11, 13). The sacred pillar (*maṣṣēbah*), which was later wholly forbidden to the worship of Yahweh (Deut 16.22), was a single stone (e.g., of basalt or limestone) erected as a pillar (cf. the verb *hṣyb*) perhaps for the purpose of commemorating the visit of a supplicant[34] (*sic* rather than a representation or symbol of a god). That sacred pillars were earlier regarded as a legitimate part of the Yahwistic cult is clear from Isa 19.19.

In the context of a sentence where 'without' is repeated no less than five times (see note c above), its absence before the word Teraphim suggests strongly that Ephod and Teraphim belong together (so Sellin; cf. Judg 17.5; 18.14, 17ff). In the well-known P tradition (Exod 28.6ff; 39.2ff) the Ephod was a mantle worn by the high-priest having a pocket for the sacred lot, the Urim and Thummim. Elsewhere the Ephod, apparently sometimes carried (1 Sam 23.6ff; 1 Sam 2.28, 14, cf. 3.18) is used for consulting Yahweh. The latest etymological and archaeological evidence suggests (so KB³, p. 75) that the term originally

[34] Cf. E. Stockton *AJBA* 1 (1968–72), pp. 34–63; the author supposes that sacred pillars represented the person of a votary or worshipper in the presence of his god, thereby, e.g., 'prolonging (his) sacrifice in a durable form', or 'standing as a permanent prayer medium (for him) in the holy place'. At Canaanite Hazor a number of sacred pillars have been found, one inlaid with carvings of suppliant hands; see Yadin in D. W. Thomas *AOTS*, pp. 248ff. In Gen 31.45 a sacred pillar is erected by Jacob to mark an agreement. For recent evidence from the Negev and from Eastern Sinai see U. Avner *Tel Aviv* 11 (1984), pp. 115ff. For the view that the pillars represented deities, see W. Robertson Smith *The Religion of the Semites* (London, 1889), pp. 265ff. For photographs, see Y. Yadin *Hazor: the Head of all those Kingdoms*, Schweich Lectures 1970 (London, 1972), pp. 43–47.

denoted a metal breast-plate attached to an image of a god (cf. Judg 8.27); thereafter it came to denote a priestly garment (e.g. 1 Sam 2.18; 2 Sam 6.14) and, finally, the high-priestly mantle of P. Where mention of Teraphim is concerned, consultation or divination also seems to be implied (cf. Ezek 21.26; Zech 10.2). That Teraphim was/were (? plural of majesty[35]) capable of being carried seems clear from Gen 31.19ff and that it/they resembled the human form is evident from 1 Sam 19.13ff. Judges chapters 17f indicate a place in a household shrine. Archaeological evidence from Tirzah (Tell el-Far'ah) suggests that pious household objects sometimes found a place also in public sanctuaries[36].

Whatever the precise designation intended by Hosea, it seems clear that the two terms are used to refer to the consultation of Yahweh in the cult, i.e. to the practice of seeking decisions or oracles from him. The rabbinic commentators (Rashi, ibn Ezra and Kimchi), no doubt influenced by later biblical law, suggest that sacrifice and Ephod depict the worship of Yahweh while sacred pillars and Teraphim indicate the Baal cult. The suggestion raises the difficult question whether Hosea sought to depict (1) a cult which was marked by usages some of which were legitimate and others idolatrous; (2) a wholly idolatrous cult (so, as a possibility in the name of 'other authorities', ibn Ezra); or (3) a cult which in his time made use of elements some of which were later repudiated.

At first it would seem likely that the rabbinic commentators are correct, for elsewhere (4.12) Hosea specifically ridicules divination practised with a piece of wood. On the other hand feasting, while clearly legitimate, is deprecated as displeasing to Yahweh in the well-known 6.6. On the whole it seems likely that Hosea is repudiating the existing cult as totally corrupt and as obscuring that knowledge of Yahweh, i.e. of his moral requirements, which deserved absolute priority (cf. 2.22, EV 20; 6.6 etc.). With this Hosea's wholesale repudiation of the existing establishment (king and princes) is consistent.

In general the prophecy seems to depict the threat of the destruction of the state and the consequent life of its people without king or cult in exile. The tone of the oracle is menacing and stern. On the other hand, a quality of inexorable realism is to be detected and with it, intrinsically, there is left open the possibility of restoration and of hope. Rudolph's conclusion that the whole is a prophecy of punishment (logical on his view of

[35] Cf. Nöldeke *ZDMG* 42 (1888), p. 476.
[36] R. de Vaux in D. W. Thomas *AOTS*, pp. 376f.

the prophetic actions of vv. 1–3) is then ill-founded[37]. Rather, the prophecy reflects the prophet's honest appraisal of the dreadful realities of the situation and, in that appraisal, his seeking a way forward rather as, some eight centuries later, another author was to see in the terrible moment when 'it was night', the revelation of God's glory (Jn 13.30f).

Text and Versions

מצבה LXX θυσιαστηρίου, Pesh. *mdbḥ'*, Vulg. *altari*, all 'altar', suggest modification of the sense in translation made to reconcile the text with the prohibition of the *maṣṣēbah* in Deut 16.22. It is unlikely that these translations imply that the Hebrew text before them read מזבח (so, e.g., Wolff); Targ. renders 'without acceptable sacrifice in Jerusalem or pillar in Samaria' (respectively, לית דדבח לרעוא and לית קמתא).

תרפים Targ. מחוי 'one telling', 'proclaiming', apparently meaning 'idolatrous oracles', cf. Jastrow, p. 758 and Cathcart, p. 35.

3.5 **Thereafter, the Israelites will again[a] seek[b] Yahweh their God (and David their king)[c] and they will rely reverently upon[d] Yahweh and his bounty (in the days to come)[c].**

[a]Here the verb שׁוב is used; the phrase may be translated 'will return and' but, when used in conjunction with another verb, it is likely to denote 'again'; cf. BDB p. 998, col 1 8, and NEB. BDB in fact gives the meaning 'repent' (*s.v.* 6 d); it is possible that this sense of the verb ('will repent and seek') was the later redactor's interpretation (see below).

[b]The origins of the verb are to be found in cultic usage where, in sanctuaries (a) god or the face of (a) god is sought, i.e. in personal communion with him, cf. 5.6, 15, and, e.g., Pss 24.6; 27.8; 105.4; Deut 4.29.

[c]Commonly regarded as a Judaean gloss; so, e.g., Wolff; see further in commentary below.

[d]The phrase is usually understood as a pregnant construction, lit. '(come) in dread to Yahweh'. Ibn Janāḥ takes the view that there are two distinct meanings of the verb פחד; the first 'to fear' and the second, in connection with which he cites this verse, 'to seek', 'call for' help

[37] Rudolph's understanding that the command 'love' has an ironic, menacing force and is intended to match the careless assertion by his contemporaries that 'Yahweh loves us despite our behaviour' is surely contrived.

(Arabic *'l'stnǧ'd, 'l'stṣr'd*). Ibn Barūn[38], too, detects two meanings for the verb, the first 'to fear' (with מן), the second 'to seek shelter in fear' (with אל) and for precisely this semantic range he compares Arabic *fz'*. It is unlikely that such views conflict fundamentally with the usual account of the phrase in question noted above. On the other hand, they suggest a wider semantic range for the verb than is usually given. It should be noted that 'to come trembling to Yahweh and his bounty' is somewhat awkward. The translation offered above 'rely reverently upon' seeks to convey the nuances of the verb detected by the two rabbinic authorities named above.

[e]Lit. 'at the end of the days'. The phrase has here an eschatological sense and is likely to have been added by the Judaean redactor, cf. Isa 2.2; Mic 4.1; Jer 23.20; 30.24; Ezek 38.16. It appears at the end of the sentence in Gen 49.1; Num 24.14; Jer 48.47.

The nature of Hosea's symbolic actions in vv. 1–3, sternly realistic as they are, clearly have as their aim the redemption of Gomer and his 'love' (v. 1) finds its expression in this sense. Rudolph's contrary view that the oracle (vv. 1–4) is wholly one of judgement and that the command 'to love' is ironic in character has been examined above. Consistent with his view, however, is the conclusion that v. 5 as a whole is an addition to Hosea's oracle made by the Judaean redactor. Rudolph's theory depends largely upon his view of Hosea's actions in vv. 1–3 and upon the consequent deduction that vv. 1–4 are a self-sufficient oracle wholly judgemental in character. Earlier, Harper had rejected v. 5 on three grounds: first, that the verse does not correspond to any evidence in vv. 1–3 that Hosea succeeded in taking back his wife; he merely placed her in seclusion. In answer to this argument, it is urged that Hosea's action (as he recorded it at the time) clearly had the redemption and restoration of Gomer in mind[39] and it is not strictly relevant whether that plan was brought to fruition or was merely recorded – but failed. Further, on the wider view, if Hosea did fail in his personal mission, then so did Yahweh in respect of the Northern Kingdom which was destroyed finally in 722/1 BC. This destruction required reinterpretation of other hopeful elements of Hosea's prophecies on a longer historical perspective and hence the appropriation of his work by Judaean circles without which his work would undoubtedly have been lost to us. That they did this suggests that a hopeful element was already in the text of chapter 3 which they received. Secondly, the tone and contents

[38] Wechter, pp. 115 and 185.
[39] Cf. Emmerson, pp. 13f.

of the verse accord with elements in chapter 2 (vv. 1–3, 9, 16f; EV 1.10–2.1; 2.7, 14f) which must be treated as of later origin. If, however, two phrases of the present verse (see below) are so regarded, what remains does not accord so evidently with (acknowledged) later material. Further, that Hos 2.9, 16f (EV 7, 14f) are late is very far from certain. Thirdly, the language of the verse points to a later time. That is likely to be true of the phrases 'David their king' and 'in the days to come', and for this reason they are here regarded as later Judaean additions. Harper's further contention that *pḥd* (in his translation 'tremble before Yahweh') occurs elsewhere only in late passages, and is therefore here late, seems to me to be questionable. Thus, he does not make clear that it is only in Mic 7.17 that the verb is construed with *'l* followed by Yahweh. It is rash to propose a theory upon the basis of a single precise parallel, particularly when a satisfactory account of the use of the verb in the present text (see note d) can be given[40]. That *ṭwb* (of Yahweh) is only found 'in later writings' is questionable not least because it is perilous to make assertions about the language of Hosea. The word itself occurs in 10.11 and (of Yahweh) reference may be made to Exod 33.19 (JE). Hence it is reasonable to conclude that its place here is authentic.

A less radical solution is to suppose (with, e.g., Wolff) that the two phrases 'and David their king' and 'in the days to come' are glosses added by the Judaean redactor in order to give longer perspective to Hosea's words and to enable the promise contained in them to find its fulfilment in the Southern Kingdom after the fall of the North in 722/1 BC. Certainly the verb *bqš* in its technical, cultic sense (note b above) is not used elsewhere with a second object following Yahweh as its first[41]; nor is it likely that the phrase should find a place between two clauses in which Yahweh is the object (note d) of nearly synonymous verbs[42]. 'In the days to come' clearly belongs to the vocabulary of Judaean eschatology (see note e above) and is therefore likely

40 Cf., with ibn Ezra, the use of the nearly synonymous verb *ḥrd* in 11.10f. See also Jer 2.19; McKane regards Hos 3.5 as evidence that the usage 'is established'.

41 Emmerson's argument that *bqš* is used in 2 Sam 3.17 with David as an object fails to meet the point that here the verb (with Yahweh as object) has a cultic sense; in 2 Sam 3.17 it does not carry this sense and in any case it is there qualified by the addition of the words 'as a king over you' thereby making the use wholly non-cultic.

42 Jer 30.9 'they will serve (עבד) Yahweh their God and David their king' is usually regarded as an exilic addition, cf. Rudolph *Jer.*, p. 191. The phrase may be dependent on Hos 3.5 (as transmitted by the Judaean redactor).

here to be added from that source. Certainly it does not fit well here with 'thereafter' at the beginning of the verse[43].

Once these phrases are recognised as additions to the text, what remains contains sentiments wholly consistent with Hosea's views. First, the purpose of his action of vv. 1–3 is clearly to effect the restoration of Gomer. Secondly, the word *bqš* 'seek' is used pejoratively in reference to idolatrous worship in 2.9 (EV 7), if there under the figure of the pursuit of lovers. Its use here shows by contrast a proper 'seeking' of Israel's true God. Thirdly, the reverent reliance (note d above) upon Yahweh and his bounty matches precisely the gracious gifts which he is to bestow following the restoration of Israel's relationship with him and her single-minded devotion to him (2.17, 24; EV 15, 22). Here, then, Yahweh's bounty[44] denotes corn, wine and oil, the staple crops of the land (2.24; EV 22; cf. Jer 31.12).

The question remains whether what is wholly consistent with Hosea's views was written by him, by him at a later time, or by another on the basis of genuine knowledge of Hosea's words and actions (as, especially, in chapter 1). In this connection an important consideration is that the piece was not written with autobiographical intent but to set forth Israel's fate and destiny. Accordingly the transition from reference to Gomer is in v. 4 complete. In vv. 1–3 there is no mention of restoration; yet restoration is clearly implied, for discipline and punishment can serve only that goal. Verse 4 clearly depicts the parallel disciplinary punishment of Israel and, again, it is legitimate to infer that that has as its goal the ultimate redemption of the state. That is clearly stated in the very different material of chapter 2 (especially vv. 16ff, EV 14ff) as well as by such texts as 11.8ff.

It is in Hosea's realistic and honest appraisal of this the nadir both of his personal situation and of his country that hope for the future was born. To that vv. 1–4 bear witness and without the necessity of referring to v. 5. In that v. 5 elucidates vv. 1–4 we may suggest that its contents go back to Hosea himself, but that they were actually committed to writing by his disciple, the author of chapter 1 and the editor of his work. If that estimate is

43 *Contra* Emmerson, p. 104. Its occurrence at the end of the sentence hardly 'forms a parallel to אחר'; rather as a concluding addition its function is further definition and the resulting 'structured and balanced' sentence is that of a highly skilled redactor. There is no need, of course, to deny that the phrase had a use before it was adopted by redactors as a technical term for use in connection with eschatology.

44 Saadya (as quoted by Kimchi) gives to the word the meaning 'glory', comparing Exod 33.19. The interpretation reflects a more theological appraisal of the text.

correct, Hosea himself will have written vv. 1–4 at a time which was singularly dark for himself and for his country. Since faith in the future is implied, that faith was 'the assurance of things hoped for, the conviction of things not seen' (Heb 11.1). It was for his disciple to set forth the substance of his master's faith and for those in Judah who eventually received it to apply it *mutatis mutandis* to themselves. They both have well served Hosea and his God.

Where the Judaean redactor (as opposed to Hosea) is concerned, Rudolph[45] is probably correct in his assessment that the redactor made of v. 5 a recapitulation of the contents of v. 4. Thus, exile is matched by repentance and return (see note a above); 'without king' is matched by return to 'David' (i.e. the true king of all Israel, as in the work of the Chronicler[46]); 'without feasting etc.' by future loyalty to Yahweh in the Jerusalem cult[47].

Text and Versions

ופחדו אל LXX καὶ ἐκστήσονται ἐπί,; Symm. καὶ ἐπαινέσωσι; Aq. πτοηθήσονται; Pesh. *wnd'wn*, respectively 'amazed at', 'praise', 'passionately excited at', 'know'; Targ. ויתנהון לפולחנא דײ 'and they will present themselves for the worship of the Lord'.

45 Relying partly on Gordis; Gordis, however, does not subscribe to the theory of a Judaean redactor and prefers to believe the words (including 'David their king') to be genuine; see especially p. 31 n.

46 Cf. Williamson *IBC*, p. 139.

47 Cf. Rudolph *Chron.*, p. ix. Associated with 'at the end of the days', 'David their king' is, in Rudolph's view, a messianic concept which implies David *redivivus* as in Mic 5.1ff; Jer 30.9; Ezek 34.23f; 37.24f.

EXCURSUS ON HOSEA'S MARRIAGE

The following piece represents an attempt to set forth the conclusions reached as a result of this study of the text and of the endeavour to write a commentary upon it. In the light of these conclusions criticisms are offered of a number of the more important variant interpretations presented by other scholars.

LITERARY CONCLUSIONS

Historically, chapter 3.1–4 was the first written notice of events in Hosea's marital life[1]. It was written by Hosea himself soon after the events described in it and preserved by him personally (see below). It sets forth Hosea's understanding that he was commanded by God to renew his love for his wife and to show that love for her by redeeming her from the trap of an adulterous and unsatisfactory relationship into which, by her thoughtless promiscuity, she had betrayed herself. He perceived at the very same time that his love was symbolic of and parallel to Yahweh's love for Israel, i.e. for the Northern Kingdom which, by its fundamental sin of syncretistic idolatry, had sunk to the depths of moral depravity, murder and bloodshed. Thereby, inexorably, the nation was doomed to destruction. The fundamental insight, *viz.* that his personal circumstances at that time reflected the love of Yahweh for Israel, belonged also to this moment. There is here no reference to his initial marriage to Gomer and to his children because the piece is an authentic first-person account written by Hosea at the time in question and making a single point. It is a self-sufficient pericope written not at the time for public consumption, but like, e.g., the notices of Isaiah's committal of his teaching to his disciples, of Jeremiah's account of the purchase of a field at Anathoth, as a testimony and marker for the intimate circle of his disciples or chosen witnesses[2]. There is no mention of the ultimate success or failure of his personal quest for the simple reason that at the time of writing he did not know how things would develop. His action

[1] 'Perhaps the most original and authentic part of the preserved material'; so AF, p. 118.

[2] Isa 8.16ff and Jer 32.6ff. The latter passage is particularly instructive as a parallel. Where Isaiah is concerned, it is noteworthy that the children whom Yahweh had given him as signs and portents (v. 18) are mentioned in the context of the intimate circle of his chosen witnesses.

was thus an action of faith and of a faith which believed (but did not certainly know) that restoration was possible.

Chapter 2 is very different in character. It contains material largely concerned with the relationship of Yahweh and Israel but explained by the ubiquitous parable of a man's love for his unfaithful wife. Here there is no explicit personal testimony; rather, appeal is made by the use of the parable to the feelings of those who receive the words; as in Isa 5 and the parable of the vineyard, appeal is made to the hearers of it. The material of chapter 2 is likely to go back to public sermons or discourses of Hosea[3] which were designed to evoke from his hearers agreement and sympathy *in re* the parable of a man's love for his wayward wife and, consequently, agreement with the analogous application of the parable to the idolatrous and corrupt nation of which the hearers were sons. In this connection there is specifically an appeal (cf. Isa 5.3) to the children of the marriage to remonstrate with their mother and, within the context in which this appeal is found, the referent is clearly the nation (mother) and its individual citizens (children).

It was said above that there is in chapter 2[4] no explicit personal testimony. It can, however, hardly be doubted that the depths of understanding shown throughout the parable reflect the experiences of a man who knew at first hand the subject of a marriage threatened by adultery and of the aspirations of a loyal husband to repair his marriage. Almost every word is chosen with great skill and reflects with unerring accuracy the realities of the subject. Thus, there is the anger which erupts from the pain of being deceived; the desire to humiliate (v. 5); to wreak vengeance even upon the innocent children of the marriage (v. 6), to proclaim that the marriage is at an end (v. 4), and to threaten execution (v. 5). There is the understanding that adulterous behaviour is often based upon foolishness and faulty reasoning (v. 7) and that even remorse can have its origins in selfishness (v. 9). Again, where attempts to mend the marriage are concerned, the author shows the whole gamut of tactics which a husband adopts in his quest: appeal to the children of the marriage to join their father in an attempt to save it (v. 4); the desire physically to isolate the wayward wife from temptation (vv. 8, 16) and above all to reason with her, to make a fresh start in trust and love (vv. 16ff).

It is perhaps conceivable that prophetic material of the two sorts so far described (i.e. chapters 3 and 2) should have origins

[3] So Rudolph, p. 60.

[4] NB the verse numbers in EV are two behind those of the Hebrew text.

which are wholly separate and totally distinct and that consequently the material in chapter 2 should have been plucked from the air without reference to particular personal experiences (such as are found in chapter 3). It is also possible that such distinct material should have been conjoined by an editor for the reason that he saw in it similarity of content. The balance of probability, however, surely suggests the opposite sense: that the parable of chapter 2 rests upon and reflects the personal experience of its author. This is particularly likely in view of the express purpose which the parable serves, i.e. to set forth the love of Yahweh for his people; it is just this purpose which Hosea indicates with great clarity and simplicity as the reason for his actions in chapter 3. For further conclusions on the nature of chapter 2, see under Composition (pp. lxviiif of the Introduction).

Turning to chapter 1, we are confronted with a third person account of the prophet's marriage to Gomer. The account is clearly retrospective in character (see on 1.2) and has been placed at the beginning of the book because, according to the author's testimony, the marriage marked the beginning of Yahweh's revelations to Hosea[5]. There is no reason to doubt the authenticity of the testimony, nor that its origins go back to the prophet himself. Since it is a third person account and retrospective in character, and since its present position reflects an editorial decision so to place it, it is reasonable to suppose that historically it was the latest of the three pieces to be written. The substance of the chapter is the report of Hosea's marriage and of the naming of the children of that marriage. The marriage is to a 'promiscuous woman' and the subsequent birth to that marriage of 'children of promiscuity' is clearly and explicitly linked to the idolatry of the nation, described as promiscuous unfaithfulness to Yahweh. Gomer and her children, then, reflect and show forth the promiscuous idolatry of the nation. More particularly the children receive names which reflect the guilt of the nation, and Yahweh's increasing unwillingness to tolerate that guilt or to continue to act on the nation's behalf. The characterisation of Gomer and of her children as 'wife and children of promiscuity' is done explicitly by reference to the sins of the nation, and the arrival of each child marks the progressive deterioration of the relationship between Yahweh and Israel.

[5] There is, of course, no need to suppose that Hosea was not a prophet before his marriage and his reception of the revelations recorded in his book; cf. Rudolph, p. 39 and Rowley *MG*, pp. 95ff.

The birth of children to Hosea and his naming them by reference to the state of the nation at the time of their birth seems to be characteristic of eighth century prophecy and in Isa 7.3; 8.3 (cf. 8.18) we have clear parallels. There is no biographical interest in the children who are simply *incarnationes verbi dei*. No more is said of them than is said of Maher-shalal-hash-baz or of Shear-jashub in Isaiah. Their names and the naming of them at specific times is all that is important. Isaiah 8.16ff, with its reference to the prophet's children as signs and portents given by Yahweh, is likely to form part of Isaiah's memoir concerning the sealing of his message among his disciples (cf. Clements, p. 100). Even if there is a public dimension to the naming of such children, the documentation of it would appear to be delivered to the prophet's intimate circle.

Where Gomer is concerned, the situation appears to be somewhat different. The narrator takes the trouble to give her name and her father's name and recounts that it was at the time of her marriage to Hosea that Yahweh began to speak to the prophet. Indeed, the substance of that first revelation was the command to marry her.

It has been noted that the account is retrospective and that reference in it to the *beginning* of Yahweh's revelation implies knowledge on the part of the author (and so presumably of the prophet on whose testimony he is dependent) of at least part of the rest of that revelation.

It is suggested that the author of chapter 1, and indeed Hosea himself, knew of Gomer's subsequent delinquent behaviour and of its disastrous results (cf. chapter 3). Retrospective understanding is documented of other early prophets (Jer 1; Isa 6) and it is to this that the evidence of chapter 1 bears witness. To the author, then, as to Hosea himself, marriage to Gomer was perceived to be at the behest of Yahweh himself since its subsequent deterioration mirrored accurately Yahweh's relationship with Israel. It is in this sense that the marriage to Gomer marked the beginning of Yahweh's revelations to Hosea; those revelations were not made in their fulness until later events prompted them. The unity of thought is to be found in the mind of the prophet as he contemplated retrospectively the history of his marriage and through the good offices of his compiler/redactor that unity of thought is presented by the book as it has come down to us.

HISTORICAL CONCLUSIONS

In the light of the literary considerations outlined above a tentative attempt may be made to outline chronologically the constituent parts of Yahweh's revelation to Hosea made through the circumstances of his personal life.

(1) Hosea married Gomer in the ordinary way. Whether or not at the time of the marriage he was conscious of Yahweh's prompting cannot be determined though, in retrospect, he believed that he was and he recalled that Yahweh's revelations started at this time.

(2) Gomer gave birth to three children to whom he gave *more prophetarum* symbolic names which conveyed at the time of their birth his understanding of Yahweh's relationship with the Northern Kingdom of Israel. The names represent a deterioration of that relationship and ultimately (Lo-Ammi) of its complete breakdown. The period during which the children were born was perhaps 750–740 BC (cf. on 9.12, 15). It is not said that any of the children were fathered otherwise than by Hosea and in the absence of any indication to that effect it is assumed that he was the father of them all. In the account of the children the reference seems to be wholly to the nation and not to the marriage.

(3) The evidence of chapter 2 suggests that at some stage Gomer indulged in promiscuous relationships outside her marriage (2.4b, EV 2b). The invitation to the children within the parable of chapter 2 to remonstrate with their mother may suggest that her perfidy began some time after their birth and when they were old enough to be apprised of the situation and for their father to enlist their help in preserving the marriage and the family. It is not unreasonable to suppose that the experiences reflected in the invitation to 'remonstrate with your mother' took place some ten years after the birth of the last child, Lo-Ammi (*c.* 735 BC).

Apart from the invitation 'remonstrate with your mother' there is in chapter 2 a lack of material which can be construed as specific instances in the history of the marriage. The rest, despite its likely origins in the form of public sermons and speeches and its point of reference in Yahweh and the nation, appears fundamentally to reflect soliloquy. The hearer or reader is shown the thoughts and (particularly) the aspirations of the husband of the parable so that he may be led to the conclusion required, *viz.* the condemnation of the nation for its idolatrous behaviour and the acknowledgement that it should return to the pure worship of Yahweh. It is, then, not surprising that the soliloquy moves from expressions of outrage and pain through the desire to isolate and coerce the wayward wife to repentance, to the ultimate wish of the husband to start his marriage anew upon a basis of mutual trust and affection[6]. The lyrical and beautiful expression of this latter is no more than an expression of hope and, applied, hope that the nation will repent and thereby find its salvation and true destiny.

Such pronouncements, then, reflect the circumstances in which Hosea's marriage was increasingly threatened by Gomer's infidelity. There is no requirement that at this stage he should have publicly revealed the circumstances and personal experience which enabled him to argue so powerfully[7]. If chapter 1 and chapter 3 had not been written and transmitted, the parable of chapter 2 would no more be regarded as reflecting specifically personal experience than would the parable of the vineyard in Isa 5 or indeed the parable of the Good Samaritan in the gospels. General knowledge of viticulture or of the road from Jerusalem to Jericho is all that is required. Here, by contrast, the parable of marriage is associated with two phases of Hosea's marital history, the one written by the prophet himself and the other (if not written on Hosea's explicit instructions) by another author whose testimony is likely to be trustworthy. The person who juxtaposed the material at his disposal chose to reveal the basis for the parable in Hosea's personal experiences. He was revealing, in other words, that the message of Hosea was inexorably bound up with the man.

(4) The darkest moments of Hosea's life are recounted in chapter 3 and here supremely the aspirations of chapter 2 find their expression in Hosea's actions. In a personal testimony written by himself, the prophet recounts his vocation to renew his efforts to love a woman now trapped in an adulterous relationship by her previous foolishness. Again, the love and the specific actions which express it are, with massive simplicity, stated to be a reflection of Yahweh's love for Israel. Since the account is written by Hosea himself and forms an independent pericope, it was not originally designed to serve the purpose to which now it has been put. Of itself it is a reflection of Hosea's ultimate insight expressed elsewhere in Hos 11.8, 'How can I give you up, O Ephraim'. Hosea's action mirrors Yahweh's desire to save his people betrayed into misery by their own

[6] Cf. Clines, pp. 83ff.

[7] Such considerations remove the ground from Rudolph's (p. 46) lively and imaginative objections to the view that Hosea's public were burdened with the secrets of Hosea's marriage.

thoughtless stupidity. The date is likely to be in the dark period between the disastrous events of 733 BC and the fall of Samaria in 722/1 BC.

(5) The final stage is that Hosea perceived that the whole of his marriage from the very beginning was instituted of Yahweh to reflect and match the latter's dealings with the nation. The nation's idolatry, its consequent corruption and ruin had been mirrored step by step by his personal circumstances. It was this retrospective insight that he communicated to the circle of his disciples and, shortly before the fall of Samaria, it was this retrospective insight which, in the unit chapters 1–3, Hosea (or his scribe/redactor) faithfully committed to writing. Essentially, it is composed of a combination of material which goes back to his public pronouncements (chapter 2) and material which is essentially private in character, originally designed to serve as a prophetic marker in the sense indicated above. (See pp. 113 and 116 above.)

TERMINOLOGY

In Hosea's own account of his love for Gomer and his redemption of her he states that she was adulterous (3.1) and that, back in his power, she would no longer act promiscuously or enter a relationship with another man (3.3). The verb translated 'act promiscuously' (*znh*) denotes the selling of sexual favours. Yet as *semper et ubique* the verb is used as a pejorative description of promiscuity (see on 3.3). In connection with the circumstances of chapter 3, where Gomer is described as 'in an adulterous relationship' and where she is forbidden any future relationship with another, the verb is likely to carry the second meaning rather than the first. Reference to Hosea's expenditure in the course of his redemptive activity refers to the financial implications of Gomer's tragic and messy relationship rather than to her husband's being driven to buy her time as a *souteneur*[8].

In the third person account of Hosea's marriage of chapter 1, Gomer is described as a 'promiscuous wife', see on 1.2. Her children too are 'children of promiscuity'. The whole phrase is characterised by zeugma and means that the author understood Hosea to have taken on a promiscuous wife and by her to have fathered 'children of promiscuity'. Recognition that the account is retrospective at once allows the conclusion that these terms refer to the whole history of the marriage and especially to its

[8] *Contra* Ginsberg, p. 56; cf. Rudolph.

significance over the years for the relationship between Yahweh and Israel. The author testifies that Hosea had eventually come to understand that the history of his marriage and of his children reflected the promiscuous idolatry of Israel and the disastrous consequences of it. The terms 'wife/children of promiscuity' are, therefore, in no sense contemporary descriptions of Gomer or of her family and they afford no evidence whatsoever as to her status or character at the time of her marriage to the prophet.

FURTHER CONCLUSIONS ON CHAPTER 1

This assessment of chapter 1 corresponds strikingly with that offered by Rudolph. For him the original form of 1:2 read 'Take for yourself a wife that she may bear children to you'[9]. To that the redactor added '(wife) of promiscuity' by reference to 2.4, EV 2 ('let her give up her brazen promiscuity') and '(children) of promiscuity' by reference to 2.6, EV 4 ('for they are children of promiscuity') and then concluded the verse by writing 'for the nation has turned from Yahweh in gross promiscuity', relating thereby the central message of chapter 2 to the notice of Hosea's marriage that he had before him.

Rudolph's assessment, coupled with the conclusions offered above, prompts a further deduction concerning the nature of chapter 1. Its origins are to be found in a testimony from Hosea himself in which he recorded simply the birth of his children and the names that he felt constrained to give them. It is again likely to have been originally a private document devised as a testimony and a marker for his disciples against the future authentication of his more public pronouncements (cf. again Isa 8.16ff and Jer 32.6ff). This the redactor or compiler of chapters 1–3 has reworked to form a third-person account[10]. By the addition of the details of Gomer's name and by incorporating Hosea's own later insight that not only the children, but the marriage itself, had become an accurate reflection of Yahweh's relationship with Israel, he has created in chapters 1–3 a unity which accurately represents the experienced and developed understanding of his master.

[9] וילדה לך ילדים, p. 48.

[10] That he did not similarly rework chapter 3.1–4 is understandable in that he was not obliged, as was the case in chapter 1, to shift its point of reference. In the latter case, the redactor needed to make the material at hand a suitable account of the beginning of Yahweh's speaking to Hosea in accordance with the way in which he now understood the contents of that initial revelation.

THE MAIN ALTERNATIVE THEORIES CONCERNING CHAPTERS 1–3

Theories which suppose that the prophet's words refer to visionary experiences and are allegorical in character

Since the Targum, a common interpretation of Hosea's dealings with Gomer and the woman of chapter 3 supposes that these are allegorical or visionary in character. The Targum (e.g.) renders 1.2 'Go prophesy a prophecy against the inhabitants of the idolatrous city who increase in sin because the inhabitants of the land surely err from the worship of the Lord'. Amongst the rabbinic commentators ibn Ezra is perhaps the most unequivocal in his support of such interpretations. For him all the notices in question refer to dreams and visions for which he compares (e.g.) Isaiah's walking naked and barefoot (Isa 20.2f) and Ezekiel's action with the brick (Ezek 4.1). All such visionary actions accord with the notice of Num 12.6 where it is said 'If (Moses) were your prophet and nothing more, I would make myself known in a vision, I would speak with him in a dream'. Hosea's reports differ from, e.g., those of Ezekiel only in that he does not explicitly state that they are visionary. It is the application of Hosea's visionary actions that is of crucial importance: they serve as an indication of the land's promiscuous idolatry. It is inconceivable that God should actually have instructed a prophet to marry a promiscuous woman and consequently all notices of promiscuity refer only to the nation.

For ibn Ezra, the dual form of the name Diblaim constitutes an allusion to the two kingdoms of Judah and Israel and at 3.2 the quantities of silver and barley mentioned contain allusions to the king and priests of the Southern Kingdom. Similarly, Jerome, whose interpretations are also allegorical in character[11], believes that Gomer of chapter 1 is a figure for the Northern Kingdom, while the adulterous woman of chapter 3 stands for the Southern Kingdom of Judah. For this he compares Ezek 23 and the portrayal there of the two nations under the figure of the grossly promiscuous sisters Oholah and Oholibah.

[11] See his comments *ad loc.* He is less insistent than ibn Ezra that God could not have prompted Hosea to have dealings with promiscuous women; for him the evidence of other OT passages as well as of the gospels indicates that *non solum meretrices sed etiam adulterae Deo placere videantur*. The ultimate significance of Hosea's actions was the conversion of a loose woman to a life of virtue; see his prologue and his comments on 1.2.

Such allegorical accounts of the material in question do not bear examination in connection with an exegesis of the book of Hosea. Allegories (as opposed to parables) require that each detail has a particular significance. In so far as the details of the accounts are invested with such meanings, it is clear that they are read into the text rather than that they belong intrinsically to it[12]. On the other hand the evidence of Jerome and of ibn Ezra may be valuable as an indication of the way in which the material in question was interpreted at a relatively early date. The reference to Ezek 23 is particularly telling and the latter may well constitute an early representation of Hosea's insights during exilic times and in the light of the history of the two kingdoms as then appreciated and understood[13].

Ibn Ezra's allegorical treatment, if extravagant, has the great merit that it emphasises the reference of the accounts in question to the relationship between Yahweh and Israel. He is right in seeing that the accounts were written for this reason and not for any biographical purpose. He is right, too, in perceiving that the fundamental insight of the *māshāl* or parable belongs to Hosea's understanding (cf. especially his very interesting – if at the same time far-fetched – view that *lqḥ* 'take (to wife)' in 1.2 involves 'take to heart', 'perceive', 'understand'[14].

Theories which see in chapters 1 and 3 different women

The clearest recent presentation of this view is that of Rudolph (cf. Davies). For him chapter 1 told of an entirely normal marriage to which were born the three children to whom Hosea gave symbolic names. Chapter 3 relates a totally different action of the prophet by which he purchased the right of *souteneur* in relation to an unnamed prostitute and kept her in isolation in order to symbolise Yahweh's punishment and isolation of Israel. In view of references in chapter 2 to Israel's whoredom (both as mother and as children, vv. 4 and 6, EV 2 and 4) the redactor of chapters 1–3 has harmonised the account of Hosea's marriage

[12] Rudolph (p. 40) in his criticisms of the allegorical method does less than justice to, e.g., ibn Ezra's ingenuity in providing interpretations of most if not all the details of chapter 1.

[13] A modification of this view is that of Marti. He believes that chapter 3 is the work of an interpolator made by reference to chapter 2 which seeks to portray the Northern Kingdom; this in contrast to chapter 1 which, as edited by him, portrays the Kingdom of Judah.

[14] For modern allegorical interpretations, cf. H. Schmidt *ZAW* 42 (1924), pp. 245ff, Budde *TSK* 96/97 (1925), pp. 2ff and Cruveilhier *RB* NS 13 (1916), pp. 345ff.

with the contents of chapter 2 by introducing 'of whoredom' to the words 'wife' and 'children' (see p. 120 above).

Rudolph's account of chapter 1 is in many respects convincing. With his view that chapter 3 refers to a totally different woman there is the fundamental objection based upon the nature of Hosea's perception, expressed in chapter 2, that Yahweh's relationship with Israel could be described in terms of a wayward wife and a loyal husband. While it is conceivable that the prophet should have dealings with two distinct women and that the second alone (who was not his wife) should have been used by him to indicate specifically Yahweh's judgement upon adulterous Israel, that supposition is surely less likely than that he should have been speaking of the same woman, *viz.* his wife. The massive unity of thought displayed in chapter 2, and especially its emphasis on the consistent love of Yahweh for Israel, coincides radically with the latter supposition and makes of the former an affront to it.

Rudolph's objections to the view that the same woman is referred to in chapters 1 and 3 rest primarily, I submit, upon mistaken estimates of the literary form, nature and transmission history of chapter 3 and of the circumstances and purpose of the eventual combination of the three chapters, see above p. 120. That the redactor of these chapters made of chapter 1 a reference to Hosea's marriage to a woman who would be promiscuous and who would reflect Israel's promiscuous idolatry, is highly significant. The natural assumption is that one who lived near Hosea in time did not gratuitously present his own individual theories; rather 'as one who has gone over the whole course of these events in detail' he 'decided to write a connected narrative so as to give authentic knowledge' (so Lk 1.1–4)[15].

Theories that Gomer's promiscuity was specifically connected with the cult

Amongst recent attempts to explain the 'promiscuous wife' and 'children of promiscuity' by reference to cultic practices, the best known is, perhaps, that of H. W. Wolff[16]. He supposes that, in connection with the cult of Baal, Israelite young women were required to lose their virginity by prostituting themselves with strangers. In support of this view, Wolff quotes the well-known passage of Herodotus (I § 199) in which it is reported that

15 Cf. AF, p. 119, for the same sense.

16 But cf. Harper, p. 258, and B. P. Church *The Private Lives of the Prophets* (New York, 1953), p. 78.

Babylonian women once in their lifetime were required to prostitute themselves with strangers in honour of the goddess of love. He notes that similar practices are recorded by Lucian *De Syria Dea* § 6 and St Augustine (in regard to the Phoenicians) *De Civitate Dei* iv 10. Turning to the evidence of the Old Testament he suggests that 'perhaps' a similar sexual cult is presupposed by Lev 19.29 and Prov 7.13ff and that in Deut 23.18f there is a reference both to professional prostitution and to a (single occurrence) sexual initiation rite. Where Hosea is concerned, 'frequent references to such a sexual cult stand in the background to his sayings' and 4.13f is especially important since, with L. Rost, he believes that the verses depict a rite of initiation whereby, in Canaan, the power of procreation is expected from Baal, since the womb is opened in his sanctuary[17].

These considerations prompt Wolff to see in 'wife of promiscuity' a reference to 'any young woman ready for marriage who had submitted to the Canaanite bridal rite of initiation'. Her children are 'children of promiscuity' since their mother had, before her marriage, acquired her ability to bear them by her participation in rites which were, in Yahweh's judgement, whoredom.

While it is possible that such practices were not unknown in the idolatrous cults of Hosea's Israel[18], the supposition that they obtained generally is largely speculative. The evidence of Herodotus concerning Babylonian customs in no way points to a bridal ritual but rather to the requirement that women were once in their lives expected to prostitute themselves. Similarly Prov 7.13ff, as is made clear by 19f, refers to a married woman, not a virgin or bride[19]. Deuteronomy 23.18 refers to professional prostitution (by both males and females) and not to single, sexual intercourse of the sort implied by the notion of initiation rites. Further, Deut 22.23ff contains specific legislation concerning the loss of virginity before marriage; it might be expected, on Wolff's theory, that it should have included an indictment of such initiation rites. In fact there is none. In Deut 22.13ff legislation concerning proof of virginity (when that is disputed by a husband) is set out: again there is no reference to initiation rites; clearly in this connection, if such rites had existed, mention of them would have been *de rigueur*.

17 See *Bertholet Festschrift*, pp. 451ff.

18 See further C. Clemen *Baudissin Festschrift* BZAW 33 (1917), pp. 89ff. The evidence of St Augustine (*op. cit.*) may be a pointer to Phoenician and so to Canaanite practices of the sort described. Lev 19.29 may be an indictment of them, but is not certainly so.

19 So G. Boström *Proverbiastudien* (Lund, 1935), pp. 117ff.

Wolff's expansive and imaginative theory is designed specifically to give an account of the phrases 'wife of promiscuity' and 'children of promiscuity'. As has been indicated, his theory is largely speculative and, since good sense can be given to the expressions in question by reference to Hosea's thought and to the redaction of the texts in question, his explanation should be rejected[20].

An alternative and widely held theory which connects Hosea's personal experiences to the cult suggests that Gomer was, whether by original status or intermittently after her marriage, a cult prostitute[21]. There are many references to cult prostitution in the Old Testament though little detail is given concerning its personnel and their status. In general it may be suggested that the theory has the advantages that, first, it links Hosea's personal experience to his public condemnation of the institutions of the cult (e.g. especially in 4.13ff) and thereby might be said to give poignant force to his general condemnation of the nation's idolatrous promiscuity, since that is what his marriage proclaims. In chapter 2 the image of the wife's infidelity seems to be indissolubly linked to cultic observances. While the parable which the prophet there employs requires only that Israel's cultic idolatry should be compared with a wife's infidelity to her husband, it is possible that Hosea used it because he knew from his personal experience a situation in which his wife's infidelity was *de facto* linked to the cult[22]. Secondly, the theory might go some way towards explaining the financial transaction of 3.2 if it be assumed that Hosea was thereby redeeming his wife (or the unnnamed woman) from the service of the cult.

On the other hand, in 4.14, where cult women are explicitly mentioned, they are given the name *qdšwt*. If Hosea (or his redactor) had wished to convey that Gomer was such a woman, it is likely that he would have used this word with its clear and unequivocal definition. Those who favour the theory in question are obliged to suggest that Hosea uses circumlocution or else that phrases such as 'wife of promiscuity' (1.2) and 'loved of a paramour' (3.1) constitute alternative technical terms defining a cult prostitute[23]. In the latter case, the arguments cannot be said

20 For similar and more detailed criticisms of Wolff, see Rudolph, pp. 44ff and his 'Präparierte Jungfrau' *ZAW* 75 (1963), pp. 65ff.

21 So, e.g., H. Schmidt *ZAW* 42 (1924), pp. 245ff, T. H. Robinson *TSK* 106 (1934–35), pp. 301ff, Fohrer *SH*, p. 21, H. W. Robinson; see further, Rowley *MG*, p. 76.

22 Cf. AF, pp. 125, 159.

23 So, e.g., Tushingham, for whom 'wife of whoredom' is a circumlocution and 'loved of a paramour' denotes that the woman is had in the cult by a worshipper whose function is that of a *r'* or deputy of the god.

to be convincing and, in the former, it is difficult to see why Hosea should have used circumlocution when explicit clarity would the better have served his purpose.

On the assumption that Gomer's infidelity was connected with cultic practices, recognition that little is known of cult prostitution prompts further questions about definition. Were such women full-time professionals? Or were they (as in Herodotus' account) only required once to submit themselves to this function? Hosea 4.13ff presents the argument that womenfolk should not be condemned for promiscuous behaviour in the cult since their menfolk had behaved even more atrociously by resorting to both common prostitutes and cult women. The verses and the argument in them suggest sexual practices which were orgiastic in character; they depict the moral degeneration of the drunken parties held at the shrines into which ordinary folk, 'daughters and sons-in-law', were caught up together with professional prostitutes and cult women. See further on 4.13 below.

If Gomer's infidelity was connected with the cult, as seems distinctly possible in view of the evidence of chapter 2, it is perhaps better to understand it in terms of the general depravity indicated by 4.13ff rather than by the supposition, for which there is no clear evidence, that she was a cult woman or indeed a common prostitute.

It has been argued above that chapter 2 indicates that Gomer betrayed Hosea by promiscuous infidelity after the birth of her children and that, according to chapter 3, she was eventually and consequently betrayed into an adulterous and unsatisfactory relationship from which Hosea was moved to redeem her. This interpretation is based upon the evidence of the texts and it seeks to restrict itself to an exegesis of the meaning of the words. Unfortunately the words of the texts do not themselves furnish any detailed evidence concerning Gomer's status, the nature of her infidelities, of the relationship from which Hosea redeemed her or of the significance of the transaction that he undertook to this end. In such circumstances speculation needs must abound and the vast literature[24] on the subject is a testimony both to the ingenuity of scholars and to the perennial interest of the subject. The fact remains, however, that we do not certainly know the answers to these questions and it is likely that we never will.

[24] See, e.g., Rowley's extensive survey.

CHAPTER 4.1–19

YAHWEH'S INDICTMENT OF ISRAEL THE RESPONSIBILITY OF THE PRIESTS THE ABUSE OF CULTIC WORSHIP BY PRIESTS AND PEOPLE

4.1 **Hear the word of Yahweh, Israelites[a], for Yahweh has an indictment[b] against the inhabitants of the land. There is in the land no moral integrity[c] whatsoever[d], no goodness[e], no knowledge of God.**

[a]I.e. the citizens of the Northern Kingdom, cf. v. 15, where Israel is contrasted to Judah.

[b]Cf. Isa 3.13 'The Lord comes forward to argue his case (לריב) and stands to judge his people' (NEB), and Mic 6.2. The word ריב here has a forensic sense as in 12.3 (EV 2) though elsewhere it is capable of denoting a less formal dispute such as a family quarrel (cf. 2.4, EV 2).

[c]אמת Cf. אמונה in 2.22 (EV 20). The words denote reliability, loyalty and integrity. For loyalty, cf. 1 Kgs 2.4; for personal and moral integrity, 2 Kgs 20.3 and 1 Kgs 3.6.

[d]כי at the beginning of the sentence in Hebrew may have an asseverative force, 'surely', 'certainly', BDB p. 472, col 2 e.

[e]חסד Cf. 2.21 (EV 19), the familiar 'loving kindness' of earlier English versions. The word characterises the actions of the person who undertakes the responsibilities of love and trust necessary for the success of society and family life (cf. Gen 21.23; 24.49 etc.). It is an essential characteristic of a solemn agreement or covenant (cf. 1 Sam 20.8) and an expression of a bride's devotion to her husband (Jer 2.2). Where God is concerned, חסד defines his gracious actions within the sphere of the covenant but also his unlimited goodness which goes far beyond expectation of adequate response (so Qyl, p. 19). Hosea uses the word to depict the ideal relationships of men in society and of man to God (cf. 10.12). Here, according to the indictment, Israelite society is totally devoid of this quality.

The opening words of the solemn indictment are familiar from the recorded words of many of the earlier prophets. Elisha uses such words in 2 Kgs 7.1 as does Micaiah ben Imlah in 1 Kgs 22.19; cf. further Num 12.6. Wolff's view that they are the redactor's words and not Hosea's rests essentially upon the judgement that 'the word of Yahweh' and 'sons of Israel' are not typically Hosea's, since the former occurs only in 1.1 and the latter in chapter 3 and 2.1ff (EV 1.10ff). However, similar words, addressed to the priests, are found in 5.1 and since a similar formula is found in many pre-exilic prophecies (Amos 3.1; 4.1; 7.16; 8.4; Mic 3.1, 9; 6.1; Isa 1.10; Jer 2.4; 7.2; 19.3; 22.2) the words may be accepted as genuine.

The solemnity of the announcement is emphasised by the formal title 'Israelites' (note a) and the weight of the indictment by the notice of the complete (note d) absence of basic moral qualities. As Kimchi observes, the land was vouchsafed as a gift to the Israelites on condition that their lives were characterised by moral integrity and justice (cf. Num 35.33f). Since Yahweh is the giver of the land and his eyes are continually upon it (Deut 11.12) and because its inhabitants have failed him, he has an indictment (*ryb*) against them. If the language is forensic, it is adapted to the requirements of the specifically prophetic announcement of divine judgement in which Yahweh is both plaintiff and judge[1].

The substance of the indictment is that the Israelites are completely lacking in moral integrity (note c) and in goodness (note e), i.e. what exceeds common decency in gracious kindliness is impossible in people who cannot act with integrity and justice (so Kimchi). Such qualities are essential to the fabric of a healthy society; their absence marks the disintegration of the state and its decline into bloodthirsty lawlessness (see the following verse). Yet the ultimate fault, upon which those already mentioned are dependent, is the absence of the 'knowledge of God'. In 2.22 (EV 20), the phrase 'to know Yahweh' was interpreted as single-minded attentiveness to him (cf. 5.4). Here the phrase is 'knowledge of God' and the reference is to the fundamental requirements of morality though, in a speech directed to Israelites, that will include their particular manifestation in Yahwism[2]. 'Knowledge of God' denotes recognition of his character and willingness to accept his demands (cf. with Qyl, 1 Chr 28.9). It is akin to the fear of Yahweh (cf. Prov 2.5) and it manifests itself in just and straight dealing, cf., with Kimchi, Jer 22.15f, 'think of your father ... he dealt justly and fairly ... he dispensed justice to the lowly and the

[1] Rightly, Rudolph; Deroche goes further and argues that vv. 1–3 do not reflect a lawsuit but a straightforward dispute between Yahweh and his people. Wolff's distinctions between proclamation formulae and judicial sentence, messenger formulae and summons to the court to listen are *de trop*. The words of the verse constitute a unity rather than a complicated texture of different forms.

[2] Cf. W. Reiss *ZAW* 58 (1940/41), p. 78, J. L. McKenzie *JBL* 74 (1955), pp. 22ff.

poor ... did not this show that he knew me?' Knowledge of God is connected with 'goodness' (*ḥesed*) in 6.6, where it is stated to be preferable to holocausts, as 'goodness' is to sacrifices.

Responsibility for the absence of the 'knowledge of God' is attributed by Hosea in no small part to the priests (cf. 4.4ff) but also to the people who choose to ignore his manifest revelations.

Text and Versions

No significant readings.

4.2 **Malicious curses[a], perjury[b], murder, robbery and adultery inundate[c] [the land] and bloodshed prompts[d] yet more bloodshed.**

[a]As the first infinitive absolute in a series of five, the word cannot properly be taken with the second (perjury) as indicating 'oaths are imposed and broken' (so, e.g., NEB, cf. Rashi). As in Judg 17.2 the meaning here is to invoke a curse upon someone from God (so Rashi, ibn Ezra and Wolff). To invoke such curses improperly is to make 'wrong use of God's name' (Exod 20.7), i.e. to relate the name and nature of God to a purpose inconsistent with it; cf. 10.4 (אלות שוא), where the context and meaning are different.

[b]The word denotes lying deception perpetrated to cheat and defraud others (cf. Gen 18.15; Lev 19.11; Josh 7.11; Zech 13.4). In particular it refers to perjury in a forensic sense and is therefore a breach of the ninth commandment 'You shall not give false evidence against your neighbour' (Exod 20.16).

[c]The five infinitives absolute are here taken as subjects of the verb פרצו which is understood to be parallel to the verb נגעו in the second part of the verse. The verb פרץ is used of wine vats bursting with wine (Prov 3.10), of children bursting forth from the womb (Gen 38.29) and of escapers bursting forth from confinement (Mic 2.13). Elsewhere the verb is used in association with the roots רבה/רבב 'to increase', 'multiply' with apparently the meaning 'break over limits' and so 'increase' (Gen 30.43; Exod 1.12; Isa 54.3, cf. Job 1.10). It is this particular sense (i.e. 'multiply') that is detected in the verb by Rashi and Kimchi[3]. The word 'land' is added in translation *ad sensum*, cf. Text and Versions below.

The massoretic punctuation suggests a different interpretation of the verse (*athnaḥ* below נאף; *zaqeph gadol* above פרצו). Here the five infinitives absolute stand alone and as opposites to the virtues listed in the previous verse, i.e. there is no integrity or goodness or knowledge of

[3] Cf. Morag, p. 504.

God (but there is) cursing, perjury etc. פרצו, then, is taken as a finite verb, used absolutely in conjunction with the previous infinitives absolute. On this interpretation a number of meanings have been detected for פרצו. First, ibn Ezra compares the noun פָּרִיצִים 'violent men' (Ezek 7.22, cf. 18.10 where such a man sheds blood) thereby suggesting the meaning 'they have acted violently'. Secondly, for ibn Janāḥ the meaning is closely related to the well-attested sense 'to breach a wall' but here denotes 'they have thrown themselves into vice' (Arabic *'nhtkw' fy 'lm''ṣy*)[4]. Thirdly, the Targum renders 'they beget sons from their neighbours' wives'. Here פרץ is understood in terms of the increase of children and as the opposite of 4.10 'they have abandoned themselves to promiscuity but they will not be fertile'.

Such interpretations, based upon the massoretic accentuation which is syntactically awkward, are less satisfactory than those based upon the view that the infinitives absolute are subjects of the verb.

[d]Lit. 'bloodshed touches/reaches to bloodshed'. The sense is that one bloodthirsty deed arrives at another[5] and so, in English, 'prompts'. Rashi, ibn Ezra and Kimchi understand the phrase more literally; thus, e.g., Rashi 'they multiply bloodshed to the extent that the blood of one victim touches the blood of the next'.

The verse matches the preceding verse: there the total absence of morality and decency is expressed; here the all-pervading prevalence of wickedness in society is described. The terms used correspond in spirit (though not, in the first two cases, in letter) to parts of the Ten Commandments. Thus, the malicious invocation of solemn curses upon the innocent is a breach of the commandment not to make wrong use of the name of Yahweh. 'Perjury' denotes false evidence in the formal situation of a law court but is used here also of deceit practised to the detriment of the other formal agreements of ordinary life (cf. 12.8, EV 7). The three following verbs correspond *verbatim* with the sixth, eighth and seventh commandments which are designed to protect a citizen's life and property. Such wholesale wickedness leads to the destruction of society and inevitably degenerates into the spiral of ever increasing bloodshed and murder.

Hosea's use of words indicates a free presentation of the substance of a number of the Ten Commandments and specifically those concerned with obligations to society. That he displays such freedom (in respect of the choice of words and of

[4] See Dozy, under *htk*.

[5] Cf. Jer 51.9; Jon 3.6. It is interesting to note that the Arabic cognate noun *nǧy'* is attested with the meaning 'effused blood'; see Lane under *ḫwḍ* (1 2 p. 822, col 3). It is possible that the root נגע and its use here need further exploration (cf. AF's tentative speculations, p. 338).

the order in which he presents them) is no evidence that the commandments had not by his time reached a fixed form (*contra*, e.g., Wellhausen, Marti). The offences listed represent the tragic consequences of the lack of 'the knowledge of God' and hence they constitute together a breach of the first commandment.

Yahweh's indictment is likely to depict the situation during the latter part of the reign of Jeroboam II rather than specifically the series of internecine plots and murders which marked the reigns of his successors (so van Gelderen). As in the case of Amos, the indictment indicates the hideous realities underlying the apparent prosperity of Jeroboam II's Israel, realities which were to play so important a part in the subsequent collapse of the kingdom. The general character of the indictment ('Hear the word of Yahweh, Israelites') militates against reserving the words to the history of the monarchy after Jeroboam II. On the other hand, Hosea manifestly has a lively sense of cause and effect in history and the initial 'bloodshed of Jezreel' (1.4) was clearly to him a cause or trigger which prompted (note d) yet more bloodshed.

Text and Versions

פרצו LXX κέχυται ἐπὶ τῆς γῆς and this suggests (e.g. Wolff, Rudolph and Borbone) that בארץ stood originally in the Hebrew text but was lost by homoioteleuton following פרצו. On the other hand ἐπὶ τῆς γῆς may have been supplied *ad sensum* since it is difficult to render the verb satisfactorily without it (see note c above); Vulg. follows LXX's choice of verb with *inundaverunt*; Pesh. *sgyw* 'have increased'; Targ. מולדין בנין 'they beget sons'; → פֶּרֶץ פָּרְצוּ or וּפָרִץ (*BHS*).

נגעו LXX μίσγουσιν, cf. Pesh. *ḥlṭw* 'have mingled' (Gelston, p. 167); Vulg. *tetigit* 'has touched'; Targ. מוספין 'they add'.

4.3 **For this reason the land shall be dried up[a] and every one who dwells in it will waste away, and with them[b] the wild animals and the birds of the air; even the fish in the water[c] will disappear[d].**

[a] Ibn Janāḥ, though he does not cite this verse, was clearly aware of a meaning for אבל distinct from 'to mourn' (for which cf. the older English versions). In Jer 4.28; 12.4 and Lam 2.8 he gives the verb the different meaning 'desolation' (Arabic *'lḫ'b w'lwḥšt*). Similarly the Targum (see below); Rashi and Kimchi elucidate the verb by the use of the Aramaic/Hebrew verb חרב 'be dried up'. The word has recently

been discussed by G. R. Driver[6] who compares the cognate Accadian verb *abalu* 'to dry up/out'. It is important to note that Driver does not distinguish two homonymous roots but argues that the common meaning 'to mourn' represents a 'gradual transition from the physical meaning to its application to a mental state' (*contra*, e.g., KB³, Wolff, Rudolph).

[b]The *beth* is *beth* of accompaniment, 'together with', cf. BDB p. 89, col 1 a. 'And with them' is translational, cf. the lit. '... with the wild animals and with the birds ...'.

[c]The word ים denotes not only the ocean but also lakes and rivers, cf. KB³ *ad loc.*

[d]I.e. by dying, cf. ibn Ezra, Kimchi.

The phrase 'for this reason' *'l kn* introduces, 'more generally than *lkn* the statement of a fact, rather than a declaration' (so BDB p. 487, col 1 f). On the basis of such considerations a number of scholars, most notably Rudolph[7] have judged the tenses of the verse to denote the present situation rather than a threat for the future (for which לכן would be appropriate, cf. 2.8, 11; EV 6, 9; 13.3). Accordingly the words are seen to depict an extraordinary drought (cf. Jer 14f) which furnishes Hosea with an occasion on which to explain Yahweh's intervention. To this view, however, there are a number of objections: first, there are occasions when *'l kn* is used of the future as Rudolph himself concedes (e.g. Amos 3.2; Isa 30.16). Secondly, Rudolph is inclined to ask (with Sellin) whether, on his view of the verse, mention of the animals really belongs to the original text. Though he does not answer the question decisively, by raising it he points to a certain awkwardness in translating the verse in accordance with his view (e.g. can *y'spw* as it stands really denote 'are in the process of disappearing'? The verb is surely too strong to allow of such a usage, for which a participle might have been appropriate).

Another treatment of this problem is presented by the theory of K. Koch *ZThK* 52 (1955), 1ff.; *VT* 30 (1962), 396ff; for him the verse reflects the thought that all deeds inevitably have implications for those who do them and that, therefore, such persons determine their own fate. In this verse, which does not expressly attribute the punishment to Yahweh but rather merely states its imminence for the land, the principle mentioned is illustrated. Rudolph objects to the theory as follows: first, the fact that Yahweh is not mentioned does not preclude fundamental belief

[6] *Gaster Anniversary Volume*, p. 75; cf. D. J. A. Clines *VT* 42 (1992), pp. 1ff.
[7] So also van Hoonacker, Harper, Mauchline.

in his involvement in the relationship between human deeds and destiny; and secondly, 4.9b explicitly and clearly links the two.

Both the foregoing interpretations have the merit that they draw attention to an element in Hosea's thinking that has been detected in the previous verse, *viz.* his strong sense of cause and effect in the sphere of ethics and nature. The massive degree to which the fabric of society has been destroyed by bloodthirsty immorality will bring upon the land the curse of Yahweh (so rightly Mays, comparing Isa 24.4ff; 33.8f). *'l kn* 'for this reason' conveys such inevitable consequence as in Amos 3.2 where the fact of Israel's election by Yahweh has, as a logical corollary (*'l kn*), the certainty of punishment in the face of her wickedness, a point emphasised there by the sequence of rhetorical questions designed to indicate the inexorable connection between cause and effect[8]. It seems best, then, to understand the verse as having a future reference and as depicting in strong language the comprehensive character of Yahweh's avenging curse. In this sense the verse is not the judicial sentence of a judge but is rather a fully theological statement about Yahweh's response to outrages perpetrated against his nature and on a land that is his[9]. Even the speechless world of nature experiences the wrath of God (Jerome).

The curse is depicted in terms of a severe drought in which the land will dry up (note a) with the consequence that its inhabitants will not find the food and support on which they depend. Hence, with the creatures of nature, they will waste away and die (cf. notes b, d). For ibn Ezra the extinction of the wild animals precludes the possibility of hunting; for Kimchi the devastation of the settled areas results in the absence from them of (scavenging) wild animals. The same privation affects the birds which are accustomed to human habitation since there they find seeds and fruit[10]. Where the fish are concerned, Kimchi speaks of the 'sea of the land of Israel' and of the absence from it of the vegetable growth which sustains their life. In view of his words it is likely that he too is thinking primarily of the lakes and rivers of the land (note c). On the other hand, ibn Ezra may be right to detect hyperbole in the mention of the fish; he notes that in the flood the fish were not killed off and hence their

[8] Cf. the frequent use of *'l kn* in the aetiological stories of Genesis; e.g., 2.24; 10.9; 11.9; 16.14 etc.

[9] Cf. Deroche, who argues that the verse represents a 'reversal of creation' motif similar in form and substance to Zeph 1.2–3; in particular the verb *'sp* is used to convey the undoing of Creation.

[10] As an alternative he suggests the possibility that mention of the birds is hyperbole, cf. Jer 9.9.

extinction here indicates wickedness greater than that of Noah's contemporaries.

Text and Versions

תאבל LXX πενθήσει, cf. Pesh. *ttb b'bl'* and Vulg. *lugebit* 'will mourn'; Targ. תחרוב 'will dry up'.

אמלל LXX omits, → בכל (*BHS* and Borbone) or → עם כל (*BHS*).

כל LXX σὺν πᾶσι ? → בכל, see preceding entry, cf. Borbone who, preferring LXX, argues that אמלל has come into MT under the influence of Isa 24.4; Jer 14.2.

השדה LXX adds καὶ σὺν τοῖς ἑρπετοῖς τῆς γῆς 'and with the creeping things of the earth' (וברמש האדמה) after 2.20.

יאספו LXX ἐκλείψουσιν can denote 'die' and is not evidence for יִסָּפוּ as Nyberg would suppose.

4.4 [a]**If no one indicts or reprimands his fellow[b] then surely[c], O priests[d], my indictment is against you[e].**

The verse is an extremely difficult one and there have been many attempts to understand it. What follows (which is not new) seeks to restore sense with the minimum emendation. In this connection I make the following assumption and deductions: first, the verse forms part of an address (by Yahweh) to the priests (cf. the second masculine pronouns and pronominal suffixes in vv. 5ff). Hence the occurrence of the word כהן is likely to be vocative. Secondly, in such an address, the people would be 'my (*sc*. Yahweh's) people' and not the priests' (cf. עמי in v. 6). Hence suspicion attaches to וְעַמְּךָ in this verse (as pointed in MT).

[a]The negative jussives are understood as implying the protasis of a conditional sentence as in 2 Kgs 6.27; GK 109h[11].

[b]איש ... איש. The first occurrence is the subject of the verb ירב, the second the object of the verb יוכח (so ibn Ezra and Kimchi; cf. Isa 3.5 and 1 Kgs 20.20). The structure is chiastic though not truly so for then both occurrences would constitute subjects of the verbs. (The latter, though a possibility, seems unlikely in that the resulting sense is weak.) The two occurrences, then, indicate 'each other' or 'anyone' and the

[11] So Sellin; Junker *BZ* NF 4 (1960), p. 166; N. Lohfink *Biblica* 42 (1961), p. 304. This interpretation removes the ground from Budde's (*JBL* 45, 1926, pp. 286ff) and Wolff's argument in favour of reading the verbs as passives, for it explains clearly the relationship between negative command in 4a and positive statement in 4b.

reference is to the total absence in society of any reprimand for wickedness.

[c]אך occurring at the beginning of the verse in Hebrew is taken as asseverative, i.e. as emphasising the truth of the whole saying (so Kimchi; cf. BDB p. 36, col 2 1. It is removed to its present position in the English translation the better to bring out the force of the argument.

[d]כהן is understood as a vocative and as a collective singular. The absence of the article in vocatives which are collective singulars is confirmed by Mic 6.8; Zech 11.2; Prov 24.15; Eccles 11.9.

[e]MT's וְעַמְּךָ כִּמְרִיבֵי כֹהֵן is emended and repointed as follows: וְעִמְּךָ מְרִיבִי כֹּהֵן. Here it is assumed that the *kaph* before מריבי was a dittograph and is, therefore, here omitted. מְרִיבִי is understood to be from a noun מָרִיב (which is not elsewhere attested) close in form to the well-attested מְרִיבָה (cf. ריב and ריבה)[12]. Amongst alternative emendations are those which see in the letters כמריבי the word כֹּמֶר 'idol-priest', (so, e.g., Sellin, Driver[13]; cf. NEB) giving ועמך כמר ריבי 'with you, false-priest, is my dispute'. Accordingly כהן has come into the text as a gloss explaining the less familiar כמר. Against this solution it is urged that the address concerns not the idol-priests (as in 10.5) but the priests of Yahweh (see v. 6).

Amongst the rabbinic commentators Rashi interprets the MT as containing negative commands like that of Amaziah in Amos 7.13 ('Do not prophesy') addressed to the priests and prophets bidding them to refrain from reproving the people. Hence, as in the Targum, 'thy (*sc.* ? the hearer's) people' are characterised as those 'who quarrel with their teachers'; similarly Kimchi, for whom the *kaph* before מריבי is *veritatis*. Accordingly the latter part of the MT is likely to have been understood as a characterisation of the attitude expressed by the negative imperatives which precede, i.e. 'thy people are truly those who contend with the priests'; similarly Aquila, Symmachus and the Vulgate, see below. Another view is suggested by ibn Ezra and, as an alternative, by Kimchi. Here the priests and the people are urged to refrain from reproof because both, being wicked (cf. v. 9), are quite disqualified from doing so. (Similarly, perhaps, the LXX and Peshiṭta.)

Yahweh's indictment of the Israelites is solemnly announced in v. 1 and the grounds for it are set forth in vv. 1 and 2. Notice of Yahweh's devastating curse upon the land follows in v. 3. Then in vv. 4–6 the ultimate responsibility for the catastrophe is traced to the priests. Since the moral anarchy of the people prevailed unchallenged and protests of conscience within society were

12 The suggestion goes back to Hermann *TSK* 52 (1879), p. 516; cf. Robinson, Lohfink *op. cit.* p. 304.

13 *JTS* 39 (1938), p. 155.

wholly absent (note b), responsibility must be placed where it belonged, i.e. on those whose function was to guard 'knowledge' (Mal 2.7) and to teach justice and the law of God (cf. Deut 33.10).

Recognition of the logical progression from the indictment of Israel to the attribution of primary responsibility for it to the priests militates against the theory of Weiser and Wolff that vv. 1–3 form one distinct unit, followed by another (beginning with v. 4) whose concern was the cult. For Hosea the perverse cult of the sanctuaries is fundamentally connected with the primary moral sickness of the state, the absence of 'the knowledge of Yahweh' (see v. 1). Since, then, the priests are responsible for the latter it is natural that Hosea, having made that clear (vv. 1–6), should depict their involvement with the former (vv. 7ff).

The priests are addressed as a collective singular (note d). Attempts to interpret the passage (vv. 4–6) in terms of an historical altercation[14] between a single particular priest (unknown to us) and Hosea are not convincing. Apart from more general considerations, where the text is concerned the interpretation usually rests upon the alleged difficulty of understanding (other than literally) mention of 'your mother' (v. 5) and 'your sons' (v. 6). However, since these expressions can be adequately explained in conjunction with the collective view (see commentary on vv. 5, 6, 14) and because the easy alternation between singular and third person plural which marks the whole passage (vv. 4–9) is only fully understandable on this view (cf. Rudolph), it is more natural to abide by what has been the dominant interpretation. With this the rabbinic commentators may be held to agree (cf. also the Targum and Qyl). For although, e.g., ibn Ezra can go so far as to speak of the 'high priest of the time of the prophet' (on v. 5) it seems clear that such references are to the contemporary high priest as typical, an assumption confirmed by the additional use, by such commentators, of the plural 'priests' (cf. ibn Ezra on 4.4, 6; Rashi on 4.4, 6; Kimchi on 4.6). The form by which a single priest is addressed is understood, then, to be a rhetorical device by which the priesthood as a class is addressed generically.

[14] So, e.g., Robinson, Weiser, Wolff, Lohfink, Mays.

Text and Versions

ועמך כמריבי כהן LXX ὁ δὲ λαός μου ὡς ἀντιλεγόμενος ἱερεύς, cf. Pesh. *w'mk 'yk khn' mthr'*, 'my (Pesh. 'thy') people are like a contentious priest'; Aq. ὡς ὁ ἀντιδικῶν ἱερεῖ, cf. Symm. ὡς ἀντίρρησις ἡ πρὸς ἱερέα and Vulg. *populus enim tuus sicut hii qui contradicunt sacerdoti* 'like he who/those who contend with the priest'; (Symm. 'like contention with a priest'); see note e above for rabbinic comments in accord with such versional interpretations. Targ. ועמך נצן עם מלפיהון 'thy people quarrel with their teachers'; → עמך ריבי כהן 'with you is my dispute, priest' (e.g. Oort, Wolff, Borbone); → עמך אני רב הכהן (*BHS*, as a possibility).

4.5 and 6 (5) **And this very day[a] you shall fall[b] (with you also the prophet by night[c]) (and I will destroy your mother[d]).** (6) **My people is destroyed[e] for lack of knowledge. Because you have rejected knowledge, I shall reject[f] you from serving me as a priest. You have forgotten the instruction of your God, and so I too will forget your sons.**

Verses 5 and 6a are as difficult as v. 4 and considerable uncertainty attaches to any attempt to understand them. It is likely that there is present at least some element of gloss or expansion. The words bracketed above have been so identified (after Wolff, see below). Amongst attempts at wholesale reconstruction of the text, that of Rudolph (following suggestions of Lohfink) is cited in Text and Versions. His attempt (like other similar ones) is, however, more ingenious than convincing mainly because there is a large element of textual emendation[15] for which there is little evidence.

[a]Cf., with Kimchi, the similar ביום ההוא in the sense 'on that very day', Deut 31.17.

[b]The words are understood to follow on from the previous phrase in a clipped expression of judgement[16]. כשל means to 'stumble' and 'fall' and is often used as an expression of misfortune or overthrow through divine judgement, cf. BDB *ad loc.* and 5.5; 14.2.

[c]Three of the words are identical to those of the Judaean gloss which concludes 5.5, כשל גם ... עם. 'By night' (לילה) seems to have been used to balance 'this very day' (היום), but with the apparent intention of expressing an antithesis 'by day' and 'by night'. Since היום does not of

[15] Seven words out of nine (v. 5) are emended.

[16] Cf. Rudolph's comment that notice of judgement placed at the beginning of the piece reflects the prophet's strength of feeling.

itself convey this meaning[17] it is likely to have been in the text received by the redactor. Mention of the 'prophet' seems to have been imported to balance mention of the priest's fall at the beginning of the verse, for elsewhere Hosea does not condemn the prophets nor, here, is there any mention of a transgression on their part. See further the commentary below.

[d]The two words ודמיתי אמך are understood to be a second gloss made in reference to and inserted before the following נדמו[18]. Suspicion attaches to the first word (ודמיתי[19]) since it has, apparently, a first person form and is immediately surrounded by second and third person forms. It cannot be said to reflect the form of what follows (6b, c) since, there, announcement of punishment in the first person follows a statement of the transgression in the second person. אמך is likely to have been written in relation to the near occurrence of the similar words עַמְּךָ (עִמְּךָ) and עַמִּי and to constitute a reference by the glossator to the mother of 2.4 (EV 2) who is, interpreted, the people. Nearby mention of sons, too, may have prompted the glossator to refer to the mother.

[e]The verb is from the root דמה III (KB[3], p. 216)[20] 'to cease', 'bring to an end', 'to destroy'. Ibn Janāḥ gives to the word here the meaning 'destruction' (Arabic *'lhl'k*); ibn Ezra and Kimchi translate it by forms of the verb כרת 'to cut off', the latter comparing Zeph 1.11 and Hos 10.15. Rashi apparently connected the verb with the roots דמם/דום 'be silent', for he comments 'like a man who sits in terror and no answer comes to his mouth'. For the evidence of the versions, see Text and Versions. The verb in the plural has a collective singular subject, cf. Isa 9.1.

[f]*Kethib* ואמאסאך, *Qere* וְאֶמְאָסְךָ. The last *aleph* is thereby judged superfluous[21] and probably represents a copyist's error. A similar form occurs in 1 Sam 15.23 without any trace of *aleph* and hence theories (e.g. van Gelderen) that the evidence points to a voluntative form with suffix are unlikely to be correct.

[17] Hence, e.g., Wellhausen's emendation: וכשלחה יומם/ביום.

[18] The appearance of the verb without conjunction suggests that it marked the beginning of a completely new sentence or phrase.

[19] There is no reason (*contra* Wolff) to question the *Qal* form (with transitive sense); for if the *Qal* of דמה (III, KB[3] = II, BDB) apparently occurs only here, the *Niphal* 'is destroyed' is well attested, cf. Rudolph, p. 97 *contra* Driver, see n.$.20 below.

[20] Cf. BDB דמה II, p. 198, col 2. Further, Lohfink, p. 362 n. 1, *VT* 12 (1962), pp. 275f, Guillaume I, pp. 21f and, especially, G. R. Driver 'A confused Hebrew Root' in M. Haran and B. Z. Luria (edd.) *Sefer Tur-Sinai* (Jerusalem, 1960), pp. 1ff.

[21] Borbone records that 95 Kennicott and de Rossi MSS do not have the *aleph*.

The opening words are closely connected to what precedes and indeed may have formed the close of what is now the previous verse. The indictment of the priest is then followed by a sharp statement of judgement '... then, O priest, my indictment is against you, and this very day you shall fall'. Thus, as in 6b and c, the transgression of the priests, indicated by the total lack in society of censure for wickedness, is followed by a summary statement of their deserved overthrow (note b). The indictment is amplified in what follows together with further definitions of the nature of their punishment. Society is doomed (note e) through lack of knowledge, i.e. of God (cf. v. 1) and of his moral requirements (cf. for the form, v. 4's statement 'if no one indicts or reprimands his fellow'). The reason for this is the priests' rejection of such knowledge and their failure to give it its due importance. The result is that Yahweh will justly reject them in depriving them of their privileged status as his priests. Again (so here parallelism) they have forgotten the instruction (*twrh*[22]) of their God; they have failed to pay proper attention (so Kimchi) to the teaching or instruction imparted to them by God in virtue of their office (cf. Deut 33.10 and Mal 2.7 'men seek instruction from his mouth'). Yahweh will therefore no longer bother to vouchsafe his providential care for their successors who, because the office was hereditary, were their sons. For similar divine repudiation of priestly dynasties, cf. the history of Eli and his sons, priests at Shiloh, 1 Sam 2ff, and Amos 7.17, the rejection of Amaziah and his sons. Thus Hosea proclaims, in Yahweh's name, the rejection of the whole contemporary northern priesthood as a specific punishment for a specific failure. There is naturally here no doctrinal repudiation of the northern priesthood, which Hosea appears to regard as legitimate[23], in contrast to the Deuteronomic historian and the Chronicler for whom legitimacy is restricted to the Jerusalem priesthood.

The glosses (indicated in the translation by brackets, see notes c and d) are likely to have been introduced by the Judaean redactor in order to elucidate the relevance of Hosea's words to a later time. For the Targum (cf. ibn Ezra and Kimchi) the 'prophet' denotes the false prophets and (so Wolff) the reference is likely to be to the false prophets who opposed Jeremiah and who, according to that prophet, were closely linked with the priests in the Jerusalem temple establishment (cf. Jer 2.8; 4.9; 5.31; 6.13; 8.10; 14.18; 18.18; 23.11). 'By night' is added

22 Hos 8.12 suggests that *twrh* could be written; Mal 2.7 suggests spoken instruction. In this context the question is unimportant.

23 Cf. A. Neher, p. 295.

somewhat mechanically and thereby seeks to invest *hywm* with the meaning 'by day' and to convey, with the complementary 'by night', the permanent and total ruin of the false priest and prophet for whom there will be no escape (so Rosenmüller)[24]. The second gloss is designed first to elucidate further the word *ndmw* 'is destroyed' by supplying a transitive form of the word, now predicated of Yahweh and designed to indicate his judgement; secondly to identify the people with the mother of 2.4 (EV 2), cf. Ezek 19.2, 10. The word 'mother'[25] is represented in all the ancient versions and is interpreted of the congregation by the Targum (cf. Jerome and Kimchi).

Jeremias, who does not recognise the second gloss (of v. 5) supposes that Hosea's words originally and in their oral form were directed against a particular chief priest whose whole family is to be punished with extinction (hence 'mother' and 'sons') for which he compares 1 Sam 15.33. Placed, however, in the present context the words are now directed against the generality of the priesthood, past and present; cf. Wolff's earlier treatment.

Text and Versions

היום LXX ἡμέρας, cf. Pesh. *b'ymm'* and Targ. ביממא 'by day'; Aq. σήμερον, cf. Vulg. *hodie* 'today'.

ודמיתי אמך LXX νυκτὶ ὡμοίωσα τὴν μητέρα σου 'I have likened your mother to night', reading וְדִמִּיתִי (from דמה I); Aq. and Theod. νυκτὸς ἐσιώπησα (Symm. νυκτὸς σιωπήσω) 'I have been silent' (from דום or דמם), cf. Vulg. *nocte tacere feci matrem tuam*, 'in the night I made your mother silent', and Pesh. *wstqt*, '(your mother) was silent'; Targ. ואבהית כנישתהון 'and I will put to shame their (MSS 'your') congregation'.

נדמו LXX ὡμοιώθη; Aq. and Theod. ἐσιώπησεν; Symm. ἐφιμώθη; Pesh. *štq*; Vulg. *conticuit*; Targ. אתפשו '(my people) act obdurately'.

ואמאסאך LXX κἀγὼ ἀπώσομαι σέ → אמאסך אני, corrupted to אמאסאך (*BHS*); Rudolph → וכשלתה יומם כשל גם בך עמי כלילה ודמיתי אמיך 'You shall

[24] Attempts to see in 'night' the time of reception of prophetic visions as opposed to 'day', the time of priestly function (so, e.g., Qyl) are highly contrived, as are those which make an *a fortiori* contrast between the natural stumbling (of the prophets) by night and the extraordinary stumbling (of the priests) by day (so, e.g., Wolff and Rudolph).

[25] *Difficilior* (*quia inepta*) *lectio potior*. A number of emendations have been proposed, notably עַמְּךָ (so Grätz) and אַמֶּיךָ 'your kindred' (Rudolph). Lohfink's theory that mention of priests, their mother and sons, reflects a three-generation curse (i.e. on the perpetrator of the sin, his living ancestors and his offspring) may have some force; cf. Jer 13.18; 22.26; Ps 109.12ff; 1 Sam 15.33.

fall in daylight: surely my people also through you fell as in the night. And I will bring to ruin your kindred'.

4.7 **In proportion as[a] they have become powerful[b], so have they transgressed against me; their prestige[c] I[d] will turn to[e] ignominy[f].**

[a]So כן ... כ; for 'this distinctively Hebrew idiom' (so Rashi), cf. Hos 10.1; 11.2; Exod 1.12; Josh 2.21.

[b]The word רבם is either an infinitive construct from רבב or a noun (so, e.g., Rosenmüller), but the presence of a verb in the following clause perhaps tips the balance in favour of the former view. The word רבב can indicate increase in numbers but also in greatness and power. The Targum (cf. Kimchi) interprets the word of the increase in riches and wealth (cf. Rosenmüller and the standard lexica *ad loc.*).

[c]כבודם The noun denotes honour, glory, prestige. The cognate adjective כבד can also signify weight of numbers (e.g. Gen 50.9; Exod 12.38), and the choice of words is deliberate, being marked by assonance.

[d]So MT which accords well with vv. 5f where divine punishment follows human transgression. On the *tiqqun sopherim* and the evidence of the Peshiṭta and Targum wrongly adduced for the (composite) reading 'they have turned my glory into ignominy' (so, e.g., AF), see Text and Versions.

[e]The verb מור in the *Hiphil*, construed with ב, denotes exchange, substitution; cf. with Kimchi, Lev 27.10.

[f]קלון is semantically the opposite of כבוד and the fundamental notions of lightness and heaviness are respectively used. קלון denotes disgrace, dishonour, cf. Isa 22.18; Prov 3.35; 13.18.

In vv. 7–10 the form of speech changes from an indictment of the priests, addressed collectively in the second person singular, to judgement upon them for their misdeeds expressed in the third person plural. Since vv. 1–6 and 7–10 both contain notice of the guilt of the priests followed by judgement upon it there is no need to doubt that the passages belong together[26]. Such grammatical changes of person are common in the prophets and not least in Hosea where different themes are also artfully combined in a single discourse (cf. on chapter 2 above). The passage 7–10 represents, then, a further description of the wickedness of the priests and it follows naturally upon the earlier

[26] *Contra*, e.g., Wolff who speaks of a traditionist's arrangement of Hosea's words. The arguments are too convoluted to be convincing and represent an excessive use of form critical analysis.

indictment of them expressed in the collective second person singular. Rather than attempting to recognise a variety of forms and thereby to identify separate sayings delivered at separate times, only later to be combined by a redactor (e.g. Wolff), it is more satisfactory to recognise the unity of the sustained rhetoric of a single author who makes use of a number of different forms and images (cf., again, chapter 2). That is not to deny that Hosea's words have been the object of redaction; it is to challenge the validity and worth of pressing form critical analysis to extremes.

The prestige and power (notes b and c) to which the priesthood in the later days of Jeroboam II attained, are matched only (note a) by its ability to offend against Yahweh. The emphasis is perhaps less upon its increase in numbers (though this is part of it) than upon its dominance of society and its consequent corruption of it. For the essential thought involved, Kimchi compares Deut 32.15 'Jeshurun grew fat and kicked'. Preoccupied with cultic festivities and their own central importance, the priests forgot their more prosaic and essential responsibilities in the propagation of justice and morality amongst the people (cf. 6.6). Their punishment will consist in Yahweh's turning their prestigious importance in society into shame and ignominy. Thus they will be disregarded and scorned by the very people who had allowed them to become their leaders and guides (so Kimchi).

The punishment is expressed by a version of *lex talionis* as in the other previous announcements and the punishment fits the crime. Here, however, the verb 'to sin' cannot be used of the punishment since Yahweh is never its subject (so Rudolph). Yet if prestige in society is the occasion of sin, then its conversion to ignominy is its punishment.

Text and Versions

חטאו לי לי is not represented in Pesh.

כבודם A *tiqqun sopherim* כבודי 'my glory' is attested first in the *Tanḥuma* list (dated after AD 800) of such *tiqqunim* and was consequently almost certainly added at a late stage. It is not mentioned in any of the early traditions from *Sifre* to the *Midrash Haggadol* and is therefore to be eliminated from the list of authentic *tiqqunim*. The reason for its invention is probably connected with tendencies which sought to harmonise the verse with Jer 2.11 and Ps 106.20 which, with almost identical words, were understood to speak of the glory of God. In these two cases earlier *tiqqunim* attest to the desire to avoid the apparently (to the scribes) blasphemous reference to the diminution of God's glory. At all events there is no evidence from this quarter to substantiate the claim that כבודי was the original reading here. It is clear that Hosea is speaking of the glory ('prestige') of the priests and, whatever certain scribes may have supposed, not at all of the glory of Yahweh. For this and a full treatment, see C. McCarthy *The Tiqqune Sopherim*, Göttingen, 1981, pp. 97ff.

אמיר Pesh. *ḥlpw* 'they have changed', cf. Targ. with חליפו; these readings are best explained 'as corruption due to translators or copyists who, without knowledge of *tiqqune* traditions, were possibly influenced by the third person forms of Jer 2.11, and Ps 106.20' (so McCarthy). I have been unable to find (e.g. by reference to G. E. Weil *Massorah Gedolah*, Rome/Stuttgart, 1971), any evidence to substantiate the assertion (e.g. by Marti and Wolff) that the 'Massorah transmitted the reading הֵמִירוּ 'als die ursprüngliche Lesart'. McCarthy (p. 101 n.) characterises such assertions as based upon 'vague references to Jewish, massoretic or *tiqqunim* traditions'. In the light of these considerations and because MT is entirely satisfactory as it stands, attempts to emend it (for such now they are seen to be) may be discounted. In the interests of completeness such emendations are: first, כבודם בקלון הֵמִרוּ 'their glory they have turned to ignominy' (so, e.g., Marti, Harper, Wolff, AF, Borbone); secondly, כבודי בקלון המירו 'my glory they have changed for ignominy' (so, e.g., M. Geiger[27] and Ginsburg[28], van Hoonacker and, apparently, as 'an alternative reading', AF).

4.8 They feed on the sin[a] of my people; and each one[b] has an appetite[c] for their transgressions[d].

[a]The word (חטאת) can denote 'sin' or, technically, the 'sin-offering'[29], the flesh of which was reserved to the priests (Lev 6.19; 7.7; 10.17). Here the parallelism (see note d below) suggests the former meaning, cf. 8.11, 13; 9.9; 10.8; 13.12, where flagrant sins are compounded and not alleviated by sacrificial worship which is characteristically self-indulgent.

[b and c]Lit. 'and to their transgression they lift up his appetite' (נפשו). The suffix is understood to be a distributive singular (so Kimchi, cf. König, 348u, v); cf. the following verse. A number of Hebrew MSS (cf. Text and Versions) read נפשם 'their appetite', but *difficilior lectio potior*. Ibn

27 *Urschrift und Übersetzungen der Bibel* (Breslau, 1857), *ad loc.*

28 C. D. Ginsburg *Introduction to the massoretico-Critical Edition of the Hebrew Bible* (London, 1897), p. 357.

29 For a recent treatment of the post-exilic institution of the sin-offering, see A. Marx *RB* 96 (1989), pp. 27ff.

Ezra[30], comparing Deut 24.15, suggests that the phrase means 'they (falsely) raise my people's expectations concerning their transgression', i.e. they lead the people to rely upon them to expiate their transgression. The interpretation is unlikely to be correct since it requires that the suffix of נפשו has a reference different from the subject of the verb ישאו and for this, elsewhere, there is no parallel. For the phrase נשא נפש, see BDB p. 660, col 2 6 a; ibn Ezra's comparison with Deut 24.15 is instructive; here the phrase conveys 'expectation'.

[b]The word (עון) denotes 'iniquity', 'transgression'. In contrast to חטאת 'sin' (see note a) it is never a sacrificial term.

The prestige which the priests enjoyed enabled them to live a life of plenty. Their concern was with the sacrificial cultus rather than with their primary responsibility (see on v. 6). The people, ignorant of the knowledge of God, were encouraged in the lavish self-indulgence of cultic worship and thus the priests fed on their sin and lived in expectation of their transgression (so ibn Ezra). Their consciences were stifled by their well-fed opulence and, now accustomed to it, they encouraged its continuance (so, essentially, Rashi).

The phrase 'they feed on the sin of my people' thus denotes a prosperous style of life and it is depicted by the particular reference to the plentiful sacrificial meat which was available to the priests in the cult. In the P code and in Chronicles the word חטאת denotes specifically the 'sin-offering' (which was primarily concerned with expiation of inadvertent cultic transgressions), the flesh of which was eaten in the sanctuary by the priest. It is possible that such sin-offerings were known in earlier times (cf. 2 Kgs 12.17 and Mic 6.7)[31], but it is unlikely that this verse refers to them (see note a above). Here the context (see vv. 4–7, 12–13) suggests that the priests and people are condemned *inter alia* for taking part in sacrificial meals which are displeasing to Yahweh; more particularly they constitute a 'sin' and a 'transgression' since they serve to obscure the moral requirements which were prior in importance. With this view Rashi seems to agree for, in his view, the 'sin' is that commonly denounced by virtually all the minor prophets[32]. Here, then, Hosea is of the same mind as Amos (see Amos 4.4f).

[30] For a more recent presentation of this view, see Junker *BZ* NF 4 (1960), p. 167 and the criticisms of it in Rudolph.

[31] See R. de Vaux *IAT* 2, p. 311 = *IAI*, pp. 429f. There is the possibility (so, e.g., Gray) that 2 Kgs 12.17 is a post-exilic gloss.

[32] So, too, Jerome; the priests devour the sins of the people by showing themselves agreeable to the crimes of the wicked.

Kimchi interprets the phrase of the sin-offering[33] and, in particular, he mentions the possibility that the situation was akin to that described in regard to the sons of Eli at Shiloh who ate the sin-offering before the proper service to Yahweh had been performed (1 Sam 2.12ff); the difficulty with this view is that the text of 1 Samuel does not refer specifically to the sin-offering. On the other hand the text furnishes a fine illustration of priestly greed and the related disregard of morality and just-dealing.

It is likely that the lavish cult which Hosea here condemns reflects the pervasive influence of Baalism upon the service of Yahweh in the later years of Jeroboam II (cf. 2.18, EV 16). The emphasis on sacrificial worship detracted from the true emphases of Yahwism, *viz.* upon just-dealing and knowledge of God.

Text and Versions

חטאת LXX ἁμαρτίας (λαοῦ μου), cf. Vulg. *peccata populi mei* (Oort *Em.* → חַטָּאת); Symm. ἁμαρτίας ὁ λαός μου ἐσθίει 'my people devour sins'.

נפשו LXX and Symm. τὰς ψυχὰς αὐτῶν; Theod. ἐν ταῖς ψυχαῖς αὐτῶν; Vulg. *animas eorum*; Pesh. *npshwn*; Targ. נפשהון; 9 Kennicott MSS read נַפְשָׁם; the reading is adopted by Borbone.

4.9 **And so[a] the same fate[b] will befall priest and people; I will punish each one[c] for his ways and repay each one[c] for his misdeeds[d].**

[a]For the word והיה, see above on 1.5; 2.1, 18, 23.

[b]Lit. 'and it will be like people like priest'. For ibn Ezra and Kimchi the repeated *kaph* is a construction of abbreviation; for it, cf. Gen 44.18; 1 Kgs 22.4; Isa 24.2 etc. The usage conveys 'the completeness of the correspondency between two objects' (BDB p. 454, col 1 2); cf. König, 371g.

[c]The third masculine singular suffixes are, as נפשו in the previous verse, distributive. Each guilty individual, whether a priest or a layman, will suffer punishment (so ibn Ezra and Kimchi).

[d]For the same phrase, cf. 12.3 below.

[33] So, too, e.g., Qyl, AF.

Verses 9f announce the punishment which will befall both priests and people. They are alike in their guilt and they will be alike in their punishment (so Kimchi). If the prior responsibility is the priests', the actual result is that the people are caught up with them in transgression and with them equally will sustain the punishment of Yahweh. The emphasis, then, is different from that of vv. 4ff; there, the particular and prior guilt and punishment of the priests is set forth; here it is the wider guilt of society with its inevitable and tragic consequences.

In these circumstances, and particularly in view of the emphasis upon the common fate of the priests and people (see notes b and c), the suggestion that v. 10 originally preceded v. 9 is discounted[34]. Verse 9 defines the mode of Yahweh's punishment and emphasises that it will befall society as a whole, thus matching accurately the opening words of the oracle (4.1) with its indictment of the Israelites as a nation. The oracle, then, conveys with considerable subtilty the interdependence in transgression of priest and people. Where Yahweh is concerned the notion of primary responsibility does not excuse the sins of those who are guilty because they have allowed themselves to be mislead. It is precisely the lack of conscientious objection to wickedness throughout society that is the main focus of Yahweh's complaint and its origin is traced to the baleful relationship between priests and people (vv. 4f, 8). Indeed, the nation as a whole is destroyed for 'lack of knowledge' (v. 6).

Recognition that this verse proclaims the identical fate of priest and people renders otiose Wolff's discussion whether the verse concerns the one rather than the other. Indeed, he is unable to resolve the question he poses other than by further proposing that the verse is a gloss upon vv. 4–6 wrongly inserted into its present place (cf. *BHS*). The primary ground for this suggestion is that *whyh* is used in 1.5; 2.1, 18, 23 (EV 1.10, 2.16, 21) to introduce an expansion upon a transmitted text. But that is not evidently the case here since there is no sign of the phrase 'on that day' characteristic of the passages cited by Wolff.

Wolff is right to see a close connection of thought between vv. 4–6 and this verse. The significance of that connection, however, lies in its portrayal of the interdependence of priest and people in transgression and then of the punishment which will befall both equally. Accordingly the verse should not be seen as a glossator's attempt to define specifically the punishment of the priests over and above that of the people, the latter independently

34 *Contra*, e.g., Rudolph. For arguments against the view that v. 10 refers to the priests alone, see below.

authenticated by 12.3 (EV 2). To do so is to miss the thrust of Hosea's argument and his indictment of the whole society of the Northern Kingdom.

Text and Versions

והיה כעם ככהן LXX καὶ ἔσται καθὼς ὁ λαὸς οὕτως καὶ ὁ ἱερεύς; Symm. καὶ ἐγένοντο ὁμοίως ὁ λαὸς καὶ ὁ ἱερεύς.

4.10 and 11 (10) **They will eat but they will not be satisfied; they have abandoned themselves to promiscuity[a], but they will not be fertile[b]. For they have forsaken Yahweh in their love of[c] (11) promiscuity[d] and wine, and new wine[e], a devotion[f] which deprives them of their understanding[f].**

[a]The *Hiphil* here is intransitive (so ibn Janāḥ and Kimchi) as opposed to its transitive (so causal) use in, e.g., Exod 34.16; Lev 19.29. Cf. 4.18; 5.3. The intransitive use is peculiar to Hosea and it is possible that it represents a northern dialectal form[35]. Since, however, the *Qal* is used elsewhere (e.g. 1.2 and 2.7) it is probably best to regard the use of the *Hiphil* as expressing 'action in some particular direction' (GK 53f, BL 294b) and hence, in this case, 'they have abandoned themselves to promiscuity'[36]. A similar comment is made by ibn Janāḥ who speaks of 'the abundance of their delight/expansiveness (Arabic *'nbs'ṭhm*) in promiscuity'[37]. Such considerations go some way, perhaps, to explaining the perfect tense (i.e. without *waw* consecutive)[38] which unusually follows the parallel consecutive perfect (ואכלו). The perfect, then, denotes that they have given themselves to a promiscuous way of life and the punishment is that they will lose their fecundity. The *Qal* consecutive perfect ואכלו denotes an aspect of ordinary life in the future which is not characterised by 'action in some particular direction'. Accordingly the form of the verse seems to be (1) (as a punishment in the future) they will not find due nourishment in life, since (2) they have abandoned

35 See Morag, p. 500 n. Morag supposes that a *Yiphil* preterite (and imperfect) existed in northern Hebrew (as in Phoenician) and that later there was a tendency for *Qal* imperfects to be confused with such *Hiphil* (or *Yiphil*) forms with consequent loss of the particular meanings of the respective themes of the verb. Morag gives no account of 'pure' *Hiphil* forms such as are found in the present verse nor does he suggest the particular nuances for *Qal* and *Hiphil*, the existence of which his theory would seem to imply.

36 Cf. שׂכל 'be prudent', *Qal*; 'act circumspectly', *Hiphil*.

37 See under פרץ, Neubauer, p. 588.

38 For the emendation יזנו see, e.g., Wellhausen and Marti. According to *BHS* 2 MSS read והזנו; Borbone lists no such reading.

themselves to promiscuity; and (3) because such promiscuity is not undertaken for the purpose of procreation[39], the absence of progeny is the punishment which will follow.

[b]See note c on 4.2. The verb means 'to break over limits', 'to increase' (Gen 30.43; Exod 1.12; Isa 54.3; Job 1.10). So, e.g., ibn Janāḥ, Rashi, ibn Ezra and Kimchi; for the evidence of the versions, see below.

[c]The verb שמר, commonly translated 'to keep', denotes here 'cleaving to', 'devoting oneself to' and the usage is peculiar to Hosea[40]. Elsewhere it is commonly used in the semantic field of ethics and religion having, as its objects, e.g., 'instruction', 'the ways of Yahweh', 'the word of Yahweh', 'statutes and ordinances', etc. Here, however, its usage is in the field of sexuality and sensual love (cf. 12.13, EV 12) and its meaning is precise, hence the translation 'love of' (cf. Peshitta below). Rashi and Kimchi[41] similarly speak of 'preoccupation with' (עסוקין/מתעסקים) the sensual vices concerned. The word matches well the use of the *Hiphil* of זנה earlier in the verse 'they have abandoned themselves (to promiscuity)'.

It is possible that the common use of שמר in the field of religion and ethics together with its nearness here to the tetragrammaton later gave rise to the verse division of the MT and the tradition whereby the word is interpreted in connection with Yahweh, cf. ibn Ezra 'they have forsaken Yahweh, i.e. in respect of keeping his way or his law' (so Kimchi), cf. the evidence of the versions below.

[d]The objects of לשמר are to be found in the following verse, *viz.* זנות, יין and תירוש; cf. the LXX, the Peshiṭta and, as noted by Kimchi, Saadya. For a defence of the verse division of MT and the translation 'they have ceased to take heed of Yahweh', see, e.g., Rudolph. Decisively against this view is the consideration that שמר is not used elsewhere with Yahweh as its object. It is noteworthy that, e.g., ibn Ezra and Kimchi feel constrained to supply objects for the verb *ad sensum* (his ways, his law). There is no need (*contra* Wolff) to question the form זנות; for it is found in, e.g., 6.10 and in Jer 3.2, 9.

[e]On תירוש (new wine), see above 2.10. Kimchi believes its mention here (beside wine) indicates its especially intoxicating character. L. Köhler, *ZAW* 46 (1928), pp. 218ff, notes that יין 'wine' and תירוש do not occur together elsewhere in the OT Since he believes that תירוש is merely the

[39] Following Kimchi's comments on 4.14 and a suggestion of Tur-Sinai (see Ben Yehuda, p. 5135), Morag (p. 504) suggests that the meaning of the phrase as a whole is that they have indulged in promiscuous and intentionally contraceptive intercourse (cf. Gen 38.9). The difficulty with this view is that the form of the verse seems to require in יפרצו a judgement upon promiscuity rather than a particular definition of it, cf. 'they will eat and not be satisfied'.

[40] Morag, pp. 501f.

[41] I.e. in their comments on v. 11 and in spite of the fact that they take לשמר with v. 10.

Canaanite term equivalent to יין he emends the text to זנונים ותירוש (so also, e.g., Wolff). Rudolph dissents from the emendation, preferring to see the language of the verse as dialectally northern. For him תירוש denotes new wine which, still opaque, was very palatable but deceptively strong and particularly intoxicating to those who did not know its character. Rudolph further suggests that the noun is derived from the root ירש 'to take possession' and that it denotes 'the drink that takes possession of someone'. Hence the noun anticipates the phrase which follows 'which deprives them of their understanding'. In support of this view is the fact that ibn Janāḥ explicitly derives the noun from the root ירש and, though he does not explain the reason for the name, he gives it the meaning new wine (Arabic *'lmṣṭ'r*), cf. Isa 65.8. Wolff's view that unfermented grape-juice is denoted does not accord with the context which requires intoxicating drink. For a full and up to date account of the word, see KB³, pp. 1591f.

[f]Lit. 'which takes away the heart'; the phrase is a short relative clause (i.e. without אשר, GK 155f–m), and the subject of the singular verb is the whole preceding phrase beginning with לשמר, cf. Rashi, ibn Ezra and Kimchi who state that each one of the vices deprives the people of their understanding. The 'heart' is the seat of thought and understanding, cf. Deut 29.3; Jer 5.21; Prov 7.7.

Verses 10 and 11 are understood to follow the sense of v. 9 and to set forth judgement upon both priest and people for, mutually interdependent, both have abandoned themselves (see notes a and c) to the profligacy of the cult. From now on their eating, as if cursed, will not bring them the satisfaction of nourishment and blessing. The punishment again fits the crime (see vv. 6f above). It is precisely because they have abused their appetites in the lavish (sacrificial) feasts to which they had allowed themselves to become accustomed that the blessing of food will be withheld (in, perhaps, famine, see on v. 3 above). For the blessing of (modest) eating, cf. Lev 26.5; Deut 8.10. Further, since priests and people (vv. 12–14) have abandoned themselves to promiscuity, their natural procreation[42], cursed henceforth, will cease. For the verb *prṣ* in the context of the blessing of progeny, cf. Exod 1.12; Isa 54.3. Wholesale preoccupation with sensuality (see note c), with drink and promiscuous sex, encouraged indeed by the sanction of supposedly Yahwistic religion, had dulled the wits of the nation and banished the ability of its people to think correctly (see note f). In fact, by their actions, they have deserted Yahweh (cf. Deut 31.16) and with him the knowledge of God that he required (cf. as so often, 6.6). Thus addiction to

42 Cf. Rudolph's similar but not identical remarks.

sensuality had made brute beasts of reasonable men (after Jerome).

The argument that the verse refers to the priests alone (so most commentaries; Marti, e.g., is an exception) usually rests upon the assumption that the 'eating' specifically follows from the reference in v. 8a to the priests 'feeding on the sin of the people' and upon the related argument that v. 9 is misplaced or a gloss. The latter argument has been countered above. In regard to the former it is urged that v. 8 in fact sets forth the mutual involvement of priest and people in the obnoxious cult for it is on the *sin of the people* that the priests feed. Further, if the priests encouraged (sacrificial) meals there is no question but that the people partook of them, as in 1 Sam 2[43]. Marti, then, is correct in seeing the punishment of v. 10 as devised for the whole people, the priests included.

With that understanding reference to promiscuity and its punishment is also consistent. It is not merely the priests who indulged in such behaviour, but priests and people as is made clear, e.g., by the reference in vv. 13f to daughters and daughters-in-law as well as by the reference in v. 15 to Israel's (*sc.* the nation's) promiscuity. Cf. also 'my people' (whether it is read with v. 11 or 12). Accordingly the theory (e.g. Harper, Mays, Wolff) that the promiscuity of this verse is specifically to be defined in terms of the priests, formally performing ritual fornication with cult prostitutes in sympathy with the *hieros gamos* is excluded. On the other hand such ideas may have infiltrated Yahwism and have given the sanction of this religion to the self-indulgence which clearly attended the cult of the hill-top shrines mentioned below (v. 13), in which the priests clearly took a leading part (again v. 13).

The verses, then, proclaim Yahweh's judgement on priest and people in accordance with the principle set forth explicitly in v. 9 and implied by the words of v. 8. The central position of the priests in the corruption of the people (all too willingly involved) reflects the centrality of the cult in the corruption of Yahwism and with it the attenuation of morality and the collapse of society itself.

43 The notion that the priests (v. 8) *alone* consumed the meat in accordance with the law of the sin-offering is excluded since, as it has been argued, there is in v. 8 no reference to the sin-offering.

Text and Versions

ולא יפרצו LXX καὶ οὐ μὴ κατευθύνωσιν 'and they will in no way prosper' (→ Wellhausen, יִתְרַצּוּ = they shall not delight themselves[44]); Symm. and Theod. καί οὐ πληθυνθήσονται, cf. Pesh. *wl' sgyw*, 'and they did not multiply'; Vulg. *cessaverunt*, i.e. 'ceaselessly'[45]; Targ. ולא יילדון בנין 'they will not beget sons'.

לשמר זנות ויין LXX τοῦ φυλάξαι πορνείαν. καὶ οἶνον κ.τ.λ.; Pesh. *wrḥmw znywt'*; these versions take זנות as the object of לשמר; Vulg. *in non custodiendo, fornicatio* etc. and Targ. ולא נטרו 'and they have not kept', agree with MT.

ויין The *waw* conjunctive is missing in 15 Kennicott/12 de Rossi MSS. In a sequence of three nouns, the second sometimes has *waw* and sometimes does not (cf. Rudolph). Ibn Ezra notes deficiency of *waws* (plural) and for this compares Hab 3.11. The presence or absence of *waw* does not constitute decisive evidence on the question of the verse division (cf. Rudolph).

לב Pesh. *lbhwn*, Targ. ליבהון 'their heart'.

4.12 **My people[a] seek revelations[b] from their [pieces of] wood[c], and their staves[d] tell them[e] [what to do]. For a promiscuous impulse[f] has led [them] astray [g]and they have betrayed their God by their promiscuity[g].**

[a]The phrase is emphatic and matches the final word of the MT, 'their God'. In the suffix 'my', the pain of Yahweh is emphatically expressed (so Rudolph)[46]. The view (so, e.g., Wolff, AF, *BHS*, Borbone, Jeremias) that the word should be read with the previous verse (so LXX, see Text and Versions), *viz.* (lit.) 'which takes away the heart of my people' is rejected since v. 11 is complete as it stands and the structure of 12a (3:3) is impaired by the removal of the word.

[b]The phrase שאל ב is technical and denotes the seeking of oracles, cf. Judg 1.1; 2 Sam 2.1; Ezek 21.26.

[c]Lit. 'his [block of] wood'. The antecedent of the third masculine suffix is the (collective singular) people. Here the view is taken that 'wood' refers sarcastically to a graven image (so Targum and ibn Ezra; cf. Jer 2.27; Hab 2.19; Isa 40.20; 44.13). It is possible, however, that since the word עץ can denote 'tree' as well as 'wood' that there is a reference to 'tree-oracles' (cf. Gen 12.6; Judg 9.37).

44 The emendation is unlikely. The Greek verb answers to, e.g., the root צלח but never to the root רצה, see Hatch and Redpath *ad loc.*

45 On the basis of this, Ruben proposes יִפָּרְצוּ; Grätz יֵעָצְרוּ.

46 Cf. Jerome, 'the people, once called by my very name'.

[d]Lit. 'his staff'. The word מקל can denote a 'branch', 'twig' (Gen 30.37; Jer 1.11) or a 'staff', 'wand'. Here the latter view is taken and the reference is understood to be to rhabdomancy. So *Sifre* Deut 18.8 (Friedmann, p. 218), 'the diviner seizes his staff and enquires, Shall I go or not go?'. So Jerome, comparing Ezek 21.26f. Alternatively, the word may again have to do with trees and perhaps specifically with the Asherah or cult-pole (cf. Deut 16.21; Judg 6.25ff etc.). The view that both words מקל/עץ denote phallus/penis ('he consults his stick, his rod directs him') is most unlikely to be correct[47].

[e]Lit. 'informs him', *sc.* of future events or what to do and what not to do (so Rosenmüller).

[f]Lit. 'a spirit (wind) of promiscuity'. The word רוח in such a phrase denotes 'movement of the mind' (Rosenmüller), 'uncontrolled or unaccountable impulse' (G. B. Gray *Numbers*, ICC, Edinburgh, 1912, p. 50). For similar phrases compounded of רוח, cf. Num 5.14 'fit of jealousy'; 1 Kgs 22.23 'lying impulse'; Isa 19.14 'perverse (NEB 'warped') attitude'.

[g]Lit. 'and they have acted promiscuously from under their God'; cf. (of an adulterous wife) Ezek 23.5. The preposition תחת implies obedience and proper subjection and מן has a privative force. The phrase denotes perfidious and high-handed rebellion. For Morag's view that the verb ויזנו may conceal a *Hiphil* (or *Yiphil*) form characteristic of Hosea, see above v. 10.

There is no need to see in vv. 11–14 a separate section (so, e.g., Rudolph) in which cultic transgressions are attacked. The verse continues logically from Yahweh's indictment of priest and people and from previous recognition that their joint abuse of the cult is the *fons et origo* of the breakdown of society and the impending doom for the whole nation (see on the verses above). Here, then, the stupidity of the worshippers, which is caused and encouraged by their addiction to sensual pleasure, is expounded. Yahweh's people, called by his very name (note a), are reduced to consulting blocks of wood and to acting at the bidding of rhabdomancy (see notes c and d) which has come to dominate their minds and has caused them, like an animal (Exod 23.4) or a drunken man (Isa 28.7), completely to lose their way (cf. Wolff).

The promiscuous impulse denotes, then, the contemporary *Zeitgeist* leading directly, in minds of those deprived of judgement, to repudiation of their God. Here is a classic definition from the eighth century BC of apostasy as promiscuity and whoredom, a definition taken up and developed by most

[47] *Contra* Ginsberg *The Prophets: Nevi'im* (Philadelphia, 1978), pp. 74f.

subsequent prophets and especially by Jeremiah and Ezekiel. It is this deranged reason which repudiates allegiance to the proper authority of God (note g) and which, for it, substitutes an easy allegiance to what is unworthy. Resort to idolatry (note c) and sorcery (note d) is analogous to the promiscuity of a faithless wife (so Kimchi). What is done self-indulgently by the nation leads to the certain doom of moral anarchy and enslavement to vice (cf. chapters 1–3).

Text and Versions

עמי LXX (καρδία) λαοῦ μου, taking 'my people' with what precedes in v. 11; see note a above.

בעצו LXX ἐν συμβόλοις 'omens', 'indications'; Pesh. *btr'yth* 'his mind', 'imagination'; Vulg. *in ligno suo*, cf. Targ. דבצלים אעיה 'his wooden image'.

מקלהו LXX καὶ ἐν ῥάβδοις αὐτοῦ ἀπήγγελλον αὐτῷ 'they were making pronouncement to him with staves'; Aq. ἐν ξύλῳ αὐτοῦ, Symm. ξύλου 'wood'; Pesh. *whwṭrh ḥwyh*; Targ. ומדמי דחטריה מחוי ליה '(and imagine that) his staff informs him', cf. Vulg. *et baculus eius adnuntiavit ei.*

התעה Third masculine plural pronouns are supplied as objects by Pesh., Targ. and Vulg., hence Grätz reads (with 2 Kennicott MSS – so Borbone) הִתְעָם and Marti הִתְעָהוּ; since LXX (in agreement with MT) does not have an object it is here supposed that the aforementioned versions supplied it *ad sensum* and that MT implied (if it did not read) הִתְעָהוּ.

4.13 **Upon the tops of the mountains they persist in their sacrificial meals[a], and upon the hills [b]they raise the smoke of their offerings[b] – under oak[c] and poplar[d] and terebinth[e], for their[f] shade is pleasant. For this reason[g] your daughters act promiscuously and your daughters-in-law[h] commit adultery[i].**

[a]The verb זבח means to kill an animal and partake in the sacral meal before and in fellowship with the god[48]. The *Piel* is intensive (so Kimchi) or iterative (e.g. Wolff) and the imperfect frequentative. For ibn Ezra the *Piel* is causative and the meaning is that 'they urge (the priests) to sacrifice ...'. Kimchi's view is here accepted as the more likely. The *Piel* is used of the abundant sacrifices made to Yahweh by Solomon (1 Kgs 8.5) and by Hezekiah (2 Chr 30.22); cf. Hos 8.13; 11.2.

48 Cf. de Vaux *IAT* 2, pp. 294, 307 = *IAI* pp. 417, 427.

[b—b]Lit. 'they send up in smoke'; for the verb קטר see on 2.15. The reference is to the smoke of the sacrificial offerings, whether or not seasoned by the addition of spices.

[c]The oak, *quercus*; a symbol of luxuriant strength (Amos 2.9).

[d]The poplar, *styrax officinalis*, mentioned elsewhere only in Gen 30.37. Rashi (cf. LXX below) thinks specifically of the white poplar, *populus alba*, probably by reference to the root לבן 'white'. The species is, however, not much found in Palestine/Israel and, when it is, it is usually cultivated[49].

[e]The terebinth, *pistacia palestina*. Ezek 6.13 speaks of the 'leafy terebinth'. The tree grows to a great age.

[f]It is likely that the feminine suffix is used to refer to the three trees not least because the oak, too, provides ample shade. For the third feminine singular suffix referring to plurals, see GK 135p.

[g]See on 4.3 above and commentary below.

[h]The word כלה denotes 'daughter-in-law' in reference to the husband's father and also 'brides', i.e., as in English, referring either to the time just before marriage or just after it (so BDB, *ad loc.*). Hence 'young wives' is appropriate provided that it is recognised that, in view of what follows (v. 14), the younger generation of young women is defined. On the term, see further L. Rost *Festschrift A. Bertholet*, pp. 451ff.

[i]The use of the verb נאף is precise for, as Rashi observes (on Exod 20.14), 'there is no adultery, except a man's wife be involved'.

The verse sets forth the connection between the self-indulgent and idolatrous worship of the sanctuaries and the moral decay of society. From the older generation to the younger the corruption is passed on; the example of the former prompts the excesses of the latter. Those who partake in such worship fail to appreciate (14b) that it is their own young, daughters and brides, who are tainted by corruption and not merely impersonal whores whom, they suppose, may be used as the objects of their lust. Again Hosea demonstrates a strong sense of the causal connections which may be perceived in the sphere of morality and human actions (cf. on 4.3).

The tops of the mountains and the hills are, from time immemorial, the natural sites for sacrificial worship. The question arises whether the trees are those associated also with the tops of the hills and which survive in modern Israel/Palestine in the *auliya* or Welis of the hill tops (e.g. Nabi Samwil, north of Jerusalem). Alternatively, the reference may be to shrines

[49] Cf. Qyl and Y. Felix, pp. 118, 247.

associated with sacred trees (e.g. the oak or terebinth at Shechem, Gen 35.4; Judg 9.6) whether or not they were city sanctuaries. The former interpretation is perhaps the more likely in view of Hosea's explicit desire to connect the aberrations of the beginning of the verse with those of its end. At all events, the phrase 'on every high hill and under every luxuriant tree' became a stereotype of licentious worship, e.g. Jer 2.20; 1 Kgs 14.23, cf. Deut 12.2 etc. and it is possible that Hosea's words were the origin of it, so W. L. Holladay *VT* 11 (1961), pp. 170ff. From these places went up the continual smoke of offerings and here the Israelites slaughtered for their frequent feastings (notes a and b). Under the pleasant shade of the trees, out of the heat of the sun, they partook of the meat, reserving, in the manner of *zbḥym*, the required portions for the altar and for the priests[50]. There gorged, inebriated with wine (v. 11), their consciences eased by the sanctions of religion, they indulged in sexual orgies with prostitutes and cult-women (v. 14), failing to perceive that such behaviour would lead to the corruption of their own young female relatives, swept up by the wind of promiscuity (v. 12). It is the causal connection[51] that Hosea emphasises and not least by the literary device in which 'their' actions in 13a, thus depicted, are shown in 13b to involve 'your very own' (with abrupt change to second masculine plural forms[52]) daughters and daughters-in-law.

Verse 13 belongs with and is elucidated by v. 14 (so rightly, e.g., Rudolph). The fundamental question arises whether the daughters etc. were involved formally in the sacral offering of their virtue in connection with the Canaanite fertility cult. For Wolff this is the case and the situation is illuminated by the well-known notice of Herodotus, Book 1 § 199, concerning such institutions in Babylonia. Arguments against Wolff's theory in relation to chapters 1–3 have been deployed above (see pp. 123ff). That the theory does not accord with the present verses is suggested by Hosea's particular argument in them; *viz.* that the cultic aberrations of the seniors of society redounded upon the young of their own families (so rightly Qyl). If Wolff's theory were correct, then the prior wickedness would be the formal requirement for all women to prostitute themselves.

50 De Vaux *IAT* 2, pp. 294ff = *IAI* pp. 417ff.

51 Ibn Ezra (cf. Kimchi) perceives the causal relation implied by *'l kn*, though by the implausible, if amusing, suggestion that the idolatry of the men-folk on the hills gave the women-folk at home an ideal opportunity to indulge in adultery and promiscuity.

52 *Contra BHS* which records a proposal to emend to third masculine plural suffixes.

According to these verses the prior wickedness, and that which consequentially gives rise to sexual wickedness, is the profligacy of the idolatrous worship of the sanctuaries.

For the second and related question which is raised by these verses, *viz*. the nature of the sexual malpractices defined in them, see on v. 14 below and consideration of the terms and language employed there.

Text and Versions

לבנה LXX and Aq. λεύκης 'white poplar'; Symm. and Theod. πεύκην (-ης) 'pine'; Vulg. *populum* 'poplar'; Targ. לבן; Pesh. *ḥwr'* 'white poplar'.

4.14 **I will not punish your daughters for their promiscuity[a] nor yet your daughters-in-law for their adultery[a]; for they themselves[b] associate[c] with prostitutes, [d]and with cult-women[d] they eat sacrificial meals. A people without discrimination[e] shall stumble in confusion[f]** or **are inflamed by lust[f].**

[a]Lit. 'because they act promiscuously', 'because they commit adultery': frequentative imperfects, as in the case of the next two verbs.

[b]Emphatic use of the masculine הם. Rudolph's emendation אדניהם 'the heads of their families' is not convincing since the emphatic use of 'they themselves' has a dramatic effect (see below).

[c]For ibn Janāḥ, the verb יפרדו denotes that they 'isolate and segregate themselves' (Arabic *ynfrdwn*, i.e. the cognate, *wyn'zlwn*), *sc*. with the prostitutes. So, e.g., BDB, KB[3]. For ibn Ezra the reference is to a number of men segregating themselves to a particular prostitute. For Kimchi, too, separation is the basic meaning, though for him the separation is specifically from the marriage bond[53]. He quotes his father's view that there is in the verb an allusion to the lustful yet distinctively infertile activity characteristic of the mule (פרד[54]) and the view of 'others' that the emphasis is upon sexual activity designed to avoid conception. The latter view has recently been advocated by Tur-Sinai (cf. Morag; *op. cit.*) who thinks of onanism (Gen 38.9), or other contraceptive intercourse, to which he sees an allusion in Prov 18.1. Such views are here discounted on the grounds that they rely ultimately

[53] Accordingly he interprets the *Piel* as causative: they separate wives from the marriage bond to have intercourse with them.

[54] Usually derived from פרד II in distinction from the homonymous root פרד I, so, e.g., BDB.

on Kimchi's father's view that the verb פרד can be interpreted by reference to the characteristics of the mule and to his confusion of what are probably two distinct roots. It is by no means likely that such complicated and contrived ideas were present in Hosea's mind. The parallelism of the verse, 'with cult-women they eat sacrificial meals', suggests that the verb denotes association more generally (sexual intercourse, though, is not excluded). Thus Rashi suggests that they associate with prostitutes in drinking wine. Rosenmüller quotes 'others' as saying that the *Piel* verb denotes the sharing (properly 'dividing') of the sacrificial meal as in 1 Sam 1.4f (though the verb פרד is not used there). Such a view is not wholly inconsistent with the etymology of the word[55].

The unique use of the *Piel*[56] in this verse together with the large number of interpretations of its meaning suggest that the usage is dialectal and that it cannot now certainly be determined. Ibn Janāḥ's view that the basic meaning is 'isolation and separation with' indicates that the word denotes an aspect of association with such women in the cult and that, by implication, such association involved or led to promiscuous sexual relations.

d—dThe word קדשות (here 'cult-women') seems to denote originally women who were consecrated as functionaries at cultic sanctuaries, cf. the LXX τετελεσμένοι, i.e. 'initiates'. Deuteronomy 23.18ff forbids any Israelite, of either sex, to become such a functionary and, apparently in association with this prohibition, gain derived from (?secular) prostitution is expressly forbidden in payment of a vow. The קדשים/ות are frequently mentioned in the OT, especially in the period of the monarchy 'when rites of foreign origin made their way into both Israel and Judah' (so S. R. Driver *Deut.*, p. 265), see 1 Kgs 14.24; 15.12; 22.47; 2 Kgs 23.7; Job 36.14. It is, then, very commonly assumed by modern scholars that the term denotes 'cultic prostitutes' who, after the manner of the Babylonian women described in Herodotus, 1 § 199, provided sexual services at temple sites in exchange for money (payable to the cult; cf. Wolff for the most uncompromising acceptance of the view that Hosea describes precisely such activities).

It should be noted that this common assumption has recently been vigorously challenged by M. I. Gruber[57] who reviews carefully the evidence of the Accadian and Canaanite cognate terms and concludes that there is no evidence to substantiate for them the meaning or

55 Cf. Arabic *frd* 'to assign or devote especially to someone' (ɪvth theme), e.g., Wehr *ad loc.* A. A. Wieder's suggestion, *JBL* 84 (1965), pp. 163f, that the word is to be illuminated by reference to the Ugaritic *ḫrd* (which occurs once only) 'to bring offerings' is unconvincing; cf., e.g., Gibson *CML*, p. 143.

56 The suggestion to read a *Niphal* (so, e.g., Grätz, *BHS*) is, in the absence of clear indications in its favour, unnecessary.

57 See *UF* 18 (1986), pp. 133–148. For his views on the biblical texts, see *Tarbiz* 52 (1983) pp. 167ff. For similar definition (and especially in regard to the payment of vows), see K. van der Toorn *JBL* 108 (1989), pp. 193ff.

function 'cultic prostitute(s)' in the literature of the people concerned. A number of functions associated with the god Adad are attested by the Accadian texts; they include (primarily) singing, acting as a midwife or wetnurse, and the mediating of purification rites. There is, moreover, no evidence that a *qadištu* was a funtionary of the cult of Ishtar, the goddess of erotic love (*contra*, e.g., BDB *ad loc.*). Where the Canaanite texts are concerned there is, again, no evidence from Ugaritic to substantiate the claim that a *qdšt* was a sacred prostitute. Rather, apart from the presence of the feminine word in personal or clan names, the masculine term seems to denote 'cultic singers' (*KTU* 1.112) and this accounts for their close association with priests in the administrative lists (*CTA* 75.1f (p. 165) and 77.1.3 (p. 166).

In the Hebrew bible the term קדשה seems to have been capable of meaning a prostitute *tout court*. In Gen 38.15, 21f, Tamar, clothed appropriately and acting as a prostitute, is described by this word without, in this instance, mention or allusion to cult or sanctuary.

Despite Gruber's protestation, we are relatively safe in accepting that there were sacred prostitutes (but called *harimtum* rather than *qadištum*)[58] associated with Babylonian temples in the early second millennium BC. Deuteronomy 23.18ff seems to imply similar activities in ancient Israel[59] though the Tamar story suggests that the word קדשה had come to mean (? also) simply a prostitute.

In the light of such considerations caution must clearly be exercised in evaluating the meaning of Hosea's words. It may be suggested that, in the context of cultic misdemeanours and in parallelism with הזנות 'prostitutes', the prophet uses the term הקדשות to denote women of loose morals who were closely associated with the syncretistic cult. His words do not necessarily imply that a sexual function was formally and *ex officio* part of their activities but rather that their presence at the sanctuaries (perhaps as singers) and their inclinations rendered them willing partners in the orgiastic practices described (cf. Rudolph's cautious remarks in interpreting their function). For a reference to sexual intercourse by Eli's sons with women ministering at the Tent of Meeting in Shiloh, see 1 Sam 2.22 and cf. Exod 38.8. A number of scholars (subscribing to the view that the word קדשות means 'cult-prostitutes') have been inclined to see in the juxtaposition of הקדשות and הזנות a distinction between public prostitutes and cult-women (so, e.g., Wolff, Rudolph). AF prefer to see the terms as 'mutually defining'. Such mutual definition may go some way towards an explanation of the established usage whereby קדשה came to denote in Hebrew simply a

[58] Cf. M. L. Gallery *Orientalia* 49 (1980), p. 338 and J. Spaey *Akkadica* 67 (1990), pp. 1ff. I am grateful to J. N. Postgate, Fellow of Trinity College, Cambridge, for guidance in assessing the Accadian evidence.

[59] Gruber's assessment of Deut 23.18ff seems to smack of special pleading; thus, that the male קדש in this text was (still) a 'cultic singer' while קדשה was (now) a 'prostitute' and that, in this way, Deuteronomy indicts together moral and cultic aberrations is surely far-fetched.

prostitute (as in the Tamar story). Euphemisms, *semper et ubique*, have a tendency to become established in language; cf. the use of the phrases 'escort services' or 'hostesses' in modern English to denote prostitution and prostitutes.

For the use of the definite article to determine a universally known, closely circumscribed, and therefore well defined class of persons, GK 126l.

[e]The phrase is a short relative; lit. 'a people who do not discriminate'.

[f]The verb לבט occurs only here and in Prov 10.8, 10 and in all three cases it is in the *Niphal*. Ibn Janāḥ compares the Arabic cognate with the sense I 'to throw to the ground' and VIII 'to tumble to the ground' (Arabic *'ltb'ṭ*), an expression which conveys 'dire lameness' (Arabic *'sw' 'l'rğ*). For ibn Ezra, too, the Arabic cognate suggests the meaning 'like a man immobilized[60] (משתבש) who does not know what to do'. Kimchi suggests the meaning 'to stumble' (כשל). The word is likely to denote, then, the fall of a lame man with its attendant confusion and panic. On this view, Hosea ends with a note of judgement and indicates the inevitable consequences of the people's foolish behaviour. An alternative interpretation is that of Morag[61]. Reviewing the evidence of comparative philology and emphasising the force of the Syriac cognate verb 'to incite', 'become excited', he believes that the reflexive denotes being overwhelmed by uncontrolled passion. Noting that the word is here found in the context of sexual misbehaviour and comparing the image of the oven in 7.4, Morag believes that such considerations point to the sense 'a people without understanding are inflamed by passion', i.e. they lose all balanced judgement and are totally in the grip of unbridled lust[62].

According to this view the phrase denotes Hosea's conclusion. The guilt of a society ('people') which has senselessly given itself to gross promiscuity lies primarily with its leaders and fathers who initiated such behaviour and who, by example, fostered it among the rising generations.

As in v. 4 above, where the prior responsibility for wickedness is laid at the door of the priests, so here responsibility for the contagious promiscuity which has infected even the young women of the Israelite family is held to be that of their seniors. Hence 'I will not punish' is relative rather than definitive and is to be understood specifically in the context of the apportionment

60 This rather than the later meaning 'confused'; see Jastrow *ad loc.* for the sense (horses' hooves) 'entangled' (in mud).

61 Pp. 504f; cf. Rudolph who, again by reference to the Syriac cognate, renders by *aufreizen* 'they are inflamed'.

62 In Proverbs, the fool, according to Morag, gives himself totally to his passionate anger and is no longer capable of balanced judgement.

of blame (so ibn Ezra)[63]. It is the fathers and seniors of the families who are to blame since they have used the cult as an opportunity to associate with prostitutes and cult-women. Examination of the language of the verse (notes c and d) suggests that there is not a reference here to sacral prostitution in the sense that sexual intercourse formally represented the 'sacred marriage' or intercourse between the heavens and earth as a prelude and a prompting of the fertility of the latter. As Rudolph observes, mention of cult-women together with regular prostitutes suggests that general depravity, prompted indeed by the feasting and wine-drinking of the sacrificial feasts, held sway on the hill tops and under the shady trees.

On the other hand, notices elsewhere (see note d) concerning the existence at sanctuaries of cult women (together with mention of them in this verse) suggest that the influence of Canaanite religion within Yahwism was considerable and extended beyond the adoption of the sacrificial practices typical of the former. The whole religion of Yahweh had, through the baleful influences and malpractices of the cult, degenerated into the worship of materialism, plenty and sensuality and hence was rightly characterised by Hosea as the worship of Baal. This indeed had been adopted by a people without discrimination (cf. v. 6); it was a nation whose foolishness had unleashed a force which destroyed family life and which would inevitably cause the nation to stumble in confusion, reducing it to the abject helplessness of a fallen cripple (note f). On the alternative view of the matter (note f) the nation's foolishness consists in its giving itself over to lustful passion, the frenzy of which has infected its whole fabric.

The view that the verse contains an indictment specifically of the priests (so, e.g., Harper, Wolff, AF, Jeremias) is here rejected. The verse forms part of the judgement upon the people as a whole for their stupidity and wickedness, a judgement which starts in v. 10 and which is defined by the more general statement of v. 9 that the whole people (priests included) would suffer the same punishment. If the priests, specifically, had been the object of the comments of this verse then 'they themselves' would scarcely be sufficient to indicate them. As it is, 'they themselves' picks up the third masculine plural references at the beginning of v. 13, a reference interrupted to great and dramatic effect by the second plural suffixes 'your very own daughters'

[63] Nyberg's suggestion that the phrase be understood as a negative question 'shall I not punish ...?' does not fit the context in which prior responsibility is set forth.

etc. That the verse concludes with the phrase 'a people without discrimination' is a further indication that the whole people is referred to by 'they themselves'.

Text and Versions

לא אפקד LXX adds καί, linking the verse more explicitly with the preceding.

יפרדו LXX συνεφύροντο, cf. Pesh. *ḥlyṭn* 'mingled with'; Aq. ἐχωρίζοντο 'separated with'; Theod. κατηριθμήθησαν 'counted, reckoned (themselves) with'; Vulg. *versabantur* 'they were occupied with'; Targ. מסתיען 'meet with'.

עם הקדשות LXX μετὰ τῶν τετελεσμένων 'with the inititates'; Aq. τῶν ἐνδιηλλαγμένων 'the sodomites'; Symm. τῶν ἀκαθάρτων 'the impure' (Jerome ἑταιρίδων 'courtesans'); Theod. βδελύγμασιν 'abominations'; Vulg. *cum effeminatis* 'with transvestites'; Pesh. *npqt šwq'*, cf. Targ. נפקת ברא 'street women'.

ילבט LXX συνεπλέκετο μετὰ πόρνης 'was entangled with a prostitute'; the first two words of the following verse were read with this verse and MT's אם as עם. For this understanding of לבט, cf. note f above. Pesh. *'pq znyt'* 'has embraced a prostitute' is somewhat similar (cf. Gelston, p. 167); Aq. δαρήσεται, cf. Vulg. *vapulabit* 'will be thrashed', 'afflicted'; Symm. παρελήφθη 'was captured'; Theod. ταραχθήσεται 'will be confounded'; Targ. אתרטיש 'will be abandoned/deserted'.

4.15 **(If you[a], Israel, behave promiscuously, let not Judah incur the punishment/guilt[b]. Do not come to Gilgal, nor go up to Bethaven, and [simultaneously][c] swear, As Yahweh lives.)**

[a]The pronoun is second masculine singular.

[b]The verb אשם comprehends the meanings (1) to commit an offence, (2) to be or become guilty, and (3) to be held guilty, bear punishment. The jussive following אל represents a plea to Judah not to follow Israel nor to learn its ways (cf. Rashi).

[c]The force of the final jussive clause is understood to denote, by parataxis, the enormity of the wickedness of idolatry undertaken simultaneously with ostensible loyalty to Yahweh. For the general sense (though in respect of formalism rather than idolatry), cf. Isa 29.13.

The verse is understood to be a gloss written by the Judaean redactor. The abrupt change to an address in the second person singular is remarkable and since, followed by a third person singular jussive, the likely sense is clumsily expressed[64], it is assumed that the redactor made use of a sentence written by Hosea in that form. It is now impossible to determine what the original sentence was but the *difficilis lectio* of the second person singular address suggests, perhaps, something like the contents of 9.1 '(Do not rejoice) Israel ... for you have behaved promiscuously ...'.

The reasons for supposing that the verse is a gloss are as follows: first, notwithstanding the second person singular address to Israel, the concern of the verse is to exhort Judah not to follow Israel's example. Accordingly the form of the sentence is, to say the least, extraordinary and highly contrived. That in itself suggests the work of a redactor or glossator who sought to redirect what lay before him to a new situation. Secondly, Hosea's concern is largely if not exclusively with Israel/Ephraim, the Northern Kingdom, and it is the editor of chapters 1–3 who is concerned to interpret Hosea's oracles in regard to Judah (cf. 1.7; 2.2; EV 1.11; 3.5). Thirdly, the condemnation of the Israelite people for their cultic corruption reaches a natural climax at the end of v. 14. In this passage condemnation of all the northern sanctuaries is subsumed and the prohibition of this verse in respect of two of them seems unnecessary to the argument (cf. Rudolph).

If, then, the verse is a gloss the words of its second part are likely to be derived from Amos 4.4 and 5.5 which are substantially similar. That Amos 5.5 is prior to this verse depends upon the consideration that Bethel is there so named but explicitly re-styled as Bethaven, whereas here it is named Bethaven *tout court*. The word-play by which the judgements upon Bethel and Gilgal are expressed in Amos 5.5 and the noticeable absence there of similar word-play judgement upon Beersheba, together with the absence of any mention of Beersheba in Amos 4.4, suggests that it was not present in the original text of Amos 5.5 but was added later to make Amos' words relevant also to southern sanctuaries. The presence in Hos 4.15 of a phrase ('swear') which uses the same root as appears in the name Beersheba suggests that the Judaean glossator had the later text of Amos 5.5 (i.e. including Beersheba) to hand and that he introduced or substituted a prohibition based upon an

[64] Thus, e.g., the omission of אתה from the phrase would give 'If Israel behaves promiscuously, let not Judah incur ...'.

element in that name[65]. It is possible also that the phrase 'seek Yahweh and live' in Amos 5.6a (containing 'Yahweh' and 'live') influenced his choice of words.

Gilgal is probably to be equated with Khirbet el-Mefjer in the Jordan valley near Jericho[66] (cf. Josh 5.2ff). It is likely that it (in common with others) was reconstituted as a sanctuary by the Israelites following the destruction of Shiloh (so Qyl, citing 1 Sam 10.8 etc.). Bethel is identified with Beitin beside the road which runs down from Ramallah to Jericho (some fifteen kilometres north of Jerusalem)[67]. The verb used ('go up') is entirely appropriate to this sanctuary high in the Ephraimite mountains which, of old, was the scene of Jacob's dream (Gen 28.12ff), and of Jeroboam I's setting up a golden calf (1 Kgs 12.29).

Its designation Bethaven 'house of wickedness' seems to derive from the judgement of Amos 5.5 and thereafter to have become a standard prophetic and deuteronomic designation of the place (see footnote 67)[68]. Hosea also uses the term *'wn* of cultic elevations (10.8) and of the inhabitants of the city of Gilead (6.8; 12.12). For Kimchi the name denotes 'evil and falsehood' (*'wn wšw'*, cf. Hos 12.12, EV 11), in view of the placement there of the golden calf.

The two sanctuaries are near the Judaean border and, in the period following the subjection of the Northern Kingdom by Assyria, it is highly likely that Judaeans were tempted to make use of these old sanctuaries (cf. Rudolph). Hence the Judaean

65 *Contra* Rudolph's view that Beersheba is original to Amos 5.5 and that it has dropped out of this text by homoeoteleuton (cf. Wellhausen, Nowack, Harper). I regard Amos 8.14 as a later addition (cf. Rudolph *Amos*) and therefore inadmissable as evidence here (*contra BHS*).

66 Cf. J. Muilenburg *BASOR* 140 (1955), pp. 11ff and K. Galling *ZDPV* 66 (1943), p. 145. Qyl (on the view that the verse is genuine) mentions the possibility that 'Gilgal' denotes the sanctuary of Dan or another near Shechem (cf. Deut 11.30), today Jaljuliya. For the latter, cf. the thesis of Sellin *Gilgal* (Leipzig, 1917). It is unlikely, on the view taken here, that Judaeans would be tempted to resort to sanctuaries so far from their borders.

67 For the view that an old alternative name for the settlement (distinguished from the sanctuary just east of the city, properly called Bethel, Gen 28.19; Josh 16.1f) was Bethon ('house of riches') which lent itself to the pejorative name Bethaven 'house of wickedness', cf. van Gelderen, p. 122. See also Schunck, p. 155 n. More recently Z. Kallai *Bethaven*, pp. 176ff, has challenged all such conclusions. He argues that the sanctuary and town of Bethel were practically identical but that Bethaven was originally a separate place, north of Michmash. The important point, however, is that Bethaven becomes (following Amos) a pejorative prophetic term for the royal cult centre Bethel. Hos 5.8 is *sui generis*; see below.

68 Josh 7.2; 18.12; 1 Sam 13.5; 14.23.

redactor appended to Hosea's general condemnation of the nefarious worship of the northern sanctuaries a warning, expressed in the words of his earlier compatriot Amos to his contemporaries, against incurring the guilt and punishment which the North had so richly deserved. Cf. Rashi (though, of course, not on critical grounds): the Judaeans must not learn the ways of the northerners; if Israel sins, then the Judaeans are not necessarily guilty and provided that they do not go to Gilgal or Bethel 'the House of Judah will I love' (Hos 1.7).

The injunction 'Do not swear, as Yahweh lives' is illustrated by Deut 6.13 'You shall fear Yahweh your God, serve him alone and take your oaths in his name', and by Jer 5.2 'Men may swear by the life of Yahweh, but they only perjure themselves' (so Rashi, ibn Ezra and Kimchi). Thus to swear 'As Yahweh lives' implies total commitment to him and to his laws and is inconsistent with participation in the worship of the idolatrous sanctuaries. As Rashi observes, 'in that they swear falsely, they invoke the name of heaven; in that they swear truly, they invoke the Baals'. The general sentiment, though not a genuine word of Hosea, is wholly consistent with the thought and with the burden of his message.

Two alternative treatments of the verse may be mentioned: (1) Wolff, taking the first two words of this verse with v. 14, regards the word 'Judah' alone as a gloss. Accordingly he emends the text to 'Israel, do not be guilty' (*t'šm* for MT's *y'šm* comparing the LXX, see Text and Versions). His solution depends upon his assumption that the verse belongs with the condemnation specifically of the priests and that it pleads with Israel not to be involved in their transgression. That assumption is, in my view, ill-founded (see on vv. 9ff) as is the assumption that the word *znh* belongs to v. 14. (2) Emmerson regards the phrase 'let not Judah incur guilt' as a Judaean gloss. Hence, Hosea's original words were 'If you, Israel, play the harlot, do not enter ... and do not swear ...'. Yet, as mentioned above, it is unlikely that Hosea would mention particular sanctuaries in the context of a general indictment of cultic transgression; and also there are considerations in favour of the priority of Amos' formulation of similar words.

Text and Versions

זנה See on the previous verse.

אל יאשם LXX μὴ ἀγνόει 'do not go wrong' (i.e. second masculine singular) is likely to follow from the initial (mistaken) taking of זנה with the previous verse. It is less likely that תאשם was in the text before the translators. Pesh. *l' tḥyb lyhwd'* '(Israel), do not render Judah guilty' takes the same process further, yielding a highly improbable sense. Aq., Symm. and Theod. μὴ (συμ)πλημμελείτω 'let not (Judah) offend', cf. Vulg. *non delinquat*, and Targ. (pl.) יתחייבון.

בית און LXX εἰς τὸν οἶκον Ὤν; Aq., Symm., Theod. (but for details and variants, see Field) ἀνωφελοῦς 'vanity'; Vulg. *Bethaven*; Targ. בית אל; Jerome expresses surprise at the LXX reading, and suggests that it is a mistake (his argument is, however, obscure; see Migne *ad loc.* and his comments, cf. Rosenmüller). The reading is, in my view, merely a matter of pronunciation, cf. Pesh. *byt 'wn*, the latter word pointed with two *zqāphās*.

4.16 **Surely Israel has become stubborn[a] like a stubborn heifer. Should Yahweh now[b] feed them as lambs[c] on a wide pasture?**

[a]Ibn Ezra connects the (double *ayin*) word סרר with סור 'to turn aside'. The סורר is the man who habitually turns aside from the way and Israel is likened to a heifer which, turning aside, is useless for ploughing. It is likely, however, that there is a distinct double-*ayin* root, cf. BDB and KB^3 *ad locc.* The sense is rebelliousness and intractability (cf. Deut 21.18, 'a son who is disobedient and out of control'). For the pausal form with *zaqeph qaṭon*, GK 29i.

[b]עתה is used to denote a conclusion in view of what has been stated (so BDB p. 774, col 2 b, cf. 1 b). Accordingly ibn Ezra (so Kimchi) sees in the whole sentence a conditional force, 'Had you not become obdurate, God would have pastured you like a sheep'. The same force is obtained by treating 16b as an interrogative phrase (so Abarbarnel, cf., e.g., Rudolph and, for questions without the interrogative particle, König, 353a, b). An alternative treatment is offered by Rashi (cf. ibn Ezra and Kimchi): Now, in view of their obduracy, God will feed them as a (single) sheep on a wide (and scanty) pasture rather than as a heifer fed on (plentiful) barley and vetch (Rashi); or as a (single) sheep which wanders bleating and distracted in a wide pasture and consequently does not feed properly (ibn Ezra and Kimchi). The former interpretation is the more likely since the verb רעה and the noun מרחב are elsewhere used of a good situation (cf. Ps 18.20; 31.9; 118.5 and, with Kimchi, the phrase in Isa 30.23).

[c]The noun כבשׂ is here understood as a collective singular (so Kimchi's father) which fits better the plural suffix of 'feed them'.

The section vv. 16–19 forms a unity in that its contents depict judgement upon Israel/Ephraim for their cultic wickedness. The form is now that of the prophetic oracle rather than a judgement expressed directly in Yahweh's name. This suggests, perhaps, that the sayings were placed here by a redactor on the basis of the catchword *hznw* 'acted promiscuously' (v. 18) which then follows *tznynh* 'acted promiscuously' (v. 14). That the redactor was dealing already with a small collection (vv. 16–19) is likely in view of apparent word connections in the verses (*srr* v. 16, cf. *sr* v. 18, and *prh* v. 16, cf. *'prym* v. 17; so Rudolph[69]). It is further likely that the addition of v. 15 (*q.v.*) directed the piece as a warning to Judah not to do as Israel/Ephraim had done.

The image of the recalcitrant heifer is usually understood to mean that she twists and bends herself when the yoke of the plough is imposed and thus becomes useless to the task (cf. the Peshiṭta, ibn Ezra and Kimchi). Jerome renders 'like a frisky (*lasciviens*) cow', i.e. frenzied as if stung by a gad-fly (cf. the LXX)[70]. His choice of words, however, may imply that he understands Hosea to mean that the behaviour of the cow is an accurate image of Israel's, a nation smitten indeed by a spirit of promiscuity and frenzied indulgence. The Targum and Rashi, too, think of rebellion induced by a surfeit of food and drink. Rudolph suggests that the specific mention of a cow implies its rebellious and wilful refusal of a bull (for which he might have compared Judg 19.2 where the behaviour of the Levite's concubine (*wtznh 'lyw*) may imply similar conduct[71]). At all events, the metaphor denotes Israel's recalcitrant behaviour and rebellion against her God (cf. with Rudolph, v. 12 and Jer 2.20).

If, then, Israel behaves in such a way, why should Yahweh feed its citizens as lambs (note c) in a wide pasture (note b)? In the circumstances (note a) he is hardly likely to respond to stubborness by reward but rather by punishment.

Weiser has seen in 16b an allusion to the motif of Yahweh as a shepherd of his people, cf. Ps 23. Accordingly the sense is: if Israel is recalcitrant then there is no reason why Yahweh should continue his providential care of his people. Another allusion is seen by Qyl: in Deut 33.17 Joseph is described as a 'first-born ox'. Hence, in a passage referring to Ephraim (of which Joseph was an ancestor), the image is particularly appropriate as an

[69] AF suggest also a word-play in *bmrḥb* (v. 16) and *ḥbwr* (v. 17).

[70] There is the possibility that the LXX (and Jerome) are here relating the phrase to the well-known Greek legend of Io, changed into a heifer and stung by a gad-fly (see, e.g., J. Schmidt *Dictionnaire de la mythologie grecque et romaine* (Paris, 1965), *ad loc.*

[71] So ibn Janāḥ on זנה in the verse.

adaptation of a traditional description. Rosenmüller similarly compares Deut 32.15 'Jeshurun grew fat and unruly ... he forsook God who made him'.

Text and Versions

סררה LXX παροιστρῶσα 'driven mad', 'frenzied'; Aq. and Theod. ἐκκλίνουσα 'shying'; Symm. ἐπιθυμοῦσα 'eager', 'desirous', cf. Vulg. *lasciviens* 'frisky', 'lascivious'; Pesh. *dmrdt mn nyr'* 'that rebels from the yoke'; Targ. דאתפטים ובעט 'that is fattened and kicks/is rebellious'; Pesh., Targ. and CD i. 13–14 add *hknh*/כין/כן after סררה, cf. Gelston, pp. 116, 118.
ככבש Pesh. *'mr'* 'lambs' (plural), perhaps influenced by *'nwn* three words earlier; the other versions, singular.

4.17 **Ephraim is yoked[a] to idolatry[b]; leave him alone[c].**

[a]The verb חבר denotes 'to bind', 'unite', 'join' and its form (uniquely here) is passive. Kimchi paraphrases with 'cleaves to', 'clings to' (דבוק), and Rashi with 'yoked to' (נצמד). The latter word is adopted here in translation to convey the notions of close association and simultaneous servitude.

[b]עצבים Lit. 'idols'. The usage here is almost *abstractum pro concreto* (cf. Rashi). The word denotes strictly the fashioned images of gods but here, as in Isa 10.11 where it is parallel to אלילים 'false-gods', it denotes such gods themselves (cf. Ps 106.36; Zech 13.2). Ibn Ezra compares Jer 22.28 and עצב נבזה 'a despised vessel' (as carved, fashioned) in order to distinguish the word from what today is regarded as the root עצב I[72]. Having done so, however, he suggests that all idolatry is toil and pain and thus elucidates a conscious word-play of Hosea (cf. Rudolph).

[c]*Hiphil* (b form) imperative second masculine singlar from the verb נוח, with the sense 'refrain from interfering with' (so BDB *ad loc.*; cf. Exod 32.10; 2 Sam 16.11; 2 Kgs 23.18). See further in the commentary below and under Text and Versions.

Ephraim is an alternative title of the Northern Kingdom since that tribe was the dominant one and from it came the first king Jeroboam I, the son of Nebat, after the division of the united kingdom (1 Kgs 11.26). It is found in parallelism with Israel (v. 16) also in 5.3, 5; 11.8. Ephraim is yoked to idolatry;

72 Cf., e.g., BDB *ad loc.* for עצב I, 'to hurt', 'pain', 'grieve' and עצב II 'to shape', 'fashion'.

constant practice has led to national addiction (note a) for which there is no remedy (so Kimchi).

The idolatry (note b) to which Israel is addicted consists of the golden calves of Bethel and Dan, Baal and Asherah (so Kimchi) or else the oracular devices mentioned in v. 12 above. It is in the frequent practice of the cultic festivals (ostensibly in the name of Yahweh) that the addiction is caught by a people who lack the discrimination to resist and repudiate it. They are enslaved by the toil and pain of their idolatry (note b).

They are to be left alone since they are beyond redemption. The closing imperative (note c) is thus an expression of intensity (cf. Jer 2.19) reflecting the degree of Israel's addiction and the prophet's despair at it[73]. As Kimchi observes the saying is true to life: as, when a man is angry with a friend who refuses to listen to his reproof, he says 'I will desist from reproving you for ever, since you do not listen'; yet within an hour he returns to the task. Accordingly attempts to determine the subject of the imperative are likely to be misleading not least since they frequently entail consequential emendation of the text. Thus Jerome, comparing v. 15, interprets the imperative as addressed to Judah imploring that country not to follow Ephraim's folly. On the basis of a similar interpretation, Marti regards the phrase as a gloss added in the same sense as v. 15. Again, Rudolph, sensing a contradiction between the warning of v. 15a and the fatalistic expression here, emends the text to read *hn(h) ḥyl* (or *yḥyl*) *lw*, 'Behold, he will writhe (in pain)'. Such endeavours seem to me to be ill-founded[74].

Text and Versions

חבור LXX μέτοχος 'partaking in', cf. Symm. ἡνώθη, Pesh. *šwtp'*, Vulg. *particeps*, Targ. אתחברו.

הנח לו LXX ἔθηκεν ἑαυτῷ σκάνδαλα 'he has made for himself stumbling-blocks' is interpretative rather than suggestive of a different Hebrew text, *contra* → הניח לו מכשול (Grätz); for van Hoonacker

[73] For Rashi (cf. Kimchi) the imperative is addressed by God to the prophet.

[74] Mays, following Aquila and Theodotion, reads הֵנִיחַ לוֹ conjoining the words with the beginning of the next verse: 'he has fallen in with a crowd of drunkards'. AF also read the text as Mays (but without including words from the following verse): 'he (*sc.* Yahweh) has abandoned them for himself'. Both suggestions seem to me to be improbable. Amongst earlier treatments of the text that of Müller *TSK* 67 (1904), p. 124 deserves consideration. Reading הנח לו and interpreting it as a short relative he finds the sense 'Ephraim is yoked to idols which he has set up for himself', cf. 2 Kgs 17.29.

σκάνδαλα is a second translation of עצבים; Aq. and Theod. ἀνέπαυσεν ἑαυτῷ (ἄρχων συμποσίου αὐτῶν) 'the ruler of their feast has ceased'; the last three words (Aq. only) derive from the following verse (*q.v.* below); for Symm. ἔασον αὐτόν, Vulg. *dimitte eum*, Pesh. *šbwqw lh*, cf. MT; Targ. שבקו להון ית פולחני 'abandon them to idolatry'.

4.18 **Their liquor at an end[a], they give themselves to promiscuity[b]; they fornicate wildly[c]; their[d] canopies[e] are canopies of disgrace.**

[a]For סור 'to come to an end', see BDB p. 694, col 1 4. The perfect is understood to have a temporal force '(when) their liquor is gone, they ...'. (cf. GK 164b). סבא 'liquor'; it is uncertain whether wine or beer is denoted (see KB[3] *ad loc.*). Rudolph avoids the question by understanding the word as an infinitive construct, 'when their carousing is finished'. The *athnaḥ* beneath סבאם suggests to Qyl that the Massoretes understood the phrase as absolute (and not temporal) and that it had the sense 'their liquor is ruined/spoiled' as in Isa 1.22 'your liquor is diluted with water'. Rashi, comparing Jer 2.21 and the root זור, detects in the verb notions of what is degenerate and loathsome (*sc.* to Yahweh). Kimchi, by reference to Aramaic סרי, gives to the verb the meaning, the liquor stinks in their mouths. On the assumption that an *ayin waw* verb with this sense existed in Hebrew (for which I find no evidence), it is possible that the sense is '(still) reeking of liquor, they give themselves ...'. At all events, the interpretation may be indicative of Hosea's meaning, *viz.* that the drinking bouts led on to licentious promiscuity.

Amongst a number of emendations (two others, e.g., are listed below under Text and Versions) mention may be made of Houtsma's[75] suggestion (cf. *BHS*) סד סְבָאִים 'a company of drinkers, they give themselves ...'. The suggestion is discounted on the grounds that the paronomasia of the verses (סרר in v. 16, צרר in v. 19) is spoilt.

[b]The infinitive absolute followed by the finite perfect is a regular expression of intensity, cf. note c below and 4.10; 5.3. The *Hiphil* is understood to be an internal *Hiphil* expressing characteristic behaviour (cf. GK 53f)[76].

[c]אהבו הבו An emphatic form (so Morag, pp. 499f), in which the second and third radical are reduplicated to make a five-letter word (*pe'al'al*). Other forms attested are חמרמרו (Lam 2.11) and יפיפית (Ps 45.3). The presence of *waw* after the first part of the word is unique. The reason may be that the form is derived from repetition of the full verb: אהבו אהבו → אהבהבו but here אהבו הבו (?Hosea's dialect).

[75] *ThT* 9 (1875), p. 60.

[76] For Morag's treatment of the verb, *op. cit.* p. 500.

According to ibn Janāḥ, who earlier had taken a similar view, the word is contracted from the forms אָהֲבוּ אָהֵב and the *tsere* in MT is an indication that the second word, though now abbreviated, is from the verb אהֵב (i.e. with its characteristic *tsere*). The printing of two words (rather than one) goes back to the manuscript tradition which had forgotten the true nature of reduplicated verbal forms[77]. As Morag indicates, Hosea, when using language of love and sexuality, has a marked tendency to use emphatic or intensive forms[78]. The translation 'they fornicate wildly' seeks to convey this force.

For Rashi, ibn Ezra and Kimchi the word הֵבוּ (*sic*) is from the root יהב and denotes 'Give!' (second masculine plural imperative). The leaders and princes (see note e below) love the command 'give' which, frequently on their lips, expresses their inordinate desire to receive bribes in return for the perversion of justice (ibn Ezra and Kimchi). For Rashi הבו (conjoined with קלון), having the same etymology, denotes an exhortation to indulge in disgraceful conduct, lit. 'Come on, let us ...' as in Gen 11.3 and Exod 1.10; thus the princes and leaders love the exhortation to disgraceful conduct. Rudolph takes a similar view and cites Gen 38.16 where הבה, masculine(!) singular imperative, is used as an invitation to a harlot. These endeavours seem to me to be too contrived to be likely. For the view that הבו is a partial dittograph, see Text and Versions.

Amongst emendations, mention may be made of Simson's suggestion to read אהוב אהבו, whereby the *figura etymologica* of the preceding phrase is reproduced (so, also, e.g., Wolff, Mays).

[d]The third feminine suffix 'her' is here interpreted as a reference to the people of Israel. The same suffix occurs in the following verse (*q.v.*) and, juxtaposed to the third masculine verbal forms, it has a collective force (GK 135p).

[e]The translation 'canopy' is advocated by Morag (pp. 500f) as appropriate to the context in which sexual love is described. The root גנן is attested with the sense 'to cover' whence the notions of protection and safety (cf. especially מגן 'shield'). In Lam 3.65 מגנת לב denotes the covering of (i.e. hard shell around, BDB) the heart. Hence Morag suggests the specific meaning 'canopy' since the well-known *ḥuppah* with this sense shows a very similar semantic development (from חפף 'to cover', 'enclose') and the cognate Aramaic *ğnwn' ğnn', ğnnyt'* all denote 'enclosure', 'canopy'. In Hosea's use of the word two particular motifs are discernible: first, a contrast between 'honour', 'prestige' and 'shame', 'ignominy' already expressed in 4.7 (*q.v.*). Isa 4.5, 'for glory shall spread over all as a covering and a canopy' (cf. *BHS* and NEB), attests to the association elsewhere of *ḥuppah* with glory. Here in Hosea

[77] Cf. Morag, p. 500 n. 42 and BL, p. 285.

[78] Cf. the similar forms: from נאף in 2.4, נאפופיה and from זנה זנונים in 1.2 and 2.4 (EV 2).

the reverse is expressed. Secondly, the word *ḥuppah* is associated with bride and bridegroom (Joel 2.16; Ps 19.6). In a context in which Hosea attacks specifically sexual promiscuity, he mockingly describes such activity as perpetrated under a 'canopy of disgrace'. One might add that the allusion here may well be to v. 13 and to the pleasant shade of the trees described there[79].

For Jerome and the rabbinic commentators (ibn Janāḥ, Rashi, ibn Ezra and Kimchi) the word denotes the kings and princes of the people[80]. The sense of the phrase is then 'her rulers are shame, ignominy'.

G. R. Driver, *JTS* 34 (1933), p. 383[81] suggests that the word is illuminated by the Arabic root *mǧn* and specifically the adjective *māǧîn* 'shameless', 'insolent'[82]. Accordingly he renders 'her impudent ones love shame'. The meaning seems to me to be weak, if not tautologous. On the other hand, if such a word existed in ancient Hebrew, Hosea's choice of מגן 'canopy' (on that view of the matter) may reflect an element of word-play in view of its juxtaposition to קלון 'disgrace'.

C. Rabin, *SH* 8 (1961), p. 389, has suggested that the word, pointed, is derived from a noun מגן with the meaning 'reward', 'gift' (cf. the rabbinic exposition of הבו, note c) for which he compares Phoenician and Aramaic evidence. Hence the translation 'shame is the reward thereof' (cf. Rudolph). The theory seems to me to produce a sense which, though in itself reasonable, is not as suited to the context as that of Morag.

Amongst emendations, mention may be made of the common suggestion (e.g. Houtsma, Grätz and NEB) that מִגְּאוֹנָם be read following the reading of the LXX (*q.v.* below), 'they have preferred ignominy to their glory'.

The verse depicts with sharp realism the carousals at the sanctuaries and their degeneration into the sexual licence in which priest and people, devoid of discrimination, allow themselves to become involved. Apart from the vocabulary (for which see above), there is no new argument or train of thought and the verse expresses, with some mockery (note e), what has been attacked earlier in the chapter.

79 Nyberg (p. 34) thinks the word מגן here denotes gardens in which idolatry was practised. Accordingly 'her' denotes a Canaanite goddess.

80 For מגן with this meaning, see the literature cited in my *Isaiah XXI*, p. 26 n. 4.

81 So KB, KB³, Wolff, Mays.

82 Driver finds other instances in Prov 6.11 and 24.34.

Text and Versions

סר סבאם LXX ᾑρέτισεν χαναναίους 'he has chosen the Canaanites'; Harper suggests that the verb is an internal Greek corruption of an original ἠρέθισε, a reading attested by Jerome (*provocavit* C.). The verb would answer to סר (from סרר) with a causative meaning 'he has made the Canaanites stubborn'. For סֹבְאִים (*sic*) = drunkards = Canaanites, cf. I. Zolli *ZAW* 56 (1938), p. 175. Aq. ἀνέπαυσεν ἑαυτῷ ἄρχων συμποσίου αὐτῶν (see on the previous verse; the first two words derive from it); Symm. ἐπέκλινε τὸ συμπόσιον αὐτῶν, cf. Theod. ἐπέκλινε τὸν οἶνον αὐτῶν 'he lay down at his feast/his (their) wine'; Pesh. omits the phrase, cf. Gelston, p. 146; Vulg. *separatum est convivium eorum* 'their feast is (to be) distinct (from yours, Judaeans)', cf. his commentary; Targ. שלטוניהון אסגיאו שיריאן אונים 'their rulers increase feasts from extortion'; it is possible that this translation (cf. Aq.) derives from a reading שׂר for סר which is likely to have been originally merely an orthographic variant. → סָבְאוּ סָבָא 'they carouse', H. Torczyner BZAW 41 (1925), p. 277, cf. Wolff.

אהבו הבו LXX ἠγάπησαν ἀτιμίαν (with קלון), cf. Pesh. *wrḥmw z'r'*; Symm. ἠγάπησαν ἀγάπην, cf. MT; Vulg. *dilexerunt adferre* (*ignominiam*) 'they love to bring (disgrace)' ? taking הבו as an infinitive from יהב, 'provide', cf. Targ. רחימו דייתי להון קלנא 'they love what brings disgrace to them'; הבו is omitted as dittography (cf. LXX and Pesh.) by, e.g., Borbone, cf. *BHS*.

קלון מגניה LXX (BQ[A]) ἀτιμίαν ἐκ φρυάγματος αὐτῆς (AQ* αὐτῶν); the word φρυάγματος suggests (cf. Jer 12.5) מִגְּאֹנָם, see note e above; Symm. οὗ ἡ βοήθεια ἀτιμία 'whose help is dishonour' (cf. the notions of protection in מגן); Pesh. ... *z'r' wdḥlt'* 'disgrace and dread (or false religion)'; the latter word has suggested the emendation מְגוֹרֶיהָ (cf. Rudolph, who rejects it); Vulg. ... *protectores eius* 'his defenders', 'rulers' (cf. note e above), cf. Targ. רברביהון 'their lords'; → קְלוֹן גַּנֵּיהֶם 'the shame of their gardens' (*BHS*).

4.19 **The wind has confined[a] them[b] in her wings[c]. They shall[d] be confounded[e] by reason of their sacrificial feasts[f].**

[a]For the verb צרר similarly construed with ב, cf. Job 26.8, 'he has confined water in his clouds'[83]. That רוח is feminine is confirmed by the third feminine singular suffix of 'wings'. The verb preceding the noun may, however, take a masculine form; GK 145o, König, 345b. For the possibility that the phrase has a metaphorical sense 'to remember', see

[83] Rabin's argument (*op. cit.* p. 398) that the meaning here is illuminated by Arabic *ṣrr* 'to sweep away' is unconvincing since such a meaning for the Arabic verb is far from certain (cf. Rudolph).

below. The use of the verb here reflects by paronomasia סרר (v. 16) and סר (v. 18).

[b]The feminine pronominal object refers to the people, cf. note d on v. 18. Hence the translation 'them' (so already Kimchi). Emendation to אתם (so, e.g., Oort, Borbone, cf. *BHS*) is unnecessary.

[c]The word כנף denotes 'wing' and also 'skirt' as an extremity of clothing (cf. BDB *ad loc.*). The Arabic cognate verb denotes 'to hedge in', 'surround'.

An alternative translation seems to be indicated by Aquila, the Peshiṭta and Symmachus (*q.v.* below), ibn Ezra and Kimchi: roughly 'as for the wind, he binds it in his skirts' (for which there is the difficulty of the third feminine singular suffix of wings/skirts, so Rosenmüller); see further below.

[d]Probably simple *waw* with imperfect rather than an expression of purpose or wish.

[e]Lit. 'they shall be ashamed' but here the opposite of Ps 25.3 'all who wait for thee shall not be confounded', i.e. disappointed, disillusioned.

[f]The feminine plural of זבח occurs only here and may reflect northern dialectal usage (cf. Nyberg, van Gelderen). Wellhausen supposes that the text represents a corruption (by haplography) of ממזבחותם 'of their altars' (cf. LXX, Peshiṭta and Targum below). Rashi suggests that the feminine form זבחה denotes the place of sacrificial meals.

For Rashi the image is that of a bird swept away by the wind which cleaves to its wings allowing the bird no rest until it has carried it far off. Thus the nation will be swept into exile by the advent of its enemies (cf. the Targum and Jeremias). Rashi also suggests that the phrase may reflect the midrashic usage[84] whereby to bind (a matter) in another's skirts or lap indicates solemnly to remember. In *Canticum Rabbah* (9b, Ct 1.7) the expression is found 'I (*sc.* God) will tie this up in thy lap (*bknpyk*)[85], i.e. I shall remember and visit this act upon thee' (Jastrow p. 1305, col 1). Accordingly for Rashi the whole expression denotes that Yahweh's anger is firm and that he is resolute in his desire for vengeance.

For ibn Ezra and Kimchi the metaphor is that of a man who binds mere wind in his clothing and, when he loosens it, he finds nothing. Hence Ephraim's addiction to idolatry will bring in the

[84] See Ben Yehuda, p. 5659.

[85] Jastrow's view that 'thy' lap is reverential for 'my' (*sc.* God's) lap would fit the metaphor here more precisely in that it is the wind which binds up Ephraim in its skirts, and solemnly remembers its wickedness.

end nothing but harm and scarcity. The difficulty attending this interpretation has been outlined above (note c).

The wind is here, as elsewhere in Hosea (cf. 13.15), an agent of Yahweh's justice and judgement. There is here no reference to the 'promiscuous impulse' (lit. 'wind of promiscuity', v. 12) *contra* Jerome's *spiritus diaboli* and, e.g., Wolff, Mays. If Rashi's estimate of the metaphor is correct, the wind (as God's agent) solemnly witnesses and remembers the wickedness of the people. Indeed they have sown the wind and shall reap the whirlwind (8.7). The verse expresses a fitting conclusion to an indictment of considerable power and sustained argument.

Text and Versions

צרר רוח אותה LXX συστροφὴ πνεύματος σὺ εἶ 'you are a whirlwind'; the last two words confirm MT (אותה); the alternative reading of some LXX MSS (Q[mbg], L[49], C[239] – so Ziegler) συριεῖ 'will whistle', represents a further development (or degeneration) of the tradition. Aq. ἐνδεσμῶν πνεῦμα αὐτῆς 'binding up her wind ...', cf. Symm. ὥσπερεί τις δήσειε τὸν ἄνεμον 'as if someone were to bind up the wind ...' (cf. note c above); Pesh. *tṣṭrr* 'will be bound up ...' (*contra* Harper); Vulg. *ligavit spiritus eam in alis suis* = MT; Targ. כמא דלית אפשר למצר רוח בכנף '(the deeds of their leaders are not right) just as it is not possible to bind wind in one's skirts'.

מזבחותם LXX ἐκ τῶν θυσιαστηρίων αὐτῶν, cf. Pesh. *mn mdbḥyhwn*; Targ. מאוגרי טעותהון 'of/from the altars of their idols', → ממזבחותם (Borbone); Vulg. *a sacrificiis suis*, cf. MT.

CHAPTER 5.1–7

THE APOSTASY OF THE NATION, ITS LEADERS AND ITS PEOPLE

5.1 **Hear this[a], O priests; pay attention, House of Israel. Harken, Royal House[b]; for yours is the [responsibility for] government[c]. Yet[d] you have become a trap at Mizpah, and a net spread upon Tabor.**

[a]I.e. what follows; not (so, e.g., Hitzig) chapter 4.

[b]Lit. 'House of the King'; the verb is plural and hence the phrase denotes the royal court with its officials. The same construction is used with the previous phrase. *BHS* notes the proposal to read שׂרי 'princes of' designed (unnecessarily) to restore concord.

[c]Such is the natural meaning of the phrase; so the Targum; cf. Gen 26.20 'the water is ours (לנו)', Hag 2.8 'mine is the silver', and especially Deut 1.17 'judgement belongs to God'; משפט denotes, amongst other things, the execution of judgement in general (BDB p. 1048, col 2 f) and here, as in 10.4, (good) government. The phrase is likely to apply to all three groups addressed, cf. לכלכם of the next verse. There seems to me to be no need to posit in לכם haplography for לכלכם (*contra* Ehrlich and Rudolph). An alternative translation is that of Rashi 'the judgement of suffering is upon you (עליכם)'. Rashi's change of preposition suggests, however, that this view is not correct and the absence of a clear parallel (משפט and ל with the sense 'upon you') also counts against it. Rudolph's advocacy of this view on the grounds that כי in 1b must have an adversative sense thus precluding a different sense for כי here (i.e. in 1a) is hardly convincing. The word is so common and its meanings so diffuse that it is only particular contexts that can prompt an estimate of its particular meanings.

[d]Lit., perhaps, 'surely'; the context requires here an adversative force (cf., e.g., Qyl and Rudolph).

Verses 1–7 are usually seen as a unit which depicts the apostasy of the leaders and the people. Verses 1f are in the form of divine speech as are vv. 3ff, but the abrupt conclusion of 2b probably indicates that they form one distinct element in the composition.

The three groups addressed form the establishment of the Northern Kingdom. The priests and the royal court (note b) are clearly defined. 'House of Israel', however, presents some problems since it is argued that, elsewhere, the term denotes the people of the Northern Kingdom as a whole (so Rudolph). For ibn Ezra it is the Sanhedrin, i.e. all the judges. Micah 3.1 reads 'Listen, you leaders of Jacob, rulers of the House of Israel'. On the basis of this very similar text, it is reasonable to suppose that the shorter form 'House of Israel' here means the establishment of the kingdom rather than its people as a whole, more particularly as the phrase is paralleled by 'Royal House'. In 1.4, too, the context in which the same phrase occurs suggests that the establishment is meant (see above on 1.4)[1].

As in Mic 3.1 the establishment of the kingdom is regarded as having the responsibility for just and good order in society: 'you leaders ... should you not know justice?' (cf. note c). In contrast (notes c and d) the leaders, all of them (note c), having failed to do what they should have done, have done what they should not have done. Specifically they have become a trap at Mizpah and a net spread on Tabor. The two terms denote fowlers' nets. The first (*pḥ*)[2], possibly a sprung trap, was apparently a smaller device than the latter (*ršt*) which, spread out, could also be used to trap, e.g., lions and gazelles (e.g. Ezek 19.8; Ecclus 27.20). From Job 18.8 it appears that the nets entrapped the feet of such animals and birds[3]. In the Psalms, the terms are frequently used to describe the machinations of the wicked (e.g. Ps 119.110) in their persecution of the righteous. The metaphor of the fowlers' traps is in itself appropriate to the mention of the hills (of Mizpah and Tabor) for it was on such wooded hills that fowlers practised their craft (so Jerome and Kimchi, cf. Rudolph). The precise reference of the metaphor is unfortunately not clear since it depends in no small part upon the interpretation of v. 2a the language of which seems to be unspecific and to refer quite generally to corruption. Accordingly reference has to be made to the context of the verses (i.e. to vv. 1–7) in which, apparently, cultic abuse is referred to, abuse which is described in detail in the previous chapter.

Howbeit, the general sense of this verse and of the metaphor in it is: just as fowlers and hunters spread their nets and set their traps on Mizpah and Tabor, so the folk of Israel are caught and trapped by you, the establishment. For your indulgence in promiscuous idolatry has betrayed you into perverting the just and good order of the state as a whole (after Rosenmüller). Recognition of the metaphorical character of the verse and of its

[1] Emendations to the text, e.g., the insertion of שׂבי 'elders' (Rudolph), נביאי 'prophets' (Richter), שׂרי 'princes' (Lindblom) are thus unnecessary.

[2] Cf. Amos 3.5; Ps 124.7; Prov 7.23.

[3] For details of the operation of these devices, cf. *AOB*, nos 181f; and *AUS* 6, 322ff, 334ff.

reference quite generally to the state and more particularly to its leaders would appear to preclude the quite specific interpretations (i.e. linked to the place-names) that have been suggested. Thus, for the rabbinic commentators (Rashi, ibn Ezra and Kimchi) the reference is to Jeroboam I's having set up military controls on Tabor and Mizpah to prevent his subjects continuing to make pilgrimages to Jerusalem (cf. 1 Kgs 12.28). I. Libny[4] has seen in *pḥ* ('trap') a reference to the 'taking' of Saul as king (*lkd*, 1 Sam 10.20f), since the verb is used both in connection with the lot and with traps (for the latter, cf. Amos 3.5 and Isa 24.18). Accordingly the metaphor has a historical reference and in particular to the election of Saul as Israel's first king at Mizpah (1 Sam 10). For a historical allusion to Hosea's time, Alt[5] has suggested that the verses refer to the period following the end of the Syro-Ephraimite War when, he assumes, the Assyrians made Mizpah and Tabor (with Shittim, see on the next verse) political centres of their province. As Rudolph rightly observes, the hypothesis fits ill with the metaphor of the traps for into them (*ex hypothesi*) the hunters (the Israelite leaders) themselves would have fallen. Notice of such a fate is not consistent with the indictment of present guiltiness which the verses set forth (cf. Wolff).

Nor does the view of the majority of modern critics (e.g. Wolff, Rudolph, Mays, AF), *viz*. that the places are mentioned as examples specifically of cultic wickedness, fit the metaphorical nature of the verse. For why should these places rather than, say, Bethel and Gilgal (4.15) be mentioned? And why are they mentioned in connection with the establishment in general and with the Royal House in particular? To such questions Rudolph (e.g.) very honestly replies that our knowledge precludes any clear answers.

Accordingly it is perhaps best to see the reference to Mizpah and Tabor as important to the metaphor of the fowlers and as naming places particularly known for their activity.

Mizpah is usually identified[6] with Tell en-Naṣbeh about thirteen kilometres north of Jerusalem on the present day road to Ramallah and near the Jerusalem airport. It was a Benjamite site and in Jeroboam II's time was part of the Northern Kingdom (cf. v. 8). As has been stated above, it was also connected with

4 See מקרא ככתבו ולשון כתבניתה, Jerusalem, 1960, p. 106; so Qyl; I have not had access to this work.

5 *KS* 2, 187 n. 1.

6 Alt *ZDPV* 69 (1953), pp. 1ff and Schunck, p. 22 n. and p. 27 and Kallai *HGB* p. 402. At the time of writing the site is marked by a rocky outcrop above the local arak factory.

Samuel and the election of Saul. Another possibility in the same area is that Mizpah denotes the present day Nebi Samwil, the high peak some seven kilometres north-west of Jerusalem (so Qyl). Others again have identified the place as the site east of the Jordan known as Mizpah of Gilead (present day El Mishrifeh[7]), cf. Judg 10.17; 11.11, 29; it is difficult, however, to believe that Hosea would have wished to refer to such a comparatively far off place.

Tabor is the beautifully rounded mountain which rises to some four hundred and fifty five metres from the Jezreel valley, twenty two kilometres along the road from Afula to Tiberias. It is the traditional site of the Transfiguration and on its summit there is today the Franciscan church of that dedication. According to Josh 19.22, cf. Judg 4.14, it fell within the boundaries of three tribes, Zebulun, Issachar and Naphtali. It is not anywhere in the Old Testament named specifically as a cultic centre[8], though its association with Deborah and the victory over Sisera may have invested it with some importance to the nation.

Text and Versions

כי לכם המשפט Targ. הלא לכון למידע דינא 'is it not your responsibility to know judgement?'

למצפה LXX translates the name by τῇ σκοπιᾷ 'look-out', 'mountain-peak', cf. OL[W] *speculae in visitatione*, Aq. τῇ σκοπεύσει, Vulg. *speculationi* and Pesh. *dwq'* (Gelston, p. 123); Symm. τῇ πλατείᾳ 'the broad place', 'street'; Targ. renders by למלפיכון 'to your teachers', interpreting √צפה 'watching' as 'instructing', cf. Isa 21.6; Hab 2.1; Ezek 3.17 (the latter quoted by Kimchi on Targ.).

תבור LXX τὸ 'Ιταβύριον; Aq. θαβώρ, cf. Pesh. *tbwr*; Symm. τὸ ὅριον 'the boundary'; Theod. τὸν δρυμόν 'copse/thicket'; Targ. טור רם 'high hill'.

5.2 **These perverse men[a] have delved[b] deep into corruption[c]; but I am [a force for] discipline to all of them[d].**

For a general note on the translation of the first part of this verse, see note e.

[7] Cf. M. Noth *ZDPV* 89 (1973), pp. 32f.

[8] Deut 33.19 may suggest Tabor but does not do so explicitly, cf. S. R. Driver *ad loc.* O. Eissfeldt presents evidence that Zeus Itaburios was worshipped on Tabor in Hellenistic times; *ARW* 31 (1934), pp. 14ff.

[a]The word שֵׂטִים is understood to be derived from the root שׂוּט/סוּט akin to שׂטה (so BDB *ad loc.*, cf. Kimchi) with the sense 'to swerve', 'fall away', 'deviate'; cf. Ps 40.5 'those falling away to falsehood'. A noun סֵטִים from the same root occurs in Ps 101.3 'the doing of deviation I hate'. In Aramaic סטי/סטא means 'to deviate', 'be faithless' (cf. Jastrow p. 972). For ibn Janāḥ the word denotes 'deviation' and for this meaning he compares Ps 101.3. Ibn Ezra also makes use of the word סטים (*sic*) to explain that those mentioned here are 'the servants of Baal'. Accordingly, since comparison with Ps 101.3 and סֵטִים is well established in rabbinic tradition, the pointing שֵׂטִים may be held to constitute an interpretation in MT made by reference to the Psalm. The pointing should perhaps be corrected to the participial form שָׂטִים (cf. Morag). Kimchi compares the noun סרה 'apostasy', 'deviation' which in Isa 31.6 is also construed with the *Hiphil* of the verb עמק. The absence of the article is understood to be in accordance with the principle of 'indeterminateness for the sake of amplification' (GK 125c), following the previous verse. Hence the translation 'these perverse men' for the literal 'perverse ones'.

[b]The *Hiphil* of עמק is construed with סרה in Isa 31.6 and with שחתו in Hos 9.9. The meaning is literally 'to make deep'. The metaphor, used here in the semantic field of deviation and perversity (so rightly Morag), is clear enough as it stands. For Morag the verb is an expression of strength and intensity. For ibn Janāḥ, however, 'going deep' denotes 'obscuring' and 'removal' (Arabic *'l'ġm'ḍ,'l'b''d*) for which he compares Lev 13.3 and Eccles 7.24. It is difficult to be quite sure of the sense that he detects, but he seems to be indicating nuances of hidden depravity; cf. ibn Ezra 'the evil in which they have gone deep is not hidden from God'; also the use of נכחד 'hidden' in the following verse.

[c]The word שחטה is understood to be an infinitive construct *Qal* (cf. אהבה from אהב, so Kimchi) from the verb שחת but here spelt deliberately in a variant way (so Morag). In Hos 9.9 the phrase 'they have delved deep into corruption (שחתו) as in the days of Gibeah' is found. Other instances of the use of the verb שחת by Hosea are 11.9 and 13.9. The variant spelling is of a sort with that attested for חתף/חטף, and for צבת/צבט within a single chapter of a book (Ruth 2.14, cf. 2.16) and may be connected here with the phonological value of the *ḥeth* which, depending on its position, influences either towards assimilation or dissimilation (the latter here). Such is Morag's view of the matter. As an alternative suggestion, attention may be drawn to the following word שטים with an initial sibilant followed by an emphatic *t* which, by assimilation, may have influenced the final radical of שחטה.

[d]Lit. 'but I am discipline to them all'. The expression is marked by ellipsis cf., with Kimchi, Ps 109.4 ('I am [a man] of prayer')[9] and, on

[9] His view of this verse is not affected by modern critical views of the phrase in the Psalm.

the assumption that Yahweh is the subject of the phrase (rather than, as Kimchi supposes, the prophet), the translation 'force for' is offered as appropriate to the context. The renderings of the LXX and Vulgate (see below) 'I am disciplining' are more likely to reflect a preference for a less abstract expression (cf. Rudolph) than to indicate a different text (*contra* Oort and, e.g., Harper, Wolff). Other interpretations or changes proposed include Ehrlich's suggestion that the word is a *Hophal* participle of סור and means 'I am removed, defunct, for all of you' and Duhm's 'I am a fetter to all of you' (for 'you', see Text and Versions below).

[e]The first part of this verse has long been regarded as difficult and then, as a consequence, corrupt. The main difficulty has been occasioned by the word שחטה which appears to be from the root שחט 'to slaughter', a meaning which, whether with men or animals as the object, ill fits the context. Morag's treatment (p. 508) of the passage is here adopted (with minor variations) on the following grounds: first, his recognition that שחטה is a variant spelling of שחתה enables the phrase in this verse to be compared with the very similar phrase of Hos 9.9. Secondly, the use of the verb העמיקו is parallelled in Isa 31.6, a verse which depicts deviation and perversity and thus confirms that 5.2a and 9.9 belong to this semantic field. Thirdly, and decisively, Morag's treatment of the verse yields for it a sense that is entirely satisfactory without recourse to emendation and the consequent elaboration of theories for which there is scarce evidence.

Amongst such emendations[10] that of Umbreit has been very widely adopted (e.g. by Wellhausen, Marti, Wolff, Rudolph, Mays). Thus he reads 'a pit of Shittim they have dug deep' (see Text and Versions) whereby reference is made to a third device of hunters and to the trans-Jordanian Moabite site associated with the worship of Baal-Peor (Num 25), the latter being mentioned in Hos 9.10[11]. Ibn Ezra had already seen in the verb העמיקו alone a reference to the deep burial or hiding of the trap mentioned in the previous verse 'so that those who go by will not see it'. Despite his suggestion, however, the verb is not attested elsewhere with traps or pits as its object and therefore the emendation, although ingenious, is unlikely to be correct. Secondly, it is not clear why Shittim should be mentioned in connection with an indictment of the contemporary establishment of the Northern Kingdom, even if 2 Kgs 14.25 is interpreted as suggesting that the eastern side of the Dead Sea belonged to Jeroboam II's dominion. The problem mentioned above in connection with Mizpah and Tabor as cultic places arises even more

[10] For a comprehensive list, see Harper.

[11] A variation on the theme is offered by G. R. Driver *JTS* 34 (1933), p. 40, who invests שחט with the meaning 'lewdness', 'corruption' after the Accadian and Syriac cognates, 'they have deepened the corruption of Shittim' (reading וְשַׁחַט הַשִּׁטִּים). The word is not elsewhere attested with this sense and the suggestion is dubious.

acutely in regard to a supposed mention of Shittim: why these places and this place rather than the known and important sanctuaries of the kingdom itself? Hosea 9.10 is clearly an allusion to a well-known incident of the time before the settlement and therefore hardly constitutes evidence that 5.2a refers to cultic wickedness on the part of the Israelite establishment in trans-Jordanian Shittim of Hosea's time.

The verse follows closely v. 1. The establishment of the Northern Kingdom, infected by the promiscuous impulse caught at the sanctuaries (v. 4), has failed the nation by neglect of its responsibility for justice and equity. As fowlers on Mizpah and Tabor enmesh birds in their nets, these men contrived the ruin of their nation. They are perverse (note a), flawed in their ethical stance, who have delved into the hidden depths of corruption (notes b and c). It is in the sphere of justice that their wickedness obtrudes, for here their corruption has borne its bitter fruit. The nation, deprived of leaders of integrity, flounders in a morass of murder, stealing and adultery (4.2). In 9.9 the 'depths of corruption' are compared with the days of Gibeah, i.e. to the outrages committed in the Benjamite city against the laws of hospitality. Of this sort, then, is the violence and depravity to which the nation has sunk by reason of its iniquitous rulers.

Yet Yahweh watches and remains constant as a force of discipline to them all (note d). Discipline denotes both instruction and chastisement and the verb from the same root is used in Deut 8.5; Prov 31.1 in connection with a father's obligations to his son. Yahweh 'disciplines' Israel in just such a sense; chastisement is not an end in itself but rather a means to inculcate obedience and wisdom, cf. Jerome 'I am your teacher and I wish to correct you and not to punish you, to save you and not to lose you'. The manner of the discipline is unfolded later in the chapter, but is found essentially in the collapse of the state and in its ruin at the hands of the Assyrian invaders. The terseness of the notice is highly effective; the words say it all and the little oracle reaches its decisive end (so Rudolph).

Text and Versions

ושחטה שטים העמיקו LXX ὃ οἱ ἀγρεύοντες τὴν θήραν κατέπηξαν 'which (*sc*. the net) the hunters of game have fixed'[12], cf. Pesh. *wṣyd' dṣydyn ṭmrw pḥ'* 'and the hunters who are hunting hide traps'; Vulg. *et victimas declinastis in profundum* 'and victims you have turned aside

12 Jerome renders the Greek *quod qui capiunt venationem confixerunt*.

into the depths', i.e. (so Jerome's commentary) the leaders have set ambushes for pilgrims to Jerusalem and sacrificed them as offerings to demons; Targ. ודבחין לטעון מסגן 'they sacrifice many victims to idols'. All these translations are interpretative and cannot be regarded as evidence for a text different from MT (cf. Rudolph). → וְשַׁחַת הַשִּׁטִּים העמיקו (Umbreit); → וְשַׁחַת בַּשִּׁטִּים (*BHS*).

מוסר LXX παιδευτής 'teacher'; Vulg. *eruditor*; Targ. ואנא מיתי יסורין 'I am bringing discipline', cf. Pesh. *'n' dyn 'rd'* 'I will instruct/chastise them', cf. Gelston, p. 145. On the basis of LXX and Vulg. Oort proposed מְיַסֵּר (cf., e.g., Wolff, *BHS*, Borbone), 'I am disciplining'; see comments above; → מוֹסֵר 'fetter' (Duhm, cf. Umbreit).

לכלם LXX ὑμῶν on the basis of which לכם or לכלכם is often proposed and the reading is held to match the imperatives of v. 1 (cf., e.g., Wolff and Rudolph). On the other hand the change of subject presupposed by העמיקו and שׂטים and its indeterminate character (note a) suggest that MT is, on that view, entirely satisfactory.

5.3 **I know Ephraim, and Israel is not hidden from me[a]. Now indeed[b], Ephraim, you have behaved promiscuously[c]; Israel is defiled.**

[a]I.e. the Israelites in their actions and deeds are not out of Yahweh's omnipresent sight, cf. Ps 69.6 'O God you know my foolishness, and my sins are not hidden from you'.

[b]כי with asseverative force; in that the Israelites are seen by Yahweh to be perverse, they merit the description which follows. With the following עתה the particle constitutes a conclusion or judgement, cf. 2.12 (EV 10); 4.16 etc.

[c]An internal or intransitive *Hiphil*, cf. on 4.10, 18 above; cf. the versions below. Kimchi prefers this understanding, though he mentions the possibility that it is a transitive, causative *Hiphil*. The difficulty with the resulting 'you have caused Ephraim to act promiscuously' is that the second masculine singular subject is obscure. The change in subject ('you have behaved ... Israel is defiled') is frequent in Hosea, cf., e.g., 4.13, 14, hence the proposal to read a third masculine singular verb (e.g. Oort, Mays) is unnecessary. Recognition of the intransitive *Hiphil* renders unnecessary Rudolph's suggestion that a *Hophal* be read.

Verses 3 and 4 are in the form of a divine saying and so are distinguishable from vv. 5–7 which are prophetic sayings. These considerations, however, do not tell against a fundamental unity of thought which may be characterised as Israel's apostasy from Yahweh, his recognition of it and the consequences that follow. Ephraim, as a synonym for Israel, denotes its dominant tribe, cf. on 4.17.

The corruption of the nation and the wicked deeds of its citizens are not hidden from the all-seeing eyes of the consistent God. He knows the nation as its owner and lord. Its people may suppose that their deeply corrupt actions are hidden (cf. note b on v. 2 above) but in reality they are not so (note a above). In fact (note b) the nation is judged to have given itself to promiscuous idolatry and together with the resulting wickedness is defiled by it. Thus the nation's relationship with its essentially clean and wholesome God is ruptured and rendered impossible. The word 'defiled' (*ṭm'*) is technical and denotes fundamentally the state of cultic impurity which is radically inconsistent with the holiness and purity of God[13]. To be defiled is to be unable to enter the presence of Yahweh. Here the state of impurity is due to the promiscuous apostasy of the nation and its inhabitants (cf. *per contra* Ps 15) rather than to the exigencies of ordinary life (such as death or childbirth). The thought is expressed elsewhere in Ps 106.39, 'they made themselves foul (*wyṭm'w*) by their acts, and by wanton deeds they acted promiscuously (*wyznw*)'.

For Rashi the verse expresses clearly that now the whole state, and not only its rulers, is guilty before God. The word 'now' (*'th*) thus marks a point of time rather than the announcement of a conclusion (note b). Rashi's view depends in part upon his use of a midrashic tradition according to which the king Hoshea removed the military controls preventing access to Jerusalem (see on v. 1 above) and, since the people did not resume worship there, at that point they incurred guilt. The details of his exegesis need not be accepted. His emphasis upon the sense of the verse, *viz.* that now the guilt of the people as a whole is expressed, is correct (cf. Rudolph). Yahweh's knowledge of that guilt and its inability to be hidden from him constitute a solemn warning which is expressed in accordance with the prophet's desperate desire that Israel will repent and come to its senses. With that desire, however, the facts of the situation are at odds and the very wickedness to which the nation is given seems to prevent its repudiation of it; see the next verse and cf., with Rudolph, Jer 6.27–30; also Rom 7.15ff.

Text and Versions

הזנית LXX ἐξεπόρνευσεν, cf. Pesh. *zny* and Vulg. *fornicatus est* which suggests to Ruben הזנה (cf., e.g., Mays, *BHS*, Borbone); Targ. טעו 'are worshipping idols'.

13 Cf. de Vaux *IAT* 2, p. 353; *IAI*, p. 460.

5.4 **Their evil deeds[a] do not permit[b] [them] to return to their God; for a promiscuous impulse[c] has affected them deeply[d]; and they do not know Yahweh.**

[a]The word 'deeds' (מעללים) in Hosea denotes specifically evil deeds (4.9; 7.2; 9.15; 12.3, EV 2).

[b]For this meaning 'to permit' for נתן, cf. with Rashi, ibn Ezra and Kimchi, Gen 20.6; 31.7; Num 21.23; cf. BDB p. 679, col 1 g. An alternative translation (cf. certain of the ancient versions, *q.v.* below) is offered by ibn Ezra: 'they do not deeds of repentance'. For this, Rosenmüller compares Eccles 1.13 'I gave my heart to seeking', and suggests that the phrase here means 'they did not give their preoccupations to repentance'. The suggestion is less satisfactory than that which makes the deeds the subject of the verb and recognises that the deeds are evil deeds (cf. note a).

[c]Cf. on 4.12 above.

[d]בקרבם Lit. 'is in them'; cf. Qyl, 'has taken hold of them'. Wolff argues against this view and urges that the spirit of promiscuity, like the nation's leaders, rules in their midst. The expression, however, surely denotes the *Zeitgeist*, mode of thought and behaviour prevalent amongst the people as a whole. For קרב as the seat of thought and emotion (*contra* Wolff), parallel to לב 'heart', cf. BDB p. 899, col 1 2.

Despite the reference to 'their God' and 'Yahweh', the verse forms part of the divine saying (cf. on 1.2; 2.22, EV 20; 4.10). The wickedness of the nation has become so compulsive that the possibility of repentance and return to the God of truth and justice is virtually precluded. The situation resembles that defined in Isa 59.2 'your iniquities raise a barrier between you and your God', cf. 'defiled' in v. 3 and, with Rudolph, Jer 13.23; Jn 8.34. The prophet's words, while they describe accurately the ruinous behaviour and attitude of the people, are also devised, by describing it, to break what seems to be a vicious circle, cf. on the previous verse, Isa 6.10 and, again, Jer 6.27ff.

The origins of the nation's malaise have been traced to the idolatrous cult and, with a brief reference to the promiscuous impulse which characterises it (cf. 4.12), the conclusion is reached in its hideous simplicity that they no longer know Yahweh, i.e. they are totally forgetful of his character and his requirements of truth, justice and moral integrity (cf. *per contra* 2.22, EV 20). Though not explicitly stated, Yahweh has no longer any alternative but the sanction of punishment (cf. Kimchi). The words, then, are full of menace and foreboding.

Text and Versions

לא יתנו מעלליהם LXX οὐκ ἔδωκαν τὰ διαβούλια αυτῶν τοῦ ἐπιστρέψαι, cf. Vulg. *non dabunt cogitationes suas ut reverantur* 'they do not dispose their counsels/thoughts that they should return ...'; Pesh. *l' šbqn lhwn ṣn'thwn dntpnwn* 'their deeds do not permit that they turn ...', cf. Targ. לא שבקין עובדיהון למתב. In the minor Greek versions only their renderings of the noun are preserved: Symm. βουλάς, Theod. γνώμην, both accusative, which suggests that these versions followed the interpretation of LXX (Aq.'s ἐπιτηδεύματα is ambiguous). Pesh.'s *lhwn* has suggested to Oettli (cf., e.g., Wolff, Rudolph, Mays) that MT has lost a final *mem* by haplography and that יתנום should be read. However, the context (with third masculine plural suffix attached to the subject and to 'God') is enough to imply such an object without writing it and Pesh.'s *lhwn* is likely to have been added *ad sensum* (cf. Borbone).

5.5 **And the pride of Israel testifies[a] against him[b] (and Israel)[c] and Ephraim will fall[d] through their[c] sin. [f](Judah also will fall[d] with them)[f].**

[a]For the rabbinic commentators (Rashi, ibn Ezra, Kimchi, cf. the LXX, Peshiṭta and Targum) ענה is identified as ענה III (BDB p. 776, col 1), an expression of affliction and submission. As an alternative Rashi quotes Dunash ben Labrat (tenth century) as saying that the verb is to be identified as ענה I (BDB pp. 772f) 'to respond', 'answer' and specifically 'to testify' (cf. BDB p. 773, col 1 3 a). This view (cf. the Vulgate below) is preferable on the grounds that the first alternative is difficult to construe with בפניו 'to his face' (note b below). For a similar expression cf., with Qyl, Isa 3.9, 'the look on their faces testifies against them' (and, with Rudolph, Ruth 1.21). For the same expression in Hosea, see 7.10.

[b]Lit. 'against his face'.

[c]For Jerome (cf. Kimchi) 'Israel' denotes the whole people, and 'Ephraim' Jeroboam I and the nation's leaders (since Jeroboam was an Ephraimite); for more recent interpretations in this sense, cf. van Gelderen, AF and H. J. Cook *VT* 14 (1964), pp. 132ff. Since Israel and Ephraim are more or less synonymous in Hosea, the widely held view that 'and Israel' is a gloss or a dittograph is here adopted. Without the words, parallelism is restored (cf., e.g., Wolff, Rudolph, Mays, *BHS*).

[d]The verb כשל denotes to stumble and fall and is often used figuratively of ruin and collapse through misfortune or divine judgement. The *Niphal* and *Qal* are used with much the same sense, though 'through their sin' may have prompted the reflexive mood, 'they have tripped themselves'. For the prophetic perfect, see note f.

[e]The suffix 'their' refers collectively to the people. There is no need to emend to עונו 'his' on the supposition that the expanded text 'Israel and Ephraim' required a consequent change (*contra*, e.g., Wolff).

[f–f]The words are regarded very commonly by modern commentators as an addition by the Judaean redactor (so, e.g., Wolff, Rudolph, Mays, Emmerson *contra* Harper and AF, cf. 1.7; 3.5; 4.15; 12.3). The perfect is likely to have been used by the redactor as a prophetic perfect (GK 106n) with the sense 'Judah, too, will undoubtedly fall'; cf. under Text and Versions below.

Verses 5–7 in the form of prophetic (as opposed to divine) speech summarise the nation's mistaken attitude and announce the judgement alluded to but not defined in vv. 3f. The words seem to be devised to counter the fatal response of the nation during the prosperity of Jeroboam II's reign which they regarded, despite the prophet's indictment of them, as evidence of the *de facto* continuance of Yahweh's favour, favour guaranteed by the offerings brought to him in the cult. It is this that Hosea characterises as the nation's arrogance, and which Yahweh is obliged to correct by judgement and punishment. The verses, then, are likely to have been placed here by, or on the instruction of, Hosea in order to set forth the full implications of Yahweh's reproof (vv. 3f).

The pride of Israel is interpreted generally by Rashi and Kimchi as the arrogance with which the people acted and transgressed God's will (Rashi) or else the glory and greatness of the nation before its humiliation (see note a) in exile (Kimchi). For Qyl pride denotes the royal establishment, the kingdom as in Isa 13.19, 'Babylon, fairest of kingdoms, proud beauty (*tp'rt g'wn*) of the Chaldaeans'. Such views may be said better to fit the interpretation (here set aside) that the verb *'nh* denotes 'affliction and humiliation'.

Another specific interpretation of the pride of Israel is that it denotes the royal sanctuary of Bethel (Amos 7.13). In Amos 6.8 the expression *g'wn y'qb* 'the pride of Jacob' is interpreted of the temple by the Targum, Rashi and Kimchi, Rashi comparing Ezek 24.21 where the Jerusalem temple is described as 'the pride (*g'wn*) of your strength'. The interpretation has recently been applied to Hos 5.5 by G. A. Danell[14] (cf. Emmerson, pp. 66f). Since, however, pride in a more general sense clearly fits Amos 6.8, this particular or specific interpretation is rejected. It should be noted that none of the rabbinic commentators mentions this interpretation in connection with Hos 5.5. That is not to say,

[14] *Studies in the Name Israel in the Old Testament*, Uppsala, 1946, pp. 117f.

however, that the idolatrous sanctuaries (of which Bethel and Dan were prime instances) were not identified as particular exemplars of Israel's pride. Indeed the next verse of Hosea speaks explicitly of cultic malpractice. That, together with, e.g., Ezek 24.21, may indicate the early fixing of the interpretative tradition represented by the Targum and rabbinic commentators on Amos 6.8[15].

Another interpretation is that the pride of Israel is Yahweh, as in Amos 8.7 (e.g. Keil, Hitzig). Accordingly the pride of Israel (*sc*. Yahweh) will indict the nation to its face. The context, however, tells against such a view in that to construe 'to his face' (note b) in such a way renders the phrase otiose. On the contrary, the expression conveys that the Israelites convict themselves by their behaviour.

It is, then, the arrogance of Israel which testifies against the nation; it is incriminated by its own attitude and behaviour. It is inevitable that Yahweh will bring about its calamitous fall and it is the sin of its inhabitants (note e) which is the catalyst.

Text and Versions

וענה LXX καὶ ταπεινωθήσεται, cf. Pesh. *wntmkk* (Gelston, p. 123) and Targ. וימאך 'will be abased'; Vulg. *respondebit* 'will answer', 'testify'.

גאון LXX and Symm. ἡ ὕβρις; Aq. and Theod. ἡ ὑπερηφανία; Vulg. *arrogantia*; Pesh. *'yqrh*, cf. Targ. יקר.

כשל LXX and Pesh. prefix 'and', hence Oort suggests וכשל; cf. note f above. → יִכָּשֵׁל בַּעֲוֹנוֹ (*BHS*).

5.6 **With their flocks and herds they go[a] to seek[b] Yahweh, but they do not find him[c]; he is quite detached[d] from them.**

[a] A frequentative imperfect (GK 107g) rather than denoting the future (so Kimchi in relation to Judah's return to the worship of the temple at the time of Josiah's reform).

[b] 'To seek (the face of) God (in a sanctuary)'; i.e. a personal communion with him by means of sacrificial feasting etc.; cf. on 2.9 (EV 7); 3.4; 4.15 and 7.10.

[15] R. E. Clements' suggestion, *God and Temple*, p. 55 n. 1, that Ps 47.5 refers to the Jerusalem sanctuary is surely ill-founded. The context clearly speaks of the land of Canaan as Jacob's pride (cf. Gunkel *ad loc.*).

[c]The object is supplied *ad sensum* (cf. the LXX below); it is not present in the Hebrew.

[d]חלץ, uniquely here without object, denotes, according to ibn Janāḥ, that Yahweh has 'vanished', 'disappeared' (Arabic *f't wz'l*). For Rashi the meaning is illustrated by 2 Sam 2.21; Judg 14.19 where the derivative noun חליצה denotes what is stripped off a person as spoil, *viz*. his clothes and equipment. Accordingly Yahweh has become detached, released from (the burden of) his people (נשמט). Ibn Barūn (Wechter, p. 85) compares the Arabic cognate *ḫlṣ* (with *mn*) 'to be free,' 'liberated from' 'to be rid of'. The sense of the verb is then clear in the context and emendation is unnecessary (e.g. Oettli's *Pual*). The sense is detachment and separation rather than withdrawal, retreat, *contra* the versions below.

The verse describes the nation's unrealistic reliance upon cultic worship as the means for ensuring the continued favour of Yahweh and the perversity of this view as, *de facto*, Yahweh cannot thus be found since now he is totally detached from such activities (note d). Mention of sheep and cattle is redolent of the saying in Exod 10.9 'young and old ... sheep and cattle; for we have to keep a pilgrimage-feast of Yahweh'. Again, for seeking and finding Yahweh, cf. Deut 4.29 'If you seek ... Yahweh your God, you will find him'. There is here no contradiction of v. 4 and the desperate wish there expressed that the folk should return to Yahweh. For here the wrong attitude prevails: it is not in sacrificial feasts that Yahweh is found but in integrity and recognition of his ethical nature and demands (cf. 6.6). For Wolff, mention of seeking and not finding Yahweh echoes the Canaanite searching for Baal in the underworld and constitutes a polemical use of such motifs. It is more likely, however, that the saying reflects the antithesis also formulated by Amos (5.4f) between resorting to Yahweh in truth and resort to the sanctuaries such as Bethel and Gilgal (cf. Mays). Again, Yahweh's total withdrawal from such sanctuaries and their worship brings the inevitable result that those resorting to them 'shall stagger from north to south, they shall range from east to west, seeking the word of Yahweh, but they shall not find it' (Amos 8.12 – so NEB).

For Jerome, ibn Ezra and Kimchi the verse follows mention of, and is thus concerned with, Judah and the worship of the Jerusalem Temple. Their view may reflect the way Hosea's words were applied by the Judaean redactors (and thereafter) to the Southern Kingdom, cf. with Kimchi, 2 Kgs 23.27.

Text and Versions

ימצאו LXX adds αὐτόν, cf. Pesh. *nškḥwnh*. The addition is *ad sensum* and does not necessarily imply that the Hebrew also had such a suffix.

חלץ LXX prefixes ὅτι, cf. Pesh. *mṭl d*; again supplied *ad sensum* rather than implying an original כי in the Hebrew; LXX ἐξέκλινεν (ἐκκέκλικεν γάρ, VL' 86, 613, OL[W]) 'has turned away'; Pesh. *prq* 'departed', cf. Vulg. *ablatus est*; Targ. יסליק שכינתיה 'he will remove his glory'; cf. ibn Ezra who compares v. 15 'I will return to my place'.

5.7 **They have been unfaithful[a] to Yahweh, for they have brought bastards to birth[b]. Now, a change of circumstances** (or) **a time of misfortune[c] will destroy[d] them with their lands[e].**

[a]The verb בגד means to act or deal treacherously and is used, e.g., of a wife deceiving her husband (cf. Jer 3.20). In 6.7 the action is explicitly related to transgressing a covenant. Hence, with Yahweh as an object, the verb means that they have, by their actions, deceived him and broken their close relationship with him.

[b]Lit. 'they have brought to birth foreign sons'. The word 'foreign' (זר) denotes a person who does not belong to a regular family group or household, cf. BDB and KB[3] *ad locc.* Hence in this context and in relation to unfaithfulness (note a), 'bastards' (cf. again KB[3]), i.e. not sons of Yahweh; cf. 'children of promiscuity' in 1.2 and contrast Deut 14.1; Hos 2.3 (EV 1).

[c]The view here taken of the meaning of חדש is derived from ibn Janāḥ's treatment of it with which the comments of ibn Ezra are consistent. The word usually denotes a 'month', the fundamental meaning of the root being 'renewal' (ibn Janāḥ); a month in Hebrew is called חדש because it is ever renewed (ibn Barūn, Wechter p. 81). The particular meaning of the word in this verse is, according to ibn Janāḥ, illustrated by its use in Jer 2.24 (בְּחָדְשָׁהּ יִמְצָאוּנְהָ). Here the image of a wild ass in the desert is set forth; she (and he) goes off in a headstrong and compulsive way and it is useless to try to stop her. Those who seek to retrieve her[16] are urged not to weary themselves in the search because at the completion of this her period (Arabic *mnthy 'ǧlh'*) they will readily find her. The time will come to her (Arabic *y'tyh wqt*) when she may be easily retrieved. It will happen with the lapse of this her period of time (Arabic *'nqr'ḍ mddth*). The Hebrew word חדש in this context, then, defines the arrival of a new

16 Such is ibn Janāḥ's view of 'those who seek her'; modern scholars (so, e.g., McKane) see in the word a reference to (male) asses' seeking of the female. The difference of interpretation does not affect ibn Janāḥ's argument concerning the meaning of the word חדש.

phase in the ass' cycle when amenability replaces intractability. According to ibn Janāḥ a similar sense is to be detected in Hos 5.7, '(Hosea) means that "the time will come upon them when they will perish"' (Arabic *sy'tyhm šhr' ybydwn*). Here ibn Janāḥ uses the Arabic word *šhr* 'new moon', 'month' but it is clear from the parallel passages cited above that he means 'new phase, new period' (Arabic *'ǧl, wqt, mddt*).

For ibn Ezra the word חדש in this verse denotes an evil month (חדש רע) which will devour the bastard sons and their lands and he states that the phrase is similar to Deut 32.35 'the day of their downfall is near'. Here too, then, חדש is interpreted more generally in terms of time than particularly of a month.

The sense detected for the word חדש by these two authorities fits the context admirably and obviates the need for emendation[17] or the somewhat contrived interpretations based on the view that the word bears its usual sense of 'month'[18]. Three observations in support of it may be added: first, the word is derived as usual from the root חדש (renew) but has here (as in Jer 2.24) a slightly different meaning; secondly, a meaning which is not dissimilar is found in the word חדשה 'a new thing' in Isa 43.19 where the sense is akin to that of a new epoch (cf. BDB *ad loc.*); thirdly, the Arabic cognate (cited for the root חדש by ibn Barūn) has, in the form of a derivative noun (*ḥdṯ*) the sense 'event', 'occurrence' and, of particular interest to the context of Hos 5.7, 'misfortune'.

In the interests of precision, and to draw out the meaning of the word the alternative translations 'a change of circumstances', 'a time of misfortune' are offered. It is likely, however, that the accompanying verb (note d below) conveys the sense of misfortune.

[d]Lit. 'eat', 'devour', 'consume', so 'to destroy' cf. BDB *ad loc.*

[17] The most common is to read החסיל 'the locust', on the basis of the LXX, see below; cf. already Jerome and, e.g., Cheyne, Wolff. Alternatively, החרס(ש) 'itch', 'disease', 'mildew', cf. Wellhausen. More recently van Hoonacker has suggested חלש (Isa 14.12) 'conqueror', and Eitan *HUCA* 14 (1939), p. 2, cf. Jeremias, מחדש 'conqueror' after Arabic *ḥdš* 'to trample', 'throw to the ground'.

[18] Amongst such interpretations the following may be listed: (1) 'A (single) month (will suffice) to devour them', i.e. a month will suffice to see the land thoroughly devastated (cf., e.g., Rudolph). (2) '(Each) month could devour them' (cf. van Gelderen). (3) 'A month shall devour them', i.e. they will be devoured within a month's time (cf. Mauchline). The latter two interpretations are unlikely since the first is too vague and the second makes Hosea pronounce calamity in an untypically short interval of time. (4) 'The new moon will devour them', i.e. either in its inherently baleful and dangerous character (so Hitzig), or the new moon festival with its child sacrifices (e.g. Nyberg, Wolff), or the new moon festival as a representative of all festivals and, therefore, of the cult as a whole (e.g. Keil and Frey). All these interpretations require not inconsiderable assumptions for which there is little or no evidence.

[c]Lit. 'their portions'. The word חלק in the context denotes portions of land or territory, cf., e.g., BDB *ad loc.* and Amos 7.4.

The behaviour of the Israelites, under the influence of the leaders of the nation, has ruptured their relationship with their God (note a). The word used describes a wife's deception of her husband and her breaking of the marriage bond. Elsewhere it is used for political treachery and revolt (see my *Isaiah XXI* pp. 11f). It is, however, the former nuance that obtrudes here and leads on to the description of the individual members of the nation as, from Yahweh's point of view, bastards. Idolatry, instigated and sanctioned by the establishment, has made of those who were privileged to be 'sons of Yahweh' a rising generation (see on 1.2 and especially 2.6, EV 4 above) of bastards (note b). Such a characterisation of the nation and its citizens may well have had its origin in Hosea's knowledge of the actual conception and birth of illegitimate children in the promiscuous activities of the cult (cf. Rudolph and, for a more thorough-going appraisal in this sense, Wolff). Accordingly they are living witnesses to the debilitating syncretism of the cults of Yahweh and of Baal (so Rudolph). Hosea's words here recall the description of his own children as 'children of promiscuity'. Whether that amounts to evidence of the illegitimacy of the children of his wife is, however, dubious. Rather it suggests that those children were, through the sins of the fathers and of the establishment, and as members of the nation, children of a wicked and adulterous generation.

Judgement follows inevitably and it is pronounced in v. 7b. A change of circumstances, a time of misfortune (note c) will speedily overtake and destroy the nation. The mode of that destruction is not specified and mention of the nation's acquisitions, i.e. its lands, fits either the devastation of natural plague (cf. the LXX below) or that of foreign invasion (so, e.g., the Targum below, cf. Jerome and Kimchi). For Jerome the reference is specifically to the invasion of Tiglath-pileser III and to the annexation by him of large parts of the Northern Kingdom in 733 BC[19]. More likely, however, is the view that vv. 5–7 belong to the end of Jeroboam II's reign and the judgement, though indeed menacing, refers to the future (cf. Rudolph). That

[19] So more recently, Alt *KS* 2, pp. 176, 187. Budde *JPOS* 14 (1934), pp. 8f, 14f, comparing references to the Syro-Ephraimite War and to Assyrian intervention in Isa 7.2ff; 9.8; 17.3; 28.3, has argued that such texts, with Hos 5.7, belong to the period before that intervention.

the events of 733 BC authenticated the prophet's words is not inconsistent with this estimation.

For ibn Ezra, Rashi and Kimchi, the month (note c) which will devour the nation is *Ab*, the traditional date of the fall of the Jerusalem temple in 587 BC. The interpretation again suggests the way in which Hosea was read in exilic times and is consistent with their view that vv. 6f, following mention of Judah at the end of v. 5, refers to the Southern Kingdom.

Text and Versions

ביהוה LXX ὅτι τὸν κύριον does not necessarily suggest כי (before ביהוה, lost by haplography, cf. Borbone) since the conjunction introduces the following clause and the existing asyndeton is striking (cf. Rudolph *contra* Borbone).

ילדו LXX ὅτι ἐγεννήθησαν αὐτοῖς suggests, perhaps, that the translators read יֻלְּדוּ; Symm. (so some witnesses to LXX, e.g., Q 26', 407) has the active ἐγέννησαν; Pesh. *'wldw* may have read הולידו; Vulg. *genuerunt*; Targ. בנין מבנת עממיא קיימו להון 'sons have they begotten of the daughters of the nations'.

חדש LXX ἡ ἐρυσίβη 'mildew', 'red-blight'; for emendations based on this, see note c above. Aq. νεομηνία; Symm. and Theod. μήν '(new) moon', 'month'; Pesh. omits 7b; Vulg. *mensis*; Targ. ירח בירח 'month by month (I will bring upon them nations)'; (cf. Jerome who interprets *mensis 'per singulos menses hostis adveniet'*). → יאֹכַל מַשְׁחִית 'destruction will consume (their portions)' or יֵאָכְלוּ מֵחֲרִישִׁית 'they will be consumed by a hot wind'(cf. *BHS*, after Oort and Gressmann).

CHAPTER 5.8–14

ISRAEL'S INTERNECINE STRIFE AS A JUDGEMENT OF YAHWEH UPON THE WICKEDNESS OF EPHRAIM AND JUDAH

5.8 **Blow the ram's horn[a] in Gibeah, the trumpet[a] in Ramah; shout the alarm[b] at[c] Bethaven: 'Benjamin, [we are] behind you'[d].**

[a]Such is the meaning of the first word; the second is the metal trumpet or bugle.

[b]The *Hiphil* of the root רוע denotes 'to raise a shout' and 'to give a blast (with trumpet or horn)'. Since it is likely that what follows is a quotation, the former of the two meanings seems the better to fit the context (cf. Jerome).

[c]The word is construed as an accusative of the place where. The construction may have been preferred to the natural construction for euphonic reasons, in order to avoid the combination of the sound ב + ב (GK 118g).

[d]The interpretation of this phrase is very uncertain and a large measure of conjecture attends any attempt at it. It is here assumed that (1) the phrase is a quotation from a national epic poem or saga on the grounds that the same phrase occurs in Judg 5.14, cf. Kallai *Bethaven*, pp. 171, 174, 180; (2) that, following the imperatives which precede it, it constitutes an order or exhortation. The interpretation of Judg 5.14 is, of course, equally uncertain (see the standard commentaries). On balance I take the view that the phrase means '(right) behind you, Benjamin', i.e. we are behind you in support[1], and that it alludes to Ephraim's support of Benjamin in the battle against Sisera (cf. Rudolph).

A plausible alternative view is that the phrase amounts to an urgent warning of danger, i.e. '(watch) your back, Benjamin' (cf. Kimchi and, e.g., Ehrlich (*Miq.*, p. 370) who quotes the Arabic usage *b'dk* to the same effect; cf. the commentary below.

[1] An interesting use in modern Hebrew of a similar phrase is recorded on the Palmach Negev-Brigade memorial at Beer Sheba. There is inscribed the time-honoured subaltern's cry to his men 'Follow me!' (אחרי).

Verses 8–14 constitute a new section which is concerned with the historical and political circumstances of the time of the Syro-Ephraimite War (*c.* 735 BC). They have been placed here to indicate the mode of the punishment threatened in the preceding verses. What God had threatened through his prophet is now fulfilled in the events of history (after Jerome). The editor of Hosea's words, in so arranging them, is likely to have represented faithfully the prophet's own understanding of prophecy and fulfilment.

The interpretation of these verses requires careful evaluation of their historical background. In particular the question arises as to the significance and situation of the Benjamite territory mentioned in them. Was Benjamin part of the Northern or Southern Kingdom at this time? And what attitude to Benjamin do Hosea's words imply?

The sounding of the ram's horn and metal trumpet signify the alarm at the approach of an enemy and constitute a signal that the population with its flocks and cattle should repair to the safety of their city and its walls (so, e.g., the Targum, Jerome and Kimchi; cf. Amos 3.6; Jer 4.5; 6.1; Joel 2.1). That this interpretation is preferable to the alternative, *viz.* that the signals constitute a call to arms or preparation for attack (as in, e.g., Num 10.9; Judg 6.34; 7.21, cf. Rudolph) is dependent upon the likely interpretation of the verse as a whole.

Gibeah, Ramah and Bethaven are all located in Benjamite territory. Gibeah is now to be identified with Jeba', two kilometres west of Er-Rām and two kilometres south of Mukhmās (Michmash)[2]. Ramah, identified with Er-Rām (cf. Kallai *HGB*, p. 403), is a peak on the same side of the road but some two kilometres further to the north. Mizpah, not mentioned in this verse, is a kilometre north along the same road but on the west side (see on 5.1 above).

Where Bethaven is concerned it seems that Hosea's usage is here different from that he otherwise employs. Elsewhere the name is used as a pejorative appellation for Bethel (see on 4.15; 10.5). Here, where he is making use of epic material and is specifically concerned with the territory of Benjamin, he refers to the Benjamite city of this name, convincingly identified by Kallai with Khirbet Tell el-'Askar, north of Michmash and adjacent to

[2] The identification was first made by E. Robinson in 1838; see J. M. Miller *VT* 25 (1975), pp. 145ff, and P. M. Arnold *Gibeah* (Sheffield, 1990). The widely held view that Gibeah is to be identified with Tell el-Fûl, on the east of the present road from Jerusalem to Ramallah, some three kilometres north of Jerusalem, must now be abandoned.

Ai[3]. Hosea's usage may reflect his predilection for 'ancient formulae and traditions' and thus be antiquarian (Kallai, p. 187). Yet his purpose is clear: he wishes to refer to the district of Benjamin with its principal towns. Of Bethel, which belonged to Ephraimite territory[4], there is no mention at all.

All three sites were of enormous strategic importance as they controlled the northern approach to Jerusalem as well as the road which ran from east to west through the Beth-horons towards the Sh[e]pelah and the Mediterranean.

The situation to which Hosea refers is the struggle of a century and more between Ephraim and Judah for control of Benjamite territory as now exemplified in the circumstances of the Syro-Ephraimite War. In *c.* 734 BC Ahaz of Judah was besieged in Jerusalem by the allies following his refusal to join a wider anti-Assyrian coalition and he consequently sought help from the Assyrians (2 Kgs 16, cf. Isa 7). Tiglath-pileser III of Assyria responded by invading Israel from the north and in 733 BC he conquered the regions on the east of the Jordan (Gilead) and west of the Jordan (Galilee) as far south as the Jezreel valley and including Megiddo. By this time he had already subjugated the coastal plain in connection with his conquest of Philistia.

In these circumstances and in view of the description in Hos 5.8 of alarm throughout the Benjamite territory (Gibeah–Ramah –Bethaven), it is reasonable to follow but modify the theory of A. Alt[5] that Judah took advantage of the situation to make incursions into Benjamite territory, until then controlled by Ephraim (cf. v. 10). That there is no other notice of such incursions is not surprising in view of the limited extent of the biblical material dealing with the Syro-Ephraimite War.

It is clear from 1 Kgs 15.16–22 that the Benjamite territory involved had been for some one hundred and fifty years the scene of tension and conflict between Judah and Israel. Benjamin's early dependence upon its stronger neighbour Ephraim is reflected in the Song of Deborah (Judg 5.14) and its attempts at achieving a measure of independence (cf. Judg 19–21) resulted only in its being further dominated, its withdrawal from the northern ten tribe grouping and its

3 So Kallai *Bethaven*, pp. 175f. The city gave its name to the 'wilderness of Bethaven' mentioned in a topographical text describing the boundary of Benjamin and Joseph (e.g. Josh 18.12). Because, following Amos, the prophets increasingly used the name as a pejorative appellation of Bethel (i.e. 'House of Wickedness'), 'the names Bethel, Luz and Bethaven became entangled' (Kallai, p. 178).

4 Cf. Kimchi's definition to the effect that Bethel belonged 'to the sons of Joseph, to Ephraim, on the border of Benjamin'.

5 For this definitive work, see his *KS* 2, 163ff.

emergence as a mere southern district of Ephraim. The Benjamite Saul restored the fortunes of the tribe and its territory which met with hostility the subsequent attempts by David to consolidate a united kingdom in Jerusalem. By the time of the division of the kingdom, Benjamin seems to have abandoned its hostility to the house of David and to have become largely dependent upon Judah which regarded the area (as controlling the northern approach to Jerusalem) as of considerable strategic importance (cf. 1 Kgs 12.20ff[6]).

1 Kings 15.15, 17 depicts an attempt by Baasha of Israel to check, by fortifying Ramah, the increasing dependence of this territory on Judah. Asa of Judah appealed to Syria for help and thus prevented the completion of the plan. 1 Kgs 15.22 suggests that Judah strengthened its position in the area by building fortress towers at Mizpah and Geba (= Gibeah). The date is *c.* 900 BC.

In *c.* 788 BC Jehoash of Israel defeated Amaziah of Judah at Beth-shemesh, attacking from the coastal plain. He is said to have plundered Jerusalem and then to have returned to Samaria (2 Kgs 14.8–14). 2 Chr 25.13[7] mentions a previous incident in which Ephraimites, hired and then dismissed by Amaziah, took the opportunity to attack the area of Beth-horon. This notice confirms the likelihood that Jehoash was able in this period to regain at least some control of the Benjamite territory.

It is difficult to estimate the attitude of the Benjamites to the two neighbouring kingdoms during this period. Hostility to both Ephraim and Judah is detectable from their history and the frequent changes to the border which ran through their territory (Schunck, p. 169) may suggest that they suffered the misfortunes common to peoples caught in territory between two more powerful and warring nations. According to Schunck it is likely that the north-eastern district of Benjamin remained, from the time of Asa, a part of the Northern Kingdom while the area mentioned by Hosea was under Judaean control.

Where the Syro-Ephraimite War is concerned, it may be concluded that in a short time, from *c.* 735 BC, the territory of Benjamin was dominated by the advance of the northern allies to the gates of Jerusalem and that, with the advent of the Assyrians, Judah took the opportunity to regain control of it (cf. again

[6] So Schunck whose findings are here generally accepted; and *contra* R. Kittel *Könige*, p. 105 who regards 1 Kgs 12.21 as secondary and as reflecting the situation after the exile.

[7] For an assessment of the essential reliability of this notice, cf. Williamson *Chronicles*, p. 328.

v. 10). In view of the divided nature of the territory at the time it is unlikely that its inhabitants were in a position to adopt any kind of united Benjamite support for either of the two sides to the dispute. The precise suggestion, then, that Hosea's reference in 5.8 depicts the alarm experienced by Benjamite towns (fundamentally loyal to the north) at the advance of hostile Judaeans (so Alt and, e.g., Wolff[8]) is unlikely to be correct. Similarly, the contrary suggestion (so Rudolph), *viz.* that Hosea's reference depicts a call to arms directed at the Benjamites (fundamentally loyal to Judah) to join a Judaean counter-attack on the north is untenable[9].

Hosea's words are best interpreted as serving to depict the alarm raised in Benjamite territory (Gibeah, Ramah, Bethaven) at the menace of the Judaeans. Benjamin is to suffer yet another military invasion with its inevitable disruption, plunder and arbitrary reprisals. Writing as a northerner, Hosea makes use of the ancient cry of solidarity preserved in the Song of Deborah (Judg 5.14) 'We Ephraimites are behind you, Benjamin!' The use of this phrase is likely to set forth feelings of sympathy with the Benjamite towns mentioned and to suggest that what Benjamin now suffers, its ally of the ancient past is also about to suffer. Long ago Ephraim was behind Benjamin lending support for their attack on Sisera; now Ephraim is behind Benjamin as another victim of invasion[10]. In this situation Benjamin depicts the inhabitants of the area caught in the crossfire[11]; the term is thus (archaically) geographic and does not define a political entity.

Such an interpretation may be said to fit the more general attitude of Hosea towards the Syro-Ephraimite War and its

8 Alt (so Wolff) assumes that Benjamin, following the Syro-Ephraimite attack on Jerusalem, is part of the Northern Kingdom. Accordingly (after Wellhausen) he emends the text of the last phrase of the verse (note d) to read 'Terrify (*hḥrydw*) Benjamin'. The emendation hardly provides a satisfactory sense since the preceding imperatives are directed to the inhabitants of the (Benjamite) cities, while this one seems to be directed at the Judaeans. For the evidence of the LXX cited by Wellhausen, see below.

9 Rudolph understands the last phrase of Hos 5.8 to be quoted ironically with (now) the sense 'Attack, Benjamin, for we Judaeans are behind you'. A variant of Rudolph's view is that of Arnold (*op. cit.*) who supposes that the alarm is to be sounded in north Judaean territory in connection with the initial Syro-Ephraimite attack. Amongst other weaknesses in Arnold's position is that he gives no satisfactory account of the reference to Benjamin.

10 So Jerome. Qyl sees in Judg 20.40f 'and Benjamin looked back' (*'ḥryw*) the possibility of an earlier conversion of the triumphal phrase of Judg 5.14 into one depicting defeat.

11 Cf. with Qyl the rabbinic addage: 'Woe to the wicked and woe for his (unfortunate) neighbour'; *Nega'im* 12.6 (Danby, p. 692).

consequences. Both Judah and Ephraim are at fault; both Judah and Ephraim will suffer (cf. 8.12). The tragedy of their internecine conflict reflects Yahweh's judgement upon their faithlessness (see the verses that follow).

The interpretation of the historical background to Hosea's words offered above is essentially a modification of Alt's theory. For Alt the place-names of 5.8 depict the main south-north route from Jerusalem towards Bethel and hence, he supposed, described a Judaean counter-attack on Ephraim following the unsuccessful initial attack on Judah/Jerusalem by the Syro-Ephraimite allies. Alt's theory represents to-date the most rigorous and systematic attempt to understand the historical background to Hosea's words. Yet it must now be abandoned on the following grounds: first, his identification of Gibeah with Tell el-Fûl is untenable and that seriously (but perhaps not fatally, cf. Miller *op. cit.* p. 160) undermines the assumption that Hosea describes a south-north route. Further, it is unlikely that Bethaven here is Bethel as Alt assumed (see above). Secondly, Alt makes a number of emendations to the MT (see, e.g., fn. 8 above) in conformity with his theory. Thirdly, he fails to do justice to Hosea's predilection for 'ancient formulae and traditions' (Kallai, loc. cit.) as clearly exemplified in the quotation of the ancient cry 'Benjamin, we are behind you'. More generally it may be said that Alt mistakenly seeks to press Hosea's words into an accurate description of contemporary events (some known and others assumed) rather than to see in them a longer perspective (cf. on 5.1–7)[12].

More plausible is the view suggested above that Hosea, using quotations from such 'established formulae and traditions', seeks to show that the events of the Syro-Ephraimite War are but the latest examples of a long history of dispute and tension between Ephraim and Judah in respect of the territory of Benjamin; that both states are and have been at fault and that their hostility and greed represent a fundamental disloyalty to Yahweh, for which both are punishable. His manifestly even-handed condemnations (cf. vv. 9–12) suggest that he grieves for 'Israel', i.e. the whole people of Yahweh, now, and long, debilitated and ruined by such internecine strife.

[12] H. L. Ginsberg, on the basis of Tadmor's attempt at an earlier dating of the prophecies of Hosea, sees in 5.8ff a reference to an otherwise unknown northward push into Benjamite territory by Uzziah of Judah in *c.* 743 BC; see *Fourth World Congress of Jewish Studies* 1, pp. 92f; for Tadmor, see *Kaufmann Jubilee Volume*, pp. 84–88. I am not persuaded by Tadmor's arguments, though what he says may constitute a pointer to the longer perspective for Hosea's words which I have sought to indicate.

Text and Versions

בגבעה LXX ἐπὶ τοὺς βουνούς translates the place-name: 'upon the hills', cf. OL[W] *super colles domino*; Pesh. *brmt'* reads Ramah here (and again for MT's Ramah); Targ. expands to 'Prophesy that the murderous nations will come against them because they made Saul of Gibeah king over them'.

ברמה LXX ἐπὶ τῶν ὑψηλῶν again translates the place-name with 'upon the heights'; Targ. expands to 'because they did not listen to the words of Samuel, the prophet of Ramah'.

בית און LXX ἐν τῷ οἴκῳ Ὤν, cf. Theod.; Aq. εἰς οἶκον ἀνωφελοῦς; Symm. ἐν βῆθ Ὤν; Pesh. *byt 'wn*, cf. 4.15 above.

אחריך בנימין LXX ἐξέστη βενιαμείν 'Benjamin is astonished, affrighted', suggested to Wellhausen החרידו 'terrify Benjamin'. Rudolph suggests that it goes back to a reading אחריד ב׳ where the verb is an Aramaic *Aphel* form meaning 'one terrifies Benjamin' → 'Benjamin is terrified'. LXX's reading is, however, more likely to represent an attempt (by reference to √חרד) to make sense of אחריך which was not understood; Aq., Symm. and Theod. confirm MT with ὀπίσω σου; Pesh. *btrk*, Vulg. *post tergum tuum*. → בבית און חרדתך ב 'in Bethaven is your terror, Benjamin' (Borbone).

5.9 **Ephraim will become[a] a devastation on the day of punishment[b]. It is an inexorable fate[c] that I have decreed[d] for them[e] among[f] the tribes of Israel.**

[a]The third feminine singular verb implies that it is the land or kingdom of Ephraim that will be devastated. For the phrase, cf. Deut 28.37. An alternative translation is 'You, Ephraim, will become ...' (i.e. the verb is taken as second masculine singular), cf. Rosenmüller.

[b]The word תוכחה is derived from the root יכח 'to reprove' and in this context Yahweh's reproof denotes punishment. 'In the day of the reproof and punishment of Israel my words are authenticated: what by the prophets I have threatened in word I now confirm by action' (Jerome).

[c]The word נאמנה is a *Niphal* participle denoting what is 'confirmed' or 'established', or physically 'steady' (cf. Exod 17.12). In the context of punishment and reproof, plagues and diseases are so described (Deut 28.59) and the sense is that their course is persistent and unremitting. The word 'fate' is added here in English *ad sensum*.

[d]Lit. 'I have made known'; I. Libny (*op. cit.* at 5.1) believes that the word denotes punishment and for this he compares Judg 8.16, 'he

disciplined those men of Succoth with ... briars' (*sic* NEB)[13]. The theory on which the suggestion is based is now generally abandoned; in any case, here the verb is construed with ב whereas in Judg 8.16 an accusative follows.

[e]The words are added in English *ad sensum*.

[f]The preposition ב construed with this verb, is best understood to denote 'among' (cf. Isa 12.4; Pss 77.15; 105.1) rather than 'against' (BDB p. 89, col 1 4 a) which, though possible[14], is less well attested.

The imminent threat of Assyrian domination and with it Judah's opportunism threatens the devastation of Ephraim. The situation is understood to constitute the reproof and punishment of Yahweh directed against a nation which had initiated the Syro-Ephraimite War. The advent of Assyria, following the unsuccessful siege of Jerusalem and attempt to replace its legitimate king (Isa 7.6b), was thus in accordance with the dictates of justice and so prompted by Yahweh himself.

Yet the fate that Yahweh had decreed for Ephraim was promulgated among the tribes of Israel (notes c, d, f). The term Ephraim is used by Hosea to denote specifically the Northern Kingdom (5.11; 7.8, 11) while Israel denotes the people of Yahweh as a whole (6.10; 7.1). Hence Yahweh's justice is revealed in the context of the whole covenant people and by reference to the old tribal unity[15]. In such a context Judah, too, was indicted for transgression (cf. v. 10 below) and liable to punishment[16]. Hence the judgement announced by Hosea in Yahweh's name is marked by impartial objectivity and conveys his grief at the tragedy of the civil strife which marred the unity and peace of Yahweh's people. Where Ephraim was concerned, no doubt Hosea saw their political and military wickedness as deriving from their fundamental idolatry; for such is the drift of his argument *passim*.

Such an assessment of the verse affords reasonable sense and consequently it is unnecessary to suppose with Rudolph that its second half (9b) is a later gloss made in reference to 'We are behind you, Benjamin' in the previous verse. According to

[13] Cf. D. W. Thomas on the verb ידע II, *JTS* 25 (1934), pp. 298ff; 38 (1937), pp. 404f; J. A. Emerton *ZAW* 81 (1969), pp. 189f; W. Johnstone *VT* 41 (1991), pp. 49ff and Emerton *VT* 41 (1991), pp. 150ff.

[14] So Rudolph with 'über'.

[15] So already Kimchi '... as I reproved them in the desert when all the tribes were united'. AF see an allusion to Judg 19–21 and Benjamin's indictment and punishment by the assembled tribes. Now Ephraim and Judah are indicted.

[16] Cf. the talmudic theodicy reproduced by Rashi in the matter of alleged divine discrimination against the Northern Kingdom.

Rudolph the characterisation of the northern tribes in the Song of Deborah is, for Hosea, normative and that of Benjamin, reinterpreted, manifests a proclamation by Yahweh which is constant and abiding (note c). Rudolph's argument is more ingenious than convincing.

Similarly, Alt's insistence (p. 160) that the perfect tense of the verb ('I have made known', note d) reflects an earlier pronouncement of Hosea, in the name of Yahweh, against the Syro-Ephraimite confederacy and its military consequences is unlikely to be correct. As Rudolph justly observes, of such a saying there is no trace in the book of Hosea and it is most unlikely that Hosea or his editor would have omitted one prophecy and included another which, without the first, is obscure.

Again the form-critical judgement that 9b is a statement (in Yahweh's mouth) appended to and authenticating a prophetic word (so, e.g., van Gelderen, Wolff) hardly seems likely in view of the consideration that v. 15 suggests that announcement of punishment did not mark Yahweh's final word. Why then should Hosea (or his redactor) later add a solemn authentication of a prophecy of imminent punishment? (cf. Rudolph).

The perfect tense (note d) in 'it is an inexorable fate that I have decreed' is, then, akin to the common formula 'Thus Yahweh has said' (כה אמר יהוה) and it has a present force (cf. the stative verbs in Amos 5.21; Jer 2.2 and Brockelmann, *Syntax* 41c). The chaos and misery associated with and consequential upon the civil war which unfolded in *c.* 735 BC represents Yahweh's intervention in reproof and punishment and Hosea, at the time of this pronouncement, attributes it to the God of Israel.

Qyl has seen in the use of the word 'tribes' (שבטי) an allusion to the rod (שבט) of punishment. Forms of the same root 'punish', 'punishment' (cf. note b) are found in close connection with 'rod' in 2 Sam 7.14 and Prov 29.15. His suggestion is unlikely to indicate that Hosea intended the primary sense 'rods of punishment' for 'tribes of Israel' yet it may point to subtilty in Hosea's choice of words.

Text and Versions

בשבטי LXX ἐν ταῖς φυλαῖς; Pesh. and Targ. *b* ...; Vulg. *in tribubus.*

נאמנה LXX πιστά 'sure things'; Pesh. *hymnwt'* 'truth'; Vulg. *fidem* 'what is sure'; Targ. אוריתא 'the law'.

5.10 **The princes of Judah are[a] men who[b] remove[c] their neighbour's boundary. Upon them I will pour out my wrath like water[d].**

[a]'Have become' and so 'are'. The perfect tense conveys a present meaning, cf. Wolff.

[b]*Kaph veritatis* (so Kimchi); Rashi explicitly denies this possibility and emphasises the comparative force of the *kaph*. For him, however, the whole phrase is used metaphorically to indicate Judah's adoption of Israelite malpractices (so Saadya, as quoted by Kimchi and, more recently, van Gelderen). On the assumption made here that the phrase has a concrete reference (*viz*. to the appropriation of land) there is little difference between comparing the Judaean princes with 'men who remove ...' and stating of them that they have become 'men who remove ...'.

[c]For this *Hiphil* form of the root נסג I, cf. GK 72ee.

[d]For the use of the definite article in comparisons, GK 126o; *contra* AF.

Judaean incursions into Benjamite territory are likely to be dated at a time shortly before 733 BC and Tiglath-pileser's annexation in that year of substantial portions of the Northern Kingdom (see above pp. 195ff). This verse suggests that the 'princes of Judah', i.e. the military commanders of the Judaean forces, used the opportunity to wrest from Ephraim land which did not belong to them. Hence they are condemned by Hosea in the language of the ancient law of Israel whereby individual citizens who stealthily (so ibn Ezra) and crookedly changed to their advantage the boundaries of their neighbours' fields (i.e. by removing the marker stones) are condemned (Deut 19.14; 27.17; Prov 22.28; Job 24.2). Accordingly judgement is pronounced against them. Yahweh will pour forth upon them, like the water of the flash-floods of Israel/Palestine, his fury (cf. Isa 8.7; Jer 14.16). For *'brh*, the punishment of Yahweh's overflowing anger, cf. Isa 9.18; 10.6.

Alt assumes that the verse was originally a self-sufficient unit containing a perfect tense of the crime committed followed by an imperfect (future) of the resulting punishment. Accordingly he sees the verse as referring to a situation later than that described in vv. 8f where a Judaean counter-attack on Ephraim is depicted as imminent and future. Thus initially Yahweh was seen by Hosea as sanctioning the Judaean counter-attack as a punishment upon Ephraim for its participation in the Syro-Ephraimite advance on Jerusalem. Yet when the military commanders of the counter-attack themselves offended the decrees of justice by appropriating land which had never been theirs, Hosea, in a later oracle, condemned that action in Yahweh's name. Hosea's understanding of the developing situation matches exactly that of Isaiah of Jerusalem who saw Assyria as the 'rod of Yahweh's wrath' but yet later condemned that nation for injustice and arrogance (cf. Isa 10.5ff).

While, however, emphasis upon the temporal force of the tenses in this verse just may point to some aspects of the underlying history and to Hosea's chronological reactions to particular events, it is more probable that we are presented with a kerygmatic unity (so Wolff) and a judgement passed upon Israel (i.e. upon the people of Yahweh) as a whole. Thus, the section from vv. 8 to 14 constitutes in its present form (whatever the history of its composition) a reasoned, impartial and mature interpretation of the Syro-Ephraimite War and its consequences. The composition bears all the marks of theological reflection and sets forth the consistency and moral integrity of the God in whose name it was recorded. Whether the composition was that of the redactor of Hosea's sayings or of Hosea himself is difficult to judge not least because, if it was the former, he has accurately set out the thought of the latter.

It is unfortunately impossible to give details of the annexation of Benjamite land by Judah since, other than this verse, there is no evidence for or about it. In 722/1 BC, following the fall of Samaria, Judah was bordered on the north by an Assyrian province and 2 Kgs 17.28 makes clear that Bethel belonged to it. It is likely then that the Ephraimite land appropriated by Judah was in the Benjamite territory south of Bethel described above and that the situation was similar to that obtaining one hundred and fifty years earlier when Judah fortified Geba and Mizpah (1 Kgs 15.22) ostensibly for reasons of security. Indeed it is possible that Hosea's condemnation of Judah's misdemeanors may have been expressed in words and attitudes remembered from the earlier incident and that it is thus gnomic in character, cf. the use of the old expression concerning Benjamin in 5.8.

Alt's general estimate of the historical background to this verse has proved to be an important milestone on the road to understanding the verse in its context. Wellhausen's view that the verse described the economic injustices, condemned in Judah by Isaiah (5.8) and Micah (2.2), whereby small farms were dishonestly incorporated into the larger ones is, as a result, largely discarded. Indeed it is unlikely that Hosea would condemn the social injustices of a neighbouring state in the context of sayings concerning a political crisis (so, e.g., Alt and Rudolph)[17].

Text and Versions

CD xx. 15–16 cites the verse.

5.11 **Ephraim is oppressed**[a] *either* **crushed by the requirements of justice** *or*[b] **all hope of justice for him is crushed**[a]. **For willingly**[c] **he followed futility**[d].

[a]The verbs (עשק and רצץ), denoting cruel oppression, imply sympathy on the part of the speaker whether or not the oppression is sanctioned by God (cf. Deut 28.33 and note b below). For רצץ of a broken reed, cf. Isa 42.3; for the LXX's understanding of these verbs in an active sense, see Text and Versions.

[b]Two translations of MT are possible. The first is made by analogy with the phrase נְשׂוּא פָנִים, lit. 'lifted up as to face' (so 'man of rank', NEB, Isa 3.3), or קְרוּעֵי בְגָדִים 'rent in respect of clothes', (e.g. 2 Kgs 18.37). Here the genitive is epexegetic or explicative (GK 128k, cf. 116k, 128x). On this view the phrase means lit. 'Ephraim ... is crushed in respect of justice'. To convey the meaning adequately the English translation 'all hope of justice for him is crushed' is offered. Alternatively, the genitive denotes cause (GK 116l) and the phrase is similar to שְׂרֻפוֹת אֵשׁ 'burnt with fire' (Isa 1.7) or מֻכֵּה אֱלֹהִים 'smitten by God' (Isa 53.4). On this view the phrase means lit. 'Ephraim ... is crushed by justice' for which the English translation 'crushed by the requirements of justice' is offered. The latter view is taken by the ancient versions (other than the LXX, see below) and by Rashi and Kimchi[18].

[c]For the asyndeton or co-ordination of the complementary verbal idea in the finite verb, GK 120g, König, 361h; cf. v. 15 below and 9.9.

[d]Following the LXX (below), the word צו is understood to be cognate with Arabic *ṣww* 'empty' and *ṣwwt* 'echoing sound'[19], and to have here the meaning 'vain follies', 'futility'. The word occurs elsewhere only in

[17] The same argument may be deployed against the suggestion that it is the Northern Kingdom (reading 'Israel' for 'Judah' with, e.g., Nowack, Marti, Harper) that is castigated.

[18] So, amongst moderns, e.g., Schmoller, Keil, Frey, Rudolph. The former alternative is adopted by, e.g., Alt and Qyl, and allowed as a possibility by Rudolph. Wolff (cf. Mays) with 'justice is crushed' departs from MT in that he appears not to recognise רצוץ as a construct.

[19] See Driver in *Essays presented to David Winton Thomas*, p. 55.

Isa 28.10, 13, where it is used to describe the shouts of the drunkards of Ephraim. The rabbinic commentators (Rashi, ibn Ezra and Kimchi) understand the word to be derived from the root צוה 'to command'. It is, then, the commands (*sc.* of mere men, of Jeroboam I, or of the prophets of Baal) that the Ephraimites have followed. For Kimchi the abbreviated form צו (rather than מצוה) is an indication of such a pejorative sense[20]. Jerome (cf. the Vulgate below) took the word to be an abbreviated form of צֹאָה 'filth' and interpreted it of idols (cf. the Peshiṭta, Targum and, possibly, the LXX below). These interpretations are scarcely satisfactory since 'commandments' (even false ones) cannot be said to fit the context and a passage clearly concerned with political folly hardly allows of the mention of idols (cf. Rudolph).

Amongst emendations proposed the following may be listed: (1) on the basis of the ancient versions (see below), e.g., Marti has proposed שׁו (as an abbreviation of שׁוא) 'vanity', a corruption of which, it is assumed, is presented by MT[21]. (2) צרו 'his enemy' was proposed by Duhm and adopted by Alt who sees in it a reference to the Syrians. (3) רצין Rezin, the Syrian king of the Syro-Ephraimite alliance; so Sellin. (4) סוא So, the Egyptian king (= Sib'u)[22].

All such emendations are somewhat arbitrary. The presupposition here adopted is that MT is likely to be correct and that some such meaning as has been proposed by Driver is plausible. It is admitted that his suggestion is far from certainly correct (since, e.g., the Arabic cognate cited is rare), but it is the best solution offered in the present state of our knowledge.

Again, from a strictly chronological point of view, the verse indicates a time slightly later than that depicted in vv. 8f. There the punishment of Ephraim is imminent; here it is an accomplished fact and, though deserved, elicits the prophet's sympathy (notes a and b). The subjugation of Ephraim at the hands of Tiglath-pileser III in 733 BC as well as the incursions of the Judaeans into Benjamite territory constitutes God's judgement upon the Northern Kingdom for entering into an anti-Assyrian alliance with Syria against their brothers of Judah (Alt, p. 176, cf. Jeremias). Their precipitate action has, as its consequence, removed all hope of justice, i.e. an outcome in which the country could live in peace and freedom; or else (see

20 For the talmudic view that צו (from צוה) denotes idolatry, cf. B *Sanhedrin* 56b; ET, p. 383 in *Neziḳin* III.

21 Wolff retains MT but sees in it a synonym for שׁוא. Driver's view is preferable as more precise.

22 So P. Humbert *OLZ* 21 (1918), p. 224ff. For arguments against the suggestion, cf. Alt, p. 174 n. and W. F. Albright *BASOR* 171 (1963), p. 66. K. A. Kitchen, p. 373 claims that the identification is unsound. For a treatment of 2 Kgs 17.4 and So, see J. Day *VT* 42 (1992), pp. 289ff.

note b) their foolish actions resulted in the oppression which God's justice demanded. Whichever is correct, the verse constitutes part of Hosea's interpretation of the history of the time and is characterised by mature reflection. As is the case in the previous verse, Hosea's particular judgement is built into what became a single consistent piece of historical judgement (see on v. 10 above). Impetuous actions in the political field led to tragic consequences, to civil war and to inevitable injustices. Thus, if Ephraim is cruelly oppressed, his own willingness to pursue futility (note d) brought it about. Judah, too, though wronged, allowed itself to commit wrongs and hence incurs divine punishment. For Ephraim, in a sense the prime mover of the disaster (11b), the prophet yet feels some sympathy: the enormity of the punishment is apparent in the reduction of the nation to a rump state upon the hills of Samaria, a semi-independent vassal of the Assyrians. That the Judaeans, by comparison, received so unequivocal a condemnation rests upon the consideration that they, like the Edomites at the fall of Jerusalem in 587 BC, took advantage of the massive misfortune of their brothers and added to it by their own treacherous opportunism (so Alt).

Text and Versions

עָשׁוּק ... משפט LXX κατεδυνάστευσεν E. τὸν ἀντίδικον αὐτοῦ, κατεπάτησεν τὸ κρίμα 'Ephraim has oppressed his opponent, he has trampled upon justice'. The interpretation is likely to derive from harmonisation with, e.g., Amos 4.1 where the two verbs are found in the active (so Alt). A number of modern scholars (e.g. Marti, Harper, NEB) have, however, suggested that active participles or infinitives absolute be read, i.e. עוֹשֵׁק/עָשׁוֹק and רוֹצֵץ/רָצוֹץ, on the grounds that passive participles do not fit the imperfect tenses of the preceding verses nor, in the case of the second, with the noun משפט (so, e.g., Harper). Since both these points are met by Alt's interpretation which affords reasonable sense, the suggestion may be discounted. → עשק א׳ מריבו (Borbone, after LXX).

רצוץ משפט LXX, see above; Vulg. *fractus iudicio*, cf. Pesh. *w'lys bdyn'* 'broken', 'crushed by judgement'; cf. also Targ. כבישין בדינהון 'oppressed by their judgements/law-suits'.

הואיל LXX ἤρξατο 'he began', cf. Vulg. *coepit*.

אחרי צו LXX ὀπίσω τῶν ματαίων 'after vanities', cf. Pesh. *btr sryqt'* (Gelston, p. 167; cf. the phrase *ṣlm' dsryqwt'* 'idols of vanity'); Vulg. *post sordem* 'after filth'. These versions imply that the word, whatever its precise etymology, denotes 'idols'. Targ. בתר ממון דשקר '(their judges have turned aside to err) after deceitful money'; cf. the variant reading (one manuscript is listed by Sperber) שחד 'bribe' (for שקר).

5.12 **For my part[a] I am to Ephraim like an emaciating disease[b]; and to the House of Judah like caries[c].**

[a]The personal pronoun אני emphasises the change of subject (as frequently in the Psalms) and indicates Yahweh's distinctive role and attitude in and behind the political disasters described.

[b]The word עש is usually translated 'moth', so called in reference to its destructive activity, cf. Job 13.28. The word in this sense is cognate to Arabic *'ṯṯ* which bears the same meaning (so ibn Barūn, cf. BDB, KB[3] *ad locc.*). Amongst the rabbinic commentators, Kimchi states that the phrase is metaphorical and means that Yahweh is in respect of Ephraim and Judah 'like a moth which consumes clothes'. The difficulty arises that a moth is not appropriate as a scourge of human beings (so, e.g., Wolff, Rudolph and Driver, *op. cit.* below). Ibn Barūn, commenting upon Ps 6.8 'my eyes waste away for sorrow' (*ASB*), where the cognate verb (עששׁ) is used, appeals to the same Arabic cognate verb *'ṯṯ* with the meaning 'was consumed', 'vexed' and, as an alternative, to a different Arabic verb *'šš* 'became emaciated', 'weak-sighted' and to the phrase *'mr't 'ššt* 'an emaciated woman'[23]. Yet another Arabic cognate verb is cited by G. R. Driver (cf. KB[3])[24], *viz. ġṯṯ* (said of a sheep or goat) 'it was' or 'became lean' or 'meagre' and the derivative noun *ġṯyṯt* 'thick purulent matter' and 'dead flesh of a wound'[25]. Accordingly he translates the word here 'pus' (so Wolff, Mays, Rudolph, Jeremias, cf. NEB).

The difficulty of unravelling the relationship between these various roots is apparent[26]. Generally speaking, however, it may be said that the Arabic cognate verbs all point to the notion of emaciation and disease (in relation to animals and human beings) and with this (in relation to wool or clothing) the well-attested meaning for (Hebrew) עש 'moth' is not inconsistent. Driver's theory that Arabic *ġṯṯ* most clearly illuminates the noun in this verse may well prove to be correct. However, the particular meaning that he suggests for the noun here, *viz.* 'pus', is questionable. For pus is a symptom and not a disease. Another noun derived from the same Arabic root is *ġṯ'ṯt* 'leanness'[27], and in the light of this, עש may be held here to denote 'leanness' 'emaciating disease' as does the well-attested word רזון from √רזה. With this view ibn Barūn's comments (if tentative) may be said to be consistent as is the parallelistic use of the word 'caries' (see below). Further, in the following verse the sickness of Ephraim is mentioned explicitly.

23 Wechter, p. 113.

24 Ed. H. H. Rowley *Studies in OT Prophecy*, Edinburgh, 1950, pp. 66f.

25 So Lane 6, p. 2229 col 2.

26 Driver makes an attempt to do so; *op. cit.* p. 67. It seems to me, however, that the situation is more complicated than his solution implies. For further comments and a defence of the tradition 'moths', see J. Barr *CPOT*, pp. 243f, 252 n., 279.

27 See Wehr *ad loc.*; cf. Lane 6, p. 2229 col 3.

[c]The noun רקב denotes 'rottenness', 'decay', and is elsewhere associated with bones (and so the body or whole being); cf. Hab 3.16; Prov 12.4; 14.30, and BDB *ad loc.* Again it is disease that is apparently described; see further the versions (and especially the Peshiṭta) below.

The change of subject (note a) introduces Hosea's theological appraisal of the tragic outcome of the Syro-Ephraimite War. It is Yahweh ('for my part'), the Lord of history, who visits upon his guilty people Israel and Judah their sins of political recklessness and impetuosity. Again the notion of Israel as the whole people of Yahweh obtrudes (cf. Wolff). If they bring upon themselves their own punishment it is because Yahweh has so willed it; his judgement rests equally upon those, whether Ephraim or Judah, who flout his will for Israel and whose behaviour is at odds with his moral consistency. Both nations are smitten, as it were, with wasting diseases (notes b and c) whose progress ravages their health and well-being (cf. with Rudolph, the opposite sense of 2.2, EV 1.11, where reunification and future harmony are depicted). Noteworthy is Hosea's even-handed emphasis upon the guilt of Ephraim and Judah as is his implicit understanding that the historical forces at work are directly under the control of Yahweh who uses them in his response to moral and political turpitude. In this respect his understanding is remarkably similar to that of Isaiah in Judah: for him, too, if Ephraim is deservedly punished for his sins (Isa 7.7–9, 16; 8.4) then Judah also merits punishment for his perversity (7.17ff; 8.5–8). The metaphor of sickness implies a deterioration of the political situation. If Ephraim's disease is in a measure already well-advanced (v. 11) then Judah's will be subject to no remission (v. 10)[28].

[28] Jerome's exegesis of a moth which devours a garment (Ephraim) and of the decay which, over a much longer period, pulverises wood (Judah), may reflect Jewish interpretation of the words in the light of a larger perspective of history. He seizes accurately, however, on an element in Hosea's thinking.

Text and Versions

כעשׁ LXX ὡς ταραχή[29], cf. Pesh. *'yk dlwḥy'*[30] 'like trouble', on the basis of which ככעס has been proposed (Vollers); Vulg. *tinea*, cf. Targ. כעשׁא 'moth'; Symm. εὐρώς 'dank decay'; Aq. βρωστήρ 'moth'.

כרקב LXX ὡς κέντρον 'like a sting', 'goad'; Pesh. *'ry'* 'elephantiasis', 'leprosy'; Vulg. *putredo*, cf. Aq. and Symm. σῆψις 'rottenness', 'decay'; Targ. רקבא, cf. MT.

5.13 **When Ephraim recognised[a] his disease and Judah his lesions[b], Ephraim went to Assyria, Judah[c] sent a delegation[d] to the Great King[e]; yet he is unable to heal you, nor can he free[f] you from your lesions.**

[a]Cf. BDB p. 907, col 1 3 and 5 b, for this sense of the verb ראה. As in Gen 42.21, the word denotes recognition by outward signs or symptoms.

[b]The noun מָזוֹר is often derived from the verb זור III, so BDB p. 266, col 2 'press (down, out)'. A wound (מכה) is so called because it is compressed in the process of healing (so ibn Ezra and Kimchi). The word is given the meaning 'disease' (Arabic *'ldw't*) by ibn Janāḥ. The word 'wound' is avoided here since what is referred to is not a wound (i.e. inflicted by enemies) but the sores and lesions of disease (cf. Rashi).

[c]Judah is supplied in translation *ad sensum*; see below in the commentary and cf. Rashi, ibn Ezra and Kimchi.

[d]The verb שׁלח 'to send' is used here without object (cf. 2 Sam 11.6). The word 'delegation' is supplied in English *ad sensum* (cf. the LXX and Kimchi). Rudolph's suggestion that וירושלם should be read for וישלח 'and Jerusalem [went to] the Great King' is implausible since Jerusalem is unlikely to stand for the kingdom of Judah. Alt's earlier suggestion (cf. *BHS*) to read בית יהודה is equally or more implausible since it diverges markedly from the MT.

[e]The phrase מֶלֶךְ יָרֵב is taken to be a title of the king of Assyria and to be a northern Hebrew dialectal rendering of the Accadian title *šarru rabū* 'the Great King'[31]; cf. 2 Kgs 18.19 where the phrase המלך הגדול 'the Great King' refers to the king of Assyria. The same phrase is found

[29] Rudolph suggests that, since 'pus' was inappropriate to Yahweh, the LXX renders by a blander word (which is not then to be taken as an internal Greek corruption of ἀράχνη 'spider'; cf. Ziegler *Bei.* p. 381).

[30] Probably in dependence upon the LXX; cf. Gelston, p. 167.

[31] So J. D. Michaelis *Supplementa*, p. 1155 and, more recently, G. R. Driver *JTS* 36 (1935), p. 295. For a full treatment of the history and significance of the title 'The Great King', see Artzi and Malamat.

in 10.6 and the evidence of the LXX and Peshiṭta (see below) confirms the MT and its word division[32]. The existence of a Syriac root *yrb* 'to be great' suggests that יָרֵב is an adjective related in form. It is possible that the phrase also constitutes a word-play since the form of the adjective is identical to the jussive *Qal* (third masculine singular) of √ריב 'to contend'. Hence Hosea may intend additionally to convey the sense 'to a king who might contend for you' (so Rudolph, cf. Jerome, referring to Judg 6.32, and the Targum, for which see below)[33].

Amongst the rabbinic commentators ibn Ezra and Kimchi state that in the phrase 'the king of Yareb' an Assyrian city is named. More recently Nyberg (pp. 38f) has suggested that Melek Yareb refers to an Assyrian deity who alone, in the mistaken view of the supplicants, can heal their disease. The latter suggestion presses too far the image of sickness and healing; the former, though it correctly identifies the king of Assyria as the reference, is likely to reflect a mistaken guess.

[f]The verb יִגְהֶה occurs only here and its sense is detected by reference to the parallel verb רפא 'to heal' (so already ibn Janāḥ). The Syriac cognate verb *gh'* denotes 'to be freed (from pain and disease)'. Ibn Ezra and Kimchi refer to Prov 17.22 where the sense 'healing' is possible for the derivative noun גֵּהָה (so, e.g., ibn Janāḥ, though he prefers for this noun the sense 'appearance'[34]). Rashi supposes that the sense 'remove' is the correct one and for this he compares the verb הגה II (BDB, p. 212) for which, he assumes, the verb here (גהה) is a variant form. The best attested sense is likely to be that indicated by the Syriac cognate and it is here assumed that the *Qal* is capable of a transitive force (cf. Rudolph *contra* Alt, the latter wishing to read a *Hiphil* form יַגְהֶה; since in Syriac the *Aphel* of *gh'* is attested with both transitive and intransitive force[35] it is unwise to press the comparison).

The verse continues to describe and to interpret the consequences of the Syro-Ephraimite War to Ephraim and Judah, i.e. to Israel as the people of Yahweh. The miserable plight of both kingdoms is described in terms of disease (cf. Isa 1.5ff; Jer 10.19; 30.12f) which is understood to be inflicted as a punishment for misguided political action (see on v. 12 above). When both kingdoms were obliged to acknowledge their pitiful state they compounded the disaster by appealing to the Assyrians, to the Great King (note e), in the vain hope that he would take up their

32 Hence the earlier suggestion that the text originally read מלכי רב may be discounted; for the suggestion, W. M. Müller *ZAW* 17 (1897), pp. 334ff.

33 Guillaume's similar (but different) attempt to invest the title with the meaning 'usurper' by reference to an Arabic cognate, though it accords with Tiglath-pileser III's illegitimate ascent to the throne, is too contrived to be convincing (I, 26f).

34 See further KB[3], p. 174.

35 See Payne Smith *ad loc.*

cause (note f). Yet he would prove unable to cure them or rid them of the lesions which scarred the lives of the nations. The implication of Hosea's words is that Yahweh alone could heal since it was he who had brought about and caused the debilitating sickness. The abrupt change of style from third person to second person plural emphasises the force of Hosea's argument and its negation of the mistaken policies of the nations with which he was concerned and whose internecine strife and mindless grasping for advantage he saw as a hideous disease.

Accordingly it is likely that the rabbinic commentators are right (see note c) in their view that the text implies, if it does not state, that Judah is the subject of the verb 'sent a delegation'. For this view specific mention of Ephraim and Judah in vv. 12, 13, 14 is telling evidence (notes c and d).

The form of Hosea's words is readily confirmed by the history of the times. In 738 BC Menahem had pacified the Assyrians with vast tribute (2 Kgs 15.19f)[36] and, as a consequence, they refrained from invading Ephraim, leaving the king secure in his land. In 732 BC following the assassination of the anti-Assyrian Pekah (2 Kgs 15.30), Hoshea paid tribute to Tiglath-pileser III and became a vassal king[37]. It is perhaps this latter situation which is uppermost (as most recent) in Hosea's mind (so Alt, cf. Wolff), though his argument is general enough to have comprised the former incident. Where Judah was concerned, Ahaz's personal visit to Tiglath-pileser III in Damascus in 732 BC (2 Kgs 16.10), made in the face of the Syro-Ephraimite threat, is clearly depicted[38]. Again it should be noted that Hosea's words represent an interpretation of the history of the times and there is no reason to suppose that the events to which he refers were strictly (or more or less) simultaneous (cf. Rudolph, *contra* Alt). It is the flawed policies of the time which he indicts; he is not seeking to provide a chronological catalogue of events.

Text and Versions

מזרו LXX τὴν ὀδύνην 'pain', cf. Pesh. *k'bwhy* and Targ. מכאוביה; Aq. ἐπίδεσιν 'bond', cf. Vulg. *vinculum*; Jerome, commenting on the latter, understands the Hebrew word to be מזור 'fetter' as in Ob 7 and

36 Cf. *ANET*, p. 283a.
37 Cf. *ANET*, p. 284a.
38 Rashi and Kimchi draw attention to 2 Chr 28.16ff and to Edomite and Philistine attacks on Judah which (so Williamson *Chronicles ad loc.*) are 'fully compatible with what is known (of them) ... at this time'. According to the Chronicler this, too, prompted Ahaz' appeal to Assyria.

interprets it of the devastation of Judah at the hands of the Syro-Ephraimite alliance. The word in Ob 7 is, however, highly problematic.

וישלח LXX adds πρέσβεις 'elders', 'ambassadors' *ad sensum*.

ירב LXX Ιαρ(ε)ίμ or Ιαρείβ (O); the word is here understood as a proper name; Pesh. *mlk' dyrb* 'king of I' (i.e. a place-name, cf. the rabbinic commentators, note e); Aq. δικασόμενον 'contending', 'judging', cf. Theod. κρίσεως; Symm. φονέα 'murderer'; Vulg. *ultorem* 'avenger'. All are likely to have interpreted the Hebrew as from the verb ריב 'to contend' in a short relative construction following מלך. The variations in renderings reflect particular attempts to meet the needs of the context; cf. the comments of Jerome and Ziegler. Targ., too, reflects this type of interpretation דייתי לאתפרעא להון 'who should come to take vengeance for them'.

5.14 **For it is I who am like a lion to Ephraim; like a lion[a] to the House of Judah. I, I alone[b], maul and go my way[c]. I carry off the prey[d] and no one can save it.**

[a]The word כפיר has traditionally been rendered 'young lion' (e.g. BDB, KB³). However, it is likely to be merely a synonym for שחל 'lion' and, since there is no synonym in English, the word is here repeated. Rabbi Johanan (B. *Sanhedrin* 95a; ET, p. 639 in *Neziḳin* III) lists six names for lions though it is not known whether they denote particular species or have some other significance. See further, L. Kopf *VT* 8 (1958), p. 207, S. Mowinckel in *Hebrew Studies presented to G. R. Driver*, p. 95 and Tur-Sinai *LS* 1, pp. 380ff. Qyl mentions two species of lions in ancient Israel, *felis leo persicus* (short-maned) and *felis leo barbaricus* (long-maned).

[b]The first person pronoun, repeated, is emphatic.

[c]The verb הלך 'to go', 'walk' is likely here to depict the lion, having made its kill, removing the carcass to his lair (cf. Rudolph, Qyl). For an imperfect with conjunctive *waw* co-ordinate with a preceding imperfect, cf. S. R. Driver *Tenses*, § 134.

[d]The word 'prey' is added in translation *ad sensum*.

The emphasis of the verse upon Yahweh's sole agency in and through the history of the times is very substantial. *ky 'nky* introduces the verse, 'for it is I'; and, in the second part, the repeated pronoun 'I' gives the sense 'I alone'. Thus it is not the mighty Assyrians who control the destiny of Ephraim and Judah and healing will not be mediated to the latter by their frantic attempts to enlist the support of the former. It is Yahweh alone who shapes their destinies in accordance with his consistent integrity; cf. the Targum for which the action of Yahweh's word (*mymr'*) is like a lion.

The change of image from emaciating sickness to the ferocious lion suggests to ibn Ezra the completeness of the devastation that Hosea depicts for the two kingdoms. It extends from the debilitating internal effect of the sickness (for him, though, the 'moth') to the external mauling and destruction of the beast of prey. The internecine strife of Ephraim and Judah, rightly interpreted, is none other than an expression of Yahweh's anger, vented by him in punishment. Yet where Ephraim's and Judah's destiny is bound up with the advance of the mighty Assyrians, Yahweh is again unleashing his fury, this time in the external sphere of world history. Here he is like a lion which mauls its prey and, unimpeded, drags it to annihilation in his lair. The substantial subjugation of the Northern Kingdom at the hands of the Assyrians in 733 BC (see on v. 11 above) clearly prompted Hosea's image of inexorable doom, already partly accomplished for Ephraim, inevitable also for Judah (v. 10). All such events are set in motion by Yahweh; while his fury continues there will be no relief. The verse, then, is not cast in the form of a threat: yet its contents, understood correctly, imply nothing but threat (so Alt).

For Yahweh under the image of the lion, 13.7f, cf., e.g., Isa 31.4. Elsewhere among the prophets Assyria (Nah 2.12ff) and Babylon (Jer 4.7) are compared with a lion.

Text and Versions

כפיר LXX λέων (πάνθηρ for שחל); Aq. σκύμνος 'whelp', cf. Pesh. *gwry' d'ry'*; Vulg. *catulus leonis*; Targ. כבר אריון.

CHAPTER 5.15

YAHWEH AWAITS THE NATION'S PENITENCE

5.15 **I shall retreat[a] to my place until, suffering punishment[b], they seek my presence[c] and, in their distress, they resort eagerly[d] to me.**

[a]Lit. 'I shall go, retreat ...'; asyndetic co-ordination, cf. GK 120g. The second verb, representing the principal idea, is cohortative and this determines the mood of the phrase as a whole.

[b]So for the verb אשם, e.g., BDB p. 79, col 2 3; cf. 10.2; 14.1. So, too, Rashi, ibn Ezra and Kimchi, though ibn Ezra mentions the possibility that the verb denotes desolation (שממה) as in Hos 14.1 and תֵּשַׁם in Gen 47.19; cf. on Hos 14.1; and, further, Ezek 6.6; Isa 6.11. These observations are consistent with G. R. Driver's view[1] that a second root אשם 'be desolate', is to be discerned in Hebrew and that it is a by-form of the roots שמם/ישם. On this view an alternative translation would run '... until, in desolation (lit. 'they are desolate and') ...' cf. the LXX below.

[c]Lit. 'my face', cf. Pss 24.6; 27.8. The sense is to resort to the presence of God in the hope that he will respond in help and blessing; compare and contrast 3.5; 5.6.

[d]The verb שחר is denominative from שחר 'dawn' and the sense is that 'they will resort to Yahweh like the dawn', i.e. 'eagerly' (so ibn Ezra). Elsewhere it is used, e.g., of wild asses seeking eagerly their food (Job 24.5). With God as its object, cf. Pss 63.2; 78.34; Isa 26.9. For the addition of a suffix to a form with paragogic *nun*, cf. GK 60e.

The verse constitutes a carefully worded transition from the oracle of judgement which precedes it to the expression of penitence which follows (6.1–3). Accordingly there is some understandable divergence of opinion as to whether the verse should be placed with what precedes it (so, after MT, e.g., Wolff, Qyl, AF) or with what follows (so, e.g., Marti, supposing the whole to be an addition by a later hand; Harper, Alt, Rudolph, Jeremias without doing so). Certainly in content the verse marks a clear break with what precedes it and, in tone and phraseology, it is akin to what follows. The words 'and no one can save it' at the end of v. 14 are clearly a climax and final phrase. The initial *'lk* of v. 15 (note a) bears all the marks of a catchword just as 'to my place' provides a literary link with the

[1] *Gaster Anniversary Volume*, pp. 75f.

image of the lion going (14b) unimpeded to his lair (cf. ibn Ezra and Rosenmüller). On the other hand, the intention that the Israelites should ultimately 'seek Yahweh's presence' here matches 'living in his presence' (6.2), as 'resorting eagerly to him' here matches 'the dawn' of 6.3 (note d). Links, too, are clearly forged between the oracle of punishment (5.13f) and 6.1–6 (see below) and this suggests that the whole piece reflects a natural development of thought from an assessment of the political and historical disasters which marked the end of the Syro-Ephraimite War to the religious attitudes alone capable of redeeming the situation. Indeed the conclusion is clear: the disasters must prompt repentance and return on the part of the people to humble reliance upon their God. Verse 15 proclaims this conclusion (from Yahweh's point of view) at the outset and serves as a herald to the expression of penitence which it is designed to evoke.

Linked, then, indissolubly both with what precedes it and with what follows, the verse depicts Yahweh, his terrible work done, retreating to his abode. The image of the lion recedes and hence, as in Mic 1.3; Isa 18.4ff, it is heaven (so the Targum, cf. Rashi and Kimchi) that is meant by 'my place', rather than the lair, initially suggested to the reader by the nature of the literary transition involved (and especially by the link word *'lk*, cf. ibn Ezra). The purpose of Yahweh's punitive action is revealed; and he can wait for the response of the people since he alone is in control. For further consideration of the implications of the verse, see Introduction, p. lxviii.

Text and Versions

יאשׁמו LXX ἀφανισθῶσι, cf. Vulg. *deficiatis* 'they be destroyed/you fail'. The change of subject in the latter is matched by *quaeratis* for בקשו, though it is not followed in the renderings of להם or יְשַׁחֲרֻנְנִי, which revert to third plural forms. The verse division in Vulg. is different and occurs at 'my presence' (*faciem meam*); as a consequence, the change of subject is not there so apparent. It is likely to have been done *ad sensum* and to match the second plural form in 6.4 where, again, Yahweh is the speaker. It is unlikely that these renderings imply יָשֹׁמּוּ or יֵשַׁמּוּ (from שמם so, e.g., Wellhausen, Procksch, Marti, Wolff); see note b above; Aq. and Theod. πλημμελήσωσι (cf. Symm. πλημμελοῦντες), Pesh. *nḥwbwn*, Targ. ידעון רחבו all imply אשׁם 'be guilty' (cf. note b).

ישחרנני LXX ὀρθριοῦσι πρὸς με, cf. Vulg. *mane consurgunt ad me* 'rise up early (and come) to me'; so also Pesh. *nqdmwn*; Targ. ויתבעון דחלתי 'they will seek the fear of me'.

CHAPTER 6.1–6

THE PENITENCE THAT MIGHT HAVE BEEN, CONTRASTED WITH THE TRUTH WHICH YAHWEH MUST CONFRONT

6.1 **Come[a], let us return to Yahweh; he[b] who has mauled us shall heal us; he who smites[c] us shall bind up our wounds[d].**

[a]Cf. Isa 2.5 for this hortatory usage of הלך.

[b]The personal pronoun הוא is emphatic. The particle כי has here virtually a conditional force 'if it is he that has mauled us, then he shall heal us'; cf. GK 159aa. The usual translation 'for', 'because' hardly suits the context since it wrongly suggests a reason for the repentance (cf. AF). The concessive force 'although' detected by AF is also scarcely correct since the sentence suggests very positively that Yahweh alone can reverse what he has done deliberately. The particle governs the two parallel clauses which follow it (i.e. 'he who has mauled us ... he who smites us'). For the two verbs (וְיִרְפָּאֵנוּ/וְיַחְבְּשֵׁנוּ) as jussives with simple *waw* expressing the 'assurance of a contingent occurrence', GK 109f.

[c]The verb יַךְ has the (shortened) form of a jussive, which has suggested to a number of scholars that וַיַּךְ should be read (the MT representing haplography of the *waw*)[1]. On the other hand ibn Ezra and Rashi detect in the form a frequentative (or present) sense. It is possible that the jussive form (i.e. without *waw* consecutive) fits the conditional nature of the expressions (cf. GK 109h, i) and, standing at the beginning of the phrase, it may also have been prompted by rhythmical (GK 109k) or euphonic considerations (i.e. before the following וְיַחְבְּשֵׁנוּ, so Qyl). The sense and emphasis, then, are potential and therefore appropriate to an expression of hope.

[d]The word 'wounds' is added in English *ad sensum*.

Verses 1–3 represent an expression of penitence, ostensibly on the part of the people or nation (cf. the first person plural verb and suffixes). The question arises whether the piece is a quotation of a formal expression of penitence uttered by (the priests on behalf of) the people or whether it is a composition of the prophet himself.

[1] So, e.g., Wellhausen, Marti, Wolff, Mays, Rudolph, Jeremias, *BHS*, Borbone.

The latter view seems to have been adopted by a number of the ancient versions (LXX, Peshiṭta, Targum) since they link the words with what precedes as follows: '... until ... they resort to me eagerly and say, "Come, let us return ..."'. Accordingly the expression of penitence in vv. 1–3 is understood to be formally part of the divine speech ('I will retreat ... until they resort to me and say "..."') and must therefore be interpreted as a statement of Yahweh's requirements in such an expression. To put the matter differently, the piece may be characterised as Hosea's depiction of and hope for true penitence on the part of his people[2]. It is, then, a somewhat extended elaboration of 5.15, and has something of the character of soliloquy (cf. Harper). On this view the reality of the situation obtrudes again in vv. 4f (an integral part of the piece); so far from the true penitence that Yahweh longs for[3], he is confronted with contrition that is merely transitory[4], with cultic worship which obscures ethical integrity and with continued acts of moral turpitude. Yahweh's reaction is accordingly one of despair (v. 4a).

On this view of the nature and form of these verses, their connections of thought and vocabulary with what precedes and with what follows (as also with other expressions of Hosea) are readily understandable and natural. Such connections are as follows: healing (*rp'*) in 5.13 and 6.1; mauling (*ṭrp*) in 5.14 and 6.1. In 6.4 there is mention of Ephraim and Judah as in 5.14[5]. In 5.13 the mighty Assyrians are quite unable to effect a cure, whereas in 6.1f Yahweh is represented as alone able to do so. The presence of Yahweh is mentioned in 5.15 and in 6.2. More generally, knowledge of God is a perennial emphasis of Hosea and mention of it in 6.3 matches the similar expressions in 2.22 (EV 20); 4.1 and 5.4. The beautiful image of 6.3b whereby the advent of Yahweh is likened to the beneficial coming of the regular rains is matched by the contrast of 4b where Israel's fecklessness is compared with the transitory mist and dew of dawn. Again generally the former comparison echoes the expressions of 2.19ff (EV 17ff) where restored relationship with Yahweh is reflected in the harmonious workings of nature.

[2] Cf. Keil, Orelli, Sellin.

[3] *Sic*; not a song of penitence invented by Hosea to caricature the inadequate penitence of his people, cf., e.g., Ewald, Cheyne, Harper.

[4] Cf. Alt.

[5] Clearly in both places, and in deliberate contrast to the tragedy of the Syro-Ephraimite War, Israel, Yahweh's whole people, is meant.

An alternative view[6] of vv. 1–3 is that they are a quotation by Hosea or his redactor of a formal expression of penitence by the people, perhaps in connection with a day of lamentation, made as a direct result of the calamities following the Syro-Ephraimite War and specifically in connection with Hosea's interpretation of them. Such a view of the matter implies that the expression of penitence was contrived or otherwise inadequate and that it prompted Yahweh's answer (vv. 4ff) which, so far from being an oracle of acceptance and hope, expresses his exasperation and despair.

According to this theory the links of content and vocabulary between 6.1–3 and what precedes it are explicable in terms of a direct (if inadequate) response by priests on behalf of the people to Hosea's preaching. In that the song of penitence is quoted by the redactor of Hosea's work it is made to serve the purpose of making intelligible Yahweh's reply of vv. 4ff, rather as the words of Amaziah in Amos 7.10ff were preserved and placed there as an introduction to Amos' words in vv. 14ff (Wolff). The words of the song of penitence are inadequate[7] either because the prophet perceived that, although spoken, they were not matched by appropriate deeds (Rudolph) or because they represent 'the popular piety which had been influenced by the Canaanization of the Yahweh cult' (Hentschke, cf. Wolff). Reference in Yahweh's answer (v. 6) to his absolute preference for loyalty over sacrifice, suggests to Rudolph that the expression of penitence (spoken by the priests on a day of lamentation) was marked, as usual, by the practice of propitiatory sacrifice.

A number of considerations suggest that this latter view of the matter is less satisfactory than the former. First, that so beautiful a piece, so attuned to Hosea's thought and marked by such clear connections with what precedes it, should have been composed by officials who were most unlikely to have been in sympathy, even for reasons of expediency, with Hosea is difficult enough to believe. It is more so when it is assumed (as on this theory it must be) that the composition found its way into the hands of Hosea's redactors who, in the interests of introducing Yahweh's answer (vv. 4ff), then inserted it without explanation or other

[6] Cf., e.g., Wolff, Rudolph, Mays. An earlier exposition of the piece as liturgical is to be found in H. Schmidt *Sellin Festschrift* pp. 112ff; cf. R. Hentschke BZAW 57 (1957), pp. 89f. Jeremias, by contrast, is inclined to see the closest parallels in (communal) exhortations to pilgrimage; cf. Isa 2.3; Jer 31.6; Ps 122.1 etc.

[7] The judgement that the expression of penitence was contrived and inadequate is dependent on the more recent fashion to label it as a formal Song of Penitence. Thus, e.g., Harper following Ewald, Cheyne and G. A. Smith.

formula. The assumption that the contents of the expression are somehow flawed is also difficult to maintain and in the light of their evident sincerity that assumption is characterised (by, e.g., Marti but in support of a different conclusion) as forced. The view that the contents reveal a corrupt Yahwism tainted by Canaanite ideas is mistaken (see below on vv. 2f); more likely is the judgement outlined above, *viz.* that Hosea, as in 2.19ff (EV 17ff), is appropriating to Yahwism elements of Canaanite religion which, properly understood, belong to it. The belief that nature reflects and responds to the proper practice of Yahwism became an important element in its profession, as is indicated by Deut 11.13ff.

A third suggestion is that the verses 5.15–6.3 are a later post-exilic addition to the text of Hosea made by reference to such texts as Jer 3.22ff (e.g. Marti). This view depends, amongst other things, upon the judgement that 5.14 marks the end of Hosea's genuine oracle of judgement which is accordingly contradicted by any expression of penitence or hope. Further it is said that the renewed condemnations of 6.4ff fit reasonably 5.14 but that the unity of thought is marred by the presence of the intervening verses.

Against this view it is urged that since the first account listed above is able adequately to explain the presence of vv. 1–3 and the connection of thought with what precedes and follows them, it is unnecessary to doubt their authenticity. 6.1 is linked by content and vocabulary with 5.11ff. If Yahweh is the source of Israel's (i.e. Ephraim's and Judah's) sickness and lesions[8] he, and he alone, can effect their cure. In vocabulary not only do 'mauling' and 'healing' occur here, as in 5.13f, but the introductory phrase 'let us return' (*nšwbh*) seems designed to match the divine statement of 5.15 'I will retreat (*'lk 'šwbh*) to my place'. The notion, perhaps, emphasises regression on the part of both parties to positions from which alone a new start is possible. Indeed Yahweh's retreat from his people is designed to prompt their return to him (in both cases *šwb*) since reason and expediency thereafter dictate it (cf. 2.9, EV 7). If they are able to acknowledge that their sorry plight is the result of his sovereign will, they can hope *de profundis* that, repentant, they may be healed by that same sovereign will (cf. Deut 32.39; Job 5.18 and, in a negative sense, Ezek 30.21).

[8] Ibn Janāḥ records that the word *ṭrp* here denotes the infliction of sickness (Arabic *'sqm w''ll*); cf. the talmudic usage *ṭryph* 'one having a fatal organic disease'; Jastrow, p. 554. The verb *nkh* is also used of the infliction of disease, cf. BDB p. 646, col 1 4.

Text and Versions

The saying is prefaced by the following words in LXX, Pesh., and Targ. λέγοντες *wn'mrwn* יימרון 'saying', 'they will say'; the words are interpretative and do not imply that לאמר was present in MT; cf. Gelston, p. 148.

לכו LXX πορευθῶμεν 'let us go', cf. Pesh. *nhpwk*. The renderings suggest attraction in translation to the following cohortative form rather than a different text.

יהוה LXX adds τὸν θεὸν ἡμῶν; → אלהינו (Borbone).

טרף LXX ἥρπακεν, cf. Vulg. *cepit*, 'snatched', 'carried off'; Pesh. *dmḥn* 'who smote us', cf. Targ. דמחנא.

יך Pesh. *wtbrn* 'and bruised us' has been cited as evidence for a *waw* consecutive reading וַיַּךְ (so Wellhausen *et al.*, cf. *BHS*, Borbone); the conjunction is not represented in LXX and Vulg. and hence Pesh. reading is regarded as translational (Gelston, pp. 185f); for my interpretation and translation, see above (note b).

6.2 **In two days[a] he will restore us to health[b]; on the third day[a] he will raise us from our sick-beds[c] that we may live on[d] in his presence[e].**

[a]The preposition מן is most likely to have the sense 'within', cf. Lev 27.17 and ibn Ezra's comment on it. The rendering 'after two days' is also possible; cf., e.g., BDB p. 581, col 2 b and c. 'The collocation of a numeral with the next above it is a rhetorical device employed in numerical sayings to express a number which need not, or cannot, be more exactly specified', GK 134s[9]. The general sense is that a short time is all that is needed for the healing process (cf. ibn Ezra and Kimchi). Convalescence will take some two days and on the third will be complete. The argument[10] that the phrase should not be classed as a number sequence (since the second component contains an ordinal number) is unconvincing.

[b]The verb חיה 'to live' is here found in the causative *Piel* theme. The *Qal* can denote 'to live' in the specific sense 'to recover', cf. Josh 5.8 and Isa 38.21 (so ibn Ezra and Kimchi). The *Piel*, then, as in Ps 41.3 denotes 'to cause to recover', 'to restore to health', cf. the LXX below.

[9] See further, W. Roth *VT* 12 (1962), pp. 300ff and, for Ugaritic parallels, Dahood *Proverbs*, p. 13.

[10] Cf. G. Sauer BWANT 84 (Stuttgart, 1963), p. 81. See also H. Bauer *ZAW* 54 (1936), p. 152 and H. L. Ginsberg *ZAW* 55 (1937), pp. 308f.

[c] יְקִמֵנוּ Lit. 'he will cause us to rise', i.e. from our sick beds; cf. (for *Qal/Peal*) Exod 21.19; Dan 8.27; Mk 5.41. In Ps 41.11 the causative *Hiphil* is an exact parallel to the usage here. The phrase 'from our sick beds' is added in English in order to convey the meaning precisely[11].

[d] The verb חיה, here in the *Qal*, has the sense 'to continue to live', 'to live on', cf. Kimchi and, with Rosenmüller, Gen 17.18[12], 'if only Ishmael might live under thy special care' (NEB; lit. 'might live in thy presence') where the sense is 'might live on and produce descendants under God's protection'. See further Isa 53.2; Jer 30.20.

[e] Lit. 'to his face'; see on 5.15 and note d above.

The verbs follow the imperfects of the preceding verse and express assurance of hope (cf. note c on v. 1). As in the previous verse it is healing that is depicted and, without doubt, the vocabulary attests to this (see notes b–d above)[13]. The verse, then, expresses the confidence in Yahweh's ready capability to effect the healing of those who turn to him in repentance and humility.

The reference to time and the number of days forms part of the expression of hope. The numeral two is found frequently in phrases denoting paucity (cf. 1 Kgs 17.12; Isa 7.21; 17.6 and Jer 3.14). In 2 Kgs 20.5, 8 Hezekiah is promised that, following his cure, he will go up 'on the third day' to the temple of Yahweh, i.e., raised from his sick bed, he will be able to enter the presence of Yahweh in thanksgiving[14]. Since again the phrase can denote a short time it is likely that Hosea's usage (with its two numbers) bears this meaning rather than the somewhat pedestrian and tautologous 'after two days he will restore us ... on the third he will raise us ...' (*contra*, e.g., Wolff). The phrase, then, reflects a rhetorical device (note a) and the sense is that in a short time[15] the healing process will be complete and, restored to health, the sick man will rise from his bed to live out the rest of

11 That the verb is used in connection with resurrection is not denied (e.g. Isa 26.19). It is the context which determines whether this meaning or 'rising from a sick bed' is correct. Here the latter is clearly intended; cf. König *ZThK* 45 (1948), p. 95.

12 Cf. Naḥmanides' comments on this verse (p. 102).

13 Cf. the important study of M. L. Barré *VT* 28 (1978), pp. 129ff. The author cites parallels in the (Aramaic) Genesis Aprocryphon as well as in Accadian medical texts which indicate that terms such as 'live' and 'arise' are there used of the recovery of the sick.

14 Ibn Ezra interprets three days specifically of the period after which a convalescent patient is relieved of his pain and suffering.

15 Cf. Barré (*op. cit.*), who cites close parallels from the prognosis sections of Accadian medical omen texts.

his life in the care and fellowship of God (note e). Of such a sort is Yahweh's potential healing of Israel ('we', 'us'); the image of the cure of sickness is applied metaphorically to the nation (all Israel, the people of Yahweh) which, ravaged by misfortune, is capable, if repentant, of speedy and full restoration to health by the agency of the God who alone controls its destiny[16].

The vocabulary and the particular expressions of this verse are, from an examination of the context, properly interpreted of sickness and healing. The Targum, however, constitutes evidence that from comparatively early times the imagery was interpreted in Jewish circles of resurrection from the dead; thus 'He will make us live for the days of comfort which will come in the future: on the day of the resurrection of the dead he will raise us up and we will live before him'. Undoubtedly such an interpretation has its roots in the common Old Testament understanding of sickness and recovery whereby the sick were thought to be (to some extent at least) within the sphere of death and cut off from the presence of Yahweh (cf., e.g., Pss 6.6; 30.10; 42 and 43; 88.11ff) and, recovered, were transferred to the realm of the living and to Yahweh's presence (cf., e.g., Pss 16.9ff; Isa 38.18f)[17]. A further contributory factor to the emergence of such a doctrine is the association of the notion of resurrection with that of national restoration (cf. Ezek 37) and it is noteworthy that the Targum seems to preserve this latter element. Similarly, amongst the rabbinic commentators, Rashi and Kimchi interpret the verse of the destruction of the first and second temples (which corresponds to the two-fold afflictions) and of the preceding exiles (i.e. of Egypt and Babylon); it is the third (i.e. present) exile from which national resurrection will take place and, with it, the building of the third temple.

Where early Christianity is concerned it is widely thought likely that this verse was one of the particular scriptures according to which Jesus 'was raised from the dead on the third day' (1 Cor 15.4)[18]. In fact, however, neither the New Testament

[16] This assessment is to be preferred to that of J. Wijngaards *VT* 17 (1967), pp. 226ff who argues from Hittite and Accadian treaty texts that the image of national death and resurrection finds its place in the context of covenant and is to be derived from the language used in connection with deposition of vassal kings who are 'killed' and, desiring reinstatement, beg to be 'raised to life'.

[17] Cf., e.g., C. Barth *Die Errettung vom Tode in den individuellen Klage- und Dankliedern des A. T.* (Zollikon, 1947), pp. 101f, 114f, and G. von Rad in *TDNT* 2, pp. 847ff (German, p. 849).

[18] Cf. J. du Pont *Biblica* 40 (1959), pp. 745f and S. V. McCasland *JBL* 48 (1929), pp. 124ff.

nor the early Fathers actually cite the verse as a proof-text and it was not until Tertullian[19] that it was so used. Here again Tertullian is careful to apply the text to the women – from the journey with spices early on Sunday morning to the tomb ('they resort eagerly to me', see note d on 5.15), to the joyful conversion of their desolation (thus 'they seemed to themselves smitten by the Lord' and thus, by 'the hope of his resurrection', they were restored and bound up on the third day, cf. 6.1). Elsewhere[20] Tertullian, quoting this verse, notes that the third day marked the reception of Jesus by God in heaven (thus, 'Come, let us return to the Lord', cf. 6.1).

All such interpretations represent later developments in the application and use of this verse and, while it is possible to detect a certain continuity in those developments, they do not constitute evidence in respect of the original meaning and intentions of the author.

The vocabulary and imagery of the verse have suggested to a number of scholars that Hosea was alluding to the pagan belief in the death and resurrection of the fertility god (Adonis, Osiris, Attis, Tammuz)[21], whether simply to discredit it (e.g. Sellin) or to indicate by reference to it a contrast with true Yahwistic belief (e.g. E. Jacob[22]). It is certainly striking that the 'third day' is mentioned in this connection by Lucian[23] (in reference to Adonis at Byblos), by Plutarch[24] (to Osiris) and by an ancient Sumerian poem[25] (to Ishtar/Inanna). On the other hand, the Ugaritic Texts do not mention three days in connection with Baal's triumphant return from the underworld; rather the time element there reflected is related to the (exceptional) droughts and eventual rainfall which the myth reflects[26]. Further, it is clear that this verse is concerned with Israel (i.e. the people) rather than with a god and that its expressions denote sickness and recovery rather

19 *Adversus Marcionem* iv 43, 1. Migne *PL* 1, cols 465f (*CC* Tert. vol 1, 1954, p. 661).

20 *Adversus Judaeos* xiii, 23. Migne *PL* 1, cols 636f (*CC* Tert. vol 2, 1954, p. 1389).

21 Cf. especially W. W. Baudissin *Adonis und Esmun* (Leipzig, 1911), pp. 403ff; Sellin, Robinson, Weiser, May *AJSL* 48 (1931/2), pp. 73ff.

22 *Ras Shamra-Ugarit et l'Ancien Testament* (Neuchâtel, 1960), p. 98.

23 *De Dea Syria* § 6.

24 *De Iside et Osiride* 13, 356c; 19, 366f.

25 S. N. Kramer *BASOR* 79 (1940), pp. 18ff. See further W. von Soden *RGG* 1. 688f.

26 So Driver *CML*, p. 20. An example of the time scale may be cited from op. cit. Baal III ii 25f (*CTA* 6.II.25f; *KTU* 1.6, p. 25), 'a day, two days, verily days, verily months passed, and the damsel Anath sought him'.

than the resurrection of a fertility god, temporarily dead[27]. In this connection mention of the interval of time is likely to have a rhetorical and proverbial character and to indicate a short interval rather than a reference to themes of mythology.

Text and Versions

יחינו LXX ὑγιάσει 'he will heal us'; Aq. ἀναζωώσει, cf. Vulg. *vivificabit nos*, Pesh. *wnḥyn* and Targ. יחיינא; Symm. ἐπιδήσει 'he will bind up, heal'; Quinta ὑγιεῖς ἀποδείξει 'restore to health'.

מימים LXX μετὰ δύο ἡμέρας, cf. Vulg. *post duos dies* 'after two days'; Pesh. does not reproduce מן and reads *ywmt'* 'in days' (Gelston, p. 155); Targ. ליומי נחמתא 'in the days of comfort'.

ביום Pesh. *wbywm'* suggests to Harper the addition of ו to ביום. MT is, however, entirely satisfactory.

יקמנו LXX ἀναστησόμεθα 'we will rise up' mistakenly harmonises the subject with that of the following verb.

6.3 So let us[a] agree[b] that we should[c] pursue knowledge[d] of Yahweh whose appearance[e] is as clear[f] as the sunlight at dawn[g]; he comes[h] to us like the rain[i], like the spring showers[i] which[j] water[k] the land.

[a]A cohortative form preceded by simple *waw* connects the verse with the preceding and introduces an exhortation to united contrition.

[b]Cf., with Kimchi, Job 34.4 where the same word denotes 'let us together establish the true good' (NEB; lit. 'let us acknowledge between us what is good'). The NEB renders the verb here 'let us humble ourselves', apparently deriving it from the supposed ידע II (= Arabic *wada'a*) 'make submissive', 'humiliate', 'chastise'[28]. E. Zolli has

[27] AF, somewhat differently, believe that the verse concerns resurrection rather than cure since Yahweh's prior role in punishment is assimilated to that of the Canaanite God of Death (Mot) and is fatal (5.14). The assessment is hardly convincing since AF give no comparable indication as to how Yahweh as the author of the resulting resurrection is to be understood.

[28] For this word see the writings of D. W. Thomas on the subject listed comprehensively by J. A. Emerton in *JSS* 15 (1970), pp. 145ff. For more recent criticism and evaluation, see W. Johnstone *VT* 41 (1991), pp. 49–62 and J. A. Emerton *ibid*, pp. 145–163. D. W. Thomas himself does not believe that his theory should be applied to this verse, *JTS* 38 (1937), p. 405; G. R. Driver, however, according to a report of a communication from him in B. Gemser *Sprüche Salomos*, 2nd edn., Tübingen, 1963, p. 111, may have done so. I am not aware of any reasoned case for the view. In any case, Driver *JTS* 38 (1937), p. 401 n. 7, proposes a quite different solution.

suggested[29] that the verb is to be understood as a form of a verb cognate to Arabic *d'w(y)* 'to call', 'implore' with the sense here 'let us urge ...'. Since an entirely suitable meaning can be given to the verb in accordance with the usual derivation (i.e. from ידע I 'to know') such variant interpretations, which also lack support in the ancient versions (but cf. Quinta below) and rabbinic commentators, should be discounted.

[c]For the asyndetic sequence of verbs in the same mood, typical of Hosea, cf. 5.15.

[d]לדעת Lit. 'to know'.

[e]The word מוֹצָא (lit. 'going forth') is used of the rising of the sun (Ps 19.7); cf. the cognate verb יצא 'to go forth', i.e. to rise (of the sun), Gen 19.23, and 'to appear' (of the stars), Neh 4.15.

[f]נָכוֹן the *Niphal* participle of כון, which is used in Prov 4.18 of broad daylight (so NEB) as firm or established 'when the sun seems motionless in the mid-heaven' (BDB p. 465, col 2 1 c).

[g]כְּשַׁחַר, lit. 'as the dawn'. The phrase is somewhat elliptical and the translation offered above seeks to draw out the meaning. The association of the word, usually rendered 'dawn', with the words 'appearance' and 'clear' (notes e and f) indicates that the arrival of strong sunlight is denoted[30]. H. G. May[31] has seen in the word a reference to the Ugaritic god Šḥr symbolising the winter solstice. It is unlikely on the view here taken of the piece that Yahweh should be compared with a heathen god.

[h]The verb וְיָבוֹא is understood to consist of a simple *waw* with frequentative imperfect and to constitute a parallel to the previous phrase 'whose appearance is ...'.

[i]The word גשם is a comprehensive term denoting rainfall and therefore includes the phenomena of Israel/Palestine, *viz.* the former and the latter rains, respectively, of winter and spring[32]. Of these the latter rain מלקוש ('spring showers') alone is here named[33].

[j]A short relative clause, without אשר. The absence of the article before מלקוש suggests that it is in the construct state before the relative clause.

[29] *Sefarad* 16 (1956), p. 30. The root has been detected in Prov 24.14 by D. W. Thomas *JTS* 38 (1937), p. 401. He gives the meaning of the word as 'ask', 'desire'.

[30] Cf. further *AUS* 1, p. 601.

[31] *ZAW* 55 (1937), p. 273.

[32] Cf. R. B. Y. Scott *ZAW* 64 (1952), p. 23. The former rains come in the period December to February and the latter rains in March and April.

[33] *Contra* van Gelderen who invests the word גשם here with the meaning 'the former rains' (יורה). In Ezra 10.9, 13 the plural word גשמים denotes the rainy season of the year (so BDB). Williamson (*Ezra-Nehemiah*) renders 'heavy rain' at v. 9 but 'rainy season' at v. 13 and thinks that in v. 9 the word is a plural of intensity.

[k]The verb is construed as a *Hiphil* form of the verb ירה akin to רוה 'to fill', 'satisfy', 'water' (so Rashi and Kimchi, cf. the Peshiṭta and Targum) from which the noun יוֹרֶה 'former rains' is to be derived (cf. KB[3] p. 416, col 2). The suggestion that יַרְוֶה be read (so Perles, *BHS*) is unnecessary. The attempt to parse the word here as the noun 'former rains' (cf. LXX and Vulgate; *q.v.* below)[34] is unsatisfactory since it is consequently impossible to construe the word 'land'. It is possible that the verb reflects the dialectal usage of the North (so Rudolph).

The verse constitutes a conclusion to the expression of penitence. The words indicate mutual exhortation on the part of the people in accordance with the reasoning which the piece (vv. 1–3) sets forth. They must acknowledge (see note b above) the necessity vigorously to pursue knowledge of Yahweh. For the form of the words, cf., with Kimchi, David's exhortation to Solomon (1 Chr 28.9) 'My son, acknowledge your father's God'.

It is likely that the concept of vigorous striving to know Yahweh is to be seen against the background of his withdrawal (see 5.15). There is also an allusion, by way of contrast, to mother Israel's futile pursuit of her lovers and her consequent resolution to return to her husband (see on 2.9, EV 7). Reason thus prompts resolution and resolution demands vigorous effort. Such effort is rewarded by success (cf., with Qyl, Deut 4.29) and the sure response of Yahweh: his appearance will be as bright and clear as the dramatic sunrise of Israel/Palestine (see note e) and his beneficial effect upon his people will be as decisive as that of the regular rain and spring showers upon that land (see note i). In the case of the former simile the emphasis is upon the prompt and decisive strength of sunlight; in the latter the emphasis is upon the effect that the life-giving rains have upon the earth, since their inception is subject to temporal variations (so Rudolph citing *AUS* 1, pp. 172f).

Knowledge of Yahweh (note d above) indicates single-minded loyalty to him and to his ethical nature (see on 2.22, EV 20 and 4.1). To pursue it is to strive vigorously to appropriate it. It is noteworthy that the verb is used elsewhere frequently in relation to ethical integrity (*ṣdq*), cf. Deut 16.20; Isa 51.1; Prov 15.9; to goodness (*ṭwb*), Ps 38.21; to peace (*šlwm*), Ps 34.15; to decency (*ḥsd*), Ps 23.6; Prov 21.21. As ibn Ezra observes, knowledge of God comprehends all such 'wisdom' (*ḥkmh*).

Wolff sees in the similes the influence of the nature-myths of Canaanite religion. On the view here adopted, *viz.* that the piece (vv. 1–3) is an expression of penitence conceived by Hosea as a

[34] Cf. also ibn Ezra.

statement of Yahweh's requirements, the similes indicate his assessment of Yahweh's capability of ready response and of his *de facto* control of nature which thus, correctly understood, witnesses to that response. In this sense, Hosea as elsewhere (especially chapter 2) seeks to appropriate for Yahweh the sphere claimed as Baal's by his opponents.

Wolff's view is bound up with his assessment of the piece as a defective expression of penitence on the part of the people. He identifies one of its defects as a faith in Yahweh tainted by Canaanite ideas. On this view of the matter, Rudolph's objection is persuasive: why, in Yahweh's 'reply' (vv. 4ff) is this defect not explicitly censured?

Again, the contents and vocabulary of the expression of penitence are wholly consistent with Hosea's thought. If the similes from the world of nature reflect elements detectable in Canaanite religion that is not surprising, for the prophet is at pains to meet the challenge of that religion and to show that the processes of nature are to be undertsood in relation to the reality of its Creator. Wolff's assessment of the similes is therefore mistaken, largely because his evaluation of the expression of penitence is incorrect.

For comparisons elsewhere between Yahweh and the brightness of sunlight, cf. Deut 33.2 (*zrḥ*); between Yahweh's teaching (by Moses) and the rain, Deut 32.2 (so ibn Ezra).

Text and Versions

ונדעה LXX καὶ γνωσόμεθα; Symm. γνῶμεν; Vulg. *sciemus*; Pesh. *wnd'*; Targ. ונילף; all denote 'know', 'learn'. Quinta παιδευθῶμεν οὖν 'let us then be disciplined'; the verb often answers to יסר and here might be taken to indicate knowledge of ידע II (see note b above); it is a further question whether this translation is correct in the context, cf. D. W. Thomas *op. cit.* above. Barthélemy *ThZ* 16 (1960), pp. 342–353 argues that it is incorrect to ascribe the reading to Quinta, cf. Emerton *op. cit.*, p. 149. Borbone omits נרדפה לדעת → 'Dobbiamo conoscere Yahweh'.

מצאו LXX εὑρήσομεν αὐτόν. The reading has suggested the emendation כְּשַׁחֲרֵנוּ כֵּן נִמְצָאֵהוּ 'when we seek him then we shall find him' (e.g. Giesebrecht, Wellhausen, Marti). It is possible that the reading has come about in reference to, e.g., Deut 4.29 where seeking Yahweh precedes finding him.

יורה LXX (ὡς ὑετὸς ἡμῖν πρόϊμος) καὶ ὄψιμος (τῇ γῇ), cf. Vulg. (*quasi imber nobis temporaneus*) *et serotinus* (*terrae*), '(like the rain to us, former) and latter, (on the earth)'; Pesh. *dmrw' l'r'* (Gelston,

p. 127), cf. Targ. דמרוי ערעא 'which saturate the earth'. Two examples of emendations and rearrangements of the text are: (1) Giesebrecht's proposal (*Beiträge*, p. 208) to read כְּשַׁחֲרֵנוּ כֵּן נִמְצָאֵהוּ 'when we seek him so we shall find him'. All the versions and the citation of the phrase in 1QH iv 6 confirm MT; for the citation, M. Mansoor *RQ* 3 (1961/2), pp. 265f. (2) NEB adds after יהוה, וּמִשְׁפָּטוֹ כָּאוֹר יֵצֵא transposing the clause from v. 5 and emending it, 'Yahweh, whose justice dawns like morning in light (and its dawning is as sure as the sunrise)'.

6.4 What am I to do with you, Ephraim? What am I to do with you, Judah? Your good intentions[a] are like the morning[b] mist and like the dew[b] which disappears early[c] in the day.

[a]For the word חסד 'goodness', 'kindness', cf. 2.21 (EV 19) and 4.1. In the present context the word is used specifically to denote the contrition of which the people were capable but which, in reality, fades to nothing (so, essentially, ibn Ezra). Accordingly, since the word here refers to intention or internal disposition, the translation 'good intentions' is offered.

[b]For the article before 'dew' כַּטַּל together with its absence before 'morning', cf. König, 299m.

[c]For the participle without article following a definite noun, cf. König, 409b. The translation 'early in the day' (משכים) answers to the literal Hebrew 'arising early'. The two participles מַשְׁכִּים/הֹלֵךְ are either juxtaposed asyndetically (GK 120g) or else the first participle משכים is a variant construction for an infinitive construct הַשְׁכִּים), cf. Ps 127.2 and P. Wernberg-Mo{/}ller *ZAW* 71 (1959), p. 65. Ibn Ezra comes to much the same conclusion by regarding the word as virtually a noun denoting 'dawn'. Accordingly the phrase means literally 'like the dew of (each) dawn which disappears'.

The prophet's soliloquy upon the theme of the penitence of which Ephraim and Judah, the people of Yahweh, were capable and which alone could bring about the redemption of their unhappy plight, is interrupted by his perception of the reality of the situation (see on v. 1). In fact there is no penitence and any residual good intentions (note a) fade as swiftly as does the morning mist (*'nn-bqr*) or the heavy dew in the heat of the summer sun of Israel/Palestine[35], cf. Isa 44.22; Job 7.9. Hosea thus depicts Yahweh as enunciating the age-old reprimand of the parent faced with wayward children 'What am I to do with you?'

[35] For descriptions see e.g. *AUS* 1, pp. 93ff and R. B. Y. Scott *ZAW* 64 (1952), pp. 21ff.

(so Jerome). For similar anthropomorphic expressions of exasperation, cf. Isa 5.4 and Mic 6.3f.

On this interpretation of the verse, Yahweh's cry of exasperation forms an integral part of the single composition which runs from the end of 5.15[36]. With the two verses that follow (i.e. 6.5f) the prophet sets forth the mind of his God as he contemplates the miseries of Ephraim and Judah following the Syro-Ephraimite War. To these indeed he has brought them and he has had no choice but to do so. The remarkable insight of Hosea consists in his suggestion that Yahweh himself shares in the misery which he is constrained to cause and the saying matches precisely the great divine *cri de cœur* of 11.8ff, 'How can I give you up, Ephraim ... ?'

An alternative view, taken by reference to form-critical methods, is to see in vv. 4ff a formal divine oracle or answer given in response to the (quoted) formal expression of penitence by (priests on behalf of) the people[37]. It seems to me that such an explanation is doubtful on two grounds: first, the expression of penitence is so well attuned to Hosea's thought and so uncompromising in its loyalty to Yahweh that it is unlikely to be mere lip service on the part of the people, then challenged by Yahweh's answer. Nor can it be said to be an expression of penitence flawed by the inclusion within it of Canaanite beliefs and ideas, for then Yahweh's retort could be expected explicitly to have attacked such views (see further on v. 1 above). Secondly, while such a form-critical account of the composition of 6.1–6 is a possibility, it is achieved at the expense of the more attractive theory that the piece is characterised by unity of thought and represents Hosea's attempt to explain the dilemma in which Yahweh himself is placed by a people to whom he is committed but whose behaviour and attitude require his wrath. With this latter view the language and sentiments of v. 5 are more consistent than with the view that they are employed in a divine retort to an expression of penitence flawed by inconsistent actions (Rudolph) or by syncretistic ideas (Wolff). Accordingly it seems to me that vv. 4–6 are better understood as a theodicy than as a divine decree or answer.

36 Cf. the similar, but not identical, views of AF.

37 So, e.g., Wolff and Rudolph applying H. Gunkel's and J. Begrich's theory originally posited in reference to the Psalms; *Einleitung in die Psalmen* (Göttingen, 1933), pp. 136ff.

Text and Versions

No significant readings.

6.5 **In the circumstances that[a] I have hewn them in pieces[b] through[c] the prophets, killed them[d] through the words of my mouth, [e]can judgement in your favour[f] be a shining light?[e]**

[a]For על כן with the sense 'because that', 'in the circumstances that', cf. with Rashi Gen 33.10 and Gen 38.26. See further the comments on 4.3. The clause prefaces the rhetorical question 'can judgement in your favour ...' cf. Rashi and note e below.

[b]The object 'them' is not present in the MT but, being found after the parallel verb 'kill', is supplied in translation *ad sensum*. The verb חצב which usually denotes hewing stone is here understood to be used figuratively of harsh treatment (cf., with ibn Janāḥ, the use of the verb רצץ 'to crush' in 2 Chr 16.10). A similar use of the verb is found in Isa 51.9 where the arm of Yahweh, in primeval battle, hews Rahab in pieces (so, again, ibn Janāḥ). In Ugaritic the cognate verb *ḫṣb* denotes 'to slay', 'to fight' and is found in parallelism with *mḫṣ* 'to smite', 'wound'; again the context is combat, here Anat's massacre of the inhabitants of the two cities[38]. For evidence of the versions see under Text and Versions below. See further in the commentary for evaluation of the sense of the word in this context.

[c]*Beth instrumenti* BDB p. 89, col 2 2 c; so the Targum and Rashi. The LXX and Peshiṭta understand the prophets as the object of the verb as does ibn Ezra for whom 'I hewed amongst the prophets' denotes 'I killed some of their prophets' (because they led the people astray)[39]. The parallel phrase 'through the words of my mouth' indicates plainly that the former view is preferable.

[d]The usual meaning of the verb הרג. For further evaluation of its meaning in this context, see the commentary. The third person masculine plural suffix 'them' is awkward, followed as it is by a second masculine singular suffix 'judgement in your favour'. Changes of suffix in the same verse are, however, not infrequent in Hosea and, according to the interpretation of the verse here followed, the final rhetorical question with the second person reference is not without force or appropriateness. The NEB emends to a second person masculine plural suffix.

[38] *CTA* 3.B.6f, 19f, 23f, 29f; *KTU* 1.3 (pp. 10f); cf. *CTA* 7.I.4, 6; *KTU* 1.7 (p. 29); cf. Gibson, pp. 147, 151.

[39] Similarly, Jerome in his comments upon the LXX. This interpretation is followed amongst moderns by, e.g., Sellin, Nyberg and Qyl.

e—eThe whole phrase is taken as a rhetorical question (cf. Rashi and Qyl) parallel to the question posed in v. 4 'What am I to do about you ...?'; see further in the commentary below.

fFor the clause cf., with ibn Ezra, Ps 37.6 '(He will make your righteousness shine clear as the light) and the justice of your cause (משפטך) like the sun at noon'. The *yodh* before the suffix (here and in many MSS at Ps 37.6) is not necessarily an indication of a plural form, cf., with Qyl, Prov 3.18 וְתֹמְכֶיהָ with its singular predicate.

The verse, according to the interpretation of it here adopted, is of a sort with v. 4 and expresses with a similar rhetorical question (note e) the divine dilemma. The penitence of which Hosea dreams is at best ephemeral and hence Yahweh is constrained to act punitively against his people. Accordingly he simply cannot do as he would like to have done and Hosea depicts such feelings with the question '(In such circumstances) can judgement in your favour be a shining light?' Or, according to Rashi's paraphrase, 'How can I show favour towards you in face of the demands of justice?' Thus the question is a variation, though more sharply defined, of the preceding 'What am I to do with you, Ephraim ... Judah?'

The events following the Syro-Ephraimite War constitute Yahweh's judgement upon his people (Israel and Judah) and their miserable plight is depicted at the end of chapter 5. Here the mode of the punishment and its origin are defined. It is by the agency of Yahweh's prophets and by the very word of his mouth that it has been effected. Whether in this respect Hosea is thinking of his own work and that of other like-minded contemporary prophets, or whether he sees the present disasters as the culmination of the condemnations of earlier prophets (Ahijah, Elijah, Micaiah ben Imlah, Amos and Isaiah[40]) is not clear. At all events the words he uses are strong ones.

The verb *ḥṣb* 'hewn in pieces' seems to have a long literary history, occurring as it does in connection with Yahweh's defeat of the monster Rahab (Isa 51.9) and, in Ugaritic, of Anat's massacre of the inhabitants of the two cities (see note b above). *hrg* 'killed them', being a common word, seems to confirm such a meaning for the earlier *ḥṣb*. Accordingly Hosea is likely to be making use of ancient mythological terms depicting divine destruction to describe Yahweh's decisive and awful contem-

40 So, e.g., Wolff and Mays. Kimchi (though he does not mention them by name) speaks of God's urgent and daily warnings with which he wearied the prophets.

porary punishment of his people[41]. The prophets, then, are agents of Yahweh since they proclaim and unleash the words of his mouth, words which have the effect of a baleful curse.

The use of such mythological language by the prophets (and the psalmist) in relation to events in the history of Israel is widely acknowledged, cf., e.g., the verb *g'r*, 'to roar', 'chide' which provides a particularly clear example since it is used of Yahweh's effective speech[42].

That the language is strong does not preclude the possibility that its use in this particular context is metaphorical. Thus G. R. Driver[43] has argued that *ḥṣb* may denote here specifically 'to denounce' and that *hrg* may denote 'to confound', i.e. by violent speech. His argument relies upon comparable ranges of meaning attested in various semitic languages for similar words (in relation to both *ḥṣb* and *hrg*). His view is reflected in the NEB translation of the verbs which seeks to convey both their strength and their metaphorical usage, 'I have lashed you through the prophets ... torn you to shreds with my words'.

Recognition of the likely grammatical form, and the nature of the vocabulary in the verse (i.e. the view of it taken by Rashi) enables the judgement that good sense can be elicited from it and that it fits the context admirably. Accordingly the many alternative accounts of it, and particularly those that resort to emendation, may be discounted. Among the most common are those which understand the last clause as having virtually a purposive or consequential sense, i.e. 'I have hewn ... killed ... so that judgement in your favour may eventually prevail' (so, e.g., ibn Ezra and Kimchi).

Secondly, a substantial number of modern commentators[44] follow the LXX, Peshiṭta and Targum (*q.v.* below) and read 'my justice' (*mšpṭy*) for 'thy justice'. The sense that emerges is then, 'I have hewn ... killed ... so that (or with the consequence that) my justice will shine forth'.

Thirdly, and more radically, Rudolph[45] seeks to stick to the literal meaning of *ḥṣb* and by substantial emendation to find in the verse a reference to Yahweh having 'hewn in stone by the

[41] For the ritual significance of Anat's slaughter of mankind interpreted as a necessary prelude to the restoration of peace and fertility, see J. C. de Moor, pp. 94ff.

[42] See Macintosh *VT* 19 (1969), pp. 471ff.

[43] *VT* 1 (1952), p. 246; cf. and contrast R. P. Gordon's observations in *VT* 40 (1990), p. 140.

[44] E.g. Harper, Wolff, Rudolph, Mays, AF, *BHS*, Borbone.

[45] He relies upon earlier suggestions by A. Klostermann *ThLZ* 26 (1905), pp. 474f and H. Schmidt *Sellin Festschrift*, p. 120.

prophet (*sc*. Moses) and taught them from the Mountain through the words of my mouth so that my ordinance goes forth as clearly as light'. (For his emendations of MT, see under Text and Versions below.)

Text and Versions

חצבתי LXX ἀπεθέρισα 'cut off'; Aq. and Theod. ἐλατόμησα, cf. Vulg. *dolavi* and Pesh. *psqt*, 'hew (stones)'; Symm. οὐκ ἐφεισάμην 'I did not spare'; Quinta ἐξέκοψα 'cut off', 'make an end of'; Targ. אזהרתנון 'I warned them' or, with Cod. Reuch., אוחרתינון 'I made them tarry', *sc*. restrained them, (through the prophets)'; LXX and Pesh. (Gelston, p. 166) understand 'the prophets' as the object of the verb (so Borbone, → נביאיכם); the translations of Symm. and Targ. suggest a weakening of the sense of MT in deference to the needs of the context; see the commentary above.

משפטיך LXX καὶ τὸ κρίμα μου, cf. Pesh. *wdyny* and Targ. ודיני 'my judgement'; Quinta ἡ δικαιοκρισία; Vulg. *et iudicia tua* 'and thy judgements'; → ומשפטי (*BHS*, Borbone).

אור LXX ὡς φῶς 'like light', cf. Vulg. *quasi lux*, Pesh. *'yk nwhr'* (Gelston, p. 122) and Targ. כניהור; → ומשפטי כאור (*BHS*, Borbone, cf. Cathcart).

The text of the verse as emended by Rudolph (on the basis of suggestions by other scholars) runs ...על כן חצבתי בְּנביא מֵהַר הֹרֵיתִים.

6.6 **For[a] it is goodness[b] that I desire, not sacrifice; knowledge of God[b] and not[c] burnt offerings.**

[a]The particle כי is understood to have its customary sense. Rudolph's view that it is כי *recitativum* accords with his understanding of the previous verse which is here discounted.

[b]Cf. 2.21f (EV 19f) and 4.1.

[c]מן is here understood to have a privative force, cf. GK 119w. An alternative view is that מן has a comparative force and that לא in the first half of the verse is a 'relative or dialectal' negation[46], i.e. 'not only'. According to this view the force of the saying is 'it is decency that I desire, not (just) sacrifice; knowledge of God rather than (just) burnt offerings'. The former view is preferred as being more consistent with Hosea's thought; see the commentary below.

46 See H. Kruse *VT* 4 (1954), pp. 385ff.

This fine saying represents Hosea's view of Yahweh's consistent and unchanging requirement of his people. Here it provides the reason why Yahweh cannot vindicate them despite his longing to do so. Thus it forms part and is the culmination of the argument which runs from 5.15 to the present point and beyond it to the catalogue of sins listed in 6.7–10.

Goodness, kindness in moral behaviour (so *ḥsd* as in 2.21, EV 19, and 4.1) and the proper recognition of Yahweh's ethical nature (so 'knowledge of God') are set in direct contrast to the cultic feasting ('sacrifice') and to the costly burnt offerings (note the plural) whereby whole animals were offered to Yahweh. Since elsewhere (5.6; 8.11ff) Hosea repudiates radically the whole sacrificial cult with its licentious feasting it is likely that here, too, this is the burden of his message. The alternative view, grammatically possible (see note c), that Yahweh's preference is for decency and knowledge of God above sacrifice and burnt offerings is less likely to fit the argument in this particular context. Qyl's preference for the latter view is likely to represent post-exilic and later Jewish views and it is significant that he quotes Isa 56.7 in support of his case that Hosea, in Yahweh's name, condemns not sacrificial worship for itself but faulty reliance upon it on the part of those in prior need of moral correction. Hosea's view-point is more of a sort with that of Amos (5.21ff), Micah (6.6ff) and Jeremiah (7.21ff) than with that of the perhaps less radical Isaiah of Jerusalem (1.10ff) – so Rudolph.

The qualities of moral integrity and of the correct devotion to Yahweh are contrasted with the cultic feasting and opulent worship which has precisely the effect of lessening those qualities in the lives of individuals and then of the nation itself (see the argument of chapters 4 and 5). It is this that has led step by step to the disastrous situation of the Syro-Ephraimite War, to the politics of coalition (5.11b), to submission to a greater nation (5.13) and to internecine strife between Ephraim and Judah (5.8, 10) – so essentially, Wolff.

Yahweh's unchanging requirement is for decency and knowledge of God, terms which are essentially complementary in meaning (cf. Jeremias). For the reason that his people have not met that covenant requirement, so far from vindicating them, Yahweh has 'hewn them in pieces through the prophets and killed them through the words of his mouth' (v. 5). Such has been his consistent policy and to it the present situation conforms. The didactic statement of the verse is axiomatic to the theodicy of which it is a part. Despite his inclinations, Yahweh cannot resolve his dilemma other than by acting in accordance with his ethical nature. It is, then, by reference to his understanding of Yahweh's nature that Hosea applies his argument to the present situation. The verse is not, as Rudolph would have it, the particular response to an argument of the people who were disposed to believe that they could ingratiate themselves with Yahweh by expressing formally (but superficially) their penitence and, additionally, by associating that expression of penitence with costly sacrificial offerings[47].

The sentiments of the verse are expressed in words which are very similar by Samuel (1 Sam 15.22) and consequently some scholars (e.g. Wolff and Mays) see in them the reflection of a didactic tradition preserved in Levitical/prophetic circles opposed to the nation's priestly and royal establishment. More generally Hosea may be said here to reflect the established values of the prophets of the Northern Kingdom (cf. Jeremias) and to have contrasted those values with those of the syncretistic cult of the eighth century establishment.

The verse is twice quoted by Jesus (Mt 9.13; 12.7) and was apparently used by him to condemn the rigid and inhumane attitudes displayed by the contemporary Pharisees.

Text and Versions

ולא LXX (B-239, Q^c, L), cf. OL^W, ἤ 'rather than', cf. Targ. מדרבח; Vulg. and Pesh. (*et non, wl'*) 'and not', cf. LXX (rel.) καὶ οὐ.

מעלות LXX ἤ, cf. the Vulg. *plus quam*; Pesh. and Targ. *mn*/מן.

47 For arguments against the view that vv. 1–3 are a quotation by Hosea of a formal expression of penitence (*Busslied*) on behalf of the people, see on 6.1 above.

CHAPTER 6.7–7.2

TREACHERY AND TREASON

6.7 But they have broken a covenant[a] in Adam[b]; there they behaved treacherously against me.

[a]The word ברית is apparently indefinite. Two of the ancient versions (see below) render the word 'my covenant' interpreting the word of Yahweh's covenant. That the reference is to that covenant is, however, far from certain (see further in the commentary).

[b]Reading with Codex 554 (de Rossi) and Wellhausen, together with most recent commentaries בְּאָדָם, the name of the town[1] mentioned in Josh 3.16 which is identified with the modern ed-Damiyeh at the mouth of the Jabbok, on the east bank of the Jordan approximately forty two kilometres north of the Dead Sea. That a place-name was indicated is virtually certain in view of the following שם 'there'[2] and of the place-names mentioned in the subsequent verses. The MT reads כְּאָדָם which appears to mean 'like Adam' or 'like man'.

The ancient versions together with Jerome and Rashi, following MT, understand the phrase to mean 'like Adam/like men they have broken my covenant'. שם, 'there', is therefore understood to denote the good land (of Israel), comparable to the garden of Eden (Rashi). Amongst modern commentators, e.g., Harper, van Hoonacker and Qyl have taken 'like man' to mean 'after the manner of man'. The interpretation is, however, contrived and yields a weak if not meaningless sense in the context. That the word constitutes a reference to Adam/Man has attracted the support of, e.g., Nyberg, Ridderbos and van Gelderen. It is doubtful, however, whether Adam could be said to have transgressed a covenant or whether his transgression of the divine command is here referred to since that is not the case anywhere else in the OT (cf. Rudolph).

Kimchi understands the phrase to constitute a comparison between the transgression by Israel of Yahweh's covenant and the transgression by a man of a covenant with his neighbour. According to this view a grammatically possible translation of MT can be secured: 'they have broken the covenant like that of a man', i.e. as though it were merely an agreement between men. Amongst modern commentators this view has found the support of, e.g., Ehrlich and Riessler. A similar but different

[1] The ancient name has been revived in modern times in the Israeli name of the nearby bridge Gesher Adam.

[2] The claim (e.g. Nyberg) that שם here bears a temporal meaning 'then' is dubious, cf. Rudolph.

view is taken by Rabbi Eliezer of Beaugency (twelfth century) who understands the clause to mean 'they have broken my covenant as though I were a mere man'.

The latter view is less satisfactory than the former which is contrived. Both views, however, depend upon the assumption, which is far from certain (cf. Rudolph and see below in the commentary), that the text speaks of Yahweh's covenant with Israel.

The question immediately arises whether vv. 7ff belong to what precedes them or whether they constitute a new section and refer to a different situation. An important consideration is that here, as distinct from 5.8–6.6, Judah is no longer apparently in the prophet's mind (6.11 is generally regarded as secondary, even by those, e.g. Wolff, who take a different view) and his attention seems to be directed exclusively to Ephraim. Accordingly it is doubtful whether the material of 6.7ff referred originally or at all to the situation following the Syro-Ephraimite War. Where the contents of the section are concerned, it seems on balance most likely that the whole section (i.e. 6.7–7.16) constitutes an indictment of the Northern Kingdom in the degeneracy of its royal and cultic establishment and is therefore a series of particular examples of the corruption more generally described in e.g. 1.4ff[3]. On the view here taken of vv. 4–6, *viz.* that they are an imaginative description of Yahweh's dilemma in the form of a soliloquy and that they constitute, therefore, a theodicy, the redactor (or Hosea editing his own words) may have written the opening word *whmh* 'but they' as a redactional link-word. This would indicate the further argument that, where Ephraim is concerned, the nation stands condemned since, in its recent history, it has consistently breached the axiomatic requirements of Yahweh (v. 6).

Wolff believes that since 'but they' never introduces a new prophetic saying, the section (6.7–10a) belongs more radically to what precedes it and is accordingly a further demonstration of the inadequacy of the people's expression of penitence. For criticisms of the theory that vv. 1–3 constitute an expression of penitence by the people, see on v. 1 above.

The verse forms part of an identifiable cluster of sayings (6.7–7.2) which, with 7.3–7 and 7.8–16, constitute a larger collection of examples. By means of them the establishment of

[3] For the view that 6.7–7.2 constitutes a retrospective judgement upon Israel's earlier history (Adam and Gilead, Judg 12.1–6; Shechem, Gen 34 etc.), cf., e.g., Sellin. It is regarded here as more likely that the prophet is concerned with recent or contemporary history (cf. Rudolph).

the kingdom of Ephraim stands condemned. The details of the events to which reference is made in the section 6.7–7.2 are unfortunately not certainly known to us. Following the suggestions of Alt[4] and G. Fohrer[5] (cf. Rudolph), it is here assumed that the prophet depicts an act of revolution against the reigning king initiated with the aid of men from the trans-Jordanian city of Gilead (v. 8); hence the movement spread to the city of Adam (v. 7) and continued westward over the Jordan via Wady Far'ah/Naḥal Tirzah[6] to Shechem (v. 9) and on to Samaria and the royal house of Israel (v. 10). According to 2 Kgs 15.25 fifty Gileadites took part in the overthrow in Samaria of King Pekahiah by his lieutenant Pekah in 736/5 BC[7]. Alt was inclined to think that either of the usurpations of the throne by Shallum or Menahem in 747 BC may be alluded to and their names 'Son of Jabesh' and 'Son of Gadi' have been understood to reflect the area of Jabesh-gilead in the tribal territory of Gad (cf. Rudolph). It is, however, safer to think of Pekah's rebellion since in that case Gileadites are explicitly mentioned by 2 Kgs while in the case of Shallum and Menahem the significance of their full names is far from certainly known[8] and it is possible that they were contenders for the throne from Ephraim and Manasseh (cf. with Gray, Isa 9.19f). In the case of Menahem (2 Kgs 15.14) his rebellion is stated to have originated in Tirzah.

Verse 7, then, is taken to refer to the beginnings of the rebellion of Pekah in 736/5 BC at Adam in Gilead (see note b above). There the current ordinance established between the monarch and people of Ephraim was breached by Pekah's plot and hatched with the active support of Gileadites. For this sense of the word 'covenant' (*bryt*) cf. BDB p. 136, col 1 I 2 and Fohrer, *op. cit.* The breach (i.e. treason) is judged by Hosea to have been an act of treachery against Yahweh their God, perceived as the guarantor (cf. Jeremias) of the particular covenant (cf. 2 Sam 5.3 and the phrase 'before Yahweh'). For the word, cf. on 5.7 above. An alternative interpretation is to see in 'covenant' a reference to the covenant established between Yahweh and his people. Such is the interpretation of two of the ancient versions which translate the word 'my covenant'[9]. If,

4 *KS* 2, p. 186 n.

5 *ZAW* 71 (1959), pp. 15f.

6 The wady is the only wide pass leading from the Jordan valley into the heart of Palestine/Samaria.

7 So already Rosenmüller.

8 Cf., e.g., Gray; also N. K. Gottwald, p. 125 and J. Day *VT* 36 (1986), p. 5.

9 Amongst moderns, cf. Wolff, Mays, Qyl, AF; cf. also Nicholson, pp. 184ff and Day *op. cit.*

however, this had been Hosea's intention one would expect him, as in 8.1, to have written 'my covenant'; the *difficilior lectio* of the MT which has, apparently, the indefinite 'covenant' is more likely to be correct[10]. In this connection it is worth recording first, that Kimchi (note b above), though he believes that the verse refers to a breach in Yahweh's covenant, understands that it does so by reference to a breach in a covenant concluded by men[11]. Secondly, J. J. P. Valeton *ZAW* 13 (1893), p. 247, has demonstrated that the breach of a covenant concluded by men invoking Yahweh's name was judged as an act of treachery against Yahweh. See further on the following verse and cf. 10.4 for condemnation of the injudicious making of numerous foreign treaties.

Text and Versions

כאדם LXX ὡς ἄνθρωπος, cf. Pesh. *'yk br nš'* 'like man', Vulg. *sicut Adam* 'like Adam'; Targ. כדריא קדמאי 'like earlier generations'.

ברית Pesh. and Targ. *qymy*, קימי, 'my covenant'; LXX and Vulg. διαθήκην/*pactum*.

6.8 **Gilead is a city[a] of evil-doers[b], [c]exposed as treacherous by bloodshed[c].**

[a]It is here assumed with Noth[12] that Gilead is the name of a city and that it is to be identified with the modern Khirbet Jal'ad, some ten kilometres north-east of Salt, and seven kilometres south of the Jabbok. The objection to this is the fact that the term Gilead usually denotes the district (so already Rosenmüller; the point is emphasised more recently by AF). However, Judg 10.17 clearly seeks to denote by 'Gilead' the specific place (as opposed to the district) where the Ammonites confronted the Israelites who, in turn, were encamped at Mizpah (*sc*. of Gilead), also identified as a site at modern Khirbet Jal'ad[13]. It is likely

[10] Cf. Perlitt, p. 143; curiously neither Nicholson nor Day address themselves to the indefinite character of the reference to 'covenant'.

[11] His argument is, of course, aided by his belief that *k'dm* means 'like a man'.

[12] *ZDPV* 75 (1959), pp. 35f, 38 n.

[13] Cf. J. Simons, pp. 229f. It seems likely that Jephthah's family home was in Mizpah (-peh) of Gilead (Judg 11.34) and that he was buried there, i.e. in his city Gilead, cf. J. Simons, p. 36 after the LXX.

that in early times this Gilead was confused with Ramoth-Gilead[14], cf. Jerome and B. *Makkoth* 10a[15], and more recently, Qyl.

This interpretation obviates the need to give קריה 'city' a different meaning (so, e.g., Michaelis[16], 'meeting place of evil doers') or to posit a comparison without the use of *kaph* (e.g. van Gelderen, 'Gilead is like a city of evil-doers').

[b]For the phrase פֹּעֲלֵי אָוֶן, cf. Ps 28.3; Prov 6.12 and Hos 12.12.

[c—c]This phrase is difficult. For the evidence of the versions, see below. According to ibn Janāḥ, the word עֲקֻבָּה (feminine of the adjective עָקוֹב) is from the root denoting 'violation', 'trickery and deception' and with its use here he compares (cf. ibn Ezra) Gen 27.36; 2 Kgs 10.19; Jer 17.9. The following preposition מן must in this context denote the immediate or efficient cause (cf. BDB p. 579, col 2 e and ibn Ezra), i.e. 'because of'. 'Blood' (דם) is likely to denote 'blood that has been shed' (so ibn Ezra; cf. the comparable usage in Ezek 22.3). Since the first phrase of the verse constitutes a characterisation of Gilead as 'a city of evil-doers' it is likely that a similar judgement of it is expressed here. The bloodshed is, then, the cause of its being styled עקבה 'treacherous', hence the translation 'exposed as treacherous', where 'exposed' (i.e. 'shown to be') seeks to convey the force of the preposition מן in the context.

A slightly different view may be suggested by reference to the talmudic tradition (Rabbi Eliezer[17]) whereby the city was so named since its inhabitants 'pursued (היו עוקבין) men to kill them'. Since the verb עקב can denote 'follow at the heel'[18], the description of the city may denote that it merited the title עקבה 'assassinatory' because of the bloodshed perpetrated by its inhabitants. This view is similar to that of Rashi who understands the phrase to denote (in paraphrase) 'full of murderous assassins'.

Amongst other interpretations which seem to me less likely are, e.g., the imaginative rendering of the NEB 'marked by a trail of blood'. Here the adjective is given the meaning 'foot-tracked' (*sc*. by blood, cf. BDB, *ad loc.*). This precise meaning is, however, posited only for this verse and is far from certainly correct. Secondly, J. Bachmann[19] (cf. Wolff, Mays, *BHS*) emends the text to read עִקְּבֵיהֶם דָּם 'their footprints are blood(y)'.

14 Now identified with Tell er-Ramith (to the SE of Irbid) by P. Lapp; see, e.g., N. Glueck in (ed.) D. W. Thomas *AOTS*, pp. 433, 452.

15 ET, p. 60 in *Neziḳin* IV. The passage seeks to place Ramoth-gilead beyond the Jordan opposite Shechem. Jal'ad matches this description more exactly than Tell er-Ramith.

16 *Supplementa*, p. 2203.

17 B. *Makkoth* 10a; ET, p. 60 in *Neziḳin* IV.

18 Cf. BDB and Jastrow *ad locc.*

19 *Alttestamentliche Untersuchungen*, Berlin, 1894, pp. 1–37.

For the likely historical background, see on the previous verse. The city of Gilead, some twenty kilometres due east of Adam, is indicted as being implicated in the bloody rebellion which is described. Again the situation best fits that of 2 Kgs 15.25 where Gileadites are explicitly mentioned as assisting Pekah's revolt against Pekahiah. If the interpretation of the verse set out above is correct (see notes to the translation), Hosea characterises Gilead as a city of evil-doers whose treachery is exposed since it is thence that assassins have come westward in support of Pekah's putsch. Indeed the guess may be hazarded that it was at Adam that Pekah (or his representatives) met the Gileadites and there made the preparations for the rebellion which constituted treason and treachery against Yahweh (see on the preceding verse).

Text and Versions

עקבה מדם LXX ταράσσουσα ὕδωρ 'which troubles the water', apparently reading מים for מדם. Rudolph suggests that the phrase is idiomatic (cf. English and German 'to fish in troubled waters') and means 'to conduct devious and base actions'. Aq. περικαμπὴς ἀπὸ αἵματος 'bent round through blood'; Symm. διώκεται ἀπὸ αἵματος 'is pursued because of blood', cf. Vulg. *subplantata sanguine* 'tripped up/overturned through blood', and Quinta ὑποσκελίζουσα καὶ δολοφονοῦσα 'tripping up and assassinating'; Theod. ἡ πτέρνα αὐτῆς ἀφ' αἵματος (?) 'her footstep is from/out of blood'. These renderings seem to represent guesses made by reference to the various connotations of the root עקב; Pesh. *wmplpl' bdm'* 'weltering in blood' appears to be pure conjecture; Targ. בנכלין אשדין דם זכי 'with guile they shed innocent blood' is characteristically free but conveys the meaning advocated by ibn Janāḥ and ibn Ezra (see above).

6.9 **Just as highwaymen[a] lie in wait[b] for a traveller[a], so does a company[c] of priests; they commit murders[d] on the road to Shechem[e]; they have perpetrated[d] a deliberate atrocity[f].**

[a]The expression אִישׁ גְּדוּדִים has been understood to be a plural of אִישׁ גְּדוּד, cf., with Rudolph, GK 124r and, with Qyl, the phrase אִישׁ יִשְׂרָאֵל construed with a plural verb in Judg 8.22. An alternative view seems to be presented by ibn Ezra and Kimchi (cf. Rosenmüller). For them the infinitive construct (see note b) is followed by both object (איש) and subject (גדודים) and, cf. GK 115k, the phrase means literally, 'like the-lying-in-wait-for-a-man of highwaymen'. This view seems preferable

since (איש/אנשי גדוד(ים is not attested elsewhere as a composite expression. The word איש 'man' is here rendered 'traveller' *ad sensum.*

ᵇThe word חַכֵּי may be understood as an infinitive construct with the orthographical variant חכי for חכה, GK 75aa; so ibn Ezra and Kimchi; (for the evidence of Quinta and the Targum, see below). An alternative view is to regard the word as a *Piel* participial (or adjectival) form without the initial מ, cf. with Rosenmüller, מָאֵן in Exod 7.27 etc. On this view, the sense obtained is identical.

According to Rashi חכי denotes, literally, '(fish-)hooks' (from the root חנך, cf. חכה, BDB p. 335, col 2). The usage here is figurative: like the hooks with which tailors fasten garments together[20], so the band of priests is united[21] and, as it were, fastened together in their resolve to rob and kill. Kimchi quotes Saadya as supposing that חכי are fish-hooks and that גדודים are the banks of a river (cf. Hebrew גדה and Arabic *ǧddt* with this meaning). Accordingly the band of priests is 'like the hooks of a fisher(man) on the banks'. Such interpretations seem to be far-fetched, though it is possible that Rashi's interpretation is consistent with the more general view that the verse conveyed the whole-hearted commitment of the priestly gang to the conspiracy mentioned.

ᶜThe word חֶבֶר seems to have a pejorative sense; so, e.g., Wolff; cf. with Qyl, Job 34.8. For this reason, perhaps, it has been usual to understand the phrase as the antecedent to the verbs which follow 'they commit murder', 'they have perpetrated outrages'. Qyl records[22] that 'some' have conjectured that the priests were the object of the verb יְרַצְּחוּ used impersonally.

ᵈA frequentative imperfect used dramatically to describe their behaviour is followed by asseverative כי and a perfect characterising that behaviour.

ᵉThe genitive שֶׁכְמָה (i.e. Shechem with *he locale*) is separated from the construct דֶּרֶךְ by the verb 'they commit murder' apparently in poetic style. The pointing שֶׁכְמָה seems to be anomalous, cf. the well-attested שְׁכֶמָה (Gen 37.14; Josh 24.1). It is possible that the Massoretes were seeking to indicate the noun שְׁכֶם 'shoulder' for which the pausal form שֶׁכֶם is attested (Ps 21.13), cf. certain of the ancient versions (*q.v.* below) and the rabbinic commentators (Rashi, ibn Ezra and Kimchi). The latter compare Zeph 3.9, where the phrase שְׁכֶם אֶחָד denotes '(with) one shoulder' (i.e. with one consent) and thus they detect the meaning here 'the priests make common cause to commit murder' (cf. the AV). While it is now generally acknowledged that a reference to the city of Shechem is required by the context and is much more probable, the prophet, with his love of word-play, may well have intended to convey this further meaning.

20 He refers to the (general) remarks of B. *Baba Bathra*, 119.

21 So he interprets שכמה; see note e below.

22 I have been unable to find a reasoned statement of this view.

[f]זִמָּה, a strong word, elsewhere denoting outrages of sexual behaviour in Judg 20.6, cf. Ezek 16.43, 58. The verb זמם, when predicated of men, denotes predominantly evil thought and purpose and hence the Targum (*q.v.* below) renders 'counsel' which Kimchi regards as a possible interpretation, i.e. 'as they have resolved upon it in their thinking, so they practise it'. The asseverative כי, which forms part of the phrase, is conveyed in the translation by 'deliberate.'

Again Hosea appears to be referring to outrages well-known to his hearers. If it is correct to see in this section reference to the details of Pekah's revolt against Pekahiah of 736/5 BC, then this verse would appear to indicate that the rebellion, initiated by armed elements from the city of Gilead, was whole-heartedly supported (notes b and e) by a conspiracy of priests (notes c and f) from Ephraimite territory. The outrageous conduct appears to have been perpetrated 'on the road to Shechem' which lies opposite the trans-Jordanian places mentioned earlier, i.e. Adam and Gilead. The road leading from the Jordan by way of Wady Far'ah/Naḥal Tirzah would seem to be indicated. The outrage consisted in murder but, unfortunately, we are not given any indication of the identity of the victims. Jerome speaks of the priests of Bethel who sought to waylay and rob pilgrims passing from the north via Shechem towards Jerusalem 'in order that they might worship more fully the golden calves of Dan and Bethel than God in his temple'. Similarly the rabbinic commentators think that robbery was the motive for the attacks.

More likely is the view that the murders were committed in the course of the rebellion. Shechem (cf. modern Tell Balāṭah near Nablus) marks the natural cross-roads between the east-west route from Adam, through Naḥal Tirza, to the coast and the north-south route from Samaria towards Bethel, the southern border of Ephraim[23]. It is axiomatic that the important highways be secured by successful insurgents, and we may suppose that the priestly party, sympathetic to the revolt, played this role. As Gileadite support played an important part in Pekah's revolt (2 Kgs 15.25), we may further suppose that the priestly conspiracy had the important task of securing the approach from the Jordan and Gilead. In that case the victims are likely to have been officials of Pekahiah's establishment.

Again we are not told whether the company of priests was associated with any particular sanctuary. Some (e.g. Wolff) have supposed that, since Shechem is never indicted by Hosea (as

[23] Cf. G. E. Wright in (ed.) D. W. Thomas *AOTS*, p. 356: 'all major roads in north-central Palestine pass by'.

were Bethel, Gilgal, Mizpah, Tabor and Samaria), it retained its old and approved character as the place of the older, uncorrupted, tribal Yahwism (cf. Deut 27.11ff; 1 Kgs 12.1). Accordingly the assault by the corrupt gang of priests is supposed to have been directed against the priestly (Levite) and prophetic opposition of Shechem and the wickedness of their crime to have been exacerbated by the fact that Shechem was one of the cities of refuge (Josh 20.7, cf. Deut 19.3).

On the other hand Hosea's indictment of the corrupt priesthood in 4.4–19 seems to consist in his portrayal of their ethical depravity which is seen to have its roots in and to be fostered by the idolatrous and syncretistic worship to which they had given themselves. Thus, the particular events referred to here are more likely to be an indication of the depths to which some of the priesthood had sunk, and their espousal of bloody revolution for short-term and selfish ends is a symptom of massive ethical corruption by those who should have known better. Such is their promiscuity (*znwt*) and it has effected the pollution of the whole state (see the following verse).

Text and Versions

וכחכי איש גדודים LXX καὶ ἡ ἰσχύς σου ἀνδρὸς πειρατοῦ, cf. Pesh. *'wšnky 'yk dgbr' gys'* 'thy strength is (like) that of a highwayman', apparently read כֹּחֲכִי כְ (cf. Gelston, p. 123); Aq. καὶ ὡς θυρεὸς ἀνδρὸς εὐζώνου 'like a shield of a well-equipped man'; Symm. καὶ ὡς φρύαγμα[24] ἀνδρὸς ἐνεδρευτοῦ/ὑποκριτοῦ 'like the insolence[25] of one lying in ambush/of a dissembler'; Vulg. *et quasi fauces virorum latronum* 'like the throat of highwaymen', reading כְּחִכֵּי; Quinta ὡς λόχος πολυχειρίας ληστρικῆς 'like the ambush of a piratical throng'; Targ. (not all authorities, see Sperber) וכמא די מסבר אנש למשרין 'as a man waits for soldiers'; LXX joins the phrase to the previous verse. 4QpIs[c] כיחכה איש גדוד (*DJD* 5, 23 ii 13, p. 24, cf. Strugnell, p. 193 and Borbone), 'as a man of robber(s) lies in wait ...', for which Allegro (*DJD* 5, p. 25 n.) compares the singular reading of the LXX.

חבר LXX ἔκρυψαν 'they hid', cf. Pesh. *'štwtpw* 'they are confederate' and Targ. אתחברו seem to have read the word as a verb: LXX, perhaps, חִבְּאוּ or חָבְאוּ (*BHS*, cf. Job 24.4); Pesh. and Targ., perhaps, חָבְרוּ (so Rudolph). According to Jerome, Theod. renders by a verb (*absconderunt*), Aq. and Symm. by nouns (*participatio/societas*).

דרך LXX (conjoining the word with the preceding) ἔκρυψαν ἱερεῖς ὁδὸν (κυρίου – so AQ) '(priests) hid the way (of the Lord)'; Pesh.

[24] For comments, see Ziegler, p. 160 and *Bei.*, p. 357.
[25] See Field 2, p. 950 n. 17.

b'wrḥ' wqṭlw lškym' '(the priests are confederate) on the road and kill at Shechem'; cf. Symm. (according to Jerome) *in via interficiebant*; Vulg. *pergentes de Sychem* 'those passing from Shechem'; Targ. באורח חדא קטלין נפשן כתף חד '(their priests) on the same way kill men with one consent', cf. the comments of the rabbinic authorities (note e above); Aq. and Theod. (according to Jerome) understand Shechem as 'shoulder', 'back'(*humeros/in dorso*).

The verse has often been considered very corrupt and a large number of emendations has been proposed. For those that follow the LXX cf., e.g., G. Fohrer *ZAW* 71 (1959), p. 15, and KB who read כְּכֹחַ 'like the strength (of robbers)'. For attempts to read חבר as a verb and for the consequent harmonising of the first word, e.g., Marti and Budde, נֶחְבְּאוּ/כֹּהֲנִים נֶחְבָּא 'as robbers conceal themselves, the priests have concealed themselves'. For earlier suggestions, see Harper. Recent commentaries have sought to interpret MT without emendation and, since it is possible to obtain reasonable sense from it, I have preferred to do the same.

6.10 **In the House of Israel[a] I have seen an outrage[b]; there is Ephraim's promiscuity[c] and there Israel has become unclean[d].**

[a]Cf. 1.4; 'the House of Israel' is likely to denote the royal establishment and, since it is here the antecedent of שָׁם in the second half of the verse, Samaria is likely to be intended as the seat of the Ephraimite monarchy. A number of scholars (e.g. Wolff, Qyl) have seen here a reference to Bethel[26] so described in the LXX version of 10.15 and Amos 5.6[27]. The Targum (which reproduces MT's 'House of Israel') interprets שעריריה of the golden calf in Bethel (cf. also ibn Ezra and Kimchi, the latter speaking also of Dan) but this is not evidence that 'House of Israel' denotes Bethel.

[b]On the *Qere/Kethib* see Text and Versions below. For similar forms, cf. Jer 5.30; 18.13; 23.14. The word שַׁעֲרִירִיָּה is compared by ibn Janāḥ, ibn Ezra and Kimchi with הַתְּאֵנִים הַשֹּׁעָרִים 'rotten figs' in Jer 29.17. Rashi notes that in Jer 5.30 it is parallel with שַׁמָּה 'horror', 'appalment'. Morag (following E. Yalon[28]) places the word in the semantic field of ethical depravity and suggests it is used to describe deviation from the natural order such as treachery and revolution. Bound up with it is the notion of mental aberration and hence it is akin to sickness (so the Habakkuk Commentary 9.1, Yalon, *op. cit.*). The evidence of the Targum is important to Yalon/Morag; see further under Text and Versions below.

[26] Or else they have emended the text to read Bethel; so, e.g., Wellhausen, Marti, Harper, *BHS* etc.

[27] See further Simons, p. 464.

[28] מגילות מדבר יהודה -- דברי לשון (Jerusalem, 1967), p. 104.

[c]Lit. 'there to Ephraim is promiscuity'. The proposal to read a verbal form, following the Peshiṭta and Targum (*q.v.* below) is not followed since it would require a consequential explanation of the following preposition ל. The root זנה and its derivatives are Hosea's principal metaphor to describe Israel's moral depravity (*contra* Jeremias who argues that the term is typical of Jeremiah on whom the verse, as an exilic addition, is dependent).

[d]Cf. 5.3 above, where the word נטמא is parallel to הזנית, 'now indeed, Ephraim, you have behaved promiscuously, Israel is defiled'. Rudolph mentions the possibility that the words are a later addition made by reference to 5.3 (cf. Wolff). On the other hand, as he also points out, the clause makes of the verse a tristich, not unusual at the end of a strophe.

The revolution reaches its climax in the murder of Pekahiah in Samaria (2 Kgs 15.25). This treacherous act of conspiracy on the part of the king's lieutenant, undertaken with the support of trans-Jordanian Gileadites and elements of the Ephraimite priesthood, may have been known at first hand to Hosea. In v. 7, it is true, 'there they acted treacherously against me' suggests that 'I have seen' here is predicated of Yahweh, at least in the text as it is received. On the other hand, 5.11; 6.8f; 7.3–6, 8–9 are not in themselves presented as sayings of Yahweh (cf. Wolff) and they can be read as the observations and reactions of the prophet to the events he describes. If this impression is correct the statement here 'I have seen' may be said to lack the emphasis required of Yahweh formally stating that he has witnessed the atrocity and wickedness (cf. and contrast, e.g., 5.3a). It is possible, then, that 'I have seen' was originally a saying of Hosea and that he was actually present at the events described or near enough to Samaria to have had accurate knowledge of them. As a result of the redactional activity (whether of Hosea or of his redactors), the saying has been incorporated into what is *in toto* a divine speech and thus 'I have seen' becomes the witness of Yahweh. In any case what was witnessed, either by Hosea or Yahweh, is characterised as an 'outrage' which manifested mental aberration or sickness of mind (see note b above). The enormity of the treachery is evidence of the nation's 'promiscuity' (*znwt*, note c), the term Hosea consistently uses to indicate the moral degeneration of the nation and its establishment and which, he argues, has its roots in unfaithfulness to Yahweh in the idolatrous cult. It is there, in Samaria, that the nation's promiscuity has revealed itself in its full enormity and it is there that the nation has become totally defiled (notes c and d above); cf. also Ps 106.39, an indication that the themes were valued in the exilic (or post-exilic) period.

Text and Versions

שעריריה *Qere* שַׁעֲרוּרִיָּה; for the *Kethib*, ibn Janāḥ (cf. Qyl) compares סגריר 'steady rain' and, for the ending יה, מאפליה 'deep darkness'[29]; LXX φρικώδη 'horrible thing', cf. the Vulg. *horrendum*; Targ. שנו 'strangeness', 'deviation' (cf. Yalon, *op. cit.* above); Pesh. *tmh'* 'an amazing thing'.

זנות לאפרים LXX πορνείαν τοῦ E. conjoining with what precedes '(I saw there) the promiscuity of Ephraim'; Vulg. *fornicationes*; Pesh. *zny 'prym* '(there) Ephraim committed fornication', cf. Targ. טעו בית אפרים 'the House of Ephraim has gone astray'. For emendations in favour of a verbal form, see, e.g., Wellhausen, Oort and Marti.

6.11a **(Also, Judah, he has prepared[a] a harvest[b] for you.)**

It is generally accepted that these words at least (cf. *BHS*) are a gloss added to the text by the Judaean redactors with the intention of applying Hosea's message at a later time to Judah. For גם 'also' as the first word of such a gloss, cf. 4.5 and 5.5. 'Judah' is a vocative in the light of the following second person singular pronoun ('for you'), cf. Kimchi.

[a]Since 11a is here understood to be a gloss, there is no reason to question MT's שָׁת 'he (*sc.* Yahweh) has prepared ...'.

[b]Such is the likely meaning for the word קָצִיר; cf. with Rashi, Jer 51.33. For ibn Janāḥ, ibn Ezra and Kimchi the word denotes a 'bough' or 'branch' as in Job 14.9. By this figure of speech 'the king' is referred to as in Isa 11.1 (so ibn Janāḥ). For Kimchi the reference is specifically to Jeroboam II who restored Damascus and Hamath to Judah (2 Kgs 14.28). The sense of the verse, then (i.e. with 11b of course included), is that, despite the respite afforded to Israel and Judah in the time of Jeroboam II, despite the restoration of the fortunes of the people (11b) and Yahweh's desire to heal them (7.1a), still they did not repent, i.e. neither Israel nor Judah repented (so Kimchi). The interpretation is far-fetched in regard to 11a and to the word קציר, though it is important as an indication of the traditional rabbinical understanding of 11b and 7.1a; see further below. As a defence of the MT it is remarkable for its ingenuity.

[29] It is possible that the ending represents the short form of the divine name, used as an intensive.

The half verse is understood to be a Judaean gloss added to Hosea's prophecies at a later time in order to make his message relevant to the Southern Kingdom. The harvest that Yahweh has prepared is a harvest of judgement (see note b above and cf. Jer 51.33). In that Judah is guilty of enormities similar in kind to those of Ephraim, that nation may expect a similar fate at Yahweh's hands. With Emmerson (p. 87) the sentiments of Jer 5.12f may be compared with the saying here under consideration, 'they have denied the Lord, saying, He does not exist. No evil shall come upon us ...' (NEB). It is to this attitude that the Judaean redactor directed the proven arguments of Hosea. The date, then, is likely to be towards the end of the seventh century.

Text and Versions

גם LXX with ἐμιάνθη Ἰσραὴλ καὶ Ἰουδά joins the first two words of MT with the preceding verse, 'Israel is defiled, and Judah ...'.

שת קציר לך LXX ἄρχου[30] τρυγᾶν σεαυτῷ '(begin to gather) the harvest for yourself (when I turn ...)'; 3 MSS[Luc] αὐτοῦ → לָהּ 'for her'(*BHS*); Quinta (ἀλλὰ καί συ Ἰούδα) παρασκεύαζε σαυτὸν εἰς τὸ ἐκθερισθῆναι 'prepare yourself for being harvested'; Vulg. *pone messem tibi* 'place the harvest for yourself'; the imperatives of these versions have prompted a number of scholars (e.g. Oort) to read the imperative שִׁת (for שִׁית) in place of MT's שָׁת; Symm. καί σοι Ἰούδα ἀπόκειται θερισμός 'for you, Judah, a harvest is stored up'; following this a number of scholars[31] have suggested that שִׁ(י)ת (pass. part.) be read; Pesh. *'bd lk qṭp'* (perhaps imperative, cf. Walton's *Polyglot*) 'make yourself a harvest'; Targ. שריאו לאסגאה חובין אף להון ימטי קיצא 'they (*sc.* the Judaeans) began to multiply sins and also to them will come the end'.

6.11b **(When I restore the fortunes of my people ...)**

The phrase is understood to be a second gloss[32] (later than the preceding) made by reference to, and interpreting the words which begin, 7.1 'When I wished to heal Israel'. It has the effect of converting the whole of v. 11 into a prophecy of weal for Judah (cf. van Gelderen and Jeremias), for whom a harvest (of

30 K. Vollers suggests that שְׁרִי (an Aramaising form) was read, cf. the Targum.
31 E.g. Cheyne, Marti, Rudolph.
32 Cf., e.g., Marti.

good)[33] is appointed when Yahweh ('I') restores the fortunes of his ('my') people. The date is likely to be exilic[34]. The phrase 'when I restore the fortunes of my people' בְּשׁוּבִי שְׁבוּת עַמִּי[35] is a technical term used throughout the prophetic literature of the eschatological restoration of Israel's fortunes, interpreted more particularly of restoration from exile[36]. It is not used elsewhere by Hosea and its occurrence in Amos 9.14 is generally regarded as late. By contrast, the phrase which follows 'when I wished to heal Israel', כְּרָפְאִי לְיִשְׂרָאֵל, seems to be an authentic saying of Hosea (*q.v.* below) with its characteristic use of the concept of 'healing' רפא in respect of ethical deviation and sickness (Morag, pp. 505ff).

Commentators have regarded the phrase as belonging to 7.1a and have translated it 'when I would reverse the fortunes of my people, when I would heal Israel, then ...' (so, e.g., NEB). Against this view are the following considerations. First, that such a lengthy and cumbersome temporal clause preceding 'then the guilt of Ephraim stands exposed' does not accord with Hosea's terse style. Secondly, the first person suffix 'when I ...', made in accordance with 'when I heal' כרפאי, does not fit the third person singular 'he has prepared' שת in 11a[37], a clear indication, in my submission, that the phrase is dependent in origin upon what follows and influences what precedes only in a contrived and imperfect way. Thirdly, the preposition ב introduces this phrase as is normally the case[38], whereas the preposition which precedes 'when I heal' is כ, an indication that, while the former was in origin dependent upon the latter, it was introduced again in a contrived and imperfect way. Fourthly, attempts to translate the phrase in question (i.e. בשובי ...) by 'when I would reverse the fortunes'[39] or by 'whenever I wished to ...'[40] or by 'the more I restored ...'[41] are inconsistent with the

33 Cf. Rudolph. Amongst the rabbinic commentators the term קציר is seen to have a good sense by, e.g., Kimchi (but see above for the precise meaning).

34 Cf. E. Janssen in FRLANT 69 (Göttingen, 1956), pp. 88, 91.

35 See especially E. L. Dietrich BZAW 40 (1925). The word שבות is derived from the root שוב; see further R. Borger *ZAW* 66 (1954), pp. 315ff.

36 Cf. the *Kethib* שבית (from the root שבה) in a number of passages in Jeremiah (29.14; 49.39) and Ezekiel (16.53).

37 The point is negated, of course, by the very common recourse to emendation; so, e.g., שַׁתִּ 'I have prepared' (e.g. Marti), in addition to others noted above on v. 11a.

38 Cf. Pss 14.7; 53.7; Jer 31.23; Zeph 3.20; *contra BHS* which, conjoining with 7.1, emends to כשובי.

39 E.g. NEB, Harper, Weiser, Mauchline, Mays, AF.

40 E.g. Wolff.

41 E.g. Sellin.

fundamental meaning of the phrase and its distinctively eschatological reference (cf. Rudolph).

For the view that the gloss includes the whole of v. 11 and 7.1a, that it has been misplaced and belongs properly with 6.1–3, see Rudolph[42]. While there may be said to be a correspondence between 6.1 and 7.1a (*rp'*), it is not immediately clear why, on Rudolph's view, 6.11b בשובי corresponds with 6.2.

Text and Versions

No significant readings.

7.1 **When I would heal Israel[a], then Ephraim's guilt stands exposed[b], even[c] the wicked deeds of Samaria; for they acted treacherously. [d]They [e]break in with the stealth[e] of a thief, they rob[f] as highwaymen in the open[g] country[d].**

[a]The phrase is interpreted as an unfulfilled wish[43], cf. 6.1; so Rashi, ibn Ezra and Kimchi (the latter on 6.11). For the verb (רפא) followed by the preposition ל, cf. 5.13 and Ps 147.3.

[b]*Waw* consecutive with a perfect is here understood to have something of a frequentative or abiding force[44], hence the translation 'stands exposed' (cf. NEB; cf. ibn Ezra 'their wickedness of heart remained before me', and Rashi 'their sins were revealed before me for they continually did wrong'). It is unnecessary to suppose (with, e.g., Nowack, cf. Harper) that a preceding verb has dropped out of the text or that the *waw* is an editorial addition made to accommodate the Judaean gloss (e.g. Marti and Rudolph).

[c]*Waw explicativum*, GK 154a n. (b).

[d—d]Lit. 'and a thief comes in/is wont to come in'. The imperfect is frequentative[45] and describes the characteristic behaviour of thieves with which the evil actions of the Ephraimites are compared[46], cf. the NEB, 'they are thieves, they break in ..., they are robbers, they strip ...'. The second phrase, like 'they acted treacherously' (note c) above describes the deeds of the Ephraimites which are like those perpetrated by highwaymen. The phrase has a complex chiastic structure which may be

42 Cf. also Lindblom *HLU*, pp. 86f.
43 Cf. the Vulgate and Peshiṭta, *q.v.* below.
44 GK 112v, 114r and 164g; cf. 'they are noted by me' in 7.2 below.
45 Cf. Rashi and ibn Ezra.
46 For *comparatio decurtata*, GK 118r n.; cf. GK 161a.

set out as follows: 'As a thief breaks in (so have they broken in), they have robbed as highwaymen (are accustomed to rob) in open country'.

[e–e]The verb בוא often has the sense 'to enter', cf. the versions and Rosenmüller's comments. 'With the stealth' is added *ad sensum* in translation so as to draw out the contrast with the highwaymen who operate 'in the open'.

[f]The verb פשט, literally 'to strip', is akin to the idiomatic English phrase 'to fleece a person'.

[g]So ibn Ezra understands בחוץ; cf. Judg 9.44. Certain of the versions think of streets (*q.v.* below); cf., with Qyl, 1 Kgs 20.34.

The dilemma facing Yahweh is again depicted by the opening words of the verse (cf. 6.4). His desire to heal his people (so 'Israel') is confronted by the manifest guilt of the Ephraimite nation and the wicked deeds perpetrated by the inhabitants of its capital Samaria. Healing, here as in 6.1, denotes restoration of the nation's fortunes following adversity though elsewhere it is defined as the healing (of the sickness) of moral perversity (14.5, EV 4). Yahweh cannot heal the nation in the former sense. Like a skilled physician he must expose the wound and express from it all the pus and rottenness (so R. Eliezer of Beaugency, twelfth century, quoted by Qyl). Accordingly the verse indicates that Yahweh's dilemma is resolved by the needs of justice and realism[47]. Only when the nation's guilt is exposed and the moral depravity to which, as a matter of plain fact, they have stooped is acknowledged (v. 2) does healing become possible. The verse indicates, then, in a remarkably subtle way, a shift in the definition of Yahweh's healing activity. It is the perverted will of men that he must change and that function cannot be accomplished by superficial means (so again R. Eliezer).

The shameful deeds perpetrated in Ephraim and Samaria were all founded in treachery and deception (note c) and the statement corresponds with that of 4.1 'there is no moral integrity'. In particular their behaviour is akin to (note d–d) that of thieves and highwaymen. Whether the statement is a general indictment of such evils in society (so, e.g., Rudolph) or whether it is another indictment of the particular events listed in 6.7ff cannot certainly be determined. In favour of the latter view is the similarity of vocabulary in 6.9 and the fact that 7.3ff is concerned *inter alia*

[47] For a similar interpretation cf., perhaps, the rendering of the Targum, *q.v.* below.

with treachery in the royal court of Samaria. At any rate, there is further correspondence with 4.2 in 'violence' and 'robbery'.

Text and Versions

כרפאי LXX joins with 6.11; similarly many commentators who take the view that 'when I restore the fortunes ...' (בשובי etc.) is authentic; cf. on 6.11b; LXX renders כ by ἐν (τῷ ἰάσασθαί με τὸν Ἰσραήλ) so prompting a number of scholars to read ב (e.g. Ewald, Marti, Borbone); Vulg. *cum sanare vellem* 'when I wished to heal', cf. Pesh. *m' d'syt*; Targ. כמתבעי חובי ישראל 'when the sins of Israel are required of them ...'.

ונגלה LXX καὶ ἀποκαλυφθήσεται 'will be revealed', cf. Targ. ויתגלין '(then the guilt of Ephraim) will be revealed'; Pesh. *w'tgly*, cf. Vulg. *revelata est* (without *et*) 'was revealed'.

ורעות LXX, Pesh., Vulg. and Targ. render with singular nouns, possibly by attraction to the singular עון above (so Rudolph); → וְרָעַת (Borbone, cf. *BHS*).

שקר Pesh. adds *qdmy* → לְפָנַי (Borbone, cf. *BHS*).

יבוא LXX πρὸς αὐτὸν εἰσελεύσεται 'to him (*sc*. Ephraim) will come in' has suggested to Oettli a corruption from πρὸς οἶκον and hence an original בַּבַּיִת (cf. הַבַּיְתָה, *BHS*); for the verb, cf. Vulg. *ingressus est* and Pesh. *''l*; Targ. ובליליא בבתיא גנבין 'and at night they steal in the houses' suggests that the terse Hebrew lends itself in translation to some expansion *ad sensum*[48]. → + עליו (before יבוא, Borbone, after LXX).

פשט LXX ἐκδιδύσκων, cf. Pesh. *wmšlḥ*, Vulg. *spolians* and Targ. קפחין has suggested (cf. the preceding frequentative imperfect) the reading פֹּשֵׁט (e.g. Rudolph, cf. *BHS*) in place of the perfect of the MT.

בחוץ LXX ἐν τῇ ὁδῷ αὐτοῦ 'in his (*sc*. Ephraim's) way'; Vulg. *foris*, cf. Pesh. *bšwq'* 'in the streets'; Targ. בדברא 'in the pasture land', *v.l.* במדברא 'desert'; → בדרכו (Borbone, after LXX).

7.2 **The while they did not reason[a] that[b] I would remember all[c] their wickedness. Now[d] their wicked deeds have trapped them[e], they are noted by me[f].**

[a]Frequentative imperfect with past reference, lit. 'they were not saying to their heart', i.e. thinking, reasoning. The preposition ל is unusual since ב 'in' is found elsewhere. It is possible that the reading (cf. the versions below) reflects northern dialectal usage.

[48] Cf. Budde *JBL* 53 (1934), p. 130.

[b]For asyndetic introduction of indirect speech, cf. König 384g.

[c]The view that כל here means 'as often as' (Brockelmann *Syntax*, § 144) is hardly appropriate (cf. Rudolph).

[d]The sense of עתה is as in 1 Sam 25.7b 'as things are', describing the reality of the situation.

[e]Lit. 'surrounded them', as those besieged in a city, cf. Eccles 9.14 and Ps 118.10.

[f]Lit. 'they are' or 'have come before my face'; cf. 'the guilt of Ephraim stands exposed' in the previous verse; for the phrase, cf. Ps 90.8. Rashi paraphrases 'all their evil is written as a record before me'.

Here, continuing the theme of v. 1, the faulty reasoning (note a) of Ephraim is contrasted with the requirement (as a prelude to 'healing') that the nation's wickedness and its consequences be realistically acknowledged and evaluated. The supposition that Yahweh does not see or pay attention to wicked deeds (cf. Ps 10.11) is, for Hosea, a mark of faulty reasoning and elsewhere (e.g. 7.1, 16) is diagnosed as the very sickness to be healed. Whatever, by their deluded reasoning, the Ephraimites may choose to suppose, the truth is that their wicked deeds are noted by Yahweh (note f above) and at the same time they have brought about inexorably the confinement (note e) of their perpetrators. The latter, indeed, are 'caught in and circumscribed by their own deeds' which render 'necessary the further punishment announced by the prophet' (5.9, 14) – so Wolff.

Text and Versions

ובל יאמרו LXX (which takes the phrase with the preceding verse) ὅπως συνᾴδωσιν ὡς συνᾴδοντες (AQ and 4 MSS) τῇ καρδίᾳ αὐτῶν 'in order that they should sing/be in accord as those singing/those in accord with their heart' represents an inner Greek corruption or a double rendering (so Vollers, Borbone), the first words being a later corruption of ὡς ᾄδοντες (so LXX *rel.*); the phrase gives no good sense[49]; Aq. καὶ

[49] Cf. Field *ad loc.* '*aliter:* Ἀ.Θ. ὡς λέγοντες ἐν τῇ καρδίᾳ αὐτῶν'. The suggestion of Vollers that an original מזמרים lay behind this reading (cf. Rudolph) seems to me to be unlikely. The meaning 'be in accord', attested for the verb by Liddell and Scott (cf. Jerome's use of *concinare* with such a meaning in his translation of the LXX), suggests the possibility that the LXX intended the sense 'in order that they should be in accord with their heart'. That the phrase is plural

μήποτε εἴπωσι ταῖς καρδίαις αὐτῶν, cf. Pesh. *wl' 'mryn blbhwn* and Targ. לא מחשבין בלבהון 'and they do not say to/in their hearts'; Vulg. *et ne forte dicant in cordibus suis* 'lest, perchance, they should say in their hearts ...'; → בלבבם (Borbone).

כל → כי 'surely', 'for' is noted as a suggested emendation (*BHS*), cf. note b above.

and follows (in the LXX) an apparently singular antecedent is a further problem. Jerome may be right in supposing that it is to be taken with what follows (cf. his translation of the LXX 'that they may be in accord with their heart, all their wickednesses I will remember').

CHAPTER 7.3–7

THE CONSPIRACY REACHES ITS CLIMAX

7.3 **By their wickedness they promote the rise[a] of a king[b], and princes by their treachery[c].**

[a]Ibn Janāḥ, though he does not quote this text[1], defines the meaning of the verb שמח by the words 'growth', 'increase', 'expansion', 'progress' (Arabic *'lnmw*) and 'enhancement', 'elevation' (Arabic *'lzy'dt*). For such meanings the Arabic cognate verb *šmḫ* 'to be high', 'lofty', 'to tower up' may be compared. In this particular context memory of the meaning is detectable in ibn Ezra's comment 'they (*sc.* the princes) crown him (*sc.* the king; ימליכוהו)'. The suggestion, dating back to Wellhausen, that יְמַשְׁחוּ 'they anoint' be read is, then, unnecessary, for a similar meaning is detected in the MT as it stands[2]. The meaning 'to (cause to) rejoice'[3], normally attested for the verb, fits the context less well, whether the resulting sense be taken as the royal establishment's cynical delight in the wicked deeds perpetrated by its subjects (so Rashi, Kimchi etc.) or as their careless *bonhommie* purposely promoted by wicked conspirators with the aid of wine (so, e.g., Rudolph who compares Judg 9.13; Ps 104.15; Eccles 10.19).

Nyberg, by reference to a different Arabic verb (*smḥ* 'be generous', 'kind') has proposed the meaning for the causative *Piel* here 'they win over the king by their wickedness' (cf. the NEB and REB). Against this view are the considerations[4]: first, it is not attested by the evidence of tradition; and secondly, it fits less well a context which seems to be concerned with palace revolution and regicide.

[b]The imperfect tense expresses behaviour by now customary (GK 107g) and which has effected (perfect) the fall of king after king (v. 7). The indefinite 'king' and 'princes' is similarly likely to have a gnomic force, cf. Hos 8.10.

[c]Either, lit. 'their lies' or, as an abstract plural, 'their lying'. The word is associated with violent crime in Nah 3.1.

[1] The context of his observations is the 'metaphorical' use of the verb in Prov 13.9.

[2] So also, tentatively, J. C. Greenfield *HUCA* 30 (1959), p. 148.

[3] That this meaning is also illuminated by reference to the same Arabic cognate is noted by L. Kopf *VT* 9 (1959), p. 276.

[4] Apart from the objections which may be directed to the alleged isogloss, Arabic *s* and Hebrew שׂ.

The section 7.3–7 seems to form a distinct unit within the larger piece (6.7–7.16; see on 6.7 above). On the view here taken of the preceding material, that it is an indictment of the establishment of Samaria for their treachery and involvement in the overthrow of Pekahiah, 7.3–7 seems, by its contents, to constitute a similar indictment (cf. Wolff). Now, however, rather than describing the movement of the rebellion from Gilead to Samaria, the scene shifts to describe the situation within the palace of Samaria. The difficulty is that the section seems to contain both particular references (especially v. 5) and more general descriptions of characteristic behaviour (see note b above and cf. v. 4). Such considerations have prompted some scholars (e.g. Procksch, Nyberg) to see here references to a number of distinct crimes. It is preferable, however, to see this piece as a unity (so Rudolph) which, by reference to particular events and to the attitudes which facilitated them, proclaims (v. 7) that the monarchy has moved inexorably towards its well-deserved end (cf. 1.4).

The verse refers to the widespread treachery and wickedness prevalent at the royal court of Samaria. It is by such means that the cause of pretenders to the throne is promoted (note a). Disaffected parties within the court await their moment and king after king (note b), with their respective supporters (for 'princes' see on 3.4 above), gain the ascendency they desire by regicide and palace intrigue. The verse reflects accurately the history of the court of Samaria between 747 and 732 BC when no fewer than five kings sat on the throne of whom four were assassinated. In view of the preceding description (6.7ff) of Pekah's revolution, and of Yahweh's judgement in v. 7, it is likely that the verse was written towards the end of the hideous process it describes and sets the scene for a description of Pekah's seizure of the throne in Samaria (735 BC). Against the view that Hoshea's seizure of the throne (732 BC) is alluded to (so Wolff) is the consideration that in 7.5 sympathy seems to be expressed for 'our king' which would be unlikely in reference to Pekah, himself a treacherous upstart.

Text and Versions

ברעתם LXX ἐν ταῖς κακίαις αὐτῶν reads MT as a plural.

ישׂמחו LXX εὔφραναν, cf. Vulg. *laetificaverunt*, Pesh. *ḥdyw* and Targ. מחדן, all 'gladden'.

מלך LXX translates with a plural βασιλεῖς (but O' singular), cf. Pesh. and Gelston, 104, p. 79.

ובכחשיהם Pesh. takes the word with what precedes.

שׂרים Pesh. takes the word (translated *šlyṭnyhwn*) with the next verse.

7.4 **All of them are treacherous[a] like an oven heated[b] by[c] a baker who[d] can cease stoking[e] it from the kneading of the dough until it is leavened[f].**

[a]Lit. 'adulterers'. The *Piel* מְנָאֲפִים is intensive. In Jer 9.1 the same phrase is clearly used metaphorically and to define treacherous behaviour in respect of Yahweh. In particular the passage goes on to mention 'lying' (Jer 9.2) as well as the whole gamut of treacherous sinfulness. The choice of the word נאף with this sense is dictated perhaps by the nearby baker (אפה) with which it constitutes a word-play. The commonly accepted view[5] that מנאפים is a corruption of a form of the verb אנף 'they are all angry' is here discounted as quite inappropriate to a description of a conspiracy which requires calculated restraint rather than passionate anger (cf. Rudolph).

[b]As ibn Ezra notes, the Massoretes accented the word בֹּעֵרָה *mil'el*, indicating recognition that the word 'oven' (תנור) is masculine. The ה ending is then paragogic and designed apparently for poetic emphasis, cf. GK 90f and, with ibn Ezra, Ps 124.4.

[c]The preposition מן expresses here that the oven is heated by the agency of the baker (so Rashi); cf. BDB pp. 579f, col 2 e. Wolff gives the preposition a privative sense 'like an oven burning without a baker; he ceases ...'; the interpretation, though perhaps possible, is less satisfactory.

[d]The verb יִשְׁבּוֹת is understood to introduce a short relative clause, cf. Rudolph.

[e]The verb מֵעִיר is a *Hiphil* participle of the verb עור I, BDB p. 734, col 2, the participle (rather than an infinitive) construed as the object of the verb ישבות, cf. ibn Ezra and, with Rudolph, GK 120b. Wutz's suggestion (p. 312, cf. Nyberg) that the word is illuminated by reference to Arabic *wġr* 'be hot' seems to me to be unlikely since there is no evident or compelling reason to suppose that the form מעיר here conceals a *pe yod/waw* root.

[f]The word חֻמְצָתוֹ is a feminine form of the infinitive construct, cf. the familiar אהבה from אהב (so, e.g., BDB; cf. König, 229d).

[5] E.g. Sellin, Frey, van Hoonacker and S. M. Paul, pp. 114ff.

This verse, together with vv. 6 and 7 which also use the simile of the oven, presents very considerable difficulties not least because the text refers to technical procedures which are now imperfectly known to us. This consideration suggests that exceptional restraint should be exercised in regard to emendation since recourse to it, though understandable, may serve only to overemphasise the licence of the commentator.

The context in which the simile is found is that of conspiracy to regicide and, on the view here adopted (see above 6.7ff), specifically that of Pekah's putsch of 735 BC. The scene is likely to be Samaria and the citadel of the royal palace (2 Kgs 15.25). Hitherto the external elements of the conspiracy outside the capital have been described. Here the culmination of the plans in the assassination of Pekahiah at his palace is depicted. Verses 4–7 seem to indicate the deadly menace of a well-founded conspiracy which awaits only the final moment of truth.

It is to this final moment that the simile of the baker's oven is directed. The type of oven referred to (*tnwr*) is known to us from archaeological discoveries at Taanach and Megiddo[6] and is more akin to the modern *tannūr* of northern Galilee, Golan and Iraq (*c*. 1900) than to the Palestinian *ṭābūn* which can be traced back only to the Arab conquests of the seventh century[7]. The *tannūr* is a cylindrical object fashioned of clay, either interred or raised above the earth, in the bottom of which a fire of wood, dried grass or dung was allowed to blaze until it became a pile of hot ashes. The dough, previously kneaded and leavened into a pancake shape, was placed through a hole in the top so that it adhered to the inner sloping walls until it was baked.

Such ovens may have belonged to individual houses (cf. Lev 26.26) and in larger cities they were grouped in particular streets for communal use (Jer 37.21; Neh 3.11). A number of texts suggest that royal palaces employed professional bakers (Gen 40.1ff; 41.10; 1 Sam 8.13). In recent times bakers' ovens are often situated in specially designed buildings (again *ṭābūn*) or huts which provide shelter and also serve to isolate the necessarily smoky operation from dwellings.

The point of the simile in all three verses which make use of it seems to consist of an allusion to the intense but quiet heat of the oven now ready for its function. The earlier blazing fire has effected over a period of time that readiness. The baker is able to desist from stoking the oven in the last part of this longer time

[6] See Noth *World*, pp. 159ff (*Welt*, pp. 125ff).

[7] So *AUS* 4, pp. 96ff, pp. 107ff; cf. A. G. Barrois *Manuel d'archéologie biblique* I (Paris, 1939), pp. 320ff.

span; the shorter time-span is described by reference to the process of kneading and leavening the dough immediately prior to the actual baking process. It is now that the oven, like the conspirators, is deceptively quiet but in fact optimally ready to fulfil its function.

Text and Versions

מנאפים Quinta εἰς τὸ μοιχεύειν ἐκπυρούμενοι 'inflamed to adultery'; on the basis of this, Oort suggested the reading כֻּלָּם מְנֻפָּחִים; for the proposal to read a form of אנף, see note a above.

בערה מאפה LXX καιόμενος εἰς πέψιν 'blazing for baking', cf. Pesh. *dyqd lm'pyt'*; on the basis of this Vollers suggests לאפות; → בער למאפה (Borbone); → כמו תנור בער הם ... 'they are like a blazing oven' (*BHS*); Vulg. *succensus a coquente* 'fired by the baker'; Targ. דאזי ליה נחתומא 'which the baker has heated for himself'; Oort, Wellhausen *et al.* read בֹּעֵר הֵם אֹפֵהוּ 'they burn like an oven, whose baker ...'.

ישבות LXX κατακαύματος 'of the burning up' (*sc.* the fire of the oven); Vollers suggests that this is an internal corruption of καταπαύματος 'desisting', cf. Quinta ἐπαύσατο; Vulg. *quievit paululum* 'it (the city) rested a little'; Pesh. *nbṭl* 'he ceases'; Targ. diverges widely, creating 'a homiletical expansion of the few words of MT' (Cathcart, p. 43 n. 9).

מעיר LXX ἀπὸ τῆς φλογός 'by the flame', suggesting to Oort מִבַּעַר; Rudolph rightly argues that LXX did not read a different text but rather understood מעיר of 'stirring up' (Jer 15.8) – here, the flames; Vulg. (*quievit paululum*) *civitas*, cf. Pesh. *mn mdynt'* 'from the city' and Targ. מקרויתון 'from their cities'.

7.5 **On the day of our king, when the princes are sick[a] with the heat of wine[b], he deploys[c] the conspirators[d] with a signal[e].**

[a]The *Hiphil* is understood to be intransitive or 'internal' (GK 53d); so, as an alternative, Qyl. Ibn Ezra (so most moderns) understands the *Hiphil* to be causative 'they make the princes sick with the heat of wine'. The latter suggestion seems less likely on the following grounds: first, the change of subject in the next line (i.e. to third masculine singular), difficult in itself, is less so if the princes are the subject of the first line and the chief conspirator of the second; secondly, it seems more likely that conspirators anticipated drunkenness on the king's day than that they induced it.

[b]For the construct state before a preposition, see König, 336w, GK 130a. The noun חֵמַת 'heat' is construed as an accusative of cause, GK 118l.

[c]The verb משך is attested in military contexts with this sense; cf. especially Judg 4.6f and 20.37 and the comments of Soggin upon these verses. According to ibn Janāḥ the word has in Judges the basic meaning 'extension' (Arabic *'nbsṭ*) but is virtually synonymous with the Hebrew verb פשט 'to attack' with which it is there associated.

On the interpretation here adopted, the subject of the verb 'he' is understood to be the chief conspirator, perhaps Pekah himself. That he is not named or otherwise defined is not unnatural in a more or less contemporary prophecy relating to specific historical events. Indeed the impersonal nature of the notice may be said to heighten the dramatic and sinister impression conveyed by the piece. For similar dramatic and impersonal notices, cf., e.g., Isa 10.28; 21.1.

[d]Ibn Ezra rightly insists that the word לֹצְצִים is to be derived from the double *ayin* root לצץ and not from ליץ/לוץ 'to scoff', for which, with reduplicated third radical, the form would have been מל(ו)צצים. Unfortunately ibn Ezra does not indicate the meaning of the verb לצץ which seems to occur only here. Arabic *lṣṣ* 'to act stealthily or secretly' may be indicated as a cognate giving precisely the meaning required by the context[8]. This account of the word is preferable to those which interpret it as a *po'lel* of ליץ[9] even with particular meanings illuminated by reference to Arabic *laḏlaḏa* 'to spy out', hence 'spies'[10] or to Arabic *lwṣ* 'to diverge' hence 'the aberrant'[11]. For the evidence of the versions, see below.

The traditional rendering of the phrase (so, e.g., Jerome, Rashi and Kimchi) 'he (*sc.* the king) has stretched out his hand with (drunken) scoffers' has the disadvantages that, first, it has to be assumed that the king is the subject of the verb, which is awkward following the impersonal 'they have made the princes ill with wine'; secondly, the resulting sense, *viz.* that the king associated himself with the drunken *bonhommie* of the princes, may be said to lack precision and force in the context.

[e]Lit. 'his hand'. The word is understood to constitute a modal accusative following the verb 'he deployed', cf. GK 118l. The hand as *semper et ubique* is associated with a command or signal, cf., e.g., Isa 49.22; Ps 10.12. For a Ugaritic parallel, *mṯk yd*, cf. Aistleitner, p. 199; yet the

[8] Cf. Lane 7, p. 2659, col 3.

[9] I.e. 'babblers', 'drunkards', 'mockers'; see H. N. Richardson *VT* 5 (1955), pp. 166f, followed by Wolff.

[10] P. Ruben *AJSL* 52 (1935/6), p. 36.

[11] T. H. Gaster *VT* 4 (1954), p. 79, followed by Rudolph and Jeremias.

context[12] in which it is found is fragmentary and (e.g. Jeremias') caution about reaching conclusions by reference to it is justified.

The verse is understood to depict precisely the events in Samaria of 735 BC when Pekah successfully assassinated Pekahiah, 'our king', and appropriated the throne for himself (see above). Here, then, the simile of the baker's oven finds its reference in the events depicted. The conspirators (note d), prepared and ready like the heated oven, are now deployed for the attack (note c) on the person of king. His 'day' is likely to denote the anniversary of his accession/coronation[13] (cf. the rabbinic commentators) rather than the anniversary of his birth. At all events his princes, i.e. the court officials with whom he is so closely associated (cf. v. 3), could on this day be expected by the conspirators to be incapable of coming to the king's assistance by reason of their over-indulgence in the festivities. Accordingly the opportunity is grasped by the chief conspirator Pekah, who gives the appropriate signal (note e) to his co-conspirators. That he is not specifically named (note c) is not unnatural in a more or less contemporary text.

That the king is sympathetically described as 'our king'[14] is taken as an indication that Pekahiah is meant since he alone in this period succeeded to the throne without treachery or violence.

[12] *CTA* 15.I.2 (p. 68); *KTU* 1.15 (p. 44).

[13] Presumably the first anniversary of his coronation or accession. 2 Kgs 15.23 records that Pekahiah reigned for 'two years'. Since this notice is likely to reflect the 'ante-dating' system of calculating regnal years, theoretically his reign may have lasted as little as 'only a few months' (Soggin *H.*, p. 226). The statement in Kings that he reigned for two years indicates that his reign extended before and after the all-important point at which a new year began (in Israel, as opposed to Judah, this point was in the seventh or eighth month). Hosea's phrase 'on the day of our king' implies, then, that he was assassinated on the first anniversary of his coronation/accession and before the next and second Israelite New Year's Day (cf. H. Tadmor *apud* Soggin *op. cit.*, p. 374). The accession date is 737/6 BC.

[14] Rudolph's argument (cf. Wolff, Mays, *BHS* and Jeremias) that 'their king' *mlkm* be read on the basis of the Targum, and because 'our king' is inappropriate on the lips of Yahweh, is hardly convincing.

Text and Versions

יום מלכנו LXX ἡμέραι τῶν βασιλέων ὑμῶν (βασιλέως, 223', 534'; A' αἱ ἡμέραι ... ἡμῶν) 'the days of your kings'; Pesh. has 'kings' without suffix in the plural; Vulg. *dies regis nostri* 'the day of our king'; Targ. יומא דמניאו עליהון מלכהון 'the day on which they appointed their king over them'.

החלו LXX ἤρξαντο 'they began', cf. Pesh. *šryw*; Vulg. *coeperunt* and Targ. שריאו. On the basis of these renderings הֵחֵלּוּ is proposed by, e.g., Dathe, Wolff, Borbone. The reading is unlikely in the context, cf. Rudolph.

חמת LXX θυμοῦσθαι 'to rage', cf. Vulg. *furere* and Pesh. *lmrgz*; Targ. למשתי 'to drink'. That all the versions have here an infinitive is a consequence of their mistaken understanding of החלו; for a justification of the versions, cf. Wolff and J. W. Wevers *ThR* 22 (1954), p. 106.

משך LXX ἐξέτεινεν 'he stretched out', cf. Vulg. *extendit*; Pesh. *ngdw* (third plural) and Targ. נגד; → משכו (ידיהם) 'they stretched out their hands' (Borbone, after 4 LXX MSS).

את לצצים LXX μετὰ λοιμῶν 'with pestilent fellows'; Aq. χλευαστῶν 'scoffers', cf. Vulg. *cum inlusoribus*; Pesh. *'m byš'* 'evil men'; Targ. סיעת שכרין 'a company of falsehood (Cathcart adopts a *v.l.* → 'company of deceivers').

7.6 **For in their conspiracy[a] they have made ready[b] their resolve[c] like an[d] oven. Their baker[e] sleeps all the night. In the morning it (*sc.* the oven) burns as [f]a blazing fire[f].**

[a]The infinitive construct of the verb ארב which denotes 'to lie in wait with hostile intent'.

[b]Lit. 'caused to come near'; a *Piel* form of the verb קרב. Rashi and Kimchi detect in the usage the sense 'to fix', 'to set', 'to make ready' the heart (see note c); cf. the Vulgate 'they have applied their heart' (see Text and Versions below). For ibn Ezra the word denotes 'to make close to', 'to approximate to' (cf. Qyl, who takes a similar view). Against this latter view is the presence of the preposition כ 'like' (the oven) which does not accord with it.

[c]Lit. 'their heart'. The word לִבָּם is likely to have been chosen in association with אֵשׁ לֶהָבָה 'blazing fire' which follows; cf. the phrase בְּלַבַּת contracted from בְּלַהֲבַת אֵשׁ in Exod 3.2. The heart here denotes the seat of resolution or determination of the will, cf. BDB p. 525, col 1 II 4 and Kimchi's comment 'the heart is the instrument of thought and denotes the resolution of the conspirator'.

[d]For the article (according to the massoretic pointing) in comparisons, GK 126o.

[e]Following the evidence of the Peshiṭta and Targum (*q.v.* below) a large number of modern commentators (e.g. Harper, Wolff, Rudolph, Mays, *BHS*, Borbone) have suggested the reading 'their anger', 'passion' (אַפֵּהֶם or אַפָּם). The context, however, suggests not passionate anger but the careful planning of a conspiracy. Hence the masssoretic pointing is here accepted. According to Kimchi 'their baker' corresponds precisely to 'their resolve/their heart', and the baker in the simile stands for the resolve/heart. The third plural suffix is, then, the key to the use of the simile[15]. In it the intention of the baker in fuelling and stoking the oven overnight is to prepare it for its function in baking bread. His work done, he can afford to sleep until the morning when he is able to bring his preparations to fruition. The oven is already hot and all he has to do is to revive the fire so as to achieve the optimal temperature (see below). In just this way the plans of the conspirators have been carefully worked out; since their determination and resolve are now complete, they await the proper moment to translate their plans into action. As Kimchi observes, 'the baker in the simile is the strength of thought. He sleeps at night and thought is not translated into action until the morning'. The essence of the meaning of the verse is well illustrated by Mic 2.1 where it is expressed without simile (the verse is quoted below).

[f—f]The expression is likely to denote the blazing mass of a hot fire, revived in the morning, prior to baking. Contrast, perhaps, אש להבה 'blazing fire' with להבת אש 'fiery flame' (e.g. Exod 3.2). Flames and smoke are, of course, inconvenient at the moment of baking; cf. *AUS* 4, pp. 89f and 104f; the verse implies, however, the addition of fresh fuel in the morning which then flares up and so quickly brings the oven to its optimal heat for baking.

The readiness of the conspirators for the moment of truth is here compared with a baker and his oven. The baker is depicted as fuelling and stoking his fire overnight in the knowledge and expectation that early in the morning the oven can readily be brought to its optimal heat and, consequently, that it will be ready for its function. Indeed his knowledge and expectation are so sure that, his preparatory work complete, he can afford to sleep until daybreak and the time for baking. The resolve of the conspirators has similarly been formed upon the basis of their

[15] Rosenmüller criticises Kimchi's interpretation on the grounds that the heart is earlier compared with the oven rather than with the baker. In my submission, however, the point of comparison in this earlier phrase is with the readying of the oven (cf. קרבו לבם) rather than with the oven itself. In other words the phrase, expanded *ad sensum*, means 'they have made ready their resolve as a baker makes ready his oven for baking'.

carefully laid plans and their confident expectation that what they have set in train will come to fruition at the appointed time. 'Their baker', then, as Kimchi observes, stands in the simile for the conspirators' determination and resolve and the pronominal suffix 'their' specifically effects the link to 'their resolve' (notes c and e). The concern of the verse is with the plans, calculations and determination of the conspirators and it is well illustrated by Mic 2.1 'Shame on those who lie in bed planning evil and wicked deeds and rise at daybreak to do them, knowing that they have the power' (NEB).

Whether the reference in the simile to the baker's sleeping at night denotes generally the interval between the completion of the conspirators' plans and their execution of them or whether, literally, to their sleeping in confidence on the eve of the festal day of 'our' king (v. 5) is difficult to judge. On balance I am inclined to the former view.

The seventeenth century scholar J. Schmidt, quoted by Rosenmüller[16], sees in 'their baker' a reference to the person of the chief conspirator (i.e. to Shallum in his conspiracy against Zechariah, 2 Kgs 15.10). The suggestion is not unattractive and could, perhaps, be referred rather (on the view here adopted) to Pekah. On the other hand, Kimchi's interpretation may be said to fit better the construction of the verse and its apparent reference to calculation and planning.

Text and Versions

קרבו LXX ἀνεκαύθησαν '(their hearts) are inflamed', cf. Pesh. *ḥm* (*lbhwn*); Aq., Symm. and Theod. ἤγγισαν, cf. Vulg. *applicuerunt* 'they have brought near/applied (their heart)'; Vollers, on the basis of LXX, reads בערו (cf. Borbone and Grätz; so also Nowack). For the view that the verb should be read as a *Qal* form 'they have drawn near' and that the verse has incorporated a marginal gloss ('their heart is like an oven') made by reference to v. 4, see Rudolph and below.

בארבם LXX (taken with what follows) ἐν τῷ καταράσσειν αὐτούς 'in their rushing down'; Vollers corrects to καταρᾶσθαι (√ארר) 'in their cursing'; Aq., Symm. and Theod. ἐν τῷ ἐνεδρεύειν αὐτούς, cf. Vulg. *cum insidiaretur eis*, Pesh. *bkm'nhwn*, Targ. באתכמניהון, all 'lying in wait'; Rudolph assumes an original בְּאֶרֶב לִבָּם 'in the ambush of their heart' to which the gloss 'their heart is like an oven' is added as an explanation by reference to v. 4.

[16] I have not had access to his work.

אפהם LXX 'Εφράιμ; Aq. ὁ πέσσων 'the baker'; Theod. ὁ πεσῶν[17]; Vulg. *coquens eos* '(the heart) baking them'; Pesh. *rwgzhwn*, cf. Targ. רגזהון 'their anger'; the renderings have prompted many scholars to read אַפְּהֶם/אַפָּם; for comments, see note e above.

בקר הוא בער LXX πρωὶ ἐνεγενήθη, ἀνεκαύθη 'in the morning it came to pass that he (*sc.* Ephraim) flared up', cf. Pesh. *wbspr' yqd hw'* apparently reading היה for הוא.

7.7 **All of them are heated like an oven. They have consumed their rulers[a]; all their kings are casualties[b]. Not one of them[c] cries out to me.**

[a] As in 13.10, the word שפטים denotes not merely officials having a judicial function but also those involved in the administration[18]. They are royal officials similar, as 13.10 makes clear, to the שרים 'princes'.

[b] For the specific sense of נפל, cf., e.g., Judg 8.10.

[c] *Sc.* those involved in successive revolutions. The view that the kings are meant (already mentioned as a possibility by Kimchi) is less likely since the verse is concerned with the characteristic attitude and behaviour of the whole establishment of Samaria.

The verse constitutes a final and more generalised comment upon the instability of the royal establishment of Samaria during its last days made again by reference to the simile of the baker's oven. Hitherto that simile had a particular reference (vv. 5f) and, on the view here adopted, it is to Pekah's putsch of 735 BC. As Rudolph observes, this verse may well belong to the period of Hoshea, the last king of the Northern Kingdom (731–723 BC) who gained the throne by assassinating Pekah. On the other hand, by Pekah's time no fewer than three recent kings had met their death through assassination, only Menahem dying of natural causes, and this record would have been enough to prompt the more general statement before us.

At all events, the whole structure of the state is destabilised by this series of bloodthirsty revolutions in which, naturally, the state officials are caught up. They are consumed (*'kl*) by the insatiable fire of repeated revolutions. Just as the fire of an oven

17 On this, see Ziegler's remarks in *Bei.*, p. 357.
18 See further W. Richter *ZAW* 77 (1965), pp. 58ff.

burns on with its own momentum[19], so the establishment ('all of them') is heated and attuned solely to revolution and counter-revolution. The prophet, then, perceives the harm that is done to the whole state by the circumstances in which one king after another is the primary casualty. The fundamental mistake is the failure of such agitators to acknowledge that their behaviour is adulterous (cf. v. 4); it is disloyalty to Yahweh, who alone could restore and heal the state. Thus ever-increasing reliance upon the next revolution and the new king is one aspect of their shortsighted foolishness and their resort to bloodthirsty violence is the means adopted to the achievement of an end which is both immoral and flawed. Again the unity of thought displayed by the prophet in the sphere of religion, politics and ethics is impressive, consistent and convincing.

Text and Versions

ואכלו את LXX[A] κατέφαγεν πύρ on the basis of which P. Ruben reads וְאָכְלָה אֵשׁ.

[19] The fire of the *ṭābūns* of contemporary Palestinian villages can last as long as three years; I am grateful for this and other information given to me privately by Dr. Fadwa Kirrish.

CHAPTER 7.8–16

EPHRAIM'S DISASTROUS FOREIGN POLICIES

7.8 **Through[a] the nations Ephraim is vitiated[b]; Ephraim has become a cake which has not[c] been turned.**

[a]The preposition is understood to be *beth instrumenti*, cf. Morag (p. 497) and note b below.

[b]The verb בלל is usually given the meaning 'to mingle', and so here 'mingles itself among the nations' (so LXX, Vulgate, Targum, Rashi, ibn Ezra, Kimchi and most modern commentators). For ibn Janāḥ, the usage is to be compared with the phrase תֶּבֶל עָשׂוּ in Lev 20.12 (of incestuous intercourse) which denotes deviation, corruption ('violation of nature', BDB p. 117, col 2). Here the verb יִתְבּוֹלָל conveys that Ephraim has become rotten, corrupt, spoiled, vitiated (Arabic *yfsd*), and changed *sc.* for the worse (Arabic *ytğyyr*). For ibn Barūn[1] the usage is illuminated by the Arabic cognate verb *blbl* 'to throw into disorder', cf. Gen 11.9. Such meanings may be said to fit this particular context and the reference to the spoiled cake better than the other sense of the verb, *viz.* 'mix', 'mingle', though the two senses are clearly related. Accordingly the associated preposition is better understood in the sense indicated in note a above.

Morag also repudiates the view that 'mix' or 'mingle' is the sense of the verb in this verse. Referring quite generally to the standard lexica[2], he believes that the verb יתבולל denotes 'Ephraim has become withered/atrophied (נבילה, כמישה) by means of nations' and for this he cites the phrase from the following verse 'foreigners have devoured his strength'. The suggestion is not unattractive, but the rather more precise etymological account offered by ibn Janāḥ and ibn Barūn is preferable and affords a sense not dissimilar to that which Morag seeks by reference to the context.

The view that the phrase denotes 'Ephraim is kneaded among the nations' (cf. Bauer and Orelli) has been revived and illuminated from Accadian evidence by S. M. Paul. Since, he claims, the root בלל is used in that language to denote both the kneading[3] and the 'mixing of populations', Paul supposes that Hosea has used the cognate Hebrew word here rather than the well-attested לוש (as in v. 4) intentionally to

[1] Wechter, pp. 75f.

[2] Cf. BDB and Marti who refer to suggestions of Nowack and Ewald that the root is here בלה or נבל rather than בלל.

[3] There seems to be but one instance and that is the result of a 'corrected reading', cf. *CAD* 2, p. 41.

effect a clever *double entendre*. The theory seems to me to be far fetched and, in the absence of clear evidence for such meanings for the Hebrew verb, unsatisfactory.

The word order of the phrase is, perhaps, somewhat unusual and is best explained as emphatic in style. The word Ephraim is marked by *zaqeph gadol* which, at the beginning of the verse, suggests an ejaculatory force, i.e. 'Ephraim! through the nations he is vitiated'. Accordingly the word is the antecedent to which the emphatic (so Qyl) הוא refers. Rudolph, following Duhm *et al.*, prefers to ignore the accent and to see in the line two distinct sentences, the second of which explains the first: 'Ephraim amongst the nations: he has muddled himself up (*sc.* with them)'. The suggestion accords with his view of the meaning of the verb which is not here accepted.

[c]The negative בלי, often found before nouns, occurs before verbs in Hos 8.7 and 9.16 (*Kethib*) and in particular before a participle, as here, in Ps 19.4.

The section 7.8–16 contains sayings concerning Ephraim and its relations with foreign nations.

The Northern Kingdom is described as disastrously weakened and debilitated by its vacillating international policies. Short-term expediency is the primary motivation of the nation's leaders and that is consistent with stupidity, immorality and, in the end, idolatry. To turn to foreign nations involves political, cultural and religious subservience (cf. 2 Kgs 16.10ff), and the energies expended by the nation in achieving it on the grounds of the supposed beneficial effects served only to spoil and vitiate its health and integrity (cf. note b above). Indeed Ephraim had become a half-baked cake, i.e. a pancake which the baker neglected to turn during the baking process[4] with the result that one side remained uncooked and the other burnt (cf. Kimchi). No doubt, as Rudolph observes, Hosea has the end result in mind. Thus, the pancake, burnt and charred by the baker's carelessness and inattention, is rendered inedible and quite useless and falls into the fire (cf. Quinta, Peshiṭta and Targum, *q.v.* below).

Amongst the rabbinic commentators ibn Ezra and Kimchi rightly understand the cake to be specifically a figure of the nation's counsel. The unturned cake, then, depicts the nation's inability to think through its policies; for reasoning which is not 'turned from one matter to another' (so Kimchi) is not securely based. Such a view of the matter has the merit that it sees in the figure a single clear and striking metaphor. With Rudolph, we

[4] Cf. *AUS* 4, pp. 35ff.

may repudiate attempts to allegorise the details (for which, see, e.g., Wolff and van Gelderen).

S. M. Paul's view that 'which has not been turned' indicates that the cake/state is 'incapable of action' seems to me to be mistaken. The metaphor pictures Ephraim as a spoiled and useless product of the baker's inattention; thus the state is similarly vitiated. The point of the metaphor is the ruin of the nation by reason of its leaders' foolishness and not its 'lethargic state' nor its 'present exhausted condition'.

The nations with whom Ephraim had foolishly involved itself are likely to be specifically the greater powers, Assyria and Egypt (cf. v. 11). Menahem had paid tribute to Tiglath-pileser III in 738 BC (2 Kgs 15.19f) thereby seeking to consolidate his grip on the monarchy that he had usurped. Pekah's rebellion of 735 BC marked the beginnings of an anti-Assyrian movement and the attempt in 733 BC, with Syria, to coerce Judah into joining the Syro-Ephraimite conspiracy. No doubt Egyptian support for Pekah was actively sought and assured[5]. In 734 BC Tiglath-pileser had led a successful campaign against Philistia and had subjugated the south-west of Palestine as far as Gaza and the Wady el Arish specifically in order to isolate the small Palestinian states from Egypt. It was in Egypt that the defeated Philistine prince Hanun took refuge. Tiglath-pileser met the Syro-Ephraimite revolt by conquering the Israelite areas of Gilead and Galilee and by crushing Damascus. Pekah, after his defeat, was overthrown by Hoshea in 732 BC and the latter immediately paid tribute to Assyria and was confirmed as a dependent vassal king. By 724 BC Hoshea himself sought, by overtures to Egypt, to rid himself of Assyrian control and this led to the final siege of Samaria and its fall in 722/1 BC. From this it is clear that the Northern Kingdom vacillated fatally between loyalty to Assyria and loyalty to Egypt during the period 738–724 BC. The time of the greatest lurches between the two was precisely in the period before, during and after Pekah's reign of 735–732 BC.

Text and Versions

יתבולל LXX συνεμίγνυτο, cf. Vulg. *commiscebatur*, Pesh. *'tḥlṭ* 'mingled together', Targ. אתערבו 'mingled itself with, had dealings with'.

עגה LXX ἐγκρυφίας, cf. Vulg. *subcinericius* 'loaf baked in ashes'; Pesh. *ḥḥwrt'* 'round loaf'; Targ. חררא 'cake'; for Quinta, see below.

[5] Cf. with Wolff, Kittel *Geschichte* 2, p. 365.

בלי הפוכה LXX οὐ μεταστρεφόμενος, cf. Vulg. *non reversatur*, Targ. (*v.l.*, see Sperber) לא איתהפכה 'not turned'; Pesh. *d'dl' 't'pyt 't'klt* 'which is consumed before it is fully baked'; Targ. דעד לא אתאכלת אתהפכת, the *v.l.* reverses the order of the last two words (adopted by Cathcart, cf. Gelston, p. 187), 'which is consumed before it is turned'. Gelston is inclined to see here an agreement in exegetical tradition between Targ. and Pesh.; Quinta ὡς ἐν σποδιᾷ πεσσόμενος ἄρτος ἀμεταστρέπτως 'like a loaf baked in the ashes without being turned'; since אכל in Aramaic/Syriac, like Hebrew, is capable of denoting consumption by fire as well as by eating, the question arises whether Pesh. and Targ. intend what is explicit in Quinta, *viz.* 'like a cake which, before it is turned/baked, is consumed (*sc.* by fire)'. Gelston and Cathcart, however, think of consumption by eating.

7.9 **Foreigners have eaten up his strength[a], but he does not acknowledge it[b]; he has become totally decrepit[c], but he does not acknowledge it[b].**

[a] As ibn Janāḥ observes, both parts of the verse use the metaphor of old age as a time of decline and decrepitude. In the metaphor, 'strength' denotes 'bodily strength'; applied to Ephraim, it denotes the resources of the state and in particular, perhaps, its financial resources, cf. ibn Ezra.

[b] For the translation of לא ידע, cf. on 2.10 above. The phrase, repeated, emphasises the ludicrous stupidity displayed in the situation, cf. Qyl. Rashi interprets the verb 'he did not pay attention' (לא שם על לבו). For the implausible view that the verb is to be compared with Arabic *wd'* in the sense 'to wrap up', 'preserve', see Hirschberg *VT* 11 (1961), p. 379.

[c] Lit. 'Yea, grey hairs are strewn on him', i.e. are profuse on him. The phrase is, as ibn Janāḥ notes, an allusion to the weakness of his condition; it is in old age, the time of decrepitude and weakness of the body, that grey hairs are profuse (Arabic *'lšyb 'kṯr šyh*). The phrase, then, is characterised by metonymy. In the interests of clarity, the essential meaning of the phrase is conveyed in the English translation above rather than the literal expression of it (cf. the Targum, below). For the adverb גם introducing a climax, cf. BDB p. 169, col 2 3.

It seems to be likely that the verb זרק has here its usual meaning 'to scatter', 'sprinkle'[6] and that the *Qal* is used intransitively 'as though it were a *Niphal* (so Kimchi, cf. on 5.6). Alternatively the verb may be pointed as a *Pual* (so, e.g., Marti). Ibn Janāḥ lists this verse with other instances where the verb denotes 'sprinkling'; he makes no mention of a different meaning and, commenting on the phrase, he states 'old age has

[6] For a Latin parallel, cf. Propertius III 4 *sparsevit et nigras alba senecta comas*.

made him grey' (Arabic *wẖṭh*), which suggests that he was merely offering a paraphrase for what is, on this view, an idiomatic figure of speech.

G. R. Driver *JTS* 33 (1932), p. 38, cf. the NEB, has postulated the existence of a second Hebrew root זרק, cognate with Arabic *zariqa* (IXth theme 'to be blue'), and *'zrq* 'blue-grey' (of, e.g., blind eyes and of horses) having the meaning here 'hoar hairs are grey upon him'. While it is clear that this Arabic word is used to denote a colour, it is not evident that it denotes the colour of or is appropriate to 'hoary hairs'. It is significant that neither ibn Janāḥ nor ibn Barūn who are quite accustomed to cite illuminating evidence from Arabic do so in this case[7].

S. M. Paul (so also AF) believes that the verse as a whole continues the metaphor of the 'inert' cake from the previous verse. In the first stich, foreigners nibble at it while it, like the state, 'remains passive and incapable of taking measures'. In the second stich, Hosea 'culls another idiomatic expression from the lexicon of bakers'. Since in Accadian 'white hairs' can denote 'mould', the phrase as a whole suggests that the cake is attacked not only by greedy mouths but also by moulds which it 'throws off' (so זרק).

The theory seems to me to be most unlikely. The preceding verse pictures a cake ruined by the inattention of the baker who fails to turn it at the correct time. In these circumstances that it should subsequently be nibbled or become mouldy is less likely than that it should be destroyed in the ashes (see above). That it should be represented as both nibbled and mouldy seems to be unlikely in the extreme.

For the emendation זרחה 'come forth', 'blossom', see Text and Versions.

Ephraim, vacillating between the great powers and indecisive about where to place his loyalty, does not appreciate that involvement with those powers in fact saps his vital strength. It is likely that financial inducements as well as formal tribute were expended upon these world powers as is well attested, e.g., 2 Kgs 15.19; 16.8; Isa 39.1. Not only so, the net effect of such financial outlay was that the state lost Gilead and Galilee by the advent of Tiglath-pileser in 733 BC. All this is expressed by the phrase 'foreigners have eaten up his strength'. Further, in a striking metaphor, the state is likened to a decrepit old man, liberally sprinkled with grey hairs, who is sinking to his demise

[7] Other suggestions which I find equally or more unconvincing are: first, J. Blau *VT* 5 (1955), p. 341, who, following Gesenius-Buhl, quotes the colloquial Arabic usage for *zrq* 'secretly to steal upon'. Secondly, J. Reider *HUCA* 24 (1953), p. 93 supposes by reference to Arabic *'zrq* that Hebrew זרק is here virtually synonymous with זרח and has the sense 'to disseminate light', 'to shine'. The Arabic word, however, is best attested as describing the colour of the sky.

(note c). The emphasis of the verse is upon the repeated 'but he does not acknowledge it' which indicates the foolishness of the leaders of the state who concern themselves with the illusion of short-term advantage and who are consequently quite unable to perceive the disastrous effects of their policies and thus the reality of the situation. The repeated phrase evokes the statement of 2.10 (EV 8) where the mother/nation 'does not acknowledge' that it is Yahweh, and not her lovers, who provides her with the produce of nature. In both cases, then, foolishness has a moral aspect. It is the failure, in the interests of short-term advantage, to allow the mind to come to a correct evaluation of the truth. For similar phrases, cf. Isa 1.3; 42.25.

Text and Versions

Pesh. adds *hkn'* 'thus' at the beginning of the verse.

גם Vulg. *sed et* 'but also'.

זרקה LXX ἐξήνθησαν, cf. Pesh. *npq* '(grey hair) has come out, blossomed on him'. The translation is a free rendering of MT and does not imply that זרחה was read (so Rudolph *contra* the original suggestion of Grätz); Vulg. *effusi sunt* 'were poured out'; Targ. חלשותא מטיתנון 'weakness overtakes them', cf. Quinta τυγχάνων.

7.10 **And the pride of Israel has testified against him[a]; yet they did not return to Yahweh their God nor, for all this[b], did they seek him.**

[a]See on 5.5 above. For the versions and the rabbinic commentators the sense is 'the pride of Israel will be brought low before his (*sc.* the enemy's) face'. Rashi understands the verb וְעָנָה as having here a past reference (cf. Isa 6.3 וקרא) as opposed to 5.5 where it has a future reference. His interpretation is interesting and suggests that he perceived that the repetition of the words was artful and deliberate (see the commentary below).

[b]Cf. Isa 9.11, 16, 20; Ps 78.32; Job 2.10.

Since the first phrase of the verse is found in 5.5 (*q.v.*) a number of modern commentators have supposed that here it constitutes an interpretative gloss made by reference to the earlier occurrence (so, e.g., Wolff, Rudolph, Mays, *BHS*). The theory is plausible in that the end of the preceding verse appears to echo the last line of 5.4 just as the second part of the present verse 'yet they did not return to Yahweh their God' echoes 'to return to their God' in 5.4 (so, e.g., Rudolph). There is no reason to suppose that the words in 5.5 are not authentic and, in view of their appropriateness to the context here (so, e.g., Wolff, Mays), we may suppose that their occurrence accurately reflects the prophet's view. Rudolph's contrary understanding, *viz.* that 'pride' is not appropriate to the context, seems to me to be mistaken: the particular foolishness which Ephraim displays is characterised by moral perversity (see on the previous verse) and that is not so far from pride.

It is, furthermore, foolish pride which prevents the nation returning in penitence to Yahweh as also their seeking him (see on 2.9, EV 7; 3.4; 4.15 etc.) despite the calamities apparent to those who had the wit to understand the situation.

It is here, too, that a link with the words of chapter 2 becomes clear. There, as we have had reason to argue, the state is depicted under the figure of the wayward mother and the language that Hosea employs suggests that what he says reflects his personal marital experience. Here, as in 2.7, 10 (EV 5, 8), the state, like the wayward mother, conducts herself in a way that is at once unreasonable and wilful; both chose not to perceive the truth of the situation. Hence the calamities instigated by Yahweh must increase (cf. on 5.4) until the nation (cf. the mother) is compelled to come to her senses and return to her husband for 'things were better for me then than now' (2.9, EV 7).

The thought is so consistent and central that the repetition of the words of 5.5 here cannot but reflect the mind of the prophet himself and we may suppose that he repeated them in order to indicate that the truth of his earlier conclusions was vindicated by these later developments and events (cf. Rashi's comments, note a above; also 5.7). If the repetition was in fact made by a redactor of Hosea's sayings, then he is likely to have acted on Hosea's instructions; and even if he did so without instructions, he has so adequately and faithfully represented the mind of his master that no importance attaches to such distinctions.

Text and Versions

וענה גאון – in most respects as in 5.5 except that, for the verb, Pesh. has *w'tmkk* (perfect rather than imperfect) and Vulg. *humiliabitur* (= ענה III) rather than *respondebit* (= ענה I) as in 5.5.

בכל זאת LXX ἐν πᾶσι τούτοις, cf. Vulg. *in omnibus his*; Pesh. omits the phrase, for which cf. Gelston, p. 133.

7.11 And so[a] Ephraim is like a dove, gullible[b], without sense[c]. They called[d] to Egypt and betook themselves to Assyria.

[a]ויהי 'and Ephraim has become ...'. For the view that the word is a redactional addition, see Wolff.

[b]The participle פּוֹתָה, from פתה, denotes 'simple-mindedness' and, in the context, 'gullible'; thus the bird is incapable of sensing danger from the fowler's snare when it alights to feed on the grain laid out as a bait (so Kimchi). For a noun from the same root used of human gullibility, cf., e.g., Prov 7.7; 14.15.

[c]Lit. 'heart'; cf. in 4.11 above.

[d]Apparently a plural form, matching the final הָלָכוּ.

Ephraim's impetuousness and lack of sense are seen in its oscillating between policies of reliance upon Egypt and Assyria. The gullibility of the dove (note b) is like that of human simpletons 'who can believe anything' (cf. Prov 14.15). Accordingly the establishment of the state can turn in hope to their very adversaries, the Assyrians (cf. 5.13) and, at the same moment (perhaps prompted by a different party), contemplate a similar overture to the Egyptians. They have not the wit to see that such vacillation brings inevitable doom and such mindless optimism can only trap them in its toils. That the dove is associated in the Song of Songs also with love (e.g. 5.2) may suggest that here the state approaches Egypt and Assyria with the easy optimism of a loose woman (cf. Ezek 23) just as *mutatis mutandis* the gullible youth is easy prey to the seductress of Prov 7.

Jerome sees a particular point in the comparison with the dove. Other birds are noted for the strong defence of their chicks and only the dove does not grieve or search for them when they are snatched from the nest. So Ephraim, deprived of lands and population, yet does not grieve nor show concern for its salvation. The interpretation matches that of the Targum, *q.v.* below.

The two verbs 'they called' and 'they betook themselves', used respectively of Egypt and Assyria, seem to reflect accurately the circumstances of the period (*c.* 733 BC). Thus, appeal to Egypt represented the alternative policy to that which was the norm, *viz.* the king[8] paying tribute to Assyria in exchange for the status of a protected client. It is likely, as has been noted, that Pekah

[8] Menahem, Pekahiah (presumably) and Hoshea (after his deposing Pekah, cf. 2 Kgs 17.3).

will have appealed to Egypt for help as Hoshea certainly did some nine years later (2 Kgs 17.4). But the call to Egypt seems in fact to have been in vain (cf. Isa 20.6; 36.6). Nonetheless, that it was made is a testimony to vacillating policies and, with the witholding of tribute to Assyria, was sufficient to precipitate the wrath of that country[9].

It is unlikely that the verse denotes a specific occasion but rather reflects the general situation immediately before, during and after Pekah's brief reign (cf. on v. 8 above).

Text and Versions

פותה LXX ἄνους, cf. Pesh. *šbrt'*, 'foolish'; Aq. θελγομένη 'spell-bound'; Symm. ἀπατωμένη 'beguiled', cf. Vulg. *seducta*; Targ. שריחתא דאתנסיבו בנהא 'a foolish[10] (dove) whose young have been snatched away'; Sperber records the *v.l.* שחירתא 'sent abroad', cf. Jastrow, p. 1551b and Cathcart, p. 44.

קראו Pesh. *'tw*, cf. Targ. אתקרבו 'they have come', 'drawn near'. Gelston (p. 188) rejects Sebök's suggestion that the Hebrew *Vorlage* was קרבו; he argues that Pesh. represents a simplification of MT and that Targ. is paraphrastic, conveying the sense 'to claim relationship' in political intrigues.

הלכו Pesh. *'zlw* 'they are gone away', cf. perhaps Targ. גלו 'exiled', 'gone away'; Gelston, however, characterises the rendering of Pesh. 'straightforward' and that of Targ. as 'paraphrastic'. He is disinclined to see a link between the two versions in this verse.

7.12 **Just as[a], when they are on their way[b], I will spread my net over them and, like birds, I will bring them down, so at[a] the very rumour of their assignations[c] I will chastise[d] them.**

[a—a]The whole verse is understood to consist of the simile of the fowler in its first half and, in the second half, of a statement of Yahweh's reaction to the actual dealings of the statesmen to which the simile is directed. The whole follows the structure of the preceding verse where simile is followed by statement of fact. These considerations tell against some modern commentators (*q.v.* notes c and d below) who seek to find

[9] So Targum; see Smolar and Aberbach, p. 203 (especially n. 480).

[10] So Jastrow *ad loc.* Kimchi understands the word to mean 'distraught', i.e. 'like a woman weeping and scratching her face'. Such a meaning for the word would give precisely the opposite sense to that detected by Jerome. Cathcart, p. 44 n. 24, raises the question whether the word may be illuminated by reference to Syriac *šryḥ* 'unrestrained', 'lascivious'.

in the second part of the verse further reference to the activities of the fowler.

The construction shares some important similarities of form with that of Isa 23.5 and, like it, is apparently designed to convey a simile. There are, however, differences. Rashi (cf. Rosenmüller) understands the phrase in Isa כאשר שֵׁמַע למצרים יחילו כְּשֵׁמַע צֹר to mean 'just like the report concerning Egypt (i.e. the ten plagues), they will squirm in terror at the report concerning Tyre'. For this, however, the unwarranted assumption must be made that כאשר ... כ is equivalent to the well-attested כאשר ... כן (for the latter, BDB p. 455, col 2 d). The pointing כְּשֵׁמַע in this verse implies that the noun שמע is in the construct state, cf. the phrase כְּשֵׁמַע צֹר in Isa 23.5. Yet the phrase here in Hosea is different and manifestly awkward in that the preposition ל intervenes between construct and absolute. It seems best, then, to suggest[11] that כְּשֵׁמַע be repointed כַּשֵּׁמַע, thereby creating a genuine nominal clause (for a parallel, cf. Isa 26.9) in which the absolute + ל is an alternative construction to the construct + absolute (cf. GK 129a, b). The rendering of the Vulgate (*q.v.* below) may be quoted in support of the proposal. The preposition ל in the phrase כשמע לעדתם is understood to convey 'at the report/rumour *concerning* their meeting', cf. Isa 23.5 and Rashi's comments upon it (i.e. the effect of the words is 'what they heard *about* Egypt'). For כ 'according to' having here virtually a temporal sense 'at', cf. Hos 13.6 and BDB p. 454, col 2 3 b.

[b]Cf. Vulgate; *q.v.* under Text and Versions.

[c]The singular noun עֵדָה is understood to be derived from the root יעד 'to appoint'. It is widely and commonly attested with the meaning 'congregation' as a 'company assembled together by appointment' (so BDB p. 417, col 1). Ibn Barūn, though he does not refer to this verse nor to עדה, compares the verb and the related noun מוֹעֵד with the Arabic cognate *w'd* which has the meanings 'to make mutual promises' (cf. Judg 20.38; Josh 11.5). The context here suggests a reference to the diplomatic meetings or appointments between the Ephraimites and the representatives of Assyria and Egypt at which mutual obligations were undertaken. The semantic range of the root and its derived noun עדה are entirely compatible with such a meaning though, in the absence of a clear parallel elsewhere in the OT, the usage may reasonably be held to be dialectal. Jerome comes near to such a view of the matter with his comment on the phrase 'all by mutual agreement (*iuncto consilio*) manufactured idols' though he understands idolatry to be the underlying transgression. The singular noun 'their meeting' is rendered by a plural in English *ad sensum*.

Amongst the rabbinic commentators (Rashi, ibn Ezra, Kimchi) the 'assembly' is that of the Israelites in Palestine to which (so ל) evil

[11] I am grateful to Gelston for making the suggestion in a private communication.

tidings will come (ibn Ezra); to that reported as warned by Jeremiah (Jer 42; so Rashi); or to the assembly in the desert reported as warned by the execrations of Deut 28 (Kimchi). For emendations made on the basis of the ancient versions, and for comments upon them, see Text and Versions.

Nyberg[12], comparing Judg 14.8 where עדה is used of a swarm of bees, supposes that the word here means a flock (of birds) and that, again, the whole verse refers to the fowler. He renders 'I will capture them at the sound of their flock (now caught in the net)'; Rudolph, rightly doubting that שמע can mean 'bustle', 'stir', 'noise', prefers to read כְּשֹׁמֵעַ and renders 'I will capture them, as one who hears their flock'.

Such suggestions seem to me to be very doubtful and, for reasons advanced under note a, I prefer to see in the second half of the verse reference to the events to which the simile of the first half is appropriate. The verse as a whole means that Yahweh will frustrate the Ephraimites' plans at the very outset of their attempt to implement them and at the very first report of their diplomatic meetings.

[d] A *Hiphil* form of the verb יסר 'to discipline', 'chastise'; cf., with ibn Ezra, the uncontracted *Hiphil* form יֵישְׁרוּ in Prov 4.25. He notes that unusually the initial *yodh* has not become *waw* as in מוסר 'discipline'[13]. The *Hiphil* here is likely to reflect dialectal usage rather than to be a mistake for the *Piel*. (For the latter view, see, e.g., Grätz, Wolff, Mays, AF). Rudolph, following C. Budde, suggests as a possibility the reading אסירם (√סור) 'I will deflect them', interpreting the second half of the verse in terms of the fowler's skill. Similarly, e.g., Marti and Nyberg (cf. Rudolph, *BHS*) read אוסרם → אאסרם (√אסר) 'I will bind (*sc.* capture) them'. The suggestion is already listed as a possibility by Rashi, though he does not thereby concede that the second half of the verse continues the simile of the fowler.

In direct and immediate response to the foolish attempts of the rulers of Ephraim to enlist the support of Egypt and Assyria, Yahweh is represented as stating that he will discipline them and frustrate their plans. R. Malbîm (nineteenth century[14]) suggests that the verse refers to the capture and imprisonment of Hoshea at the hands of Shalmaneser, king of Assyria, in 724 BC (2 Kgs 17.4f), following his refusal to pay tribute and his attempts to enlist the support of the Egyptian king, So. Whether that was Hosea's original intention is questionable as it seems more likely that the words, like those of the preceding verses (*q.v.*), are directed to the vacillating policies of the period during, before

[12] Cf., for similar treatments, Weiser, Bruno, van Gelderen and Mauchline.
[13] Cf., with R. Eliezer of Beaugency, Gen 8.17: *Qere* היצא; *Kethib* הוצא; cf. GK 70b.
[14] מקראי קודש 4, Jerusalem, 1956, *ad loc.*

and immediately after Pekah's reign. Yet it is likely that Hosea's words were seen (by him or by his redactor) to have a particular application and fulfilment in the events of 724 BC.

The threat expressed by the verse is, however, more general and predicative in its intent. It expresses the view that the very first impetuous steps (note a) taken towards enlisting foreign help will activate immediate and inexorable doom in the toils of the trap laid by the fowler, i.e. by Yahweh, and the very mention of diplomatic assignations (note c) will be sufficient to activate Yahweh's chastening (note d) of his disloyal and recalcitrant people. In other words, the policy of seeking foreign intervention, adopted for short-term advantage and for that reason characterised by frequent changes of loyalty, has necessarily within it the seeds of destruction. Indeed the state is caught like a bird in the tangled web of Yahweh's net, its ability to fly frustrated in its forcible confinement to the ground. It is likely that the methods of the fowler involved the use on the ground of decoys to which, with the accompanying grain, the flying birds were enticed, thereby enabling the fowler to spring his net over them, cf. on 5.1 above. The imagery is singularly appropriate to the historical realities.

Text and Versions

כאשר ילכו LXX καθὼς ἂν πορεύωνται 'just as they journey'; Vulg. *et cum profecti fuerint* 'when they have set out'; Pesh. *l'tr dn'zlwn* 'wherever they shall go', cf. Targ. באתר דיהכון 'in the place where they go'.

איסרם LXX παιδεύσω, cf. Vulg. *caedam*, Pesh. *w'rd'* and Targ. יסורין איתי; all witness to √יסר 'discipline'.

כשמע לעדתם LXX ἐν τῇ ἀκοῇ τῆς θλίψεως αὐτῶν 'at the report of their distress', has suggested the readings לְצָרָתָם or לְרָעָתָם (cf. Marti followed by *BH*, Wolff, Mays). → (מ)שם על רעתם (Borbone cf. *BHS*); Aq. κατὰ ἀκοῆς τῆς συναγωγῆς 'concerning the report of (their) meeting'; Ziegler (*Bei.*, p. 357) corrects to ... ἀκοήν τῇ συναγωγῇ '(according to the) report to their meeting'; Symm. μαρτυρίας, cf. Pesh. *'yk šm'' dshdwthwn* '(according to the report) of their witness', on the basis of which לְעֵדֻתָם has been proposed (Sebök, cf. Gelston, p. 122); AF, adopting the reading עֵדוּתָם render 'oath', 'covenant' → 'treaties', which is very dubious; Vulg. *secundum auditionem coetus eorum* 'according to the report of their meeting', cf. note a above; Targ. על דשמעו לעיצתהון 'because they listened to their counsel' which, Rudolph suggests, implies the reading בִּשְׁמֹעַ לַעֲצָתָם. It seems to me more likely that the rendering represents an ingenious attempt to make sense of MT by reference to the context; cf., with Cathcart (p. 44, n. 29), Targ. v. 6 'they have drawn near to the counsel of sinners'.

7.13 **Woe to them, for they have flown far[a] from me; destruction upon them[b], for they rebelled against me. I wished to redeem them[c], but what they have done is to speak lies about me[d].**

[a]The verb נדד, meaning 'to flee', 'wander', is used elsewhere of birds and of other animals who have, as a result of disaster, wandered far and lost their way (cf. Isa 16.2; Jer 4.25; 9.9). Hence the image of the preceding verses continues.

[b]Following the phrase 'Woe to them', the words are probably to be construed as a wish, cf. Wolff's 'down with them'.

[c]A conative imperfect, cf. Rashi, ibn Ezra, and Kimchi. 'It was in my heart and thoughts to redeem them' (ibn Ezra). Rudolph rightly finds this confirmed by the following perfect, *contra* van Gelderen who argues for a frequentative imperfect. A number of commentators understand the words as a question 'should I redeem them, when ...?' (e.g. Nowack, Harper, Wolff). Against this is the consideration advanced by van Hoonacker, cf. Rudolph: the close similarity of v. 15b with 13b, where 15b is clearly indicative and not interrogative.

[d]Lit. 'they have spoken lies about/against me'. The third person pronoun is emphatic in Hebrew and the translation, expanded in English, seeks to convey that emphasis. 'About' or 'against' are both possible translations. The difference in the context is marginal.

Yahweh's cry of exasperation (cf. 9.12) suggests the climax of the collection of sayings (so Wolff). It is elicited in the circumstances that Ephraim, again under the figure of a bird, has flown far from the only real source of its protection. Indeed such impetuous and foolish migration (whether to Assyria or to Egypt) constitutes the rebellion elsewhere attested of sons against their father (Isa 1.2), or of subjects against their legitimate king (1 Kgs 12.19). He, Yahweh, was inclined to redeem them (cf. 13.14), to rescue them from the toils of their impending doom. Yet for their part, all they had done was to speak calumnies against him. As a parallel instance, Rashi cites Jer 43.2 'they said to Jeremiah "You are lying; Yahweh, our God, has not sent you to forbid us to go to Egypt"'. For ibn Ezra the calumny consists in their affirming that all Yahweh wanted was their doom; and for Kimchi, that Yahweh was quite indifferent to wicked and immoral actions. The lies, then, were a denial of the power and authority of Yahweh in contemporary history (cf. Jer

5.12) and they were amply exemplified in the nation's craven attempts to ingratiate itself with the world powers and in its preoccupation with materialistic comfort together with muddled notions of its origin (cf. on the following verse).

Text and Versions

נדדו LXX ἀπεπήδησαν 'they have started away from'; Pesh. *ndw* 'they have turned (from me)'; Vulg. *recesserunt* 'they have withdrawn'; Targ. אתרחקו 'they have taken themselves afar'.

שד להם LXX δείλαιοί εἰσιν 'they are wretched'; Theod. ταλαιπωρία 'distress'; Pesh. *byšt' 'yt' 'lyhwn* 'I will bring calamity upon them'; Vulg. *vastabuntur* 'they will be ravaged', cf. Quinta ἐκπορθήσονται; Targ. בזוזין איתי עליהון 'I will bring plunderers against them', cf. perhaps Aq. προνομὴ αὐτοῖς 'a foray against them'; on the agreement between Pesh. and Targ. (and for the possibility that *byšt'* in Pesh. is a corruption of *bzt'*), see Gelston, pp. 185f.

7.14 **Nor have they cried out to me in sincerity[a]. Rather they howl about[b] their couplings[c], they lacerate themselves[d] concerning corn and new wine. They rebel[e] against me.**

[a]Lit. 'with their heart'; cf., with Qyl, Jer 3.10; Ps 119.10.

[b]The preposition על, in view of the following phrase, is taken to mean 'about', 'concerning' rather than 'upon' (as in Ps 149.5).

[c]מִשְׁכְּבוֹת Lit. 'place of lying', 'couch', 'bed'. For its use to denote sexual intercourse, cf. Judg 21.11f; Lev 18.22; 20.13; Isa 57.8; Ezek 23.17 etc. This meaning seems more appropriate to the context than 'they howled upon their beds (cf. *per contra* Ps 149.5) since the action is clearly public, cf. Rudolph. For the evidence of the versions, see below.

[d]Reading, with 13 MSS, cf. the LXX (*q.v.* below), יִתְגּוֹדְדוּ (so *BHS*, Borbone); cf. 1 Kgs 18.28 and most modern authorities. Very considerable uncertainty attaches to MT's יִתְגּוֹרָרוּ. Ibn Janāḥ lists this occurrence under both roots גור and גרר, thereby indicating uncertainty about the matter. Under the root גור he cites Lam 2.22; Hab 1.15 and Joel 1.17 together with the present verse, investing all of them with the meaning 'gathering' (Arabic *'lğm'*). With this assessment ibn Ezra and Kimchi appear to agree (e.g., 'they associate to eat and to drink'; so ibn Ezra on this verse). Rashi, too, refers to Joel 1.17 but supposes that the present verse refers to the gathering of grain in silos and so to its plentiful amount (cf. the Targum). Under the root גרר ibn Janāḥ cites Pss 56.7; 140.3 and Prov 21.7. He comments that, if this is correct, then the third radical, in these occurrences, has been weakened and that the

meaning is not at variance with that listed under גור. Unfortunately he is not more precise and gives no Arabic translation of גרר.

In Jer 5.7 where MT reads יִתְגֹּדָדוּ 'they thronged' (Rashi) or 'gashed themselves' in a harlot's house (see McKane, *ad loc.*) the variant reading יתגוררו is attested by two of de Rossi's manuscripts and in Jer 47.5, 2QJer records the same variant for MT's תִּתְגּוֹדָדִי. These readings, together with the evidence of the present verse, suggest the possibility that we are presented with genuine variants and in all cases the *Hithpo'el* of גרר may have been capable of a meaning not dissimilar to that of גדד. In this connection the well-attested cognate noun מגרה 'a saw' may afford some evidence, as also talmudic Hebrew גרר 'to scrape' or 'scratch' as well as 'to drag' (cf. Arabic *ǧrr*) and Aramaic גרר which, with similar meanings, may also denote (in the *Ithpa'el*) 'to stimulate one another'[15]. In the absence of clearer evidence, however, I have thought it prudent to adopt the alternative reading יתגודדו. The possibility remains that the verb גדד may have constituted a variant or early translation of גרר at a time when it was no longer understood; cf. on 2.8 (EV 6); 7.15f and 8.13.

Amongst other attempts to justify the MT reading, mention may be made of Jerome (cf. Symmachus) who sees in the verb a reference to rumination and hence to the prolonged enjoyment of material wealth and plenty (cf. Ezek 16.49). For this meaning he is clearly relating the verb to the well-attested noun גרה 'cud' and he remarks that the choice of the verb here (with the sense 'to ruminate') is made in order to emphasise that their preoccupation is appropriate to that of brute beasts. The solution is more ingenious than convincing (cf. Rudolph).

J. D. Michaelis (*Supplementa*, p. 286) suggests that the verb is to be illuminated either by reference to the Vth theme of Arabic *ǧwr* to which he gives the meaning 'they prostrate themselves concerning' or, by comparison with Hos 10.5, where the verb גור in the *Qal* denotes 'fear'[16], 'they fear for themselves concerning'. The first idea may be said to be doubtful since, though the Arabic verb does mean 'to lie down', it is better attested with the sense 'to be brought to the ground, felled (as by a spear)'[17], and no parallel occurrences in Hebrew are cited. The second idea amounts to a possibility and, as Michaelis remarks, the Peshiṭta (*q.v.* below) may give it some support. On the other hand it is not clear why, on this view of the matter, Hos 10.5 uses a *Qal* and this

[15] So Jastrow, p. 273, col 1; it should be noted that there appears to be some MS confusion between the Aramaic roots גרר and גרד which have similar meanings. H. L. Ginsberg SVT 16, pp. 75ff, favouring the reading יתגוררו, supposes that it is a form of the root גור and means 'they fornicate', for which he compares Aramaic גור with similar meanings. Since the word in Aramaic is a euphemism (so Jastrow) doubt must attach to the theory.

[16] Cf. BDB p. 158, col 2 for גור III 'to dread'.

[17] Cf. Lane 2, p. 483, col 1.

text a *Hithpo'lel* form when both contexts require much the same meaning. Again no parallel instances are cited.

[e]In view of the following preposition בִּי 'against me' it is preferable to read יָסֹרוּ (from סרר) changing the pointing but not the consonantal text (so Houtsma and most moderns). MT's יָסוּרוּ (from סור) is interpreted by ibn Ezra 'they speak rebellion (סָרָה) against me'. As Rashi observes, the verbs סור and סרר are very close in meaning.

The verse continues and illuminates the sense of the preceding 'they have spoken lies about me'. So far from calling upon Yahweh in sincerity (note a), they are preoccupied with self-interest and with the loss of their material well-being. Hence their religious practices, even in their distress, are marked by the trappings of Canaanite syncretism. They howl not in penitence but in regret at the loss of their orgiastic opportunities (note c) and they lacerate themselves (note d) in response to the loss of their agricultural produce. The latter action was undertaken by the prophets of Baal on Mount Carmel (1 Kgs 18.28) and it is proscribed in Deut 14.1 in connection with the cult of the dead. It is probable that it also had some connection with orgiastic sexual rites, cf. Jer 5.7; Zech 13.6[18], and, in view of the likely sense of the preceding phrase, it is to this that Hosea alludes. At all events these practices indicated rebellion against Yahweh (note e) and a total failure rightly to appraise the situation. Once again it is flawed reasoning as the fundamental aspect of idolatry and immorality that Hosea emphasises (note a). Thought, speech and action are interconnected and the lies spoken against Yahweh are consistent with the behaviour and insincerity of the liars. The sentiments of the verse match 6.4 and Yahweh's *cri de cœur* 'your good intentions are like the morning mist and like the dew which disappears early in the day'.

The dearth of agricultural products is likely to reflect the situation of 733 BC and Tiglath-pileser's invasion (cf. 7.9) by which the Jezreel valley, the most important source of grain, was annexed to the Assyrian province of Megiddo, leaving Pekah only the district of Samaria. That tribute in kind was also paid then and in the years following is clear from 12.2 (EV 1).

Text and Versions

בלבם LXX αἱ καρδίαι αὐτῶν as the subject of וזעקו and apparently ignoring ב.

[18] Cf. B. Otzen *Deuterosacharja ad loc.*

על משכבותם LXX ἐν ταῖς κοίταις αὐτῶν, cf. Vulg. *in cubilibus suis*; Pesh. *'l mškbhwn* (singular) 'on their bed(s)'; the word κοίτη is capable of a pejorative sense, 'lasciviousness; cf. Rom 13.13[19]; Aq., Symm. ἀλλὰ ἀσελγῶς ἐλαλήσαν 'but they have spoken wantonly'; (for doubts about the attribution of this to Aq., see Ziegler *Bei.*, p. 357); Targ. על ערסתהון 'upon their bed' or, more likely, 'concerning their sexual intercourse'; → מִזְבְּחֹתָם 'beside their altars' (Harper); → מִשְׁכְּנוֹתָם 'concerning their dwellings' (Rudolph).

יתגוררו LXX κατετέμνοντο 'they cut themselves'; Aq. περιεσπῶντο 'they stripped themselves' (cf. perhaps, Aramaic נגד); Ziegler *Bei.*, p. 357, suggests an original κατεσπάσθησαν; Vulg. *ruminabant*, cf. Symm. ἐμηρυκῶντο 'they ruminated', see above; Pesh. *mtktšyn* 'they strove', 'struggled', cf. Gelston, p. 120; for Michaelis' use of this rendering, see above (note d); Targ. הוו כנשין '(the grain and wine which) they were gathering', cf. Cathcart, p. 45 n. 36.

יסורו בי LXX ἐπαιδεύθησαν ἐν ἐμοί on the basis of which (e.g.) Vollers reads יָסְּרוּ and Wünsche יִוָּסְרוּ 'they are/will be disciplined'; Symm. ἐξέκλιναν ἀπ' ἐμοῦ 'they have deviated from me', cf. Quinta ἀπέστησάν μου, Vulg. *recesserunt a me*; Pesh. *mrdw by*, cf. Targ. מרדו במימרי 'they have rebelled against me (my Memra)'; on the *v.l.* *'ly* in Pesh., see Gelston, p. 74.

7.15 **For my part[a] I sought to support them[b], but they devised evil against me[c].**

[a]The pronoun אני is emphatic.

[b]Lit. 'I have strengthened their arms'. Ibn Janāḥ gives to the word יִסַּרְתִּי the meaning 'I have strengthened' (Arabic *šddt*). Similarly[20] G. R. Driver *JTS* 36 (1935), p. 295 argues that it carries this sense, being a northern dialectal form of Aramaic אשר 'to be strong'. חִזַּקְתִּי is, then, a gloss added at a later stage to elucidate the meaning of the rare יסרתי. The view that יסרתי here is authentic rather than חזקתי is strengthened by the evident word-play made by it with יסורו at the end of the preceding verse. The evidence of the LXX, which has one verb for MT's two, is not in itself decisive. This analysis of the word is confirmed by the very similar phrase of Job 4.3 where the same two verbs are found in parallelism. 'To strengthen a person's arms' is a regular idiom for encouragement and support. The translation adds

19 Cf. Jerome: 'their meetings are well called *cubilia* or bestial debauchery'.

20 Kimchi seeks to link the verb with √אסר 'to bind', suggesting that the notion of binding is connected with that of strengthening. His theory is unlikely to be correct, yet it indicates the same instinct as is displayed by ibn Janāḥ and Driver. See further Barr *CPOT*, p. 322.

'sought to' to convey the longer perspective indicated by the context, cf. the conative imperfect of v. 13 above.

Ibn Ezra and Rashi understand the verb in terms of its usual meaning 'to discipline', 'chastise'. Hence, with two verbs, the discipline was imposed for the purpose of encouragement; cf. the evidence of the versions, below.

[c]Cf. Nah 1.9.

The contrast between the truth of the situation, *viz.* that Yahweh has always encouraged and supported (note b) his people and their perverse ingratitude, is set forth. The sense is very similar to v. 13 above 'I wished to redeem them but what they have done is to speak lies about me'. For his part, Yahweh appeals to his consistent support in the nation's history (cf. 11.3) and thus authenticates his claim that he wishes to be their God (Rudolph).

By contrast the nation, even in its hour of greatest danger, is wilfully set upon a mistaken evaluation of the truth. In fact, they are powerless to harm their creator; what they can do is to think perversely and disloyally and the tragic result is their own destruction (so Jerome).

Text and Versions

LXX begins v. 15 with ἐπαιδεύθησαν ἐν ἐμοί κἀγώ, cf. on v. 14 above.

יסרתי LXX κατίσχυσα 'strengthened', i.e. one verb for the two in MT; it is possible that חזקתי is translated here rather than יסרתי, cf. Hatch and Redpath (p. 751), who note that the Greek verb frequently answers to חזק but not to יסר (cf. *BHS* which deletes יסרתי); it is possible to argue that LXX translated the familiar verb leaving untranslated יסרתי which was not understood; Symm. ἐπαίδευον αὐτούς, cf. Vulg. *erudivi*; Pesh. *rdyt* (for the *v.l.* *'rdyt* see Gelston, pp. 72ff), Targ. מיתי יסורין – all 'discipline', 'training', 'chastisement'.

7.16 **Time and again[a] they change their minds[b] but never to higher things[c]; they have become a faulty[d] bow. Their emissaries[e] will fall by the sword, a consequence of their offensive words[f] (this is their blasphemy[g]) in the land of Egypt.**

[a]The verb יָשׁוּבוּ (note b) is a frequentative imperfect which the English phrase seeks to convey.

[b]The verb שׁוב is very common, and has a wide range of possible meanings, of which the fundamental one is 'to return'. For the evidence

of the versions, see below. Rashi and ibn Ezra interpret the verb specifically of return to Egypt, mentioned later in the verse; similarly Rudolph, though in conjunction with emendation of the following words. For Qyl (cf. Morag) the reference is to returning in repentance. In connection with any attempt to determine the meaning of the verb, much depends upon the view taken of על which follows. On the view here adopted, *viz.* that it means 'higher things', the verb is understood to denote reversion, changing of mind or a course of action (BDB p. 997, col 2 5 e), cf. Job 6.29. The reference is to the frequent changes of national policy, especially in regard to alliances with Assyria or Egypt.

[c]לא על lit. 'not (to) what is above'. Commenting upon Hos 11.7 and the similar phrase אל על, ibn Janāḥ refers to 2 Sam 23.1 where David is described as הֻקַם עָל 'established on high' (lit. 'as to height'). In Hos 11.7 אל על means that Ephraim is called to the highest level, i.e. to 'true piety' (Arabic *'ly drğt 'lyt yryd 'ltqwy*). Similarly, and apparently independently, Morag argues that in Hos 11.7 אל על denotes 'to the highest level' (הדרגה העליונה) and thus the phrase means 'they have repented but not to the highest level of behaviour'. Rashi, too, believes that על denotes 'height', 'elevation' though he paraphrases 'they returned to Egypt but there was no benefit for them' (ולא להועיל להם). Kimchi understands על to be an adjective like עליון and it is thus a reference to God as 'the most high'[21]. Accordingly 'when trouble comes, they revert to calling upon idols and not to me who am higher than everything'. Morag (cf. Qyl) adopts this theory as an alternative, thus, 'they have repented but not to God', or (as a question and answer), 'Do they repent? Not to God!'[22].

It seems to me that על is more likely to be a noun denoting 'what is above' than to be a name of God, for it is difficult to see why Hosea should wish to use such a rare name when elsewhere he employs the usual names and expressions. On the other hand if ibn Janāḥ's view is correct, then 'what is above', i.e. the highest level of morality and behaviour, is appropriate to the character of Yahweh himself and thus clearly points to him. The sense may be accurately illustrated by reference to Col 3.1 τὰ ἄνω ζητεῖτε 'seek those things which are above'.

A number of scholars have sought to emend the text, many taking a lead from Rashi's paraphrase ולא להועיל (see below).

[d]Lit. 'slack'. There are three roots רמה meaning, respectively, (1) to shoot; (2) to beguile, deceive; and (3) to be loose, slack (cf. BDB *ad loc.*). It is to the third that G. R. Driver (*Nötscher Festschrift*, p. 53) points by citing an Accadian parallel phrase in elucidation of this occurrence as well as of that in Ps 78.57. What is depicted is a bow which has become too pliant and is thus slack and inefficient at

21 For more recent statements of this theory, cf. Nyberg, p. 58 and AF.

22 A variant understanding is that of AF who, assuming that the preposition אל is missing, render 'they return to No-God'.

propelling its arrows over the expected distance. Earlier Rosenmüller had pointed to the same root thinking, though, that the bow was slack by reason of a broken string. For the evidence of the versions, see below. Jerome, Rashi and Kimchi (cf. BDB) understand the expression by reference to the second root, explaining that the bow is treacherous because, when its user 'wishes to shoot northwards, it shoots southwards' (Rashi, cf. Kimchi). Jerome suggests that the bow, being treacherous, wounds its user (cf. Qyl); so Ephraimites 'wound their own Lord with the arrows of blasphemy'. For a modern defence of this etymology, cf. Rudolph. It is not unlikely that Hosea uses the phrase intentionally to make possible a *double entendre*: the bow in the simile is a faulty one and the people to whom the simile refers are deceitful.

[e]Lit. 'princes', 'officials'. The context suggests emissaries as in Isa 30.4 (so Rudolph).

[f and g]'Their offensive words' Lit. 'the זעם of their tongue'. The word זַעַם is usually given the meaning 'indignation', 'anger' and, in regard to God, the working out of his anger in a malevolent curse[23]. It is likely, however, that it has a range of meaning akin to the verb נער[24], i.e. from sounds denoting disgust or anger to condemnation and cursing. Here ibn Janāḥ gives it the meaning '(what is) repulsive, repugnant, disgusting' (Arabic *'lqbyḥ*) and he states that the phrase as a whole means that they direct offensive speech against God. Kimchi suggests the link between this and the well-known meaning 'indignation' by his comment, 'their proposal to turn to Egypt for help is the זעם of their tongue in that they rile (זועמים) God with such words'. For the evidence of the ancient versions, see below. Amongst them the Peshiṭta's rendering 'the audacity of their tongue' comes close to capturing the meaning. It is the hybris of the speakers that is depicted. For a similar approach, cf. Nyberg, p. 60.

Rudolph rightly perceives that neither 'indignation' nor 'curse' will fit the context and hence, by reference to Arabic *zġwm* 'a stammer', supposes that the reference here is to the broken Egyptian speech of the envoys of Ephraim in Egypt as they seek to present their request for help (cf. Qyl). Following the earlier suggestion of Oort (cf. Harper), Rudolph argues that the phrase זוֹ לַעְגָם is a gloss but a gloss that correctly explains the meaning of זעם; for forms of the root לעג, usually meaning 'to deride', are found depicting (the stammering of) foreign speech in Isa 28.11 and 33.19 (cf. BDB *ad loc.*).

Rudolph is almost certainly correct in supposing that these words represent an interpretative gloss[25] on the phrase זַעַם לְשׁוֹנָם in circumstances that its true meaning was at the time not readily perceived. Yet his particular view of the matter is mistaken. Following

23 Cf. especially KB[3]; Wolff seeks, to my mind unsuccessfully, to find this meaning in the present verse.

24 For which, see A. A. Macintosh in *VT* 19 (1969), pp. 471ff. The word זעם is deserving of detailed study.

25 He follows G. R. Driver 'Linguistic and Textual Problems' (1938), p. 157.

ibn Janāḥ's definition of the phrase זעם לשונם as 'offensive, repulsive speech', it is possible to see in the gloss זו לעגם a precise translation of it. For the word לעג then has its well-attested sense 'derision' and its use here is precisely matched by that in Job 34.7 where it denotes derision directed against God, i.e. blasphemy. Rashi and Kimchi understand the phrase in terms of the derision that the Ephraimites will eventually suffer in Egypt as a result of their appeal to that country for help. This judgement was made, of course, without the possibility of their perceiving that זו לעגם was an interpretative gloss; but even after this possibility was recognised, their interpretation became very widespread amongst later commentators (cf. e.g. Rosenmüller, Wolff, Mays and, as one possibility, Qyl).

It has been suggested more recently that the form of the feminine demonstrative pronoun זוֹ is an example of Hosea's northern dialectal usage (so, e.g., Kutscher *Language*, p. 31, and Rendsburg, p. 89). On the view of the phrase adopted here the words זו לעגם are not Hosea's and consequently זו cannot be regarded as an instance of the prophet's northern usage.

More particularly, it should be noted that the familiar feminine demonstrative זאת is found close by in Hos 7.10. זֹה (feminine) is attested in one of the Elisha stories with a northern provenance (2 Kgs 6.19), though there the form clearly agrees with the feminine noun (עיר) which follows it[26]. Here, in Hos 7.16, the antecedent (זעם) is masculine and if a variant form of the demonstrative זה was in fact written, זוּ and not זוֹ would be expected. On this argument the received pointing זוֹ may reflect later (massoretic) predilection for the form (under the influence of mishnaic Hebrew where it is common). זוּ is not uncommon in biblical Hebrew and is used both as a demonstrative and, more commonly, as a relative (cf. BDB *ad loc.* and BL, p. 265d). Either force is not inappropriate in introducing an explanatory gloss (i.e. 'this is' or 'which is ...'); its brief form may have been a factor in its deployment for this purpose.

The form זו (זוּ or זוֹ) is not attested in the inscriptions of the eighth or seventh centures BC but, on the contrary, the familiar forms זה and זאת are found (see Davies *AHI*, pp. 342f). זֹה is common in later biblical Hebrew (cf. Ecclesiastes *passim* and Ezek 40.45)[27].

[26] Cf. Judg 18.4 (northern provenance) but also 2 Sam 11.25 (southern provenance).

[27] The only other occurrence of the form זוֹ in the bible is in Ps 132.12 where its antecedent is feminine. Rendsburg's view that this psalm (notwithstanding its emphasis on David and its mention of Judaean place-names) is a northern composition seems to me to be unlikely in the extreme. Further its date, like the other psalms in the collection 'the Songs of Ascent' is, in all probability, post-exilic.

The evil that the Ephraimites have devised against Yahweh (v. 15) is explained by the present verse. Once again it is perverse thinking that is indicted in his name. Integrity and right thinking would impel them to revert in penitence to Yahweh and to consider accurately the demands of morality and consistency (notes b and c). In fact their wilful and stupid determination to ingratiate themselves with Assyria and Egypt and to enlist their support is flawed by the very fluctuations of their policy; for at one moment it is a pro-Assyrian policy that is favoured and, at the next, a pro-Egyptian policy. The apparent demands of the moment prompt them to change their minds with meretricious ease (note b), and the one thing that is constant is their refusal to revert to loyalty to their God and to 'the things that are above' (note c). The precise force of the simile 'they have become a faulty bow' (note d) is not easy to determine. Thus, the point of reference may be to the fluctuations in foreign policy which, being so frequent, have the effect of weakening the state and rendering it like a faulty bow, incapable of fulfilling its function. For Qyl the reference is to the slack bow which cannot project its arrows (in trajectory) upwards and so the simile illuminates the preceding statement, *viz.* that the Ephraimites do not return to God above (*contra* Rashi who explicitly denies that the simile is connected with what precedes it). If Hosea uses the phrase to convey also the notion of deceit (note d) yet further possibilities become apparent. Thus, for Kimchi the bow deceives because the trajectory of its arrow is different from that intended by its user; so the Israelites at times revert to the right path but in a moment they lapse again from it (cf. Rosenmüller). Rudolph takes a similar view and perceives in the simile the nuance of *ḥṭ'* 'to sin', but with its basic meaning of 'missing the mark' (cf. also ἁμαρτάνειν). At all events, gross deceit characterises the actions of the nation and, in that they are compared to a faulty bow, they are described as now incapable of their proper function; cf., with Harper, the vineyard of Isa 5.

The emissaries of Ephraim who went to Egypt for help are guilty of blasphemous words (notes f and g), i.e. their request for help constituted blasphemy against Yahweh himself. Rashi supposes that Hosea saw in that request a direct repudiation of the faith of the exodus itself. Thus, in connection with his promise that Yahweh will fight for Israel, Moses states 'for as sure as you see the Egyptians now, you will never see them again' (Exod 14.13f). The interpretation is instructive in that it gives a possible indication of the radical nature of the blasphemy of which Ephraim was guilty. The emissaries themselves will, as a direct result of their blasphemy, suffer death by the sword whether as a result of Egyptian treachery (cf. Rudolph) or because such, whether at Assyrian or Egyptian hands, is the inevitable result of two-faced perfidy (cf. v. 7 above)[28].

Specific mention of recourse to Egypt fits the policy of Pekah and the (later) policy of Hoshea (724 BC). We may suppose that, in common with the rest of chapter 7, Hosea originally spoke of Pekah's pro-Egyptian policy, following his predecessor's subservience to Assyria (cf. v. 11). His words will have been seen (whether by the prophet himself or by his disciples) to have had renewed significance when Hoshea reversed his own policy of subservience to Assyria by renewed overtures to Egypt in 724 BC.

Text and Versions

ישׁבו LXX ἀπεστράφησαν, cf. Symm. ἀνέστρεψαν, Quinta ἀπέστησαν, Vulg. *reversi sunt*, Pesh. *'thpkw* 'they turned back'; Targ. תבו למרד 'they reverted to rebellion'.

לא על LXX εἰς οὐθέν, cf. Pesh. *'l l' mdm* 'for nothing'; Vollers supposes that על לא was read and Rudolph comments that 'nothing' was taken as a reference to idols; Symm. εἰς τὸ μὴ ἔχειν ζυγόν, cf. Quinta ἵνα διάγνωσιν ἄνευ ζυγοῦ, Vulg. *ut essent absque iugo*, reading עֹל 'yoke'; Jerome comments that they have wilfully reverted to an existence without the restraints (the yoke) of the law. Targ. paraphrases thus תבו למרוד מן אוריתא לא על דאבאישית להון '(they have again rebelled) against the law not because I made it burdensome to them'; while לא על confirms MT, the paraphrase may constitute evidence that the 'yoke' tradition was also known here. Newcome proposes לא יועיל, cf. Grätz ללא יועיל '(they return) to what does not profit'; Rudolph expands in view of the later reference to Egypt לעם לא יעל 'to a people who do not benefit (them)'; Marti believes that לא על is a corruption of לבעל(ים) '(they have returned) to the Baal(im)', cf. *BHS* (which suggests לבליעל 'to Belial' as another possibility).

[28] N. Wyatt *SJOT* 6 (1992), pp. 87f has made the interesting suggestion that *l'gm* is a cipher ('perversion' is his word) for *'glm* 'their calf' and that Hosea is indicting by this phrase the calf-cult of Samaria (cf. 8.5, 6; 10.5), the cult of El. Accordingly Hosea rebukes his contemporaries for clinging to the ancient formulation of the tradition by which El was their saviour at the exodus. Wyatt does not recognise the phrase *zw l'gm* as a gloss and he proposes to emend the preceding phrase *z'm lšnm*. On the view here adopted, Wyatt's reading of the text is fundamentally mistaken. Nonetheless his particular treatment of *zw l'gm* is telling in that it accords with similar condemnations made by means of word-play in the book of Hosea (e.g. 8.9; 13.15). Whether, on my view of the verse, the Judaean redactors were themselves capable of creating a particular condemnation, similar in form to others devised by the prophet himself, deserves consideration.

רמיה LXX ἐντεταμένον 'strung (tight) for shooting'; Quinta διάστροφον, cf. Symm. ἀνεστραμμένον 'twisted backwards' (? so 'shooting backwards'), cf. Ps 78.57 where נהפכו occurs in MT; Vulg. *dolosus*, cf. Pesh. *nkylt'* and Targ. נכילא 'treacherous'.

זעם LXX ἀπαιδευσίαν 'boorishness'; Pesh. *mrḥwt'* 'audacity'; Vulg. *furore* 'madness', 'rage'; Targ. עמקות 'trickery', 'insidiousness'; Aq. and Symm. ἐμβρίμησεως/ιν ? 'raging'; for an instance of the cognate verb as a translation of Hebrew נער, see p. 479 n. 4 of my article (*op. cit.* above).

לעגם LXX ὁ φαυλισμὸς αὐτῶν 'their disparagement'; Aq. μυχθισμός 'jeering'; Symm. ὃ ἐφθέγξαντο 'what they spoke loudly'; Quinta ἐβλασφήμησαν; Vulg. *subsannatio eorum* 'their mocking'; Pesh. *'wrzlhwn* 'their entanglement', 'trickery'; Targ. עובדיהון 'their doings'; → וְזָל לַעֲגָם 'and their blasphemy will end ...'(*BHS*).

CHAPTER 8.1–14

EPHRAIM IS PUNISHED FOR CULTIC APOSTASY AND UNFAITHFULNESS TO ITS GOD IN RESPECT OF FOREIGN ALLIANCES

8.1 **Put the ram's horn[a] to your mouth[b]! [c]One like a vulture[d] swoops against Yahweh's land[e][c]; it is because they have transgressed my covenant and rebelled against my teaching.**

[a]Cf. on 5.8.

[b]חכך lit. 'thy gums'. The word seems to denote specifically the palate or roof of the mouth in contrast to the tongue (cf. Ezek 3.26; Job 29.10) but is used also for the organs of speech and of taste. In Ct 5.16; 7.10 it denotes virtually the mouth as 'an element in personal sweetness and beauty' (cf. BDB p. 335, col 1 d), i.e. as the organ of kissing (KB^3 p. 300, col 2). What is meant here is the mouth as used in blowing the ram's horn; cf. Kimchi's remark 'the horn is placed on the mouth (פה) since the sound passes by way of the חך after it leaves the throat'. The phrase as a whole, lit. 'to thy mouth with the ram's horn!' (i.e. to blow it), is marked by ellipsis, cf. with Qyl, Gen 18.6 where 'hasten' means 'hasten and take'.

[c—c]Lit. 'like a vulture against (על) Yahweh's land'; again the phrase is marked by ellipsis. A fuller form of the figure may be seen in Deut 28.49 'May Yahweh raise against (על) you a nation from afar ... who will swoop like a vulture'. The word 'swoops' is added above *ad sensum* and by reference to this text. The simile apparently illustrates the imminent arrival of a foreign invader (cf. the Targum, Rashi, ibn Ezra, Kimchi). The preposition על in the simile indicates the vulture above; applied, it suggests the hostile approach of the enemy (so essentially Jerome).

[d]The word נשר covers a number of species of large birds of prey. Here the emphasis is upon its predatory character (cf. Jer 49.22; Ezek 17.3) and, with Qyl, we may suggest *gyps fulvus* or the 'griffon vulture'.

A radically different account of the phrase is given by Tur-Sinai (*Job*, p. 551) for whom כַּנֶּשֶׁר should be pointed כְּנַשָּׁר or כְּנֹשֵׁר (he prefers the former) and, regarded as cognate with Arabic *nšr*, 'herald'. Accordingly the phrase as a whole means 'Put the trumpet to thy mouth as a herald against Yahweh's house'. The suggestion wins the approval of Barr (*CPOT*, p. 27) though he rightly notes that the Arabic/Hebrew isogloss would require כנשר. However, reference to Arabic dictionaries reveals no noun *nšr* with the meaning 'herald'. Lane translates the verb *nšr* 'to scatter', 'spread', 'strew' and it is found in the phrase 'to disseminate news', but only with the addition of the noun *ḫbr* 'news'. The suggestion, then, rests upon somewhat doubtful evidence and, since it is not supported by ancient tradition, it is discounted in favour of the traditional interpretation.

[e]Lit. 'the House of Yahweh'. The reference cannot be to the Jerusalem Temple (*contra* the Targum, Jerome, Rashi, ibn Ezra and Kimchi) nor to that of Samaria (*contra* Frey) but to Yahweh's land, cf. with Rosenmüller, 9.8, 15; Jer 12.7. Harper notes in this connection that the Northern Kingdom is called 'the House of Omri' in Assyrian inscriptions. The presence of the phrase within a speech on Yahweh's lips indicates its fixed, stereotyped character (cf. Rudolph). Emmerson (p. 133), following Tur-Sinai's rendering of נשר, believes that Bethel is the target of Hosea's proclamation, though she admits that in 9.15 בית denotes the land.

Yahweh is the speaker and the prophet is addressed (cf. note b, 'thy gums'). The opening phrase recalls that of 5.8, though in the latter text the verbs are plural and the call to sound the alarm is addressed more generally to the people of Benjamin. The present verse is likely to be more metaphorical in character (cf., with Rudolph, Isa 58.1, and also the evidence of the versions below). Jerome comments that Hosea is 'to raise his voice so that it sounds like a trumpet to the end that the majority who had sinned should hear it'. The Targum with the vocative 'O prophet' and the command 'say "behold like an eagle ..."' clearly takes a similar view (see further below). Wolff's contrary view of the matter, *viz.* that a military commander is addressed, is based upon his argument that nowhere else in the complex of chapters 4–14 is the prophet addressed. The argument is hardly convincing since it is based on too heavy a reliance upon generalised form-critical observations.

The urgent warning that the prophet must sound is the imminent and speedy approach of the enemy, cf. v. 3. This is expressed by the simile of the vulture swooping from above upon its prey. So Yahweh's land lies under the threat of imminent attack. The enemy is not named but the situation appears to be broadly similar to that envisaged in the previous chapter. In that the present sayings link nefarious foreign policy with idolatry and specifically that of Samaria alone, it is possible that the saying is to be placed after the loss of Galilee in 733 BC and with it the sanctuary of Dan. Assyria, then, is likely to constitute the threat that is proclaimed.

The reason for the imminent calamity is stated: Israel had transgressed Yahweh's covenant and had rebelled against his moral instruction. The latter word (*twrh*) seems to include written instruction, cf. v. 12 below, and, combined with mention of Yahweh's covenant (note 'my' covenant), is likely to include the ten commandments and other similar material (cf. 4.2). It is probable that Hosea here refers to (at least an early or emerging form of) the 'Mosaic' covenant and thus to Israel's fundamental constitution as Yahweh's people. It is this that the kingdom has repudiated by its manifold idolatry, treachery and immorality. The contrary view of the matter, *viz.* that Hosea is unlikely to have known 'covenant' or 'instruction' in this highly formal sense and, therefore, the words cannot be his but are rather a later addition is advocated by Wellhausen[1], cf. Marti, Harper, Nowack, Perlitt. Such arguments seem to me to be contrived and *a priori* in character; cf. Nicholson's arguments (*GP*, p. 187); Nicholson is inclined to the view that Hosea coined the notion of a 'theological' covenant.

Text and Versions

אל חכך שפר LXX εἰς κόλπον αὐτῶν ὡς γῆ 'into their lap/bosom, like land'; Jerome, understandably, regards the meaning as uncertain though he notes that some authorities understand the word 'lap' as the lower part of a garment as well as of the gulf of the Adriatic sea. Wicked teachers either 'retain in their clothing all things, even earthenware ones, needful for their desires' or 'search out in their port of refuge no precious goods but only earthenware ones'. It is scarcely surprising that he prefers to follow *veritatem Hebraicam*. On the basis of LXX, Vollers proposes אל חיקם כעפר and Houtsma, comparing Job 31.33, אל חֻבָּם כעפר; the Hebrew text before LXX must in any case be regarded as corrupt; Symm. ἐπὶ φάρυγγί σου κερατίνῃ 'upon thy throat of horn'; Vulg. *in gutture tuo sit tuba*, cf. MT; Pesh. *pwmk 'yk qrn'* 'thy mouth like a horn' (nothing corresponding to MT's אל, cf. Gelston, p. 133); Targ. נביא בחכך אכלי כד בשופרא אימר 'O prophet, shout with thy palate as with a horn and say ...'.

כנשר Wellhausen → כי נשר; Halévy → כַּצֹּפֶה, cf. Procksch → כְּשֹׁמֵר and *BHS* → כַּנֹּצֵר 'like a/the watchman'; Pesh. adds *w*, i.e. '(thy mouth like a horn) and like a vulture ...'.

על LXX ἐπί; Vulg. *super*; Pesh. *'l*; Targ. וישרי על '(like an eagle that flies, so a king with his army goes up) and encamps against ...'.

[1] *Prolegomena*, p. 443.

8.2 **Yet it is to me[a] that they cry out[b], [c]'My[d] God, we know[e] you, we, your people Israel'[c].**

[a]The inversion of the normal word order so that לי 'to me' opens the verse is emphatic and, in the context, implies a strong contrast with what precedes it. Wolff argues that, since the preposition אל is used with the verb 'cry out' in 7.14, the preposition לי here must denote 'in respect of me' as in Isa 15.5 and Jer 48.31. The use of ל is, however, so well-attested with verbs of speech that his argument may be regarded as over-ingenious; further, the resulting sense is somewhat awkward: 'Of course they lament over me, "My God! We know you!"'

[b]A frequentative imperfect, cf. Rudolph. Qyl suggests the possibility that it is a jussive having the sense here 'O that they would call out to me!'

[c—c]Lit. 'My God, we know you, Israel'. The word order presents some difficulty though it is defended by Kimchi as being in accordance with the usage מאוחר מוקדם as in Ezek 39.11 and Ps 141.10. Accordingly for Rashi, ibn Ezra and Kimchi, Israel is the delayed subject of the verb 'they cry out'. The absence of the word 'Israel' in the LXX and Peshiṭta has led some scholars to suppose that in the MT it is an early gloss explaining the identity of 'we', the subject of the verb, or else it is a dittograph of Israel in v. 3 (so, e.g., Grätz, Nowack, Marti). On the former view, if that is a correct assessment, then the gloss is likely to be accurate. In such circumstances it is better to retain the reading and to regard it as in apposition to 'we' (so Jerome). The translation above is expanded to convey the sense, cf. the Targum (below). Amongst other suggestions, Qyl (cf. van Hoonacker) records the possibility that the sense is 'To me they call out "My God"', to which God (or Hosea) replies 'But we know you, Israel'. To this van Gelderen (cf. Rudolph) objects that God does not use the royal 'we' except when speaking to others in the heavenly court. That Hosea should reply in such exalted language is most unlikely. Torczyner[2] has suggested that 'Israel' here and the tetragrammaton in the previous verse are wrongly placed and should exchange places (there → 'House of Israel'; here → 'we have known thee, Yahweh'). These suggestions are, in my view, more ingenious than convincing[3].

[d]The pronominal suffix has a distributive force, i.e. each one makes this confession, cf. Rosenmüller.

[e]A stative perfect having the force of a present tense.

Despite the fact that Ephraim had manifestly transgressed Yahweh's covenant and rebelled against his instruction (v. 1) the nation, confronted with disaster, was hypocritical enough to

[2] *Marti Festschrift*, p. 277.

[3] So also Wellhausen's emendation ידעתיך 'I knew thee'.

reiterate its confession of loyalty to Yahweh. Indeed that expression of loyalty may well have sycophantically and purposefully made use of the ancient covenantal name, Israel (note c–c) in order that each of those (note d) who enunciated it might ingratiate himself with his God (after Jerome, cf. Rudolph). The sentiments are those of 7.14 'nor have they cried out to me in sincerity', and are similar to those of Isa 1.15ff.

'My God, we know you.' The confession implies that Ephraim claims to acknowledge Yahweh as God of Israel and that their loyalty to and love for his ethical and consistent nature was intact. For 'knowledge of Yahweh' cf. 2.22 (EV 20); 4.1, 6; 6.6 etc. For 'My God' as a confession of allegiance, cf. 2.25 (EV 23). In fact, their insincerity is perceived by Yahweh whose resolution is unswerving; for they have abandoned what is good and their enemy's progress is inexorable, v. 3. In that they have abandoned what is good, they can no longer lay any claim to the title bestowed by him who is good (again after Jerome).

Text and Versions

לי → אלי (Borbone).

יזעקו Pesh. adds *w'mrw* 'and said', cf. Targ. ואמרין; cf. next entry.

אלהי LXX ὁ θεός, preceded by λέγοντες in Q^{mg}, cf. OL^{CS}, indicating direct speech; Pesh. *'lhn* 'our God'; Vulg. *deus meus*; Targ. ארי לית לנא אלה בר מנך 'that there is for us no God except for you'; Oettli (so Borbone) and Marti read אלהים/אלהינו respectively by reference to LXX and to Pesh.

ישראל 1 Kennicott MS and 1 de Rossi MS do not have the word; LXX and Pesh. have nothing corresponding to the word, either because it was not in the text before them (e.g. Wolff) or because they did not perceive how to construe it (cf. Rudolph); Targ. ארי אנחנא עמך ישראל '(Redeem us) for we are thy people, Israel!' *BH*, cf. *BHS*, considers the emendation ידענוך אלהי־ישראל; Borbone omits ישראל.

8.3 **Israel has banished[a] what is good[b]; the enemy shall put him[c] to flight[d].**

[a]Cf., with Qyl, Ps 77.8 and 1 Chr 28.9. זנח is taken by BDB and KB[3] to be cognate with an Arabic *znḥ* apparently 'to repel'. It should be noted, however, that neither Lane nor Dozy makes any reference to such a word. For ibn Barūn's assessment of the evidence from Arabic, see on v. 5 below. N. G. Schroeder, quoted by Rosenmüller, seeks to illuminate the word by reference to Arabic *znḫ* 'to become rancid', 'to sink down'

and he interprets the phrase 'Israel, becoming putrid, sinks down in regard to goodness'. 'Goodness' here refers both to piety and to prosperity; the debasement of the one effects that of the other. The theory is, as Rosenmüller observes, somewhat forced. Ibn Janāḥ, commenting on 8.5 (but not on this verse) understands the word there to denote 'to be remote', 'to depart'; see further on 8.5 below. On the assumption that the word has the same meaning in both verses and that here it is transitive (with 'goodness' as its object), the likely meaning is 'removal afar off', 'banishment'. The word is attested in talmudic Hebrew with the sense 'to loathe' and, in the *Hiphil*, 'to declare rejectable/unclean' (cf. Jastrow, p. 406).

[b]For Jerome, ibn Ezra and Kimchi the adjective 'good' refers to God; cf. Qyl who quotes Ps 73.1, 'God is indeed good to Israel'. More precise, however, is the view that Israel has repudiated what has been clearly revealed as God's prescribed will with its attendant blessing of good fortune, cf. with Rudolph, Amos 5.14. AF, following Dahood's assertion that 'the Good One' is virtually a personal name for God and arguing that elsewhere he is usually the subject of the verb, propose the reading 'The Good One rejects Israel'. The interpretation seems to me to be most unlikely since the objective suffix in the phrase 'shall put him to flight' clearly refers to Israel as its antecedent and that is more appropriate to a judgement upon Israel's act of folly than to a (banal) statement of the background to the disaster depicted. Further, no clear reason for Hosea's use of the supposed name 'the Good One' in this context is given.

[c]For the suffix וֹ instead of the more usual הוּ, cf. with ibn Ezra and Kimchi, Jer 23.6; also GK 60d. The LXX (see below) understands the enemy to be the object of the verb and this interpretation is followed by Duhm, Nyberg and van Gelderen who, emending the pointing, invest the phrase with the meaning 'they diligently pursue the enemy'. While the contrast between repudiation of what is good and active pursuit of political alliance ('the enemy') would be attractive (cf. Rudolph), it seems most unlikely that the word איב 'enemy' would carry this sense.

[d]For the verb רדף, usually rendered 'to pursue' with the sense 'to put to flight' *sc.* a defeated foe, cf. with BDB, Amos 1.11 and Deut 32.30.

The nation might claim the title 'Israel' in association with its attempt to ingratiate itself with its God (see on the previous verse) but since in fact 'Israel' had utterly repudiated what was good it forfeited the right to the title bestowed by its Lord (after Jerome). Accordingly the enemy will bring upon them abject defeat. The verse suggests that the nation has made a disastrous exchange (so Wolff); in repudiating what was for their good, *viz.* the ordinances and requirements of the covenant with the attendant blessings of peace and security, they had gained nothing but their own inevitable doom. The identity of the enemy is not explicitly revealed and the reference is of a sort with that of the vulture in v. 1 above. To Hosea's hearers, no doubt, the reference was clear. At all events it is the moral stupidity of the nation which has brought about its doom and that stupidity was manifested in palace revolts and idolatry (vv. 4–7), in mistaken foreign policy (vv. 8–10), in the perverted cult (vv. 11–13) and in reliance upon mere human resources (v. 14); so Rudolph.

Text and Versions

LXX prefaces the verse with ὅτι; hence Grätz proposes the addition of כי to MT.

זנח ישראל טוב LXX 'I. ἀπεστρέψατο ἀγαθά 'Israel has turned away from good things', cf. Pesh. *ṭ'' 'ysryl ṭbt'* 'has disregarded goodness' and Targ. טעו בית ישראל מבתר פלחני דבדיליה אנא מיתי עליהון טובא 'Israel has strayed from my service in respect of which I brought good upon them'; Vulg. *proiecit I. bonum* 'Israel has abandoned the good'.

אויב ירדפו LXX ἐχθρὸν κατεδίωξαν 'they have pursued an enemy', on the basis of which יִרְדְּפוּ or יְרַדְּפוּ in the sense '(vigorously) to follow' as in 2.9; 6.3; 12.2 is proposed by Duhm, Nyberg and van Gelderen; the other versions make the enemy the subject of the verb.

8.4 They[a] have crowned kings[b] without my prompting[c]; they have promoted officials[d] without my knowledge. Their silver and gold they made into idols[e] for themselves, to the end that[f] it[g] will be lost.

[a]The pronoun הם is not emphatic but introduces a circumstantial clause, cf., with Harper, GK 142a, b; it also serves to effect a contrast to 'my' (in reference to Yahweh); so Rudolph.

[b]המליכו lit. 'made kings', the usual and traditional interpretation of the *Hiphil* form. G. R. Driver[4], comparing Neh 5.7, and by reference to the Aramaic verb מלך, proposes the meaning 'they have taken counsel'; similarly, he sees in the MT's השירו a verb cognate with Arabic *'šr/šwr* with much the same meaning. The suggestion lacks any supporting evidence from tradition and is to be discounted, cf. Rudolph.

[c]ולא ממני lit. 'and not from me', where the preposition מן denotes the source or author of the action in question, cf. 2 Sam 3.37.

[d]השירו lit. 'they have made princes' where the *Hiphil* form of the denominative verb שרר is parallel to the preceding 'they have crowned

[4] *Nötscher Festschrift*, p. 50.

kings'. For *Hiphil* forms of double *ayin* verbs assimilating to those of hollow root verbs, cf. GK 67v. Such is the interpretation of the ancient versions, Jerome, Rashi, ibn Ezra and Kimchi. An alternative view is noted by Rashi and ibn Ezra according to which the verb is a *Hiphil* form of the root סור (הסירו) written with שׂ rather than ס, cf. 9.12 below[5]. One Kennicott MS and 2 de Rossi MSS read ס. The resulting sense is 'and they have demoted (lit. 'removed') them without my knowledge' and the parallelism becomes antithetical. The reading deserves serious consideration since it is based upon MS evidence and gives good sense. The balance of probability, however, may be said to tilt in the direction of the meaning 'promoted officials' on the grounds that the indictment is directed against the establishment of godless government rather than against removal of some of its elements.

[e] Accusative of the product, GK 117ii.

[f] The conjunction למען always denotes purpose and never consequence. 'Sometimes in rhetorical passages, the issue of a line of action, though really undesigned, is represented by it ironically as if it were designed', cf. Isa 30.1; 44.9; so BDB p. 775, col 2 n. 1. Cf. Jerome's 'they have not so acted in order to perish but because they have so acted for this reason they will perish' – though he understands the people rather than the silver and gold to be the subject of the verb.

[g] The subject is collectively the silver and gold, so Rashi, ibn Ezra and (as an alternative) Kimchi. The ancient versions render with plural verbs suggesting that the idols or the people are the subject. Kimchi, as an alternative, understands 'their name' to be the implied subject, cf. Rosenmüller for whom the subject is the state or its members.

Verses 4–7, spoken in Yahweh's name, link indissolubly the sins of idolatry and political apostasy. 'These are the kings established by men and the gods manufactured by men' (so Harper). The reproach constitutes an explanation of Israel's repudiation of what is good (v. 3). As in 7.7, political apostasy is marked by treachery and deceit and by a series of palace revolts. It is done in stupidity for apparent short-term advantage and its origins are in human weakness. Kings and royal officials are promoted (notes b–d) in rapid succession by the will of frail men and without any reference to Yahweh and the possibility of his initiative through his loyal servants. For the formulation of Yahweh's choice in the law of kingship, cf. Deut 17.15.

[5] Qyl's observation that, on this view of the word, we may have an instance of Ephraimite dialectal usage, *viz.* שׂ for ס, seems to me to be unlikely, for the root סור is well attested in biblical Hebrew. What is more likely (on this view) is that we have evidence of a variant spelling of the same word, cf. English 'quire/choir' and Hebrew סוך/שׂוך.

There can be no doubt that Hosea has in mind the contemporary situation and the palace revolts of his time. The question arises whether he also refers to the whole history of the kingship in Ephraim from the time of Jeroboam I. Hosea 1.4 already demonstrates his independence of thought in that he can repudiate the House of Jehu despite its being sanctioned by the tradition of Elisha's support (2 Kgs 9.1ff). Accordingly the divine sanction of Jeroboam I's reign recorded in 1 Kgs 11.29ff would not be enough to prevent his conclusion that the kingship of the Northern Kingdom was totally unacceptable to Yahweh (cf. Rudolph). Jerome, ibn Ezra and Kimchi understand Hosea's words as referring to Jeroboam I's accession and the latter is careful to note that Ahijah the Shilonite did not explicitly sanction that accession but merely predicted what would happen. For them, of course, the classic sin of Jeroboam was his secession from the Davidic monarchy and his establishment of an idolatrous kingdom in the North. Amongst modern commentators, e.g., van Gelderen and Östborn favour the view that this was indeed Hosea's opinion of the matter. In fact nothing is said here of the Davidic monarchy and the ready applicability of what is said to Hosea's time may suggest that the prophet was primarily concerned to show that the government of the kingdom was, in his day, typically godless in its constitution. The reference to 'our king' in 7.5 may possibly afford evidence that Hosea was not against the northern monarchy *per se*, but against the majority of its exemplars or, more precisely, against the mode of, as well as the reasons for, their successive exaltation to office. That his words were, however, capable of a longer historical perspective may depend upon two considerations: first, their intrinsic accuracy, especially in the diagnosis that idolatry and political apostasy were closely related; and, secondly, their authentication in the end of the Northern Kingdom, viewed from Judah as Yahweh's final judgement upon it.

If perverse and arbitrary foolishness marked the nation's activities in relation to its government, the very same characteristics were displayed in their recourse to idolatry. The two aspects of godless behaviour arise from the deranged reason of their practitioners. The material resources of the state had been expended on the worship of idols, on the syncretistic cult where preference for profligate self-indulgence found full expression and, rationalised, was understood to be productive of plenty. For a similar indictment, but in respect of the mother/Israel, and for the availability of precious metals, see on 2.10 (EV 8) above. In fact the resources of wealth and in particular the silver and gold used to adorn the idolatrous artefacts (the verb *'ṣb* from which 'idols' is derived, means to 'shape' or 'fashion') are totally wasted and lost (note g), since the idols are destined to be removed (cf. 6b) and the action in making them contains within it that inevitable consequence (note f).

The mention of idols in the plural in this verse matches Hosea's similar use of the plural in 4.17; 13.2; 14.9. Wolff supposes that the reference is not only to the calf images of Bethel and Dan but also to the many statuettes used in private sanctuaries throughout the land for which he compares Judg 8.22ff and 17f[6]. For Rudolph the prophet's ironic treatment of idolatry is continued in the verses which follow when the principal example of such idolatry (the 'calf') is subjected to the same ironic attack. It seems to me likely that the present verse, being concerned to link idolatry in general with political apostasy, marks the beginning of an attack which then has more particular focus in the verses which follow.

Recognition of Hosea's fundamental diagnosis, *viz.* that idolatry and political apostasy against Yahweh are indissolubly linked, renders most unlikely the radically different view advocated by Nyberg and Cazelles. For them the verbs of this verse allude to the nation's confession of the kingship of Baal and of his divine court of princes (Nyberg) or of other idols (Cazelles[7]). The evidence of 7.7, with which the words of the present verse are so closely parallel, together with the clearly attested historical circumstances in which Jeroboam I combined idolatry with the establishment of his independence (1 Kgs 12.28f), constitute powerful arguments in favour of the traditional interpretation of the verbs and of the verse, cf. Wolff and Rudolph.

Text and Versions

הם המליכו LXX ἑαυτοῖς ἐβασίλευσαν, cf. Vulg. *ipsi regnaverunt* 'they have ruled for themselves/they themselves have ruled'; such renderings appear to have understood the *Hiphil* as internal rather than causative; Pesh. (but without the pronoun) *'mlkw* could be either and Targ. אנון אמליכו is most likely to be causative, cf. Jastrow, p. 791 and Cathcart.

השׂירו LXX ἦρξαν 'they ruled', cf. Vulg. *principes extiterunt* 'they acted as princes', Pesh. *w'šlṭw* 'they ruled', Targ. רביאו 'they became great'; these versions again understand the *Hiphil* as internal; for Targ. cf. Jastrow, p. 1441a; he records a *v.l.*, a *Pael*, which could mean 'promote', 'appoint', cf. Cathcart.

[6] See further B. Gemser 'Bilder und Bilderverehrung' *RGG* 1, pp. 1271f.
[7] *CBQ* 11 (1949), pp. 14ff.

ולא ידעתי LXX καὶ οὐκ ἐγνώρισάν μοι, cf. Pesh. *wl' 'wld'wny* 'and have not informed me'.

למען יכרת LXX ὅπως ἐξολεθρευθῶσιν, cf. Vulg. *ut interirent* 'in order that they may be destroyed/perish'; Pesh. *dn'bdwn* 'that will come to nought' (*sc*. idols, cf. Gelston, pp. 72ff and 122); Targ. בדיל דישתיצון 'in order that they be consumed (*sc*. idols)'. It is likely that LXX and Vulg. understand the subject of the verb to be the idolaters, cf. the neuter plural εἴδωλα, preceding in LXX, which cannot take a plural verb, and Jerome's comments upon the phrase (see note f above); → יכרתו (Borbone).

8.5 Your calf, Samaria, is clean gone[a]. My anger has flared up against them[b]. How long will they be incapable[c] of innocence[d]?

[a]The transitive meaning 'to reject' normally given to the verb זנח is unsatisfactory in this verse not least because no object for it is apparently expressed. Ibn Ezra, who gives to it this meaning (מאס), is obliged to supply the object, thus 'Thy calf, O Samaria, has rejected thee'. The solution is grammatically strained and requires the unlikely assumption that Hosea could predicate action of an idol. Amongst modern commentators the problem has usually been resolved by resort to emendation; e.g. Wolff reads זְנַח (imperative) or זָנֹחַ (infinitive absolute) 'Reject thy calf, O Samaria'; Rudolph (cf. Mays) זָנַח 'rejected is thy calf'; Harper, following Oort, emends to אזנח, Marti to זנחתי 'I will reject/have rejected thy calf, Samaria'; the same sense is obtained by NEB which, as an alternative, reads זָנֹחַ[8]. For the evidence of the versions, see below.

Ibn Barūn[9], commenting upon Lam 3.17 ותזנח משלום נפשי (NEB 'peace has gone out of my life') states that the verb זנח is, by metathesis[10], cognate to Arabic *nzḥ*, which has the meaning 'to be remote'. Ibn Janāḥ, though he makes no comment upon comparative philology, states that the verb in this verse is intransitive and has the same meaning, *viz*. 'thy calf is remote', 'has departed' (Arabic *b'd wǧl'*). For this intransitive use he too compares Lam 3.17. For the verb in the *Qal* with a transitive sense, *viz*. 'to make remote', he cites Lam 2.7; 3.31; Ps 88.15; Zech 10.6. A *Hiphil* form[11] used intransitively is to be found in Isa 19.6 where וְהֶאֶזְנִיחוּ נהרות means 'the rivers are gone away, are cut off, have run dry' (Arabic *b'dt w'nqṭ't wnḍbt*). Kimchi, too, translates the verb

[8] Cf. Huesman *Biblica* 37 (1956), p. 294.

[9] Wechter, pp. 55, 79.

[10] For ibn Barūn's treatment of this phenomenon, see Wechter, p. 183. A clear example may be cited: שרקים = Arabic *šqr* 'sorrel horses'. See further Brockelmann *Grundriss* 1, pp. 267–278 and Barr *CPOT*, pp. 96ff.

[11] Cf. GK 53p. Ibn Janāḥ regards the presence of the *aleph* as evidence of a *forma mixta*.

with forms of the root רחק 'to be distant' though he is uncertain as to the subject. He gives as alternatives: (1) 'thy calf has removed thee afar off, O Samaria', i.e. 'because of it thou art far from thy land' and (2) intransitively 'thy calf is far from thee, O Samaria', i.e. it has been destroyed and removed from Samaria by the King of Assyria, cf. v. 6.

Such accounts of the meaning of this verse seem to me to be the most convincing. They are dependent on a number of considerations of which the most fundamental is the recognition that זנח is here used intransitively as opposed to v. 3 above where the same verb is used transitively. The second person suffix attached to the word 'calf' suggests that the word 'Samaria' is vocative and cannot be the object of זנח. Attempts to understand Yahweh or God as the (unexpressed) subject of the verb ('God has rejected thee, Samaria, for the sin of the calves' – so Rashi, cf. AF) are forced and unsatisfactory, not least because Yahweh speaks in the first person in the very next phrase.

Reference to the texts cited above (and especially Lam 3.17 and Isa 19.6) suggests that the phrase denotes effective disappearance together with a complete rupture of association or relationship ('thy calf'), cf. v. 3 above and the transitive use of the verb. It is difficult to find precisely the right English word and 'clean gone' is offered on the understanding that it must be glossed thus: 'your calf, Samaria, has no effective presence for you, it is shown up as of no account whatsoever'.

N. G. Schroeder, as in v. 3 above, suggested that the verb is cognate to Arabic *znḫ* 'to be rancid' and the suggestion is adopted by the NEB 'your calf-gods stink, O Samaria'. The suggestion was already regarded as dubious by Rosenmüller. For further comments, see on v. 3 above.

[b]The plural suffix 'them' is taken by ibn Ezra to refer to the calves and Samaria, and by Kimchi as referring either to the two calves or to Israel who made them. Since one calf only is mentioned the suffix is likely to refer to the inhabitants of Samaria.

[c]The verb יוכלו, usually 'to be able', is used transitively as in Isa 1.13 and has the sense here 'to be (in)capable of'.

[d]The noun נִקָּיֹן denotes 'innocence'; in Amos 4.6 it has the more physical sense of purity; hence Rudolph's suggestion that the phrase means 'how long will they be incapable of making a clean sweep?' Similarly Rashi suggests that the phrase denotes '... innocence, i.e. "from that filth"' (*sc.* idolatry). Ibn Ezra connects the interrogative phrase with what precedes it and comments 'my anger will be against them until they become pure'.

From a general indictment of idolatry and political apostasy the prophet focuses Yahweh's wrath upon the official idolatry of the state and in particular the calf-image set up in Bethel by Jeroboam I, later and correctly regarded by the Deuteronomic historian as the *fons et origo* of all apostasy and the cardinal sin of the Northern Kingdom (1 Kgs 12.29f *et passim*). Reference to 10.5 confirms that Samaria stands for the whole Northern Kingdom and is not itself the site of a calf-image (so already Kimchi). 2 Kings 10.25ff records that Jehu destroyed and desecrated the Baal temple built there by Ahab (1 Kgs 16.32) and it is most unlikely that a calf-image associated with Yahweh would have been subsequently erected there (cf. Wolff) or have survived in the private shrines of the older inhabitants of the city (so Alt[12]). That one calf only is mentioned is likely to reflect the period following the subjugation of northern Galilee by Tiglath-pileser III in 733 BC when the other site of calf-worship, Dan, would already have been lost. In any case Dan seems to have had something of secondary importance (so Kimchi on 10.5, cf. Rudolph).

The calf is 'your calf', the calf of Samaria, the Northern Kingdom; not imported from foreign peoples, it is 'from Israel and of Israel' (*quia ex Israel et ipse est*, cf. the Vulgate of the next verse; cf. Jerome and Kimchi). The reference, then, is not to thorough-going Baalism in which the calf, a 'young bull at the peak of its youth' compared with Baal or El, is the official state cultic symbol (so Wolff). Rather the reference is to syncretism between Yahweh on the one hand and to Canaanite idolatry on the other. Yahweh had brought Israel out of Egypt and it is he who was to be worshipped under the figure of a golden calf as an expression of the particular national aspirations of the Northern Kingdom in its resolution to be free of the House of David and the Jerusalem cult (cf. 1 Kgs 12.27ff). It is this debasement of authentic Yahwism, effected in the supposed interests of northern nationalism and reflecting the general political and ethical corruption with which it is associated, that Hosea attacks in the name of his God.

It is not possible here to enter into discussion of the vexed question of the relationship between the account of Jeroboam I's apostasy (1 Kgs 12.27ff) and the thematically parallel account in Exod 32 of Aaron's initiation of a calf-cult at Sinai. In general I am inclined to accept Noth's view[13] that the latter account is ultimately dependent upon the former whether or not the latter contains residual elements of an authentic event at Sinai. At any

12 *KS* 3, pp. 294ff.
13 *Exodus*, p. 246 (*ATD* 5, p. 202).

rate Noth argues persuasively that Exod 32 may legitimately be used to clarify the nature of Jeroboam's artefacts[14].

When Hosea says here in Yahweh's name 'your calf, Samaria, is clean gone' (note a above) he means that the very constitution of the Northern Kingdom, epitomised in its national cultic symbol to which indeed its aspirations and beliefs were directed, had proved worthless; made by human hands, it was destined for destruction and with it the whole fabric of the state which had trusted in it. It is thus syncretistic idolatry which characterises the cardinal sin of Ephraim as a nation and to it the moral turpitude and chaos which marked its national life was indissolubly linked. Such considerations depend very heavily upon a correct understanding of the meaning of the verb *znh*.

As has been indicated above, the 'calf of Samaria' was located in Bethel which, as in Amos 7.13, is the official national shrine, the cultic centre to which the nation's very independence and constitution were linked.

If, then, Hosea's primary motive is to repudiate the 'calf of Samaria' as the exemplar of the official religion of Ephraim, the question arises whether his words are original and formative of, e.g., the condemnation by the Deuteronomic historian of Jeroboam I's institution of the calf-cult in 1 Kgs 12.27ff. To this question a number of further questions are linked. First, are his words ironical in tone (so especially Rudolph) or are they factual, in the sense that the realities of Canaanite religion are described by them (so especially Wolff)? Secondly, what precisely lies behind the calf image? Was it a pedestal upon which Yahweh was understood (invisibly) to stand in much the same way as was the ark in Jerusalem[15]? Or was it a staff surmounted by a small calf image used as a standard in cultic processions (so Eissfeldt[16])? Thirdly, if the main thrust of Hosea's argument here is rightly understood to be an attack upon the religion of the state, what was Hosea's attitude to the very independence of the North?

The answers to such questions are of course extremely difficult and unlikely ever certainly to be known. Some considerations may be offered (not in the order that the questions above are posed). First, neither Exod 32 nor 1 Kgs 12 gives any support to Eissfeldt's suggestion of a small calf image mounted on a

14 *UP*, pp. 157ff (= *Traditions*, pp. 142f). Cross argues that Exod 32 represents a (northern) polemic against the Bethel cult and its Aaronide priesthood; *CMHE*, p. 73.

15 See, e.g., Von Rad *Theology* 1, p. 58 (*Theologie* 1, p. 66).

16 *KS* 2, pp. 291ff; cf. Cross *op. cit.*, p. 73, n. 117.

standard and for it Eissfeldt can adduce only one example from Mari (*op. cit.*, p. 300). By contrast a bronze figurine of a calf (17.5 cms long and 12.4 cms high), found at a cultic site[17] in northern Samaria and dating to the time of the Judges, is thought by Mazar to have been an object of worship. This suggests that Jeroboam I made use of iconography long known in the North. Secondly, the evidence of Exod 32.8 and of 1 Kgs 12.28 'these are thy gods' suggests that such images were so closely associated with 'their' divinities that they became themselves objects of worship (so Cross, loc. cit.) and consequently Hosea could object (in relation to the calf of Bethel) 'it is No-god' (8.6). In this case Jeroboam I's deliberate imitation of the calf-cult is likely to have represented a conscious attempt to unify the Canaanite and Israelite elements in his kingdom by the device of combining in the official state religion important elements of the distinctive religions of both cultures[18].

Hosea's condemnation of the 'calf of Samaria' is based upon and closely related to his general indictment of the moral bankruptcy of the kingdom and his perception that Ephraim was on the verge of total collapse. On the basis of this perception the national policy of syncretism, undertaken earlier for political ends, is seen by him to be totally bankrupt. It represents faulty reasoning and issues in the outrageous naming of Yahweh 'my Baal' (2.18, EV 16); it causes the nation, like an unfaithful wife, to vacillate between husband and lover and eventually, torn apart, to become ever more enslaved to the immediate promptings of selfishness and irresponsibility.

By contrast, Ephraim's proper place is as an integral part of 'Israel', i.e. Yahweh's covenant people; as such Yahweh, despite his anger and hurt, has no wish to surrender the Northern Kingdom to oblivion (11.8). Accordingly Hosea seems to have proposed no specifically political solution such as, e.g., a return by the North to loyalty to the Davidic sanctuary of Jerusalem[19]. Indeed, it is possible that earlier he hoped for a return to stability on the part of the northern monarchy in the shape of its existing exemplars (cf. on Hos 7.5) and for repentance to pure Yahwism on the part of the cultic hierarchy (6.1–6).

If, then, Hosea concludes that syncretistic idolatry is the fundamental cause of the nation's ills, it seems to me likely that

[17] See Mazar, pp. 27–40; the site lies between Dothan and Tirzah. For a treatment of this evidence specifically with regard to Hosea and Yahwism, see Wenning and Zenger.

[18] E.g. Fohrer *Religion*, pp. 132f (*Geschichte*, p. 124).

[19] Emmerson, p. 133 (cf. on 8.1 note e above) suggests that Hosea's polemic was not directed against Bethel as a legitimate sanctuary.

he was the first to depict explicitly the 'calf of Samaria' at Bethel as epitomising the idolatry which he indicts (*contra* Rudolph). He was led to disassociate the artefact from what it had been manufactured to represent and thus to equate it with the idols of silver and gold that had proliferated in the many sanctuaries and settlements of the land (v. 4 above). It had failed in its purpose, and the purpose of those who made it had failed. The calf and the state of which it was an emblem were on the verge of annihilation; the one was a mere human artefact, the other, in its degeneracy, a hideous product of human sinfulness and folly.

So clear and perceptive was Hosea's insight that, following the final collapse of the Northern Kingdom in 722 BC, his words became normative as an explanation for that collapse. Subsequently the Deuteronomists applied the lesson that they inherited from Hosea and characterised the apostasy of Jeroboam I as the cardinal sin of Ephraim and by reference to it they judged all his successors in the history which eventually they edited.

This understanding of Hosea's words in no way detracts from the supposition that he was dependent upon the strict prohibition against idolatry expressed in the second commandment. Rather his words represent an application of this aspect of pure Yahwism specifically to the constitution of the nation with its official adoption of syncretism for political ends. Exod 20.5 makes clear that idolatry will always provoke the anger of a jealous God, a God who will brook no rivals. Accordingly Hosea implies that the imminent collapse of the state is the direct result of the working of Yahweh's anger, which has flared up against its inhabitants (note b). The calf-image, the emblem of Ephraim, is totally discredited and manifestly worthless. Yet even in the face of this overwhelming evidence the Ephraimites seem incapable of drawing the correct conclusions. Thus, with a phrase so familiar from other expressions of lament (*'d mty* 'how long?'; Pss 6.4; Isa 6.11; Hab 2.6 etc.), Yahweh turns, as if to a third party, with his cry of exasperation 'How long will they be incapable of innocence?' i.e. 'What is this madness that, when I offer an opportunity for penitence, they are unwilling to come to their senses?' (so Jerome; for 'innocence', see note d).

Text and Versions

זנח LXX ἀπότριψαι, cf. Theod. ἀπόῤῥιψαι 'reject', 'get rid of!' on the basis of which Vollers reads זְנַחְי and Grätz, cf. Wolff and Borbone, reads זְנַח; some MSS (L' 407, 613) present the alternative reading ἀπόρριψον 'disown!'; Aq. ἀπώθησαν 'they put aside (thy calves)'; Symm. ἀπεβλήθη 'he/it was rejected', cf. Vulg. *proiectus est* and Quinta ἀποβλητός σου, on the basis of which Rudolph (cf. Jeremias) reads זֻנַּח; Pesh. *ṭ'w* 'they have erred (through thy calf)', cf. Targ. טעו בתר עגלא 'they have erred after the calf (of Samaria)'.

נקין LXX καθαρισθῆναι, Aq. ἀθῳωθῆναι, Symm. καθαρθῆναι, Vulg. *emundari*, Pesh. *lmzk'* and Targ. למזכי, all infinitives 'to be/become pure, free of faults'.

8.6 **For indeed[a] it was of Israel; the craftsman fashioned it, it is no god. The calf of Samaria will surely be ousted[b].**

[a]The pronoun הוא is prefixed with *waw* and Rashi, comparing Ezek 47.11 ולא, describes it as pleonastic. The conjunction, however, is likely to have emphatic force, cf. GK 154a n. (b), and the inversion of the word order may serve as a rhetorical device to emphasise 'Israel'. Such an account of the phrase is in accordance with the massoretic accentuation where *zaqeph qaton* above והוא links the pronoun with what precedes it. For Rashi the sense of 'from/of Israel' is that the materials used in the manufacture of the calf came from donations of the Israelites; for ibn Ezra the phrase suggests that its manufacture was brought about through Israel's (and Jeroboam I's) counsel and deliberation. Jerome (cf. Rudolph who cites König, 375g) appears to understand the *waw* as meaning 'also' (*quia ex Israel et ipse est*) and suggests that repudiation of the calf by Israel should match its manufacture by Israel. The suggestion, though grammatically possible, is more an account of the rhetorical and explicative nature of the clause than a satisfactory account of the conjunction *waw*.

Following the evidence of the LXX (see below) Wolff understands כי מישראל to belong to the preceding verse and to be a hopeful interjection 'But they are from Israel'; והוא then belongs to what follows. The solution is somewhat strained and a hopeful interjection (with unexpressed subject) to the effect that Israel's true nature precludes idolatry scarcely fits the context. Amongst other emendations to the consonantal text or pointing, mention may be made of Nyberg's suggestion (adopted by Rudolph and Jeremias) that the text be read מַיִשְׂרָאֵל וְהוּא (for מה־ישראל) and rendered 'what has Israel to do with it?' i.e. what have Israel and the calf in common? The suggestion is attractive since the words are given a sense which follows well the question posed at the end of the preceding verse as well as the statements which follow. On the other hand the absence of the preposition ל, attested in the comparable and well-known expression מה לי ולך (cf. 14.9), tells against the suggestion and, since it is possible to give an account of the MT as it stands, it is here discounted.

[b]The word שְׁבָבִים is a *hapax legomenon* and very considerable uncertainty as to its meaning has long been prevalent. For the evidence of the versions, see below, and for the differing views of a number of early rabbinic commentators, see Wechter, p. 234.

In general the word has been interpreted by reference to the following words:

(1) The root שוב in its *Po'lel* form. Ibn Janāḥ lists Hos 8.6 in his account of the root שבב (i.e. double *ayin*) comparing Ezek 38.4; Mic 2.4 and, in particular, Jer 50.6 (quoting the *Qere* שובבום). He gives to the form the meaning 'to drive out', 'banish', 'expel' (Arabic *ṭrd*). In Jer 50.6 the meaning is that 'the mountains have expelled them' and hence, in the words that follow, 'they walk from mountain to hill and forget their resting place'. Similarly, the phrase here under review means that the calf of Samaria will be 'banished, removed from its home and, with its worshippers, taken off into captivity'. This account seems to have been known to Jerome some six centuries earlier; for he repudiates it with the words '*sababim* is written here, i.e. with *yodh* as the penultimate letter and not, as some falsely suppose, *sababwm*, i.e. with a *waw* in that position'. Since the latter form is attested by the MT only in Jer 50.6 it is clear that, like ibn Janāḥ, he knew of a tradition which interpreted Hos 8.6 by reference to Jer 50.6. It is clear (for he says so) that ibn Janāḥ is also influenced by Hos 10.5 and by the phrase there predicated of the calf (or its glory) 'it is removed' – גלה. He does not parse the word שבבים as it occurs in the present verse, being content to paraphrase with the passive participle 'banished' (Arabic *mṭrwd*).

If ibn Janāḥ's assessment is correct it is probable that the form should be referred to the *Po'lel* of the root שוב rather than to a double *ayin* root שבב. Comparative philology gives no indication of any double *ayin* cognate with meanings even remotely similar to that detected by ibn Janāḥ for these forms (see below), and the evidence of Ezek 38.4 (cf. BDB) suggests that the *Po'lel* of שוב might be capable of such a meaning. We may tentatively suppose that the *Po'lel* had something of a privative sense such as 'to deprive of the possibility of return' → 'to banish' and that שבבים in Hos 8.6 is a derived abstract plural noun[20]. The phrase will then have the literal meaning 'the calf of Samaria will become banishment' → 'will be ousted'.

(2) Notwithstanding this account of the word which he attributes to his mentor R. Judah Ḥayyuz, ibn Janāḥ says that he is inclined to prefer a second explanation, i.e. that of the Targum which apparently renders 'will become chips of boards' (for the text of the Targum, see below). The sense of the root שבב is, then, akin to the well-known שבר 'to break', 'demolish' and this sense, attested for Hos 8.6, is thought to be preserved in the talmudic comment on Exod 19.8 to the effect that the

[20] The word may be repointed שֹׁבְבִים cf., e.g., קֽוֹמְמִיּוּת from the root קום, BDB p. 879, col 2.

peoples' words which Moses brought back to God were such as 'break (משבבין) men's minds' (B. *Shabbath* 87a; ET, p. 413 in *Mo'ed* I).

With this approach Rashi (cf. Kimchi) and many modern commentators are in agreement. Rashi believes the word to be an Aramaism and with it he compares the Aramaic expression שיבא מכשור 'a chip of a beam' as it occurs in B. *Sanhedrin* 7b (ET, p. 28 in *Neziḳin* III), cf. perhaps Mt 7.3ff and the 'mote' and 'beam' of Jesus' parable.

The suggestion is at first sight attractive. In Exod 32.20 (cf. Deut 9.21) Moses is said to have 'ground the calf-image to pieces', an expression not dissimilar in meaning, though it should be noted that he is also said to have burned the image (see below). On the other hand, the notice of Exod 32.20 (if later than Hosea) may denote primarily a *quasi* liturgical action designed to bring punishment on the guilty by means of the water contaminated by the dust of the crushed image which the Israelites were made to drink[21].

It must be emphasised that very considerable uncertainty characterises many of the elements in this general approach. First, it is not clear what precisely the words of the Targum denote; thus, e.g., Jastrow (p. 919a) understands them to denote 'gold foils or veneers for boards'. Secondly, the late Hebrew verb שבב is better attested with the sense 'to chastise', 'discipline' than 'to chip', 'chisel' (cf. Jastrow *ad loc.*) and the talmudic verbal form משבבין (see above) is rendered 'chastise' (the heart of man) by a number of authorities (so ibn Janāḥ, cf. Jastrow). Further, the debate recorded in B. *Shabbath* 87a explicitly raises the question whether the word משבבין is indeed correct, some parties to the debate claiming that it should be מושכין 'draw/attract' or משיבין 'refute'. Moreover, despite ibn Janāḥ's claim, the passage itself does not appear to refer at all to the view that the word can mean 'to break'.

Thirdly, the reading שיבא in *Sanhedrin* 7b is not certain and (e.g.) Goldschmidt in fact prints the word שיכא with שיבא in the margin. Moreover שיבא, the Aramaic noun in question (if it is the correct reading), is better attested in connection with ploughs and ploughing and with the meaning 'incision', 'groove' (cf. Jastrow, p. 1556). The sense 'chip', 'mote' etc. is then not as firmly grounded as many modern commentators and authorities (e.g. BDB, KB, Wolff, Rudolph) are inclined to suppose.

(3) Ibn Barūn compares שבבים with Arabic *sbb*, for which Wechter gives the meaning 'to cut', 'wound' (i.e. a person). While such meanings are not unknown, the word, according to Lane (4, p. 1284 col 2), is better attested with meanings such as 'to revile', 'vilify', 'upbraid' (cf. the sense 'to chastise' attributed to the talmudic verb mentioned above). It is difficult to see how ibn Barūn's comparison could be applied unless, perhaps, his suggestion means that the 'calf will

21 Cf. Noth *Exodus ad loc.*; for a recent treatment, D. Frankel *VT* 44 (1994), pp. 330–339.

become (the object of) vilification'. That, however, is uncertain and without supporting evidence from other sources ibn Barūn's suggestion does not at present commend itself.

(4) Jerome in the Vulgate (see below) renders the phrase 'spiders' webs' and, in his commentary, states that the calf will dissolve into oblivion just as spiders' webs are blown to pieces by the wind. It is possible that his interpretation is illuminated by reference to the cognate Syriac word *šbb* which means 'to descend (upon a rope)' (cf. Barthélemy *ThZ* 16, 1960, p. 344). The theory is too uncertain to commend itself.

(5) Ibn Ezra asserts that the word is to be compared with Hebrew שביבים, apparently 'sparks', 'flames' (cf. Job 18.5). In this connection BDB tentatively cite Arabic *šbb* 'to blaze up'. The suggestion has recently been revived by Albright *BASOR* 84 (1941), p. 17 n. 36, and Osty. According to this view the phrase means the calf 'will be consigned to the flames'. As has been noted above, Exod 32.20 records that Moses initially burnt the golden calf before grinding it into pieces. Yet apart from the assumption that, on this view of the word in Hosea, there is an anomalous isogloss between Hebrew and Arabic *š*, some doubt may be said to attend the suggestion that burning specifically was envisaged by Hosea as a likely fate for the calf of Samaria.

On balance it seems to me likely that Hosea wished to express the view that the calf of Samaria, the emblem of the Northern Kingdom, was man-made and worthless and that it was destined shortly to lose its place of honour. With this, the evidence of Hos 10.5 seems to agree. Accordingly it is unlikely that his words depict a particular fate, such as burning or reduction to chips or splinters. If this assessment is correct then the phrase שבבים יהיה is parallel to גלה ממנו in 10.5 and, like it, denotes 'will be removed', 'ousted' (*sc.* from its place of honour). Ibn Janāḥ's initial philological account of the word שבבים (i.e. that of R. Judah) and the modification of it set out above, *viz.* that we are confronted with a *Po'lel* form of the root שוב, is, then, judged the best account of the matter in the present state of our knowledge. For evidence of the ancient versions, see below.

The strong interrelation between the Northern Kingdom, here named by reference to its capital Samaria, and its official emblem, the calf, is again emphasised. For the nation it was indeed the god which had brought them out of the land of Egypt and so given them their independence and constitution. The calf, the product of the nation's and of Jeroboam I's considered plan, was thus the object of the nation's aspirations and worship. In this sense it was 'of Israel' (note a), the very epitome of the nation's own estimate of its identity, and in no way imported or imitated from the example of foreign peoples (so Jerome and Kimchi). Yet in fact it was a mere human artefact (cf. 13.2), no different from the many idolatrous artefacts which had multiplied throughout the land as a result of the nation's recent opulence (v. 4). It was not a god at all and, with the advent of the Assyrians and the imminent collapse of the whole fabric of the nation, it would shortly be ousted from its place of honour (note b), as totally discredited as the nation which had spawned it. See further on the previous verse.

Text and Versions

כי מישראל והוא LXX ἐν τῷ Ἰσραήλ· καὶ αὐτό, i.e. conjoining the first element with v. 5 and in disagreement with the verse-division of MT; Pesh. *mṭl dmn 'ysr'l hw*; cf. Targ. ארי מישראל והוא (but cf. Cathcart, p. 46); Vulg. *quia ex Israel et ipse est*; a number of modern commentators have followed the punctuation of LXX and then emended כִּי מִיִּשְׂרָאֵל to בית ישראל or בני ישראל (Halévy, *BHS*, Borbone) as the subject of the plural verb of the preceding verse; the evidence of Pesh. has prompted a number of scholars to omit the conjunctive *waw* of והוא, e.g., Wellhausen, cf. Marti; but see note a above and Gelston's important note (p. 138).

יהיה 4QpHos[b] היה (see also Borbone and cf. Gelston, p. 115).

שְׁבָבִים LXX διότι πλανῶν (so also Theod.) ἦν ὁ μόσχος σου Σαμάρεια 'because thy calf was deceiving, O Samaria'; cf. Quinta ῥεμβεύων 'is roving'; Symm. ἀκατάστατος 'unstable', 'unsettled'[22]; Pesh. *lṭ'ywt' hw' 'glky* 'thy calf, O Samaria, has become straying, error', cf. Gelston, p. 167; Aq. (so Jerome) *errantibus* 'for those who stray'; these versions may point to the *Po'lel* of שׁוב as indicated in note b (1) above though, naturally perhaps, understood of apostasy rather than of separation or expulsion; Vulg. *aranearum telas* 'spiders' webs' (see note b (4) above); Targ. נסרי לוחין ?'chips of boards', but see note b (2) above; 4QpHos[b] reads שו]בבי[ם; so Strugnell, p. 202, cf. Borbone; if this is correct, then it may afford evidence for a *Po'lel* form, see note b (1) above; Allegro prints שי]בבי[ם but gives ו as an alternative to י.

עגל → עגלך 'thy calf' (Borbone).

8.7 **Indeed, they sow[a] the wind and reap[a] the whirlwind[b]; [c]their endeavour produces no standing corn[dc], a growth[e] which produces no grain[f]. [g]Even if it does, foreigners consume it[g].**

[a]Frequentative imperfects.

[22] For the variant reading ἀκαταστάτων attested by Jerome and for comments, cf. Ziegler *ad loc.*

[b]The form of the noun סוּפָתָה with pleonastic *taw* (so ibn Ezra and Kimchi) is a survival of the old accusative case, GK 90f.

[c—c]Lit. 'it has no standing corn'. The preposition ל with third masculine singular suffix (in the lit. translation 'it') is understood to refer to the seed which 'they' have sown (so Rashi, cf. Qyl). The sense, then, is that their endeavour in sowing is doomed to failure (so, again, Rashi). Rudolph prefers to understand the first phrase as a relative clause which here precedes rather than follows the noun צמח to which it refers, and hence facilitates the rhyme צֶמַח/קָמָה. The words mean 'growth (צמח) which does not come to standing corn produces no grain'. The interpretation is ingenious and amounts to a possibility. On the other hand, it seems to me more likely that the line is constructed of two parallel clauses rather than of a main clause and a subordinate one. Rashi's solution has the merit that it makes it possible to see a connection between 7a and 7b – a connection which Rudolph's theory obliges him to deny.

For Rosenmüller, cf. Harper, the preposition לו refers to Israel and hence 'Israel has no standing corn'. The interpretation is hardly convincing. It attempts a solution to the problem which is not unlike Rashi's.

[d]The word קָמָה from the root קום, denotes fully grown standing corn (cf. the Vulgate). It does not denote 'ears of corn' (*contra* van Hoonacker).

[e]צמח, 'growth', i.e. germinating seed, and so the whole process of growth; cf. Gen 19.25; Ezek 16.7; Ps 65.11.

[f]Cf., with Rudolph, Isa 47.2; corn ready for grinding into flour is denoted.

[g—g]The phrase has been regarded as a later addition (Marti, cf. Rudolph) on the grounds that it laboriously and unnecessarily adds an element ('foreigners') which does not belong to the theme of natural calamity. Rudolph, following Procksch and Frey, accordingly suggests the emendation קדים 'eastwind' for זרים 'foreigners', the addition of a suffix to the preceding verb and the repointing of the following verb, thereby achieving a second rhyming pair (i.e. יַעֲשֵׂהוּ/יְבַלְעֵהוּ). The latter suggestion is more ingenious than convincing. Marti's argument carries some force and it may be supposed that if the phrase is not original, it was added early by Hosea or his redactor and in the light of historical circumstances, cf. vv. 1 and 3 (so Wolff).

The prophet appears to be using two proverbial sayings. The first describes the inevitable consequences of human folly by reference to sowing and reaping (cf. Prov 22.8; Job 4.8; Gal 6.7) and the second, more directly agricultural in origin, conjoined with the first, makes the verse as a whole into a specific judgement upon Israel's foolish idolatry (cf. Kimchi). The creation of an oracle of judgement is emphasised by the last phrase 'even if it does (produce grain) foreigners consume it'. Whether or not that phrase was original (note g above) it accords with the general sense of the verse and the movement of thought to which the juxtaposition of its elements bears witness (cf. Mays).

The first saying goes further than the familiar equation 'a man reaps what he sows'. Here, as in Ecclus 7.3 where sowing the furrows of unrighteousness has compound and accelerating (seven times) effect, the wind strengthens inexorably to a whirlwind. The wind (*rwḥ*) that Israel sows is, as so often in the Wisdom literature, 'vanity', 'emptiness', almost 'chaos' (cf. Isa 41.29). The context in which the verse is found suggests that Hosea has in mind the fundamental sin of idolatry from which, as he consistently argues, moral and institutional anarchy ultimately derive. When the nation by its actions sows such chaotic vanity it is not surprising that it reaps a veritable whirlwind, the latter (as in Prov 1.27) being a figure of doom, destruction and terror.

The juxtaposed saying has all the appearance of being derived from a farmer's *bon mot*[23] marked as it is by word-play and even rhyme[24]. The connection with the first saying is effected by the preposition *lw* (note c) whose antecedent is the sowing. The two phrases of the line are thus parallelistic, and depict sowing (again note c) which affords no standing corn, growth which produces no grain. Where the application of the saying is concerned, juxtaposed with what precedes, the meaning is that moral turpitude and folly produce only more of the same. Further, however, and in relation to the nation's commitment to idolatry, made *inter alia* to facilitate the fertility of the land (cf. 2.7, EV 5), the saying is given by Hosea a particular and literal application: it thus becomes an oracle of judgement. The crops will fail, and they will do so because the whole agricultural endeavour is associated with the calf of Samaria, as indeed is the political management of the state of Samaria (cf. the following verse and v. 4 above). Hosea thus detects a fundamental continuity between the natural world and the sphere of human morality, between the land and its wayward inhabitants (cf. 4.1ff). That continuity, of course, reflects the nature of Yahweh

[23] Cf., e.g., Eccles 11.4 and, outside the bible, the Gezer Calendar (see Mauchline in Thomas *DOTT*, pp. 201f and Davies *AHI*, no. 10, p. 85).

[24] For analysis of an echoing effect constructed by certain of the letters, cf. Qyl.

as Israel's consistent God and as the true lord of the land that he gave to her.

The closing phrase 'even if ... foreigners' serves to press home the inexorable quality of the curse that the Israelites bring upon themselves and may reflect the particular circumstances in which that curse was seen to work itself out (cf. 7.9 and note g above).

Text and Versions

כי רוח יזרעו LXX ὅτι ἀνεμόφθορα ἔσπειραν 'because they sowed (seeds) blasted by the wind' (after Jerome), cf. Liddell and Scott, p. 132b; Targ. בית ישׂרעל דמן לדרוח זרע 'the House of Israel is like the man who sows the wind (and reaps the whirlwind)'.

וסופתה יקצרו LXX καὶ ἡ καταστροφὴ αὐτῶν ἐκδέξεται αὐτά (αὐτό, *v.l.*) 'and their destruction will await these things' (? what follows, i.e. the failed crops); Symm. συσσεισμὸν θεριοῦσι 'they will reap the whirlwind', so Vulg.; Theod. καταιγίδα ἐθέρισαν 'they reaped the tempest', cf. Pesh.

קמה rightly, LXX δράγμα; Vulg. *culmus stans*.

לו Wellhausen (so Marti, Harper, cf. *BHS*, AF) reads לה, referring to קמה; but the difficulty then arises that there has to be consequential amendment of יעשׂה (→תעשׂה/תעשׂהו etc. – so Marti, cf. *BHS*); AF, who take קמה as a verb, render 'If it grows, there will be no sproutage on it. It will not make a meal'; but this presents the difficulty that the implied subject זרע 'seed' is masculine.

אולי יעשׂה Targ. מא אם יקנון נכסין 'What if they acquire business? (Foreigners will plunder it)'; the rendering may represent accommodation to the city life of Alexandria.

8.8 **Israel is lost[a]: because of[b] the nations they have now become like a worthless[c] vessel.**

[a]נבלע lit. 'is swallowed up'. To this, the primary meaning of the verb, the specific meaning for this verse is, according to ibn Janāḥ, connected. It denotes here 'vitiation', 'decay', 'undermining destruction' (Arabic *fs'd, 'fs'd, 'hl'k*). Other meanings, again connected with the primary notion of 'swallowing', are 'enclosure', 'covering', 'concealment' (cf. Job 10.8, 11 where תַּלְבִּישֵׁנִי, 'thou dost clothe me' illustrates the meaning of תְּבַלְּעֵנִי 'thou dost conceal me on every side'). In the light of this analysis of the word, it may be suggested that Hosea means that Israel is 'swallowed up', i.e. decayed, lost from view or, to use English idioms, 'undermined', 'vitiated' by reason of her involvement with the world powers of the day. Since the word does not denote total destruction,

Rudolph's objection to the term as too strong to describe the political situation in which the nation had, as a result of the Assyrian annexation of its territories in 733 BC, lost international respect, falls to the ground and with it his proposal to read נבצע 'is robbed', 'dismembered'. Rather the verb, properly understood, denotes precisely what Rudolph describes: the nation, by its vacillating and inconsistent approaches to the great powers, has exhausted all its integrity and in this sense is ruined and lost. The meaning is very similar to that expressed in 7.8 above[25].

[b]The preposition ב may be understood to denote 'among', i.e. 'in the sight of' (so Kimchi). In view of the evidence of the closely parallel 7.8, it is perhaps preferable to understand it as *beth instrumenti* 'through', 'because of'.

[c]Lit. 'in which is no pleasure'. The noun חפץ has also the sense 'value', 'worth', cf. Prov 3.15; 8.11 (so Wolff). The phrase occurs also in Jer 22.28 and 48.38 where, again, it is connected to כלי 'vessel'.

In words very similar to those he uses in 7.8, Hosea states that Israel, through her vacillating attempts to ingratiate herself with the great powers of Egypt and Assyria, has exhausted her integrity and is thus lost; she is vitiated (note a) and her role in international relations played out. The perfect tense of the verb, necessarily interpreted as a prophetic perfect on the view that what is denoted is total destruction (so, e.g., Rosenmüller, cf. Rudolph), is, on a correct understanding of its meaning, a straightforward historic perfect which matches the following 'they have become'. With a change of subject to third person plural the Israelites are further described as having become like a worthless vessel or pot, discarded as now useless. In Jer 22.28 the metaphor illuminates the passive participle *nbzh* 'despised' (cf. Kimchi here). Such a vessel, whether because it is somehow flawed or stained (cf. Jerome), is thrown out and smashed (cf. Jer 48.38) as it is no longer the object of affection (cf. Rosenmüller). What is said here reflects the decision made in regard to the pot, *viz.* that it is now useless. Hence the simile accurately reflects the sense 'is lost' detected for the verb *nbl'* (note a).

Again the situation is that of 735–732 BC, cf. on 7.8 above.

[25] J. Barth *Beiträge Jesaia* (Karlsruhe, 1885), pp. 4f suggests that one root בלע is a by-form of בלל or בלה (cf. KB[3] בלע III). G. R. Driver *ZAW* 52 (1934), p. 52 acknowledges the formal possibility of the theory but prefers to relate the occurrence of the word נבלעו in Isa 25.7 to Arabic *blġ*. See further G. R. Driver in *Essays presented to D. W. Thomas*, p. 52. The evidence adduced here for Hos 8.8 may serve to strengthen Barth's theory.

Text and Versions

נבלע LXX κατεπόθη; Vulg. *devoratus est*; Pesh. *'tbl'*, 'swallowed down' (n. b. Syriac *'tbl'* can mean 'to be struck', 'wounded' as well as 'to be swallowed up'); Targ. אתבזיז 'is plundered'.

היו Oettli and Marti propose היה.

אין חפץ בו LXX ἄχρηστον 'useless', cf. Pesh. *dlyt bh ḥšḥw* and Targ. דלית צרוך ביה; Vulg. *inmundum* 'unclean', 'foul'.

8.9 For it was of their own accord[a] that they came[b] to Assyria; a wild ass[c] following its own nose[d]: Ephraim [e]is full of its love-affair[e].

[a]The pronoun המה is emphatic (lit. 'it was they') and serves to indicate that the action was of their own choosing (cf. van Hoonacker, van Gelderen, Wolff; and, with Rudolph, 8.4 above).

[b]Kimchi notes that the verb עלה normally denotes 'going up' *to* Israel and that here the expression is unusual in that the going up is *from* Israel; for this he compares Exod 1.10. As an alternative he quotes Saadya as suggesting that the verb means 'to arrive', 'come' (באו) as though from the Aramaic verbs עול/עלל 'to enter', 'arrive' (cf. Qyl).

Rudolph, noting that Nineveh is only 250 metres higher than sea level and that no heights lie on the road from Israel/Palestine, is inclined to doubt the sense 'go up'. Accordingly he applies to this text G. R. Driver's theory, *ZAW* 69 (1957), p. 76, posited by reference to other texts, that עלה was capable of the sense 'to go north'. The theory is also suggested by Qyl in the name of ibn Ezra (he gives no reference).

It seems to me that Saadya's account is the more satisfactory and, accordingly, Hosea's usage here is again likely to be dialectal.

[c]Such is the traditional translation of the term פרא. L. Köhler *ZAW* 44 (1926), pp. 59ff, argues for the zebra and against this view P. Humbert *ZAW* 62 (1949/50), pp. 202ff, vigorously defends the traditional translation. The animal is identified by Qyl (cf. Humbert, p. 205) with *Equus Hemionus* 'of the equine family but no higher than a donkey'. The word with Ephraim constitutes a word-play – פרא/אפרים.

[d]בודד לו lit. '(going) alone for itself', i.e. wilfully. The colloquial English expression 'to follow one's nose' signifying independent action is also adopted here in reference to Jer 2.24 where the wild ass is described as 'snuffing the wind' in its lust (cf. also Gen 16.12) and to Rashi who comments 'it goes of its own accord from place to place, snuffing the wind as it wanders'.

[e—e]See on 2.14 (EV 12) above. Ibn Janāḥ lists the verb התנו under the root תנה (cf. AF) though he gives the verb here a meaning consistent with the notion of giving, cf. נתן: 'they have given their love to Assyria' (Arabic *bḏlw' wddhm l'šwr*). Morag, comparing the Arabic cognate verb *tny* (IVth theme) with the sense 'to celebrate', 'praise' together with instances of the verb תנה in Hebrew having the same meaning (cf. Judg 5.11; 11.40; Ps 8.2), argues persuasively that in the context of love the primary meaning is to celebrate or praise (*sc*. a girl or the act of love). Morag adduces evidence to suggest the merging of *Hiphil* and *Qal* forms in Hosea's northern dialect and hence what is apparently a *Qal* form of the same verb in the following verse may not in fact be so[26]. At all events the *Hiphil* does not appear to have any particular significance (cf. the *Hiphil* forms of זנה, unique to Hos 4.10; 5.3, used with the same sense as the *Qal* elsewhere in the bible). *BHS* mentions the proposal to read נתנו.

The word אהבים is an abstract plural and denotes 'love', 'love-affair', cf. the similar (but not identical) form in Prov 7.18 and BDB p. 13, col 1. Morag suggests (p. 498) that the rare (plural) form is dialectal and has a pejorative sense.

Israel's ruinous bankruptcy in the sphere of politics (see on the previous verse) is the result of the actions of the nation itself. It was the Ephraimites themselves who took the initiative in appealing to Assyria for help (see note a) and in this they are characterised as a wild ass who follows his own nose (note d) as he traverses the desert in search of a mate. It is likely that the term is used generically rather than as depicting a particular animal which breaks away from the herd (cf. Rudolph). That Ephraim is so described seems to be confirmed by the word-play constituted by the proximity of the words 'wild ass' (*pr'*) and 'Ephraim' (*'prym*). The contrary view is noted by Qyl (for earlier advocates of the view, cf. Harper); thus Assyria is described because it was an arrogant nation intent on its own purposes and totally wilful like the wild ass (cf. the Babylonians, similarly described, in Ezek 23.20). Apart from the evidence of the word-play, however, a further consideration against this view is that the metaphor accurately reflects the emphasis of the preceding phrase, *viz*. that it was the Israelites who took the initiative in the matter.

The 'coming' to Assyria (note b) is likely to reflect dialectal usage though it has been suggested that the word (lit. 'go up') is used here sarcastically by Hosea (so Qyl as a possibility) since the verb is properly used of the approach *to* Israel/Palestine. At

26 The argument is developed by reference to the *yp'yl* preterites (initial *yodh*) in Phoenician corresponding to the Hebrew *hp'yl* and to the tendency of imperfects of the Ist and IVth themes of verbs in Arabic dialects to merge with consequent loss of distinguishable meanings; see *op. cit*., p. 500 n. 44.

all events, for Kimchi the reference is to Menahem's tribute paid to Tiglath-pileser in 738 BC (so Deden, Rudolph etc.) which was to lead inexorably to the disastrous Assyrian invasion of 733 BC. On the other hand, the connection established between this verse and the preceding suggests that Hosea had in mind specifically Hoshea's tribute paid to Assyria in 732/1 BC, soon after he had deposed Pekah – tribute paid, with the intention of securing his position[27] (so, e.g., Wolff). If that supposition is correct then the previous example (*viz.* of Menahem) may also have been in Hosea's mind as a disastrous precedent. In both cases the payment[28] was made for the specific purpose of winning Assyrian support for a usurper to the throne.

The action was, for Hosea, meretricious and foolish. Thus he describes it in terms of an affair, an adulterous affair which is conducted in breach of the nation's required loyalty to Yahweh as her husband[29]. Thinking themselves secure in their newly forged relationship with Assyria and without considering the eventual consequences of it, the Ephraimites are 'full of their love affair' (note e–e); they are self-satisfied and stupidly smug. In this sense the Ephraimites have become veritable *pr'ym* (wild asses) for whom irresponsible freedom and arbitrary wilfulness are the dominant instincts (cf. Rudolph). Hoshea's action in paying tribute and expecting thereby protection from Assyria represents a volatile change of policy from that of Pekah's pro-Egyptian stance and thus particular mention of Assyria here is not inconsistent with mention of love-affairs with nations (plural) in the following verse. Indeed R. Meir Löb ('Malbim', nineteenth century) has a point in his assertion that amorous involvement with Assyria was simultaneous with similar involvement with Egypt (cf. Wellhausen's proposal to read 'Egypt' for 'Ephraim'; see further under Text and Versions)[30].

27 Noth *History*, p. 261 (*GI*, p. 236) and Tiglath-pileser, Annals III, 1 1 17f; cf. *ANET*, p. 284.

28 Cf. Noth *History*, p. 258; *GI*, p. 233.

29 For the metaphor of whoredom used in reference to breaches of treaties in Assyrian inscriptions, cf. the treaty between Assurnirari V (755–746 BC) and Arpad; *AO* 8 (1932–3), p. 23.

30 Dalley's suggestion (p. 40) that Hos 8.8f reflects the Samaritans' mercenary activities in hiring their equestrian officers to the Assyrian army, though in itself instructive, does not accord with Hosea's emphasis upon the volatile nature of Ephraim's particular overtures to both Egypt and Assyria.

Text and Versions

עלו LXX ἀνέβησαν, cf. Vulg. *ascenderunt* and Pesh. *slqw*; Targ. גלו 'they were exiled (to Assyria)'.

פרא בודד לו LXX ἀνέθαλε καθ' ἑαυτόν 'has shot up by himself' (reading the verb פרח/יִפְרַח); cf. Nyberg, who, by reference to Accadian *pir'u*, renders פרא 'shoot', 'sprout', which hardly fits the context; Aq. ὄναγρος μονάζων ἑαυτῷ, cf. Theod. and Quinta ... καθ' ἑαυτόν, Vulg. *onager solitarius sibi Ephraim* and Pesh. *'yk 'rd' yḥydy'* 'a wild ass alone' – Pesh. and Quinta adding *'yk*, ὡς, 'as a wild ass ...'; Symm. καὶ οὐκ ἀνέθαλεν ἐν ἐμοί 'and Ephraim did not spring up in me (?)'; Targ. על דהליכו ברעות נפשהון כערד מרוד 'since they went on their own accord like an ass running wild'.

אפרים Wellhausen emends to מצרים 'Egypt': they have gone up to Assyria, to Egypt ...'; LXX, Aq., Symm., Theod. and Vulg. take the word with what precedes; Targ. and Pesh. with what follows.

התנו אהבים LXX δῶρα ἠγάπησαν 'they have loved gifts' → אתנים אהבו (Vollers, cf. Borbone), cf. Pesh. *'prym mwhbt' rḥm* 'Ephraim loves gifts' (Gelston, p. 166); Vulg. *munera dederunt amatoribus*, cf. Ezek 16.33, 'they have given gifts to lovers'; Targ. בית ישראל אתמסרו ביד עממיא דרחימו 'the House of Israel is delivered into the hands of the peoples that they loved'.

8.10 **Yet though[a] they are delighted by their affairs[b] among the nations, now I shall make an end of them[c] and they shall soon[d] show weakness[e] because of the oppression[f] of [g]the king of princes[g].**

[a]For גם כי having an affirmative and concessive force, cf. BDB p. 169, col 2 6.

[b]The word יתנו, here with ellipsis of אהבים, is the same as that in the preceding verse (cf. Morag and cf. note e on 8.9). Construed in a concessive clause (note a) the sense conveyed is that the Ephraimites may suppose themselves to have secured their future well-being but in fact it is Yahweh's intervention against them that is determined. Literally, the phrase means 'though they have related-their-appreciation (of their love-affairs)'; in the context the sense is that self-satisfaction in meretricious manoeuvres is illusory. For comments on the apparent inconsistency (noted by Kimchi) in the use of the *Qal* of the verb in this verse, and of the *Hiphil* in v. 9, see on the latter verse. It is thus possible that יתנו represents a preterite *Hiphil* rather than an imperfect *Qal*. At all events, whether the tense is a preterite ('they have related') or an imperfect ('they relate'), the meaning is virtually identical.

[c]אקבצם lit. 'I will gather them'. The 'gathering' for Rashi has a future

reference to Yahweh's redemptive activity; for ibn Ezra, they will be gathered in Egypt in punishment, and for Kimchi it is the nations who will be gathered to effect Israel's exile (cf. Ezek 16.37). Such meanings are hardly satisfactory.

A number of modern commentators have adopted a view not dissimilar to that of ibn Ezra: the word is used metaphorically to depict God's gathering of Israel for indictment and punishment; so, e.g., Nyberg, comparing Hab 2.5; Zeph 3.8; Wolff, citing Mic 4.12; Ezek 22.19f; Mays, Joel 4.2 (EV 3.2). As Rudolph rightly argues, the suggestion is unsatisfactory since gathering in this sense is not appropriate to Ephraim, as yet largely unscattered and in place. And if gathering is a prelude to judgement, then, since gathering is a neutral word, that would need to be said explicitly. Rudolph is accordingly driven to emendation, reading אקצבם 'I will cut them off'. The suggestion is more ingenious than convincing since such a meaning is not clearly attested in biblical Hebrew for the verb.

Perhaps the best solution is that suggested by Qyl. He notes that in 9.6 the verb is parallel to קבר 'to bury' and he goes on to suggest that the verb קבץ has in both verses a meaning similar to that known from the verb אסף, *viz.* 'to gather', but also 'to remove', 'to destroy', cf. Nah 2.11; Joel 2.6 and ibn Janāḥ's comments under the root *p'r* (Neubauer, p. 560). Following this suggestion I have rendered 'I shall make an end of them'. For further comments on Hosea's choice of this particular word, see the main commentary below.

It may be noted finally that some authorities, understanding the verb to have only a favourable sense (cf. Rashi's view above) and, noting that the rest of the verse is minatory in tone, cut the knot and deem the whole of v. 10a to be a later gloss referring to the redemption of the exiles in the diaspora (so, e.g., Marti, Harper etc.). There is some force to this argument though I prefer to conclude that Hosea intended the verb to have a minatory sense (cf. 9.6) and that only later was it interpreted in a redemptive sense. Rashi's original comment, then, may constitute evidence of the later (exilic) interpretation of Hosea's words.

[d]For the temporal force of the adverb מעט, cf. 1.4. Rudolph suggests as a possibility that לא has fallen out of the text following ויחלו and that the consequent sense 'not a little' is litotes for 'very', cf. Isa 10.7. The suggestion is hardly convincing.

[e]The MT understands the verb וַיָּחֵלּוּ as a *Hiphil* of the root חלל with *waw* consecutive, 'and they began'. Even if a simple *waw* is read 'so that they will begin' no adequate sense seems to be afforded. Ibn Ezra and Kimchi valiantly suggest that a modal infinitive following 'to begin' can be supplied *ad sensum* from the context (they suggest 'to complain', יתלונו ויתרעמו). Building upon ibn Ezra's comparison with Ezek 9.6, Rosenmüller supposes that 'to begin' was capable of the sense 'to begin (*sc.* in the context) to be oppressed', rather as in Ezek 9.6 'to begin' (in the context) means 'to begin to exterminate'. Alternatively, Rosenmüller

suggests that מעט represents a modal infinitive construct (cf. the form שְׁכַב in 2 Kgs 14.22) following the verb, giving 'they begin to be minished'. Other scholars have suggested changes in the pointing in order to find in the consonants a form of the verb חיל 'to writhe', 'suffer' (cf. again ibn Ezra, Rashi – on the next verse – and AF; Rudolph reads וְיָחִילוּ), or of the verb יחל 'they will have little in which to hope' (וְיֹחִלוּ, so van Gelderen).

Since the collapse of the moral order of the state and consequently of its whole fabric is characteristically described by Hosea in terms of sickness (cf. 5.13; 6.1ff; further Morag, pp. 505ff) it is perhaps best to see in the consonants a form of the verb חלה 'to be weak', 'sick' and, with van Hoonacker, to read וְיָחֵלּוּ 'and they will soon show weakness'; for a comparable use of the *Hiphil*, cf. 7.5.

[f]משׂא lit. 'load', 'burden'. It seems likely in the context that tribute and taxation are denoted, cf. 2 Chr 17.11 and then, more generally, oppression (cf. Rudolph). Van Gelderen's suggestion that the other sense of the word, *viz.* 'oracle' applies in this case is doubtful since he makes the questionable assumption that here 'oracle' has the somewhat different meaning 'judgement', 'sentence'.

[g]מלך שׂרים Lit. 'king, princes'. For Kimchi the phrase is marked by asyndeton, cf. Exod 1.2; Hab 3.11 etc. and denotes 'king and princes'. This, following a construct (מַשָּׂא) presents difficulties and it is more likely that מלך is itself a construct. Thus the phrase מלך שׂרים denotes 'the king of princes' and is designed to indicate the mighty power of the Assyrian monarch whose 'princes are kings' (Isa. 10.8). The usage, then, is not dissimilar to that of Ezek 26.7 where the king of Babylon is described as 'king of kings'[31] (so, e.g., Rosenmüller, Harper, Rudolph, Qyl, Mays etc.). Nyberg and H. Cazelles *CBQ* 11 (1949), pp. 21ff, seek to interpret the phrase of gods and images; for comments on their theory, see on 8.4.

The verse belongs closely with the two preceding ones. The description in v. 9 of the Ephraimites' meretricious dealings with Assyria prompts the opening words of the present verse. They may (note a) congratulate themselves (note b) upon their latest political *volte-face* and upon their ingratiating themselves with Assyria in the foolish expectation that their future safety was thereby assured; but in reality what they have done is to activate Yahweh's destructive punishment of their action ('I will make an end of them', note c). If Hosea sees Yahweh's (proper) jealous reaction behind what is now to happen, that constitutes his theological appraisal of the political and historical realities.

[31] *sar sarrani* frequently occurs as a title for Assyrian kings from Tiglath-pileser I to Ashurbanipal; see Wolff *ad loc.*

Menahem's payment of tribute to Assyria in 738 BC had led, one way or another, to the disastrous invasion of 733 BC and to the dismembering of the state. Now Hoshea, in 732/1 BC, reversing Pekah's pro-Egyptian policy, had made the same mistake. Both kings had acted with the selfish intention of securing their own places on the throne (see on v. 9 above); they and their establishment had failed to see that their involvement with the 'king of princes' (note g), the greatest world power of the day, would lead shortly (note d) only to humiliation and shame, the fate indeed of the discarded pot (v. 8).

The verse emphasises the contrast between what is apparent and what is real (notes a and d, together with the word 'now'). Ephraim's capacity for self-delusion is characterised as the short-sighted self-satisfaction of the adulterous lover. The reality, with Yahweh (no less) as their God, is the immediate inception of the destructive consequences of the foolish act. The moment, then, of smug self-congratulation is the very moment ('now') that Yahweh resolves to make an end of them (note c). The choice of the verb, together with the preceding phrase 'among the nations' may serve to indicate the geographical dimension of the Ephraimite endeavour (i.e. embassies despatched to Assyria by Hoshea following so closely those despatched to Egypt by Pekah) which prompts Yahweh's specific reaction. In 'gathering' them in ('rounding them up', NEB) he reduces their endeavours to nothing and so makes an end of the state; very shortly its weakness will become apparent (note e) and it will be effected by the harsh oppression (note f) of the very nation to whom they had turned in facile attempts to ingratiate themselves.

Text and Versions

יתנו LXX παραδοθήσονται, cf. Pesh. *nštlmwn* 'they will be handed over' (Gelston, p. 166), has suggested the reading יֻתְּנוּ/יֻתַּן (Harper); Vulg. *cum mercede conduxerint* 'they will have hired (nations)'; Targ. אם ישוון בית־ישראל דחלתי על לבהון 'if the House of Israel take fear of me to heart'.

עתה Pesh. omits.

אקבצם LXX εἰσδέξομαι αὐτούς 'I will admit, receive them'; Aq. and Symm. συνάξω 'gather', cf. Vulg. *congregabo eos* and Pesh. *'knš 'nwn*; Quinta περιστοιχιοῦμαι αὐτούς 'I will entrap them'; Targ. אקריב גלותהון 'I will return' (lit. 'bring near') their captivity'; → אֲפִיצֵם (Oettli, cf. *BHS*) 'I will scatter them'.

ויחלו LXX καὶ κοπάσουσιν 'and they shall abate, grow weary', on the basis of which Wellhausen, cf. *BHS*, Borbone, proposes וְחָדְלוּ/וְיֶחְדְּלוּ 'and they shall cease' (from anointing); Aq. καὶ λιτανεύσουσιν 'they shall entreat' (√חלה II, cf. Ziegler *Bei.*, p. 358); Symm. καὶ μενοῦσιν 'they shall tarry, remain', cf. Theod. καὶ διαλείψουσι, Vulg. *et quiescent* 'and they will be at rest' (? 'they will abate', cf. LXX; does this point to √חלה?), cf. Pesh. *wnttnyḥwn* 'and they shall have rest' (Gelston, pp. 127ff); Targ. יחכמון '(if) they show wisdom'.

ממשא LXX and Theod. τοῦ χρίειν on the basis of which many scholars have proposed מִמְּשֹׁחַ '(they grow weary of, abate) from anointing ...' (so, e.g., Oort, Grätz, Marti, *BHS*, etc.); for criticisms see Rudolph; Symm. ἀπὸ φόβου 'from fear of'; Ziegler prefers the reading φόρου 'tribute'; Aq. ἀπο ἄρματος, cf., with Ziegler *Bei.*, Vulg. *ab onere* and also Pesh. *mn šql'* 'from the taxation/burden of'; Targ. מרות 'dominion'.

מלך Symm., Pesh. and Targ. render in the plural.

שׂרים LXX, Pesh., Vulg., Aq., some MSS of Targ. and many Kennicott and de Rossi MSS join this word to the previous with the conjunction 'and' (so *BHS*, Borbone).

8.11 **[a]When he already[b] had altars so as to sin[c], Ephraim multiplied[d] altars so as to sin[c].[a]**

[a—a]The two parts of the verse are inverted in translation. The interpretation is that of ibn Ezra (cf. Kimchi): 'Ephraim already has altars so as to sin which he inherited from his fathers, and why now does he multiply these more?'

[b]Lit. simply, 'there were to him altars, so as to sin'.

[c]The preposition ל attached to the infinite construct qualifies or limits the idea expressed by the principle verbs (cf. BDB p. 517, col 1 7 b). A very similar expression is found in Josh 22.16 '... in your building for yourselves an altar so as to rebel against Yahweh'. Orelli (cf. Nyberg, Rudolph, Mays and Jeremias) reads the first infinitive construct in MT as a privative *Piel* לְחַטֵּא (or as an infinite absolute, לְחַטֹּא, cf. Harper) and gives it the meaning 'to atone for sin', cf. Lev 6.19. The resulting phrase is then a play on words and has the sense 'Ephraim has multiplied altars to atone for sin; they have become altars to (promote) sin'. Such a meaning for the *Piel* of חטא is certainly attested only in later texts (P) and the notion of altars designed specifically for atonement sacrifices is hardly 'consistent with this period' (so Harper). Jeremias' attempt[32] to see in the word-play of the verse an allusion to an assumed root חוט, 'den Willen erforschen' (cf. Accadian *ḫiāṭu*) is far-fetched and unsupported by ancient tradition.

32 For the evidence (adduced in regard to Gen 31.39) see O. Loretz *ZAW* 87 (1975), p. 208 and S. E. Loewenstamm *ZAW* 90 (1978), p. 410.

[d]The word הרבה is preceded by כי which has here an asseverative force (cf. Wolff). Attempts to give it the meaning 'for', 'because' and to link the verse with what precedes (so, e.g., Rashi, 'for the reason that he has multiplied, I will make him writhe ...'; cf. Rosenmüller) are hardly satisfactory.

Verses 11–13 form a section devoted to an attack on the sacrificial cult. As in v. 4, where Hosea turns from internal politics to idolatry, so here he turns from foreign politics to the cult; in both cases the effect of the juxtaposition is to link the two elements. The fundamental error, as always, is disregard of Yahweh and ethical realities in foolish lack of thought (cf. vv. 1b and 3a).

Ibn Ezra's understanding of the force of the argument in this verse is here adopted (note a–a). In a situation where there were already many cultic centres (cf. 2 Kgs 17.9f), what the Ephraimites did was to multiply them yet more. As Kimchi rightly observes, the dynasty of Omri had done much to further the proliferation of syncretistic cult centres; Jeroboam's activities in the same cause were to become a veritable paradigm. Now, *pari passu* with their meretricious attempts to ingratiate themselves with the world powers, at home they pressed on with the proliferation of yet more sacrificial centres (cf. 4.7; 10.1). Verses 5.6 and 6.6 (so Rudolph) indicate their thinking: sacrificial worship of Yahweh served to keep him content. By performing it, the Ephraimites believed that they won for themselves freedom from concern with his more difficult ethical demands (cf. v. 12) and freedom to behave licentiously (4.13). It is not that such sacrificial worship was formally directed to atonement, that being an emphasis of later times; cf. my comments on 4.8. There the priests are said to 'feed on the sin of my people', i.e. their preoccupation with self-indulgent feasting in the cult prompted them to ignore their prior function to impart 'knowledge of God'; cultic self-indulgence obscures Yahweh's moral requirements. This, then, is the argument of the present verse. 'Each new altar fosters sin since it strengthens yet more deviation from the will of God' (so Rudolph). In his attack on the proliferation of altars Hosea is seen by Wolff as 'showing a close affinity to the fathers of Deuteronomy', which later promulgated the law of the single sanctuary (Deut 12.5ff). If this assessment has some value, it is necessary to point out (cf. Rudolph) that the motive for the Deuteronomic reform was somewhat different from that which prompted Hosea to condemn the proliferation of altars in the eighth century BC.

Text and Versions

לחטא (1st occurrence) LXX εἰς ἁμαρτίας conjoined with what follows: ἐγένοντο αὐτῷ θυσιαστήρια ἠγαπήμενα 'well-loved altars have become sins for him'; Vollers supposes that the last word is derived from v. 13 (i.e. הבהבי); Wellhausen (cf., e.g., Marti) omits לחטא; Vulg. *ad peccandum* 'for sinning'; Pesh. *lḥṭyt'* 'to sin', cf. Targ. למחטי; → לְחֵטְא, conjoining with what follows (*BHS*).

לחטא (2nd occurrence) LXX appears to omit, but adds ἠγαπημένα (see above); Symm. εἰς ἁμαρτίαν 'into sin'; Vulg. *in delictum* '(altars have become for him) an offence'; Pesh. *lḥṭh' rb'* '(have become) a great sin'; Targ. לתקלא '(have become) a stumbling-block'; a number of scholars (e.g. Oort, *BHS*, Borbone) omit the last two words as a repetition (so LXX L').

8.12 **Though I write[a] for him the principal requirements[b] of my law, they are considered as those of an alien god[c].**

[a]*Kethib*, אכתוב; *Qere*, אֶכְתָּב with *maqqeph*. The verb 'to write' has, in the context, the connotation of permanence, hence the sense is virtually 'to prescribe'; cf. with Rudolph 2 Kgs 17.37; 22.13.

[b]The plural verb in 12b requires the finding of a plural antecedent in the first half of the verse. Since the term תורה in Hosea is a singular concept (cf. 4.6; 8.1), the antecedent must be found in the word רבו (*contra*, e.g., Wellhausen, Rudolph). The *Kethib* is here interpreted as a third plural perfect *Qal* of רבב construed as a short relative clause '(the things) which are great or many (in respect of) my law', so Kimchi, cf. Qyl. That the verb may denote what is 'great', 'important', 'weighty' as well as what is 'numerous' is clear from Gen 18.20; Isa 6.12. The *Qere*, רֻבֵּי appears to be the construct plural of the noun רוֹב. The form does not occur elsewhere and consequently, e.g., Wellhausen reads רב תּוֹרֹתַי 'the abundance, greatness of my laws'. Commenting upon the *Qere*, Kimchi compares Esth 1.8 where the cognate adjective רַב denotes 'every important person' and Qyl, similarly, compares Jer 39.13 'all the important officials of the king of Babylon'.

A number of scholars have read the *Kethib* as the construct noun רִבּוֹ 'myriad (precepts)'; e.g. Marti, Rudolph, Jeremias. Rudolph construes the noun adverbially 'ten thousand times over' and, following Keil, sees in the *Qere* a reflection of massoretic dissatisfaction with unacceptable exaggeration. C. Brockelmann[33] reads the word רַבּוֹ, i.e. as the noun רב with the old nominative case ending.

33 *Handbuch der Orientalistik* III (Leiden-Cologne, 1964), p. 62.

Hosea's choice of this word is clearly dictated by the *Hiphil* form in the preceding verse 'Ephraim multiplied altars' (cf. Wolff). In his wish to contrast Ephraim's proliferation of altars with Yahweh's moral requirements, however, there need be no presumption that he believed that such requirements were in turn prolific. Indeed the contrary is likely to be the case. Thus Hosea's words constitute a word-play made possible by the well-attested meanings of the roots רבב/רבה; the contrast is between the proliferation of altars on the one hand, and the weighty requirements of Yahweh's law on the other.

[c]The participle/adjective זר is singular and can therefore hardly be related to the plural subject of the verb נחשבו. A number of modern commentators appear to understand the word as a collective neuter, i.e. 'alien thing' (so, e.g., Wolff, Mays); the interpretation is questionable since the masculine adjective is not so used elsewhere. More plausible is the view (cf. Qyl) that the phrase is marked by ellipsis and means 'they are considered as (those of) an alien'. Since Yahweh is the speaker, the word 'god' is added *ad sensum*, cf. Ps 44.21; in Isa 17.10 זר, used absolutely, apparently has this meaning.

Ephraim's multiplication of altars and cultic sites is matched by the nation's disregard of the 'weightier matters of the law' (note b; cf. Mt 23.23). So preoccupied was the nation with self-indulgence in the cult that Yahweh's moral instruction was judged as if it came from a totally alien culture and authority (note c). That the verse represents Yahweh as having written the principal requirements of his teaching matches mention of his writing the ten commandments (Exod 24.12; 34.1; Deut 9.10). What is emphasised is the authoritative nature of his moral law; it is prescribed by Yahweh himself and hence comes its primacy and sovereign importance. The same emphasis may be detected in 4.1 (where there is a clear allusion to the ten commandments), 4.6f; 6.6; 8.1. The contrasting attitudes of Ephraim, i.e. to cultic worship on the one hand and to the requirements of Yahweh's moral law on the other, are well captured by Hosea's word-play upon forms of the root *rbb/rbh* (*hrbh/rbw* – note b). The notion that Ephraim considered Yahweh's law as if from an 'alien' source implies also that the nation regarded it as unauthorised (cf. the use of *zr* in definition of unauthorised incense or altar fire, Exod 30.9; Lev 10.1). It is, then, the flagrant disregard of Yahweh's authority that is portrayed. Ephraim had deluded itself that Yahweh, soothed by lavish cultic offerings, could be diverted from expecting the obedience due to the moral requirements of his law.

For their part the Ephraimites sought Yahweh in the sacrificial cult not because they wished to acknowledge the truth but because they could eat their fill (after Jerome, who quotes Jn 6.26).

Text and Versions

אכתוב Pesh. *wktbt* 'and I wrote' = ? וָאֶכְתּוֹב.

רבו תורתי LXX πλῆθος, καὶ τὰ νόμιμά μου '(I will write down for him) a great amount, and my laws ...' (see below); Aq. πληθυνομένους νόμους 'myriad laws'; Symm. πλήθη νόμων μου 'the myriads of my law'; Pesh. *swg" dnmwsy* 'the multitude of my laws' (cf. Gelston, p. 119); Vulg. *multiplices leges meas* 'my manifold laws'; Targ. סגיות (אוריתי) 'the multitude (+ of my laws' – with MSS); → דברי תורתי 'the words of my laws'(Grätz *Gesch.* II i, p. 469); → רֹב־תּוֹרֹתַי 'the multitude of my laws' (Hitzig, Wellhausen, Marti, *BHS*); → תּוֹרֹתָי retaining רבו with various explanations = 'the multitude of my laws' (Wolff, Rudolph); → רב. ותורתי (Borbone).

כמו זר נחשבו LXX (καὶ τὰ νόμιμά μου) εἰς ἀλλότρια ἐλογίσθησαν '(and my laws) are accounted as alien', so, with minor variations, Aq. and Symm.; see also on next verse; Vulg. *quae velut alienae conputatae sunt* 'which are accounted as alien'; Pesh. *w'yk nwkryt' ḥšb 'nyn lmly* 'and like alien things he (*sc.* Ephraim) accounted my words'; Targ. ואנון כעממי אתחשיבו 'but they are accounted as foreign (lit. 'the gentiles').

8.13 **In his [Ephraim's] frequent[a] sacrifices [b](they continually slaughter and eat meat)[b], Yahweh has no pleasure. Now he will remember their guilt and punish their sins. They shall return to Egypt.**

[a](1) This translation of the *hapax legomenon* הבהבי is based upon ibn Janāḥ's assessment of the word. He lists the root as a quadriliteral (Neubauer, pp. 183f) and states that he believes it to be illuminated by the Arabic adjective *hbhbyy'*, used to describe a cook who roasts meat (Arabic *'lṭbb'ẖ 'lḏy yšwy*). For this meaning he compares (so Rashi and ibn Ezra) the mishnaic verb הבהב which is attested with the sense 'to scorch', 'singe', cf. Jastrow, p. 329 col 1. He continues by raising the question whether Hosea's usage is not also illuminated by other meanings of the Arabic adjective, *viz.* (of a man or a camel) 'fast', 'swift', 'nimble' (Arabic *sry'*). He concludes that the phrase in question may have the meaning 'sacrifices that go on incessantly, in uninterrupted sequence or are frequent' (Arabic *mtd'rkt, mtt'b't 'y kṯyrt*).

Reference to Lane's lexicon (8, p. 2873, col 2) indicates that the Arabic adjective in question is derived from the verb *hbb*, which has the sense 'was brisk, lively or sprightly'; the reduplicated form *hbhb* also means 'he was quick' or 'swift'. The adjective 'quick', 'swift' (camel) is also attested in the sense 'one who serves well', 'anyone who does well a small thing'; according to some, specially a 'cook', and a 'roaster of meat ... butcher'. From this account it seems clear that in Arabic the notion of speed and efficiency is prior, and that the meaning 'butcher', 'cook' is a particular derivation of this.

Since one of the ancient versions (Symmachus; see below) is consistent with ibn Janāḥ's second interpretation of the word in question, and since it is doubtful if the versions show evidence of influence from the post-biblical word (i.e. 'to roast'; so Barr *CPOT*, p. 234) it is concluded that ibn Janāḥ's view is the most likely in the present state of our knowledge. A further consideration against the view[34] that the word denotes here 'my roast, burnt offerings' is that advanced by Rudolph, *viz.* why should so well-known an institution be described here by so rare a term?

If ibn Janāḥ's interpretation is substantially correct, then it is necessary to assume that the word הבהבי represents an absolute noun following the construct זבחי. At all events it is unlikely that the word contained a first person suffix in a verse in which Yahweh is elsewhere mentioned in the third person. Accordingly it is necessary to assume that the final *yodh* was a corruption of an original *waw* made, perhaps, in connection with other (and on this view, mistaken) views of the meaning of the word (see on Kimchi below). It is noted that the *yodh* is not represented in any of the ancient versions. The text, then, is emended to a noun הַבְהָבוֹ or (as an abstract plural) הַבְהָבָיו 'sacrifices of his (Ephraim's) speed' → 'his frequent sacrifices'. For the third singular in the first half of a verse, followed by the third plural in the second, cf., e.g., 8.8 above.

b—b A further consideration in favour of ibn Janāḥ's second interpretation is the view here proposed that the three following words represent an early gloss whose function was to translate the rare word הבהבי (cf. on 2.8, EV 6; 7.14ff above). Certainly the phrase 'they slaughter/sacrifice meat' is awkward in that the verb is usually used of animals where, so to speak, 'meat' is the end product. Further the pointing of וַיֹּאכֵלוּ, i.e. with *waw* consecutive (lit. 'and they ate'), can hardly be correct. The phrase has all the appearance of a pedestrian gloss whose function was explanation. The two imperfects are frequentative (the second read with simple *waw*) and the phrase means 'they (continually) slaughter, *sc.* meat, and eat' or 'they continually slaughter and eat meat'[35].

34 Adopted by a number of modern scholars, e.g., Orelli, J. J. Glück *VT* 14 (1964), p. 370.

35 Gelston, in a private communication, has drawn my attention to a number of passages in the book of Job where a copulative *waw* appears to be attached to the second word in a clause rather than, as might be expected, to the first. If this

[a](2) It remains to review the other principal interpretations of the phrase: first, Kimchi supposes that the word is derived from the root יהב ('to give') with reduplication of the second and third radicals. The meaning of the word is 'my gifts' (מתנותי), i.e. 'the gifts that they deem to be given to me', 'sacrificial gifts accorded to me'[36]. The phrase as a whole, he explains, has a force similar to the שלמים 'peace-offerings' where the emphasis, in practice, was upon the worshippers' eating the flesh. The theory is ingenious but hardly convincing and there remains the problem of a first person reference to Yahweh in a verse which otherwise speaks of him in the third person. Secondly, Rudolph compares the Arabic word *hbb* with the meanings 'to blow', 'breathe', 'to long for', 'be greedy for'. He sees another instance of the same word in Prov 30.15 where הב הב denotes the voracious greed of the horseleech with its twin suckers. Accordingly he renders Hosea's phrase 'they offer sacrifices of voracious greed', reading a noun הַבְהָב to which a *yodh* has been added by dittography. Rudolph considers further whether the word, with this sense, may not be derived from the well known verb אהב 'to desire', 'love' and in this connection he draws attention to Theodotion and the Targum (see below) as well as to D. W. Thomas' theory, *ZAW* 57 (1939), pp. 57ff, that אהב is ultimately connected with the root הבב.

The suggestion is ingenious and worthy of consideration. It is not possible here to enter into a detailed discussion of the many issues raised by Rudolph's treatment. There remain, however, some considerable doubts; first, reference to Lane's lexicon suggests that the only meaning which comes remotely close to that claimed for it by Rudolph (*viz.* 'to be greedy' etc.) is 'excited with lust' (of a stallion-camel or goat). Since that meaning is consistent with the notions of 'agitation', 'liveliness', 'sprightliness' (of the wind, humans, animals etc.) clearly attested for the verb, it is questionable whether Rudolph is right in his assertion that the word can denote 'greed'. Secondly, Prov 30.15 is notoriously obscure and doubt must attend any interpretations of it and so, *a fortiori*, any deductions made from it. Finally, there are a number of proposed emendations of which, perhaps, the most widely adopted is that of Duhm and Marti (cf. Wolff and Mays): זבח(ים) אהבו וְיִזבחו 'sacrifice(s) they love and sacrifice; meat (they love) and eat it'.

If Ephraim had multiplied altars (v. 11), here the nation is represented as indulging in uninterrupted, continuous, sacrificial feasting (note a). The explanatory gloss or early translation (note b) makes plain that Kimchi's observation is substantially correct:

usage is confirmed, then בשר in Hos. 8.13 could be taken as the object of the following ויאכלו. The passages in Job to which Gelston draws attention are: 4.6 (ותם דרכיך is the subject and תקותך the predicate, the *waw* being prefixed to the subject תם in second place); 5.27; 10.8; 14.20; 19.23; 39.12.

36 Amongst moderns, cf., e.g., Rosenmüller, Bauer, Ridderbos, König (*Wörterbuch*), BDB.

the sacrifices were of a sort with the *šlmym* 'peace-offerings' where, even if the intention was fellowship with God, the practical emphasis was upon devouring meat in lavish feasting. In this Yahweh has no pleasure just as, on the other side, the Ephraimites regard the principle requirements of his law as quite alien. The rupture between the two parties to the relationship is thus complete; the Ephraimites had shown no understanding of the requirements of their God and he, for his part, is consequently obliged to repudiate them. As in v. 10 *'th* 'now' represents the moment of judgement and it is expressed in relation to the whole attitude portrayed in vv. 11–13, *viz.* the constant ignoring of Yahweh's commands in favour of a withdrawal to the illusory comfort of the cult (after Rudolph). Thus Ephraim's guilt is now firmly in Yahweh's mind; it is evident to him; he 'remembers' it. So convinced, he is resolved to punish them for their sins. The verbs here are likely to reflect forensic usage[37] and they are used similarly in 7.2; 9.9 and in Jer 14.10. Yahweh's pronouncement is, then, like that of a judge who finds proven an indictment and who pronounces sentence on the culprit. As in 4.8 'guilt/transgression' is parallel to 'sins' and the terms imply 'offences in any sphere of life which render the culprit culpable and punishable' (so Wolff; cf. further 12.9, EV 8; 13.12; 14.2f).

That the specific punishment or sentence is recorded in the final phrase 'they shall return to Egypt' seems clear on a number of grounds: first, mention of Egypt and the nearby use of the verb *šwb* 'return' concludes the section 7.8–16 and it is likely that this prompted Hosea's redactor to add here the section 8.1–13 which has a similar ending (cf. Rudolph); secondly, 9.3 (cf. 11.5) uses the verb *šwb* 'return' in relation to Egypt, thereby suggesting an established theme of Hosea; thirdly, Deut 28.68, which is likely to be dependent upon Hosea, provides a clear presentation of the same theme; fourthly, the use of 'they' *hm(h)* as an indication of guilt is typical of Hosea (so Wolff; cf. 3.1; 4.14; 6.7; 7.13; 8.4, 9; 9.10; 13.2). For the contrary view, *viz.* that the words are a later addition, see Marti.

The question arises whether the sentence means that Yahweh will reverse his classical saving event[38], *viz.* the exodus from Egypt (cf. Deut 28.68) or whether the reference is to a more literal punishment of exile in Egypt, parallel indeed to the references to exile in Assyria (9.3, cf. 8.1, 3, 7, 10)[39]. In 7.16

37 Cf. B. S. Childs *Memory and Tradition in Israel* (London, 1962), pp. 32ff.

38 So especially Wolff, followed by Rudolph.

39 So, e.g., Harper.

Ephraim is stated not to have turned back (*šwb*) to higher things but rather to have offended Yahweh in Egypt by grossly disloyal overtures to that country. Verses 7.11ff. place this condemnation within the context of Ephraim's vacillating foreign policy. Chapter 8 seems to be more concerned with the threat from Assyria (1, 3, 7, 10) and this raises the further question whether Hosea is not referring to a new captivity (i.e. in Assyria) by reference to the classical captivity in Egypt. In answer to such questions, it seems likely that Hosea's words are framed by reference to the political realities of his time, in particular to the probability (cf. on 7.16) that Pekah made overtures to Egypt in 733 BC and, perhaps additionally, to Hoshea's overtures in 727 BC. Thus the term *šwb* 'return' is likely to evoke a 'return' to pro-Egyptian policy[40], contrasted indeed to the fundamental failure to 'return' to Yahweh (7.16). Mention of such a switch, in the context of material which mentions predominantly the disastrous results of a pro-Assyrian policy, may have been required by Ephraim's dilemma: thus, if she were to avoid annihilation at Assyria's hands, she must turn again to Egypt. At all events there can be no doubt that for Hosea the punishment fits the crime; or rather, the punishment is dictated in the very terms which were appropriate in describing the crime. If they do not 'return to higher things' (7.16) then they 'return' to Egypt (for help); so to Egypt they shall 'return'[41], i.e. to the classical slavery of exile from which, as a nation, they were born.

Text and Versions

זבחי הבהבי LXX θυσιαστήρια τὰ ἠγαπημένα 'well-loved altars', joined to v. 12; on this basis Vollers reads זבחים אהובים and Duhm, Marti, cf. Mays, *BHS* more boldly זֶבַח אָהֵבוּ (see note a (2) above); → כי אם יזבחו זבח (Borbone); Symm. θυσίας ἐπαλλήλους 'sacrifices one after another'; the rendering seems to be supported by ibn Janāḥ's treatment of the word, see note a (1) above; Aq. θυσίας φέρε φέρε 'sacrifices. Offer! Offer!', understanding הב הב as repeated imperatives of √יהב, cf. Vulg. *hostias adfer adfer*; for Kimchi's similar views, see under note a (2) above; Pesh. *dbḥ' dgbyt'* 'sacrifices of tributes'; Targ. דבחין דמגבן מן אונים 'they sacrifice what they seize by force'; Theod. θυσίας μεταφορῶν ? 'sacrifices of transferences' (*sc*. of ownership).

40 Cf., e.g., Jerome.

41 Jeremiah similarly makes play with the various nuances of the verb *šwb* cf. Jer 3.1; 4.4; 8.4ff, so Rudolph; we may add 4.8.

יזבחו Pesh., Aq. and Theod. construe with the preceding phrase; LXX διότι ἐὰν θύσωσιν θυσίαν (OL[S] plural) 'wherefore if they sacrifice a sacrifice (the Lord will not ...)'.

בשׂר ויאכלו LXX καὶ φάγωσιν κρέα, cf. Pesh. *wbsr' 'klyn* 'and eat flesh', on the basis of which Oettli reads ובשׂר יאכלו, but see fn. to note b.

יהוה לא רצם deleted as a gloss in *BHS*.

יזכר/ויפקד → אֶזכר//ואֶפקד, cf. 8.12 (*BHS*).

מצרים ישׁובו LXX adds καὶ ἐν Ἀσσυρίοις ἀκάθαρτα φάγονται after 9.3 (so Borbonne).

8.14 **And Israel forgot his creator[a] and built castles[b]; and Judah multiplied walled cities. But I will send fire upon his[c] cities, and it will consume the fortresses of each of them[d].**

[a]עשׂהו Cf., with Kimchi, Deut 32.6, where Israel's God is his 'father' who 'created him' and 'established him'; further, 1 Sam 12.6, where God 'made (i.e. gave you – so NEB) Moses and Aaron'; Kimchi comments 'Israel forgot Him who made him great and multiplied him'.

[b]The word היכלות can denote 'temples' (cf. the versions below) but the point here is clearly fortification (so ibn Ezra) and this is made clear from the second half of the verse (so Rudolph). The word is thought to be a loan word, *via* Accadian, ultimately from Sumerian *egal* 'great house', cf. BDB *ad loc.* G. A. Rendsburg argues (pp. 47ff) that the sense 'palace' as opposed to 'temple' is distinctive of northern Hebrew. Some scepticism is in order.

[c]The suffix is likely to denote Israel's (i.e. Ephraim's and Judah's) cities; see further under note d below. The association of Israel with castles and Judah with walled cities is stylistic and not literal (so, e.g., Wolff, Rudolph).

[d]Lit. 'her fortresses'. The antecedent to the feminine suffix is ערים 'cities' and the singular suffix has a distributive force, cf. König, 348g, h and, with *BHS*, Amos 1.7; 10.14.

The verse has been regarded as a late addition on the grounds that its contents are not of a sort with what precedes; that Judah is mentioned only here in the chapter (cf. *BHS*); that the notion of Yahweh as 'creator' is later than Deutero-Isaiah; and that 14b appears to be a quotation of Amos 1.4 (see, e.g., Wellhausen, Marti and Jeremias).

An alternative and better treatment is that of Wolff and Rudolph who understand the verse as a genuine oracle of Hosea, earlier than 8.1–13, but added at this point by Hosea's redactor in conformity with Hosea's own ideas and intentions. The interpretation is made possible in the light of the following considerations. First, reference to the building of fortified cities and castles hardly fits the period, *c.* 735 BC onwards. Attention at this time was directed largely if not exclusively to international politics and defence policy was associated with attempts to win the protection of foreign powers[42]. More likely is the supposition that the verse reflects the prosperous times of Jeroboam II and his contemporary in Judah, Uzziah, to whose many fortified buildings 2 Chr 26.9ff refers.

The argument that 14b contains a formula used by Amos (1.4, 7, 10, 14; 2.2) is not conclusive against the authenticity of 14b: the formula has all the marks of stereotype (cf., with Rudolph, Num 16.35; 21.28; Judg 9.15); in Amos it is used to define specifically the punishment of foreign atrocities whereas building operations by Israel are condemned as part of Amos' attack on the immorality of the luxurious rich; in this connection he states that the buildings will never be enjoyed since they will be destroyed (3.15; 5.11; 6.8). Hosea, on the other hand, condemns Israel's building operations as an indication that the nation has rejected its creator, and it is to this offence that he applies the stereotype of destruction by fire.

Kimchi's assessment of the meaning of the term 'creator' (note a) does much to counter the argument that the term was not used until the time of Deutero-Isaiah (44.2; 51.13; 54.5). If Deut 32.6 can describe Israel's God as his father, who has created and established him, then this description is close indeed to Hos 11.1 and 13.4, where the exodus is seen as an act of paternal love which brought into being and constituted the nation.

Verse 14, then, reflects Hosea's condemnation of (all) Israel's reliance upon her own resources (cf. 1.5) and, with it, refusal to turn to her God. The particular circumstances within the period of Jeroboam II and Uzziah of Judah which prompted Hosea to utter it are not known to us. In that the saying contains the word 'multiplied' Hosea (or, more likely, his redactor) was furnished with a catchword which prompted him to link the saying with v. 11 where 'Ephraim multiplied altars'. The link, prompted indeed by the catchword, is not, however, solely dependent upon

42 *Contra* Emmerson (p. 76) who refers the verse with its mention of Judah to the situation of the Syro-Ephraimite war; her view that 'palaces' reflects Ephraimite monarchical independence from Judah and 'walled cities' Judaean hostility to Ephraim is far-fetched and is based *inter alia* upon a mistaken view of the meaning of *hyklwt*, see note b above.

it, for there is clearly unity of thought as between the verse and the material that precedes it: Ephraim's history of arrogant self-delusion and lack of proper reliance upon her God is reflected in her false estimate of politics, both internal and external, and in her misuse of the cult and her fundamental idolatry, as well as in the earlier reliance of all Israel (including Judah) upon the strengthening of military fortifications and defences. Such reliance was one factor which contributed to and was of a sort with the present disastrous *Zeitgeist* in Ephraim where Yahweh was forgotten, cf. 2.15 (EV 13).

Text and Versions

היכלות LXX τεμένη 'sacred precincts'; cf. Vulg. *delubra* and Targ. היכלין לטעותא 'temples for idols'.

ארמנתיה LXX τὰ θεμέλια αὐτῶν 'their foundations'; → ארמנתיהן (Grätz).

CHAPTER 9.1–9

THE EFFECTS OF YAHWEH'S SENTENCE OF JUDGEMENT

The section has been seen (by, e.g., Wolff and Rudolph) as a collection of Hosea's own words delivered to those assembled for a particular celebration of the great autumnal festival. The date is considered to be in the short time following the Assyrian invasion of 733 BC and the period of rapid internal revolutions which ended with Hoshea's consolidation of the throne in 731 BC. Exuberant rejoicing at a successful harvest, on this view, marks the resumption of carefree attitudes and self-deception concerning the realities of the situation. It is pointed out that the setting is not known (so Rudolph) and that it could have been any one of Bethel, Gilgal, Shiloh or Samaria (so Wolff; he opts tentatively for the last).

Considerable difficulties are presented by this general view. Not least among them is that occasioned by the perplexing changes of personal pronouns within the section. If the words reflect an oracle delivered by Hosea at a particular festival, it is difficult indeed to understand why so many of them are in the third person (singular and plural). It seems unlikely that Wolff is correct in pressing such evidence to his conclusion that the whole piece reflects a public verbal dispute from which Hosea's own words, by the express intention of his disciples, alone were recorded; or that Hosea speaks his words about Israel in the third person specifically to his disciples but in the presence of the culpable, as though to an assembled court. His conclusions are as unconvincing as his reasoning is tortuous.

A further problem is identified by Rudolph in respect of v. 1 in which verbs and a pronominal suffix are second singular masculine but refer to Israel's rôle as a promiscuous woman. He notes that, without changing the consonantal text (other than by adding a *yodh* to *tśmḥ*, which *yodh* could have been lost by haplography), it would be possible to change the pointing and read second singular feminine forms. He is inclined, however, to follow the third feminine singular form of v. 2 (*bh*), and to consider the more radical solution of reading third feminine singular forms throughout v. 1. The difficulties which Rudolph describes are, perhaps, more apparent than real (see on v. 1 below) though they emphasise the importance of the endeavour to furnish a satisfactory account of the section.

In attempting such an account the following points may be made: first, the majority of the verses are in the third person[1], and appeals in the second person (vv. 1, 5, 7b) appear to be interjections based upon the contents of the material which follows or precedes them. The substance of the section, then, consists of the threats and judgements pronounced in the third person by the prophet as opposed to chapters 8 and 9.10f where divine speech constitutes the predominant form. Secondly, the piece as a whole seems to be linked redactionally to chapter 8 by the repetition (or near repetition) in vv. 3b and 9b of what is said in 8.13b (cf. Rudolph). There the phrase 'now he will remember their guilt and punish their sins. They shall return to Egypt' marks the moment of Yahweh's decisive intervention in response to the nation's political treachery and simultaneous infatuation with the cult. Now, reference to the contents of the judgements of 9.1–9, written in the third person, suggests the theme that henceforth the Ephraimites will no longer worship Yahweh on his land in thanksgiving for his gifts of plenty in the harvest; rather they will lead the miserable life of captivity in Egypt or Assyria. Indeed 'the days of reckoning, of retribution are come' (v. 7); the phrase indicates the effect of Yahweh's intervention, announced so powerfully in 8.13b. Ephraim's self-indulgent reliance upon the cult is replaced by a situation in which there can be no more cult at all for the covenant is abrogated and with it the blessings of harvest and well-being.

Hosea's words have all the hallmarks of a meditation upon the implications of Yahweh's sentence of judgement in 8.13b into which he has placed (in vv. 1, 5 and 7b) appeals to Israel to take to heart the effect that the punishment will have upon what was the covenant people. The phrases in the second person, then, express the anguish of Hosea for his lost nation. If this estimate of the piece is correct, then it follows that attempts on the basis of the opening words 'rejoice not, Israel ...' to find recollections of a speech made by Hosea on a particular occasion are mistaken. Rather, the piece is meditative and systematic in character, communicated perhaps to the company of his disciples in common with (the very different) chapter 1. That accords with the element of personal experience which obtrudes so briefly in vv. 7f. The reaction of the nation to his announcement of Yahweh's sentence of judgement (whether that of chapter 8 or more generally) is itself the object of retrospective meditation and is judged to constitute an occasion of further self-destructive sinfulness.

[1] Thus: vv. 2–4, singular and plural; vv. 6, 7, 9 plural; v. 8, singular.

9.1 **Do not give yourself, Israel, to exuberant rejoicing[a] like other peoples[b]. For [c]you have acted promiscuously in betrayal of your God[c]. You loved the presents[d] given you [e]on every threshing-floor heaped with corn[e].**

[a]Lit. 'Israel, do not rejoice unto exuberance', the jussive תשׂמח being masculine singular. The expression is confirmed by Job 3.22 where השׂמחים אלי גיל has a similar but, in that particular context, different sense. The root גול/גיל is interpreted by Saadya and ibn Janāḥ (on Ps 2.11) by reference to the Arabic word *ṭrb* and is given by them the meaning 'physical agitation' manifested both by the happy, exhilarated person and also by the sad, afflicted person (for the latter, see 10.5 below). For a full discussion of the evidence, see A. A. Macintosh *JTS* NS 27 (1976), pp. 1ff. For other treatments involving emendation, see Text and Versions below.

[b]Lit. 'like the peoples'. The point of the comparison is that other peoples have not acted in the deceitful way that Israel has done and, therefore, are entitled to rejoice as she is not (so ibn Ezra, Kimchi; cf. Jer 2.10f). There is no need to understand the phrase (so Wellhausen, Wolff) as denoting the 'heathen', nor yet to emend the text to read גיל כנענים '(do not rejoice) with Canaanite joy' (so Richter, followed by Rudolph), notwithstanding the fact that the word גיל is often associated with Canaanite practices and therefore seems to have been avoided by a number of biblical writers (so Wolff).

[c—c]Lit. 'you have whored away from your God', the personal pronouns being singular.

[d]אתנן is used here collectively; it is to be derived from the root תנה as is the rarer אתנה and means the fee or 'present' given to a prostitute; see on 2.14 (EV 12) and 8.9f above.

[e—e] Lit. 'upon all threshing-floors of grain'.

The verse is in the form of a second singular masculine negative command, 'Do not give yourself to exuberant rejoicing' followed by the reason 'for you have acted promiscuously ...'. Within the context, however, of a meditative exploration of the effect of Yahweh's sentence of judgement (see above), the words have the effect of distinct assurance (GK 109e, 110c), 'you shall not (any more) give yourself to rejoicing', 'there will be no more rejoicing'. Rather than constituting a quotation of the prophet's word to an assembled company, then, the verse expresses the prophet's considered view of the effect of Yahweh's judgement upon his people.

Exuberant rejoicing (note a) is likely to reflect the uninhibited worship of ancient Israel (Deut 16.14; Lev 23.40) particularly at the great autumnal festival, 'the feast of Yahweh' (cf. Judg

21.19; Lev 23.39) as it is called in v. 5 below. It is this, the natural rejoicing over the harvest, that is to cease for the reason that the produce of the land will become attenuated or will fail and its inhabitants will have no opportunity or occasion to give thanks to their God. Verses 3f make it clear that it is the expression of thanks to Yahweh that is to cease (cf. Mays). The view, then, that mention of exuberant worship reflects, in this instance, Hosea's condemnation of the syncretistic, Canaanite quality of the cult is mistaken (*contra*, e.g., Wolff, Rudolph). That the people are here styled 'Israel' seems to confirm this assessment, for by the term the prophet described the nation as a cultic covenant community before Yahweh (cf. with Wolff, 4.15; 8.2f, 6; 9.10; 10.1; 11.1; 12.14, EV 13; 13.1; 14.2).

If Israel's worship is to cease, that is because, unlike other nations (note b), Israel alone has behaved outrageously in deceiving its God. It is the unique crime of Israel which is here the cause of its unique punishment. Israel has forfeited its identity, its place as a nation among other nations and, with it, its opportunity to express its identity in praise of its God.

Israel's crime is the crime of fundamental disloyalty, expressed by Hosea by means of his all-important analogy with a (and his) wife's unfaithfulness. Since 'Israel' defines the covenant people of Yahweh expressed in terms of the eponymous forefather, it is natural that the masculine gender should be used. The comparison or metaphor is constituted by subsequent use of the verbs used in the masculine but appropriate to the activities of an unfaithful wife (*contra* Rudolph). The essential fact is that Israel (Yahweh's people) has acted with outrageous infidelity and in that respect is like a faithless wife (cf. 4.15). The whole construction has some similarity with the more clearly attested syntax of *comparatio decurtata* (GK 118r). There is no need to question the phrase as a possible gloss (cf. *BHS*).

As the unfaithful wife of the comparison enjoys the 'presents' (note d) of her lovers (cf. 2.7, 10, 14; EV 5, 8, 12), Israel had been maliciously disposed to regard the corn of the threshing-floors as an expression of appreciation to her (*sic* emphasising the metaphor) on the part of her lovers, the Baals. Hence the autumnal festivals on which Yahweh's people should properly have thanked him for his bounty, had become occasions of despicable ungratefulness (so Rudolph). It is for this reason (cf. 2.9–13, EV 7–11) that from now on there will be no possibility of thanking Yahweh for he will no longer vouchsafe to grant in the harvests what had been, all along, his own gracious gifts.

The threshing-floor is mentioned as the place where the corn-harvest reached its final stage. Frequently built on higher ground so as to facilitate the wind's action in winnowing, threshing-floors were naturally places associated with achievement and merriment (cf. Ruth 3.3f, 6f). Rashi (cf. AF) may have a point in his supposition that such places at such times were naturally (if reprehensibly) scenes of prostitution. More doubtful is the suggestion of Marti and Wolff (cf. Kimchi) that threshing-floors served as formal cultic sites; for this there is no clear evidence (cf. Rudolph). Hosea's point is that Israel's meretricious attitude was displayed and fostered by the facile exuberance of these places. Here was nurtured the carefree preoccupation with immediate self-gratification which led Israel to forget Yahweh and promiscuously to attribute the immediate blessings of harvest to her (*sic*) appreciative lovers, the Baals (cf. 2.7, EV 5).

Text and Versions

אל־גיל LXX μηδὲ εὐφραίνου 'neither exult', cf. Vulg. *noli exultare*, Pesh. *wl' tdwṣ* and Targ. לא תבועון; → אַל תָּגֵל (Marti, so *BHS* and Borbone); Harper omits אל גיל as gloss; → אַל גִּיל לָךְ 'you shall have no joy', Eitan *HUCA* 14 (1939), p. 2; Rudolph omits אל as a dittograph and sees in שמח/גיל a *figura etymologica* by which the noun שמחה, cognate with the verb שמח, is replaced by the synonym גיל; it is difficult to see why such a figure of speech should have been coined and the evidence of Job 3.22 is more telling, see note a above.

כעמים Some MSS of Kennicott and de Rossi read בעמים; the reading does not require a substantially different translation; for 'in company with' (e.g. BDB p. 89, col 1 III 1 a) is little different from 'like'; all the versions imply כעמים.

על כל Pesh. *mn kwl* 'from every'.

דגן Not apparently represented in Pesh.; Gelston's suggestion (p. 133) that the omission may be more apparent than real finds some support in the fact that *'dr* is attested with the meaning 'corn' as well as threshing-floor, cf. Payne-Smith *ad loc.* Harper omits דגן as a dittography of גרן in v. 2.

9.2 **Threshing-floor and vat[a] will not give attention to them[b], and the new wine[a] will disappoint[c] them[d].**

[a]See on 2.10 above. Kimchi notes that גרן 'threshing-floor' implies a single specific end-product, i.e. bread, whereas יקב 'vat' was used both for storing (eating) grapes and the wine pressed from grapes. Mention, then, of תירוש 'new wine' serves as an additional stipulation. Wolff, Mays, Rudolph, noticing the same phenomena, understand יקב 'vat' as

an allusion here to the storing of olive oil (cf. Joel 2.24) so that the verse alludes to the three staple end-products, bread, wine and olive oil. Reference to *AUS* 4, 207 (cf. Barrois I, p. 330) suggests caution. In 2.11 (EV 9), 7.14 corn and wine are mentioned without oil.

[b]The meaning given to ירעם accords with the root styled רעה III by BDB p. 946, col 2. Though he does not mention the present verse, ibn Janāḥ discusses the word רעה in Hos 12.2 giving it the meanings[2] 'thought', 'review', 'attention' (Arabic *'lfkr w'ltfqqd w'lr''yt*). The third of these translations makes use of the cognate Arabic root *r'y* which is clearly attested as having such meanings (see Lane 3 p. 1108, col 3) in addition to that attested for רעה I 'to pasture', 'graze' (of flocks etc., cf. BDB p. 944, col 2). Ibn Janāḥ recognises that this meaning is like that of the Aramaic noun רעיונין 'thoughts' in Dn 2.29 and with this Rudolph (independently) appears to agree by his tentative suggestion that the verb here is an Aramaism, akin to Hebrew רצה 'to favour'. The evidence from ibn Janāḥ, however, may be held to suggest that Hosea's usage reflects his own Hebrew dialect rather than an Aramaism and that that usage may be illustrated by reference to the Arabic and Aramaic roots *r'y*[3]. Ibn Ezra appears to confirm the interpretation of ibn Janāḥ by his comment (on 9.1) that threshing-floor and wine-vat will not pay attention to them (יכירם). The meanings so commonly attested for standard Hebrew רעה, *viz.* 'to pasture', 'tend', 'feed', 'graze' (i.e. according to BDB, רעה I) hardly fit a context in which threshing-floor and (especially) wine-vat are the subjects. With the meaning 'feed', 'graze' the verb is usually intransitive and if an object is supplied it denotes what is grazed, i.e. consumed (BDB p. 945, col 1 2). The active meaning is properly 'to pasture', 'tend' (i.e. a flock or animals) and there is no evidence for the sense 'to nourish', 'provide for'; when this meaning is claimed for the phrase in question, commentators (e.g. Rudolph) are obliged, in the absence of any clear parallel, to resort to special pleading[4]. It is not surprising, then, that some other commentators (e.g. Nyberg, Wolff) have sought to derive the word from רעה II 'to associate with' (BDB p. 945, col 2) and have suggested: 'threshing-floor and wine-vat will not befriend them'. Again there is no clear parallel for such an alleged meaning and the suggestion is significant rather for its attempt to find a suitable meaning than its inherent plausibility.

[2] He cites also Eccles 1.14; 2.22. Cf. also Hos 10.15.

[3] The question arises whether modern lexica are right in distinguishing homonymous roots; it is arguable in the light of this evidence that at least רעה I and III are the same root having different but related meanings (i.e. 'think' → 'pay attention' (to animals) → 'tend', 'pasture', 'graze'). For ibn Barūn's comments on the root, see Wechter, p. 120; see also Barr *CPOT*, pp. 281f.

[4] Cf. G. W. Ahlström *VT* 11 (1961), p. 116, who sees in threshing-floor and wine-vat mere symbols of fertility gods who, then, are appropriate subjects of the verb 'to tend', 'pasture' with the people as its object.

[c]The verb כחש followed by the preposition ב indicates that the paucity of the product will disappoint the expectations of the people, cf., with ibn Janāḥ, Hab 3.17.

[d]Lit. 'her'. The third feminine singular pronominal suffix is used in reference to the collective notion of the nation (cf. Kimchi) perhaps under the influence of the verb 'you have acted promiscuously' in 9.1 (e.g. Wolff, Rudolph); Kimchi cites 2 Kgs 3.4 as another similar instance. All the ancient versions (see Text and Versions) translate by a third masculine plural pronoun in simplification *ad sensum*, as above.

The verse describes in poetic form the effects of Yahweh's imminent action in withholding the fertility of his land (cf. 2.11; EV 9). Threshing-floor and wine-vat[5] will cease to furnish Yahweh's people with the benefits to which they were accustomed; in this sense they will no longer show consideration or pay attention to the people's needs; they will not fulfil their function (see note b). Similarly, the new wine, the product of the wine-vats, will disappoint the people's expectations (note c) by reason of its poor quality. The same thought is expressed in full form by Hag 2.16 'if a man came to a wine-vat to draw fifty measures, he found but twenty' (so Kimchi). If Yahweh is the instigator of this failure of the land's fertility, the mode of his action is not made explicit. For Kimchi the verse points simply to the operation of Yahweh's curse. Qyl, quoting Deut 28.38f and 33, suggests as alternatives the action of pests or of foreign invaders. The contents of the following verse may be said to favour the latter. At any rate, the verse depicts an aspect of the inevitable consequences of Yahweh's breaking his covenant with his people. As the God of the land, he is the controller of its fertility and he will withhold what previously he had graciously given to his people (cf., again, 2.10f, EV 8f).

Text and Versions

לא ירעם LXX οὐκ ἔγνω αὐτούς 'did not know them' (cf., perhaps, note b above); Wellhausen, Marti, Harper *et al.*, cf. *BHS*, propose יְדָעֵם/יֵדָעֵם on the basis of this reading; Vulg. *non pascet eos* 'will not feed them'; Pesh. *l' nsb'wn* 'they will not be satisfied (from the threshing-floor)', cf. Targ. לא יתזנון 'they will not be nourished (from threshing-floor.)'; both versions, being free renderings, necessitate the introduction of the preposition מן 'from'.

[5] Properly a trough dug out of the rock and connected by a channel to the treading trough (*gt*); the grape-juice flows from the latter into the former; *AUS* 4, pp. 354ff and illustration 103.

יכחש LXX ἐψεύσατο (αὐτούς) 'deceived (them)', cf. Vulg. *mentietur*; Pesh. *wmšḥ' nkdb* 'and oil (*sic*) shall deceive (them)'; Targ. לא יסופיק '(wine) will not be sufficient (for them)'.

בה All the ancient versions render by a third masculine plural.; Bab. Cod. reads בם and hence a large number of scholars adopt this reading (cf. Harper *ad loc.*); but see note d above.

9.3 **They shall not stay[a] in Yahweh's land. Ephraim shall go back to Egypt, and in Assyria they[b] shall eat heathen[c] food.**

[a]For this sense of the verb ישב, cf., with Qyl, Exod 23.33.

[b]The plural verb יאכלו follows the singular collective in the preceding clause as frequently (cf. 7.11; 8.5, 8; 9.16 and GK 145g).

[c]Lit. 'unclean'; for the translation 'heathen', see below.

Alienation from Yahweh will have as its consequence not merely the failure of the land's fertility but the eviction from it of its wayward inhabitants. Ephraim is no longer Israel (cf. v. 1), Yahweh's people. The land, however, is Yahweh's as Hosea here states quite explicitly and for the first time among the prophetic writings (cf. 8.1, where it is called the 'House of Yahweh'). Since it is his land his control is complete, over both fertility and inhabitants. The indissoluble connection between Yahweh and his land is here properly stressed and, as Kimchi observes, the consequence of the people's folly is that the land will evict them, 'will spew them forth' in the words of Lev 18.25. Accordingly the Ephraimites will be obliged to return to Egypt in explicit reversal of the theme of the exodus, cf. with Kimchi, Exod 14.13; Deut 28.68; see on 8.13 above. It is likely that the historical realities of the time (again, see on 8.13 above) prompted Hosea to define specifically the implications of his theme (see p. 275 above) and, for the first time, he explicitly mentions Assyria as an alternative place of exile, a new exemplar of the classical 'house of bondage'. 'To eat unclean food in Assyria' emphasises the people's utter exclusion from Yahweh's land of joy and gladness and the sentiment is akin to that expressed in Ps 137.1–4. For unclean food in a foreign land, cf. Ezek 4.13; for a foreign land described as an 'unclean' (NEB rightly 'heathen') land', cf. Amos 7.17.

Text and Versions

לא ישבו LXX οὐ κατῴκησαν 'they did not dwell', reading יָשְׁבוּ.

וישב LXX κατῴκησεν 'dwelt', reading יָשַׁב, surprisingly in view of 8.13 where the verb is rendered correctly. The mistake probably arose in view of 3a.

9.4 **They shall not pour out libations of wine to Yahweh; their sacrifices[a] shall not be performed[b] in his honour[c]. [d]Theirs is food[d] of mourning[e]; all who partake of it will render themselves unclean. ([f]For their food shall serve merely to satisfy their appetite[g]; it will not come into Yahweh's house[f].)**

[a]The accent *segholta* is placed upon the word לו, indicating that the word 'sacrifices' should be read with what follows it, i.e. 'their sacrifices are like bread of mourning'. Accordingly in the MT (cf. LXX, Vulgate, ibn Ezra and Kimchi) the subject of the verb יערבו is presumably to be understood from the preceding phrase (i.e. 'libations'): 'they shall not pour libations and (even if they did) they would not be pleasing to him' (so ibn Ezra, cf. Kimchi). It seems better, however, to follow the Peshiṭta (cf. perhaps the Targum) and to take 'sacrifices' as the subject of the verb יערבו though the construction of the following phrase is, admittedly, difficult (see d–d below).

[b]The ancient versions and the rabbinic commentators are unanimous in understanding the verb to mean 'their libations or sacrifices (see note a above) will not be pleasing to him'. (For ערב III with this sense, see, e.g., BDB p. 787, col 1). Malachi 3.4 and Jer 6.20 (NB 'your sacrifices', i.e. with suffix, are the subject) furnish telling evidence in favour of this view of the matter. It seems likely that the phrase reflects technical, cultic language[6] and that 'to be pleasing to God' means here 'done correctly in his honour' (so ibn Janāḥ on Mal 3.4, Arabic *wyḥsn 'ndh*). Accordingly, on this view of the phrase, Hosea means that the Ephraimites' sacrifices (i.e. slaughtering for meat) will not be done in Yahweh's honour since, banished from the land, they will eat meat without the possibility or intention of worshipping ('pleasing') him (*contra* Rudolph's arguments).

An alternative translation is that based on G. R. Driver's suggestion[7] that the verb, comparable with the Old South Arabian and Syriac cognates, was capable of the meaning 'to offer' (gifts/sacrifices). He renders 'they will not offer their sacrifices to him'. In this connection, Driver draws attention to the LXX's rendering of the phrase מִי עָרַב אֶת לִבּוֹ in Jer 30.21. On this latter phrase (he makes no comment on Hos

[6] Cf., with Wolff, von Rad *Theology* I, p. 261 (EV only).
[7] See H. H. Rowley (ed.) *OTP*, pp. 64f.

9.4) ibn Janāḥ comments that its meaning is 'who has arranged, set in order, corrected his heart (so as to be fit to approach God)'. If Driver's theory is correct[8], the nearest approximation to Hosea's usage (and it is only an approximation) is likely to be found in these words of Jeremiah.

On balance, it seems to me better to follow the traditional understanding of the verb. At least one particular consideration favours this course, 'their sacrifices' (i.e. with suffix) seems somewhat clumsy and *de trop* in Hebrew as the object of the third person plural verb. By contrast the same verb, having 'sacrifices' (with pronominal suffix) as its subject is clearly attested elsewhere.

[c]Lit. 'to/for' him; see note a above.

[d—d]When 'sacrifices' is taken with the preceding phrase (notes a and b) the difficulty immediately arises that there appears to be no subject of which the phrase in question is the predicate. Accordingly, since Kuenen's[9] time, לָהֶם has frequently been emended to לַחְמָם 'their food is like food of mourning' (cf. *BHS*). A second solution (cf. Wolff, Qyl and possibly the Targum) is to understand 'sacrifices' to be the implied subject with which the phrase in question is somewhat loosely juxtaposed. The difficulty presents itself that the suffix to the following participle 'those that eat it' is clearly singular and is unlikely to refer to (plural) sacrifices as an antecedent.

It is here assumed that the כ preceding 'bread', 'food' is *kaph veritatis* (GK 118x) and that the word להם denotes possession. The phrase will have the literal meaning 'to them is veritable bread of mourning', i.e. 'theirs is food of mourning'. For the terse, emphatic nature of phrases construed with *kaph veritatis*, cf. 1 Sam 20.3; Lam 1.20; Isa 13.6; Hos 5.10.

[e]The word אונים is understood to be an abstract plural noun having the sense 'mourning'. Ibn Janāḥ derives the word from a root און[10] and compares for this sense Gen 35.18; Job 21.19; Deut 26.14 (so, for Deut 26.14, ibn Ezra and Kimchi). Rudolph and Qyl prefer to follow Gesenius-Buhl in deriving the word from the root אנה I 'to mourn' (BDB p. 58, col 1) on the grounds that this verb is more clearly attested with this sense. Accordingly a noun אֻנָּה is posited with the meaning '(time of) mourning' or else the word is parsed as the plural masculine participle 'those in mourning' (so Rudolph, cf. the Vulgate). In view of the well-attested phenomenon of by-forms of the type הום/המה it seems

[8] It seems to me that some doubt attaches at least to his appeal to Syriac, since the meaning he adduces ('delivered goods after sale') is hardly close to 'offer', 'present (sacrifices)'.

[9] *National Religions*, pp. 312f.

[10] Cf., e.g., BDB p. 19, col 2; p. 20, col 1.

rash (particularly in respect of Hosea) to dismiss the possibility that the root און was capable of the meaning clearly attested for אנה[11].

[f–f]The words are regarded as an exilic addition to the text, see below.

[g]Lit. 'for their food is for their appetite'. For נפש with the force 'throat', 'appetite', cf., e.g., Wolff on 4.8.

The theme of alienation from Yahweh and his land is developed in relation to cultic matters and to food (cf. on 3.4 above). No longer will the Ephraimites, banished from Yahweh's land, be able to worship him, 'to eat and drink before him' (Exod 24.11), i.e. to enter into joyful fellowship with him by means of cultic meals which included, as an important element, the use of wine (cf., with Qyl, Num 15.2ff). To be exiled from the land necessarily involves being cut off from the worship of the God of the land. It is thus impossible to offer such worship in a heathen (i.e. unclean) land where other gods hold sway. The sentiment is accurately reflected in the later cry of misery, 'How shall we sing Yahweh's song in a strange land?' (Ps 137.4). In these circumstances all eating and drinking is divorced from the joyful worship of Yahweh and, as the gloss (see below) of 9.4b rightly comments, these activities will serve only to satisfy the physical appetite (note g) of the exiles. Indeed their food in exile may be characterised as in all respects (note d–d) 'food of mourning'. As may be inferred from Num 19.11ff; Deut 26.14, death rendered a whole household unclean and its members were, for the time being, cut off from the holiness of Yahweh's presence. Accordingly the food brought (Jer 16.7) to a household in mourning was consumed in a totally secular way and served merely to satisfy the physical needs of its members. The exiles' food and drink will, then, constantly and invariably partake of the joyless, secular character of the mourning institutions known to them from their days in the land. Such meals necessarily render unclean the partakers; they are debarred *ipso facto* and necessarily from the presence of Yahweh. The alienation is total and complete. To be exiled from the presence of Yahweh in his land is to be sentenced to a living death.

Mention of 'Yahweh's House' in 4b has generally led to the conclusion that the words (note f–f) are a later gloss. There can be no doubt that *byt yhwh* denotes the temple and that Hosea, knowing a multiplicity of open-air sanctuaries, could not have spoken of any one in such terms. Elsewhere (8.1; 9.15) Hosea

[11] It is worth recording that ibn Barūn (Wechter, p. 69) compares אנה with Arabic *'nn* 'to groan', 'moan'.

uses the phrase to denote Yahweh's land, but this meaning can hardly be said to fit the context here. More likely, then, is the view that the words as a whole are an explanatory gloss which serves to expound the meaning of Hosea's words but in the light of later experience and understanding (cf. Rudolph). Jeremiah 29.5ff constitutes evidence that the prophets in exilic times could envisage ordinary life in exile conducted in patient discipline and without the possibility of the cultic worship of Yahweh. Deut 12.15ff is clear evidence for the growth from Josiah's time of the legitimation of the secular slaughter of meat for food[12]; such was a necessary part of the law of the single sanctuary. Exodus 23.19 and Lev 23.9ff make use of the phrase under consideration in respect of the first-fruits which, offered to God, sanctified the whole subsequent produce. Commenting, then, on Hosea's words, the glossator seeks to turn them to fit the cultic codes of the exile whose contents and purpose were to inculcate reverence for the House of Yahweh in Jerusalem and to nourish hope in its restoration to its proper function (cf. Ezek 40ff)[13]. The daily food of exilic times is thus merely for nourishment and such disciplined use of it is alone consistent with the hope that one day the whole produce of the land of Israel will be sanctified and used in Yahweh's worship in his reconstituted, holy Temple.

Text and Versions

לא יערבו לו (זבחיהם) LXX οὐχ ἥδυναν αὐτῷ (OL^S *eis*) 'they have not pleased him', cf. Vulg. *non placebunt ei* (Jerome 'they will not please him, neither what they offer nor those who make the offering. Heathen sacrifices are bread of mouring'), taking 'offerings' with what follows, cf. MT; Pesh. *l' nbsmwn lh dbḥyhwn* 'their offerings will not please him', cf. Targ. לא יתקבלון לרעוא קורבנהון ודבחיהון (כלחים) 'their offerings will not be received with favour. And their sacrifices will be like (abominable bread)', where 'offerings/sacrifices' are taken as the subject of the verbs answering to יערבו.

(כלחם) אנים LXX (ἄρτος) πένθους, cf. Pesh. *d'wlṣn'* '(bread of) mourning', 'affliction'; Vulg. *lugentium* 'of mourners'; Targ. מרחק 'unclean', 'abominable' (cf. Cathcart, p. 48 n. 11).

להם → לַחְמָם 'their bread' (*BHS*, cf. note d).

לנפשם Targ. interprets 'since their offerings for (על; Kimchi, 'on behalf of', 'in atonement for') their own souls will not atone for them in the sanctuary of the Lord'.

[12] Cf. von Rad *Theology* 1, p. 83 (*Theologie*, p. 91).
[13] Cf. von Rad *Theology* 2, p. 296 (*Theologie*, pp. 308ff).

9.5 **What preparations will you make[a] on[b] festal days[c], at the time[b] of Yahweh's festival[d]?**

[a]So Qyl (cf. Wolff) comparing Exod 10.25 where עשה ליהוה means to prepare sacrifices for Yahweh. Rudolph prefers the more general and literal sense, 'What will you do ...?' on the grounds that 'prepare' is suitable only to priests who are not specifically addressed here. The objection is over-scrupulous. In the context of Hosea's strong assurance that (cultic) worship of Yahweh will henceforth be quite impossible for all (cf. AF), it is natural that he should use words without pedantic accuracy. For ibn Ezra mention of Yahweh's festival specifically implies sacrifices and picks up the reference to them in the previous verse.

[b]*lamedh temporis* cf., with Rudolph, König, 331f.

[c]Cf. on 2.13, note e. The term is more general than that which follows and, being indefinite, is used collectively (cf. Rudolph). The nation's major festivals are in the prophet's mind.

[d]From the more general to the specific; here the phrase is definite and, unlike 2.13, חג refers to the festival of Yahweh, i.e. the great autumnal festival. Since this festival lasted more than one day, יום is here likely to denote 'time', cf. BDB p. 399, col 2 6.

The abrupt change from third person plural to second person represents the prophet's *cri de cœur* designed to bring home to the Ephraimites the tragic effect for them of exile and alienation from Yahweh and his land (see the introductory remarks to chapter 9). The rhetorical question has the effect of a strong denial (so AF) 'in exile you will make no preparations for the joyful worship of Yahweh since there this is totally precluded'. As the festivals come round, with their appointed times and seasons, the people will feel the full force of their exile and its concomitant sense of desolation. In particular the time (notes b and d) of the great autumnal festival, the festival of Yahweh (cf. Lev 23.39; Judg 21.19), normally a time of special rejoicing (Lev 23.40; Deut 16.14; Judg 21.21) and lasting a number of days, will serve to emphasise to the Ephraimites their utter dereliction.

Rashi (cf. Kimchi) sees in the words further menace; thus, the יום מועד 'festal-day' is, by reference to the root יעד 'to appoint', capable of suggesting 'the time fixed for the enemy to be assembled against you' and חג 'feast', with its inherent notion of sacrifice/slaughter, denotes the slaughter that God has 'appointed for you'.

Text and Versions

No significant readings.

9.6 **For, [a]behold, they may have[a] fled[b] destruction, yet[a] Egypt will make an end[c] of them, Memphis[d] will bury them. [e]For all their vaunted silver[e], thistles[f] will be their successors, thorns in their dwellings[g].**

[a—a]The particle הנה introduces a 'truth upon which some proposal or suggestion is to be founded', BDB p. 244, col 1 b (*a*). The sense is not far from the conditional 'if they have fled.', so BDB p. 244, col 2 (top).

[b]*Sic ad sensum*; הלך מן lit. 'to go (away)', 'depart from', BDB p. 231, cols 1 (bottom), 2 (top).

[c]Cf. on 8.10 above.

[d]מף This Egyptian city, capital of Lower Egypt, lay some 20–30 kms south of Cairo on the west bank of the Nile, opposite modern Helwan. The name *mn-nfr*, pronounced conventionally *men-nefer*, applied originally to the pyramid of Pepi (Phiops) I and means '(Pepi is) established and perfect'. Thereafter the name spread over the entire city. In Assyrian it is called Mêmpi and in Greek (so LXX) Μέμφις. Elsewhere in the OT it is called נֹף/'Noph', probably a contraction, i.e. *(Men-)nóf(er)*, but close to the official pronunciation[14]. For Hosea's מף/'Moph' and a similar variation between נ/*n* and מ/*m* in a proper noun, Kimchi draws attention to the name כמהם/כמהן in 2 Sam 19.38, 41. König (*Wörterbuch*) suggests that Hosea uses the form of the name with מ/*m* in order to contribute further to the noticeable alliteration in the verse.

[e—e]מחמד לכספם lit. 'the proud glory pertaining to their silver'. The phrase is understood to be of a sort with and parallel to the הנה clause (note a) at the beginning of the verse, i.e. 'their silver may be their proud boast, yet thistles ...'. For a similar terse nominal clause employing the preposition ל see 9.4 (note d) above. The noun מחמד and other cognate nouns are rendered 'proud glory', 'vainglorious pride' by ibn Janāḥ (Arabic *'lfhr 'lmf'hr*), citing 1 Sam 9.20; Ezek 23.6; 1 Kgs 20.6; Lam 1.11; Isa 44.9; Jer 3.19. (He does not mention Hos 9.6.)

Such an interpretation of the phrase seems to me to fit the style of Hosea as well as the grammatical structure of the verse and to afford a reasonable sense. For the rest, very considerable diversity has marked attempts to understand the phrase. Amongst the rabbinic authorities

[14] For an up-to-date discussion, see *Lexikon der Ägyptologie* IV (Wiesbaden, 1982), pp. 24f. I am grateful to my colleague J. D. Ray for information on the subject.

Rashi and Kimchi (cf. Qyl) understand the phrase to refer to the Ephraimites' houses (cf. the Targum), repositories of their valued silver, which thistles and thorns will take over. The difficulty arises that the third plural suffix 'will inherit them' (above, 'will be their successors') does not seem to fit a singular antecedent ('the glory of their silver') which, in any case, has to be understood as an *abstractum pro concretis*. More recently the noun has been emended to the plural מחמדי and (with the following ל deleted) interpreted as 'idols of silver' or as 'treasure houses' (see, e.g., Harper *ad loc.*); in which case, why are silver idols mentioned or why are treasure houses to be inherited by thistles rather than by robbers? On the basis of the LXX's rendering מחמד as a place name (*q.v.* below) Robinson has suggested implausibly that the word represents the Egyptian city Tahpanhes (cf. Jer 43.7ff)[15]. *BH* proposes that the phrase be read as the object of the verb 'Memphis will bury their costly treasures'; yet קבר 'bury' is elsewhere never used of inanimate objects.

Rudolph, referring to a discussion of the root כסף by G. R. Driver, *WO* 2 (1954), pp. 26f, suggests that the word does not mean 'silver' in this particular context, but 'shame', 'disillusionment', a sense attested for the cognate verb in late Hebrew and Aramaic. Driver does not mention Hos 9.6, though it is likely that NEB's 'the sands of Syrtes shall wreck them' reflects his view that the basic meaning of כסף is 'to break'. Rudolph, reading מחמדם, renders the phrase in question 'their object of longing (*sc.* Egypt) will become their shame'. The suggestion is not supported by any ancient or rabbinical tradition and seems to me contrived and implausible as, *a fortiori*, is that of the NEB.

[f]The word קמוש is transmitted sometimes with *shin* and sometimes (as here) with *sin*. For identification of the species, see *AUS* 1, p. 372; 2, p. 318.

[g]Lit. 'tents'; cf. with Qyl, Num 24.5 and Ps 132.3 for the wider sense 'dwelling-places'. Sellin and Wolff's view that festal, cultic tents are meant is unlikely in view of their brief time of employment, with which mention here of the growth of thorns and thistles is hardly consistent (cf. Rudolph).

In his meditation upon the total rupture of the covenant relationship, Hosea sets forth the inexorable quality of the fate which confronts the Ephraimites. Their attempts to evade the coming disaster will be quite frustrated and those who flee to Egypt to avoid it will meet there their end (note c); their burial in Memphis (note d), for two thousand years the famed site of pyramids and immense burial grounds, will mark their annihilation in the oblivion of exile from Yahweh's land. Their

[15] Cf. the NEB's 'sands of Syrtes' for a similar geographical interpretation.

financial resources, in which so fondly they put their trust (note e–e) as a means of ingratiating themselves with the Egyptians, will not prevent this outcome and the ruins of their homes in the land will be taken over by thistles and thorns.

The verse appears to be a meditative expansion of the terse judgement of 8.13b 'they shall return to Egypt' (*q.v.* above). That punishment fitted the particular crime of switching to a pro-Egyptian policy in the face of the Assyrian threat. Accordingly here, the coming disaster, from which the Ephraimites seek to flee, reflects the disastrous Assyrian invasion of 733 BC and Hosea's conviction that Hoshea's *volte face* of *c.* 727 BC in favour of Egypt will bring only more of the same. The reference to 'all their vaunted silver' is likely to reflect the official payments to the Egyptians (cf. 12.2, EV 1) (to which no doubt the citizens were made to contribute, cf. 2 Kgs 15.20) parallel to those made by Menahem and Hoshea to the Assyrians in 738 and 732 BC. Certainly 12.9 (EV 8), cf. 13.15, furnishes evidence of Ephraimite riches and their boastful reliance upon them in the period of Hoshea's pro-Egyptian phase. At all events, resumed and increased Assyrian dominance of the land will, in Hosea's view, necessarily preclude all possibility of return on the part of those who were now tainted in Assyrian eyes by their Egyptian dalliance (cf. again 12.2, EV 1).

Text and Versions

משד Pesh. *bbzt'* 'through robbery, plunder', cf. Targ. מן קדם בוזין 'through plunderers'; LXX πορεύονται ἐκ ταλαιπωρίας (Αἰγύπτου) 'they go from the distress (of Egypt)', taking 'Egypt' with שד 'destruction'; → אשור ... המה 'they have gone to Assyria' (Borbone); → ילכו אשור (*BHS*); LXX [AQ] πορεύσονται 'they will go'.

תקבצם LXX καὶ ἐκδέξεται αὐτοὺς Μέμφις 'and Memphis will receive them', taking Memphis as the subject of the verb.

מף LXX Μέμφις; Vulg. *Memphis*; Pesh. *mps*; Targ. למפיס יתקרבון (Cod. Reuch. and printed rabbinic bibles יתקברון) 'they will be brought to Memphis' (alt. 'at Memphis they will be buried'); cf. Cathcart, p. 48, n. 15.

תקברם LXX καὶ θάψει αὐτοὺς (Μαχμάς) 'and M. will bury them', understanding מחמד as a place-name and as subject of the verb; for the place-name, LXX evidently thought of the familiar מכמס, i.e. Michmash in Benjamin, north of Jerusalem, which hardly fits the context (for Robinson's theory, see note e above).

מחמד לכספם LXX see above for מחמד; לכספם LXX τὸ ἀργύριον αὐτῶν ὄλεθρος κληρονομήσει αὐτό ([AQ] omit αὐτό) 'destruction will inherit it', where 'destruction' reflects unfamiliarity with קמוש, cf. Pesh. *rgt' ds'mhwn nwkry'* 'foreigners will inherit their desired silver'; Vulg. *desiderabile argenti eorum* 'what is desirable of their silver', Targ. בית חמרת כספהון 'the house of their desired silver'; 3 Kennicott and 1 de Rossi MSS read לנפשם for לכספם, a reading favoured by P. Ruben; for מחמד Aq. ἐπιθύμημα, cf. Symm. τὰ ἐπιθυμήματα 'desired thing(s)'; see further Ziegler *Bei.*, p. 358; → מחמדי כספם (Borbone).

קמוש see above for LXX; Vulg. *urtica* 'nettles', cf. Targ. קרסולין; for Pesh., see above and Gelston, p. 158.

חוח Targ. חתולין '(wild) cats'; according to Jastrow a corruption of חרולין 'nettles', cf. Cathcart, p. 48 n. 18.

9.7 **The days of reckoning have come[a], the days of retribution have come[a] – [b]Israel will perceive[c] [whether] [d]'the prophet is a knave, the inspired man, deranged[bd]' – because of the magnitude of your guilt[e] and your great enmity[e].**

[a]The repetition of the verb באו is emphatic; for similar repetition, cf. 6.4; 7.9; 11.8. Wolff's suggestion that the second instance represents a corruption of an original קרבו (after the Peshiṭta, see below) is unlikely.

[b–b]Ibn Ezra specifically connects the advent of the days of reckoning with Israel's calumny against Yahweh's prophet; for him the next phrase, with the second person singular suffix ('your guilt'), denotes distributively the guilt of each Ephraimite. This treatment is perhaps the most satisfactory of the many that have been proposed. Accordingly it is necessary to understand the words b–b as parenthetical (cf. Qyl), the main sentence consisting of the judgement and the reason for it 'the days of reckoning have come ... because of the magnitude of your guilt'. Associated with that main sentence is the meditative aside (see the introductory remarks to 9.1–9 above) that Israel will perceive on the days of reckoning that their characterisation of the prophet is a distortion of the truth. See further in the general commentary below and note the Vulgate's imperative 'Know Israel that ...'.

[c]The verb ידע 'to know' is given one of its well-attested and straight forward meanings, cf. BDB p. 393, col 2 c. For the plural form predicated of Israel, cf. 8.2 above. By reference to the LXX's reading (see below) van Hoonacker (cf. Wolff) proposes the reading יָרֵעוּ 'Israel will shout' which is then followed by a quotation of their shouted words. The suggestion is dubious, not least because this verb is elsewhere attested with the rather different sense 'to raise a shout' (i.e. in battle, in triumph, in joy etc.). Rudolph (cf. Harper) prefers to take the verb with what precedes rather than with what follows and argues that a quotation (see note d) may stand without specific introduction. Following the prophetic perfects ('will surely come'), he understands the

phrase to mean that 'Israel will experience it' (German *erfahren*). Taking a similar view, D. W. Thomas (cf. the NEB)[16] has proposed that ידע here has the meaning 'shall be humiliated'. Serious doubts have now been expressed concerning the essential validity of the theory of which his interpretation of this verse is part (for references, see 6.3 above). Moreover, where the general approach is concerned, two difficulties present themselves: first, it is difficult to understand on the massoretic punctuation why two prophetic perfects should be followed by an imperfect; secondly, while Rudolph's argument that a quotation without introduction is quite intelligible in a prophetic text has some force, that view raises in turn the question of the connection between the quotation and what follows it. To solve that problem Rudolph is driven to emendation (see below). The NEB, on the other hand, does not recognise the presence of a quotation, rendering 'then the prophet shall be made a fool ... by your great guilt'. Here the introduction of 'be made' is without warrant in the absence of a verb in the Hebrew and the sense obtained (in connecting the words with what follows) is obscure, if not meaningless.

[d—d]The words are understood to be a quotation of the hostile sentiments of Hosea's opponents (cf. ibn Ezra, Kimchi and many modern commentators).

[e]The noun משטמה occurs only here and in the following verse. The cognate verb appears to be a variant form of the root שטן (cf. BDB p. 966, col 1) and means 'to bear a grudge', 'cherish animosity'. The view[17] that the noun has the basic meaning 'fetter' (cf. Syriac *swṭm'* and the apparent parallelism with פח 'trap' in the following verse, *q.v.*) is hardly convincing since that meaning in no way fits the context of this verse (cf. Rudolph).

A number of scholars have found in the last line a complete sentence, 'because of the magnitude of thy guilt, the animosity is great'. This is achieved by emendation (so Wolff, cf. Borbone) reading רבה המשטמה, (cf. Rudolph רב המשטמה) or by understanding the conjunction *waw* to denote here 'indeed'[18]. Accordingly the animosity is Yahweh's response to Israel's guilt (Rudolph, cf. Rashi and Kimchi) or else it is the people's animosity towards Yahweh, the very evidence of their guilt (so Wolff). Such an approach seems to me to be unnecessarily contrived and to produce meanings which are in themselves so convoluted that they require very considerable further explanation.

The interpretation adopted here (following the lead of ibn Ezra) affords a sense for the whole verse which is readily intelligible but without recourse to emendation. It requires only the addition of 'your' *ad sensum* for MT's 'a great antagonism' and the reasonable supposition

[16] See *JTS* 41 (1940), pp. 43f.

[17] See Marti; also R. R. Schärf *Die Gestalt*, pp. 33ff.

[18] So apparently Kimchi; cf. L. Prijs *BZ* NF 8 (1964), p. 106 and Qyl.

that the force of the preposition על is continued over to the second phrase. That the adjective רבה may precede the noun is clearly attested; see GK 132b.

The moment of truth has come. The nation's perfidious disloyalty to Yahweh has brought upon it the days of reckoning and of retribution, indubitably, finally (note a). For Hosea there was the bitter-sweet knowledge of his own vindication. His convictions about the truth of the situation had been proved correct (note c). Yet the nation's final, unforgivable sin (cf. Mk 3.29) was to seek to repudiate Yahweh's message through Hosea by a vicious calumny (note b). They had suggested (note d) that the prophet was a knave (*sic*; *'wyl* denotes not mere stupidity but moral perversity, cf. Prov 1.7; 15.5; Ps 14.1); that his function as one inspired by God's spirit had degenerated into mad perversity. It seems clear that the title 'man of the spirit' is used quite factually and, parallel to the title 'the prophet', denotes one inspired by God's spirit (cf. Rudolph). The phrase is akin to the familiar 'man of God' (e.g. Judg 13.6; 1 Sam 9.6; 1 Kgs 12.22 etc.) and should be distinguished from the usage attested in, e.g., Ezek 13.3; Mic 2.11 where *rwḥ* 'spirit' implies vain or contrived falsehood. Yet in the light of this evidence the authentic title lends itself well to the formulation of the calumny. The message of Yahweh which Hosea, at his inspiration, proclaimed has been discredited by his perverted people and characterised as the wild, helpless panic of madness (cf. Deut 28.28, 34).

This accusation was, of course, made in respect of other prophets both before Hosea (2 Kgs 9.11) and after him (Jer 29.26), as Rudolph rightly observes. From his people's point of view, however, Hosea's perversity lay in his unreasonable and wilful attempts to undermine the nation's morale and self-confidence and the reaction was akin to that shown to Amos (7.10) and to Jeremiah (29.25ff).

The time now had come. It had come because of the magnitude of Ephraim's guilt and because of the great enmity that its people had displayed towards Yahweh (notes b and e). An essential manifestation of that animosity towards their God was the blasphemous assertion that his prophet was a knave and a madman. The structure of the verse is, as ibn Ezra rightly perceives, beautifully contrived and reflects again the powerful unity of thought so typical of Hosea.

Text and Versions

באו (second occurrence) Pesh. *qrbw* → קרבו (Borbone).

ידעו LXX καὶ κακωθήσεται 'will be afflicted', upon the basis of which is proposed יָרִיעַ/יָרֵעוּ 'will shout' (van Hoonacker, cf. Wolff, see note c); D. W. Thomas' explanation (see note c), in itself attractive, is less likely to be correct than the supposition (cf. *BHS*) that the LXX read וְיֵרְעוּ or וְיֵרַע לְ (from √רעע)[19]; Aq. and Theod. καὶ ἔγνω, cf. Symm. καὶ γνώσεται; Vulg. *scitote* (imperative); Pesh. *nd'*; Targ. ידעון, all 'know'.

על רב עונך ורבה משטמה LXX ὑπὸ τοῦ πλήθους τῶν ἀδικιῶν σου ἐπληθύνθη μανία σου 'because of the multitude of your transgressions (? עֲוֹנֶיךָ – Vollers), your madness has increased'; Pesh. (for the latter phrase) *'tytrt šryḥwtk*; both versions (so Targ.) apparently fail to reproduce ו (see note e); Vulg. *propter multitudinem iniquitatis tuae et multitudo* (*v.l.* *-inem*) *amentiae*, 'because of the multitude of your wickedness, there is also (*v.l.* and) abundance of madness'; Targ. על דסגיאו חובך תקיפו חטאך 'in that (the false prophets) increased your guilt (and) multiplied your sin'; for solutions involving the transfer of משטמה to the next verse, Nowack and NEB; Borbone (cf. LXX, Pesh., Targ.) → על רב עונך רבה משטמך 'through your great guilt, great will be your affliction'; for rearrangements of the text and עונך → עונם, see *BHS*.

9.8 [a]Ephraim stands in confrontation with my God[a]. (Prophet)[b] A fowler's[c] snare is on all his[d] paths and in the House of his[d] God is nothing but[e] enmity[f].

[a—a]The words are amongst the most difficult in the prophecies of Hosea and many modern scholars have felt constrained to resort to emendation (see below). However, MT is confirmed by all the ancient versions, and it seems best to assume that the problems arise because of our unfamiliarity with Hosea's dialectal usage (cf. note b).

Although he does not discuss this verse, ibn Janāḥ argues that the verb צפה, with its very familiar participial sense 'watchman', was capable also of a number of related meanings such as 'to have an eye on something, to turn one's face to something/body, to confront him/it' (Arabic *ṭl'*, Vth theme, and *qbl*, Xth theme), cf. Lam 4.17. He notes that in Ps 5.4 the verb צפה is closely associated with ערך and argues that it has a similar meaning. אערך־לך denotes 'I will face/confront thee in prayer'; the following ואצפה continues this sense 'and I will confront, be opposite, face (thee)' (Arabic *'q'bl w'ḥ'ḏy w'w'zy*). The verb צפה is also found in Job 15.22 with a specifically hostile sense 'he is confronted by the sword' (so ibn Janāḥ; Arabic *mqbl 'lsyf*). Where the preposition עם

[19] See J. A. Emerton *JSS* 15 (1970), pp. 152f, cf. *VT* 41 (1991), p. 148.

(which follows the verb) is concerned, the most likely usage seems to be that found in Deut 18.13 'You shall be whole with (עם) the Lord your God'. Accordingly the participle צֹפֶה is understood to denote here Ephraim's improper, hostile attitude to Hosea's God (cf. Deut 9.24) and, in particular, the nation's futile opposition to him in the face of the final rupture of the covenant relationship.

[b]The word נביא is taken to be a (mistaken) gloss (cf. Wolff) which seeks to interpret the participle צֹפֶה understood (as by all the ancient versions and by later tradition) in its usual sense of 'watchman' (for which see, e.g., Rashi, ibn Ezra, Kimchi; cf. Qyl). Its place, following the word 'my God' may also serve to interpret the first person pronominal suffix. Suspicion attaches to the word not least because it stands without the definite article and because, following so closely the first person reference 'my God', and understood to refer to the prophet (Hosea) in the third person, the resulting sense is extremely forced if not ludicrous.

For the numerous attempts to solve the problems of these words, reference may be made to R. Dobbie *VT* 5 (1955), pp. 199ff, and to Harper. The word צפה is not infrequently invested with the sense 'to lie in wait', 'watch insidiously' (cf. Ps 37.32) and, accordingly, the MT might seem to suggest 'Ephraim keeps insidious watch in the presence of my God, as for a/the prophet ...'. Apart from the reasons stated above, this is far from satisfactory since the sense 'to lie in wait', even if allowed, can scarcely be followed by the preposition עם. Nor do interpretations based upon reading צֹפֵה as a construct offer much improvement; e.g. Wolff, 'The watchman of Ephraim is with (my) God' (for variations, see Mays, AF). Resort to more robust emendation seems to raise as many problems as it solves; e.g., Dobbie's 'Ephraim spies on the life (אֶל־חַיֵּי) of the prophet'; but what has become of עם? Rudolph (cf. earlier, Oettli) suggests 'Ephraim opens its mouth. The people of my God are against the prophet. Traps ...' (reading פצה פה, עַם for עם and inserting אל (for על) and ה־ before נביא); are not these changes very considerable? and is the resulting sense worth the cost of making them?

[c]The word יקוש occurs only here in this form; cf. the common adjectival forms גדול, קרוב (so Qyl).

[d]The suffixes refer to the antecedent 'Ephraim'. As Rudolph rightly perceives, 'the House of his God' can scarcely refer to the prophet (Hosea) since he would be unlikely so to describe cultic sites with their syncretistic improprieties.

[e]'Nothing but' is added in translation *ad sensum*.

[f]The word משטמה is translated as in the preceding verse. The view (Marti and R. R. Schärf, see v. 7, note e) that the word denotes here 'fetter', 'trap' is based upon the 'clear' parallelism with פח 'trap' and is facilitated by reference to the Syriac cognate *swṭm'* bearing this meaning. Since, however, such a meaning does not fit the occurrence in the preceding verse (*q.v.*), it is more likely that the generally accepted

'animosity', 'hatred', 'enmity' is intended in both cases. Accordingly the enmity shown by Ephraim to Yahweh is matched here by his enmity towards his erstwhile people, with whom (note a) he is in direct confrontation.

In his reflections upon the final rupture of Israel's relationship with Yahweh, Hosea perceives that his nation has now placed itself in direct confrontation (note a) with his God. The use of the phrase 'my God' is significant and testifies to the unity of thought as between Yahweh and his prophet (cf. v. 17). Hosea's convictions reflect the mighty will and resolution of his God; and his words allow his vocation as the mediator of that divine will to obtrude (cf. Jer 1.10). Yahweh and his erstwhile people now stand totally opposed to one another. The prophet perceives that the superior will of Yahweh will inevitably prevail. His people are consequently doomed; on every path they could conceivably take in their international political machinations Yahweh has placed his lethal traps (cf. 7.12).

The 'House of (Ephraim's) God' is unlikely to refer to cultic sites (cf. note d) in general or to constitute an allusion to Bethel (so Kimchi, cf. as a possibility, Qyl and Rudolph). Hosea's unequivocal condemnation of such sites (cf. 4.15; 8.11ff) renders it unlikely that he would speak (even sarcastically) of them in this way. Rather the phrase refers to the 'land of Yahweh' (as in 8.1, cf. 9.3 and 9.15), i.e. the area in which he holds sway and where, heretofore, his people might have enjoyed the benefits of his care and protection. Now, however, their guilt and enmity (9.7) have provoked him and, within his own sphere, the nation, alienated from him, will encounter only his devastating hostility. The thought reflects the collapse of the political structure of the nation as well as the curse upon the fertility of the land which necessarily follows upon the rupture of the covenant relationship (cf. chapter 7, and 8.7). Confrontation reflects the enmity shown by both parties, yet one alone will prevail. At home and abroad the trap is sprung and doom for Ephraim is inevitable.

Text and Versions

צפה אפרים עם אלהי LXX σκοπὸς 'E. μετὰ θεοῦ 'the watchman of Ephraim is with God', cf. Vulg. *speculator E. cum Deo meo*; Pesh. *dwq' 'prym 'm 'lhy* 'Ephraim is a watchman with my God'; Targ. מסכן בית ישראל דיתקיים להון פולחן טעותא 'the House of Israel arranges for their preservation of idol-worship'; → צָפָה פָּה (Oettli, cf. Rudolph), cf. note b above; עם → עַם (Grotius, cf. Rudolph); אלהי → אלהים (Borbone); → אֹהֶל

נָבִיא (Sellin, *BHS*); נביא is reproduced in all the versions; Targ. לנבייהון 'for their prophets (snares are spread)'.

משׂטמה LXX μανίαν (κατέπηξαν) '(they planted firmly) madness', taking the initial verb (העמיקו) of the following verse with this verse; Targ. מסגן תקלא 'they increase offence/snares'.

אלהיו → אלהים (Borbone, cf. LXX, Pesh.).

9.9 [a]**They have sunk deep into corruption**[a] **as at the time of**[b] **Gibeah**[c]. **He will remember their guilt, he will punish their sins.**

[a—a]Cf. on 5.2 above where a very similar phrase occurs. The verb העמיקו is used almost adverbially in both verses. In 5.2 the infinitive construct שחטה is strictly the object of העמיקו; here a finite verb is co-ordinated without copula to the first verb which serves to define the manner of the second; GK 120d–h.

[b]Lit. 'days of'.

[c]The place name is frequently found with the article; since the meaning is 'hill' the usage is similar to that in English 'The City' (i.e. of London).

The verse concludes and summarises (cf. AF) Hosea's meditation. The second half repeats the words of 8.13 with its overtones of a judicial finding to the effect that the indictment is proved. Ephraim's guilt is now in Yahweh's mind, it is evident to him 'he remembers it'.

In summarising Ephraim's guilt Hosea repeats (with minor variation) his phrase of 5.2, yet now he brings it into relation with one of the most notorious past outrages of the nation. The reference is made *tout court* by mention of the town of Gibeah in Benjamin (for the location of the site, see on 5.8 above) where the basic laws of hospitality and of common decency were flouted by the multiple rape and murder of the Bethlehemite concubine (Judg 19ff). It seems clear that the story was well enough known in Hosea's time for the prophet to be able to allude to it simply by using the name 'Gibeah'[20]. A salient

20 P. M. Arnold (*op. cit.* at 5.8) supposes that in this verse (and in 10.9), Hosea refers not to the Benjamite outrage but to Ephraim's unwarranted and sinful attack on a brotherly tribe. In this connection he assumes that Judg 19f reflects later rationalisation of this 'war crime' by the incorporation of an (originally distinct) sexual outrage story, so that Ephraim no longer commits a crime but rather delivers its just punishment (*op. cit.*, p. 116). The theory is here discounted as unlikely. Apart from the many assumptions that Arnold makes, it is urged that Hosea is wont to see an essential unity between moral (and sexual) turpitude and

feature of the Benjamite outrage was the collusion in it of the citizens of Gibeah (cf. Kimchi and more recently Rudolph) and, accordingly, Hosea's words serve to emphasise the wholesale involvement of the state of Ephraim in the present destructive immorality and apostasy. As has been emphasised in respect of 5.2, the word 'corruption' belongs to the semantic field of perversity and moral sickness and it is typical of a number of Hosea's sayings (see Morag, pp. 505ff.); indeed the particular phrase compounded of the verb 'they have sunk' (note a–a), is unique to his prophecies. What Hosea here offers is a very strong condemnation, in summary form, of the moral bankruptcy and turpitude of his nation. By the repetition of the formula of Yahweh's certain knowledge and appraisal of the situation, he suggests that the coming punishment (cf. v. 7) will be as devastating as that which came so near to obliterating the whole tribe of Benjamin following the outrage at Gibeah (cf. Mays).

A number of modern scholars have seen in the verse a comparison between Hosea's personal treatment at the hands of his contemporaries and the injustice suffered by the Levite in the Gibeah episode (cf. Wolff, Rudolph and Mays). Rudolph suggests that Hosea records sentiments akin to those expressed in 1 Pet 2.23: Jesus 'committed himself to him that judgeth righteously'. Here, where the name of Yahweh is not mentioned as self-evident, there is a similar expression of faith in God's concern with justice. The argument has some force as an indication both of an aspect of Hosea's faith in the overwhelming righteousness of his God and of an element of self-vindication that that faith afforded him. Yet the particular conclusion, *viz.* that Hosea speaks here of his own ill-treatment at the hands of Ephraim, is based upon the premise that the suffixes of v. 8b refer to the prophet. It is argued here that they refer to the nation rather than to the 'prophet' (see note d on verse 8).

Rashi (cf. ibn Ezra) records that some authorities see in the reference to Gibeah an allusion to Israel's paradigmatic sin in elevating Saul to the monarchy, since Gibeah was the residence of Saul (1 Sam 10.26; 11.4). While Hosea certainly condemns the institution of Israel's monarchy (3.4; 8.4, cf. 9.15), the inauguration of Saul's kingship was at Gilgal, not at Gibeah, and hence an allusion to that event would be too obscure to be likely.

the degeneration of the nation as a whole; cf., e.g., his reference to Baal-Peor in 9.10. Ephraim's present turpitude is thus compared specifically to the notoriously degenerate actions of Benjamin at Gibeah.

Text and Versions

העמיקו LXX reads the verb with the preceding verse, *q.v.*; Vulg. *profunde peccaverunt* 'they have sinned deeply', correctly understanding the syntax, cf. the next entry.

שחתו LXX ἐφθάρησαν 'they have gone to ruin'; Wellhausen (cf. *BHS*) reads העמיקו שַׁחְתּוֹ *sic* 'in the house of his God, they have made deep a pit for him', transferring the two words to the end of verse 8.

הגבעה LXX τοῦ βουνοῦ translating the proper name; cf. perhaps Pesh. *drmt'*, although the place Ramah is not far from Gibeah, cf. 5.8.

יזכור Pesh. *mkyl ntdkr*; → עתה יזכור (Borbone).

CHAPTER 9.10–17

WHAT MUST BE, CONTRASTED WITH WHAT WAS AND WHAT MIGHT HAVE BEEN

9.10 **Like grapes in the desert[a], I found[b] Israel, like an early fig on a fig tree (at its beginning[c]) I caught sight[d] of your fathers. But they arrived at Baal-Peor[e] and gave themselves[f] to shame[g]. So they became detestable[h] like the object of their desire[i].**

[a] 'In the desert' belongs to 'like grapes' and not (*contra* Kimchi's father) to 'I found'; cf. with, e.g., ibn Ezra, Marti, Harper, Rudolph, the parallel phrase 'like an early fig on a fig tree'.

[b] Cf., in the light of the following 'caught sight of' (note d), Prov 18.22.

[c] The third feminine singular suffix appears to refer to the 'fig tree'. The word בראשיתה, not reproduced in the Peshiṭta, mars both the structure and parallelism of the verse and is frequently understood to have been a gloss indicating 'at the beginning (of its yearly fruitful season)', cf. Rashi; it seems to have been added in order to define more precisely the 'early fig', the word for which (בכורה) occurs in all only four times in the Hebrew bible.

[d] ראיתי lit. 'I saw'; Rashi comments 'thus your fathers appeared to me in my sight so that I loved them'. The familiar verb is attested with the sense 'to gaze at with pleasure', BDB p. 908, col 1 8 a 5 (ii).

[e] Ostensibly the name of the deity of Peor, the 'Baal of Peor', and so it might be assumed that the translation 'they came to the Baal of Peor' was correct. Since the term Beth-Peor also occurs it is suggested (so BDB, cf. Rudolph) that both terms are abbreviations of a full Beth-Baal-Peor. Accordingly, in view of the apparent accusative of place following the verb באו, the phrase is understood to be a reference to the place (on which, see the commentary below).

[f] The verb נזר, attested with the sense 'to dedicate or consecrate oneself to' implies also and necessarily 'separation' (so ibn Janāḥ, who uses the Arabic word *'l''z'l'*, cf. Rashi) from something else (cf., e.g., Lev 15.31). In the context (so typical of Hosea) where unfaithfulness to Yahweh is implied, the translation 'gave themselves to' is offered, with its overtones of sexual infidelity.

[g] A pejorative description of the god Baal. It has been thought (e.g. Harper) that בשׁת replaces an original 'Baal' as elsewhere names compounded of 'Baal' are commonly altered in this way. However, it is

at least equally possible that Hosea himself coined the usage; for, first, the name Baal has already been mentioned in this verse; secondly, the usage is found in the text of Jeremiah (3.24f; 11.3) who is in other respects clearly indebted to Hosea's thought. Thus, Hosea may well have been the originator of what has become a traditional description (cf. Wolff and Rudolph).

[h]שקוצים, a plural noun 'objects of disgust/detestation'.

[i]The word is best understood as a noun אֹהַב with suffix, 'the object of their love/desire', cf. BDB p. 13, col 1. Rosenmüller understands the word as an infinitive construct with suffix, 'according to their loving' which is difficult to construe satisfactorily. Further, the infinitive construct of the verb אהב is attested in the form אהבה in v. 15, as commonly elsewhere. An alternative explanation of the word as an infinitive construct is that of Kimchi's father, who takes the phrase to mean 'as (my) loving of them, so they have become detestable', i.e. 'in proportion as I love them, now I detest them'. The interpretation, though ingenious, is not convincing since an objective suffix without reference to the subject is harsh. In this context the word belongs to the field of love in the sense of sexual desire, cf. Morag, p. 502. Cf. Prov 7.18.

Using the form of divine speech, Hosea meditates upon the early apostasy of his people. The words cannot be understood as a report by Hosea of an audition with Yahweh (so Wolff, citing Amos 7.1–6 and Isa 6.8ff) for then the second singular suffix would have been used (cf. Rudolph). Nor is it likely that we are presented with an address to the (prophet's) hearers, for the third plural suffixes which follow (vv. 11ff) hardly fit that supposition. More likely is the view that Hosea's meditation upon the implications of Yahweh's sentence of judgement (9.1–9) is here continued but in a different key and with an altered emphasis. For further observations see on the verses which follow and especially on v. 16.

Divine speech in v. 10a with its use of the second plural suffix ('your fathers') serves to emphasise the intensely personal relationship of Yahweh with his people which had its origins and consummation in the desert. Indeed the words represent a lyrical expression of Yahweh's falling in love with Israel at that time and should be compared with the expression of 2.16ff (EV 14ff) where the hope of a second, renewed espousal in the desert is entertained. The words, then, seek to emphasise the continuity in Yahweh's mind between the Ephraimite nation in its present dereliction and the Israel (in the persons of its fathers) whom he had once made his own. The language used is so clearly appropriate to what today is called falling in love (cf. notes b and d) that a third person pronoun ('I saw their fathers', cf.

certain of the versions, see below), conforming to what follows, would be impersonal and out of place. Thus Hosea, with consummate artistry, faithfully relays this his insight into the mind of Yahweh. It is against this commitment of himself in love to Israel that the perfidy of Ephraim's ancestors is placed. Indeed the strongly adversive '(but) they', refering to the fathers, constitutes a bridge to Yahweh's reference to Ephraim in the third person plural that follows (vv. 11ff). No longer is the relationship characterised by the warm familiarity of 'I : you'; now, the relationship ruptured, Yahweh's 'I' speaks coldly only of 'them'.

Yahweh's first sight of his people, his providential finding of them (again, notes b and d) is compared with the intense pleasure experienced by the traveller who finds grapes in the desert or to the person who savours the exquisite freshness of a fig ripe in early summer. Where the former simile is concerned, ibn Ezra comments that the pleasure consists, at least partly, in the unexpected nature of the discovery in a place where there is no cultivation (cf. Sellin, for whom the phrase is pure hyperbole). Rudolph, for similar reasons, supposes that reference is to grapes growing in oases of the desert (cf. the Targum). However, those who know the Negev are today inclined to the view that viticulture was possible and long known in the desert and the widespread presence of what the Bedouin call 'Tululat al Aynab' ('grape cairns') may constitute evidence for this (see on 2.17 above). At any rate grapes grown in desert areas at the present time are described as small and exceptionally sweet. Where the second simile is concerned, reference is to the small figs which can appear as early as May-June and thus are two months in advance of the main season for ripe figs. Again, they are regarded as a great delicacy in view of their sweet freshness; cf. Isa 28.4, where it is said that they are so delicious that they are consumed while yet in the hand (further, Jer 24.2 and Mic 7.1)[1].

If Israel is compared with grapes in the wilderness, but also to early ripe figs (note a), there can be no doubt that Yahweh's finding her refers to the time of the sojourn in the wilderness (cf. with ibn Ezra, Deut 32.10). To say this is not to be committed to the view of Wolff, cf. R. Bach in *ThLZ* 78 (1953), col 687, that

[1] *AUS* 1, pp. 379 and 419. Where grapes in the desert are concerned, I am grateful to my intrepid friend Ora Lipschitz who has tasted grapes grown in the region of Kadesh-Barnea. I have myself picked grapes grown in the gardens of the Bedouin Jabaliyeh tribe in the mountains surrounding St Catherine's Monastery in Sinai.

Hosea is here dependent upon the traditions of a divergent group who saw Israel's origins not in the exodus but in Yahweh's discovery of her in the desert. Rather as the evidence of 2.16ff (EV 14ff) indicates, Hosea saw the wilderness period as the honeymoon between Yahweh and his people (cf. Jer 2.2), a time when nothing disturbed the blissful unity of their relationship. To this the title used here 'Israel' also bears witness, cf. 11.1 and 12.14 (EV 13); 'Israel' denotes Yahweh's people bound to him in the covenant relationship; Ephraim, by contrast, denotes the present reality, the geographical Northern Kingdom in its imperfection and frailty (cf. Wolff).

Yahweh's idyllic relationship with Israel was limited and short-lived (ibn Ezra) by reason of the early apostasy of the fathers as they moved from the desert towards the cultivated land and thus came into contact with the fertility cult, of which the sanctuary of Baal-Peor (note e)[2] furnished an outpost (cf. Rudolph). The apostasy is recorded starkly and emphasised by the strong adversative '(but) they'. The incident in question is related in the Pentateuch in Num 25[3] and it seems likely that the specific mention there of the initiative of Moabite women in seducing the Israelites into the worship of Baal implies licentious worship of the Canaanite cult to which Hosea takes so great exception. In Num 25.3 Israel is described as binding itself (√*ṣmd*) to Baal-Peor; here Hosea uses the word *nzr* which conveys (note f) that the fathers gave themselves to the deity ('shame'; note g) in gross infidelity to Yahweh. Moreover, his choice of word here may well reflect the usage in 4.14 where the Ephraimites 'associate with the prostitutes', i.e. isolate and segregate themselves with such persons (see note c on 4.14). This seems to be a more likely account of the word than that advocated by, e.g., Rudolph who sees in Hosea's use of it a bitter irony in that a *nāzîr*, Nazirite, was one who consecrated himself to a particularly whole-hearted and uncompromising service of Yahweh (Num 6; Amos 2.11f). To find such an allusion largely on the basis of etymology and in the absence of any support from, e.g., the rabbinic commentators is altogether unlikely.

2 Identified by O. Henke *ZDPV* 75 (1959), pp. 155ff, with Khirbet 'Ajun Musa, 7 kilometres west-south-west of Ḥesban, east from the northern end of the Dead Sea.

3 For an attempt to find in this verse an allusion, not to the idolatry of the fathers in the wilderness period, but to Israelite idolatry at Peor after the settlement and surviving to the eighth century BC, see G. R. Boudreau 'Hosea and the Pentateuchal Traditions. The Case of the Baal of Peor' in *History and Interpretation. Essays in Honour of John H. Hayes* (ed.) M. P. Graham, W. P. Brown and J. K. Kuan (Sheffield, 1993), pp. 121–132.

The promiscuous infidelity of Israel's fathers rendered them detestable, unclean (note h), like filth in Yahweh's sight. This opprobrium they shared with the object of their lust (note i), the Baal of Peor. The thought, as Jerome observes, is akin to that expressed in Ps 135.18 'they that make (idols) become like them, and so is everyone that trusts in them'. For Jerome, too, the name Baal-Peor should be understood as the idol of lust, akin to the Latin Priapus, and, *sensu obsceno*, particularly *habens in ore*[4], *id est, in summitate, pellem; ut turpitudinem membri virilis ostenderet*[5]. His interpretation, though somewhat far-fetched, may be held accurately to convey the general force of Hosea's strong words and the obscenity which, in the name of his God, he perceived in this act of idolatrous infidelity. Amongst the rabbinic commentators Rashi, ibn Ezra and Kimchi understand that the uncleanness was incurred physically by the fathers' intercourse with Moabite women which led necessarily to the idolatrous worship of Baal-Peor, their god.

Text and Versions

כענבים Targ. כגופן דשתיל על מבוע דמיין 'like a vine planted beside a water source'.

כבכורה LXX ὡς σκοπόν 'like a watchman'; despite σῦκον 'fig' in a number of MSS, Field argues, by reference to Nah 3.12 and to the usage πρόδρομοι for 'early figs', that the rendering σκοπόν denotes an 'early fig' and that it is not a mistake; for the view of Theophylact of Achrida that the fig is a 'first object of sight', see Ziegler, p. 95.

בראשיתה LXX πρόιμον 'early'; Vulg. *in cacumine eius* 'in its top'; Jerome (commentary) sees here a reference to the patriarchs as the head of the nation; Pesh. appears to omit the word, see Gelston, p. 133; Targ. דבאול מאבבה 'which ripens in early season'.

אבותיכם LXX, Pesh. and Vulg., third person plural suffix, → אבותיהם (Borbone); but cf., e.g., BDB p. 3, col 1 for the view that אבותיהם (rather than אבותם) is late; the view would tell against Borbone's proposal if he is relying on the similarity of MT to this form.

בעל־פעור LXX Βεελφεγώρ; Vulg. *Beelphegor*.

[4] For the verb *p'r* used of the open mouth, cf. Isa 5.14. The cognate Arabic root is *fġr* and not *f'r* as BDB supposes. The LXX and Vulgate transliterate in accordance with the clear perception that the middle radical was *ghain* and not *'ain*.

[5] Cf. perhaps the famous painting from the Villa dei Misteri at Pompeii; see E. Simon *Augustus: Kunst und Leben in Rom* (Munich, 1986), plate 21.

ויהיו שקוצים כאהבם LXX, cf. Symm. καὶ ἐγένοντο οἱ ἐβδελυγμένοι ὡς οἱ ἠγαπημένοι where, in a number of MSS and OL[CS], the position of the participles is inverted; Syro-Hex. ἐγένοντο ὡς οἱ ἐβδελυγμένοι οἱ ἠγαπημένοι, suggesting the sense 'the loved became as the detested'; Symm. ἐβδελυγμένοι ὅσῳ ἠγαπήθησαν 'detested in proportion as they were loved' (cf. Kimchi's father's view, above); Aq. καὶ ἐγένοντο βδελύγματα ὡς ἠγάπησαν 'they became abominations as ? (the things) that they loved', cf. Vulg. *et facti sunt abominabiles sicut ea quae dilexerunt*, Pesh. *whww lṭnpwt' 'yk drḥmw* and Targ. והוו שקוצין כדרחימו.

9.11 Ephraim is like[a] a flock of birds[b] which flies away[c] (their population)[d]; no more[e] giving birth, no pregnancy, no conception[f].

[a]The simile is understood to be used directly and the phrase to constitute a terse allusion to the imminent rapid loss of the nation's population. An alternative interpretation, worthy of consideration, is that of Rashi, who supposes that the simile represents a wish on Hosea's part, i.e. 'would that they would flutter away from the nest like a bird which ceases to bring up her young ... for what point is there in their bringing them up when I will eventually bereave them of such grown sons?' His interpretation has the merit that it accords with the concessive ('even if') sentiments of the following verse. On the other hand, as an indicative the phrase furnishes a clear introduction to what follows.

[b]עוף is a collective noun, used in comparisons with the article (GK 126o, p). The word 'flock' is added in English *ad sensum*.

[c]A *Hithpo'lel* form, found only here.

[d]The word כבודם is understood to be an (early) exegetical gloss expounding correctly the terse simile. Its function is similar to that of the translational glosses detected elsewhere in the prophecies (e.g. 2.8; 7.14ff; 8.13). This judgement is based on the following considerations: (1) the word is not easy to construe; if the suffix refers strictly to Ephraim (so most commentators), then the word would be expected before the simile rather than after it and to follow the word 'Ephraim', understood as a *casus pendens*; (2) the first half of the line appears to be over-long if the word was originally present. The word, often translated 'glory', denotes here the strength of the state measured in terms of its population, cf. with Qyl, Isa 5.13 where it is found in parallelism with המון 'crowd', 'multitude' (of a whole population) and, with Rudolph, Gen 31.1. For further considerations in favour of understanding the word as a gloss, see the commentary below.

[e]The preposition מן is understood here as privative, GK 119w. The alternative view, *viz.* that Ephraim (like birds) flies away from fecundity

(so Orelli, van Gelderen) is less likely not least because the terms are hardly appropriate to a simile referring to birds.

[f]The argument is understood to be cumulative: no more giving birth, no pregnancy ('womb'[6], cf. Isa 46.3), nor even conception. Rudolph argues in a contrary sense, seeing in the words as usually translated an anticlimax which, in any case, does not accord with the sense of vv. 12 and 16b where the possibility of conception and birth is expressly entertained. Accordingly he gives to the word לדה the sense 'to beget' rather than 'to bear' and to הריון 'pregnancy' rather than 'conception'. The argument seems unnecessarily contrived with regard to what is clearly a highly terse and poetic expression. For the infinitive לדה in place of the more common לדת, cf. GK 69c, m.

In contrast to the magical moment when Yahweh found his people (v. 10) and thereby created the potential for their flourishing prosperity in the land (cf. the sentiments of 2.1f, 25; EV 1.10f, 2.23), now, as a result of their long history of wicked apostasy, the nation will suffer the punishment of dismemberment and dispersal. Its fundamental strength, the very resources of its population (see note d), will fly away as a flock of birds. Whether the simile is directed to the speed with which this privation comes (so ibn Ezra) or alludes to abandonment of nests and so to the exclusion of reproduction (so Rashi) is not clear. Wellhausen and others have seen in the expression as a whole a word-play upon Ephraim (*'prym*): no longer is it compounded of *pry* 'fruit', i.e. fecundity, cf. 13.15 and Gen 41.52, but evokes *'brym* 'wings'. Again, for Wolff, cf. Qyl, the word *kbwd* 'glory' (note d) is chosen deliberately as a contrast to the 'shame' of Baal-Peor (v. 10). This view does not necessarily conflict with that advocated above, *viz.* that the word is an early exegetical gloss. Indeed it is possible that the glossator chose this particular word to indicate ('glory' →) 'population' for just such reasons. Since in v. 10 'shame' refers to Baal, 'glory' as a true contrast would require that Yahweh was indicated (so, as a possibility, then discounted, AF). Yet the tenor of what follows clearly indicates the punishment of depopulation and loss of fecundity and hence the term must have a related meaning.

If Ephraim's resources of population are said to fly away like a flock of birds, no doubt the prophet has in mind principally Yahweh's sentence of judgement pronounced in 8.13, and his own meditations upon its implications in 9.3, 6 etc. The land, under Yahweh's control, will 'spew them forth' (Lev 18.25) and

[6] For Dahood's (unnecessary) attempt to find a verbal form here, see *Biblica* 44 (1963), p. 301.

the population will be dispersed. That, however, does not exhaust the matter. The prophet perceives further that Yahweh has effective control over the reproductive capacity of his erstwhile people and thus, dispersed, the latter will no longer be able to renew their numerical strength. It is the fecundity of Ephraim as a nation that is at an end. Here Hosea undoubtedly sees a punishment fitted to the crime of a nation which had sought the blessings of fertility in the cultic exuberance whose poisonous influences actually produced the very opposite (cf. Rudolph).

Text and Versions

No significant readings.

9.12 **Even if[a] they should bring up their sons, I will render them[b] childless, without population[c]. [d]There is nothing but woe for them[d] in my abandoning them[e].**

[a]A concessive clause styled a 'counterfactual concession' (German *irreale Synchorese*) by H. Gese *VT* 12 (1962), pp. 436f.

[b]The antecedent is the 'sons', the next (attenuated) generation, cf. Rudolph.

[c]I.e. the same privative sense of מן, detected in the previous verse, cf. Isa 6.11. אדם means 'human beings' and not 'grown men' which precludes the interpretation of the Targum (see below), cf. ibn Ezra and Kimchi 'I will bereave (the parents) ... so that they (the children) do not become grown men'. Qyl (in the name of 'others') mentions as an alternative interpretation the view that the phrase is elliptical and means 'from (the land designated for) man', and for this he cites Prov 30.14. The former view, however, has the merit that it accords better with the general sense of the oracle, see the commentary below.

[d–d]כי גם אוי להם lit. 'surely even woe to them'. אוי is an impassioned expression of grief upon which the adverb גם lays particular stress (cf. BDB p. 169, col 1 2). Marti (cf. Rudolph) prefers to take the adverb with 'for them' and in the sense 'also', thereby indicating that the sons are specifically included in the deprivation. For Kimchi the phrase as a whole indicates the extent of the deprivation which then evokes this reaction from the onlookers who (presumably in Yahweh's name, cf. the first person suffix, 'my abandoning') make the exclamation. For the form and sentiment he compares Deut 31.17. If Kimchi sees in the phrase an exclamation by onlookers, Marti understands it to be a gloss where כי 'for' is designed to introduce the explanation that the privation would affect the children as well as (so גם) the fathers and not as a substitute for the latter. The suggestion is worthy of consideration because it seeks, if in the end unconvincingly, to resolve the difficulties presented by the form and content of the phrase; see further in the commentary below.

[e]בשורי מהם lit. 'when I turn aside from them'. Jerome, Rashi, ibn Ezra and Kimchi all understand the word to be from the well-attested root סור 'to depart', 'turn aside' occurring here with the variant (or dialectal) spelling שׂ for ס; cf. GK 6k[7]. In 8.4 השׂירו is from the root שׂרר and in 4.16, cf. 9.15, סרר is found. The root סור, spelt normally, appears in 2.4, 19 as also probably in 4.18 which raises the question why a form with variant spelling should occur here. Some authorities have detected another instance in 8.4 (*q.v.*), but this is far from certain. Returning to 9.12, it must be said that very considerable uncertainty attaches to שׂורי and that in the present state of our knowledge we simply do not know its meaning. Accordingly, in the absence of any other clear traditions concerning its derivation, it is probably best to adopt the view advocated by the authorities cited above. The verb, then, means 'to depart' and, used of God, implies the withdrawal of his care and protection, cf. Deut 31.18.

Amongst the many suggestions made by modern scholars mention may be made of the following: (1) to read בשׁורי (Hitzig, cf. Wolff) where either the root שׁור I 'to travel' is understood (→ 'when I go away from them'), or else שׁור II 'to look, behold' (→ 'when I look away from them'); (2) to read the same consonants and to compare Arabic *ṯ'r* 'take vengeance' for which support is seen in the Peshiṭta (see below, so Nyberg, cf. *BHS*). Without other instances or supporting evidence the suggestion is unlikely to be correct; (3) to read, on the evidence of the LXX, בשׂרם הם 'they are their flesh' (Prätorius, cf. Sellin, Bruno) or הם בשׂר מהם (Rudolph), 'they are flesh of their flesh', where flesh denotes, as often, kindred. Accordingly the phrase serves to emphasise that the privation will affect the children as well as the parents (cf. note d above).

The verse begins with a counterfactual concession (note a) which is designed to emphasise the inexorable quality of the nation's imminent collapse. There is no need to detect here a logical flaw in that the loss of fecundity is followed at once by a concession involving mention of grown-up children, i.e. without mention of the newly born. Upon the basis of this consideration indeed, e.g., Marti and Rudolph propose to rearrange the text so that v. 16b, inserted here, supplies the link. However, v. 16b in its traditional place may be held merely to repeat, but with emphasis on small children, the same counterfactual concession that occurs here.

[7] The reading בסורי is attested in 4 Kennicott MSS (cf. Borbone).

The demise of Ephraim is set forth in terms of the loss of its population. Dispersed as a result of the folly of the nation and its leaders, and then so dispersed by the decisive action of Yahweh (see on v. 11), the nation will no longer renew its strength by its parents bringing to it the young who will grow up to be its citizens. It is here that the counterfactual concession finds its place and, *per contra*, alludes to the factual possibility of individuals (who had been citizens of Ephraim) bringing children to birth. If this happens, reasons Hosea in Yahweh's name, the children themselves, now further removed from full citizenship of Ephraim, exemplars of an attenuated, residual identity, will in no way reverse the process. On the contrary with them the inexorable demise of the nation will reach its sad conclusion.

The second part of the verse, again spoken in Yahweh's name, appears (see note e and NB the uncertainty attaching to the translation) to constitute a reminder of the reason behind the nation's demise. That is conveyed by an impassioned expression of grief (note d) and that it is placed on Yahweh's lips (cf. 7.13) serves the prophet's purpose, i.e. his attempt, in the meditation of which the verse forms a part, to set forth the mind of his God. It is God's complete detachment and separation from his people (cf. 5.6) which is the decisive and effective cause of their calamity; in that he will no longer be Yahweh to them (1.9), their fate is determined. The totality of his election, support and care of his people is withdrawn from the moment (8.13) of his final irrevocable decision. No longer (as in 5.15) is envisaged temporary withdrawal for the purpose of redemption; now the covenant is abrogated and (cf., again, 1.9). Yahweh is no longer Yahweh for a people who are no longer his people. The expression, with its emphasis upon the demise of the nation and of the population of which it was constituted, accurately reflects the prophet's other statement linked indeed to the person of his son Lo-Ammi as well as, *mutatis mutandis*, to the prophecy of recapitulation attached to it, with its emphasis upon the restoration of the nation and the resurgence of its population (2.1f; EV 1.10f). For a similar statement reflecting the name Lo-Ruḥamah, cf. 9.15 below.

The first person suffix ('in my abandoning them') serves again to make the contrast to the wonderful moment when Yahweh found his people like grapes in the desert (9.10). Thus, the intensity of Yahweh's pain in abandoning his people matches his original joy in finding them. The pronoun in '(there is nothing but woe) for them' is likely, then, to refer to the whole people and not merely to the children of the counterfactual concession (for which, cf. Marti, van Hoonacker) or to the parents (for which, cf. van Gelderen, Wolff).

Since it is possible to find in v. 12b a sense which fits the context (as well as the wider argument of Hosea) reasonably well, Marti's suggestion that the words are a gloss may be discounted.

Text and Versions

ושכלתים LXX ἀτεκνωθήσονται 'they will be deprived of children'; Vulg. *absque liberis eos faciam* 'I will render them childless'; Pesh. *'gyz 'nwn* 'I will bereave them'; Targ. ואתכילנון, cf. MT.

מאדם LXX ἐξ ἀνθρώπων 'from men' = ? 'among men', cf. Vulg. *in hominibus* and Pesh. *mn bny 'nš'*; Targ. מלמהוי גברין 'from becoming men'.

בשׂורי מהם LXX and Theod. σάρξ μου ἐξ αὐτῶν 'my flesh is from them', reading בְּשָׂרִי; for emendations based on this reading, see note e above; Aq. and Symm. ἐκκλίναντός μου ἀπ' αὐτῶν 'when I turn away from them', cf. Vulg. *cum recessero ab eis*; Pesh. *mtpr' 'n' mnhwn* 'I am taking vengeance on them'; for Nyberg's interpretation of this evidence, see note e above; Sebök corrects the reading to *mtprq* or *mtprš* to agree with the orthography שׂור in MT[8]; Targ. בסלקותי שכינתי מנהון 'when I remove my presence from them'; cf. Cathcart.

9.13 Ephraim (when I caught sight of him)[a] became[b] a palm-shoot[c] transplanted in a meadow[d]; yet[e] Ephraim has[f] now[g] to present his sons to the executioner[h].

[a]The words in brackets are understood to be an early gloss referring to v. 10, 'I caught sight of your fathers'. The words are designed to elucidate the contrast inherent in this section (see on the preceding verses) between Ephraim's potential at the time of election and its present terrible situation. A number of modern commentators have found the phrase difficult to construe (e.g. ראה followed by the preposition ל) or as suspiciously prosaic (e.g. Harper, Rudolph). To recognise it as a gloss which refers to v. 10 and (correctly) elucidates the contrast implicit in the verse removes such difficulties.

[b]The preposition ל is understood to be used as normally with the verb היה and to convey the notion of transition (BDB p. 512, col 1 4). Here, in the terse elliptical style of an oracle, the preposition is used without

[8] Borbone supposes that the Peshiṭta read (or understood) a form of the root שׂוב.

the verb, cf., e.g., Prov 10.7. The usage fits well with what follows, note f.

[c]The suggestion that the word צוֹר is here illuminated by Arabic *ṣwr* (*ṣawrun*) '(small) palm trees' goes back to A. J. Arnold[9]. A form of the same word (צורי) seems to appear in B. *Abodah Zarah* 75a (ET, p. 359 in *Neziḳin* IV) and in B. *Shabbath* 90b (ET, p. 431 in *Mo'ed* I) apparently in the sense of '(ropes woven from the bands of) palm bark'. Lane (4 p. 1744, col 3) notes that *ṣawrun* can denote 'root' (of a palm) and hence 'shoot', 'root' is suggested here. The passive participle 'planted', 'transplanted' which follows is always used of plants or trees and this provides corroborative evidence in favour of Arnold's view. That the word is construed as feminine (cf. שתולה) reflects the fact that the female of the species produces fruit (cf. Qyl) or else that it is a mere shoot, K. Albrecht *ZAW* 16 (1896), p. 105. Jerome and the rabbinic commentators see in the word a reference to Tyre initially planted on a pleasant site but later to be inundated by the sea. The theory has recently been revived by J. K. Kuan *PEQ* 123 (1991), pp. 104–108. The resulting sense is (*pace* Kuan) hardly convincing; it is difficult to see why Hosea should refer to Tyre, even as a symbol of prosperity and ease (so Rashi, cf. Keil and van Gelderen). A change of pointing (צוּר for צוֹר) yields the sense 'rock' (cf. Theodotion), but this cannot be said to yield a suitable sense, particularly as the subject of '(trans)planted'. Duhm's suggestion that כאשר be read as כאשל, which gives the resulting sense, 'Ephraim I saw as a tamarisk on the rock, transplanted into a meadow', is again more ingenious than convincing. For one (of the many) further emendations and suggestions, see Text and Versions below.

[d]The word נוה denotes a 'meadow', as green (cf. Ps 23.2) and well-watered. Palm trees, particularly, need well-watered roots.

[e]ואפרים is an emphatic repetition conveying the sense 'yet this very same Ephraim' (cf. Rudolph).

[f]Infinitive construct with ל expressing obligation, compulsion, cf. Kimchi and GK 114h, k; cf. also note b above; further, I. Eitan and C. R. Krahmalkov[10].

[g]Cf. notes a and e. The word is supplied in translation *ad sensum* to draw out the contrast to the time 'when I caught sight of him'.

[h]Certain of the ancient versions (see below) appear to take the consonants הרג as an abstract '(to) slaughter' and they are followed by, e.g., Harper; MT's 'killer' → 'executioner' is more forceful and is retained.

[9] C. W. Justi *Blumen althebräischer Dichtkunst* (Giessen, 1809), pp. 536ff.

[10] Eitan *AJSL* 45 (1928–29), p. 202; Krahmalkov *Rivista degli Studi Orientali* 61 (1987), p. 73.

The verse presents again the vivid contrast between the time of Israel's election in the desert (v. 10) and, on the other hand, the imminent future with the death throes of the state. When Yahweh fell for Israel, when he caught sight of their fathers (v. 10), all the potential for a glorious future was brought into being. At this point Ephraim, the nation which was to be an exemplar of this dream, could be described as a palm-shoot (note c) transplanted into an ideal place for growth, a well-watered meadow (note d). Here indeed the prophet may be alluding to the imagery of the Blessing of Joseph (cf. Qyl), the father of Ephraim; e.g., 'Joseph is a fruitful tree by a spring with branches climbing over the wall' (Gen 49.22, NEB). Such blessings are characterised by their emphasis on the fecundity of the nation in a fruitful land (cf. Gen 49.25f; Deut 33.13ff). Now, however, through the nation's wilful stupidity, the reverse is all that Yahweh can contemplate. The very same nation will be obliged to bring forth its precious sons to the executioner, to the merciless hatred of its enemies. Here, no doubt, the prophet in Yahweh's name sees the results of dispersal and the vulnerability of those who managed to live through it. As Kimchi rightly explains, Ephraim is a collective term denoting the nation; 'his sons' is distributive and refers to the individual members, those who managed to survive. At all events, the verse depicts the demise of the state with its resources of population and the inexorable quality of Yahweh's punishment which reaches out to the individual members of the state, lost indeed without it, and thus meeting their inevitable doom, unable to perpetuate their future.

Amongst the rabbinic commentators, Rashi (cf. ibn Ezra) follows the Targum and detects in the language of the second part of the verse an allusion to the sacrifice of children to idols. This is unlikely to be correct, at least in a literal sense. Yet the language may reflect a further insight of Hosea, *viz.* that the fathers of the nation can be said to have sacrificed their sons to idolatry in their unending revolutionary civil wars and in their clash with the might of Assyria (cf. Rudolph). For the rest, it must be emphasised that the verse, together with those that precede it, is, properly understood, a meditation presented as that of Yahweh himself (*contra*, e.g., Mays). Accordingly, as Rudolph observes, the lamentation expresses the misery felt by Yahweh himself at the necessary punishment of his people. Things could have been quite different; yet that they are as they are is the responsibility of Ephraim.

Text and Versions

כאשר ראיתי → אַיָּלָה '(E. is) a hind (whose young they make prey)', van Hoonaker, cf. *BHS*.

לצור שתולה בנוה LXX εἰς θήραν παρέστησαν τὰ τέκνα αὐτῶν (παρέστη O/[Luc], αὐτοῦ [Luc]), '(E.) has presented its children as prey'; on the basis of this a number of modern commentators have reconstructed the Hebrew text, e.g., לַצַּיִד שָׁתוּ לָהֶם בָּנֶיהָ//לַצַּיִד שָׁתְלָה בָנֶיהָ 'whose young they make prey/whose young she has transplanted(?) for the hunter' (cf. Houtsma, Wellhausen, Marti, Wolff, *BHS*, Borbone); undoubtedly the LXX read the Heb. text in some such way, cf. J. K. Kuan *op. cit.*, note c above; Aq. and Symm. ὡς ἀκρότομον πεφυτευμένην ἐν κατοικίᾳ 'as a rock planted in a settlement'; Theod. εἰς πέτραν πεφυτευμένοι οἱ υἱοὶ αὐτῆς '(E.), her sons are planted as a rock'; Vulg. *Tyrus erat fundata in pulchritudine* '(E.) was a Tyre grounded in excellence'; Pesh. *lṣwr dštyl' bbnynyh* '(E. was) (as if thou hadst seen *sic*) Tyre planted in its buildings'; Targ. דמיא לצור באצלחותה בשליותה 'like Tyre in her prosperity and ease'.

אל הרג LXX εἰς ἀποκέντησιν, cf. Pesh. *lqtl'* 'for slaughter'; accordingly → אֶל הֶרֶג (Vollers, Borbone) or לַהֲרֵגָה (Wellhausen, Marti); Aq. + πρὸς μέ; Vulg. supports MT; Targ. חבו לקטלא לפלחן טעותא בניהון '(The Ephraimites) have sinned by slaughtering their sons for idol-worship'.

9.14 **Give to them, Yahweh – what[a] are you to give? Give to them miscarrying[b] wombs, breasts shrivelled up[c].**

[a]The interrogative pronoun מה is given its usual meaning, *contra* Rudolph who, citing König, 382a, 884a, understands it as introducing an indirect question with a sense akin to a relative particle, 'Give to them what you will'; cf. the earlier discussion and repudiation of this view by Rosenmüller.

[b]משכיל lit. 'causing bereavement', hence, here, 'miscarrying' (cf. BDB, *ad loc.*); some MSS read משכיל 'successful' which is clearly a mistake in the context. For a similar confusion, cf. Jer 50.9.

[c]The verb צמק occurs only here; in Targum Pseudo-Jonathan to Num 6.3 it is used to render יבשים 'dried up' and the noun צמוקים in Hebrew denotes raisins as 'dried out' (cf. ibn Ezra's similar comment).

Rashi, ibn Ezra and Kimchi all see in the words a prayer of Hosea. So horrible is the vision of the Ephraimites' bringing forth their sons to the executioner that the prophet is prompted to intercede with Yahweh that his just punishment may be effected by the more merciful death of the foetus or of the newly-born. Thus the greater pain of parents' handing over their grown children to death will be obviated.

It is here argued that this whole section represents a meditation of Hosea's upon the full implications of Yahweh's just repudiation of his people, for the most part spoken from Yahweh's point of view and in his name. The nation's heinous offences have necessarily brought about its total alienation from its God and the effects are seen to be horrific. The sense of grief on Yahweh's part is clearly and incisively expressed by Hosea (cf. on vv. 10 and 13). Accordingly it is not surprising that the prophet, perceiving the logical outcome of events and its terrible consequences for his countrymen, should be moved to share that grief and to express his own horror at what is to happen. His words, then, form a natural part of his meditation and are neither (in a precise sense) 'imprecation' nor 'deprecation' (Harper's words). The prophet is not expressing his own wish and prayer – 'what would I have thee give?' (so Harper, cf. Keil, Sellin, AF); rather, seeing the full consequences of Yahweh's alienation from his erstwhile people, prayerfully but passionately he seeks the least of the evils which must necessarily come (cf. 2 Sam 24.14). His words imply a full understanding of Yahweh's ways but reflect a natural human and prophetic wish to intercede (cf. with Rudolph, Jer 12.1); he requests not the abrogation of Yahweh's punishment but that it should be accomplished specifically through barrenness as the most merciful means of its achievement (cf. Jer 20.18; Job 3.11f, 16 and Lk 23.29). As has not infrequently been observed (e.g. Wolff, Rudolph), we are fortunate indeed to have here a brief glimpse of the inner thoughts of Hosea, of his deep appreciation of the moral consistency of his God and of his wrestling to reconcile it with an equally deep appreciation of the grief and reluctance of that same God. At this point, indeed, Hosea's mind is perfectly attuned to that of Yahweh and it is not surprising that some (cf. Wolff, Qyl)) have seen a dialogue between Hosea and Yahweh which, in fact, represents the dilemma of the latter; so, e.g., Qyl: to Hosea's 'Give to them, Yahweh', Yahweh responds 'what would you give them?' and receives Hosea's reply 'miscarrying wombs' etc.

Mention here of the 'miscarrying wombs' and of 'shrivelled breasts' may well represent a reversal of the traditional blessing of Joseph, the father of Ephraim, as expressed in Gen 49.25, 'the blessings of the breast and of the womb'; cf. on the preceding verse.

Text and Versions

No significant readings.

9.15 **All their evil[a] [had its roots[b]] in Gilgal; there indeed[a] I came to hate them[c]. Because of the wickedness of their actions I will banish them from my house[d]; I will[e] love[f] them no more; all their officials are intractable[g].**

[a]On the assumption that רעה denotes ethical evil (cf. 7.2), כי later in the verse must be asseverative. An alternative view (cf. Oort) is that the word means evil in the sense of 'distress', 'calamity'; on that view כי is explicative and the phrase as a whole means 'all their calamity derived from (lit. 'in') Gilgal because there I began to hate them'; see further in the commentary below.

[b]The phrase is added in English *ad sensum*, there being no verb in the Hebrew.

[c]The verb שׂנאתים is inchoative with the sense 'I formed or conceived hatred for them' (cf. Harper).

[d]I.e. the land of Israel, cf. 8.1 and Jerome's commentary *sed domum Dei vel terram sanctam appellabimus*.

[e]אוֹסֵף a jussive form of the first person instead of a cohortative, for which cf. BL p. 279, n. 1 and König, 191c, g.

[f]Infinitive construct אהבה of אהב without ל, cf., with Rudolph, Gen 4.12.

[g]Cf. note a on 4.16 and, for the word-play, Isa 1.23.

For ibn Ezra mention of Gilgal (for its location near Jericho, cf. on 4.15 above) constitutes a reference to the situation immediately following the crossing of the Jordan when the fathers first set foot in the land. Accordingly the phrase expresses elliptically a similar contrast to that of v. 10 above. Entry into the land (Gilgal) should have elicited in the Ephraimites a proper sense of gratitude for Yahweh's providential care of their fathers; in fact their wickedness and its consequences had prevailed to the extent that now Yahweh will banish them from the land, the gateway to which was Gilgal (cf. the Entry of Hope in 2.17; EV 15).

This interpretation depends to some extent on the related question concerning the meaning of *r'tm* 'their evil' for it may denote 'all their calamity' or 'all their moral evil' (see note a). If the essential force of the verse presents a contrast similar to that of, e.g., v. 10, the distinction may not be as important as first appears to be the case. For in reality the nation's calamities are a sign of and punishment for their moral evil. What could have been is contrasted to what was (cf. AF). Since, in Hosea's thinking, past and present are so strongly connected, the evil afflicting Ephraim and perpetuated by it goes back to the very beginnings of its presence upon the land.

For Jerome, cf. Kimchi, Gilgal constitutes a reference to the rebellious inauguration of the kingship of Saul (1 Sam 11.14f) which happened at Gilgal. Certainly such an interpretation accords with Hosea's explicit teaching that the monarchy, connected with idolatry, was a prime exemplar of the nation's apostasy (cf. 3.4; 7.3–7; 8.4; 10.3, 7, 15, etc.). The frequent use of the word *r'h* also characterises the account of 1 Sam 12 (cf. Qyl's exposition of the occurrences)[11]. The theory has been championed by a number of modern commentators, e.g., Wolff, E. Jacob[12], Mays. Yet doubts remain (cf. Rudolph): first, as a simple reference to Saul and the inauguration of the kingship, the phrases could not be more obscure; secondly, the reference to the 'officials' scarcely serves to confirm such a reference, but rather has a contemporary ring (see below); and thirdly, while Hosea has a lively sense of the formative character of past events, it seems unlikely that eviction from the land should depend upon an event so far in the past when clearly the guilt of the present generation is in his mind.

More likely is the view that the trigger for Hosea's mention of Gilgal is an event, now not known to us, in the recent past and of a sort with the notices of 5.1ff, and especially 6.7ff. That allusion alone is necessary accords with the supposition that that event was well known to Hosea and to his hearers. We cannot even be sure which Gilgal Hosea has in mind. Reference in the latter part of the verse to 'intractable officials' (cf. 7.3) may imply the sort of revolutionary situation depicted in 6.7ff where Pekah's revolt is described as originating in trans-Jordanian Gilead and spreading through the place Adam, arriving at Shechem and Samaria. The traditional Gilgal, near Jericho, is distant from Adam by only some twenty five kilometres, and it is possible that an event (and perhaps a cultic one, cf. 4.15; 12.12, EV 11) connected with that revolution took place there. Alternatively, another Gilgal (modern Jiljaliyah) is situated some seventeen kilometres south of Shechem and may have played some part in such or similar events. Whatever this particular

[11] Cf. further Sellin's finding of striking verbal similarities between vv. 15, 17 and 1 Sam 15; but also Rudolph's criticisms.

[12] *EvTh* 24 (1964), p. 284.

event it seems likely that it prompted Hosea to frame words which saw a deeper significance in the name of the place and depicted the sort of contrast detected by ibn Ezra.

Another indication that the words were initially prompted by a particular situation is Yahweh's assertion that he will no longer love his people. The words are very similar to those of 1.6f with its reference to Hosea's daughter Lo-Ruḥamah. On the view here adopted of the nature of chapter 1, Hosea's daughter represents an historical marker in his life when he perceived that Yahweh would no longer extend to his people his love and forbearance. Indeed, it was then that his displeasure was conceived. The extremely tentative estimate of the date of Lo-Ruḥamah's birth, 747–740 BC (p. 23), may suggest an event associated with the revolution of Shallum or of Menahem in the year 747 BC. In a meditation concerned with Yahweh's final decision to repudiate his people, it is not inappropriate that he should look back to the beginnings of the contemporary disastrous situation. For further consideration of this verse and its relation to 12.12 (EV 11), see on the latter verse.

An allusion to one of the themes of chapter 2 has also been detected (so already Rosenmüller) in some of the phrases of the verse; the verb, 'I will banish them' is used of divorced women (cf. Lev 21.7, etc., Ezek 44.22); such women, 'thrust forth', are said to be the object of their husbands' hatred or revulsion (Deut 24.3, cf. 21.15; 22.13) where this term implies at least the end of the husband's love. The phrase 'from my house', while in the context it clearly means the land of Israel (note d), also accords well with a description of divorce, cf. Gen 21.10.

Text and Versions

רעתם LXX αἱ κακίαι αὐτῶν, cf. Pesh. *byšthwn*, 'evils' (plural) is as ambiguous as MT (note a above); Vulg. *nequitiae eorum*, cf. Targ. בישתהון suggests 'moral evil'.

כי all the versions understand the usage as explicative.

רע LXX τὰς κακίας, again plural.

סררים LXX ἀπειθοῦντες 'disobedient'; Vulg. *recedentes*; Pesh. *mrwdyn*, cf. Targ. מרדין; of these Vulg. appears to think of √סור, the others of √סרר; cf. note a on 4.16.

9.16 **Ephraim is blighted[a]; their roots are[b] withered; they cannot[c] produce fruit. Even if[d] they bring to birth, I will slay their precious children[e].**

[a] So BDB נכה *Hophal* 7; this verb, usually rendered 'to smite', is used in respect of grass in Ps 102.5 and of a worm attacking a gourd in Jon 4.6. Since the metaphor refers back to, and reverses the sense of, that in v. 13, the word 'blighted' is chosen as appropriate to a tree.

[b] Lit. 'their root is withered'. English, perhaps, requires a plural.

[c] The negative בלי *Kethib*, cf. 8.7, here effects a rhyme with פרי 'fruit'; the *Qere* is בַּל.

[d] A counterfactual concession, cf. note a on v. 12 above.

[e] Lit. 'the precious things of their womb'. For the word מחמד, 'precious', as described by ibn Janāḥ, see on 9.6 above. The phrase denotes the children as precious to their parents and in whom the latter take pride.

Reverting to the metaphor of Ephraim as a palm-shoot (see on v. 13) Yahweh describes the nation's present situation; the shoot is blighted (note a) and, its roots withered, it is now incapable of producing fruit. The passive verb 'is blighted' corresponds to the passive participle in v. 13 'transplanted', and hence the form of the first half of the verse presents the opposite sense to the (unfulfilled) promise of v. 13. It appears that the words belong to the semantic field of sowing and planting (cf. Morag, p. 497) and hence the death of the palm-shoot is likely to be the result of a viral infection or of pests rather than that of lightning, storm or heat (so as possibilities, e.g., Rosenmüller; cf. Harper, Rudolph) and certainly not that of human felling. At any rate, the roots, although planted in a well-watered meadow (v. 13), wither and dry out so that there can be no possibility of the palm's fruiting. Accordingly Ephraim (*'prym*) can be characterised as fruitless (*pry bly y'śwn*); the pun conveys the nation's fate and serves to negate the traditional blessing of Ephraim formulated in Gen 41.52, and of Joseph in 49.22ff.

The metaphor refers again to the nation's demise and to the denial of all possibility of the renewing of its resources of population (vv. 11f). As in v. 12, the thoroughness of the fate, willed and decreed by Yahweh, is expressed by the same counterfactual concession; the metaphor recedes and Yahweh's threat appears in its stark reality. The transition is facilitated perhaps by the common description of children in Hebrew as 'the fruit of the womb', so Rosenmüller. Yahweh will personally bring about the death of any children born to individual members of the erstwhile nation notwithstanding the pride and joy that the latter may have in the former.

Since Wellhausen first made the suggestion, many scholars have thought that v. 16 is misplaced and finds its proper place between vv. 11 and 12. The ground for this supposition is that, in its present position, v. 16 interrupts the link between v. 15, with its historical reference and its mention of the punishment of disinheritance, and v. 17 which continues the same theme (cf. Harper). Placed between vv. 11 and 12, however, this disadvantage disappears and, positively, a 'perfect link' (cf. Harper) between vv. 11 and 12 is forged. In particular, 16b mentions children brought to birth and this makes a logical connection between 11b where loss of fecundity is followed in the MT *tout court* by mention in 12a of grown children (cf. Rudolph).

Variations on Wellhausen's theme are: (1) Marti's view that 16b alone should be placed between vv. 11 and 12; (2) Rudolph's view that 16a should be placed between vv. 10 and 11, while 16b should be placed between vv. 11 and 12.

Rudolph addresses himself to the further question as to how the disorder in the MT may have taken place. He argues that by homoioarcton a scribe overlooked both 16a (which, like v. 11, begins with a mention of Ephraim) and 16b (which, like 12a, begins with a counterfactual concession). Thereafter he wrote the two parts of v. 16 in the margin and then, at a later stage, the parts were inserted together in the present position.

Finally, the rearrangement is alleged (by Harper and Rudolph) to restore the strophic structure, thus: three distinct strophes (10; 16a 11; 16b 12) are now visible, each composed of two parts; the first alone has a third or additional part, 'they became detestable like the objects of their desire', which effects a special emphasis. Verse 13 has two doublets, while v. 14 is a tristich (so Rudolph).

Such rearrangements of the MT seem to me contrived and unnecessary and the alleged advantages the result of pure rationalisation. If rationalisation is to be employed, then, e.g., Wolff or AF may be said to have produced a comparable justification of the structure of MT as it stands. Apart from such detailed attempts to find form and structure (e.g. Wolff's 'audition account') in the section, the view here adopted, *viz.* that the piece is essentially a meditation by Hosea (placed largely on Yahweh's lips) seems to meet many of the difficulties that are alleged to be present. In particular v. 16 resumes the themes earlier proposed in the section (for 16a, cf. 13a; for 16b, cf. 12a). So far from breaking the link between vv. 15 and 17, the verse serves to emphasise the unity of Hosea's thought in that he manifestly seeks to connect the more factual description of the nation's plight (e.g. vv. 15, 17) with his estimate of the intentions and motivation of Yahweh which provide the reasons for it. Indeed his words express most poignantly the divine sorrow and regret that what from the beginning could have been has not been possible; that the nation's culpability dictates and requires the divine response (v. 17), and that from the earliest times the roots of the malaise were discernible (v. 10). The prayerful interjection of v. 14 (cf. v. 17) serves to express the prophet's own deep understanding of the mind of Yahweh and his sympathy with it (cf. on v. 14 above). Here indeed the form is not so far removed from the so-called confessions of Jeremiah (in chapters 15 and 20 of that book) and we are presented with a remarkable insight into a prophet's penetrating appreciation of moral and theological truths and the immense grief that he felt as a result of that appreciation. There can be no doubt that the experiences of his personal life are here reflected – if only at some remove – and that they contributed not a little to the profundity of his expression.

Text and Versions

הכה אפרים שרשם יבש LXX ἐπόνεσεν 'E. τὰς ῥίζας αὐτοῦ ἐξηράνθη 'Ephraim is afflicted in his roots and dried up' (so Jerome; printed editions of the LXX suggest '... is afflicted, dried up in his roots'); Aq. and Symm. ἐπλήγη (τῷ 'E. ἡ ῥίζα αὐτοῦ.) ? 'E.'s root is smitten'; Pesh. *mḥ' 'prym 'qr' wybš*, 'Ephraim has smitten the root and it has withered'; Vulg. *percussus est Ephraim, radix eorum exsiccata est* 'Ephraim is smitten, its root dried up'; Targ. expands to 'the House of Israel is like a tree whose root below is smitten (דלקא, *v.l.* דיקלא 'is parched') and its branches above wither'.

9.17 **My God must[a] reject them, for they have not listened to him; so they shall[b] become fugitives among the nations.**

[a]Rashi insists that the verb ימאסם is not a jussive (i.e. a curse) 'let my God reject them', but rather is an announcement of the inevitable future. Thus the imperfect here expresses 'obligation or necessity according to the judgement of another person' (GK 107n), i.e. of Hosea.

[b]The simple *waw* prefixed to the verb יהיו indicates that it is a jussive and expresses the 'assurance of a contingent occurrence' (cf. GK 109f).

As in v. 14 above, the prophet reacts to the thought-processes which he has perceived in the mind of his God and to which he has himself given expression. 'My God' is notable and prompts ibn Ezra (cf. Kimchi) to comment that the description emphasises that he is no longer the nation's God, since he has now repudiated it. More particularly the description recalls v. 8 where it is also used and where it serves to emphasise the unity of thought between Yahweh and his prophet. Here the verbs convey the prophet's wholesale concurrence in Yahweh's obligation (note a) to repudiate his people and his acknowledgement of the necessary consequences (note b). Again, then, Hosea perceives his vocation to be the mediator of the mighty will and resolution of Yahweh. In v. 14 there was an element of intercession which yet did not demur from acceptance of the divine will; here Hosea expresses unreserved concurrence with the logic of Yahweh's resolution (cf. Rudolph).

The nation's guilt consists essentially in its inability to listen to Yahweh. It was this consistent failure which precluded the great possibilities which, at the beginning, Yahweh had lovingly foreseen for the nation (v. 13, cf. 16). Even before they had set foot on the land (v. 10, cf. v. 15), their failure to listen was apparent, and recent events (again v. 15), conforming to the pattern, provoked the final exasperation of Yahweh.

Yahweh's rejection of his people spells the end of the nation (cf. 3.4, and Jerome's similar comments); the result is that its erstwhile members will inevitably become rootless fugitives cast forth from the land (cf. v. 15, 'I will banish them from my house') for whom, in the words of Deut 28.65, there will be 'no repose and no rest for the sole of their feet'.

From Jerome's time (see his commentary) the words of this verse have evoked in the minds of commentators the plight of the 'eternal Jew'[13]. For Jerome, indeed, the destruction of the state marks not only God's repudiation of the nation and its rulers for their rejection of Christ but his utter rejection of the subsequent endeavours of the Jews in matters of scriptural knowledge and teaching. Specifically he 'banished them from his house' and will never go on to cherish them again (*eiecit eos ... et non addet, ut ultra diligat eos*). The words are interesting in

[13] So, e.g., Sellin, Weiser, Wolff, H. Braun *ZThK* 48 (1951), p. 36. The very expression is, of course, strictly anachronistic (and even misleading) in respect of Hosea's words, for he was speaking of Ephraim; and the Ephraimites, as a matter of fact, never became 'eternal Jews' for they disappeared from history in 722/1 BC. Without taking Judah into consideration, this prophecy of Hosea, a prophecy of unrelieved woe, was fulfilled by events.

that they seem to be devised to refute the contrary view, *viz.* that in exile is preserved for the Jews the hope of redemption.

This more hopeful view is advocated by Rudolph. For in respect of Hosea and the words of this verse, what appears to be a final judgement of Yahweh upon his people is, in the end, a device to bring them back in repentance. Rudolph regards this evaluation as confirmed by Hosea's other formulations in which he proclaims, e.g., the recapitulation of the judgement of woe conveyed by his children's names (2.3, EV 1) and the wonderful renewal of the broken relationship between Yahweh and his people (2.17ff, EV 15ff; 11.8ff).

Rudolph's assessment is surely correct in respect of Hosea's developed thought in the completed book that bears his name. Whether the assessment is correct in regard to Hosea's meditation at the time of its formulation is another matter. The words and expressions point to a particular mood of the prophet and his deep appreciation of the inexorable logic of Yahweh's position. The finality of the statement 'they have not listened' points to dark times indeed and to coming disaster. Whether Wolff is correct in seeing such words as an indication of Hosea's own rejection and his bitterness at it in the time after 733 BC is hard to determine. The further question of transition from woe to weal is a vexed one and to it commentators have long given their attention (cf. on 2.1f, EV 1.9ff, above). That it happened in respect of Hosea's writings is indubitable; that it happened in Hosea's own lifetime is most likely; yet the words of the present piece suggest in themselves that it had not happened yet.

Text and Versions

אלהי LXX ὁ θεός, → אלהים (Borbone, cf. 1 Kennicott MS); → אלהיהם (cf. *BHS*).

CHAPTER 10.1–8

THE DEMISE OF THE STATE, ITS CULT AND ITS KING

10.1 **Israel is a damaged[a] vine whose[b] fruit fails[c] him. [d]At the time that his fruit should have been prolific[d], he was prolific with[e] altars; when his land should have been at its best[d], they excelled[f] with sacred pillars.**

The verse is amongst the most difficult in the book of Hosea and very considerable uncertainty attends any attempt to interpret not only the individual words but also the syntax that is employed and the simile or metaphor that is thereby formulated.

[a]The evidence of Nah 2.3 (EV 2) suggests that the word בוקק is inherently applicable to vines (so Rashi, cf. ibn Ezra on Nah 2.3). It seems likely, then, that the word is technical and that, for this reason, it is especially difficult to be precise about it. From early times (cf. the LXX, Peshiṭta and Vulgate) the word has been understood to denote healthy and luxuriant growth and many modern commentators and lexica have followed this line of interpretation. Thus Michaelis, in justifying it, draws attention to the Arabic cognate *bqq* with meanings (amongst others) such as 'be prolific (of a woman bearing children)', 'be copious (of rain)'[1]. Reference to Lane's lexicon suggests that the comparison may be sound but that it is not certainly so. Plants are said to come forth (*bqq*) but this is clearly connected to another fundamental meaning of the Arabic verb, *viz.* 'to cleave/split', so that such plants, coming forth, split the earth. In the fourth theme a valley is said to 'put forth its plants or herbage' (*'bqq 'lw'dy*), but this expression may also have a similar explanation behind it.

By contrast, the rabbinic commentators (Rashi, ibn Ezra, Kimchi) are agreed that the word denotes the poor quality or deficiency of the vine. For this Kimchi compares Nah 2.11 (EV 10) and the words בוקה/מבוקה which occur there. Ibn Barūn compares these particular words with Arabic *bwq* 'he came with or brought misfortune, disaster' (so Lane 1, p. 276, col 2, cf. Wechter) and *b'qthm 'lbw"yq* 'misfortunes overtook them'. Ibn Janāḥ specifically compares בוקק in the present verse with

[1] BDB p. 132, col 2, making a similar comparison, distinguishes two roots בקק, the first (I), occurring only here, with the sense 'to be luxuriant'. R. Gordis *JQR* 27 (1937), p. 49, and, independently, Morag are inclined to think of one root that is in the class *Aḍdād* (i.e. having opposite meanings); thus (e.g., Morag), both 'emptying out/destruction' and (uniquely here) 'fulness/abundance'. For another treatment, see P. Humbert *ZAW* 62 (1949/50), p. 200.

בקקים בקקום in Nah 2.3 though unfortunately he does not translate these phrases. Nah 2.3, as has been indicated, also clearly refers to vines and the words there seem to depict the destruction of the state under the figure of such a metaphor ('plundering hordes have stripped them bare', NEB). A further cross-reference to Nah 2.3 is provided by ibn Ezra who (on that verse) states that the transitive verb בְּקָקוּם means that the Israelites will be made like the vine (גפן בוקק) of Hos 10.1.

The reference to and comparison with Nah 2.3 made by ibn Janāḥ and ibn Ezra seems to me to amount to strong evidence in favour of a meaning for the word בוקק denoting poor quality, deficiency or damage (cf. 9.17) rather than to healthy and luxuriant growth. The antiquity of this alternative view is suggested by the evidence of Aquila, Symmachus and the Targum. For further indications in its favour, see the treatment of the rest of the verse.

If this judgement is correct, and the usage of Hos 10.1 is of a sort with that attested by Nah 2.3 and also by Nah 2.11 (so Kimchi), the question of the etymology and derivation of the word must be addressed. Here it may be suggested that KB³ is right in its supposition that the root בקק as it occurs in Nah 2.3 should be compared with Arabic *bwq* (mentioned above) and with Syriac (and Mandaic) *bqq* 'to be worm-eaten', 'rotten', 'decayed'[2]. Further, the evidence of Nah 2.11 suggests that the root occurred in Hebrew in two forms, i.e. as a hollow root but also with reduplicated third radical (cf. המם/הום or, as a *Po'lel* from the root קום, קומם cf. GK 72m). Ibn Ezra, in his comments on Nah 2.3 is inclined to the view that בקק is strictly a transitive verb though he suggests that, like שוב, it could be either transitive (as in Nah 2.3) or intransitive (as in Hos 10.1)[3]. From this it may be deduced that the form בוקק, applied specifically to vines, means that they display damage, deficiency and decay (cf. שובב from שוב) or else that others (בֹּקְקִים) are the bringers of damage, deficiency and decay to them (cf. קומם from קום). The former sense is to be detected in Hos 10.1, the latter in Nah 2.3[4]. The translation 'damaged', proposed above, seems best fitted to the generality of the evidence; cf. further, for the general image (but without בקק), Ezek 19.12. For comments on the gender of גפן see note b below.

[b]The words are understood as a short relative clause with ellipsis of אשר; lit. 'a damaged vine of which the fruit fails it/them'. Generally speaking the word גפן is feminine and the present instance, where it is construed in the masculine, is held to be unique in the OT and thus another indication of the dialectal character of Hosea's Hebrew (so, e.g., Rudolph, Morag). The matter is not easy, for there are a number of instances where masculine pronouns refer to גפן – even sometimes

[2] Cf. K. J. Cathcart *Nahum in the light of North-West Semitic* Biblica et Orientalia 26 (Rome, 1973), pp. 84f.

[3] Ibn Janāḥ clearly addresses himself to the same problem for he wonders whether בוקק does not stand for בקק.

[4] For the forms בּוֹקָה and מְבוּקָה in Nah 2.11, cf. (from שוב) שׁוּבָה and מְשׁוּבָה.

alternating with feminine pronouns (Ezek 17.6f; 19.11; cf. 2 Kgs 4.39 with its northern features). Such usage may be capable of other explanations (GK 135o), but at least it constitutes evidence which requires cautious evaluation.

It is further the case that the metaphor by which Israel is described as a vine is expressed very tersely and succinctly; accordingly, since Israel (masculine) is uppermost in the prophet's mind, his particular usage may reflect that emphasis (so, e.g., BDB, Mauchline, Wolff). Certainly, in the second part of the verse, where the climax is expressed, it is Israel who multiplies altars etc. and the action is understood metaphorically as the 'fruit of his actions' (so the Targum, cf. Kimchi)[5]. The antecedent of לו, then, is likely to refer here both to the tenor and to the vehicle of the metaphor (i.e. the vine which is Israel).

[c]The most commonly attested meaning for the verb שוה is 'to be like', 'resemble' (so שוה I, according to BDB). Such a sense has been detected here by Jerome, Rashi, ibn Ezra and Kimchi as well as, more recently, by Wolff. Thus the fruit of the vine 'resembles' it or 'is appropriate' to it in its character as בוקק. BDB distinguishes a second root שוה which has the meaning 'to set', 'place' and specifically here 'to make', 'produce'. A similar view of the matter has recently been advocated by Morag, though for him such a meaning reflects a natural semantic development from the notion of 'equality' and hence to posit a second root is not necessary. Psalm 18.34 = 2 Sam 22.34 'who makes (משוה) my feet like a hind's feet', gives an indication of the link. Here in Hos 10.1 as in talmudic Aramaic, Mandaic and dialectal Arabic, the usage has developed in such a way that the point of comparison becomes unnecessary and the verb expresses action pure and simple. Accordingly the line means 'Israel was a luxuriant vine (so בוקק) which produced (abundant) fruit for itself'. The verb is thus synonymous with the well known עשה 'to produce' as it occurs in Hos 9.16.

Ibn Janāḥ knows this view but he is insistent on repudiating it as supplying an interpretation which is 'weak and feeble'. He does so on two related grounds: first, it is necessary to make the unwarranted assumption that the initial reference is to the past, 'Israel was a בוקק vine which produced fruit'; and, secondly, that only in the second part of the verse does the present situation obtrude. On his view, בוקק and ישוה describe the present situation and the meaning of both terms, clearly interlocking, denotes the present adverse state of the vine, Israel (cf. Hos 8.7; 9.2; 9.17).

[5] For attempts to see in בוקק a predicate of Israel as the subject 'Israel despoils/reaps the vine', 'Israel was luxuriant as a vine', etc., cf. Halévy, G. R. Driver *Nötscher Festschrift*, p. 55, H. Torczyner *Marti Festschrift*, p. 278. The word order tells against such interpretations, some of which, in any case, fail to do justice to the metaphorical character of the text (*contra*, e.g., Sellin; cf. Rudolph).

Ibn Janāḥ's argument has some considerable force and tells against the approach of BDB and Morag, at any rate as it affects this particular verse.

Reference to the Arabic cognate verb *swy* and its attested sense (VIIIth theme) 'to be (of a man) mature, of full vigour' or (of food) 'to be thoroughly cooked', 'to be ripe' has prompted Nyberg (cf. Rudolph) to see in the word this latter meaning; thus 'Israel is a luxuriant vine which brings fruit to ripeness'. The suggestion has its merits not least (though Nyberg does not mention the fact) because the meanings 'to boil', 'cook', 'to grow ripe' are clearly attested for another Hebrew verb, *viz.* בשל; this latter is specifically used of the ripening clusters of grapes on a vine in Gen 40.10. There are, however, objections: thus Morag indicates that the meaning 'properly cooked' is more likely to be derived from the notions of completeness, correctness, connected with that of equality inherent in the Arabic verb (cf. the colloquial English 'to come up to scratch'). The colloquial Arabic meaning 'to be ripe' is thus closer to the well-attested sense 'to be cooked' or 'ready for eating' rather than to the notion of a tree or plant bringing its fruit to ripeness.

Ibn Janāḥ believes that the verb is to be derived from the root elsewhere well-attested as a noun under the radicals שוא 'emptiness', 'nothingness', 'vanity'[6]. Accordingly the verb, occurring only here, has exactly the same force as יכחש in Hos 9.2 'new wine will disappoint them', cf. Hab 3.17. The theory is attractive since it fits the context admirably and accords with the best attested meaning for בוקק (note a above). Further it facilitates an interpretation of the verse as a single metaphor depicting the adverse state of the nation under the figure of a vine and thus obviates the necessity of seeing in the first part a reference to the past ('Israel was a vine ...') and in the second part a reference to a more recent, and perhaps even the present, situation (so, e.g., Wolff, Rudolph, Mays). While undoubtedly such a contrast may be detected in 9.10, 13, the participial בּוֹקֵק followed by the imperfect יְשַׁוֶּה cannot be said to suggest such a contrast here; rather the imperfect suggests a temporal sense akin to that expressed by the imperfect of 9.11.

[d—d]The preposition כ prefixed to infinitives construct (so rightly, e.g., Rosenmüller, Nyberg, Rudolph) denotes, of time, 'at', 'about', 'when', 'at the time of' (BDB p. 454, col 2 3 b, cf. especially Hos 13.6). For the hypothetical sense 'should have' cf. Isa 10.15. The phrases כרב ... ל and כטוב ... ל, closely parallel to each other, mean (literally) 'when there was multiplying in respect of his fruit ...', 'when there was prospering in respect of his land ...'

[e]The perfect הרבה expresses the reality of Israel's fruitfulness and its

[6] Ibn Janāḥ regards the final *aleph* as (radically) superfluous and for this he compares the pronouns הוא and היא. For the close relation between roots *lamedh he* and *lamedh aleph*, GK 75oo.

(obnoxious) nature. The preposition ל which follows is dictated by the construction of the sentence and follows the grammatically unexceptionable ל ... כרב; by the construction of the sentence it is not (*contra* Rosenmüller, Wolff and Rudolph) a pure dative with the sense 'he multiplied (fruit) for the altars'. The words mean literally 'he gave multiplicity in respect of (the, so MT) altars'.

[f] Again, the sense of the verb היטיבו here is best defined by reference to the preceding clause כטוב לארצו and to the earlier parallel הרבה; the contrast is between goodness, excellence predicated of the land and then of the (obnoxious) excellence of the Israelites. היטיב in this sense is clearly attested, cf. BDB p. 405, col 2 3. Amongst other (related) meanings of the verb is 'to prepare', 'make ready', cf. (of lamps) Exod 30.7 and perhaps 'to build', cf. Ps 51.20 (of Zion)[7]. The notion of conscientious preparation is sometimes consistent with adornment, beautification (cf. 2 Kgs 9.30) but that is scarcely the emphasis in this instance.

The verse, like 9.11, depicts the immediate situation; it is unlike 9.10 and 13 which draw a contrast between the past and the present; on the other hand, a contrast between what might have been and present realities is clearly discernible in the second half of the verse. Accordingly the verse, though strictly different from some of those which precede it, fits well with the general sense already expressed. The tragedy of Israel's predicament is the more poignant in the light of what might have been (cf. on 6.1–6 and 9.16 above). Indeed the very use here of the term 'Israel' rather than 'Ephraim' conveys an ideal; it denotes the object of Yahweh's care and concern, the centre of his plan and purpose.

Israel, so defined, is now blighted and damaged (note a, cf. 9.16). This thought is expressed by a tersely worded metaphor in which, at all points, the referent (Israel) obtrudes (note b). The metaphor of the vine is frequently used by the prophets (cf. with Rudolph, Jer 2.21; Ezek 15.2ff; 17.6ff; further Ps 80.9f; Isa 5.1ff; 27.2 and Jer 12.10) and is found elsewhere in Hosea at 9.10 and 14.8 (EV 7). Here the vine, which is Israel, is blighted and damaged and the grapes that it might have been expected to produce in abundance disappoint the expectations of those who believed themselves to be Israel (notes b and c). Again the land, both the soil of the vine and the home of Yahweh's people, was potentially ideal for the fruitful growth of the vine and for the well-being of the nation. Yet that nation's endeavour was misdirected and effected the discreditable proliferation of altars

7 The Peshiṭta uses the *Ethpa'al* of *ṭwb* to render Hebrew נצב (cf. מַצֵּבָה) at Exod 33.8; cf. Qyl.

and sacred pillars (see on 3.4) which indicate, by metonymy, the syncretistic and idolatrous cult now so widespread (see further on 8.11 above). At this point, then, Hosea indicates that it is the nation's wilful idolatry which has spoiled and damaged the vine; that the very reason for the failure of its vintage is the nation's misplaced and disloyal endeavour; that the nation's disappointment at the failure of the ideal, conveyed by the title Israel, is its own making (so essentially, ibn Janāḥ; cf. ibn Ezra and, as an alternative, Rashi).

Text and Versions

בוקק LXX εὐκληματοῦσα, cf. Vulg. *frondosa* 'abundant in leaves', 'leafy', and Pesh. *dšbwq'* '(vine of) shoots', cf. the rendering of שׂרקה 'choice vine' in Gen 49.11; Aq. ἔνυδρος 'watery', i.e. which over-extends itself in growth (see Jerome's commentary); Symm. ὑλομανοῦσα 'run to wood', i.e. directing its growth to abundant shoots rather than to fruiting (cf. Jerome); Targ. בזיזא 'despoiled'.

ישוה LXX εὐθηνῶν 'flourishing'; on the basis of this Eitan *HUCA* 14 (1939), p. 3, reads יֹשֶׁה and, comparing Arabic *wšy*, renders 'abundant'; Aq. and Symm. ἐξισώθη, cf. Vulg. *adaequatus est* 'became equal'; Pesh. *d'bdt* 'which produced'; Targ. פירי עובדיהון גרמו להון דיגלון 'the fruits of their actions brought about (their exile)'.

כרב פריו → לו פריו (cf. *BHS*).

למזבחות → מזבחות (cf. *BHS*).

כטוב לארצו → לו ארצו (cf. *BHS*).

היטיבו LXX ᾠκοδόμησεν 'he was built'; Aq. ἐσπούδασε 'he was zealous (about pillars)'; Vulg. *exuberavit* 'he has been abundant (with images)'; note the singular in these versions for MT's plural; Targ. איטיבו 'they have excelled (with their pillars)'; → היטיב (Borbone, cf. *BHS*).

מצבות → למצבות (Borbone; cf. and contrast *BHS* which, as a possibility, deletes ל from למזבחות).

10.2 **[a]They have dissimulated in their hearts[a], they must bear the punishment[b]. It is this[c] which will break[d] their altars, it will smash their sacred pillars.**

[a—a]Lit. 'their heart has dissimulated'. The phrase is not easy and considerable difficulty attaches to any attempt to interpret it. The verb חלק may be derived from either of two roots, the first indicating 'division' (BDB חלק I), the second 'smoothness', 'slipperiness' (BDB

חלק II) and so 'flattery' and then 'dissimulation'. Amongst the rabbinic commentators Rashi, ibn Ezra and Kimchi favour the first of the alternatives (cf. the versions) and interpret the phrase of the Ephraimites' alienation and schism from Yahweh. As a variant, e.g., Bauer, Hitzig, RV, have understood the division of the heart of the Israelites, halting between their affection for Baal and Yahweh.

Generally recent commentators have long (cf. Rosenmüller) favoured the second root (so, e.g., Wellhausen, Marti, Harper, Wolff, Rudolph, Mays, RVmarg.) understanding the phrase of the false, deceitful zeal of the people whose offerings, ostensibly brought to honour Yahweh, were in fact devoted to Baal, the greater object of their affection. For Rudolph the etymology is, in the end, unimportant; both alternatives issue in the same general sense: the people are indicted for their breach of the first commandment.

This approach raises a second question: the precise denotation of the word 'heart' (לב) in this context. To it, surprisingly, few commentators have turned their attention. It seems likely that the word here denotes either the thinking or reflection of the nation (cf. BDB p. 524, col 2 3 c) or else its moral character (cf. BDB p. 525, col 1 6), a reflection of its inclination, resolutions and determination of the will (col 1 4). It seems most unlikely that the nation's affection or zeal as, e.g., divided between the service of Yahweh and Baal, is intended; 'heart' cannot be said to be capable of such a meaning here (*contra*, e.g., Wolff, Rudolph) for it is only by the use of particular verbs (e.g. Deut 6.5) that that meaning is conveyed (cf. BDB p. 524, col 2 II 2). Hosea, when he deals with the subject is generally insistent that moral perversity is connected with and attributable to faulty and perverse reasoning (cf., e.g., 2.7, EV 5; 4.14f; 7.13ff) and it seems likely that here too he makes such a point. Where the verb חלק is concerned, Harper is right to draw attention to its usage in Ezek 12.24 where it denotes 'dissimulation' and, interestingly in view of ibn Janāḥ's treatment of ישוה in Hos 10.1 (note c to that verse), it is in parallelism with שוא 'falsehood', 'deceit'.

[b]יאשמו For ibn Ezra and Kimchi (cf. LXX and Vulgate, below) the verb אשם represents a by-form of the verb ישם/שמם 'be desolate', 'devastated' (cf. on 5.15 above) and for this they compare Hos 14.1 and Gen 47.19. The evidence of 4.15 (*q.v.*); 5.15; 13.1, however, suggests that the sense 'bear punishment' may be held the better to fit this particular context (cf. most moderns). Certainly the rendering 'they will be devastated' is unconvincing in anticipation of what follows, i.e. the (more particular) destruction of altars and sacred pillars (cf. Rudolph). The Targum, with a double translation, appears to have known both interpretations.

[c]Rashi, ibn Ezra and Kimchi all suppose that the pronoun הוא refers to the 'heart' (cf. note a–a); it is thus the nation's dissimulation (as here understood) and the resulting guilt which will entail the destruction of the altars etc. An alternative view of the matter is that the pronoun refers to Yahweh, cf. 'my God' in 9.17 (so Rosenmüller). Jerome (cf.

Qyl) similarly understands Yahweh as the referent, though he goes on to suggest that Yahweh affects his purpose specifically through the agency of the nation's enemies (cf. the Targum).

Amongst less likely interpretations are those of Nyberg, cf. Östborn, p. 89, for whom the pronoun refers to Baal; and Marti, for whom Israel itself is meant, i.e. seeing the false cult under sentence of destruction and judging it to be worthless, the nation, disillusioned, itself brings about the cult's final destruction (cf. Isa 2.20). Marti's suggestion depends not a little on his supposition that v. 2a is a later gloss and this facilitates referring the pronoun to the antecedent 'Israel' of v. 1. Yet even if the supposition is accepted, it is strange indeed that Israel, represented by a third person pronoun, should destroy Israel's, now 'their', altars. To meet such objections, Marti is driven to gratuitous emendation. See further on the problem in the commentary below.

[d]The verb is denominative from עֹרֶף 'neck' and means strictly, to slaughter an animal by breaking its neck (cf. Exod 13.13; Deut 21.4 etc.). The usage here, where altars are the object, is metaphorical (so ibn Janāḥ and the rabbinic commentators)[8]. There is no reference to breaking the four horns of the altars, as in Amos 3.14 (*contra*, e.g., Wellhausen, Marti, Wolff); rather the verb expresses that the altars, constructed of numerous stones, will be radically damaged, i.e. rendered useless in respect of their function. Michaelis' theory that the verb is illuminated by reference to Arabic *'rf* 'knew', 'recognised', 'was aware of' is hardly convincing (cf. Rosenmüller's further criticisms).

The verse appears to be constructed with such care that its character seems almost contrived. Accordingly the question arises whether it is an early gloss; or rather an early explanation and commentary on the difficult verse which precedes it. Immediately apparent is the repetition of the words 'altars' and 'sacred pillars' each with third person plural suffixes, the latter matching the final third person plural verb of the preceding verse ('they excelled'). While third person plural forms appear in v. 2a, it is striking that the opening phrase is grammatically third person singular; and equally, and more so, that the third phrase of the verse is emphatically (note c) third person singular. It seems likely, then, that the complicated combination of metaphor and referent which characterises v. 1 is reflected here. Accordingly 'their heart has dissimulated' (note a) may be taken to refer to the singular (damaged) vine; 'they must bear the punishment', in which the verb is now plural, showing its reference to the people, to the vine's disappointing produce and then to the

[8] See H. Tawil *JNES* 32 (1973), pp. 481ff, for a discussion of Aramaic הרג used 'with respect to destroying a physical object' and for the possibility, ערף in this verse compared, of 'a broader pattern of figurative usage'.

nation's aberrant cultic behaviour; while the emphatic third person singular ('it is this/it is he who') matches the third singular reference to the vine ('when it should have produced much fruit', 'when its soil should have excelled') but yields a sense which is dramatically new. For now the vine's flaw, the people's dissimulation, itself brings about the withering of its fruit, the destruction of their monstrous cultic artefacts. The choice of the pronoun (note c) allows also the understanding that if wilful perversity naturally entails ruin then it is because Yahweh so wills it: it is he that is the architect and controller of the moral order.

Marti's argument that v. 2a is an intrusive gloss has some merit but, in view of his particular interpretation, is open to serious objection (note c). Nevertheless, what he says raises important issues in respect of v. 2 and prompts the sort of interpretation attempted above. On this view of the matter v. 2, if contrived, yet reflects very accurately the sense of v. 1. If, then, it is a gloss it is an accurate gloss; if an interpretation, an authentic one. Accordingly it seems likely that it comes from Hosea himself; and if not, then from the hand of the compiler of his oracles, one who accurately understood his master.

It is argued (note d) that the destruction of the altars under the figure of 'the breaking of their necks' is essentially a metaphor. For some commentators, however, the phrase has a deeper significance. Thus, Wolff understands Yahweh's destruction of the altars as involving profanation; they are treated 'like animals that are not sacrificed in the legitimate cult' (cf. Exod 13.13). Rudolph suggests that the phrase, evoking the ancient ritual of the breaking of the heifer's (*'glh*) neck (Deut 21.4ff), implies, so to speak, the destruction and cessation of the national cult of the calf. Such interpretations seem somewhat over-ingenious and contrived. It is enough that the verse sets forth the imminent and total destruction of Israel's prolific cultic centres, the epitome and fruit of the nation's perverted thinking and the (false) manifestations of the well-being to which it aspired. For the removal of sacred pillars as a metonym of the nation's cult and establishment, cf. 3.4; here the monarchy is also mentioned as it is in 10.3.

Text and Versions

חלק לבם LXX ἐμέρισαν καρδίας αὐτῶν 'they have divided their hearts', on the basis of which Vollers proposes חִלְּקוּ; Aq. and Symm. ἐμερίσθη καρδία, cf. Vulg. *divisum est cor eorum*; Pesh. *'tplg lbhwn* and Targ. אתפליג לבהון 'their heart is divided'; changes in pointing include חָלַק (Oort, Harper) and חֻלַּק (Oettli, Borbone); → + לָקַח מיהוה (cf. *BHS*).

יאשמו LXX ἀφανισθήσονται, cf. Vulg. *interibunt*; 'they will be destroyed'; Aq., Symm. and Theod. πλημμελήσουσι, cf. Pesh. *nthybwn*; Targ. יחובון 'they will offend', 'be guilty'.

הוא Targ. כען איתי עליהון סנאה 'now I will bring upon them an enemy' suggests a double translation of יאשמו and an interpretation of הוא in terms of Yahweh, see notes b and c above.

יערף LXX κατασκάψει 'raze to the ground', cf. Pesh. *nsḥwp*; Vulg. *confringet* 'break in pieces'; Targ. יחור קדלהון (דאיגריהון) 'he will twist the neck (of their altars)'; by reference to LXX, → יערה or יערער (Vollers).

10.3 **Then they will[a] acknowledge[b]: we have no king; we have shown no respect whatsoever[c] for Yahweh. And as for the king, what can[d] he do for us?**

[a]For עתה of 'a time ideally present' (i.e. from Hosea's point of view), BDB p. 774, col 1 c. The imperfect tense again denotes the imminent future, cf. 2.12, EV 10; 8.10 and the preceding verse.

[b]Cf. BDB p. 56, col 1 2 and see the commentary below.

[c]כי is used asseveratively.

[d]Cf. GK 107r, *contra* Rudolph who understands the imperfect as frequentative: 'what does he do for us?'

Kimchi rightly characterises the verse as a confession on Israel's part, though for him it was made 'in their exile'. It is not necessary to follow him in this latter supposition, for the words bear all the marks of Hosea's own estimate of what his nation will shortly (note a) be driven to recognise. Accordingly Marti's supposition (cf. Harper) that the phrase 'we have shown no respect ...', at least, is an exilic gloss (because such sentiments were evidently not those of eighth century Ephraimites) may be discounted.

The punishment shortly to befall Israel, the punishment which would entail the destruction of its exuberant cultic self-expression, will bring the people to the acknowledgement that the royal establishment which, like the cult, afforded them some guarantee of safety and well-being (cf. Rashi) is now virtually defunct if not quite so. The words seem closely to mirror the terse statement of 3.4 where the removal of (*inter alia*) king and sacred pillars marks the disruption of the national establishment.

The element of penitence and confession obtrudes in the statement 'we have shown no respect for Yahweh' which is an acknowledgement that that failure has brought about the impotence of the national establishment, now virtually destroyed.

If the words of the verse have been rightly evaluated as Hosea's estimate of the sentiments that his people will shortly be driven to express, the question arises whether that estimate reflects the historical realities of the period. Verse 7 describes the monarchy as foam swept away by flood water. Verse 6 seems to refer to disastrous switches of foreign policy and to the consequences of withholding tribute; and v. 4 to treachery and revolts in respect of the monarchy. Accordingly Wolff would seem to be correct in his estimate that the verse is to be set against the reign of Hoshea (731–725 BC). He had assassinated Pekah and been confirmed as a dependent vassal king by Tiglath-pileser, paying tribute to the latter until some years later (? 724 BC), presumably after a time of exploratory negotiations, he ceased to do so, seeking a renewed alliance with Egypt. According to 2 Kgs 17.4 he was captured and imprisoned by Tiglath-pileser's successor Shalmaneser V. These events would seem to have a close affinity with Hosea's words and it is not unreasonable to suppose that the prophet, from the time of Pekah's overthrow, was able to perceive accurately the way things were going.

The two statements about the king in the verse are superficially contradictory; thus 'we have no king' and 'what can the king do for us?' The problem is perceived by Kimchi, who supposes that the former phrase is hyperbole and conveys the sense 'it is as if we have no king', indicating that the king has no longer any effective power. This interpretation has the advantage that the second phrase 'what can the king do for us' is seen to be merely a variant of the first. It also accords with the statement of v. 7 which depicts the king of Samaria as swept away by events which he cannot control. Again such statements match accurately the particular situation which obtained during the reign of Hoshea.

Kimchi's observations allow a coherent exposition of the verse. Alternatives which are less satisfactory are as follows: first, the view that the words have a past reference and indicate a repudiation of the institution of the monarchy, cf. 1 Sam 8 (so Sellin). It is inconceivable that 'then they will acknowledge' (note a) can be taken of the past. Secondly, the view that the quotations of the verse are those of Hosea's contemporaries and have a strictly present reference. It seems most unlikely, however, that Hosea's contemporaries would have said 'we have shown no respect for Yahweh'; rather, they claimed that they did so, cf. 8.2; 7.14. In the light of this consideration a number of commentators have supposed that the verse reflects a dialogue between Hosea and his contemporaries (so, e.g., van Hoonacker, van Gelderen), thus, to the people's words 'we have no king' or 'have we no king?' (i.e. why do we derive no benefit from him?), Hosea replies 'When we show no respect for Yahweh, what can the king do for us?' To this Rudolph properly objects that it is not likely that Hosea would thus identify himself with his contemporaries. Van Gelderen's supposition that such identification is like that of Isaiah with his Judaean contemporaries (Isa 6.5) is unlikely, since that obtained in the period before and not during his ministry (so again Rudolph).

Text and Versions

כי לא Pesh. has no equivalent כי.

10.4 **They have made[a] promises[b], invoked unprincipled oaths[c], concluded[c] treaties. So their government[d] sprouts[e] like[d] poisonous weeds[f] on the furrows of the field[g].**

[a]The evidence of the LXX (see below) has suggested to a number of commentators that an infinitive absolute should be read here in conformity with those which follow. Further it is argued (e.g. Rudolph) that since the verse answers the question 'what can the king (i.e. singular) do for us?' (v. 3), a plural form is out of place. However, it may be urged that the following infinitives absolute serve to express the continuation of the preceding finite verb (GK 113z); and further, that if the verse is indeed concerned primarily with the actions of the king, that concern is rather generally with the institution than with a particular exemplar (see further below). The third person plural verb דִּבְּרוּ is, then, retained and its subject is understood to be the monarchy in general or the establishment of the state of which the monarchy was the head.

[b]For the particular sense of the noun דברים 'promises' in this context, cf., with Qyl, Ps 105.8 (similarly AF). Rudolph's definition of the phrase in terms of empty speech unaccompanied by action points to the same conclusion.

[c]Cf. a above and GK 113ff. The infinitive absolute אָלוֹת in place of the expected אָלֹה (cf. 4.2) is usually explained as an attraction to the following כָּרֹת, cf. Rashi and GK 75n. Ibn Ezra suggests that, since the word takes a form similar to that of an infinitive construct, it may just possibly be such, the *qametz* replacing *shewa* by reason of the gutteral

first letter (for a similar view, but as one possibility, see Rosenmüller). The balance of probability, however, points to the word as an infinitive absolute (GK 113ff). On this view it may be suggested that we are confronted with a Judaean alternative form adopted here in accordance with the principle indicated above. In support of this view attention may be directed to the form שָׁתוֹת (alongside שָׁתוֹ) in Isa 22.13 and to ראית (? רָאִית, *Qere* רָאוֹת) in Isa 42.20. In view of the occurrence of אָלֹה in 4.2, we may suppose that the Judaean redactors modified the form here because of the near occurrence of כָּרֹת, leaving that in 4.2 unchanged[9].

A more radical solution is to regard the word as a construct plural noun (cf. the Vulgate and, with Rosenmüller, Deut 29.20). On this view, the phrase is in apposition to 'promises' and is the object of the verb, i.e. 'they have made promises, unprincipled oaths'. Yet to see the word as an infinitive absolute permits what follows ('they concluded treaties') to be construed similarly. If the word is a noun, it is not easy to construe the following phrase satisfactorily. In 4.2, the verb implies malicious curses rather than perjury; here, however, oaths – so often associated with treaties undertaken without integrity – are indicated; for שוא in this context, cf. the third commandment (Exod 20.7; Deut 5.11).

[d]Precise definition of the term משפט in this verse is very difficult. For Rashi, cf. Kimchi, the term denotes (God's) judgement of discipline and punishment. As an alternative Rashi suggests that, in the context of broken agreements and the collapse of the structure of society, it is specifically litigation that flourishes, with resulting bitterness for the afflicted and poor. For ibn Ezra the term denotes 'their' perverted justice; justice which is sweet but which, as in Amos 5.7, has turned bitter.

Ibn Ezra's assessment suggests the possibility that משפט denotes justice in the sense of (good) government (cf. Isa 42.1, 3). In the context of an attack upon the monarchy and the establishment for their treacherous duplicity in foreign policy, the government of the nation, which should have a proper concern for its well-being and safety, is shown to be flawed; it is turning into (cf. Amos 5.7; 6.12), and here 'grows as', a poisonous weed which will infest the ploughed furrows of the land. On this view the phrase is metaphorical and may be held to convey the sense that 'government will proliferate in the manner of a poisonous weed along the furrows ...' (GK 118s, w). According to this approach it is the phrase as a whole that is characterised by irony or litotes rather than the particular word משפט and the use of the verb ופרח is dictated within the metaphor rather by ראש (poisonous weed) than by משפט (government). Such considerations tell against the objections reasonably formulated by Rudolph against the view that משפט denotes here 'justice' but with the sense of 'injustice'. Qyl offers much the same interpretation

[9] The argument represents an attempt to give more precision to an idea posited by Rabin (p. 125). That the influence of the Judaean redactors is to be detected specifically in morphology, cf. Morag, p. 491.

by supposing that the word שוא governs and influences all the phrases of the verse and thus here משפט stands for משפט שוא 'perverted justice'. For further comments, see notes e and f below.

The main alternative interpretation of משפט is that of Rashi and it is followed by a number of modern commentators, most notably by Rudolph (cf. Ewald, Cheyne, Harper). According to this view, the last clause of the verse represents God's judgement upon the monarchy for wickedness described earlier in the verse. משפט denotes divine judgement (BDB p. 1048, col 2 f) as the necessary consequence of wicked actions and policies. Such judgement is in some sense (see note f) bitter or poisonous to the land and its inhabitants. The problem presented by this view is that it is difficult to accept that Hosea would characterise (divine) judgement as poisonous, even by reference to its effect upon the wicked. Elsewhere (5.11, on one view) Ephraim is described as crushed according to the requirements of divine justice; but that justice itself should act as a poison against (cf. Rashi) the nation seems somewhat inconsistent with Hosea's understanding of the nature of divine punishment. Further, it should be noted that (e.g.) Rudolph is driven to interpret the word כראש, both in respect to syntax and to meaning, in a way which differs considerably from the traditional understanding (note f) and also to regard 'upon the furrows of the field' as a gloss added later to the text by reference to 12.12 (EV 11).

[e]ופרח *waw* consecutive with the perfect is here taken as frequentative, i.e. expressing present action 'as the temporal or logical consequence' of other, repeated actions (GK 112m). Nowack, who favours the view that משפט (note d) denotes 'justice', 'right' and thus cannot be said to flourish as poisonous weeds, proposes the emendation והפכו ... ל 'they turn justice to poisonous weeds' after Amos 6.12. For Rudolph's view of the meaning of פרח see note f.

[f]For Rashi ראש denotes a poisonous herb, identified tentatively by Qyl, and amongst other possibilities, with *papaver somniferum*. Elsewhere the word, spelt רוש or ראש, denotes poison in general and its use is always figurative, cf. BDB *ad loc.* For Kimchi, what is denoted is the poisonous fruit of a particular root or plant (cf. Deut 29.17).

Rudolph is emphatic that ראש elsewhere (even in Deut 29.17) never certainly denotes a plant but rather 'poison', 'venom' and the view that it means a plant here is wholly dependent upon the presence of the following words 'upon the furrows of the field'. Since משפט is properly the subject of the verb the resulting sense of MT is awkward and thus suspect; he concludes that 'upon the furrows of the field' was added as a later gloss by reference to 12.12 (EV 11) where its occurrence is original and satisfactory and in mistaken explanation of the verb פרח understood in the sense 'to grow', 'sprout' (√I in BDB). For Rudolph פרח denotes to 'break out' (√II in BDB) as of leprous or malignant ulcers (cf. Exod 9.9f; Lev 13.20, 25); the preposition כ conceals another preposition, *viz. beth instrumenti*, because the point of the comparison is not with משפט but with the wickedness previously described in v. 4a. In the light of such considerations Rudolph renders 'judgement has broken out as through the agency of poison(ous substance)', i.e. as if in a human body. The number of assumptions and alterations to the text necessary to achieve this interpretation is very considerable; moreover, inconsistency results in that, though Rudolph understands the poisonous substance specifically of the king's wickedness, yet he continues to understand משפט as the actual subject of the verb (cf. his note c, p. 193 and his comments on p. 194).

It seems best to follow Rashi in his assumption that ראש was capable of denoting a poisonous plant which infests and takes over all that land which, properly cultivated, was capable of produce (cf. Rosenmüller).

[g]שׂדי archaic for שׂדה. For על, see on 12.12.

The verse is most likely to constitute an answer to the question raised in the preceding 'what can the king do for us?' (*contra* Marti who regards v. 5 as the proper continuation of v. 3). The answer, however, is made by reference to the current record of the monarchy and serves to emphasise the answer strictly required by the rhetorical question 'what can the king do?' 'Nothing' (cf. again Marti's comments). The kings and the national establishment had in the period immediately prior to and including the reign of Hoshea continually (note a) involved themselves in promises (note b) which they were unable or unwilling to keep, i.e. in foreign policies which they could not or would not sustain (cf. Isa 8.10; 36.5). Their precarious position led them to invoke all too speedily unprincipled oaths in connection with such policies thus perpetuating and increasing the evil web of intrigue which crippled every possibility of stable government (cf. Rudolph). Thirdly, as in 12.2 (EV 1; cf. 5.13; 8.9), they have contracted formal alliances with the great powers, the disastrous consequences of which are now generally apparent. It is this that is meant rather than the covenant between king and people (so Fohrer[10], cf. Wolff, Mays); in 6.7, where the latter is clearly the subject of Hosea's condemnation, it is the breach (*'brw*) of covenant that is set forth, not, as here, its being made or concluded.

In the second half of the verse the effect on the nation of such foolishness is set forth. The complicated syntax of the phrase with, again (cf. 10.1), its close binding of tenor and vehicle, conveys the contrast between what might have been and the present reality (so Rosenmüller). *mšpṭ* 'justice' is, as always, a positive concept and denotes here 'proper government' (note d);

[10] *ZAW* 71 (1959), p. 17.

similarly the phrase 'the furrows of the field' suggests the fruitfulness of successful agriculture blessed by divine providence (cf., with ibn Ezra, Ps 65.11). The perverse foolishness of the nation's monarchy and establishment has not caused proper government of the nation to flourish as 'the ripe corn fields, nor even as barley which feeds the animals; nor as vines whose fruit yields new wine, nor as trees whose apples turn the moisture of the ground into various juices' (so Jerome). Rather, the fields are infested with, as it were, poisonous government; with a 'type of weed which is characteristically able, through its branches and foliage, to propagate yet more weeds and which, unless it is remorselessly dug up and removed, is capable of reducing all the cultivated land to bush' (again, Jerome, here abbreviated).

It is apparent that Hosea, by such speech, perceives a close, even necessary, connection between the moral turpitude of the nation's rulers and the inevitable deterioration of the agriculture of the land (cf. 4.2f). Since that perception is essentially theological in character, there remains some force, at least, in the alternative interpretation of *mšpṭ* mentioned above (note d) in the name of Rashi, *viz.* that it conveys the notion of Yahweh's judgement of discipline and punishment. As in 4.2f, punishment is the inevitable consequence of wrong-doing; that is the way that Yahweh, God of his people and Lord of his land, has arranged the world. If the nation's leaders have, by their turpitude, effected the wholesale deterioration of proper government, that is tantamount to unleashing Yahweh's malevolent curse, which affects not only the people but the land upon which they depend. Careful examination of Hosea's complex formulation suggests, however, that the notion of divine judgement is to be glimpsed behind and through a description of the nation's ruin which portrays the more apparent ethical and political realities of the time.

Text and Versions

דברו LXX λαλῶν 'speaking' suggests the reading דבר → דֹּבֵר (agreeing with the 'king' of the previous verse, so Harper, relying on the punctuation of LXX) or, more probably, דַּבֵּר in conformity with the following infinitives absolute (so Wellhausen, *BHS*, Borbone and many others); Vulg. *loquimini*, 'you speak'; Pesh. *mllw*, cf. Targ. ממללין agreeing with MT.

דברים → כזבים 'lies', after 7.13 (Grätz).

אלות שוא LXX προφάσεις ψευδεῖς, cf. Pesh. *d'llt' dglt'* '(words) of false allegations' (cf. Gelston, p. 167); an accurate interpretation, cf.

note c above, rather than implying עלות, an Aramaism with a similar meaning (Vollers); Symm. ὅρκους ματαίους 'vain oaths'; Vulg. (*verba*) *visionis inutilis* '(words) of vain vision'; Targ. ימן לשקר 'they swear falsely'; on Aq. θρασεῖς, προπετεῖς see Ziegler *Bei.*, p. 359.

כרת LXX διαθήσεται 'he will make (a covenant)', upon the basis of which → כָּרַת (Oort, cf. on דברו above); Vulg. *et ferietis* 'and you (cf. on דברו) make (a treaty)' (*sc.* with falsehood, cf. Jerome).

ופרח → יפרח (LXX ἀνατελεῖ, Borbone, but see note e).

כראש Some Hebrew MSS read בראש (cf. Harper); LXX ὡς ἄγρωστις 'like grass, weed' = Latin *gramen* (Jerome); Symm. and Theod. ὡς λάχανον (χλωρόν) 'like garden-herb', 'vegetable', all reading כדש(א), Ziegler *Bei.*, p. 348; Vulg. *quasi amaritudo* 'like bitterness'; Pesh. *'yk y'r'* 'as a briar'; Targ. כריש חוין בישין 'like the poison of venomous snakes', cf. Cathcart *ad loc.* and W. McKane *VT* 30 (1980), pp. 480ff.

משפט LXX κρίμα, cf. Vulg. *iudicium*; Pesh. *dyn'* 'judgement'; Targ. דין שקרהון 'judgement for their lie'; → מִשְׂפָּח 'bloodshed' (Oettli, cf. Isa 5.7; cf. Fohrer *op. cit.*).

תלמי שדי LXX χέρσον 'dry ground'; cf. Pesh. *bḥql' d'r'' byrt'* 'in the field of the barren land'; Vulg. *sulcos* 'furrows'; Targ. על תחומי חקלן 'on the limits (of the fields)'.

10.5 The inhabitants[a] of Samaria fear for[b] the calf cult[c] of Bethaven; its people lament[d] over it and its priests show their distress[e] for it, for its wealth[f] now lost to it[g].

[a]The singular expression has a distributive force (cf. König, 256a), cf. Isa 5.3; the plural verb which accompanies it is thus in order, GK 145b-g. The word שְׁכַן is the construct of שָׁכֵן, cf. with Qyl זְקַן from זָקֵן.

[b]The verb יגורו, construed with ל, apparently means 'to be in dread concerning', cf. √גור III (BDB, pp. 158f). With the sense 'to fear', 'be afraid of' the verb is construed with מפני, מן, and similarly when it denotes fear in the sense of worship as in Ps 22.24; 33.8 (so Rosenmüller). The latter sense (cf., e.g., Aquila, the Vulgate, Targum and more recently Wolff) hardly fits this particular context.

[c]The noun עגלות, uniquely here, appears to be in the form of a feminine construct plural. The reading is well-attested (cf. certain of the versions below) and emendation is too easy a solution (cf. AF). Amongst the rabbinic commentators, Rashi and ibn Ezra speak of the (plural) calves at Bethel; Kimchi of the calves of Bethel and Dan, spoken of by Hosea as if both were in Bethel for that was the principal site of the cult, cf. Amos 7.13; 1 Kgs 12.32. The use of the feminine gender is, according to Kimchi, derogatory, implying that they were mere artefacts. More likely is the approach of Rudolph (cf. Keil, Orelli) whereby the feminine

plural ending is understood as an abstract plural and the word as denoting 'calfery' → 'the calf cult'[11]. For similar usage, cf. perhaps עשתרת 'increase (of flocks)', Deut 7.13 etc. The presence in what follows of third masculine singular pronouns 'its people', 'over it', 'for it' etc. is *constructio ad sensum*, whereby the idol itself is in the prophet's mind.

[d]אבל A stative, rather than a prophetic (so Rosenmüller) perfect, cf. GK 106g.

[e]The verb יגילו, normally 'to rejoice', is also capable of the meaning 'to show distress', 'fear'. Both Saadya (on Ps 2.11) and ibn Janāḥ argue for the latter meaning in this verse; for a treatment of the word, see Macintosh in *JTS* 27 (1976), pp. 1ff and especially p. 3. For the difficult interpretations based upon the view that the verb גיל here means 'rejoice', see the commentary below.

[f]The noun כבוד can denote 'honour', 'glory', 'prestige'. In 1 Sam 4.22 the word is, as here, the subject of the verb גלה and 'glory has departed from Israel' alludes to the capture of the Ark. Here, in view of the reference to the payment of tribute in the following verse, it is likely that כבוד means specifically 'wealth' as in Gen 31.1; Isa 10.3; 61.6; Nah 2.10 etc. Such an understanding also makes sense of the emphatic expression 'moreover it itself' (i.e. the calf) as it occurs in the next verse (cf. Qyl, Rudolph).

[g]Lit. 'for it has departed from us/it'. The suffix of ממנו has been taken as a first person plural and consequently the phrase, on that view, amounts to a quotation, cf. with Rosenmüller, 1 Sam 4.21; Isa 24.11; Jer 48.7. More likely is the view that the suffix is third person singular masculine though on this view it is difficult to judge precisely the identity of the antecedent. Amongst the possibilities are the calf (for the masculine, cf. note c above), Bethaven, or the people; for the latter, cf. with Rosenmüller 4.7 and 9.11. The presence of the third masculine singular pronoun in v. 6, which apparently refers to the calf, renders this (i.e. the calf) the most probable antecedent (cf. Rudolph) despite the admitted awkwardness. The knot is cut by Wellhausen *et al.*, cf. Harper, who understand the whole phrase to be a later gloss.

Chapter 10 vv. 5 to 8 depict the severe straits into which the national calf cult of Bethel is reduced, and the despairing reaction to the situation on the part of the population of Samaria, the royal and political capital of the Northern Kingdom. The language of v. 5 is marked by a plethora of *lameds* (cf. Amos 5.5) conveying, by alliteration, frenzied ululation (cf. Qyl). As Rudolph observes, the verse is also characterised throughout by

[11] For F. F. Hvidberg's emendation לעגלת understood as '(they fear) together with the heifer (i.e. the goddess Anat) of Bethaven', see *Weeping and Laughter*, p. 99 n. 3; for criticisms, see Rudolph.

strong sarcasm. A god's function is to help his worshippers; here the worshippers are reduced to fearful and distressed (note e) concern for their idol. Yet that is the natural consequence of a situation in which the nation is no longer Yahweh's but the nation of the calf ('its people'). The words imply the situation set forth by Hosea's third child Lo-Ammi (1.9), cf. 9.15 in relation to 1.6. Bethel is named contemptuously as Bethaven (as in 4.15, cf. Kallai *Bethaven*, p. 178) and its priests labelled *kmrym*, a term reserved in the OT (e.g. 2 Kgs 23.5; Zeph 1.4) for the officials of an idolatrous cult. Finally the wealth (note f) of Bethel's calf, now lost, denoted by the term *kbwd* ironically evokes Israel's repudiation of Yahweh, its true glory, cf. Ps 106.20. The distress of the people of Samaria and of the cultic personnel of Bethel clearly reflects a historical occasion when the sanctuary suffered from the ravages of foreign domination of the land. 1 Kings 15.18 (cf. 2 Kgs 18.16) indicates clearly that, in connection with the necessity of paying heavy tribute, resort was made to the resources of the sanctuaries and thus *kbwd* here is likely to denote physically the wealth of the sanctuary of Bethel, whether that of the treasury (so, e.g., Qyl) or of the gold overlay of the calf itself (cf. Sellin). For Kimchi the glory of the calf is lost when its form was smashed, the residual gold (from the overlay) then being sent to Assyria as tribute (cf. v. 6). The situation is unlikely to reflect that of Menahem's tribute in 738 BC since 2 Kgs 15.20 implies that he was able to raise it by taxing wealthy land-owners. It is more likely that the verse reflects Hoshea's payment of tribute over a number of years from 731 BC (2 Kgs 17.3f), the burden of which may well have prompted him to lay hands on the treasures of the national shrine. At all events, the reaction of the nation is clear from the verse; both priest and people, whether in Samaria or Bethel, perceive the event as the loss of the nation's fundamental prestige much as, in 1 Sam 4.22, the loss of the Ark to the Philistines was marked by an earlier sense of Israel's desolation.

For a number of recent scholars, the verse is understood to reflect the ritual lamentation and exultation which accompanies the death (and resurrection) of Baal[12]. To this cultic language is added the last phrase, an ironic notice to the effect that cultic lamentation is now replaced by lamentation for an historical calamity.

The theory is based to a considerable extent upon the view that the verb *gyl* denotes 'rejoicing' which is unlikely to be correct

12 Hvidberg, *op. cit.*, p. 100; cf. Pedersen, 3/4, pp. 470 and 713; similarly, e.g., Wolff and Mays.

(see note e). In any case, mention of 'rejoicing' hardly fits a context in which lamentation is *ex hypothesi* the final attitude adopted. To make it do so would require a different expression, e.g., to the effect that rejoicing had finally given over to lamentation (cf. Rudolph). Amongst the rabbinic authorities who assume that *gyl* denotes 'rejoicing' such a sentiment is indeed detected, though they interpret it upon an historical plane; e.g. Rashi, 'its priests who continually rejoice over it, now lament over its lost glory' (cf. ibn Ezra and Kimchi). These authorities are driven to understand that the phrase in question is a relative clause, i.e. 'its people lament over it and its priests, who rejoice(d) over it ...' (cf. AV). This approach is, however, hardly convincing and can scarcely be held to constitute evidence for language reflecting cultic reaction to the vicissitudes of Baal. Indeed an alternative explanation of 'rejoicing', transmitted by Jerome in the name of the Hebrew tradition, may be held to indicate the extent to which ingenuity has been deployed to justify it; thus, the priests of Bethel rejoiced when the calves were sent to Assyria since that event precluded the discovery of an earlier fraudulent substitution of bronze calves for the golden ones.

Text and Versions

לעגלות LXX τῷ μόσχῳ, cf. Theod. τὸν μόσχον and Pesh. *l'gl'*, suggests a singular reading לעגל to a number of scholars (e.g. Wellhausen, Marti, Wolff, *BHS*, Borbone); Aq. τὰς δαμάλεις, cf. Vulg. *vaccas* and Targ. לעגליא seems to confirm MT.

בית־און LXX τοῦ οἴκου Ὤν; Aq. τοῦ οἴκου ἅς (Theod. τοῦ οἴκου ὄν = Ὤν (Ziegler).

יגורו LXX παροικήσουσιν 'dwell near', cf. Pesh. *nhwwn twtb'*; see √גור I, BDB, p. 157, cf. Gelston, pp. 143, 167; Theod. ἐφοβήθησαν, cf. Aq. ἐσεβάσθησαν 'fear' (with direct object, i.e. calf, calves); Vulg. *coluerunt*, 'worship', cf. Targ. פלחו; for comments on Aq., see Ziegler *Bei.*, p. 359.

שְׁכַן LXX κατοικοῦντες 'dwellers' (plural), cf. Pesh. *'mwr'*; on the basis of which → שֹׁכְנֵי (a number of scholars, see Harper; so Borbone, cf. *BHS*).

אבל Wellhausen *et al.* (see Harper, cf. *BHS*) read יאבל with future reference; *BHS* compares Symm. πενθήσει.

כמריו LXX καθὼς παρεπίκραναν αὐτόν 'just as they provoked him', seeing in the word כ and the root מרה, cf. Vollers; the word is taken by Pesh. with what precedes, (*'mh*) *wkwmrwhy* '(its people) and priests'.

עליו omitted by Borbone.

יגילו LXX ἐπιχαροῦνται, cf. Vulg. *exultaverunt*, Pesh. *nḥdwn*, Targ. יבועון, all 'rejoice'. (For Jerome's understanding of 'rejoice', see the commentary above.) LXX and Pesh. seem to understand the session of Samaritans at Bethel as for the purpose of mourning, to which is contrasted present or future rejoicing; e.g. LXX 'the inhabitants of Samaria shall dwell near the calf of the house of On: because its people had lamented over it. And just as they have provoked him, they will rejoice over its glory because it is removed from it ...'. Amongst numerous emendations, → יחילו 'will writhe' (Oort and Grätz); → ילילו 'will howl' (Wellhausen, Marti, cf. *BHS*).

10.6 **Moreover the calf itself[a] will be taken[b] to Assyria as tribute for the Great King[c]; disgrace[d] is all that Ephraim gains; Israel will be disgraced by reason of its aspirations[e].**

[a]אותו The sign of the accusative construed with a passive verb, cf. GK 121b. An alternative explanation is that את, originally a particle of emphasis, is here used quite properly as a sign of the nominative; see P. P. Saydon *VT* 14 (1964), pp. 192ff and J. Macdonald *VT* 14 (1964), pp. 264ff. The third masculine singular suffix appears to refer to the calf and, in the interests of clarity, the word is included in the translation above.

[b]יובל Cf., with Kimchi, Isa 18.7.

[c]I.e. the king of Assyria, cf. on 5.13 above.

[d]The noun בשנה, placed emphatically at the beginning of the phrase, appears to be a modified form of בושה 'shame', 'disgrace' with *nun* added to the root. According to ibn Janāḥ the word constitutes a reference to the cult which is disparaged by means of the modified form. For the usage he compares Jer 3.24. The phrase denotes literally 'Ephraim will receive/receives disillusionment'. For לקח in this sense cf., with Wolff, Jer 20.10 and Ezek 36.30. Qyl rightly paraphrases shame 'will be the lot of Ephraim' (תפל בחלקו של אפרים). For the addition of *nun* before a feminine ending, ibn Ezra compares שִׁבְעָנָה בָנִים in Job 42.13. The latter instance, though its authenticity is not infrequently questioned (e.g. GK 97c), together with the form here under discussion, may indicate an established dialectal usage. Rudolph's change of the pointing (see Text and Versions) enables him to posit the sense, 'In the year that he (*sc*. the Great King) captured Israel ...'. The change, however, is arbitrary and the resulting construction of the phrase (i.e. with a short relative) forced.

[e]מעצתו In view of the previous phrase as rightly interpreted by ibn Janāḥ, עצה is understood to denote the aspirations and goals of the Northern

Kingdom, represented and expressed by the state cult of the calf. As Rashi and Kimchi observe, the cognate verb יעץ is used of Jeroboam's policy in setting up the cult, 1 Kgs 12.28. The noun occurs in Ps 14.6 (where it is the object of the *Hiphil* of בוש) and denotes 'plans', 'aspirations' (cf. ASB 'they frustrate the poor man in his hopes'), cf. Ps 106.43 'their own designs' (so ASB). Cf. further, Deut 32.28; Isa 29.15; 30.1; and for a different but related noun, Jer 7.24; Mic 6.16.

Many commentators have expressed unease about the reading, usually on the assumption that it denotes here, as frequently, 'counsel', 'plans' and so specifically (state) policies – so, e.g., Wolff, cf. de Boer SVT 3 (1955), pp. 49f. Since the oracle is concerned with the removal of the calf and not with state policies, Wellhausen's proposed emendation מֵעֲצַבּוֹ '(will be ashamed) of its idol' is frequently adopted. A variant is that of Rudolph (cf. AF and Jeremias) who takes עצה to mean 'wood', 'wooden image', a *nomen unitatis* for the familiar עץ ('will be ashamed of its wooden image'). However, ibn Janāḥ's recognition that בשנה in the preceding phrase constitutes a reference to the calf renders it likely that עצה is the correct reading and that it denotes here the plans or aspirations of the state as represented in its national calf cult. For such thoughts, see chapter 8 above and especially 8.6.

An alternative explanation of עצה, made by reference to philological considerations, is that of G. R. Driver[13] who, comparing Arabic *'ṣy*, posits a noun עצה II 'disobedience', 'rebellion' here and in a number of other places. The resulting 'Israel will be ashamed of its rebellion' is, however, somewhat banal and telling criticisms of Driver's theory as 'unnecessary' are expressed by, e.g., KB^3, p. 821.

The verse follows closely what precedes it. As Kimchi observes, the particle *gm* ('moreover') serves to amplify and expand the reference to the cult's lost wealth in v. 5. It is not just that Bethel will lose its wealth in connection with the harsh tribute demanded by the Assyrians; rather the severity of that demand will eventually entail the surrender to them of the very calf itself. If, then, the Assyrians receive as tribute the calf, the very emblem of the Northern Kingdom, the symbol of its aspirations and identity (cf. 8.6 above), devised as such from the moment of its separate constitution by Jeroboam I, that inevitably signals the end of all that had been created. Ephraim's calf is shown to be its disgrace (note d). If Assyria is to receive the physical calf image, Ephraim will be left with what in truth that image represented: disgrace, disillusionment, shame. Israel's aspirations for the future, its whole national policy (note e), tied to and expressed by the national cultic symbol, will bring about nothing but disgrace, disillusionment, shame. The thought is generally

[13] *WO* 1 (1947–52), pp. 412f; *JSS* 13 (1968), p. 45.

well expressed in Jer 48.13[14] 'Israel was betrayed (*bšw*) by Bethel, a god in whom he trusted' (NEB).

Text and Versions

אותו לאשור LXX αὐτὸν εἰς Ἀσσυρίους δήσαντες ? 'binding it (they take it) to/for[15] the Assyrians', apparently translating אשור twice (in the second instance seeing in the word a form of אשר/אסר and understanding אותו as an object (so Targ. and Pesh.).

יובל LXX ἀπήνεγκαν (with מנחה as its object), cf. Pesh. *nwblwn* and Targ. יובלון 'they have brought/will bring'; the renderings are deemed more likely to be *ad sensum* than to imply a reading יובילו (*contra*, e.g., Wellhausen, Marti, cf. Borbone, *BHS*); Vulg. *delatus est*.

מנחה LXX and Pesh. plural (but a *v.l.* in Pesh. singular).

מלך ירב LXX τῷ βασιλεῖ Ἰαρείμ/Ἰαριμ; Vulg. *regi ultori* understanding a form of √ריב; so Aq. and Theod. δικάζοντι, Symm. ὑπερμαχοῦντι and Targ. מלכא דייתי לאתפרעא 'the king who will come to take vengeance (for them)'; see further on 5.13 above.

בשנה אפרים יקח LXX ἐν δόματι Ἐ. δέξεται ? 'in a house Ephraim will receive (and Israel will be ashamed)'[16]; Jerome renders this (*tulerunt munera regi Jarib*) *in domo. Ephraim suscipiet confusionem*, understanding ἐν δόματι with what precedes and apparently reading αἰσχύνην; Vulg. *confusio Ephraim capiet* construing בשנה as the subject; Pesh. *bhtt' nqbl 'prym*, cf. Targ. בהתא דבית אפרים יקבלו 'the House of E. will receive shame'; → בַּשָּׁנָה 'in the year (that he captured Ephraim)' (Michaelis, cf. Rudolph; see note d above); Marti (normalises) → בֹּשֶׁת.

מעצתו LXX ἐν τῇ βουλῇ αὐτοῦ 'in its counsel', cf. Targ. ממלכי עצתהון 'of the counsels of their advisers'; Vulg. (*confundetur Israhel*) *in voluntate sua* ('will be confounded) in its design'; Pesh. *btr'yth* 'in its belief', 'opinion'; → מֵעֲצַבּוֹ 'of its idol' (Wellhausen, Marti, *et al.*); see further, note e above.

14 For the deity Bethel as distinct from the place of that name, cf. *ANET*, p. 534a.

15 See Arndt and Gingrich, p. 229, col 1 g.

16 Muraoka's suggestion that בְּאֶתְנָה (*sic*– he points it) rather than בשנה was in the *Vorlage* of the LXX seems to be most implausible both in itself and because, on this view, he makes no attempt to explain the preposition ב; see p. 211 of his article 'Hebrew Hapax Legomena and Septuagint Lexicography' in (ed.) C. E. Cox *VII Congress of the International Organization for Septuagint and Cognate Studies, Leuven, 1989* (Atlanta, Georgia, 1991).

10.7 **As for Samaria, its king[a] will fade away[b] like foam[c] on the surface of water.**

[a]The third feminine suffix must refer to Samaria which is accordingly a nominative absolute, cf. with Rosenmüller, Eccles 2.14 and Jon 2.7. Alternatively, the nouns are conjoined asyndetically, cf. Hab 3.11 and מלך שׂרים in Hos 8.10. In the light of such considerations, the proposal to remove the *athnaḥ* to Samaria and to read the participle as a feminine (נִדְמָה – so, e.g., Wellhausen, Rudolph, *BHS*) is discounted.

[b]נדמה Cf. on 4.5 and 10.15. The root is דמה II; the form (as pointed) is a *Niphal* participle used as *futurum instans* (but without הנה) conveying an imminent event, GK 116p. Its masculine form (as pointed) indicates that it is predicated of מלכה 'its king'. The essential meaning of the verb is 'to come to an end', 'be ruined', 'perish' and the view taken of the meaning of קצף in the following simile (note c) naturally influences the precise meaning and translation in the context. Attempts to interpret the verb by reference to דמה I 'is likened to' (so, e.g., Abarbanel) or to דמם 'is silenced' (so Rashi) are discounted.

[c]The word קצף is a *hapax legomenon*. Two accounts of the word have long been known to tradition: first, that the noun is related to the familiar verb קצף 'to be angry' whose fundamental meaning is, according to ibn Janāḥ, 'boiling with rage' (Arabic *'lġly'n b'l'ġḍ'b*). In the present text the fundamental meaning obtrudes and the word קצף here means the 'agitation' or 'boiling' of water through the force of the wind (Arabic *'stš'ṭt 'lm' 'y ġlynh bqwwt 'lryḥ*). This view appears to be reflected in some of the versions (Aquila, Symmachus, Vulgate and Targum) as well as by Rashi who renders by (French) *écume*. Secondly, ibn Ezra and Kimchi refer to Joel 1.7 where, as Kimchi explains, the phrase תאנתי לקצפה means that the fig is stripped of its bark (קליפת העץ) by locusts who then devour it. Here, then, קצף may denote, on Kimchi's explanation, a piece of bark stripped from a tree (again קליפת העץ). It seems likely that some such view of the word underlies the translations offered by those of the ancient versions not listed above (see Text and Versions). More recently, J. Blau *VT* (1955), p. 343, cf. BDB, has drawn attention to the Arabic root *qṣf* 'to break off' and *qṣyf* 'broken', 'fragile', 'brittle' (of a plant, see Lane *Supplement*, *ad loc.*) and this consideration has prompted a number of modern commentators to render the word 'chip', 'flotsam' or the like. Thus, e.g., Rudolph, while he acknowledges that both possibilities (i.e. 'foam' or 'chip') furnish a striking image, is inclined to favour the second alternative.

The appeal to Arabic *qṣf* may not be as decisive as Rudolph supposes. It is not made by Arabic speaking lexicographers such as ibn Janāḥ and ibn Barūn. Further, Joel 1.7 does not certainly mean that the fig tree is reduced to broken pieces; rather, on Kimchi's view, it means that the wood is peeled or stripped of its bark. Moreover, ibn Janāḥ in his explanation of the root קצף, as it occurs both in Joel and here in Hosea, offers an alternative view which may well be correct. Thus, the Arabic word *šyṭ* provides an accurate parallel to the semantic range of קצף since it is capable of the meanings 'singeing', 'scorching' as well as 'boiling', 'agitation'. It is the former sense that should be detected in Joel 1.7 – the fig-trees are scorched (by fire).

Two other considerations are relevant: first, the verb, associated with the image, *viz.* נדמה (see note b), may be held better to fit the first possibility for קצף: thus foam or froth on the waters rapidly dissolves and vanishes (so Jerome), cf., with Rudolph, Exod 32.20. Secondly, the explicit phrase 'on the surface of water' also fits better the first possibility for קצף. The second possibility would require some such phrase as 'by water', i.e. flotsam swept to destruction by rushing water, or floods.

The fact that vv. 5, 6 and 8 all refer to the imminent end of the cult has prompted a number of recent scholars to interpret the 'king' here as a title of the calf/Baal (so Nyberg, cf. Rudolph, Mays, AF). Comparison of Jer 19.5 with Jer 32.35 suggests that *melek* could be used interchangeably with Baal and, it is assumed, what happened in the south is likely to have happened in the north[17].

On the other hand, it may be urged that Hosea is speaking of the whole establishment of the kingdom and that for him the cultic emblem of the state, the calf of Bethel, is inextricably connected with the royal establishment of Samaria (cf. on 8.4). If the inhabitants of Samaria were to fear for the calf cult of Bethel (v. 5) then it is not unreasonable to suppose that Hosea saw in the imminent demise of the cult at Bethel the end of its guarantor and protector, the monarch resident in Samaria. It is then the monarchy in Samaria which is so shortly (note b) to vanish, dissolved like the foam on the surface of water, the 'white-horses' of the sea (of Galilee?) on a windy day (note c and cf. Jerome on 10.15). A similar image is offered by Hosea in 10.15 where the end of the monarchy ('the king of Israel') is portrayed as imminent and irrevocable (again the verb *ndmh* is used): it will come as speedily as the Palestinian dawn. Despite the fact that the same verb is predicated of the king in 10.15, none of the scholars named above is disposed to argue that there, too, the 'king' denotes Baal/the calf. It should be noted, moreover, that 10.15 also contains a reference to the destruction

17 For the general question of the title Molech, see Eissfeldt in *RGG* IV (1960), cols 1089f, and J. Day *Molech. A god of human sacrifice in the OT*, Cambridge, 1989, pp. 56ff. Day argues against the supposition that Molech is another name for Baal (p. 35) and denies that Molech has any mention in the prophecies of Hosea (pp. 75ff).

of Bethel and this (unless it is emended, see below *ad loc.*) appears to confirm the impression that Hosea both there and here saw the destruction of the state in terms of the parallel demise of the calf cult of Bethel and of the monarchy in Samaria.

Amongst the rabbinic commentators, Kimchi supposes that the verse reflects specifically the impotence of Hoshea ben Elah following his imprisonment by Shalmaneser V in 725 BC (2 Kgs 17.4); the situation thus marked the inevitability of the final *dénouement*. The suggestion is not without its merits.

Text and Versions

נדמה LXX ἀπέρριψεν Σ. βασιλέα αὐτῆς, cf. Pesh. *šdt š. mlkh* 'Samaria has expelled her king' (Gelston, p. 168); Vulg. *transire fecit Samaria regem suum* 'Samaria has made her king to vanish'; Targ. בהיתת ש במלכה 'Samaria is ashamed of her king'; some codices of de Rossi point נִדְמָה.

כקצף LXX and Theod. ὡς φρύγανον, cf. Pesh. *'yk gl'* 'like firewood', 'stick', 'chip'; Vulg. *quasi spumam* 'foam', cf. Aq. ὡς ἀφρόν, Symm. ὡς ἐπίζεμα 'boiling'[18], and Targ. כרתחא (but see Jastrow p. 1464, col 2).

10.8 **The sanctuaries[a] of Aven[b], the very sin of Israel[c], shall be destroyed; briers[d] and thistles[d] shall grow up upon their altars. And they[e] shall say to the mountains, Cover us; and to the hills, Fall upon us.**

[a]The word במות properly denotes man-made cultic platforms composed of field-stones. They were apparently used directly for sacrifices or alternatively had altars built upon them. For a detailed study of the literary and archaeological evidence, see P. H. Vaughan *The Meaning of 'bāmâ' in the Old Testament* (Cambridge, 1974). In the circumstances that poetic parallelism may be either synonymous or synthetical it is not possible here to determine whether Hosea means to use the word as a synonym for 'altars' or, synthetically, as their base (cf. Vaughan, p. 69 n. 27). The general sense, however, is clear. The word 'sanctuaries' is offered in English translation as an approximation to what is meant.

[b]The word און meaning 'wickedness' is that used by Hosea in his pejorative name for Bethel, i.e. Bethaven, cf. 4.15; 5.8; 10.5; Amos 5.5f. The question arises whether the word should here be taken as a common or as a proper noun. Rashi and Kimchi (cf. the LXX and Targum) understand it as a reference to Bethel and so the various sanctuaries and

[18] Jerome: *volens ostendere ferventis ollae superiores aquas.*

altars in that place are designated. Ibn Ezra, cf. Jerome, Wolff, Rudolph, Mays, understands the word as a common noun and consequently thinks of the 'sanctuaries of wickedness' (i.e. of idolatry, cf. Jerome) situated throughout the Northern Kingdom, of which Bethel was the prime example (so, e.g., Qyl). In the context of this particular passage, with its explicit reference to Bethel (v. 5) and to the calf cult, it seems likely that the balance of probability favours the first alternative (cf. Kallai *Bethaven*, p. 178). Wellhausen (cf. Marti *et al.*) suggests that the words און חטאת are later glosses (→ 'the sanctuaries of Israel shall be destroyed') which reflect (Judaean) opposition to all but the Jerusalem Temple. More likely, however, is Rudolph's assessment, *viz.* that such texts as these were eventually to form the grounds for the Deuteronomic law of the central sanctuary in Jerusalem.

[c]The words חטאת ישראל are in apposition to 'sanctuaries of Aven' (cf. Rosenmüller).

[d]קוץ is identified with *Notobasis Syriale* and דרדר with *Notobasis Silybum*, cf. Qyl; for עלה 'grow up', cf. Isa 5.6.

[e]Ibn Ezra quotes R. Moses the Priest (twelfth century) to the effect that it is the sanctuaries and altars which, figuratively, give voice; for which Josh 24.27 is compared. As an alternative, he quotes Japhet (tenth century) to the effect that it is the worshippers at the sanctuaries who speak. For Rashi and Kimchi it is the Israelites in general who give voice to the cry of calamity and distress.

The section comes to an end with a powerful cry of despair, whether that is spoken by the inhabitants of the Northern Kingdom or, figuratively, by the sanctuaries (note a) and altars themselves (note e). The coming destruction of the whole fabric of the state by the Assyrian invaders will bring to an end all use of the sanctuaries and of Bethel in particular (note b). It is, indeed, places such as this which epitomise and constitute the fundamental sin of Israel (notes b, c); here in the syncretistic worship and the exuberant self-indulgence of the people (cf. 9.1) Yahweh was not accorded the worship that was his due and consequently the first commandment was broken (so Rudolph, cf. v. 2 and 8.11, 13). The sanctuaries and altars will thus be justly destroyed and, unfrequented, their ruins given over to the ravages of the wild. Briers and thistles will grow up amongst the stones (cf., with Rosenmüller, Isa 32.13) and thus remove from sight the vestiges of what once they had constituted.

The cry of despair, quoted in Lk 23.30, cf. Rev 6.16, is not made to the mountains and hills as the site of the sanctuaries (*contra* Rudolph, cf. Qyl), for that view rests upon a misconception concerning the meaning of *bmwt* (note a). Rather the cry is a simple request for obliteration to the end that the nation's enemies will not see the people in their shame (Rashi) or that they will suffer no more the multitude of calamities and distress which had befallen them (Kimchi). They preferred simply to die than to discover what would bring their death (Jerome).

Text and Versions

במות LXX βωμοί 'platforms', 'altars'; Vulg. *excelsa* 'heights', 'elevations'; Pesh. *prk'* '(idol) sanctuaries'; Targ. במה 'altar'.

און LXX Ὢν; Vulg. *idoli*; Pesh. *d'wn*; Targ. בית אל.

חטאת LXX and Targ., plural.

עלינו Pesh. and Targ., third masculine plural suffixes.

CHAPTER 10.9–15

THE FAILURE OF THE NATION TO FULFIL ITS DESTINY ITS INEVITABLE FALL TO FOREIGN MIGHT

10.9 **Israel, you have sinned from[a] the time of Gibeah. It is there[b] that they adopted their position[c]. Surely[d] war will overtake them as[e] in Gibeah – war prosecuted against[f] perverse[g] men.**

[a] So most of the older commentators and all the ancient versions. Ibn Ezra argues that מן has a comparative force as in Ps 119.98, 100 and consequently the phrase means 'you have sinned more than at the time of Gibeah'. This view is adopted by, e.g., Rosenmüller and Rudolph and they justify it on exegetical grounds, for which, see the commentary below.

[b] The position of the word שם is emphatic.

[c] Cf. 2 Kgs 23.3 and the phrase ויעמד כל־העם בברית, 'all the people pledged themselves to the covenant' (NEB; lit. 'took their stand in the covenant'). Rashi, ibn Ezra and Kimchi comment that the words refer to the prophet's generation who stand with their ancestors, adopting the same attitude and refraining from any form of contrition (cf. Jerome). The words mean, then, that at Gibeah Israel's fundamentally perverse character was formed and that the nation's present iniquity indicates that that character persisted thereafter unchanged.

[d] Modern commentators have widely taken the view that the negative phrase לא־תַשִּׂיגֵם is a rhetorical question (cf. Latin *nonne*) conveying an emphatic positive statement (e.g. Orelli, Harper, Wolff, Rudolph, Mays)[1]. *BHS*, suggesting הֲלֹא as a possibility, clearly incline to a similar view. It is possible that ibn Ezra and Kimchi may be searching for a similar solution in their comments that the people suppose that war will not overtake them when in fact it most certainly will.

[e] As ibn Ezra observes, the words conceal a comparison and consequently (lit.) 'in Gibeah' may be characterised as *comparatio decurtata* (GK 118r). He comments 'they do not fear that war will overtake them as it once overtook the Benjamites', i.e. in Gibeah. Ibn Ezra further suggests that the order of the words (i.e. delayed subject 'war') is of a sort with that in Gen 27.27 where אשר ברכו belongs in sense with בני rather than with שדה.

[1] See further R. Gordis *VT* 5 (1955), p. 89 and G. R. Driver *Journal of the Ancient Near Eastern Society of Columbia University* 5 (1973), pp. 107–114.

[f]Since the verb נשׂג is never construed with על, the phrase by which על is introduced belongs with 'war' (cf. Rashi, Rosenmüller). The main alternative view is to suppose that the phrase has been misplaced and belongs properly with שם עמדו 'there they took their stand against the sons of wickedness' (so, e.g., Ruben, Nowack, Rudolph *et al.*). Yet recognition of the way in which the verse is constructed (see ibn Ezra's view, note e) renders such emendation unnecessary.

[g]Kimchi supposes that MT's עלוה stands by metathesis[2] for עולה 'injustice' and with this view the LXX, Peshiṭta and Vulgate seem to agree (cf. amongst moderns, e.g., Rudolph; for the MSS evidence, see Text and Versions). The phrase בני עולה occurs in 2 Sam 3.34; 7.10. Rashi understands the word in the MT as a derivative of עלה 'to go up' (cf. the Targum) with the sense 'pride' (בני גאוה) since the Benjamites made themselves 'high and mighty' (עליונים). Amongst other attempts to defend MT, mention may be made of A. Schultens[3] who compares Arabic *ġlw* 'to exceed the proper bounds', 'to go too far' and suggests the rendering 'sons of insolence', i.e. of hybris; for Michaelis[4], Syriac *'ly* 'to act perversely', 'wickedly' provides evidence in favour of MT's reading. It is possible that some such theory[5] is correct and that the view represented by Kimchi, together with the fact that some Hebrew MSS read עולה (see Text and Versions, cf. Rudolph) reflects attempts to harmonise Hosea's (dialectal) language with the better known עולה. The general sense, however, is clear.

Chapter 10.9f are usually regarded as originally a separate oracle in the form of divine speech directed against Israel and beginning with a reference to the atrocity of Gibeah, cf. 9.9. As there, the reference is not to Saul's accession to the monarchy (*contra* the Targum, Wellhausen *et al.*) but to the Benjamite outrage reported in Judg 19ff (so already Rashi and Kimchi)[6]. Since there all Israel is depicted as waging war upon the Benjamites, Rudolph argues that Israel as a nation cannot here be represented as having sinned 'since the time of Gibeah'. Accordingly he favours ibn Ezra's view that *mn* has a comparative force and that the phrase means 'Israel, you have sinned more than at the time of Gibeah' (see note a above). The evidence of 9.9, however, suggests clearly that Hosea regarded the atrocity perpetrated by the Benjamites as (one of) the classical sins of Israel with which

2 For a recent evaluation of the phenomenon, see Barr *CPOT*, pp. 97f.

3 *Haririi eloquentiae Arabicae principis tres priores consessus* (Leipzig, 1731), I p. 15.

4 *Supplementa*, p. 1912.

5 See further C. Rabin *SH* 8 (1961), p. 396.

6 For P. M. Arnold's theory that Hosea refers not to the Benjamite outrage but to Ephraim's war-crime in attacking Benjamin, see on 9.9 fn.

the nation's subsequent behaviour was all too consistent. That in 9.10 he dates the nation's perversity from the time of the entry is hardly inconsistent with this view (*contra* Rudolph) but rather forms part of an *a fortiori* argument. In 9.9 the prophet's point is that the nation's perversity is now as great as that manifested at Gibeah and that that will indubitably prompt Yahweh to intervene decisively. Here much the same point is made: if the Benjamite atrocity at Gibeah resulted in war being waged against perverse men (notes d–f) then his contemporaries, similarly perverse, should expect that war, similarly prosecuted, will overtake them too. It was thus at Gibeah that Israel took its stand; here 'the character of the contemporary nation was established' (Mays) and, established, remained thereafter fundamentally unaltered by any trace of contrition (note c).

The change from the address to Israel in the second person singular in the first part of the verse, to comment about Israel ('they') in the third person plural is typical of Hosea's oracles (cf. 8.1–14 above) and occasions no surprise or difficulty. Rather than reflecting the language of the court (so Wolff), the device is rhetorical in character and serves to reinforce the essential connection or identity seen by Hosea between events then and now (note e and cf. Rudolph).

Text and Versions

מימי LXX ἀφ'οὗ 'from when'; Vulg. *ex diebus* 'from the days', cf. Pesh. *mn ywm'* and Targ. מיומי.

הגבעה LXX οἱ βουνοί '(from when) the hills were'; cf. Pesh. *drmt'*.

חטאת LXX and Vulg. ἥμαρτεν/*peccavit*; i.e. third person singular; Pesh. second person singular; Targ. second person plural; → חַטַּאת '(from the days of Gibeah is Israel's) sin', (Wellhausen, cf. Harper, *BHS* – citing a few MSS); → חָטָא 'Israel sinned' (Borbone).

עמדו LXX ἔστησαν 'stood', cf. Vulg. *steterunt* and Pesh. *nqwmwn*; Targ. קמו מרדו 'they stood in rebellion' (cf. NEB) and adds 'in setting up the king over them' etc.; → מָרְדוּ (cf. *BHS*).

עלוה LXX ἀδικίας 'injustice', cf. Pesh. *d'wl'* and Vulg. *iniquitatis*; Targ. סליקו is obscure. Rudolph has seen in it evidence that עלוה was understood as a form of the verb עלה; but this is very uncertain. Cathcart renders 'father with sons went up' (i.e. to war), in reference to Judg 20.3, 18 etc. עולה is adopted by Borbone following the *v.l.* of 46 Kennicott and 15 de Rossi MSS (cf. *BHS*).

10.10 **It is my wish[a] that[b] I discipline[c] them; and so nations will be gathered against them, [d]because they have bound themselves[e] to two wicked attitudes[d].**

The verse is amongst the most difficult in Hosea's prophecies. Rather than resorting to emendation, I have preferred to follow the general approach of the rabbinic commentators and, in particular, that of ibn Janāḥ. Accordingly the last part of the verse is understood to contain an allusion to Israel's wickedness under a metaphor of ploughing, akin to those which present themselves in the following verses and especially to the phrase in v. 13 'wickedness is what you have ploughed'.

[a]באותי Cf. Rashi and Jerome, 'in accordance with my good pleasure'. Most modern commentators (cf. *BHS*, NEB, Wolff, Mays etc.), by reference to the LXX (see Text and Versions), read (ו)בָאתִי 'I have (will) come'. The resulting sense is, however, hardly satisfactory and, e.g., Wolff's assertion that Yahweh has come as commander-in-chief of the nations is far-fetched. Moreover, the perfect tense, even taken as a prophetic perfect, is difficult to construe in the context (cf. Rudolph). König, 401m (cf. Rudolph) prefers to read an infinitive construct *Piel* בְּאַוֹּתִי and to take the phrase with the question posed in the previous verse 'shall not war overtake them as in Gibeah – because I am concerned to chastise them?' The suggestion depends upon a reordering of the words of v. 9 which is not here accepted; in any case the particular difference in respect of באותי is minimal (cf. אהבה as an infinitive construct, GK 45d).

[b]A purpose clause, cf. GK 165a, König, 415s.

[c]With the versions and rabbinic commentators, the word ואסרם is understood to be an imperfect form of the verb יסר. For the form with *dagesh forte*, see GK 60a, 71 and cf. Morag, p. 491.

[d–d] It is, in ibn Janāḥ's view, most likely that the word עונתם (*sic*, the *Qere*)[7] is related to the words מענה (1 Sam 14.14) and מעניה (*Qere* Ps 129.3) which both mean 'furrow' and are derived from a root ענה (cf. II in BDB, pp. 775f)[8]. These nouns denote properly 'a furrow made by a ploughman around a place which he intends to plough and called in Arabic *lǧnt*'[9]. The verb אסר 'to bind' is attested of the harnessing of cows to a wagon in 1 Sam 6.7 and this is its sense in the present verse. The phrase as a whole means 'in their being harnessed to their two ploughing beasts'. Though this is the apparent (Arabic *ẓ'hr*) meaning, the phrase in fact conveys the making of the *lǧnt* since that action is

[7] It is worth recording that Michaelis (*Supplementa*, p. 1895) in support of the *Kethib* draws attention to Arabic *'yn* which is attested with the meaning 'plough' or 'plough-share' (cf. Lane 5, pp. 2217f for the somewhat technical details).

[8] For further comments on these nouns and the root ענה, see Morag, p. 495; for the form, cf. with Rosenmüller, שׁאוה from the root שׁאה.

[9] The word is a loan-word derived from Latin *elix* 'trench', cf. Dozy, *ad loc.*

comprised in the more general reference to ploughing. Ibn Janāḥ, then, understands the words to convey essentially the notion of intention or resolution by making the *lğnt*. In the context it is the nation's persistence in two wicked attitudes or policies (Arabic *'ṣr'rhm*[10] *'ly mḏhbyn*) that is set forth and, where the reference to 'two' is concerned, specifically the policies of Judah and Ephraim in their apostasy.

This last assumption seems unlikely and dependent, to some extent at least, upon the reference to Judah in the following verse which, in common with most moderns, I understand to be a later gloss. For the rest, ibn Janāḥ's view is reflected in the comments of ibn Ezra and Kimchi, although their accounts of the matter are, by comparison, incomplete. Amongst the versions, the Targum (see Text and Versions) understands the verb אסר of binding oxen, though עינת (*sic* the *Kethib*) in terms of עין 'eye' but then, עינת 'eyes', *sc*. 'rings of a yoke', through which ropes are passed (cf. Rashi, who speaks of ropes going down on each side of the eyes of the ox).

The LXX, Peshiṭta and Vulgate appear to have read עֲוֹנֹתָם, 'their wickednesses' and with this the *Qere* may be, but is not certainly, in agreement. It is this view which is taken by the majority of modern commentators. The sense is not unreasonable in the context and is, in the end, close to that advocated by ibn Janāḥ (i.e. 'their wicked policies'). It seems preferable, however, to suppose that *difficilior lectio potior* and that the versions named above have attempted to find the proper meaning by an easier route. Certainly the noun עון 'wickedness' is not elsewhere construed with אסר 'to bind' and it is noteworthy that these versions understand the latter in terms of the root יסר 'to chastise' with which 'wickedness' fits more naturally. Amongst other attempts at elucidating the phrase, mention may be made of Nyberg who takes the *Kethib* עינתם to mean not 'eyes' but 'springs'[11] and שתי not as the numeral two but as an infinitive construct of שתה 'to drink' (cf. כחכי in 6.9). He compares באסרם with the Arabic adverbial phrase *b'srh* 'entirely'[12]. Accordingly the words mean that the nations are gathered against them, all of them ('in hordes', NEB) to drink of their springs. Much of this depends upon Nyberg's view that vv. 9f constitute a fragment reflecting Israel's nomadic past when the search for water sources was particularly important. As Rudolph comments, it is not easy to see why such a fragment should find itself in the book of Hosea nor in a context which is concerned with imminent doom occasioned by enemy invasion.

[e]The preposition ב with infinitive construct is interpreted as having a causal force, cf. BDB p. 91, col 1 V. 2. The suffix is objective and not subjective; 'in their binding' → 'in their being bound', cf. GK 115c.

10 Reading *'ṣr'rhm* for Neubauer's apparently mistaken *'ḏr'rhm*.

11 So, earlier, A. Schultens *Animadvertiones* quoted by Rosenmüller (I have not had access to this work).

12 Cf. also Guillaume I, p. 19.

The verse fits and continues the argument of v. 9. That the classical outrage perpetrated by the Benjamites in Gibeah should evoke the response of a punitive gathering of Israel against them was a reflection of Yahweh's essential preoccupation with justice. The subsequent iniquity of Israel, conforming indeed to the classical outrage of Benjamin, evoked in him the same response. It was, then, his good pleasure that he should discipline them (notes a–c) and the present gathering of the hostile nations against Ephraim matches the gathering against the Benjamites. The use of the verb *'sp* seems to reflect its use in the tradition formulated in Judg 20.11, cf. 14, 'All the Israelites to a man were massed against the town'. That 'nations' in the plural are mentioned may reflect the use of various nationals in the Assyrian army (cf. 2 Kgs 17.24 for the resettlement of various peoples) or else, as in 7.8, indicate that it is heathen foreigners who will shortly execute Yahweh's purposes (cf. Wolff, Rudolph, Mays) and be the agents of the fighting which will shortly overtake Ephraim (v. 9 and cf., with Rudolph, Judg 20.42).

The last phrase of the verse is particularly difficult (see note d–d) but, on the view here adopted, the prophet seeks by a complex metaphor to convey his belief that the impending doom is the result (note e) of the people's persistence in the evil attitudes to which, from the time of Gibeah, they had so firmly tied themselves. In this respect they were like the ploughman with his team of oxen who, prior to ploughing a field, marked out his task with delimiting furrows. It is this which constitutes the two-fold nature of the nation's perfidy: 'not only do they consider wickedness, they perpetrate it' (so ibn Janāḥ, cf., but from a different standpoint, Rudolph). Indeed, the words may be seen to convey a sense not far removed from 'there they have adopted their position' (v. 9 and see note c there; cf. Wolff). Where the vehicle of the metaphor is concerned, the agents of the ploughman's intention and of his effecting it are the twin ploughing beasts who made both the initial delimiting furrows and also the furrows of the completed plough. The essentially two-fold character both of ploughing and of its agents serves, then, to convey forcibly the two-fold nature of the nation's wickedness.

This account of the matter (substantially that of ibn Janāḥ), though complicated, has the merit that it yields a sense fundamentally agreeable to the context and to the thought of the prophet. Other attempts to understand the nation's double guilt (reading עֲוֹנֹתָם), if simpler, are in the end less satisfactory. Thus Jerome interprets the twin wickednesses of the idolatry of Micah (Judg 17) and of Jeroboam I in making the golden calves or (alternatively) of the latter's two calves at Bethel and Dan. Neither the context nor Hosea's words can be said to confirm such apparent conjectures nor the more recent variations upon them, e.g., idolatry (AF) or idolatry on the one hand and the crowning of Saul on the other (e.g. Harper and Mays).

Text and Versions

באותי ואסרם LXX (NB Swete includes these two words with v. 9) ἦλθεν παιδεῦσαι αὐτούς 'he came to chastise them', hence → (וּבָאתִי) בָּאתִי וְאֲיַסְּרֵם 'I have (will) come to chastise them' (many moderns, e.g., Oort, Marti, Wolff, Mays, cf. *BHS*, seeing ἦλθεν as an inner Greek corruption of an original ἦλθον, so Ziegler; Vulg. *iuxta desiderium meum corripiam eos* 'according to my wish I shall censure them'; Pesh. *bk'ty 'rd' 'nwn* 'in my censure I will chastise them'; Targ. במימרי איתיתי עליהון יסורין 'through my Memra I brought chastisements upon them'; → אאסרם 'I will bind them' (Halévy, cf. Qyl, √אסר; → בגערתי איסרם 'I will chastise them with my rebuke' (Borbone).

באסרם LXX ἐν τῷ παιδεύεσθαι αὐτούς 'when they are disciplined', cf. Vulg. *cum corripientur*, Pesh. *m' dmtrdyn* suggest to, e.g., Wellhausen, Oort, Oettli, Harper, Wolff, Mays, AF, *BHS*, Borbone, forms of √יסר such as ב/ליסרם or בהוסרם; Rudolph justly comments that a form of √אסר is inherently more probable as constituting a word-play, באסרם/ואספו/ואסרם, so typical of Hosea's style; Targ. כמיסר 'as one binds', i.e., understanding a form of √אסר.

לשתי עינתם *Qere* (so many MSS) עונתם; LXX ἐν ταῖς δυσὶν ἀδικίαις αὐτῶν 'on account of (Arndt and Gingrich, p. 260 b) their two wickednesses', cf. Vulg. *propter duas iniquitates suas*, Pesh. *'l trtyhyn sklwthwn*; → עֲוֹנֹתָם (from עָוֺן, most moderns); Targ. על תרתין עונתיה 'to its two rings' (*sc*. of the yoke, cf. Jastrow, *ad loc*.).

10.11 **Yet Ephraim was a biddable[a] heifer who loved[b] threshing; it was I[c] who happened upon[d] her fine[e] neck; I shall harness[f] Ephraim that (Judah) he[g] should plough[h], that Jacob should engage in[i] harrowing[j].**

[a]מלמדה Cf. the cognate noun מלמד 'an ox-goad' in Judg 3.31; for the negative image, Jer 31.18, 'an untrained calf'.

[b]אהבתי A participial form in the construct with *yodh compaginis* and retracted tone; cf. GK 90k, l.

[c]ואני is emphatic.

[d]Considerable uncertainty attaches to the phrase עברתי על. Ibn Ezra states

that, in conformity with the practices of good ploughmen, 'I have cared for her fine neck', cf. Kimchi. By contast, Rashi who does not address himself to the question directly, seems to see in the words a reference to harsh treatment. Similarly, Jerome argues that the verb, predicated of God, would seem to imply the bringing of adversity and thus, here, of the taming of the beast by the imposition of a yoke. Amongst more recent commentators, Rudolph (cf. NEB, AF) proposes to repoint the word as a *Piel* עִבַּרְתִּי and to assume that על is haplography for עֹל עַל 'I have made to pass a yoke over ...'. The difficulty presents itself that no such meaning is attested for the *Piel* of the verb. Qyl assumes that the *Qal* has a causative force and that the phrase is elliptical with the meaning 'I passed my hand over (*sc.* stroked) her neck'. Again no parallel can be adduced.

Wolff gives to the verb עבר its usual meaning 'to pass by' and supposes that the phrase implies not passing by, and so sparing (so, e.g., Harper) the animal's neck; but rather passing by and so discovering in appreciation that fine neck. This seems to me to be the correct approach. עבר is clearly attested in the sense 'to come upon', 'light upon' (cf. BDB p. 717, col 1 h). Reference to the Arabic cognate verb *'br* (VIIIth theme)[13] suggests the meanings 'to acknowledge a quality in someone', 'to esteem, value or respect someone' and 'to have regard to someone'. This is precisely the sense sought by Wolff and it fits the context well. It is possible that the same sense underlies the use of the verb in Deut 24.5, where לא יעבר עליו לכל דבר may mean 'one will not have respect to him in any matter', i.e. he shall not be looked at for any (public) duty (cf. NEB). In the interests of caution, however, I have suggested a translation consistent with attested usage in Hebrew yet not inconsistent with the possibility that such further connotations are here present.

[e]טוב Not so much beautiful as, from a ploughman's point of view, well-formed and apt for his purpose, cf. Wolff. Accordingly the phrase may be rendered 'the firmness of her neck'[14].

[f]The first person imperfect form ארכיב has something of a consequential force, cf. with GK 156d, Ps. 103.5. The transition from what precedes is explained by Qyl in terms of what Yahweh resolved in the particular circumstances earlier depicted. The verb in the *Hiphil* denotes, according to ibn Janāḥ (see under the root ענה), the 'fastening or mounting of the yoke' (Arabic *trkyb 'lmqrnt*) to or upon the heads of the animals in question[15].

[g]The MT reads 'Judah'. Reference to Judah in this particular context is unlikely and is therefore understood to be a gloss inserted by the

[13] So Wehr, *ad loc.*; cf. Lane 5, p. 1937.

[14] For an unconvincing attempt to understand the words as a short relative clause 'her whose neck was perfection', see Nyberg and cf. Rudolph's criticisms.

[15] Cf. Mowinckel *VT* 12 (1962), p. 285 n.; see also S. P. Brock *VT* 18 (1968), p. 396.

Judaean redactor (cf. Emmerson, pp. 83ff, Rudolph and Davies). A number of scholars have supposed 'Israel' was the original reading; see further in the commentary below.

[h]יחרוש For the subordination of the complementary verbal idea in the imperfect, i.e. the imperfect without *waw* expressing purpose, cf. GK 120c.

[i]The translation 'engage in' is an attempt to convey the force of the ethic dative לו, used to 'give emphasis to the significance of the occurrence in question *for* a particular subject', GK 119s.

[j]ישדד The function was, according to Kimchi, 'to break up the clods after ploughing, to level the soil and prepare it for sowing'; see further *AUS* 2, pp. 189ff and 354; cf. Isa 28.24f; Job 39.10.

The metaphor of the Northern Kingdom hitched, like twin ploughing beasts, to twin wicked attitudes (see on the previous verse) leads Hosea to contrast with it, in a similar metaphor, Yahweh's gracious election of his people. In 9.10 he found Israel as grapes in the wilderness; here he states that he came across her (note d) as a biddable heifer already used to and enjoying the work of threshing. This work was not onerous since it could be accomplished without a sledge (*AUS* 3, p. 107) and the animal was relatively free (Jer 50.11) and able to browse (Deut 25.4). Seeing this 'cheerfully industrious young animal' (Wolff), Yahweh is moved to appreciate (again note d) her well-formed neck (note e) with its promise of aptitude for the more responsible and mature work of ploughing. Consequently he resolves that she is his choice for the work which he plans (cf. v. 12) and in direct speech (note f) he announces that this is his intention for her.

The essential contrast presented by vv. 10 and 11 is, then, between the nation's promise as the object of Yahweh's gracious election and the failure which its persistent waywardness effected, cf. the contrast between vv. 12 and 13 below. As Kimchi comments (on v. 10), 'I thought that they would plough well, but they have ploughed badly'.

Recognition of the nature of the contrast expressed by the prophet renders unnecessary and misleading attempts to see in the reference to ploughing a punishment or judgement imposed by Yahweh and then, as a consequence, to interpret *'br 'l* in a hostile sense (e.g. Wellhausen, Marti). Similarly the attempt (e.g. Harper) to see a contrast between Yahweh's initial action of restraint in passing by, in sparing the animal (note d), only thereafter to punish her, is mistaken and involves, in any case, emendation of the text (he supplies *w'th* before *'rkyb*).

Where the application of the metaphor of the heifer is concerned, Hosea undoubtedly wishes to contrast Israel's ready obedience and attentiveness to Yahweh (cf. 2.17, EV 15) at the time of her election in the desert (cf. 9.10; 11.1) with the nation's failure in her subsequent history to fulfil her early promise. Yahweh is represented, then, as believing in his people, as supposing that they were capable of fulfilling his purposes for them in the more difficult conditions which would obtain after the wilderness period, when they would be exposed to the temptations presented by the land of Canaan. Rudolph may be right in supposing that 'biddable' (note a) contains an allusion to Israel's reception of the law on Sinai. Certainly the rabbinic commentators sense that Yahweh taught Israel from the beginning to bear the yoke of his commandments (ibn Ezra). At any rate Rudolph is right to emphasise the religio-ethical contents of Hosea's words and in particular the weighty responsibility that Israel incurred as a result of her election, cf. on vv. 12 and 13 below, 'To whomsoever much is given, from him much shall be required' (Lk 12.48). It remains to draw attention to the consistency apparent between the passage under consideration and the material in chapters 1–3 which treat of the prophet's wife and her failure to fulfil her vocation in marriage. For 'heifer' as a term of affection for a wife/daughter, cf. Judg 14.18 and 2 Sam 3.5.

The MT furnishes the word 'Judah' as the subject of the phrase 'that he should plough' (note g) which is here regarded as a gloss added by the Judaean redactor. The decision so to regard it depends upon the consideration that its appearance here in a passage concerned with the Northern Kingdom is out of place. Further, as Rudolph rightly observes, if Judah is represented as ploughing, to what end is Ephraim said to be harnessed (cf. note f)? Wolff has sought to defend the reading on the grounds that reference to Judah is appropriate to a passage concerned with the settlement of the land by Israel (here 'Jacob') as a whole. The argument is scarcely convincing in view of the considerations outlined above. More likely is the view that Hosea's perspective is restricted to that of the Northern Kingdom and its imminent collapse. Mention of Jacob, parallel to Ephraim, serves to emphasise the historical perspective (cf. the Targum in Text and Versions) and the call of the nation as a whole (cf. ibn Ezra), of which Ephraim was only a part (cf. Rudolph). That 'Israel' not 'Judah' was the original reading (so Nowack, Harper, Nyberg) is, in the light of these considerations, a distinct possibility. Yet to vary the name (i.e. Ephraim to Israel) within the space of a few words, when the parallel 'Jacob' conveys what is necessary, seems clumsy.

Text and Versions

ואפרים LXX does not reproduce *waw* (cf. 3 Kennicott MSS); in the light of the interpretation of the words set out above, the force of *waw* is adversative, 'yet' and *waw* is likely to be authentic (*contra* Borbone).

מלמדה LXX δεδιδαγμένη, cf. Vulg. *docta*; Pesh. *mlpt'*, 'taught'; Targ. דמלפין לה 'which men teach (to plough)'; Wellhausen omits the word as a gloss.

לדוש LXX νεῖκος, *v.l.* νῖκος, 'strife', 'dispute before a judge'; Vollers suggests that לדין was read (cf. Borbone).

עברתי LXX ἐπελεύσομαι 'I will come down upon', cf. Vulg. *transivi* and Pesh. *'brt*; Targ. ('I redeemed them from slavery in Egypt') אעדיתי 'I removed (the hard yoke from their necks)'; → הֶעֱבַרְתִּי עֹל עַל (Marti, cf. *BHS*) or עִבַּרְתִּי עֹל עַל (Halévy, Rudolph) 'I passed a yoke over (her neck)'.

ארכיב LXX ἐπιβιβῶ 'I will place on' (? captivity, cf. Jerome); Vulg. *ascendam* 'I will mount Ephraim' (*sc.* her neck, back); Pesh. *'rkb*, cf. MT; Targ. אשריתי 'I caused to live (*sc.* in the land)', cf. Cathcart, p. 52, n. 32.

יחרוש LXX παρασιωπήσομαι 'I will pass over Judah in silence'; Aq. and Theod. ἀλοήσει 'he will thresh'; Symm. ἠροτρία 'he was ploughing'; Vulg. *arabit*, cf. Pesh. *wndrk* 'he will tread', 'thresh', reading ? ידוש (so Sebök); Targ. אחסינית יתהון אחסנא 'I have given them their inheritance'.

ישדד LXX ἐνισχύσει 'will strengthen', 'prevail'; Pesh. *nbwz* 'will plunder', cf. Gelston, p. 143; Vulg. *confringet* 'will harrow'; Targ. דקיימית לאבוהון יעקב '(the inheritance) that I swore to Jacob, their father'; NB that Targ. of this verse paraphrases extensively and it is not entirely clear which particular Hebrew words/phrases are represented by its particular readings.

10.12 **[a]Your sowing shall be in accordance with what is right; your reaping in accordance with goodness; give yourselves to ploughing[a] the fallow. [b]And then there is the season[b] to seek Yahweh till[c] he comes to rain down[d] blessing[e] for you.**

[a—a]Lit. 'sow according to ... reap according to ... plough ...'. In order to avoid awkwardness in English translation and to seek to convey the full sense, two of the imperatives are not reproduced in English. For ל and לפי denoting the principle with regard to which an action is accomplished, see BDB p. 516, col 1 j (b), cf. under פה, 6 c (1). Ethic datives (GK 119s) follow 'sow' and 'plough' and give emphasis to 'the significance of the recurrence in question *for* a particular subject'.

[b—b]ועת Lit. 'and (there is) a season'; the *waw* has its full copulative force and consequently the phrase means neither 'it is high time' nor 'there is still time'(*contra* LXX[Luc], cf. Rudolph).

[c]עד 'to the point that' (cf. BDB p. 725, col 1 1 b); here the force is virtually purposive (cf. König 396f).

[d]וירה Cf. 6.3, note k; so Rashi and ibn Ezra. For the *Hiphil* וירה 'send (i.e. throw) rain', Rashi compares Exod 15.4 and throwing the Egyptians into the sea. For the evidence of the versions and the view that the verb means 'to teach', see Text and Versions.

[e]צדק Lit. 'righteousness', 'correctness'; see further in the commentary below.

The contrast delineated in vv. 10f between the nation's failure to fulfil its vocation (v. 10) and Yahweh's prior gracious election of Israel (v. 11) is repeated in vv. 12f. Here the order is reversed and the religio-ethical substance of the agricultural metaphor obtrudes more clearly. The imperatives of the verse suggest that the words denote Yahweh's charge to Israel which follows the particular description of her election in v. 11. Israel's vocation, as Yahweh leads her towards the land is, naturally, to break up the fallow, i.e. 'to dislodge the twitch in the season of heat for a number of days before sowing' (so Rashi)[16]. The success of the venture, however, is wholly dependent upon Israel's preserving a proper relationship with Yahweh, who summons her to her task. The concepts of 'what is right' and 'goodness', to which the activities of sowing and reaping are here tied, are descriptive of that proper relationship just as, *mutatis mutandis*, they characterise the image of the marital relationship between Yahweh and his people in 2.21f (EV 19f). There these qualities are acknowledged as Yahweh's gifts which indicate the nature of the marriage that he offers and they are concomitants to it; once Israel's relationship with Yahweh is established then the life of the nation will be characterised by these same qualities. Here the agricultural operations, breaking up the soil (cf. Jer 4.3), sowing and harvest are images for the ethical conduct expected of the nation as it settles in the land. That conduct is to be in accordance with the norms (so Rosenmüller) of 'what is right' (*ṣdqh*) and 'goodness'

[16] Cf. *AUS* 2, p. 201.

(*ḥsd*, for which see on 4.1; 6.4, 6; 12.7, EV 6). Moreover, proper conduct as indicated by the work of agriculture depends, like it, upon a steadfast attitude of trust in the divine partner to the enterprise. The farmer's industry comes to nothing if God does not send the former rains (*ywrh*) to water the seed. Accordingly prayerful dependence upon God ('seeking Yahweh'), following the initial enterprises of ploughing and sowing, properly constitutes the farmer's next step ('and then there is the season ...', note b). The response of the divine partner reflects his gracious 'righteousness' (note e) and at the proper time he visits the land with his blessing of rain (cf. Joel 2.23 and Isa 45.8).

In 8.7, 'sowing' and 'reaping' are used as an image for the like consequences of like actions. Here, however, 'sowing' and 'reaping' (with the 'ploughing of the fallow') suggest a totality of enterprise not least since, in the verse which follows and depicts the contrast, 'reaping what is wrong' is not a consequence but an integral part of 'ploughing wickedness' (cf. Harper and Rudolph).

That the verse begins with direct speech on Yahweh's lips and then continues to refer to him in the third person is perhaps prompted by the requirements of the fixed phrase 'to seek Yahweh' and in any case accords with Hosea's usage elsewhere (cf. 1.2 etc.). 'Seeking (the face of) Yahweh' (here *drš*, but cf. *bqš* in 3.5; 5.6, 15) denotes the adoption of an attitude of prayerful trust in him. That the phrase is elsewhere used of resort to him in time of need through the agency of a prophet (cf. 1 Kgs 22.5ff; 2 Kgs 3.11; 8.8ff; 22.13ff) scarcely amounts to evidence that, in the context of a general description of Israel's relationship with Yahweh, this is the particular meaning here (so Wolff insistently). More probable is the view (so Rudolph) that the phrase emphasises, in this particular context, the nation's need to persist in its acknowledgement that Yahweh, and not Baal, is the guarantor of the success of its vocation and endeavour (cf. 2.10, EV 8)[17].

Text and Versions

ל(צדקה) LXX εἰς; Vulg. *in*; Pesh. may well have taken ל as an indication of the object, cf. Gelston, pp. 144f; Targ. עבידו לכון עובדין טבין 'do good deeds', so interpreting the whole clause.

[17] For the view that the verse and especially the last part of it makes use of Canaanite imagery, cf. T. Worden *VT* 3 (1953), p. 296 and Mays, quoting *ANET*, pp. 136f.

לפי חסד LXX εἰς καρπὸν ζωῆς 'to the fruit of life' on the basis of which → לפרי חסד (Harper); Vulg. *in ore misericordiae* 'in the mouth of mercy', cf. Pesh. *pwmh dṭybwt'* and Gelston, p. 144; Jerome explains the phrase to mean simply 'reap in mercy'; Targ. הליכו באורחא דזכו 'walk in the path of righteousness'.

נירו לכם ניר LXX φωτίσατε ἑαυτοις φῶς, cf. Pesh. *'nhrw lkwn šrg'* 'light a lamp for yourselves'; cf. Borbone and √נור 'give light', BDB p. 632, col 2, and √ניר I 'to till', BDB p. 644, col 2 and Gelston, p. 143; Vulg. *innovate vobis novale* 'initiate the ploughing of fallow land'; Targ. קיימו לכון אלפן אוריתא 'establish for yourselves learning of the law'.

ועת LXX γνώσεως 'of knowledge'; → דַּעַת '(the grounds/soil of) knowledge'/'(the light of) knowledge' (Oort, Wolff, Borbone); → לָדַעַת 'to know (to seek ...)' (*BHS*); LXX[Luc] ὡς ἔτι καιρός 'for there is still time'; Vulg. *quoniam est tempus*, cf. Pesh. *mṭl dzbn'hw* 'for it is time'; so → כִּי עֵת (cf. *BHS*), but see note b above.

לדרוש LXX ἐκζητήσατε (imperative); → דִּרְשׁוּ (Rupprecht); Wolff retains MT, but sees in it virtually an imperative force, 'break up the ground of knowledge in seeking (lit. and seek) Yahweh'.

עד יבוא וירה LXX ἕως τοῦ ἐλθεῖν γενήματα 'until the produce (of righteousness come to you)'; → פרי for וירה (Oort, Wellhausen *et al.*); וירה is rendered 'and teaches' by Wolff (cf. Vulg. and Pesh. below); he regards the phrase as a late Jewish interpretative break with Hosea's metaphor. The notion that LXX's γενήματα implies פרי is by no means certain; similarly Nyberg's contention that it presupposes a form of √הרה 'be pregnant'. More likely is Rudolph's view that the rendering is merely translational and, I would add, perhaps made by reference to the sentiments of Isa 45.8. Vulg. *cum venerit qui docebit* 'when he comes who will teach (you righteousness)'; the phrase is interpreted christologically by Jerome and it is likely that the title of the Qumran 'Teacher of Righteousness' (מורה צדק) has its origins here and in Joel 2.23, cf. G. R. Driver *The Judaean Scrolls*, p. 256; C. Roth *VT* 13 (1963), p. 91; J. C. von Kölichen *ZAW* 74 (1962), pp. 326f; see further B. *Bechoroth* 24a; Pesh. similarly *'d 't' wmḥw'* 'until he comes and declares (righteousness to you)'; Targ. כען יתגלי וייתי 'now he will reveal himself and bring (you righteous deeds)', cf. Cathcart, p. 53 n. 33.

צדק Pesh. adds the third masculine singular suffix.

לכם LXX ὑμῖν 'to you' (B. ἡμῖν 'to us').

10.13 **Wickedness is what you have ploughed[a], you have reaped what is wrong[b]; you have consumed the produce[c] of deceit. For you trusted in your policy[d] and in the number of your warriors.**

[a]The verb חרשׁ probably here comprises sowing, so Kimchi; cf. *AUS* 2, pp. 180f.

[b]For the ending *-ātāh*, cf. 8.7, note b.

[c]פרי Lit. 'fruit'.

[d]בדרכך Lit. 'in thy way'; for 'way' denoting 'course of life', or 'actions', 'undertakings', see BDB p. 203, col 1 5. A large number of authorities follow the evidence of the LXX (some MSS, see Text and Versions) and read בְּרִכְבְּךָ 'in thy chariotry' which makes a good parallel to 'thy warriors' (so, e.g., Wellhausen, Marti, Wolff, NEB, Borbone, *BHS*). However, MT yields a reasonable sense and I have preferred to retain it as the *difficilior lectio* (cf. Rudolph). S. Bartina *Verbum Domini* 34 (1956), pp. 202ff compares Ugaritic *drkt* 'dominion', 'power' and finds such a meaning here. The suggestion lacks support in tradition or clear parallel (cf. Davies, p. 248).

Despite the clarity of Yahweh's charge to Israel at her election, the nation has, from the beginning, acted in exactly the opposite sense (so Kimchi). Its policies and actions from those early days have been characterised by wickedness and wrong. The agricultural metaphors, from ploughing to sowing (note a above), reaping and harvest convey, as in the previous verse, the totality of the nation's enterprises from its election to the present day. Rudolph's contention that in this verse (13a) the present generation is addressed in contrast to v. 12, where the generation of the wilderness receives Yahweh's charge, is clearly mistaken; for the contrast consists not in the persons addressed (for who, other than the present generation, is the object of all Hosea's prophecies?) but rather in the nation's behaviour throughout its history seen against the background of Yahweh's gracious initiative in calling it to fulfil his purposes. The agricultural metaphor, then, naturally expresses the time span in which the nation's wickedness has so consistently been perpetrated. 'Wickedness' is set forth as the opposite of 'what is right' (v. 12); 'wrong' as the opposite of 'goodness' (v. 12); the whole suggests all that is opposed to the will of Yahweh, i.e. policies and actions that are deeply disordered (cf. Rudolph). Accordingly the end product, the harvest (note c) of the nation's endeavours is characterised by 'deceit'; it is worthless and yields no benefit to those who consume it (cf. with Rashi, 9.2). No doubt that is because their wickedness and wrong constitute deceit practised against Yahweh himself (again, Rashi, cf. Jerome), for it is in the nature of the prophet's particular formulation here that what characterises punishment characterises guilt also, cf., with Qyl, Isa 3.11 'Woe betide the wicked! with him all goes ill, for he reaps the reward that he has earned' (NEB). In light of such considerations it is not necessary to follow Ruben, Guthe (cf. Rudolph) in reading *w'kltm* (see Text and Versions) whereby the last phrase is made simply a threat of punishment 'and you shall consume ...'. As Harper rightly observes, the agricultural forms are not intended to designate consequence but represent the whole gamut of wickedness, wrong and disaster.

The change from second person plural to second person singular in the second half of the verse has long prompted many scholars to see in 13b the beginning of a new rhetorical unit or strophe (e.g. Harper, Wolff, Rudolph)[18]. Amongst the rabbinic commentators, Kimchi understands the new subject to be Hoshea whose reign saw the final devastation of Samaria and the end of the Northern Kingdom. There is perhaps something to be said for this approach. The references in the first half of the verse, and in v. 10, to the consistent wickedness of the nation since its very election suggests that the prophet is now ready to address himself to present realities, to the predicament of his nation seen against the background of its consistent past wickedness. Certainly the 'number of your warriors', 'your people' (v. 14) as well as the explicit mention of the nemesis of the king of Israel (v. 15) appear to corroborate Kimchi's view[19]. The theme of the half-verse is, moreover, consistent with the principle enunciated in v. 9, *viz.* that nemesis followed the atrocity at Gibeah and will necessarily do so in the present situation. Indeed, the section 13b–15 *more prophetarum* offers an interpretation of the current historical events which seeks to confirm the validity of that principle.

For Rudolph, 13b–15, with its change in vv. 13f to a second person singular reference, is a separate section added by a redactor on the basis of a catch-word ('war' in vv. 9 and 14); the section 11–13a (added to 9f by reason of the catch-word *'lwh/'wlth*) belongs to the period after Jeroboam II, when the nation had already experienced the first Assyrian incursions; 13b–15 belong to an earlier period, i.e. the hey-day of prosperity

[18] For earlier appraisals, including theories to the effect that later insertions may be detected, cf. Wellhausen, Volz, Nowack *et al.*

[19] Wolff's theory that the section reflects Hosea's response to an objection posed directly to him by an important representative of the royal court of Samaria amounts to a speculative variation of Kimchi's interpretation; the latter is better because it is simpler.

under Jeroboam II. While his account of the matter represents a possibility, I have preferred to suppose that there is a connection between the two passages and that this juxtaposition, whether accomplished by Hosea or by a redactor, represents accurately the mind of the prophet (cf. Wolff, p. 183). Certainly, e.g., Mays, who like Rudolph, regards the passage as originally distinct, none the less suggests that Hoshea's reliance upon the military resources of the nation at the time of his rebellion against Assyria (2 Kgs 17.4) fits as the background to 13b–15. Even at the fall of Samaria in 722/1 BC, Sargon II was able to appropriate as many as fifty Israelite chariots into his own army (*ANET*, p. 284).

Hoshea, then, the contemporary exemplar of the nation's consistent wickedness, is indicted by the prophet for his unwarranted confidence in his own policy (note d) and in his military resources. His policy is radically consistent with the nation's long-held commitment to fake attitudes, in 'making flesh their right arm' (Kimchi), in its wilful failure to rely in trust upon its God. For similar sentiments, cf. Amos 6.13; Isa 31.1; Hos. 8.14.

Text and Versions

חרשתם LXX ἵνα τί παρεσιωπήσατε 'why have you passed over in silence (godlessness)?' Harper (cf. *BHS*) wonders whether למה, a dittograph from לכם, was read; for חרשׁ II 'be silent' as opposed to חרשׁ I 'to plough', cf. BDB, pp. 360f; Pesh. *dbrtwn* and Vulg. *arastis* 'ploughed'; Targ. אתעשתון 'you have devised for yourselves (oppression)' interprets the metaphor.

אכלתם → וַאֲכַלְתֶּם 'and you shall eat', 'consume' (Ruben and Guthe, cf. *BHS*).

בדרכך LXX ἐν τοῖς ἁμαρτήμασιν, probably a harmonising correction (Rudolph) or corruption (Harper) of the reading of LXX[AQ] τοῖς ἅρμασιν 'chariots' on the basis of which → בְּרִכְבְּךָ 'in thy chariotry' (e.g., Manger, Wellhausen, Wolff, Mays, NEB, *BHS*, Davies, Borbone); Vulg. *in viis tuis* 'in thy ways', cf. Pesh. *b'wrḥtkwn* (plural suffix) and Targ. באורחתך (singular suffix).

גבוריך LXX δυνάμεώς σου, cf. Pesh. *gnbrwtkwn* '(the multitude) of thy/your strength'; Targ. גיברך, cf. Vulg. *fortium tuorum* 'of thy warriors'; → גְּבוּרָתְךָ (Vollers).

10.14 **The tumult of war will arise against[a] your people[b], and all your fortresses shall be destroyed[c], as Shalman destroyed Beth-arbel in the day of battle, [d]mothers butchered[e] with[f] their children[d].**

[a]ב 'against' rather than 'amongst'; BDB p. 878, col 1 2 suggests אל as the more usual preposition but Mic 7.6 and Ps 27.12 indicate that ב was an alternative; see further note b below.

[b]בעמך A plural reading (i.e. בעמיך) is attested in a number of MSS and accepted by, e.g., Kimchi in the sense 'your tribes'; with this ב 'among' amounts to a possibility. The singular reading of other MSS is, however, preferable. The plural reading may have arisen by attraction to the plural 'fortresses'. See further under Text and Versions below.

[c]The singular verb יוּשַּׁד is construed with כל as its subject, cf. König, 394d; the mood is properly the passive of the *Qal*, GK 53u.

[d—d]The phrase is simply juxtaposed; it amounts to a short relative clause without אשר and may be rendered 'when mothers were ...'. The word 'mother' is singular but its use is akin to indeterminateness for the sake of emphasis or amplification; GK 125c. *BHS* suggests the possibility that the phrase is a later addition; the tentative suggestion is here discounted.

[e]The verb רטש, often rendered 'to dash in pieces', is used of the wounds inflicted by arrows (Isa 13.18) and of the destruction of children by their being dashed to pieces (Isa 13.16, cf. Ps 137.9). The translation 'butchered' offered above is not precise but seeks to convey the sense in English. Rashi and Kimchi mention as an alternative view of the verb that it means 'abandoned' and they cite Exod 23.11 where רטש in the Targum answers to MT's נטש. Aramaic רטש can mean 'to abandon', 'forsake' and it is therefore likely that the interpretation is made by reference to Aramaic rather than to Hebrew usage. That there is some confusion in the matter seems clear from the fact that in the Targum Ps 137.9, רטש answers to MT's נפץ and thus there seems to mean 'to dash in pieces' (cf. Jastrow p. 1472, col 1).

[f]For על with the sense 'together with' in this stereotyped expression, cf., with ibn Janāḥ, Gen 32.12 (EV 11). Kimchi suggests a more literal meaning since, in such circumstances, mothers are wont to throw themselves over their children in order to protect them.

In accordance with the principle that the prophet has established in reference to Gibeah, *viz.* that, by divine decree, war overtakes perverse men (v. 9), he now announces the imminent advent of the horrors of war to the king and his people (note b). If trust in the king's own policies and in the strength of his military forces is misplaced and wrong, that fact will be made manifest in the brutal realities of foreign invasion. The tumult of war will confront his people and, all his cherished fortresses destroyed, nothing will avail to stop it. The end result will be typified in the awful realities of total war when even mothers with their children are the objects of the cruel bloodlust of the conquerors. To lend force to his terrible depiction of such realities, the prophet appeals to his hearers' knowledge of events at Beth-arbel when that city was destroyed by Shalman. If his hearers certainly knew of the event to which he refers, it is unfortunately certain that we do not. Nor, apparently, does tradition offer any satisfactory guide. Perhaps the most plausible suggestion is that the Moabite king Salamanu is intended. His name is known from a tribute list of Tiglath-pileser III[20] and 2 Kgs 13.20b mentions Moabite raids and incursions into the Northern Kingdom; further Amos 2.1–3 reports Moabite atrocities in the south of the trans-Jordanian region. Beth-arbel has been identified[21] with modern Irbid, fifteen kilometres north-west of Tell Ramit (Ramoth-gilead) in northern Gilead across the Jordan and opposite Beth-shean.

Amongst the views of earlier commentators, mention may be made of that of Jerome who sees in Shalman a reference to Salmana (*sic*), the Midianite king killed by Gideon (Judg 8.21), otherwise known as Jerobaal (*sic*), of which Arbel here is an abbreviated form: '... just as Salmana was destroyed by the house of him who took vengeance on Baal' (so he renders the half verse) alludes to 'the book of Judges where Gideon says to Salmana "Your sword has made women childless and your mother of all women shall be childless too"'. His argument is not aided by the fact that the quotation comes not from Judges but from 1 Sam 15.33 where the speaker is Samuel and Agag is addressed. For the rest, as Rosenmüller comments, Jerome's argument is facilitated by the similarity in sound to the Latin ear between the two names. In fact, of course, they are marked by very considerable differences: צַלְמֻנָּע/שַׁלְמַן.

Amongst the rabbinic commentators, ibn Ezra and Kimchi's father consider the possibility that the reference is to the Assyrian king Shalmaneser and (so Kimchi's father) Beth-arbel is Samaria 'ambushed' (cf. the root *'rb* and the Targum) by God. The argument has subsequently been developed (so, e.g., Rosenmüller, cf. Davies, referring to 2 Kgs 17.3) and not least in

[20] Cf. *ANET*, p. 282; A. H. van Zyl *The Moabites* (Leiden, 1960), pp. 23f, 149f, 183.

[21] Cf. Noth *PJ* 37 (1941), p. 92 and N. Glueck *AASOR* 25–28 (1951), pp. 153ff. Other suggested identifications are: (1) Khirbet Irbid, north-west of Tiberias and below the Horns of Ḥattin in the modern (Israeli) Biq'at Arbel, referred to in 1 Mac 9.2 as Arbela; (2) the Assyrian Arbela, which lies 100 kms east-south-east of Mosul and is today called Erbil; for references, see Harper. The latter is too far removed from Israel/Palestine to be convincing.

the supposition that the name is a variant like Pul for Tiglath-pileser (e.g. 2 Kgs 15.19). Shalmaneser V (726–722 BC) may have attacked Galilean Beth-arbel on his way to Samaria or at an earlier stage in his reign (cf. 2 Kgs 17.3) but this seems to be too late for mention in the prophecies of Hosea[22]. If Hosea, in keeping with his predilection for older formulae and traditions (cf. on 5.8), is citing an instance from earlier Assyrian campaigns in the region of Galilee, it is possible to suppose that Shalmaneser III (859–824 BC) may have crossed the Jordan in connection with his attack on Damascus in 838 BC, following his invasion of Lebanon in the years immediately before (cf. Orelli, but NB the revision of dates since he wrote)[23].

For an assessment of the historical background to the verse as a whole, see on v. 13 above.

H. G. May (cf. 6.3 and 10.15) is disposed to wonder whether in the name Shalman there is an allusion to the Canaanite god Shalem just as, in v. 15, there is (so he believes) an allusion to the god Shaḥar. Yet May, regarding the texts as 'very corrupt', gives no translation or further explanation.

Text and Versions

וקאם For the use of *aleph* to indicate the long *a* vowel, common in Arabic, but rare in Hebrew, cf. GK 9b, 23g, 72p.

בעמך 14 Kennicott MSS read בְּעַמֶּיךָ; Kimchi seems to be aware of the variant reading for he explicitly supports the plural reading. The singular reading (cf. all the versions) is probably correct (cf. Rudolph); Aurivillius (see Rosenmüller) supposes that the plural reading represents a tendency to intensify the meaning, thus the terrors of war will affect all the people of Israel, all its tribes; → בְּעָרֶיךָ 'in thy cities' (Wellhausen, cf. Marti and *BHS*).

יושד → יוּשַּׁדוּ (Borbone, cf. *BHS*).

כשד LXX ὡς ἄρχων 'like a ruler'; Aq. ὡς προνομή 'like a foray ...'; Symm. καθὼς ἠφανίσθη 'as (Salman) was destroyed', cf. Vulg. *sicut vastatus est* (Salman); Pesh. *'yk bzt' dšlm'*, and Targ. כביזת שלמא.

שלמן The massoretic tradition presents variant pointings: שַׁלְמָן/שַׁלְמַן/שָׁלְמָן, cf. Rudolph; LXX Σαλαμάν (Σαλαμα – Q); Vulg. *Salman* (*v.l. Salmana*, cf. OL[S]); Pesh. and Targ. *šlm'*/שלמא, interpretative; (1 Targ. MS שלמנא); → שָׁלוֹם (Cheyne[24] and many moderns; Cheyne also

[22] I.e. assuming the authenticity of the words; for arguments for regarding the reference as an interpolation, see, e.g., Marti.

[23] Cf. M. C. Astow *JAOS* 91 (1971), pp. 383–389.

[24] See *Expositor* 5/6 (1897), p. 364.

reads בית ירבעם for בית ארבאל, see next note, and thinks that the incident recorded in 2 Kgs 15.10 is in mind.)

בית ארבאל LXX[B] (cf. OL[S]) ἐκ τοῦ οἴκου Ἰεροβοάμ 'of the House of Jeroboam'[25]; LXX[A] ...Ἰεροβαάλ '... of Jerubaal'; the latter is likely to be a corruption of an original transcription of ארבאל, the former a further (inner) corruption of the latter; Aq. τοῦ οἴκου τοῦ δικάζοντος 'of the house of one judging/pleading' (cf. √ריב); Vulg. *a domo eius qui iudicavit Baal*; Symm. ἐν τῷ οἴκῳ τοῦ ἀρβεήλ transcribes; Pesh. *byt 'yl* 'Bethel' represents an unlikely attempt based upon the last two letters of MT's ארבאל to harmonise with Bethel in v. 15; Targ. בכמנא 'in an ambush', cf. Theod. ἐνέδρου (√ארב, cf. Ziegler *Bei.*, p. 359).

רטשה LXX ἠδάφισαν, cf. Pesh. *šqpw* 'they dashed to the ground'; impersonal third plural active for MT's passive, cf. Gelston, p. 137.

10.15 **Just so[a] men[b] will deal[c] with you, Bethel[d], because of your wicked policy[e]. At dawn[f] the king of Israel will be utterly swept away[g].**

[a]The adverb ככה is somewhat more emphatic than כה 'thus'; so BDB p. 462, col 1. Luther (cf., e.g., van Hoonacker) sees an antecedent for the word in כשר in v. 14, i.e. 'like Shalman's destruction ... so ...'. However, the כשר clause belongs with the first half of v. 14, and v. 15 refers back to the whole of v. 14. Further the construction ככה ... כ is only elsewhere attested in the late Eccles 11.5 (so Rudolph).

[b]The third person masculine singular of the verb עשה is understood to be used impersonally (cf. the Peshitta and GK 144b) rather than as an indication that Yahweh (so presumably the LXX) is the unexpressed subject. Halévy (cf. Rudolph, *BHS*) rightly seeks this sense but by unnecessary resort to emendation; he reads יֵעָשֶׂה 'it will be done (to you)'. A third possibility is that suggested by the Vulgate and Jerome, for whom Bethel is the subject; i.e. Bethel, the site of the wicked and idolatrous cult, will bring upon you, Ephraimites, the fate that has been depicted in the previous verse. Against this view is the consideration that the cause of the coming disaster is apparently expressed by the words which follow, *viz.* 'because of your wicked policy'.

[c]The perfect is a prophetic perfect, GK 106n.

[d]The name is understood to be in apposition to לכם. For discussion of the emendation בית ישראל 'House of Israel' for MT's 'Bethel', made by reference to the LXX and widely adopted by modern authorities, see the commentary below.

[25] The reading is the basis for the conjecture (Sellin, Procksch in *BH*) that בית ירבעם was original.

[e]רעת רעתכם Apparently '(because of) the wickedness of your wickedness'; the phrase is often taken as a superlative expression, the only one where both nouns are singular (GK 133i). Parallels such as 'Song of Songs', 'Holy of Holies', etc., have suggested to Ehrlich (cf. Rudolph) that the second word should be pointed רָעֹתֵ(י)כֶם. G. R. Driver[26] points the (second) word רְעֻתְכֶם '(the wickedness of) your purpose', thereby avoiding 'ugly paronomasia'. Ibn Janāḥ does not refer to this verse but in connection with רעה in Hos. 12.2 (EV 1) he suggests that the word denotes 'thought', 'review', 'consideration' (Arabic *'lfkr w'ltfqqd w'lr''yt*) and is akin to Aramaic רעיון (cf. Dan 2.29 etc.). The similarity between ibn Janāḥ's account of possible meanings for רעה and Driver's independent assessment of this verse is striking and suggests that the latter scholar sensed the meaning, though he resorted unnecessarily to emendation. In his treatment of the matter, Driver notes that רעות is elsewhere attested only in the late Hebrew of Ecclesiastes but he is able to adduce evidence in favour of the existence of the word as early as the eighth century BC, thereby anticipating objections to the theory adduced by, e.g., Gispen and Rudolph. *BHS* suggests the possibility that the phrase is a later addition, a suggestion here discounted.

[f]From the context it would appear that בשחר 'at dawn' denotes the very beginning of the advent of battle. The reference, then, is to the speed and immediacy with which the king will be removed. Thus Jerome compares 10.7, where Samaria's king is represented as disappearing (again from the root דמה II) as swiftly as foam upon the surface of water. Here, in a different image, the king's disappearance will be as swift as the Palestinian dawn which minimises the transition between night and day. Jerome's words, together with the Vulgate, have suggested to a number of scholars (e.g. Cappellus, see Rosenmüller, Rudolph) that Jerome read כַּשחר, a reading attested by some Kennicott and de Rossi MSS and by the LXX[Luc]. The reading is adopted by, e.g., Oort, Grätz and Rudolph. Where the Vulgate and Jerome are concerned, the interpretation of the evidence is complicated (see Text and Versions) and it is not certainly the case that Jerome read כַּשחר; rather it is probable that his translation, like the other authorities cited, is interpretative. The rabbinic commentators appear to have read בַּשחר and the reading is confirmed by the margin of the Massora (ל). The combination of the notions of immediacy and speed are, of course, combined in the widely attested adverbial usage השכם (cf. in Hos 6.4), lit. 'rising early', and it seems likely that a similar sense is to be detected in בשחר here. While he does not mention this verse, for Job 24.5 and Prov 13.24 ibn Janāḥ compares the (denominative) verb שחר with השכם and suggests that they have the same meaning; cf. further

[26] *JTS* 47 (1946), pp. 163f.

Isa 58.8. Accordingly, since adequate sense for בשחר here can be detected, the reading is retained.

[g]For the *Niphal* of √דמה II, see on 4.5f and 10.7. The perfect is a prophetic perfect.

The verse expresses the conviction that the wicked policies (note e) of the Northern Kingdom will bring upon it inexorably the same (note a) horrible fate as befell Beth-arbel. Such is the stark reality of the war predicted in specific terms by v. 14 and established in v. 9 as the inevitable result of perversity. If the agents of the action against Israel are human (note b), the (impersonal) third singular verb may yet suggest that it is Yahweh who wills it. It is against the nation as a whole ('you') that the punitive war will be unleashed. Further definition of the nation as an establishment is provided by the twin references to 'Bethel' (in apposition to 'you', note d) and to the 'king of Israel', i.e. to the site of the national cult and to the royal house of Samaria. The LXX reads for 'Bethel', 'House of Israel' and this is adopted by a large number of modern commentators[27] (see Text and Versions) on the grounds that Hosea prefers to use the pejorative name 'Bethaven' for the cultic site. Yet, with the instance of Beth-arbel in his mind, it is not unlikely that Hosea would express his conviction that the same fate would befall Bethel, prominent as a symbol of his nation (cf. AF). Here, too, the characteristic wickedness of the place is specifically expressed in the words that follow, 'your wicked policy', and hence it may have been unnecessary to use the pejorative term. Hosea 12.5 (EV 3) provides clear evidence that Hosea was capable of using the name Bethel as well as Bethaven, cf. Kallai *Bethaven*, p. 178 and his note 38.

The cause of the nation's imminent suffering is its 'wicked policy' (note e) and this has already been explained in the contrast expressed in vv. 12f between a dutiful response to the charge of Yahweh and the nation's *de facto* repudiation of him in favour of false attitudes and confidence in their own military and political resources. In particular Bethel, the site of the 'calf of Samaria' (8.5f), is the epitome of the nation's repudiation of the first commandment of which, indeed (cf. 8.4, 9), the wicked policies of the monarchy and the establishment were symptoms.

So it is that the king of Israel (NB the use of the official title) will, as in v. 7a, be swept away to oblivion. The phrase 'at

27 There are differences, however, in the understanding of the term; for Wolff it denotes the royal dynasty of Samaria; for Rudolph, the people of the Northern Kingdom as a whole; see on 5.1 above.

dawn' conveys the immediacy and speed with which he will meet his fate (note f). Amongst the rabbinic commentators, the phrase is understood more literally; thus, ibn Ezra suggests that the people will be destroyed in the night and then the king on the following morning; for Rashi, the king will be stupefied[28] by sleep, i.e. rendered helpless, in the daytime as if it were night; for Kimchi (after his father) the phrase refers to the very dawn of Hoshea's reign when he was arrested by Shalmaneser V. Such interpretations seem contrived and are likely to be based upon a faulty assessment of the meaning of *bšḥr* (note f).

The motif of God's help at dawn (e.g., Ps 46.6) has suggested to Wolff[29] that here God's punishment (rather than help) for Israel is presented in similar terms. Since it is likely that the language of speed and immediacy contributed to the emergence of the motif[30], the suggestion may amount to a possibility. The more thorough-going mythological approach of H. G. May *ZAW* 55 (1937), p. 275, that here (as in 6.3) there is a reference to the dawn god Shaḥar is discounted.

For the historical background to the verse, cf. on vv. 7 and 13 above.

Text and Versions

עשה LXX ποιήσω 'I will do'; → אֶעֱשֶׂה (e.g., Wellhausen, Grätz, Marti, Borbone, *et al.*), but see notes b and c above; Pesh. *'bdw* 'they did', cf. note b above.

בית־אל LXX οἶκος τοῦ Ἰσραήλ; → בית־ישראל (Wellhausen, Grätz, Wolff, Rudolph, Mays, Borbone, cf. *BHS*).

רעת רעתכם LXX (ἀπὸ προσώπου) (+ ἀδικίας, B) κακιῶν ὑμῶν; OL[S] *malitiae iniquitatium*; Vulg. *malitiae nequitiarum vestrarum*; Pesh. *byšwt byšwtkwn*; the last two understand both words of רעה 'evil thing'; Targ. בישות עובדיכון 'the evil of your deeds'; → (מפני) רעתכם (Borbone, cf. LXX).

בשחר Some Kennicott and de Rossi MSS כַּשחר; LXX ὄρθρου 'at dawn'; LXX[Luc] ὡς ὄρθρος 'like dawn', cf. perhaps Vulg. *sicuti mane*; Aq. ἐν ὄρθρῳ, cf. Pesh. *bšpr'* 'at dawn'; Targ. בסופא בצפרא 'in the end, at dawn' (the second word is omitted by a number of authorities, cf. Cathcart, p. 53, n. 42. In the Vulg. the phrase as a whole is rendered *sicuti mane transit pertransiit rex I.* In his commentary Jerome compares

[28] He is clearly thinking of √דמם I (BDB, p. 198) rather than דמה.

[29] He refers to J. Ziegler's essay in *Friedrich Nötscher Festschrift*, pp. 281ff; Ziegler, however, does not discuss this verse.

[30] See Ziegler *op. cit.*, p. 282.

the phrase explicitly with v. 7 and writes *diversis figuris eumdem explicat sensum*. On this verse: *sicut enim ortus aurorae, et diluculum, et principium diei, quod appellatur mane, inter noctis solisque viciniam transit celeriter; ita ut finiatur nox et clarescat dies: sic rex I. ...*'. This extremely detailed definition hardly fits the reading כַּשחר which would, as in v. 7 (כקצף), have been easily explained. Rather its very detail and in particular the definition *inter noctis solisque viciniam* suggests that Jerome seeks to interpret the reading בַּשחר but by reference to the simile of v. 7 which has accordingly influenced his translation and comments[31]. At all events it seems questionable to cite Vulg. as evidence for the reading כַּשחר[32]. Emendations, include בשׂערה (for בסערה) 'in the storm' (Oort, Wellhausen, Marti, cf. *BHS*) and כענן שׁחר 'like the mist of dawn' (Ruben).

נדמה נדמה For Vulg., see above; LXX and Vulg. connect this clause with 11.1, as does Rashi.

[31] The rendering *sicuti mane transit* followed by *pertransiit* suggests that he interpreted the infinitive absolute as such but also as a finite verb connected with שׁחר. Such ingenuity fits better a *difficilior lectio*.

[32] For a contemporary account of the variant readings and for an explanation which is similar to Jerome's, cf. Cyril of Alexandria's comments.

CHAPTER 11.1–11

CONSISTENT LOVE AND CONSISTENT INGRATITUDE

Chapter 11 presents a more or less coherent whole. It begins with an historical retrospect which is perhaps more intense (cf. Wolff) than those of preceding sections (cf. 9.10 and 10.9). References to earlier oracles may be detected in vv. 2, 4, 5, 7 and 11 and, consequently, Wolff's assertion (cf. Rudolph) that there are no connections between these oracles and others is to be rejected. In particular the themes of the chapter may be styled: vv. 1–4, Yahweh's consistent love is confronted by Ephraim's ingratitude; vv. 5f, Assyrian dominance and invasion is the inevitable consequence of the nation's ungrateful foolishness; v. 7, the nation's foolishness has robbed it of all possibility of a satisfactory response; vv. 8f, Yahweh's gracious intervention and his decision to show unmerited compassion; vv. 10f, originally an indication that Yahweh's decision would have, as its result, miraculous freedom of the nation from involvement with Egypt and Assyria and its restoration to the land; this theme is later reworked to constitute a full (Judaean) statement of Yahweh's redemption of the diaspora (see below).

11.1 **When[a] Israel was a lad, I loved[b] him; and I[c] called my son from[c] Egypt.**

[a]Modern commentators usually detect this sense for כי, comparing, e.g., Isa 43.2 (Rosenmüller) and Gesenius-Buhl *ad loc.* (Rudolph). The ancient versions (see Text and Versions) understand the conjunction in a causal sense connecting the phrase with what has been said in 10.15 (so Rashi), i.e., 'all this has befallen Israel because I loved him from his childhood'. Ibn Ezra and Kimchi invest כי with a temporal sense and interpret the phrase as a whole of the training and discipline applied to Israel from its childhood as by a loving father (cf. Deut 8.5) and hence they establish the connection between punishment (10.15) and its origin in *quasi* parental love. Jerome, somewhat differently, understands the conjunction to convey that Yahweh loved Israel because the latter was, as it were, a helpless lad held captive in Egypt. Such interpretations are prompted largely by the belief that 11.1 has an integral connection with 10.15, a view that is not here accepted. Further, and in any case, all three rabbinic commentators, irrespective of their views on כי, interpret

the two words נער ישׂראל as a circumstantial clause with a temporal sense, 'when Israel was a child'. It seems best then to regard כי as a temporal conjunction introducing the circumstantial clause.

[b]The *waw* consecutive verbal form ואהבהו begins the main clause (cf. Qyl). The sense here is 'I set my love upon him', i.e. then the relationship of love began and the summons to leave Egypt with the status of Yahweh's son.

[c—c]The phrase as a whole and the preposition מן are understood to have a local sense (cf. v. 2a). Kimchi (cf., e.g., van Hoonacker, Sellin) supposes that a temporal sense may be detected, *viz.* 'from (the time) of Egypt I began to call him my son' (cf. the Targum below). It is likely that this interpretation is prompted (1) by reference to Exod 4.22 where, in an address to Pharaoh, God refers to Israel as 'my son, my first-born' and (2) is facilitated by the temporal sense given to כי (note a). Yet קרא with ל denotes 'call', 'summon', as opposed to the usage of v. 2a, where the sense (קרא with *dativus commodi*) is artfully varied. (By contrast, when קרא is used in the sense 'to name' it is construed with ל of the person and an accusative of the appellation.) Indeed, the point is conceded by Kimchi when he gives as alternative renderings of the phrase in question 'I called him because he was my son' and 'I called (to Pharaoh) on behalf of Israel, my son'. Kimchi has an exegetical point, see further below.

The nation's perfidious and vacillating policies (cf. vv. 2a and 5) are indissolubly bound up with the people's persistent idolatry; see v. 2b. By contrast, from the very beginning Yahweh's gracious actions are marked by consistency and love. For at the time of its bondage in Egypt, the nation was a mere child, small and vulnerable (so, after Jerome; cf. Jer 1.6), incapable of independent action (cf. with Rudolph, 1 Kgs 3.7). At this particular moment Yahweh chose to set his love upon Israel and, freeing him from servitude to others, to adopt him as his own son. The beginnings of the nation are, then, here depicted as due entirely to Yahweh's grace and not at all to its own inherent attractiveness or fitness for its vocation (cf. and contrast 9.10; 10.11). This motif seems to be in Hosea's mind here rather than that of the wilderness period where *n'wrym* 'youth' (2.17, EV 15) depicts the age of young maturity and fits well the metaphor of Israel as Yahweh's bride. Here the cognate noun *n'r* is used because it is capable of meaning not only 'boy', 'child' but also 'servant' and thus conveys the notion of Israel's pitiable state of bondage to Egypt. In that Hosea here traces back Yahweh's relationship with the nation to the very beginning, and thus behind the time of the wilderness, his choice of metaphor is naturally different. Yahweh's love for Israel and his adoption of the nation as his son depicts the same gracious initiative and that is exemplified by the all-important and decisive rescue from servitude in Egypt. By that decisive action, Israel's special relationship with Yahweh is constituted and from that moment the nation becomes Yahweh's son. Thus Kimchi's attempt to see in v. 1b and the preposition *mn* a temporal sense (note c), though strictly inaccurate, serves to convey an important element in Hosea's thought.

The central importance and originality of the metaphor of Israel as Yahweh's son has rightly been emphasised by modern scholars. Certainly the motif of God as Israel's loving father becomes central in Deuteronomy (cf., with Wolff, 4.37; 7.8, 13; 10.15; 23.6). As the words of v. 3 imply, the emphasis is upon Yahweh's loving care, expressed in terms of training and education, rather than upon the notion of a father as pro-creator. The image is likely to be a natural one (so Rudolph) rather than the result of Hosea's conscious attempt to rebut the notion of Baal as a father god (so Wolff) or of his conscious borrowing of ideas from the wisdom tradition of courtly circles (so again, but tentatively, Wolff).

Verse 1b is cited by Mt 2.15 in connection with the story of the flight of the Holy Family to Egypt and specifically to their (and thus Jesus') return thence. Jerome quotes the objection raised by Julian the Apostate (332–63) to the effect that what was written about Israel has been transferred by Matthew to Jesus so that he might take advantage of the gullibility of gentile believers. Jerome retorts that since Matthew first published his gospel in Hebrew, Jews alone would be able to read it; hence he cannot be accused of setting out to deceive gentiles. Further, that if he had wished to deceive Jews he was either a fool or incompetent because they would readily perceive any fabrication or bogus interpretation. For the rest, he argues that the use of the prophecy is essentially typological and of a sort with, e.g., St Paul's use of Sinai/Hagar, Sion/Sarah in Gal 4. A type, for Jerome, reveals a part of the truth; if the totality were to have been realised in the type, then that would no longer be type but historical fact. See further Rudolph's similar conclusions, 'Jesus, according to God's plan, the goal and consummation of Israel's history should in his life recapitulate its beginning.'

Text and Versions

LXX and Vulg. connect the verse with 10.15; cf. the last entry there.

כי LXX ὅτι (*v.l.* διότι) 'for the reason that', 'because'; Aq., Symm., Theod. ὅτι; Vulg. *quia*; Pesh. *mṭl dkd*; Targ. ארי; for the double translation of Pesh., cf. Gelston, p. 173.

ממצרים Targ. וממצרים קריתי להון בנין 'and from the time of Egypt I called them sons', cf. Cathcart, p. 54, n. 2.

קראתי LXX (cf. Aq. and Theod. ἐκάλεσα) μετεκάλεσα, cf. Vulg. *vocavi* (with acc.) 'I summoned'; Pesh. *qryth* (Gelston, p. 145), cf. Targ. קריתי להון 'I named him/them (my son, sons)'; Symm. κέκληται '(my son) was called'.

לבני LXX τὰ τέκνα αὐτοῦ 'his children', cf. Targ. בנין and OL[S]; Aq. and Theod. (τὸν) υἱόν μου, cf. Symm. υἱός μου, Vulg. *filium meum*, Pesh. *bry*: all 'my son'. Rudolph supposes that the readings of the LXX and Targ. arise from the desire to avoid the possibility of Christological interpretation. For the reading לו בני, cf. Winckler, p. 182. Wellhausen (cf. Harper) reads לו כדי '... him. The more ...', conjoining with the following verse.

11.2 They have made their own[a] call [*sc.* to Egypt] and likewise[b] they have withdrawn from them[c]. They continue[d] to make sacrifices for the Baals and to burn incense[d] to idols.

The verbs of the first half of the verse (קראו ... הלכו) are strikingly similar to those of 7.11b and it is here assumed that the prophet is repeating them. In the case of the second verb it is likely that he also makes allusion to 9.6 and the phrase הלכו משד. For a similar quotation in chapter 11, cf. v. 5 with 8.13 and 9.3. The sudden transition (v. 2) to the third person plural is interpreted by Jerome, the Targum and the rabbinic commentators of the prophets (in particular Moses and Aaron, but not exclusively so) through whom Yahweh's call (v. 1b) to his people was mediated. Accordingly the people's deviation (so הלכו מפניהם) is understood to be proportional to the insistence of the prophetic summons. Modern commentators, for whom the transition of subject is altogether unacceptable, resort to emendation by reference to the LXX (so, e.g., Oort, Marti, Wolff, Mays, Rudolph, AF; see Text and Versions). The resulting sense is 'the more I called, the further they went from me' (so NEB).

[a]להם, *dativus commodi* which (GK 119s) gives 'emphasis to the significance of the occurrence in question *for* the particular subject'.

[b]For the sense of כן 'in the same measure', cf. with ibn Janāḥ, Rashi and Kimchi, Exod 1.12. Qyl compares Ps 48.6, where כן comes to have virtually the force of simultaneous reaction. On the view here taken of the nature of this part of the verse as a quotation, it is this latter meaning that is conveyed.

[c]הלכו Lit. 'they have betaken themselves', cf. 7.11; 'from them', i.e. from the Egyptians, *sc.* to the Assyrians.

[d]The imperfects are frequentative. The contrast with the preceding perfect tenses should be noted; see the commentary below.

The third person plural verbal forms are understood to be a quotation, cf. the use of the perfect, note d to 7.11, 'they called to Egypt and betook themselves to Assyria'. The quotation is incomplete since 'from them' here replaces 'to Assyria' in 7.11b, and 'to Egypt' is understood here. By alluding to the saying of 7.11b the prophet seeks to emphasise the contrast between Yahweh's gracious call to Israel his son, and Israel's craven overtures to Egypt beginning with that of *c.* 733 BC. Since 'Egypt' provides the connecting theme the prophet does not need to mention it in v. 2a. Rather, by the use of the ethic dative *l* he emphasises the nation's contemporary call to Egypt and with the words 'they have withdrawn from them' depicts an exodus which is a travesty of that instigated by Yahweh's original gracious action. These latter words may themselves constitute an allusion to the opening words of 9.6 'they have fled (*hlkw*) destruction'. There the words denote withdrawal to Egypt from the threat of disaster at the hands of the Assyrians and constitute, in turn, a meditative expression of the judgement of 8.13b 'they shall return to Egypt'. Here, by contrast, the words depict withdrawal from Egypt to which, now, 'they will not return' (11.5) but rather will have to surrender themselves to the king of Assyria (11.5). Accordingly the words of the verse constitute a modification of the earlier judgement (i.e. 9.6 and 8.13b) and may reflect the later stage of the growing ascendancy of Assyrian power during the reign of Hoshea (cf., with Rudolph, 9.3). With Wolff, the words may be dated at the beginning of the reign of Shalmaneser V (727 BC) when Israel's renewed call to Egypt prompted Assyria's retaliation (cf. 2 Kgs 17.4).

If the words reflect a revised judgement on the part of the prophet of the particular mode of Yahweh's punishment, the particular fault of the nation which prompted that judgement is consistent and consistently indicted. It is the nation's vacillating policy of turning from one power to another without regard at all for Yahweh their God. As elsewhere (cf. 8.10ff), the roots of this fundamental disloyalty are traced to the nation's persistent (note d) and self-centred addiction to idolatry, to their faithless resort to the Baals (for the plural, cf. 2.15, 19; EV 13, 17) and to the worship of graven images (here a reference to the calf-images, so Rudolph). At all events the emphasis (again, note d) seems to suggest a reference to the persistent idolatry of the Northern Kingdom from the time of Ahab (so Jerome) rather than to the paradigmatic instance of Israel's early apostasy at Baal-Peor (*contra* Wolff, cf. Mays, AF). For 'sacrifices', see on 8.13 above; for 'burning incense', on 2.15 (EV 13). The interpretation of v. 2 here offered differs from that of the majority of commentators, rabbinic and modern. For the former, the third person plural verbs are interpreted first of the prophets (see introductory note to the translation) through whom Yahweh's call to Israel was mediated and, secondly, of the nation's persistent deviation from that call. Amongst modern commentators, emendation makes the same interpretation easier. At all events the verse is seen as a retrospective look at Israel's persistent faithlessness in response to Yahweh's initial act of grace. The interpretation offered here has the merit that it accords with that of v. 5 (and of v. 11) where, again, earlier themes of the prophet are modified and that, without recourse to somewhat strained exegesis or to emendation, it is able to see in the juxtaposition of vv. 1 and 2, a telling contrast between the initial call of Yahweh and the nation's present grotesquely foolish stance.

Text and Versions

קראו LXX καθὼς μετεκάλεσα (A μετεκαλέσατο) 'as I called (them)', → כְּקָרְאִי (Oort, Marti, Wolff, Mays, Rudolph, AF, *BHS*, NEB, Borbone etc.) or קָרוֹא (Rudolph); or 'the more I called them' (Wellhausen, cf. on previous verse); Pesh. adds *'yk d*, cf. *BHS* and Gelston, p. 166; Vulg. as MT; Targ. שלחית נביי 'I sent my prophets (to teach them)'.

מפניהם LXX ἐκ προσώπου μου· αὐτοί, 'from my face. They ...' (cf. Pesh. *mn qdmy*) → מִפָּנַי and הֵם with what follows (Michaelis, Oort, Wellhausen, Marti, Wolff, Rudolph, *BHS*, NEB, Borbone; on Pesh., Gelston, p. 122); Vulg. *a facie eorum*, 'from their face', cf. MT; Targ. ואנון טעו מקביל אפיהון 'but they erred from them' (*sc*. the prophets).

The differences between LXX and MT seem to me to have arisen from the need to interpret the apparently obscure MT in the context of the preceding verse rather than from a text which differed from MT.

11.3 **It was I[a] who applied myself assiduously[b] to Ephraim, taking them[c] in my[d] arms; but they did not appreciate that I protected[e] them.**

[a]ואנכי The pronoun is emphatic and, with the conjunction, makes a contrast with the third person plural subject of the preceding verse.

[b]The word תרגלתי, *hapax legomenon*, is understood to be a verb by the majority of the versions and commentators. Kimchi records the view of his brother, Moses Kimchi (d. 1150), that the word is a noun, in form akin to תפארת. Unfortunately he gives no indication as to its meaning[1]. Ibn Janāḥ offers two explanations made on the assumption that the word is to be parsed as a *Tiphel* (cf. GK 55h) used in place of the normal *Hiphil*. First, the usage is akin to that attested for the rabbinic Hebrew adjective רגיל 'in the habit of', 'wont to', 'usual', 'common', 'habitual'. Accordingly the *Tiphel* form here means 'I accustomed myself in respect of Ephraim to take them in my arms' (Arabic *'n' 'wwdt 'prym ''ḥḏhm*). Such is the account ibn Janāḥ provides under the root רגל. In the course of his explanation of the next-but-one word קחם (under √לקח) he renders by the third theme of the same Arabic verb (*'wd*) in place of the second theme (i.e. *''wdt* for *'wwdt*). The verb in this theme means 'to apply oneself anew', 'to be zealous', 'active'[2] and hence the rendering suggested above, 'I applied myself assiduously to Ephraim ...'. Secondly, ibn Janāḥ suggests that the verb means 'I lifted their feet from the ground' (Arabic *rf't 'rǧlhm mn 'l'rḍ*). Here the *Tiphel* has almost a privative sense and is directly connected with the regular sense of the root רגל 'foot'. For this meaning ibn Janāḥ compares the Arabic phrase *trǧǧl 'lnh'r* 'the dawn advanced, rose up'. It is possible that this latter interpretation was known to Jerome, who compares Deut. 1.31 and 32.11 where Israel is 'carried' (√נשא) by Yahweh 'as a man carries his son' or else 'as an eagle ... carries (its young) upon its wings'. Accordingly for Jerome (cf. the Vulgate in Text and Versions) the verb clearly conveys parental concern and care; he renders '*ego quasi nutritius*' and he brings out the sense which he thinks is intended by paraphrasing (cf. Symmachus), '*Ego, inquit, qui pater eram, nutritius factus sum*' i.e. 'I, a father, became as it were a tutor'. Such considerations raise the question whether the verb, whatever the precise etymological explanation, denotes in a more general sense 'to bring up', 'to bring to maturity' (cf. Isa 1.2), a sense clearly attested in the Arabic cognate root *rǧl* (cf. the tenth theme and the well-known noun *rǧl* 'a man'). That, however, remains uncertain. For the rest, ibn Ezra and Kimchi suggest, by reference to the root רגל (again *Tiphel* for *Hiphil*), that תרגלתי means 'I taught to walk', i.e. to use his feet, an interpretation which is widely accepted by most subsequent authorities. Yet whether this particular meaning is correct is open to doubt[3] not least because it hardly accords with the prior image (v. 1) of Yahweh summoning his son (to walk) from Egypt (cf. AF's telling criticisms). On the other hand the interpretation, understood as one possible etymological explanation amongst many others, may point once again to the more general notion of upbringing or parental

[1] For an assessment, see Rosenmüller *ad loc.* AF, amongst moderns, regard the word as a noun for which they hazard the meaning 'guide'.

[2] Cf. Dozy and Wehr *ad locc.*

[3] Ben Yehuda *Thesaurus*, p. 7898.

education. Amongst alternative explanations of the verb offered more recently, mention may be made first of Tur-Sinai's theory that the word is to be referred to Accadian *tarcullu* 'to bind'[4]; accordingly the phrase means (in reference to Ephraim's predisposition to idolatry) that 'I bound his feet', i.e. to inhibit such activity. The theory may derive some support from the LXX (see Text and Versions) and from the reference to 'ropes', 'cords' in the following verse; yet it hardly fits the emphatic 'I' (note a) which more naturally introduces an act of grace rather than one of inhibition. Secondly, M. D. Goldman[5] proposes the meaning 'to suckle', referring to Num 11.12 (where somewhat similar but not identical actions are predicated of Moses) and by appeal to the cognate Arabic verb *rǧl*. The suggestion is questionable in respect of the Arabic evidence (the usage is rare, restricted to animals and capable of explanation by reference to well-attested meanings of the verb) and, predicated here of Yahweh, most unlikely (cf. Rudolph's criticisms).

[c]If the text is to be retained, the word קחם must be understood as an unusual form of the infinitive absolute *Qal* of לקח (cf., perhaps, Ezek 17.5) with third person plural suffix (? קָחֵם) where the suffix replaces the expected אֹתָם, cf. GK 113g; so ibn Janāḥ. For infinitives absolute expressing the particular mode of an action, cf., with Rosenmüller, Jer 7.13; 22.19. For Rashi and Kimchi the verb is a form of the perfect *Qal* with suffix, the *lamedh* being omitted (i.e. קָחָם for לְקָחָם) and the subject is Moses. The interpretation is explicitly made by reference to Num 11.12 and may be characterised as far-fetched. Modern commentators are disposed to emend the text by reference to the versions (see Text and Versions).

[d]The MT has a third person singular suffix. The reading is judged corrupt in view of the preceding and following third person plural suffixes and in the light of the evidence afforded by the four main ancient versions. Even ibn Janāḥ is moved to characterise the reading as a corruption. Accordingly זרועתי is read. The corruption is likely to have arisen as a result of (mis)understanding the verb תרגלתי as having the meaning 'to teach to walk'; in the process of that activity Yahweh is depicted as taking the child by *his* (i.e. the child's) arms since in Yahweh's arms the child could scarcely learn to walk (cf. Rudolph's comments, but from a different perspective). For לקח associated with נשא and the preposition על, cf. Deut 32.11.

[e]The verb רפא is usually rendered 'to heal'. Reference to Exod 15.26 and 2 Chr 30.20 suggests, however, that the word was capable of a prophylactic sense and then, further, of conveying more generally the

[4]פשוטו של מקרא vol. 3 2 (Jerusalem, 1967), p. 431; for a similar view, cf. Ben Yehuda, p. 7898.

[5]*Australian Biblical Review* 4 (1954/5), pp. 91f.

notion of salvation[6], cf. Jer 17.14; see further in the commentary below. G. R. Driver *JTS* 39 (1938), p. 162, comparing Arabic *rf'*, invests the word with the meaning 'I bound/harnessed them (with leading-strings)', cf. NEB and see further on the following verse. The suggestion is most improbable.

The verse presents again the motif of the two that precede it. On the one hand, Yahweh's gracious initiative marked the very beginnings of the nation. It was he ('I', note a) who had applied himself unstintingly (note b) to the care and nurture of his son. Such assiduous care is expressed in the particular metaphor which follows: Yahweh was like a father who constantly lifts his son into his arms when weariness or danger threatens in the course of a journey, cf. with Jerome, Deut 1.31; 32.11 and, with Qyl, the slightly different image of the care of the parent eagle in Exod 19.4, cf. Deut 32.11. On the other hand, Ephraim chose not to recognise that it was Yahweh who had provided such gentle protection (note e). Here the choice of the verb *rp'* clearly constitutes a word-play upon Ephraim (*'prym*), though it should be noted that in v. 3a too the nation is called Ephraim rather than Israel (as in v. 1). For Kimchi the use of the name Ephraim is significant in that it emphasizes the idolatrous record of the nation, a very sign of its base ingratitude. Certainly the words 'they did not appreciate' mirror precisely the wilful ingratitude of the nation under the figure of a faithless wife in 2.10 (EV 8). It is likely, too, that Hosea's use of the verb *rp'* recalls the usage of Exod 15.26 where Yahweh's protective care[7] assures the Israelites (if faithful) that they will not undergo the sufferings inflicted upon the Egyptians[8]. At all events the words, like those of vv. 1f, refer to Yahweh's gracious initiative in effecting the exodus and so creating his nation rather than to his care of the nation in the subsequent wilderness period[9]. It is the nation's subsequent ingratitude and faithlessness which, contrasted with Yahweh's initial gracious act, gives the longer historical

[6] Ibn Janāḥ suggests that the roots רפא and רפה are in places confounded. The question arises (but is not here answered) whether the verb here and elsewhere may be illuminated by Arabic *rfh* (second theme) 'to afford a pleasant/comfortable life', 'to act gently and courteously with some one' (so Wehr *ad loc.* and Lane 3, p. 1128, col 3).

[7] Cf. J. Hempel in *NAG*, 1958/3, p. 282. Morag lists the usage as belonging to the semantic field of deviation and correction, sickness and restoration to health. The usage here, it seems to me, is somewhat different to the other instances in Hosea's writings.

[8] So Rudolph consistently with his argument that Exod 15.26 is from the hand of the Yahwist rather than the Deuteronomist; see BZAW 68 (1938), pp. 32f.

[9] *Contra*, e.g., Mays.

perspective to the saying and gives to it its striking relevance to Hosea's times.

Text and Versions

תרגלתי LXX συνεπόδισα 'I bound their feet', see note b above; Symm. ἐπαιδαγώγουν 'I trained', 'nurtured', see note b above; Theod. κατὰ πόδας 'I was at his heals' (cf., with Field, LXX at Isa 41.2); Vulg. *quasi nutritius*, see note b above; Pesh. *dbrt* 'I led', cf. Targ. דברית.

קחם LXX ἀνέλαβον αὐτόν 'I took him up'; Vulg. *portabam eos*; Pesh. *wqblt 'nwn* 'I received them', cf. Targ. נטילתנון; on the basis of such evidence the following emendations are proposed: אֶקָּחֵם 'I was wont to take them' (e.g. Ewald, Cheyne, Oort, Wellhausen, KB[3], NEB, Marti, cf. Borbone); וָאֶקָּחֵם 'and I took them' (e.g. Wolff, cf. Gelston, p. 126); לקחתִים/ו 'I took them/him' (e.g. Halévy); קַחְתָּם (infinitive construct), 'taking them' (e.g. Grätz); Rudolph, seeking the same sense as that afforded by an infinitive absolute, reads מִקָּחָם, i.e. the noun מִקָּח with suffix construed as an accusative of manner, 'taking of them (by the arms)', cf. GK 118m.

זרועתיו LXX, Vulg. and Pesh. have a first person singular suffix; so many commentators (e.g. Wellhausen, Grätz, Marti, Wolff, KB[3], NEB, *BHS*, Borbone); Targ. has no suffix; see note d above.

רפאתים LXX ἴαμαι αὐτούς 'heal', cf. Pesh. *'syt 'nwn*; Vulg. *curarem eos* 'care for'; Targ. מן קדמי מתרחם עליהון 'from me they were loved'; see note e; Nowack → גִּדַּלְתִּים/רוממתים 'I brought them up' after Isa 1.2.

11.4 **I sought[a] to lead them forth[b] with bonds of friendship[c], with ropes of love. I was for them like[d] [e]those who lift the yoke from their jaws[e], [f]so that I may proffer them[g] their fodder[f].**

[a]The imperfect, in view of the meaning of the verb (note b), is more likely to be conative in force than frequentative; cf. König, 181 and Rudolph.

[b]The verb משך appears to have a wide range of meanings, all connected with the fundamental sense of pulling or drawing out (so ibn Janāḥ). The context, i.e. Yahweh's calling Israel from Egypt (v. 1), here under the figure of a ploughing animal (cf. 10.11), suggests that the closest parallel to the sense of the verb here is to be found in Exod 12.21, where sheep are extracted and taken (from the flock). See further note c below.

[c]בחבלי אדם Lit. 'bonds of man'. The phrase is clearly metaphorical[10] in intention and, together with the synonymous phrase which follows, conveys the sense, the bonds of close human relationship (so ibn Janāḥ; Arabic *'lṣlt w'lsb'b*). Accordingly 'friendship' is offered as a suitable rendering. In Jer 31.3 much the same sense is expressed and the verbs משך and אהב 'love' are closely connected to each other. There, apparently[11], Yahweh has drawn to Israel his kindness (חסד) and so bound his חסד to her (cf., and contrast, AF on Hos 11.4).

[d]For the construction, cf. 5.10 above. Here the construction has the force of a simile; i.e. I was to them like those good farmers who ... (cf. the Targum and Rashi).

[e—e]MT is here retained and with it the traditional and well-attested sense for עֹל, i.e. 'yoke'. For the yoke being 'upon their jaws' (על לחיהם), cf., but of a halter, Isa 30.28[12]. In so far as this is so, the reference must be strictly to that part of the equipment, designed for steering an animal, which encircles the front part of the head, see *AUS* 2, p. 100 and cf. pp. 105, 109 and illustrations 37 (of a camel) and 41. What is, as an integral part of the equipment of the yoke, 'upon the jaws' must be removed (and with it perhaps, the whole yoke), so that the animal may feed unimpeded, see note f below and *AUS* 2, pp. 99f. Amongst the rabbinic commentators, ibn Ezra, Rashi and Kimchi are agreed that the participial form מרימי denotes the lifting off, i.e. removal of, the yoke, though they differ in their interpretation of על לחיהם; for ibn Ezra the yoke is lifted time and again from the jaws; for Kimchi the yoke, lifted from the neck, is suspended beside the jaws and is thus idle and out of use. For Rashi the ploughman removes the yoke by hand (standing) 'beside the jaws', or else he lengthens the shafts of the yoke (cf. the Targum) so that (presumably, cf. Kimchi) it hangs idle beside the jaws.

For Rudolph the verb implies lifting onto rather than removal. When the animal enters the yoke, the ploughman shows his consideration by lifting the apparatus to a point close to its jaws (cf. Kimchi and Rashi's interpretation of עַל), i.e. so that his hands make friendly contact with the beast in the process. The interpretation is laboured and unconvincing. The reference to feeding and fodder which follows suggests strongly that the prior removal of the yoke is what Hosea intends, cf. note f.

[10] For the opposite view, cf. G. R. Driver *JTS* 39 (1938), pp. 161f and Hirschberg *VT* 11 (1961), p. 373. Driver gives to both אדם and אהבה the meanings 'leather', cf. NEB margin. The theory is nicely characterised by Rudolph as 'ledern'. For further criticisms, see Barr *CPOT*, p. 154.

[11] The construction is not entirely clear; for ibn Janāḥ the second person singular direct object in משכתיך is an elegant substitute for an indirect object.

[12] The argument that מרימי in the sense of 'removal' requires מעל rather than על (so, e.g., van Gelderen and Gispen, Wolff) is not convincing; the evidence of Isa 30.28 suggests that the phrase על עַל לחיהם here is almost equivalent to a short relative clause.

Difficulties in understanding the complexities of the technical language and reluctance to see a change of metaphor in v. 4 from that of v. 3 have prompted van Hoonacker to propose a radically different account of the verse, an account which has been widely adopted (e.g. Wolff, Mays, Qyl, NEB etc.). For such commentators the verse continues the image of the father's care of his child; accordingly MT's עֹל 'yoke' is a corruption of[13] an original עוּל/עֻל 'child', 'suckling' and the phrase as a whole means 'I was to them as those who lift a child to their cheek'. The suggestion is highly implausible on a number of grounds. First, the plural forms ill accord with the singular child (cf. AF) and with the image of a single father (cf. the first person forms of v. 3). The point is met by NEB (cf. *BHS*) but by resort to emendation (see Text and Versions). Secondly, the phrase 'to lift to the cheeks' is most unlikely and, indeed, prompts H. G. May *AJSL* 2 (1931/2), p. 89, to make a consequential emendation חיקם 'their lap', 'bosom'; thirdly, there is not a shred of evidence to support the theory from the ancient versions, the rabbinic commentators or any other traditional source. Wolff's (cf. NEB) attempt to make of the opening phrase a reference to the guidance of young children or even to walking harness ('leading-strings', so NEB), has been characterised by Rudolph as an untimely recollection of an outing from a kindergarten.

Even more far-fetched are the theories of J. Reider *VT* 2 (1952), p. 121 and of Procksch. The former renders 'and I was to them as foam of the sea which caresses their cheeks (and gently I shall place confidence in him)'; the latter 'I will become as former rain upon their fields'. Both involve substantial changes to the text and the resulting renderings may be said to be (respectively) ludicrous or arbitrary.

f—f The verb ואט is parsed as an apocopated form of the *Hiphil* of נטה with, apparently, the sense 'to offer', 'proffer', cf. 1 Chr 21.10[14]. Preceded by a simple *waw*, the phrase is linked to what is said about the yoke and so expresses purpose. The word אוכיל is understood to be a noun of the form אופיר, so the minor Greek versions, ibn Ezra and Kimchi; cf. Marti, Rudolph, who are tempted to read the familiar אָכל(ו) '(his) food'[15]. As an alternative, ibn Ezra suggests that ואט is an adverb (√אטט) having the sense 'gently' (so, e.g., Ewald, van Gelderen and Gispen). Accordingly אוכיל is a *Hiphil* form of אכל (for the metaplastic

13 The corruption is understood to have arisen because of the mention nearby of cords and ropes.

14 Here *Qal*; for Hosea's use of *Hiphil* forms where *Qal* forms are usual in Judaean Hebrew, cf. Morag, p. 500 n.

15 The possibility arises that אוכיל is an early translational gloss (cf. on 8.13 above) explaining the particular sense of ואט עליו: 'so that I might sustain them (*sc.* with fodder), i.e. cause them to eat'. If this is correct it must be assumed that Hosea uses the verb with a sense akin to the well-attested phrase מטה לחם 'staff of bread' normally explained as figurative for sustenance afforded by bread. It is possible that the verb נטה as it occurs in Amos 2.8 also implies 'feeding'; see Kimchi's comments *ad loc.*

אוכיל for אאכיל, GK 68i) and the sense of the phrase is of the sort 'and gently towards him I proferred food'. The construction is, as Harper observes, 'harsh beyond measure' (for further criticisms, see Marti, Wolff and Rudolph), even if לא is taken from the beginning of v. 5 (cf. the LXX in Text and Versions) and read as לו.

A different sense is given to the verb נטה especially by those who see in the verse a continuation of the image of father and son. The *Qal* וָאֵט is read and this has the sense 'to incline oneself towards', 'to stoop down to' (cf. Ps 40.2). Accordingly the phrase is characterised by asyndeton (cf. 9.9; 10.11, 13) and means 'I bent down to him to feed him' (so, e.g., Wolff, cf. NEB). The theory is already discussed and rejected by Jerome.

[g]The change to a singular (indirect) object אליו is stylistic; at this point the beast of the metaphor obtrudes; cf. GK 145m.

Hosea's second image of Yahweh's gracious election of his people is expressed not by that of father and son but by that of the good farmer (Targum and Rashi) and his beast. The image recalls that of 10.11f where the prophet similarly expresses the notion of Yahweh's purposes for his people and the vocation which results from his election of them. The change of image does not amount to grounds for suspicion and for consequent attempts to adapt the text to exclude any change of image (*contra*, e.g., Wolff, Mays, Qyl, NEB; see note e–e). It is a feature of Hosea's art to present consecutively a number of different images (cf., e.g., 9.10f, grapes, birds, end of fecundity) and, further, at times to confound them (e.g. 2.17ff, EV 15ff, renewed marriage and entry into the land). The connection with what precedes is tender care, whether that is expressed in terms of parent and child or of the good farmer with his beast. Here, then, Yahweh is depicted as leading Israel forth (note b) as a considerate farmer, from time to time, leads his beast away from the rigours of ploughing for rest and refreshment. His attitude is indeed humane and his actions are marked by the characteristics of human friendship (note c) and affection. Thus Israel was not led by the halters and ropes of coercion, associated indeed with the response of resistance and struggle. Rather, from the beginning, Yahweh acted with the gentleness and consideration which mark the way a man leads his friend (so Kimchi). Accordingly Yahweh had sought to draw his people into a relationship of friendship and familiarity (notes b and c, cf. note b on 11.3).

In the second part of the verse the image in the prophet's mind obtrudes and Yahweh is specifically compared with (note d) such considerate farmers as free their beasts from the paraphernalia of the yoke (note e–e) in order (note f–f) to facilitate their feeding. The purpose clause resumes the use of the first person singular ('I'), thereby skilfully emphasising the force and reference of the simile. It was, then, to feed his people, to sustain them that Yahweh led them forth from the servitude of Egypt. For Jerome indeed (cf. the Targum) the saying alludes to the Manna and Yahweh's providential care of his people in the wilderness (Exod 16). Accordingly the verbal form *w'ṭ* is interpreted of God's providing food from heaven (cf. the minor Greek versions and the Peshiṭta). That view seems inherently plausible and does not exclude the corollary that Yahweh's providential care of his people was extended to the cultivated land where he was the provider of the nation's corn, wine and oil (2.10, EV 8). As in the preceding verse, the prophet's words, devised to express and emphasise Yahweh's initial paradigmatic graciousness, are none the less capable of a longer perspective and thus of establishing a consistent theology.

Text and Versions

בחבלי אדם LXX ἐν διαφθορᾷ ἀνθρώπων 'in the ruin of men', rendering חֶבֶל as though it belongs to חבל II, 'act (ruinously) corruptly', cf. BDB, p. 287; cf. Mic 2.10 and the cognate noun חֲבָל, Dan 3.25; 6.24; Vulg. *in funiculis Adam*, cf. Pesh. *bḥbl' dbny 'nš'* 'with the ropes of Adam/sons of man'; Targ. במגדת בנין רחימין 'with a harness of beloved sons'; a number of emendations have been proposed: חֶסֶד (Wellhausen), אֱמֶת (Procksch), אֹדָם from a root אדד/ידד 'love' (Nyberg).

אמשכם LXX ἐξέτεινα 'I stretched them out, (i.e. in bonds of love)'; Vulg. *traham eos* 'I will draw them', cf. Pesh. *ngdt 'nwn* and Targ. נגדתינון.

אהבה LXX adds μου, → אהבתי (Borbone).

כמרימי LXX ὡς ῥαπίζων ἄνθρωπος 'like a man striking (upon the jaws)', apparently, as in Isa 50.6, a reference to plucking the hair of the beard, cf. Rudolph; → כְּמֹרֵט (Houtsma), כְּמַכֵּה אָדָם (Vollers, Marti); LXX appears to have interpreted the verse of divine correction; Aq. ὡς αἴρων 'like one taking off'; Symm. ὡς ὁ ἐπιθείς 'like one who imposes'; Vulg. *quasi exaltans*, cf. Pesh. *'yk hw dmrym* 'like one who lifts' (singular); Targ. כאיכרא טבא דמקיל 'like a good farmer who makes light'; → מרים (NEB, cf. *BHS*).

על LXX appears to omit; Vulg. *iugum* 'yoke', cf. Pesh. *nyr'*; Targ. בכתף תוריא 'upon the shoulder of the oxen'; → עול (*BHS*, Borbone; see note e).

על לחיהם LXX ἐπὶ τας σιαγόνας αὐτοῦ 'upon his jaws', cf. Vulg. *super maxillas eorum*; Pesh. *mn qdlhwn* 'from their neck'; Targ. ומוריך

בלחותא 'and who lengthens (or 'loosens', Jastrow, p. 702) on the cheeks (? the shaft of the yoke, cf. Rashi and note e–e); → על לחיו (Borbone); → לְחָיָיו (*BHS*, cf. LXX); → לְחָיֵי (so, apparently, NEB).

ואט אליו אוכיל LXX καὶ ἐπιβλέψομαι πρὸς αὐτόν, δυνήσομαι αὐτῷ 'and I will look upon him (*sc.* hostile sense), I will prevail over him'; ואט → וְאֵבֵט (Houtsma, Oort); Aq. καὶ ἔκλινα πρὸς αὐτὸν βρώματα, cf. Symm. ἐξέκλινα ... τροφήν and Theod. ... βρῶσιν 'I extended to him food'; Vulg. *et declinavi ad eum ut vesceretur* 'I extended to him (food, cf. Jerome) that he might feed'; cf. Pesh. *w'rknt lhwn w'klw* '... to them, and they ate'; Targ. אסגיתי להון טובא למיכל '(when they were in the desert) I increased goods for them to eat'; ואט → וְאֵט 'and I bent down' (Oettli, Marti, Rudolph, cf. NEB), see note f–f; many scholars conclude that the LXX reads לו with this verse, against MT's לא at the beginning of the next (e.g. Houtsma, Wellhausen, Oettli, Harper, Wolff, Rudolph, Mays, *BHS*, Borbone, cf. NEB); see note f–f above.

11.5 **He will not return to the land of Egypt, [a]rather it is Assyria who is his king[a]: because they refused to repent.**

[a—a]The phrase is emphatic and הוא expresses a contrast with what immediately precedes. Many modern scholars argue that the negative has no place at the beginning of this verse since, if it is retained, the sentiments of the verse contradict not only verse 11 but also 8.13 and 9.3 where it is said or implied that, as a punishment, Israel will return to Egypt. In support of this contention, appeal is made to the evidence of the LXX (see on v. 4 above). Alternatively, the phrase is taken as a question and ו is translated 'and/or', e.g., 'Shall he not return to Egypt, and/or will not Assyria become his king?' (cf. NEB, see further below). The difficulty immediately arises that no account is given of the pronoun הוא and consequently on grammatical grounds the proposal is rejected. See further in the commentary below.

In v. 2 Hosea makes use of phrases from previous prophecies in order to depict a contrast between Yahweh's gracious call to Israel, his son, and the nation's craven overtures to Egypt during the reign of Hoshea. It was there argued that v. 2 represents a modification of an earlier judgement (8.13b and 9.6). Here, then, the words 'He will not return to Egypt, rather it is Assyria who is his king' are likely to reflect the situation following Hoshea's abortive attempt to revolt from Assyria by turning to Egypt for help (2 Kgs 17.4). The verse records the final prevalence of Assyria and its indisputable supremacy in the period following Hoshea's revolt. As far as Ephraim is concerned, the situation has resolved itself: Assyria has become the sole dominating power. It is possible that the turn of phrase constitutes an allusion to the nation's loss of its own king Hoshea, arrested and imprisoned by the Assyrians[16].

At all events 'return' to Egypt is now finally precluded. Egypt is no longer an option for the Ephraimites (so Jerome, cf., but somewhat differently, Kimchi). The words 'he will not return to Egypt' clearly echo the judgmental sayings of 8.13 and 9.3, 6 where Ephraim's overtures to Egypt are deemed punishable by exile in that land. Here, however, Hosea, *more prophetarum*, seeks to modify earlier prophecies in the light of the actual development of events (cf. Jer 1.13ff) and the final supremacy of Assyria (cf. Mays). Accordingly the return to Egypt, interpreted now of the nation's recent reversion to a pro-Egyptian policy, is precluded and Assyria has become the sole agent of the nation's punishment. With such an account of these words the play upon the verb *šwb*[17], apparent in the last phrase of the verse, is consistent. The nation's inevitable surrender to the power of Assyria is the result of her wilful refusal to turn in repentance (*sc.* to Yahweh; cf. Jer 3.12, 22; 4.1; 8.4f).

It is possible that yet another of the prophet's thoughts is detectable in his skilful use of these words. For ibn Ezra 'return to Egypt' constitutes, in the mind of those who wish to do so, a prelude to return to Yahweh's land. This view fits the context of the previous verses, where Israel's very existence is shown to be dependent upon Yahweh's action in bringing his people from Egypt and where the nation, by its perverse appeal to Egypt, had made a travesty of that initial and decisive action. Accordingly 'he will not return to Egypt' may convey the further sense that, by refusing to return to Yahweh, the nation will not return to the place and possibility of renewed exodus and redemption. This account of the verse may be said to provide a coherent and satisfactory explanation of Hosea's earlier pronouncement 'they shall return to Egypt' (8.13; 9.3, 6). To a large number of modern scholars, however, it is inconceivable that the verse should contradict this earlier pronouncement. Accordingly (see note a–a) either they emend the text so as to remove the negative (e.g. Wellhausen, Harper, Mays, Rudolph) or else they interpret it as expressing a question expecting the answer 'yes', i.e. 'shall he not return to Egypt?' (so already Lackemacher, see Rosenmüller

16 Or else (so Rudolph) the nation's involuntary subservience to Assyria as king is contrasted to the kingship of Yahweh which they had forfeited.

17 For similar use of the cognate noun *mšwbh* in different senses, cf. Morag's treatment (pp. 506f) of Hosea's usage.

and, more recently, Gordis *VT* 5 (1955), p. 89; cf. Wolff, AF)[18]. Apart from the grammatical consideration offered above (note a–a), it seems to me inherently more likely that the prophet's argument (word-play included) is of the form 'because they have refused to return (i.e. repent) he/they will not return' than that it is of the form 'because they have refused to return (repent) he/they shall certainly return'.

Text and Versions

לא See on the preceding verse and commentary above; Vulg., Pesh. and Targ. reproduce the negative.

ישוב LXX κατῴκησεν 'lived' (? = יֵשֵׁב, cf. 9.3); Vulg. *revertetur*, cf. Pesh. *nhpkwn* and Targ. יתובון (both plural).

אל ארץ LXX Ἐφράιμ ἐν (? = אפרים ב).

הוא Nowack thinks the word is a survival of a verbal form of which מלכו was the object; → יהיה (Grätz).

מלכו Pesh. *-hwn* 'their', cf. Targ.

מאנו LXX οὐκ ἠθέλησεν 'he was unwilling', cf. Vulg. *noluerunt* and Pesh. *l' ṣbw* (Gelston, pp. 167f).

לשוב LXX ἐπιστρέψαι, cf. Vulg. *converti*, Pesh. *lmhpk*, Targ. למתב 'turn'; Symm. μετανοῆσαι 'repent'.

11.6 The sword will fall upon[a] his cities[b], it will destroy and consume[c] his villages[d], [e]the very result of their policies[e].

[a]The verb חול, usually to 'whirl', 'twist', 'writhe', 'dance', construed with על or ב following, appears to have the sense 'to leap upon' and 'to pounce upon', 'attack' (Arabic *wṯb* – so ibn Janāḥ, comparing Jer 23.19 and Lam 4.6). The meaning is, he argues, similar to that attested for the Arabic cognate *ḥwl* 'to leap on to the back of a horse' (cf. Lane 2 p. 673, cols 2 and 3). For ibn Ezra and Kimchi 2 Sam 3.29 is compared, where the blood of Abner will alight upon Joab's head. For the differing interpretations of the versions, see below.

[b]The familiar and traditional interpretation of the word עיר 'city' is here retained. NEB's 'blood-spattered altars' derives from suggestions of T. H. Gaster and G. R. Driver, who compare the word עיר as it occurs here (and in certain other places) with Arabic and Ugaritic *ġr* 'blood-daubed stone'. The suggestion hardly fits the context and has won little

[18] Somewhat similarly J. A. Soggin *BO* 9 (1967), p. 42, and Kuhnigk detect in *l'* an instance of emphatic *lamedh* with the sense 'Surely they will return ...'.

acceptance. For references and a full (and critical) treatment, see E. W. Nicholson *VT* 27 (1977), pp. 113ff.

[c]Lit. 'it will destroy (וכלתה) his villages and consume' (ואכלה). The verbs כלה (*Piel*) and אכל are found in parallelism in Jer 10.25. The evidence of this latter verse, with its multiplicity of verbal forms, suggests that the verb אכלה, here standing alone and following כלתה with an object, has simply an emphatic force and is characterised by hendiadys (cf., e.g., 12.5). See further note e–e below.

[d]The word בדיו has been interpreted in a wide variety of ways. First, it is understood to denote 'warriors' (Targum; cf. the Vulgate and Rashi, גבורים), for which Jer 50.36, where בדים and גבורים are closely associated, is compared. This meaning has been understood as a figurative use of a literal meaning 'bars', 'bolts' (cf. Rosenmüller). The theory is marked by a number of uncertainties and is here discounted. Secondly, M. J. Elhorst[19], G. R. Driver[20] and Nyberg (cf. KB^3) have suggested the meaning 'oracle-priests' (NEB, 'prattling priests'). Already ibn Janāḥ had detected such a meaning for the word in Jer 50.36 and in Isa 44.25. Yet it is difficult to perceive why such officials should be mentioned in the present context (cf. Rudolph). Thirdly, Wolff renders 'braggarts', referring to בדד II (BDB p. 95, col 1) and the expression 'idle talk' in Job 11.3. Again the theory seems implausible in the context.

For ibn Ezra and Kimchi the word denotes properly 'branches' (so, clearly, Ezek 17.6). Ibn Ezra makes no further comment but Kimchi goes on to explain that the usage is here figurative and denotes 'villages' since 'villages are to cities what branches are to trees'. That such a figurative use is possible seems clear also from ibn Janāḥ's account of the meaning בד, 'branch'. Thus, the nerves and sinews of the body are termed בדים since they spread out from the brain, like branches from a tree. In Job 18.13 there is an instance where בדים has this particular meaning and in Job 41.4 (referring to Leviathan or the crocodile) the same meaning conveys the strong constitution of its body. Unfortunately ibn Janāḥ makes no reference to Hos 11.6. However, the context, with its reference to cities, suggests that Kimchi's view, as further illuminated by that of ibn Janāḥ, provides the best solution to the problem (cf. Symmachus in Text and Versions). Thus, the main areas of habitation, the cities, will fall to the sword; and at the same time the smaller dependent communities, the villages and outlying suburbs, will be totally consumed (note c) in the course of such wholesale attacks. For other suggestions, involving emendation, see Text and Versions.

[e—e]Rashi notes that the word ממעצותיהם is marked by both *sillûq* and *ṭiphḥā*, indicating that its sense is absolute (i.e. restricted to itself) and is not directly related in construction to what precedes it; for parallels, cf. Exod 30.31 and Lev 21.4. Accordingly the words represent a terse

[19] *ZAW* 30 (1910), pp. 266f.; he does not mention Hos 11.6.
[20] *WO* 2 (1954–59), pp. 19f, cf. *Nötscher Festschrift*, p. 54.

explanation of the cause of the impending havoc to be wrought by the sword[21]. This view of the matter runs contrary to that of a number of modern commentators who suppose that, because the preceding two verbs have objects, the same must be true of ואכלה and that, consequently, the word ממעצותיהם represents a corruption of an original noun in the accusative (so, e.g., Oort, Valeton, Wellhausen, Marti, Rudolph; for details, see Text and Versions below). See also note c above.

The emerging ascendancy of Assyria and its unhindered domination of Ephraim will inevitably bring the horrors of war to the cities and dependent hamlets (note d) of the country. Such a blood bath will be the direct consequence of the nation's foolish and immoral policies and in particular of Hoshea's fatal turn to Egypt (cf. on v. 2 above). Indeed, such policies, traced to the nation's persistent addiction to idolatry, bring upon them the reward that is their due. The thought is expressed elsewhere with proverbial force: sowing the wind inevitably entails reaping the whirlwind (8.7). The nation's refusal to turn in repentance to Yahweh is decisive and his patience is at an end. 2 Kings 17.4f (cf. Noth *History*, pp. 261f, *GI*, pp. 237f) indicates that Shalmaneser V occupied the majority of the remaining territory of Ephraim, capturing Hoshea but leaving unconquered for the moment the capital Samaria. These observations accord well with the text of this verse and suggest that Hosea is speaking of the beginnings (at least) of the terrible process. The verse may reflect a date *c.* 724 BC.

Text and Versions

וחלה LXX καὶ ἠσθένησεν, cf. Pesh. *ntkrh* 'became weak' (Gelston, p. 143) appears to derive the word from √חלה I (BDB, p. 317); Symm. καὶ τραυματίσει 'will wound', apparently from חלל I (BDB, p. 319); Vulg. *coepit* 'began' apparently from חלל III (BDB, p. 320) – if his etymology is strictly wrong, Jerome (commentary) records *irruet* 'attacks', 'rushes upon' (Aq.) as an alternative translation (perhaps √חול, cf. Gelston); Targ. ותחול 'whirls', 'is impending'.

בעריו all versions 'cities' etc.

בדיו LXX ἐν ταῖς χερσὶν αὐτοῦ, '(the sword came to an end) in his hands', cf. Pesh. *mn 'ydyhwn* 'from their hands' (cf. Gelston, pp. 167f);

[21] G. R. Driver *Nötscher Festschrift*, p. 54, proposes a new word מעצה 'disobedience' and thus here 'disobedient deeds'. The theory is questionable and unnecessary (cf. Rudolph).

Symm. τοὺς βραχίονας αὐτοῦ '(it will bring to an end) his arms'; whether such readings presuppose a form of יד seems to me to be doubtful; it is more likely that the renderings represent a (mis)understanding of the tradition that בדים meant extremities/limbs of the body (cf. ibn Janāḥ's views as explained above); Vulg. *electos eius* 'his choice men', cf. Targ. גיברוהי 'his warriors'; Jerome (Commentary) supposes that such a meaning is akin to Symm.'s 'arms' and is thus a metaphorical use (cf. Latin *caput/capita*). Emendations: עוֹרוֹ 'his skin' (Duhm); בריחיו 'his bars' or בַּחֻרָיו 'his choice men' (Grätz and Oettli); בניו 'his sons' (Gardner, cf. *BHS*); בריו 'his forts' (Behler *Angelicum* 20, 1943, p. 108); בְּדָיוֹ 'sufficiently' (Rudolph); בדיו is omitted by Wellhausen, Marti and Harper as a corrupt expansion of the text, and Wellhausen and Harper also omit וכלתה for the same reason, while Marti retains וכלתה and omits וחלה.

ואכלה LXX καὶ φάγονται, cf. Pesh. *wn'klwn* 'and they (plural) will eat'; → ואכלו (Borbone); LXX, Pesh. and Vulg. construe with what follows; → וַאֲכָלָתַם 'and will consume them' (cf. *BHS*).

ממעצותיהם LXX ἐκ τῶν διαβουλίων αὐτῶν, cf. Symm. διὰ τὰς διαβουλίας αὐτῶν, Pesh. *mn tr'ythwn*, all 'counsels'; cf. also Targ. ממלכי עצתהון 'because of the counsels of their advisers'; Vulg. *capita eorum*, '(it will consume) their chief points'; cf. Jerome *vel capita vel consilia eorum*. Emendations: בעצמותיהם 'their bones' (Ruben, Sellin); מצדותיהם (Oort, Valeton, cf. *BHS*) or במבצריהם 'their fortresses' (Wellhausen, Harper, cf. Marti); מַעֲשֹׂתֵיהֶם 'their preparations' (Rudolph); *BHS* raises the possibility that the last two words of the verse constitute a variant reading.

11.7 **My people dither[a] in respect of returning[b] to me[c]. Summoned[d] to higher things[e], [f]he will not raise himself[f].**

[a]תלואים Lit. 'are hung', from the root תלא, a variant form of תלה, GK 75rr. Morag (p. 507) suggests that a metaphorical sense attaches to the meaning 'hang' or 'swing to and fro' and that it belongs to the semantic field expressing lack of confidence or stability. For a comparable usage he compares Deut 28.66, 'your life shall be quite uncertain (lit. 'hang') before you ... and you will have no confidence in your life' (my translation). This sense seems to have been detected by the Targum (see Text and Versions) as well as by Rashi and Kimchi and it is clearly attested in talmudic Hebrew (Jastrow p. 1671, col 1 2). For Jerome the phrase implies that the wretched people 'know not what to do and are ignorant of which way to turn'. The explanation is preferable to others which suppose, for example, that the verb can mean 'to be bent on' (i.e. rebellion from me, see note b) for which there is no clear evidence (*contra* Ewald, Wolff, AF, Davies, AV, RV, NEB) or that the meaning

is literal and denotes atrocities committed by the Assyrians (*contra* Oort, van Hoonacker). For emendations, see Text and Versions.

[b]Despite ibn Ezra's assertion that משובה always has a pejorative sense, (i.e. 'apostasy', so BDB p. 1000, col 1) and the evidence of 14.5, where the word clearly has this sense, Morag's contention that here Hosea uses משובה to denote 'repentance' is accepted. The sense is, as Morag acknowledges, unique in the bible and indicates the dialectal or special character of Hosea's Hebrew. Rudolph takes a similar view of the matter, supposing that, because the cognate verb שוב is capable of the opposite meanings 'return/repent' and 'return/apostatise', such meanings cannot be excluded for the noun. The interpretation is supported by the Peshiṭta, Targum and by Rashi. The contrary views of ibn Ezra and Kimchi are contrived and thus less satisfactory. For the former, the nation engages in apostasy from Yahweh ('me') 'like a man suspended in the air who can go neither up nor down'; for the latter, the nation is suspended between distress and respite by reason of its apostasy from Yahweh ('me').

[c]The suffix has a dative sense, cf., with ibn Ezra, Ps 5.8; Isa 56.7.

[d]יקראהו Lit. 'they summon him', i.e. an impersonal third person plural active verb. For Rashi, ibn Ezra and Kimchi the prophets are the unnamed subject of the verb. For the direct object following קרא, see BDB p. 895, col 2, 5 c.

[e]See on 7.16 above. For ibn Janāḥ אל על denotes 'the highest level', i.e. 'true piety' (cf. Morag).

[f—f]The verb ירומם is derived from the root רמם (cf. BDB p. 942, col 1) by ibn Janāḥ who sees other occurrences in Job 17.4 and Ps 66.17. It has here an intransitive sense; so ibn Janāḥ, cf. Morag. For the latter, the expression 'raising himself' suggests in the context resolute striving (for the things that are above, cf. Kimchi's father). The same understanding may well lie behind the rendering of the Targum 'they have not walked erect' (i.e. in integrity) and ibn Ezra's paraphrase 'they do not lift their heads'. Nor is it far removed from Rashi's 'the people do not exalt (i.e. take seriously) the message of the prophets'. Kimchi alone speaks of the exaltation of God. The idea has recently been revived by, e.g., AF who render 'he (*sc.* the people) did not exalt the Only One', whereby יחד is interpreted as a name of God. The latter suggestion is fanciful, unparalleled and without support in tradition.

The adverb יחד, lit. 'in union', 'together', suggests 'all as one man' (Kimchi), 'with one accord' (ibn Ezra), cf. BDB p. 403, col 1 b; the people in its entirety will not raise itself to higher things; cf. with Rosenmüller, Isa 22.3 and Ps 14.3. The emphatic sense is difficult to render satisfactorily in English.

The verse constitutes the all-important transition between what precedes it (the inevitability of Yahweh's punishment following the nation's wilful refusal to repent) and what follows (his magnanimous and gracious change of heart). Here indeed Hosea, like St Paul after him, delves deeper into the nature of human sinfulness and rebellion against God. Yahweh's people ('my' people) have betrayed themselves by their own stupidity (v. 6) into a position where their stability and self-confidence have been completely eroded. Thus, even when faced with the privations and horrors of the Assyrian invasion, they are unable to bring themselves to do the one thing which they were urged to do (note d) and which would redeem the situation, *viz.* to turn in repentance (note b) to their God. Indeed the good which they would (here, to which they were summoned), they do not (cf. Rom 7.18ff). They are wretched, pitiable just because their sinfulness has led them to a position in which they dither, wracked by indecision (note a), incapable of extricating themselves from the morass and raising themselves to seeking (note f–f) the higher realms of true piety (note e). The verse displays a remarkable unity of thought with the parable or *māshāl* which, in chapter 3, Hosea recorded from the experience of his personal life. His wife had, by thoughtless behaviour and despite his warnings, betrayed herself into the trap of an adulterous relationship from which she could not readily escape (see on 3.1 and especially 3.2 above). At this point Hosea felt impelled to take steps to rescue her. He did so, on his own explicit testimony, at the prompting of Yahweh. Indeed he understood that his personal situation reflected accurately that experienced by Yahweh in respect of his people. To this proposition the words of the present verse provide eloquent testimony. In the end it is pity and love which moves Yahweh to take the initiative (see the verses which follow); he desires to rescue his people from the ills they had so richly deserved, just as pity and love prompted Hosea to rescue his wife, unworthy of it though she was. Again, the truth, *mutatis mutandis*, is that expressed by St Paul: it is precisely when he is at his most wretched and undeserving that God in Christ takes the initiative (Rom 7.24ff; 5.8).

Text and Versions

ועמי LXX third person singular suffix.

תלואים LXX (so Symm.) ἐπικρεμάμενος (Aq. -οι) 'hang over', cf. Vulg. *pendebit*; Pesh. *tlyn* 'hang' (plural), Targ. פליגין (plural) 'are divided', 'undecided'. Emendations include: נלאה 'are wearied' or הלאני 'have wearied me' (Oettli, cf. Harper); נלוים 'are joined' *sc.* to idols (Marti); מתלאים from √לאה, cf. and contrast Nyberg, 'take pains' (Rudolph); חוֹלְאִים למשובתָם 'are sick in respect of their rebellion' (cf. *BHS*).

למשובתי LXX ἐκ τῆς κατοικίας αὐτοῦ (*v.l.* παροικίας) 'from their dwelling-place'; → למושבו √ישב (Vollers); Aq., Theod., Symm. τῇ ἐπιστροφῇ μου/ἐπιστροφὴν αὐτοῦ/ εἰς τὸ ἐπιστρέφειν πρὸς με 'to, towards my (his) turning/turning towards me'; Vulg. *ad reditum meum* 'to my returning'; Pesh. *lmtb lwty*, 'to return to me'; Targ. למתב לאוריתי 'to return to my law'. Emendations include: ממשובתיו/במשובתיו 'because of/with his rebellions' (Oettli, Harper, *BHS*); אל־עצבים 'to idols' (Marti).

ואל על LXX καὶ ὁ θεὸς ἐπί 'and God as regards (his honoured things will be wrath)'; Aq. καὶ πρὸς ζυγόν 'and to the yoke (he will call him)', cf. Theod. καὶ εἰς ζυγόν; Symm. ζυγὸς δέ 'but the yoke (will happen to him)'; Vulg. *iugum autem*; → עֹל (e.g. Oort, Oettli, Harper, Rudolph); Pesh. *wl'lh'* 'to God (they will call)'; Targ. במרועא קשיא 'with heavy affliction (are met)'. Emendations include: אל בעל 'to Baal' (Ruben, Marti, Wolff, Mays, *BHS*). For Kimchi's view (cf. more recent statements by Nyberg, AF) that על = עליון 'the Most High' and for comments, see on 7.16 above.

יקראהו LXX τὰ τίμια αὐτοῦ (= יְקָרָיו Harper); Aq., Theod. καλέσει αὐτόν 'he (singular) will call him'; Symm. συναντήσει αὐτῷ); Vulg. *inponetur ei, v.l. eis*; Pesh. *nqrwn* (plural), see above; Targ. יתערעון 'are met (with)'. Emendations include: יקרא/ו (Grätz, cf. Wolff, *BHS*); יַקְרְאֵהוּ 'he will appoint him (to the yoke') (Harper); ואלי עַל על יקראו 'they call to me concerning the yoke' (Rudolph).

יחד לא ירומם LXX θυμωθήσεται, καὶ οὐ μὴ ὑψώσῃ αὐτόν 'he will be wrath, and in no wise will exalt him' = יחרה ולא ירוממהו (Vollers); Aq. and Theod. ἅμα, οὐχ ὑψώσει αὐτούς 'all at once, he will not exalt them'; Symm. ὁμοῦ, ὃς οὐκ ἀρθήσεται 'all at once, which will not be removed', cf. Vulg. *simul quod non auferetur*, → יְרוּמָם (Oort, Rudolph); Pesh. *wnrn' 'yk ḥd' wl' nttrym* 'and he pays attention likewise yet does not raise himself'; Targ. כחדא לא יהכון בקומא זקופא 'altogether they do not go in an erect stature'. Emendations include הוא חדל לרחמו 'since he ceased to love them' (Harper, cf. *BHS*); יחד לא יְרִמֻּהוּ 'which (i.e. the yoke) together they cannot remove' (again, Rudolph).

11.8 **How[a] can I hand you over, Ephraim? How[a] can I deliver you up[b], O Israel? How[a] can I make you[c] like Admah or surrender you[d] to the fate of Zeboim? My own heart recoils[e]; at once[f] my compassion is aroused[g].**

[a]איך An expression of bewilderment as well as of grief, cf., with Qyl, Gen 44.34; with Rudolph, Gen 39.9; Ps 137.4.

[b]The meaning of the word אמגנך is tolerably clear, since it is fixed by the parallelism of the preceding phrase (cf. ibn Janāḥ). A similar usage is found in Gen 14.20 '(God) has delivered (מִגֵּן) your enemies into your hand' (Rashi, ibn Ezra and Kimchi). Theories concerning the etymology of the word are less certain. Some authorities associate the verb with the root גנן, understand it as a denominative from מגן 'shield', 'protection', and think the *Piel* has a privative force, hence 'to deprive of protection' and thus 'to deliver up' (so Jerome, commenting on Theodotion). BDB p. 689, col 1, compares the similar usage of the *Piel* of סגר 'to shut', having the particular meaning 'to shut off all escapes' and hence 'to deliver up'. On this view מגן similarly denotes 'covering' (*sc*. all escape routes) and hence 'to deliver up'. More likely is the view of KB[3]: a separate root מגן (i.e. not derived from גנן) is to be distinguished, akin to the Ugaritic root *mgn*[22] 'to present (gifts)', 'to seek' (*sc*. by the handing over of gifts). Ibn Janāḥ similarly lists the word under the root מגן.

[c]The verb אתנך, from נתן, is the same as that rendered 'hand you over' in the first line. Here, however, it is paralleled by the verb שׂים lit. 'to place', 'set' (note d) and consequently the well-attested sense 'make (you)' is adopted. The two uses to which the verb is put are artistic.

[d]אשׂימך Lit. 'make you like'; cf. 2.5 (EV 3); Jer 6.8; Ezek 21.32. 'Surrender you to the fate of' is offered as an English variant in this context.

[e]Cf. Lam 1.20 and Exod 14.5. The verb נהפך here denotes remorse, realisation that the preceding thoughts are intolerable. The preposition על emphasises the personal subject of the emotion upon whom, as it were, that emotion acts (so BDB p. 753, col 2 d). The translation 'within me' (AV, NEB) is, as BDB observes, strictly incorrect. Wolff's supposition that על has a hostile sense ('my heart turns against me') is also highly questionable (cf. Rudolph).

[f]יחד Cf. v. 7, note f. The sense 'all at once' is easier to appreciate in the Hebrew, since 'compassion' is plural. S. Talmon's theory, *VT* 3 (1953), p. 139, that יחד here denotes 'covenant' (> 'my heart is turned in favour of covenant') requires emendation (the addition of ל before יחד) and is, in any case, most unlikely; cf. the criticisms of J. C. de Moor *VT* 7 (1957), p. 352 and of J. Maier *ZAW* 72 (1960), p. 14 n.

[g]נכמרו נחומי Ibn Ezra and Kimchi compare the familiar phrase of Exod 32.14: 'Yahweh relented (וינחם) and spared his people the evil with which he had threatened them' (NEB). The cognate noun נחום accordingly means here 'compassion and remorse', cf., with Rudolph, Ps 90.13; Judg 21.6, 15. It is unnecessary to emend the text; see Text and

22 Cf. Aistleitner, pp. 178f and Gibson, p. 150.

Versions for a suggested emendation. According to ibn Janāḥ the verb כמר is capable of two quite distinct meanings: (1) 'to be excited', 'aroused' (as here) and (2) 'to become dried out' (as in Lam 5.10). The semantic range, he notes, is exactly paralleled by the Arabic verb *hyǧ*. He is insistent that the context must determine which meaning is required and his opinion thus differs from that of Rashi, ibn Ezra and Kimchi, who specifically compare Lam 5.10 with this verse and suppose (Rashi and Kimchi) that כמר is an Aramaism with the meaning 'to become hot'. Ibn Janāḥ's view is preferable since the Aramaic verb כמר is clearly attested with the sense 'to dry out', 'to shrink' (i.e. meat in the heat of the sun; cf. Jastrow *ad loc.*).

The central importance of the words of this verse has long been recognised. Thus, George Adam Smith (p. 297) describes the passage as the 'greatest in Hosea – deepest if not highest of his book – the breaking forth of that inexhaustible mercy of the Most High'. Indeed from the form-critical point of view, the sudden appearance of direct speech seems to emphasise the importance of these words to Hosea himself (cf. Rudolph).

It has been argued that the exclamation 'How can I ...' should be understood in a minatory way, and that the negative particle in v. 9 (*l'*) denotes a question expecting an affirmative answer. Thus, 'despite my instinctive reluctance to destroy you (i.e. How can I ...), shall I not execute my fierce anger?' (v. 9). The suggestion – e.g. Marti, Nyberg and G. S. Glanzman *CBQ* 23 (1961), pp. 227ff – hardly commends itself since it does not accord with v. 8b ('my heart recoils, at once my compassion is aroused'). That there is a menacing tone in the exclamation ('How can I ...') should not be denied; indeed the horror of what is actually contemplated in Yahweh's mind triggers the reaction of compassion and pity. Jerome is right to dwell upon the natural (parental) dilemma in which harsh punishments must be set against feelings of compassion and sympathy. His conclusion that the dilemma is resolved in favour of punishment[23] may be influenced by his knowledge that Ephraim was in fact destroyed in 722/1 BC and by the longer perspective of the divine purpose which arose from his Christian belief. Certainly he is aware of contemporary Jewish views that the punishment of Ephraim did not constitute the end of the promise to Israel and with this

[23] His view depends also on his prior judgement that the second question of the verse means 'How can I (possibly) protect you, Israel?' (cf. the LXX). That rendering is more likely to reflect later interpretation made *ex eventu* than the intention of Hosea's words. On the Targum, see below. Jerome's argument recalls the legendary statement of the schoolmaster about to inflict corporal punishment, 'this is going to hurt me more than it hurts you'.

should be compared the view of the Targum with v. 9 and rabbinic commentators (Saadya, Rashi, Kimchi on v. 9), that Jerusalem was to become the recipient of that promise.

Such views, then, are likely to provide clues to the interpretation of Hosea's oracles after the collapse of Samaria and Ephraim. Yet the plain sense of the verse as Hosea intended it (cf. note a) presents the agonising dilemma with which Yahweh is confronted and it is expressed, as ibn Ezra rightly observes, in highly anthropomorphic terms. Justice dictates that Ephraim's persistent wickedness should lead to its total destruction (cf. v. 6b). Indeed, the inexorable process is imminent and the Assyrian sword is about to descend upon the nation's cities and settlements (6a). That process cannot but lead to the annihilation of Ephraim, to its sharing the legendary fate of Admah and Zeboim (on which see below). If Ephraim has brought such a fate upon itself, that is clearly consistent with the will of its creator. Yet, as he contemplates the terrible consequences of what he has willed, his own heart recoils in horror and his compassion is aroused. He cannot bring himself to do what he contemplated (cf. v. 9).

That Hosea's words reflect an answer to a challenge posed by his hearers to the effect that radical inconsistency characterises a message which speaks of inexorable judgement but also of hope (so Rudolph) seems to me to be less plausible than another, older supposition. As has been suggested above, v. 7 presents a striking parallel with Gomer's situation during the dark days indicated by chapter 3. There Hosea represents himself as impelled by Yahweh's command to take a new initiative of love and compassion in the face of the miserable state to which Gomer had sunk. Further, in chapter 2, the father of the parable is represented as reviewing his reactions to his unfaithful wife and concluding finally that the repair of his marriage is the only option ultimately open to him[24]. Accordingly the present verse reflects very precisely Hosea's own experience[25] and the dilemma facing him in his personal life. It is here that the conflict between justifiable feelings of hurt and anger and radical compassion is at its most acute. It seems clear that knowledge of his God (cf. Rudolph) prompted Hosea to dare to suppose that his own experience was analogous to or, more precisely, that it

24 Cf. Clines' study of the structure of Hosea 2.
25 Cf. Rowley *MG*, pp. 94f.

partook of the very essence of Yahweh's experience[26]; it was, so to speak, a 'sacrament' of that divine experience. For another such 'sacrament' involving a prophet's wife, cf. Ezek 24.15ff. That such an account of the verse conflicts (cf., e.g., Marti) with the historically later oracles of the final destruction of Samaria (13.12ff) cannot be denied. In this respect the matter raises wider and fundamental problems; thus it must be said frankly that Hosea's estimate of Yahweh's graceful intervention was misplaced; for Samaria fell and Ephraim, as a matter of fact, became as Admah and Zeboim. The final outcome was tragedy. Whether that, too, was mirrored in Hosea's personal life we cannot know; for we are not told. Such considerations have led some commentators (see especially Jerome's classical statement) to conclude that the words of the verse must reflect Yahweh's decision in favour of punishment; accordingly not a little ingenuity is deployed to interpret the text in this way. On the other hand, the whole text of Hosea's prophecies reveals that at a very much earlier stage his message was deemed relevant to the Southern Kingdom of Judaea and that, accordingly, on a longer perspective of history, Yahweh's gracious compassion, so definitively expressed in this verse, might yet prevail[27]. For the rest, following the fall of the Southern Kingdom, Hosea's words must increasingly have taken on the nature of canonical scripture and those who received them did so (and do so), in some sense at least, as those who are privileged, by God's providence, to join their faithful predecessors (Heb 11.39f). Amongst the latter were, of course, the prophets (Heb 11.32) and Hosea, one of them, was nothing if not a man of faith.

Admah and Zeboim were apparently cities near the Dead Sea not far from the more notorious Sodom and Gomorrah. They are referred to in Gen 10.19; 14.2, 8 and in Deut 29.22f. Genesis 18f do not record their destruction through Yahweh's fury as does Deut 29.22f. The question why Hosea mentions Admah and Zeboim rather than the apparently better known Sodom and Gomorrah cannot be answered. The question is addressed by Jerome who ingeniously supposes that they are mentioned because their guilt was less and thus the judgement upon them

26 *Contra* Clements *PT*, pp. 29f; Clements' statement that prophetic signs are 'a way of giving giving dramatic and visible expression to their message' seems to me to do less than justice to the nature of such 'signs'. It is to the essential unity between signs and what such signs signify that the prophetic tradition points. For Yahwism the will of God is, of course, prior; the signs coincide with, set forth, reveal and effect that will. Cf., e.g., the definition of Fohrer *HIR*, p. 241; *Geschichte*, p. 242.

27 See Introduction, pp. lxxf.

reflects a measure of the divine compassion whereby punishment is devised rather to provoke penitence than to satisfy anger. Jerome, too, notes that Sodom and Gomorrah are associated specifically with judgements upon Judah and similar considerations have prompted a number of modern scholars to suppose that Admah and Zeboim reflect a peculiarly northern tradition (e.g. Harper).

Text and Versions

איך אתנך Pesh. *'ykn' 'sy'k* 'how can I support you?'

אמגנך LXX ὑπερασπιῶ σου 'shall I shield you?', cf. Vulg. *protegam te*; Aq. ὅπλῳ κυκλώσω σε 'shall I cover you with a shield?' (cf. Ziegler *Bei.* p. 360); Theod. ἀφοπλίσω σε 'shall I disarm you (i.e. remove your shield)?'; Symm. ἐκδώσω σε 'hand you over'; Vulg. *v.l. expugnabo* 'subdue'; Pesh. *''drk* 'shall I assist you?' (*v.l.'yqrk* 'honour you'; cf. Gelston, p. 147); Targ. אשיצינך '(how) shall I destroy you?'

כאדמה LXX conjoins with what follows, i.e. with MT's אשימך.

אשימך Pesh. omits.

כצבאים Only here spelt with *aleph* in place of *yodh*; i.e. in Gen 14.2, 8; Deut. 29.22: צביים *Kethib*, צבוים *Qere*; Gen 10.19 צְבֹיִם; Qyl notes that *aleph* is found in every one of the first ten words of the verse thereby creating assonance.

יחד LXX ἐν τῷ αὐτῷ, cf. Vulg. *pariter* 'at the same time' and Symm. ἐν τούτῳ; Pesh. wanting (Gelston, p. 133); Targ. כחדא 'at once'; Borbone omits.

נכמרו LXX συνεταράχθη 'is disturbed', cf. Vulg. *conturbata est*; Pesh. *wglw* 'are moved' (Gelston, p. 184), cf. Targ. מתגוללא from גלגל, Jastrow, p. 244.

נחומי LXX ἡ μεταμέλειά μου 'my regret', 'repentance', cf. Vulg. *paenitudo mea*; Pesh. *rḥmy* 'my tendernesses', cf. Targ. רחמת, Aq. and Symm. παράκλησίς μου, Theod. τὰ σπλάγχνα τοῦ ἐλέους μου; → רַחֲמַי (Wellhausen, Grätz, Marti, Harper, *BHS*, Borbone etc.), cf. Gen 43.30; 1 Kgs 3.26; see note g above.

11.9 **I will not give effect to my fierce anger, nor will I turn back[a] to destroy Ephraim. For I am God and not a man[b]; the Holy One in your midst, [c]yet not associated with any city[c].**

[a]For Jerome and Rashi the verb אשוב means here to change, i.e. from my attitude of clemency (so Jerome) or to revoke any promises (so Rashi, who compares Lev 26.44). The sense is that listed by BDB under 'to

change one's course of action' (p. 997, col 2 5 e). The usage is akin to that of 2.11 (EV 9) where the verb denotes reverse action (cf., e.g., Rosenmüller, Marti, Ehrlich).

[b]NB איש 'a man'.

[c—c]ולא אבוא בעיר Lit. 'yet I do not enter a city', i.e. associate myself with it, cf. Gen 49.6; Josh 23.7 and BDB p. 98, col 1 f. Such is the view of Rabbi Isaac ben Moshe Saul, quoted with approval by ibn Janāḥ. The phrase complements 'the Holy One in your midst' and means that this latter description does not imply 'that any place can contain me' (Arabic *w'n knh l' yḥyṭ by mk'n 'ḥtyǧ 'ly hḏ'*). Jerome appears to take much the same view and he understands *et non ingrediar civitatem* to mean that 'I am not one of those who inhabit cities, who live by human laws, who suppose that cruelty is justice ...'. R. Lowth[28], approving this view of the matter, notes that the phrase in question is parallel and synonymous with '(I am God) and not a man' and argues that the verb אבוא has a frequentative force as do those, e.g., in Ps 22.3, 8. For Saadya (quoted by ibn Ezra and Kimchi) and Rashi the reference is to God's predilection for Jerusalem and his refusal to allow his presence to be associated with any other city. Such thoughts are most unlikely to have been in Hosea's mind. Rashi quotes 'others' as understanding בעיר as an expression of hatred (לשון שנאה) and for this he compares 1 Sam 28.16, 'and he became your adversary' (ערך; so, e.g., NEB). N. G. Schroeder[29] takes a similar view and he compares the Arabic cognate root *ġwr* used to denote 'fervent anger'. More recently G. R. Driver[30], in reference to Jer 15.8 but not to this verse, also compares this Arabic word though with the meaning 'invade', 'invasion', 'attack', 'raid'. Rudolph tentatively suggests that such a meaning may be detected here, though he prefers to emend. BDB (cf. KB[3]) suggests that עיר is a noun derived from the root עור I and with the meaning 'agitation' (*sc.* of anger) and Guillaume[31] (comparing Arabic *'yr*) proposes 'reviling' (cf. NEB 'threats'). This approach accordingly leads to translations of the sort 'I will not come with/in agitation/attack/anger/threats'. Apart from manifest uncertainty attaching to the many philological possibilities, such approaches seem to me to be unsatisfactory, because the structure and parallelism of the verse indicates that the phrase belongs with 'the Holy One in your midst' and does not constitute a separate and third negative promise following 'I will not give effect ...' and 'I will not turn back ...'. For proposed emendations to the text, see Text and Versions.

28 *De Sacra Poesi Hebraeorum* (Oxford, 1763), p. 241.
29 *Observationes*, chapter 2, 13, p. 25.
30 *JQR* 28 (1937/38), p. 113.
31 *Abr-Nahrain* 2 (1960/61), p. 27.

The questions of the previous verse are here answered[32]. Yahweh cannot give free rein to his anger as if the latter, like the forces of nature, once unleashed, was incapable of being checked (after Rudolph). The harshness of Yahweh's judgement is designed to provoke penitence and piety. Man punishes to destroy: God intervenes for the purpose of correction (after Jerome). Accordingly Yahweh will not turn back to destroy his nation (note a). Here there is no intention to refer to an earlier destruction (as for example in the flood, so Rosenmüller in the name of 'others', comparing Isa 54.9); rather the word *šwb* implies a change of conduct, i.e. in this case, to an activity incompatible with the gracious action described in v. 1 where Yahweh called his people into existence (Procksch, Sellin, Wolff, Rudolph). So Hosea's words express his belief in the radical consistency of his God who does not, like a man, change his mind or fall prey to the promptings of (even just) anger. Such, too, is the import of his momentous description of Yahweh as the Holy One. He is ineffably majestic, characterised by absolute moral purity, isolated from all sin and the destroyer of all that is sinful (so Rudolph). Further, the essentially moral character of his holiness embraces the quality of love and compassion and it is in him, and in him alone, that such loving compassion finds expression in the face of his people's sinfulness. This great God is a reality; he is present in the midst of his people and is able to control the dire historical circumstances into which, by their own folly, they had betrayed themselves. Yet that description needs qualification; he is God and not a man (cf. Num 23.19); the reality of his presence (in the midst of his people) is not confined to any particular city (note c–c). The description may suggest a telling contrast. Indeed, the Israelites were disposed to reduce and confine their glorious God to the national calf-cult of Bethel (see on 8.5f and 10.5 above). Yet such perceptions were now confronted by the deprivations wrought by the Assyrians upon the nation and its official sanctuary. For Hosea, who had prophesied just such correction with judgement, it is precisely the right moment to proclaim a proper definition of Yahweh's mysterious, compelling and abiding presence (cf. with Rosenmüller, Isa 12.6). The definition is akin to that of St Augustine, 'O Thou, who art everywhere and everywhere are wholly present, who art not absent even when far off ...'[33].

32 *Contra* AF who suppose that *l'* is used asseveratively.
33 E. M. Macnutt *The Prayer Manual* (London, 1963), p. 58.

Text and Versions

חרון LXX κατὰ τὴν ὀργήν 'according to', translational rather than → כחרון (*contra* Grätz, Harper).

לא אשוב LXX οὐ μὴ ἐγκαταλίπω 'I will not leave (that Ephraim be obliterated'), → אעזב (Schleusner), → אשׁאיר (Vollers); Vulg. *non convertar*, cf. Pesh. *wl' 'hpwk*, 'I will not change'; Targ. לא יתוב '(my word) will not again (destroy)'.

בקרבך Pesh. takes this with ולא איש.

ולא אבוא בעיר The versions reproduce a literal translation except for Targ. with ולא אחליף בקריא אוחרי עוד ית ירושלם 'I will never exchange (Jerusalem) for any other city'. Emendations include: → לְבָעֵר 'to burn', 'exterminate' for בעיר (Hitzig, Oort, Mays); → ולא אוֹבֶה לְבָעֵר 'I am not willing to exterminate' (G. A. Smith); → ולא אֲבָעֵר (MT dittography of א/ב) 'and I will not exterminate/will I not exterminate?' (Wellhausen, Marti, cf. *BHS*); → ולא אבוא אֲבָעֵר 'and I come not so as to ravish' (Rudolph, with co-ordination of the two verbs).

11.10 and 11 **(They shall follow[a] Yahweh, who[b] roars like a lion. He[c] it is that roars so that those who are his sons[d] shall come trembling[e] from the west[f].)** (11) **They will be roused[e] like a bird from Egypt, like a dove from the land of Assyria. And I will restore them[g] to their homes. Oracle of Yahweh.**

[a]Lit. 'they will go after', cf. Deut 13.5.

[b]GK 155g, *contra* Rudolph; see the commentary below.

[c]כי used asseveratively, *contra*, e.g., Rudolph who, in association with his particular understanding of the development of the text, gives it a temporal sense.

[d]בנים, indeterminateness for the sake of amplification, GK 125c. For the versions, see Text and Versions below.

[e]יחרדו The usual translation is 'to tremble' and consequently in this context (cf. Gen 42.28; 1 Sam 13.7; 16.4) the usage is considered pregnant and rendered 'come trembling' (cf. BDB, KB[3]). For ibn Janāḥ, the fundamental meaning is 'to be roused', 'stirred up' (Arabic *'l'nz''ğ*), i.e. the opposite of 'permanence', 'stability', 'rest', 'stillness' (Arabic *'lqr'r*); cf., perhaps, 2 Kgs 4.13 where the word denotes 'anxious care' (for Elisha). So defined, the verb comprises the notion of hurried movement from a place as opposed to docile fixedness in it. Such a meaning fits well with the notion of Yahweh's intervention and, under the simile of the lion in the expanded text (see below), of the roar which rouses his people to follow him in trembling obedience. For

Kimchi the verb is defined in terms of motion, movement (תנועה). See further, Text and Versions.

[f]מים Lit. 'the sea' (i.e. the Mediterranean Sea) meaning, as often, the west; cf., e.g., Gen 12.8. For the possibility that 'sea' means here the 'sea of affliction' (Zech 10.11) and is used in a mythological sense, see below.

[g]וְהוֹשַׁבְתִּים A *Hiphil* of the root ישב, 'I will make them dwell', cf. the Vulgate. The reading וַהֲשִׁבוֹתִים (*Hiphil* of שוב) is suggested by the LXX, Peshiṭta and Targum and with this the preposition על (= אל) fits better. Both forms occur in Jer 32.37. See further Text and Versions.

The two verses are generally held to display signs of editorial activity. In their present form they serve to define the way in which Yahweh's compassionate change of heart will be seen to take effect. That change of heart will bring about the return of his sons (note d) from exile in the west (v. 10, cf. note f) as well as from Egypt and Assyria (v. 11). The exiles will follow Yahweh back to their homeland (vv. 10 and 11); they will be roused (note e) as if by a lion's roar and so, like birds, they will fly back, again to inhabit their homes.

Three main approaches are listed: first, the verses are seen to resemble later post-exilic texts such as Isa 49.17f; 60.8ff; Zech 10.10. This consideration prompts certain commentators to regard them as later additions to Hosea's writings (so, e.g., Marti, Harper). Against this view is the consideration that Hosea is likely to have given at least some indication of the effect of the divine change of heart (cf. Rudolph). Secondly, a number of more recent scholars (e.g. Wolff, Rudolph, Mays, Emmerson) have understood v. 11 to be substantially genuine and v. 10 alone to be a later addition. Verse 10 is formed on the basis of the word *yḥrdw* in v. 11 which is reproduced and to it is added the explanatory gloss of v. 10. In favour of this view it is urged: (1) that Yahweh speaks in the first person in vv. 9 and 11, whereas in v. 10 he is referred to in the third person; (2) reference to Egypt and Assyria (v. 11) reflects the situation of Hosea's times and his earlier references (8.13; 9.3, 6) to these countries, whereas there is no question of any contemporary diaspora in the west (i.e. the coastlands of the Mediterranean, v. 10); (3) v. 11, with its reference to a dove, reflects a conscious attempt to recapitulate the judgement of 7.11 where Ephraim is described as a gullible dove and the nation calls to Egypt and betakes itself to Assyria. Here, in reversal of 7.11, the movement is *to* the land and indicates resettlement in it (cf. 2.17, 20; EV 15, 18); (4) the words 'lion' (*'ryh*) and 'roar' (*š'g*) in

v. 10 are regarded with suspicion since, for 'lion', Hosea elsewhere uses other terms (cf. 5.14; 13.7); the verb 'roar' is held to reflect specifically Judaean (cultic) usage (cf. Amos 1.2; 3.4, 8; Joel 4.16; Jer 25.30) and to convey the notion of Yahweh's 'solemn summons to his people' (so Emmerson pp. 44f; Wolff). By contrast Hosea's own use of the image of the lion is solely connected with judgement and punishment (5.14; 13.7). Thirdly, a variant to this approach is that of Rudolph who addresses himself to the question: why should the later addition (v. 10) have been placed before rather than after the verse which it is designed to illuminate? In answer he supposes that the words 'like a lion which roars' (*sic*, relative clause without *'šr*) were authentic but belonged originally to the end of v. 9 (i.e. 'like a roaring lion I come not to despoil'). The words 'they shall follow Yahweh', too, are genuine but originally introduced the notice of homecoming in (the present) v. 11. The present order of phrases in the two verses reflects the concern of the glossator who sought to give a positive significance to the roaring lion. This he accomplished, first, by inserting 'He roars that his sons should come trembling from the west', linking the words with v. 11 by repeating the word *yḥrdw*; and, secondly, by moving the phrase 'like a roaring lion' to its present place after 'they shall follow Yahweh'.

Review of the verses and of the arguments set out above suggests that the second theory is the most likely to be correct. In favour stands Rudolph's argument that it is likely that Hosea gave some indication of the effect which the divine change of heart (vv. 8f) would leave upon his nation. The words which appear best to fit Hosea's thinking and imagery are those of v. 11.

As ibn Ezra observes (so more recently Emmerson) the verse appears to reverse the sentiments of 7.11. There Israel was like a gullible dove who called to Egypt and at the same time betook herself to Assyria. Involvement with these foreign nations was understood by Hosea to have the likely effect that those who undertook it would finish by living as exiles in the countries concerned, far from their own homeland (cf. 8.13; 9.3, 6). Thus Kimchi observes that these countries are specifically mentioned because the Israelites supposed that they were the source of help; in fact they stumbled there and consequently were exiled to them. Here, by contrast, through Yahweh's final resolution not to allow his nation to share the fate of Admah and Zeboim (v. 8), his people will be roused (note e) from Egypt and from the land of Assyria and restored (note g, contrast 9.6) to their own homes. Chapter 9.6, in reference to Egypt, suggests not so much forcible deportation as voluntary flight while, in the case of Assyria, 2 Kgs 15.29 (cf. Noth *History*, p. 261, *GI*, pp. 237f) suggests forcible deportation of the urban upper classes to the eastern part of the Assyrian empire (or to Mesopotamia) in Pekah's time (733 BC); this policy is likely to have been renewed following Hoshea's revolt of 727 BC and certainly later brought to full fruition with the fall of Samaria in 722/1 BC (cf. 11.5 as reflecting the final supremacy of Assyria at this time, see above). At all events it is likely that Hosea saw at this time (i.e. the mid-720s BC) the gathering collapse of the nation, some of whose prominent citizens had betrayed themselves into self-imposed exile in Egypt, while others, in steadily increasing numbers, were being forcibly deported to Assyria (including, perhaps, the king Hoshea, 2 Kgs 17.4). In such circumstances, it is likely that Hosea perceived the effect of Yahweh's change of heart at the eleventh hour in terms of the restoration of the nation's leading citizens, roused indeed by his intervention to return as wandering birds to their nests or as doves to their dove-cotes (cf. Kimchi, who compares Prov 27.8 and Isa 60.8)[34].

Essentially, then, Hosea saw Yahweh's intervention as bringing an end to the nation's involvement with Egypt and Assyria, together with the baleful results of that involvement. Verse 10 is to be understood as a later gloss which explains and expands Hosea's somewhat terse language in v. 11. The initial phrase 'they shall follow' expresses what is understood to be the fundamental meaning of v. 11. The verb *yḥrdw*, seen now by the glossator to convey the notion of 'trembling', seemed to require explanation (cf. Wolff) and hence the reference to the agent, *viz.* the lion (cf. Amos 3.8), a figure for Yahweh himself who induces the trembling, obedient return of his sons. The final phrase 'from the west' (note f) may reflect an attempt to include those exiled in the coastlands of the Mediterranean in later times (cf. Isa 11.11). Alternatively, 'from the sea' may constitute a mythological/typological reference to the 'sea of affliction' associated in Zech 10.10f with redemption from Egypt and Assyria (cf. Isa 11.15).

Rudolph's ingenious and complicated assessment of v. 10 is rejected on the following grounds: first, his assessment that 'they shall follow Yahweh' is genuine rests upon the judgement that the clause is a deliberate antithesis of 11.2, 'they went from me'. In order to achieve this, Rudolph is driven to emend 11.2; secondly, and similarly, his conclusion that 'like a lion which

34 That 'their homes' continues the simile of the birds and means 'their nests' (so Sellin, comparing Ps 84.4) is unlikely (cf. Wolff and Rudolph).

roars' is genuine but belongs to the end of v. 9 involves prior emendation of the last word of (the present) v. 9. With Emmerson's suggestion (cf. Wolff) that the reference in v. 10 to the lion and its roar reflects Judaean (cultic) tradition there need be no fundamental disagreement. In particular, however, her assertion that the phrase, especially in the light of Amos 3.8, reflects a specific form, *viz.* 'Yahweh's summons to his people' seems to be misconceived. Amos 3.8 (cf. 1.2; 3.4) suggests the notions of cause and effect: if a lion roars then people fear; and so, similarly, if Yahweh has spoken, the prophets must prophesy what he commands. The lion's roar, then, serves to convey the notion of Yahweh's majestic, irresistible command. It is that which, in the glossator's view, explained why exiles should be said by Hosea to come trembling, or be aroused, from Egypt and Assyria. It is the glossator who has created here a 'solemn summons to his people' and he may have extended or been understood to have extended (see above) that summons to include exiles in the west (cf. Isa 11.11; Zech 8.7).

In short the interpretation of these verses is as follows: Hosea perceived that, despite the apparent collapse of the nation and the privations resulting from the Assyrian invasions of *c.* 725 BC (v. 6), Yahweh could not bring himself to allow Ephraim to share the fate of Admah and Zeboim (v. 8). His resolution not to destroy Ephraim, together with his consistently holy nature (v. 9) would have the effect that those who stupidly involved themselves with Egypt and Assyria (vv. 7, 11) and who, as a result, found themselves exiled there (8.13; 9.3, 6; 11.5) would be roused to return and to occupy their own homes as doves returning to their dove-cotes. Thereby the nation's 'refusal to repent' (v. 5b) is superseded by Yahweh's gracious initiative since he rouses them both from the moral torpor which had prompted them to become involved with these nations and from its inevitable consequences in their exile from their land (v. 11). To this terse statement of Hosea a later glossator, relying on specifically Judaean phrases and concepts, has prefixed[35] his explanatory interpretation in the way suggested above. The effect of his work is to create in vv. 10f an expression of the later Judaean 'eschatology of salvation' (so Wolff) with its notion of Yahweh's call to his sons exiled far and wide to follow him and to return to Zion (cf. Isa 11.11, 16; 27.13; 43.5f; 49.11f; 60.8ff; Mic 7.12, etc.).

[35] For a (probable) example of a gloss *preceding* the phrase it is designed to elucidate, cf. Isa 63.11 (i.e. 'Moses and his people' precedes 'shepherd and his flock').

Nowack and, more recently, Wolff have questioned the authenticity of the concluding formula 'Oracle of Yahweh' on the grounds that there are no other occurences in the section beginning in 4.1. Against this contention it may be urged (with Rudolph) that it would be entirely natural for Hosea to conclude so important and significant an oracle with a notice that it came on Yahweh's authority. Nowack's contention that the other occurrences (in 2.15, 18, 23; EV 13, 16, 21) are in verses that are not authentic or are under suspicion of so being, is not here adopted.

Text and Versions

Verse 10

ילכו LXX πορεύομαι; → אֵלֵךְ (Ruben).

ישאג (first occurrence) Aq. plural; Pesh. *dnhm* 'that roars'; → אשאג (Ruben).

כי הוא ישאג Absent in 3 Kennicott and 3 de Rossi MSS.

ויחרדו LXX καὶ ἐκστήσονται 'and they will be out of their wits'; Symm. καὶ σεισθήσονται 'they will be shaken'; Vulg. *et formidabunt*, cf. Pesh. *wnzw'wn* 'and they will tremble/be terrified'; Targ. ויתכנשן 'and they will be gathered'.

בנים מים LXX τέκνα ὑδάτων 'children of waters' (= בְּנֵי מַיִם, cf. Harper)[36]; υἱοὶ ἀπὸ θαλάσσης – οἱ λ.; Vulg. *filii maris* 'sons of the sea'; Pesh. *bny' mn 'm'* 'sons from the people' → *ym'* 'from the sea' (Gelston, pp. 83, 94f); Targ. גלותא ממערבא 'the exiles from the west (will be gathered)'; Emendations include: בנים מעמים (Grätz); בנים מאיי ים (Nowack after Isa 11.11); בָּנִים מִיָּם (Marti). Borbone omits מים citing 1 Kennicott MS.

Verse 11

יחרדו LXX^{AQmarg} ἐκπτήσονται 'they will fly out'; LXX^{BQ*} ἐκστήσονται 'they will be out of their wits'[37]; Vulg. *et avolabunt* 'and they will fly away'; Pesh. *wndwlwn* 'and they will be aroused/come out hastily' or 'with trepidation'; Targ. דאתי בגלאי '(like a bird) which comes openly' (Cathcart p. 55, n. 24).

[36] I.e., according to Vollers, p. 256, the Greeks.

[37] Jerome renders *formidabunt* 'they will be terrified'. It may be the LXX^{A} has understood the true meaning of √חרד; cf. note e above and Liddell and Scott *ad loc.*

והושבתים LXX καὶ ἀποκαταστήσω αὐτούς, cf. Pesh. *w'hpk 'nwn* and Targ. ואתיבינון 'and I will return them'; → וַהֲשִׁבוֹתִים (Grätz, *BHS*, Borbone, see note g above); Vulg. *et conlocabo eos* 'and I will make them dwell' (cf. MT).

CHAPTER 12.1–15

EPHRAIM AND ITS PATRIARCHAL ANCESTOR JACOB: CORRECTION WITH JUDGEMENT

NB The English Versions add 12.1 to chapter 11 as 11.12; hence the numbering of the verses for the rest of chapter 12 is one behind that of MT. Elsewhere in the Commentary the differences are noted but not in the commentary on this chapter.

12.1 **Ephraim has surrounded me[a] with deceit and the House of Israel with treachery; (and Judah)[b] still he seeks to gain the mastery[c] with God and with the Most Holy[d] remains immovable[e].**

[a]For the sense of the verb סבב here cf. with Rosenmüller, Ps 17.11 and with Qyl, Jon 2.6.

[b]MT reads ויהודה 'and Judah'. The LXX and the Peshiṭta connect the word with what precedes. The word is here regarded as a redactional modification and the conjecture is offered that והוא was read in the original text (cf. 5.13; 7.9; 8.6). Lipschitz, in a private communication, has suggested that ויעקב was original, in conformity with Hosea's predilection for triple nomenclature. See further on v. 2 below.

[c]The verb רד apparently from √רוד has long been recognised as the crux of the verse. The rendering and interpretation here adopted is that of Aquila (ἐπικρατῶν) and ibn Janāḥ who, under √רוד[1] appears to have given the word a similar meaning, *viz.* 'to make oneself master', 'to overwhelm' (Arabic *'styl'*) for which he compares Gen 27.40; Jer 2.31 and (as a possibility) Judg 19.11 (presumably, 'the day had greatly prevailed', i.e. became master of them). According to this view of the matter the line, having the force almost of a relative clause following 'Ephraim and the House of Israel', seems to constitute a reference to Jacob's wrestling at the Jabbok (Gen. 32.25ff, EV 24ff), cf. vv. 4f. The √רוד is normally given the meaning 'to wander restlessly', 'to roam' (so BDB, cf. KB), an interpretation here adopted by most modern

[1] The reading is attributed to the glossator of the Rouen MS by Neubauer, who explicitly recognises the value of such glosses. The similarity in meaning with Aquila's rendering is striking.

commentators. Since at least the seventeenth century[2], however, appeal has been made to the Arabic cognate verb *rwd* which has a wide variety of meanings. Apart from 'to move about', 'to prowl' it conveys the notions of 'having in mind', 'desiring', 'coveting', 'seeking' as well as 'striving' (i.e. for something)[3]. BDB lists the Ethiopic cognate with the meaning 'to run upon', 'to attack'. Amongst the rabbinic commentators Rashi and ibn Ezra understand the verb to have a sense akin to that attested for רדה i.e. 'domination', 'dominion', 'rule'[4], and they suppose that Judah (cf. note b) ruled with God, i.e. in the fear of God. Such a sense is forced and unsatisfactory in the context, yet it may reveal some memory of the true sense of the verb.

In the light of this evidence it is suggested that רד (√רוד) was capable of the sense 'to seek to dominate', 'to seek the mastery of'. It is likely to be similar in meaning to the verb שׂרה 'to persist', 'exert oneself' as it occurs in Gen 32.29 (EV 28), where it is used to explain the name Israel, and in Hos 12.4. It is probably related to, or is a by-form of, the well-attested √רדה 'to dominate', 'rule'[5] (cf. המה/הום; דמה/דום). The word is parsed as a participle, cf. the adverb עד 'still' with which it is closely associated.

[d]The plural word קדושים is understood to be a plural of majesty and, parallel with אל 'God', refers to him as in Prov 9.10; 30.3; cf. Josh 24.19 (so Kimchi). For אל parallel with (the singular) קדוש, see 11.9 above. Other interpretations of the word depend in large measure upon the view that is taken of רד (note c). Thus, if Judah is 'restive with God' then he can be said to be 'loyal to idols he counts holy' (e.g. NEB, AF and cf. note e below). For קדושים of idols, cf. Ps 16.3. Again, if Judah 'still roams or goes with God' (Wolff, cf. Mays) then he can be said to be 'loyal to the Holy One' (Mays) or 'to holy ones' (Wolff). For the term used of the pious[6], cf. Ps 34.10. It is such considerations which lead Wolff to interpret the term of the Levites and prophets, associated with Hosea, who find refuge in Judah. Since, in my view, these interpretations depend upon mistaken or forced understandings of רוד, they are here discounted. For emendations, see under Text and Versions.

[e]The *Niphal* participle נאמן usually has the force 'faithful'. Here, however, it is parallel to רד (note c) and has a meaning akin to that of Deut 28.59, where illnesses and plagues are described as persistent, i.e. there can be no expectation of their remission or of their being healed (so ibn Janāḥ, though he does not mention Hos 12.1). Recognition that

2 For references, see Rosenmüller *ad loc.*

3 Cf. Wehr, p. 366 and Lane 3, pp. 1183f.

4 Cf. Rosenmüller.

5 Jerome supposes that the root is ירד which is, he explains, capable of denoting both 'descent' and 'strength'; it is the latter sense that is reflected in Aquila's rendering.

6 Jerome interprets the word of angels or, alternatively, of patriarchs, prophets and others who are loyal to the service of God.

the word was capable of a pejorative sense accords with the understanding of the verb רד set out in note c above. This evidence should be given full weight, even though the generality of translators and commentators have taken the word נאמן in its well-attested and favourable sense. As a consequence 'faithfulness' has been interpreted of Judah (as opposed to Ephraim) because it was faithful with the Holy One (Kimchi, cf. Harper, Mays) or with the holy patriarchs and prophets (Jerome) or, on a pejorative view of the meaning of רד, because it (wandered in respect of God and) was faithful with idols (cf., e.g., NEB, AF). The rendering offered here 'remains immovable' seeks to convey the notion of persistent (cf. עד 'still'), unrelenting intractability.

The verse stands at the beginning of the section as a terse and summary statement of the continuity between Ephraim's present behaviour and that of its eponymous ancestor Jacob. Yahweh is the speaker (*contra* Wolff, who supposes that the prophet is the speaker) and he complains that Ephraim/Israel has surrounded him (note a) with deceit and treachery so that wherever he goes or wherever he looks he is confronted with such enormities (cf. with Qyl, Jer 9.5, EV 6). He dwells in their midst (11.9) yet is surrounded on all sides by the deceit (4.2; 7.3) and treachery (12.8) which have brought about the nation's manifest disintegration. The sentiment, expressed anthropomorphically in respect of Yahweh, refers to the all too human capacity for treachery which is based on self-delusion (cf., with Rudolph, v. 2). The root of such attitudes is often attributed by Hosea to idolatry, yet here, not the outward symptoms (e.g. Baal worship) but the inner fault is emphasised. In the second part of the verse that fault is traced back to the deceitful ambition of Jacob, the father of the nation. The sentence, expressed in the third person singular, forms a sort of relative clause which refers to Ephraim/Israel (notes b and c) and contends that the nation's present ('still') attitude and behaviour reflect and represent the patriarch's overbearing and treacherous ambition (cf. Gen 27.35 and *mrmh* 'treachery'). The nation, then, still seeks to dominate, to prevail (note c) in its dealings with God himself; it persists in its implacable striving (note e) with the Holy One (note d) and thus shares the thrusting ambition of Jacob who wrestled with God at the Jabbok (Gen 32).

Hosea's words appear to reflect in form those of the all-important Gen 32.29. Thus here the plural noun *qdwšym* together with the repeated preposition *'m* matches Gen 32.29 where Jacob is said to have vied with (*'m*) God (*'lhym*) and with (*'m*) men (*'nšym*) and prevailed, cf. vv. 4f. Again the verbal forms here appear to be virtually synonymous with those of Gen 32.29: *rd* corresponds to *śryt* in Gen 32.29 and *n'mn* to *wtwkl*. The emphasis here, however, is upon the nation's present activity rather than upon the paradigm of Jacob, and Hosea's words and expressions are designed to characterise the former by alluding to the latter. Thus it seems likely that Hosea is making free use of the tradition known to us from Gen 32. For him the nation's behaviour constitutes aggression solely against God (*'l* and *qdwšym*, note d) whereas in the paradigm of Jacob aggressive behaviour is directed both against God and men and is marked by success (NB the *waw* before *twkl* in Gen 32.29). Hosea's point about the nation is that it perpetuates Jacob's aggressive behaviour but that its motivation, unlike Jacob's, is flawed (cf. v. 2) and therefore doomed to failure.

The introduction of the word 'and Judah' (note b) is here taken to be the work of the Judaean redactor who sought, in harmony with the full description, Ephraim/House of Israel, to extend the saying to his own nation. Whether he understood Hosea's words in the pejorative sense intended by the prophet and thereby sought to extend to his nation the same warning or whether, through unfamiliarity with Hosea's dialect or because he was consciously reinterpreting these words, he was disposed to see in them a favourable message (e.g. 'Judah still rules with God and remains faithful to the Holy One', Rashi and Kimchi) is difficult to determine with precision. Certainly by the time of the versions and the rabbinic commentators it is apparent that such a favourable sense was detected and the contrast with Ephraim/Israel clearly established; thus, 'Judah was secure with God and firm in its worship of him in spite of Ephraim's worship of the calves' (so Kimchi). To this tendency the word *n'mn* with its normally good connotations (e.g. the Vulgate's *fidelis*) is likely to have contributed substantially.

Text and Versions

LXX and Vulg. connect the verse with chapter 11.

סבבני LXX (but Q[c], plural), Pesh. and Vulg. singular verb, → סְבָבַנִי (Borbone); Targ., plural, cf. MT; Targ. אסגיאו קדמי בכדבין '(those of the House of Israel) have multiplied lies before me' cf. Cathcart, p. 56 n. 1.

ויהודה LXX and Pesh. conjoin with what precedes, see note b above.

עד רד עם אל LXX νῦν ἔγνω αὐτοὺς ὁ θεός 'now God knew them' (= עַתָּ(ה) יְדָעָם אֵל, Scholz, cf. Rosenmüller, Rudolph); Vulg. *(Judas) autem testis descendit cum Deo* 'however as a witness (Judah) went down with[7] God' (= עַד יָרֵד, cf. Rudolph); Pesh. *'dm' dnḥt 'mh d'lh'* 'until the people of God go down' (= עַד יָרֵד עַם אֵל Sebök); Targ. עד דגלא עמא דאלהא מארעהון 'until the people of God were exiled from their land', cf. Cathcart.

רד Aq. ἐπικρατῶν, see note c above.

אל → אלים or בעל, cf. *BHS*.

ועם קדושים נאמן LXX καὶ λαὸς ἅγιος κεκλήσεται θεοῦ 'and a holy people will be called of God' (= וְעַם קדוש נאמן לאל, Vollers), cf. Pesh. *'m' qdyš' wmhymn'* 'a holy and believing people' and Targ. מתקרן עמא קדישא בכין הוו קיימין '(those who worshipped before me in the sanctuary) were called the holy people, therefore they are enduring/were established'; Vulg. *et cum sanctis fidelis* 'and faithful with the holy ones'.

A large number of emendations have been proposed of which a few are here noted: for עד רד עם אל, עד יָדוּעַ (Marti); מֹרֵד עם אל (Oettli); for ועם קדושים נאמן, ועם קדושים יֵאָמֵר (Grätz); וְעִם קְדֹשִׁים נִצְמָד, C. H. Cornill *ZAW* 7 (1887), pp. 286ff, cf. Wellhausen, Oettli; וְעַם קָדוֹשׁ לֹא נאמן (Halévy); וְעַם קָדוֹשׁ יְמָאֵן אָמֵן (König 348d, cf. Rudolph).

12.2 **Ephraim concerns himself[a] with wind; he pursues an east wind. [b]Everyday he multiplies lies and havoc; [c]they make a covenant with Assyria, and at the same time[c] oil is transported to Egypt.**

[a]See on 9.2 above for a consideration of Hosea's use of the verb רעה.

[b]For *zaqeph qaton* as the stronger disjunctive, GK 15f, cf. and contrast the LXX and Peshiṭta.; see Text and Versions below.

[c—c]The repeated *waw* expresses a simultaneous action (so, rightly, Rudolph, cf. Kimchi).

The verse is linked closely to v. 1 where Ephraim's deceit and treachery are said to confront Yahweh on all sides. The second line of the present verse indicates the inevitable connection between such treacherous behaviour and the disintegration of the state in havoc (cf. Kimchi, *contra* a number of modern scholars who wish to emend שד 'havoc' on the basis of the LXX; see Text and Versions). Deceit and treachery, here 'lies', are not only outwardly destructive but they result from the deep malady of self-deception. This is what Hosea means by saying that Ephraim concerns himself (note a) with wind, i.e. vanity, chaos,

[7] Jerome comments: 'Judah alone, versed in God's worship and laws, endured and is able to descend with him or to be strong with the Strong: *rad enim et descensionem et fortitudinem significat...*'.

moral and institutional anarchy (see on 8.7 above; also Prov 15.14; Isa 44.20; Jer 22.22) and chases after, as if to embrace (cf. 2.9, EV 7), the east wind. The latter is no mere synonym dictated by the needs of parallelism; rather, matching 'havoc' in the following line[8], it denotes the notorious Sirocco blowing up from the desert (cf. 13.15) today widely known in Israel/Palestine by its Arabic name *Ḥamsīn*. It is 'the most severe of winds and injurious to men' (Kimchi) by reason of its dust, violence and scorching heat whose debilitating effect is so widely attested (cf. Ezek 17.10; Jon 4.8; Isa 27.8)[9]. The phrase is marked by strong alliteration with four-fold repetition of *resh* (so Wolff).

The particular manifestation of such self-deceptive and self-destructive behaviour is described in the second half (so *BHS*) of the verse: Ephraim enters into a covenant relationship with Assyria and simultaneously (note c) takes steps to ingratiate himself with Egypt, Assyria's adversary and object of its suspicions. Israel, a veritable land of olive oil (so Kimchi comparing Isa 57.9; Ezek 27.17), was in a position to supply a commodity particularly valued in Egypt because the olive tree is quite foreign there. The notice that oil is transported to Egypt suggests primarily inducement (so Rashi and Kimchi)[10] and the change of subject ('they' in relation to Assyria; 'is transported' in relation to Egypt) indicates, perhaps, the factions within the establishment, some of which favour the one policy and some the other. At all events the behaviour of Ephraim as a single nation necessarily attracts the censure of treachery since it consists of simultaneous and morally inconsistent actions. Inconsistency and treachery are certainly portrayed as pure human folly; yet the juxtaposition of vv. 1 and 2 ('Judah' excluded, see above) suggests that, for Hosea, such foolish behaviour constitutes an affront to Yahweh himself since he is surrounded on all sides by it (*contra* Rudolph). Recognition of the fundamental unity of thought between verses 1 and 2 as here depicted tells against Wolff's assertion that the emphasis upon 'Ephraim' in this verse is intelligible only if it follows 'Judah' in verse 1b. On the contrary, it adds cumulative force to the argument, posited on other grounds, that 'Judah' is a late addition.

[8] This rather than Egypt and Assyria, as Wolff suggests. Wolff's view is dependent upon his decision to regard the words 'he multiplies lies and havoc' as an interpretative gloss.

[9] Cf. *AUS* 1, pp. 103ff.

[10] *Contra* D. J. McCarthy *VT* 14 (1964), pp. 215ff, who supposes that 'to transport oil' is a synonym for 'to conclude a treaty'.

The reference to a covenant with Assyria and to the offering of inducements to Egypt fits well the time of Hoshea who, despite on accession paying tribute to Tiglath-pileser III and being confirmed as a vassal king, by 725 BC felt himself secure enough with Egypt (cf. 2 Kgs 17.4) to withhold tribute from Shalmaneser V. The situation described in the verse, then, pertains to the years c. 732–725 BC. (The year of Shalmaneser V's accession is 726 BC.)

Text and Versions

רעה רוח LXX πονηρὸν πνεῦμα· '(Ephraim is) an evil wind'; Aq. and Symm. ποιμαίνει ἄνεμον, cf. Vulg. *pascit ventum* 'E. grazes the wind', cf. Pesh. *r'' rwḥ'*; Targ. (cf. 8.7) דמן לדרוח זרע '(the House of Israel) is like he who sows wind'; → רצה 'desires' (Marti, but cf. Rudolph).

כל היום LXX and Pesh. conjoin with preceding phrase, cf. note b above with what follows.

ושד LXX καὶ μάταια; → ושוא 'deceit', 'fraud' (so, e.g., Oort, Wellhausen, Marti, Harper, Rudolph, Borbone); Vulg. *vastitatem*, cf. Pesh. *wbzt'*, and Targ. וביזתא support MT.

ירבה Pesh. *'sgyw* → ירבו (plural; so, e.g., Wellhausen, Marti, Harper).

יכרתו LXX and Vulg. singular, making Ephraim the subject.

יובל LXX ἐνεπορεύετο, cf. Vulg. *ferebat* 'E. was importing' (? = יֹובַל, Halévy); Pesh. *'wblw* 'they carry', cf. Targ. מובלין; → יֹובִלוּ (e.g. Wellhausen, Oort, Marti, Wolff, Mays, *BHS*; some transfer here the *waw* from the beginning of v. 3).

12.3 **So[a] Yahweh has a dispute with Israel[b]; he can but[c] punish Jacob for his conduct[d], he will repay him for his misdeeds[e].**

[a]Cf. note b. It is possible that *waw* was here interpreted by the redactor in the sense 'also', i.e. Yahweh has also a quarrel with Judah, whether or not the *waw* was removed (either accidentally or on purpose) from the end of v. 2 (cf. Text and Versions on v. 2). On the other hand *waw* is attested with the force 'so', 'then' (BDB p. 254, col 2 4) and this follows well what is said in the preceding verses (cf. the Vulgate which renders ergo, 'therefore').

[b]MT (so the versions) reads 'Judah'. The view is here adopted that the original reading was 'Israel' but that the Judaean redactor made the change in order to extend the prophecy to include his own country; see notes a and c and the commentary below.

[c]The infinitive פקד with ל expresses obligation (cf., with Rudolph, König 399 z – β) and the *waw* is likely to be authentic. The connection with what precedes, so defined, suggests again that Israel/Jacob was originally the object of Yahweh's indictment rather than Judah and Jacob.

[d]Lit. 'according to his ways', cf. Jer 17.10; 32.19; Ezek 18.30.

[e]Cf. 4.9 above, where the same words occur. For a finite verb used with the same force as a preceding infinitive construct, cf., with Rudolph, König, 413a – e.

The nation's moral perversity and senselessness requires (note c) Yahweh to indict and to punish it. Since the section is concerned to show the continuity between the nation's present behaviour and that of its eponymous ancestor, Israel (*sic*, note b) is here styled also 'Jacob'. (For the Northern Kingdom so styled, cf. Isa 9.7f, EV 8f; 17.3f; Mic 1.5). The deceit and trickery perpetrated by Jacob of old are set forth laconically in the verses that follow, as is also Yahweh's mysterious and prevailing corrective to that deceit. Here, following the description of the nation's perversity (v. 2a), its symptoms (v. 2b) and the way it is perceived by Yahweh (v. 1), the present verse expresses the divine reaction that must inevitably follow. That v. 4 so clearly refers to both names of the patriarch (Jacob/Israel) points strongly to the intrusive nature of the word 'Judah' in the MT.

For the Judaean redactor the words suggested that the prophecy 'conveyed to Judah the words of God's dispute *in re*: the doings of their brothers and their disregard of Yahweh's punishing Jacob for his misdeeds'. Rashi's words seem to me to constitute a remarkably accurate account of the nature of the MT and thus to facilitate a reconstruction of the history of its formulation. Central to the latter is the supposition, suggested indeed by the coherence of the piece, that Hosea wrote 'Israel' and that his redactor emended the word so as to read 'Judah' (note b above). In the resulting text the term 'Jacob' comes to denote the whole people of Yahweh, descended indeed from the patriarch but now exemplified, following the destruction of Ephraim, in the kingdom of Judah (cf. Jer 9.3; Isa 43.28).

Text and Versions

וריב *waw* is omitted by Nowack, Oort, Wolff, *BHS*; see on the previous verse.

יהודה → ישׂראל (Oort, Nowack, Oettli, Wolff, Mays, cf. *BHS*).

ולפקד 7 Kennicott MSS and LXX omit *waw* (so Wellhausen, Grätz, Nowack, Wolff, cf. *BHS*); Vulg. *et visitatio* 'and punishment (upon Jacob)'; Pesh. *wntb'*, → ויפקד 'and he will punish' (Borbone); Targ. ולאסערא, cf. MT.

כדרכיו Vulg. joins with the following verb.

12.4 **Even[a] in the womb he supplanted[b] his brother and in his prime[c] he strove[d] with[e] God.**

[a] Supplied in translation *ad sensum*.

[b] עקב Lit. 'he grasped the heel', cf. Gen 25.26 and the etymology of the proper name Jacob there set forth. The verb is a denominative from עקב 'heel' but has connotations of deceit and trickery, cf. on 6.8 above and Gen 27.36; Jer 9.3 (EV 4). The English word 'supplant' (cf. Vulgate) is chosen *ad sensum*.

[c] אונו Lit. 'his manly vigour', cf. Gen 49.3. It is possible that Hosea chose the word because in sound and form it also suggested the noun אָוֶן 'trouble', 'sorrow', 'wickedness'; see further in the commentary and the evidence of the LXX below.

[d] Cf. Gen 32.29 (EV 28) and note c to v. 1 above. The sense of the verb שׂרה is akin to that detected for the verb רוד in that verse, *viz.* 'to seek to gain the mastery', 'to dominate'. The mode of this endeavour is depicted in Gen 32.25 (EV 24) as wrestling (√אבק).

[e] Hebrew את; in Gen 32.29 (EV 28) the synonymous preposition עם is used.

Jacob, now the patriarch rather than the Northern Kingdom (as in the previous verse), had from the beginning consistently shown the characteristics of unscrupulous ambition and his very name was seen to reflect the fact. Recalling the incident of Gen 25.26 where, at birth, Jacob is stated to have been grasping the heel (*'qb*) of his twin Esau, Hosea uses the verb *'qb* in an allusive sense (note b) but also recalls by it the usage of Gen 27.36, where Esau complains how well his brother Jacob is named since 'twice now he has supplanted me (*wy'qbny*)'. Rudolph's supposition that Hosea, recalling an incident connected with the moment of birth, concluded that the ambitious act took place even earlier, i.e. within the womb, seems to me to smack of over-interpretation. 'In the womb', especially in a poetic text, denotes rather 'from the very beginning', cf., with ibn Ezra, Jer 1.5. At all events, Hosea's phrase clearly constituted a reproach for Jacob as opposed to the received text of Gen 27 in which v. 36 was clearly read as an initial fulfilment of the prophecy of v. 29, a prophecy of Jacob's eventual superior greatness. Yet Hosea's reproach accords well with the judgement of Isaac within the Genesis text, *viz.* that Jacob had come to him *bmrmh* 'deceitfully', (v. 35, cf. Hos 12.1), as it does with Esau's complaint of v. 36 quoted above. Such considerations tell against Ackroyd's suggestion that *'qb* here has the sense 'to overtake' and expresses solely the favour in which Yahweh held Jacob and his consequent congenital superiority[11].

In the second part of the verse Hosea again reproaches the patriarch Jacob, this time by reference to the incident at the Jabbok (Gen 32.25ff, EV 24ff) where, by his wrestling, he gained his alternative name 'Israel'. The words *śrh 't 'lhym* differ from those used in Gen 32.29 (EV 28) only in that the verb is here third person singular (rather than second person singular) and *'t* is used in place of the synonymous *'m.* The form of Gen 32.29 (EV 28) also seems to be reflected in Hos 12.1b though there the words, predicated rather of Israel the nation, are different (see above). If at birth Jacob was so named for his infant ambitiousness then, in his maturity (note c), he was named Israel for his arrogant (cf. the Peshiṭta and Targum) attempt to dominate (note d) God for himself. The word *b'wnw* may have been chosen by reason of its similarity in form and sound to the word *āwen* which denotes 'trouble', 'wickedness' (note c)[12]. The *double entendre*[13], then, may suggest that Jacob's conflict with the divine presence was to be associated with the precarious situation in which he knew he must face the brother he had wronged (cf. Ackroyd, p. 249). Certainly such a motif is to be detected in the use made of the ancient legend of the Jabbok by the author of Genesis (cf. S. R. Driver *Genesis*, pp. 296f). The word *'wn* is, as Davies points out, something of a key word for this chapter; cf. vv. 9 and 12.

Text and Versions

עקב LXX ἐπτέρνισεν 'he grasped by the heel'; Vulg. *subplantavit* 'he tripped up'; cf. Pesh. *nkl* 'he defrauded'; Targ. דיסגי '(was it not said) that he would become greater (than his brother)?', cf. Gen 25.23 and Cathcart, p. 56.

[11] Such views appear to have been known to ibn Ezra who is at pains to refute them.

[12] Cf., with Wolff, Ps 36.4, where *'āwen* is parallel to *mrmh* 'deceit'.

[13] So Gertner, p. 276, n. 1; cf. Rudolph.

ובאונו LXX καὶ ἐν κόποις αὐτοῦ 'and in his troubles' (אָוֶן, see note c and commentary); Vulg. *et in fortitudine sua*, cf. Pesh. *wb'wšnh* and Targ. ובתוקפיה 'in his strength'.

שׂרה LXX ἐνίσχυσεν πρός 'he proved mighty towards'; Vulg. *directus est cum*, cf. Aq. κατώρθωσε 'he prospered (towards)', √ישׁר; Pesh. *'trwrb* 'he behaved arrogantly (before)', cf. Targ. אתרברב 'he claimed superiority'.

אלהים LXX θεόν, cf. Pesh. *'lh'*; Vulg. *angelo*, cf. Aq. ἄγγελον and Targ. מלאכא.

12.5 But [a]ISRA-EL [i.e. God gained the ascendancy][a, b] and prevailed[c]; he [Jacob][d] wept and implored the favour of him [e]who encountered him at Bethel and there spoke with us[e, f].

Any interpretation of this verse is fraught with very considerable difficulties and what follows is no more than an attempt to make sense of what has come down to us. In addition to the literature quoted, attention is drawn to the articles by Eslinger, Bentzen and S. L. McKenzie listed in the Bibliography.

[a—a]It is assumed that the first two words reproduce the name Israel (so rightly M. Gertner, p. 278), here intended to convey a particular meaning, but a meaning different from that of the preceding verse and of Gen 32.29 (EV 28). Following the pointing of MT the verb may be derived from the root שׂרר which has here a meaning akin to that in Judg 9.22 'and Abimelek ruled'[14]. The sense, then, is that God gained (note the *waw* consecutive) the ascendancy (see below on the subject of the verb) and the word is virtually synonymous (cf. Gertner, p. 278) with the following וַיֻּכָל. An alternative but similar interpretation is that of NEB which, with '(the divine angel) stood firm', reads וַיִּשַׁר[15] from the root שׁרר 'to be firm' (BDB p. 1057, col 1). The latter view presents the difficulty that elsewhere no verb from this root is attested.

Amongst the rabbinic commentators, ibn Ezra and Kimchi appear to assume a root שׂור 'to wrestle'[16] (a by-form of שׂרה?) for which, however, in biblical Hebrew, there is no evidence. Authorities which assume

[14] The pointing of MT need not, on this view, be emended (*contra* Gertner, וַיָּשַׂר); apart from the evidence of Judg 9.22, other double *ayin* verbs are attested with imperfects in *a*, e.g. מרר, רעע. Gertner's article, pp. 272ff, repays study, for in it there are important observations. His conclusions, however, are justly criticised by Rudolph as over-ingenious and as presenting a message so convoluted that Hosea's hearers would not have understood him. To speak of 'aggadic paraphrase' or 'prophetic midrash' and consequently to liken Hosea's utterance to those of later Haggada and Midrash is, as Rudolph also observes, wildly anachronistic.

[15] See Brockington, *ad loc.*

[16] Cf. dictionaries of modern Hebrew and that of Ben Yehudah.

(contrary to MT) a repetition of the verb שׂרה in the preceding verse, include the LXX and the Targum (see Text and Versions). For all these authorities, as for MT, the word אל is understood not as the noun אֵל 'God' but as the homonymous preposition אֶל 'to', 'unto'. The resulting sense 'he strove/wrestled unto the angel' (note b) hardly affords a reasonable sense even if it is assumed that אל replaces the more appropriate prepositions עם (Kimchi) or את in order to create an instance and interpretation of the proper name Israel/ישׂראל. The problem is not infrequently resolved by recourse to emendation (see Text and Versions).

A further difficulty occasioned by MT arises from the vexed question as to the subject of the verbs in the verse. Again, there has been considerable variety of interpretation. For example, ibn Ezra understands Jacob to be the subject of the verb וישׂר 'he wrestled', but the angel to be the subject of the following ויכל 'he prevailed' (*contra* Kimchi for whom Jacob is the subject of both verbs) as of the following 'he wept and implored his favour' (so Rashi and Kimchi)[17]. While it is true that the narrative of Gen 32.25ff (EV 24ff) presents a series of rapid changes of the subject (without benefit of noun or proper noun), and while it is conceivable that Hosea consciously reflects this phenomenon, it seems most unlikely that in so terse a statement changes of subject should be so frequent that they occur even within short phrases.

Such considerations prompt the following conclusions: first, the reading אל, widely attested and corroborated, is likely to be authentic; it represents, however, not the preposition אֶל (as in MT) but the noun אֵל 'God' (cf., e.g., Nyberg, Gertner, Wolff). Secondly, because there is no evidence of another (intervening) preposition, 'God' is likely to be the subject of the verb. Thirdly, the verb וישׂר, chosen for its similarity in form to שׂרה in the previous verse, carries a meaning akin to that of ויכל which follows (see note c). On מלאך 'angel', see note b below. For further considerations see the commentary.

[b]The word מלאך 'angel' is understood to be an (early) gloss interpreting (correctly) the word אל, cf. Gertner, pp. 277, 281, Holladay, p. 56, and Wolff. It should be noted that the word is not used elsewhere by Hosea and does not occur in Gen 32. Jacob's adversary at the Jabbok is there described as 'a man', 'a person' (אישׁ); that he was later very generally defined as an angel in Jewish tradition is, of course, understandable. NEB retains the reading, understanding the word to be in apposition to אל which it repoints אֵל (see Brockington); hence the rendering 'the divine angel'.

[17] It is possible that Rashi sees the angel as the subject of 'he wept' but Jacob as the subject of the following 'he implored favour'; for, in respect of the second verb, he cites 'I will not let you go unless you bless me'. On the other hand he states that the angel was trying to get away.

[c]ויכל Cf., for the sense, Gen 32.26, 29 (EV 25, 28) and note a above. It is here assumed that God is the subject and that Hosea concludes that he was the ultimate victor.

[d]For Rashi, ibn Ezra and Kimchi the angel is the subject of these verbs. It is more likely, however, that Jacob is the subject (as in v. 4) and that his weeping supplication is the result of God's gaining the ascendancy, cf., with Jerome, Gen 32.27 (EV 26) and Jacob's statement 'I will not let you go unless you bless me'; cf. Wolff's similar argument.

[e—e]Lit. '... (who) at Bethel encountered ...'. The last two clauses of the verse, juxtaposed to what precedes them, are understood to constitute short relative clauses without אשר (GK 155f–m). The antecedent is the pronominal suffix in לו 'to him', i.e. God. This interpretation has the merit that, first, it accounts for the two imperfect verbal forms which, following perfect tenses, are otherwise difficult to explain[18]. The imperfects are thus frequentative (see ibn Ezra) and refer to Yahweh's encounters with Jacob at Bethel and to the promises made both to him and to the nation (note f) of which he was the eponymous ancestor. Secondly, it forms a coherent and satisfactory way of understanding the words of v. 6 in which Yahweh of Hosts is solemnly identified as the God who revealed himself to Jacob (cf. the Targum's rendering of ימצאנו in the present verse) and to the nation at Bethel.

[f]So MT עמנו. Modern commentators have very commonly emended the text so as to read 'with him', appealing to certain LXX traditions and to the Peshiṭta (see Text and Versions below). Recognition of the force of the imperfects within relative clauses in v. 5b (note e) facilitates the view that the *difficilior lectio* of MT is authentic. For a similar figure of speech involving שם and a change to the first person plural ('we') cf., with Rosenmüller, Ps 66.6. Morag (p. 491) thinks that עמנו represents a dialectal form of the third masculine singular suffix, cf. Dahood's view; see Text and Versions.

If Jacob, the ancestor of the state, had manifested from birth the traits of ruthless ambition, the adversary whom he confronted in his prime proved himself to have the mastery. Hosea, having recalled the traditional interpretation of the name Israel (see on v. 4 above) now spells out another interpretation of it and one more likely to be in accord with what we now suppose to be its meaning[19]. Prefaced by *waw* consecutive 'Israel' indicates that God gained the ascendancy (note a—a); it was he who

[18] Rudolph argues in the opposite sense: 5b is quite distinct from 5a and introduces a new reference, this time to Gen 28.11ff. The imperfects are, then, of a sort with the historic present of lively narrative.

[19] Cf. BDB and KB[3] *ad locc.* Perhaps 'Let El persist, prove himself master', etc?

'prevailed' (note c). In Gen 32.26 (EV 25) it is stated that Jacob's adversary could not initially 'prevail' and then, in interpreting the name Israel, that Jacob had 'gained the mastery (שׂרית)' with God and men (32.29, EV 28) and 'prevailed (ותוכל)'. Hosea boldly takes this term and predicates it not of Jacob but of God and, notwithstanding Gen 32.29, his interpretation matches the conclusion of the Genesis story whereby, at sunrise, with dislocated hip, Jacob limps away from the scene towards the inevitable meeting with Esau as 'an altered man' (so S. R. Driver *Genesis*, p. 297). Accordingly Hosea may be said to have re-interpreted the two words ישׂראל and יכל in such a way that, though he changes their import, he does no violence whatever to the tradition preserved in Gen 32.

Nor, indeed, does Hosea's statement that Jacob (note d) wept and implored the favour of his mysterious adversary. Though neither of the verbs is found in Gen 32 they accord well both with Hosea's particular definition of the divine ascendancy and also with Gen 32.27 (EV 26), i.e. Jacob's insistence that, following his incapacity, he should yet receive God's blessing (so already Jerome and Rashi). Whether Hosea relies in this respect upon a tradition distinct from that which has come down to us in Gen 32 is a matter for speculation (cf. Rudolph). For present purposes, however, it is sufficient to note the congruity between Hosea's terse formulation and the account of Gen 32. W. L. Holladay, pp. 57ff, has proposed a different solution, preferring to see in the weeping and supplication a reference to Jacob's dealings with Esau in Gen 33 (see vv. 4 and 9f). Accordingly Hosea's words are marked by chiasmus and 'he wept and entreated his favour' refer back to the opening words of v. 4 'in the womb he supplanted him'. The theory is ingenious rather than convincing; for, as Rudolph justly observes, Hosea's hearers would have been hard pressed to follow so convoluted a saying. Holladay's reasoning may point to consciousness on Hosea's part that the incident at the Jabbok was connected with Jacob's need to be reconciled with his brother[20]. Yet, as S. R. Driver properly emphasises, in Genesis 'God is Jacob's real antagonist, not Esau; it is God whom his sins have offended'.

For Hosea, the adversary whom Jacob is constrained to entreat with tears is none other than the God who (note e), at Bethel, encountered[21] Jacob and vouchsafed to him the promise that he and his numerous descendants would return to occupy the land

[20] The point was seen by Rashi who states that the angel was the guardian of Esau and was stirring Jacob's conscience in respect of the stolen birth-right.

[21] For *mṣ'* with connotations of election, cf., with Wolff, 9.10.

(Gen 28.13ff) and who reiterated that promise in the course of a second appearance (Gen 35.1ff)[22]. In such encounters (note e) this God revealed himself to be Yahweh, the God of Hosts (see v. 6 below), the God of the nation whose ancestor was Jacob. Yahweh's encounter with and revelation of his promises to the patriarch are, then, naturally defined as extending to the patriarch's descendants (so Jerome, cf. Saadya as quoted by Kimchi, and Mays) and thus Hosea affirms that 'there (in Bethel) he spoke with us' (note f). In accordance with his intention the prophet is clearly concerned not to rehearse the Jacob saga for its own sake but to use it in his assessment of the nation's present predicament. In short he is at pains to emphasise that the God who prevailed over Jacob, correcting him with judgement, was the same Yahweh who graciously bestowed his promises upon the patriarch and his descendants.

The last two clauses of the verse, then, belong with what follows in v. 6, and constitute the identification (crucially important to Hosea) of the adversary who disciplined the wayward Jacob and Yahweh, the gracious God who made the promises at Bethel. Where the contemporary nation is concerned Hosea is at pains to convey the analogous truth, *viz.* that the God who forcefully prevails over an Ephraim which has provoked him with its wilful greed and selfish wickedness is none other than the gracious God who desires to implement those ancient promises. 'With us', then, constitutes the point at which Hosea's rehearsing of the story of Jacob begins to be applied to contemporary Ephraim (cf. Rashi's comments on v. 6, noted below).

It seems clear that Bethel in this verse is viewed favourably by Hosea as the site of Yahweh's revelation of himself to the patriarch. Accordingly, and in this connection, it lives up to its name as the 'House of God' (Gen 28.17, so ibn Ezra). Elsewhere (4.15; 5.8; 10.5; cf. 10.8) Hosea, following Amos, characterised the site as Bethaven 'House of wickedness', in recognition of the idolatry that came to be associated with the national shrine (for the LXX, see Text and Versions).

Text and Versions

וישׂר LXX καὶ ἐνίσχυσεν (as in v. 4, Aq.); Aq., Theod. καὶ κατώρθωσε (as in v. 4; see further Ziegler *Bei.*, p. 360); Symm. κατεδυνάστευσε 'he

22 *Contra* Rudolph (cf. Mays) who supposes that the reference, quite separate from what precedes it, is solely to Gen 28.

got control', cf. Vulg. *et invaluit* and Pesh. *w'tmṣy*; Targ. ואתרברב (as in v. 4). Many commentators assume (cf. ibn Ezra and Kimchi) a form from a √שׂור, a by-form of √שׂרה (GK 72t).

אל מלאך LXX μετὰ ἀγγέλου 'with an angel'; Aq., Theod. μετὰ θεοῦ 'with God'; Symm. τὸν ἄγγελον 'the angel'; Vulg. *ad angelum* 'to the angel'; Pesh. *ḥyl ml'k'* 'power over the angel', cf. Targ. עם מלאכא 'with the angel'; אל → את (e.g. Wellhausen, Oettli, Marti, Harper, cf. *BHS*); → עם אלהים (Borbone).

ויכל Pesh. omits; on the form in MT, cf. GK 53u and 69r.

בכה ויתחנן LXX ([Luc] excepted) plural verbs, = בכו ויתחננו (Vollers); Pesh. *wb''* for both words, omitting בכה, cf. Targ. ובעא; Rudolph accounts for the omission of *bk'* in Pesh. as an inner-Syriac corruption in view of the similar *wb''* which immediately follows.

לו LXX μου = ? לִי; the reading, with the preceding, excludes Jacob as the subject of the weeping supplication (cf. Rudolph).

בית־אל LXX ἐν τῷ οἴκῳ Ὢν = בית־און, assimilating the reading to 4.15; 5.8; 10.5, 8 (Grätz, Wolff, cf. Rudolph); Ziegler, p. 130, argues that און is the original reading on the grounds that otherwise LXX would have transcribed βαιθηλ as frequently elsewhere. LXX[A]... οἴκῳ μου, cf. Tertullian *Adversus Marcionem*, 4, 39 (*in templo meo*) and Ziegler, p. 129.

ימצאנו ימצאוני 1 Kennicott MS, cf. LXX εὕροσάν με, 'they found me'; Aq., Symm., Theod., Vulg., Pesh., Targ., third singular suffix. Targ. אתגלי עלוהי 'he revealed himself to him' (cf. Cathcart, p. 56 n. 10).

עמנו LXX πρὸς αὐτόν (αὐτούς B-V, OL[S]), = עמהם (Vollers); Vulg. *nobiscum*, cf. MT; Pesh. *'mh* (cf. LXX[A Luc] πρὸς αὐτόν → עִמּוֹ (e.g. Wellhausen, Marti, Harper, *BHS*, Wolff, Rudolph, NEB *et al.*); M. Dahood, *Ugaritic-Hebrew Philology* (Rome, 1965), p. 32, has suggested that MT conceals עִמֶּנּוּ 'with him'; cf. Morag's assessment in note f above.

12.6 **Truly[a] Yahweh, the God of Hosts[b], Yahweh is his name[c].**

[a]Cf. BDB p. 253, col 2. The force of *waw* here serves 'to introduce an appeal to a fact *confirmatory*' of the identification made by the relative clause of the preceding verse (see there note e). Since the phrase serves to confirm an identification already made, 'God of Hosts' is unlikely to be the predicate of Yahweh (first occurrence) but to be in apposition (*contra* Rudolph).

[b]The familiar Sabaoth, cf. Isa 6.3 and Gen 2.1. The traditional rendering is here retained. For more recent literature and the various theories concerning its form and meaning, see KB[3], pp. 934f.

[c] זכר Lit. 'remembrance'; the memorial by which one is remembered, hence 'name', cf. BDB p. 271, col 1 (2 a); cf. Amos 4.13; 5.8; 9.6 where שמו 'his name' occurs in a parallel formulation. Pss 102.13; 135.13 suggest that the phrase is liturgical in origin.

The God who encountered Jacob at Bethel and who there spoke through him to the nation, is here solemnly identified by Hosea as Yahweh, the God of Hosts, the mighty transcendent Lord 'of the celestial sphere of the stars in the heavens' (Kimchi). Hitherto in this section the prophet has made use of the old traditions (not so different from those in the present book of Genesis) of the intimate, if mysterious, contacts between God and the patriarch. He has been at pains to suggest that the vicissitudes of that relationship are parallel to and archetypal of the relationship between Ephraim and the God whose mighty power controlled and informed the historical situation in which the nation found itself. Something of the same point is made by Kimchi who notes that El Shaddai or Elohim (the names by which God revealed himself to Jacob) depict a God who is immanent in the lives of his people, while the name Yahweh defines a transcendent, holy God necessarily insistent upon the nation's obedience to the moral law of his creation.

Such considerations, together with the assessment of the phrase 'and there spoke with us' (v. 5), suggest that the verse, following the prophet's rehearsal of the paradigm of Jacob, forms the opening of his urgent appeal to the nation to learn the lesson of that paradigm. The appeal (see v. 7) is couched in terms which consciously reflect the words of the ancient promise to Jacob at Bethel (Gen 28.15, cf. and contrast the comments of Hitzig and Rudolph). Specific and solemn mention of Yahweh in his full name and title serves dramatically to confirm the identification already suggested less specifically in the previous verse (note e) and to proclaim the weight of the authority behind the prophet's appeal. It is these two elements which prompt Hosea to speak of Yahweh in the third person, deliberately repeating the name for emphasis, rather than resorting to the expedient of divine speech (cf. Rudolph).

In these circumstances the older view (e.g. Wellhausen, Volz and, more recently, Wolff) that the verse is a late gloss or inserted doxology is discounted[23]. While it is true that this is the only occasion that Hosea makes use of the title and that it is

23 So (cf. Ackroyd, pp. 256ff) the interpretation of P. A. H. de Boer *NThT* 1 (1946/47), p. 163; C. W. Reines *JJS* 2 (1950/51), p. 156 and H. L. Ginsberg *JBL* 80 (1961), pp. 343ff.

possible that 'doxological insertions' are to be found in Amos (so Wolff), the nature and structure of the piece as here construed are consistent with the view that the verse is genuine. Certainly, in the context, Hosea's solemn rehearsal of the divine name and title allows the possibility that he is interpreting the tetragrammaton in terms of God's intervention in Israel's history (cf. on 1.9 above) and that he is referring to the moral responsibilities of the nation which derive from it (cf. and contrast Rudolph who supposes that for Hosea the name here denotes 'He will cause', 'make to happen').

The verse, so interpreted, may constitute particular evidence from the eighth century BC (cf. Isa 6.3) for what has been described as the prophetic preference for the title 'Yahweh (God) of Hosts'. Von Rad has suggested that the title had its origins in Shiloh in the eleventh century BC and that it is closely connected with the Ark, the tribal league and cultic festivals of covenant renewal[24]. The particular notion of covenant renewal as an early institution connected with a tribal league or amphictyony is now questioned by such recent treatments of the subject as those of Perlitt and Nicholson; see *GP* pp. 55 and 85f; for the relevant literature on the subject, *GP* p. 55. Nicholson is disposed to the view that the eighth-century prophets and, in particular, Hosea were instrumental in establishing the definitive notion of a covenant relationship between Yahweh and Israel. In essence this means that if Yahweh had appropriated Israel as his own, then Israel was commanded to live in exclusive allegiance and total commitment to him (Nicholson, p. 209). Whatever the solution to the fundamental question of the origin of the covenant (cf. on 6.7, 8.1), it may be suggested that use of the traditions of Jacob's dealings with God as a paradigm of Ephraim's relationship with 'Yahweh, the God of Hosts' was an important contribution to the developing understanding of the notion of covenant. The word itself is not, of course, used; yet the God of the Jabbok and of Bethel had, to adapt Nicholson's words, 'appropriated Jacob as his own'. The consequence, at times painful, was that Jacob was tamed into a commitment and allegiance characterised by the distinct requirements of moral integrity. By identifying Jacob's God with Yahweh, the God of Hosts, Hosea depicts a God who claims the allegiance of Jacob's descendants and who requires of them commitment to justice and moral integrity (so essentially Rashi). Such a definition points forward to what was to become in its fullness the Deuteronomic theology of Covenant.

[24] *Theologie* 1, pp. 27f; *Theology* 1, pp. 18f.

Further, whatever is the solution to the vexed problems of the origins[25] of the title 'Yahweh, the God of Hosts', Hosea's use of it here constitutes the means by which, somewhat like JE in the Pentateuch, he is able to define Yahweh as the great God who controlled contemporary history but yet whose actions could be discerned in the lives of the patriarchal ancestors of the nation[26].

For the suggestion that 6a contains an allusion to Exod 12.41 ('hosts') and 6b to Exod 3.15 (*zeker*) see Gertner, p. 279; his view is challenged (on widely different grounds) by both Wolff and Rudolph.

Text and Versions

יהוה זכרו LXX ἔσται μνημόσυνον αὐτοῦ '(the Lord God the almighty) will be his memorial' interprets the second occurrence of the tetragrammaton as יִהְיֶה; Pesh. *'tdkrh* and Theod. ἐμνήσθη take זכרו as a third masculine singular verbal form with (Pesh.) third masculine singular suffix.

12.7 **For your part[a] you shall return[b] through the help[c] of your God. Observe goodness[d] and justice[e] and look[f] to your God continually.**

[a]The second masculine singular pronoun, prefaced with the conjunction *waw*, is emphatic and introduces the perspective of Ephraim/Israel as the person addressed (cf. the frequent ואני in the Psalms).

[b]The verb תשוב is imperfect referring to the future and expresses a promise. In the phrases that follow, however, imperatives are used and such (or a jussive תשב) would be required for the sense suggested by, e.g., Harper, 'you must/should return'.

[c]*Beth instrumenti*, cf. 12.14; Rashi, ibn Ezra and Kimchi (so AV, RV) understand the preposition in the sense 'to', detecting in the verb the notion of repentance. However, Rashi and ibn Ezra seem also to have detected *beth instrumenti* for they speak of God as a helper in the process of repentance and restoration. Kimchi compares the verb with the expression 'in returning (בשובה) and rest you will be saved' (Isa 30.15) thereby suggesting that turning to God alone affords sanity and peace (cf. also Qyl).

[25] See further O. Eissfeldt 'Jahwe Zebaoth' in *Miscellanea academica Berolinensia* II 2, Berlin, 1950, pp. 128ff, reprinted in *KS* 3, pp. 103–123; B. N. Wambucq, *L'épithète divine Jahvé Sebaoth* (Bruges, 1947).

[26] cf. Alt *KS* 1, pp. 62f; ET, pp. 61f.

[d]חסד, see 2.21; 4.1; 6.4, 6.

[e]משפט, see on 2.21; 5.1, 11; 6.5; 10.4.

[f]The *Piel* of the verb קוה, generally rendered 'hope', implies anticipation and expectancy, cf. Isa 5.2, 4 for instances in respect of viticulture. The cognate noun קו 'stretched line', 'rope' suggests the notion of tension[27] and consequently the attitude required is akin to that described in Rom 8.24f where hope is defined in terms of disciplined patience.

The verse is composed of a promise and an exhortation and it marks the first climax of the prophet's use of the paradigm of Jacob. The promise reflects that of Gen 28.15 'I will bring you back to this land' (*Hiphil* of *šwb*; cf. Gen 28.21 for the *Qal*), where Yahweh speaks to Jacob. Here 'you' (note a) refers collectively to the descendants of Jacob (so Kimchi) but they are so addressed by allusion to the original promise made to Jacob at Bethel (cf. the device 'and there spoke with us' in v. 5). Since in this verse Hosea, not Yahweh, is manifestly the speaker, God is referred to in the third person and the prophet continues, by the use of imperatives, to exhort the contemporary nation to responsible behaviour.

The promise of Gen 28.15 assures Jacob that God will eventually lead him back to the land from his flight to Paddan-aram undertaken in the face of Esau's fury. Since there (in Genesis) God is the agent of Jacob's return, here return is promised 'through the help of God' (note c). No doubt the return promised to the contemporary nation suggested the restoration of Ephraim/Israel to the land following the deprivations by Tiglath-pileser III in 733 BC (see on v. 12) and in the face of the obvious threat of more such deprivations following Hoshea's revolt of *c.* 725 BC. Yet the word *šwb* (and its cognate nouns) clearly denotes repentance for Hosea, i.e. turning to God in penitence and trust (see on 6.1; 7.16; 11.5, 7). Such a sense is detected here by Rashi, ibn Ezra and Kimchi and it prompts them to see a double sense in the preposition *b*, *viz.* return to God in repentance, achieved through his all-sufficient help.

In his exhortation Hosea addresses the nation with two second person singular imperatives. As in the preceding promise, the device enables him to allude to the history of Jacob. For the latter, by his action in stealing Esau's birthright, had ruptured not simply the relationship of love and trust within the family group

[27] So, e.g., Wolff. See further P. A. H. de Boer 'Étude sur le sens de la racine qwh' *OTS* 10 (1954), pp. 225ff and J. van der Ploeg *RB* 61 (1954), pp. 481ff. C. Westermann *ThV* 4 (1952), p. 57, n. 69, concludes that this verse is not authentic; his arguments are met by Wolff.

(on *ḥsd*, note d) but had also transgressed the laws by which society was justly ordered (*mšpṭ*, note e, cf. Rudolph). Just as Jacob, chastened by God, was led to forswear such behaviour and then to rely in trust upon his gracious promise, so the nation is urged at this the decisive hour to turn in penitence to the observance of common decency and justice and, in so doing, to wait with tense expectancy (note f) for the gracious and providential intervention of the sole author of such salvation.

Hosea seems to present the incidents of the history of Jacob in an order at variance with that of Genesis. Thus his reference to the divine promise at Bethel in Gen 28.15 marks the climax of a piece in which he has earlier referred to the all-important struggle at the Jabbok related in Gen 32. It is unlikely, however, that this consideration should prompt the conclusion that he is using a tradition at variance with that presented to us in Genesis. Rather he interprets the tradition with a prophetic emphasis on the ethical dimension and its relevance to the contemporary situation which was his concern. His critique of Jacob bears all the marks of balanced judgement and a fine sense of the consistency which characterises sound moral perception. Hosea's treatment of the Jacob saga, then, suggests that he allows himself the sort of freedom that he uses in connection with the Decalogue (cf. 4.2, so Rudolph) and that his piece represents 'a homiletic arrangement' (Gertner, p. 275), a 'sermon rather than an historical narrative'; so Vriezen *OTS* 1 (1942), p. 77. With Rudolph, I conclude that Hosea knew the story of Jacob in a form very similar to what has come down to us in Genesis (P material, of course, excluded).

Text and Versions

באלהיך LXX ἐν θεῷ σου, cf. MT; Vulg. *ad Deum tuum*; Pesh. *lwt 'lhk*, → אֱל־ א׳ (Oettli), לא׳ (Grätz); Targ. בפלחנא דאלהך 'in the service of thy God'; → בְּאֹהָלֶיךָ (*BHS*, cf. Marti), cf. v. 10, 'in/to thy tents (thou shalt dwell/return)'.

תשוב LXX ἐπιστρέψεις 'thou shalt turn', 'repent', cf. Vulg. *converteris*, and Pesh. *'tpny* (imperative); Targ. תתקף 'thou shalt be strong'; → תִּשָּׁבַע 'thou shalt swear' (Wellhausen); → תֵּשֵׁב 'thou shalt dwell' (Marti, cf. entry above).

קוה LXX ἔγγιζε 'draw near', a scribal mistake for ἔλπιζε, so Ziegler, cf. Borbone.

12.8 **Canaan[a] employs[b] fraudulent scales; he has an appetite[c] for extortion[d].**

[a]Here the name of the indigenous population with whom, following the exodus and entry into the land, Israel was to come into contact (cf. Qyl). It is unlikely that the word here denotes specifically 'merchants', 'traders' for which כנעני is generally used (e.g. Zech 14.21; Prov 31.24; Job 40.30). While Zeph 1.11, cf. Ezek 16.29; 17.4 suggest that כנען 'Canaan' was also capable of this meaning, the occurrence of Ephraim in the next verse indicates that the usage here is gentilic (cf. Rudolph). Isa 23.11 suggests that the Phoenician area of Tyre and Sidon originally bore the name Canaan[28].

[b]בידו Lit. 'in his hand'.

[c]אהב Cf. BDB p. 13, col 1 2, and 10.11 above.

[d]The verb עשק is used of unjust oppression and of oppression specifically by extortion; Lev 5.21, 23 (EV 6.2, 6); 19.13; Deut 24.14. Cf. 5.11.

Verses 8–10 constitute a unity and are concerned with Yahweh's indictment of the contemporary nation. The theme of ambitious ruthlessness, particularly in relation to the acquisition of wealth, links the piece with the prophet's review of the vicissitudes of Jacob (NB *mrmh* 'deceit', 'fraud', 'treachery' in this verse and cf. Gen 27.35). Rudolph argues that the section reflects historically the long period of prosperity under Jeroboam II and was therefore originally a separate and earlier prophecy in contrast to the residue of chapter 12 which, with its reference (v. 2) to alliances with Assyria and overtures to Egypt, is to be dated to Hoshea's reign. Yet retrospective review of Ephraim's relatively recent history accords well with the prophet's insistence that the nation shares the faults of its ancestor. That Hosea should attribute the nation's contemporary plight to the false values which it had entertained during the long and prosperous reign of Jeroboam II is understandable precisely for this reason. Mention of 'Canaan' (note a) constitutes a statement made by reference to history: the contemporary nation is judged to have been infected in recent years[29] with values and perceptions characterised by reference to the indigenous people with whom it came into

[28] See B. Maisler *BASOR* 102 (1946), pp. 7ff, Noth *Welt*, p. 45 (*World*, p. 52) and Lemche, pp. 135–139, 146 and 156.

[29] This understanding naturally renders unnecessary the supposition (e.g. Frey and Wolff) that a short period of prosperity, for which there is no evidence, occurred between the death of Jeroboam II and the fall of Samaria.

contact following the exodus[30]. If the identity of Israel is defined by reference to (the exodus from) Egypt (v. 10), then its sickness is defined by reference to Canaan. The word-play constituted by the juxtaposition of *b'lhyk tšwb* (7a) and *'wšybk b'hlym* (10b), which Rudolph perceives as the particular reason for the insertion of vv. 8–10 after v. 7, may equally or better be interpreted as a natural device used by the prophet the better to make his point and to be integral to the composition of the chapter as a whole.

Ephraim, then, is indicted for having appropriated the values and mores of Canaan, i.e. the ruthless sharp practices of the merchants for whom the name Canaan became virtually synonymous (note a). 'Fraudulent scales' as instruments of ruthless extortion are proverbial in the prophets and the Wisdom literature (e.g. Amos 8.5; Prov 11.1; 20.23; cf. Mic 6.11) and were prohibited in the Law (cf. Deut 25.13; Lev 19.36). The term used here (lit. 'scales of deceit') constitutes the opposite of correct or standard scales (*m'zny ṣdq*, Lev 19.36; Job 31.6; cf. Prov 16.11). In that Ephraim, like Canaan, had developed an appetite for (note c) extortion (note d), the nation's behaviour was the exact reverse of that required by the exhortation of the preceding verse 'Observe goodness and justice' (so Kimchi). As Mays rightly comments 'the old Jacob of greed and trickery lives on' in Hosea's contemporaries.

Text and Versions

כנען Targ. לא תהון כתגרין 'do not be like merchants'; → ככנעני(י) 'like Canaan/a merchant' (Sebök and Grätz), yet, as Rudolph rightly insists, there is then no expressed subject of the verse.

לעשק LXX καταδυναστεύειν 'to exploit', 'oppress'; Vulg. *calumniam* 'sharp practice'; Pesh. *wlmṭlm* 'and to oppress', 'defraud', cf. Targ. למינס (Cathcart, p. 57, n. a); → לְעַקֵּשׁ 'to pervert' (Buhl, Lippl, Weiser); לעקב 'to defraud' (Wellhausen, Marti, Harper, cf. *BHS*).

12.9 **[a]And Ephraim protests: certainly[a] I have become rich and come by[b] my[c] fortune[d]; [e]in respect of all my enterprises no man can detect in me[e] [f]the guilt which merits the description sin[f].**

[a—a]Lit. 'And (*sc.* in these circumstances) Ephraim said...'. The following

30 Cf., with Jerome, in reference to Jerusalem, Ezek 16.3 'An Amorite was your father: a Hittite your mother', and Isa 1.10 'Hear the word of the Lord, you rulers of Sodom'.

direct speech is introduced by the adverb אך which, while it clearly has an asserverative force, conveys also here a contrast with what precedes, cf. BDB p. 36, col 2 note. The verb 'protests', then, is used here *ad sensum*.

[b]מצאתי Lit. 'found', 'happened upon', i.e. with the connotation 'unexpectedly', cf. Gen 44.8 and BDB p. 593, col 2 3 a. The verb conveys the sense that Ephraim had attained wealth by an element of good fortune or, as Rudolph insists (see below), through divine favour. The rendering (e.g. NEB) 'I have made my fortune' suggests to me undue emphasis on personal endeavour (*contra* Kimchi, who cites Deut 8.17).

[c]לי i.e. *dativus commodi*, GK 119s.

[d]Cf. Job 20.10. און denotes both 'strength'/'power' (cf. v. 4) and 'wealth'/'fortune', cf., with Qyl the synonymous noun חיל. The Arabic cognate root *'wn* with meanings such as 'to enjoy a life of ease and plenty', 'to be at rest, at ease' illuminates the interpretation of the LXX which renders 'relief', 'respite' (see Text and Versions). Rashi quotes R. Simeon to the effect that the word denotes 'sovereignty', 'rights of ownership' (exercised over a slave) as in the talmudic usage (B. *Gittin* 43b; ET, p. 188 in *Nashim* IV) כתב עליו אונו. Accordingly the saying in 9a reflects the attitudes of Jeroboam I who, as an Ephraimite, claimed sovereignty over all Israel together with its wealth and reserves. Since, however, Rashi also provides a straightforward account of the word as 'strength in prosperity', R. Simeon's interpretation may be set aside.

[e—e]כל יגיעי 'all my enterprises' represents anacoluthon or else is to be defined as an accusative of respect. When it is construed as the subject of the verb no adequate sense is given to the latter (cf. Rudolph). Ibn Ezra and Kimchi rightly perceive that the subject of the verb ימצאו is the impersonal (third person) plural.

The noun יגיע denotes 'toil', 'labour' as well as the results, i.e. 'produce', 'wealth', 'what is acquired'; cf. Isa 45.14; 55.2. The English word 'enterprises' is used to convey the sense of the word in this particular context.

The verb ימצאו (cf. and contrast note b) denotes here 'detection', BDB p. 593, col 1 2 b. The following preposition לי is *dativus incommodi*, GK 119s. A variant interpretation of the phrase is offered by Rashi in reference to the Targum (Text and Versions). He detects in the verb מצא here, as in Num 11.22, the meaning 'to be sufficient' (ספק) and supposes accordingly that v. 9b represents the penitent conclusion to which Ephraim should have come. Thus, 'all my wealth will not be sufficient to atone for my guilt in that I have sinned', cf. the Peshiṭta in Text and Versions. A similar interpretation is offered by, e.g., Marti, Harper, RSV and NEB (though with emendation of the text by reference to the LXX, see below).

Rashi's interpretation is open to the objection that, though it invests מצא with a meaning which is possible (cf. Num 11.22; Judg 21.14; Jos 17.16; Zech 10.10 and BDB, KB[3] *ad locc.*), the resulting sense for the phrase is explicitly hypothetical and, therefore, unlikely. The interpretations based on the LXX are open to the same objection and also require that the phrase is a reproach uttered by Yahweh (through his prophet – so the Targum) rather than a continuation of Ephraim's protestation (cf. Wolff and Rudolph *contra*, e.g., Harper). ואנכי at the beginning of v. 10 clearly marks the beginning of Yahweh's speech.

f—f Lit. 'the guilt which (is) sin'; for the expression cf., with Kimchi, טוב אשר יפה i.e. what is 'good and proper' (Eccles 5.17, EV 18; so NEB). Kimchi understands the expression to mean that there could be detected in Ephraim neither guilt nor sin, where sin is less than guilt since it can result from inadvertence. Alternatively he suggests (by reference to Lev 22.14) that Ephraim's oppression of others was unwitting and hence the claim that he was not guilty of (conscious) sin against God. Since from Hosea's point of view the protestation represents rationalisation or special pleading, the expression is understood as a carefully formulated definition and hence the English rendering offered above (cf. Rudolph, Mays).

Hosea, following his indictment of the nation for adopting the values and mores of Canaan, furnishes an account of his contemporaries' reaction to that charge. The highly contrived nature of the speech with its use of word-play (*'wn* in a; *'wn* in b; *mṣ'* in both a and b) suggests that the formulation, though it accurately reflects the attitudes of contemporary Ephraim, is Hosea's. The protest (note a—a) smacks of rationalisation and special pleading. The affluence of the nation in recent history (see on v. 8) is to be attributed to good fortune rather than to any conscious resort to extortion. Indeed, as Rudolph insists, the protest comes close to a theological appraisal of the situation: the very fact of the nation's affluence points to divine approval with gracious oversight of minor breaches of propriety. Accordingly, there can be no possibility of anyone (note e—e) detecting in this matter guilt which merited the description of sin against Yahweh (note f—f).

From Hosea's point of view the nation's affluence during the long reign of Jeroboam II had contributed significantly to Ephraim's moral and, now, physical collapse. To his contemporaries Hosea's argument was defective since the earlier absence of divine intervention suggested that nothing had been done which merited the description of sin against Yahweh. Hosea's judgement is thus based upon a longer historical perspective and one which (cf. v. 10), in the name of his God, he takes back to the momentous events of the exodus. In conformity with the rest of the chapter, it seems likely that Hosea's use of words reflect the story of Jacob. In Gen 31.36ff (E) Jacob protests his innocence to Laban making use of the following words common to Hos 12.9: *mṣ'* 'detect' (v. 37, cf. vv. 32ff); *ḥṭ't* (v. 36); *ygy'* (v. 42). For Qyl, Ephraim's words are a parody of Jacob's protest of innocence. Yet Jacob was (unwittingly) guilty in Gen 31 of the specific crime with which he was charged and had, moreover, enriched himself considerably at Laban's expense before making off with his acquisition. If he was not actually guilty of any crimes, there can be no doubt that his actions were consistent with the crooked traits in his character, detectable since birth, which proved more than a match for the unattractive self-interest of Laban and which were not mitigated until the critical moment of confrontation at the Jabbok. Hosea's perception, then, is that the nation's preoccupation with the vigorous acquisition of wealth derives from a moral fault comparable with that of their eponymous ancestor and that, like it, it stands indicted by the God of the nation and its ancestor.

Text and Versions

און לי LXX ἀναψυχὴν ἐμαυτῷ 'respite for myself', see note d above; Aq. ἀνωφελὲς αὐτῷ 'what is unprofitable to him'; Vulg. *idolum mihi* '(I have found) an idol for myself' and Pesh. *ly k'b'* 'troubles' think of אָוֶן rather than אוֹן, cf. on v. 4 above; → הון לי (Grätz).

יגיעי LXX οἱ πόνοι αὐτοῦ 'his toils', → יגיעיו (Wellhausen, Grätz, Marti, Harper, RSV, NEB, Borbone, cf. *BHS*); Targ. prefaces this half of the verse with 'O prophet, say to them...'.

לא ימצאו LXX οὐχ εὑρεθήσονται 'will not be found', cf. Pesh. *l' spq'*, 'will not suffice', cf. Rashi's interpretation (note e—e above); Vulg. *non invenient* 'will not effect, devise; Targ. לא יתקיים '(all your riches) will not endure'.

לי עון LXX αὐτῷ δι' ἀδικίας 'for him by reason of the wrongs', = לו בעונים (Harper); Pesh. *ly lḥṭy'* 'for me for the sin', = לו לְעָוֹן (Harper), → לו לְעָוֹן (cf. Grätz, Marti, *BHS*); → לעון (Oettli, Marti); → לו על (Borbone).

אשר חטא LXX ἃς ἥμαρτεν 'which he has committed', → אשר חָטָא (Wellhausen, Grätz, Marti, Harper, RSV, NEB, cf. *BHS*, Borbone).

12.10 **But I am Yahweh your God from the [time of][a] the land of Egypt. Again I will make you dwell in tents [b]as in the days of the assembly[b].**

[a]The force of the preposition is likely to be virtually temporal, i.e. from the time of the exodus from the land of Egypt and thereafter, cf. 13.4 (note c). Two of the ancient versions (Peshiṭta and Targum) add a relative clause 'who brought you from' (see Text and Versions), but this is likely to represent a tendency to harmonise the text with the full Pentateuchal formula (e.g. Exod 13.14; Deut 6.12; 16.1), cf. Gelston, p. 173 and Cathcart, p. 57 n. 16[31].

[b—b]Considerable uncertainty has attended the translation of this phrase. מועד has the (connected) meanings 'appointed time' and hence 'assembly', 'meeting' as well as 'festival'. The latter sense is clearly correct in 9.5, *q.v.*, and it is reproduced here by three of the ancient versions (LXX, Vulgate and Peshiṭta, see Text and Versions). Amongst the rabbinic commentators, ibn Ezra and Kimchi interpret the phrase of the 'assembly of, or exodus from, Egypt', while Rashi speaks of the 'first assembly' 'when Jacob was an upright man and lived in tents' quoting Gen 25.27. Ibn Janāḥ (who does not discuss this verse) defines the word as having the primary meaning 'the gathering of people, when they meet one another'.

Modern versions and commentators have generally interpreted the phrase of 'the days of the festival(s)', seeing an allusion to Israel's dwelling in tents at them and particularly at the great autumnal festival (so, e.g., Jerome, Rosenmüller, Keil, Rudolph, Mays). For the exegetical possibilities based on this view of the phrase, see the commentary below.

The expression 'as in the days of (כימי)', however, suggests a reference to the past rather than to particular festal seasons of the present, cf., with Wolff, 2.5, 17 (EV 3, 15); 9.9; 10.9. Accordingly the Targum renders 'as in the days of old'. It seems likely, then, that Hosea's phrase denotes the assembly of Israel (*sc.* almost its constitution as a nation) brought about by the exodus from Egypt, as the rabbinic commentators cited above perceive. For Qyl (cf. AF) the expression is illuminated by the familiar Tabernacle or Tent of Meeting.

Over against his characterisation of Ephraim as having adopted the outlook and mores of Canaan (v. 8) and his perception of Ephraim's rationalisation of that charge (v. 9), Hosea proclaims the reality, consistency and sovereignty within the moral sphere of Israel's God. That sovereignty goes back beyond the time of the historical contact of Israel with Canaan to the exodus from

[31] For the possibility, unlikely in my view, that the clause fell out of the tradition behind MT by homoioteleuton, see Fuller, p. 349.

Egypt itself (cf. note a and 11.1). The thought is similarly expressed in Lev 18.2f where the formula[32] 'I am Yahweh your God' constitutes the ground for the specific rejection of Canaanite (and Egyptian) mores. The words of 10a are those of Yahweh himself (cf. 13.4) and are clearly recognisable as the introductory formula to the Decalogue and to other weighty statements of his moral requirements, most notably for this verse, those relating to business transactions and proper weights and balances (cf. Lev 19.35f). For Yahweh majestically to intone the formula suffices: the implications of his name and status as the nation's God ('thy God', second person singular suffix) are regarded by Hosea as sufficient for those to whom his words are directed. Their conduct is flawed and their rationalisation and self-justification shown to be what they are. Accordingly Yahweh will once again make the nation (again 'thee', second person singular suffix) dwell in tents, i.e. he will deprive them of the settled existence in the land with its opportunities for commercial affluence and will cause them to resort to the simpler life of the desert which they had known and experienced at the time of their creation and constitution as a nation following the exodus. This seems the most likely meaning of the phrase 'in the days of the assembly'. Certainly it agrees with the sentiments expressed more lyrically in 2.16 (EV 14), i.e. the necessity for Israel to return to the desert for re-education and reconstitution; *contra* Rudolph, cf. J. L. McKenzie *CBQ* 17 (1955), pp. 293f. If Hosea perceives this to be Yahweh's essential requirement, that does not preclude the possibility or even likelihood that he saw the mode by which it was to be effected in terms of the fate of exiles, deported by the Assyrians from their homes in the land (cf. on 2.16, EV 14; 9.6) and reduced to living in the less permanent shelter of tents.

Less likely is the supposition (see note b, where authorities are cited) that Hosea here makes reference to the Booths of the New Year Festival (Lev 23.39ff; Deut 31.10 and 1 Kgs 12.32). Such festive and voluntary manifestations are hardly in keeping with Hosea's solemn theme or with his manifest dislike of exuberant festivals of local or Canaanite origin. Cheyne and Rudolph, in answer to this objection, suppose that the reference to festive Booths is here ironic; thus 'to dwell in tents as in the days of festival' means that they will now be obliged to dwell in tents for reasons quite different from those associated with the festal occasions. The theory is implausible not least because Hosea is manifestly thinking of the exodus (v. 10a) and there is no

[32] Cf. Zimmerli *IBY/IAY*, pp. 24–40/14–28.

evidence whatsoever for any custom of dwelling in tents at commemorations of this event (cf. Wellhausen, Harper *et al.*)[33].

Yahweh's solemn announcement that the nation will have to revert to dwelling in tents is to be construed both in terms of punishment and of redemption[34] (cf. again the commentary on 2.16 above). For Kimchi *'d* 'again' implies that what Yahweh did in the past, now *mutatis mutandis* he will do in the immediate future. The element of punishment is perceived in the nation's (no doubt) painful reduction to the simple and unsophisticated life which she had known before in the days following the exodus. Yet, freed from the chains of her sins and vices, there is born the possibility for her to revert to the attitude of trustful dependence upon Yahweh and thus be led back purified to the land which he had given (so, essentially, Jerome, ibn Ezra and Kimchi)[35].

Text and Versions

מארץ LXX prefixes ἀνήγαγόν σε 'I led you up ...', cf. Pesh. with *d'sqtk* and Targ. דאפיקתך; → + העליתיך (Oort, Borbone). This verse is not preserved in the extant portions of 4QXII[c]; see further Fuller, pp. 347–349, 357.

כימי מועד LXX[AQ] καθὼς ἡμέρα (-ραι[B]) ἑορτῆς 'according to the day(s) of festival', cf. Vulg. *in diebus festivitatis*, Pesh. *'yk ywmt' d'd''d'*; Targ. כיומי קדם 'as in the days of old' interprets (rightly) MT; emendations based upon it are unnecessary, e.g. → קדם (Marti); עולם (Grätz); עד (Perles, *Analekten*); מֵעַד (NEB, cf. Brockington).

12.11 **I spoke continually[a] by[b] the prophets; it was I who promoted abundant[c] revelation[d]; by means of the prophets I revealed my mind[e].**

[a] *Waw* consecutive with perfect is understood to denote frequentative

[33] There are no reasons to postulate the existence of a tent festival in Hosea's time, *contra* H.-J. Kraus *Worship*, p. 132, *Gottesdienst*, pp. 156ff; cf. de Vaux *IAI*, p. 497, *IAT* 2, p. 400.

[34] Cf. G. Fohrer *ThZ* 11 (1955), p. 177 and R. Rendtdorff *ThLZ* 85 (1960), pp. 835f. On 12.10, see also R. Fuller *RB* 98 (1991), pp. 343–357.

[35] Rudolph's rejection of the notion that v. 10 contains an element of promised redemption forms part of his repudiation of the arguments of those scholars (e.g. Sellin, Mauchline, Frey) who wish to understand v. 11 as a promise for the future. With that repudiation there is no disagreement. Where v. 10 is concerned, however, it seems inconceivable that Yahweh's solemn pronouncement together with explicit mention of Egypt does not contain an element of hope.

action in the past, GK 112dd. See further in the commentary below.

[b]For על with the verb דבר, cf. 2.16. Wolff is right to see in the preposition the authority of the speaker. Since Yahweh commissions the prophet to speak, the force of the preposition is not dissimilar to ביד 'by means/agency of' which follows.

[c]הרביתי Lit. 'multiplied', 'increased'; the perfect tense is not inconsistent with the frequentative force of the other two verbs of the verse since, with the emphatic 'it was I', the verb expresses Yahweh's resolution to promote an abundant and on-going phenomenon (cf. Rudolph).

[d]חזון is normally rendered 'vision'. It means here God's disclosure of words which prophets are enabled to perceive (√חזה, cf. with Rudolph, Amos 1.1; Isa 2.1).

[e]The verb דמה I 'to be like', 'resemble' (BDB, pp. 197f) in the *Piel* means 'to liken', 'compare' but also 'to think', 'imagine', 'devise'. Ibn Janāḥ (who does not discuss this verse) finds in the adjectival form דומיה (Ps 65.2) the sense 'suited', 'adapted', 'fit', 'appropriate' (Arabic *l'yqt*). From the fundamental notion of comparison, then, there is to be detected here the sense of thought consisting of appropriate analogy and reasoning, devised for the purpose of instruction in regard to truth and morality. For Rashi (cf. ibn Ezra) the verb indicates that God revealed himself (נראיתי, cf. certain of the versions below) by various analogies or parables in order that his words might be readily received. Kimchi cites as a particular example of this mode of divine revelation the parable of the vineyard in Isa 5. The rendering offered above seeks to convey the overall sense, *viz.* that Yahweh, by means of the prophets (cf. Lev 10.11) has continually (cf. note a) revealed accurately and aptly his thinking or mind[36], a mind characterised by moral consistency[37].

A number of commentators refer to the homonymous root דמה II (BDB p. 198, col 2) and render 'through the prophets I shall destroy/have destroyed', comparing 4.5f; 10.7, 15 (e.g. Mays, cf. van Hoonacker in Text and Versions). The rendering hardly fits a context in which the subject is God's self-disclosure and, in any case, a *Piel* or causative form is not elsewhere attested (4.5 is dubious, see above and cf. G. R. Driver *Sepher Tur-Sinai*, ed. M. Haran and B. L. Luria, Jerusalem, 1960, p. 9).

If Israel's constitution as a nation under the sovereignty of Yahweh goes back to the exodus from Egypt, the implications of that constitution and sovereignty continued to be discernible in the work of a succession of prophets whose function had been to

36 The Syriac cognate noun *dmw* (see Payne Smith, *ad loc.*) is instructive in that it conveys the notions 'form', 'shape', and (?Platonic influence) 'archetype', 'idea'.

37 See further, A. R. Johnson *The Cultic Prophet*, p. 42 and KB^3 under דמה I.

perpetuate at his prompting Yahweh's words to his people. The context of the saying is the continuity perceived between Jacob's short-comings and those of his descendants in the contemporary nation. Rationalisation of its attitudes on the nation's part (v. 9) cannot obscure Yahweh's manifest persistence down the years in conveying to his people the realities of his moral nature and requirements. The prophets are those of the history of the Northern Kingdom (cf. on 6.5) whose work is continuous with that of him who was perceived to be the first, i.e. Moses (v. 14). By such prophets as Ahijah, Elijah and Amos, Yahweh spoke to his people; he himself facilitated their perception of his abundant verbal revelations (note d), cf. and contrast the statement of 1 Sam 3.1; indeed, it was by the agency of the prophets that he revealed his mind, i.e. they were empowered accurately to perceive and convey the coherent nature of his moral instruction (note e).

If the relationship between such sentiments and the pronouncement of v. 10a with its temporal connotation is reasonably clear, the relation to v. 10b and Yahweh's declaration that the nation will have to revert to dwelling in tents is less so. For some commentators (e.g. Weiser, cf. Sellin, Mauchline, Frey) the opening verb is rendered as a future, i.e. '(I will make you dwell in tents) and I will speak by the prophets...'. Yet this interpretation is inconsistent with the perfect form (*hrbyty*) which follows, whereas a frequentative understanding is not (note c). For Rudolph the solution is to be found in the rearrangement of the verses, and v. 11 (with frequentative interpretation) is understood to elucidate v. 14 after which it is properly placed. Yet the nature of prophetic speech hardly requires such rigorous insistence upon logical connections. If Hosea, in Yahweh's name, is disposed to emphasise his initial sovereignty at the exodus, that thought is capable of generating in his mind two divergent thoughts, i.e. the necessity for Israel again to dwell in tents as at the beginning, and then the theme of Yahweh's later persistence in communicating his will. Verse 10b is, then, likely to be something of an aside, even a species of cross-reference to an idea that the prophet has expressed elsewhere (2.16, EV 14). Verse 11, on the other hand, continues the fundamental theme of the passage.

Text and Versions

ודברתי LXX καὶ λαλήσω (future); Vulg. *et locutus sum*, cf. Pesh. *wmllt* and Targ. ומלילית (perfects).

על LXX πρός 'to'; Vulg. *super*, cf. MT; Pesh. and Targ. *'m*/עם; → אֶל (Borbone, with 2 Kennicott MSS).

חזון LXX ὁράσεις, cf. Pesh. *ḥzwny* '(my) visions' (plural); Vulg. *visionem*; Targ. נבואן 'prophecies', cf. Cathcart, p. 57, n. 18.

אדמה LXX ὡμοιώθην = אֲדַמֶּה 'I represented myself' (Vollers, cf. Isa 14.14), so Vulg. *adsimilatus sum* and Pesh. *'tdmyt* (Gelston, p. 123); → אֲדַמֶּה (Rudolph); Targ. שלחית 'I sent (word)'; → אֲדַמֵּם (van Hoonacker, see note e above); → אֵרָאֶה 'I will appear' (H. L. Ginsberg *JBL*, 80, 1961, p. 343, cf. Rashi, note e).

12.12 **If Gilead was characterised as evil[a], they [b]are now quite discredited[b]. If[c] at Gilgal they sacrificed bulls[d], then their altars have become like stone-heaps upon[e] the furrows of the fields[e].**

[a]Lit. 'If Gilead was wickedness/evil'. The phrase is understood to refer to the fuller expression of 6.8, *q.v.* (cf. Jerome).

[b—b]The inhabitants (lit.) 'have become a lie/treachery'; cf. again 6.8 and the occurrence there of the passive participle עקבה 'exposed as treacherous'. A verbal form of the root שוא occurs in 10.1.

[c]The sense of אם 'if' is understood to carry over into the second part of the verse.

[d]Such is the straightforward meaning of the MT and for an appraisal of the likely point of the statement, see the commentary below. For the evidence of the versions and proposed emendations, see Text and Versions.

[e—e]The phrase occurs also in 10.4. It is difficult to be certain about the force of the preposition על which is capable of a variety of meanings. In both verses, however, the context seems to imply something detrimental to the furrows and the success of the agricultural venture which, by metonymy, they represent (cf. Jerome's comments quoted at 10.4).

The verse serves to illuminate, by reference to particular events of contemporary history, the nature and effect of Yahweh's revelation of his will by means of prophetic activity (see on the previous verse). The places here mentioned indicate, then, the wicked acts perpetrated in them together with the manifest frustration of them at Yahweh's hands. The events at Gilead and Gilgal are respectively described elsewhere in 6.8 and 9.15 and the language of 12a suggests that the present verse constitutes a cross-reference to these other notices, rather as 10b refers to 2.16 (EV 14; see note a above).

According to the interpretation of 6.8 set out above, Gilead was a city associated with the beginnings of Pekah's revolt against Pekahiah in 736 BC (cf. 2 Kgs 15.25). Hosea makes his point in the form of a conditional sentence: if Gilead was at the time condemned (presumably by prophets such as Hosea himself) as evil and treacherous, subsequent history had vindicated that judgement (cf. the similar comments of ibn Ezra and Rashi). For, even within Pekah's short reign, the area of trans-Jordanian Gilead (see note a to 6.8) was totally in Assyrian hands[38] and, as Kimchi has it 'if Gilead began to do evil, so they were the first to be exiled'.

The second part of the verse with its reference to Gilgal is likely to have the same form as the first half (note c). We may suppose that the reference to the sacrifice of bulls (note d) constitutes not so much an attack upon idolatrous cult practice as an indication of cultic practices associated with the inauguration of a particular (this time, treacherous) enterprise. For notice of a similar action, but in respect of Elisha's mission, cf. 1 Kgs 19.21 and, further, perhaps Judg 6.25ff. Reference to 9.15 and to the interpretation of it there set out, suggests that Gilgal, being reasonably close to Adam/Damiyeh, may also have played a part in Pekah's revolt with its Gileadite connections (cf. Kimchi's note that Gilgal is a near neighbour of Gilead, the Jordan alone intervening).

A further possibility (cf. again on 9.15) is that the inauguration of Shallum's and/or of Menahem's short reigns in 747 BC was associated with sacrificial practices of the sort mentioned in 1 Sam 11.15 in connection with the inauguration at Gilgal of Saul's reign. Gilgal, then, may have become the site at which claimants to the throne of the Northern Kingdom thought it appropriate to invoke divine and human support for their ventures. At all events, the apodosis to this second conditional sentence reveals that the altars at which such ventures were solemnly initiated had been reduced to 'stone-heaps on the furrows of the fields', an impediment to the fertility of the land (note e). Thus the image of the devastated altars conveys forcibly the total failure of the ventures associated with them as well as their baleful effect.

Here it should be noted that the sentiments of 9.15, though they overlap with those of the present verse, are very different. There Gilgal, associated with the theme of Yahweh's banishing his people from their land, enables Hosea poignantly to allude to

38 Cf. Alt *KS* pp. 2, 202ff; the Assyrian province of *Gal-'a-za* was probably named after the administrative headquarters in the city of Gilead.

the original entry and possession of the land. The punishment itself may well have been triggered by the particular and contemporary misdeeds at Gilgal which Hosea had in mind. Here, then, is the point of contact between the two verses. For the rest the present verse is not concerned with the contrasting themes of Gilgal's significance set forth in 9.15; rather it depicts, in a straightforward way, how history has shown Yahweh's ability to bring to naught the contemporary misdeeds associated with Gilgal.

If the form and content of the verse have been correctly assessed, Rudolph's uncertainty as to whether we have here a further reference to the nation's disregard of the prophet's warnings concerning cultic impropriety or the beginning of an announcement of punishment for it is shown to be unfounded; for it is neither. Indeed, Rudolph's misunderstanding may be held to originate in the general and long-standing tradition amongst exegetes, both ancient and modern, that the verse is concerned specifically with cultic malpractice. Moreover, this has given rise to other consequential difficulties and proposals to meet them. Thus, since to sacrifice bulls is not in itself reprehensible, the assumption is made that the MT is in some way corrupt; that it conceals, e.g., notice of sacrifice at Gilgal to (rather than of)) bulls (*sc.* calves) or to demons (for details, see Text and Versions). Such considerations are hardly convincing not least because Gilgal is nowhere associated with calf worship and because the term *šwrym* (notwithstanding Ehrlich's appeal, *Miq.*, to Ps 106.20) is not used elsewhere to describe the notorious calves of Bethel and Dan[39].

The specific nature of the verse's references suggests that Hosea alludes to particular events known indeed to his hearers[40] rather than that he formulates a more general condemnation of sanctuaries associated with idolatrous malpractice. His use of language suggests a highly contrived saying which has the effect of drawing a contrast between the new-found innocence of the patriarch Jacob and the wickedness of his own contemporaries (cf. Qyl). For it was in the hill-country of Gilead that Jacob

[39] Emmerson (pp. 139–145) proceeds rather differently and reading אוֹן for MT's אָוֶן renders 'though Gilead was wealthy, they have become nothingness'. What was, then, originally a statement to the effect that wealth and costly sacrifices could do nothing to save Gilgal, has become in MT a (later) Judaean objection to the Gilgal sanctuary characterised as 'iniquitous' in contrast to Jerusalem.

[40] The evidence of the LXX and Targum which speak respectively of 'rulers' and 'oppressors' may preserve an echo of the real sense of the verse. See Text and Versions.

protested his innocence to Laban and, thereafter, beside the heap of stones of which Laban says 'this heap (*gl*) is witness (*'d*)', so interpreting the name Gilead (Gen 31.48), he ratified his covenant by eating (? a sacrificial meal, cf. S. R. Driver *Genesis*, *ad loc.*) with his kinsman (Gen 31.36–53). By contrast, Jacob's descendants, Hosea's contemporaries, had turned a name associated with peace and reconciliation into a symbol of treachery and wickedness. Closely associated with such treachery in Gilead is the lavish 'black mass' by which that treachery was ratified in Gilgal. By describing the altars of Gilgal as reduced to heaps (of stones), Hosea seeks to show that Gilgal shares radically with Gilead the effects of Yahweh's curse. The intricate word-play Gilead/Gilgal/*gallîm* should, in this connection, be noted.

Text and Versions

אם גלעד און LXX, cf. Theod., εἰ μὴ Γ. ἔστιν, אין for און; Vulg. *si G. idolum* 'if (in) G. is idolatry'; Pesh. *bgl'd k'b'* → בגלעד (Wellhausen, Nowack, Marti); אם → עם (*BH*, cf. *BHS*); גלעד → גַּל עַל (Rudolph); Targ. אם בגלעד הוו אנוסין 'If in Gilead were oppressors'; cf. Gelston, p. 187.

אך שוא היו LXX, Pesh., Vulg. (cf. Jerome's commentary), Targ., Aq. and Symm. take with what follows; שוא Pesh. *lsryqwt'* 'vanity', 'idol', cf. Targ. לטעון, *contra* Harper, who mistakenly supposes that it answers to שורים; cf. Gelston, p. 187; היו → עשׂו (Wellhausen, Marti, Harper).

בגלגל שורים זבחו LXX ἐν Γαλαάδ (cf. OL[S], *v.l.* Γαλγαλ) ἄρχοντες θυσιάζοντες 'rulers sacrificing in Gilead', = בגלגל שרים זבחים (Vollers); Vulg. *in Galgal bubus immolantes* 'in Gilgal those sacrificing to bulls/oxen', → לשורים (Grätz, Ehrlich *Miq.*, G. R. Driver[41]); → לשדים 'to demons' (Hitzig, Wellhausen, Marti, Harper, *BHS*); Pesh. *wbglgl' (lsryqwt') dbḥtwn twr'* 'and in Gilgal you sacrificed bulls (to idols)', cf. Targ. בבית גלגלא תורין (לטעון) דבחו 'in the House of Gilgal they sacrificed bulls (to idols)'. It seems clear that the notion of sacrifice to idols arises from MT's שוא.

מזבחותם Pesh. second masculine plural suffix.

גלים LXX χελῶναι 'tortoises', cf. Theod. on Eccles 12.6 and Nestle *ExpT* 14 (1902/3), p. 189. (Tortoises are attested, e.g., on the lower slopes of Mt Tabor).

[41] *JTS* 39 (1938), pp. 162f.

12.13 **Jacob fled to the district of Aram[a]. Israel toiled [b]to win a wife[b]. [c]To a wife he devoted himself[c].**

[a]The phrase שדה ארם occurs only here. It clearly answers to the expression Paddan-aram of Gen 25 and may be a Hebrew rendering of it (so BDB p. 804, col 2; cf. Harper). שדה may also have the force 'inheritance' (cf., with Rosenmüller, 2 Sam 9.7) and thus denote the inheritance of Aram, son of Shem (Gen 10.22), from whom the whole people and region of Syria are named.

[b—b]באשה Lit. 'for a wife', *beth pretii.*

[c—c]ובאשה שמר, a further example of the dialectal character of Hosea's Hebrew. For a treatment of the word שמר, see Morag, pp. 502ff and the similar usage in 4.10f above. For שמר with *beth* cf. 2 Sam 18.12. The sense is 'to cleave to', 'to love', cf. the English usage of the marriage service in the Book of Common Prayer 'to keep thee only unto her'. Morag observes that the phrases 'Israel toiled to win a wife, to a wife he devoted himself' match precisely the statements of Gen 29.18 where the motifs of toil (עבד) and love (אהב) are explicitly combined. He argues that Hosea prefers the word שמר here because he is emphasising the beautiful and delicate nature of Jacob's love for Rachel. Elsewhere he uses the root אהב (other than when he describes Yahweh's love for Israel) specifically of physical desire (cf. 2.7, 9, 12, 14, 15; EV 5, 7, 10, 12, 13; 4.18; 8.9; 9.10). The inverted order of words in the phrase, with באשה in first place, suggests emphasis upon 'the woman' as the object of Jacob's great devotion and commitment.

It is likely that the ancient versions (the Targum explicitly so, see below) understood שמר to be used elliptically with the meaning 'to win a wife (again *beth pretii*) he kept sheep/the flock'. Certainly this is the view of Jerome and the rabbinic and modern commentators. Rosenmüller cites 1 Sam 17.20 as an example of שמר used absolutely in this sense. The interpretation, though manifestly of great antiquity, is less satisfactory than that of Morag. The latter has the advantage that, first, it accords with Gen 29.18 as with Hosea's use of the same verb in 4.10f and, secondly, that it avoids a sense which is repetitive and weak. Where 1 Sam 17.20 is concerned, unlike the present verse, the sense is clearly facilitated by the context and an explicit reference earlier in the verse to flocks.

The verse is understood (with Jerome and Rashi) to be an abrupt reversion to the theme of Jacob. Its very abruptness suggests that it marks a new emphasis, that a different lesson is to be taught on the basis of another aspect of the vicissitudes of the Patriarch. In vv. 4–7 the point and emphasis is upon Jacob's ruthless ambition and Yahweh's correction of him. Yahweh's discipline of Jacob is shown to have its place within the context of the promise made at Bethel, *viz.* that Jacob (and his descendants) would possess the land. Here the emphasis is upon Jacob's 'penance', i.e. his flight from the land of promise to far-off Paddan-aram as a necessary consequence (so Rashi and Mays) of his unscrupulous behaviour in relation to Esau. If Jacob fled to Paddan-aram, it was Israel (i.e. Jacob as touched and altered by Yahweh, cf. v. 5 and see below for the use of the name 'Israel' here) who devoted himself in love (note c) to a woman; it was Israel who served Laban to win as his wife the woman who was to be the mother of the nation. This single-minded love and his repeated efforts in the service of Laban to win Rachel as his wife form an important part of the redemptive process to which, through Yahweh's providence, he was subjected[42]. Indeed, the process was of a sort with (and anticipated) the decisive conflict at the Jabbok.

Here it should again be noted (cf. on v. 7 above) that Hosea makes free use of the traditional material concerning Jacob. Since his emphasis is upon the ethical dimension of the Jacob saga and its relevance to the contemporary situation, there need be no surprise that in this chapter the incident at the Jabbok (Gen 32) is mentioned before Jacob's sojourn with Laban in Syria (Gen 29). Indeed, Hosea's argument of v. 10 that the contemporary nation will have to undergo the penance (the purpose being both punitive and redemptive) of 'living again in tents' may have prompted the thought that Jacob had once been obliged to undergo a similar penance when he fled from the land of promise. That flight, under Yahweh's providence, was to furnish, in Rachel, an essential factor in the creation of the nation Israel. Again, Hosea's use of the name Israel in connection with the winning of Rachel is deliberate and has the effect of linking the Patriarch with his descendants (cf. Jerome) – descendants who, brought from Egypt by Yahweh and preserved by his care (v. 14), were to become Israel in its fulness.

Hosea's choice of words (again, note c) leaves no doubt that he regarded Jacob's love for and devotion to a woman as a critically important feature of the Patriarch's redemption under Yahweh's providence. The new-found attitude of unselfish devotion matches Yahweh's own gracious commitment to his people (NB the use of the root *šmr* in this verse of Jacob's devotion to Rachel and in the verse that follows of the preservation of his people); indeed it is seen as a personal,

42 Cf. Ackroyd's similar findings, p. 247; it is noteworthy that Ackroyd comes to such conclusions without the benefit of Morag's all-important and, in my view, correct assessment of the verb *šmr*. The rabbinic commentators are unanimous in seeing divine providence as the theme of the verse.

'sacramental' reflection of Yahweh's essential love for Israel. That this is Hosea's view of the matter is not, of course, surprising in the light of his own personal perceptions of the significance of marital love and devotion (see the Excursus on Hosea's marriage above).

Hosea is not disposed to spell out the implications for the contemporary nation of his insights into their ancestor's redemption. It is enough for him to delineate the mode of that redemption and thereby to suggest that an attitude of humility and faithful commitment is a fitting response to Yahweh's gracious initiative.

The interpretation offered here necessarily rests upon the view taken of the meaning of Hosea's words. Most modern commentators follow a different assessment of their meaning and hence they are led to see in the verse a reference to Jacob's continuing intransigence and wilful disregard of Yahweh's promptings (e.g. Wolff, Rudolph). In particular, Jacob's flight to Paddan-aram suggests the contemporary nation's reliance upon foreign alliances (so Wolff *contra* Rudolph) and his menial service, in keeping sheep for the purpose of winning a wife, serves as a model of the contemporary nation's predilection for sexual relationships within the cult, regarded indeed as more important than the proper worship of Yahweh[43]. According to this view, Hosea's words are ironical in tone and devised to indict the contemporary nation by reference to the shortcomings of their ancestor. It seems to me preferable, however, to see in vv.13f the hopeful themes of penitence and divine grace, themes which serve further to emphasise Hosea's urgent plea to his nation; see further on v. 14.

Text and Versions

ובאשה שמר LXX καὶ ἐν γυναικὶ ἐφυλάξατο, cf. Vulg. *et in uxore servavit* (cf. for ויעבד *et servivit*) and Pesh. *w'l 'py 'ntt' nṭr*, all 'and for a wife he kept watch'; Targ. ובאיתתא נטר ענא '... and for a wife he kept sheep', cf. Grätz who adds צאן to MT.

[43] Cf. Vriezen *OTS* 1 (1942), p. 76; cf. Wolff, Rudolph, Mays.

12.14 **And by[a] a prophet Yahweh brought Israel up from Egypt; and by[a] a prophet [Israel] was preserved.**

[a]The verse is closely bound to v. 13 by the repetition of the verb שמר (here in the *Niphal*) at its conclusion. Cf., with Morag, p. 502, the use of the same device in 8.7f (נבלע/יבלעהו). Similarly the two-fold use of the preposition *beth* echoes its two-fold use in v. 13 and, again, serves to link the verses indissolubly. The artistry consists in the variation of the theme of the verb (from *Qal* to *Niphal*) which allows related but different meanings in each verse. Similarly in regard to the use of the preposition ב; though it reflects the form of the preceding verse, it here is construed with a different verb (העלה) and another form of the same verb (נשמר), and so it has here the force of *beth instrumenti* (so ibn Ezra and Kimchi); נשמר should be compared with the usage of Ps 37.28 where נשמרו, the antithesis of נכרת, denotes preservation as opposed to annihilation (cf. Morag). In 2 Kgs 6.10 נשמר also denotes preservation and survival.

The verse is linked indissolubly with the preceding verse (see note a above). By the skilful use of the root *šmr* and by reproducing the two-fold occurrence of the preposition *beth*, Hosea seems to suggest that Yahweh's providential care of the nation ('Israel') through a prophet is of a sort with Jacob's ('Israel's') devotion to a woman for whom he toiled in order to win her as his wife. If mention of the Patriarch's devotion precedes that of Yahweh's decisive act of grace in creating the nation, that does not imply that Yahweh's action is derived from the example of Jacob. For as I have tried to show, though Jacob is the subject of the verbs of v. 13, the verse reflects the view that Yahweh's prevenient grace was at work in the vicissitudes of the Patriarch's life. If the repeated *b'šh* of v. 13 matches the repeated *bnby'* of v. 14, the prophet seems to suggest that particular human beings are chosen vessels of Yahweh's grace. Or, to define the matter from a grammatical standpoint, the clear emergence of *beth* in v. 14 as *instrumenti* must reflect backwards upon its initial use as *pretii* in v. 13, more particularly as the subject of v. 14 is Yahweh himself.

At all events, and in the light of the interpretation of *šmr* in v. 13 here adopted, it is mistaken to find in the two verses a sharp contrast between, on the one hand, Jacob's reprehensible behaviour and, on the other, Yahweh's powerful yet gracious action (*contra*, e.g., Lindblom *HLU*, p. 105 n., cf. Wolff, Rudolph and Mays). The connection between the two verses, achieved in the way outlined above (note a), points not to contrast of behaviour but rather to the essential consistency of the divine purpose (see further below).

The prophet by whom Yahweh brought Israel up from Egypt and by whom Israel was preserved is clearly Moses, just as in v. 13 the woman for whom Jacob toiled and to whom he devoted himself is clearly Rachel. Yahweh's preservation of Israel by the agency of Moses is presumably a general reference to his care during the forty years in the desert following the exodus (cf. ibn Ezra, Kimchi and Rosenmüller who compares Deut 8.3ff, 15f).

Other links between vv. 13 and 14 have been detected. Thus, Ackroyd (p. 247) suggests that 'Laban's imposition of servitude – like Pharaoh's treatment of Israel in Egypt – looks like the defeat of God's purposes. But it is not...'. To my mind, while Ackroyd is right to see in both verses the theme of divine providence, the emphasis is rather upon its mediation through human agency than upon an alleged common denominator of servitude (cf., from a very different standpoint, Rudolph's criticisms, p. 230 n. 24). Secondly, Qyl suggests that Hosea's words in the two verses constitute an allusion to Moses' flight to Midian prior to the exodus, similar in character to Jacob's flight to Paddan-aram; for both were employed in keeping sheep. Flight may just possibly be detected as a motif common to both references since, in Hosea's earlier statement (see v. 10), that is a fate which threatens the contemporary nation. Yet the idea smacks of over-interpretation not least because, on the view here adopted, the sense of the verb *šmr* is not correctly evaluated.

The interpretation of the verses as here set forth rests upon the prior conclusions concerning the meaning of Hosea's words. A number of modern scholars, on a different view of the meaning of the text of v. 13, are disposed to find in 14b a further instance of the contrast between Jacob's reprehensible behaviour and Yahweh's gracious action. Thus, Jacob's wilful preoccupation with keeping sheep to win a woman is contrasted with Moses' whole-hearted service of Yahweh in which he tends Yahweh's people specifically by the proclamation of the Law and of the Decalogue (cf. Wolff, Rudolph, Mays); accordingly 'the "ministry" and proclamation of divine law is placed in antithesis to the false "practices" of the sex rites' (Wolff) and the nation is urged to look 'to Yahweh of the exodus and not to the cult centres of patriarchal founding' (Mays). The repeated mention of 'a woman' in v. 13 and of 'a prophet' in v. 14 has prompted AF to detect in the former a reference to Jacob's two wives[44] and in

[44] Cf. Jerome who seems to think that the first woman is Rachel and the second Leah. Since he is concerned to set forth an allegory in which Rachel represents the Church and Leah the Synagogue, his views suggest over-interpretation.

the latter, following Albright[45], a reference to Moses and Elijah or, perhaps, Samuel. AF further suppose that the lines 'came to [Hosea] ready-made'. The theory is hardly convincing not least because, as AF themselves admit in respect of the two wives, 'Hosea does not extract any particular point from this fact'. Further, while AF allow (on, e.g., vv. 4f) that Hosea can deliberately reverse or alter received tradition, they are adamant that here he woodenly reproduces what he has received (vv. 13 and 14) even though 'they contain particulars which did not all apply to his purpose'. These arguments are unconvincing in themselves; they are the more so when their authors go on to suggest that in some part (v. 14) Hosea's purpose becomes clear, *viz.* to show Israel's continual hostility to the prophets and that he refers specifically to Elijah or Samuel as well as to Moses. On AF's view it is hard to envisage on Hosea's part a more clumsy or obscure mode of communication.

It is likely that this verse presents the oldest literary reference to Moses as a prophet and that Deut 18.15ff (cf. Deut 34.10) reflects the influence of Hosea's writing upon the Deuteronomic tradition; cf. Wolff and Rudolph. That Hosea should have coined this title for Moses is questionable (so Rudolph *contra* Wolff).

Text and Versions

ב(נביא) (first occurrence): LXX ἐν; Symm. διά; Vulg. *in*.
בנביא (both occurrences): Pesh. plural, 'prophets'.

12.15 **Ephraim [a]has displayed flagrant provocation[a]. His blood-guilt [b]will be evident upon him[b] and [c]his Lord will repay him the dishonour that he has done to him[c].**

a—a הכעיס ... תמרורים Lit. 'has given provocation in respect of conspicuousness'. The verb הכעיס (in the *Hiphil*) is used absolutely (i.e. without object) in 2 Kgs 21.6, cf. 1 Kgs 21.22. תמרורים is understood to be an abstract plural used adverbially (König, 332e, cf. 262f). Ibn Ezra defines the word as meaning 'openly' (בגלוי) for which he compares Jer 31.21 where the same word, parallel to ציונים 'sign-posts' appears to denote 'heaps of stones' (so ibn Janāḥ on מרר), erected beside a road as sign-posts because they are high and conspicuous (cf. Kimchi on Jer

45 *Samuel and the Beginnings of the Prophetic Movement* (Cincinnati, 1961), p. 9.

31.21)[46]. As an alternative Kimchi notes the possibility that the word is to be derived from the root מרר 'bitter' and denotes 'bitter vexation'; it is this interpretation that is followed by most modern commentators (cf., with Qyl, the phrases מספד תמרורים and בכי תמרורים 'bitter mourning/weeping' in Jer 6.26 and 31.15). For the evidence of the versions, see below. 'Open provocation' is preferred to 'bitter provocation' here on the grounds that the phrases which follow imply open, conspicuous retribution (see on b—b below).

b—b The verb יטוש (√נטש) is understood, with ibn Janāḥ (cf. the versions), to be used here intransitively with דמיו construed as its subject. For דמים (plural) construed with a singular verb, cf. Deut 19.10 and, especially, Ezek 18.13. Ibn Janāḥ, defines the meaning of the verb here by reference to the cognate noun נטישות 'tendrils' (of a vine, Isa 18.5) as spreading out. Accordingly the phrase means that 'his sins spread out over him and are (thus) manifest' (Arabic *wḫnn'h mntšr 'lyh ẓ'hr*). Ibn Ezra and Kimchi (the latter with God as the subject and blood-guilt as the object) compare 1 Sam 30.16 and the phrase והנה נטשים על פני כל הארץ 'behold they were spread out over all the land'; thus Kimchi defines the meaning of the word as 'spreading out' (התפשטות).

Most modern commentators follow Kimchi in understanding אדניו 'his Lord' in the third phrase of the verse as the (delayed) subject of יטוש with דמיו 'blood-guilt' as its object. The sense given to the verb is not that advocated by Kimchi, but rather 'to leave', 'let alone', 'abandon', 'forsake' (cf. BDB and KB[3]), and the phrase is rendered (e.g. Harper) 'his bloodshed he will leave upon him'. However, while such meanings are clearly attested for the verb נטש, they cannot be said to fit this particular context. For what is the force of abandoning, leaving guilt upon Ephraim? Ibn Janāḥ's definition of the matter has the merit that it accords well with other comparable phrases and in particular with the legal formula of Lev 20.9, 11, 12, 13, 16, 27[47]: 'His/their blood be upon him/them', cf. 2 Sam 1.16, the purpose of which is to convey the notion that 'his blood (i.e. the traces of the blood shed by him) is still upon him – as visible evidence of the deed he has done' (so Noth *Leviticus*, on Lev 20.9). It is the open, manifest nature of Ephraim's conviction that is expressed.

c—c וחרפתו ישיב לו אדניו Lit. 'his Lord will return his reproach to him'. The suffix of חרפתו refers to Ephraim (cf. 'his blood-guilt' above) and the word denotes the reproach or dishonour that the nation has done to 'his Lord'. For the verb ישיב, cf. v. 3 and 4.9 above.

[46] A further instance of the same root is found by ibn Janāḥ and ibn Ezra in Dan 11.11 where the verb is taken to mean that the king 'exalted himself' in rebellion. Kimchi's view that תמרורים means altars (cf. v. 12) in respect of which Ephraim provoked God is, perhaps, too specific (but see the commentary below). In that he thinks of altars because they were 'high and conspicuous' his etymological point is the same as that of the other rabbinic authorities cited.

[47] Cf. further H. Graf Reventlow *VT* 10 (1960), pp. 311–327.

The concluding verse of the chapter summarises the culpability of the contemporary nation. Thus the prophet brings himself back from his meditation upon the history of Jacob, its paradigms of personal morality and its message of discipline, correction and hope; he returns to a sober, factual estimate of the situation that obtains in the dark days of the reign of Hoshea. His nation has flagrantly (note a—a) provoked the anger (of God). The absence of any expressed object for the verbal expression 'displayed provocation' is attested elsewhere (note a—a) but has inclusive force; it is Yahweh, as well as the prophets through whom predominantly he acts (cf. vv. 11f), whom the nation had provoked to anger (cf. Rudolph). By his/their intervention, Ephraim will stand convicted manifestly and clearly (note b—b) of its murderous crimes. And he who is the Lord of the nation will cause and effect the repayment to it of the gross dishonour and reproach that he has suffered at its hands (note c—c), cf. v. 3 above. Thus the openness of the provocation is matched in all respects by the openness of the retribution. If the first phrase ('blood-guilt') is redolent of the juridical formula oft repeated in Lev 20, the latter phrase ('dishonour') conveys the sentiments expressed in 2 Sam 12.14 concerning the gross dishonour done to the divine name by David in his dealings with Uriah the Hittite (so Rosenmüller).

For Wolff the phrase 'will repay him' 'rounds off the sketch of the lawsuit speech'. While the phrases (especially 'blood-guilt') certainly reflect juridical language, they serve rather to depict the nature of God's reaction and intervention, and specifically through the agency of his prophets (cf. vv. 11f above). Thus, the nation's murderous behaviour has been noted by the nation's Lord and the nation's Lord will not tolerate the dishonouring of his name. Such sentiments are surely essentially theological in nature in that they seek to expound God's ways with Israel in the times of the prophet. To see in them exclusively the form and language of the lawsuit is restrictive and fails to do justice to the argument of the chapter as a whole with its emphasis on the role of the prophets.

It seems likely that the murderous behaviour ('blood-guilt') of Ephraim and the dishonouring of Yahweh's name refer specifically to the events associated with Gilead and Gilgal and known to Hosea's hearers (v. 12 above; so tentatively Rudolph). On this view of the matter the sense of the verse is much the same as that of v. 12; the Lordship of Yahweh (v. 15) is detected in his confounding the schemes associated with the two places mentioned (v. 12) and in his indictment of the nation which sanctioned them (v. 15). In that Kimchi detects in *tmrwrym* an allusion to the altars of v. 12, he may well preserve an accurate memory of the integral connection between the two verses and of Hosea's great artistry.

The notion of 'provocation' was to become a favourite with Deuteronomy, Jeremiah and the Deuteronomist (cf. Wolff).

Text and Versions

הכעיס Vulg. + *me*, → הכעיסני (e.g. Oettli).

תמרורים LXX καὶ παρώργισε, cf. Pesh. *wmrmr* 'and provoked to anger', → וַיְמָרְרֵהוּ (e.g. Oettli, cf. Borbone); Vulg. *in amaritudinibus suis* 'by his bitter deeds', cf. Jerome... *et amaritudine sua (me) amarum fecit esse, qui dulcis sum* ('... and by his bitter/harsh behaviour made me, who am kind, bitter/harsh'); Targ. מוספין למחטי 'they continue to sin'.

ודמיו All versions render with a singular noun; → ודמו (Borbone).

עליו יטוש LXX ἐπ' αὐτὸν ἐκχυθήσεται, cf. Pesh. *'lwhy nt'šd*, '(his blood) will be poured out on him' (cf. Gelston, pp. 167f); Vulg. *super eum veniet* '(his blood) will come upon him', cf. Targ. עלוהי יתוב '(the guilt of innocent blood which he shed) will return upon him'.

אדניו LXX without suffix.

ON THE ORDER OF VERSES IN CHAP. 12

The commentary above follows the received order of verses of chapter 12. The chapter is understood to consist of a meditation by the prophet upon the theme of the continuity between the nation's present guilt and that of its eponymous ancestor who was the object of Yahweh's redemptive discipline and correction. That theme is detected from the very beginning of the chapter where in v. 1, the redactional allusion to Judah removed, a reference to the nation of Ephraim as the 'House of Israel' allows the prophet at once (in the second part of the verse) to refer to the Patriarch who bore that name. Verse 2 characterises contemporary Ephraim's behaviour as deceitful and leads to verse 3, where notice is given of the inevitability of Yahweh's punishment. That said, the prophet is led to reflect (v. 4) on the paradigm of Jacob and his congenital ruthlessness and immorality which, under divine providence, was decisively corrected; a necessary prelude to the definitive (v. 6) promise to the same Jacob and his descendants (v. 5). Verse 7 contains the first exhortation to the nation to turn in penitence. Verses 8–10 return to the theme of Ephraim's (Jacob-like) guilt, now expressed in terms of the nation's economic ruthlessness with, again, notice of Yahweh's corrective intervention (v. 10). Verse 11 relates the mode by which Yahweh, through the prophets, had persistently kept to this task; v. 12 depicts a particular example of Yahweh's revelation of his all-powerful will in contemporary history. An abrupt return to the theme of Jacob (v. 13) allows the prophet to develop a related theme: Jacob's penance (i.e. his flight to Paddan-aram) became the occasion by which he was enabled to lose himself in unselfish love for and devotion to a woman, a love and devotion (v. 14) which reflects Yahweh's devoted love (mediated through Moses) for his people. In the final verse (15) the prophet returns to a factual statement of the contemporary situation: he implies that the precondition for any hope of redemption for the nation lies in open acknowledgement and recognition of its manifest culpability.

Since the days of Grätz, Oettli and Halévy there have been a number of attempts to rearrange the order of verses in accordance with what is perceived to be the chapter's correct, logical structure. Rearrangements that have been suggested include the following: Grätz: 1–11, 13, 15, 12, 14; Oettli: 1–5, 13f, 7, 6, 8–12, 15; Halévy: 1–10, 13, 11f, 14f; Harper: 1a, 2–4a, 8–11, 15, 12, the remaining verses being additions; Rudolph: 1–7, 13f, 11f, 15 and 8–10. The number and variety of such suggested rearrangements is very considerable and hence little confidence can be placed in them. It seems better to attempt to interpret the text as it is received and more particularly since it is possible to see in it a coherent structure and a consistent argument[48].

48 For different assessments of the structure of the chapter (as received), cf., e.g., Wolff and AF.

CHAPTER 13.1–14.1

THE FINAL RUPTURE

13.1 [a]When Ephraim spoke disruption[b] (he was then dominant[c] in Israel), he incurred guilt[a] through Baal and that was his undoing[d].

The first part of the verse constitutes one of the most difficult passages in Hosea's prophecies and the translation is offered without any strong conviction as to its accuracy. The fact remains that we have no clear indications as to the force of the words רתת and נשא as they occur in the verse and all attempts to resolve the problem are tentative and conjectural.

[a—a]The construction is akin to (but not identical with) that found in 7.1. The temporal clause is followed by the *waw* consecutive form ויאשם and the intervening phrase is thus judged parenthetical.

[b]The word רתת is a *hapax legomenon* in the bible. It occurs, however, in 1QH iv 33[1]. Ibn Janāḥ refers to Exod 15.15 where MT's רעד 'trembling' is rendered in the Targum by רתיתא. He seems to suppose that it is a by-form of the noun רטט (Jer 49.24) with the same meaning (so his entry under √רתת). Ibn Ezra states explicitly that the word is an Aramaism and has the meaning 'fear'. This view was clearly known to and adopted by the ancient versions (other than the LXX, see below) as well as by the majority of rabbinic and modern commentators[2]. On this interpretation the words are construed 'When Ephraim spoke (there was) trembling'. Accordingly Kimchi, for example, paraphrases 'before Ephraim sinned, fear of him subdued all the surrounding peoples, for, when he spoke, trembling seized his hearers'. This interpretation is perhaps that most widely adopted in modern times. The difficulty at once presents itself that the construction of the words is harsh, unparalleled and hence implausible (so, e.g., Nowack, Rudolph).

Ibn Janāḥ, in addition to what has been reported above, also states that the word is somewhat like Arabic *rtyt* with the meaning 'an ache', 'ailment', 'pain in the joints'. In his description of the noun רטט in Jer 49.24 he suggests that this is its proper meaning and that רתת in Hos 13.1 is like it. Unfortunately he does not explain the matter further or translate the phrase before us. However, if his philological assessment is correct, it may be suggested that רתת has a range of meanings similar to the well-known root עצב which denotes physical pain (Gen 3.16; Prov

[1] רעד ורתת אחזוני 'shaking and *rtt* have seized me'.

[2] So, e.g., BDB, p. 958; cf. Marti, Harper, Wolff, Mays.

10.22; 1 Chr 4.9) but also the pain, hurt or strife and disruption caused by words (e.g. Prov 10.10; 15.1)[3].

Amongst other attempts to explain the word by reference to Arabic, perhaps the most plausible is that of Ehrlich (*Miq.*; so, apparently independently, Rudolph) who compares Arabic *rtt* with the meaning 'to stammer' (cf. the noun *aratt*[un] 'stammerer')[4]. The resulting sense 'when Ephraim spoke haltingly' denotes childish imperfection of speech and thus the phrase is akin to 11.1 'when Israel was a child, I loved him'. Apart from the inherent uncertainty of this conjecture, the resulting sense is hardly convincing. For what is the force of the statement 'when Ephraim spoke as a small child, then was he a prince (נָשִׂא, see note c below) in Israel'? To refer to נזיר אחיו 'prince among brothers' (Gen 49.26, so Rudolph) is to raise further problems and uncertainties. Apart from this, the appeal to 11.1 is hardly convincing; for there the theme is Yahweh's loving dealings with his son (cf. 11.3f); there is no hint in the present verse of Yahweh's and Israel's early history.

Three scholars[5] have referred to Arabic *rtt* with the meaning 'prince', 'chief'[6]. The resulting sense either requires consequential emendations or produces what is virtually tautologous (so Rudolph). Yet the possibility arises that, if this view of רתת is correct, the words נשא הוא constitute a translational gloss (cf. 7.14ff; 8.13) which serves to explain the obscure word. Accordingly the line would be interpreted 'When Israel spoke (as) a *rtt* (gloss: it is/it means "a chief") in Israel, then he incurred guilt through Baal...'. Again, however, the construction is somewhat harsh and for רתת with the meaning 'prince' there is no evidence from ancient or rabbinic tradition. Such considerations suggest that the solution proposed on the basis of ibn Janāḥ's second explanation is preferable.

[c]נשא No satisfactory meaning can be attributed to this third masculine singular perfect *Qal* (construed with ב?) and accompanied by הוא 'he'. Rashi and ibn Ezra interpret the verb in a passive or reflexive sense 'he was exalted', 'exalted himself', i.e. as though נִשָּׂא (*Niphal*) was read. Kimchi retains the *Qal* form ('he lifted') and assumes ellipsis of 'his head'; thus he also supports the sense 'exaltation'. Another possibility, widely adopted, is that suggested by Sebök (cf. the Peshiṭta), who understands the word to be the familiar noun נָשִׂא/נָשִׂיא 'prince'. The occurrence of the pronoun הוא following נשא suggests the conclusions (1) that the latter is to be construed as a noun or participle and (2) that the phrase forms a parenthesis before the clause 'he incurred guilt' (see note a). On the view here adopted of רתת (note b), the participial form נֹשֵׂא is

3 Cf. Ewald, who conjectures that the word means 'alarm', 'uproar'.

4 Cf., perhaps, the NEB 'when the Ephraimites mumbled their prayers'. Nyberg interprets the stammering of a heathen oracle.

5 Zolli *RSO* 32 (1957), pp. 371ff; Hirschberg *VT* 11 (1961), p. 379; Guillaume II, p. 32; III, p. 10.

6 Cf. Lane 3 p. 1024, col 3: '*A chief in eminence*, or *nobility* and in *bounty*, or *gifts*'.

judged preferable and constitutes a reference to Ephraim's pre-eminence 'in Israel' following Jeroboam I's establishment of the Northern Kingdom. Accordingly the parenthetical phrase amounts to an explanation or expansion of what precedes it, i.e. Ephraim caused disruption in that (or because) he made himself at the time the dominant force in Israel. For a similar (but different) view to the effect that the words נָשָׂא הוּא are a parenthetical explanation (this time of רתת meaning 'prince'), see note b above.

[d]Lit. 'he died'. The usage suggests that Ephraim 'was accounted dead' (ibn Ezra) and that the strength of the kingdom was, as a consequence of the guilt incurred, terminally affected (cf. Rashi and Kimchi). The figure of speech is similar to that of 7.9 (so Qyl).

'Ephraim' here constitutes a reference to the beginning of the Northern Kingdom under Jeroboam I (so Jerome, Rashi, ibn Ezra and Kimchi). The verse clearly stands in contrast to v. 2 with its contemporary reference 'and now they sin yet more'. Accordingly Ephraim's 'speech' denotes the fundamental decision to proclaim the independence of the ten tribes from the united Israel of the Davidic monarchy (1 Kgs 12.16ff). Ephraim's policy and action, then, are exemplified in the person of its first king (cf. ibn Ezra and, with Wolff, 1 Kgs 11.26; 12.20). Ephraim's speech and intention were harmful and disruptive (note b) in the circumstances that he had become the dominant force (note c) within Israel as a whole. His bid for independence was, of course, reflected in the cultic dispositions which he felt constrained to make and, in particular, in the institution of the worship of bulls/calves in Bethel and Dan (1 Kgs 12.26ff). Whatever the precise form and significance of the calves[7], there can be no doubt that their introduction reflected a strong syncretistic element in the worship at these places of 'the god(s) who brought up Israel from Egypt' (cf. 1 Kgs 12.28). Such syncretism advanced apace under the dynasty of Omri, and Ahab is explicitly recorded as having founded a Baal temple in Samaria (1 Kgs 16.31f), an action representing, perhaps, an attempt to give equal rights to his Israelite and Canaanite subjects[8]. For further discussion of the significance of the bull/calf cult in the Northern Kingdom, see on 8.5ff above.

For Hosea this early confounding of Yahweh and Baal in cultic worship represents the decisive fault by which his nation incurred

[7] For assessments and literature, cf. Noth *History*, pp. 232f, (*GI*, pp. 212f) and Fohrer, pp. 132f (*Geschichte*, pp. 124f).

[8] So Fohrer p. 133 (*Ges*., p. 124).

the guilt[9] which was punishable by and led inexorably to its demise and death (note d). The verse represents an early expression of a point of view which was to assume paradigmatic importance in the work of the Deuteronomic historian; for him Jeroboam's sin, imitated by all subsequent kings of the Northern Kingdom, was the supreme and decisive act of folly and disloyalty to Yahweh. From Hosea's standpoint the nation's demise and death, though inevitable following the initial culpable fault, is a process which is evident in the history of his times. Again, the statement in 7.9 'Ephraim has become totally decrepit' (cf. 8.8f) witnesses to similar observations on the realities of the nation's predicament. The situation following 733 BC and the mauling of the nation at the hands of Tiglath-pileser III no doubt constituted the single greatest symptom of its terminal degeneration[10].

For the opinion, based upon a different understanding of the meaning of the words of v. 1a, that Hosea refers to Ephraim's early pre-eminence following Jacob's blessing (Gen 48) and in v. 1b to the early apostasy to Baal on the borders of the promised land (Num 25.1–9), see, e.g., Rudolph. Other commentators have suggested that Hosea sees the pre-eminence of Ephraim in relation to (the Ephraimite) Joshua (e.g., Wolff, cf. Josh 24.30) or within the period of the Judges (e.g. Harper, as one of these possiblities, cf. Judg 8.1f; 12.1). Apart from the prior question of the precise meaning of the words of the text, and indeed of what the correct reading is, it seems more likely that Hosea's concerns are with the immediate history of his nation rather than with the remote and obscure aspects of its tribal antecedent (cf. Wolff).

Text and Versions

כדבר LXX κατὰ τὸν λόγον, cf. Aq. κατὰ τὸ ῥῆμα 'according to the word/speech' (= כַּדָּבָר, Harper); Symm. ἐν τῷ λαλεῖν, cf. MT.

רתת LXX δικαιώματα '(self) justifications' (on which Jerome comments that he does not know what is intended); = חֻקֹּת, דָּתוֹת 'statutes', 'decrees' (Vollers); Symm. Theod. τρόμον 'trembling', cf. Aq. φρίκην; Pesh. *r't hw'* 'he was trembling', = רָתַת 'E. trembled' (Sebök), cf. Targ. רתיתא אחיד להון 'trembling seized them (i.e. nations)' and Vulg.

[9] For guilt involving punishment, cf., with Wolff, Zimmerli *Ezechiel* I, p. 508 (ET, I p. 456).

[10] For weakness, illness and oppression described as (symptoms of the prevalence of) death, see von Rad *Theology* I, pp. 387ff (*Theologie* I, pp. 385ff).

horror (invasit Israhel) 'trembling (invaded I.)'. Suggested emendations include: תּוֹרוֹת/תּוֹרָתִי 'my law/'laws' (cf. *BHS*); דַּעַת 'knowledge' (Oort).

נשא הוא LXX αὐτὸς ἔλαβεν '(Ephraim) himself undertook/assumed (justifications)'; Aq. ἔλαβεν αὐτός 'himself received (shivering)'; Vulg. *invasit*, see above; Pesh. *whw' rb'* 'and he was a great one' = נָשִׂיא הוּא (Sebök, cf. *BHS*); Targ. מתרברבין הוו 'those who were great'; → נָשָׂא (Oort, Marti *et al.*, cf. *BHS*), cf. note c above.

ויאשם LXX καὶ ἔθετο (αὐτὰ τῇ βάαλ) 'and he regarded (them – *sc.* ?justifications – to Baal)', → וַיְשִׂימֵם (Vollers).

וימת → וַיָּמֻתוּ מְתָיו 'his men died' (Rudolph).

13.2 **And now [a]they sin yet more[a]; they make[b] for themselves molten images[c] out of their silver, [d]idols in accordance with their skill[d]. It is all the work of craftsmen. Of them[e] they say[f]: [g]True worshippers[g] kiss calves.**

[a—a]The frequentative imperfect יוספו construed with לחטא and עתה clearly denotes the present time; the phrase thus constitutes a contrast with the preceding verse and its reference to Ephraim's initial idolatry, *contra* Rudolph, who, following Gesenius-Buhl, invests עתה with the meaning 'nevertheless' and suggests that either this is a case of *waw* consecutive and the imperfect, even though *waw* is separated from the verb by עתה (König, 386h), or the text should be emended to יָסְפוּ (perfect).

[b]See GK 111t for the use of the imperfect with *waw* consecutive (ויעשו) following an imperfect used in the sense of the present; cf. Hos 8.13 for another example.

[c]מסכה is a collective singular, cf. 2 Kgs 17.16.

[d—d]כתבונם עצבים Ibn Ezra and Kimchi record the opinion that תבונם is a (? dialectal) variant or shortened form (so Kimchi, cf. GK 91e) of תבונָתָם, which would be expected; for it they compare Ps 49.15 where צורם occurs for צוּרָתָם. Rashi (cf. Text and Versions below) supposes that the word represents תבניתם 'according to their shape' (cf. Oettli). The difficulty arises that Hosea nowhere speaks of idols in human form, but only of calf images (so, e.g., Marti, cf. Rudolph). The proposal to read כתבנית עצבים 'according to the model of idols' (e.g. Oort, Wolff, cf. *BHS*, NEB) raises the question whether the 'likeness of idols', to which the molten images are then to conform, implies too sophisticated or implausible a distinction between the two artefacts (cf. Rudolph, ? *molten images* of Yahweh, *idols* of Baal).

The phrase כתבונם עצבים is best taken as in apposition to מסכה מכספם; it is thus a synonymous second object for the verb 'they make for themselves'. With this understanding (so Wolff) the following כלה 'all of it' (i.e. the singular suffix denoting the whole enterprise) agrees.

[e]I.e. the idols; cf. Gen 20.13 for this use of ל.

[f]See S. A. Meier *Speaking of Speaking*, SVT 46 (1992).

[g–g]The phrase זבחי אדם is interpreted, with Kimchi, as meaning 'the sacrificers of (i.e. among) men', i.e. those who wish to sacrifice among men. For the usage, compare GK 128l and the very similar phrase of Isa 29.19 (so, e.g., Rosenmüller) 'the poorest of men', and, for the superlative sense (here 'true'), cf. GK 132c, 133h. זבח denoting slaughter within the context of worship and feasting is here rendered 'worship' in order to avoid later extraneous ideas (cf. 4.13). Ibn Ezra and Rashi suppose that the phrase means 'the slaughterers of men (kiss calves)' and refers to human sacrifice. For Rashi, such worshippers alone were worthy, in the opinion of the idolatrous priests, to kiss calves since they had offered the most costly of gifts. For ibn Ezra the words, richly ironic, describe the complete reversal of ethical standards in that, instead of kissing their friends, they murder them and, instead of killing calves (for food), they kiss them.

Modern commentators generally follow one or other of the interpretations so far mentioned. Ehrlich (*Miq.*, cf. Rudolph), on the basis of the LXX (see Text and Versions), suggests the interpretation '... to them, they say, Offer sacrifices! (i.e. reading זִבְחוּ for זבחי). Men kiss calves'.

The words 'and now' together with the following frequentative imperfect (note a) indicate that the prophet speaks in this verse of his contemporaries' behaviour (so Rashi and ibn Ezra, cf. Wolff). In all respects their continuing idolatry conforms to Ephraim's initial *infelix culpa*, the paradigmatic sin of the first king of the independent nation. The nation is thus trapped in the meshes of the idolatry with which, from the beginning, it was associated. As with a disease (see notes b and d to v. 1), the morbid symptoms break out ever more widely in the body of the state. The more ruinous the effects the more the citizens exacerbate those effects by renewed commitment to their cause. Whether Hosea has in mind the renewal and increase of the national commitment to idolatry at the hands of Ahab (1 Kgs 16.31f) and then of Jehu (so Rashi, cf. 2 Kgs 10.31), or whether he thinks specifically of his contemporaries and their doings in, e.g., Gilgal and Gilead as elsewhere (cf. 6.7; 8.4ff, 11; 12.12) is not entirely clear. The nature of his argument, however, suggests that he depicts a long and consistent devotion to idolatry which reaches to the moment when he speaks.

At all events, the continued manufacture of molten images (note c), of cunningly contrived idols (note d), while in fact merely the work of craftsmen, is consistently encouraged by the promptings of those whose words are heeded; their message urges on the syncretism which promotes easy self-indulgence and with it moral decay. Those who desire to worship, to do so well and to good effect (note g–g), should make calves the object of their devotion (for 'kissing' as a manifestation of commitment and loyalty to Baal, cf. 1 Kgs 19.18). For Hosea the words are, no doubt, heavily ironic (cf. ibn Ezra) and, following his characterisation of the whole enterprise as merely the work of craftsmen, intended to emphasise its folly. Yet for those whose words he parodies, the calves, their gods, are an expression and manifestation of the national self-awareness as well as of its aspirations and hopes (cf. on 8.5 above). The plural of the description is likely to match the proliferation of idolatry described at the beginning of the verse and thus Wolff (cf. on 8.4) may be right in supposing that we have here a description of bronze statuettes overlaid with silver, copies, perhaps, of the definitive exemplar at Bethel, increasingly disseminated in the Northern Kingdom (cf., on Judah, Isa 2.8).

For Kimchi (cf., e.g., Rudolph, Qyl, cf. Mays) the verse alludes rather to Jeroboam I's golden calves at Bethel and Dan which exemplified more particularly Ephraim's inclination to idolatry, traceable indeed to the time of the Judges. He notes that Jeroboam's calves were golden rather than silver (cf. Exod 32.2ff) and supposes that Hosea means by the term 'silver' the financial resources of Ephraim devoted to Jeroboam's enterprise. Reference to 8.4, where both gold and silver are mentioned in connection with the construction of idols, suggests that mention of silver alone here does not allow of particular inferences. Rudolph appeals to 8.4, 6, which he supposes to be notices similar to the present one, and thus concludes that, since the former refers to Jeroboam's idolatry, so does the latter. Yet 8.4, 6 are concerned with a multitude of idols in relation to the prime exemplar 'of Samaria' (for which, see *ad loc.*). Here unlike 8.4, 6, the notice contains a distinct historical perspective and is concerned to reveal the proliferation of idolatry over a period of time. It seems more plausible, then, to assume a contrast between Jeroboam I's idolatry (v. 1) and that, increased, of Hosea's own time (v. 2). The underlying unity of thought as between the present notice and that of 8.4ff is not in question.

Text and Versions

ועתה LXX omits (but cf. OL[S]).

כתבונם LXX κατ' εἰκόνα (εἰδώλων), cf. Vulg. *quasi similitudinem* (*idolorum*) 'according to the pattern (of idols)'; Pesh. *bdmwthwn*, cf.

Targ. כדמותהון 'in/according to their (own) likeness', cf. Cathcart, p. 58 n. 3; → כתבניתם (Sebök, Grätz, Oettli, cf. Rashi); → כתמונת (Guthe); → בתבונה (Halévy); → כתבנית (Borbone, *BHS*).

כלה LXX συντετελεσμένα 'completed', → כָּלָה (Harper); Pesh. omits.

להם LXX takes with what precedes, i.e. 'completed work for them'; → אלהים (Grätz, Harper, cf. *BHS*); Davies deletes (dittography).

זבחי LXX θύσατε, cf. Symm. θυσιάσατε and Vulg. *immolate* 'sacrifice!'; → זִבְחוּ (e.g. Ehrlich, Rudolph, cf. *BHS*).

אדם LXX ἀνθρώπους, cf. Vulg. *homines* 'men' (accusative); Pesh. follows MT with *(dbḥy) bny 'nš'*; Targ. (דבחין) לעובד ידי אנשא '(they sacrifice) to the work of human hands'.

ישקון LXX ἐκλελοίπασιν '(for calves) have failed/are deceased', cf., perhaps, 8.5; Vollers thinks of √שפק; Theod. προσκυνήσετε 'you will worship', cf. Symm. προσκυνησάτωσαν, cf. Vulg. *adorantes*; Aq. καταφιλοῦντες, cf. Pesh. *mnšqyn* 'kissing (calves)' and, perhaps, ibn Ezra's comments; → (דם עגלים) יַשְׁקוּן 'they give (them) to drink (of calves' blood) (Eitan *HUCA* 14, 1939, p. 4). Ehrlich and Rudolph take אדם with the last two words and render 'men kiss calves'.

13.3 **Accordingly[a] they[b] will be [c]like the morning mist and like the dew which disappears early in the day[c]; as chaff whisks away[d] from the threshing-floor and like smoke from the aperture[e].**

[a]לכן, 'that being so', here introduces a statement of fact rather than, as frequently, a (divine) declaration and is thus more akin to על כן (so ibn Ezra); for similar instances, cf. Num 16.11; 1 Sam 27.6; Pss 16.9; 73.6, 10.

[b]The reference is to the fate of the idols of v. 2 (cf. 8.5f; 10.7) rather than to that of the Ephraimites (so rightly Sellin and Rudolph against most other commentators). The following verse, introduced with 'but I', clearly proclaims, in contrast to ephemeral human artefacts, the abiding reality of Yahweh, the living God. Announcement of Ephraim's punishment follows later (vv. 7ff).

[c—c]The words occur in identical form in 6.4 to which, for an account of the translation, reference may be made.

[d]The form יסער is an intransitive *Poel* with a meaning akin to that of the transitive *Qal* of the closely related root שׂער II as it occurs in the *Qal* in Ps 58.10 (EV 9) and in the *Piel* (ibn Janāḥ – *Niphal*) in Job 27.21. For a *Piel* (ibn Janāḥ – *Niphal*) with *samech*, cf. Zech 7.14. The verbs in these passages denote '(complete) removal' rather than the 'whirling, stormy motion' attested elsewhere. Such is ibn Janāḥ's very satisfactory account of the matter and, in conformity with it, the translation 'whisks away' (cf. LXX and Peshiṭta below) is offered. On this view of the

matter there is no need to repoint as a passive *Poal* (for which see Text and Versions; cf. the comments of ibn Ezra and Kimchi). For threshing-floors in the form of exposed flat rocks situated on a hillside and so easily struck by the wind, cf. 2 Sam 24.18; 2 Chr 3.1 and *AUS* 3, pp. 126ff.

[e]Chimneys are not known; see *AUS* 7, p. 74 for a description of smoke in Palestinian houses emitted either through the door, through apertures in the walls ('windows') or near the roof. The word elsewhere denotes the windows of heaven (e.g. Gen 7.11), through which comes the rain, the openings of dove-cotes (Isa 60.8) and of the eyes (Eccles 12.3).

In the light of his understanding of the idols of Ephraim as mere human artefacts, quite ridiculous as objects of devotion, Hosea asserts (note a) that they (note b) are destined to vanish into oblivion. He does so by using four similes: the first two are precisely those he uses in 6.4 (*q.v.*) to describe the nature of Ephraim's good intentions; the third ('chaff') is found frequently elsewhere (e.g., Isa 17.13; 41.15; Ps 1.4), though the verb here is somewhat unusual and perhaps dialectal (note d); for the fourth there is no complete parallel, though smoke symbolises what is transitory in, e.g., Ps 37.20; Isa 51.6. The juxtaposition of the similes has a cumulative effect and 'the strophe as a whole is very strong' (Harper). Such strength serves well in antithesis to what follows: the solemn (first person) declaration of Yahweh's sole and abiding authority as creator and champion of his people.

Text and Versions

4QXII[c], as reconstructed by Fuller (Plate IV), reads וחס]דכם as the first word of the verse; cf. 6.4 and Fuller, p. 345.

יסער LXX ἀποφυσώμενος 'blown away'; Vulg. *turbine raptus* 'whisked away by the whirlwind'; Pesh. *dpr*ḥ 'which flies away'; Targ. דנסבא רוחא 'which the wind blows'; → יְסֹעַר (*Poal*, so Grätz, Oettli, Marti, Rudolph, *BHS*, NEB; see note d).

מארבה LXX[B], cf. OL[S], ἀπὸ δακρύων '(like vapour) from tears'; LXX[MSS], cf. Symm., Theod. ἀπο ἀκρίδων/τῆς ἀκρίδος = מֵאַרְבֶּה '(like vapour) from locusts'/'(? like a beetle) from locusts'/'(like a shadow) of a locust', i.e. ?as thin and insubstantial, cf. Jerome who regards δακρύων as an inner Greek corruption of ἀκρίδων; LXX[AQ*] ἐκ καπνοδόχης, cf. Aq. ἀπὸ καταράκτου '(like smoke) from a smoke-hole', for which see Jerome and cf. Vulg. *de fumario*, Pesh. *mn kwt'* and Targ. מכות נורא.

13.4 **But[a] I am Yahweh your[b] God from the [time of the][c] land of Egypt; you[b] know no god apart from me; except for me[d] there is no saviour.**

[a]The stark antithesis requires 'but' in English for the Hebrew conjunction ו.

[b]Second person singular.

[c]The preposition מן has here a temporal sense and denotes the *terminus a quo*, cf. BDB p. 581, col 1 4 a. Ibn Ezra speaks of 'your God from ancient times'. A similar (but fuller) usage is found in Deut 9.24 'from the day I first knew you'. For מן (used with שם) having literally a spatial but effectively a temporal sense, cf. 2.17 (EV 15) above.

[d]The only occurrence of בלת in the bible with the first person singular suffix.

The ephemeral character and worthlessness of Ephraim's idols are sharply contrasted with the consistent reality and power of Yahweh, who, from the time (note c) of the exodus, was *de facto* the nation's God. The thought is solemnly expressed by use of the pronouncement (in the first person), placed on Yahweh's lips, which echoes the similar solemn pronouncement at Sinai in Exod 20.2. Here, as there, (note b) the second person singular ('you/your') conveys powerfully the notion of Israel's personal relationship with Yahweh. Certainly, and having regard to the context, the indicative phrase 'I am Yahweh your God' implies clearly that the nation should have had no truck with other gods. Similarly the following statement 'except for me there is no saviour' implies that Ephraim was foolish indeed to suppose that there was. Accordingly it seems best to interpret *l' td'* as strictly a frequentative imperfect, 'you know no god...' rather than as a strong prohibition 'you must know no god...' though that is clearly the implication of such an indicative statement (cf. Kimchi's careful comment and Wolff, *ad loc.* under 'Form'). To know Yahweh denotes experience of him and of his actions which are the ground and cause of the ensuing relationship; cf. on 2.22 (EV 20) above and Deut 13.3, 7 (EV 2, 6). The participial form 'saviour' recalls the use of the verb in the summary statement of Exod 14.30 'that day the Lord saved Israel from the power of Egypt' (NEB). For the use of such phrases in the later prophecies of Deutero-Isaiah, cf. Isa 43.11; 45.21.

Text and Versions

אלהיך LXX, with which the fragmentary 4QXII[c] appears to agree, adds at this point 'who established the heavens and created the earth, whose hands created all the host of heaven; but I did not show them to you so that you might follow them; but I brought you up...'. The material is clearly secondary, as Jerome already notes. Rather than being doxological in character, it reflects an expansive explanation of the MT in the manner of the Targums. In part the need for such expansion may be traced to the perception that the indicative mode conceals an element of exhortation and admonition; see the commentary above. For a reconstruction of the text of 4QXII[c], see Fuller, pp. 343–357 and Plate IV. Fuller concludes that the archetype which generated MT also generated a hyparchetype to which, independently, both LXX and 4QXII[c] may be traced. 4QXII[c], then, furnishes evidence that the LXX reading was known in Hebrew and would seem to nullify Davies' theory that the addition constitutes 'an Alexandrian Jewish warning against astrology'.

מארץ מצרים LXX καὶ ἐγὼ ἀνήγαγόν σε ἐκ..., cf. Pesh. *d'sqtk mn...* 'and I (Pesh. 'who') brought you up from...', and Targ. דאסיקתך, → + אשר הוצאתיך (Harper), → + העליתיך (Oort, Borbone), but cf. Gelston, p. 173.

13.5 **It was I[a] who knew[b] you in the desert, in a land of baking heat[c].**

[a]The pronoun אני, preceding the verb, is emphatic.

[b]Cf. the commentary on 13.4 above and again 2.22 (EV 20). The renderings of the LXX, Peshiṭta and the Targum (see Text and Versions below), 'I pastured you/I attended to your needs' have prompted some scholars to emend MT (e.g. Wolff, Rudolph, Mays; see below) or to suppose that ידע has here the extended sense 'to care for'; e.g., Ehrlich (*Miq.*), NEB; see also D. W. Thomas *JTS* 35 (1934), pp. 300f and 49 (1948), pp. 143f.

In the light of 2.22 (EV 20) and 13.4 the rendering 'to know' is here retained since it allows of a more general and fundamental notion, i.e. Yahweh's establishment and maintenance of a relationship of love with Israel; it is indeed a notion which overlaps to some extent with that of choice and so of the chosen people (cf. BDB p. 394, col 1 2 and KB[3] p. 374, col 1 7[11]). No doubt the notion of Yahweh's care for his people also overlaps with the prior (as I think) notion of his 'knowing' them;

[11] For a discussion of the word in the context of treaties, see H. B. Huffman *BASOR* 181 (1966), pp. 31ff; for a more recent evaluation, see Nicholson *GP*, p. 80.

indeed, this very point seems to be implicit in the comments of Rashi and Kimchi who define Yahweh's knowing Israel in terms of his attention to their needs in the desert. Rudolph argues that, in view of the renderings of the LXX and Peshiṭta, MT's ידעתיך is to be regarded as a corruption of רעיתיך (*'Ich habe dich geweidet'*) which arose as a result of the nearby occurrence of תדע (in v. 4). The argument is scarcely convincing. On the contrary, it may be urged that the context and the nearby occurrence of מרעיתם in v. 6 prompted these versions to emphasise *ad sensum* a particular nuance of the verb ידע (of which Rudolph appears to be unaware). From the philological point of view, there seems to be no need to suppose that ידע 'to know' and ידע 'to care for' are separate (homonymous) roots (cf. KB[3] p. 374, col 1 7).

[c]The noun תלאבות occurs only here and has, since ibn Janāḥ at least, been explained by reference to the Arabic cognate root *lwb* (so also, e.g., Kimchi). He describes the use of the verb as denoting a man who is thirsty but also those places which are hot and dried out by the unrelenting strength of the sun. More particularly the derivative noun *l'bt* is used to denote such places and is synonymous with (Arabic) *'lḥrrt*. The latter term (according to Lane 2, p. 539) means 'a stony tract, of which the stones are black and worn and crumbling, as though burned with fire'. In the light of this evidence it is assumed that תלאבות here is a plural of local extension (GK 124b) which describes those rugged, inhospitable tracts of desert typically littered with (baked) stones. The reference is thus primarily to the character of the land rather than to its propensity to induce thirst or hunger in those who travel through it, though that is, of course, its effect (cf. on the versions below). 'Land of drought' (so, e.g., Harper, Wolff, Mays, AF) is, then, discounted. KB[3], by reference to Accadian *la'abu*, suggests 'a land of fevers', which is unlikely and unsupported by any ancient tradition.

Following the decisive event of the exodus (v. 4), Yahweh himself (note a) took the initiative in entering a committed and loving relationship (note b) with his people. There in the desert, a land of baking heat (note c), Israel experienced that total dependence upon Yahweh which the circumstances and his initiative dictated. There can be no doubt that, though the sentence is formally constructed from Yahweh's point of view, it is the benefit which Israel experienced that is in the prophet's mind. Hence the plausible, if particular, interpretation of the verb 'I knew you' attested by some of the ancient versions (cf. note b): Yahweh's loving possession of his people was manifested in his devoted care of them (cf. the Good Shepherd who 'knows' his sheep in Jn 10.14).

For Jerome vv. 4 and 5 must be interpreted in relation to 12.13f (EV 12f); there a distinct link is forged between Jacob/Israel, the patriarch, and Israel the nation, rescued from slavery through the agency of Moses. On the view here adopted as to the meaning of the verb *šmr* in those verses, Jerome's insight is the more significant. Thus Jacob's devotion to a woman is mirrored by Yahweh's providential care of his nation by Moses. Here in vv. 4f Israel, alone in the inhospitable desert (note c), enters into the mystery of her loving relationship with Yahweh. Thus, the sentiments expressed by Hosea in 2.16ff (EV 14ff) are clearly reflected here and the relationship between Yahweh and Israel is set forth in terms which are not far removed from those pertaining to the love of a man for a woman and to his commitment to her. If Yahweh's relationship with Israel is like this, and even very like this, it is not, of course, precisely so (cf. on 2.22, EV 20, above). The agency of Moses (in 12.14; EV 13) suggests that knowledge of Yahweh (in 13.4) involves instruction (*tôrā*) and that his knowledge of Israel (in this verse) implies his imparting to her the gifts of justice, kindness, compassion and steadfastness (2.21, EV 19), gifts which were intended to characterise the life of the nation. In this insight lies Hosea's recognition that the exodus and the Wilderness are connected and that the nation which Yahweh redeemed from Egypt was, in the desert, instructed in his ways (so essentially Jerome; cf. Wolff).

Text and Versions

ידעתיך LXX ἐποίμαινόν σε, cf. Pesh. *r'ytk* 'I pastured', 'fed you'; Vulg. *cognovi te* 'knew' (*sive pavi* 'fed' – so Jerome); Targ. סופיקית צורכיכון 'I attended to your needs', cf. R. P. Gordon *NT* 16 (1974), pp. 285–287; → רעיתיך (Sebök, Wellhausen, Grätz, Marti, Wolff, Rudolph, Mays, Borbone, cf. *BHS* and note b above); Nowack and Oettli add this word before בארץ.

תלאבות LXX ἀοικήτῳ (? = לא בית Tov, pp. 137f), cf. Vulg. *solitudinis* 'uninhabited'; Pesh. *ḥrbt' dl' ytb'* 'dry and without inhabitant' (on which see Sebök); Targ. דהויתון צריכים בה לכל מדעם 'in which you were needful for everything'.

13.6 **According as they were pastured[a], they were filled; and filled[b], they became arrogant[c]. For this reason they have forgotten me.**

[a]Lit. 'according to their pasturage'. The noun מרעית serves here as an infinitive (cf. König, 233d, Nyberg); for this reason it is followed

closely by the *waw* consecutive (finite) verbal form וישׂבעו (cf. GK 114r and König, 366h).

[b]The construction of the verse suggests a series of consequences: A has the effect B and B, effected, effects C. Accordingly the perfect verbal form שׂבעו serves to state the particular circumstance (being satiated) which gave rise to the ensuing arrogance. It is, then, unnecessary to emend the word so as to read an infinitive absolute (see Text and Versions) or to delete it (cf. *BHS*).

[c]וירם לבם Lit. 'their heart became exalted'; the phrase denotes 'reckless elation' (so BDB p. 926, col 2 2 b).

Yahweh's 'pasturing' (note a) of Israel indicates his care in bringing his people to the land of Canaan, to a safe and abundant pasturage (so Rashi, ibn Ezra, Kimchi). For the figure, cf. Isa 63.12ff. It was there that satiety led inexorably to careless arrogance and to reckless self-satisfaction (note c). The end result was that Israel quite forgot Yahweh, the sole author and cause of the plenty the nation had enjoyed. These thoughts are strikingly similar to those formulated in 2.15 (EV 13) where Israel, the faithless wife, forgets Yahweh her husband, the *de facto* provider of all her bounty. The nation's forgetting Yahweh stands in stark contrast to his knowing her in the desert (v. 5) and to her earlier knowledge of him (v. 4). If knowledge of Yahweh in its theological sense has an ethical dimension and involves instruction and therewith the gracious bestowal of the gifts of justice and kindness, then the forgetting of him implies the exact reverse, i.e. that godless anarchy, bloodshed and internecine strife (cf. vv. 10f) will characterise the life of an Israel whose arrogance has prompted her to such fatal forgetfulness.

The notion of satiety and the danger of forgetting Yahweh to which it may lead is an important theme in the exhortations of the book of Deuteronomy (see 6.12ff; 8.7ff; 11.15f; 31.20; 32.15ff) and a number of commentators have suggested that Hosea's words played a crucial element in their formulation (e.g. Wolff, Mays).

Text and Versions

כמרעיתם LXX κατὰ τὰς νομὰς αὐτῶν 'according to their pasturage' is conjoined with the words which precede, cf. Symm. κατὰ τὴν νομὴν αὐτῶν; Vulg. *iuxta pascua sua*; Pesh. *wr'yt 'nwn* 'and I pastured them'; → כמו רְעִיתִים 'as I pastured them' (e.g. Halévy, Borbone, cf. *BHS*); → כרעותם 'according to their pasturing' (e.g. Wellhausen, Nowack, Marti); Targ. כד זנתינון 'when I nourished them'.

שבעו LXX εἰς πλησμονήν 'to satiety', → שָׂבוֹעַ (infinitive absolute, e.g. Oort, Harper, Rudolph); Pesh. *wmlw krshwn* 'and they filled their belly' (either וישבעו or שבעו is not reproduced); Vulg. *et saturati* (*v.l.* + *sunt*) 'and (were) filled'; Targ. סבעו מסבע 'they were satisfied with satisfaction', representing both וישבעו and שבעו.

לבם LXX καρδίαι, plural.

13.7 and 8 (7) **So I have[a] become like a lion to them; like a leopard beside a well-trodden[b] path.** (8) **I will[c] attack them like a she-bear robbed of her young[d] and I will[c] cleave open their rib-cage[e]; [f]I will[c] devour them there[g] like a lion[f], [h]a wild beast which will rip them in pieces[h].**

[a]With ibn Ezra, the *waw* consecutive form indicates the evils which, as a result of their waywardness, have befallen Israel.

[b]For ibn Janāḥ and ibn Ezra the word אשור is parsed as a passive participle of the verb אשׁר 'to walk ahead', 'advance' (cf. BDB p. 80, col 2). The road or track is thus 'walked upon', 'well-trodden', an indication of its frequent use and of the ample prey it affords to the waiting leopard. Ibn Janāḥ quotes his mentor R. Judah (Ḥayyuj) as understanding the word to be a form of the root שור II 'to look', 'gaze' (cf. BDB p. 1003, col 2) as it occurs in, e.g., Num 24.17 (so Rashi)[12]. The view is adopted by many modern commentators and translators who offer such renderings as 'to watch for', 'lurk', 'be in wait'. Ibn Janāḥ, however, regards the view as mistaken (the *aleph* being an integral part of the root) and he judges the resulting interpretation poor and weak (cf. Rudolph's criticisms). Amongst more recent philological endeavours, mention may be made of Eitan's view (pp. 4f), that the word is illuminated by Aramaic שור 'to leap', 'run', 'jump' (Jastrow, p. 1530, col 1) and Arabic *swr* 'to leap', 'assail', 'attack' (IIIrd theme). The suggestion amounts to a possibility, though there remain the difficulties (1) that an imperfect tense following so closely a *waw* consecutive imperfect is strange, as is (2) the absence of an object (see further note c below). For telling criticisms of Guillaume's appeal (II, p. 33) to Arabic *syr* 'to travel', 'walk', see Rudolph.

That certain of the versions interpret the phrase of the 'way to Assyria' may suggest that Hosea's figure of speech was chosen in order to allude, under the figure of feral ambush, to the privations of Ephraim imposed by the Assyrians and to the leading into captivity of its citizens by the road (now well-trodden) to that land (so, e.g., Qyl, cf. Jerome's comments); moreover the use of שם 'there' in the following verse is consistent with this view. While it should be noted that the interpretation

[12]Cf., for this view, Jer 5.26 and, on this, J. A. Emerton in AOAT 212, pp. 125–133.

is contradicted by the pointing, i.e. the *shin* is marked by *raphe* not *dagesh* (so Rashi), nonetheless that there is such an allusion is eminently plausible.

[c]The imperfect tenses of this verse follow the *waw* consecutive imperfect of the previous verse as part of the whole unit (5–8) in which Yahweh's change of attitude is depicted (so rightly Rudolph). Thus he knew Israel in the desert (v. 5); they forgot him (v. 6) and so he has become (v. 7) their cruel adversary who will (v. 8) fully implement that function. To suppose that אשור in v. 7 is an imperfect and forms part of the sequence (see note b) is not satisfactory since the phrase of which it is part is closely connected with the preceding phrase and is governed by the all-important 'so I have become'.

[d]The LXX and Vulgate rightly interpret דב שכול of a she-bear which, robbed of her cubs, was known as especially ferocious. For the use of the masculine form to denote animals which are strong, cf. GK 122e.

[e]So most authorities and commentators. The root סגר I, with the meaning 'close', 'enclose', here suggests the pericardium (so ibn Janāḥ, cf. Rashi and Rosenmüller) or, more generally, what encloses the heart, the breast or rib-cage (e.g., Marti, Wolff, Rudolph, NEB). By contrast Ehrlich compares Joel 2.13, 'rend your hearts and not your garments', and reasons that the phrase gains its force only on the assumption that 'rending' (√קרע) is strictly appropriate to clothing. Hence he supposes that the word here denotes a coat of mail, or breast-plate (cf. Exod 25.7), called in Arabic *ǧwšn*, devised to afford protection from the claws and teeth of just such wild animals. The theory is not without its merits and deserves consideration though, in the absence of further evidence in its favour, the traditional view is here retained. For Nestle's emendation, see Text and Versions.

[f—f]The fact that not Yahweh ('I') but 'wild animal(s)' is the subject of the last clause of the verse has prompted a number of scholars to follow the LXX, which has here a third person plural verb, and to emend the pointing. Further, reversion to the image of the lion is questioned on stylistic grounds (i.e. repetition) and hence Duhm's emendation 'dogs' (see Text and Versions) which is adopted so as to produce 'dogs shall devour them, wild animals shall tear them in pieces' (so, e.g., Wolff, Rudolph, Mays, cf. *BH*). For the appropriateness of MT, see the commentary.

[g]שם 'there', i.e. on the spot and so almost 'at once'; but also, perhaps, resuming the allusion to Assyria (cf. note b).

[h—h]The change of subject in this clause (to the third singular feminine) is consistent with Hebrew poetic usage (GK 144p; cf., e.g., Ct 1.2), though it is difficult to determine whether thereby a circumstantial clause is formed, i.e. 'while/as if wild beasts rip them in pieces' (cf. Rosenmüller and Harper) or whether a short relative clause (GK 155f–m), the force of the *kaph* continuing from the previous clause (cf. Qyl), i.e. 'like wild beasts which will rip them in pieces' (cf. Lam 3.1 and AF). Another possibility, related to the latter, is that the phrase 'wild beast' stands in apposition to 'lion', thus: 'I will devour them like a lion – a wild beast which will rip them in pieces'. (For apposition in general, see GK 131.) חית השדה may be interpreted either as a singular or a collective singular.

The verses depict the terrible nature of Yahweh's reaction to Ephraim's reckless ingratitude and consequent disregard of him (v. 6). The remorseless intensity of the language (cf. Amos 5.18f) and of the construction of the sentences is noteworthy. The time span stretches from the settlement to the present situation and on to the immediate future with its final dénouement (notes a and c). Here the kindly, loving God of the exodus and wilderness has turned himself (note a) into the furious destroyer of his nation. Like a lion or a leopard (the latter is known to this day in Israel/Palestine) which, with feline cunning, knows where to await his prey (note b), he is ready to impose his final destruction. Its mode will be akin to the action of the she-bear (note d), deranged with fury at the loss of her cubs (cf. 2 Sam 17.8; Prov 17.12; cf. 2 Kgs 2.24; Lam 3.10 etc.), whose claws, at a stroke, reduce her victim to a split carcass, internal organs laid bare (note e). Reverting to the image of the lion (note f—f), Hosea is enabled to press even further the totality of the coming destruction. For the lion is (note h) an animal which, to satisfy its hunger, consumes its dead victim by ripping it to pieces. Mention of the she-bear, then, serves to convey the force and fury of the fatal attack (cf. Kimchi), while that of the lion conveys the totality of the destruction (cf. Jer 50.17). The earlier reference to lion and leopard is indicative of Yahweh's deadly deliberation and resolve. To seek to create a sequential interpretation (lion, leopard, bear; and then dogs and wild beasts as scavengers) by emendation (note f) and by investing 'there' with a fully temporal sense (e.g. Mauchline, Rudolph) seems to me to miss the aspectual force of Hosea's words.

Hosea's description of the calamity inflicted and to be inflicted (note c) on Ephraim by Yahweh is conveyed in a series of powerful similes. There can be no doubt but that, interpreted, those similes depict the destruction of the nation by the Assyrians, a destruction largely effected but, in the future, to be completely so. Similarly, for example, in Isa 5.29, the threat to Judah at the hands of the Assyrian foe is described in terms of the growling rapacity of ferocious lions. It is possible that Hosea by his use within a simile of the particular word *'šwr* (note b) and by similar use of the adverb 'there' (note g) makes very clear to his hearers the nature of the threat and punishment which, in the name of his God, he announces so powerfully.

Text and Versions

ואהי LXX καὶ ἔσομαι, cf. Vulg. *et ero* 'and I will be'; → וְאֶהְיֶה (e.g., Wellhausen, Nowack, Oettli, Marti, *BHS*); the renderings are likely, however, to arise from a harmonising tendency (Keil, Wolff); Pesh. and Targ. follow MT.

אשור LXX Ἀσσυρίων, cf. Vulg. *Assyriorum* and Pesh. *d'twr* (Gelston, pp. 123, 167f) 'of (the) Assyria(ns)', → אַשּׁוּר (Wellhausen, Oettli); Targ. כמין (על שבילא) 'lying in wait (on the path)', cf. Cathcart, p. 59, n. 13; → אֶשְׁקֹד, cf. Jer 5.6 (Grätz, Nowack, Marti).

(8) כדב שכול LXX and Vulg. use feminine forms.

סגור לבם LXX συγκλεισμὸν καρδίας αὐτῶν 'enclosure of their hearts', cf. Pesh. *mqrm' dlbhwn* 'their pericardium'; Vulg. *interiora iecoris eorum* '(I will break asunder) the interior of their liver', i.e. all their vital parts (Jerome); Targ. רשע לבהון 'the wickedness of their heart', cf. the comments of Rashi and Kimchi, 'the heart closed up from the understanding to return to me'; סגור → כְּגוּר, Nestle *ZAW* 25 (1905), pp. 204f, followed by van Hoonacker, 'like a (lion's) whelp', which in the light of Gen 49.9; Deut 33.22 can show ferocity (so Rudolph *contra*, e.g., Sellin).

ואכלם LXX καὶ καταφάγονται αὐτούς 'and they will devour them', = וַאֲכָלָם (Nowack, *BHS*); → וַאֲכָלֵם (Marti, Rudolph, Mays, Borbone); → יֹאכְלוּם (Wolff); Pesh. *wn'kwl 'nwn* (Gelston, p. 123) 'and he will devour them', with לביא as subject, = וְיֹאכְלֵם or וַאֲכָלֵם (Sebök); Vulg. and Targ. reproduce the first person of MT.

שם omitted by, e.g., Meinhold and Marti.

כלביא LXX σκύμνοι δρυμοῦ '(lion) cubs of the forest'= כַּלְבַיָּא (Aramaism, Cappellus), → כפירי יער (e.g. Oettli, Marti); ; → כְּלָבִים 'dogs' (Duhm, *BH*, Wolff, Rudolph, Mays, cf. *BHS* and see note f above).

חית השדה Plural in LXX and Vulg.; singular in Pesh. and Targ.; Targ. חית שינא 'ferocious (lit. toothy) beast', *contra* Cathcart, p. 59 n. 18.

13.9 **Your[a] destruction[b], Israel, is my doing[c]; I, [d]your[a] erstwhile helper[d].**

[a]Singular suffix.

[b]The word שחת is understood (cf. the LXX and Vulgate) to be a noun in form comparable to דְּבַר/שְׁלָם (so, e.g., Ehrlich *Miq.*, Qyl). On the

assumption that the word is to be parsed as a third singular *Piel* perfect, the difficulty arises as to the identity of the subject. Kimchi assumes that the calf of earlier chapters is intended. For Ridderbos, van Gelderen and Gispen כי בי בעזרך is rendered 'that you are against me and my help' and then forms the (composite) subject of the verb '... has destroyed you, Israel'. Both interpretations are unconvincing (for criticism of the latter, see Rudolph). Davies, citing Williams *Syntax* 160 and following NJPS, suggests an impersonal construction 'One has destroyed you' → 'you are undone'; but the suggestion is made on the assumption that the following *by* is to be emended. To follow the first person rendering of the Peshiṭta (see Text and Versions) and to emend at least the pointing (cf. *BHS*) so as to obtain 'I destroyed/I will destroy you' (cf. note c) amounts to a possibility but generally suffers from the difficulty that, without further emendation, no sense can be made of what follows. AF's combination of this latter proposal with Rashi's interpretation of בי (note c) is ingenious and worthy of consideration. The suspicion remains, however, that the Peshiṭta's rendering represents a harmonising of the *difficilior lectio* of the MT.

[c] כי בי; the preposition is *beth intrumenti* and means 'by me' (BDB p. 89, col 2 2 c), hence the rendering 'is my doing'. The particle כי is used asseveratively and is inserted before the predicate בי (cf. GK 148d and, e.g., Gen 18.20). Ehrlich supposes that כי represents an initial scribal mistake (כי for בי) which thereafter retained its place in the text as capable of some such meaning. Rashi (cf., e.g., Qyl, AF) suggests that בי בעזרך is an elliptical expression and conveys the sense 'you have rebelled against me, my help'. The difficulty remains that, on this view, no satisfactory account is given of the word שחת (note b). AF constitute an exception. They combine Rashi's view with a first person reading of שחת as a prophetic perfect and translate 'I will destroy you, Israel, for (you rebelled) against me, against your helper'. The proposal deserves serious consideration, though in my view it is too uncertain (cf. note b) to be judged definitely preferable to a more straightforward account of MT which affords reasonable sense.

[d—d] בעזרך is understood to be in apposition to the preceding בי, i.e. (lit.) 'by me – by your help' (so, again, Ehrlich). Somewhat similarly, for Kimchi בי and בעזרך are indissolubly combined by the repeated preposition *beth* and for this he compares Job 18.8 as well as the repeated *kaphs* which signify 'the completeness of the correspondency between two objects' (BDB p. 454, col 1 2). עזרך 'your help' is *abstractum pro concreto* (BDB p. 740, col 2). 'I' and 'erstwhile' are added in English *ad sensum*.

The verse constitutes Yahweh's terse, heartfelt expression of the tragedy of Israel's plight, a plight which reflects the inexorable logic of his own position. He who had been, had resolved to be, Israel's helper (note d) now became, in the face of the nation's behaviour, the very cause of its destruction. The statement is thus a summary of what has been said in the preceding verses (4–8) and enables the prophet, in Yahweh's name, to develop the theme of the total collapse of the royal establishment of the nation in the verses that follow.

Text and Versions

שחתך LXX τῇ διαφθορᾷ σου '(who will aid) in your ruin?'; Vulg. *perditio tua* 'your ruin!'; Pesh. *ḥbltk* 'I have destroyed you' (? harmonising tendency), → שִׁחַתְךָ (so, e.g., Nowack, Oettli, Marti, Wolff, Rudolph, Mays, AF, NEB, cf. *BHS* and Borbone); → אֲשַׁחֶתְךָ (cf. *BHS*); Targ. כד מחבלין אתון עובדיכון 'when you corrupt your deeds'.

כי בי בעזרך LXX τίς βοηθήσει, cf. Pesh. *mnw n'drk* 'who will help you?' → כִּי מִי בְעֹזְרֶיךָ//בְעֶזְרֶךָ//יעזרך (cf. Oettli, Sebök, Marti, Harper, Wolff, Rudolph, Mays, *BHS*, NEB, Borbone); Vulg. *tantummodo in me auxilium tuum* 'only in me is your help'; Targ. הוי בסעדכון '... (but when you return to my law, my word) is your help'.

13.10 and 11 **So much, then, for[a] your king [b]who was to save you[b] in all your cities[c]; and for your rulers[d] of whom you said: Give me king and princes.** (11) **I give you[e] kings[f] in my wrath and I remove[e] them in my fury.**

[a]The evidence of the versions (cf. the LXX and Peshiṭta at verse 14 and 1 Cor 15.55) suggests that the word אהי is an interrogative particle meaning 'where?'. To this view ibn Janāḥ subscribes explaining that the word displays metathesis in relation to the usual form אַיֵּה. Since the Arabic cognate is of the form *'yy* and since substitution of *he* for medial *yodh* is not attested, some considerable doubt attaches to the theory and to the blander statement that the word is a dialectal variant (so, e.g., GK 150l, as one possibility, Wolff, Rudolph, *et al.*). A simpler expedient is to assume that the word is a scribal mistake for the familiar אַיֵּה (so, e.g., KB/KB[3] and many commentators). Against this, however, is the fact that the word again occurs in this form twice in v. 14 and it is implausible to suppose that such a mistake should occur three times in the same chapter (so, e.g., Ehrlich). Accordingly, it is suggested that the word is related to Syriac *'h'* and constitutes, strictly speaking, an interjection of derision[13]. Hence 'so much, then, for' in the English translation. For אפוא as an enclitic particle, see BDB p. 66, col 1 1. This view has the merit that it meets the needs of v. 14 (*q.v.*) and may go

[13] For *'alaph* in Syriac and *yodh* in Hebrew, cf., e.g., *'n'* and אני; for *'h'*, see Payne Smith, p. 46. Another form listed there is *'h* with the same sense.

some way to account for the versional rendering 'where?' which, here and in v. 14, is also capable of conveying derision. Amongst the rabbinic commentators, Rashi, ibn Ezra and Kimchi insist that the word is an apocopated form of the first person imperfect of the verb היה and means 'I will be', though their interpretations imply that they invested the phrase also with the sense 'where?' i.e. אפוא as איפה (so explicitly, e.g., Kimchi); the resulting interpretations (all of which differ from one another) are tortuous and unconvincing; e.g., Kimchi 'I will be for ever, but where is your king?'

[b—b]ויושיעך Simple *waw* with the jussive having voluntative or potential force, GK 109i; cf. the parallelistic paraphrase in '... of whom you said, give me...'.

[c]עריך A number of commentators have questioned the reading (why is salvation restricted to cities? – so Rudolph) and have emended the text in various ways (see Text and Versions). Yet 'cities' are naturally the object of an invader's privations[14] and the phrase in question is quite intelligible as a comprehensive expression of the hope for a national defence policy under the leadership of the royal establishment. For Davies' treatment, see under Text and Versions.

[d]The word שפטיך, traditionally rendered 'judges'. Here, however, the word denotes more generally royal officials as the parallelistic phrase of 10b and שרים 'princes' suggests (see on 3.4; 7.7 etc.)[15]. If an administrative function attaches to such judges, then that reflects the view that equity was a fundamental aspect of proper monarchical government, cf. Jer 21.12; Isa 11.3ff.

[e]The imperfects are frequentative, cf. 4.13; 11.2b etc. and GK 107e, g.

[f]The indefinite singular מלך, constructed with the frequentative imperfects (note e), serves as a *nomen unitatis* and is thus rendered by a plural in English.

In the light of the considerations expressed above, *viz.* that Yahweh alone could help Ephraim and that he had now turned against his people, the royal establishment (note d) of the nation is derided (note a) as totally incapable of providing any redemption from the terrible circumstances in which Ephraim is now placed. The words are on Yahweh's lips as are those that precede them. The king of v. 10 is likely to have been Hoshea and to this Hosea's choice of words 'who was to save you', with its play upon the etymology of the king's name, alludes. In general the hope placed in the person of a king may be

[14] Cf. Sennacherib's statement (*ANET*, p. 288) 'I laid siege to forty six of his (*sc.* Hezekiah's) strong cities, walled forts.'

[15] Cf. W. Richter *ZAW* 77 (1965), pp. 40ff, 58ff.

illuminated (so Rudolph) by Lam 4.20 '... we had thought to live among the nations, safe under his (*sc.* the king's) protection'. More particularly, the deposition in sequence of one Ephraimite king and the enthronement of his successor marked, during the prophet's time, the desperate attempts of the nation to find the right policy *vis à vis* Assyria and Egypt. Hoshea had ascended the throne following the debacle of Pekah's policy and of the Assyrian invasions of 733 BC. Hoshea, after initially paying tribute to Tiglath-pileser III, at some stage following the latter's death in 726 BC refused to continue to do so and changed to a pro-Egyptian policy (2 Kgs 17.4). As a consequence he was captured by Shalmaneser's forces in 725 BC and the stage was set for the final siege of Samaria. If Hosea's words of v. 10a, set as they are within the context of his strongest descriptions of the visible effect of Yahweh's wrath (vv. 7–9 and note c above), reflect the particular circumstances of the middle years of the decade 730–720, they are consistent also with his indictment of the earlier manifestations of woeful national instability. In chapter 7, under the figure of the oven, he had characterised as grossly immoral the nation's addiction to revolution and counter-revolution, exemplified in the circumstances of Pekah's accession. Short-sighted foolishness and resort to bloodthirsty violence were the symptoms of a fundamental disloyalty to Yahweh. Now that Yahweh's patience was finally exhausted, the pattern of national behaviour, so firmly established, is seen to be the result of his anger, the very mode of its operation (v. 11). Hence the state received what it deserved. Again for Hosea there is an inexorable connection between culpable immorality and the destructive force that it looses; and that connection reflects the will of the God whom he served, cf. 7.2.

The evidence of 7.3, 7 and 8.4 with their references to a royal establishment of officials and statesmen ('rulers' and 'princes') suggests that the demand of v. 10b 'Give me king and princes' refers to the history of the Northern Kingdom (so already, e.g., Jerome and Kimchi – but as one possibility) and, as I suppose, more particularly to the period of Hosea's experience and ministry (cf. Emmerson, p. 107 and Gelston, 'Kingship', pp. 82ff). However, from the time of Jerome (cf. ibn Ezra and Kimchi), at least, that demand, together with the statement 'I give' of v. 11, has been associated with the demand to Samuel for a king recorded in 1 Sam 8.6 and to the subsequent ascent of Saul to the throne. Where the repudiation of the monarchy is concerned ('I remove') the authorities quoted offer variant interpretations; thus, the reference may be to the whole institution of the monarchy (Israel and Judah) ending with the last (Judaean) king, Zedekiah; or else, as has been said, to the demise of the Ephraimite monarchy in the person of Hoshea. Jerome, it should be noted, seems to be aware of the problems raised by such considerations and he observes that the imperfect tenses of v. 11 indicate that the oracle (understood to be essentially Samuel's) has a prophetic, future reference.

Amongst modern commentators the matter is seen differently by, e.g., Wolff; for him Hosea's words reflect acquaintance with that tradition, later taken up into the Deuteronomic history, which told how the kingship was wrested from Yahweh (i.e. in Samuel's time)[16]. Examination of Jerome's observations, as well as those of Kimchi, suggests that in giving Hosea's words so long a perspective, they are reproducing interpretations of Hosea's pronouncement which are old and even very old but which have their origin in later understandings of the relevance of his words, words seen now to be true in relation to the whole institution of the monarchy in Israel and Judah. Hosea's own perception is naturally more limited in its scope. The evidence of 2.2 (EV 1.11, *q.v.*) suggests that he was favourably (if tentatively) inclined to the notion of a properly constituted single monarchy which would serve to unite once again the whole people of Israel[17] and hence it is unlikely that his words in vv. 11f were intended to run counter to that view (cf. Rudolph's similar arguments). Rather his words undoubtedly reflect his own experience and insight, *viz.* that the radical instability of the Ephraimite monarchy in his times, caused indeed by disloyalty to Yahweh (cf. 8.4), had become a symptom and vehicle of the latter's furious anger. 'What, then, they did without Yahweh became, through him, a judgement upon Israel' (Nowack). That Hosea's insight should, in time, have been extended in the understanding of his readers so as to constitute an indictment of the whole institution of the monarchy as it was exemplified in Israel and Judah, is a necessary corollary to its transmission through Judah and on into the canon of classical prophecy. Whether Hosea included in his insight Jeroboam I, and thus the monarchy of Ephraim in its entirety, is difficult to judge (cf. on 8.4 above). The devastating finality of the words that he places on the lips of Yahweh (v. 11) suggests that this was indeed the conclusion to which inexorably he was driven. If incontrovertibly he witnesses the end, then he perceived that the shadow of the end fell upon the beginning. If the kings of Ephraim are

[16] He relies on the treatment of A. Weiser *Samuel*, FRLANT 81 (Göttingen, 1962), pp. 25ff; for a different view, see S. Herrmann *ThLZ* 89 (1964), pp. 819ff.

[17] Cf. Gelston's judicious treatment, 'Kingship', pp. 77ff.

manifestly taken away in Yahweh's fury then it was in his wrath that they were given in the first place. Hosea's judgement as expressed in v. 11, particularly when it is compared with his earlier pronouncements upon the same subject (7.3, 7, and 8.4)[18], has a note of finality, of a developed and radical conclusion. Thus the logic of Hosea's view points to a repudiation of the whole institution of kingship in Ephraim. It is possible that Hosea did not spell out the implications of such logic, or that he only saw the full force of his words at a later stage; it is virtually certain, however, that his readers in Judah will have seen that force and seen in it a warning for their own monarchy. Such is the very nature of prophetic endeavour and of the development of the ideas which were to contribute in no small way to the later Deuteronomic view of the monarchy as a whole.

Text and Versions

אהי LXX ποῦ 'where?', cf. Vulg. *ubi*, Pesh. *'ykw* and Targ. אן, → אַיֵּה (e.g., Harper, *BHS*, Borbone and many commentators).

אפוא LXX οὗτος 'this (king of yours)'; Vulg. *maxime nunc*, cf. Pesh. *hkyl*, Targ. כען 'then', 'now' etc.

ויושיעך LXX καὶ διασωσάτω σε 'and let him save you', cf. Targ. ויפרקינך; Vulg. *salvet*, cf. Pesh. *nprqk* (without 'and').

בכל Pesh. *wlkwlhyn* '(let him save you) and all (your cities)', see next entry.

בכל עריך → וכל שָׂרֶיךָ 'and all your princes' (Houtsma and, e.g., Wellhausen, Marti, Harper, Wolff, cf. *BHS*); → מִכָּל צָרֶיךָ 'from all your enemies' (e.g. Grätz, Davies, the latter investing עריך with the meaning 'your enemies, cf. KB[3] p. 829, col 2; Rudolph, Mays, cf. *BHS*, retain בכל and offer the dubious rendering 'that he may help you against all your enemies').

ושפטיך LXX κρινάτω σε 'let him judge you' = יִשְׁפָּטְךָ (Vollers), → וְיִשְׁפְּטֻךָ plural (Houtsma and, e.g., Wellhausen, Marti, cf. *BH*); Pesh. *wdynk* singular (*v.l.* plural, Gelston, p. 84); Halévy transfers 'and your judges' so as to precede 'in all your cities', cf. NEB.

אשר אמרת Pesh. *dš'ltny w'mrt* 'whom you asked of me. And you said...' → שאלת ממני ואמרת (Sebök).

[18] Cf. Gelston, p. 83, who detects (in vv. 10f) 'a certain inconsistency with 8.4'; the inconsistency, if such there be, reflects the development of Hosea's thought rather than an inherent 'paradox' (Gelston, p. 84) resulting from Yahweh's simultaneous acquiescence to the demand for kingship and his repudiation of the nature of that demand as exemplified in 1 Sam 8.

שרים singular in LXX, Pesh., Targ. (*v.l.*).

(11) אתן LXX καὶ ἔδωκα 'and I gave', cf. Pesh. *wyhbt*, Targ. מניתי.

13.12 **Ephraim's iniquity is bound up in a bundle[a]; his sin is kept on record[b].**

[a]'In a bundle' is added *ad sensum*. Kimchi rightly compares Job 14.17 'my offence is secured in a bag' (בצרור).

[b]So NEB *ad sensum*. The verb צפן means 'treasured', 'stored', etc.

Hosea depicts the indelible nature of his nation's iniquity and sinfulness. The record is secure, as if written on a parchment deposited in a bundle of archives, tied and perhaps sealed for long preservation (cf. Isa 8.16 and Deut 32.34). For Rudolph, the Dead Sea Scrolls provide a good example of this. Perhaps even better, because more personal, is that of the second century Jewish woman Babata whose thirty five personal documents were found carefully tied by string in a leather pouch in the Cave of Letters in Naḥal Ḥever near Ein Gedi[19]. Davies thinks that the phrase derives from the careful storing of treasure rather than from the preservation of written documents; and W. G. E. Watson *VT* 34 (1984), pp. 242–247, suggests that, as in Accadian incantations, the binding is more technical and refers to 'the effects of unabsolved sin'. Yet the evidence of Isa 8.16, cf. Jer 32.14, suggests the preservation of a written record.

Though the phrases are construed in the passive, there can be no doubt that Yahweh is in the thoughts of the prophet. He was not disposed to be indulgent (Rashi) or forgetful (ibn Ezra) towards his people but rather had stored up in his heart (ibn Ezra) their wholesale wickedness, cf. 8.13 and 9.9. If the history of the recent past manifestly revealed his ferocious anger (vv. 7f), the indelible nature of the nation's record required that that anger could not be mollified; the time for appeasement was past (cf. on v. 14 below).

'Iniquity' and 'sin' are found in parallelism elsewhere in 4.8; 8.13; 9.9, cf. 12.9 where *ḥṭ'* is used for 'sin' and the two terms are brought into a still closer relationship with each other, offering a definition which is particularly useful. *'wn* 'iniquity' denotes wickedness which renders its perpetrator guilty and punishable. *ḥṭ't* 'sin' is perhaps more theological and accordingly can denote cultic offences against God (cf. 10.8).

[19] Y. Yadin *Bar Kokhba* (Jerusalem, 1971), pp. 222ff.

Text and Versions

צרור LXX συστροφὴν (conjoining with v. 11; LXX[Luc] reads the nominative συστροφή) '(and I took the) gathering, collection (of wickedness)', cf. 4.19 where צרר is also rendered by this noun.

13.13 **Labour pains[a] come[b] upon him. [c]He is not a clever son[c]. [de]When the time comes[d] he will have no success in giving birth[e].**

The translation and interpretation of the verse here set forth owes much to the treatment of it by Ehrlich (*Miq.*). The following considerations are important: first, the verse is predicated of the masculine Ephraim and not of the woman in labour; for she is the vehicle and not the tenor of the comparison. Other instances where males are described as in a dire situation comparable to that of a woman in childbirth are Isa 37.3 (the men of Judah) and Jer 30.6; in both cases the image is clearly used because it is inherently surprising to the ear of the hearer and so consequently powerful in its effect. Secondly, the term משבר בנים denotes not 'the breach of the womb' (*contra* Kimchi), but rather the final stage, following labour pains, of giving birth. In this connection it should be noted that Rashi (cf. the Targum and ibn Janāḥ) defines the term as the place of delivery (ibn Janāḥ), the *sella parturiensis* (Rashi). Consequently the phrase in this particular context has virtually a temporal sense (so explicitly ibn Janāḥ) and denotes the last stages of giving birth.

A number of commentators (e.g. Kimchi, Rosenmüller, Harper, Wolff, Rudolph, Mays, cf. NEB) have supposed that the verse reflects a popular understanding of unsuccessful labour. Thus the 'son who is not clever' refers to the foetus who does not present himself to the breach of the womb at the proper time. As Ehrlich observes, however, there is the consequent difficulty that in a single verse the vehicle of the comparison changes from the woman in labour to that of the foetus in her womb. Rudolph (cf. NEB) seeks to meet such objections by supposing that לו denotes, not that labour pains come *upon him* (*sc.* Ephraim), but rather have come *in respect of him* (i.e. of the foetus in the simile). Here Rudolph supports J. L. McKenzie's view, *CBQ* 17 (1955), p. 296, that 'the mother is mentioned merely to complete the metaphor, and corresponds to nothing in the prophet's mind'. Such considerations, however, suggest special pleading and a rationalising tendency. Reference to Isa 37.3 makes plain that the metaphor is that of the fruitless and terrible pains of unsuccessful labour (cf. and contrast Isa 66.7–9 and Jn 16.21) which is here applied to the nation, Ephraim.

[a]חבלי יולדה Lit. 'the pains of a-woman-giving-birth'.

[b]יבאו A frequentative imperfect describing the current disastrous state of the nation, cf. (with Wolff) 5.4; 7.2, 16.

[c—c]Ephraim the nation is described and not the (male) foetus of the woman in labour. The language used is that familiar from Proverbs (e.g. 10.1; 13.1; 15.20, cf. 1 Kgs 5.21, EV 7; 2 Chr 2.11, EV 12) where the positive expression indicates an astute, teachable young man adapted to a successful and harmonious life.

[d—d]The word עת is construed as an accusative *temporis* with the sense 'at the (right) time', cf. 10.12.

[e—e]Lit. 'surely at the (right) time he will not endure/survive at the birth of sons'. כי is asseverative and the form of the phrase is that of the well-known כי לא תאמנו of Isa 7.9 'surely ye shall not be established' (RV).

The verb יעמד (from √עמד 'to stand') is invested by commentators with a number of meanings all of which depend, to some extent at least, upon the view taken of the phrase as a whole (e.g., when interpreted of the foetus, 'he will not present himself'). On the view here adopted it seems right to assume for it the well-attested meanings 'to abide', 'endure', 'persist', 'hold one's ground' (see BDB p. 764, col 1 3 c d f and 4). Thus Ephraim, tormented as if by labour pains, will not endure or survive to the time when giving birth would normally afford relief (cf., again, Isa 37.3). Hence the point of the statement is that the persistent torment is a prelude only to doom and failure (cf. Isa 26.17f). This treatment of the verse, though dependent upon Ehrlich's main contention, nevertheless differs from it. Ehrlich connects the final phrase more closely with what precedes it and suggests that Ephraim is not a clever son since otherwise he would not remain so long in a situation (in which men feel themselves to be) like a woman in the last phase of labour. The difficulty is that כי is not elsewhere attested with the sense 'since otherwise' (*denn sonst*).

The terrible consequences of the indelible record of Ephraim's guilt (v. 12) are expressed by the powerful metaphor of a woman in labour, racked with excruciating pain whose endeavours are doomed to failure. The sense conveyed is precisely contrary to that expressed in Jn 16.21 (cf. Isa 66.7–9) where, in successful birth, the pain is replaced by joy for that 'a man is born into the world'. Elsewhere, too, the prophets use the image of labour pains to depict the circumstances of national defeat and exile (cf. Mic 4.9f; Isa 26.17f). Yet here explicitly (see notes to the translation above), the utter depths of Ephraim's suffering will be manifested in its unproductive failure. Death (cf. v. 14f) is the sole fate which awaits the nation in the last terrible years of Hoshea's reign and the pains which it now suffers (note b, cf. Wolff) are a prelude to that hopeless fate.

If the vehicle of the metaphor is the notion of labour pains doomed to failure, the tenor (*viz.* Ephraim) is defined further by the parenthetical definition, 'he is not a clever son'. The words are derived from the very core of the old wisdom tradition (note c) and, by contrast to it, suggest that Ephraim is unteachable (cf. Kimchi), insensitive to moral concerns and ill-equipped for success (cf. with Jerome, 7.11). Yet the words allow of a further interpretation. For, at the beginning, when Yahweh loved his young son, he sought to lead him forth (from Egypt) with bonds of friendship (*ḥbly 'dm*, 11.4). Here with a reference in word-play to that saying, the nation is to be oppressed with labour pains (*ḥbly ywldh*). Accordingly the use of the word 'son' forms a connection between the nation perceived initially as the object of Yahweh's love (11.1–4) and the nation, at its end, as the object of divine fury. It is this 'son', on whom was set so much affection, who now, through his stupidity and immorality, is doomed not to survive to the birth of 'sons' (note e). Thus, the theme and counter-theme, the tenor and the vehicle of the comparison, are woven together by Hosea with extraordinary skill. The tenor is defined in concepts drawn from the wisdom tradition; the vehicle is of a sort with the dire warnings of the prophetic tradition. The verse in itself constitutes a testimony to his literary skill as well as to his use of that skill in the articulation of his prophetic message[20]. It is worth noting that the LXX (see below) is likely to have perceived something of the strong ironic force of the phrase 'he is not a clever son' (cf. Jerome's comments *ad loc.*).

Text and Versions

יולדה Pesh., cf. Targ. *'yk dyldt'* 'like those of a woman in travail'.

הוא → והוא (Nowack, Marti, cf. *BHS* which records that this is the reading of a few MSS).

בן לא חכם LXX (οὗτος) ὁ υἱός σου ὁ φρόνιμος '(this is) your so clever son!'; ὁ (2) → οὐ (Cappellus, Schleusner, Vollers, Ziegler, with Q[a]), but cf. Jerome's comments to the effect that the rendering ὁ correctly conveys the irony of the MT; for לא חכם Aq. ἀνόητος, cf. Symm. and Theod. οὐ σοφός 'unwise'; Pesh. *mṭl d...* 'because (he is not a clever son)', linking the words with what precedes or with what follows; Gelston (private communication) suggests that *mṭl d* may reflect כי (see next note) which is not otherwise represented in Pesh.

כי עת LXX διότι, (LXX[Luc], O' + νῦν), cf. Vulg. *nunc enim*, Pesh. *mkyl*, Targ. כען (*v.l.* + ארי) 'wherefore/so now'; → כי עַתָּ(ה) (e.g., Scholz,

[20] See further A. A. Macintosh 'Hosea and the wisdom tradition' in *Essays in honour of J. A. Emerton*, pp. 127f.

Sebök, Borbone, cf. G. R. Driver *JTS* 39, 1938, p. 164); → כָּעֵת (Grätz, Nowack, Marti); → כְּעִתּוֹ (cf. *BHS*) 'at the (his) time'. For arguments against such changes, cf. Rudolph.

יעמד LXX ὑποστῇ, Vulg. *stabit* 'stand' (cf. Jerome 'endure'); Pesh. *nqwm* 'remain', 'stand firm'; Targ. is very free.

במשבר LXX ἐν συντριβῇ, cf. Vulg. *in contritione* 'in the crushing/pain', etymological renderings predicated of Ephraim rather than the woman (cf. Jerome); Pesh. *bḥbl'* 'in the birth pangs (of sons)'; Targ. כאיתא דיתבא על מתברא וחיל לית לה למילד 'like a woman who has positioned herself on the birthstool but has no strength to give birth' (cf. Cathcart, p. 59, n. 26).

13.14 **Shall I[a] redeem them from the hand of Sheol? Shall I[a] ransom them from death, [so that they should say[b]] 'so much for[c] your ravages[d], O Death! so much for[c] your destruction[e], Sheol[f]!'? [g]No, relief[h] is excluded from my view[g].**

[a]The two initial clauses of the verse are understood to be rhetorical questions expressed without the *he* interrogative; cf., e.g., Gen 27.24, GK 150a b (so most modern commentators). The ancient versions together with Jerome and the rabbinic commentators apparently understood the clauses as statements rather than questions which are then construed with the adversative phrases which follow (note c). In this connection the imperfect tenses are variously interpreted: for Rashi and ibn Ezra they are frequentative and convey the sense 'in the past, I redeemed them but now I will be the agent of their destruction'. For Kimchi the tenses have a conditional force, 'I would have delivered them but now...'. According to Jerome they convey simply a divine promise, an expression of God's gracious intention according to which the death of Christ becomes the death of Death. Most such interpretations depend upon the judgement that אהי denotes 'I will be/become' and that is unlikely to be correct (note c). See further, Harper's judicious review.

[b]Ibn Janāḥ records the view that Hosea is here quoting the exultant sentiments of those who have escaped death and he compares Isa 28.15, where those who deny the creator's power are represented as saying 'we have made a treaty with Death and signed a pact with Sheol' (NEB). Accordingly, I conclude that the phrases form a part of the rhetorical questions that precede them. The connection is made explicit in the English translation.

[c]On the particle אהי see on 13.10 above. The word is rendered 'where' by the LXX and Peshiṭta (cf. 1 Cor 15.55) which is not inconsistent with the view here adopted, *viz.* that it is a particle of derision. A number of the ancient versions (see Text and Versions) together with

Jerome, Rashi, ibn Ezra and Kimchi (cf. Rosenmüller) understand the word to be an apocopated form of the verb היה with the meaning 'I will be/become'. Accordingly the two clauses are adversative, '... but I will be' (*sc.* the agent of Death and Sheol to them'), or, with Jerome, 'I will be the death of Death'. The interpretation is unlikely to be correct, not least because apocopated forms of the first person without *waw* consecutive are most unusual and the resulting sense is forced and implausible.

Many modern commentators (e.g., Wellhausen, Nowack, Ehrlich (*Miq.*), Wolff, Rudolph, Mays, NEB), investing the particle with the sense 'where?', suggest that in this particular context it conveys a command, i.e. 'come here with!', cf. the NEB 'Oh, for your plagues, O Death..!'. The difficulty arises, however, that such a sense for אהי scarcely fits 13.10 where the word occurs in a phrase whose form is recognisably similar. Where the resulting sense is concerned, if Hosea wished to depict Yahweh as solemnly urging death to do its worst, it is most unlikely that he would use an interrogative particle which, in another verse of the same chapter, appears to have a derisive force.

[d]The plural (many MSS have the singular, see Text and Versions) of the noun דֶּבֶר, usually rendered 'plague', 'pestilence', cf. BDB *ad loc.* The noun is found in parallelism with קטב 'destruction' in Ps 91.6 (noted already by ibn Ezra and Kimchi). KB's 'thorns' (cf. KB[3]) is rightly discounted by J. Blau *VT* 7 (1957), p. 98. For the versions, see Text and Versions.

[e]For the form קָטָבְךָ, GK 93q. Against KB's view (cf. KB[3]) that the word denotes 'thorns' see, again, J. Blau. For etymological possibilities, see Cathcart, p. 60 n. 28.

[f]For 'Sheol', unusually masculine, cf. König, 249f.

[g—g]Lit. 'compassion is hidden from my eyes', i.e. from my view, intention. The first person singular suffix 'my eyes' refers back to the first person singular verbal forms 'shall I redeem/ransom...' earlier in the verse. Accordingly the phrase is understood to be an answer to the questions posed; hence in English the translation, 'No; ...'.

[h]The rabbinic commentators (Rashi, ibn Ezra and Kimchi) insist that the noun נֹחַם (a *hapax legomenon*) is derived from the root נחם, apparently (see Rashi) against the view that it is from the root נוח (*sc.* 'their rest is hid from my sight'). There remains, however, some difference of opinion as to whether the word denotes strictly 'repentance', i.e. change of heart (cf. ibn Ezra, who refers to the *Niphal* of the verb predicated of God in, e.g., Jer 26.3; 42.10) or 'comfort', 'compassion' (cf. ibn Janāḥ, Kimchi). In this particular context, it is argued, repentance or change of heart necessarily implies comfort or compassion and hence the distinction should not be pressed (so Rudolph *contra* Harper and Sellin).

Further examination of the evidence, however, suggests that the real question is whether the noun defines the relief or comfort which

Yahweh might feel (were he to relent) or the comfort, compassion which he might show to his people (were he to relent). For Rashi and ibn Ezra the former is the true meaning since the phrase as a whole means 'I will not relent/be consoled concerning the evil' (*sc.* which I have set in motion); לא אנחם על הרעה הזאת. For similar verbal phrases, where comfort, i.e. peace of mind[21], is intended, cf. Ezek 14.22; 32.31. Kimchi, too, compares the *Niphal* of the verb נחם to illuminate the noun as it occurs here; but since he speaks of the comfort 'which I was offering (שהייתי מנחם) for their ills', now quite excluded, he seems to be thinking of Yahweh's compassion for his people.

On balance it seems right to follow Rashi and ibn Ezra's understanding of the phrase and to assume that Hosea makes reference to the thought processes of Yahweh (cf. AF). With this view Jerome and Ehrlich (*Miq.*) seem to agree, though they both think the sentiments are strictly those of the prophet rather than those of Yahweh. For Jerome the words mean 'I cannot be consoled – whatever I have devised in my mind is unable to lessen my grief'. Similarly Ehrlich supposes that the words mean 'I can know no consolation' (לא אדע נחמה).

The terrible pains which Ephraim now suffers, the more unbearable because they serve no purpose (v. 13), can naturally lead to nothing but extinction and death. It is fanciful, if not plainly wrong (cf. the exegesis of v. 13), to interpret (with Wolff) the womb (v. 13) as a grave and place of death, or Yahweh, in the estimate of Hosea's hearers, as the 'true midwife' with authority over death. Rather the connection between the present verse and its predecessor is formed by Hosea's insight into the mind of his God. Yahweh would dearly have wished (note a) to ransom his people from the clutches of imminent death and of the shadowy abode of Sheol to which they were destined; so that, indeed, thus redeemed, they might have exclaimed 'so much for your ravages, O Death! so much for your destruction Sheol!' (note b). Yet that possibility, a real temptation to a loving God, is quite excluded. He simply cannot, in the circumstances, bring himself to relent (note h); what he could conceive as a possibility cannot be allowed to mitigate his own grief (again, note h). Such are the complex implications of the laconic statement 'relief is excluded from my view'. With it should be compared that other divine *cri de cœur* which Hosea postulates in 11.8: 'how can I hand you over, Ephraim?' If there Yahweh's compassion and remorse is aroused, here, of purpose,

[21] For a treatment of √נחם as having the fundamental meaning 'breathing', cf. D. W. Thomas *ExpT* 44 (1932–33), pp. 191f: 'The underlying idea here will be that of relief gained by taking a deep breath (cp. the phrase "a sigh of relief")'.

the possibility of relief, of relenting, is excluded from view, deliberately put out of his mind, cf. Isa 65.16.

The central phrases of the verse 'so much for your ravages, O Death! so much for your destruction, Sheol!', with the personification of death, raise the question whether Hosea is here making use of traditional Canaanite thought and mythology (cf. Wolff). It is not unlikely that this is so; yet the evidence is scanty and any estimates necessarily hypothetical. Certainly ibn Janāḥ thinks of the words as a quotation (note b). Yet more important than their past history is the use that has been made of them since at least the time of St Paul (1 Cor 15.55) within the Christian tradition. Certainly St Paul's treatment of the words owes something to the fact that the initial clauses of the verse are likely to have been understood in the LXX not as questions but as statements. Further he may also have been influenced by the tradition (see Text and Versions) that *'hy* (note c) denotes 'I will be' (cf. Rudolph). Jerome, who explicitly states that 'he cannot and dare not differ from St Paul', follows that tradition with his *ero mors tua o mors* whereby Christ, in his death and resurrection, becomes the death of Death. Again, 1 Cor 15.54f is constructed by reference to Isa 25.8 as well as to the present text (see, again, Text and Versions). Yet St Paul, following the LXX in rendering *'hy* by 'where?', is, on the view here taken of the words of the MT, taking up and adapting something suitable for his purposes from the Old Testament, and, by coincidence, echoing its original force (cf. note c). For Hosea the possibility raised by this cry must deliberately be excluded (note g). For St Paul the same cry, recorded in scripture, will, in the light of the new evidence afforded by the resurrection of Christ, find its proper fulfilment (γενήσεται, 1 Cor 15.54) at the general resurrection.

Text and Versions

אפדם LXX, cf. Vulg. and Pesh. translate by future/imperfect tenses; Symm. and the Targ. by aorist/perfects (cf. note a above); similarly in respect of אגאלם (the rendering of which by Symm. has not survived).

אהי...אהי LXX ποῦ *bis*, so Quinta (2° *deest*) 'where', cf. Pesh. *'yk' hy hkyl* (on *hkyl* see Gelston, p. 84) and *'w 'ykw*; → אַיֵּה (e.g., Grätz, *BHS*, Borbone); Aq. and Symm. ἔσομαι *bis* 'I will be', cf. Vulg. *ero*, *bis*; Theod. καὶ ἔσται (ἡ δίκη σου ἐν θανάτῳ) 'and (thy sentence) will be (in death)' and καὶ (πληγή σου ἐν ᾅδῃ) 'and (your calamity in the grave)'; Targ. כען יהי מימרי בהון לקטול 'but now my Memra will be against them to kill'; cf. on 13.10; + *v.l.* ופתגמי למחבלא 'and my decree will be to destroy'; it is not clear what (if anything) in Targ. corresponds to אהי...אהי.

דבריך 96 Kennicott MSS and 32 de Rossi MSS have דברך singular; LXX, cf. Theod. ἡ δίκη σου 'thy sentence/punishment', = ריבך (Vollers), is likely to be a free rendering, cf. Symm. πληγή σου 'thy calamity'; Vulg. *mors tua* 'thy death' (note d, cf. Rudolph); Pesh. *zkwtk* 'thy victory', cf. 1 Cor 15.55 (Gelston, pp. 154f); νίκη (so a few LXX MSS here) 'victory' arises from νῖκος of Aq. and Theod. at Isa 25.8, quoted in 1 Cor 15.54; Aq. ῥήματά σου, cf. Quinta οἱ λόγοι σου 'thy words'; Targ. מימרי 'my Memra', see above and Cathcart, p. 60, n. 28; on the first person suffix ('my word against you') see Kimchi.

קטבך LXX τὸ κέντρον σου (cf. 1 Cor 15.55) 'sting', cf. Aq. δηγμοί σου, Vulg. *morsus tuus*, Pesh. *'wqsky* (cf. ? Syriac *qwrṭb'* 'thorn', Rudolph); Theod. πληγή σου 'thy calamity'; Symm. ἀκηδία 'neglect', 'despair' – according to Jerome ἀπάντημα 'meeting'; Targ. (*v.l.*, see above) פתגמי 'my decree'.

נחם LXX παράκλησις 'encouragement', 'comfort', cf. Vulg. *consolatio*, Pesh. *bwy"*; Targ. אסליק שכינתי מנהון 'I will remove my presence from them'.

מעיני → מעינו (Rudolph, see note a to next verse).

13.15 **Since he is the one who[a] behaves wilfully[b] among[c] brothers[d], an east wind shall come, a mighty wind[e], rising up from the desert, so that his water-source[f] will fail[g] and his spring run dry. It is the one which[h] will despoil the store of every costly treasure.**

[a]The third masculine singular pronoun הוא appears to be emphatic. Since there is no obvious antecedent, the referent is likely to be concealed within the phrase itself; see note b. Rudolph believes the antecedent to be Death/Sheol mentioned in the previous verse and in that connection he emends עיני there to עינָו 'his eyes'. Connecting the first phrase of this verse to the end of v. 14, he interprets the whole: 'sympathy is hidden from his (*sc.* death's) eyes; for he separates (note b) even between brothers'. The interpretation represents something of a *tour de force* exercised upon what is admittedly a very difficult and uncertain text. Yet as many uncertainties present themselves as those that are resolved by this approach. Amongst them may be cited emendation of the text, the continued personification of death, the uncertainty of the philological account of יפריא and the somewhat forced rendering that results.

[b]Ibn Janāḥ (cf. Rashi, as a possibility) suggests that the verb יפריא (a *hapax legomenon*) is related to the well-attested noun פרא 'a wild ass'. The noun is used in Gen 16.12 and by Hosea in 8.9 (cf. Jer 2.24) to illustrate, by reference to this animal, arbitrary and wilful behaviour. According to this view the form here is an internal *Hiphil* of a

denominative verb which conveys, by means of a word-play on Ephraim (אפרים), that such behaviour is characteristic of the nation (cf. AF). It is possible that some support for this view is detectable in the Targum (see Text and Versions). Rashi, ibn Ezra and Kimchi understand the verb to be a by-form of פרה 'to be fruitful' and suggest that the phrase continues the reference to thriving in a good pasturage (v. 6 above). The suggestion is adopted by many modern authorities, though generally in conjunction with the emendation אחו 'reeds' for אחים 'brothers'; thus the manifest fruitfulness is 'among the reeds' or (with further emendation) 'like reeds amidst water' (e.g. Wellhausen, Marti, Harper, Wolff, Mays, NEB). The interpretation is not without its attraction in that, e.g., it fits with the following reference to the east wind which has the effect of destroying such fruitfulness at its source; and just possibly it allows (so Wolff) a reference to Egyptian alliances (since the word for 'reed' is Egyptian), destroyed by the harsh east wind (Assyria). Yet a fatal objection may be seen in the use of the preposition בין/בן (note c) which, emendation excluded, properly finds its place in reference to ruptured personal relationships rather than to a geographical location (so Ehrlich *Miq.*). Nevertheless it is possible and even likely that Hosea uses the verb יפריא 'behaves wilfully' as an allusion to and a parody of the verb פרה 'to be fruitful', the latter being an interpretation of the name Ephraim, cf. Gen 41.52. Indeed such a parody may possibly (but cf. GK 75nn) have been facilitated for Hosea by considerations of dialect. In 11.7 there is an instance of a *lamedh aleph* form used instead of the more familiar *lamedh he*. By analogy פרא may have constituted a legitimate variant of פרה as well as being homonymous with the root פרא 'wild ass' (so Z. Kallai in a private communication).

Another treatment is that of Rosenmüller (cf. Rudolph) who compares the Arabic verb *pry* and posits the meanings 'to cut', 'separate', 'divide'. However, reference to, e.g., Lane suggests that the semantic range of the Arabic verb is considerably wider than is suggested by 'cutting' and 'dividing' and that it has to do with the *effect* of such actions amongst others. At all events the meaning suggested by Rosenmüller for the Hebrew word may be characterised as dubious and not clearly supported by reference to Arabic *pry*. It should be noted that no rabbinic tradition alludes to this view of the matter.

[c]MT reads בן. Here, preceding אחים, the word must be understood as the preposition בין written defectively (for another instance in Job 16.21, see J. Barr *Variable Spellings*, p. 145). In Gen 49.22 (to which Kimchi refers) the phrase בן פרת occurs as a favourable interpretation of the name 'Ephraim' (*sic*, rather than the later 'Joseph', see note 23 below). Since it is likely that Hosea's יפריא parodies the name Ephraim (see note b), the suggestion is offered that the prophet consciously refers to and also parodies the word בן as it occurs in Gen 49.22[22]. While the meaning

[22] For mention of fountains in both verses (though using different words), see the commentary below.

of the phrase in Genesis is clearly favourable to Ephraim, its precise meaning is not certainly known (for possibilities, see, e.g., Westermann *Genesis*, *ad loc.* and J. A. Emerton in *Essays presented to D. W. Thomas*, pp. 91ff). It is clear, however, that 'between' was not intended in Genesis. For Ehrlich's comments on the proper meaning of בן/בין here in Hosea, see note b above.

[d]The word אַחִים, as pointed, denotes 'brothers'. Coupled with the preposition בין the resulting phrase seems to have to do with personal relationships, cf. Prov 6.19 '(the Lord hates) ... one who stirs up quarrels between brothers'. The word here, as frequently, has a social as well as a familial reference. The actual form of the saying (i.e. concerning Ephraim in the third person singular) suggests that the contemporary nation in relation to its neighbours is pictured as if in terms of the eponymous son of Joseph and his relationship with his brothers (cf. Gen 48.19). At all events, as in Prov 6.19, the phrase indicates that self-assertiveness, deceit and violence break the brotherly bonds of confidence and loyalty between a man and his neighbour (cf. McKane *Proverbs*, *ad loc.*), and 'hence the brotherhood of Israel' (Rashi).

The rabbinic commentators (Kimchi is an exception) all mention the view that the word here should be compared with אחו 'reeds' as it occurs in Gen 41.18. The interpretation is accepted by a large number of modern commentators and authorities who emend אחים to אחו while others repoint אחים to achieve the same end (see note b above and Text and Versions below). It seems to me likely that it arose as a consequence of interpreting יפריא of 'showing fruitfulness'. If the latter is discounted then the possibility of reading אחים 'reeds' falls with it.

[e]Kimchi, perhaps rightly in the context, interprets the phrase 'a wind of Yahweh' as an intensive expression, for which he compares Ct 8.6. He also allows that the phrase may indicate divine agency, and for this he cites 1 Chr 5.26. Since Yahweh is not the subject in the verse, and the phrase is found in a parallel clause, it seems likely that the intensive use is here predominant. For the phenomenon, cf. e.g. D. W. Thomas *VT* 3 (1953), pp. 209ff.

[f]The word מקור, lit. a spring or fountain (as dug), allows of a more general sense, *viz.* the 'source of life and vigour', cf. Jer 51.36 and BDB p. 881, col 1, 1 d.

[g]וְיֵבוֹשׁ, an imperfect form of the root בוש, usually 'to be ashamed', 'confounded', is defended as a possibility by ibn Ezra who supposes that the resulting phrase indicates that 'his waters fail' (יכזבו, cf. Isa 58.11), i.e. as a result of the harsh wind. See also, perhaps, the observations on the cognate noun בשנה in 10.6 above. Kimchi derives the verb of MT from the root יבש 'to be dry' though his arguments are convincingly challenged by Ehrlich (*Miq.*). In a fragment from the Dead Sea Scrolls (4QXII, Testuz, p. 38), ויבש is read (i.e. without *waw*) which may be the reading of MT, though written defectively (cf. Borbone who interprets in

this way the same reading in a number of Kennicott MSS) or else it points (so, e.g., Wolff, Rudolph, Davies) to a form of the root יבש. Most modern commentators emend (see Text and Versions). MT's וְיֵבוֹשׁ is, however, the *difficilior lectio* and what ibn Ezra has to say points to the possibility that the word, predicated of a spring or water-source, was capable of the meaning 'to fail'. That it is near in form to the more familiar וייבש suggests that Hosea may have chosen the word deliberately and with poetic skill.

[h]Again, an emphatic use of the third masculine singular pronoun והוא which is designed to match that used of Ephraim (note a). The antecedent within the verse is the east wind and yet the phrase alludes, no doubt, to the Assyrian foe who plunders the resources of the nation. If the reference to Ephraim is effected by word-play (note b), it is not unreasonable to suppose that here too such a reference is made, perhaps by the sibilants of the verb ישסה as well as by the noun אוצר, not so far in form from אשור (Assyria). Certainly there is good reason to suppose that the Isaiah tradition was disposed to name Assyria by reference to the appropriate epithet שודד 'the devastator' (Isa. 21.2), see my *Isaiah xxi*, pp. 12ff.

The verse continues Hosea's expression of Yahweh's reaction to the inevitable demise of his people. Ephraim has behaved all along with gross selfishness and disregard of 'the brotherhood of Israel' (Rashi, see note d). Such wilfulness, such headstrong behaviour, so described (note b), parodies the very name of Ephraim. In this connection Hosea is likely to have alluded to the old saying concerning Ephraim[23] preserved in Gen 49.22. Whatever the precise meaning of the difficult phrase *bn prt*, it is there repeated twice and, the second time, with the addition of the words *'ly 'yn* 'beside a fountain'. If in Jacob's blessing Ephraim is celebrated for its success in flourishing as a tree or a vine (see the literature cited in note c) in an ideal situation, here, in a parody of that blessing, Ephraim now faces the reverse: extinction by the removal of the source and fount of all its nourishment. The mighty wind (note e) roaring in from the desert is the Sirocco, commonly called in contemporary Israel/Palestine by its Arabic name the *ḥamsīn* (because, reputedly, it lasts for fifty days). This wind, bearing sand and dust, can block the natural springs and water-sources, cf. D. Baly *Geography*, pp. 67–70. Yet the image, common in prophetic literature for Yahweh's intervention in judgement (cf., e.g., Isa 21.1; Jer 13.24), has a more particular reference: it is to the advent of the

[23] Cf. Zobel *Stammesspruche*, pp. 5, 21f and de Geus *Tribes*, p. 90; MT's 'Joseph' is likely to have been a later substitution.

Assyrians, storming forward at Yahweh's behest (note e) from their land to the east of Ephraim. The point of reference is made clear by the allusion to the one (note h) who plunders the nation of all its resources (human as well as material, so Ehrlich *Miq.*), reduces it to impotent failure (note g) and thus to ultimate extinction. In large part the nation had already been exposed to this experience (so Rudolph). Again Hosea's artistry in his use of metaphor and the simultaneous presentation of a number of images are noteworthy.

Text and Versions

בן So *BH* and *BHS*; older printed editions, בין; Kennicott lists 12 MSS as reading בן.

בן אחים LXX ἀνὰ μέσον ἀδελφῶν 'between brothers', cf. Vulg. *inter fratres*, Pesh. *byt 'ḥ'*; Targ. מתקרן בנין '(they) are styled sons', understanding בן as 'son(s)', cf. Barr *Variable Spellings*, p. 145; → כבין אחו 'as between reeds' (Nowack, Oettli, cf. *BHS*); → בין אחו (Marti) 'between reeds'; → כבין מים אחו 'like reeds amidst water' (Wellhausen); → אָחִים 'reeds', plural postulated by BDB, cf. NEB אחוים (Brockington); → עין חיים 'a living spring' (Gardner, cf., for חיים, Rudolph).

יפריא LXX διαστελεῖ 'tears asunder' = יפריד (Schleusner, Vollers, Borbone, cf. *BHS*), cf. Vulg. *dividet*, Pesh. *nprwš*; Targ. ועובדין מקלקלין אסגיאו 'they have multiplied disgraceful deeds', cf. note b above; → יפריד 'divides' (Sebök, Grätz).

יבוא LXX ἐπάξει 'he will bring' = יביא (Vollers), cf. Vulg. *adducet*, with κύριος/*Dominus* as subject) and Targ. איתי 'I will bring up', → יביא (Grätz).

קדים רוח LXX καύσωνα ἄνεμον (inverted in AQ, cf. OL[CS]) 'a burning wind', cf. Vulg. *urentem ventum* (Yahweh has become the subject, see previous note); Targ. מלך דתקיף כרוח קדומא 'a king who is mighty like the east wind'; Pesh. as MT.

יהוה See previous notes; Targ. במימרא דיוי 'through Y 's word'.

עלה LXX ἐπ' αὐτόν 'on him' = ? עלה/עליו.

ויבוש 4QXII? ויבש (Testuz, p. 38); LXX καὶ ἀναξηρανεῖ 'and he will dry up', cf. Vulg. *et siccabit*, Pesh. *wtḥrb* (wind as subject); Targ. ויחריב (king as subject); → ויבש/וייבש/ויוביש (Wellhausen, Grätz, Nowack, Marti, cf. *BHS*); → יֵיבַשׁ or ? וְיָבֵשׁ (Harper, Wolff, Rudolph, Mays, Borbone); see further, note g above.

מקורו LXX, Vulg., Pesh., plural.

ויחרב LXX ἐξερημώσει 'he will lay waste' (LXX[Luc] + καὶ, cf. Vulg. *desolabit*; → ויחריב (Wellhausen, Grätz, Nowack, Marti, cf. *BHS*); Pesh. *wtwbš* '(the wind) will dry up'.

מעינו LXX and Pesh., plural.

ישסה LXX καταξηρανεῖ 'he will dry up' (? internal corruption of καταξανεῖ 'he will despoil', Vollers); Vulg. *diripiet* 'he will despoil', cf. Pesh. and Targ. *nbwz* יבוז; → יְשַׁאֶה (*BHS* as a possibility).

אוצר LXX τὴν γῆν αὐτοῦ 'his land', → ארצ(ו) (Grätz, cf. Rudolph, *BHS*); → אוצרו (Oort, cf. Rudolph).

כל LXX καὶ πάντα 'and all ...', → וכל (Grätz).

כלי LXX, Pesh., Targ., plural.

14.1 (EV 13.16) **Samaria shall bear her guilt[a], for she has rebelled against her God; they shall fall by the sword, their children shall be dashed in pieces, their[b] pregnant women ripped open[c].**

[a]Ibn Ezra and Kimchi refer the form תאשם to the root שמם 'to be desolate', 'destroyed'. Rashi, by contrast, cites the familiar root אשם 'to be guilty'. For the evidence of the versions, see Text and Versions; and for G. R. Driver's suggestion that a second root אשם means 'to be desolate', see on 5.15 above. On this view of the matter, emendation to a form of שמם (see Text and Versions) is unnecessary. Since Hosea uses the verb אשם in the sense 'to bear guilt' elsewhere (cf. 4.15; 5.15; 10.2; 13.1), and since the rendering 'Samaria's guilt shall be revealed' (so Rashi) fits the following 'for she has rebelled ...', the decision between the two interpretations is difficult to resolve. For 'Samaria shall be desolate' also fits the phrases in the second part of the verse. The matter is made more difficult by the consideration that אשם denotes 'be guilty' but also 'bear punishment for guilt' (cf. BDB p. 79, col 2 3; cf. Wolff on 4.15), and with that 'desolation' is also consistent (cf. the phrases in the second half of the verse).

Despite arguments in favour of 'desolation' (so, e.g., Rosenmüller), I prefer to settle for the supposition that the first half of the verse sets forth the assurance that Samaria must bear her guilt together with the reason for it, and that the second half indicates the terrible implication of that punishment.

[b]The suffix is third masculine singular despite the fact that Samaria is earlier construed with feminine verbs; Kimchi compares Jer 11.16; cf. GK 135o. *BHS* raises the question whether the last phrase of the verse is an addition and Davies whether the phrase is preserved here from another (lost) oracle.

[c]The verb יבקעו, predicated of women, is nonetheless masculine. For the aversion to third feminine plural verbal forms, GK 145u. Qyl considers that attraction to the other masculine verbal forms also plays a part.

The verse probably belongs to the preceding piece rather than to the rest of chapter 14. The judgement is confirmed by reference to Testuz's fragment from the Dead Sea Scrolls, where a space occurs between (MT's) 14.1 and 14.2. Accordingly, Yahweh's assertion that Ephraim shall bear her guilt and punishment (note a) picks up the initial judgement of 13.1 that Ephraim's guilt arose from the nation's idolatrous involvement with Baal.

Specific mention of Samaria (elsewhere only in 7.1; 8.5; 10.5, 7), together with the prophecy of the horrific fate of its inhabitants, suggests that the words reflect the period when the three year siege of the capital was fast approaching or had already begun. Samaria is not mentioned by metonymy for the nation as a whole (*contra* Jerome and Qyl) but simply because, standing in the central highlands of Ephraim, it was, since 733 BC, all that remained of the state.

Compared with the highly metaphorical and allusive phrases of the preceding verses, this one is remarkable for its dispassionate and terrible objectivity. So much so, indeed, that it is tempting to postulate that the words are a *vaticinium ex eventu*. If that is not the case, then they reflect Hosea's recognition that the end is inevitable and imminent.

If the sentiments are Hosea's, formally the words mark the end of the reflection of his God, of a speech by Yahweh. This judgement is not affected by mention within the verse of '(her) God' in the third person; for that serves merely to emphasise the heinous nature of Ephraim's rebellion (cf. Rudolph and my comments on 1.7). More significant is the change from allusive speech to direct and brutal objectivity. If the verse is a *vaticinium ex eventu* then its words have been cast in a form which fits what precedes it. Yet death by the sword (cf. 7.16), the depraved slaughter of children (cf. 10.14) and the unspeakable treatment of pregnant women (cf. 2 Kgs 15.16; Amos 1.13) is typical of warfare in the ancient near east and Hosea's words may well reflect his perception that this is the reality of the imminent end of Samaria. On that view, the lapse to brutal objectivity is another instance of the prophet's artistry; there can be no more agonised prevarication on Yahweh's part: this is the end and this is the reality of the end; this is what the end means.

For Wolff and Rudolph, Ephraim's fundamental rebellion has the effect that the forces of death and destruction are unleashed in the person of the Assyrians by Yahweh (Rudolph) or else they are the result of the nation's calamitous involvement with Baal – the god of fertility who brings Ephraim to death (Wolff). Whether such considerations are precisely correct is open to question (in the case of Rudolph, they depend very considerably upon his particular interpretation of 13.14f); yet at least they point to Hosea's clear convictions concerning the realities of cause and effect in the sphere of morality.

Wolff is disposed to think that 13.1–14.1 represents Hosea's reflections upon the fate of Samaria, delivered on the southern border of Ephraim to which he had been driven in circumstances reflected in chapter 12.1b. The evidence on which this conclusion is reached is, however, dubious (cf. my translation of 12.1b with Wolff's), and, in the absence of further evidence, it is perhaps better not to speculate upon so elusive a subject. For the term 'to rebel', cf. Deut 21.20 and Ps 78.8; for the theme, 11.1ff.

Text and Versions

תאשם LXX ἀφανισθήσεται 'will be destroyed', cf. Vulg. *pereat*; Pesh. *tt*ḥ*yb* 'incurred guilt', cf. Targ. תחוב; → תֵּשַׁם (Grätz), → תֵּשַׁם (Marti) and see note a above.

יפלו LXX πεσοῦνται αὐτοί, + הם/המה (Oort, Grätz); Vulg. *pereat* 'she shall perish' (singular; *v.l. pereant*).

והריותיו LXX καὶ αἱ ἐν γαστρὶ ἔχουσαι αὐτῶν 'and their women who are pregnant', cf. Pesh. and Targ. which have third person plural suffixes; → הריותים (Borbone *sic*, misprint for והריותם?).

CHAPTER 14.2–9

HOSEA'S PRAYER *DE PROFUNDIS*

NB The English Versions add 14.1 to chapter 13 as 13.16; hence the numbering of the verses for the rest of chapter 14 is one behind that of MT. Elsewhere in the Commentary the differences are noted but not in the commentary on this chapter.

Chapter 14.2–9, which concludes the prophecies of Hosea, constitutes a prayer said over Israel (*sic* v. 2) in Hosea's name. Somewhat as in chapters 1–3, where prophecies of woe are balanced by prophecies of weal, the redactor of Hosea's prophecies, following sustained pronouncements of doom and particularly that of Samaria's terrible and imminent end (13.1–14.1), sets forth what he knows to have been the essential purpose of his master's message: Hosea's desire that Israel should recognise the truth of the situation. There can be no salvation without repentance (so Rudolph). This, Hosea's prayer for Israel, is manifestly consistent with the totality of the prophet's endeavour and there is no reason to doubt that, whatever its redactional history, it reflects accurately his deepest aspirations[1].

Recent scholars have seen the form of the prayer as reflecting elements which are known from liturgical expressions of penitence. Thus, the requirement to return to Yahweh with no gift other than sincere repentance matches the classical expression of Ps 51 (cf. Rudolph). The following oracle of salvation in the first person (v. 5) is held to reflect the so-called 'audition accounts of divine decrees' (cf., with Wolff, Pss 85.9ff, EV 8ff, and 126.5f). Yet vv. 2–4 do not themselves constitute a penitential liturgy, but rather a prophetic summons to repentance (cf. Jer 3.22; 4.1). Further, the oracle of salvation (v. 5) is not formulated in direct speech to the people (contrast Jer 3.22) but it is said of them in the third person (Wolff and Rudolph). Such

[1] Among the few recent scholars to question the authenticity of the passage (as Hosea's) is Lindblom *PAI*, pp. 283f, and his early monograph *HLU*, pp. 109f. Lindblom is right, however, to emphasise the importance of the relationship of the passage to the fall of Samaria. More recently Jeremias has denied vv. 2–4 to Hosea. His arguments are countered by Davies.

considerations suggest that the words reflect prayer; and, because the contents and imagery are so consistent with what is known of Hosea's thought, the prophet's personal prayer for his people; cf. 6.1–3 above and the conclusion there reached that that expression of penitence reflects Hosea's estimate of Yahweh's requirement in the matter.

If the piece is or reflects a prayer of Hosea's, its tentative and wistful beauty may well indicate the terrible circumstances to which his nation had been reduced in the years immediately before the fall of Samaria (so Wolff, Mays, etc.). Yet Rudolph may have a point in his contrary assertion that the principle of Ephraim's inevitable destruction was known to and promulgated by Hosea over many years before 722/1 BC and, consequently, that the prophet's instinct to call his nation to repentance is correspondingly of longer standing. The fact remains, however, that Hosea's redactor has placed this passage immediately after 13.1–14.1 and in so doing has given particular significance to the message contained in it. It is possible and even likely that this redactor knew, not of the imminent end of Samaria, but of its actual end, and hence his composition constitutes a prayer for the future of 'Israel' (cf. v. 2), i.e. Israel comprising survivors and/or Judah. His achievement has, then, a significance and perspective which transcends the work of the master, the master whose message was entrusted to him. But if he has, in chapters 1–3, passed to us a connected narrative 'so as to give authentic knowledge' (Lk 1.3; see above p. 123), it is likely that, in his completion of his master's prophecies, he reflects accurately that master's perception and aspirations as well as the consistent purpose of him who inspired both of them.

14.2 **Go back[a], Israel, right back to[b] Yahweh your[c] God; for you[c] have stumbled[d] through your[c] sin[e].**

[a]The word שׁובה, lit. 'return', 'go/come back' implies here repentance, reversion to what is right, cf. 2.9, EV 7; 6.1. Jerome observes 'Israel is constrained, as though sick, to resort to a physician to obtain healing'. For Morag's placing Hosea's use of the root שׁוב and its derivatives within the semantic field of ethical deviation and its treatment as sickness (pp. 506f), cf. especially 14.5.

[b]The preposition עד with the verb שׁוב occurs elsewhere at, e.g., Deut 4.30; 30.2; Amos 4.6 and Joel 2.12. The sense conveyed is 'slowly but surely' (ibn Ezra), i.e. from the helplessness of the fallen state 'to contact with the throne of glory' (Kimchi after the Rabbis). It is not that the preposition עד is here stronger than אל (the latter occurs in 3a; cf.

Rudolph *contra* Keil); rather, construed with the verb שוב, it denotes the steady deliberation and seriousness of purpose necessary from the beginning to complete the large task.

[c]The personal pronouns are singular.

[d]Cf. 5.5; כשל 'to stumble' denotes the lack of strength which incapacitates and topples previously fit and active men; cf., with Ehrlich *Miq.*, Neh 4.4, EV 10 (of labourers) and Ps 31.11, EV 10 (of a sick man, where עון is also found). For other instances of כשל with עון, see BDB p. 506 (מכשול), col 1 2 c.

[e]עון, 'guilt', 'sin'; cf. on 5.5 and 12.9 above.

The call to repentance is that of the prophet, since God is referred to in the third person. His words reflect the enormity of the gulf that now exists between Israel and Yahweh (note b). There is now no chance of rescuing the nation from imminent judgement, for the calamity has already taken place. Israel is fallen, has totally collapsed (note d). It has happened by reason of the nation's sin and guilt (note e).

The prophet's words, while they define the terrible truth of the matter, are at the same time tender in what they convey. The summons is to Israel (rather than to Ephraim), i.e. to the object of Yahweh's ancient love (cf. 11.1 etc.). And it is to 'your' God (note c) that Israel is bidden to return. Again the preposition *'d* (note b) implies that the way back leads to 'contact with the throne of glory' (so Kimchi). To be sure, 'your God' also implies that Israel's guilt consisted in a contemptible disregard of Yahweh (cf. Rudolph) and the preposition implies that the way back is a long one. Such use of words on two levels again testifies to Hosea's artistry and to the profundity of his insight.

Israel's guilt has reduced the nation to impotent helplessness. From that position all that the nation can do is to begin the long road back to where in truth it belongs (cf. 2.9, EV 7). 'As one who is sick, Israel should return to her physician so as to be restored to health; that, as one who has collapsed, she can begin again to stand' (so Jerome). Accordingly the prophet's words urge the nation to recognise that all is lost and then, *mirabile dictu*, to perceive that that very exigency impels its folk to do what all along they should have done. Repentance, then, implies confession that the nation's terrible fate was self-induced. That confession, once made, is enough to redeem a situation which, without it, appears irredeemable.

Text and Versions

יהוה אלהיך The full expression is found in 12.10 (EV 9); 13.4; *BHS* raises the question whether one of these words is an addition.

כשלת LXX ἠσθένησας 'you were weak'; Vulg. *corruisti* 'you have collapsed'; Pesh. *'ttqlt* 'you have stumbled', cf. Targ. אתקילתא.

14.3 Take with you[a] words and go back to[b] Yahweh. Say[c] to him, [d]Forgive all our iniquity[d] and accept[e] what pleases[f] [you]; that we may[g] requite [you][h] with our confession as if with young bulls[h].

[a]The verbs and pronouns change in this verse to the second person plural.

[b]The preposition אל is the usual one, cf. note b to v. 2. For statistics, see Holladay *šûbh*, p. 78.

[c]I.e. adopt this formula of confession and attitude of mind; cf., *mutatis mutandis*, Isa 48.20; Jer 31.7; Ps 66.3 etc.

[d—d]The word order כל תשא עון is unusual, though parallels are adduced in GK 128e; cf. Kimchi, who cites Ezek 39.11 מקום שם קבר. According to this view, the construct כל, separated from the absolute, has virtually an adverbial force, i.e. 'wholly'. Ibn Ezra prefers to suppose that כל refers to all (of us) whose iniquity is forgiven and who return to God. In other words, כל is an absolute and defines the beneficiaries of divine forgiveness, i.e., literally, 'in respect of all (of us), forgive iniquity' (cf. Rashi). However the grammatical structure is defined[2] , the phrase is characterised by hypallage, cf., with Rosenmüller, Ezek 24.17; 39.11, and represents an impassioned plea which the translation offered above seeks to convey. Nyberg's attempt (cf. Brockelmann *Syntax* 144) to invest כל with the sense 'as often as' is dependent upon his further understanding that נשא can mean 'impute', 'charge', for which there is no evidence (cf. Rudolph). For Grätz's suggestion to read בל on the basis of the LXX ('will you not forgive iniquity?'), see Text and Versions.

[e]Cf., with Ehrlich *Miq.*, the usage of the verb לקח in Exod 22.10.

[f]For ibn Ezra the word טוב implies comparison, i.e. what is better than a holocaust, i.e. a good confession (דיבור טוב) or a confession of praise (cf. Rashi, as one possibility). Such considerations suggest that טוב here denotes what is good and lovely (cf. Ps 133.1) and specifically what is good and pleasing in the sight of God (cf. 1 Sam 15.22 and Mic 6.8); cf. further BDB pp. 373f, col 2 2.

[2] Cf. D. N. Freedman *Biblica* 53 (1972), p. 536.

Rashi and ibn Ezra quote rabbinic authorities to the effect that the meaning is 'accept our limited good works', i.e. the little good that we can offer (cf. van Hoonacker). The suggestion is, however, somewhat casuistic and implausible. Implausible, too, is the suggestion that the words denote 'adopt a good attitude', i.e. 'be again good, *sc.* to us' (so Hitzig, Orelli *et al.*).

A number of recent commentators (Wolff, Rudolph, Mays, cf. NEB which emends to טֻב, Brockington, p. 250) have followed Gordis 'Hosea XIV 3', pp. 89f[3], in supposing that the word טוב here, as in Neh 6.19[4] and, perhaps, Ps 39.3 (EV 2), denotes 'word', 'speech', cf. Aramaic טיבא 'rumour', 'report'. Accordingly they render 'accept the speech we offer' or 'accept our plea' (so Rudolph, adding the first person plural suffix). The suggestion is, to my mind, unconvincing. The interpretation of the rabbinic commentators cited above suggests with reason that טוב in this particular context clearly implies speech; but such reasonable estimates of the context do not warrant the further conclusion that טוב actually denotes 'speech'. It is enough that its well-attested meaning 'good/what is good' implies, in this context, speech that is good.

[g]Simple *waw* with the cohortative, following an imperative, expresses intention or intended consequence, GK 108d. The sense of the phrase is here closely connected with what precedes it and hence Rudolph is right in asserting that it is a co-ordinate rather than a subordinate phrase. It is, as Qyl observes, essentially a prayer.

[h—h]The verb שלם in the *Piel* denotes the payment of a debt or obligation; in relation to God 'vows' are frequently found as an object but also 'praises' or 'thank-offerings' (e.g. Ps 56.13, EV 12, *contra* Gordis' qualified assertion that the object of payment is not expressed after the verb). For ibn Ezra שפתינו is an accusative of respect, i.e. 'as to our lips/with the confessions of our lips' and for this he compares Ps 3.8, EV 7, (cf. GK 118 ll). פרים 'young bulls' is construed as the direct object of the verb and serves as an intensive[5] emphasising the costly sincerity of the confession to be offered (so essentially Rashi and Kimchi). A similar but not identical view is taken by Ehrlich (*Miq.*) for whom the two nouns are in apposition (cf. Num 24.8) and the resulting sense is 'that we may requite you with bulls which consist of the words of our lips'.

A large number of modern scholars have judged such explanations too contrived and have, by reference to the LXX (cf. Heb 13.15) and the Peshiṭta (see Text and Versions), understood the word פרים to represent the noun פרי 'fruit'. The *mem* is sometimes explained as an enclitic

[3] See also A. Geiger *Urschrift und Übersetzungen der Bibel* (Frankfurt, 1928), p. 44 and Barr *CPOT*, pp. 16f.

[4] For H. G. M. Williamson's criticisms of Gordis' view of טובתיו in this verse, see his *Ezra. Nehemiah* (Waco, 1985), p. 250, n. a to 6.19.

[5] The essential point is confirmed by ibn Ezra when he supposes, as an alternative explanation, that there is an ellipsis of *kaph* before פרים.

mem, as attested in Ugaritic[6], or as belonging originally to (מ)שפתינו (so Procksch). The resulting sense 'we will pay the fruit of our lips' is then compared with Isa 57.19 נוב שפתים, a figure of praise and thanksgiving, and to Prov 13.2; 12.14, the (wholesome) consequences of speech. Yet, as Rudolph observes, the contrast between (sacrificial) offerings and verbal confession forms the background to the beginning of the verse and consequently the suspicion remains that MT's פרים 'young bulls' is authentic. Further, the evidence of the LXX and of the Epistle to the Hebrews may not warrant the conclusions that have so readily been drawn from it. Thus, in Heb 13.15 'fruit of lips' (NEB 'tribute of lips') is understood to be identical (τοῦτ' ἔστιν) with 'the sacrifice of praise'. For S. Bochart's reservations on the use of the LXX as evidence for the MT, see Text and Versions.

For various emendations designed to facilitate the understanding of the text on the basis of one or more of the ideas set out above, see Text and Versions below.

Hosea's exhortation to repentance continues in this verse though in place of 'Israel', addressed in the second person singular, plural forms are now used. The call to repentance is thus clearly directed to individuals and every member of Yahweh's people must understand himself to be responsible for accepting it (cf. Rudolph). To appear before Yahweh empty-handed was prohibited by the ancient rules of the cult (Exod 23.15; 34.20) and by this, clearly, sacrificial gifts of animals were enjoined. Yet, as Hosea has already made abundantly clear (4.8; 5.6; 6.6; 8.13), Israel's God required in this respect the prior qualities of sincerity and obedience (cf. Kimchi). Hence Hosea expresses the wish that his people will take as their offering simply their words, i.e. their sincere confession and expressed repentance. They are to pray God (note c) that he will forgive their sin and totally remove their guilt. They are to do so fervently and in words which reflect their submission to him (note d—d); cf. Ps 51.19 (EV 17) and, in the Christian tradition, *qui tollis peccata mundi, miserere nobis*. The plea reflects, then, Hosea's conviction (again note c) that Yahweh alone can effect what his people should ask him to effect. In so doing, they will be inviting Yahweh to accept what alone pleases him (note f); they will be requiting Yahweh with a verbal confession in every way equal in his sight to the costly sacrifice of young bulls (so ibn Ezra, Rashi and Kimchi, cf. note h). The three elements of the prayer following 'say to him' are juxtaposed (note g) to form a litany, a litany which will cause those who recite it to come to share the

[6] So Gordis; cf. R. T. O'Callaghan *VT* 4 (1954), p. 171, though he reads פְּרִי; see Text and Versions.

conviction of the prophet who teaches them its words (cf. Mays). Thus behind the prayer *of* the people is the prophet's prayer *for* his people, the latter infusing and giving shape to the former.

Text and Versions

יהוה LXX and Pesh. add τὸν θεὸν ὑμῶν, *'lhkwn* 'your God'.

כל תשא LXX ὅπως μὴ λάβητε 'so that you may not accept (our iniquity)'; μή = בַּל (Vollers, Grätz, Gordis, O'Callaghan, Wolff, understanding the phrase as asseverative, i.e. *nonne*, 'dost thou not forgive...?' cf. NEB, reading כי לא, Brockington); Pesh. *dnšbwq* '(say to him) that he should forgive...', cf. Targ. קריב קדמך למשבק 'it is your disposition to forgive' and Theod. ἱλασθῆναι; Aq. πᾶσαν ἄρατε (ἀνομίαν), cf. Vulg. *omnem aufer (iniquitatem)* (as MT); LXX[Luc] δύνασαι πᾶσαν ἀφαιρεῖν (ἁμαρτίαν) → תּוּכַל תִּשָּׂא 'thou art able to forgive' (Rudolph, citing König 361i, cf. Oort, Valeton and Borbone); cf. Smolar and Aberbach, p. 214 on this verse and Ezek 24.7f.

וקח LXX and Pesh. plural; → וְנִקְחָה 'that we may receive good' (Oort, Valeton, Oettli, cf. *BHS* ונקח after Targ. ונתקבל); → לְקַח (Borbone, *sic*).

טוב LXX ἀγαθά '(accept) good things', cf. Pesh. *ṭbt'*; Vulg. (*accipe*) *bonum*; Targ. ונתקבל הא כטבין 'that we may be received as good men'.

ונשלמה Pesh. *wnprw'kwn* 'and he will recompense you'.

פרים LXX καρπόν, cf. Pesh. *p'r'* 'fruit', = פְּרִי (so, e.g., Wellhausen, Valeton, Marti, Borbone, *BHS*), or פְּרִים with enclitic *mem* (Gordis, Wolff, Mays, AF)[7]; Rudolph expands to מהפרים פרי '... not with bulls but with the fruit...'; S. Bochart (*apud* Rosenmüller) challenges all such interpretation of the evidence of LXX on the grounds that καρπός may denote an 'offering' and for this he cites (ὁλο)κάρπωμα and (ὁλο)κάρπωσις as answering frequently in the LXX to עֹלָה 'holocaust', 'burnt-offering'. It seems likely that LXX and Pesh. merely seek to simplify somewhat the complex figure of speech in MT. Vulg. *vitulos* 'calves'; Targ. כתורין 'like bullocks'.

שפתינו LXX χειλέων ἡμῶν 'our lips' (*v.l.* Q* ὑμῶν 'your'), cf. Vulg. *labiorum nostrorum*; Pesh. *dspwtkwn* '(the fruit of) your lips'; → משפתינו '(the bulls/fruits of) our herds/pens' (Duhm, van Hoonacker, cf. NEB → פרים מִשְׁפְּתֵינוּ, also O'Callaghan, who retains an enclitic *mem* on פְּרִי with no *mem* prefixed to שפתינו; for שפתים = משפתים, see BDB p. 1046, col 1); the suggestion is rejected on two grounds: first, it is not certain that משפה can mean 'herds/pens', cf. BDB who list only the dual and presume that the word is masculine; secondly, that Hosea should at this juncture envisage actual sacrifices is unlikely in view of 5.6; 6.6

7 For instances of the phrase and others like it in the Qumran writings, see M. Mansoor *RQ* 3 (1961–62), p. 391.

(see further Rudolph); NEB margin → פְּרִי מִשְּׂפָתֵינוּ 'fruit from our lips'; Targ. מלי ספותנא 'the words of our lips', cf. R. P. Gordon *Studies in the Targum*, p. 57.

14.4 **Assyria cannot[a] save us; we will[a] not ride on horses and no more shall[a] we say 'Our gods[b]' to the work of our hands. It[c] is [d]by your aid[d] that the fatherless is cared for[e].**

[a]The verbs, within the context of a prayer which expresses and seeks to inculcate a particular attitude of faith, display a range of the meanings attested for the imperfect; cf. GK 107n and 107w.

[b]It is difficult to decide whether the word אלהינו is to be taken as a singular (i.e. a plural of majesty) or as a plural, cf. 1 Kgs 12.28; see further below.

[c]The relative particle אשר refers back to Yahweh, the subject of the second person singular verbs in v. 3 ('forgive', 'accept'), see BDB p. 82, col 1 3; similarly Rashi who comments 'you alone will constitute our hope, you the carer of orphans' (המרחם). A similar but not identical suggestion is set forth by Ehrlich (*Miq.*). An alternative view is implied by Theodotion, the Vulgate, the Peshiṭta and, perhaps, the Targum (see below) which render 'for', 'because'. For אשר used elliptically in this sense, cf. GK 158b. In the end not much turns upon the question which is preferable since, on the latter view, the antecedent of בך is the same and the general sense differs only marginally. For a defence (*contra*, e.g., Harper) of the view that the following phrase is correctly placed here, rather than at the end of v. 3, see the commentary below.

[d–d]For the preposition ב with this sense, see BDB p. 89, col 2 2 c.

[e]See on 1.6 for the verb רחם.

Hosea's convictions, so firmly held over the momentous years of his ministry, are, so he prays, to be taken up and incorporated in Israel's confession to Yahweh. In expressing their submission to him, Hosea's countrymen are formally to repudiate the attitudes which infused and prompted their sinful behaviour. The chief amongst them were, first, their meretricious involvement with foreign alliances. In this, apart from its fundamental disloyalty to Yahweh, Ephraim had shown tragic stupidity in oscillating between pro-Assyrian and pro-Egyptian policies, cf. on 7.11f; 8.9f. Now, penitent, they are to affirm that Assyria cannot (note a) save them. In the following phrase, 'we will not ride on horses', the reference is likely to be to despatch riders with their urgent pleas for help to Assyria or to Egypt (so Kimchi). Rashi and ibn Ezra, comparing Isa 31.1, suggest that the phrase implies reliance specifically upon horses from Egypt which, according to Deut 17.16 and the evidence of Assyrian records (see Dalley), constituted a plentiful source of the animals. Accordingly, since chariotry rather than cavalry characterised the use of horses in Samaria of the eighth century BC[8], the phrase represents a general repudiation of reliance upon military resources (so Rudolph, comparing 8.14; 10.13). But the explicit reference to *riding* on horses (contrast Isa 31.1 which speaks of reliance upon horses) suggests that, like 7.11f and 8.9f, the reference complements the assertion 'Assyria cannot save us', i.e. in these circumstances we will not again send despatches by mounted horsemen. For such despatch riders, cf., e.g., 2 Kgs 9.17ff and, for evidence from Assyria, Dalley, p. 37.

Secondly, Hosea requires and expects his countrymen to repudiate the idolatry which, in his view, had marked the fundamental sickness of Ephraim. It is difficult to be certain whether his hearers are bidden to repudiate idols in the plural (cf., e.g., 2.15, EV 13), or to repudiate the 'calf of Samaria' in the singular (note b and cf. the interpretations of the versions). The latter is described in 8.6 as the object of the nation's aspirations and the expression of its identity (see on 8.6) and, historically, the principal exemplars had been situated in Bethel and Dan (1 Kgs 12.29). At all events, Israel's confession should acknowledge that idolatry depends upon worshipping human artefacts and to do so constitutes an 'open invitation for the worshipper to suppose that he has the deity at his disposal' (Mays).

Within the context of Hosea's earnest prayer for Israel to pronounce a confession of faith in Yahweh, it is natural that the negative elements should be complemented by a positive affirmation. Accordingly, in acknowledging their submission to Yahweh, the penitent are to recall in personal and intimate terms (cf. Kimchi, 'we know') that 'it is by your aid that the fatherless is cared for' (notes c, d and e). The phrase, then, reflects a prayer to the Help of the helpless: for Israel has stumbled through sin (v. 2) and, quite lost and helpless, can only turn back to his God (so, essentially, Rashi, ibn Ezra and Kimchi). Where the contents of the phrase are concerned, Jerome and the Targum are surely correct in seeing there an allusion to the exodus. In 11.1 Israel is portrayed as Yahweh's (adopted) son and that marks the beginning of the special, intimate relationship between

[8] Cf. 1.7 (note d) and *Bibl. Real.* p. 425. For a full treatment of the Assyrian evidence, see S. Dalley *Iraq* 47 (1985), pp. 31ff; she concludes that Samaria was distinctive for possessing chariotry without cavalry.

Israel and its God. Yet that relationship had been ruptured by Israel's (or Ephraim's) tragic and wilful sinfulness (see 1.6; 1.9; cf. 9.15 and 14.2); hence Israel is styled an orphan 'since he had lost God, his father' (Jerome). Through its stupidity the nation had, then, inevitably reverted to the pitiable condition of an orphan, a condition from which, at the exodus, Yahweh had graciously redeemed it (*contra* Rudolph). Yahweh's attitude of tender care (note d) is, then, appropriately described in terms of the care displayed to the helpless orphan by those who foster him. The use of the verb *rḥm* matches its use in 2.25 (EV 23) and Hosea's prophecy of the restoration of the relationship between Yahweh and his people. For 'orphan(s)' as a figure of the helplessness of defeat, cf. Lam 5.3; for Yahweh as the protector of orphans, Pss 10.14; 68.6, EV 5; Deut 10.18.

A number of modern commentators are disposed to regard the phrase 'it is by your aid that the fatherless is cared for' as a gloss (e.g. Marti, Wolff) or as displaced from v. 3 (e.g. Harper). The judgement, however, rests upon a failure to perceive the nature of the passage as a prayer or confession addressed to Yahweh in which the recalling of his characteristic goodness naturally finds a place (cf. Psalms, *passim*); further, there is a failure to appreciate how admirably this particular *cri de cœur* follows upon a confession of those sins which have reduced the people to the necessity of making it (cf. the rabbinic commentators).

Text and Versions

Pesh. begins the verse with *w'mrw* 'and say ...'.

סוס Targ. רכבי סוסון 'horsemen'.

נרכב LXX ἀναβησόμεθα 'mount', cf. Vulg. *ascendemus*; Pesh. *nrkb* 'ride'; Targ. נתרחיץ 'we will (not) rely' (harmonising with Isa 31.1).

אלהינו LXX θεοί ἡμῶν 'our gods', cf. Vulg. *dii nostri* and Pesh. *'lh'* (with *seyame*), Targ. אלהנא 'our god'.

אשר בך LXX ὁ ἐν σοί '(he) who (is) in you'; Theod. ὅτι ἐν σοί 'because in you', cf. Vulg. *quia*, Pesh. *mṭl d'nt* and Targ. ד 'for'; Vulg. *quia eius qui in te est* 'since (you will take pity on the orphan) who is in you' (i.e. ? who is yours).

ירחם LXX ἐλεήσει '(he who is in you, he) will pity', = יְרַחֵם (Vollers); Vulg. *misereberis* 'you will take pity'; Pesh. *mrḥm 'nt* 'you care for'; Targ. מן קדמך אתרחם 'from before you there came compassion'. A fragment from the Dead Sea Scrolls appears to confirm MT with ירוחם, Testuz, pp. 38f, cf. Theod. ἐλεηθήσεται.

יתום Targ. על אבהתנא דהוו במצרים הא כיתמין '.... upon our fathers who were in Egypt like orphans'; יתום is omitted as a corrupt dittograph of ירחם (Oort and Grätz); → יִתּוֹם (√תמם) '(he who finds compassion from you), will be safe and sound', i.e. become תָּמִים (so Rudolph, following F. Delitzsch *Die Lese- und Schreibfehler im AT*, Berlin, 1920, p. 75, and Bruno).

14.5 **I will heal their delinquency[a]; I will love them generously[b]. For my anger has abated[c] from him[d].**

[a]See on 11.7 (note b). Morag, p. 506, rightly understands the noun משובה in this verse as belonging to the semantic field of moral deviation described as sickness; cf. Jer 3.22.

[b]The noun נדבה is used as an adverbial accusative, describing the nature of the love, GK 118m, q.

[c]The root שׁוב lit. 'to turn back'; BDB p. 997, col 2 6 f.

[d]The singular suffix relates to the whole nation, Israel; the plural suffixes which precede relate to individuals (so Kimchi; cf. vv. 2 and 3 above). There is no need to emend (cf., e.g., Rudolph), nor to regard the change in numbers as evidence that the clause as a whole is a gloss (*contra*, e.g., Wolff, cf. *BHS*).

The form of divine speech which is used in vv. 5–9 reflects Hosea's understanding of and faith in the God of Israel and his gracious readiness to accept the repentance of his people. The use of the third person pronouns ('their', 'them', 'him') within the divine speech facilitates the identification of the piece as part of Hosea's prayer; for God is not addressing his people directly (other than in the exception of v. 9b, where, at the very end of the piece, direct personal contact is highly appropriate) and so the words attest to Hosea's own meditation, to revelation vouchsafed to him (so, explicitly, Rashi; Wolff says that the passage 'is in the style of an audition account of a divine decree'; cf. on v. 2 above).

The opening words testify to the generous and ready warmth of Yahweh's response to penitence. The same point is made magnificently elsewhere in the parable of the prodigal son (Lk 15.11ff), whose father 'saw him while he was still a long way off', whose 'heart went out to him' and who 'ran to meet him' with the embrace of full acceptance and reconciliation (after NEB). If the prodigal son, coming to his senses and resolving to go home, believed himself to have a difficult task, in the end he was surprised by joy. So, too, Hosea's Israel, helpless and fallen, had apparently a long road to tread (cf. v. 2); yet here the situation would, in Hosea's teaching, be transformed by the immense generosity (note b) of Yahweh's response of love.

Yahweh's open-hearted generosity will have another simultaneous effect upon Israel; the nation's delinquency (note a), as if a disease (cf. 6.1), will be healed in the warmth of that love. It is important to note that it is Israel's repentance which effects the crucial abatement of Yahweh's anger as well as the near-simultaneous release of his loving generosity (so the Targum, the Peshiṭta, the Vulgate, Rashi and Kimchi). Repentance resides in the very words which Israel brings (v. 3), the recognition and frank confession by the people that they had been delinquent in very specific ways (v. 4). Thus the healing that Yahweh bestows is not for Hosea that of a general human weakness; it is the healing of Israel's rebellion (so Rudolph), the nation's wilfulness of spirit which is like 'a sickness of the body' (so ibn Ezra). Yahweh's healing of Israel is, then, intensely personal and marks the repair of the ruptured relationship between the nation and its God (cf. the Targum). The same point is well made by Malachi (3.7 NEB): 'If you will return to me, I will return to you, says the Lord of Hosts'.

The element of recapitulation reflected by the words of the verse is noteworthy and constitutes important evidence of the continuity between this prayer of Hosea's and his earlier prophecies. Thus, 'I will love them generously' marks the reverse of the dire 'my God must reject them' (9.17); 'my anger has abated' the reverse of the decisive 'my anger has flared up against them' (8.5). Further, where the healing of Israel's delinquency is concerned, a contrast with the nation's recent attitudes is also clearly drawn: thus, in 6.1–3 the prophet had given expression to a prayer that his people would adopt an attitude of contrition, yet his God had detected in them good intentions as transitory as the morning mist (6.4). Again, in 11.7 Ephraim dithered in respect of repentance to God and would not raise himself in answer to the summons to piety. Here, by contrast, Hosea prays that recognition of utter helplessness will lead Israel to true repentance (vv. 3f) and that, in answer to it, Yahweh will apply his healing love. Thus the healing of the nation's delinquency (*mšwbtm*) is rendered possible by the return to God (cf. *mšwbty*, 11.7).

Text and Versions

ארפא Targ. אקבילינון 'I will accept them (in their repentance)'.

משובתם LXX τὰς κατοικίας αὐτῶν 'their dwelling-places', √ישב, cf. 11.7, = מוֹשְׁבֹיהֶם (Vollers); Vulg. *contritiones eorum* 'their penitence', cf. Pesh. *tybwthwn*, Targ. בתיובתהון (Cathcart, p. 61 n. 9).

נדבה LXX ὁμολόγως 'confessedly' 'openly', cf. Vulg. *spontanee* and Targ. בנדבא '(I will have compassion on them when they) freely (repent)'; Pesh. *ndryhwn* '(I will love/delight in) their vows'.

ממנו LXX ἀπ' αὐτῶν 'from them', Pesh. *mnhwn* and Targ. מנהון; LXX[B] ἀπ' αὐτοῦ 'from him', cf. Vulg. *ab eo* (*v.l. eis*); → מהם (Halévy, Borbone, *et al.*).

14.6 **I will be like the dew to Israel, that he may flower like the lily[a] [b]and that he may strike root[b] like the trees of[c] Lebanon.**

[a]So the traditional rendering. Dalman *AUS* 1 p. 360, and *PJ* 21 (1925), pp. 90f, notes that the word is more general and comprises all large blooms with cup-like flowers, such as irises and tulips.

[b]ויך שרשיו Israel is understood to be the subject of the singular verb ויך as it is of the preceding 'that he may flower'. The verb itself is from the root נכה, usually rendered 'to strike', and is used elsewhere, for example, of the thrusting of a fork into a cauldron (1 Sam 2.14) or of a spear into a wall (1 Sam 19.10). This is the only instance of its use in connection with the roots of plants and the usage seems to be mirrored precisely by that of English. Ibn Janāḥ and Kimchi appear to suggest that the root(s) are the subject of the verb, but closer examination suggests that what they say represents explanation rather than close paraphrase. For ibn Janāḥ the verb means that his roots 'spread under the earth, i.e. they extend far off in the way that the verb מחה is used in Num 34.11' (Arabic *tnbsṭ 'ġṣ'nh...'y tḍrb...*). Kimchi, quoting the same text, states that 'the roots will strike (יכו השרשים) all over the place'. It is thus the specific comparison with the text of Numbers which prompts these authorities, in explanation, to speak of the roots as the subject.

[c]Lit. 'like Lebanon'. By metonymy the expression means 'like the trees of Lebanon'; so the Targum, cf. Jerome, Rashi, ibn Ezra and Kimchi. There is no need to emend to 'as the poplar' (see Text and Versions) or to suppose that Lebanon is here the name of a tree (cf. Rudolph *contra* Nyberg).

With a series of similes the prophet dreams of the effect that Yahweh's love will have upon Israel once it is repentant and submissive to him. He will be like the dew which has so necessary a function in Israel/Palestine during the rainless season of summer. Indeed, without its copious regularity, fruits such as melons and grapes would not grow (*AUS* 1/2, pp. 514ff). In that Yahweh will have this effect (*'hyh*, see below), his action reflects his very name (cf. on 1.9 above); in such a mode of love he comes to their aid and meets their need. Above all he can bring life and vigour to his people (cf. Isa 26.19, where dew is used in connection with the notion of resurrection) so that Israel shall flower with all the glory of the 'lilies of the field' (cf., with Rudolph, Mt 6.28f), the flowers (note a) which flourish so strikingly in the wadies of the desert and among the thorn-bushes (Ct 2.1f, cf. *AUS* 1/2, pp. 257f). Yet Israel's glory will not be transitory like theirs for, by contrast (so ibn Ezra and Kimchi), he will strike roots like the legendary (e.g. Ps 104.16) trees of Lebanon (note c), whose great age and height are dependent upon the fact that their root system is deep and well-established (cf. ibn Janāḥ, note b above).

Again the verse is marked by recapitulation: 'I will be' reverses 'I will not be' of 1.9 (*q.v.*). Dew here is the agent of life and vigour, whereas in 6.4 and 13.3 it constitutes a symbol of the ephemeral character of the Ephraimites and their good intentions. The roots of repentant Israel here extend and flourish; in 9.16 Ephraim's roots are withered (note that a different form of the verb used here for 'that he may strike root' is found in 9.16 for 'Ephraim is blighted').

Text and Versions

אהיה Targ. יהי מימרי (כטלא) 'my Memra will be (like the dew)'.

ויך 4QXII? reads יך without *waw*, Testuz, p. 38; LXX καὶ βαλεῖ (τὰς ῥίζας αὐτοῦ) 'and he will throw', 'push out', cf. Pesh. *wnrm'*; OL (see Oesterley, cf. Jerome) *et mittet radices suas*; Targ. has for this and the two following words ויתבון על תקוף ארעהון כאילן לבנן דמשלח עוברתיה 'they will dwell in their fortified land like the tree of Lebanon which puts forth its branches'; Vulg. *et erumpet (radix eius)* '(his root) (subject) will break forth'; → וְילכו 'shall go', 'spread' (Wellhausen, Nowack); → וְיֹר, √ירה, cf. LXX (Borbone, cf. *BHS*); → ויט (cf. *BHS*).

כלבנון LXX ὡς ὁ Λίβανος; Vulg. *ut Libani*; Pesh. *'yk dlbnn* 'like (trees of) Lebanon'; Targ., see previous entry; → כַּלִּבְנֶה 'as the poplar' (cf. 4.13, so Oort, Valeton); Wellhausen, Nowack, Marti omit the word as a dittograph from either v. 7 or v. 8.

14.7 **His fresh shoots[a] shall spread[b], that his vigour[c] may be like the olive, that his fragrance may be like that of[d] Lebanon.**

[a]ינקותיו from the root ינק 'to suck', cf. English 'sucker'; the noun denotes the fresh shoots, the new growth of branches. Since the noun is identical to the feminine singular active participle *Qal* of ינק while the masculine singular active participle *Qal* means 'children', 'sucklings', the Targum and Rashi are able to interpret the phrase of the multiplication of Israel's 'sons and daughters'.

[b]For the verb הלך ('to go') used of plants with the meaning 'grow out', 'spread', cf. Jer 12.2 and BDB p. 232, col 2 3.

[c]הודו Lit. 'his glory = magnificence'; in relation to the olive it defines 'the abiding strength of its sap' which enables it to have 'verdant foliage all the year long' (so Kimchi).

[d]Virtually the same phrase occurs in Ct 4.11.

A further series of similes builds upon those of the previous verse. The olive, even in advanced age, is known for its perennial fruitfulness and for 'the rich abundance of its fresh branches and crisp foliage as well as its strong trunk' (*AUS* 4, p. 164), cf. Jer 11.16, 'an olive-tree, leafy and fair' (NEB, following the LXX). The simile, applied, may be suggestive of Israel's children and young people (note a). In this respect it is possible that the phrase constitutes a recapitulation of 9.12, 'I will render them childless'. The second simile is attested elsewhere in Ct 4.11, where the context is clearly erotic. Here, in Hosea, Israel's restoration to Yahweh's favour and blessing is described in terms of the wholesome and personal self-confidence of the person who basks in the sensual appreciation of the relationship of love.

Lebanon, the vehicle of the simile, is a district 'of shrubs and herbs which fill the air with pleasant fragrance and particularly so when the stroller treads upon them' (*sc.* the herbs – so H. Guthe *RE*[3] 11, p. 436, quoted by Wolff).

Text and Versions

ילכו LXX πορεύσονται 'will go', cf. Vulg. *ibunt*; Pesh. *wnšwḥwn* 'will flourish', 'sprout'; Targ. יסגון בנין ובנן '(sons and daughters) will multiply'; → יצלחו 'will thrive', 'prosper' (Grätz).

הודו LXX (ὡς ἐλαία) κατάκαρπος '(like a) fruitful (olive)', a free rendering (so Wolff).

כלבנון LXX ὡς Λιβάνου 'like that of Lebanon', cf. Vulg. *Libani* and Pesh. *'yk dlbnn*; Targ. כריח קטורת בסמיא 'like the scent of spicy incense' (see Cathcart, p. 61 n. 14), with which LXX may be compared, if a proper noun is not intended here, cf. OL (Oesterley) *sicut thuris*; → כלבונה 'like incense' (Newcome, Grätz, cf. *BHS*).

14.8 **Those who dwell in[a] his[b] shadow [c]shall again[d] revive the growth of corn[c]; that they may flourish as the vine, that his renown[e] be like the wine of Lebanon.**

[a]For the construct before a preposition in elevated style, GK 130a.

[b]The pronominal suffix is understood of Israel, referred to from v. 6c onwards as a luxuriant tree (so ibn Ezra, cf. Rashi). For Kimchi the referent is God, and a similar understanding here prompts a number of modern commentators (see Text and Versions below) to emend MT so as to read צלי 'my shade', 'appropriate in the context of divine speech' (so Wolff). Yet first person pronouns do not otherwise appear until v. 9 where, in so doing, they contribute to the climactic effect of the verse. Further, while vv. 5–9 approximate to divine speech, they are not precisely this but rather form part of Hosea's prayer (see on vv. 2 and 5 above).

[c—c]The *Piel* of חיה is clearly attested in connection with the raising and preservation of progeny (cf. Gen 7.3; 19.34; Isa 7.21); yet some (e.g. Rudolph) have expressed doubts as to whether the verb can be used in connection with seed which is not that of animals. Two considerations, however, may be urged against such objections: first, this possibility is allowed by the rabbinic commentators ibn Ezra and Kimchi, for whom the phrase, so understood, carries the consequential implication that the corn will flourish *mirabile dictu* as the vine, i.e. perennially and without renewed sowing. Secondly, the noun דָּגָן 'corn' is probably related to דָּגוֹן, the proper name of a Philistine god (cf. the Ugaritic god *dgn*)[9] and its use here may be understood, by a trope of metonymy, to define the whole agricultural enterprise, just as עשׁתרת, which is to be related to the name of the fertility goddess Astart, defines the successful breeding of flocks (Deut 7.13). For alternative treatments based on emendation, see Text and Versions below.

[d]For שׁוב as an auxiliary verb denoting repetition or restoration, BDB p. 998, col 1 8; cf. Hos 2.11 (EV 9) and especially (for restoration) Deut 23.14 (EV 13). For the separation of the auxiliary verb and the following main verb by its subject, cf. Josh 2.23; 2 Kgs 13.25 (*contra*

[9] Cf. BDB *sub* √דגן and W. F. Albright *Archaeology*, pp. 74, 220, n. 115; for a recent article on the Philistine god, K. Holter *SJOT* 1 (1989), pp. 141ff.

Rudolph). Reference to Pss 71.20; 85.7 (EV 6) confirms the combination of שוב and חיה in a single phrase.

[e] As in v. 5b, where there is a similar change from plural to singular, the suffix refers to Israel. The phrase, in parataxis, constitutes another optative clause. The noun זכר is rich in meaning and its position in the poetical structure of the piece deepens the philological appreciation. As ibn Janāḥ observes, the phrase is parallel to that of v. 7, 'that his fragrance may be like that of Lebanon'. The same authority notes that זכר here belongs to the same semantic field as the Arabic root *'rf*, where a derived noun has the meaning 'fragrance', 'scent' and the verb (Vth theme) denotes 'discovery, recognition, appreciation and approval'. He clinches his argument in respect of the Hebrew root זכר by reference to Ps 20.4 (EV 3) where יזכר מנחותיך means 'may he (God) accept your offerings', i.e. 'recognise and appreciate their good fragrance' (Arabic *yt'rf ysthsn 'rfh'*). Ibn Ezra and Kimchi more briefly and by reference to אזכרה in Lev 2.2 also invest the word זכר here with the sense 'fragrance'. Now since זכר as 'fragrance' anticipates the vehicle of the simile, זכר as it pertains to the tenor (Israel) is capable also of its more usual denotation, *viz.* that by which one is remembered, one's name (cf. 12.6 and BDB p. 271, col 1 2). Accordingly, and in this context, the word זכר denotes Israel's renown, its good name which is recognised and appreciated as a goodly fragrance (cf. Kimchi).

An alternative explanation is recorded by Rudolph; according to this the suffix of זכרו is taken to refer to the vine (also masculine in 10.1) and thus the words constitute a relative clause, i.e. '... like the vine whose renown/scent is as the wine of Lebanon'. Yet the structure and parallelism of both v. 7 and the present verse militate decisively against this view; thus, the pronoun לו in v. 7 clearly refers to Israel and the two *kaphs* of v. 8, like those of v. 7, introduce separate similes.

The people of Ephraim/Israel, living under the protection of the restored state (note b), will resume the successful cultivation of the land (notes c and d). The whole, the nation and the nation's citizens, will flourish like the vine and their renown, their good reputation (note e), will receive the widespread recognition and appreciation that is accorded to the fragrant wine of Lebanon (so Kimchi). The wine of Lebanon is not mentioned elsewhere in the bible, though Ezekiel (27.18) speaks of the wine of Ḥelbon, a district twenty five kilometres north of Damascus, at the foot of Mount Hermon. Since Lebanon in biblical usage comprises what is strictly the Antilebanon (Noth *WAT*, p. 51; ET, pp. 59f), this notice may be taken as evidence to support the validity of Hosea's simile (cf. Rudolph). Pliny (*Nat. Hist.* 14.74) praises the wines of Tripoli, Tyre and Berytus and Kimchi quotes Asaph the Physician to similar effect. The reference is naturally to viticulture on the slopes and valleys rather than on the mountain heights themselves.

Recapitulation is once again detectable in Hosea's phrases. Israel, the damaged vine of 10.1, here flourishes anew in its people; the revival of successful agriculture (note c) reverses the condemnation of 8.7, 'their endeavour produces no standing corn, a growth which produces no grain'. Similar condemnation and exact recapitulation are also to be detected in 2.11 and 23f (EV 9 and 21f).

Hosea's usage in respect of agriculture (note c) shows again how closely he sails to the wind of the fertility cult. Yet the use of *dgn* 'corn-growing' is clearly as demythologised as is that of *'štrwt* 'the breeding of flocks' in Deuteronomy. The third person plural verbs indicate that the Israelites, restored to their God, will themselves be the agents of the revival of the land's fertility. Thus, for Hosea (as for later prophets, such as II Isaiah) the redemption of the people of Israel and their restored relationship with Yahweh are to be reflected in the fertility and harmony of the natural world (cf. Kimchi). Hosea's view is naturally at variance with the perceptions of the fertility cult; yet those perceptions, radically redefined, constitute the orthodoxy which Hosea is at pains to set forth (cf. on 2.10, 18ff; EV 8, 16ff).

Text and Versions

ישבו Pesh. *wntbnwn* 'and they will be rebuilt', but read with MSS *wntpnwn* = MT (Gelston, p. 95) 'and they will turn'; Targ. יתכנשון מביני גלותהון 'they will be gathered from among their exiles'.

ישבי LXX καὶ καθιοῦνται 'and they will sit', cf. Pesh. *wntbwn* and Targ. יתבון; → (וְ)יֵשְׁבוּ/וְיָשְׁבוּ 'they will (again) dwell/they (will return) and dwell' (e.g., Wellhausen, Marti, Harper, Wolff, Rudolph, Mays, NEB, *BHS*, where this proposal is wrongly associated with the previous word, Borbone).

בצלו → בצלי 'in my shadow' (e.g., Wellhausen, Marti, Rudolph, Mays, cf. NEB and *BHS*); see note b above.

יחיו LXX ζήσονται 'they will live' = יִחְיוּ (Vollers), cf. Pesh. *wnḥwn*, Vulg. *vivent* and Targ. ייחון; → וְחָיוּ/יִחְיוּ (e.g. Rudolph); Targ. + subject מיתיא 'the dead will live'.

דגן LXX, as an apparent addition, καὶ μεθυσθήσονται σίτῳ 'and they will be intoxicated with grain' = + ירוו 'they will be saturated' (Vollers and Perles, taking ירוו as a corruption of יחיו, Nowack, as a conflate reading, Marti, Coote, as an authentic longer reading)[10]; Q[a], cf. OL[S], στηριχθήσονται 'they will be established'; → וְדָגְנוּ 'and they will be full of corn' (e.g. Nyberg); → וְיִדְגּוּ/ודגו 'and they will multiply' (e.g. Rudolph, cf. van Hoonacker); (cf. previous entry) → יֶחֱדוּ בְּגַנִּי 'they will rejoice in my garden' (*BH*); → יהיו כגן 'they will be like the garden' (e.g. Oettli); Vulg. *tritico* '(they will live) by wheat', cf. Pesh. *mn 'bwr'*.

יפרחו LXX singular verb; → וְיִפְרְחוּ (גֶּפֶן) (cf. *BHS*).

זכרו Pesh., plural suffix; *BH* raises the question whether the word is a place-name; if the *athnaḥ* is moved and the preceding word is repointed כְּגֶפֶן, this would give '(like a vine of) Zikro'.

לבנון → חלבון 'Ḥelbon', cf. Ezek 27.18 (Grätz, Halévy, Sellin).

14.9 **Ephraim [will confess] '[a]What need have I any more of idols[a]?' [Yahweh] 'I shall be attentive[b] and watch[c] over him'. [Ephraim] 'I am like a luxuriant[d] juniper[e]'. [Yahweh] 'It is from me that your fruit will be assured[f].'**

The verse is understood (with Qyl) to represent a dialogue between Yahweh and Ephraim constructed according to the principle enunciated in Y. *Soṭah* 9.7 (23d – 24a)[11] by which rapid change of subject is, in certain places, a feature of biblical style. The principle 'speech is not restricted to one subject' (מה שאמר זה לא אמר זה) is inferred from such passages as Gen 38.25f; Num 13.27–30; Judg 5.28–31.

While it is generally accepted that Yahweh is the speaker of 9b and 9d, there has been disagreement as to the identity of the subject in 9a and 9c. Thus, where 9a is concerned, it is natural to suppose that 'Ephraim' is a vocative and that Yahweh is the speaker (cf. the Vulgate and Jerome and, perhaps, ibn Ezra). Yet the resulting sense is rightly challenged on the grounds that Yahweh *ex hypothesi* never had anything to do with idols and hence the exclamation is otiose (cf., e.g., Rudolph). Further the presence of *zaqeph gadol* over 'Ephraim' militates against its being an integral part of the following phrase (cf. Rosenmüller). In the light of such considerations many modern commentators, by reference to the LXX, have cut the knot by emending the text (לו for לי) and, understanding 'Ephraim' as a *casus pendens*, render 'As for Ephraim, what has he anymore to do with idols?' (See Text and Versions, below).

A more satisfying account of 9a is that offered by Ehrlich (*Miq.*). By reference to usage in Arabic poetry as well as in the Talmud he notes that a rhetorical question can be used with adjectival force so that it forms the predicate of a noun, effecting a portrayal and a description of

[10] For a full discussion, see R. B. Coote 'Hos 14:8: They who are filled with grain shall live' *JBL* 93 (1974), pp. 161–173.

[11] Cf. Schwab, pp. 333f.

its essential quality[12]. Accordingly Ephraim is here described by the question that follows; the rhetorical question posed by the nation expresses the attitude that now it has adopted. What, then, the prophet intends to convey is as follows: 'Ephraim('s attitude is): what need more have I of idols?'

Where 9c is concerned, it is natural to suppose that the subject is Yahweh because that is the case in 9b and because 9c, like 9b, opens with the same pronoun, 'I'. On this view of the matter Yahweh likens himself to a juniper which, bending, makes its branches accessible to Ephraim (Rashi) so that, though essentially high and holy, he dwells also with the contrite and lowly (Kimchi). Since the juniper is not a fruit tree, the following promise of abundant fruit is essentially miraculous (Kimchi) or else indicative of the munificence of Yahweh (the tenor of the simile) towards his people (Rashi; cf. Rudolph, who compares 2.10, EV 8). Accordingly the tree to which Yahweh compares himself has been identified with the 'tree of life' (cf., with Wolff and Rudolph, Gen 3.22), evergreen and luxuriant, the source of all Israel's livelihood (cf. Mays).

The difficulty, to which virtually all modern commentators refer, remains that nowhere else in the bible is Yahweh likened to a tree and it seems most unlikely that Hosea would be inclined to make such use of the simile. The consideration is scarcely diminished by the supposition that the prophet is formulating 'polemical theology' (Wolff) and redefining ideas which belong to the Canaanite fertility cult (Mays)[13]. For elsewhere in this chapter it is Ephraim who is likened to the luxuriant, arboreal growth of Lebanon (vv. 6f) in which, indeed, a number of species (lily, olive, vine) are subsumed (*contra* Harper). Further, Ezek 31.3–9ff suggests a nation (this time Assyria[14]) likened to a stately and luxuriant tree, blessed by Yahweh's creative care, which is 'the envy of all the trees in Eden, the garden of God' (v. 9, NEB).

In these circumstances it is better to follow the interpretations of the Vulgate and Targum (see Text and Versions below) and ibn Ezra, for whom the figure of the tree is used of Ephraim and not of Yahweh.

If, as suggested, 9a and 9c are sentiments expressed by Ephraim and 9b and 9d responses of Yahweh, the verse has the structure of a rapid dialogue expressing the climax of love and mutual understanding which, in Hosea's prayer, will mark the ultimate reconciliation between

[12] For the definition of the 'unavoidable result of an action' by such methods, cf. B. *Shabbat* 75a (ET, p. 357 in *Mo'ed* I) and Jastrow p. 1200, col 2.

[13] For the possibility that Ephraim, likened to a tree, represents a redefinition of Canaanite (and Israelite) notions of the goddess Asherah and her cultic symbol, the tree (Deut 16.21), see the Commentary below.

[14] I.e., on the assumption that the text is sound; cf. NEB and contrast *BHS*. If the piece refers to Pharaoh alone, then, clearly the whole Egyptian nation is indicated by metonymy, cf. Zimmerli *ad loc.* under *Ziel*, vol. 2, pp. 761f, ET vol. 2, p. 153.

Ephraim and its God. It marks, then, the glorious finale (תפארת הסיום) of his prophetic utterances.

[a—a]As distinct from most modern commentators, Ehrlich (*Miq*., p. 394) is right to distinguish between the expression which occurs here, as also in Jer 2.18 (מה לך ... ל), and the more common expression in which *waw* precedes the second ל. The latter, commonly מה לי ולך, implies a dismissive question regarding the relationship or connection between A and B; the former implies a dismissive question concerning the need that A has of B (cf. ibn Ezra).

[b]The tenses of the (two) verbs are understood to be prophetic perfects, cf. GK 106n, cf. Rashi, ibn Ezra and Kimchi. For ענה in Hosea, see on 2.17 above. In corroboration of what is there said it should be noted that ibn Ezra, in elucidation of this verse, also compares Eccles 10.19. For the verb without suffix, cf. 2.17. An alternative is to understand the suffix of the second verb as serving also for the first (cf. GK 117f). The commonly held view that ענה here means 'I answered him', 'responded to him' (so, e.g., Rashi, Harper, Wolff, Rudolph, Mays, NEB, AF), is unsatisfactory since that meaning does not fit the occurrences in 2.17, 23f. Morag's view that the verb here (together with that which follows it, note c below) belongs to the semantic field of growth and to the preparation of the soil (i.e. for the successful growth of Israel under the figure of a shoot) is suggestive (see the commentary below), not least because his view of the meaning of the phrase as a whole comes close to the precise and comprehensive definition of ענה offered by ibn Janāḥ. Thus Morag understands the two verbs as having the general sense 'I have attended to (טיפלתי) his shoot, I have prepared his soil and watered it'. Yet strictly speaking the verbs, with Yahweh as the subject in the first person and with Ephraim as the object in the third person, are more likely to denote an aspect of dealings between persons (cf. on 2.17 above) than to dealings between Yahweh and Ephraim, portrayed as a shoot. The evidence adduced by ibn Janāḥ to the effect that the verb, predicated of the earth in 2.24, can have the particular sense 'to produce/bring forth' is indicative of an extended or metaphorical usage in 2.23f in which inanimate subjects are (to some extent) personalised.

[c]ואשורנו; for the verb שור II 'to behold', 'regard', see BDB p. 1003, col 2. Morag rightly notes that the semantic range of the verb comprises notions of protection and guarding, for which he cites evidence from comparative philology (Arabic, Hebrew and Aramaic); cf. English 'to look after', 'watch over' (so essentially Rashi, ibn Ezra, Rosenmüller). Such considerations tell against the judgement (e.g. Rudolph) that the meaning 'to behold', 'regard' is weak and the consequent preference for emendations (see Text and Versions) or for alternative philological theories (e.g. Driver[15], who repoints to a form of √שרר, cf. NEB 'and I

[15] *Studies in Old Testament Prophecy* H. H. Rowley (ed.) (Edinburgh, 1950), pp. 67f.

affirm it', by reference to Accadian and Syriac, and following 'I answer [him]' for עניתי).

[d]For רענן, strictly 'luxuriant', 'dense' rather than 'green', see D. W. Thomas SVT 16 (1967), pp. 387ff. Cf., further, Morag *Tarbiz* 41 (1971–72), pp. 14–23 and Watson *Biblica* 53 (1972), p. 197n.

[e]ברוש, probably the *juniperus phoenicea*, so LXX, cf. KB³, p. 148. This species is often mentioned in parallelism with ארז the 'cedar', cf. KB³, p. 83; further, Qyl.

[f]נמצא lit. 'will be found'; i.e. 'will be gained', 'secured', cf. BDB p. 594, col 1 h; again, a prophetic perfect (cf. note b above).

The last authentic words of Hosea's prophecy constitute a fitting finale to his work, to his ultimate aspiration and concern. They are a *tipheret haḥatymah*[16], a glorious conclusion. Hosea's prayer concludes with a vision of the total unity that shall be between Israel and her God. This vision is expressed in words of the ecstatic dialogue (see introductory note to the verse), elsewhere familiar from the Song of Songs, where the voices of man and woman alternate in a wholly complementary fashion. Ephraim will finally repudiate her addiction to the idols of Canaan with a confession which implies penitence and a renewal of fidelity. Yahweh's response is immediate, for he loves those who love him (cf., with Jerome, Prov 8.17); now he is free to offer his fully attentive protection (notes b and c and NB the prophetic perfect). The tempo increases and Ephraim, basking in the assurance of such protection, proclaims that now her condition is like that of a luxuriant juniper (notes d, e), a symbol of abiding youth and vigour, cf. the tree of Ezek 31.8. Finally, Yahweh's exclamation assures the nation that he is the source of her fruit. Here, no doubt, the word *pry* again alludes by word-play to the very name of Ephraim (*'prym*); so Wolff and Rudolph, cf. 9.16. For Kimchi, the fact that the juniper is not a fruit tree indicates the miraculous quality of Yahweh's generosity (see introductory note to the verse). Yet the reference is more plausibly to the tenor rather than to the vehicle of the simile. Thus Ephraim's fruit depicts quite generally its vitality and prosperity and not merely its human, animal and agricultural fruit (cf. Rashi, Rudolph, Sellin).

Morag's contention that the two verbs (here, 'I shall be attentive and watch over', notes b and c) belong to the semantic field of growth and allude to the necessary preparation for it of

[16] For the term, see D. Yellin *Introduction to the Hebrew Poetry of the Spanish Period* (Jerusalem, 1978), p. 90.

the soil is not here accepted precisely in the form that it is offered. The verbs, it seems to me, belong primarily to the field of personal relationships. Yet the evidence adduced by ibn Janāḥ and Morag allows of some connection between the first verb (*'nh* note b) and notions of natural growth from the soil (see on 2.23f above). It is typical of Hosea's artistry that he should choose words which allude to one of his central perceptions: that the fertility of the land is inexorably bound up with the love of Yahweh for his people and with the single-minded commitment to him to which they are called (cf. on 2.16ff, EV 14ff).

A further possibility arises in connection with Wellhausen's famous emendation of the text according to which he finds a reference to the goddesses Anat and Asherah (see Text and Versions). While there is no evidence to support the emendation itself, it remains possible that Hosea's choice of words (notes b and c) was designed to allude to the concept of god and consort, now redefined in terms of the relationship between Yahweh and his people[17].

Two further subtleties may be noted: first, 'I will watch over him' (*'šwrnw*) creates by word-play an antithesis to 'Assyria cannot save us' (*'šwr l' ywšy'nw*, v. 4); secondly, 'from me your fruit will be assured' is a recapitulation of 9.16 'they cannot produce fruit' and 10.1 'Israel is a damaged vine whose fruit fails him'.

Text and Versions

אפרים LXX τῷ 'E., see below; Pesh. *wn'mr* 'and (Ephraim) will say' (Gelston, p. 148), cf. Targ. יימרון; + ואמר (Borbone); Vulg. *E.* (*quid mihi*) (vocative); Jerome's rendering of LXX (OL) *quasi vinum Libani E.* (i.e. with v. 8).

לי LXX αὐτῷ (in apposition to τῷ 'E.) and with καί before 'idols', i.e. 'What has Ephraim to do with idols?'; → לוֹ (most moderns, e.g., Wellhausen, Marti, Harper, Wolff, Rudolph, Mays, NEB, cf. *BHS* and note a above).

עניתי LXX ἐγὼ ἐταπείνωσα αὐτόν 'I have humbled him', cf. Pesh. *mkkth*; = עִנִּיתִיו, √ענה III in BDB (so, e.g., Oort, Oettli); → עֲנִיתִי (Borbone *sic*); Vulg. *exaudiam* 'I will listen attentively' (√ענה II in BDB); Targ. אקביל צלותיה 'I will accept his (Israel's) prayer'; 1 Kennicott MS reads

[17] Cf. P. R. Ackroyd 'Goddesses, Woman and Jezebel', p. 253; Margalit *VT* 40 (1990), pp. 283f and J. Day *JBL* 105 (1986), p. 405; Day has also drawn attention to Isa 27.9, dependent, as he supposes, upon Hosea, which specifically condemns Asherim, *JTS* NS 31 (1980), p. 315.

אענהו; for Wellhausen's famous emendation, see next entry; → עֲנִיתִיו (cf. *BHS*).

ואשורנו LXX καὶ ἐγὼ κατισχύσω αὐτόν (B omits ἐγώ) 'I will prevail over him' (not 'strengthen', *contra*, e.g., Wolff), understanding a form of √שרה I (cf. LXX at 12.4f; so rightly Rudolph); Vulg. *et dirigam eum* 'I will arrange him (as)', i.e. make him like (a fir-tree); → וַאֲאַשְּׁרֶנּוּ (Grätz, cf. *BHS*, but with the sense 'I will bless him', Rudolph, cf. √ √אשר I and II in KB³), cf. Pesh. *'šbḥywhy* 'I will praise him'; Targ. וארחים עלוהי 'and I will pity him'; → ואשירך 'and I will praise thee' (Borbone); → ואֲשִׁיבנו (cf. *BHS*).

Wellhausen daringly proposes the emendation (אני) עֲנָתוֹ וַאֲשֵׁרָתוֹ '(I am) his Anat and Asherah'. While recent discoveries at Kuntillet 'Ajrud and at Khirbet el-Qôm[18] confirm the possibility of his (*sc.* Yahweh's) Asherah, there cannot be said to be any evidence or indication that the text of Hos 14.9 ever made mention either of Anath or of Asherah, cf. M. Weinfeld[19].

ברוש LXX ἄρκευθος 'juniper'; Aq. ἐλάτη 'fir', cf. Vulg. *abietem* (note the accusative case whereby the noun is taken as the object of the preceding verb; see above); Pesh. *qṭrq'*, 'cypress', 'pine'; Targ. במימרי אעבדיניה כבירון שפיר 'by my Memra I will make him like a beautiful cypress'.

רענן LXX πυκάζουσα 'thickly covered'; Aq. εὐθαλής 'flourishing'; Vulg. *virentem* 'vigorous', 'green'; Pesh. *'byṭ'*, 'thick/dense', 'leafy', 'shady'; Targ. שפיר 'beautiful'.

פריך Targ. סליח לתיובתהון 'pardon for their backslidings'; → פִּרְיוֹ (cf. Oort, Marti, *BHS*).

18 A. Lemaire 'Les inscriptions de Khirbet el-Qôm et l'Ashérah de Yhwh', *RB* 84 (1977), pp. 595–608, and 'Date et origine des inscriptions hébraiques et phéniciennes de Kuntillet 'Ajrud', *SEL* 1 (1984), pp. 131–143; for a select bibliography, see Margalit, *op. cit.*, pp. 296f.

19 שנתון למקרא ולחקר המזרח הקדום 4 (1980), p. 281. For a suggestion based on Wellhausen's emendation, see Margalit, cited above, n. 14. For a recent defence and treatment of Wellhausen's theory, see O. Loretz 'Anat-Aschera (Hos. 14.9) und die Inschriften von Kuntillet 'Ajrud' *SEL* 6 (1989), pp. 57–65, and a revised version of the same article in M. Dietrich and O. Loretz *Jahve und seine Aschera* (Münster, 1982), pp. 173–182.

CHAPTER 14.10

EPILOGUE

14.10 **Whosoever[a] is wise, let him understand these matters; whoever discriminating, let him take note[b] of them. For the ways of Yahweh are straight and just men walk on them while transgressors stumble on them.**

[a]The pronoun מִי, strictly an interrogative pronoun, is used here virtually as an (indefinite) relative pronoun, so Rashi, cf. König 382b, 390p. Thus what is literally rendered 'Who is wise? Let him understand' is equivalent to 'Whosoever is wise, let him understand ...' (cf. BDB p. 567, col 1 g). Inadmissible is the view that the two clauses taken together constitute a question, i.e. 'Who is so wise that he understands these things?' (cf. GK 166a), as if the unlikelihood of the proposition is expressed or deplored (so Rudolph *contra* Wolff).

[b]BDB p. 393, col 2 1 b.

The verse, replete with the language of the Wisdom literature (see below), is added to the collected prophecies of Hosea ('these matters') and suggests to the reader the lesson that he should draw from them. That lesson is formulated in the statement 'the ways of Yahweh are straight' and by this is meant his providential control of history effected in accordance with his consistent ethical nature; so ibn Ezra and Kimchi who contrast the unjust complaint quoted by Ezekiel (18.25) 'the way of the Lord is not equal' (AV)/'the Lord acts without principle' (NEB); see further Exod 33.13; Ps 107.43; Jer 9.11 (EV 12). The view that the 'ways of Yahweh' depict his ethical requirements or commands (so, e.g., Frey, Wolff, Mays) cannot be correct in the light of the antithetical propositions which follow, 'just men walk on them while transgressors stumble on them'. In other words, just men, attuned to Yahweh's ethical will and conforming their lives to it, are enabled to proceed along his ways with success, i.e. they perceive and recognise the ethical basis which underlies his ordering of the world and of history (cf. Deut 32.4). Transgressors, denying this basis and consequently refusing to conform their lives to it, stumble on the ways of Yahweh, suffering utter ruin (cf. Prov 10.29).

This verse is similar to other wisdom additions, cf., e.g., Eccles 8.1; Ps 107.43 and (in prophetic literature) Jer 9.11 (EV 12).

Psalm 1, as a prologue to the way in which the Psalter should be read, affords another parallel. In these texts also there is found or implied the catechetical challenge (note a) and the didactic proposition which follows it. Here the proposition contains both the vocabulary and the antithetic structure which typifies the Wisdom tradition (cf., with Wolff, Prov 10.29; 24.16b). Yet the writer seems to have picked up particular words from the text of Hosea's prophecies: thus 'to stumble' (4.5; 5.5; 14.2) and 'to transgress' (7.13; 8.1); even wisdom and understanding form part of Hosea's own perceptions (e.g. 13.13; 4.14). Accordingly what is clearly contrived is nonetheless carefully and sensitively contrived; its thought is essentially continuous with the material which it seeks to elucidate[1].

The personal nature of the appeal for wise understanding indicates that the epilogue belongs to a time long after Hosea. The reader to whom the exhortation is addressed is no longer able to read Hosea's words with immediate understanding. He needs, for example, to be reminded of their original circumstances and for that reason 1.1, with its indication of the historical context, was also added to the work. For the rest it is clear that the reader to whom the appeal is made is involved in the study of what has become, to all intents and purposes, scripture; and, studying it, he is urged to appreciate and to digest the lessons that it teaches for himself and for his own time. The period in question is likely to be the exilic or, more probably, the post-exilic (so, e.g., Wolff).

Text and Versions

בם (first occurrence) Targ. וצדיקיא דהליכו בהון ייחון בהון בחיי עלמא (First and Second Rabbinic Bibles בה for בהון) 'and the righteous who walk in them (*v.l.* on it) will live through them (*sc.* the ways of Yahweh) in the life to come'. The two pronouns may suggest a distinction between the course through life of the righteous and their adherence to the ways (*sc.* the laws) of Yahweh (cf. Rashi and Rudolph).

יכשלו LXX ἀσθενήσουσιν 'they will become weak', cf. 5.5 (note d) and BDB p. 505, col 2 *Niphal* 2.

[1] For contrasting views on this point, cf. G. T. Sheppard *Wisdom as a Hermeneutical Construct* (BZAW 151, Berlin & New York, 1980), pp. 129ff, the review of this by R. P. Gordon *VT* 32 (1982), p. 376, and C. L. Seow.

APPENDIX
THE VOCABULARY OF HOSEA

The following Table of Vocabulary lists a number of words in Hosea's prophecies which, in my opinion, display some peculiarities *vis-à-vis* Standard Biblical Hebrew. In using it, the following points should be noted:

Column 1 References in Hosea (Hebrew Text).

Column 2 Words and Forms.

Column 3 Meanings.

The sense detected for the forms in question is given approximately. Reference should be made to the commentary for a more precise account.

Column 4 An indication of where biblical parallels predominate and other comments.

No attempt has been made at comprehensive listings. The intention is merely to provide a rough indication of where parallels predominate. In particular instances exact references are supplied; for those not listed see the commentary and BDB.

Column 5 Roots. The (Roman) numerical additions, where appropriate, are those used by BDB.

Column 6 Significant cognates.

No comprehensive account is given; rather the intention has been to give some indication of the language which comes closest to illuminating Hosea's (Hebrew) usage; cf. on column 4 above. Reference should also be made to BDB and KB[3].

Column 7 Main or significant authorities.

Column 8 Categories.

The significant words of Hosea's vocabulary are divided into four categories which may be useful but are certainly not comprehensive; they are:

A Words whose roots are known (and even well-known) but whose particular forms show some peculiarity, whether of morphology, use of phonemes or of grammar.

B Words whose roots are known (and even well-known) but whose meanings in the text of Hosea vary either considerably or somewhat from what is regarded as normal (i.e. in 'Standard Biblical Hebrew').

C Rare words (often *hapax legomena*) whose meanings are fixed or confirmed by reference to cognate languages.

D Aramaisms or possible Aramaisms.

1	2	3	4	5	6	7	8
1.2	זנונים	whoredom/promiscuity	Nah Ezek	זנה	—	Morag, pp. 500, 503. Cf. Introduction, p. lvi	A
1.6	רחמה	forbearance/care	Ps 18.2	רחם	Aramaic	—	A
	נשׂא	annihilate	Job	נשׂא	—	ibn Janāḥ	B
2.4	נאפופיה	adulteries	*Hapax*	נאף	—	Morag, p. 500 n.	A
2.7–15	מאהבי(ה)	lovers	Jer Ezek	אהב	—	Morag, pp. 502f. Cf. Introduction p. lvi	A
2.7, 11	פשתי	flax	*Hapax* (form)	פשת	—	AAM	A
2.8	שׂך	obstruct	Job	I שׂוך/II סוך	Arabic	Rashi	A
2.11	והצלתי	snatch away/take from	—	נצל	Aramaic	Greenfield	D
2.12	נבלתה	lewd behaviour/ vile corruption	*Hapax* cf.? Nah Job (√III)	III? II? נבל	—	ibn Janāḥ (√III) ibn Ezra/Jerome (√II)	A B
2.14	אתנה	present/gift	*Hapax* (form)	II תנה	Aram/Arabic	ibn Janāḥ, Morag	A B

1	2	3	4	5	6	7	8
2.15	חליתה	necklace	*Hapax* (form); but cf. Ct Prov	חלה III	—	ibn Ezra	A
2.17, 23f	√ענה	be attentive/occupied with; grow/sprout (24)	Eccles	ענה II	Aram/Arabic	ibn Janāḥ	B
3.2	ואכרה	gain (legal) possession	—	נכר I	—	ibn Ezra, Morag	B
4.10, 18; 5.3	הזנו	abandon oneself to promiscuity	Intrans. *Hiphil* unique to H.	זנה	—	ibn Janāḥ, Morag	A
4.10	לשמר	devote	cf. 12.13	שמר	—	Rashi, Kimchi, Morag	B
4.14	יפרדו	associate	*Piel* unique to H.	פרד I	Arabic	ibn Janāḥ	A B
4.16[1]	עתה	now (asyndeton)	—	—	—	S. R. Driver, *Intro.* p. 306, cf. BDB	A
4.17	חבור	yoked to	*Hapax* (passive)	חבר	—	Rashi, Kimchi	A
4.18	אהבוהבו	fornicate wildly	*Hapax* (reduplication)	אהב	—	ibn Janāḥ, Morag	A B
	מגניה	canopies	*Hapax*	גנן	Aramaic	Morag	B

[1] Cf. also 5.7; 7.2; 8.8, 13; 10.2.

1	2	3	4	5	6	7	8
4.19	זבחותם	sacrificial feasts	*Hapax* (fem.)	זבח	—	—	A
5.6	חלץ	detach/separate	without object, unique to H.	חלץ I	Arabic	ibn Barūn	B
5.7	חדש	change of circumstances/time of misfortune	Jer	חדש	Arabic	ibn Janāḥ, ibn Barūn	B
5.11	צו	futility	Isaiah 28	צוו	Arabic	G. R. Driver	C
5.12	עש	emaciating disease	—	עשש	Arabic	ibn Barūn, G. R. Driver, AAM	?B ?C
5.13, 10.6	ירב	Great (King)	—	ירב	Syriac	Michaelis, G. R. Driver	?C ?D
5.13	יגהה	be free from pain/disease	*Hapax*	גהה	Syriac	ibn Janāḥ, AAM	C
6.5	חצבתי	hew in pieces	Isaiah 51.9	חצב	Ugaritic	ibn Janāḥ	B
6.9	חכי	lie in wait	form unique to H.	חכה	—	ibn Ezra, Kimchi	A
7.3	ישמחו	promote the rise	—	שמח	Arabic	ibn Janāḥ, AAM	C
7.5	החלו	be sick	*Hiphil* unique to H. in this sense	חלה I	—	BDB	A

1	2	3	4	5	6	7	8
7.8	יתבולל	be vitiated	Lev 20.12	I בלל	Arabic	ibn Barūn, ibn Janāḥ	A B
7.12	איסרם	chastise	Prov 4.25 (for form); *Hiphil* unique to H.	יסר	—	ibn Ezra	A
	עדתם	assignation	Judg 20.38, Josh 11.5	יעד	Arabic	ibn Barūn, AAM	B
7.14	יתגוררו	lacerate themselves (?)	—	גרר/גור	Mish Heb/Aram	ibn Janāḥ, AAM	C
7.15	יסרתי +gloss חזרתי	support, strengthen	Job 4.3	יסר (posited)	Aramaic	ibn Janāḥ, G. R. Driver	C
7.16	זעם +gloss זו לעגם	offensiveness	—	זעם	—	ibn Janāḥ	B
8.3, 5	זנח	remove/banish	Lam Pss Zech	I זנח	Arabic (*nzḥ* metathesis)	ibn Janāḥ, ibn Barūn	C
8.6	שבבים	banishment	*Hapax* but cf. Ezek 38.4 for √	שוב	—	ibn Janāḥ, AAM	A B
8.8	נבלע	undermined/vitiated	Job 10.8	I בלע	—	ibn Janāḥ	B

1	2	3	4	5	6	7	8
8.9	עלו	come/arrive		עלל (posited)/ עול (√ posited)	Aramaic	Saadya	B ?C
8.9f	התנו/יתנו	be full of/delighted with	Judg Ps 8.2	II תנה	Aram/Arabic	ibn Janāḥ, Morag	A B
8.9	אהבים	love-affair	Prov	אהב	—	Morag, p. 498	A B
8.10	אקבצם	remove/destroy	Nah Joel	קבץ	—	Qyl	B
8.13	הבהבי +gloss יזבחו בשר ויאכלו	speed	*Hapax*	הבהב	Mish Heb/Arabic	ibn Janāḥ	C
9.2	ירעם	give attention to	Eccles Dn cf. 10.15 12.2	III רעה	Aram/Arabic	ibn Janāḥ	C ?D
9.8	צפה	confront	Ps 5.4 Job 15.22	צפה	—	ibn Janāḥ	B
9.10	אהבם	object of desire	Prov 7.18	אהב	—	Morag	A B
9.11	יתעופף	fly away	*Hapax* (form)	I עוף	—	BDB &c	A
9.12	שׂורי	?withdraw/depart	—	שׂור/סור	—	Jerome, Rashi, ibn Ezra, Kimchi	?A
9.13	צור	palm-shoot	*Hapax*	?VI ?II צור	Mish Heb/ Arabic	A.J. Arnold	C

1	2	3	4	5	6	7	8
9.14	צמקים	shrivel	*Hapax*	צמק	Aram	ibn Ezra	D
10.1	בוקק	damage	Nah	?III בקק/בוק	Arabic	ibn Janāḥ, ibn Barūn, ibn Ezra	C
	ישוה	fail	*Hapax*	I שוא(ה)	—	ibn Janāḥ	A B
10.2	חלק	dissimulate	Ezek 12.24	II חלק	—	Harper	B
10.5	עגלות	calf cult	*Hapax*	עגל	—	Rudolph	A B
10.6	בשנה	disgrace/disillusion	Job 42.13 cf. 13.15	בוש	—	ibn Janāḥ, ibn Ezra	A
10.7	קצף	foam	*Hapax*	I קצף	—	ibn Janāḥ	B
10.9	עלוה	perversity	*Hapax*	II(?) עלה	?Arabic ?Syriac	Schultens, Michaelis	C
10.10	*Q* עונתם	policies/attitudes	*Hapax*	II ענה	Aram/Arabic	ibn Janāḥ	A B
10.11	עברתי	happen upon	?Deut 24.5	עבר	Arabic	Wolff, AAM	B
10.15	רעתכם	policy	Dn cf. 9.2, 12.2	III רעה	Aram/Arabic	ibn Janāḥ, G. R. Driver	C ?D
11.3	תרגלתי	apply oneself assiduously	*Hapax* (form)	רגל	Mish Heb	ibn Janāḥ	A B
	קחם	take	*Hapax* (form)	לקח	—	ibn Janāḥ	A

1	2	3	4	5	6	7	8
11.4	ואט	proffer	Gen 24.14 1 Chr 21.10	נטה	—	AAM	A B
11.6	בדיו	villages	Ezek Job	בדד I	—	ibn Janāḥ, Kimchi	B
11.7	משובתי	return/repentance	sense unique to H.	שוב	—	Morag	B
11.8	אמגנך	deliver up	Gen 14.20	מגן	Ugaritic	KB3	C
11.11	יחרדו	be roused	cf. 2 Kgs 4.13	חרד	—	ibn Janāḥ	B
12.1	רד	seek to dominate	Gen 27.40 Jer 2.31	רוד	Arabic	ibn Janāḥ, AAM	C
12.2	רעה	give attention to	cf. 9.2	רעה III	Aram/Arabic	ibn Janāḥ	C ?D
12.9	און	wealth	Job 20.10	און II	Arabic	Rashi	B
12.13	שמר	devote	cf. 4.10	שמר I	—	Morag	B
12.15	תמרורים	flagrantly	Jer 31.21 Dn 11.11	מרר ?II	—	ibn Janāḥ	A B
	יטוש	be evident	1 Sam 30.16	נטש	—	ibn Janāḥ, ibn Ezra	A B
13.1	רתת	disruption	*Hapax* but cf. Jer 49.24	רתת	Arabic	ibn Janāḥ	C

1	2	3	4	5	6	7	8
13.2	תבונם	skill	*Hapax* (form)	בין	—	ibn Ezra, Kimchi	A
13.3	יסער	(completely) remove	Job 27.21 Zech 7.14	סער/ II שׂער	—	ibn Janāḥ	A B
13.5	תלאבות	baking heat	*Hapax*	לוב	Arabic	ibn Janāḥ	C
13.10, 14	אהי	So much for!	H. only	—	Syriac	AAM	C
13.14	נחם	relief	*Hapax*	נחם	—	Rashi, ibn Ezra	A B
13.15	יפריא	behave wilfully	*Hapax*	II פרא	—	ibn Janāḥ	A B
	ויבוש	fail	cf. 10.6	בוש	—	ibn Ezra	B
14.6	ויך	strike root	sense unique to H.	נכה	—	ibn Janāḥ, Kimchi	B
14.8	זכרו	fragrance	Ps 20.4	זכר	—	ibn Janāḥ	B
14.9	עניתי	be attentive	cf. 2.17, 23f	II ענה	Aram/Arabic	ibn Janāḥ, ibn Ezra, cf. Morag	B

INDEX OF AUTHORS

NB Standard works and those referred to *passim* are listed in the Bibliography.

SELECT INDEX OF SUBJECTS

NB For more general themes the table 'The chapters and their contents' should be consulted.